David Jobber
Principles and Practice of
Marketing

sixth edition

David Jobber

Principles and Practice of
Marketing

sixth edition

The **McGraw·Hill** *Companies*

London   Boston   Burr   Ridge,   IL   Dubuque,   IA   Madison,   WI   New   York   San
Francisco   St. Louis   Bangkok   Bogotá   Caracas   Kuala   Lumpur Lisbon   Madrid   Mexico
City   Milan   Montreal   New   Delhi   Santiago   Seoul   Singapore   Sydney   Taipei   Toronto

Principles and Practice of Marketing, 6th edition
David Jobber
ISBN-13 978-0-07-712330-7
ISBN-10 0-07-7123301

**McGraw-Hill
Higher Education**

Published by McGraw-Hill Education
Shoppenhangers Road
Maidenhead
Berkshire
SL6 2QL
Telephone: 44 (0) 1628 502 500
Fax: 44 (0) 1628 770 224
Website: www.mcgraw-hill.co.uk

British Library Cataloguing in Publication Data
A catalogue record for this book is available from the British Library

Library of Congress Cataloging-in-Publication Data
The Library of Congress data for this book has been applied for from the Library of Congress

Acquisitions Editor: Rachel Gear
Senior Development Editor: Leonie Sloman
Marketing Manager: Alice Duijser
Head of Production: Beverley Shields
Text design by Hard Lines
Cover design by Adam Renvoize
Printed and bound in Italy by Rotolito Lombarda

ISBN-13 978-0-07-712330-7
ISBN-10 0-07-712330-1

The **McGraw·Hill** Companies

Brief Table of Contents

Detailed Table of Contents

Vignettes

Marketing Ethics and Corporate Social Responsibility in Action

Case Guide

This guide shows the key concepts covered in each of the cases in both the book and the Online Learning Centre so you can easily pick out which cases are relevant to a particular part of your course. Go to www.mcgraw-hill/textbooks/jobber to find a pdf of this guide, and search by company, industry or topic to find the ideal case to use.

Chapter	Case number	Case title and author	Key concepts covered
1	Case 1	Coca-Cola *vs* Pepsi: Cola Wars in a Changing Marketing Environment *David Jobber, Professor of Marketing, University of Bradford*	marketing-orientation, competition, leading brands, positioning
	Case 2	H&M Gets Hotter: Fashion at its Fastest *David Jobber, Professor of Marketing, University of Bradford*	marketing-orientation, effectiveness and efficiency customer value, fashion industry
	OLC case	Nokia: Re-connecting People *Tony Rowe, Principal of Marketing Mentors, and Tony Lindley, Managing Director of Tony Lindley Consultants Ltd.*	global marketing, technology, internal-orientation, mobile telecoms industry
2	Case 3	Vulnerable Volvo: Can the Volvo Brand Succeed in the New Competitive Landscape? *Conor Carroll, Lecturer in Marketing, University of Limerick*	brands, market share, competition, marketing environment, SWOT, strategic options, car industry
	Case 4	Heron Engineering: A Strategy for Storage *David Shipley, Emeritus Professor of Marketing, University of Dublin, Ireland*	organizational behaviour, marketing environment, technology, planning
	OLC case	Daloon Spring Rolls *Poul Faarup, Associate Professor, University of Southern Denmark*	marketing planning, SWOT, 4 P's, food industry
3	Case 5	Sony Shockwave: In Search of the Next Hit Product *Conor Carroll, Lecturer in Marketing, University of Limerick*	product innovation, SWOT, marketing environment, strategic options
	Case 6	Marketing Environment: PEEST Analysis Exercise *David Jobber, Professor of Marketing, University of Bradford*	elements of marketing environment analysis, legal, political, technology, economics, social and physical environment
	OLC case	The Future of Books: Gutenberg, the Kindle and Beyond *Tony Lindley, Managing Director of Tony Lindley Consultants Ltd.*	marketing environment, impact of technology, digital revolution, evolution of education, distance learning

13	Case 25	A Glass and a Half: Cadbury Gets the Love Back for Dairy Milk *Marie O'Dwyer, Lecturer in Marketing, Waterford Institute of Technology, Ireland*	advertising objectives, virtual advertising, television advertising
	Case 26	White Horse Whisky: Developing a New Advertising Strategy *Ann Murray Chatterton, Director of Training and Development at the Institute of Practitioners in Advertising*	advertising, branding, repositioning, drinks industry
	OLC case	Tracking BT Advertising Campaigns *Laura Evans, Managing Consultant, TNS IT & Telecoms, Trent Cottle, Head of Communications Insight, BT, Clive Nancarrow*	advertising awareness, television advertising, marketing communication tools, advertising effectiveness
14	Case 27	Selling in China: Harnessing the Power of the *Guanxi* *David Jobber, Professor of Marketing, University of Bradford*	international marketing, cultural issues, self reference criteria
	Case 28	Bottling It in Europe: Glastex Sells its Glass Bottling Equipment to Europe *David Jobber, Professor of Marketing, University of Bradford*	key account management, personal selling, industrial marketing, international marketing
	OLC case	Kompass Ireland: Finding Ways to Improve Salesforce Performance *Fergal Maher and Conor Carroll, Lecturer in Marketing, University of Limerick*	sales force, sales strategies, customer types, promotions
15	Case 29	Guinness' Rewards: An Award-Winning Relationship Marketing Programme *Marie O'Dwyer, Lecturer in Marketing, Waterford Institute of Technology, Ireland*	relationship marketing, direct marketing, sales promotion, drinks industry
	Case 30	CRM at Tesco: From Understanding to Engaging Customers *Colin Gilligan, Emeritus Professor of Marketing, Sheffield Hallam University and Visiting Professor of Marketing, Newcastle Business School*	relationship marketing strategies, CRM programmes, loyalty schemes, grocery retailers
	OLC case	Nectar: Loyalty Brings Sweet Rewards *Conor Carroll, Lecturer in Marketing, and Sara Kate Hurley, Research Assistant, University of Limerick*	customer loyalty, loyalty programmes
16	Case 31	Wispa: It's Back! *Marie O'Dwyer, Lecturer in Entrepeneurship, University of Limerick*	social networking, brand re-launch strategy, communication tools, marketing communication strategy, nostalgia brands
	Case 32	Beckham and Ronaldo: Sports Celebrity Sponsorship *David Jobber, Professor of Marketing, University of Bradford*	sports marketing, sponsorship, measuring effectiveness
	OLC case	JK Rowling: A Marketing Wizard *Luciana Lolich, Lecturer in Marketing, Dublin Business School*	promotional strategy, marketing communication strategy, promotional mix, word of mouth

17	Case 33	ASOS: Setting The Pace in Online Fashion *David Jobber, Professor of Marketing, University of Bradford*	online fashion retailing, customer service, promotion strategy, SWOT analysis
	Case 34	iTunes: Facing the Threat of Nokia *Conor Carroll, Lecturer in Marketing, University of Limerick*	digital technologies, halo effect, distribution of digital products, digital download industry
	OLC case	Leisure, Travel and the Internet *Justin O'Brien, Teaching Fellow, Royal Holloway, University of London*	distribution channels, disintermediation, distribution technology, cost transparency, travel industry
18	Case 35	Google: Staying Ahead of the Game? *Fiona Ellis-Chadwick, Senior Lecturer in Marketing, Open University*	competitive advantage, differentiation, online resources and competencies
	Case 36	Giftmaster: Moving Retail Online *Joseph Coughlan, Research Fellow, Dublin Institute of Technology*	search engine marketing, online retailing
	OLC case	Infiltrating an e-Community: Marketing to the Machinima Virtual Community *Tony Garry, Senior Lecturer in Marketing, and Tracey Harwood, Senior Research Fellow and National Teacher Fellow, De Montfort University*	one-to-one marketing, consumer behaviour, opinion leaders, formers and followers, virtual marketing, virtual communities
19	Case 37	The Wii Fits Us All! Nintendo Regains Video Game Supremacy *Loïc Plé, Assistant Professor, IÉSEG School of Management, France*	competitor analysis, competitive advantage, marketing mix, computer games industry
	Case 38	General Meltdown: What Caused General Motors' Bankruptcy? *Conor Carroll, Lecturer in Marketing, University of Limerick*	competitive advantage, competitive forces, recovery strategy, global automobile markets
	OLC case	The Going Gets Tough for Wal-Mart and Asda *David Jobber, Professor of Marketing, University of Bradford*	competitive advantage, international acquisitions, retail information systems, global supermarket operations
20	Case 39	Airbus *vs* Boeing: The Battle for Air Supremacy *Conor Carroll, Lecturer in Marketing, University of Limerick*	competitive marketing strategy, barriers to entry, aircraft manufacturing, risk factors.
	Case 40	Displaying Strategy: Finding a Competitive Advantage for Data Display *Michele O'Dwyer, Lecturer in Marketing, Waterford Institute of Technology, Ireland*	competitive advantage, advertising, technology
	OLC case	DSG International: Managing Multiple Brands in a Multi-Channel World *Robert Anslow, John Naughton, Conor Carroll, Lecturer in Marketing, and Sara Kate Hurley, Research Assistant, University of Limerick*	international marketing, structure of competition, e-commerce, channel strategy, consumer electronics

21	Case 41	Internal Marketing: Influencing the Board at Hansen Bathrooms *David Jobber, Professor of Marketing, University of Bradford*	pricing strategy, internal marketing, personnel management, new products
	Case 42	Munster Rugby: Implementing Change *Conor Kelleher, Lecturer in Marketing, Waterford Institute of Technology, Ireland*	internal customers, CRM, operational control, sports marketing.
	OLC case	Portland & Hackett, *Caroline Tynan, Professor of Marketing, Andrew Smith, Associate Professor in Marketing, and Matt Caldwell, Knowledge Transfer Partnership Associate, University of Nottingham*	strategic marketing planning, Mckinsey 7-S framework, internal marketing, implementation
22	Case 43	Build-A-Bear: A Custom-made Experience *Loïc Plé, Assistant Professor, IÉSEG School of Management, France*	customized products, toy retailing, customer service, emerging markets
	Case 44	Services Marketing in a Recession: The Tale of Five Supermarkets *David Jobber, Professor of Marketing, University of Bradford*	marketing strategies, service marketing, economic downturn, supermarkets
	OLC case	Gucci, Louis Vuitton, & Vertu: Marketing Lessons from some of the World's Most Exclusive Brands *Conor Carroll, Lecturer in Marketing, Sara Kate Hurley, Research Assistant, and Ann Treacy, University of Limerick*	luxury brands, brand personality, product exclusivity, experiential marketing
23	Case 45	IKEA: Building a Cult Global Brand *David Jobber, Professor of Marketing, University of Bradford*	international marketing, cult branding, adaptation, standardization
	Case 46	Made in China: Marketing Tsingtao Beer Internationally *Adrian Pritchard, Senior Lecturer in Marketing, Coventry University*	brand positioning, international branding, distribution rights, brand heritage
	OLC case	Going International with McDonald's *Justin O'Brien, Teaching Fellow, Royal Holloway, University of London and Eleanor Hamilton, Associate Dean for Undergraduate Studies, Lancaster University*	global positioning, international markets, barriers to success, diversification, 7 P'S

Preface to the 6th edition

Marketing is a vibrant, challenging activity that requires an understanding of both principles and how they can be applied in practice. The sixth edition of my book attempts to capture both aspects of the multidiscipline. Marketing concepts and principles are supported by examples of international practice to crystallize those ideas in the minds of students who may have little personal experience of real-life marketing.

My objective, then, was to produce a tightly written textbook supported by a range of international examples and case studies. In my experience, all types of students enjoy applying principles to real-life marketing problems. This is natural, as marketing does not exist in a vacuum; it is through application that students gain a richer understanding of marketing.

Becoming a successful marketing practitioner requires an understanding of the principles of marketing together with practical experience of implementing marketing ideas, processes and techniques in the marketplace. This book provides a framework for understanding important marketing issues such as understanding the consumer, marketing segmentation and positioning, brand building, pricing, innovation and marketing implementation, which form the backbone of marketing practice.

Marketing, as I have said, does not exist in a vacuum: it is a vibrant, sometimes energy-sapping profession that is full of exciting examples of success and failure. Moreover, marketing practitioners need to understand the changes that are taking place in the environment. Marketing-orientated companies are undergoing fundamental readjustments to their structure to cope with the accelerating rate of change. If you wish to enter the marketing profession then an acceptance of change and a willingness to work long hours are essential prerequisites.

Marketing in Europe has never looked stronger. International conferences organized by the European Marketing Academy and national organizations such as the Academy of Marketing in the UK make being a marketing academic challenging, rewarding and enjoyable. We should always value the companionship and pleasure that meeting fellow marketing academics brings. The growth in the number of students wishing to study marketing has brought with it a rise in the number of marketing academics in Europe. Their youth and enthusiasm bode well for the future of marketing as a major social science.

Most students enjoy marketing: they find it relevant and interesting. I hope that this book enhances your enjoyment, understanding and skills.

How to study

This book has been designed to help you to learn and to understand the important principles behind successful marketing and how these are applied in practice. We hope that you find the book easy-to-use and that you are able to follow the ideas and concepts explained in each chapter. As soon as you don't grasp something, go back and read it again. Try to think of *other* examples to which the theory could be applied. To check you really understand the new concepts you are reading about, try completing the exercises and questions at the end of each chapter. You can also test your understanding and expand your knowledge by exploring the Online Learning Centre.

To assist you in working through this text, we have developed a number of distinctive study and design features. To familiarize yourself with these features, please turn to the Guided Tour on pages xxi–xxiii.

New to the 6th edition

As always, recent events are reflected throughout this book. Here is a brief summary of the **key content changes** for this edition:

- **Brand new coverage of marketing metrics:** marketing managers are increasingly being asked to justify their marketing investments. In Chapter 21 Marketing Implementation, Organization and Control, the topic of marketing metrics is covered in detail. Even more information on this hot topic is provided on the website.

- **Fully revised coverage of Marketing Ethics and Corporate Social Responsibility:** ethical issues have become increasingly prevalent across all elements of marketing. In accordance with this, companies are expected to demonstrate corporate social responsibility in all of their business functions. Chapter 6 Understanding Marketing Ethics and Corporate Social Responsibility provides a thorough grounding to these key issues, which are also addressed in specific marketing contexts through dedicated sections found at the end of many chapters in the book and a suite of brand new Marketing Ethics and Corporate Social Responsibility in Action boxes throughout the book.

- **A fully revised and restructured Digital Marketing chapter:** since the previous edition, marketing applications of digital technology have continued to progress. Chapter 19 Digital Marketing has been revised to include all forms of digital marketing, including search engine optimization and affiliate marketing, and an expanded discussion on planning, implementing and evaluating digital marketing strategies. In every chapter there are brand new Digital Marketing vignettes showing how marketers are making use of new opportunities, such as social networking sites, widgets and the enhanced capacities of mobile phones.

- **Brand new vignettes, case studies and advertisements throughout the book:** The principles of marketing cannot be fully grasped without solid examples of how these apply in practice. That is why in every chapter you will find a wealth of examples to support the concepts presented. These include current advertisements, and vignettes spanning Marketing in Action, Digital Marketing and Marketing Ethics and Corporate Social Responsibility in Action, as well as Pause for Thought boxes that ask you to apply the principles learnt for yourself. Two case studies at the end of each chapter provide more in-depth examples. These features will not only help you to absorb the key principles of marketing, but will also allow you to make links between the various topics and demonstrate the marketing mix at work in real-life situations.

- **An exciting new package of supporting online resources**, including new video resources and cases, as well as a rich choice of activities designed to help students develop and apply their understanding of marketing concepts. See pages xxiv–xxvi for further details.

Guided Tour

Real marketing

Throughout the text, marketing principles are illustrated with examples of real marketing practice. The following features encourage you to pause to consider the decisions taken by a rich variety of companies.

3.2 Digital Marketing

Twittering Around the World

Twitter is a free-to-join social networking group, created in 2006. It has rapidly and currently has roughly 4–5 million users. Twitter enables members of the netw through quick and frequent online exchanges called 'tweets'. Tweets are text-ba 140 characters), which are displayed on the user's profile page and sent to oth as 'followers'. A typical tweet might explain what I am doing right now (e.g. 'S

Digital Marketing vignettes demonstrate how organizations have used new technologies in their marketing strategies.

9.1 Marketing Ethics and Corporate Social Responsibility in Action

Offsetting the Offsets

In an attempt to maintain positive brand associations, and to cope with new and s corporations are currently trying to reduce their environmental footprint through t such as carbon offsetting, energy efficiency and 'take-back' schemes. For exampl a system, on a trial basis, that asks consumers to dispose of excessive packaging aims to help consumers reduce household waste as well as examine what types

Marketing Ethics and CSR in Action vignettes examine ethical dilemmas and examples of how companies can engage in corporate social responsibility.

1.2 Pause for Thought

Think of a product that you consider is successful in the marketplace. Is its marke sense that product, price, promotion and distribution send a consistent, well-thou message to consumers?

Pause for thought boxes ask you to stop and think how you would act if faced with a real decision, typical real-life marketing practices.

16.1 Marketing in Action

Money-Off Promotional Blunders

Some of the world's best-known retail names have been caught up in promotion whose UK website advertised an Olympus digital camera for £98.70 rather th where a £287 iPaq handheld computer was mistakenly priced at £7.32; and on its DX3700 digital cameras advertised on its website was mispriced at £10

Perhaps the most renowned promotional blunder was Argos's £2.99 television.

Marketing in Action vignettes provide additional practical examples to highlight the application of concepts, and encourage you to critically analyse and discuss real-world issues.

▲ Green & Black's defends its position in the organic chocolate market by supplying Milk, Dark 70%, White and Creamy Milk brand varieties.

Real advertisements demonstrate how marketers have presented their products in real promotions and campaigns.

Full colour advertisements are included in every chapter and videoclips from television and online campaigns are available on the Online Learning Centre. Look out for the **Ad Insight** boxes.

Ad insight

Go to the website to see Honda's TV ad promoting its environmentally-friendly credentials

Each chapter concludes with two **case studies**. These up-to-date examples encourage you to apply what you have learned in each chapter to a real-life marketing problem.

You can test yourself by trying out the **questions** at the end of each case study section.

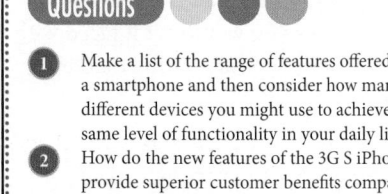

Questions

1. Make a list of the range of features offered by a smartphone and then consider how many different devices you might use to achieve the same level of functionality in your daily life.

2. How do the new features of the 3G S iPhone provide superior customer benefits compared to the earlier model?

3. Explain how smartphones are changing our daily lives and business activities.

4. Discuss how convergence might influence the development of future models of the iPhone.

This case was written by Fiona Ellis-Chadwick, Senior Lecturer in Retail Management, Open University.

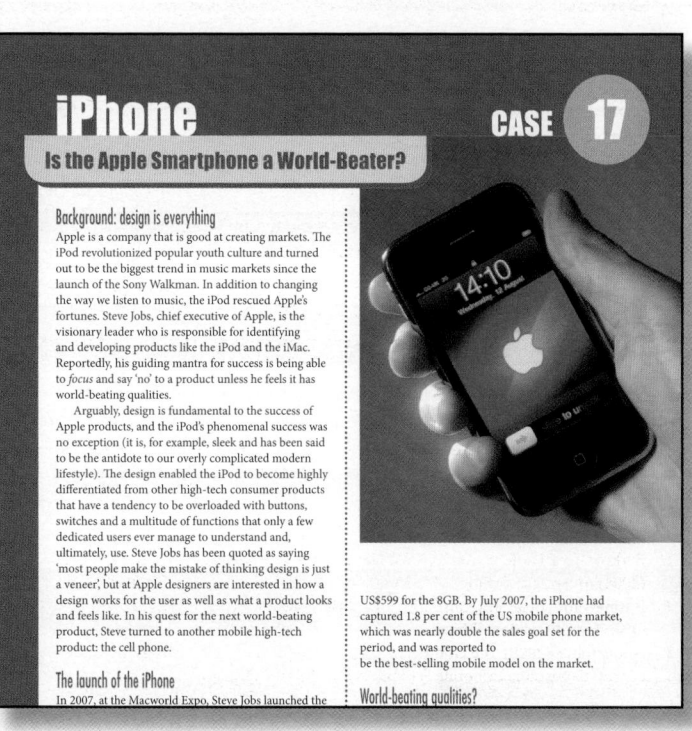

iPhone

Is the Apple Smartphone a World-Beater?

CASE **17**

Background: design is everything

Apple is a company that is good at creating markets. The iPod revolutionized popular youth culture and turned out to be the biggest trend in music markets since the launch of the Sony Walkman. In addition to changing the way we listen to music, the iPod rescued Apple's fortunes. Steve Jobs, chief executive of Apple, is the visionary leader who is responsible for identifying and developing products like the iPod and the iMac. Reportedly, his guiding mantra for success is being able to *focus* and say 'no' to a product unless he feels it has world-beating qualities.

Arguably, design is fundamental to the success of Apple products, and the iPod's phenomenal success was no exception (it is, for example, sleek and has been said to be the antidote to our overly complicated modern lifestyle). The design enabled the iPod to become highly differentiated from other high-tech consumer products that have a tendency to be overloaded with buttons, switches and a multitude of functions that only a few dedicated users ever manage to understand and, ultimately, use. Steve Jobs has been quoted as saying 'most people make the mistake of thinking design is just a veneer', but at Apple designers are interested in how a design works for the user as well as what a product looks and feels like. In his quest for the next world-beating product, Steve turned to another mobile high-tech product: the cell phone.

The launch of the iPhone

In 2007, at the Macworld Expo, Steve Jobs launched the

US$599 for the 8GB. By July 2007, the iPhone had captured 1.8 per cent of the US mobile phone market, which was nearly double the sales goal set for the period, and was reported to be the best-selling mobile model on the market.

World-beating qualities?

Studying effectively

At the beginning of each chapter, the main **learning objectives** are listed to show you what topics are covered in the chapter. Keep these aims in mind to help focus your reading and then check your understanding in the **review** at the end of the chapter.

Review

1 **The nature of the marketing environment**
- The marketing environment consists of the microenvironment (customers and suppliers) and the macroenvironment (economic, social, political, leg technological forces). These shape the character of the opportunities and th yet are largely uncontrollable.

LEARNING OBJECTIVES

After reading this chapter, you should be able to:

1 describe the nature of the marketing environment
2 explain the distinction between the microenvironment and the macroenvironment
3 discuss the impact of political and legal, economic, ecological/physical environmental, social/cultural and technological forces on marketing decisions
4 explain how to conduct environmental scanning

Key Terms

consumerism organized action against business practices that are not in the interests of consumers

corporate social responsibility the ethical principle that an organization should be accountable for how its

ecology the study of li

environmental scann analysing the marketi

Use the **Key Terms** list at the end of each chapter to look up any unfamiliar words, and as a handy aid for quick revision and review.

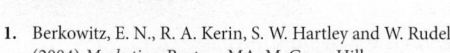

Study Questions

1 What are the advantages of market segmentation? Can you see any advantage market as homogeneous and marketing to the whole market with one market

2 Choose a market you are familiar with and use benefit segmentation to identi likely profiles of the resulting segments?

Use the **study questions** to review and apply the knowledge you have acquired from each chapter. These questions can be undertaken either individually or as a focus for group discussion in seminars or tutorials.

References

1. Berkowitz, E. N., R. A. Kerin, S. W. Hartley and W. Rudelius (2004) *Marketing*, Boston, MA: McGraw-Hill.
2. Business for Social Responsibility Issue Briefs (2003) Overview of Business Ethics, www.bsr.org.
3. Anonymous (2008) The Good Consumer, Economist Special Report on Corporate Social Responsibility

4. Bokaie, J. (2008) Beh 21 May, 14.
5. Franklin, D. (2008) J Report on Corporate
6. Naughton, J. (2006) (Great Firewall of Chi

Use the **references** at the end of the chapter to research an idea in greater depth.

Technology to Enhance Learning and Teaching

Visit www.mcgraw-hill.co.uk/textbooks/jobber today

For students: Online Learning Centre

The Online Learning Centre (OLC) is your gateway to a host of downloadable resources and activities designed to accompany the book.

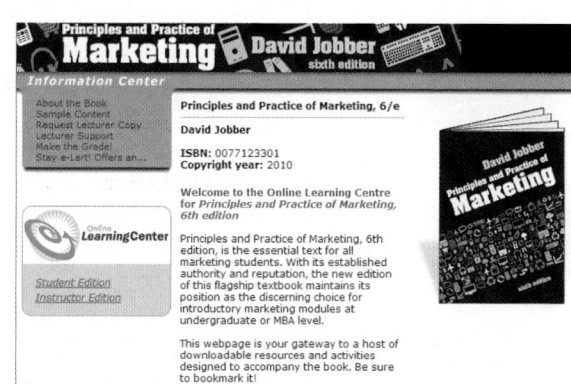

Help achieving top grades

- **Marketing skills personal development plan:** to help develop your marketing skills in four core areas: decision-making, communication, analysing and team working.
- **Tools to improve your study skills:** tips and book suggestions to help you write better essays, manage your time effectively and revise for exams.

Help for class assignments

- **Ad Insight video clips:** over 40 TV and cinema adverts, linked directly to topics in the book. Look out for the Ad Insight margin notes that refer you to the relevant clip, and answer the questions to develop your understanding of how these campaigns employ the concepts explained in the chapter.

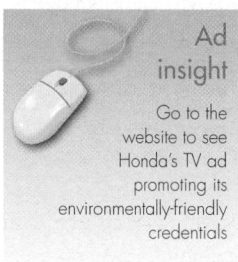

- **23 extra cases** and advice on how to approach assignments based on case studies and why this is a useful way to learn.
- **Internet marketing exercises** show you how to use companies' websites to gain insights into their digital marketing strategies and activities.
- **Ethical dilemma exercises** that enable you to test your understanding of ethical issues in marketing.
- **Marketing accountability and metrics:** provides an extended guide to this hot topic.
- **Marketing plan:** a template and completed example.
- **Weblinks** to the organisations mentioned in each chapter to support further research.

Revision aids

- **Self test questions** provide immediate feedback on your understanding
- **Audio summaries** of each chapter can be downloaded to help you revise key concepts.
- **Searchable glossary** to help you learn essential marketing terminology.

For Lecturers
Online Learning Centre

This collection of resources has been put together to help lecturers adopting this text save time when preparing their teaching and to help them engage and challenge their students so that they get more out of their course.

Visit www.mgraw-hill.co.uk/textbooks/jobber to access to a wealth of media to use in your lectures and tutorials, and ideas to use in assignments and assessments.

- **Teaching notes for all 69 cases** help guide discussion around the case questions
- **Video Ads:** recent TV and cinema adverts highlight marketing practice. Questions and suggested answers are provided to help stimulate student discussion.
- **Tutorial activities** designed to be completed and discussed within an hour – ideal for use in small groups and fully supported by teaching notes.
- **Exam questions and solutions**
- **Example solutions** to the study questions at the end of each chapter, case study questions and the Internet exercises.
- **Extra marketing examples** illustrating the concepts covered in each chapter.
- **PowerPoint slides** covering the main concepts in each chapter and supporting each of the end-of-chapter cases.
- **Artwork from the book** to illustrate lecture presentations or handouts.
- **Marketing skills personal development plan** provides ideas to help students develop core marketing skills and improve their employability.
- **Market research project:** can be used or adapted as an ongoing project over several tutorials.

McGraw-Hill EZ Test Online

This easy-to-use online testing tool accessible to busy academics virtually anywhere – in their office, at home or while travelling – and eliminates the need for software installation. Lecturers can choose from question banks associated with their adopted textbook or easily create their own questions. They also have access to hundreds of banks and thousands of questions created for other McGraw-Hill titles.

A bank of hundreds of multiple choice questions and essay titles is available to lecturers adopting this book. Questions are provided for each chapter and graded by difficulty and tagged by topic to help you to select questions that best suit your needs.

Multiple versions of tests can be saved for delivery on paper or online through WebCT, Blackboard and other course management systems. When created and delivered though EZ Test Online, students' tests can be immediately marked, saving lecturers time and providing prompt results to students.

To register for this FREE resource, visit **www.eztestonline.com**

Marketing Showcase

We are excited to offer an exclusive set of new video cases to lecturers adopting this text. Each video illustrates a number of core marketing concepts linked to the book to help students see how marketing works in the real world. This fantastic video resource will add real value to lectures, providing attention-grabbing content that helps students to make the connection between theory and practice.

What do the videos cover?

The videos offer students insights into how different organizations have successfully harnessed the elements of the marketing mix, including discussions about new product development, pricing, promotion, packaging, market research, relationship and digital marketing.

How can I use them?

To ensure maximum flexibility for teaching purposes, the videos have been edited to focus on key topics so that short extracts can be easily integrated into a lecture presentation or be delivered in a tutorial setting to spark class discussion. Each video is accompanied by teaching notes and discussion questions to ensure painless preparation for teaching.

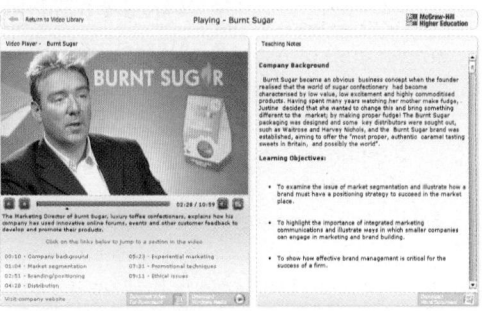

Custom Publishing Solutions: Let us help make our content your solution

Our **custom publishing solutions** offer the ideal combination of content delivered in the way which best suits lecturer and students. Lecturers can select just the chapters or sections of material they wish to deliver to their students from a database called Primis at **www.primisonline.com**

Primis contains over two million pages of content, including US and European material, from:

- McGraw-Hill Education textbooks
- Open University Press academic and study skills books
- Cases and articles from Harvard Business School, Insead, Ivey, and Darden
- Taking Sides – debate materials.

There is also the option to include additional material authored by lecturers in the custom product – this does not necessarily have to be in English.

We will take care of everything from start to finish in the process of developing and delivering a custom product to ensure that lecturers and students receive exactly the material needed in the most suitable way. Please contact your local McGraw-Hill representative with any questions or alternatively contact Warren Eels at **warren_eels@mcgraw-hill.com**.

About the Author

David Jobber is an internationally recognized marketing academic. He is Professor of Marketing at the University of Bradford School of Management. He holds an honours degree in Economics from the University of Manchester, a master's degree from the University of Warwick and a doctorate from the University of Bradford.

Before joining the faculty at the Bradford Management Centre, David worked for the TI Group in marketing and sales, and was Senior Lecturer in Marketing at the University of Huddersfield. He has wide experience of teaching core marketing courses at undergraduate, postgraduate and post-experience levels. His specialisms are industrial marketing, sales management and marketing research. He has a proven, ratings-based record of teaching achievements at all levels. His competence in teaching is reflected in visiting appointments at the universities of Aston, Lancaster, Loughborough and Warwick in the UK, and the University of Wellington, New Zealand. He has taught marketing to executives of such international companies as BP, Allied Domecq, the BBC, Bass, Croda International, Rolls-Royce, Royal & Sun Alliance and Rio Tinto.

Supporting his teaching is a record of achievement in academic research. David has over 150 publications in the marketing area in such journals as the *International Journal of Research in Marketing*, *MIS Quarterly*, *Strategic Management Journal*, *Journal of International Business Studies*, *Journal of Management*, *Journal of Business Research*, *Journal of Product Innovation Management* and the *Journal of Personal Selling and Sales Management*. David has served on the editorial boards of the *International Journal of Research in Marketing*, *Journal of Personal Selling and Sales Management*, *European Journal of Marketing* and the *Journal of Marketing Management*. He has also acted as Special Adviser to the Research Assessment Exercise panel that rated research output from business and management schools throughout the UK. In 2008, he received the Academy of Marketing's Life Achievement award for distinguished and extraordinary services to marketing.

Acknowledgements for the 6th Edition

I should like to thank my colleagues (past and present) at the University of Bradford School of Management for their stimulating insights and discussions. In particular, I should like to thank Martin Haley, Helen Preece and Sally Chan for their contributions to the website. I should also like to thank Conor Carroll from Limerick University for his outstanding contribution to the cases that appear in the book and on the website.

Thanks also to the contributors to the case competition. Their efforts appear both in the book and on the website. Fiona Ellis-Chadwick continues to make major contributions especially by deploying her talents to helping with the revision to the Digital Marketing chapter. Thanks also go to Fiona and David Bird for supplying most of the Digital Marketing vignettes. I am also indebted to Caroline Moraes for writing most of the Marketing Ethics and Corporate Social Responsibility vignettes.

I shall never forget the work of the tireless Chris Barkby, Dee Dwyer, Lynne Lancaster, Jackie Parker, Jo Cousins and Carole Zajac from Bradford School of Management and everyone from McGraw-Hill for their secretarial and administrative support. Finally, my thanks go to Janet Jobber for her help with researching the case material.

David Jobber

Publishers' Acknowledgements
McGraw-Hill would also like to thank the following people for their contributions to the text:

Sally Chan, *University of Leeds*
David Edmundson-Bird, *Manchester Metropolitan University*
Fiona Ellis-Chadwick, *Open University*
Martin Haley, *University of Bradford*
Caroline Moraes, *University of Birmingham*
Helen Preece, *University of Bradford*

We would like to thank the following people for their work on the cases:

Robert Anslow, *University of Limerick*
Ian Brace, *TNS UK*
Susan Bridgewater, *University of Warwick*
Matthew Caldwell, *University of Nottingham*
Marylyn Carrigan, *Open University*
Conor Carroll, *University of Limerick*
Ravi Chandran, *a major airline*
Trent Cottle, *BT*
Joseph Coughlan, *Dublin Institute of Technology*
Belinda Dewsnap, *Loughborough University*
Fiona Ellis-Chadwick, *Open University*
Laura Evans, *TNS IT & Telecoms*

Poul Faarup, *University of Southern Denmark*
Tony Garry, *De Montfort University*
Colin Gilligan, *Sheffield Hallam University and Newcastle University*
Eleanor Hamilton, *Lancaster University*
Tracey Harwood, *De Montfort University*
Graham Hooley, *Aston University*
Sara Kate Hurley, *University of Limerick*
Conor Kelleher, *Waterford Institute of Technology, Ireland*
Aileen Kennedy, *Dublin Institute of Technology*
Tony Lindley, *Tony Lindley Consultants Ltd and University of Bradford*
Luciana Lolich, *Dublin Business School*
Sheena MacArthur, *Glasgow Caledonian University*
Caroline Moraes, *University of Birmingham*
Anne Murray Chatterton, *Institute of Practitioners in Advertising*
Clive Nancarrow, *University of West England*
John Naughton, *University of Limerick*
Justin O'Brien, *Royal Holloway, University of London*
Marie O'Dwyer, *Waterford Institute of Technology, Ireland*
Michele O'Dwyer, *University of Limerick*
Daragh O'Reilly, *University of Sheffield*
Ken Peattie, *Cardiff University*
Loïc Plé, *IÉSEG School of Management, France*
Adrian Pritchard, *Coventry University*
Nina Reynolds, *University of Bradford*
Tony Rowe, *Marketing Mentors*
David Shipley, *Trinity College, University of Dublin*
Andrew Smith, *University of Nottingham*
Siobhan Tiernan, *University of Limerick*
Anne Treacy, *University of Limerick*
Caroline Tynan, *University of Nottingham*
Roisin Vize, *Dublin Institute of Technology*

Our thanks go to the following reviewers for their feedback on the fifth edition:

Efthymios Constantinides, *University of Twente*
Nnamdi Madichie, *University of East London*
Malcolm McDonald, *Cranfield University*
Tony McGuiness, *Aberyswyth University*
Nina Michaelidou, *University of Birmingham*
Stan Paliwoda, *Strathclyde University*
Lorna Stevens, *University of Ulster*

Finally, we are grateful to the following organisations for their permission to reproduce advertising or product images.

Part 1: Premier Foods, p.6 Toyota Motor Europe SA/NV, p.12 BSH Home Appliances, p.17 Apple Europe, p.30 iStockphoto/FuatKose, pp.33 & 35, H&M Hennes & Mauritz UK & Ireland, p.45 ABB Asia Brown Bovari, p.51 *The Economist*, p.52 Nielsen Media, p.42 Volvo Car Corporation, p.64 Volvo Ocean Race, p.66 iStockphoto © Thomas Vogel. **Part 2:** Toyota Motor Europe SA/NV, p.82 Hitachi Europe, p.83 BSH Home Appliances, p.88 innocent drinks, p.101 Sony Computer Entertainment UK, p.104 Sony Europe, p.107 iStockphoto

© Floria Marius Catalin, iStockphoto © Darko Radanovic, iStockphoto/Andrew Manley, iStockphoto © Catalin Plesa, and Alamy © David Bleaker Photography.com/Alamy, p.111 Virgin Media, p.118 Audi UK, p.127 Rolex and Unilever, p.141 Alamy © Peter Scholey/Alamy, p.144 Sony Europe, iStockphoto © Charles Taylor, iStockphoto © Devon Stephens and iStockphoto/redmal, p.151 Microsoft Corporation, p.153 Xerox Europe, p.154 Mercedes-Benz UK © Daimler AG, p.173 Scandinavian Airlines SAS International, p.177 iStockphoto/YinYang, p.188 Honda, p.195 Green & Black's, p.196 Unilever, p.208 Microsoft, p.213 New Media, p.214 The Fairtrade Foundation, p.221 Waitrose, p.242 Conquest Research and Consultancy, p.243 iStockphoto/Alex Nikada, p.255 Apple, p.257 Alamy © An Qi/Alamy, p.265 Nielsen Media, p.271 Unilever, p.276 Michelin Tyre, p.278 Nielsen Media, p.286 Land Rover and Rainey Kelly Campbell Roalfe/Y&R, p.294 Dell, p.296 Freud Communications, p.297 McDonald's. **Part 3:** Omega SA, p.307 Lego Bionicle, p.312 News International Syndication, p.315 Unilever, *The Guardian*, p.316 Cadbury's, p.325 Lucozade Sport GBM, p.329 Sony Australia and Euro RSCG, p.348 New Media, p.351 Alamy © Alex Segre/Alamy, p.356 Cadbury's, p.358 Nokia, pp.377 & 378 Unilever, p.380 and 381 Intel Corporation, p.387 Dyson, p.391 Nike, p.397 Anheuser-Busch InBev NV/SA, p.404 Philips. Philips trademarks are owned by Koninklijkc Philips Electronics NV, p.408 UKTV, p.415 BMW Group, p.418 Alamy © CW Images/Alamy, p.429 Travelodge, p.433 Nielsen Media, p.439 P&O Ferries, p.454 Alamy © Ian Miles-Flashpoint Pictures/Alamy, p.458 Alamy © TadhgD/Alamy, p.470 Land Rover and Rainey Kelly Campbell Roalfe/Y&R, p.471 Premier Foods Limited, pp.472 & 473 Nielsen Media, p.475 Diageo, p.480 KFC, p.496 Cadbury's, pp.497 & 498 Cadbury's and Falon, p.500 iStockphoto © Alex Branwell, p.542 Jupiter Images © Getty Images, p.544 iStockphoto/Kevin Miller, p.561 Virgin Holidays, p.566 Direct Line, p.568 Nielsen Media, pp.578–580 Diageo, p.582 Alamy © Ashley Cooper/Alamy, p.589 New Media, p.590 Honey Monster Foods, p.592 Caffe Nero, p.594 Specsavers, p.600 Coca-Cola Great Britain, Rugby Football Union, Steve Borthwick and Mother London, p.608 Omega, pp.614–617 Cadbury's, p.619 Alamy © Trinity Mirror/Mirrorpix/Alamy, p.623 Alamy © David Krausby/Alamy, p.628 Sainsbury's and Abbott Mead Vickers BBDO, p.646 UPS, p.657 Alamy © Chris Batson/Alamy, p.659 Apple Europe, p.663 Nokia, p.668 Robetboom, p.669 Nokia, p.677 Mercedes-Benz UK © Daimler AG, p.685 Apple Europe, p.696 Google, p.699 iStockphoto/MorePixels. **Part 4:** innocent drinks, p.717 Coors Brewers, p.721 Apple Europe, p.722 Bang & Olufsen, p.723 Levi Strauss, Bartle Bogle Hegarty and Joseph Rodriguez, p.731 Alamy © Juice Images/Alamy, p.735 Alamy © Maksymenko 1/Alamy, p.744 Marks and Spencer, p.746 Nielsen Media, p.752 Nokia, p.756 Green & Black's, p.764 iStockphoto © Dan Barnes, pp.766 & 768 Data Display. **Part 5:** Oxfam GB (Adapted by the publisher with the permission of Oxfam GB, Oxfam House, John Smith Drive, Cowley Oxford OX4 2JY, UK www.oxfam.org.uk. Oxfam GB does not necessarily endorse any text or activities that accompany the images, nor has it approved the adapted images.), p.777 Alamy © Trinity Mirror/Mirrorpix/Alamy, p.816 iStockphoto © Maciej Noskowski, p.818 Corbis © Christian Liewig/Liewig Media Sports/Corbis, p.835 Tesco, p.843 Nielsen Media, p.855 Oxfam GB (Reproduced with the permission of Oxfam GB, Oxfam House, John Smith Drive, Cowley Oxford OX4 2JY, UK www.oxfam.org.uk. Oxfam GB does not necessarily endorse any text or activities that accompany the advertisement.), pp.865 & 867 Build-a-Bear Workshop, p.867 Alamy © Alex Segre/Alamy, p.892 Lavazza, p.905 Alamy © Archimage/Alamy, p.908 IKEA.

Every effort has been made to trace and acknowledge ownership of copyright and to clear permission for material reproduced in this book. The publishers will be pleased to make suitable arrangements to clear permission with any copyright holders whom it has not been possible to contact.

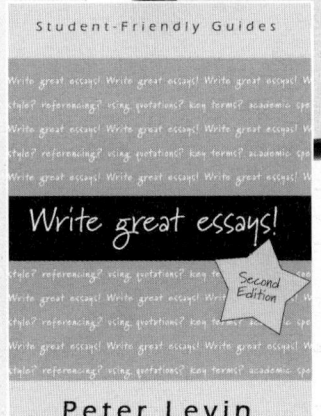
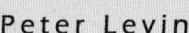

Fundamentals of Modern Marketing Thought

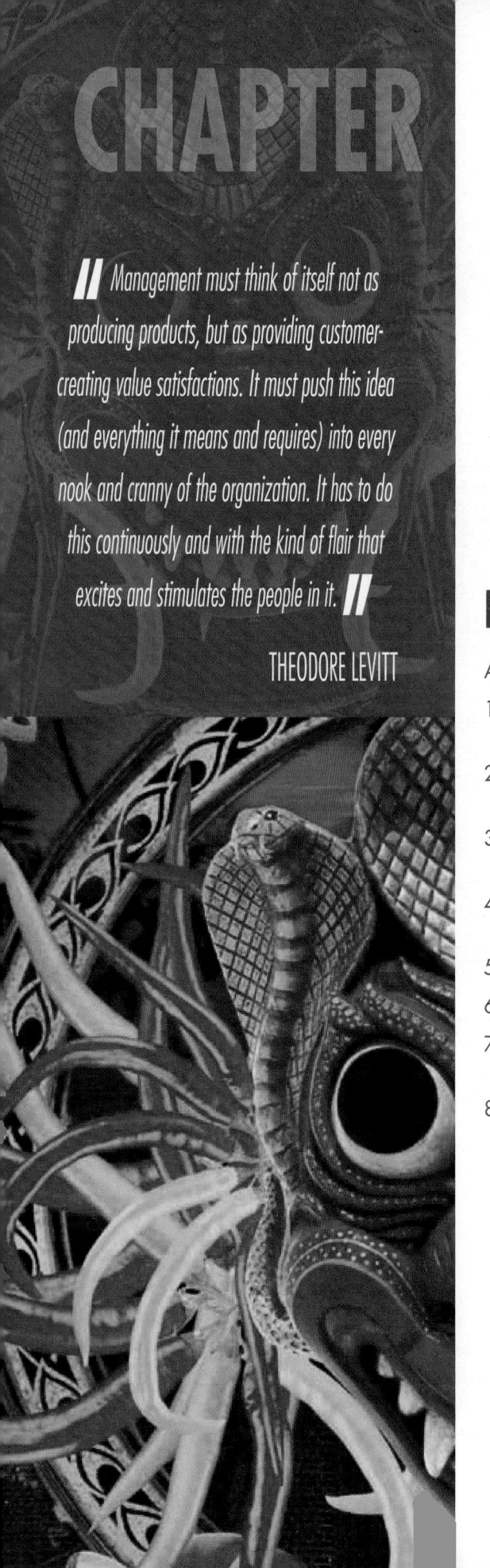

CHAPTER 1

Marketing in the modern organization

> *Management must think of itself not as producing products, but as providing customer-creating value satisfactions. It must push this idea (and everything it means and requires) into every nook and cranny of the organization. It has to do this continuously and with the kind of flair that excites and stimulates the people in it.*
>
> THEODORE LEVITT

LEARNING OBJECTIVES

After reading this chapter, you should be able to:

1. define the marketing concept and identify its key components and limitations

2. compare a production orientation and a marketing orientation

3. differentiate between the characteristics of market-driven and internally driven businesses

4. compare the roles of efficiency and effectiveness in achieving corporate success

5. describe how to create customer value and satisfaction

6. describe how an effective marketing mix is designed

7. discuss the criticisms of the 4-Ps approach to marketing management

8. explain the relationship between marketing characteristics, market orientation and business performance

In general, marketing has a bad press. Phrases like 'marketing gimmicks', 'marketing ploys' and 'marketing tricks' abound. The result is that marketing is condemned by association. Yet this is unfortunate and unfair because the essence of marketing is value not trickery. Successful companies rely on customers returning to repurchase; the goal of marketing is long-term satisfaction, not short-term deception. This theme is reinforced by the writings of top management consultant, the late Peter Drucker, who stated:[1]

> Because the purpose of business is to create and keep customers, it has only two central functions—marketing and innovation. The basic function of marketing is to attract and retain customers at a profit.

What can we learn from this statement? First, it places marketing in a central role for business success since it is concerned with the creation and retention of customers. Second, it implies that the purpose of marketing is not to chase any customer at any price. Drucker used profit as a criterion. While profit may be used by many commercial organizations, in the non-profit sector other criteria might be used such as social deprivation or hunger. Many of the concepts, principles and techniques described in this book are as applicable to Action Aid as to Renault.

Third, it is a reality of commercial life that it is much more expensive to attract new customers than to retain existing ones. Indeed, the costs of attracting a new customer have been found to be up to six times higher than the costs of retaining old ones.[2] Consequently marketing-orientated companies recognize the importance of building relationships with customers by providing satisfaction and attracting new customers by creating added value. Grönroos has stressed the importance of relationship building in his definition of marketing in which he describes the objective of marketing as to establish, develop and commercialize long-term customer relationships so that the objectives of the parties involved are met.[3] Finally, since most markets are characterized by strong competition, the statement also suggests the need to monitor and understand competitors, since it is to rivals that customers will turn if their needs are not being met.

Marketing exists through exchanges. **Exchange** is the act or process of receiving something from someone by giving something in return. The 'something' could be a physical good, service, idea or money. Money facilitates exchanges so that people can concentrate on working at things they are good at, earn money (itself an exchange) and spend it on products that someone else has supplied. The objective is for all parties in the exchange to feel satisfied so each party exchanges something of less value to them than that which is received. The idea of satisfaction is particularly important to suppliers of products because satisfied customers are more likely to return to buy more products than dissatisfied ones. Hence, the notion of customer satisfaction as the central pillar of marketing is fundamental to the creation of a stream of exchanges upon which commercial success depends.

The rest of this chapter will examine some of these ideas in more detail and provide an introduction to how marketing can create customer value and satisfaction.

The Marketing Concept

The above discussion introduces the notion of the marketing concept—that is, that companies achieve their profit and other objectives by satisfying (even delighting) customers.[4] This is the traditional idea underlying marketing. However, it neglects a fundamental aspect of commercial life: competition. The traditional marketing concept is a necessary but not a sufficient condition for corporate achievement. To achieve success, companies must go further than mere customer satisfaction; they must do better than the competition. Many also-ran products on the market could have been world-beaters in the mid-1990s. The difference is competition. The modern **marketing concept** can be expressed as:

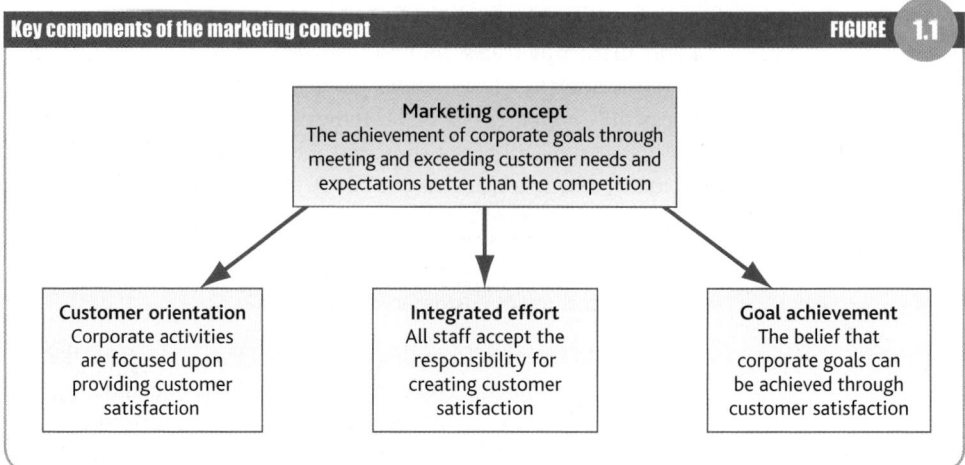

Key components of the marketing concept   **FIGURE 1.1**

The achievement of corporate goals through meeting and exceeding customer needs and expectations better than the competition.

To apply this concept, three conditions should be met. First, company activities should be focused upon providing customer satisfaction rather than, for example, producer convenience. This is not an easy condition to meet. Second, the achievement of customer satisfaction relies on integrated effort. The responsibility for the implementation of the concept lies not just within the marketing department. The belief that customer needs are central to the operation of a company should run right through production, finance, research and development, engineering and other departments. The role of the marketing department is to play *product champion* for the concept and to coordinate activities. But the concept is a business philosophy not a departmental duty. Finally, for integrated effort to come about, management must believe that corporate goals can be achieved through satisfied customers (see Fig. 1.1).

Marketing versus Production Orientation

There is no guarantee that all companies will adopt a **marketing orientation**. A competing philosophy is production orientation.* This is represented by an inward-looking stance that can easily arise given that many employees spend their working day at the point of production.

Production orientation manifests itself in two ways. First, management becomes cost-focused. It believes that the central focus of its job is to attain economies of scale by producing a limited range of products (at the limit, just one) in a form that minimizes production costs. Henry Ford is usually given as an example of a production-orientated manager because he built just one car in one colour—the black Model T—in order to minimize costs. However, this is unfair to Mr Ford since his objective was customer satisfaction: bringing the car to new

---

*This, of course, is not the only alternative business philosophy. For example, companies can be financially or sales orientated. If financially orientated, companies focus on short-term returns, basing decisions more on financial ratios than customer value; and sales-orientated companies emphasize sales push rather than adaptation to customer needs. Some textbooks even allude to the existence of eras of business orientation—production, product, selling and marketing—each with its own time zone, and this has entered marketing folklore. However, research has shown that such a sequence is based on the flimsiest of evidence and is oversimplified and misleading.[5] We shall concentrate on the fundamental difference in corporate outlook: marketing versus production orientation.

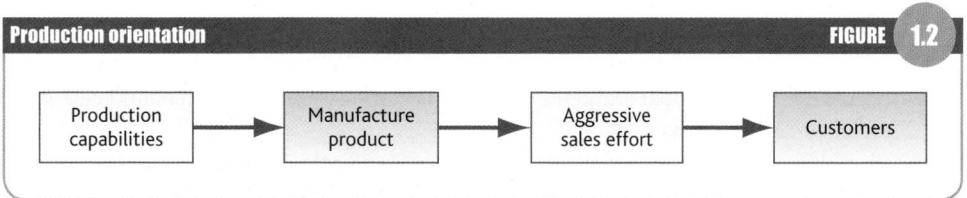

FIGURE 1.2

Production orientation

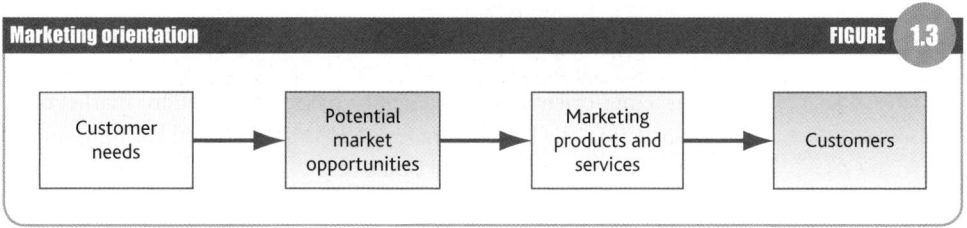

FIGURE 1.3

Marketing orientation

market segments through low prices. The real production-orientated manager has no such virtues. The objective is cost reduction for its own sake, an objective at least partially fuelled by the greater comfort and convenience that comes from producing a narrow product range.

The second way in which production orientation reveals itself is in the belief that the business should be defined in terms of its production facilities. Levitt has cited the example of film companies defining their business in terms of the product produced, which meant they were slow to respond when the demand to watch cinema films declined in the face of increasing competition for people's leisure time.[6] Had they defined their business in marketing terms—entertainment—they may have perceived television as an opportunity rather than a threat.

Figure 1.2 illustrates production orientation in its crudest form. The focus is on current production capabilities that define the business mission. The purpose of the organization is to manufacture products and aggressively sell them to unsuspecting customers. A classic example of the catastrophe that can happen when this philosophy drives a company is that of Pollitt and Wigsell, a steam engine producer that sold its products to the textile industry. It made the finest steam engine available and the company grew to employ over 1000 people on a 30-acre (12-hectare) site. Its focus was on steam engine production, so when the electric motor superseded the earlier technology it failed to respond. The 30-acre site is now a housing estate. Contrast the fortunes of Pollitt and Wigsell with another company operating in the textile industry at about the same time. This company made looms and achieved great success when it launched the type G power loom, which allowed one person to oversee 50 machines. Rather than defining its business as a power loom producer, the company adopted a marketing orientation and sought new opportunities in emerging markets. In 1929 the type G power loom patent was sold to fund the creation of a car division. The company was Toyota.[7]

Marketing-orientated companies focus on customer needs. Change is recognized as endemic and adaptation considered to be the Darwinian condition for survival. Changing needs present potential market opportunities, which drive the company. For example, the change towards ethical consumption has created opportunities for existing companies, such as Nestlé's launch of Partners' Blend, as well as opportunities for the creation and growth of new companies such as Cafédirect. Within the boundaries of their distinctive competences market-driven companies seek to adapt their product and service offerings to the demands of current and latent markets. This orientation is shown in Figure 1.3.

Marketing-orientated companies get close to their customers so that they understand their needs and problems. For example, Dürr AG, the German paint and assembly systems manufacturer, gets close to its customers by assigning over half its workforce to the sites of its customers, such as Ford and Audi. When personal contact is insufficient or not feasible, formal marketing research is commissioned to understand customer motivations and behaviour.

Part of the success of German machine tool manufacturers can be attributed to their willingness to develop new products with lead customers: those companies who themselves are innovative.[8] This contrasts sharply with the attitude of UK machine tool manufacturers, who saw marketing research as merely a tactic to delay new product proposals and who feared that involving customers in new product design would have adverse effects on the sales of current products. Marketing orientation is related to the strategic orientation of companies. Marketing-orientated firms adopt a proactive search for market opportunities, use market information as a base for analysis and organizational learning, and adopt a long-term strategic perspective on markets and brands.[9]

Marketing in Action 1.1 describes how a move to a marketing orientation has laid the foundations for success at Toyota.

Market-Driven versus Internally Orientated Businesses

A deeper understanding of the marketing concept can be gained by contrasting in detail a market-driven business with one that is internally orientated. Table 1.1 summarizes the key differences.

Market-driven companies display customer concern throughout the business. All departments recognize the importance of the customer to the success of the business. Nestlé, for example, has placed the customer at the centre of its business philosophy by giving the company's head of marketing responsibility for the company's seven strategic business units. Marketers also control strategy, research and development, and production.[10] In internally focused businesses convenience comes first. If what the customer wants is inconvenient to produce, excuses are made to avoid giving it.

Market-driven businesses know how their products and services are being evaluated against those of the competition. They understand the choice criteria that customers are using and ensure that their marketing mix matches those criteria better than that of the competition.

Businesses that are driven by the market base their segmentation analyses on customer differences that have implications for marketing strategy. Businesses that are focused internally segment by product (e.g. large bulldozers versus small bulldozers) and consequently are vulnerable when customers' requirements change.

A key feature of market-driven businesses is their recognition that marketing research expenditure is an investment that can yield rich rewards through better customer understanding. We saw in Marketing in Action 1.1 how Toyota based its new marketing strategy on a customer research survey. Internally driven businesses see marketing research as a non-productive intangible and prefer to rely on anecdotes and received wisdom. Market-orientated

The new Avensis with Toyota Optimal Drive.

You'll be impressed even before you drive it.

Today Tomorrow Toyota

◀ Toyota's Optimal Drive technology provides customer benefits of enhanced performance, lower emissions and better fuel economy.

1.1 Marketing in Action

Marketing Orientation Brings Success to Toyota

Toyota GB is the national sales and marketing company responsible for sales and after-sales service for Toyota cars and commercial vehicles in the UK. Its success is reflected in sales growth in every year since 1992 until the onset of the economic recession. Despite a consistent upward trend, the decade has seen the implementation of two fundamentally different philosophies. From 1992 to 1997, Toyota's market share grew from 2.6 per cent to 3.3 per cent as a result of a 'push' strategy fuelled by the achievement of short-term sales targets and focused on selling low-cost Japanese-designed cars. The approach was supported by a major tactical incentive programme but with little marketing or brand investment.

Despite this short-term success, Toyota GB management considered the strategy unsustainable as low-price competitors began to match its offer, resulting in lower profit margins.

Based on a major customer research survey, the company began to be marketing led. The brand values of Toyota cars were mapped out, and the emphasis moved from the aggressive selling of cars to understanding what the Toyota brand meant to customers and how the company could better meet their needs. The marketing research budget was increased by a factor of four and the company worked much more closely with its Japanese parent and European cousin to ensure that new models were aligned more effectively to the requirements of the European customer. One consequence of this is the successful launch of the European-designed Yaris. Other aspects of marketing changed too: expenditure was moved from tactical incentives to media advertising ('Today, Tomorrow, Toyota') and Toyota GB worked with its dealers to transfer the new values and culture to the car showroom.

Toyota GB has also improved the service it provides for its customers. With an average owner's purchase cycle of about 3.7 years and lengthening intervals between services, contact between Toyota and its customers (through its dealers) was sparse. The company decided to review its customer communication channels, resulting in the creation of a single customer database that forms the backbone of all Toyota communications. Communications are further enhanced by a revamped website, customer magazine, customer experience surveys and the Toyota Club for premium customers.

The result is that customer perception of Toyota cars has moved from 'cheap and reliable' to 'a quality car at competitive prices'. Toyota's commitment to innovation has resulted in Toyota Optimal Drive technology (see illustration). Market share has risen to almost 5 per cent over the past five years, together with a healthy rise in profit margins. Toyota's brand loyalty is now over 50 per cent, making it the market leader in retained business.

Paul Philpott, marketing director of Toyota GB, says there are four key learning points from this story: (i) make marketing the number one priority in your company; (ii) put the views of your customers before your own; (iii) invest for the future; and (iv) be patient.

Toyota GB's success has been mirrored globally. The company's marketing expertise and innovative culture, which is reflected in its ground-breaking petrol-hybrids, including the Prius and Lexus, has resulted in it becoming the world's biggest car maker, surpassing General Motors in 2008.

Based on: Simms (2002);[11] Anonymous (2005);[12] Anonymous (2005);[13] Clark (2009)[14]

Marketing-orientated businesses	TABLE 1.1
Market-driven businesses	**Internally orientated businesses**
Customer concern throughout business	Convenience comes first
Know customer choice criteria and match with marketing mix	Assume price and product performance key to most sales
Segment by customer differences	Segment by product
Invest in market research (MR) and track market changes	Rely on anecdotes and received wisdom
Welcome change	Cherish status quo
Try to understand competition	Ignore competition
Marketing spend regarded as an investment	Marketing spend regarded as a luxury
Innovation rewarded	Innovation punished
Search for latent markets	Stick with the same
Being fast	Why rush?
Strive for competitive advantage	Happy to be me-too
Efficient and effective	Efficient

businesses welcome the organizational changes that are bound to occur as an organization moves to maintain strategic fit between its environment and its strategies. In contrast, internally orientated businesses cherish the status quo and resist change.

Attitudes towards competition also differ. Market-driven businesses try to understand competitive objectives and strategies, and anticipate competitive actions. Internally driven companies are content to ignore the competition. Marketing spend is regarded as an investment that has long-term consequences in market-driven businesses. The alternative view is that marketing expenditure is viewed as a luxury that never appears to produce benefits.

In marketing-orientated companies those employees who take risks and are innovative are rewarded. Recognition of the fact that most new products fail is reflected in a reluctance to punish those people who risk their career championing a new product idea. Internally orientated businesses reward time-serving and the ability not to make mistakes. This results in risk avoidance and the continuance of the status quo. Market-driven businesses search for latent markets: markets that no other company has exploited. 3M's Post-it product filled a latent need for a quick, temporary attachment to documents, for example. The radio station Classic FM has become successful by filling the latent need for accessible classical music among people who wished to aspire to this type of music but were somewhat intimidated by the music and style of presentation offered by Radio 3. A third example is the online auction site eBay, which exploited the latent market consisting of individuals who wished to sell products directly to other people and required a forum in which to do so. Finally, Nintendo identified a latent market for electronic games with the launch of its Brain Training software for the Nintendo DS, targeted at older people. Internally driven businesses are happy to stick with their existing products and markets.

Intensive competition means that companies need to be fast to succeed. Market-driven companies are fast to respond to latent markets, innovate, manufacture and distribute their products and services. They realize that strategic windows soon close.[15] Dallmer, chief executive of a major European company, told a story that symbolizes the importance of speed to competitive success.[16] Two people were walking through the Black Forest where it was rumoured a very dangerous lion lurked. They took a break and were sitting in the sun when one of them changed out of his hiking boots and into his jogging shoes. The other one smiled and, laughing, asked, 'You don't think you can run away from the lion with those jogging shoes?' 'No,' he replied, 'I just need to be faster than you!' Internally driven companies when they spot an opportunity take their time. 'Why rush?' is their epitaph.

A key feature of marketing-orientated companies is that they strive for competitive advantage. They seek to serve customers better than the competition. Internally orientated companies are happy to produce me-too copies of offerings already on the market. Finally, marketing-orientated companies are both efficient and effective; internally orientated companies achieve only efficiency. The concepts of efficiency and effectiveness are discussed in the next section.

Ad insight

Go to the website to see how Panasonic markets its Lumix camera in a competitive market

Efficiency versus Effectiveness

Another perspective on business philosophy can be gained by understanding the distinction between efficiency and effectiveness.[17] **Efficiency** is concerned with inputs and outputs. An efficient firm produces goods economically: it does things right. The benefit is that the cost per unit of output is low and, therefore, the potential for offering low prices to gain market share, or charging medium to high prices and achieving high profit margins, is present. For example, car companies attempt to achieve efficiency by gaining economies of scale and building several models on the same sub-frame and with the same components. However, to be successful, a company needs to be more than just efficient—it needs to be effective as well. **Effectiveness** means doing the right things. This implies operating in attractive markets and making products that consumers want to buy. Conversely, companies that operate in unattractive markets or are not producing what consumers want to buy will go out of business; the only question is one of timing.

The link between performance and combinations of efficiency and effectiveness can be conceived as shown in Figure 1.4. A company that is both inefficient and ineffective will go out of business quickly because it is a high-cost producer of products that consumers do not want to buy. One company that has suffered through a combination of inefficiency and ineffectiveness is General Motors. The inefficiency is the result of the legacy of paying healthcare costs to its current and retired workers—this adds $1500 to the cost of each of its cars; the ineffectiveness stems from a history of making unreliable and undesirable cars.[18]

A company that is efficient and ineffective may last a little longer because its low cost base may generate more profits from the dwindling sales volume it is achieving. Kodak is an example of an efficient and ineffective company. It is an efficient producer of photographic film but has become ineffective as consumers have moved to digital photography.[19] Firms that are effective but inefficient are likely to survive because they are operating in attractive markets and are marketing products that people want to buy. Mercedes used to fall into this

Efficiency and effectiveness   FIGURE **1.4**

	Ineffective	Effective
Inefficient	Goes out of business quickly	Survives
Efficient	Dies slowly	Does well Thrives

category, with its emphasis on over-engineering pushing up costs and lowering efficiency, while still making cars that people wanted to buy (driving an S500 has been likened to 'being wrapped in a freshly laundered silk sheet and blown up the road by a warm wind')[20] and so achieving effectiveness. The problem is that their inefficiency is preventing them from reaping the maximum profits from their endeavours. Many small companies that operate in niche markets fall into the effective/inefficient category. One example is Porsche, which is a highly effective maker of premium-priced aspirational sports cars. Its small size relative to other car manufacturers renders the company inefficient by comparison. It is this inefficiency that has led to Porsche acquiring Volkswagen to give it the scale to reduce costs and fund the research and development needed to produce innovative, technology-leading new models.[21] It is the combination of both efficiency and effectiveness that leads to optimum business success. Such firms do well and thrive because they are operating in attractive markets, are supplying products that consumers want to buy and are benefiting from a low cost base.

Toyota is an example of an efficient and effective company. Its investment in innovative manufacturing practices and modern technology ensures efficiency, while its ability to build cars that people want to buy (see Marketing in Action 1.1) proves its effectiveness.

Another company that has thrived through a combination of efficiency and effectiveness is Zara, the Spanish fashion chain. By using its own highly automated manufacturing and distribution facilities, seamstresses in 350 independently owned workshops in Spain and Portugal, and low advertising expenditures (its shops have always been its primary marketing tool), Zara has achieved high levels of efficiency. It is also highly effective through its ability to match fashion trends that change quickly by means of an extremely fast and responsive supply chain. The result is that Zara has become the world's largest clothing retailer.[22]

The essential difference between efficiency and effectiveness, then, is that the former is cost focused while the latter is customer focused. An effective company has the ability to attract and retain customers.

Limitations of the Marketing Concept

A number of academics have raised important questions regarding the value of the marketing concept. Four issues—the marketing concept as an ideology, marketing and society, marketing as a constraint on innovation, and marketing as a source of dullness—will now be explored.

The marketing concept as an ideology

Brownlie and Saren argue that the marketing concept has assumed many of the characteristics of an ideology or an article of faith that should dominate the thinking of organizations.[23] They recognize the importance of a consumer orientation for companies but ask why, after 40 years of trying, the concept has not been fully implemented. They argue that there are other valid considerations that companies must take into account when making decisions (e.g. economies of scale) apart from giving customers exactly what they want. Marketers' attention should therefore be focused not only on propagation of the ideology but also on its integration with the demands of other core business functions in order to achieve a compromise between the satisfaction of consumers and the achievement of other company requirements.

Marketing and society

A second limitation of the marketing concept concerns its focus on individual market transactions. Since many individuals weigh heavily their personal benefits while discounting the societal impact of their purchases, the adoption of the marketing concept will result in the production of goods and services that do not adequately correspond to societal welfare. Providing customer satisfaction is simply a means to achieve a company's profit objective and does not guarantee protection of the consumer's welfare. This view is supported by Wensley, who regards consumerism as a challenge to the adequacy of the atomistic and individual view of market transactions.[24] An alternative view is presented by Bloom and Greyser, who regard consumerism as the ultimate expression of the marketing concept compelling marketers to consider consumer needs and wants that hitherto may have been overlooked:[25] 'The resourceful manager will look for the positive opportunities created by consumerism rather than brood over its restraints.'

Companies are responding to the challenge of societal concerns in various ways. Marketing Ethics and Corporate Social Responsibility in Action 1.1 describes how company and government collaboration resulted in a social marketing campaign to control obesity. Other companies are responding to society's concern for the environment (see the illustration overleaf from Bosch).

 **1.1 Marketing Ethics and Corporate Social Responsibility in Action**

Using Social Marketing to Combat the Obesity Crisis

Overeating has become a pressing health issue in many developed countries—for example, in the UK, where 9000 premature deaths per year are linked to obesity. Government data suggest that obesity-related illnesses will cost the tax payer £50 billion by 2050, and up to 90 per cent of today's children will be obese or overweight by the same year if current trends continue. In an attempt to raise public awareness of the link between obesity and life-threatening diseases such as coronary heart disease and diabetes, the UK Government financed a £75 million social marketing campaign, which drew an additional £200 million worth of services and marketing support from a variety of companies and organizations, including supermarkets, large food producers, health clubs, the London Marathon, voluntary groups and a wide-ranging media coalition. Rather than shocking people into healthier lifestyles, the Change4Life TV campaign used light-hearted animation to inform consumers of the threats posed by sedentary lifestyles, and drew particular attention to the need for children to eat more healthily and become more active.

The campaign is a social marketing effort aimed at employing the power of marketing tools and concepts to achieve specific behavioural goals for increased societal welfare. Although the initiative has been welcomed by most stakeholders, some have criticized the government's choice to engage in corporate partnerships, as food corporations and supermarkets are seen as part of the issue. Indeed, some of the food companies supporting the campaign are junk food manufacturers, which in turn have been accused of 'back-door' marketing targeted at school children. Also, a few supermarkets have been blamed for pushing foods high in salt, fat and sugar as cheap and credit crunch-friendly options for hard-pressed consumers. As a result, critics have suggested that the use of legislation to protect children from junk food marketing, food reformulation and effective nutritional labelling enforcement would be far better investments than the Change4Life campaign. Others, however, have argued that such private partnerships will be positive in that they will put junk food companies under the spotlight, while making them subject to public scrutiny due to their commitments to a health-related cause. Time will show the effectiveness of such partnerships and social marketing in the fight against obesity.

Based on: Boseley (2009);[26] Sweeney (2009);[27] Watts (2009);[28] National Social Marketing Centre[29]

▲ Bosch reduces energy consumption (an environmental concern) while offering cost savings to consumers.

Marketing as a constraint on innovation

In an influential article, Tauber presented a third criticism of marketing—that is, how marketing research discourages major innovation.[30] The thrust of his argument was that relying on customers to guide the development of new products has severe limitations. This is because customers have difficulty articulating needs beyond the realm of their own experience. This suggests that the ideas gained from marketing research will be modest compared to those coming from the 'science push' of the research and development laboratory. Brownlie and Saren agree that, particularly for discontinuous innovations (e.g. Xerox, penicillin), the role of product development ought to be far more proactive than this.[31] Indeed technological innovation is the process that 'realizes' market demands that were previously unknown. Thus the effective exploitation and utilization of technology in developing new products is at least as important as market-needs analysis.

However, McGee and Spiro point out that these criticisms are not actually directed at the marketing concept itself but towards its faulty implementation: an overdependence on customers as a source of new product ideas.[32] They state that the marketing concept does not suggest that companies must depend solely on the customer for new product ideas; rather the concept implies that new product development should be based on sound interfacing between perceived customer needs and technological research. Project SAPPHO, which investigated innovation in the chemical and scientific instrument industries, found that successful innovations were based on a good understanding of user needs.[33] Unsuccessful innovations, on the other hand, were characterized by little or no attention to user needs.

Marketing as a source of dullness

A fourth criticism of marketing is that its focus on analysing customers and developing offerings that reflect their needs leads to dull marketing campaigns, me-too products, copycat promotion and marketplace stagnation. Instead, marketing should create demand rather than reflect demand. As Brown states, consumers should be 'teased, tantalized and tormented by deliciously insatiable desire'.[34] This approach he terms 'retromarketing', and says that it is built on five principles: exclusivity, secrecy, amplification, entertainment and tricksterism.

Exclusivity is created by deliberately holding back supplies and delaying gratification. Consumers are encouraged to 'buy now while stocks last'. The lucky ones are happy in the knowledge that they are the select few, the discerning elite. Short supply of brands like Harley-Davidson (motorcycles), certain models of Mercedes cars and even the BMW Mini has created an aura of exclusivity.

The second principle of retromarketing—secrecy—has the intention of teasing would-be purchasers. An example is the pre-launch of the blockbuster *Harry Potter and the Goblet of Fire,* which involved a complete blackout of advance information. The book's title, price and review copies were withheld, and only certain interesting plot details were drip-fed to the press. The result was heightened interest, fed on a diet of mystery and intrigue.

Even exclusive products and secrets need promotion, which leads to the third retromarketing principle of amplification. This is designed to get consumers talking about the 'cool' motorbike or the 'hot' film. Where promotional budgets are limited, this can be achieved by creating outrage (e.g. the controversial Benetton ads, including one showing a dying AIDS victim and his family) or surprise (e.g. the placing of a Pizza Hut logo on the side of a Russian rocket).

Entertainment is the fourth principle, so that marketing engages consumers. This, claims Brown, is 'modern marketing's greatest failure' with marketing losing its sense of fun in its quest to be rigorous and analytical. The final principle of retromarketing is tricksterism. This should be done with panache and audacity as when Britvic bought advertising time to make what appeared to be a public service announcement. Viewers were told that some rogue grocery stores were selling an imitation of its brand, Tango. The difference could be detected because it was not fizzy and they were asked to call a freefone number to name the outlets. Around 30,000 people rang, only to be informed that they had been tricked ('Tango'd') as part of the company's promotion for a new, non-carbonated version of the drink. Despite attracting censure for abusing the public information service format the promotion had succeeded in amplifying the brand extension launch and reinforcing Tango's irreverent image.

Creating Customer Value and Satisfaction

Customer value

Marketing-orientated companies attempt to create **customer value** in order to attract and retain customers. Their aim is to deliver superior value to their target customers. In doing so, they implement the marketing concept by meeting and exceeding customer needs better than the competition. For example, the global success of McDonald's has been based on creating added value for its customers, which is based not only on the food products it sells but on the complete delivery system that goes to make up a fast-food restaurant. It sets high standards in quality, service, cleanliness and value (termed QSCV). Customers can be sure that the same high standards will be found in all of the McDonald's outlets around the world. This example shows that customer value can be derived from many aspects of what the company delivers to its customers—not just the basic product.

Customer value is dependent on how the customer perceives the benefits of an offering and the sacrifice that is associated with its purchase. Therefore:

Customer value = perceived benefits − perceived sacrifice

Perceived benefits can be derived from the product (for example, the taste of the hamburger), the associated service (for example, how quickly customers are served and the cleanliness of the outlet) and the image of the company (for example, whether the image of the company/product is favourable). If one of those factors—for example, product benefits—changes then the perceived benefits and customer value also change. For instance, the downturn in the fortunes of McDonald's a few years ago was largely attributed to the trend towards healthier eating. This caused some consumers to regard the product benefits of its food to be less, resulting in lower perceived benefits and reduced customer value. In an attempt to redress the situation McDonald's has introduced healthy-eating options including salad and fruit.[35]

A further source of perceived benefits is the relationship between customer and supplier. Customers may enjoy working with suppliers with whom they have developed close personal and professional friendships, and value the convenience of working with trusted partners.

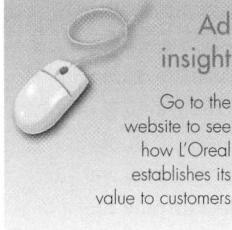

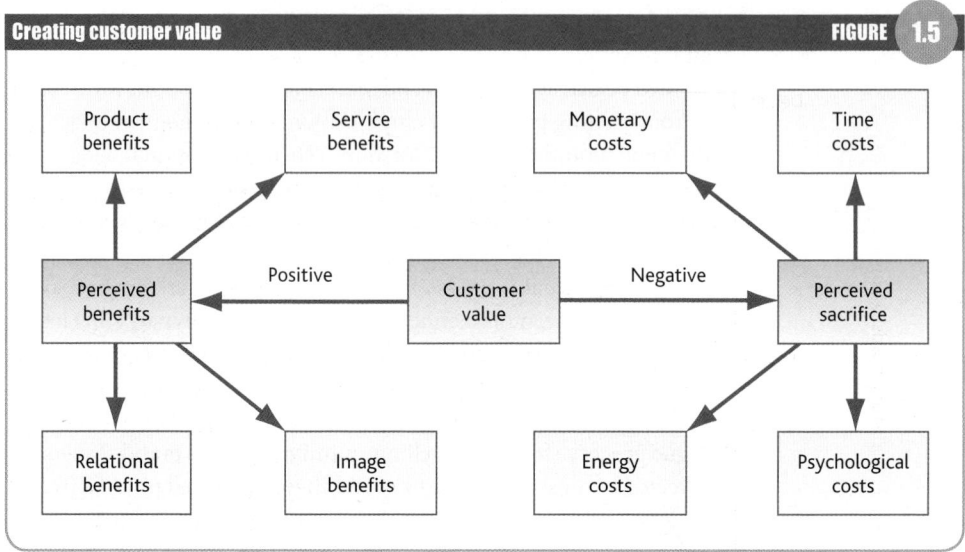

Creating customer value   FIGURE 1.5

Perceived sacrifice is the total cost associated with buying a product. This consists of not just monetary cost but the time and energy involved in purchase. For example, with fast-food restaurants, good location can reduce the time and energy required to find a suitable eating place. But marketers need to be aware of another critical sacrifice in some buying situations. This is the potential psychological cost of not making the right decision. Uncertainty means that people perceive risk when purchasing. McDonald's attempts to reduce perceived risk by standardizing its complete offer so that customers can be confident of what they will receive before entering its outlets. In organizational markets, companies offer guarantees to reduce the risk of purchase. Figure 1.5 illustrates how perceived benefits and sacrifice affect customer value. It provides a framework for considering ways of maximizing value. The objective is to find ways of raising perceived benefits and reducing perceived sacrifice.

Customer satisfaction

Exceeding the value offered by competitors is key to marketing success. Consumers decide upon purchases on the basis of judgements about the values offered by suppliers. Once a product has been bought, **customer satisfaction** depends upon its perceived performance compared to the buyer's expectations. Customer satisfaction occurs when perceived performance matches or exceeds expectations. Successful companies, such as Canon, Nokia, Toyota, Samsung, H&M, Apple and Virgin, all place customer satisfaction at the heart of their business philosophy. Companies facing difficulties, such as General Motors, Chrysler, Gap and Kodak, have failed to do so as customers' needs and expectations have changed.

An example of a company that is flourishing as a result of creating customer satisfaction is ASOS, the online fashion retailer. It is succeeding by satisfying young women's desire to replicate the look of their favourite celebrities. The company does this by offering affordable versions of celebrity styles, showing online how to copy the designer looks of magazine favourites such as Victoria Beckham, Lindsay Lohan and Jennifer Lopez at a fraction of the cost.[36] Expectations are formed by suppliers' marketing activities, discussions with other people and post-buying experiences. All these play a part with ASOS, including its website, which allows visitors to view dresses from several angles and watch models display the clothing along the catwalk.[37]

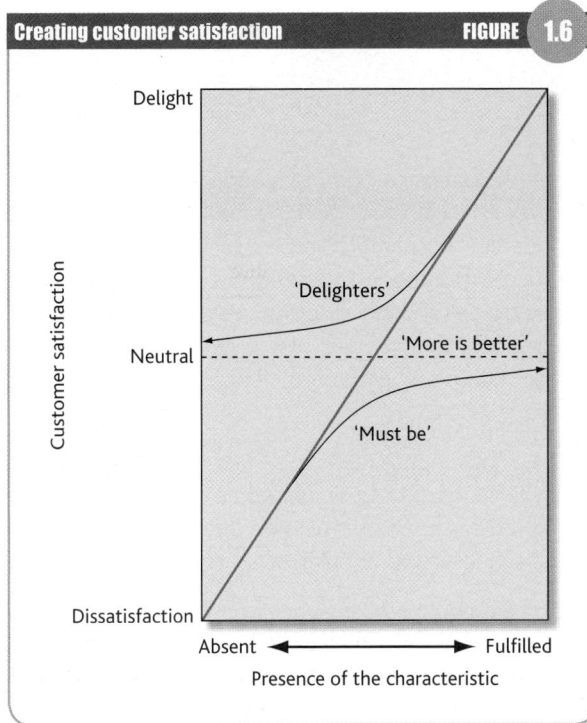

Creating customer satisfaction   FIGURE 1.6

Customer satisfaction is taken so seriously by some companies that financial bonuses are tied to it. For example, two days after taking delivery of a new car, BMW (and Mini) customers receive a telephone call to check on how well they were treated in the dealership. The customer is asked 15 questions, with each question scored out of 5. The franchised dealership only receives a financial bonus from BMW if the average score across all questions is 92 or better (5 is equivalent to 100, 4 to 80, and so on). Customer satisfaction with after-sales service is similarly researched. Aspiring dealerships have to be capable of achieving such scores, and existing dealerships that consistently fail to meet these standards are under threat of franchise termination.

This makes a great deal of sense as higher levels of customer satisfaction are associated with higher levels of customer retention, financial performance and shareholder value.[38]

In today's competitive climate, it is often not enough to match performance and expectations. Expectations need to be exceeded for commercial success so that customers are delighted with the outcome. In order to understand the concept of customer satisfaction the so-called 'Kano model' (see Fig. 1.6) helps to separate characteristics that cause dissatisfaction, satisfaction and delight. Three characteristics underlie the model: 'Must be', 'More is better' and 'Delighters'.

'Must be' characteristics are expected to be present and are taken for granted. For example, in a hotel, customers expect service at reception and a clean room. Lack of these characteristics causes annoyance but their presence only brings dissatisfaction up to a neutral level. 'More is better' characteristics can take satisfaction past neutral into the positive satisfaction range. For example, no response to a telephone call can cause dissatisfaction, but a fast response may cause positive satisfaction or even delight. 'Delighters' are the unexpected characteristics that surprise the customer. Their absence does not cause dissatisfaction but their presence delights the customer. For example, a UK hotel chain provides free measures of brandy in the rooms of its adult guests. This delights many of its customers, who were not expecting this treat. Another way to delight the customer is to under-promise and over-deliver (for example, by saying that a repair will take about five hours but getting it done in two).[39]

A problem for marketers is that, over time, delighters become expected. For example, some car manufacturers provided small unexpected delighters such as pen holders and delay mechanisms on interior lights so that there is time to find the ignition socket at night. These are standard on most cars now and have become 'Must be' characteristics as customers expect them. This means that marketers must constantly strive to find new ways of delighting. Innovative thinking and listening to customers are key ingredients in this. Marketing in Action 1.2 explains how to listen to customers.

The importance of customer satisfaction is supported by studies which show that higher levels of customer satisfaction lead to higher financial (profits and sales) performance,[40] greater customer loyalty[41] and the willingness of customers to pay higher prices.[42]

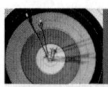
1.2 Marketing in Action

Listening to Customers

Top companies recognize the importance of listening to their customers as part of their strategy to manage satisfaction. Customer satisfaction indices are based on surveys of customers, and the results plotted over time to reveal changes in satisfaction levels. The first stage is to identify those characteristics (choice criteria) that are important to customers when evaluating competing products. The second stage involves the development of measurement scales (often statements followed by strongly agree/strongly disagree response boxes) to quantitatively assess satisfaction. Customer satisfaction data should be collected over a period of time to measure change. Only long-term measurement of satisfaction ratings will provide a clear picture of what is going on in the marketplace.

The critical role of listening to customers in marketing success was emphasized by Tom Leahy, chief executive of Tesco, the successful UK supermarket chain, when talking to a group of businesspeople. 'Let me tell you a secret,' he said, 'the secret of successful retailing. Are you ready? It's this: never stop listening to customers, and giving them what they want. I'm sorry if that is a bit of an anticlimax ... but it is that simple.'

Marketing research can also be used to question new customers about why they first bought, and lost customers (defectors) on why they have ceased buying. In the latter case, a second objective would be to stage a last-ditch attempt to keep the customer. One bank found that a quarter of its defecting customers would have stayed had the bank attempted to rescue the situation.

One company that places listening to customers high on its list of priorities is Kwik-Fit, the car repair group. Customer satisfaction is monitored by its customer survey unit, which telephones 5000 customers a day within 72 hours of their visit to a Kwik-Fit centre.

Another more hands-on approach to listening to customers is that taken by Feargal Quinn, founder of the highly successful Dublin-based supermarket chain Superquinn. He devotes a portion of every week to walking around his supermarkets talking to customers. 'Believe me, when you do experience the emotional strength of a customer's reaction, you are much more likely to do something about it,' he says.

A strategy also needs to be put in place to manage customer complaints, comments and questions. A system needs to be set up that solicits feedback on product and service quality, and feeds the information to the appropriate employees. To facilitate this process, front-line employees need training to ask questions, to listen effectively, to capture the information and to communicate it so that corrective action can be taken.

The Internet is providing other ways of listening to customers. Consumers write blogs, which can contain positive and/or negative comments about companies and brands. A blog is a personal commentary, a collection of thoughts and comments, which creates a kind of personal diary on the Internet. Companies can listen to what is being said about them and their brands by using a blog search engine such as Technorati, which also identifies the writer of the blog. This means that companies not only have a major research tool but also a means of responding to comments—both positive and negative.

Companies can also launch websites to solicit customers' ideas. Dell did this after it received a flood of criticism over poor customer service, while also reaching out to online bloggers. The feedback led to a customer services overhaul and a fall in negative buzz. Finally, Google listens to customers by releasing most products in 'beta' (which means they are not quite finished), allowing users to suggest improvements. This approach has led to the refinement of such products as Google News, Gmail and the Chrome browser.

Based on: Jones and Sasser Jr (1995);[43] Morgan (1996);[44] White (1999);[45] Roythorne (2003);[46] Ryle (2003);[47] Mitchell (2005);[48] Wright (2006);[49] Jarvis (2009)[50]

Developing an Effective Marketing Mix

Based on its understanding of customers, a company develops its **marketing mix**. The marketing mix consists of four major elements: product, price, promotion and place. These '4-Ps' are the four key decision areas that marketers must manage so that they satisfy or exceed customer needs better than the competition. In other words, decisions regarding the marketing mix form a major aspect of marketing concept implementation. The third part of this book looks at each of the 4-Ps in considerable detail. At this point, it is useful to examine each element briefly so that we can understand the essence of marketing mix decision-making.

Product

The **product** decision involves deciding what goods or services should be offered to a group of customers. An important element is new product development. As technology and tastes change, products become out of date and inferior to those of the competition, so companies must replace them with features that customers value. As new products are developed that give greater benefits than old ones market leadership can change. For example, the Sony Walkman was the market leader in portable music players. Following its launch, the Apple iPod soon outsold the Walkman, however, as it had the advantages of being able to download music and hold thousands of songs on a much smaller device From the first iPod, Apple has developed a product range to cater for diverse customer needs (see illustration).

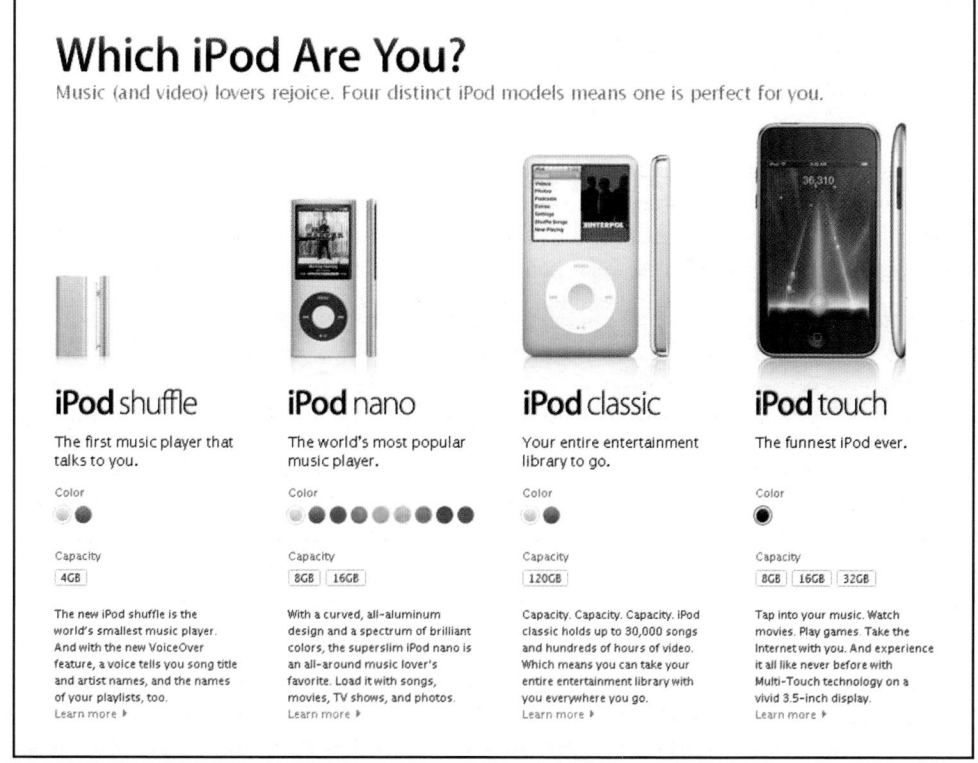

▲ Apple has extended the iPod brand to cater for diverse customer requirements.

Product decisions also involve choices regarding brand names, guarantees, packaging and the services that should accompany the product offering. Guarantees can be an important component of the product offering. For example, the operators of the AVE, Spain's high-speed train, capable of travelling at 300 kmph, are so confident of its performance that they guarantee to give customers a full refund of their fare if they are more than five minutes late.

1.1 Pause for Thought

Think of a product that you have bought recently. What features pleased you? Were there any surprises that delighted you? Were there any disappointments? Imagine you are a consultant for the company that supplies the product. Given your experiences with the product, have you any recommendations for improving its ability to give customer satisfaction?

Price

Price is a key element of the marketing mix because it represents on a unit basis what the company receives for the product or service that is being marketed. All of the other elements represent costs—for example, expenditure on product design (product), advertising and salespeople (promotion), and transportation and distribution (place). Marketers, therefore, need to be very clear about pricing objectives, methods and the factors that influence price setting. They must also take into account the necessity to discount and give allowances in some transactions. These requirements can influence the level of list price chosen, perhaps with an element of negotiation margin built in. Payment periods and credit terms also affect the real price received in any transaction. These kinds of decisions can affect the perceived value of a product.

Because price affects the value that customers perceive they get from buying a product, it can be an important element in the purchase decision. Some companies attempt to position themselves as offering lower prices than their rivals. For example, supermarkets such as Asda (Wal-Mart) in the UK, Aldi in Germany, Netto in Denmark and Super de Boer in the Netherlands employ a low-price positioning strategy. Another strategy is to launch a low-price version of an existing product targeted at price-sensitive consumers. For example, Apple launched the Mac mini, a basic version of the Macintosh computer. With this low-priced machine Apple believes it can tempt people who have bought an iPod (and become fans of the company) to ditch their Windows-based PCs and switch to the Mac mini.[51]

Promotion

Decisions have to be made with respect to the **promotional mix**: advertising, personal selling, sales promotions, public relations, direct marketing and online promotion. By these means the target audience is made aware of the existence of a product or service, and the benefits (both economic and psychological) it confers to customers. Each element of the promotional mix has its own set of strengths and weakness, and these will be explored in the second part of this book. Advertising, for example, has the property of being able to reach wide audiences very quickly. Procter & Gamble used advertising to reach the emerging market of 290 million Russian consumers. It ran a 12-minute commercial on Russian television as its first promotional venture in order to introduce the company and its range of products.[52] Advertising can be a powerful tool in a recession. While its competitors cut back on advertising expenditure during the Great Depression of 1929, Procter & Gamble increased its spend. The company dominated share of voice in radio advertising, bringing market leadership during the 1930s and the creation of the platform that has led to its continuing success to the present day.[53]

The Internet is of increasing importance as a promotional tool. A great advantage of the Internet is its global reach. This means that companies that did not have the resources to promote overseas can reach consumers worldwide by creating a website. In business-to-business markets, suppliers and customers can communicate using the Internet and purchases can be made using e-marketplaces. The Internet has also proven to be a powerful communication tool, sometimes replacing traditional media. For example, Arctic Monkeys, a UK rock band, built up their fan base online before signing a record deal, by placing demo tracks on their website and MySpace, a social networking site that allows downloading and sharing among music fans. The band's popularity soared through viral word of mouth, resulting in number-one single and album hits.[54]

However, social networking sites do pose challenges to marketers, as Digital Marketing 1.1 explains.

1.1 Digital Marketing

What Opportunities do Social Media Environments Offer?

The marketer's use of social media environments is still in its infancy. Social networking environments, such as Facebook and Twitter, provide opportunities for organizations to engage in a direct dialogue with individuals rather than just attempt to market to them.

The promise of an economically viable, direct, one-to-one dialogue between customers and companies seems to be a nirvana that marketers have been seeking for years. Examples of this include GlassesDirect, which uses the Twitter application to publicly respond to direct queries from customers browsing its website. This creates a kind of on-the-fly FAQ (frequently asked questions) as well as demonstrating a swift level of customer response. Microsoft employees actively use their staff blogs to engage with software developer customers, by opening up the process of software design for others to see and comment on. But environments such as Facebook and Twitter do have emerging problems that companies are finding difficult to grasp.

Social networkers appear to resent direct marketing via the environment they choose to use to communicate with others. The Twitter developers have a policy of resisting non-relevant direct marketing (and actively close down the accounts of 'Twitter-spammers'). In addition, the 'conversation' between social networkers may not be in the best interests of the company. Many Facebook groups have been set up by users to complain vociferously about organizations: HSBC famously reversed a policy decision on student debt after thousands of graduates and undergraduates of British universities joined a group to voice their opposition to the action.

Used well, social media environments can be a new channel into difficult-to-reach markets. But many organizations are still learning the hard way that such environments can actually be very negative places to engage with customers.

Useful further reading: Charles (2007)[55]

Place

Place involves decisions concerning the distribution channels to be used and their management, the locations of outlets, methods of transportation and inventory levels to be held. The objective is to ensure that products and services are available in the proper quantities, at the right time and place. Distribution channels consist of organizations such as retailers or wholesalers through which goods pass on their way to customers. Producers need to manage their relationships with these organizations well because they may provide the only cost-effective access to the marketplace. They also need to be aware of new methods of distribution that can create a competitive advantage. For example, Dell revolutionized the distribution of computers by selling direct to customers rather than using traditional computer outlets. Music, too, is increasingly being distributed by downloading from the Internet rather than being bought at music shops.

Following this trend, Radiohead offered fans the opportunity to pay whatever they liked to download their new album, and the rock band Nine Inch Nails released theirs as a free download from the band's website.[56]

Key Characteristics of an Effective Marketing Mix

There are four hallmarks of an effective marketing mix (see Fig. 1.7).

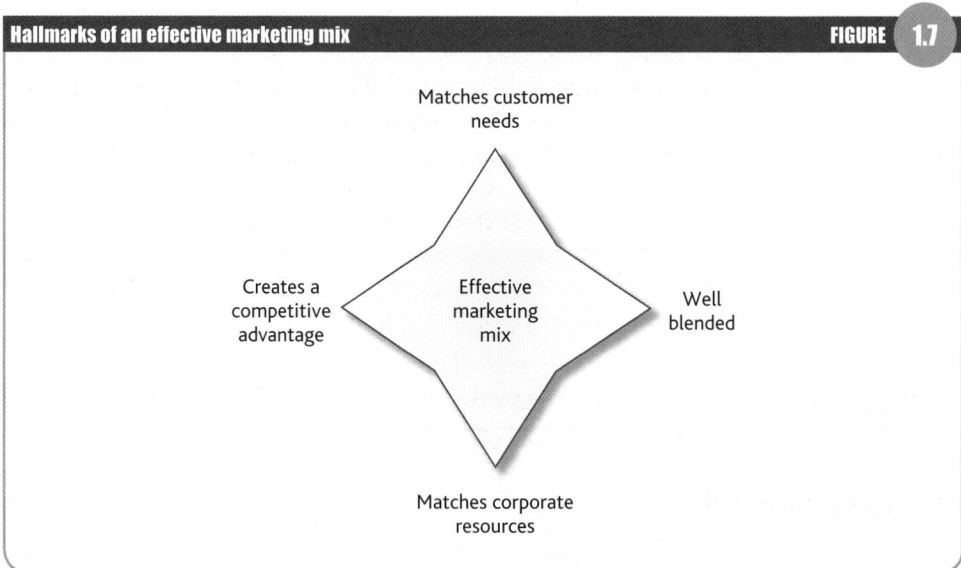

Hallmarks of an effective marketing mix   FIGURE **1.7**

The marketing mix matches customer needs

Sensible marketing mix decisions can be made only when the target customer is understood. Choosing customer groups to target will be discussed in Chapter 8, which examines the process of market segmentation and target marketing. Once the decision about the target market(s) is taken, marketing management needs to understand how customers choose between rival offerings. They need to look at the product or service through customers' eyes and understand, among other factors, the choice criteria they use.

Figure 1.8 illustrates the link between customer choice criteria and the marketing mix. The starting point is the realization that customers evaluate products on economic and psychological criteria. Economic criteria include factors such as performance, availability,

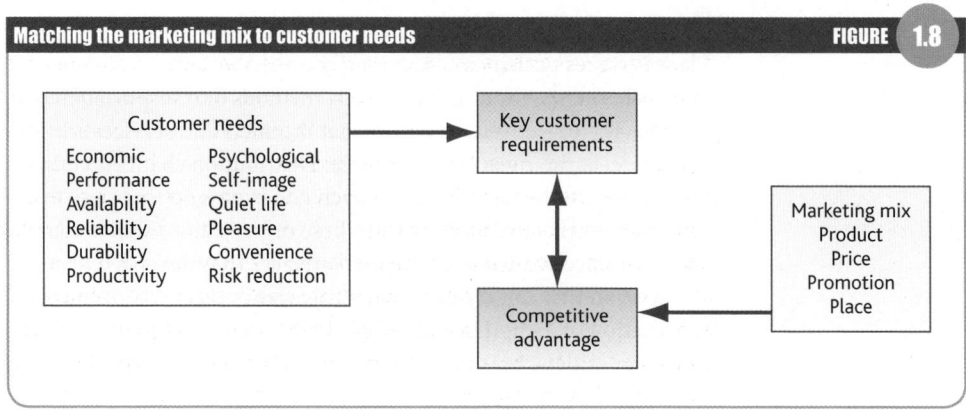

Matching the marketing mix to customer needs   FIGURE **1.8**

reliability, durability and productivity gains to be made by using the product. Examples of psychological criteria are self-image, a desire for a quiet life, pleasure, convenience and risk reduction. These will be discussed in detail in Chapter 4. The important point at this stage is to note that an analysis of customer choice criteria will reveal a set of key customer requirements that must be met in order to succeed in the marketplace. Meeting or exceeding these requirements better than the competition leads to the creation of a competitive advantage.

The marketing mix creates a competitive advantage

A **competitive advantage** may be derived from decisions about the 4-Ps. A competitive advantage is the achievement of superior performance through differentiation to provide superior customer value or by managing to achieve lowest delivered cost. The example of the Apple iPod is an example of a company using product features to convey customer benefits in excess of what the competition is offering. The iPod's small size and its ability to download and store music can, therefore, be regarded as the creation of competitive advantages over the previous market leader in portable music players, the Sony Walkman. Aldi, the German supermarket chain, achieves a competitive advantage by severely controlling costs, allowing it to make profits even though its prices are low, a strategy that is attractive to price-sensitive shoppers. Marketing in Action 1.3 explains how Cobra beer has gained a competitive advantage.

1.3 Marketing in Action

Spare the Gas with Cobra Beer

Before Cobra beer, British Asian curry eaters faced a problem: what drink to order with a curry. Often Asian cuisine overpowered the taste of wine, and standard beers or lagers were too gassy. Cobra beer's competitive advantages were its 'less gassy' nature and its Indian heritage. Positioned as an Indian lager, Cobra has seen massive growth since its launch in 1989 and is now regarded as a natural accompaniment to Asian meals. It is now available in a selection of ranges, including the double-fermented King Cobra, Cobra Light, Cobra 0% and the Cobra Bite range of fruit-flavoured premium beers. The company has also signed new deals to offer the drink in bottles, cans and on draught.

It is now available in bars, pubs and restaurants in almost 50 countries around the world. Its success is based on marketing fundamentals: meeting a customer need (a less gassy, suitable accompaniment for Asian food); better than the competition (wine and standard beers and lagers).

Based on: Fernandez (2008)[57]

The strategy of using advertising as a tool for competitive advantage is often employed when product benefits are particularly subjective and amorphous in nature. Thus the advertising for perfumes such as those produced by Chanel, Givenchy and Yves St Laurent is critical in preserving the exclusive image established by such brands. The size and quality of the salesforce can act as a competitive advantage. A problem that a company such as Rolls-Royce, the aeroengine manufacturer, faces is the relatively small size of its salesforce compared to those of its giant competitors Boeing and General Electric. Finally, distribution decisions need to be made with the customer in mind, not only in terms of availability but also with respect to service levels, image and customer convenience. The Radisson SAS hotel at Manchester Airport is an example of creating a competitive advantage through customer convenience. It is situated five minutes' walk from the airport terminals, which are reached by covered walkways. Guests at rival hotels have to rely on taxis or transit buses to reach the airport.

The marketing mix should be well blended

The third characteristic of an effective marketing mix is that the four elements—product, price, promotion and place—should be well blended to form a consistent theme. If a product gives superior benefits to customers, price, which may send cues to customers regarding quality, should reflect those extra benefits. All of the promotional mix should be designed with the objective of communicating a consistent message to the target audience about these benefits, and distribution decisions should be consistent with the overall strategic position of the product in the marketplace. The use of exclusive outlets for upmarket fashion and cosmetic brands—Armani, Christian Dior and Calvin Klein, for example—is consistent with their strategic position.

1.2 Pause for Thought

Think of a product that you consider is successful in the marketplace. Is its marketing mix well blended in the sense that product, price, promotion and distribution send a consistent, well-thought-out and appealing message to consumers?

The marketing mix should match corporate resources

The choice of marketing mix strategy may be constrained by the financial resources of the company. Laker Airlines used price as a competitive advantage to attack British Airways and TWA in transatlantic flights. When they retaliated by cutting their airfares, Laker's financial resources were insufficient to win the price war. Certain media—for example, television advertising—require a minimum threshold investment before they are regarded as feasible. In the UK a rule of thumb is that at least £5 million per year is required to achieve impact in a national advertising campaign. Clearly those brands that cannot afford such a promotional budget must use other less expensive media—for example, posters or sales promotion—to attract and hold customers.

A second internal resource constraint may be the internal competences of the company. A marketing mix strategy may be too ambitious for the limited marketing skills of personnel to implement effectively. While an objective may be to reduce or eliminate this problem in the medium to long term, in the short term marketing management may have to heed the fact that strategy must take account of competences. An area where this may manifest itself is within the place dimension of the 4-Ps. A company lacking the personal selling skills to market a product directly to end users may have to use intermediaries (distributors or sales agents) to perform that function.

Criticisms of the 4-Ps Approach to Marketing Management

Some critics of the 4-Ps approach to the marketing mix argue that it oversimplifies the reality of marketing management. Booms and Bitner, for example, argue for a 7-Ps approach to services marketing.[58] Their argument, which will be discussed in some detail in Chapter 22 on services marketing, is that the 4-Ps do not take sufficient account of people, process and physical evidence. In services, people often *are* the service itself; the process or how the service is delivered to the customer is usually a key part of the service, and the physical evidence—the décor of the restaurant or shop, for example—is so critical to success that it should be considered as a separate element in the services marketing mix.

Rafiq and Ahmed argue that this criticism of the 4-Ps can be extended to include industrial marketing.[59] The interaction approach to understanding industrial marketing stresses that success does not come solely from manipulation of the marketing mix components but long-term relationship building, whereby the bond between buyer and seller becomes so strong that it effectively acts as a barrier to entry for out-suppliers.[60] This phenomenon undoubtedly exists to such an extent that industrial buyers are now increasingly seeking long-term supply relationships with suppliers. For example, car manufacturers have drawn up long-term contracts with preferred suppliers that provide stability in supply and improvements in new component development. Bosch, the German producer of industrial and consumer goods, conducts quality audits of its suppliers. These kinds of activities are not captured in the 4-Ps approach, it is claimed.

Nevertheless, there is no absolute reason why these extensions cannot be incorporated within the 4-Ps framework.[61] People, process and physical evidence can be discussed under 'product', and long-term relationship building under 'promotion', for example. The important issue is not to neglect them, whether the 4-Ps approach or some other method is used to conceptualize the decision-making areas of marketing. The strength of the 4-Ps approach is that it represents a memorable and practical framework for marketing decision-making and has proved useful for case study analysis in business schools for many years.

Marketing and Business Performance

The basic premise of the marketing concept is that its adoption will improve business performance. Marketing is not an abstract concept: its acid test is the effect that its use has on key corporate indices such as profitability and market share. Fortunately, in recent years, two quantitative studies in both Europe and North America have sought to examine the relationship between marketing and performance. The results suggest that the relationship is positive. We will now examine each of the studies in turn.

Marketing characteristics and business performance

In a study of 1700 senior marketing executives, Hooley and Lynch reported the marketing characteristics of high- versus low-performing companies.[62] The approach that they adopted was to isolate the top 10 per cent of companies (based on such measures as profit margin, return on investment and market share) and to compare their marketing practices with the remainder of the sample. The 'high fliers' differed from the 'also-rans' as follows:

- more committed to marketing research
- more likely to be found in new, emerging or growth markets
- adopted a more proactive approach to marketing planning
- more likely to use strategic planning tools
- placed more emphasis on product performance and design, rather than price, for achieving a competitive advantage
- worked more closely with the finance department
- placed greater emphasis on market share as a method of evaluating marketing performance.

Marketing orientation and business performance

Narver and Slater studied the relationship between marketing orientation and business performance.[63] Marketing orientation was based on three measures: customer orientation, competitor orientation, and degree of inter-functional coordination. They collected data from 113 strategic business units (SBUs) of a major US corporation.

The businesses comprised 36 commodity businesses (forestry products) and 77 non-commodity businesses (speciality products and distribution businesses). They related each SBU's profitability, as measured by return on assets in relation to competitors over the last year in the SBU's principal served market, to their three-component measure of market orientation.

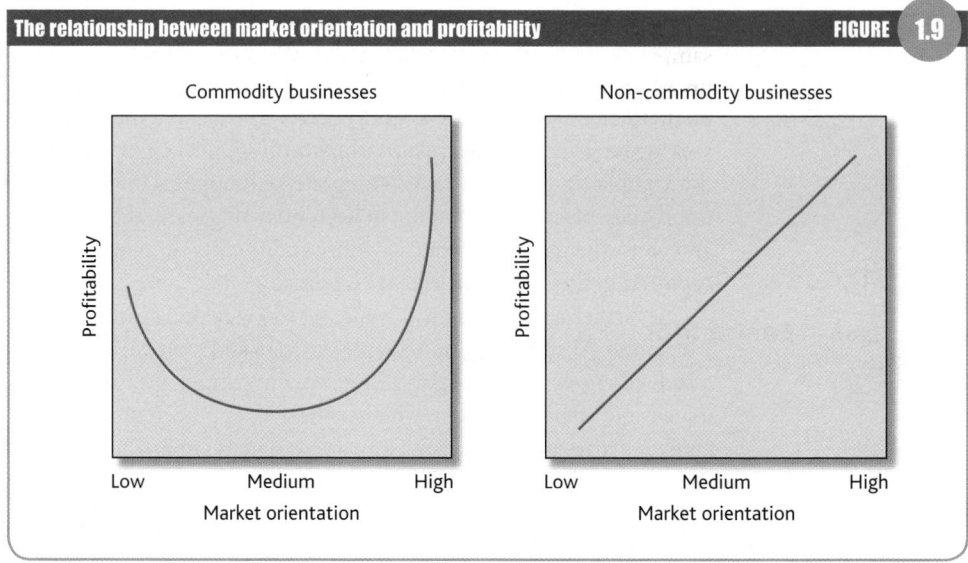

The relationship between market orientation and profitability   FIGURE **1.9**

Figure 1.9 shows the results of their study. For commodity businesses the relationship was U-shaped, with low and high market-orientation businesses showing higher profitability than the businesses in the mid-range of market orientation. Businesses with the highest market orientation had the highest profitability and those with the lowest market orientation had the second highest profitability. Narver and Slater explained this result by suggesting that the businesses lowest in market orientation may achieve some profit success through a low cost strategy, though not the profit levels of the high market-orientation businesses, an explanation supported by the fact that they were the largest companies of the three groups.

For the non-commodity businesses the relationship was linear, with the businesses displaying the highest level of market orientation achieving the highest levels of profitability and those with the lowest scores on market orientation having the lowest profitability figures. As the authors state, 'The findings give marketing scholars and practitioners a basis beyond mere intuition for recommending the superiority of a market orientation.'

A number of more recent studies have also found a positive relationship between market orientation and business performance. Market orientation has been found to have a positive effect on sales growth, market share and profitability,[64] sales growth,[65] sales growth and new product success,[66] perception of product quality[67] and overall business performance.[68]

Finally, a study by Kirca, Jayachandran and Bearden analysed the empirical findings from a wide range of studies that sought to identify the antecedents and consequences of marketing orientation.[69] Their findings showed that a marketing orientation led to higher overall business performance (higher profits, sales and market share), better customer consequences (higher perceived quality, customer loyalty and customer satisfaction), better innovative consequences (higher innovativeness and better new product performance) and beneficial employee consequences (higher organizational commitment, team spirit, customer orientation and job satisfaction, and lower role conflict). Their analysis of the antecedents of marketing orientation showed the importance of top management emphasis on marketing, good communications between departments and systems that reward employees for market success for the implementation of marketing orientation.

So, what overall conclusions can be drawn from these studies? In order to make a balanced judgement their limitations must be recognized. Most were cross-sectional studies based on self-reported data. With any such survey there is the question of the direction of causality. Perhaps some respondents inferred their degree of marketing orientation by reference to their performance level. However, this clearly did not occur with the commodity sample in the Narver and Slater study.[70] What these studies have consistently and unambiguously shown is a strong association between marketing and business performance. As one condition for establishing causality, this is an encouraging result for those people concerned with promoting the marketing concept as a guiding philosophy for business.

When you have read this chapter

log on to the Online Learning Centre at www.mcgraw-hill.co.uk/ textbooks/jobber to explore chapter-by-chapter test questions, links and further online study tools for marketing.

Review ● ● ●

1 **The marketing concept: an understanding of the nature of marketing, its key components and limitations**
- The marketing concept is the achievement of corporate goals through meeting and exceeding customer needs better than the competition.
- It exists through exchanges where the objective is for all parties in the exchange to feel satisfied.
- Its key components are customer orientation, integrated effort and goal achievement (e.g. profits).
- The limitations of the concept are that the pursuit of customer satisfaction is only one objective companies should consider (others, such as achieving economies of scale, are equally valid), the adoption of the marketing concept may result in a focus on short-term personal satisfaction rather than longer-term societal welfare, the focus on customers to guide the development of new products will lead to only modest improvements compared to the innovations resulting from technological push, and the emphasis on reflecting rather than creating demand can lead to dull marketing campaigns and me-too products.

2 **The difference between a production orientation and marketing orientation**
- Marketing orientation focuses on customer needs to identify potential market opportunities, leading to the creation of products that create customer satisfaction.
- Production orientation focuses on production capabilities, which defines the business mission and the products that are manufactured. These are then sold aggressively to customers.

3 **The differences between market-driven and internally orientated businesses**
- Customer concern vs convenience.
- Know customer choice criteria and match with marketing mix vs the assumption that price and performance are key.
- Segment by customer differences vs segment by product.
- Marketing research vs anecdotes and received wisdom.
- Welcome change vs cherish status quo.
- Understand competition vs ignore competition.
- Marketing spend is an investment vs marketing spend is a luxury.
- Innovation rewarded and reluctance to punish failure vs avoidance of mistakes rewarded and a failure to innovate is conspicuously punished.
- Search for latent markets vs stick with the same.
- Recognize the importance of being fast vs content to move slowly.
- Strive for competitive advantage vs happy to be me-too.
- Efficiency and effectiveness vs efficiency.

④ The differing roles of efficiency and effectiveness in achieving corporate success
- Efficiency is concerned with inputs and outputs. Business processes are managed to a high standard so that cost per unit of output is low. Its role is to 'do things right'—that is, use processes that result in low-cost production.
- Effectiveness is concerned with making the correct strategic choice regarding which products to make for which markets. Its role is to 'do the right things'—that is, make the right products for attractive markets.

⑤ How to create customer value and satisfaction
- Customer value is created by maximizing perceived benefits (e.g. product or image benefits) and minimizing perceived sacrifice (e.g. monetary or time costs).
- Customer satisfaction once a product is bought is created by maximizing perceived performance compared to the customer's expectations. Customer satisfaction occurs when perceived performance matches or exceeds expectations.

⑥ How an effective marketing mix is designed
- The classical marketing mix consists of product, price, promotion and place (the '4-Ps').
- An effective marketing mix is designed by ensuring that it matches customer needs, creates a competitive advantage, is well blended and matches corporate resources.

⑦ Criticisms of the 4-Ps approach to marketing management
- Criticisms of the 4-Ps approach to marketing management are that it oversimplifies reality. For example, for services marketing three further Ps—people, process and physical evidence—should be added and, for industrial (business-to-business) marketing, the marketing mix approach neglects the importance of long-term relationship building.

⑧ The relationships between marketing characteristics, market orientation and business performance
- Research has shown a positive relationship between business performance, market orientation and marketing characteristics (although for commodity businesses the relationship was U-shaped).

Key Terms

competitive advantage the achievement of superior performance through differentiation to provide superior customer value or by managing to achieve lowest delivered cost

customer satisfaction the fulfilment of customers' requirements or needs

customer value perceived benefits minus perceived sacrifice

effectiveness doing the right thing, making the correct strategic choice

efficiency a way of managing business processes to a high standard, usually concerned with cost reduction; also called 'doing things right'

exchange the act or process of receiving something from someone by giving something in return

marketing concept the achievement of corporate goals through meeting and exceeding customer needs better than the competition

marketing mix a framework for the tactical management of the customer relationship, including product, place, price, promotion (the 4-Ps); in the case of services three other elements to be taken into account are process, people and physical evidence

marketing orientation companies with a marketing orientation focus on customer needs as the primary drivers of organizational performance

place the distribution channels to be used, outlet locations, methods of transportation

price (1) the amount of money paid for a product; (2) the agreed value placed on the exchange by a buyer and seller

product a good or service offered or performed by an organization or individual, which is capable of satisfying customer needs

production orientation a business approach that is inwardly focused either on costs or on a definition of a company in terms of its production facilities

promotional mix advertising, personal selling, sales promotions, public relations, direct marketing, and Internet and online promotion

Study Questions

1 What are the essential characteristics of a marketing-orientated company?

2 Are there any situations where marketing orientation is not the most appropriate business philosophy?

3 Explain how the desire to become efficient may conflict with being effective.

4 How far do you agree or disagree with the criticism that marketing is a source of dullness? Are there any ethical issues relevant to the five principles of 'retromarketing'?

5 To what extent do you agree with the criticisms of the marketing concept and the 4-Ps approach to marketing decision-making?

References

1. Drucker, P. F. (1999) *The Practice of Management*, London: Heinemann.
2. Rosenberg, L. J. and J. A. Czepeil (1983) A Marketing Approach to Customer Retention, *Journal of Consumer Marketing* 2, 45–51.
3. Grönroos, C. (1989) Defining Marketing: A Market-Oriented Approach, *European Journal of Marketing* 23(1), 52–60.
4. Houston, F. S. (1986) The Marketing Concept: What It Is and What It Is Not, *Journal of Marketing* 50, 81–7.
5. Lawson, R. and B. Wooliscroft (2004) Human Nature and the Marketing Concept, *Marketing Theory* 4(4), 311–26.
6. Levitt, T. (1969) *The Marketing Mode*, New York: McGraw-Hill.
7. Morgan, O. (2006) Toyota's Spin to Pole Position is Just a Start, *Observer*, 2 April, 4.
8. Parkinson, S. T. (1991) World Class Marketing: From Lost Empires to the Image Man, *Journal of Marketing Management* 7(3), 299–311.
9. Morgan, R. E. and C. A. Strong (1998) Market Orientation and Dimensions of Strategic Orientation, *European Journal of Marketing* 32(11/12), 1051–73.
10. Benady, A. (2005) Nestlé's New Flavour of Strategy, *Financial Times*, 22 February, 13.
11. Simms, J. (2002) Building Brand Growth, *Marketing*, 26 September, 26–7.
12. Anonymous (2005) The Car Company in Front, *Economist*, 29 January, 73–4.
13. Anonymous (2005) Loyalty Winner, *Marketing*, 1 June, 14.
14. Clark, A. (2009) Our Friends Electric, *Guardian*, 12 January, 23.
15. Abell, D. F. (1978) Strategic Windows, *Journal of Marketing*, July, 21–6.
16. Anonymous (1989) Fortress Europe, *Target Marketing* 12(8), 12–14.
17. Brown, R. J. (1987) Marketing: A Function and a Philosophy, *Quarterly Review of Marketing* 12(3), 25–30.
18. London, S. (2005) Rotten Cars, Not High Costs are Driving GM to Ruin, *Financial Times*, 23/24 April, 11.
19. Teather, D. (2005) Kodak Cuts 10,000 More Jobs as its Film Business Weakens, *Guardian*, 21 July, 20.
20. Smith, G. (2005) Four Wheels, *Guardian* G2, 15 March, 26–7.
21. Anonymous (2008) In the Driving Seat, *Economist*, 8 March, 82.

22. Keeley, G. and A. Clark (2008) Zara Bridges Gap to Become World's Biggest Fashion Retailer, *Guardian*, 12 August, 23.

23. Brownlie, D. and M. Saren (1992) The Four Ps of the Marketing Concept: Prescriptive, Polemical, Permanent and Problematical, *European Journal of Marketing* 26(4), 34–47.

24. Wensley, R. (1990) The Voice of the Consumer? Speculations on the Limits to the Marketing Analogy, *European Journal of Marketing* 24(7), 49–60.

25. Bloom, P. N. and S. A. Greyser (1981) The Maturity of Consumerism, *Harvard Business Review*, Nov–Dec, 130–9.

26. Boseley, S. (2009) Matter of Life and Death: Wallace and Gromit Makers get Animated over UK Obesity Crisis, Guardian.co.uk, 2 January (retrieved 6 April 2009 from www.guardian.co.uk/politics/2009/jan/02/wallace-gromit-obesity-ad-health).

27. Sweeney, M. (2009) Government in £275m Anti-obesity Drive, Guardian.co.uk, 2 January 2009 (retrieved 6 April 2009 from www.guardian.co.uk/media/2009/jan/02/change4life-obesity).

28. Watts, R. (2009) Taking a Wrong Turn in Tackling Obesity, Guardian.co.uk, 2 January 2009 (retrieved 6 April 2009 from www.guardian.co.uk/society/joepublic/2008/dec/31/change4life-campaign-obesity).

29. National Social Marketing Centre (2009) (retrieved 6 April 2009 from www.nsms.org.uk/public/default.aspx).

30. Tauber, E. M. (1974) How Marketing Research Discourages Major Innovation, *Business Horizons* 17 (June), 22–6.

31. Brownlie and Saren (1992) op. cit.

32. McGee, L. W. and R. L. Spiro (1988) The Marketing Concept in Perspective, *Business Horizons*, May–June, 40–5.

33. Rothwell, R. (1974) SAPPHO Updated: Project SAPPHO Phase II, *Research Policy*, 3.

34. Brown, S. (2001) Torment Your Customers (They'll Love It), *Harvard Business Review*, October 83–8.

35. Dickinson, H. (2005) Forget Supersizing, Think Downsizing, *Marketing*, 7 December, 13.

36. Finch, J. (2008) Nick Robertson: Wannabe Celebs Provide the Silver on Screen, *Guardian*, 18 April, 31.

37. Armstrong, L. (2009) asos.com: As Seen on the Screens of the Fashion Savvy, *The Times*, 21 January, 28.

38. See Mittal, V. and W. Kamakura (2001) Satisfaction, Repurchase Intent, and Repurchase Behaviour: Investigating the Moderating Effect of Customer Characteristics, *Journal of Marketing* 38 (February), 131–42; Zeithaml, V. A. (2000) Service Quality, Profitability, and the Economic Worth of Customers: What We Know and What We Need to Learn, *Journal of the Academy of Marketing Science* 28 (Winter), 67–8; and Anderson, E., C. Fornell and S. K. Mazvancheryl (2004) Customer Satisfaction and Shareholder Value, *Journal of Marketing* 68 (October), 172–85.

39. White, D. (1999) Delighting in a Superior Service, *Financial Times*, 25 November, 17.

40. See Anderson, E. W., C. Fornell and D. R. Lehmann (1994) Customer Satisfaction, Market Share and Profitability:

Findings From Sweden, *Journal of Marketing* 58 (July), 53–66; Anderson, E. W., C. Fornell and R. T. Rust (1997) Customer Satisfaction, Productivity, and Profitability: Differences Between Goods and Services, *Marketing Science* 16 (Z), 129–45; Reichheld, F. and E. W. Sasser Jr (1990) Zero Defections: Quality Comes to Services, *Harvard Business Review* 68 (September/October), 105–11; and Rust, R. T. and A. J. Zahorik (1993) Customer Satisfaction, Customer Retention and Market Share, *Journal of Retailing* 69 (Summer), 193–215.

41. See Anderson, E. W. and M. W. Sullivan (1997) The Antecedents and Consequences of Customer Satisfaction for Firms, *Marketing Science* 12 (Spring), 125–43; and Bolton, R. N. and J. H. Drew (1991) A Longitudinal Analysis of the Impact of Service Changes on Customer Attitudes, *Journal of Marketing* 55 (January), 1–9.

42. Homberg, C., N. Koschate and W. D. Hoyer (2005) Do Satisfied Customers Really Pay More? A Study of the Relationship Between Customer Satisfaction and Willingness to Pay, *Journal of Marketing* 69 (April), 84–96.

43. Jones, T. O. and W. E. Sasser Jr (1995) Why Satisfied Customers Defect, *Harvard Business Review*, Nov–Dec, 88–99.

44. Morgan, A. (1996) Relationship Marketing, *Admap*, October, 29–33.

45. White, D. (1999) Delighting in a Superior Service, *Financial Times*, 25 November, 17.

46. Roythorne, P. (2003) Under Surveillance, *Marketing Week*, 13 March, 31–2.

47. Ryle, S. (2003) Every Little Helps Leahy Tick, *Observer*, 13 April, 18.

48. Mitchell, A. (2005) The Path to Success is Simple—Why Do So Few Stay the Course, *Marketing Week*, 19 May, 20–1.

49. Wright, J. (2006) *Blog Marketing*, New York: McGraw-Hill.

50. Jarvis, J. (2009) How the Google Model Could Help Detroit, *Business Week*, 9 February, 33–6.

51. Anonymous (2005) A Man's Best Friend, *Economist*, 2 April, 8–10.

52. Freeman, L. and L. Wentz (1990) P&G's First Soviet TV Spot, *Advertising Age*, 12 March, 56–7.

53. Ritson, M. (2008) History Will Repeat Itself, *Marketing*, 15 October, 20.

54. Smith, D. and A. O'Keeffe (2006) TV: So How Will You Watch It? *Observer*, 12 March, 24–6.

55. Charles, J. (2007) Facebook Protest Forces Interest Rate Climbdown, Timesonline.co.uk, 31 August (retrieved from www.timesonline.co.uk/tol/money/student_finance/article2358640.ece).

56. O'Flaherty, K. (2008) Keeping a Fresh Spin On Things, *Marketing Week*, 22–3.

57. Fernandez, J. (2008) Will the Sale of Cobra Beer Enable it to Achieve Worldwide Growth? *Marketing Week*, 4 December, 9.

58. Booms, B. H. and M. J. Bitner (1981) Marketing Strategies and Organisation Structures for Service Firms, in

Donnelly, J. H. and W. R. George (eds) *Marketing of Services*, Chicago: American Marketing Association, 47–52.

59. Rafiq, M. and P. K. Ahmed (1992) The Marketing Mix Reconsidered, *Proceedings of the Marketing Education Group Conference*, Salford, 439–51.

60. Ford, D., H. Håkansson and J. Johanson (1986) How Do Companies Interact? *Industrial Marketing and Purchasing* 1(1), 26–41.

61. Buttle, F. (1989) Marketing Services, in Jones, P. (ed.) *Management in Service Industries*, London: Pitman, 235–59.

62. Hooley, G. and J. Lynch (1985) Marketing Lessons from UK's High-Flying Companies, *Journal of Marketing Management* 1(1), 65–74.

63. Narver, J. C. and S. F. Slater (1990) The Effect of a Market Orientation on Business Profitability, *Journal of Marketing* 54 (October), 20–35.

64. Pelham, A. M. (2000) Market Orientation and Other Potential Influences on Performance in Small and Medium-Sized Manufacturing Firms, *Journal of Small Business Management* 38(1), 48–67.

65. Narver, J. C., R. L. Jacobson and S. F. Slater (1999) Market Orientation and Business Performance: An Analysis of Panel Data, in R. Deshpande (ed.) *Developing a Market Orientation*, Thousand Oaks, CA: Sage Publications, 195–216.

66. Slater, S. F. and J. C. Narver (1994) Does Competitive Environment Moderate the Market Orientation Performance Relationship, *Journal of Marketing* 58, January, 46–55; Im, S. and J. P. Workman Jr. (2004) Market Orientation, Creativity, and New Product Performance in High Technology Firms, *Journal of Marketing* 68 (April), 114–32.

67. Pelham, A. M. and D. T. Wilson (1996) A Longitudinal Study of the Impact of Market Structure, Firm Structure, and Market Orientation Culture of Dimensions of Small Firm Performances, *Journal of the Academy of Marketing Science* 24(1), 27–43.

68. Pulendran, S., R. Speed and R. E. Wilding II (2003) Marketing Planning, Market Orientation and Business Performance, *European Journal of Marketing* 37(3/4), 476–97. For a review of the literature on market orientation and business performance see C. R. Cano, F. A. Carrillet and F. Jaramillo (2004) A Meta-Analysis of the Relationship between Market Orientation and Business Performance: Evidence from Five Continents, *International Journal of Research in Marketing* 21(2), 179–200.

69. Kirca, A. H., S. Jayachandran and W. O. Bearden (2005) Market Orientation: A Meta-Analytic Review and Assessment of its Antecedents and Impact on Performance, *Journal of Marketing* 69(2), 24–41.

70. Narver and Slater (1990) op. cit.

Coca-Cola *vs* Pepsi

Cola Wars in a Changing Marketing Environment

For most companies, owning the number one brand name in the world (valued at over $67 billion by the Interbrand consultancy), having global brand recognition and earning $4.8 billion profits on sales of $21.9 billion a year in 2005 would spell success on a huge scale. But Coca-Cola is not 'most companies'. In the face of strong competition and a changing marketing environment, the fortunes of Coca-Cola have turned in recent years.

Once a Wall Street favourite, Coca-Cola created a global brand by the expert marketing of something as humble as brown carbonated water laced with caffeine and vegetable extracts. For decades the company outperformed its arch-rival PepsiCo such that in early 2000 Coca-Cola's market capitalization was $128 billion, almost three times that of PepsiCo, which was valued at $44 billion. By December 2005 all that had changed: PepsiCo had nudged ahead with a market capitalization of $98.4 billion against Coca-Cola's $97.9 billion. For the first time in the history of the two companies PepsiCo was valued more highly than its old enemy. Suddenly, the 'real thing' was second best.

Coke's problems

Many observers date Coke's problems back to the death in 1997 of Roberto Goizueta, its charismatic and highly successful chief executive, who delivered double-digit annual profit growth. His success over PepsiCo led him to treat that company with contempt. He once said, 'As they become less relevant, I don't need to look at them any more.' Since his death, however, the company's shares have lost a third of their value, and profit growth has collapsed to the low single digits. His successors reigned during a time of bungled takeovers, disastrous product launches, contamination scares, and constant feuding between factions within the management and boardroom. A classic illustration of Coke's problems was the scandal involving the launch of Dasani, a bottled mineral water that turned out to be distilled tap water. When the harmful chemical bromate was found in a batch the brand was withdrawn in the UK.

However, other people attribute the roots of Coke's failings to Goizueta's single-minded devotion to cola. His philosophy was that nothing could beat the low-cost, high-profit-margin business of producing syrupy concentrate for bottlers, under licence, to transform into the world's favourite drink. While Coca-Cola focused on carbonated colas, PepsiCo diversified away from sugary fizzy drinks into a powerful portfolio of non-carbonated products. In 1998, it bought the fruit juice business Tropicana, which it has built to be the number one fruit juice brand in the USA. Three years later it bought Quaker Oats, thereby acquiring the energy drink Gatorade, which has also been built into a major brand. (Coca-Cola pulled out of the Quaker Oats bidding war believing its price to be too high.) PepsiCo also owns Aquafina, the leading bottled water brand in the USA. The fruit juice, energy drink and bottled water sectors have all experienced double-digit growth in recent years. It has continued its acquisition programme with the purchase of the South Beach Beverage Co, which manufactures the SoBe healthy drinking range, and has launched SoBe Life Water, which it claims contains the full recommended daily amount of vitamin C together with vitamins E and B, and no preservatives or artificial flavourings. Its bottling partner Pepsi-Americas has also bought Ardea Beverages, which markets the Nutrisoda range containing amino acids, vitamins, CoQ10, herbs and minerals. In contrast to Coke, the culture at PepsiCo was reported to be more dynamic and customer focused, and less bureaucratic.

Where Coke has focused on soft drinks Pepsi has interests in the snack food business (it bought the Frito-Lay snack food business in 1965), owning such brands as Doritos, Walkers Crisps, Quavers, Lay's Potato Crisps and Wotsits (see Table C1.1). The result is that PepsiCo generates about 23 per cent of its worldwide profits from the stagnant carbonated drinks sector, while Coca-Cola relies on fizzy drinks for 80 per cent of profits. Coca-Cola always seems to be playing catch-up,

Cola wars: who owns what		TABLE C1.1
Coca-Cola brands	**PepsiCo brands**
Coca-Cola	Pepsi
Coke Zero	Diet Pepsi
Diet Coke	Gatorade
Powerade	Tropicana
Minute Maid	Aquafina
Dasani	Lipton Iced Tea
Fanta	Frappuccino
Lilt	Mountain Dew
Sprite	Walkers crisps
Calypso	Lay's potato crisps
Oasis	Quaker Oats
Just Juice	Quavers
Kia Ora	Doritos
Five Alive	Wotsits
Malvern water	Sugar Puffs
	7-Up

having launched Minute Maid fruit juice to challenge Tropicana, Dasani to take on Aquafina, and Powerade, an energy drink, following the success of Red Bull and Gatorade in this sector.

PepsiCo's diversification programme and its brand-building expertise has made it the world's fourth largest food and beverage company, ranking behind Nestlé, Kraft and Unilever. Its sales were more than $43 billion compared with Coke's $32 billion in 2008; it has 16 brands that each generate more than $1 billion of annual revenue; and it owns 6 of the 15 top-selling food and drink brands in US supermarkets—more than any other company, including Coke which has two. Coke, on the other hand, is market leader in carbonated drinks (43 per cent versus 32 per cent).

Life since Mr Goizueta has also seen Coke criticized for its fall in marketing investments, including advertising and marketing research, in an effort to maintain short-term profits, and the lack of iconic

brand-building advertising. Its culture has also been questioned and its high-rise headquarters in central Atlanta is known in the industry as 'the Kremlin' because of the political intrigue and bureaucratic culture that pervades its corridors.

A new era?

In response to its problems, Coca-Cola brought an ex-employee, Neville Isdell, out of retirement to become chairman and chief executive in 2004. One of his first acts was to allocate an additional $400 million a year to marketing and innovation. This was in recognition of the under-investment in brands and product development. Emerging markets such as China and India are also being targeted more aggressively. He also briefed advertising agencies around the world in an attempt to create new iconic campaigns to revive the core brand and reconnect with consumers. In the face of research that showed the proportion of Americans agreeing that cola is 'liked by everyone' falling from 56 per cent in 2003 to 44 per cent in 2005, and those agreeing that the drink was 'too fattening' increasing from 48 per cent to 59 per cent, Coke has increased investment in sugar-free brands such as Diet Coke and Sprite Zero. Sugar-free colas have also been launched, such as Coke Zero, which comes in black cans and bottles and is targeted at calorie-conscious young males who have failed to connect with Diet Coke, believing that it lacks a masculine image. The brand is designed to compete with PepsiMax, which is also a diet cola targeted at men. Overall, marketing spend for the category has doubled. Isdell has also overseen the acquisition of a number of small water and fruit juice companies in Europe.

Isdell resisted the temptation to follow Pepsi with the acquisition of a snacks company. Instead his strategy was to focus on building a portfolio of branded drinks. Following this strategy, Coca-Cola has purchased the US firm Energy Brands, which owns Glaceau, a vitamin-enhanced water brand, and has bought a stake of between 10 and 20 per cent of innocent, the market leader (68 per cent) of fruit smoothie drinks in the UK. Innocent has built a reputation for making only natural healthy products, and using only socially and environmentally aware products. At the time of the deal (2009), innocent operated in the UK, Ireland, France, Scandinavia, Germany and Austria. Coca-Cola has also launched an energy drink, Relentless, aimed at men aged 18–40.

Meanwhile, PepsiCo has introduced its own labelling system in the USA to identify healthier products, using criteria set by an independent board of health experts. Now 40 per cent of sales derive from products with the green 'Smart Spot' given to healthier brands such as sugar-free colas and baked rather than fried crisps. Most of its research and development is focused on healthier products such as Tropicana-branded fruit bars, which provide the nutritional equivalent to fresh fruit. Sales of Smart Spot products are growing at twice the rate of those without the designation, and account for over half of Pepsi's product portfolio.

Continuing its focus on healthy drinks, PepsiCo has launched Pepsi Raw, a premium cola, on to the UK market. The product, which uses cane sugar rather than high-fructose corn syrup, and no artificial preservatives, colours or flavourings, was positioned as the first 'natural' cola. Pepsi has followed its launch with the creation of PurVia, which uses stevia—a South American herb used to create natural sugar substitutes—as a zero-calorie sweetener. It was first used in flavours in PepsiCo's water brand SoBe Life. Coca-Cola followed this launch with its own equivalent, Truvia. The company has also launched Pepsi Extra Cold, which is sold in pubs and bars, so that consumers can be guaranteed a cool drink of draught Pepsi.

Both companies have also attempted to arrest the decline in the carbonated soft drinks sector by launching a flurry of new products such as lime- and cherry-flavoured colas. Nevertheless colas have come under attack for their contribution to obesity. One UK school removed Coca-Cola fizzy drinks from its vending machines when it identified that its pupils were drinking on average three cans a day—equivalent to more than one and a half times a child's recommended daily sugar intake. In the United States, Arnold Schwarzenegger (of *Terminator* fame), now governor of California, recently passed legislation banning the sale of all carbonated drinks in schools across California.

Other ethical controversies have been encroaching upon Coca-Cola's global hold on the drinks market. A French entrepreneur, Tawfik Mathlouthi, launched Mecca-Cola, designed to benefit from increasing concern at American foreign policy and anti-American sentiment around the world. His aim is to encourage Muslims to choose Mecca-Cola rather than Coca-Cola. Coca-Cola, like other American brands, has felt the negative impact of US boycotts and anti-globalization sentiments targeted at US brands. Mecca-Cola has already been launched in France, Britain, Germany, Belgium, Italy, Spain and Scandinavia. Another alternative to US colas is ZamZam Cola (an Iranian brand), which is selling well in Iraq, Saudi Arabia, Pakistan and Africa.

Under Mr Isdell, Coca-Cola achieved steady international sales and profit growth. In 2008 he returned to retirement and was succeeded by Muhtar Kent.

References

Based on: Devaney, P. (2006) As US Tastes Change, Coca-Cola's Supremacy Drip, Drip, Drips Away, *Marketing Week*, 6 April, 30–1; Teather, D. (2005) Bubble Bursts for the Real Thing as PepsiCo Ousts Coke from Top Spot, *Guardian*, 27 December, 26; Ward, A. (2005) A Better Model? Diversified Pepsi Steals Some of Coke's Sparkle, *Financial Times*, 28 February, 21; Ward, A. (2005) Coke Gets Real: The World's Most Valuable Brand Wakes Up to a Waning Thirst for Cola, *Financial Times*, 22 September, 17; Sweeney, M. and C. Tryhorn (2009) The Day Innocent Lost its Innocence, *Guardian*, 7 April, 3; Bokai, J. (2008) Soft Drinks Eye Herbal 'Sugar', *Marketing*, 6 August, 2; Bokai, J. (2008) Soft Drinks Eye Premium Boost, *Marketing*, 19 March, 2.

Questions

1. Compare Coca-Cola's response to the changing marketing environment before the arrival of Neville Isdell to that of PepsiCo.

2. Assess both companies in terms of their level of marketing orientation.

3. How would you position Coca-Cola and PepsiCo on the efficiency–effectiveness matrix? Justify your answer.

4. What advantages, if any, does PepsiCo's greater diversification give the company over Coca-Cola?

5. Assess Coca-Cola's part-ownership of innocent drinks from the point of view of both companies.

6. What future challenges is Coca-Cola likely to face?

The case was written by David Jobber, Professor of Marketing, University of Bradford, and Marylyn Carrigan, Senior Lecturer in Marketing, Open University.

H&M Gets Hotter

Fashion at its Fastest

Stefan Persson, chairman of Swedish retailer Hennes & Mauritz (H&M), vividly remembers his company's first attempt at international expansion. It was 1976, the year H&M opened its London store in Oxford Circus. 'I stood outside trying to lure in customers by handing out Abba albums' he recalls with a wry laugh. Persson, then 29, son of the company's founder, waited for the crowds. And waited. 'I still have most of those albums,' he says.

But Stefan is not crying over that unsold vinyl. In a slowing global economy, with lacklustre consumer spending and retailers across Europe struggling to make a profit, H&M's pre-tax profits hit £1.7 billion in 2008, a 10 per cent increase on the previous year, on sales of £7.4 billion. At current sales levels, the chain is the largest apparel retailer in Europe. This is not just a store chain; it is a money-making machine. Table C2.1 compares H&M with Gap and Zara, its closest rivals.

Marketing at H&M

If you stop by its Fifth Avenue location in New York or check out the mothership at the corner of

The clash of the clothing titans				TABLE C2.1
	Style	**Strategy**	**Global reach**	**Financials**
H&M	Motto is 'fashion and quality at the best price' Translates into cutting-edge clothes	Production out-sourced to suppliers in Europe and Asia Some lead times are just three weeks	Has 1800 stores in 35 countries Largest sales are to Germany, followed by the UK and Sweden	Pre-tax profits were £1.7 billion (€1.9 billion) in 2008 on sales of £7.4 billion (€8.4 billion)
Gap	Built its name on wardrobe basics such as denim, khakis and T-shirts	Outsources all production An average of nine months for turnaround	Operates 3100 stores (including Banana Republic and Old Navy) in the USA, Europe, Japan and Canada	Pre-tax profits were £864 million (€986 million) in 2008 on sales of £9.7 billion (€11.1 billion)
Zara	Billed as 'Armani on a budget' for its Euro-style clothing for women and men	Bulk of production is handled by company's own manufacturing facilities in Spain	Runs 1520 outlets Sales breakdown: 44% Europe (excl. Spain) 31% Spain, 11% the Americas, 10% Asia	Parent Inditex Group's pre-tax profits were £1.9 billion (€2.2 billion) on sales of £9.1 billion (€10.4 billion)

Data: Company reports, Santander Central Hispano, BNP Paribas, Goldman Sachs & Co

Regeringsgatan and Hamngatan in Stockholm, it's easy to see what's powering H&M's success. The prices are as low as the fashion is trendy, turning each location into a temple of 'cheap chic'. At the Manhattan flagship, mirrored disco balls hang from the ceiling, and banks of televisions broadcast videos of the body-pierced, belly baring pop princesses of the moment. On a cool afternoon in October, teenage girls in flared jeans and two-toned hair mill around the ground floor, hoisting piles of velour hoodies, Indian-print blouses and patchwork denim skirts—each £16 or under. (The average price of an H&M item is just £10.) This is not Gap's brand of classic casuals or the more grown-up Euro-chic of Zara. It's exuberant, it's over-the-top, and it's working. 'Everything is really nice—and cheap,' says Sabrina Farhi, 22, as she clutches a suede trenchcoat she has been eyeing for weeks.

The H&M approach also appeals to Erin Yuill, a 20-year-old part-time employee from New Jersey, who explains, 'Things go out of style fast. Sometimes, I'll wear a dress or top a few times, and that's it. But I'm still in school and I don't have a lot of money. For me this is heaven.'

H&M is also shrewdly tailoring its strategy to the US market. In Europe, H&M is more like a department store—selling a range of merchandise from edgy street fashion to casual basics for the whole family. Its US stores are geared to younger, more fashion-conscious females. H&M's menswear line, a strong seller in Europe, hasn't proved popular with the less-fashion-conscious American male. So a number of US outlets have either cut back the selection or eliminated the line. And while the pricing is cheap, the branding isn't. H&M spends a hefty 4 per cent of revenues on marketing.

Behind this stylish image is a company so buttoned-down and frugal that you can't imagine its executives tuning into a soft-rock station, let alone getting inside a teenager's head. Stefan Persson, whose late father founded the company, looks and talks more like a financier than a merchant prince. A penny-pinching financier, at that. 'H&M is run on a shoestring' says Nathan Cockrell, a retail analyst at Credit Suisse First Boston in London. 'They buy as cheaply as possible and keep overheads low.' Fly business class? Only in emergencies. Taking cabs? Definitely frowned upon. To rein in costs, Persson even took away all employees' mobile phones in the

1990s. Today, only a few key employees have cell-phone privileges.

But that gimlet eye is just what a retailer needs to stay on its game—especially the kind of high-risk game H&M is playing. Not since IKEA set out to conquer the world one modular wall unit at a time has a Swedish retailer displayed such bold international ambition. H&M is pressing full-steam ahead on a programme that brought its total number of stores to 1800 by the end of 2008—a 50 per cent increase in the past three years.

Yet H&M is pursuing a strategy that has undone a number of rivals. Benetton tried to become the world's fashion retailer but retreated after a disastrous experience in the USA in the 1980s. Gap, once the hottest chain in the States, has lately been choking on its relatively slow reaction time to changing fashion trends and its failure to attract young shoppers, and has never taken off abroad. Body Shop and Sephora had similar misadventures.

Nevertheless, Persson and his crew are undaunted. 'When I joined in 1972, H&M was all about price,' he says. 'Then we added quality fashion to the equation, but everyone said you could never combine [them] successfully. But we were passionate that we could.' Persson is just as passionate that he can apply the H&M formula internationally.

> **//** While the pricing is cheap, the branding isn't. H&M spends a hefty 4 per cent of revenues on marketing. **//**

What's that formula, exactly? Treat fashion as if it were perishable product: keep it fresh, and keep it moving. That means spotting the trends even before the trendoids do, turning the ideas into affordable clothes, and making the apparel fly off the racks. 'We hate inventory,' says H&M's head of buying, Karl Gunnar Fagerlin, whose job it is to make sure the merchandise doesn't pile up at the company's warehouses. Not an easy task, considering H&M stores sell over 600 million items per year.

Although H&M sells a range of clothing for women, men and children, its cheap-chic formula goes down particularly well with the 15-to-30 set. Lusting after that Dolce & Gabbana corduroy trenchcoat but unwilling to cough up £600-plus? At £32, H&M's version is too good to pass up. It's more Lycra than luxe and won't last for ever. But if you're trying to keep *au courant,* one season is sufficient. 'At least half my wardrobe comes from H&M,' says Emma Mackie, a 19-year-old student from London. 'It's really good value for money.'

▲ H&M works with high profile designers to create exclusive lines. They used London taxi cabs to advertise the collection designed by Matthew Williamson.

H&M's high-fashion, low-price concept distinguishes it from Gap, Inc., with its all-basics-at-all-price-points, and chains such as bebe and Club Monaco, whose fashions are of the moment but by no means inexpensive. It offers an alternative for consumers who may be bored with chinos and cargo pants, but not able—or willing to trade up for more fashion. H&M has seized on the fact that what's in today will not be in tomorrow. Shoppers at the flagship store agreed, particularly the younger ones that the retailer caters to.

In 2004 H&M commissioned Karl Lagerfeld, Chanel's designer, to create the limited-edition Lagerfeld range, which included a £70 sequinned jacket and cocktail dresses for under £55. The range, which was offered in the USA and 20 European countries, sold out within two hours in some stores. This was followed in 2005 by the Stella McCartney collection. McCartney, the British designer whose clothes normally retail for hundreds and sometimes thousands of pounds, designed 40 pieces for H&M, including camisoles, skinny jeans and tailored waistcoats. The average price was £40 per item, around 15 times cheaper than her own prices. The limited edition was a resounding success, with customers queuing from as early as 6.30 am to get first pick of the clothes

Since then, many other top names have lined up to work with H&M, including Robert Cavalli, Kylie Minogue and Madonna. In 2009, Matthew Williamson, who has designed dresses for Sienna Miller, Keira Knightley and Penelope Cruz, reworked his most popular designs—kaftan dresses, beaded cardigans and print frocks—for the retailing giant. His designs sold out within hours of hitting the stores.

Design at H&M

H&M's design process is as dynamic as its clothes. The 95-person design group is encouraged to draw inspiration not from fashion runways but from real life. 'We travel a lot,' says designer Ann-Sofie Johansson, whose trip to Marrakech inspired a host of creations worthy of the bazaars. 'You need to get out, look at people, new places. See colours. Smell smells.' When at home, Johansson admits to following people off the subway in Stockholm to ask where they picked up a particular top or unusual scarf. Call it stalking for style's sake.

The team includes designers from Sweden, the Netherlands, Britain, South Africa and the USA. The average age is 30. Johansson is part of the design group for 15 to 25 year olds, and one style they designed for the autumn was Bohemian: long, crinkled cotton skirts with matching blouses and sequinned sweaters for a bit of night-time glamour. H&M's design team were not pushing a whole look. They know H&M's customers ad-lib, pairing up one of its new off-the-shoulder chiffon tops with last year's khaki cargo pants for instance. The goal is to keep young shoppers coming into H&M's stores on a regular basis, even if they're spending less than £16 a pop. If they get hooked they'll stay loyal later on, when they become more affluent.

Not all designs are brand new: many are based on proven sellers such as washed denim and casual skirts, with a slight twist to freshen them up. The trick is striking the right balance between cutting-edge designs and commercially viable clothes.

To deliver 500 new designs to the stores for a typical season, designers may do twice as many finished sketches. H&M also has merchandise managers in each country, who talk with customers about the clothes and accessories on offer. When they travel, buyers and designers spend time with store managers to find out why certain items in each country have or haven't worked. In Stockholm, they stay close to the customers by working regularly in H&M's stores. Still, Johansson and her crew won't chase after every fad: 'There are some things I could never wear, no matter how trendy,' she says. Hot pants are high on that list. It's safe to say they won't be popping up at H&M anytime soon.

H&M's young designers find inspiration in everything from street trends to films to flea markets. Despite the similarity between haute couture and some of H&M's trendier pieces, copying the catwalk is not allowed, swears Margareta van den Bosch, who heads the H&M design team. 'Whether it's Donna Karan, Prada or H&M, we all work on the same time frames,' she says. 'But we can add garments during the season.'

Cutting lead times and costs

Working hand in glove with suppliers, H&M's 21 local production offices have compressed lead times—the time it takes for a garment to travel from design table to store floor—to as little as three weeks. Only Zara has a faster turnaround. But Zara has nearly 300 fewer stores. In addition, Zara's parent, Inditex, owns its own production facilities in Galicia, Spain, allowing Zara to shrink lead times to a mere two weeks. Gap, Inc. operates on a nine-month cycle, a factor analysts say is to blame for its chronic overstock problem.

H&M's speed maximizes its ability to churn out more hot items during any season, while minimizing its fashion faux pas. Every day, Fagerlin and his team tap into the company's database for itemized sales reports by country, store and type of merchandise. Stores are restocked daily. Items that do not sell are quickly marked down in price to make room for the next styles. Faster turnaround means higher sales, which helps H&M charge low prices and still log gross profit margins of 58 per cent.

All major fashion retailers aim for fast turnaround these days, but H&M is one of the few in the winners' circle. To keep costs down, the company outsources all manufacturing to a huge network of 900 garment shops located in 21 mostly low-wage countries, primarily Bangladesh, China and Turkey. 'They are constantly shifting production to get the best deal,' says John Tisell, an analyst at Enskilda Securities in Stockholm.

References

Based on: Capell, K., G. Khermouch and A. Sains (2002) How H&M Got Hot, *Business Week*, 11 November, 37–42; Wilson, M. (2000) Disposable Chic at H&M, *Chain Store Age*, May, 64–6; Jones A. and E. Rigby (2005) A Good Fit? Designers and Mass Market Chains Try to Stitch Their Fortunes Together, *Financial Times*, 25 October, 17; Fisher, A. (2009) Woman Who Gave Us the A-List Look, *Observer*, 22 March, 21; Venkatraman, A. (2008) Basic Instinct, *Marketing Week*, 21 August, 27.

Questions

1. To what extent is H&M marketing orientated? What evidence is there in the case to support your view?
2. Into which cell of the efficiency–effectiveness matrix does H&M fall? Justify your answer.
3. What is the basis of the customer value H&M provides for its customers?
4. What are the marketing benefits to H&M of commissioning Karl Lagerfeld, Stella McCartney and Matthew Williamson to design limited-edition clothing ranges?
5. What challenges are likely to face H&M in the future?
6. Do you consider the marketing of disposable clothes contrary to societal welfare? Justify your opinion.

This case was compiled by David Jobber, Professor of Marketing, University of Bradford.

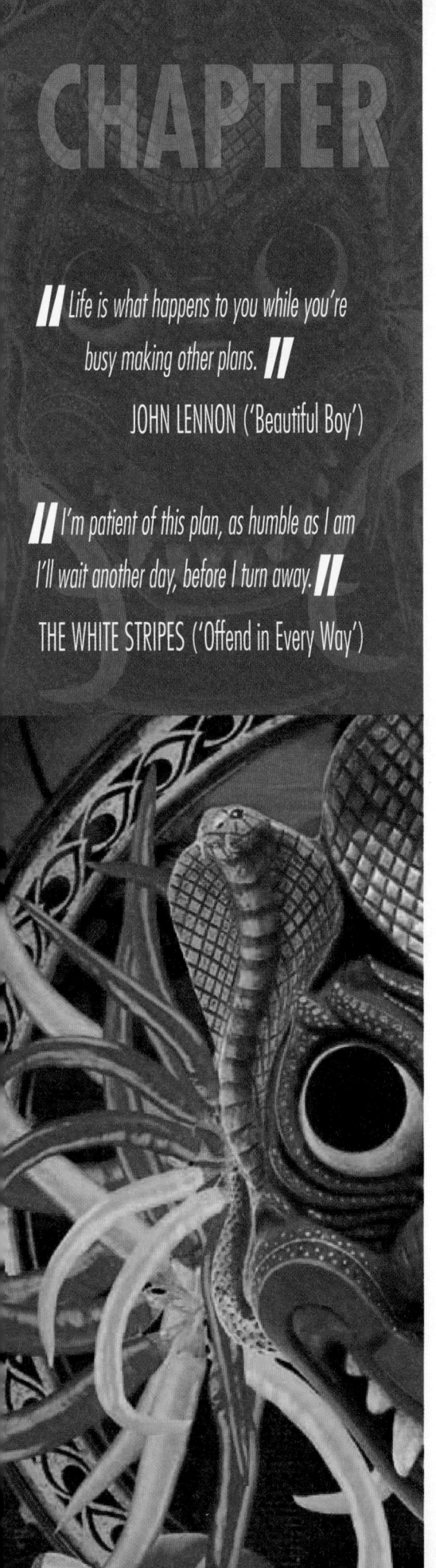

CHAPTER 2

Marketing planning: an overview of marketing

Life is what happens to you while you're busy making other plans.

JOHN LENNON ('Beautiful Boy')

I'm patient of this plan, as humble as I am I'll wait another day, before I turn away.

THE WHITE STRIPES ('Offend in Every Way')

LEARNING OBJECTIVES

After reading this chapter, you should be able to:

1 describe the role of marketing planning within businesses

2 identify the key planning questions

3 discuss the process of marketing planning

4 describe the concept of the business mission

5 explain the nature of the marketing audit and SWOT analysis

6 discuss the nature of marketing objectives

7 identify the components of core strategy and the criteria for testing its effectiveness

8 explain where marketing mix decisions are placed within the marketing planning process

9 discuss the importance of organization, implementation and control within the marketing planning process

10 describe the rewards and problems associated with marketing planning

11 discuss the recommendations for overcoming marketing planning problems

In Chapter 1 we saw that commercial success follows companies that can create and retain customers by providing better value than the competition. But this begs the question 'Which customers?' The choice of which customer groups to serve is a major decision that managers have to make. Furthermore the question 'How should value be created?' also needs to be addressed. This involves choices regarding technology, competitive strategies and the creation of competitive advantages. As the environment changes, so businesses must adapt in order to maintain strategic fit between their capabilities and the marketplace. The process by which businesses analyse the environment and their capabilities, decide upon courses of marketing action and implement those decisions is called **marketing planning**.

Marketing planning is part of a broader concept known as *strategic planning*, which involves not only marketing, but also the fit between production, finance and personnel strategies and the environment. The aim of strategic planning is to shape and reshape a company so that its business and products continue to meet corporate objectives (e.g. profit or sales growth). Because marketing management is charged with the responsibility of managing the interface between the company and its environment, it has a key role to play in strategic planning.

In trying to understand the role of marketing planning in strategy development the situation is complicated somewhat by the nature of companies. At the simplest level a company may market only one product in one market. The role of marketing planning would be to ensure that the marketing mix for the product matches (changing) customer needs, as well as seeking opportunities to use the companies' strengths to market other products in new markets. Many companies, however, market a range of products in numerous markets. The contribution that marketing planning can make in this situation is similar to the first case. However, there is an additional function: the determination of the allocation of resources to each product. Inasmuch as resource allocation should be dependent, in part, on the attractiveness of the market for each product, marketing is inevitably involved in this decision.

Finally a company may comprise a number of businesses (often equating to divisions) each of which serves distinct groups of customers and has a distinct set of competitors.[1] Each business may be strategically autonomous and thus form a **strategic business unit** (SBU). A major component of a corporate plan will be the allocation of resources to each SBU. Strategic decisions at the corporate level are normally concerned with acquisition, divestment and diversification.[2] Here, too, marketing can play a part through the identification of opportunities and threats in the environment as they relate to current and prospective businesses.

Despite these complications, the essential questions that need to be asked are similar in each situation. These questions will now be discussed.

The Fundamentals of Planning

Planning can focus on many personal as well as business issues. We can produce a career plan, we can plan our use of leisure time or we can plan for our retirement. In each case the framework for the planning process is similar and can be understood by asking the questions posed in Table 2.1. Let us first examine planning in the context of a person developing a career plan. Then the process of planning in a business context will be explained.

The starting point is asking the basic question 'Where are we now?' This may involve a factual statement and a value judgement as to the degree of success achieved against expectations. The answer will depend upon 'facts' as perceived by the individual. The next

Key planning questions	TABLE 2.1
1 Where are we now?	
2 How did we get here?	
3 Where are we heading?	
4 Where would we like to be?	
5 How do we get there?	
6 Are we on course?	

question, 'How did we get here?', focuses on an analysis of significant events that had a bearing on the achievements and shortcomings identified earlier. To illustrate the process so far, the answer to the first question could be 'assistant brand manager in a fast-moving consumer goods company for five years with experience in developing advertising, sales promotion and new product variations'. Our self-assessment of this situation may be negative: five years is too long in this position. Our assessment of how we got there might include the gaining of academic (degree) and professional qualifications, and the use and development of personal skills, which we assess are communicational and analytical.

The next question, 'Where are we heading?', focuses on the future, given that we make no significant changes in our actions. If we proceed as we have done in the past, what are the likely outcomes? Our assessment of this may be that we proceed to brand manager status at our company in three years' time and product manager in 10. But 'Where would we like to be?' This question allows us to compare our prediction of the future with our aspirations. It is a key planning question. If our aspirations match our predictions based on current behaviour, we shall proceed as before. We are satisfied that we shall achieve brand manager status in three years and become a product manager in 10.

However, if we want to become a brand manager in one year and a product manager in five, we need to change our behaviour. Our assessment of the situation is that current actions are insufficient to achieve where we would like to be. So we need to ask 'How do we get there?' We begin thinking creatively; we identify options that make sense in the light of our aspirations; we consider changing jobs; we ponder working more effectively; we assess the likely impact of working longer hours; we look at the methods of successful people in our company and analyse the reasons for their success. Out of this process we decide on courses of action that give us a better chance of achieving our aspirations than current behaviour. Thus answering the question 'How do we get there?' provides us with our strategy. Finally, after putting into practice our new actions, we periodically check our position by asking 'Are we on course?' If we are, then the plan remains unaltered; if not, then we modify our plan.

In business the process is essentially the same in theory. However, the practice is much more complex. Businesses are comprised of individuals who may have very differing views on the answers to these questions. Furthermore, the outcome of the planning process may have fundamental implications for their jobs. Planning is therefore a political activity and vested interests may view it from a narrow departmental view rather than a business-wide perspective. A key issue in getting planning systems to work is tackling such behavioural problems.[3] However, at this point in the chapter it is important to understand the process of marketing planning. A common approach to the analysis of the marketing planning process is at the business unit level (see, for example, Day)[4] and this is the level adopted here.

The Process of Marketing Planning

The process of marketing planning is outlined in Figure 2.1. It provides a well-defined path from generating a business mission to implementing and controlling the resultant plans. In real life, planning is rarely so straightforward and logical. Different people may be involved at various stages of the planning process, and the degree to which they accept and are influenced by the outcomes of earlier planning stages is variable.

However, the presentation of the planning process in Figure 2.1 serves two purposes. First, it provides a systematic framework for understanding the analysis and decision-making processes involved in marketing planning and, second, it provides a framework for understanding how the key elements of marketing discussed in subsequent chapters of this book relate to each other. The stages in marketing planning will now be discussed in some detail, and finally they will be related to the basic planning questions listed in Table 2.1.

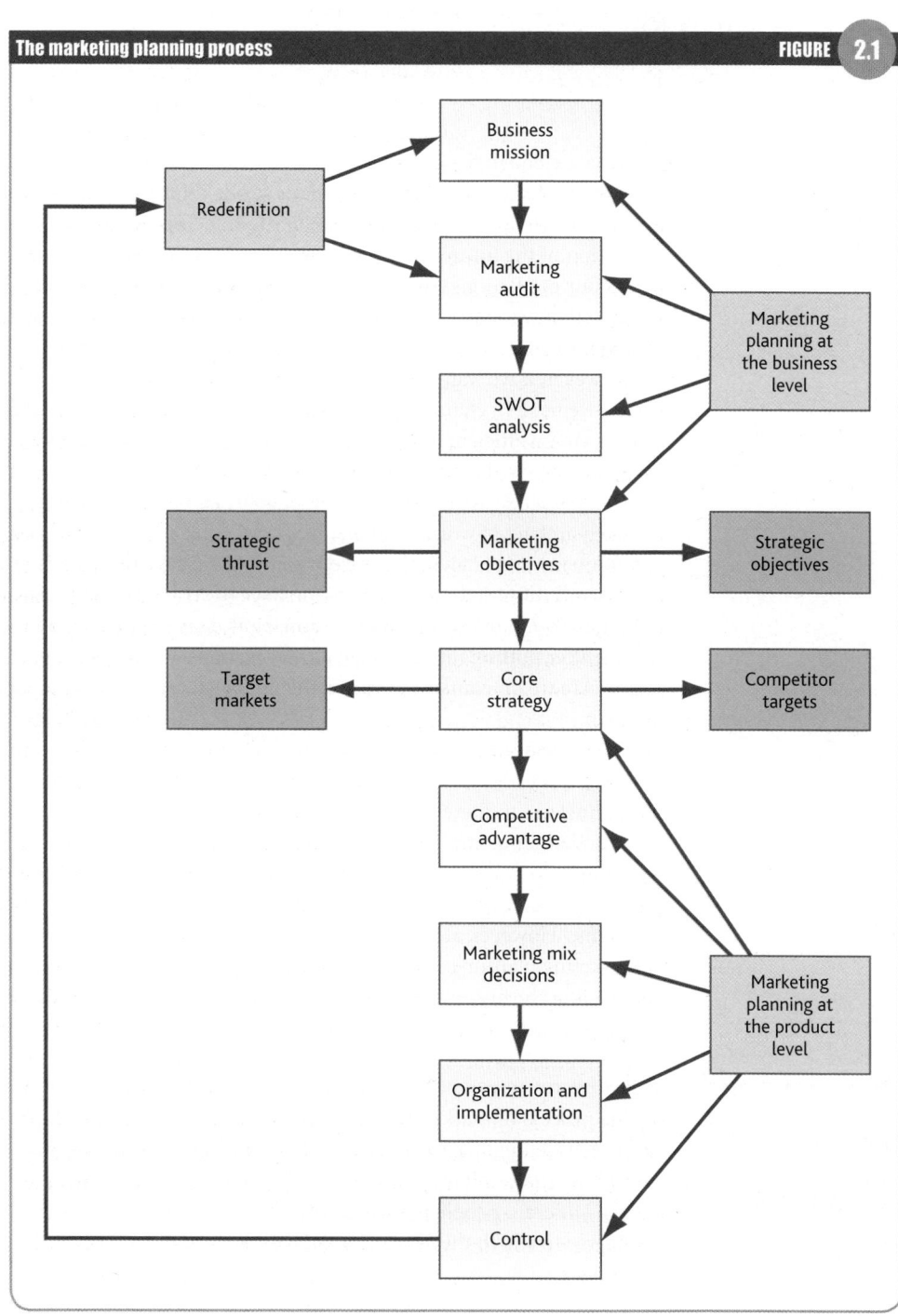

The marketing planning process   FIGURE 2.1

Business mission

Ackoff defined **business mission** as:

> A broadly defined, enduring statement of purpose that distinguishes a business from others of its type.[5]

This definition captures two essential ingredients in mission statements: they are enduring and specific to the individual organization.[6] Two fundamental questions that need to be addressed are 'What business are we in?' and 'What business do we want to be in?' The answers define the scope and activities of the company. The business mission explains the reason for its existence. As such it may include a statement of market, needs and technology.[7] The market reflects the customer groups being served; needs refer to the customer needs being satisfied, and technology describes the process by which a customer need can be satisfied, or a function performed.

The inclusion of market and needs ensures that the business definition is market focused rather than product based. Thus the purpose of a company such as IBM is not to manufacture computers but to solve customers' information problems. The reason for ensuring that a business definition is market focused is that products are transient but basic needs such as transportation, entertainment and eating are lasting. Thus Levitt argued that a business should be viewed as a customer-satisfying process not a goods-producing process.[8] By adopting a customer perspective, new opportunities are more likely to be seen. In IBM's case this has led to it taking advantage of opportunities in consultancy and services within the information technology sector, and has limited its capacity to manufacture computers by selling its personal computer division to Lenovo.[9]

While this advice has merit in advocating the avoidance of a narrow business definition, management must be wary of a definition that is too wide. Levitt suggested that railroad companies would have survived had they defined their business as transportation and moved into the airline business. But this ignores the limits of the business competence of the railroads. Did they possess the necessary skills and resources to run an airline? Clearly a key constraint on a business definition can be the competences (both actual and potential) of management, and the resources at their disposal. Conversely, competences can act as the motivator for widening a business mission. Asda (Associated Dairies) redefined its business mission as a producer and distributor of milk to a retailer of fast-moving consumer goods partly on the basis of its distribution skills, which it rightly believed could be extended to products beyond milk.

A second influence on business mission is environmental change. Change provides opportunities and threats that influence mission definition. Asda saw that changes in retail practice from corner shops to high-volume supermarkets presented an opportunity that could be exploited by its skills. Its move redefined its business.

The final determinants of business mission are the background of the company and the personalities of its senior management. Businesses that have established themselves in the marketplace over many years, and that have a clear position in the minds of the customer, may ignore opportunities that are at variance with that position. The personalities and beliefs of the people who run businesses also shape the business mission. This last factor emphasizes the judgemental nature of business definition. There is no right or wrong business mission in abstract. The mission should be based on the vision that top management and its subordinates have of the future of the business. This vision is a coherent and powerful statement of what the business should aim to become.[10]

Four characteristics are associated with an effective mission statement.[11] First, it should be based on a solid understanding of the business, and the vision to foresee how the forces acting on its operations will change in the future. A major factor in the success of Perrier was the understanding that its business was natural beverages (rather than water or soft drinks). This subtle distinction was missed by major competitors such as Nestlé, with grave marketing consequences. The vision of its business was also crucial to the success of Nokia. Established in 1865 by Fredrik Idestam as a paper manufacturer, it expanded into a conglomerate operating in industries such as paper, chemicals and rubber. The vision of management in the early 1990s transformed the company by redefining its mission. Nokia abandoned life as a conglomerate to focus on mobile phone technology, a strategic decision that has led to it becoming one of Europe's most successful companies and the world leader in mobile phones.[12]

Second, the mission should be based upon the strong personal conviction and motivation of the leader, who has the ability to make his or her vision contagious. For example, it was Walt Disney who founded his company's mission statement 'To make people happy', which is both contagious and motivating for staff.[13] Another example is Google's mission to organize the world's information and make it universally accessible and useful. It must be shared throughout the organization. For example, when Komatzu challenged Caterpillar in the bulldozer market, its mission statement was 'to beat Cat'.

Third, powerful mission statements should create the strategic intent of winning throughout the organization. This helps to build a sense of common purpose, and stresses the need to create competitive advantages rather than settle for imitative moves. Finally, mission statements should be enabling. Managers must believe they have the latitude to make decisions about strategy without being second-guessed by top management. The mission statement provides the framework within which managers decide which opportunities and threats to address, and which to disregard.

A well-defined mission statement, then, is a key element in the marketing planning process by defining boundaries within which new opportunities are sought and by motivating staff to succeed in the implementation of marketing strategy.

Marketing audit

The **marketing audit** is a systematic examination of a business's marketing environment, objectives, strategies and activities, with a view to identifying key strategic issues, problem areas and opportunities. The marketing audit is therefore the basis upon which a plan of action to improve marketing performance can be built. The marketing audit provides answers to the following questions.

- Where are we now?
- How did we get here?
- Where are we heading?

Answers to these questions depend upon an analysis of the internal and external environment of a business. This analysis benefits from a clear mission statement since the latter defines the boundaries of the environmental scan and helps decisions regarding which strategic issues and opportunities are important.

The internal audit focuses on those areas that are under the control of marketing management, whereas the external audit is concerned with those forces over which management has no control. The results of the marketing audit are a key determinant of the future direction of the business and may give rise to a redefined business mission statement. Alongside the marketing audit, a business may conduct audits of other functional areas such as production, finance and personnel. The coordination and integration of these audits produces a composite business plan in which marketing issues play a central role since they concern decisions about which products to manufacture for which markets. These decisions clearly have production, financial and personnel implications, and successful implementation depends upon each functional area acting in concert.

External marketing audit checklist	TABLE 2.2
MACROENVIRONMENT	
Political/legal: EU and national laws; codes of practice	
Economic: economic growth; unemployment; interest and exchange rates; global economic trends (e.g. the growth of the Chinese and Indian economies)	
Ecological/physical environmental: global warming; pollution; energy and other scarce resources; environmentally friendly ingredients and components; recycling and non-wasteful packaging	
Social/cultural: changes in world population, age distribution and household structure; attitude and lifestyle changes; subcultures within and across national boundaries; consumerism	
Technological: new product and process technologies; new materials	
MICROENVIRONMENT	
Market: size; growth rates; trends	
Customers: who they are, their choice criteria, how, when and where they buy; how they rate us vis-à-vis the competition on product, promotion, price and distribution; how customers group (market segmentation), and what benefits each group seeks; trends	
Competitors: who are the major competitors (actual and potential); their objectives and strategies; strengths and weaknesses; size, market share and profitability; entry barriers to new competitors; trends	
Distributors: channel attractiveness; distributor decision-making unit, decision-making process and choice criteria; strengths and weaknesses; power changes; physical distribution methods; trends	
Suppliers: who they are and location; strengths and weaknesses; power changes; trends	

A checklist of issues that may be examined in a marketing audit is given in Tables 2.2 and 2.3. External analysis covers the macroenvironment and the microenvironment. The **macroenvironment** consists of broad environmental issues that may affect business performance. These are political/legal, economic, ecological/physical, social/cultural and technological forces. Auditing these issues is known by the acronym PEEST analysis. Table 2.2 lists the key topics that fall within each area and an in-depth examination of them will be undertaken in Chapter 3, which deals with the marketing environment.

The **microenvironment** consists of the actors in the firm's immediate environment that affect its capabilities to operate effectively in its chosen markets. The key actors are customers, distributors, suppliers and competitors. Microenvironmental analysis will consist of an analysis of issues relating to these actors and an overall analysis of market size, growth rates and trends (see Table 2.2).

Microenvironmental analysis consists of *market analysis*, which involves the statistical analysis of market size, growth rates and trends, and **customer analysis** of buyer behaviour—how they rate competitive offerings, and how they segment.

Internal marketing audit checklist	TABLE 2.3
Operating results (by product, customer, geographic region)	**Marketing mix effectiveness**
Sales	Product
Market share	Price
Profit margins	Promotion
Costs	Distribution
Strategic issues analysis	**Marketing structures**
Marketing objectives	Marketing organization
Market segmentation	Marketing training
Competitive advantage	Intra- and interdepartmental communication
Core competences	**Marketing systems**
Positioning	Marketing information systems
Portfolio analysis	Marketing planning system
	Marketing control system

It continues with **competitor analysis**, which examines the nature of actual and potential competitors, and their objectives and strategies. It also seeks to identify their strengths and weaknesses, size, market share and profitability. Finally, entry barrier analysis identifies the key financial and non-financial barriers that protect the industry from competitor attack.

The next element of microenvironmental analysis is **distribution analysis**, which covers an examination of the attractiveness of different distribution channels, distributor buyer behaviour, their strengths and weaknesses, movements in power bases, and alternative methods of physical distribution. Finally, **supplier analysis** examines who and where they are located, their strengths and weaknesses, power changes and trends in the supply chain.

The internal audit allows the performance and activities of the business to be assessed in the light of environmental developments. Operating results form a basis of assessment through analysis of sales, market share, profit margins and costs. **Strategic issues analysis** examines the suitability of marketing objectives and segmentation bases in the light of changes in the marketplace. Competitive advantages and the core competences on which they are based would be reassessed and the positioning of products in the market critically reviewed. Core competences are the principal distinctive capabilities possessed by a company, which define what it really is good at. An example of a company that has invested in its core competences in printer, copier and camera technologies is Canon: 8 per cent of its sales revenues is invested in R&D to maintain and extend its success in these markets.[14] ABB is another company that invests in its core competences in power technology. The illustration shows that the payoff is the capability to increase energy efficiency by 25 per cent. One danger that companies face is moving away from their core competences into areas where their skills

Increasing energy efficiency by 25%?

A complete power and automation solution from ABB has helped the largest aluminum refinery in Europe to increase its energy efficiency by 25 percent, boosting productivity at the same time. With research and development geared toward improving performance and resource conservation, we're constantly working to save energy and money. And the environment. www.abb.com/energyefficiency

Certainly.

Power and productivity for a better world™   ABB

▲ By investing in core competences, companies like ABB can meet the needs of customers – and the environment.

and capabilities do not provide a competitive advantage. Management can become distracted, leading to poor performance, as Marketing in Action 2.1 describes.

Finally, **product portfolios** should be analysed to determine future strategic objectives.

Each element of the marketing mix is reviewed in the light of changing customer requirements and competitor activity. The **marketing structures** on which marketing activities are based should be analysed. Marketing structure consists of the marketing organization, training, and intra- and interdepartmental communication that takes place within an organization. Marketing organization is reviewed to determine fit with strategy and the market, and marketing training requirements are examined. Finally, communications and the relationship within the marketing department and between marketing and other functions (e.g. R&D, engineering, production) need to be appraised.

Marketing systems are audited for effectiveness. These consist of the marketing information, planning and control systems that support marketing activities. Shortfalls in information provision are analysed; the marketing planning system is critically appraised for cost-effectiveness, and the marketing control system is assessed in the light of accuracy, timeliness (Does it provide evaluations when managers require them?) and coverage (Does the system evaluate the key variables affecting company performance?).

Marketing systems can be vital assets. For example, marketing information systems at British Airways, Qantas and Singapore Airlines provide knowledge regarding repeat passengers' preferred seats, newspapers, food and drinks, allowing customization of their offerings.

This checklist provides the basis for deciding on the topics to be included in the marketing audit. However, to give the same amount of attention and detailed analysis to every item would grind the audit to a halt under a mass of data and issues. In practice, the judgement of those conducting the audit is critical in deciding the key items to focus upon. Those factors that are considered of crucial importance to the company's performance will merit most attention. One by-product of the marketing audit may be a realization that information about key environmental issues is lacking.

All assumptions should be made explicit as an ongoing part of the marketing audit. For example, key assumptions might be:

- inflation will average 3 per cent during the planning period
- VAT levels will not be changed
- worldwide overcapacity will remain at 150 per cent
- no new entrants into the market will emerge.

2.1 Marketing in Action

Focusing on Core Competences: Back to Basics for Lego and Linn

Both Lego, the Danish toy maker best known for its Lego brick, and Linn Products, the British premium-priced hi-fi equipment maker, have suffered financial losses in recent years. A major contributory factor for both companies was a move away from their core competences.

For Lego its mistake was to diversify into the manufacture of clothing, bags and accessories—areas that required very different skills to the manufacture and marketing of toy bricks. The result was an overcomplicated product portfolio and an overstretching of the Lego brand. Lego's remedy was to refocus on its core brick-based product range and place more emphasis on its key target group: boys aged five to nine.

Linn also made the mistake of stretching its product portfolio further than its competences could handle. Over the years, it grew into one of the world's leading producers of top-of-the-range audio equipment but plunged into loss making because it spread itself too wide. As well as making audio systems for homes, it had moved into distributing high-definition television sets for Loewe, the German-based maker of upmarket domestic electrical equipment.

As Ivor Tiefenbrun, the company founder and chairman, stated, 'We had started to do things that were not our prime purpose.' The answer was to refocus on Linn's core business, which meant divesting television distribution.

The moral of these tales is not that diversification is wrong per se (as Nokia has proven), but that it should be undertaken only when the core competences to succeed are in place or can be acquired.

Based on: Marsh (2008);[15] Siburn (2008)[16]

The marketing audit should be an ongoing activity, not a desperate attempt to turn round an ailing business. Some companies conduct an annual audit as part of their annual planning system; others operating in less turbulent environments may consider two or three years an adequate period between audits. Some companies may feel that the use of an outside consultant to coordinate activities and provide an objective, outside view is beneficial, while others may believe that their own managers are best equipped to conduct the analyses. Clearly there is no set formula for deciding when and by whom the audit is conducted. The decision ultimately rests on the preferences and situation facing the management team.

SWOT analysis

A **SWOT analysis** is a structured approach to evaluating the strategic position of a business by identifying its strengths, weaknesses, opportunities and threats. It provides a simple method of synthesizing the results of the marketing audit. Internal strengths and weaknesses are summarized as they relate to external opportunities and threats (see Fig. 2.2).

When evaluating strengths and weaknesses, only those resources or capabilities that would be valued by the customer should be included.[17] Thus strengths such as 'We are an old established firm', 'We are a large supplier' and

Strengths, weaknesses, opportunities and threats (SWOT) analysis		FIGURE 2.2

		Source
Strengths	Weaknesses	Internal (controllable)
Opportunities	Threats	External (uncontrollable)

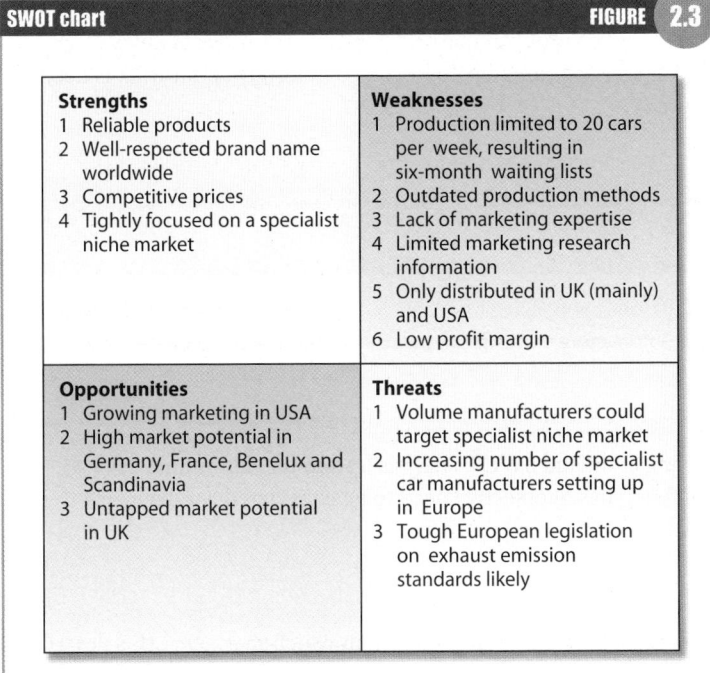

SWOT chart FIGURE 2.3

Strengths	Weaknesses
1 Reliable products 2 Well-respected brand name worldwide 3 Competitive prices 4 Tightly focused on a specialist niche market	1 Production limited to 20 cars per week, resulting in six-month waiting lists 2 Outdated production methods 3 Lack of marketing expertise 4 Limited marketing research information 5 Only distributed in UK (mainly) and USA 6 Low profit margin
Opportunities	**Threats**
1 Growing marketing in USA 2 High market potential in Germany, France, Benelux and Scandinavia 3 Untapped market potential in UK	1 Volume manufacturers could target specialist niche market 2 Increasing number of specialist car manufacturers setting up in Europe 3 Tough European legislation on exhaust emission standards likely

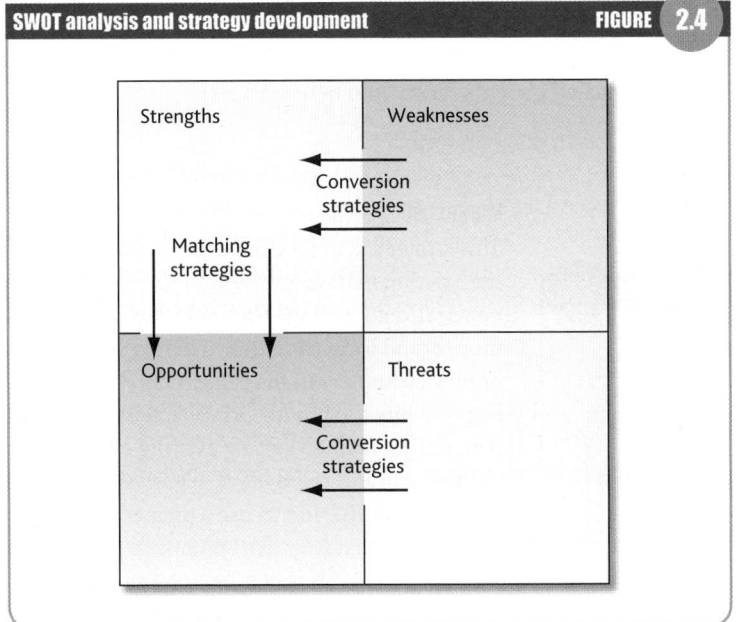

SWOT analysis and strategy development FIGURE 2.4

'We are technologically advanced' should be questioned for their impact on customer satisfaction. It is conceivable that such bland generalizations confer as many weaknesses as strengths. Also, opportunities and threats should be listed as anticipated events or trends *outside* the business that have implications for performance. Figure 2.3 shows an example of a SWOT chart for a specialist, low-volume US sports car manufacturer.

Once a SWOT analysis has been completed, thought can be given to how to turn weaknesses into strengths and threats into opportunities. For example, a perceived weakness in customer care might suggest the need for staff training to create a new strength. A threat posed by a new entrant might call for a strategic alliance to combine the strengths of both parties to exploit a new opportunity. Because these activities are designed to convert weaknesses into strengths and threats into opportunities they are called conversion strategies (see Fig. 2.4). Another way to use a SWOT analysis is to match strengths with opportunities. An example of a company that successfully matched strengths with opportunities is Next, the UK clothing retailer, which saw an opportunity in the growing demand for telemarketing services. One of Next's strengths was the fact that it had run its own call centres for more than a decade to service its own home shopping operation. The result is that Next has created a profitable business running call centres for other companies.

Using the SWOT chart for the specialist sports car manufacturer (Fig. 2.3), conversion strategies might include building a new manufacturing facility to raise production levels to 50 cars per week and to incorporate more modern production methods, establishing a marketing function and (if marketing research supports it) raising price levels. The company could also seek to eliminate the threat of tougher European standards on exhaust emissions by redesigning its engines to meet them. Marketing strategies might include building on the company's strengths in producing reliable products and possessing a well-respected global brand name to establish distribution in Germany, France, Benelux and Scandinavia, while building sales in the USA and UK (opportunities). Given the company's lack of marketing expertise, the geographic expansion would need to be carefully planned (with full input from the newly created marketing department) at a rate of growth compatible with its managerial capabilities and production capacity. International marketing research would be conducted to establish the relative attractiveness of the new European markets to decide the order of entry. Such a phased entry strategy would enable the company to learn progressively about what is needed to market successfully in Europe.

2.1 Pause for Thought

Why do you think marketing managers find SWOT analysis so useful?

Marketing Objectives

The results of the marketing audit and SWOT analysis lead to the definition of **marketing objectives**. Two types of objective need to be considered: strategic thrust and strategic objectives.

Strategic thrust

Ad insight

Go to the website to work out M&S's marketing objectives

Objectives should be set in terms of which products to sell in which markets.[18] This describes the **strategic thrust** of the business. The strategic thrust defines the future direction of the business. The alternatives comprise:

- existing products in existing markets (market penetration or expansion)
- new/related products for existing markets (product development)
- existing products in new/related markets (market development)
- new/related products for new/related markets (entry into new markets).

Figure 2.5 shows these alternatives in diagram form.

Market penetration

This strategy is to take the existing product in the existing market and to attempt increased penetration. Existing customers may become more brand loyal (brand-switch less often) and/or new customers in the same market may begin to buy the brand. Other tactics to increase penetration include getting existing customers to use the brand more often (e.g. wash their hair more frequently) and to use a greater quantity when they use it (e.g. two spoonfuls of tea instead of one). The latter tactic would also have the effect of expanding the market.

Product development

This strategy involves increasing sales by improving present products or developing new products for current markets. New product replacements that fail to provide additional benefits may disappoint, as with the Vista version of Microsoft Windows, which was intended to replace XP. Many users did not

Strategic thrust alternatives   FIGURE 2.5

	Markets	
	Existing	New/related
Existing	Market penetration or expansion	Market development
New/related	Product development	Enter new markets

(Products)

change systems, preferring the XP product.[19] Product development may take the form of brand extensions (e.g. Anadin Extra, Maximum Strength and Soluble) that provide slightly modified features for target customers.

Market development

This strategy is used when current products are sold in new markets. This may involve moving into new geographical markets. Many consumer durable brands, such as cars, consumer electronics and household appliance brands, are sold in overseas markets with no or only very minor modifications to those sold at home. An alternative market development strategy is to move into new market segments. Marketing in Action 2.2 discusses how Tesco has used both strategies with great success.

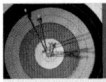

2.2 Marketing in Action

Market Development at Tesco

Tesco is the UK's most successful supermarket chain and accounts for a staggering £1 of every £8 of consumer spending in British shops. The traditional Tesco supermarket was the large superstore offering large food and non-food (e.g. clothing, consumer electronics goods, petrol, CDs) product ranges. These superstores tend to be on the edge of town, with free parking and facilities that include cafés and petrol stations. They target customers who want big, trolley-based family shopping. This one-stop-shopping experience, backed by a good-quality, value-for-money positioning strategy based on the 'Every Little Helps' strap-line ensured healthy sales and profit growth for many years.

In an effort to continue this growth, Tesco embarked on a market development strategy based on entering a new market segment. This was the convenience shopper who wishes to 'top up' their shopping or replace home essentials such as milk or bread. Two new store formats were created, both small but differing in terms of location. Tesco Metro stores allow convenience shopping in town centres, while Tesco Express stores are usually found at petrol stations, providing drivers and local customers with a convenient place to shop for groceries. Both stores carry the same grocery products, albeit a smaller range, than their superstore counterparts.

Tesco has also pursued market development through moving into new geographical markets with similar products. It has expanded into the USA, China, India, South Korea, Thailand, Hungary, Poland and Turkey as it seeks to compete globally with Wal-Mart. Although overseas expansion has sometimes been met with difficulties—most notably in the USA—Tesco's two-pronged market development strategy of seeking to serve new market segments at home and moving into new geographical markets abroad has been highly successful in maintaining sales and profit growth.

Based on: http://www.imaginerecruitment.com;[20] Singh (2008)[21]

Entry into new markets

This strategy occurs when new products are developed for new markets. This is the most risky strategy but may be necessary when a company's current products and markets offer few prospects for future growth. When there is synergy between the existing and new products, this strategy is more likely to work. For example, Apple's experience and competences in computer electronics provided the platform for designing a new product, the iPod, targeting a different market: young people who want downloadable music on a portable music player.[22] This, in turn, has been followed by the launch of the iPhone, which has placed Apple in a strong position in the market for smartphones.[23] Intel also believes it has the core competence required to move into smartphones, as Digital Marketing 2.1 describes.

2.1 Digital Marketing

Intel Enters the Mobile Phone Market

Intel, the world leader in microprocessors, is entering the mobile phone market. Its decision is based on its core competence in processor development and design, which can help it make inroads into mobile phones as smartphones become more like computers. It views smartphones as offering the value proposition of full Internet access that happens to have a voice capability. It also believes that it is easier to add voice to a small computer than vice versa—hence its confidence in entering what is, for the company, a new market.

Entry will be spearheaded by Intel's low-power Atom microprocessor, which has been developed for smartphones. When the Atom was launched, Intel expected PC manufacturers to launch a new category of portable computers known as mobile Internet devices—iPhone-like mini PCs designed for mobile Internet access—and based on Atom chips. Based on the new microprocessor, Intel hopes to become a major player in mobile communications.

Based on: Nuttal and Taylor[24]

Strategic objectives

Alongside objectives for product/market direction, **strategic objectives** for each product need to be agreed. This begins the process of planning at the product level. There are four alternatives:

1 build
2 hold
3 harvest
4 divest.

For new products, the strategic objective will inevitably be to build sales and market share. For existing products, the appropriate strategic objective will depend on the particular situation associated with the product. This will be determined in the marketing audit, SWOT analysis and evaluation of the strategic options outlined earlier. In particular, product portfolio planning tools such as the Boston Consulting Group Growth–Share Matrix, the General Electric Market Attractiveness–Competitive Position Model and the Shell Directional Policy Matrix may be used to aid this analysis. These will be discussed in detail in Chapter 10, which deals with managing products.

The important point to remember at this stage is that *building* sales and market share is not the only sensible strategic objective for a product. As we shall see, *holding* sales and market share may make commercial sense under certain conditions; *harvesting*, where sales and market share are allowed to fall but profit margins are maximized, may also be preferable to building; finally, *divestment*, where the product is dropped or sold, can be the logical outcome of the situation analysis.

Together, strategic thrust and strategic objectives define where the business and its products intend to go in the future.

Core Strategy

Once objectives have been set, the means of achieving them must be determined. **Core strategy** focuses on how objectives can be accomplished and consists of three key elements: target markets, competitor targets and establishing a competitive advantage. Each element will now be examined and the relationship between them discussed.

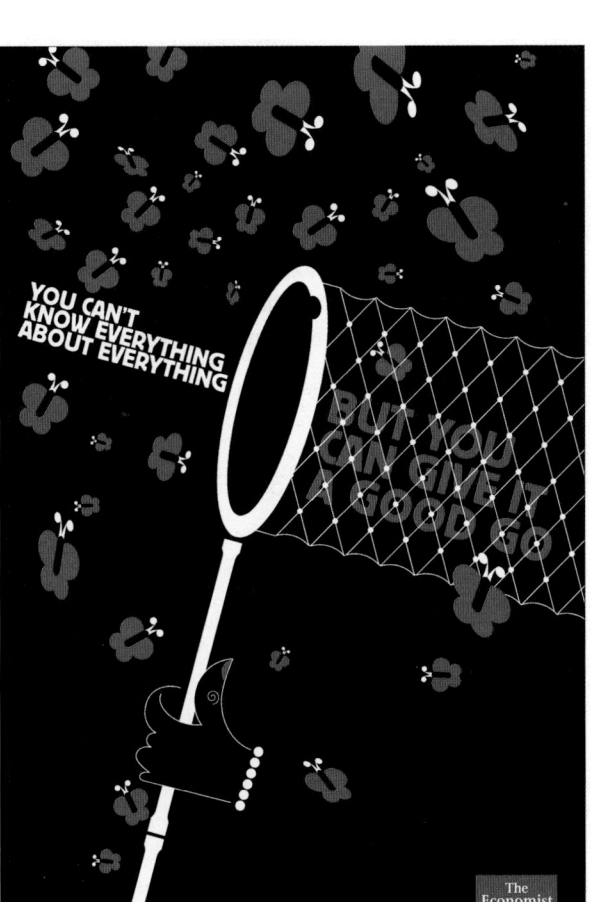

YOU CAN'T KNOW EVERYTHING ABOUT EVERYTHING

The Economist

▲ An important part of marketing planning is target marketing: *The Economist* targets professionals who wish to be perceived as knowledgeable and intelligent.

Target markets

A central plank of core strategy is the choice of **target market(s)**. Marketing is not about chasing any customer at any price. A decision has to be made regarding those groups of customers (segments) that are attractive to the business and match its supply capabilities. The illustration for *The Economist* shows how it targets professionals who aspire to be thought of as knowledgeable and intelligent.

Usually, the choice of target market will emerge as a result of the SWOT analysis and the setting of marketing objectives (strategic thrust). For example, the marketing audit upon which SWOT analysis is based will include market segmentation analysis and, when considering the strategic thrust of the business, decisions regarding which markets to serve must be made. However, if this is defined only in broad terms—for example, 'enter the business personal computer market'—there will be a number of segments (customer groups) of varying attractiveness and a choice has to be made regarding which segments to serve.

One way of segmenting such a market is into large, medium and small customers. Information regarding size, growth potential, level of competitor activity, customer requirements and key factors for success is needed to assess the attractiveness of each segment. This may have been compiled during the marketing audit and should be considered in the light of the capabilities of the business to compete effectively in each specific target market. The marketing audit and SWOT analysis will provide the basis for judging capabilities.

For existing products, management should consider its current target markets. If the needs of customers have changed, this should be recognized so that the marketing mix can be adapted to match the new requirements. In other cases, current target markets may have decreased in attractiveness, so products will need to be repositioned to target different market segments. The process of market segmentation and targeting is examined in depth in Chapter 8.

2.2 Pause for Thought

Why is target marketing a central plank of marketing planning?

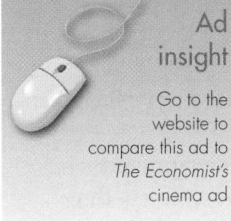

Ad insight

Go to the website to compare this ad to *The Economist's* cinema ad

Competitor targets

Alongside decisions regarding markets lie judgements about **competitor targets**. These are the organizations against which the company chooses to compete directly. Weak competitors may be viewed as easy prey and resources channelled to attack them. The importance of understanding competitors and strategies for attacking and defending against competitors is discussed in Chapters 19 and 20, which examine in detail the areas of competitor analysis and competitive strategy.

GET THE DENTIST CLEAN
FEELING THAT LASTS*

NEW COLGATE TOTAL ADVANCED CLEAN
Get rid of plaque as easily as you can peel back the panel below.
Colgate Total Advanced Clean provides 12 hour antibacterial
protection plus a new advanced cleaning silica system, that fights
plaque between dentists visits.

REMOVE PLAQUE BUILD UP.

▲ Colgate Total attempts
to be better than the
competition by providing
a new advanced cleaning
silica system that fights
plaque.

Competitive advantage

The link between target markets and competitor targets is the establishment of a competitive advantage. A competitive advantage is the achievement of superior performance through differentiation to provide superior customer value, or by managing to achieve lowest delivered cost. For major success, businesses need to achieve a clear performance differential over competition on factors that are important to target customers. The most successful methods are built upon some combination of three advantages:[25]

1 *being better*—superior quality or service (e.g. BMW, Singapore Airlines)
2 *being faster*—anticipate or respond to customer needs faster than the competition (e.g. Zara)
3 *being closer*—establishing close long-term relationships with customers (e.g. IBM).

Colgate Total attempts to be better for those target consumers who are concerned about plaque (see illustration).

Another route to competitive advantage is achieving the lowest relative rate cost position of all competitors.[26] Lowest cost can be translated into a competitive advantage through low prices, or by producing standard items at price parity when comparative success may be achieved through higher profit margins than those of competitors. Achieving a highly differentiated product is not incompatible with a low cost position, however.[27] Inasmuch as high-quality products suffer lower rejection rates through quality control and lower repair costs through their warranty period, they may incur lower total costs than their inferior rivals. Methods of achieving competitive advantages and their sources are analysed in Chapter 19.

Tests of an effective core strategy

The six tests of an effective core strategy are given in Figure 2.6. First, the strategy must be based upon a *clear definition of target customers and their needs*. Second, an understanding of competitors is required so that the core strategy can be based on a *competitive advantage*. Third, the strategy must *incur acceptable risk*. Challenging a strong competitor with a weak competitive advantage and a low resource base would not incur acceptable risk. Fourth, the strategy should be *resource and managerially supportable*. The strategy should match the resource capabilities and managerial competences of the business. Fifth, core strategy should be derived from the *product and marketing objectives* established as part of the planning process. A strategy (e.g. heavy promotion) that makes commercial logic following a build objective may make no sense when a harvesting objective has been decided. Finally, the strategy should be *internally consistent*. The elements should blend to form a coherent whole.

Marketing mix decisions

Marketing managers have at their disposal four broad tools with which they can match their offerings to customers' requirements. These marketing mix decisions consist of judgements about price levels, the blend of promotional techniques to employ, the distribution channels and service levels to use, and the types of products to manufacture. Where promotional, distribution and product standards surpass those of the competition, competitive advantage

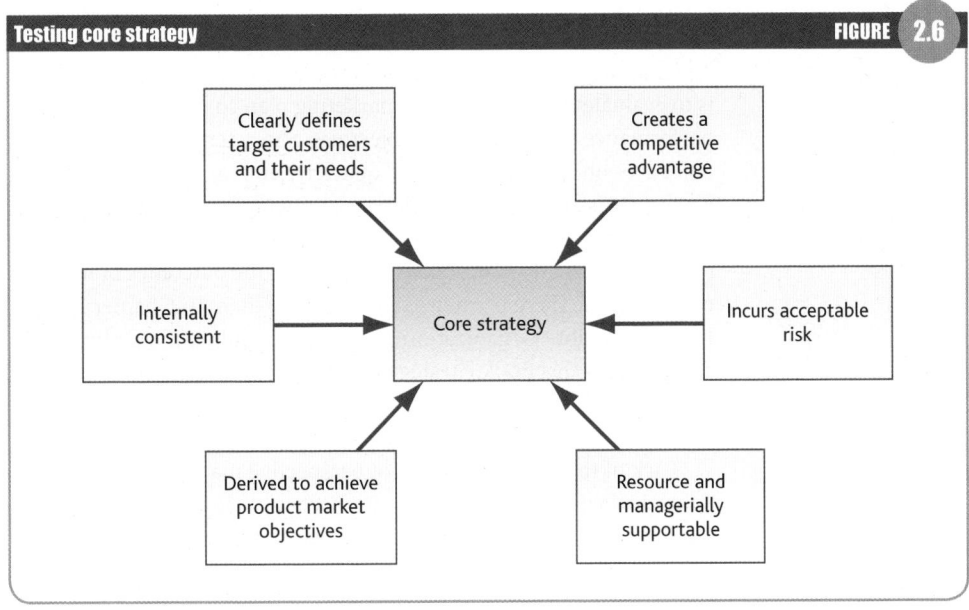

Testing core strategy FIGURE 2.6

may be gained. Alternatively, a judgement may be made only to match, or even undershoot, the competition on some elements of the marketing mix. To outgun the competition on everything is normally not feasible. Choices have to be made about how the marketing mix can be achieved to provide a superior offering to the customer at reasonable cost.

A common failing is to keep the marketing mix the same when moving from one target segment to another. If needs and buying behaviour differ, then the marketing mix must change to match the new requirements. The temptation, for example, to use the same distribution outlets may be great but, if customers prefer to buy elsewhere, a new distribution system, with its associated extra costs, must be established.

Organization and implementation

No marketing plan will succeed unless it 'degenerates into work'.[28] Consequently the business must design an organization that has the capability of implementing the plan. Indeed, organizational weaknesses discovered as part of the SWOT analysis may restrict the feasible range of strategic options. Reorganization could mean the establishment of a marketing organization or department in the business. A study of manufacturing organizations by Piercy found that 55 per cent did not have a marketing department.[29] In some cases marketing was done by the chief executive, in others the sales department dealt with customers and no need for other marketing inputs was perceived. In other situations, environmental change may cause strategy change and this may imply reorganization of marketing and sales. The growth of large corporate customers with enormous buying power has resulted in businesses focusing their resources more firmly on meeting their needs (strategy change), which in turn has led to dedicated marketing and sales teams being organized to service these accounts (reorganization). Organizational issues are explored in Chapter 21.

Because strategy change and reorganization affects the balance of power in businesses, and the daily life and workloads of people, resistance may occur. Consequently marketing personnel need to understand the barriers to change, the process of change management and the techniques of persuasion that can be used to affect the implementation of the marketing plan. These issues are dealt with in Chapter 21.

Control

The final stage in the marketing planning process is **control**. The aim of control systems is to evaluate the results of the marketing plan so that corrective actions can be taken if performance does not match objectives. Short-term control systems can plot results against objectives on a weekly, monthly, quarterly and/or annual basis. Measures include sales, profits, costs and cash flow. There is a growing need for marketing managers to assess the payoff from their investments and justify them. This has resulted in the use of marketing metrics, which are quantitative measures of the outcomes of marketing activities and expenditures. There is extensive coverage of them in Chapter 21, Managing Marketing Implementation, Organization and Control, and on the Online Learning Centre that accompanies this book. Strategic control systems are more long term. Managers need to stand back from week-by-week and month-by-month results to critically reassess whether their plans are in line with their capabilities and the environment.

Lack of this long-term control perspective may result in the pursuit of plans that have lost strategic credibility. New competition, changes in technology and moving customer requirements may have rendered old plans obsolete. This, of course, returns the planning process to the beginning since this kind of fundamental review is conducted in the marketing audit. It is the activity of assessing internal capabilities and external opportunities and threats that results in a SWOT analysis. This outcome may be a redefinition of the business mission, and, as we have seen, changes in marketing objectives and strategies to realign the business with its environment.

So how do the stages of marketing planning relate to the fundamental planning questions stated earlier in this chapter? Table 2.4 illustrates this relationship. The question 'Where are we now and how did we get here?' is answered by the business mission definition, the marketing audit and SWOT analysis.

'Where are we heading?' is forecast by reference to the marketing audit and SWOT analysis. 'Where would we like to be?' is determined by the setting of marketing objectives. 'How do we get there?' refers to core strategy, marketing mix decisions, organization and implementation. Finally 'Are we on course?' is answered by the establishment of a control system.

Key questions and the process of marketing planning	TABLE 2.4
Key questions	**Stages in marketing planning**
Where are we now and how did we get here?	Business mission Marketing audit SWOT analysis
Where are we heading?	Marketing audit SWOT analysis
Where would we like to be?	Marketing objectives
How do we get there?	Core strategy Marketing mix decisions Organization Implementation
Are we on course?	Control

The Rewards of Marketing Planning

Various authors have attributed the following benefits to marketing planning.[30,31,32]

1   *Consistency*: the plan provides a focal point for decisions and actions. By reference to a common plan, decisions by the same manager over time, and by different managers, should be more consistent and actions better coordinated.

2   *Encourages the monitoring of change*: the planning process forces managers to step away from day-to-day problems and review the impact of change on the business from a strategic perspective.

3   *Encourages organizational adaptation*: the underlying premise of planning is that the organization should adapt to match its environment. Marketing planning, therefore, promotes the necessity to accept the inevitability of change. This is an important consideration since adaptive capability has been shown to be linked to superior performance.[33]

4   *Stimulates achievement*: the planning process focuses on objectives, strategies and results. It encourages people to ask, 'What can we achieve given our capabilities?' As such it motivates people to set new horizons for objectives when they otherwise might be content to accept much lower standards of performance.

5   *Resource allocation*: the planning process asks fundamental questions about resource allocation. For example, which products should receive high investment (build), which should be maintained (hold), which should have resources withdrawn slowly (harvest) and which should have resources withdrawn immediately (divest)?

6   *Competitive advantage*: planning promotes the search for sources of competitive advantage.

However, it should be realized that this logical planning process, sometimes called *synoptic* planning, may be at variance with the culture of the business, which may plan effectively using an *incremental approach*.[34] The style of planning must match business culture.[35] Saker and Speed argue that the considerable demands on managers in terms of time and effort implied by the synoptic marketing planning process may mean that alternative planning schemes are more appropriate, particularly for small companies.[36]

Incremental planning is more problem-focused in that the process begins with the realization of a problem (for example, a fall-off in orders) and continues with an attempt to identify a solution. As solutions to problems form, so strategy emerges. However, little attempt is made to integrate consciously the individual decisions that could possibly affect one another. Strategy is viewed as a loosely linked group of decisions that are handled individually. Nevertheless, its effect may be to attune the business to its environment through its problem-solving nature. Its drawback is the lack of a broad situation analysis and strategy option generation, which renders the incremental approach less comprehensive. For some companies, however, its inherent practicality may support its use rather than its rationality.[37]

Problems in Making Planning Work

Empirical work into the marketing planning practices of commercial organizations has found that most companies did not practise the kinds of systematic planning procedures described in this chapter and, of those that did, many did not enjoy the rewards described in the previous section.[38] However, others have shown that there is a relationship between planning and commercial success (see, for example, Armstrong and McDonald).[39,40] The problem is that the *contextual difficulties* associated with the process of marketing planning are substantial and need to be understood. Inasmuch as forewarned is forearmed, the following is a checklist of potential problems that have to be faced by those charged with making marketing planning work.

Political

Marketing planning is a resource allocation process. The outcome of the process is an allocation of more funds to some products and departments, the same or less to others. Since power bases, career opportunities and salaries are often tied to whether an area is fast or slow growing, it is not surprising that managers view planning as a highly political activity. An example is a European bank, whose planning process resulted in the decision to insist that its retail branch managers divert certain types of loan application to the industrial/merchant banking arm of the group where the return was greater. This was required because the plan was designed to optimize the return to the group as a whole. However, the consequence was considerable friction between the divisions concerned because the decision lowered the performance of the retail branch.

In another European bank, the introduction of a series of market-based products was blocked by managers of existing product-orientated offerings who feared their launch would mean them losing their jobs. Both these examples demonstrate how political factors can be a barrier to marketing planning initiatives.

Opportunity cost

Some busy managers view marketing planning as a time-wasting ritual that conflicts with the need to deal with day-to-day problems. They view the opportunity cost of spending two or three days away at a hotel thrashing out long-term plans as too high. This difficulty may be compounded by the fact that people who are attracted to the hectic pace of managerial life may be the type who prefer to live that way.[41] Hence they may be ill at ease with the thought of a long period of sedate contemplation.

Reward systems

The reward systems of many businesses are geared to the short term. Incentives and bonuses may be linked to quarterly or annual results. Managers may thus overweight short-term issues and underweight medium- and long-term concerns if there is a conflict of time. Thus marketing planning may be viewed as of secondary importance.

Information

To function effectively a systematic marketing planning system needs informational inputs. Market share, size and growth rates are basic inputs into the marketing audit but may be unavailable. More perversely, information may be wilfully withheld by vested interests who, recognizing that knowledge is power, distort the true situation to protect their position in the planning process.

Culture

The establishment of a systematic marketing planning process may be at variance with the culture of the organization. As has already been stated, businesses may 'plan' by making incremental decisions. Hence the strategic planning system may challenge the status quo and be seen as a threat. In other cases, the values and beliefs of some managers may be hostile to a planning system altogether.

Personalities

Marketing planning usually involves a discussion between managers about the strategic choices facing the business and the likely outcomes. This can be a highly charged affair where personality clashes and pent-up antagonisms can surface. The result can be that the process degenerates into abusive argument and sets up deep chasms within the management team.

Lack of knowledge and skills

Another problem that can arise when setting up a marketing planning system is that the management team does not have the knowledge and skills to perform the tasks adequately.[42] Basic marketing knowledge about market segmentation, competitive advantage and the nature of strategic objectives may be lacking. Similarly, skills in analysing competitive situations and defining core strategies may be inadequate.

How to Handle Marketing Planning Problems

Some of the problems revealed during the market planning process may be deep-seated managerial inadequacies rather than being intrinsic to the planning process itself. As such the attempt to establish the planning system may be seen as a benefit to the business by revealing the nature of these problems. However, various authors have proposed recommendations (as follows) for minimizing the impact of such problems.[43,44]

1 *Senior management support*: top management must be committed to planning and be seen by middle management to give it total support. This should be ongoing support, not a short-term fad.

2 *Match the planning system to the culture of the business*: how the marketing planning process is managed should be consistent with the culture of the organization. For example, in some organizations the top-down/bottom-up balance will move towards top-down; in other less directive cultures the balance will move towards a more bottom-up planning style.

3 *The reward system*: this should reward the achievement of longer-term objectives rather than exclusively focus on short-term results.

4 *Depoliticize outcomes*: less emphasis should be placed on rewarding managers associated with build (growth) strategies. Recognition of the skills involved in defending share and harvesting products should be made. At General Electric, managers are classified as 'growers', 'caretakers' and 'undertakers', and matched to products that are being built, defended or harvested in recognition of the fact that the skills involved differ according to the strategic objective. No stigma is attached to caretaking or undertaking; each is acknowledged as contributing to the success of the organization.

5 *Clear communication*: plans should be communicated to those charged with implementation.

6 *Training*: marketing personnel should be trained in the necessary marketing knowledge and skills to perform the planning job. Ideally the management team should attend the same training course so that they each share a common understanding of the concepts and tools involved and can communicate using the same terminology.

Online **Learning Centre**

When you have read this chapter

log on to the Online Learning Centre at www.mcgraw-hill.co.uk/textbooks/jobber to explore chapter-by-chapter test questions, links and further online study tools for marketing.

Review ●●●

1 **The role of marketing planning within business**
- Marketing planning is part of a broader concept known as strategic planning.
- For one-product companies, its role is to ensure that the product continues to meet customers' needs as well as seeking new opportunities.
- For companies marketing a range of products in a number of markets, marketing planning's role is as above plus the allocation of resources to each product.
- For companies comprising a number of businesses (SBUs), marketing planning's role is as above plus a contribution to the allocation of resources to each business.

2 **The key planning questions**
- These are: 'Where are we now?', 'How did we get there?', 'Where are we heading?', 'Where would we like to be?', 'How do we get there?' and 'Are we on course?'

3 **The process of marketing planning**
- The steps in the process are: deciding the business mission, conducting a marketing audit, producing a SWOT analysis, setting marketing objectives (strategic thrust and strategic objectives), deciding core strategy (target markets, competitive advantage and competitor targets), making marketing mix decisions, organizing and implementing, and control.

4 **The concept of the business mission**
- A business mission is a broadly defined, enduring statement of purpose that distinguishes a business from others of its type.
- A business mission should answer two questions: 'What business are we in?' and 'What business do we want to be in?'

5 **The nature of the marketing audit and SWOT analysis**
- The marketing audit is a systematic examination of a business's marketing environment, objectives, strategies and activities, with a view to identifying key strategic issues, problem areas and opportunities.
- It consists of an examination of a company's external and internal environments. The external environment is made up of the macroenvironment, the market and competition. The internal environmental audit consists of operating results, strategic issues analysis, marketing mix effectiveness, marketing structures and systems.
- A SWOT analysis provides a simple method of summarizing the results of the marketing audit. Internal issues are summarized under strengths and weaknesses, and external issues are summarized under opportunities and threats.

6 **The nature of marketing objectives**
- There are two types of marketing objective: (i) strategic thrust, which defines the future direction of the business in terms of which products to sell in which markets; and (ii) strategic objectives, which are product-level objectives relating to the decision to build, hold, harvest or divest products.

7 **The components of core strategy and the criteria for testing its effectiveness**
- The components are target markets, competitor targets and competitive advantage.
- The criteria for testing its effectiveness are that core strategy clearly defines target customers and their needs, creates a competitive advantage, incurs acceptable risk, is resource and managerially supportable, is derived to achieve product–market objectives and is internally consistent.

8 **Where marketing mix decisions are placed within the marketing planning process**
- Marketing mix decisions follow those of core strategy as they are based on an understanding of target customers' needs and the competition so that a competitive advantage can be created.

9 **The importance of organization, implementation and control within the marketing planning process**
- Organization is needed to support the strategies decided upon. Strategies are unlikely to be effective without attention to implementation issues. For example, techniques to overcome resistance to change and the training of staff who are required to implement strategic decisions are likely to be required.
- Control systems are important so that the results of the marketing plan can be evaluated and corrective action taken if performance does not match objectives.

10 **The rewards and problems associated with marketing planning**
- The rewards are consistency of decision-making, encouragement of the monitoring of change, encouragement of organizational adaptation, stimulation of achievement, aiding resource allocation and promotion of the creation of a competitive advantage.
- The potential problems with marketing planning revolve around the context in which it takes place and are political, high opportunity cost, lack of reward systems tied to longer-term results, lack of relevant information, cultural and personality clashes, and lack of managerial knowledge and skills.

11 **Recommendations for overcoming marketing planning problems**
- Recommendations for minimizing the impact of marketing planning problems are: attaining senior management support, matching the planning system to the culture of the business, creating a reward system that is focused on longer-term performance, depoliticizing outcomes, communicating clearly to those responsible for implementation, and training in the necessary marketing knowledge and skills to conduct marketing planning.

Key Terms

business mission the organization's purpose, usually setting out its competitive domain, which distinguishes the business from others of its type

competitor analysis an examination of the nature of actual and potential competitors, and their objectives and strategies

competitor targets the organizations against which a company chooses to compete directly

control the stage in the marketing planning process or cycle when the performance against plan is monitored so that corrective action, if necessary, can be taken

core strategy the means of achieving marketing objectives, including target markets, competitor targets and competitive advantage

customer analysis a survey of who the customers are, what choice criteria they use, how they rate competitive offerings and on what variables they can be segmented

distribution analysis an examination of movements in power bases, channel attractiveness, physical distribution and distribution behaviour

macroenvironment a number of broader forces that affect not only the company but the other actors in the environment, e.g. social, political, technological and economic

marketing audit a systematic examination of a business's marketing environment, objectives, strategies, and activities with a view to identifying key strategic issues, problem areas and opportunities

marketing objectives there are two types of marketing objective: strategic thrust, which dictates which products should be sold in which markets, and strategic objectives, i.e. product-level objectives, such as build, hold, harvest and divest

marketing planning the process by which businesses analyse the environment and their capabilities, decide upon courses of marketing action and implement those decisions

marketing structures the marketing frameworks (organization, training and internal communications) upon which marketing activities are based

marketing systems sets of connected parts (information, planning and control) that support the marketing function

microenvironment the actors in the firm's immediate environment that affect its capability to operate effectively in its chosen markets—namely, suppliers, distributors, customers and competitors

product portfolio the total range of products offered by the company

strategic business unit a business or company division serving a distinct group of customers and with a distinct set of competitors, usually strategically autonomous

strategic issues analysis an examination of the suitability of marketing objectives and segmentation bases in the light of changes in the marketplace

strategic objectives product-level objectives relating to the decision to build, hold, harvest or divest products

strategic thrust the decision concerning which products to sell in which markets

supplier analysis an examination of who and where suppliers are located, their competences and shortcomings, the trends affecting them and the future outlook for them

SWOT analysis a structured approach to evaluating the strategic position of a business by identifying its strengths, weaknesses, opportunities and threats

target market a market segment that has been selected as a focus for the company's marketing mix

Study Questions

1. Is a company that forecasts future sales and develops a budget on the basis of these forecasts conducting marketing planning?

2. Explain how each stage of the marketing planning process links with the fundamental planning questions identified in Table 2.1.

3. Under what circumstances may *incremental* planning be preferable to *synoptic* marketing planning, and vice versa?

4. Why is a clear business mission statement a help to marketing planners?

5. What is meant by core strategy? What role does it play in the process of marketing planning?

6. Distinguish between strategic thrust and strategic objectives.

References

1. Day, G. S. (1984) *Strategic Marketing Planning: The Pursuit of Competitive Advantage*, St Paul, MN: West, 41.
2. Weitz, B. A. and R. Wensley (1988) *Readings in Strategic Marketing*, New York: Dryden, 4.
3. Piercy, N. (2002) *Market-led Strategic Change: Transforming the Process of Going to Market*, Oxford: Butterworth-Heinemann.
4. Day (1984) op. cit., 48.
5. Ackoff, R. I. (1987) Mission Statements, *Planning Review* 15(4), 30–2.
6. Hooley, G. J., A. J. Cox and A. Adams (1992) Our Five Year Mission: To Boldly Go Where No Man Has Been Before . . . , *Journal of Marketing Management* 8(1), 35–48.
7. Abell, D. (1980) *Defining the Business: The Starting Point of Strategic Planning*, Englewood Cliffs, NJ: Prentice-Hall, Ch. 3.

8. Levitt, T. (1960) Marketing Myopia, *Harvard Business Review*, July–August, 45–6.

9. Ritson, M. (2005) Lenovo is All Over the Place, *Marketing*, 8 June, 22.

10. Wilson, I. (1992) Realizing the Power of Strategic Vision, *Long Range Planning* 25(5), 18–28.

11. Day, G. S. (1999) *Market Driven Strategy: Processes for Creating Value*, New York: Free Press, 16–17.

12. Davidson, H. (2002) *The Committed Enterprise*, Oxford: Heinemann.

13. Sanghera, S. (2005) Why So Many Mission Statements are Mission Impossible, *Financial Times*, 22 July, 13.

14. Anonymous (2002) Hard to Copy, *Economist*, 2 November, 79.

15. Marsh, P. (2008) Sound Strategist Gets Back on Track, *Guardian*, 29 October, 16.

16. Siburn, J. (2008) Lego Renaissance Builds on Key Strengths, www.telegraph.co.uk.

17. Piercy, N. (2008) *Market-led Strategic Change: Transforming the Process of Going to Market*, Oxford: Butterworth-Heinemann, 259.

18. McDonald, M. H. B. (2007) *Marketing Plans*, London: Butterworth-Heinemann, 2nd edn.

19. Anonymous (2008) After Bill, *Economist*, 28 June, 92–4.

20. http://www.imaginerecruitment.com/jobs/featured/tesco.

21. Singh, S. (2008) Is India the Gateway to Global Domination for Tesco?, *Marketing Week*, 21 August.

22. Helmore, E. (2005) Big Apple, *Observer*, 16 January, 3.

23. Allison, K. (2008) Apple Unveils iPhone Grand Plan, *Financial Times*, 10 March, 23.

24. Nuttal, C. and P. Taylor (2008) Intel to Re-Enter Mobile Market, *Financial Times*, 2 June, 25.

25. Day (1999) op. cit., 9.

26. Porter, M. E. (1980) *Competitive Strategy: Techniques for Analysing Industries and Competitors*, New York: Free Press, Ch. 2.

27. Phillips, L. W., D. R. Chang and R. D. Buzzell (1983) Product Quality, Cost Position and Business Performance: A Test of Some Key Hypotheses, *Journal of Marketing* 47(Spring), 26–43.

28. Drucker, P. F. (1993) *Management Tasks, Responsibilities, Practices*, New York: Harper and Row, 128.

29. Piercy, N. (1986) The Role and Function of the Chief Marketing Executive and the Marketing Department, *Journal of Marketing Management* 1(3), 265–90.

30. Leppard, J. W. and M. H. B. McDonald (1991) Marketing Planning and Corporate Culture: A Conceptual Framework which Examines Management Attitudes in the Context of Marketing Planning, *Journal of Marketing Management* 7(3), 213–36.

31. Greenley, G. E. (1986) *The Strategic and Operational Planning of Marketing*, Maidenhead: McGraw-Hill, 185–7.

32. Terpstra, V. and R. Sarathy (1991) *International Marketing*, Orlando, FL: Dryden, Ch. 17.

33. Oktemgil, M. and G. Greenley (1997) Consequences of High and Low Adaptive Capability in UK Companies, *European Journal of Marketing* 31(7), 445–66.

34. Raimond, P. and C. Eden (1990) Making Strategy Work, *Long Range Planning* 23(5), 97–105.

35. Driver, J. C. (1990) Marketing Planning in Style, *Quarterly Review of Marketing* 15(4), 16–21.

36. Saker, J. and R. Speed (1992) Corporate Culture: Is it Really a Barrier to Marketing Planning?, *Journal of Marketing Management* 8(2), 177–82. For information on marketing and planning in small and medium-sized firms see Carson, D. (1990) Some Exploratory Models for Assessing Small Firms' Marketing Performance: A Qualitative Approach, *European Journal of Marketing* 24(11), 8–51, and Fuller, P. B. (1994) Assessing Marketing in Small and Medium-Sized Enterprises, *European Journal of Marketing* 28(12), 34–9.

37. O'Shaughnessy, J. (1995) *Competitive Marketing*, Boston, Mass: Allen & Unwin.

38. Greenley, G. (1987) An Exposition into Empirical Research into Marketing Planning, *Journal of Marketing Management* 3(1), 83–102.

39. Armstrong, J. S. (1982) The Value of Formal Planning for Strategic Decisions: Review of Empirical Research, *Strategic Management Journal* 3(3), 197–213.

40. McDonald, M. H. B. (1984) The Theory and Practice of Marketing Planning for Industrial Goods in International Markets, Cranfield Institute of Technology, PhD thesis. A more recent study has also confirmed that marketing planning is linked to commercial success: Pulendran, S., R. Speed and R. E. Wildin II (2003) Marketing Planning, Marketing Orientation and Business Performance, *European Journal of Marketing* 37(3/4), 476–97.

41. Mintzberg, H. (1975) The Manager's Job: Folklore and Fact, *Harvard Business Review*, July–August, 49–61.

42. McDonald, M. H. B. (1989) The Barriers to Marketing Planning, *Journal of Marketing Management* 5(1), 1–18.

43. McDonald (2002) op. cit.

44. Abell, D. F. and J. S. Hammond (1979) *Strategic Market Planning*, Englewood Cliffs, NJ: Prentice-Hall.

Vulnerable Volvo

Can the Volvo Brand Succeed in the New Competitive Landscape?

Over the years Volvo had developed an image of being stodgy, and designing cars resembling large boxes on wheels for county gentry. A typical Volvo owner was seen to be middle-aged, with 2.5 kids and a golden retriever dog barking in the boot. This image of functionality over styling prevailed. A newer suite of car models attempted to move Volvo away from these traditional, 'boxy' lines. Volvo developed a suite of cars that seemed to turn around the fortunes of the company, and deliver stable revenues and profits for the firm. Volvo became one of the most successful automotive brands for its parent, Ford Motor Corporation. However, sales for Volvo were down by 18.3 per cent in 2008, and are continuing to underperform in 2009, given the global economic turmoil. This unprecedented downturn has lead to leading companies filing for bankruptcy, and the demise of several automotive brands. Volvo hopes that a suite of newer models will help turn around its performance. Is Volvo a fading star or is this just a blip in the performance of a stellar company?

Volvo is a relatively small car manufacturer, with less than 1 per cent of global market share. Volvo lost more than $1.5 billion in 2008—a colossal figure in any industry. The Volvo name is over 90 years old and has become an international icon for Sweden. In 1999, AB Volvo sold Volvo cars to Ford Motor Company for $6.45 billion, much to the chagrin of many Swedes. Many feared that Volvo would lose its unique appeal and that the brand would be destroyed by the takeover. AB Volvo continues to make commercial trucks and buses. The Volvo brand is managed under a unique dual-partnership brand committee to ensure that the brand's equity is protected. Ford wanted a slice of the luxury car market to compete successfully against the likes of the increasingly successful Toyota and Lexus brands. Volvo was part of Ford's four-pronged strategy to enter the luxury car marque sector. It formed the Premier Automotive Group (PAG) by buying Volvo, Land Rover, Aston Martin and Jaguar. Volvo consistently made large profits for the group, ranging from $750 million to $1 billion per year, whereas other investments, such as Jaguar, continued to haemorrhage money for Ford. In 2008, Ford bailed out of this aspirational initiative by

fire-selling the Jaguar, Aston Martin and Land Rover brands. It sold Jaguar and Land Rover to Indian car manufacturer Tata for $2.3 billion. Volvo is up for sale too, as Ford wants to concentrate on its core brands, but no suitor has yet emerged. It was bought for $6.4 billion in 1999, but is now (2009) estimated to be worth only $3.5 billion. When Ford bought Volvo, it bought not only a successful brand but a unique culture, which has never been forced into becoming just another Ford subsidiary. Volvo maintained its independence but, at the same time, benefited from platform sharing, shared research and development, and combined buying power.

The Volvo brand was primarily about two key aspects: big estate cars, and safety. Over the years Volvo developed a reputation for big estate cars that would last for long periods of time. Entry-level models were somewhat affordable, with high-end models priced at a premium, with big engine options. The company sells basic models and has a whole host of optional extras and accessories, ranging from metallic paint, leather seats and roof racks to grocery holders. All these optional extras help boost the final selling price, and provide a certain level of customization, which is sought after by Volvo customers. Now, Volvo has four main types of model: the S-Type (saloons), the V-Type (estates), the XC (SUVs), and the C-Type (coupes). Its XC range became the company's biggest seller, being particularly successful in America, where big cars typically equated with big success. Now, with rising petrol prices, Volvo's SUV market is under threat. Furthermore, consumers are moving away from Volvo's large engines, seeking more fuel-efficient options. The

Volvo at a Glance	TABLE C3.1
Headquarters based in Göteborg, Sweden	
Volvo has a presence in over 120 countries	
Sold through a network of 2400 dealers: 1500 in Europe and 400 in the USA	
Employs 20,000 people, many based in Sweden	
Mission statement: 'We design cars for a better life'	
Sold 458,323 in 2007; 374,297 in 2008	
Manufacturing plant in Göteborg, Sweden, and Ghent, Belgium	
Has established manufacturing sites through partnerships in other export markets, such as China, where it hopes to sell 10,000 a year	
Brand values include safety, modern Scandinavian design, environmental care, premium quality, customer experience and driving dynamics	

Volvo market by country, 2007 and 2008		TABLE C3.2
Country	**2007**	**2008**
United States	106,125	73,078
Sweden	62,229	47,775
Britain	30,003	33,341
Germany	32,329	27,053
Russia	21,077	21,043
Netherlands	20,253	16,742
Italy	20,290	16,653
Belgium	13,991	12,872
China	12,460	12,640
France	13,497	11,745
Others	126,069	101,355
Total	*458,323*	*374,297*

USA is the firm's largest market, with sales equating to 19.5 per cent of total sales, but sales have collapsed by 31 per cent due to the economic crisis, and the market's focus on eco-friendly alternatives rather than large, gas-guzzling SUVs like the XC-90. In these developed markets, growth is flat; however, in emerging markets such as those in Asia, prospects seem good.

Competition in the global automotive market is fierce. The company's key competitors would be Volkswagen's Audi, General Motors' Saab, Toyota's Lexus, Mercedes-Benz and BMW. The industry is faced with continued economic turmoil, with Volvo's nearest Scandinavian rival, Saab, being abandoned by the bankrupt General Motors. The industry is faced with some notable challenges: the impact of globalization, increasing regulation, growing environmental/energy concerns, rising fuel prices, rising commodity prices, calls for more safety initiatives, greater taxation of the automotive trade, manufacturing overcapacity, pressure on margins, and changing socio-cultural influences. Some auto makers—such as General Motors and Ford—are faced with crippling debt and ebbing market share. Companies have to adapt or face death.

Toyota is becoming the world's largest and most successful car manufacturer—however, it isn't immune either, recording its first ever corporate loss in 2008, of $4.4 billion. It is achieving huge success through its winning combination of value for money, fuel-efficient, reliable cars. This is what the industry is labelling 'guzzler fatigue', where consumers are migrating to smaller, more fuel-efficient cars. In addition, governments are putting in place taxation structures that penalize large cars with higher CO_2 emissions. Governments are providing tax incentives for consumers who buy fuel-efficient hybrid and Flexi-Fuel cars, and possibly other incentives such as free road tolls, parking and so on. With the rising price of oil in the US market, all the major automotive players have seen sales shrink, as consumers move towards more fuel-efficient cars. Volvo is now offering Flexi-Fuel (a combination of petrol and ethanol) in certain geographic markets. This provides consumers with a more eco-friendly alternative and cheaper oil prices. These cars produce 80 per cent less carbon gas emissions.

Volvo states that its vision is 'to be the world's most desired and successful premium car brand', whereas in its mission statement it aims to 'create the safest, most exciting car experience for modern families'. This continued emphasis on creating a luxury automotive brand means that research and development is crucial, and that Volvo needs to create models that exude quality, performance and safety. An interesting aspect of this mission statement is the company's focus on the

Volvo's product range		TABLE C3.3
	Description	
C30	Small hatchback	
S40	Mid-sized saloon (entry level), prices from £15,700	
S60	Mid-sized saloon	
S80	Large luxury saloon	
V50	Mid-sized estate, second most popular seller	
V70	Large estate, V stands for versatile.	
XC60	New crossover small premium utility launched in 2008	
XC70	Cross-country sport utility vehicle (SUV)	
XC90	Large SUV, most popular seller, prices from £33,000 to £54,000	
C70	Turbo-charged convertible	

▲ Volvo sponsors events such as the Volvo Youth Sailing ISAF World Championships that complement its core target market.

family sector, particularly in light of declining birth rates in Europe, smaller families and more couples choosing to remain childless. Many cars on the road today are used by single occupants, commuting to work. The firm sees its future as delivering 'safe', 'premium' and 'exciting' driving, suitable for families. However, in a radical departure from this philosophy, it has launched a new sporty hatchback called the S30, destined to compete against high-end versions of VW's Golf. A key challenge for Volvo is to attract younger drivers to the car marque, as its target audience of 15 years ago is downsizing and migrating to smaller, more fuel-efficient cars as they approach retirement. Luring the next generation of Volvo drivers is essential to ensuring long-term success. Volvo's design philosophy is that 'good design is not only a matter of styling the surface. It is just as important to make the product easy to understand and use. If the product is not functional, it can't be beautiful.' However, sales have yet to capture the market's imagination, with only 40,000 units sold.

The company's overall long-term aim is to sell 600,000 cars annually. It ceased assembly operations in South Africa and has now started ramping up production in China. The company has established over 40 state-of-the-art dealerships in the country. It has even

decided to sell in India, too, initially selling its premium ranges in three dealerships. The company sponsors the internationally known Volvo Global Ocean Race, the Volvo Youth Sailing Championship and golf events that complement its core target market. This has proved an excellent brand platform, with exciting media coverage lasting several months, and the company has been able to leverage experiential marketing opportunities through such events and competitions. Volvo has created a museum to showcase its brand philosophy; it is called the 'Volvo Experience' and is full of interactive exhibits that showcase the company, its brand and its achievements. In order to be successful in the premium sector, it believes that customers' satisfaction with the Volvo brand experience is vital. This can be achieved through excellent, superior product performance and excellent dealership service.

Despite the takeover by Ford, Volvo has maintained much of its independence. It benefits from shared R&D expenditure and buying power. Furthermore the company benefits from platform sharing, where the costly vehicle undercarriage is shared between diverse models—for example, its V50 estate shares the same platform as a Ford Focus and a Mazda. Volvo believes that success can be achieved through strategic positioning and operational effectiveness (e.g. shared technologies, cost advantages). Its emphasis is on design, safety and sustainability. The company has launched the DRIVe initiative, aimed at reducing the carbon emissions of its popular models. Furthermore it also aims to launch a plug-in hybrid in 2012.

Volvo has launched Volvo Vision 2020, where the firm aims to differentiate itself from its competitors. The central plank of this strategy is an ongoing commitment to the environment and to safety. There has been a transfer from the concept of the 'common good' to the 'private good', where a fun, exciting driving experience is created for the customer. By doing this, the firm aims to create a brand that is well respected and trustworthy. It aims to create cars that are exciting to drive, and that drivers feel good about driving. In relation to the environment, the firm plans to improve energy efficiency and health-related technology through the incorporation of recycled materials, alternative fuel types and reduced emissions. The continued emphasis on safety aims to focus on preventive and protective safety through reducing accidents, fatalities and injuries. Volvo has placed great emphasis on creating a safer world, in relation to the environment and driving. This will represent Volvo's core positioning strategy, but will it yield increased dividends in a market where competitors are mimicking this strategic focus?

The company is extremely proud of its innovations in car safety enhancements, being a pioneer of the safety cage, crumple zones, side impact protection, antilock brakes, whiplash protection and airbags. Volvo invests heavily in safety research and development; its Göteberg safety centre is world renowned. The company continues to innovate with blind spot and collision warning systems. Yet branding a car as just 'safe' is never going to win over large numbers of would-be consumers. Performance, styling, reliability, handling and value for money are all vitally important. Volvo's core positioning statement of producing the safest cars in the market remains, yet more and more of its competitors (e.g. Renault) have also successfully integrated safety into their customer propositions. Volvo needs to offer something else to consumers.

The company uses the tag-line 'Volvo. For Life'. A key question remains for Volvo: will it maintain its tried and tested marketing formula, or will the firm have to pursue a radical rethink of its business philosophy in the wake of a changing marketing environment? The company is under threat from the changing automotive landscape, but how will it adapt?

Questions

1. Outline and discuss the macro- and microenvironmental factors that are influencing Volvo's strategy.

2. Conduct a SWOT analysis on Volvo cars.

3. Outline the strategic options available to Volvo Auto Division, recommending what you believe to be the best option available and giving reasons for your answer.

This case was written by Conor Carroll, Lecturer in Marketing, University of Limerick.

Heron Engineering

A Strategy for Storage

Established in 1899 and based in Manchester, Heron was the global market leader in the industrial stacking and storage business when John Toft was appointed marketing director for its European division. The European market alone was estimated to be worth around £275 million and Heron had generated some £100 million sales revenue and £24 million gross profits in it during the financial year to March 2008. However, the market had changed noticeably in recent years and Toft's first responsibility was to review the overall marketing situation and, if necessary, propose a new long-term marketing plan for the European region.

To help with his review, Toft had held a briefing meeting in February 2009 with his predecessor, Peter Box, who had retired the week before. Box had begun by explaining that Heron had divided the market geographically into the Western European (WE) region and the Central and Eastern European (CEE) region, and that, in each geographic region, it served a low-technology storage products sector and a high-technology storage systems sector.

The low-technology sector consisted of customers for shelving brackets and simple storage units into which trays and small pallets could be placed by hand. The simple storage units were often used by supermarkets to stock and display bread and other items in-store. However, the vast majority of customers in this sector were in the manufacturing, wholesaling and distribution industries. The prime customer choice criterion in this sector in both WE and CEE was price, while product availability was also very important. Product functionality was also important to customers although minimum acceptable standards for this were met by all suppliers in the market.

The high-technology sector was made up of customers seeking to buy high-value sophisticated storage and materials handling systems. These consisted of advanced mechanical storage units, conveyor systems, overhead lifting and carrying technologies, and so on, for use in factories, airports, docks, warehouses and other large facilities. Customers in WE applied product functionality and systems customization as their prime supplier selection criteria. However, they also valued having close relationships with suppliers and the benefits these provide, such as easy contact, empathy, trust, advice, training in systems usage and help in

crises. In many CEE countries, customers faced difficulties in being able to pay for the high-cost sophisticated storage systems due to hard currency shortages and inaccessibility to international credit. Consequently, the main choice criteria among these customers were attractive financing and systems functionality. Customers also regarded price as important, as well as customization and local contact with suppliers.

Approximately 65 per cent of Heron's 2008 European revenue had been generated in WE with the remainder in CEE. Around 65 per cent of the WE revenue was gained from sales of high-technology systems, whereas some 65 per cent of CEE revenue was for sales of the low-technology products. There had been a marked inter-regional contrast in market growth rates and Heron's market share performance over the last 10 years. In WE, market growth had been negligible and, as competition had intensified, Heron's shares had fallen from over 50 per cent in 1998 to around 40 per cent in 2008 in both the high- and low-technology sectors. Conversely, demand for storage technologies had grown strongly in CEE during the decade following the collapse of the former communist regimes in the region. Moreover, Heron had been among the first western firms to enter the CEE market and had achieved an approximately 50 per cent market share in both technologies by 2000. After that time, however, Heron's sales volume had stabilized and, as the market continued to grow, the company's market shares had fallen to about 30 per cent in both the high- and low-technology sectors.

Peter Box explained to John Toft that he had been neither surprised nor alarmed by the changes in Heron's market shares in CEE. Numerous local producers of the low-technology products had emerged after 1998. These firms had achieved much lower costs and prices than Heron, and it had to be expected that they would win some market share in this very price-sensitive market. Also, from 1998 several other WE companies had been offering high-technology systems in CEE and it had been inevitable that they would gain some success. Even so, Box had felt content that Heron remained the market leader in both technologies in CEE and was the only firm in that region offering the full range of high- and low-technology products.

Peter Box had expressed some concern about the reduction of Heron's market shares and profits in the mature WE market as this had always been the company's main business. However, he had also felt that the demise was understandable. He had admitted that Heron had been focusing most of its attention on achieving growth in CEE during the last 10 years and had perhaps been slow to react to changing competitive conditions in WE.

Throughout the decade, WE-based rivals had been attacking aggressively in the high-technology sector, while rivals in CEE had been exporting low-technology products into WE at very low prices. Nevertheless, Box had contended that the division was in better shape at the end of the decade than it had been at the beginning. Heron had become firmly established in CEE. Moreover, with the right strategy, the company would be able to re-establish its former position in WE.

// Heron had been focusing most of its attention on achieving growth in Central and Eastern Europe, and had been slow to react to changing competitive conditions in Western Europe. //

In summarizing Heron's competitors, Peter Box had noted that whereas WE rivals were strong in high-technology systems, they were weak in low-technology products. Conversely, CEE competitors were strong in the low-technology sectors but lacked the technological capability needed to produce the high-technology systems. Box then opined that he did not anticipate any further shrinkage of Heron's market shares and that, indeed, the share trends could easily be reversed. The low-technology competitors produced only crude, simple products with far less functionality than Heron's range. The CEE rivals' low-cost situation did enable them to produce what he described as 'cheap and nasty' products, which might be of interest to some customers and distributors. Nevertheless, although these firms were price-sensitive, Box was confident that Heron's global reputation, extensive and high-quality product range, and its own wide distribution network provided the necessary basis for a market share recovery exercise in both CEE and WE.

Box had been similarly optimistic about Heron's potential for rebuilding high-technology market shares in both regions. The company's high-quality products offered more functionality and productivity than those of other WE firms. Allied to Heron's outstanding reputation and other competences, this provided a strong competitive base. Most of the WE rivals were more willing than Heron to customize their offerings to meet customer requirements. Further, they each had a wide network of sales offices throughout Europe, which they had used in 'going to extraordinary lengths to buy their way into customers' favours' by forming local relationships with them. They had started to offer very generous financial terms, systems training and a host of other 'customer bribes to ingratiate themselves'. However, these were very costly activities, Box had noted, and Heron had been able to undercut its rivals' prices in the high-technology sector in both geographic regions.

In line with industry convention, Heron used distributors for sales of low-technology products in both WE and CEE. Distributors had been selected on the basis of being financially sound and having storage products experience, established customer contacts, stocking facilities and service capabilities. Heron offered slightly smaller distributor margins than its rivals. However, Heron endeavoured to keep distributors motivated by providing company information, product training, catalogues and advertising support in the English, German and French languages, two months' trade credit and other supports. However, many of the distributors were often difficult to communicate with and did not appear to push sales energetically.

All the distributors were independent companies and all had exclusive rights to distribute Heron's products in their local areas. A problem was that many distributors had often sold products at prices above or below those stipulated by Heron. Also some of them had been violating their neighbours' exclusivity rights by attacking their territories. Further, many of Heron's distributors had started to carry competitor products and some others had switched their loyalties to rivals entirely. Due to this, local producers had collectively established wider market coverage than Heron in CEE although Heron had managed to retain the widest coverage in WE.

Heron handled its high-technology business directly. For this purpose, the company had established sales offices in Paris, Brussels, Frankfurt, Milan, Vienna, Warsaw and Moscow to build and maintain customer contacts. These offices were staffed by indigenous technological salespeople who provided customers with technical assistance and advice about storage systems design. Heron had three technically qualified key account managers, based in Manchester, to make sales calls throughout Europe and to assist personnel in the regional sales offices as required. Heron's headquarters also accommodated an effective research and development department and a department responsible for tendering and financing.

Heron maintained a continuous product innovation policy to preserve its strong reputation for product functionality and quality. The company also utilized a cost-plus pricing method. Sales personnel were allowed some freedom to adjust prices to meet local demand and

competitive conditions. However, company policy precluded acceptance of any orders for sales with profit margins less than 12 per cent above full average costs.

After his meeting with Peter Box, John Toft felt very dispirited. Despite the optimism that had been displayed by his predecessor, Toft wondered whether his division of the company was in dire trouble. He also wondered about what, if anything, he could do to remedy the situation.

 Propose a long-term marketing plan for Heron's high-technology and low-technology businesses in the two European regions.

This case was prepared by David Shipley, Emeritus Professor of Marketing, Trinity College, University of Dublin, Ireland. The name of the company, financial data, market characteristics and other matters have been disguised.

Marketing Analysis

PART 2

CHAPTER 3

The marketing environment

" *Change is the only constant.* **"**

A. TOFFLER

LEARNING OBJECTIVES

After reading this chapter, you should be able to:

1 describe the nature of the marketing environment

2 explain the distinction between the microenvironment and the macroenvironment

3 discuss the impact of political and legal, economic, ecological/physical environmental, social/cultural and technological forces on marketing decisions

4 explain how to conduct environmental scanning

5 discuss how companies respond to environmental change

| The marketing environment | FIGURE 3.1 |

A marketing-orientated firm looks outwards to the environment in which it operates, adapting to take advantage of emerging opportunities and to minimize potential threats. In this chapter, we will examine the marketing environment and how to monitor it. In particular we will look at some of the major forces acting on companies in their macro- and microenvironments.

The **marketing environment** consists of the actors and forces that affect a company's capability to operate effectively in providing products and services to its customers. As we saw in Chapter 2 it is useful to classify these forces into the macroenvironment and the microenvironment (see Fig. 3.1). The macroenvironment consists of a number of broad forces that affect not only the company but also the other actors in the microenvironment. Traditionally four forces—political/legal, economic, social/cultural and technological—have been the focus of attention, with the result that the term PEST analysis has been used to describe macroenvironmental analysis. However, the growing importance of ecological/physical environmental forces on companies has led to the acronym being expanded to **PEEST analysis**. The microenvironment consists of the actors in the firm's immediate environment that affect its capabilities to operate effectively in its chosen markets. The key actors are customers, competitors, distributors and suppliers. The macro- and microenvironments shape the character of the opportunities and threats facing a company and are largely uncontrollable.

This chapter will focus on the macroenvironmental forces—political/legal, economic, ecological/physical, social/cultural and technological—that affect marketing decisions. Later in the chapter the four dimensions of the microenvironment—customers, competitors, distributors and suppliers—will be introduced and then examined in greater detail throughout the book. The influence of customers on marketing decisions will be discussed in Chapters 4 and 5 and the changing nature of the supply chain examined in Chapter 5. Distribution and competitive forces will be analysed in Chapters 17, and 19 and 20 respectively.

Political and Legal Forces

Political and legal forces can influence marketing decisions by setting the rules by which business can be conducted. For example, smoking bans in public places can have dramatic short- and long-term effects on the demand for cigarettes. Because of politicians' power to affect business activities, companies try to cultivate close relationships with them, both to monitor political moods and also to influence them. Sometimes, sizable contributions to the funds of political parties are made in an attempt to maintain favourable relationships. Never has the relationship between political forces and business been more apparent than in the recent 'credit crunch', which has forced governments to financially support banks and, in the case of the British Government, acquire Northern Rock.[1]

In Europe, companies are affected by legislation at EU and national levels. We will first examine EU-wide laws before discussing the impact of national laws on business life.

European Union-wide laws

EU laws exist at two levels: (i) regulations that are binding on member states and (ii) directives that are binding only through enactment of a law within the member state in line with the directive. A major influence at European level is EU competition, which is based on the belief that business competitiveness benefits from intense competition. The role of competition policy, then, is to encourage competition in the EU by removing restrictive practices and other anti-competitive activities. This is accomplished by tackling barriers to competition through rules that form a legal framework within which EU firms must operate. The objects of these legal rules are to:

- prevent firms from colluding by price fixing, cartels and other collaborative activities—competition is encouraged by preventing firms joining forces to act in a monopolistic way
- prevent firms from abusing a position of market dominance—they are discouraged from taking such actions as monopoly and discriminatory pricing, which could harm small buyers with little bargaining power
- control the size that firms grow to through acquisition and merger—the objective is to prevent firms acquiring excessive market power through acquiring, or merging with, other firms within defined markets, and thereby reaping monopolistic profits
- restrict state aid to firms—it can be in a nation's interest for its government to give state aid to ailing firms within its boundaries; on a broader scale this can give artificial competitive advantages to recipient firms, which may, for example, be able to charge lower prices than their unsupported rivals; recipients may also be unfairly shielded from the full force of the competitive pressures affecting their markets.

We will now review each of these rules to illustrate the impact they have made on firms' activities.

Collusion

The European Commission, whose job it is to enforce EU rules, has had considerable success in disbanding and fining cartels. For example, cartel partners ABB Løgstør, Henss/Isoplus, Sigma and six other firms were fined for price fixing, market sharing and bid rigging in the European insulated heating pipe market. More recently, BA was fined £270 million for conspiring with Virgin Airways (who escaped prosecution because it alerted the regulators about the price fixing) to fix the price of passenger fuel surcharges on transatlantic flights;[2] and glass manufacturers, Saint-Gobain, Pilkington, Asahi Glass and Soliver, were fined a total of over £1000 million for illegally fixing the price of glass used in the car industry.[3] Such actions are having a real impact on firms' behaviour, as Marketing in Action 3.1 explains.

The success the European Commission has had in locating and punishing those firms that collude acts as a major deterrent through both the severity of the fines imposed and the bad publicity that results.

Abuse of market dominance

Market dominance has also been successfully challenged, as when Italian cigarette producer and distributor AAMS was found to be abusing its dominant position for the wholesale distribution of cigarettes in Italy. AAMS was protecting its own sales by imposing restrictive distribution contracts on foreign manufacturers, which limited the access of foreign cigarettes to the Italian market.[4] However, the most high-profile case is that against Microsoft, which was fined £340 million for its alleged misuse of its near monopoly in operating systems to squeeze out rivals by bundling Media Player into the Windows operating system.[5] This was

3.1 Marketing in Action

The European Commission's Crusade Against Cartels

Both in the USA and the EU the battle against price-fixing cartels has never been so strongly fought. In the USA, auction houses Sotheby's and Christie's were convicted of fixing the prices they charge clients. For many years America has been obsessed by bringing down price-fixing cartels but the message is now spreading, with new measures against anti-competitive cartel behaviour such as bid rigging and deals to carve up market share being adopted from Sweden to South Korea.

Since 2000, the European Commission has crusaded with renewed vigour against cartels including those in the vitamins, airline, cigarette, glass, carbonless paper, graphide electrodes, citric acid, amino acid, monochloroacetic acid and banking industries. Such actions have stretched its resources to the limit, which is one reason it has published a Green Paper designed to encourage customers and competitors to place private claims for damages resulting from anti-competitive practices, an action that moves it towards the US anti-trust regime, which relies heavily on private litigation.

One of the driving forces behind the EC's efforts to drive out anti-competitive behaviour is the desire to create a genuine single market in Europe, where geographic 'market sharing' is seen as highly damaging. Companies are responding by educating themselves. Roche, for example, has put thousands of its managers through training to teach them to follow the law.

Based on: Ritson (2002);[6] Buck (2005);[7] Murphy and Yuk (2008)[8]

followed by a £650 million fine for failing to disclose complete and accurate technical information on 'reasonable terms' to allow rivals to develop products that would work with Windows.[9]

Acquisitions and mergers

The laws relating to acquisitions and mergers are designed to prevent firms building up excessive market power through acquiring, or merging with, other companies within a market, resulting in monopolistic profits. Action can take the form of the blocking of mergers or acquisition—such as the prevention of the merger between Swedish truck, bus and coach builders Scania and Volvo—or approval subject to strict conditions—such as the requirement that Nestlé sell a number of Perrier brands to encourage a third force to emerge in the French mineral water market to compete with Nestlé and BSN.

State aid

The giving of financial aid to companies by member states can provide unfair advantages such as the ability to charge lower prices than their unsupported rivals. EC approval of state aid is usually given as part of a restructuring or rescue package for ailing firms. The general principle is that such payments should be 'one-offs' to prevent uncompetitive firms being repeatedly bailed out by their governments. This has not always applied, however, with Air France being given financial assistance several times.[10] Overall, though, the level of state aid given to firms in most of the EU member states is declining.

National laws

In addition to EU laws, member states also have the right to make their own legislation governing business practice. This can mean inconsistencies across Europe. For example, national laws governing advertising across Europe mean that what is acceptable in one country is banned in another. For example, toys cannot be advertised in Greece, tobacco advertising is illegal in Scandinavia, the UK and Italy, alcohol advertising is banned on television in France and at sports grounds, and in Germany any advertisement believed to be in bad taste can be prohibited. This patchwork of national advertising regulations means that companies attempting to create a brand image across Europe often need to make substantial changes to advertising strategy on a national basis.

Supplementing the work of the European Commission are national bodies set up to investigate anti-competitive practices. For example, the Competition Commission in the UK, the Bundeskartellant in Germany and the Competition Council in France provide national protection against anti-competitive behaviour. These investigations can lead to heavy fines. For example the Financial Services Authority, which overseas the UK financial services industry, fined Shell £17 million under national market abuse provision relating to the overstating of oil reserves.[11]

Self-regulation also occurs at national level, with industries drawing up codes of practice to protect consumer interests, sometimes as a result of political pressure. Examples of such regulatory bodies in the advertising industry are the Deutscher Werbat (Germany), Stichting Reclame Code (Netherlands), Marknads Etiska Radet (Sweden) and the Advertising Standards Authority (UK). The Code of Advertising Standards and Practice drawn up by the Advertising Standards Authority is designed to keep advertising 'legal, decent, honest and truthful'. Similarly, the marketing research industries in many European countries have drawn up codes of practice to protect people from unethical activities such as using marketing research as a pretext for selling.

Marketing management must be aware of the constraints on its activities made by the political and legal environment. Such staff must assess the extent to which they feel the need to influence political decisions that may affect their operations, and the degree to which industry practice needs to be self-regulated in order to maintain high standards of customer satisfaction and service. Above all, companies need to ensure that their activities are in accord with EU and national laws and codes of practice.

Economic Forces

The *economic environment* can have a critical impact on the success of companies through its effect on supply and demand. Companies must choose those economic influences that are relevant to their business and monitor them. We will examine four major economic influences on the marketing environment of companies: economic growth and unemployment, interest and exchange rates, the move by 10 central and eastern European countries to join the EU, and the growth of the 'Bric' economies (Brazil, Russia, India and China).

Economic growth and unemployment

The general state of both national and international economies can have a profound effect on a company's prosperity. Economies tend to fluctuate according to the business cycle, although more enlightened economic management in recent years has reduced the depth of the contraction in some countries. Most of the world's economies have gone through a period of significant growth since the mid-1990s, driven partly by productivity gains brought about by developments in computing and telecommunications technologies. This growth was followed by an economic slump in 2009, referred to as the 'credit crunch'. During periods of boom, well-managed companies experience an expansion in the demand for their products, while slump may bring a decline in sales as consumers became wary of discretionary expenditures. A major marketing problem is predicting the next boom or slump. Investments made during periods of high growth can become massive cash drains when consumer spending falls suddenly. The problems facing some of the world's leading technology firms, such as Cisco

Systems, Compaq (since acquired by Hewlett-Packard) and Intel, in recent years were partly caused by this trap.

Within an economy, different sectors experience varying growth rates, leading to changing degrees of market attractiveness. Undoubtedly, the services sector has experienced the fastest growth and become the dominant force in most western economies. For example, among the 25 EU countries, services account for over 70 per cent of gross domestic product, which is a measure of the total value of goods and services produced within an economy.

Low growth rates are reflected in high unemployment levels, which in turn affect consumer spending power. The recent recession has caused unemployment rates to rise and consumer spending to fall. This has led to calls for state aid for ailing companies—for example, in the motor car industry—to help them through the slump.

Interest and exchange rates

A key monetary tool that governments use to manage the economy is interest rates. Interest rates represent the price that borrowers have to pay lenders for the use of their money over a specified period of time. Most western economies lowered interest rates during the credit crunch to encourage borrowing and lending, in an effort to avert a major slump in consumer and business demand.

An exchange rate is the price of one currency in terms of another (e.g. an exchange rate of £1 = €1.20 means that £1 buys €1.20). Fluctuations in exchange rates mean that the price a consumer in one country pays for a product and/or the money that a supplier in an overseas country receives for selling that product can change. For example, if the exchange rate between the pound sterling and the euro changes, such that a pound buys fewer euros, a German car manufacturer who receives payment in euros will receive fewer euros if the price of the car remains unchanged in the UK. In an attempt to maintain a constant euro price, the German car manufacturer may raise the UK pound sterling price to UK distributors and consumers. The following example illustrates these points.

At £1 = €1, a German car manufacturer would receive €10,000 for a £10,000 car. If the exchange rate changed to £1 = €0.5, the German car manufacturer's receipts would fall to €5000. To maintain euro receipts at €10,000 the UK price would have to rise to £20,000.

The exchange rates between most European countries are now fixed, thus avoiding such problems. However, the rates at which major currencies such as the US dollar, the euro, the pound sterling and the yen are traded are still variable. As seen in the example above this can have significant implications for sales revenues and hence the profitability of a firm's international operations. For example, as the value of the US dollar fell during 2004 amid concerns about the inclining US trade deficit and the cost of the Iraq war, losing about one-third of its value against the pound and the euro, the profitability of some European firms trading in the USA fell as their receipts in pounds and euros fell at constant US dollar prices. For example, it is estimated that Heineken's operating profits in the USA fell from £250 million to £84 million between 2002 and 2006 largely because of the fall in the value of the dollar during this period.[12] During the credit crunch, the pound fell against the dollar. This meant that UK goods and services exported to euro zone countries could be sold cheaper, or, if sold at the same price, would realize higher sterling profit margins.

Central and eastern Europe

The move by eight central and eastern European countries to join the EU in May 2004, and their earlier change from centrally planned to market-driven economies has far-reaching marketing implications. The EU is a massive, largely deregulated market in which barriers to the free flow of goods, services, capital and people among the member states are removed. One objective is to lower the costs of operating throughout Europe and to create an enormous free market in which companies can flourish. As we have already seen, competition is encouraged through the enactment and enforcement of laws designed to remove restricted practices and other anti-competitive activities.

The eight central and eastern European EU members that joined the EU in 2004 are the Czech Republic, Slovakia, Hungary, Latvia, Lithuania, Estonia, Poland and Slovenia. Their combined population is about 75 million within the EU's total of 454 million, although Poland alone accounts for 39 million.[13] In 2007, Romania and Bulgaria also joined the EU. The strengths of these economies are high economic growth that is double that of western Europe, low wages that are often competitive with those in China and India, an abundance of engineers and technical graduates, workers who have a flexible mind-set and 'can do' attitude, low corporate income taxes, and easy access to wealthy western European and Russian markets. Weaknesses are a shortage of trained managers, corruption and bureaucracy in some of the countries, poor-quality roads in some countries (e.g. Poland) and, by western standards, low levels of wealth.[14]

The strengths of these economies, boosted by EU membership, have led to considerable inward investment. Today the region is attracting foreign investment at the rate of £21 billion a year, which places it second only to China in the international competition for capital. For example, LG Philips, the liquid crystal display producer spent £246 million to make flat-screen televisions in Poland, creating 3200 jobs. Investment in knowledge-driven industries ranging from telecoms to pharmaceuticals is also gathering pace. For example, the region's growing ranks of highly skilled workers mean that it is shaping up as the next outsourcing destination for engineering and software development after China and India.[15] The region is also fast becoming a manufacturing centre for the production of cars, with companies such as Toyota, Ford, GM, Fiat, Audi, Volkswagen, Renault, Citroën, Suzuki and Kia having at least one car plant in the region.

Clearly, the rise of central and eastern European economies not only poses threats to western European firms in terms of potential new competition, but also opportunities. First, as we have already seen the region's strengths make it an attractive location for new investment. Second, the eight new EU members have a combined population of 75 million and a gross domestic product of £473 billion, making it a sizeable target market. These statistics need to be tempered by the fact that many of the individual countries are small (Poland dominates, with 39 million consumers) and poor. However, all these economies are growing and opportunities exist from the privatization of industries such as energy generation and railways.[16]

China and India

Why are western nations watching the economies of China and India like hawks? First, both economies are growing at high and consistent rates, although both, like other major economies, have suffered during the recent recession. For the past 20 years, China's economy has been growing at an average of 9.5 per cent and India's at 6 per cent. Second, both nations possess considerable strengths, traditionally in low-cost labour but increasingly in technical and managerial skills. China possesses strengths in mass manufacturing, and is currently building massive electronics and heavy industrial factories. India, on the other hand, is an emerging power in software, design, services and precision industry. These complementary skills are persuading some electronics multinationals to have their products built in China with software and circuitry designed in India. Furthermore, the skills base in both countries is likely to grow, with China and India graduating a combined half a million engineers and scientists a year.[17]

Third, China and India not only pose threats to western companies, they also provide opportunities. Chinese consumers are spending their growing incomes on consumer durables such as cars, a market that has reached 3 million, and mobile phones where China has the world's biggest subscriber base of over 500 million, and computers, where over 200 million people browse the Internet on broadband connections.[18] Both have vast populations, with 1.3 billion people in China and 1 billion living in India. As Carl Leaver, Marks & Spencer's international strategy director, remarked, 'If one in eight of the Chinese population ends up wearing M&S knickers, we will be very happy.'[19] In India, the consumer market is also growing rapidly. For example, since 2000 the number of mobile phone subscribers has rocketed from 5.6 million to 80 million, and Internet users total over 20 million. Over half of India's 1 billion people are under 25.[20] Western companies such as Microsoft, Procter & Gamble, Coca-Cola, BP, Vodafone, Tetley, Siemens and GlaxoSmithKline have seen the potential of these markets (particularly China) and sought to develop them, usually with the aid of local partners.

While both countries possess considerable strengths, they also have weaknesses. First, neither country has a strong track record in global brand building. A survey of *Financial Times* readers conducted by McKinsey, the management consultancy, to find out what businesspeople around the world consider are the top Chinese brands rated Haier, a white-goods and home appliances company first and Lenovo, a computer company, famous for buying IBM's personal computer division, second. Neither company is a major global player in their respective markets.[21] India, similarly, does not possess major global brands. However, the conglomerate Tata is building a global presence with its purchase of Jaguar and Land Rover from Ford, the acquisition of Corus (steel) and the growth of Tata Consultancy Services, Asia's largest software company.[22] Second, both countries suffer from the risk of social strife—resulting from the widening gap between rich and poor, as well as corruption. Third, both countries have paid a steep ecological price for rapid industrial and population growth, with millions of deaths attributed to air and water pollution each year.[23] Fourth, wage levels are rising fast, particularly in skilled areas, reducing their advantage in low labour costs. Fifth, bureaucracy can make doing business in both countries difficult. China, in particular, has been a destination for western goods and foreign investment but great care needs to be taken when entering the Chinese market, as Marketing in Action 3.2 explains.

3.1 Pause for Thought

To what extent do you believe China and India pose threats to European firms?

Russia and Brazil

Like China and India, Russia and Brazil had been growing at impressive rates before the recent recession. Russia's economy has benefited from 7 per cent growth and Brazil's 5 per cent. Surprisingly for an ex-communist state, Russia has one of the lowest income tax rates in the world: a flat rate of 13 per cent. Also all Russians own their own homes, having been given their own flat or house free as the Soviet era ended (most of these, however, are in a poor state of repair). Wealth tends to be centred around Moscow and there are cash-rich consumers present, as the fact that Russia is the fourth biggest consumer of luxury goods after the USA, Japan and China testifies.[24]

Russia's economy is largely dependent on oil and gas. It vies with Saudi Arabia as the world's largest oil producer, and has the world's largest gas reserves. It is also rich in gold, with the fourth largest reserves. Russia's large population of 140 million, which has rapidly become richer, has attracted international food and drink companies such as Unilever, PepsiCo, Kellogg, Kraft, Nestlé, Coca-Cola and Carlsberg, which have entered by acquisition. For example, PepsiCo purchased the Russian food and drinks group Lebedyansky for over £1 billion.[25]

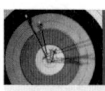

3.2 Marketing in Action

Doing Business in China

Marketing in any overseas country is difficult because of differences in culture, and local laws and regulations. China is particularly troublesome, with many companies—such as Whirlpool, a US white-goods manufacturer that lost more than £26 million in a series of joint ventures, and food multinational Kraft, which was forced to close its loss-making dairy business after eight years—finding life uncomfortable in the Chinese market.

In order to succeed, overseas companies need to recognize a number of guidelines. First, they must appreciate the diversity of the market. A country with 1.3 billion people speaking 100 dialects is vastly diverse, and the need to segment the market is essential. For example, Samsung discovered that consumers living in humid Guangdong Province needed larger refrigerators than those in the more temperate north, so it started marketing bigger fridges in the south. P&G has targeted consumers in less affluent rural districts with a budget detergent called Tide Clean White, while targeting richer city consumers with the more expensive Tide Triple Action. To understand customers, domestic and multinational companies are conducting focus groups and surveys. For example, the Grey Global Group, a Chinese advertising agency, has segmented Chinese consumers into 11 categories based on their lifestyle and aspirations. These groups range from independents who do not follow consumer trends to shoppers on the cutting edge.

Western firms often enter China by means of a joint venture, but they need to be aware of the different business scenarios there. In China there is no effective rule of law governing business. One potential drawback is that western companies can fall prey to the theft of intellectual property. Other problems that western companies complain about include the siting of projects in inappropriate locations so local authorities can charge inflated land use costs, and inflation of costs by joint venture partners. Bureaucracy and governmental interference can also bring difficulties. Thames Water reportedly had to pull out of a 20-year water treatment project in Shanghai after the government ruled that the guaranteed rate of return to investors was illegal. Technical problems can also hamper joint ventures. For example, Chrysler ended its small car venture with Cherry Automobile because of their failure to bring the cars' safety and environmental performance up to western standards. For Ericsson, the world's largest telecommunications equipment producer, entering into a contract with China's two biggest mobile phone companies—China Mobile and China Unicom—the rewards of a joint venture could be enormous. The deal is worth $1.44 billion to help supply China's mobile networks.

Western companies also need to understand the importance of *Guanxi* networks. *Guanxi* is a set of personal relationships/connections on which a person can draw to obtain resources or an advantage when doing business. *Guanxi* is one reason why working with a Chinese partner is usually better than going it alone. When entering into business relationships the Chinese seek stability and trust more than intimacy. They want to feel comfortable that western companies will not spring surprises that may hurt them, but they do not need to feel that they are the company's best friend. It is claimed that the failure of Rupert Murdoch's NewsCorp to penetrate China is largely because the company did not spend enough time and effort on building *guanxi*.

The media also have to be handled with care. Severely restrained in reporting domestic politics and social issues, Chinese media feel much freer to attack foreign companies. Chinese reporters need to be educated about the western company's business, treated with respect, and regular contact to develop personal relationships is recommended.

Based on: McGregor (2005);[26] Roberts and Rocks (2005);[27] Singh (2005);[28] Anderlini and Reed (2008);[29] Bulkley (2008);[30] Ibison (2008)[31]

Working in Russia can be highly profitable for western companies, but can be fraught with problems, as the battle for control of the TNK-BP joint venture showed. Although BP managed to keep 50 per cent of the ownership, it was forced to sacrifice its chief executive and agree to international expansion, even when that meant competing with existing BP interests.[32]

Brazil's industry is linked to agri-business and other primary products. Its main output arises from sugar, steel, oil and iron. It also has an important technological sector that ranges from submarines to aircraft, and is involved in space research. Its economy has benefited from high levels of foreign investment by such companies as Procter & Gamble, IBM, Ford, DuPont, Anheuser-Busch InBev and PepsiCo. Its two largest companies are Petrobas (oil and gas) and Vale (mining). It is also a major producer of ethanol, a sugar-based biofuel. Growth in the economy has led to rising demand for cars, mobile phones, computers and televisions. It has a large population of 190 million. However, like the other Bric nations, Brazil has not developed significant brand-building capabilities.[33]

Companies need to be aware of the economic forces that may affect their operations and be wary of assuming that a benign economic environment will last for ever. Sudden changes in growth, interest and/or exchange rates can alter the economic climate quickly so that contingency plans are needed to cope with economy-induced downturns in demand. Firms also need to monitor the international economic environment, including the change to market-driven economies and the move into the EU by central and eastern European countries, and the opportunities and threats posed by the rise of China and India as major economic forces.

Ecological/Physical Environmental Forces

Ecology is the study of living things within their environmental context. In a marketing context it concerns the relationship between people and the physical environment. Environmentalists attempt to protect the physical environment from the costs associated with producing and marketing products. They are concerned with the environmental costs of consumption, not just the personal costs to the consumer. Five environmental issues are of particular concern. These are combating global warming, pollution control, conservation of energy and other scarce resources, use of environmentally friendly ingredients and components, and the use of recyclable and non-wasteful packaging.

Global warming

Concerns about global warming and the problems associated with climate change have arisen as a result of a quadrupling of carbon dioxide emissions over the last 50 years. More extreme weather conditions, such as hurricanes, storms and flooding, which are reported to be associated with carbon dioxide-induced climate change, are already impacting industries such as insurance, agriculture and oil. BP, for example, took a billion-dollar battering from Hurricane Katrina in the USA.[34] To avoid irreversible environmental consequences it has been agreed internationally that two forms of preventative action are required:[35]

1 reduction of CO_2 emissions
2 a ban on the use of chlorofluorocarbons (CFCs).

The purpose is to prevent further depletion of the ozone layer, which lets through increased levels of ultraviolet radiation with potentially harmful health and environmental effects. Governmental response through the Kyoto international agreement, changes in consumer behaviour, and individual action taken by companies such as GE, BP and Bayer to reduce harmful emissions, is required to achieve the objective. Car manufacturers also have a responsibility to reduce their carbon footprint. Marketing Ethics and Corporate Social Responsibility in Action 3.1 discusses how Honda is responding to the challenge. Hitachi is also taking steps to reduce its carbon footprint, as illustrated in its advertisement.

3.1 Marketing Ethics and Corporate Social Responsibility in Action

Honda Fights Back

When consumers think of petrol-electric hybrid cars, the Prius usually springs to mind. Not only has this car built Toyota's environmentally friendly image, it has also sold over 1 million worldwide. Honda, by contrast, like many of its rivals, has lagged behind in the race to build successful hybrid cars. In a major strategic move Honda has decided to make major investments in hybrid technology to expand its range of hybrids. It hopes to sell 500,000 hybrid cars a year by 2012, up from only 55,000 in 2007.

What are Honda's specific plans? First, it intends to launch a dedicated hybrid model. Unlike Toyota, with its dedicated hybrid Prius, other manufacturers usually make hybrid versions of petrol-only cars. Second, it intends to build hybrid versions of the Jazz, a new Civic hybrid, and a hybrid based on its CR-Z concept sports car.

A problem for hybrid sales has been a price gap of around £3000. Using different technology from Toyota, Honda hopes to reduce that to around £1000. Although not as powerful as Toyota's hybrid technology, the Honda system is lighter and so its new models should offer higher mileage.

Honda has clearly seen the opportunities provided by cleaner technology and is prepared to back its judgement by heavy investment.

Based on: Reed and Soble (2008);[36] *Rowley (2008)*[37]

▲ This Hitachi advertisement communicates how the company is quietly helping to preserve the planet by reducing its CO_2 emissions by 100 million tons by 2025.

Pollution

The manufacture, use and disposal of products can have a harmful effect on the quality of the physical environment. The production of chemicals that pollute the atmosphere, the use of nitrates as a fertilizer that pollutes rivers, and the disposal of by-products into the sea have caused considerable public concern. In recent years the introduction of lead-free petrol catalytic converters, and the launch of hybrid cars such as the Toyota Prius and the Honda Civic, has reduced the level of harmful exhaust emissions.

Denmark has introduced a series of anti-pollution measures, including a charge on pesticides and a CFC tax. In the Netherlands higher taxes on pesticides, fertilizers and carbon monoxide emissions are proposed. Not all the activity is simply cost raising, however. In Germany, one of the marketing benefits of its involvement in green technology has been a thriving export business in pollution-control equipment.

Energy and scarce resource conservation

The finite nature of the world's resources has stimulated the drive towards their conservation. Energy conservation is reflected in the demand for energy-efficient housing and fuel-efficient cars, for example. In Europe, Sweden has taken the lead in developing an energy policy based on renewable resources. The tax system penalizes the use of polluting energy sources such as coal and oil, while less polluting resources such as peat and woodchip receive favourable tax treatment. In addition, it is planning to become the world's first oil-free economy by 2020, not by building nuclear power stations but by utilizing renewable resources such as wind and wave power, geothermal energy and waste heat. The plan is a response to warnings that the world may be running out of oil, global climate change and rising petrol prices. The UK is also responding by committing to generate 10 per cent of its electricity from renewable sources by 2012.[38] Companies are also making more energy-efficient products. For example, Siemens manufactures energy-efficient fridge freezers (see illustration).

An opportunity that is arising over the need to reduce reliance on oil is the development of biofuels. Fuels based on ethanol have the potential to replace petrol. Already the Saab 9-5 BioPower and a version of the Ford Focus can run on either petrol or ethanol. A problem is that ethanol-based fuel costs 20 pence a litre more than unleaded petrol, but as petrol rises in price and ethanol production costs fall this may change. If so, Europe has the capacity to

One of the most energy efficient fridge freezers in the world. That's because it's a Siemens

Free 5 Year Guarantee
call bill, parts and labour

The KG49NP93GB Fridge Freezer is one of the most energy efficient A+ rated Fridge Freezers in the world. Now that really is cool.
For a free brochure call (UK) 0844 892 9044, (Republic of Ireland) 1890 626 041, (Northern Ireland) 00353(1) 8505021 or visit
www.siemensappliances.co.uk or www.siemens-appliances.ie

The future moving in.   SIEMENS

◀ Siemens makes energy-efficient fridge freezers.

provide around 40 per cent of the fuel it needs for transport from ethanol fermented from crops (e.g. corn and sugar beet) and biodegradable waste. However, the penetration of biofuels as a source of clean power has been hampered by fears of food shortages (as biofuel crops replace traditional food crops) and deforestation.[39]

Another concern of environmentalists is the consumption of wood. Forest depletion by the deforestation activities of companies and the effects of acid rain damage the ecosystem. Consumers' desire for soft and hardwood furniture and window frames is at odds with the need to preserve forests. Trees' leaves absorb carbon dioxide and their roots help to stabilize slopes: a landslide in the Philippines that cost many lives was allegedly caused by illegal logging. A solution is the replanting of forests to maintain the long-term stock of trees.

Environmentally friendly ingredients and components

Environmentalists favour the use of biodegradable and natural ingredients and components when practicable, and PETA (People for the Ethical Treatment of Animals) campaigns against cruelty to animals. Companies have responded to the challenge by launching products such as the Estée Lauder Origins skincare and cosmetics range of vegetable-based products containing no animal ingredients. Plastic products and components have been the target of criticism because of their non-biodegradability, but biodegradable polymers are now available. For example, Biopol was developed by ICI, which claims it is the first fully biodegradable commercial plastic. Its applications include disposable nappies, rubbish bags, and paper plates and cups that are coated with a thin plastic film.

Concern has also been expressed over the use of genetically modified (GM) ingredients in food products since the health implications are uncertain. Pressure from consumer groups and the media have forced Monsanto, a pioneer in genetic modification, to stop further development, supermarkets to banish such products from their shelves, and countries such as Austria, France, Germany, Greece, Italy and Luxemburg to impose import bans.

Recycling and non-wasteful packaging

Germany took the lead in the recycling of packaging when it introduced the Verpackvo, a law that allows shoppers to return packaging to retailers and retailers to pass it back to suppliers. In response, suppliers promised to assume responsibility for the management of packaging waste. Over 400 companies have created a mechanism called the Dual System Deutschland (DSD). Consumers are asked to return glass bottles and waste paper to recycling bins and are also encouraged to separate other recyclable materials such as plastics, composite packaging and metals, and place them in yellow bags and bins supplied by the DSD. Collection takes place every month and is, together with separation of the refuse, paid for by the DSD and the cost eventually absorbed by the packaging manufacturers. Recycling is also important in Sweden, where industry has established a special company to organize the collection and sorting of waste for recycling, and in Finland where over 35 per cent of packaging is recycled.

Companies can promote recycling by, for example, using recycled paper for burger containers rather than styrene, which is non-biodegradable. Not only is cutting out waste in packaging environmentally friendly, it also makes commercial sense. Thus companies have introduced concentrated detergents and refill packs, and removed the cardboard around some brands of toothpaste, for example. The savings can be substantial: in Germany, Lever GmbH saved 15 per cent of paper, carton and corrugated board; 30 per cent by introducing concentrated detergents; 20 per cent by using lightweight plastic bottles; and the introduction of refills for concentrated liquids reduced the weight of packaging materials by half. Henkel has introduced special 22-gram 'light packs', which are polyethylene bottles that save 270 tons of plastic a year.

Marketing managers need to be aware of the environmental consequences of their decisions and activities, and recognize the dangers to the reputations of their companies and brands of environmentally irresponsible actions. They should also consider communicating their environmentally conscious credentials. For environmental groups, marketing provides the tools to spread awareness of their campaigns, as Digital Marketing 3.1 explains.

3.1 Digital Marketing

Friends of the Earth Uses Digital Marketing to Raise Awareness of Environmental Campaigns

Activists and environmental organizations have led the way in drawing attention to the impact of business and trade on the health of the planet. Since the early 1970s, Friends of the Earth—'the grassroots environmental network'—has campaigned hard in this area and has become the UK's most influential campaigning organization, which promotes environmentally sustainable societies at local, national, regional and global levels. The organization focuses its activities on environmental issues, which have social, political and human rights implications. Campaigns reach into many different areas of activity (e.g. car fuel efficiency, agro-fuels, climate change and energy consumption, nuclear power, trade and globalization). Ultimately, Friends of the Earth seeks to influence the government and business to make policy changes that will benefit the planet.

Friends of the Earth has faced many tough challenges and conflicts when campaigning for business to change procedures. Cadbury Schweppes shareholders were left with a bitter taste in their mouths when Friends of the Earth campaigners handed out chocolate bars outside their annual general meeting to raise awareness of Cadbury's (and other food producers') use of palm oil in the manufacturing process. The campaign specifically aimed to highlight how this hidden ingredient is damaging the environment, and Friends of the Earth wanted the re-labelling of products so consumers are more informed about what they are buying (e.g. 'WARNING: May contain traces of deforestation and exploitation').

Digital interactive media have provided a communication channel that enables Friends of the Earth to successfully attract attention and develop its global network with current and new supporters (currently, approximately 1 million supporters across five continents). Its innovative use of new media and digital technologies includes live interactive discussion groups and real-time opinion polls on current climate issues; it uses viral marketing tools such as e-cards to connect with a wider audience through links to friends and family, and e-commerce solutions to collect donations.

Arguably, the most innovative online campaign is 'the big ask'. Friends of the Earth created an online march by asking the public to post video clips online to appeal to the UK Government to make important decisions about climate change laws. The campaign was very successful as it contributed to the government's decision to form a new coalition looking at climate change. A series of 'big ask' live concerts raised awareness of climate issues, which highlighted that three-quarters of UK citizens support laws reducing carbon emissions. In 2008, in conjunction with a gig by the band Razorlight, pressure was put on the government to say *yes* to including aviation and shipping in the carbon emissions bill.

Digital technologies and online marketing have enabled Friends of the Earth to communicate campaign issues to a much wider audience, and in doing so to elicit more support and influence on environmental policy.

Based on: Friends of the Earth Europe;[40] *Friends of the Earth Trust (2004)*[41]

We shall explore in more detail how marketing should respond to environmental issues in Chapter 6, which deals with understanding Marketing Ethics and Corporate Social Responsibility.

Social/Cultural Forces

Three key *social/cultural forces* that have implications for marketing are the changes in the demographic profile of the population, cultural differences within and between nations, and the influence of consumerism. Each will now be examined.

Demographic forces

Demographic forces concern changes in populations in terms of their size and characteristics. **Demography** is important to marketers because it helps to predict the size and growth rates of markets, and the need for products such as schools, one-person housing and homes for the elderly. Three major demographic forces are world population growth, the changing age distribution and the changing structure of households in western countries.

World population growth

Overall, the global population is expanding at an increasing rate. However, the rate of growth is uneven across the world. In particular, the population in developed economies is expected to be stable or shrinking, whereas countries of Africa, India, 'other Asia' and Latin America are expected to account for over 90 per cent of the projected population increase during the twenty-first century (see Fig. 3.2).[42] As these countries grow more youthful, the developed countries will play host to an ageing population. In 2025, half the population of Europe will be over 45 years old. For the next decade, the world population is expected to grow by an average of 97 million per year.

The changing world population distribution suggests that new markets outside the developed economies may provide attractive opportunities, although the extent to which this force progresses will depend on a concomitant rise in income levels in the less developed world. The problem is that the major growth is predicted to be in countries that are already poor. Concern for their well-being is growing among people in the developed world. One response is the social marketing of family planning and birth control. Companies such as Hewlett-Packard and Citibank are increasingly focusing their attention on these so-called 'pre-markets' (i.e. those not yet sufficiently developed to be considered consumer markets). For example, Hewlett-Packard aims to sell, lease or donate a billion dollars worth of computer equipment and services to these under-served markets.[43]

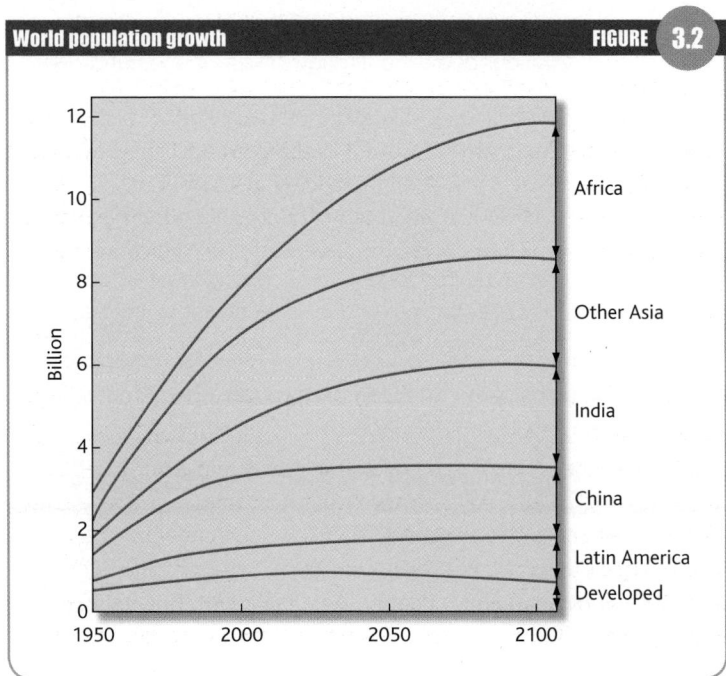

World population growth   **FIGURE 3.2**

Age distribution

A major demographic change that will continue to affect the demand for products is the rising proportion of people over the age of 45 in the EU, and the decline in the younger age group. The rise in over-45s creates substantial marketing opportunities because of their high level of per capita income. They have higher disposable income and higher levels of savings than younger people, tend to benefit from inheritance wealth, and are healthier than ever before. In France, for example, the average per capita disposable income for households headed by a retired person is now higher than the average for all households, and people over 60 (who constitute 18 per cent of the population) consume more than 22 per cent of the French gross domestic product (GDP).

Another demographic change is the growth in the numbers of retired people in Europe. This is partly because people are living longer but also because of early retirement. For example, although the official UK retirement age is 65 and likely to rise, early retirement schemes and redundancies have meant that a high proportion of people below this age group are, in effect, retired—for example, over 30 per cent of men aged 55–64 have already left the labour market. High disposable income, coupled with increasing leisure time, means that the demand for holidays and recreational activities such as golf, fishing and walking should continue to increase. Also there should be increasing demand for medical products and services, housing designed for elderly couples and singles, and single-portion foods. Understanding the needs of the over-45s presents a huge marketing opportunity, so that products can be created that possess the differential advantages valued by these people. In reality it is likely that there are a number of subgroups according to age band, which will allow market segmentation to be used. The overall implication of these trends is that many consumer companies may need to reposition their product offerings to take account of the rise in 'grey' purchasing power.

Household structure

Changes in household structure and behaviour that have marketing implications are the rise in one-person households, households with no children and the growth in dual-income families.

More people are living alone by choice, through divorce or bereavement. This suggests that a key market segment is people who demand products that meet their particular needs, such as one-bedroom houses or apartments, and single-portion foods. The proportion of couples who have no children has also increased. This may reflect a desire to maintain high standards of living for longer. The implication is an increase in the attractiveness of markets where couples are likely to spend their disposable income, such as restaurant meals, luxury holidays and designer clothing.

Households are also changing behaviour regarding employment. In many European countries there has been a growth in dual-earner families. In the UK, for example, over half of couples with dependent children are double-income families. The rise of two-income households means that this market segment has high disposable income, leading to reduced price sensitivity and the capacity to buy luxury furniture and clothing products (e.g. upmarket furniture and clothing) and expensive services (e.g. foreign holidays, restaurant meals). Also, the combination of high income and busy lives has seen a boom in connoisseur convenience foods. Marks & Spencer, in particular, has catered for this market very successfully. Demand for homecare facilities has also risen.

Cultural forces

Culture is the combination of traditions, taboos, values and attitudes of the society in which an individual lives. A number of distinctive subcultures in the UK provide a rich tapestry of lifestyles and the creation of new markets. The Asian population, for example, has provided restaurants and stores supplying food from that part of the world. This influence is now seen in supermarkets, where Asian foods are readily available. The free movement of workers around the EU has also encouraged the growth of subcultures—for example, the flow of workers from central and eastern Europe to older, established EU countries. To meet the needs of the Polish community in the UK, for example, Tesco now runs a groceries website in the Polish language.[44]

Subcultures can also span national boundaries. For example, the existence of a youth subculture across Europe has allowed brands such as Levi's jeans, Coca-Cola, Pepsi and MTV to be marketed with only modest adaptation to local tastes. Young consumers spend considerable time communicating with others via the Internet. The existence of social networking sites such as Facebook and MySpace means that they can share information, post photographs and download music. These sites provide huge opportunities and challenges for marketers to reach young audiences.

3.2 Pause for Thought

Do you believe European firms could do more to market successfully to different cultures within and between nations?

Attitudes towards food among some sections of society in Europe are also changing. Pressures toward healthy eating have prompted moves towards food with less fat, sugar and salt, and health labelling. For example, the Nestlé-branded cereal range targeted at children has been reformulated with 10 per cent less sugar. New brands focusing on their healthy credentials have emerged, like innocent (see illustration).

Market segments have appeared based on the concept of ethical consumption, leading to demand for fair trade and organic products, and avoidance of companies and brands that are associated with dubious labour practices. The growth in healthy eating and ethical consumption has prompted the acquisition of Green & Black's chocolate by Cadbury, and Ben & Jerry's by Unilever.

Successful non-European marketing depends on knowing the cultural differences that exist between European consumers. The German preference for locally brewed beer has proved a major barrier to entry for foreign brewers, such as Guinness, which have attempted to penetrate that market. The slower than expected take-off of the Euro Disney complex near Paris was partly attributed to French consumers' reluctance to accede to the US concept of spending a lot of money on a one-day trip to a single site. Once there, the French person, being an individualist, 'hates being taken by the hand and led around'.[45]

Cultural differences also have implications for business-to-business

◀ The innocent brand has been remarkably successful, tapping into the healthy living lifestyle. It has extended its product line from smoothies to vegetable pots.

marketing. Within Europe, cultural variations affect the way business should be conducted. Humour in business life is acceptable in the UK, Italy, Greece, the Netherlands and Spain but less commonplace in France and Germany. These facts of business life need to be recognized when interacting with European business customers.

A study by Mole examined business culture in the EU and the USA.[46] Management styles were analysed using two dimensions: type of leadership and organization. Figure 3.3 shows the position of each of the 13 nations according to these two characteristics. Individual leadership (autocratic, directive) is to be found in Spain and France, whereas organic leadership style (democratic, equalitarian) tends to be found in Italy and the Netherlands. Systematic organization (formal, mechanistic) is found in Germany, Denmark and the Netherlands, while organic companies (informal, social) are more likely to exist in Spain, Italy, Portugal and Greece.

Based on the Mole survey, Wolfe describes business life in Italy, Spain and the Netherlands.[47] As Figure 3.3 shows, Italian organizations tend to be informal, with democratic leadership. Decisions are taken informally, usually after considerable personal contact and discussion. Italian managers are flexible improvisers who have a temperamental aversion to forecasting and planning. Interpersonal contact with deciders and influencers in the decision-making unit (DMU) is crucial for suppliers. Finding the correct person to talk to is not easy since DMUs tend to be complex, with authority vested in trusted individuals outside the apparent organizational structure. Suppliers must demonstrate commitment to a common purpose with their Italian customers.

In Spain, on the other hand, business is typified by the family firm where the leadership style is autocratic and the organizational system informal. Communications tend to be vertical, with little real teamwork. Important purchasing decisions are likely to be passed to top management for final approval, but good personal relationships with middle management are vital to prevent them blocking approaches.

Leadership in the Netherlands is more democratic, although organizational style tends to be systematic, with rigorous management systems designed to involve multilevel consensus decision-making. Buying is, therefore, characterized by large DMUs and long decision-making processes as members attempt to reach agreement without conflict or one-sided outcomes.

Management styles in the EU and the USA   FIGURE 3.3

Consumerism

Consumerism takes the form of organized action against business practices that are not in the interests of consumers. Organized action is taken through the consumer movement, which is an organized collection of groups and organizations whose objective is to protect the rights of consumers. Pressure from the consumer movement, environmentalists, individuals who engage in ethical consumption and the media has resulted in many organizations adopting corporate social responsibility as a guide to their business practices. **Corporate social responsibility** (CSR) refers to the ethical principle that an organization should be accountable for how its behaviour might affect society and the environment. The importance of CSR is reflected in the large proportion of Chapter 6 (Understanding Marketing Ethics and Corporate Social Responsibility) that is devoted to coverage of this topic.

The consumer movement has had notable successes, including improvements in car safety, the encouragement of fast-food restaurants to provide healthy-eating options, health labelling of food products, and the banning of smoking in public places in some European countries including Ireland and the UK.

Some consumer organizations, such as the Consumers' Association in the UK, campaign for consumers and provide information about products, often on a comparative basis that allows consumers to make more informed choices between brands.

Marketing management should not consider the consumer movement a threat to business but an opportunity to create new product offerings to meet the needs of emerging market segments. For example, in the detergent market brands have been launched that are more environmentally friendly, and food companies have reduced the fat and salt content of some of their products.

Changes in social and cultural aspects of the marketing environment need to be monitored and understood so that marketing management is aware of the changing tastes and behaviour of consumers. Such changes can create demand shifts that can act as either opportunities or threats for European companies.

Technological Forces

Technology can have a substantial impact on people's lives and companies' fortunes. Technological breakthroughs have given us body scanners, robotics, camcorders, the Internet, mobile phones, computers and many other products that have contributed to our quality of life. Many technological breakthroughs change the rules of the competitive game: the launch of the computer and word-processing software has ruined the market for typewriters; the growth of e-mail spelt the decline of the fax machine; the rise of the compact disc decimated the market for cassette tapes.

Heavy investment in new technology can pay handsome dividends. ICI, for example, invested heavily in the biotechnology area and is the market leader in equipment used for genetic fingerprinting, and Apple's investment in the technology supporting its iPod has made it global leader in the mobile music market. The key to successful technological investment is market understanding not technological sophistication for its own sake. Marketing and R&D staff need to work closely together to achieve this aim. The classic example of a high-technology initiative driven by technologists rather than pulled by the market is Concorde. Although technologically sophisticated, management knew before launch that it never stood a chance of being commercially viable. By contrast the development of the Airbus A380, the world's biggest passenger plane, has been market based, taking into account the need for greater passenger comfort on long-haul flights, the higher revenues accruing from a larger number of passengers per flight, and recognition that over the next 20 years around 70 per cent of flights will be from just 25 airports, many of which are so congested they are unable to take any more planes. By using aircraft like the A380 the predicted increase in passenger demand can be accommodated using the same number of planes.[48]

A lack of investment in high-potential technological areas can severely affect the fortunes of companies. For example, Sony—once regarded as a leader in high-tech product innovation—has lost ground due to its lack of early investment in flat-screen television, liquid crystal display and portable audio systems, which allowed Apple to supersede the Sony Walkman with its iPod, which not only allows high-quality mobile listening but also the downloading of music, and for Samsung to gain a competitive advantage in flat-screen televisions.

Besides investment in technological areas that have high market potential, companies need capabilities in identifying how technology developed in one field can be exploited in another market. For example, Teflon, which has been a major marketing success in the coating of non-stick frying pans, was first developed as a coating on the nose cones of space rockets. A more recent technology transfer success story is of Visco foam, which was developed by NASA for the space programme to absorb the tremendous forces that astronauts are subjected to during lift-off. It has been used to create Visco memory foam beds that adjust to body position minimizing pressure points and maximizing body support.

As we have seen, technological change can provide opportunities for new product development and also threats to existing markets. Technology also affects the way in which marketing is conducted. Developments in information technology have revolutionized marketing practices. Information technology describes the broad range of processes and products within the fields of computing and telecommunications. The Internet and mobile phone technology have allowed companies to use new channels of communication and distribution (e.g. music downloads) to reach consumers. The importance of these developments is reflected in Chapter 18, on digital marketing, which explores how these advances are providing new opportunities for marketers. Salesforce automation is improving the efficiency of salesforces, and these are described and the implications examined in Chapter 14, on personal selling and sales management. A whole new industry, customer relationship management (CRM), has emerged in recent years, founded on database technologies to enable companies to improve communications and relationships with consumers. CRM issues are discussed in Chapter 15, on direct marketing.

Marketing-led companies seek not only to monitor technological trends but also to pioneer technological breakthroughs that can transform markets and shift competitive advantage in their favour. They also seek to use technology to improve the efficiency and effectiveness of their marketing operations.

The Microenvironment

The microenvironment consists of the actors in the firm's immediate environment that affect its capabilities to operate effectively in its chosen markets. Those actors—customers, competitors, distributors and suppliers—will now be introduced and will be analysed in more depth throughout the book.

Customers

As we saw in Chapter 1, customers are at the centre of the marketing philosophy and effort, and it is the task of marketing management to satisfy their needs and expectations better than the competition. The starting point is an understanding of them and this is considered in Chapter 4 (Understanding Consumer Behaviour) and Chapter 5 (Understanding Organizational Buying Behaviour). The techniques for gathering and analysing customer and other marketing information are discussed in Chapter 7, on marketing research. Furthermore, the grouping of consumers to form market segments that can be targeted with specific marketing mix offerings is the subject of Chapter 8 (Market Segmentation and Positioning).

Changing customer tastes, lifestyles, motivations and expectations need to be monitored so that companies supply the appropriate targeted marketing mix strategies that meet their needs. Changes in consumer behaviours also need to be monitored. For example, consumers are using social network sites like Twitter to communicate—a fact not lost on marketers, as Digital Marketing 3.2 explains. Marketers should also seek out the latest customer needs that currently have not been met. The discovery of these can result in lucrative unserved markets in which first-mover advantage can be a vital asset, as was demonstrated by 3M's Post-it brand.

3.2 Digital Marketing

Twittering Around the World

Twitter is a free-to-join social networking group, created in 2006. It has rapidly grown in popularity worldwide and currently has roughly 4–5 million users. Twitter enables members of the network community to connect through quick and frequent online exchanges called 'tweets'. Tweets are text-based posts (no longer than 140 characters), which are displayed on the user's profile page and sent to other users who have signed up as 'followers'. A typical tweet might explain what I am doing right now (e.g. 'Sitting in my home office writing a mini case study for *Principles and Practice of Marketing*'). Users of Twitter can control who can access their messages (e.g. close circle of friends, work colleagues or anybody) and tweets can be sent and received via the Twitter website, short message service (SMS) or external applications. Increasingly, individuals and companies are providing links to Twitter trails from their websites.

In countries all around the world, people follow Twitter trails, which are relevant and of interest, to access information and stay informed about world events or news updates from friends.

World leaders, celebrities and pop icons have been quick to recognize Twitter as a powerful communication network. President of the United States, Barack Obama, used Twitter to gain support during the presidential election campaign. Indeed, he was reportedly the most followed person on Twitter at the time, with over 144,000 followers. Many other world leaders are now holding press conferences via Twitter. High-profile celebrities also use Twitter. Virgin's Richard Branson has an account to recruit prospective employees; pop star Britney Spears gives fans updates of her whereabouts. British tennis player Andy Murray is also a regular tweeter; he informed his fans not long after his loss in the Australian Open Tennis Championship: 'Just bak from dinner. Bumpd in2 the guys from The Prodigy in hotel lobby. Tuf 2day. Fernando playd gr8 5th.'

The potential influence of Twitter and similar online social networking groups is constantly growing. For example, Twitter users came together online in a 'Twestival', a global online meeting involving Twitterers from over 170 cities around the world. Marketers should be aware of the potential significance of Twitter in influencing consumer behaviour.

Based on: Mzimba (2009)[49]

Competition

Competitors have a major bearing on the performance of companies. For example, when competitors price-cut the attractiveness of the market can fall and their ability to innovate can ruin once highly profitable brands. Marketing history is littered with brands that were once successful (e.g. Olivetti typewriters, Amstrad computers and Lotus software) but are now defunct because rivals developed and marketed better alternatives. No longer is it sufficient to meet customer needs and expectations—success is dependent on doing it better than the competition.

Marketing-orientated companies not only monitor and seek to understand customers but also research competitors and their brands to understand their strengths, weaknesses, strategies and response patterns. In this book, the importance of these issues is reflected in a section being devoted to such analysis and the strategies that can be employed to anticipate and combat competitive moves. These matters are discussed in Chapter 19 (Analysing Competitors and Creating a Competitive Advantage) and Chapter 20 (Competitive Marketing Strategy).

Distributors

Some companies, such as those providing services, dispense with the use of distributors, preferring to deal directly with end-user customers. The others use the services of distributors such as wholesalers and retailers to supply end users. As we shall see in Chapter 17, on distribution, these channel intermediaries perform many valuable services, including breaking bulk, making products available to customers where and when they want them, and providing specialist services such as maintenance and installation.

Distributors can reduce the profitability of suppliers by putting pressure on profit margins. For example, large retailers such as Wal-Mart and Tesco have enormous buying power and can demand low prices from their suppliers, a fact that has been criticized in the media when applied to small farmers.

Distribution trends need to be monitored. For example, the trend towards downloading music has hit traditional music outlets that sell CDs, and the growth of the Internet-based sellers such as Amazon has impacted on traditional bricks-and-mortar booksellers. As the attractiveness of distribution channels changes so suppliers must alter their strategies to keep in touch with customers.

Suppliers

The fortunes of companies are not only dependent on customers, competitors and distributors, they are also influenced by their suppliers. Increases in supply costs can push up prices, making other alternatives more attractive. For example, increases in the price of aluminium make plastic more attractive. Also, as with distributors, powerful suppliers can force up prices. The rise in the price of gas has been blamed on powerful European suppliers who, it is alleged, restricted supply in order to force prices higher.

Companies need to monitor supply availability, such as shortages due to labour strikes or political factors, as these can cause customer dissatisfaction and lost sales. They also need to be sensitive to alternative input materials that can be substituted for those of existing suppliers if the latter's prices rise or availability diminishes significantly.

The importance of suppliers is reflected in discussion of their relationship with customers in Chapter 5, which focuses on organizational buying behaviour. Many customers are increasingly forming partnerships with selected suppliers in order to enhance value delivery.

All the elements of the microenvironment need to be monitored and assessed so that opportunities can be exploited and threats combated. This forms an essential ingredient in maintaining strategic fit between a company and its marketing environment.

Environmental Scanning

The process of monitoring and analysing the marketing environment of a company is called **environmental scanning**. Two key decisions that management need to make are what to scan and how to organize the activity. Clearly, in theory, every event in the world has the potential to affect a company's operations, but to establish a scanning system that covers every conceivable force would be unmanageable. The first task, then, is to define a feasible range of forces that require monitoring. These are the *potentially relevant environmental forces* that have the most likelihood of affecting future business prospects. The second prerequisite for an effective scanning system is to design a system that provides a fast response to events that are only partially predictable, emerge as surprises and grow very rapidly. This is essential because of the increasing turbulence of the marketing environment. Ansoff proposes that environmental scanning monitors the company's environment for signals of the development of *strategic issues* that can have an influence on company performances.[50]

Figure 3.4 provides the framework for corporate response, which is dependent on an analysis of the perceived impact, signal strength and urgency of the strategic issue.

There are four approaches to the organization of environmental scanning, as follows.[51]

A framework for analysing and responding to environmental (strategic) issues · FIGURE 3.4

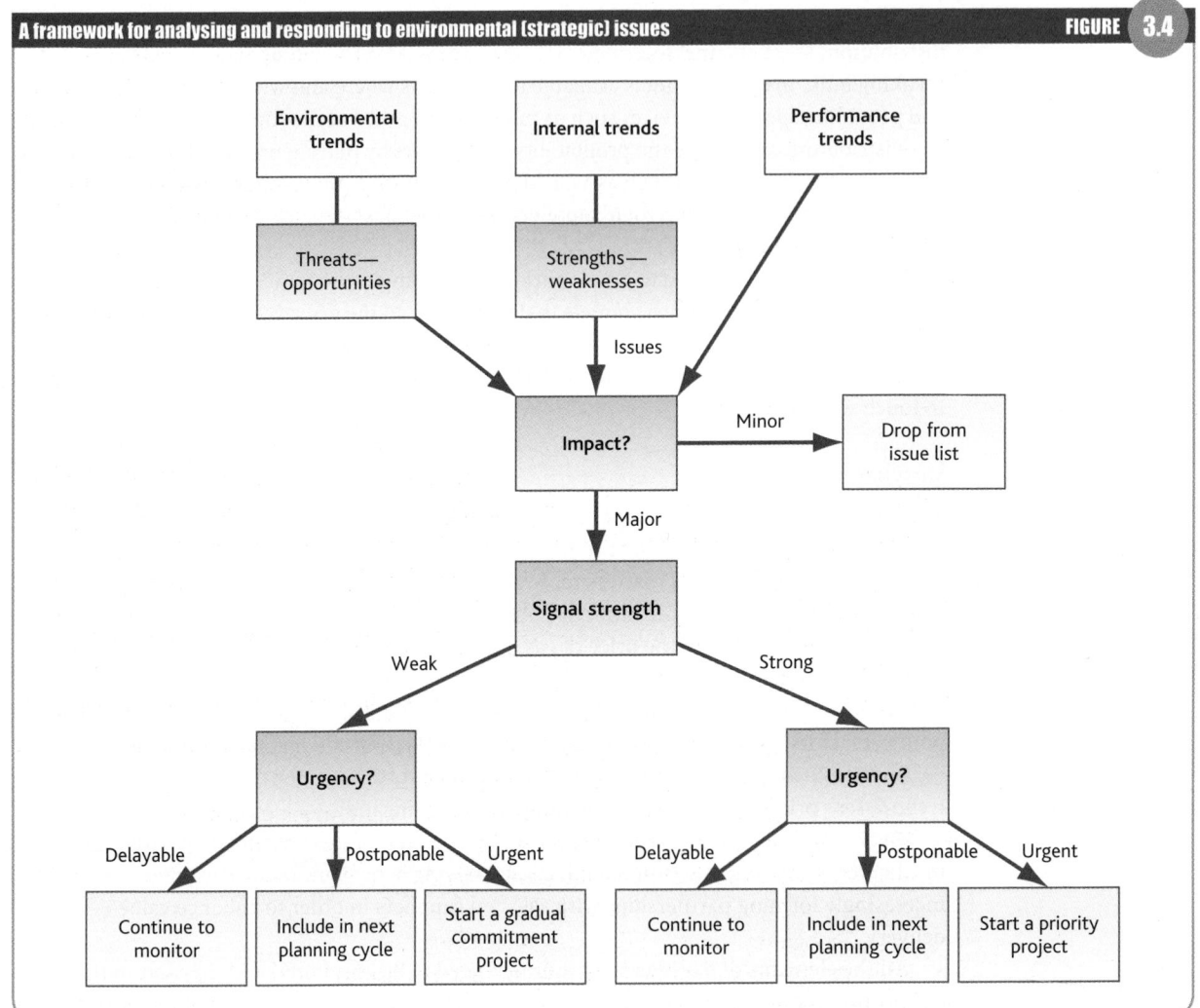

1 *Line management*: functional managers (e.g. sales, marketing, purchasing) can be required to conduct environmental scanning in addition to their existing duties. This approach can falter because of line management resistance to the imposition of additional duties, and a lack of the specialist research and analytical skills required of scanners.

2 *Strategic planner*: environmental scanning is made part of the strategic planner's job. The drawback of this approach is that a head office planner may not have the depth of understanding of a business unit's operations to be able to do the job effectively.

3 *Separate organizational unit*: regular and ad hoc scanning is conducted by a separate organizational unit and is responsible for disseminating relevant information to managers. General Electric uses such a system, with the unit's operations funded by the information recipients. The advantage is that there is a dedicated team concentrating its efforts on this important task. The disadvantage is that it is very costly and unlikely to be feasible except for large, profitable companies.

4 *Joint line/general management teams*: a temporary planning team consisting of line and general (corporate) management may be set up to identify trends and issues that may have an impact on the business. Alternatively, an environmental trend or issue may have emerged that requires closer scrutiny. A joint team may be set up to study its implications.

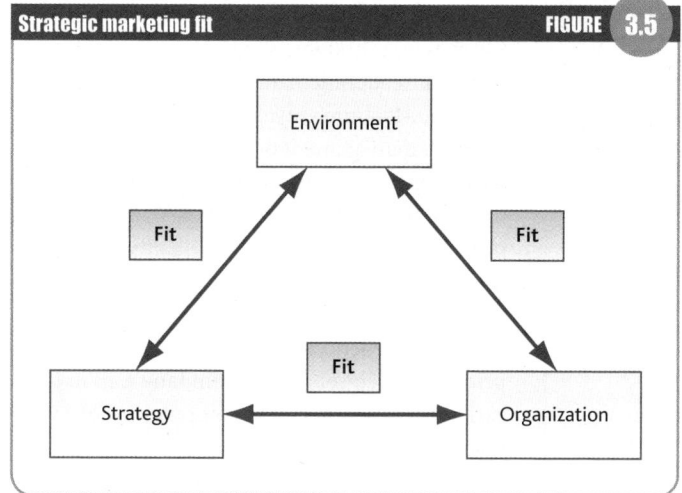

Strategic marketing fit   FIGURE 3.5

The most appropriate organizational arrangement for scanning will depend on the unique circumstances facing a firm. A judgement needs to be made regarding the costs and benefits of each alternative. The size and profitability of the company and the perceived degree of environmental turbulence will be factors that impinge on this decision.

Brownlie suggests that a complete environmental scanning system would perform the following tasks:[52]

- monitor trends, issues and events, and study their implications
- develop forecasts, scenarios and issues analysis as input to strategic decision-making
- provide a focal point for the interpretation and analysis of environmental information identified by other people in the company
- establish a library or database for environmental information
- provide a group of internal experts on environmental affairs
- disseminate information on the business environment through newsletters, reports and lectures
- evaluate and revise the scanning system itself by applying new tools and procedures.

Formal environmental scanning was researched by Diffenbach, who found that practitioners believed it provided the following benefits:

- better general awareness of, and responsiveness to, environmental changes
- better strategic planning and decision-making
- greater effectiveness in dealing with government
- improved industry and market analysis
- better foreign investment and international marketing
- improved resource allocation and diversification decisions
- superior energy planning.

Environmental scanning provides the essential informational input to create strategic fit between strategy, organization and the environment (see Fig. 3.5). Marketing strategy should reflect the environment even if this means a fundamental reorganization of operations.

Responses to Environmental Change

Companies respond in various ways to environmental change (see Fig. 3.6).

Ignorance

Because of poor environmental scanning, companies may not realize that salient forces are affecting their future prospects. They therefore continue as normal, ignorant of the environmental issues that are threatening their existence, or opportunities that could be seized. No change is made.

Delay

The second response is to delay action once the force is understood. This can be caused by *bureaucratic decision processes* that stifle swift action. The slow response by Swiss watch

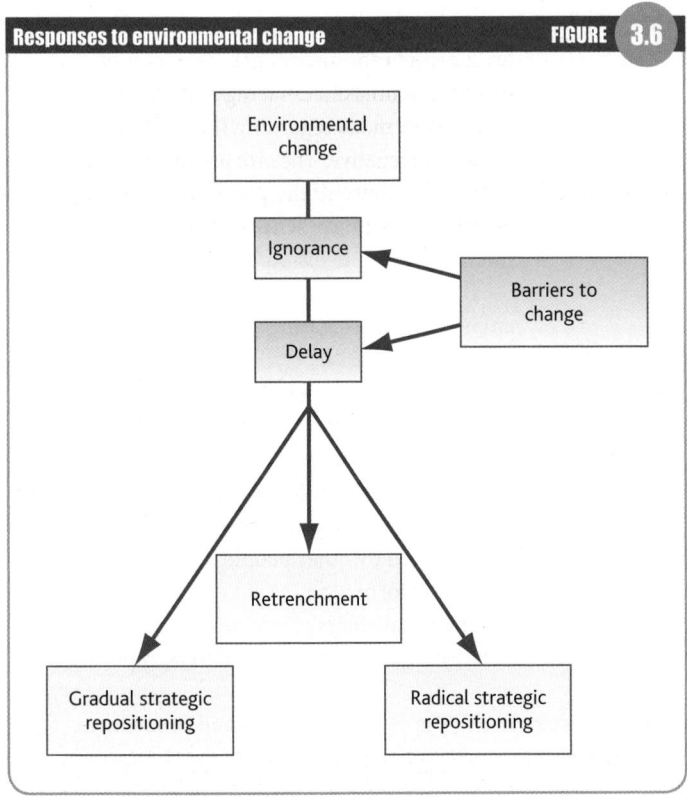

Responses to environmental change   FIGURE **3.6**

manufacturers to the introduction of digital watches was thought, in part, to be caused by the bureaucratic nature of their decision-making. *Marketing myopia* can slow response through management being product rather than customer focused. For example, Compaq grew to sales of £2 billion in eight years based on processes that produced high-quality products. Manufacturing concentrated on quality, sacrificing speed and economy to ensure product excellence. Compaq's quality-at-any-price approach served the company well in the early days of the personal computer industry when customers worried about product usability. As PCs became commodities and nimble rivals like Dell grew, competition shifted to value for money. Compaq continued to rely on well-honed processes that churned out quality products but at a price that meant they gathered dust on dealers' shelves.[53] A third source of delay is *technological myopia*, where a company fails to respond to technological change. An example is Kodak's slow response to the emergence of digital technology in cameras. The fourth reason for delay is *psychological recoil* by managers who see change as a threat and defend the status quo. These are four powerful contributors to inertia.

Retrenchment

This response tackles efficiency problems but ignores effectiveness issues. As sales and profits decline, management cuts costs; this leads to a period of higher profits but does nothing to stem declining sales. Costs (and capacity) are reduced once more but the fundamental strategic problems remain. Retrenchment policies only delay the inevitable.

Gradual strategic repositioning

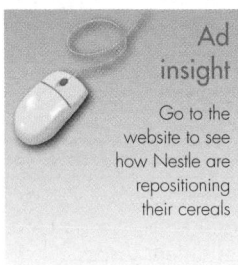

This involves a gradual, planned and continuous adaptation to the changing marketing environment. Tesco is a company that has continually repositioned itself in response to changing social and economic trends. Originally a supermarket based on a 'pile it high, sell it cheap' philosophy, it has maintained its low price positioning while moving to higher-quality products. It has also expanded the range of products it sells (including CDs, electrical goods, financial services and clothing) to provide one-stop shopping, and has expanded into new market segments (Tesco Express convenience stores) and international markets including the Far East, the USA and central and eastern Europe.

Radical strategic repositioning

Radical strategic repositioning involves changing the direction of the entire business. An example is Nokia, which radically repositioned from being a conglomerate operating in such industries as paper, chemicals and rubber into a world leader in mobile phones. Samsung also successfully repositioned by transferring itself from a copy-cat producer of cheap televisions and microwave ovens into a technology company marketing mobile phones, flat-screen televisions, and memory chips that are used in digital cameras, mobile phones and portable music players such as the iPod nano.[54] Radical strategic repositioning is much riskier than gradual strategic repositioning because, if unsuccessful, the company is likely to fold.

This chapter has explored a number of major forces occurring in the marketing environment, and has discussed methods of scanning for these and other changes that may fundamentally reshape the fortunes of companies. Failure to respond to a changing environment has the same effect on companies as lack of adaptation by animals: extinction.

Online **Learning**Centre

When you have read this chapter
log on to the Online Learning Centre at www.mcgraw-hill.co.uk/textbooks/jobber to explore chapter-by-chapter test questions, links and further online study tools for marketing.

Review

1 The nature of the marketing environment
- The marketing environment consists of the microenvironment (customers, competitors, distributors and suppliers) and the macroenvironment (economic, social, political, legal, physical and technological forces). These shape the character of the opportunities and threats facing a company and yet are largely uncontrollable.

2 The distinction between the microenvironment and the macroenvironment
- As can be seen above, the microenvironment consists of those actors in the firm's immediate environment that affect its capabilities to operate effectively in its chosen markets.
- The macroenvironment consists of a number of broader forces that affect not only the company but also the other actors in the microenvironment.

3 The impact of political and legal, economic, ecological/physical environmental, social/cultural and technological forces on marketing decisions
- Political and legal forces can influence marketing decisions by determining the rules by which business can be conducted. In Europe, marketing decisions are affected by legislation at EU and national levels. EU laws seek to prevent collusion, prevent abuse of market dominance, control mergers and acquisitions, and restrict state aid to firms. National laws also affect marketing decisions by regulating anti-competitive practices. Marketers who apply ethics to their decision-making should have no problem working within this legal framework. They should also decide the extent to which they feel the need to influence political decisions that may affect their operations.
- Economic forces can impact marketing decisions through their effect on supply and demand. Key factors are economic growth, unemployment, interest and exchange rates and changes in the global economic environment such as the entry of central and eastern European countries into the EU, and the rise of the Chinese and Indian economies. Marketers need to have contingency plans in place to cope with economic downturns, and to be aware of the opportunities and threats arising from changes in the global marketing environment.
- Ecological/physical environmental forces are concerned with the environmental costs of consumption. Five issues that impact marketing decisions are combating global warming, pollution control, conservation of energy and other scarce resources, use of environmentally friendly ingredients and components, and the use of recyclable and non-wasteful packaging. Marketers need to be aware of the environmental consequences of their actions, and the opportunities and threats associated with ecological issues.

- Social/cultural forces can have an impact on marketing decisions by changing demand patterns (e.g. the growth of the over-50s market) and creating new opportunities and threats. Three major influences are changes in the demographic profile of the population, cultural differences within and between nations, and the impact of consumerism.
- Technological forces can impact marketing decisions by changing the rules of the competitive game. Technological change can provide major opportunities and also pose enormous threats to companies. Marketers need to monitor technological trends and pioneer technological breakthroughs. They should also seek to use technology to improve marketing operations.

4 How to conduct environmental scanning

- Two key decisions are what to scan and how to organize the activity.
- Four approaches to the organization of environmental scanning are to use line management, the strategic planner, a separate organizational unit and joint line/general management teams.
- The system should monitor trends, develop forecasts, interpret and analyse internally produced information, establish a database, provide environmental experts, disseminate information, and evaluate and revise the system.

5 How companies respond to environmental change

- Response comes in five forms, which are: ignorance, delay, retrenchment, gradual strategic repositioning and radical strategic repositioning.

Key Terms

consumerism organized action against business practices that are not in the interests of consumers

corporate social responsibility the ethical principle that an organization should be accountable for how its behaviour might affect society and the environment

culture the combination of traditions, taboos, values and attitudes of the society in which an individual lives

demography changes in the population in terms of its size and characteristics

ecology the study of living things within their environment

environmental scanning the process of monitoring and analysing the marketing environment of a company

marketing environment the actors and forces that affect a company's capability to operate effectively in providing products and services to its customers

PEEST analysis the analysis of the political/legal, economic, ecological/physical, social/cultural, and technological environments

Study Questions

1 Choose an organization (if you are in paid employment use your own organization) and identify the major forces in the environment that are likely to affect its prospects in the next five to 10 years.

2 What are the major ecological/physical environmental forces acting on marketing? What are their implications for marketing management?

3 What are the major opportunities and threats to EU businesses arising from the move to market-driven economies of former eastern bloc countries?

④ Generate two lists of products and services. The first list will identify those products and services that are likely to be associated with falling demand as a result of changes in the age structure in Europe. The second list will consist of those that are likely to see an increase in demand. What are the marketing implications for their providers?

⑤ How does technological change affect marketing? What should marketing management do to take account of technological forces?

⑥ Evaluate the marketing opportunities and threats posed by the growing importance of the socially conscious consumer.

References

1. Wachman, R. (2009) Turn Failed Banks Back into Mutuals, Labour Told, *Observer*, 8 February, 1.
2. Milmo, D. (2008) Former BA Bosses Face Price-Fixing Charges, *Guardian*, 7 August, 26.
3. Tait, N. and P. Hollinger (2008) Record EU Fine for Glass Cartel, *Financial Times*, 13 November, 27.
4. Mercado, S., R. Welford and K. Prescott (2001) *European Business: An Issue-Based Approach*, Harlow: FT Pearson.
5. Helmore, E. (2004) Do Not Pass Go Says EC, *Observer*, 28 March, 3.
6. Ritson, M. (2002) Companies Walk a Tightrope as EU Free Trade Law Begins to Bite, *Marketing*, 7 November, 16.
7. Buck, T. (2005) EU Targets Cartels in Antitrust Overhaul, *Financial Times*, 21 December, 1.
8. Murphy, M. and P. K. Yuk (2008) Record Fine Over Price Fixes, *Financial Times*, 13 July, 1.
9. Tait, N. and K. Allison (2008) Brussels Hits Microsoft with €899m Antitrust Fine, *Financial Times*, 28 February, 27.
10. Johnson, D. and C. Turner (2000) *European Business*, London: Routledge.
11. Macalister, T. (2006) Shell Faces New Damages Claim, *Guardian*, 10 January, 23.
12. Jones, A. and J. Mackintosh (2005) Taking the Hit: European Exporters Find the Dollar's Weakness is Hard to Counter, *Financial Times*, 3 May, 17.
13. Watts, N. (2006) Migrant Workers from East Helping to Boost EU Fortunes, says Report, *Guardian*, 9 February, 22.
14. Ewing, J. and G. Edmondson (2005) Rise of a Powerhouse, *Business Week*, 12/9 December, 42–60.
15. Ewing and Edmondson (2005) op. cit.
16. Bartram, P. (2004) Targeting the New Ten, *Marketeer*, May, 22–5.
17. Engardio, P. (2005) A New World Economy, *Business Week*, 22/29 August, 32–8.
18. Bulkley, K. (2008) Partnerships Are Key, *Media Guardian*, 29 September, 1; Anonymous (2008) Alternative Reality, *Economist*, 2 February, 69.
19. Branigan, T. (2008) Rush for Yorkshire Pud and Cotton Socks, *Guardian*, 3 October, 21.
20. Ramesh, R. (2009) After the World's Cheapest Car, India Launches £7 Laptop, *Guardian*, 3 February, 19.
21. McGregor, R. (2005) China's Companies Count Down to Lift-off, *Financial Times*, 30 August, 9.
22. Ramesh, R. (2008) Making a Difference: The Philanthropic Industrial Powerhouse Rising in the East, *Guardian*, 27 March, 31.
23. Engardio, P. (2005) Crouching Tigers, Hidden Dragons, *Business Week*, 22/29 August, 40–1.
24. Connon, H. (2008) Brazil and Russia: Giants of a New Economic World Order, *Observer*, 25 August, 6–7.
25. Wiggins, J. (2008) Multinationals Eat into the Russian Market, *Financial Times*, 18 June, 22.
26. McGregor, J. (2005) How China Learned to Love Capitalism, *Observer*, 6 November, 4.
27. Roberts, D. and D. Rocks (2005) Let a Thousand Brands Bloom, *Business Week*, 24–6.
28. Singh, S. (2005) Western Brands Vie to Fulfil Eastern Promise, *Marketing Week*, 21 April, 24–6.
29. Anderlini, J. and J. Reed (2008) Chrysler Ends Small Car Deal with Cherry, *Financial Times*, 10 December, 23.
30. Bulkley (2008) op. cit.
31. Ibison, D. (2008) Ericsson Clinches Deals With China Duo, *Financial Times*, 15 April, 24.
32. Hoyos, C., E. Crooks and C. Belton (2008) Strained Relations Thaw over TNK-BP, *Financial Times*, 5 September, 19.
33. Connon (2008) op. cit.
34. Macalister, T. (2006) BP to Make Biggest Profit in UK History, *Guardian*, 12 January, 26.
35. Charter, M., K. Peattie, J. Ottman and M. J. Polonsky (2002) *Marketing and Sustainability*, Cardiff: Centre for Business Relationships, Accountability, Sustainability and Society (BRASS) in association with the Centre for Sustainable Design.
36. Reed, J. and J. Soble (2008) Honda to Lift Hybrid Production As Fuel Prices Rise, *Financial Times*, 22 May, 30.
37. Rowley, I. (2008) Honda Goes Whole Hog For Hybrids, *Business Week*, 28 July, 62–3.

38. Vidal, J. (2006) Sweden Plans to be World's First Oil-free Economy, *Guardian*, 8 February, 16.
39. MacAlister, T. (2008) Brazil Disputes Cost of Sugar in the Tank, *Guardian*, 10 June, 23.
41. www.foeeurope.org/about/english.htm.
41. Friends of the Earth Trust (2004) Cadbury's Shareholders Find Palm Oil Leaves a Bitter Taste, Foe.co.uk, 21 May 2004 (retrieved from www.foe.co.uk/resource/press_releases/cadburys_shareholders_find_20052004.html).
42. Brown, P. (1992) Rise of Women Key to Population Curb, *Guardian*, 30 April, 8.
43. James, D. (2001) B2-4B Spells Profits, *Marketing News*, 5 November, 13.
44. Anonymous (2008) Poles Apart, *Economist*, 30 August, 33–4.
45. Writers, F. T. (1992) Queuing for Flawed Fantasy, *Financial Times*, 13/14 June, 5.
46. Mole, J. (1990) *Mind Your Manners*, London: Industrial Society.
47. Wolfe, A. (1991) The 'Eurobuyer', How European Businesses Buy, *Market Intelligence and Planning* 9(5), 9–15.
48. Edemariam, A. (2006) Wings of Desire, *Guardian*, 23 February, 6–17.
49. Mzimba, L. (2009) Why Celebrities Love Twittering, *BBC News*, 22 January 2009, http://news.bbc.co.uk/1/hi/entertainment/7851383.stm (accessed 2 April 2009).
50. Ansoff, H. I. (1991) *Implementing Strategic Management*, Englewood Cliffs, NJ: Prentice-Hall.
51. Brownlie, D. (2002) Environmental Analysis, in Baker, M. J. (ed.) *The Marketing Book*, Oxford: Butterworth-Heinemann.
52. Brownlie, D. (2002) op. cit.
53. Sull, D. (2005) Ingrained Sullen Breeds Failure, *Financial Times*, 3 October, 12.
54. Fifield, A. (2008) Samsung Sows for the Future With its Garden of Delights, *Financial Times*, 4 January, 17.

All is not well in the Sony dynasty. The company's performance in recent years has been less than stellar for this global brand icon. The Sony brand was once a byword for innovation; now it is seen as failing to tap new opportunities, being complacent and over-reliant on past successes. Its share price has fallen by two-thirds in the space of five years, and its credit rating has been downgraded. Its pioneering electronics division is struggling, sales have plummeted and profits are in decline. Aggressive competitors are stealing market share in key markets where once it dominated. Now the company is being criticized for its lack of focus, and failing to avail itself of strategic windows of opportunity that its competitors have rapidly exploited. In the wake of this 'Sony shockwave', the company has initiated a raft of changes to turn around its performance, including radical cost-saving initiatives to stop the haemorrhaging of profits. The restructuring involves supply chain cost reductions, headcount reductions and manufacturing site realignment. The biggest surprise is that, although earning huge revenues from the variety of industries in which it operates, Sony's income from its core electronics business is collapsing, with a 17 per cent decrease, and the firm is losing millions. So what is happening at Sony? Faced with intensification of price competition, a strong currency and the global economic slowdown, can it reinvent itself?

Following the ravages of the Second World War, Akito Morita and Masaru Ibuka joined together to form a small electronics firm that would go on to become a global colossus. In the ramshackle remains of a bombed-out department store in Tokyo, the pair started to make radio components and repair radios. Morita was the consummate salesman, while Ibuka was a technical expert; they formed a perfect partnership. Both guided the firm for over 50 years. Among the company's first engineering forays was an electric rice cooker and electric heated seat cushions. In the early years, the company set upon an innovation focus, always looking for potentially lucrative markets and exploiting new technology. The founders would frequently visit other countries with a view to exploiting new opportunities, such as Ibuka visiting the USA in 1952 and bringing back the idea of exploiting new transistor technology

and developing radios. This became the launch pad for Sony's early success, when people bought hundreds of thousands of transistor radios to listen to the new rock'n'roll. The company went from strength to strength through a combination of leading-edge technology products and miniaturization. Sony became the embodiment of post-war Japanese industry: entrepreneurial, creative, pioneering and highly successful. The company was always at the forefront of technology, entering untested new markets, and creating one hit product after the next.

From these humble beginnings, Sony now has become a highly respected global brand name, manufacturing audio, video, communications and information technology products for both consumer and industrial markets worldwide. The Sony brand has

Sony at a glance	TABLE C5.1
Headquarters based in Tokyo, Japan	
Sony employs over 171,300 people worldwide	
Annual sales exceed over $78 billion dollars per year; revenue was down 12.9%	
One of the world's most valuable brands	
Pioneers of ground-breaking technology such as the Walkman, PlayStation, transistor radios, tape recorders, video recorders, CD players and video cameras	
Owns second largest music company in world	
Large investment in the motion picture and television industry, with Sony Pictures	

developed into a highly respected and sought-after brand, instantly recognizable the world over. Its products have the reputation for being highly innovative, extremely reliable and possessing high quality standards. The company has evolved to become more than just an electronics business. It has a large presence in the music, movie and television business, banking, insurance and Internet services. The company has several key divisions within the group (see Table C5.2). Some of these divisions are owned outright, while others are joint ventures with leading multinationals. For example, the firm merged its mobile phone business with Swedish telecommunications giant Ericsson. This 50:50 joint venture, called Sony Ericsson, aims to leverage the core competences of both firms, in an effort to beat market leader Nokia in the mobile telephone market. The new venture is performing well, with its range of phones equipped with high-end camera and Walkman-branded capabilities turning the mobile phones into portable digital music devices. It is hoped that these devices will be the future 'iPod killer' and help

Sony regain the portable music market that it once dominated. However, the venture is experiencing rapid losses, coupled with the stellar success of Apple's iPhone and the continued strong performance of Nokia. The division needs a hit, but nothing has captured the public's imagination.

One of the biggest areas of concern for Sony is its electronics business. This accounts for nearly 70 per cent of it revenues and is the cornerstone of the business. In 2008, Sony's electronics division decreased 17 per cent on revenues. This sent shockwaves around the world's investment community and highlighted that there was something inherently wrong within Sony. At present the firm is over-reliant on the success of its PlayStation games console business, involved in intense price competition, experiencing ever tightening price margins (prices have deflated by 30 per cent in some cases), and losing ground to competitors. The company's sales of its Cybershot digital cameras, Vaio laptops and Handycam camcorders are seeing decreased demand. The company is still yearning for a blockbuster product that will

The major divisions of Sony	TABLE C5.2
Name	**Details**
Sony Electronics	Manufactures a wide variety of electronic products for both consumer and industrial markets. Products include DVD players, plasma screens, digital audio players, semiconductors, camcorders, notebook computers and a variety of other electronic products
Sony Computer Entertainment	Markets the Sony PlayStation family of products and produces gaming content for these devices. Over 70 million PlayStations have been sold
Sony DADC	Manufactures media storage discs such as CD, DVD, Blu-Ray and Universal Media Discs
Sony Ericsson	A 50:50 joint venture with Swedish firm Ericsson focused on the mobile telephony industry. Joint venture established in October 2001. The division develops innovative mobile phones integrating camera, digital audio and gaming technology. Uses linkages with Sony BMG and Sony Pictures with regard to content. Employs 5000 staff worldwide. Sales are down 19%. Losses €489 million in 2008
Sony Music Entertainment	Second largest music publisher in the world. A music colossus, owning several music labels in a variety of genres. Artists on roster include Beyonce, Jennifer Lopez, Outkast, Bruce Springsteen, Leona Lewis and Rod Stewart. Owns huge back catalogue of masterworks, including Elvis Presley, Johnny Cash and Louis Armstrong
Sony/ATV Music Publishing	Joint venture with the late Michael Jackson, who owned a treasure trove of a music back catalogue including music from the Beatles, Bob Dylan and Jimi Hendrix. The firm owns and administers the copyright of these songs

Sony milestones	TABLE C5.3

1946—Founded by Masaru Ibuka and Akito Morita in post-war Tokyo, using a bombed-out department store and employing 20 people. Called the company Tokyo Tsuchin Kogyo KK (Tokyo Telecommunications Engineering Corporation)
1954—Produces Japan's first transistor radio
1958—Name is changed to Sony (serived from *Sonus*, Latin for sound)
1962—Releases the world's smallest transistor television
1968—Manufactures Trinitron colour television
1971—Sells the first video cassette recorder
1975—Launches the ill-fated Betamax home video recorder; loses format war to VHS standard
1979—Launches the Sony Walkman, the personal portable stereo that becomes a worldwide phenomenon
1983—Releases the first consumer camcorder
1988—Launches American acquisitions phase, diversifying by buying CBS Records
1989—Acquires Columbia Pictures, which now forms Sony Pictures
1995—Enters the games console market with the first Sony PlayStation
1999—Founder Akito Morita dies, aged 78
2000—PlayStation 2 launched
2001—Sony Ericsson venture launched
2004—Sony BMG Music Entertainment launched after successful merger
2005—Launches PlayStation Portable, the PSP
2005—Bought the famous MGM movie studio for $5 billion as part of a consortium
2005—Welshman Sir Howard Stringer appointed as chairman and CEO of Sony
2006—Launches the PlayStation 3. Forecasts a 10-year life cycle for the latest console
2007—Cancelled the Sony Connect music distribution platform
2008—Announced a 95 billion yen (£590 million) loss
2009—Demoed the motion-sensitive 'Sony PlayStation Wand' for the PlayStation 3

revitalize it. Its Bravia television screens are performing well; however, all other electronic product categories are facing enormous pressure and declines. Its iconic status as the world's leading electronic brand is losing its lustre; other firms have taken the lead, such as its Korean arch-rival Samsung and the rejuvenated Apple Computers. It has tried to take the lead in new platforms like e-readers, only to be surprisingly trounced by Amazon.com with its Kindle device due to wireless connectivity and abundance of content.

Some blame Sony's current problems on its past successes, making it complacent with regard to the changing needs of the market. The company is facing intense competition from several key competitors in several diverse markets in which it operates. In televisions, where it was once so dominant, it lost impetus by failing to provide a viable LCD screen and plasma screen offering. Competitors like Samsung devoured the market, while Sony continued to focus on the traditional bulky televisions. Sony completely missed the market. In the mid-1990s it decided to stay out of the LCD market because it felt that the technology was simply not good enough. It failed to invest in LCD manufacturing capabilities. In trying to catch up with the market, as demand for flat-screen televisions took off, Sony had to buy in LCD screen technology from competitors, as it didn't have the expertise or production capacity itself. Losing market leadership in the television sector could have done very serious detrimental damage to the Sony brand and sales of other products. Typically, a television in the home was the centrepiece, where other electronics peripherals would be attached, such as camcorders and DVD players. Consumers bought devices that worked well with their television. Having a Sony-branded television had a knock-on effect for the sales of other peripherals.

In other markets, it is feeling the pressure of intense competition on multiple fronts. Competitors are offering very good-quality technology products at competitive price points. Apple iPods have become this generation's new Walkman. While Apple pioneered the market, Sony was more concerned with the piracy and copyright issues associated with the digital music revolution. It was reluctant to manufacture devices that could impinge on its music business. The company has ultimately failed to rekindle the Walkman brand as a digital music device. It is fighting Dell, Acer, Asus, Toshiba and HP in its mobile computing business. Nikon and Canon have retaken the lead in the digital photography market. It faces strenuous competition in the games console market with the recent launch of the Microsoft Xbox 360 and Nintendo's Wii in the next-generation games console market. Nokia, Samsung and now Apple dominate the mobile telephone market. Traditionally Sony was regarded as a premium brand because of its reputation for quality, higher specifications, reliability and innovation. This strong reputation enabled it to charge consumers premium prices. Consumers are now being enticed by the competition's high-quality and competitive pricing, leaving Sony unable to justify its higher prices. Sony needs to develop the 'must have' consumer electronics gadgets that consumers want. The company is now

▲ Sony is focusing on its 'champion products', including the Bravia LCD television shown here.

focusing intensively on several 'champion products' including PlayStation 3, PSP (PlayStation Portable), Walkman, OLED and Bravia LCD televisions.

The company has widely diversified from being solely an electronics firm. The purchase of Columbia Pictures cost Sony $3.4 billion dollars in 1989, and it purchased CBS Records for $2 billion; both were bold moves for an electronics company. This was during the heady days of the Japanese 'bubble' economy. Sony felt it wanted to create a global entertainment empire combining technology with the best entertainment content. The acquisition of CBS Records and Columbia Pictures garnered a mixed reception by industry commentators, with many questioning whether a technology firm that specialized in gadgets knew anything about the entertainment industry. The company decided to diversify into entertainment, in the hope that synergies could emerge between both the hardware and software aspects of the business. Sony now had the opportunity to set the standards and provide content that works on its devices. Convergence is seen as the 'holy grail', however the vision and successful integration of both Sony's hardware and entertainment division remains elusive. The entertainment divisions are providing a substantial contribution to the business—both have operating margins of in excess of 8 per cent—however, critics of the strategy see it as sidetracking the business and losing focus on its central business: electronics. Also success can be fickle in these sectors, depending on notoriously unreliable blockbuster movies and a new record superstar to emerge.

In the music arena, the industry is consolidating even further. Sony Music Entertainment has an estimated 25.2 per cent share of the music market. The division has an impressive roster of talent and is now the second largest music label behind Universal Music Group. With Sony possessing so much clout in the music business, it has the ability to set digital standards in the burgeoning online download market. The strategy of owning the content and the technology has yet to yield its full potential. Some question the logic behind the strategy, citing that Apple's success in becoming the dominant player in the digital music landscape was not due to it owning a record label. Some commentators view the entertainment division as an unnecessary distraction for Sony, and feel that it curtailed the development of digital technology because it was too concerned with the effects on piracy and the copyright of its Entertainment Division. Other rival electronics firms have no such qualms (e.g. trying to placate their entertainment divisions) and have developed hit products quickly. The music business itself is facing enormous challenges as sales are falling and most revenue is generated through touring rather than album sales.

One of the main challenges facing Sony is leveraging the content that it owns through its entertainment ventures with its hardware technology. It had to abandon its Sony Connect initiative as an alternative music distribution channel similar to iTunes. This was due to a lack of popularity in comparison to rivals. The market wanted content that was 'DRM free', where consumers could transfer content with ease to multiple devices. Innovation within Sony remains the core challenge. For the company to maintain its product leadership status, and command a price premium, developing products that are cutting edge and that the market wants is pivotal to its future. The company is investing heavily in Organic Light Emitting Diode (OLED) technology, which it hopes will set standards in high-definition, flat-screen technology. Furthermore it is abandoning pet R&D projects, like robotic dogs.

Back in the early 1980s, Sony lost a bitter technology standard war, which damaged its brand and resulted in thousands of disgruntled Sony customers. Sony backed the losing video recording technology: Betamax. Betamax was indeed a superior product, however the mass market chose a rival format, VHS, which became the industry standard for all video tapes. Now Sony has won the latest format war, with its Blu-Ray format winning the war to be the next generation of DVD. Blu-

Some blame Sony's current problems on its past successes, making it complacent with regard to the changing needs of the market.

Ray boasts greater storage capacity, can record, possesses anti-piracy technology and has the ability to deal with high-definition broadcasts. Sony beat its Japanese rival, Toshiba, which with its partners was backing HD-DVD (an alternative format). Sony won due to the support of all the major movie studios.

This Blu-Ray format victory for Sony could prove decisive. In an effort to encourage the adoption of the Blu-Ray disc, Sony integrated the technology into its PlayStation 3 console release. This Trojan horse move, it hoped, would provide the much needed impetus to gain mass-market support. Success on the Blu-Ray disc is a big gamble for Sony; it hopes to gain lucrative royalties from sales of the technology, more sales for its movie business as consumers buy Blu-Ray movie discs, and to sell copious amounts of Blu-Ray electronics players. However, this may prove futile as more consumers are downloading content thought their broadband connection, rather than using disc storage.

The other big gamble for Sony was the most recent launch of its PlayStation console—PlayStation 3—which it hoped would give the company a much needed boost. Six years had elapsed since the launch of PlayStation 2, which had sold 75 million units. The games industry is very cyclical, with new consoles fighting for market dominance. Microsoft and Nintendo have both launched their respective next-generation consoles. The PlayStation 3 launch date was delayed on several occasions due to delays with production. The new console is equipped with the latest technology, such as the super-fast 'cell' computer processor and Blu-Ray disc format. The company placed a lot of hope in the new 'cell' processor technology, which will be used in other Sony products too. This latest technology came with a big price tag, which initially put off consumers. The delayed launch also gave rival games console brands more sales momentum that could curtail Sony's success.

Sales for the games console have been less than stellar due to strong competition from Microsoft and Nintendo. Although the PlayStation 3 was the most technologically sophisticated, rivals have exploited different gaps in the market to enormous success. The Nintendo Wii, with its fun innovative gameplay, has less graphical finesse, but its addictive gameplay became a runaway surprise success. Furthermore, the Xbox 360 continues to thrive thanks to a strong games portfolio, and online gaming capability (with over 20 million online subscribers). In addition, the company faces strong competition from Nintendo and Apple in the handheld gaming market. The future of gaming relies on immersive games like the *Grand Theft Auto* series, addictive gameplay, games that cater for divergent markets (e.g. Nintendo sells 54 per cent of its DS consoles to females), and motion-sensitive technology (where physical movement is captured on-screen in gaming environments).

In the wake of the 'Sony shockwave', and after several years in charge, the Sony president stepped down and, for the first time, a non-Japanese executive took over the reins of Japan's leading company. Sir Howard Stringer, a Welsh-born US citizen, who had headed up Sony's Entertainment Division, was the surprise choice for the role. The former television producer, who speaks little or no Japanese, has the onerous task of turning around the fortunes at Sony. He transformed their entertainment operations and now it is hoped that he will find the same magic for the core business. Sony was seen by many as top heavy in terms of top management, too bureaucratic, and as not possessing enough cohesion between divisions. The firm has undertaken several initiatives to turn around the business. These have focused on cutting costs, removing layers of management, greater coordination of expenditure on research and development, and streamlining the business, consolidating important business activities such as warehousing and information technology. The new Sony chief bemoans the fact that Apple has a higher market value based on a small handful of products, whereas Sony has thousands.

It is not all doom and gloom in the Sony camp, however: its Entertainment Division is doing well, and the brand still enjoys massive retailer support. Sony has adopted a new tag-line for its business, using the slogan 'like.no.other'. Sony's brand status is being eroded by strong competition, with competitors such as Samsung, LG and Toshiba investing in high-profile global sponsorships and brand advertising. However, the Sony brand is still as strong as ever. When Sony launched its Bravia series of LCD screens, it released a classic television advert where over 250,000 brightly coloured balls were released down the hills of San Francisco. This new sub-brand is helping Sony regain its lead in this market sector. The company, under its new revitalization plan, has decided to reduce its product portfolio by a fifth, consolidate its manufacturing sites through

closures, reduce its global workforce and focus on high growth markets. Sony is tempted to sell off non-core activities such as Sony Life Insurance and Sony Chemicals, but ironically these businesses are contributing a healthy profit to the business.

The company, under a new management initiative, wants greater cross-company collaboration, removing the silos that developed within the company, hindering the cross-fertilization of ideas, and inhibiting growth and innovation. It is hoped that this will remove duplication of effort and improve coordination of activities. Its new chief executive wants the company to renew its focus on world-class technological innovation, with products and services focused around the needs of customers. Its new chief executive and president, Sir Howard Stringer, believes that the future for Sony lies in the company exploiting new projects, new strategies, new ideas and new alliances. He is in the process of radically overhauling the business, making it less bloated by altering a top-heavy management structure, removing bureaucracy and making it more reactive to the needs of the marketplace. The company has set up five different strategy committees focusing on product, production, technology, procurement and sales. The Welshman has a number of challenges facing him at the helm of Sony: he has to stem the losses at Sony's electronics business, make a greater profit, improve the coordination between Sony's disparate divisions, renew the focus on research and development, and figure out where Sony is headed in the next five years.

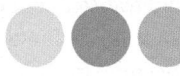

Questions

1. Discuss the importance of product innovation to the future success of Sony, in regard to the changing marketing environment.

2. Conduct a SWOT analysis of Sony.

3. What are the strategic options available to Sony, in the wake of the 'Sony shockwave'? Recommend a course of action for Sony, giving reasons for your answer.

This case was written by Conor Carroll, Lecturer in Marketing, University of Limerick.

For each of the following products, assess which of the political/legal, economic, ecological, social/cultural and technological environments has had the most impact in recent years.

1 Tobacco
2 Soft drinks
3 Mobile phones
4 Cosmetics
5 Housing

This exercise was prepared by David Jobber, Professor of Marketing, University of Bradford.

CHAPTER 4

Understanding consumer behaviour

You can be through with the past, but the past isn't through with you.

PAUL THOMAS ANDERSON
(from the film *Magnolia*)

The things you own end up owning you.

JIM UHLS (from the film *Fight Club*)

LEARNING OBJECTIVES

After reading this chapter, you should be able to:

1   define the dimensions of consumer buyer behaviour

2   describe the role of the buying centre (who buys) and its implications

3   describe the consumer decision-making process (how people buy)

4   discuss the marketing implications of need recognition, information search, evaluation of alternatives, purchase and post-purchase stages

5   compare the differences in evaluation of high- versus low-involvement situations

6   describe the nature of choice criteria (what are used) and their implications

7   explain the influences on consumer behaviour—the buying situation, personal and social influences—and their marketing implications

I n Chapter 2 we saw that a fundamental marketing decision was the choice of target customer. Marketing-orientated companies make clear decisions about the type of customer to whom they wish to aim their product offerings. Thus an in-depth knowledge of customers is a prerequisite of successful marketing—it influences the choice of target market and the nature of the marketing mix developed to serve it. Indeed, understanding customers is the cornerstone upon which the marketing concept is built.

In this chapter we will explore the nature of consumer behaviour and, in Chapter 5, organizational buying behaviour will be analysed. We shall see that the frameworks and concepts used to understand each type of customer are similar although not identical. Furthermore, we shall gain an understanding of the dimensions we need to consider in order to grasp the nuances of buyer behaviour and the influences on it.

Understanding consumer behaviour is important because European consumers are changing. While average incomes rise, income distribution is more uneven in most nations, household size is gradually decreasing in all EU nations, more women have jobs outside the home, the consumption of services is rising at the expense of consumer durables and demand for (and supply of) health, green (ecological), fun/luxury and convenience products is increasing. Examples of luxury or fun goods are 'gourmet', exotic and ethnic food, especially in Denmark, the UK and Germany, expensive off-roaders and two-seater cars, and other expensive brands such as Rolex, Cartier and Armani. Concern for the environment and European legislation has led to an increase in recyclable and reusable packaging, while concern for value for money and increasing retailer concentration has led to an increase in market share for private-label (own-label) brands.[1]

One change in consumer behaviour that has had a dramatic effect on the fortunes of Lego is the move away from traditional toys by children. They are losing interest at a younger age as toys are replaced by mobile phones, mp3 music players, video consoles and computer games. This trend has resulted in a series of losses at Lego, although refocusing on its core competences, and the success of its *Star Wars* computer game is helping to redress the situation.[2] The lesson is that companies need to have a deep understanding of their customers and be sensitive to their changing behaviours. This chapter provides the foundations upon which such an understanding and sensitivity can be gained.

The Dimensions of Buyer Behaviour

C onsumers are individuals who buy products or services for personal consumption. Organizational buying, on the other hand, focuses on the purchase of products and services for use in an organization's activities. Sometimes it is difficult to classify a product as being either a consumer or an organizational good. Cars, for example, sell to consumers for personal consumption and organizations for use in carrying out their activities (e.g. to provide transport for a sales executive). For both types of buyer, an understanding of customers can be gained only by answering the following questions (see also Fig. 4.1).

1 *Who* is important in the buying decision?
2 *How* do they buy?
3 *What* are their choice criteria?
4 *Where* do they buy?
5 *When* do they buy?

These questions define the five key dimensions of buyer behaviour.

Answers to these questions can be provided by personal contact with customers and, increasingly, by the use of marketing research. Chapter 7 examines the role and techniques of marketing research.

Buyer behaviour as it relates to consumers will now be examined. The structure of this analysis will be based upon the first three questions listed above: who, how and what. These are often the most intractable aspects of buyer behaviour; certainly, answering the questions where and when do customers buy is usually much more straightforward.

Consumer Behaviour

Who buys?

Many consumer purchases are individual. When purchasing a Mars bar a person may make an impulse purchase upon seeing an array of confectionery at a newsagent's counter. However, decision-making can also be made by a group such as a household. In such a situation a number of individuals may interact to influence the purchase decision. Each person may assume a role in the decision-making process. Blackwell, Miniard and Engel describe five roles, as outlined below.[3] Each may be taken by parents, children or other members of the **buying centre**.

1   *Initiator*: the person who begins the process of considering a purchase. Information may be gathered by this person to help the decision.
2   *Influencer*: the person who attempts to persuade others in the group concerning the outcome of the decision. Influencers typically gather information and attempt to impose their choice criteria on the decision.
3   *Decider*: the individual with the power and/or financial authority to make the ultimate choice regarding which product to buy.
4   *Buyer*: the person who conducts the transaction. The buyer calls the supplier, visits the store, makes the payment and effects delivery.
5   *User:* the actual consumer/user of the product.

One person may assume multiple roles in the buying group. In a toy purchase, for example, a girl may be the *initiator*, and attempt to *influence* her parents, who are the *deciders*. The girl may be *influenced* by her sister to buy a different brand. The *buyer* may be one of the parents, who visits the store to purchase the toy and brings it back to the home. Finally, both children may be *users* of the toy. Although the purchase was for one person, in this example marketers have four opportunities—two children and two parents—to affect the outcome of the purchase decision. The advertisement for Virgin Media's broadband service targets all members of the household decision-making unit.

Much of the research into the roles of household members has been carried out in the USA. Woodside and Mote, for example, found that roles differed according to product type, with the woman's influence stronger for carpets and washing machines while the man's influence was stronger for television sets.[4] Also the respective roles may change as the purchasing process progresses. In general, one or other partner will tend to dominate the early stages, then joint decision-making tends to occur as the process moves towards final purchase. Joint decision-making is more common when the household consists of two income-earners.

As roles change within households so do purchasing activities. Men now make more than half of their family's purchase decisions in food categories such as cereals, food and soft drinks.[5] Women, however, still purchase the majority of men's sweaters, socks and sports shirts in the USA.[6] Working-woman families spend more on eating out and childcare.[7] However, they do not spend more on time-saving appliances, convenience foods or spend less time on shopping when income and life-cycle stage are held constant.[8] Working women are forming a growing market segment for cars.

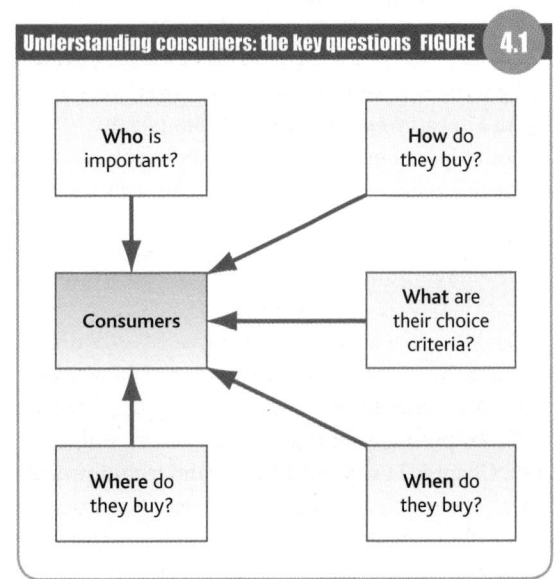

Understanding consumers: the key questions FIGURE 4.1

- **Who** is important?
- **How** do they buy?
- **Consumers**
- **What** are their choice criteria?
- **Where** do they buy?
- **When** do they buy?

Broadband that keeps the whole family up to speed.

We're all demanding more from the internet, from live gaming, to streaming your favourite TV shows, to chatting online. So you need broadband that can cope. The power of our fibre optic broadband means the whole family can enjoy being online at the same time. It's enough to keep everyone happy.

0800 952 0856
virginmedia.com
visit Virgin Media stores

Virgin media
POWERFUL STUFF

▲ Virgin Media targets its advertising at all members of the household decision-making unit, with the customer benefit of multiple online usage.

Teenagers also play an important role in an increasing range of products, including cars and household appliances, and may be seen as the household experts when considering high-technology products such as video recorders and compact disc players.[9]

The marketing implications of understanding who buys lie within the areas of marketing communications and segmentation. An identification of the roles played within the buying centre is a prerequisite for targeting persuasive communications. As the previous discussion has demonstrated, the person who actually uses or consumes the product may not be the most influential member of the buying centre, nor the decision-maker. Even when the user does play the predominant role, communication with other members of the buying centre can make sense when their knowledge and opinions may act as persuasive forces during the decision-making process. The second implication is that the changing roles and influences within the family buying centre are providing new opportunities to creatively segment hitherto stable markets (e.g. cars).

How they buy

How consumers buy may be regarded as a decision-making process beginning with the recognition that a problem exists. For example, a personal computer may be bought to solve a perceived problem, e.g. lack of access to the Internet. Problem-solving may thus be considered a thoughtful reasoned action undertaken to bring about need satisfaction. In this example, the need was fast and accurate calculations. Blackwell, Miniard and Engel define a series of steps a consumer may pass through before choosing a brand.[10] Figure 4.2 shows these stages, which form the **consumer decision-making process**.

Need recognition/problem awareness

In the computer example, *need recognition* is essentially *functional*, and recognition may take place over a period of time. Other problems may occur as a result of routine depletion (e.g. petrol, food) or unpredictably (e.g. the breakdown of a television set or video recorder). In other situations consumer purchasing may be initiated by more *emotional* or *psychological* needs. For example, the purchase of Chanel perfume is likely to be motivated by status needs rather than any marginal functional superiority over other perfumes.

The degree to which the consumer intends to resolve the problem depends on two issues: the magnitude of the discrepancy between the desired and present situation, and the relative importance of the problem.[11] A problem may be perceived but if the difference between the *current and desired situation* is small then the consumer may not be sufficiently motivated to

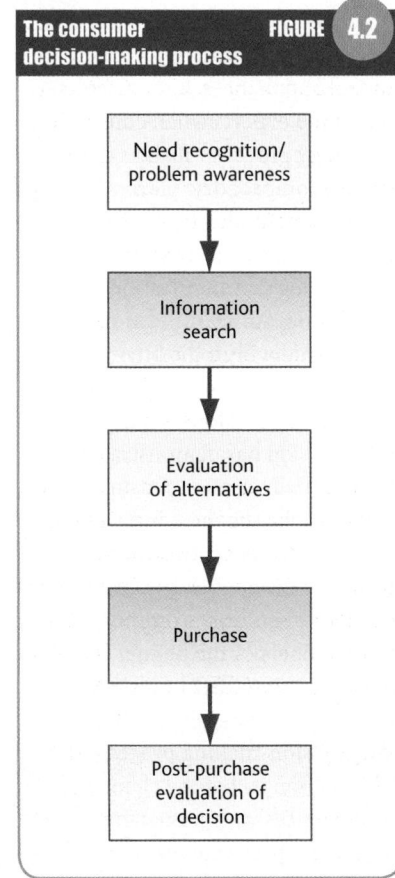

The consumer decision-making process   FIGURE 4.2

- Need recognition/problem awareness
- Information search
- Evaluation of alternatives
- Purchase
- Post-purchase evaluation of decision

move to the next step in the decision-making process. For example, a person may be considering upgrading their mobile phone from their existing model to a smartphone model. The smartphone may be viewed as desirable but if the individual considers the difference in benefits to be small then no further purchase activity may take place.

Conversely, a large discrepancy may be perceived but the person may not proceed to information search because the *relative importance* of the problem is small. A person may feel that a smartphone has significant advantages over a mobile phone, but that the relative importance of these advantages compared with other purchase needs (for example, the mortgage or a holiday) are small.

The existence of a need, however, may not activate the decision-making process in all cases. This is due to the existence of *need inhibitors*.[12] For example, someone may want to buy an item on eBay but may be inhibited by fear of paying for but not receiving the good. In such circumstances, the need remains passive.

There are a number of marketing implications of the need-recognition stage. First, marketing managers must be *aware of the needs* of consumers and the problems that they face. By being more attuned to customers' needs, companies have the opportunity to create a competitive advantage. This may be accomplished by intuition. For example, intuitively, a marketing manager of a washing machine company may believe that consumers would value a silent machine. Alternatively, marketing research could be used to assess customer problems or needs. For example, group discussions could be carried out among people who use washing machines, to assess their dissatisfaction with current models, what problems they encountered and what their ideal machine would be. This could be followed by a large-scale survey to determine how representative the views of the group members were. The results of such research can have significant effects on product redesign. Second, marketers should be *aware of need inhibitors*. For example, eBay has recognized that overcoming the need inhibitor lack of trust in being sent the product is important. To overcome this need inhibitor, eBay introduced its PayPal system, which acts as financial insurance against non-receipt of goods, and has developed a feedback system that allows buyers to post information on their transactions and their experiences with particular vendors.

Third, marketing managers should be aware that needs may arise because of *stimulation*. Their activities, such as developing advertising campaigns and training salespeople to sell product benefits, may act as cues to needs arousal. For example, an advertisement displaying the features and benefits of a smartphone may stimulate customers to regard their lack of a computer, or the limitations of their current model, to be a problem that warrants action. As we have seen, activating problem recognition depends on the size of the discrepancy between the current and desired situation, and the relative importance of the problem. The advertisement could therefore focus on the advantages of a smartphone over a mobile phone, to create awareness of a large discrepancy, and also stress the importance of owning a top-of-the-range model as a symbol of innovativeness and professionalism (thereby increasing the relative importance of purchasing a computer relative to other products).

Not all consumer needs are readily apparent. Consumers often engage in exploratory consumer behaviour such as being early adopters of new products and retail outlets, taking risks in making product choices, recreational shopping and seeking variety in purchasing products. Such activities can satisfy the need for novel purchase experiences, offer a change of pace and relief from boredom, and satisfy a thirst for knowledge and the urge of curiosity.[13]

Information search

If problem recognition is sufficiently strong the second stage in the consumer decision-making process will begin. **Information search** involves the identification of alternative ways of problem solution. The search may be internal or external. *Internal search* involves a review of relevant information from memory. This review would include potential solutions, methods of comparing solutions, reference to personal experiences and marketing communications. If a satisfactory solution is not found, then *external search* begins. This involves *personal sources* such as friends, the family, work colleagues and neighbours, and *commercial sources* such as advertisements and salespeople. *Third-party reports*, such as blogs and product-testing reports in newspapers and magazines and on the Internet, may provide unbiased information, and *personal experiences* may be sought such as asking for demonstrations and viewing, touching or tasting the product.

The objective of information search is to build up the **awareness set**—that is, the array of brands that may provide a solution to the problem. Using the smartphone example again, an advertisement may not only stimulate a search for more unbiased information regarding the advertised smartphone, but also stimulate an external search for information about rival brands.

Information search by consumers is facilitated by the growth of Internet usage and companies that provide search facilities, such as Yahoo! and Google. Consumers are increasingly using the Internet to gather information before buying a product, for example, most in-store car and mobile phone purchases only take place after consumers have researched brands online. Of growing importance are recommendation and review sites, as Digital Marketing 4.1 explains.

 **4.1 Digital Marketing**

Recommendation and Review Sites

One of the significant outcomes of the 'powerful consumer' phenomenon is the role of personal recommendation as part of the marketing process.

According to Bazaarvoice/Jupiter Research, 70 per cent of Internet shoppers find the personal ratings and reviews section of a retail website the most useful to them, particularly when both positive and negative reviews of a product are shown. In the USA, more than 60 per cent of respondents (according to Edelman) trust reviews from 'a person like themselves' more than an expert in the field or an academic. This is most significant for purchases such as travel, recreation and leisure, where 82 per cent of US consumers checked a personal review before making a purchase decision, according to Opinion Research.

In this field, sites such as TripAdvisor lead the way in the use of personal customer reviews. Hotels, cities, airlines and even excursions are rated by previous travellers, and Opinion Research's findings show how important consumers find these ratings.

So powerful are TripAdvisor's commentaries, and so important are they to the customer decision-making process, that many travel firms, such as Kuoni, now include the TripAdvisor reviews on their own websites as part of the process of increasing sales likelihood, because both good and bad reviews are shown.

Amazon has an interesting take on personal reviews, in that it encourages other customers to say if they found particular reviews useful. The reviews that are found to be most useful are found nearer the top of the list of reviews (whether positive or negative).

The implication for manufacturers is that the need to produce excellent products that people want becomes all the more important. With poor reviews that people trust, it isn't long before a product might simply not sell because of a few bad, but trusted, reviews.

Useful links: www.eMarketer.com (March, April, July 2008)

Evaluation of alternatives and the purchase

The first step in *evaluation* is to reduce the awareness set to a smaller set of brands for serious consideration. The awareness set of brands passes through a screening filter to produce an **evoked set**: those brands that the consumer seriously considers before making a purchase. In a sense, the evoked set is a shortlist of brands for careful evaluation. The screening process may use different choice criteria from those used when making the final choice, and the number of choice criteria used is often fewer.[14] One choice criteria used for screening may be price. Those smartphones priced below a certain level may form the evoked set. Final choice may then depend on such choice criteria as ease of use, speed of connection to the Internet and reliability. The range of choice criteria used by consumers will be examined in more detail later in this chapter.

Although brands may be perceived as similar, this does not necessarily mean they will be equally preferred. This is because different product attributes (e.g. benefits, imagery) may be used by people when making similarity and preference judgements. For example two brands may be perceived as similar because they provide similar functional benefits, yet one may be preferred over the other because of distinctive imagery.[15]

A key determinant of the extent to which consumers evaluate a brand is their level of *involvement*. Involvement is the degree of perceived relevance and personal importance accompanying the brand choice.[16] When a purchase is highly involving, the consumer is more likely to carry out extensive evaluation. High-involvement purchases are likely to include those incurring high expenditure or personal risk, such as car or home buying. In contrast, low-involvement situations are characterized by simple evaluations about purchases. Consumers use simple choice tactics to reduce time and effort rather than maximize the consequences of the purchase.[17] For example, when purchasing baked beans or breakfast cereal, consumers are likely to make quick choices rather than agonize over the decision.

This distinction between high- and low-involvement situations implies different evaluative processes. For high-involvement purchases the Fishbein and Ajzen theory of reasoned action[18] has proven robust in predicting purchase behaviour,[19] while in low-involvement situations work by Ehrenberg and Goodhart has shown how simple evaluation and decision-making can be.[20] Each of these models will now be examined.

Fishbein and Ajzen model: this model suggests that an attitude towards a brand is based upon a set of **beliefs** about the brand's attributes (e.g. value for money, durability). These are the perceived consequences resulting from buying the brand. Each attribute is weighted by how good or bad the consumer believes the attribute to be. Those attributes that are weighted highly will be that person's choice criteria and have a large influence in the formation of attitude. **Attitude** is the degree to which someone likes or dislikes the brand overall. The link between personal beliefs and attitudes is shown in Figure 4.3a. However, evaluation of a brand is not limited to personal beliefs about the consequences of buying a brand. Outside influences also play a part. Individuals will thus evaluate the extent to which *important others* believe that they should or should not buy the brand. These beliefs may conflict with their personal beliefs. People may personally believe that buying a sports car may have positive consequences (providing fun driving, being more attractive to other people) but refrain from doing so if they believe that important others (e.g. parents, boss) would disapprove of the purchase. This collection of *normative beliefs* forms an overall evaluation of the degree to which these outside influences approve or disapprove of the purchase (*subjective norms*). The link between normative beliefs and subjective norms is shown in Figure 4.3a. This clearly is a *theory of reasoned action*. Consumers are highly involved in the purchase to the extent that they evaluate the consequences of the purchase *and* what others will think about it. Only after these considerations have taken place does purchase intention and the ultimate purchase result.

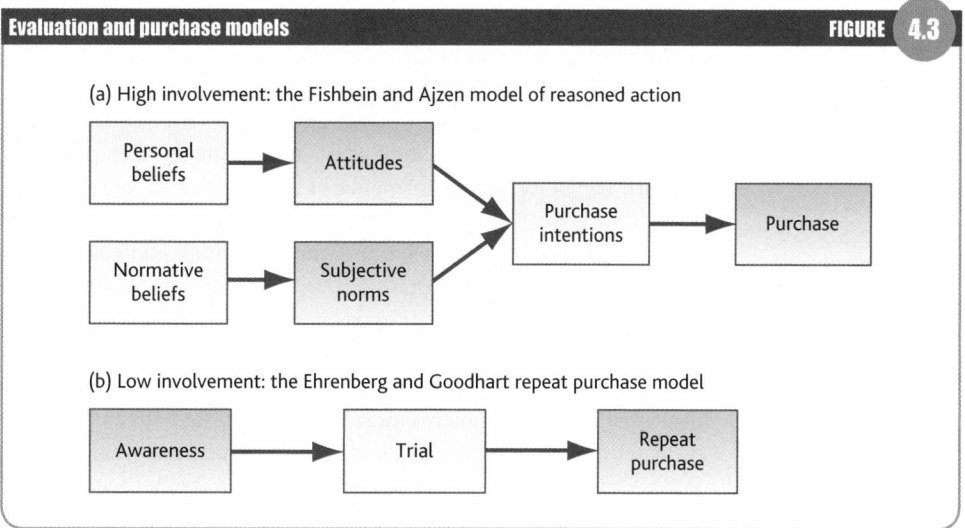

Evaluation and purchase models   FIGURE 4.3

(a) High involvement: the Fishbein and Ajzen model of reasoned action

(b) Low involvement: the Ehrenberg and Goodhart repeat purchase model

The Fishbein and Ajzen model can be illustrated by using the smartphone again. Having conducted the search for information, the evoked set comprises an iPhone and BlackBerry. The buyer believes that buying an iPhone would result in a significant cost saving and that both models are virtually identical on other attributes (e.g. reliability, design and speed). Cost savings are very important to this person and so is rated as a very good attribute to possess. The buyer, therefore, has a more favourable attitude towards the iPhone. Furthermore, a close friend, whose opinion the buyer regards as important, owns an iPhone, rates it highly and would strongly approve of such a purchase. Therefore, subjective norms also favour the iPhone. This leads to a purchase intention to buy the iPhone and subsequently its purchase. If the friend was perceived to disapprove of the iPhone purchase, the decision would depend on the relative strengths of the attitude and subjective norm components. When attitudes outweigh subjective norms, the iPhone would be purchased and, for the opposite case, the BlackBerry would be chosen.

Ehrenberg and Goodhart model: in low-involvement situations the amount of information processing implicit in the earlier model may not be worthwhile or sensible. A typical low-involvement situation is the *repeat purchase* of fast-moving consumer goods. The work of Ehrenberg and Goodhart suggests that a very simple process may explain purchase behaviour (see Fig. 4.3b). According to this model, awareness precedes trial, which, if satisfactory, leads to repeat purchase. This is an example of a behavioural model of consumer behaviour: the behaviour becomes *habitual* with little conscious thought or formation of attitudes preceding behaviour. The limited importance of the purchase simply does not warrant the reasoned evaluation of alternatives implied in the Fishbein and Ajzen model. The notion of low involvement suggests that awareness precedes behaviour and behaviour precedes attitude. In this situation the consumer does not actively seek information but is a passive recipient. Furthermore, since the decision is not inherently involving, the consumer is likely to satisfice (i.e. search for a satisfactory solution rather than the best one).[21] Consequently any of several brands that lie in the evoked set may be considered adequate.

Distinguishing between high- and low-involvement situations: the distinction between these two purchasing situations is important because the variations in how consumers evaluate products and brands lead to contrasting marketing implications. The complex evaluation outlined in the high-involvement situation suggests that marketing managers need to provide a good deal of information about the positive consequences of buying. Messages with *high information content* would enhance knowledge about the brand; because the consumer is actively seeking information, high levels of repetition are not needed.[22] Print media and websites may be appropriate in the high-involvement case since they allow detailed and repeated scrutiny of information. Car advertisements often provide information about the comfort, reliability and performance of the model, and also appeal to status considerations. All of these appeals may influence the consumer's beliefs about the consequences of buying the model. However, persuasive communications should also focus on how the consumer views the influence of important others. This is an area that is underdeveloped in marketing and provides avenues for further development of communications for high-involvement products.

The salesforce also has an important role to play in the high-involvement situation by ensuring that the customer is aware of the important attributes of the product and correctly evaluates their consequences. For example, if the differential advantage of a particular model of a car is fuel economy the salesperson would raise fuel economy as a salient product attribute and explain the cost benefits of buying that model vis-à-vis the competition.

For low-involvement situations, as we have seen, the evaluation of alternatives is much more rudimentary, and attitude change is likely to follow purchase. In this case, attempting to gain *top-of-mind awareness* through advertising and providing positive *reinforcement* (e.g. through sales promotion) to gain trial may be more important than providing masses of information about the consequences of buying the brand. Furthermore, as this is of little interest, the consumer is not actively seeking information but is a passive receiver. Consequently advertising messages should be *short* with a small number of key points but with *high repetition* to enhance learning.[23] Television may be the best medium since it allows passive reception to messages while the medium actively transmits them. Also, it is ideal for the transmission of short, highly repetitive messages. Much soap powder advertising follows this format.[24]

Marketers must be aware of the role of emotion in consumer evaluation of alternatives. A major source of high emotion is when a product is high in symbolic meaning. Consumers believe that the product helps them to construct and maintain their self-concept and sense of identity. Furthermore, ownership of the product will help them communicate the desired image to other people. In such cases, non-rational preferences may form and information search is confined to providing objective justification for an emotionally based decision. Studies have shown the effects of emotion on judgement to be less thought, less information-seeking, less analytical reasoning and less attention to negative factors that might contradict the decision.[25] Instead, consumers consult their feelings for information about a decision: 'How do I feel about it?' Consequently, many marketers attempt to create a feeling of warmth about their brands. The mere exposure to a brand name over time, and the use of humour in advertisements, can create such feelings.

Impulse buying is another area that can be associated with emotions. Consumers have described a compelling feeling that was 'thrilling', 'wild', 'a tingling sensation', 'a surge of energy', and 'like turning up the volume'.[26]

Post-purchase evaluation of the decision

The art of effective marketing is to create customer satisfaction. This is true in both high- and low-involvement situations. Marketing managers want to create positive experiences from the purchase of their products or services. Nevertheless, it is common for customers to experience some post-purchase concerns; this is called **cognitive dissonance**. These concerns arise because of uncertainty about making the right decision. This is because the choice of one product often means the rejection of the attractive features of the alternatives.

Dissonance is likely to increase in four ways: with the *expense* of purchase; when the decision is *difficult* (e.g. many alternatives, many choice criteria and each alternative offering benefits not available with the others); when the decision is *irrevocable*; and when the purchaser has a tendency *to experience anxiety*.[27] Thus it is often associated with high-involvement purchases. Shortly after purchase, car buyers may attempt to reduce dissonance by looking at advertisements, websites and brochures for their model, and seeking reassurance from owners of the same model. Volkswagen buyers are more likely to look at Volkswagen advertisements and avoid Renault or Ford ads. Clearly, advertisements can act as positive reinforcers in such situations, and follow-up sales efforts can act similarly. Car dealers can reduce *buyer remorse* by contacting recent purchasers by letter to reinforce the wisdom of their decision and to confirm the quality of their after-sales service.

However, the outcome of post-purchase evaluation is dependent on many factors besides this kind of reassurance. The quality of the product or service is obviously a key determinant, and the role of the salesperson acting as a problem-solver for the customer rather than simply pushing the highest-profit-margin product can also help create customer satisfaction, and thereby reduce cognitive dissonance.

Choice criteria

Choice criteria are the various attributes (and benefits) a consumer uses when evaluating products and services. They provide the grounds for deciding to purchase one brand or another. Different members of the buying centre may use different choice criteria. For example, a child may use the criterion of self-image when choosing shoes, whereas a parent may use price. The same criterion may be used differently. For example, a child may want the most expensive video game while the parent may want a less expensive alternative. Choice criteria can change over time due to changes in income through the family life cycle. As disposable income rises, so price may no longer be the key criterion but is replaced by considerations of status or social belonging.

Table 4.1 lists four types of choice criteria and gives examples of each. Technical criteria are related to the performance of the product or service, and include reliability, durability, comfort and convenience. Convenience is often synonymous with ease of use and Apple products have often been leaders in this area. For example, it was Apple's Macintosh that led the way in icon-based graphical interfaces that are now standard in PCs; it was the iPod that made digital mobile music players user friendly; and it was the iPhone that first introduced an elegant, easy-to-use touchscreen.[28]

Economic criteria concern the cost aspects of purchase and include price, running costs and residual values (e.g. the trade-in value of a car). The advertisement on the next page for the Audi TT TDI announces the higher fuel economy (and hence lower running costs) of the new model, as well as its more responsible credentials (an ethical consideration). Social criteria concern the impact that the purchase makes on the person's perceived relationships with other people, and the influence of social norms on the person. The purchase of a BMW car may be due to status considerations as much as any technical advantages over its rivals. Choosing a brand of trainer may be determined by the need for social belonging. Nike and Reebok recognize the need for their trainers to have 'street cred'. The need to project success gives rise to celebrity endorsements where a product is associated with a high-flying sportsman, film star, television personality or team. That is why Nike paid £300 million to ensure that Manchester United wears its shirts and shorts for 13 years.[29] Social norms such as convention and fashion can also be important choice criteria, with some brands being rejected as too unconventional (e.g. fluorescent spectacles) or out of fashion (e.g. 'shell' tracksuits).

Personal criteria concern how the product or service relates to the individual psychologically. Self-image is our personal view of ourselves. Some people might view themselves as 'cool' and

Choice criteria used when evaluating alternatives		TABLE	4.1
Type of criteria	**Examples**	**Type of criteria**	**Examples**
Technical	Reliability	Social	Status
	Durability		Social belonging
	Performance		Convention
	Style/looks		Fashion
	Comfort	Personal	Self-image
	Delivery		Risk reduction
	Convenience		Ethics
	Taste		Emotions
Economic	Price		
	Value for money		
	Running costs		
	Residual value		
	Life-cycle costs		

The new TT TDI.
A sports car that
drinks responsibly

No, we haven't really
reduced the fuel cap.
We have however, reduced
the amount of fuel the car
consumes. Audi's injection
technology is so precise
hardly a drop is wasted.
The result is 53.3 mpg or
600 miles per tank, which
just goes to prove a little
can go a very long way.

Visit audi.co.uk or
watch the Audi Channel
on Sky Guide 884.

The new, more fuel
efficient Audis.

successful, and only buy fashion items such as Hugo Boss or Burberry clothes which reflect that perception of themselves. Risk reduction can affect choice decisions since some people are risk averse and prefer to choose 'safe' brands; an example is the purchase of designer labels, which reduces the risk of being seen wearing unfashionable clothing. Ethical criteria can also be employed. For example, brands may be rejected because they are manufactured by companies that have offended a person's ethical code of behaviour. Research has shown that consumers weigh up the ethical arguments for buying products against other more personal criteria.[30] For example, for many young consumers the importance of image, fashion and price outweighs ethical issues as an influence on purchase behaviour.[31] Another problem is deciding the extent to which a particular brand is truly ethical, as Marketing Ethics and Corporate Social Responsibility in Action 4.1 discusses.

◀ Audi advertises both the fuel efficiency and responsible credentials of its TT TDI model.

4.1 Marketing Ethics and Corporate Social Responsibility in Action

Is Ethical Consumption Always Ethical?

The market for ethical products has proven durable even in the recent economic downturn. Ethical products that appeal to consumers' emotions as well as economic sensibilities have proved particularly popular. Some of the products currently deemed ethical include fairly traded foods and drinks that guarantee a fair deal to producers in developing countries, organic or local produce, vegetarian products, cruelty-free animal products, recycled and recyclable products, energy-efficient electrical appliances, green energy and rechargeable batteries, eco travel and transport, sweatshop-free fashion, ethical finance and cloth nappies.

Although advocates of ethical consumption believe that we have the political power to influence the marketplace through our individual consumer choices, in practice the extent to which such ethical alternatives are preferable to 'normal' products and services is debatable. For example, some commentators will argue that the premium prices paid for fairly traded goods are not necessarily fully transferred to the farmers under such agreements. Also, although sweatshop working conditions in developing countries are seen as unethical by most western consumers, some will suggest that such workers would otherwise be unemployed. Green claims are also confusing, and it is difficult to determine what the preferable choices are. Organic may be seen as the greener and healthier food option, but many scientific studies cast doubts on such conclusions. Furthermore, recycling and recyclables may seem like they do not negatively affect the environment but, as with all physical activities, recycling consumes energy. Thorough product lifespan analyses in product-specific contexts are necessary for the benefits of green options to be assessed.

Although ethical consumption is important in shaping and maintaining empowered ethical consumer identities and markets, there is much uncertainty about the choices to be made, and at times ethical trade-offs occur (i.e. products are not always organic as well as fair trade). This, in turn, generates much inconsistency with regard to what it is possible to achieve. Although people feel empowered and responsible for environmental issues at an individual level, this is coupled with the insecurity of not knowing what the 'right choices' are, and such contradictions pose huge challenges to policy-makers and marketers alike.

Based on: Micheletti (2003);[32] Cooper (2005);[33] Connolly and Prothero (2008);[34] Co-operative Bank (2008)[35]

Emotional criteria can be important in decision-making. The rejection of new-formula Coca-Cola in 1985, despite product tests that showed it to be preferred on taste criteria to traditional Coca-Cola, has been explained in part by emotional reactions to the withdrawal of an old, well-loved brand.[36] Many purchase decisions are experiential in that they evoke feelings such as fun, pride, pleasure, boredom or sadness. Research by Elliot and Hamilton showed that a decision about out-of-home leisure activities such as going for a drink, a meal, to the cinema, a disco or to play sport is affected by the desire to 'do something different for a change' and 'do what I'm in the mood to do', both of which reflect emotional criteria.[37] In another survey of consumers, 31 per cent claimed that many of their purchases were motivated by a desire to 'cheer themselves up'.[38] The importance of experiences to consumers has led to the growth in experiential consumption, as Marketing in Action 4.1 explains.

Concern about store design and ambience at shops such as H&M and Zara reflects the importance of creating the right feeling or atmosphere when shopping for clothes. Saab ran a two-page advertising campaign that combined technical and economic appeals with an emotional one. The first page was headlined '21 Logical Reasons to Buy a Saab'. The second page ran the headline 'One Emotional Reason'. The first page supported the headline with detailed body copy explaining the technical and economic rationale for purchase. The second page showed a Saab powering along a rain-drenched road. Another brand that

4.1 Marketing in Action

Experiences and Consumer Behaviour

What drives fans of the Pet Shop Boys to pay £2200 for two tickets to see them perform live in London? Why did thousands of tickets for an Arctic Monkeys tour priced at £14 sell for over £60 each on eBay? What explains the demand for 112,000 Glastonbury Festival tickets, which took less than four hours to sell? And how come tickets for Led Zeppelin's gig at London's O$_2$ arena sold for over £7000? The answer lies in the concept of experiential consumption.

A Pet Shop Boys CD can be bought for around £10 so what extra were those two fans seeking that persuaded them to pay £1100 per ticket? We can imagine that the experience of seeing them play live engendered feelings of nostalgia, fun and pleasure at attending a rare event (the 'tour' consisted of only two gigs). They may also have valued the experience of being with a crowd of like-minded fans, all of which would contribute to the feeling of excitement at being there.

In a world that can often seem bland, consumers are willing to pay premium prices for experiences that can arouse the emotions. The implications for marketers are that products that tap into this trend—such as music concerts, football matches, white-water rafting and piloting an aircraft—are likely to grow in demand in the future.

Based on: Smith (2005);[39] *Gibson (2008)*[40]

has successfully appealed to emotions is Absolut Vodka, one of the world's biggest spirits brands. Its clever, simple ads—featuring the now famous clear bottle and tag-lines such as 'Absolut Bangkok'—have appealed to consumers' sense of fun. Gordon Lundquist, the Swedish company's president, claims that it is Absolut's wit rather than its taste that is the reason for the brand's success. 'Absolut is a personality,' he says 'We like certain people but some people are just more fun and interesting.'

When a product scores well on a combination of choice criteria the outcome can be global success. For example, the success of the BlackBerry derives from the convenience of being able to access e-mails and websites on the move (technical), and the status (social) and high self-image (personal) that is associated with owning one. The popularity of the iPod can also be understood by its high performance, access to a large library of music via iTunes, stylish looks (technical), affordability (economic), and the status (social) and high self-image (personal) associated with owning one.

Marketing managers need to understand the choice criteria that are being used by customers to evaluate their products and services. Such knowledge has implications for priorities in product design (e.g. are style/looks more important than performance) and the appeals to use in marketing communications, which should be linked to the key choice criteria used by buying centre members.

Influences on Consumer Behaviour

As we saw when discussing the evaluation of alternatives, not all decisions follow the same decision-making process. Nor do all decisions involve the same buying centre or use identical choice criteria. The following is a discussion of the major influences on the process, buying centre and choice criteria in consumer behaviour. They are classified into three groups: the buying situation, personal influences and social influences (see Fig. 4.4).

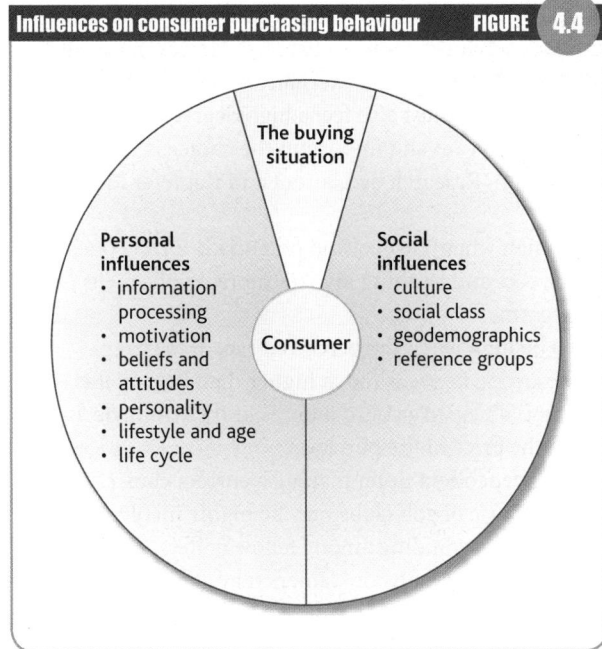

Influences on consumer purchasing behaviour   FIGURE **4.4**

The buying situation

Three types of buying situation can be identified: extended problem-solving, limited problem-solving, and habitual problem-solving.

Extended problem-solving

Extended problem-solving involves a high degree of information search, and close examination of alternative solutions using many choice criteria.[41] It is commonly seen in the purchase of cars, video and audio equipment, houses and expensive clothing, where it is important to make the right choice. Information search and evaluation may focus not only on which brand/model to buy but also on where to make the purchase. The potential for cognitive dissonance is greatest in this buying situation.

Extended problem-solving is usually associated with three conditions: the alternatives are differentiated and numerous; there is an adequate amount of time available for deliberation; and the purchase has a high degree of involvement.[42]

Figure 4.5 summarizes these relationships. High involvement means that the purchase is personally relevant and is seen as important with respect to basic motivations and needs.[43] Differentiation affects the extent of problem-solving because more comparisons need to be made and uncertainty is higher. Problem-solving is likely to be particularly extensive when all alternatives possess desirable features that others do not have. If alternatives are perceived as being similar, then less time is required in assessment.

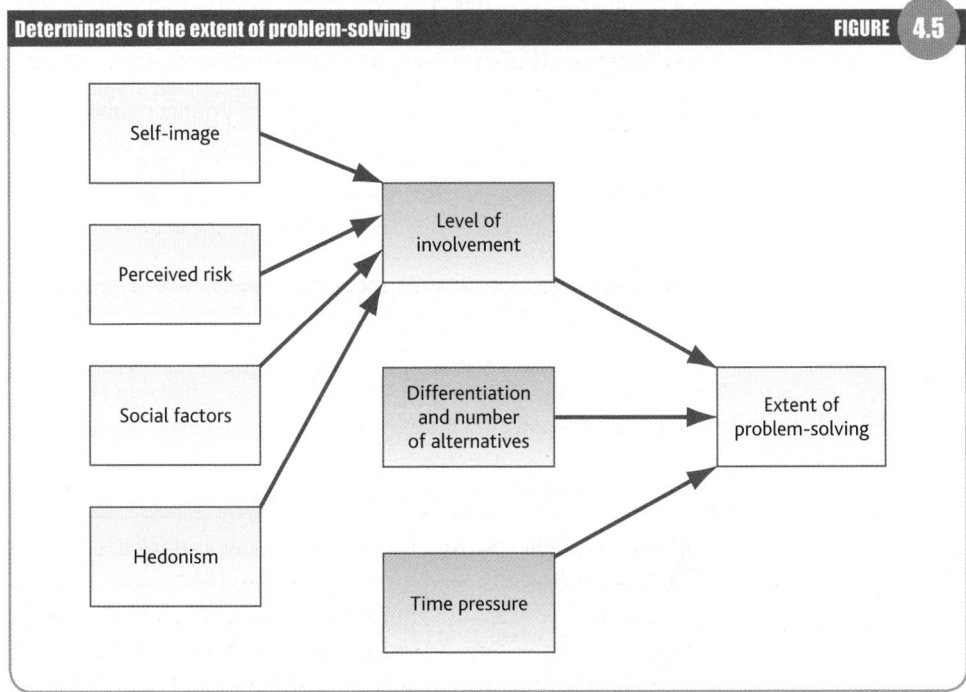

Determinants of the extent of problem-solving   FIGURE **4.5**

Extended problem-solving is inhibited by time pressure. If the decision has to be made quickly, by definition, the extent of problem-solving activity is curtailed. However, not all decisions follow extended problem-solving even though the alternatives may be differentiated and there is no time pressure. The decision-maker must also feel a high degree of involvement in the choice. Involvement—how personally relevant and important the choice is to the decision-maker—varies from person to person. Research by Laurent and Kapferer identified four factors that affect involvement.[44]

1 *Self-image*: involvement is likely to be high when the decision potentially affects one's self-image. Thus purchase of jewellery, cars and clothing invokes more involvement than choosing a brand of soap or margarine.

2 *Perceived risk*: involvement is likely to be high when the perceived risk of making a mistake is high. The risk of buying the wrong house is much higher than buying the wrong chewing gum, because the potential negative consequences of the wrong decision are higher. Risk usually increases with the price of the purchase.

3 *Social factors*: when social acceptance is dependent upon making a correct choice, involvement is likely to be high. The purchase of golf clubs may be highly involving because the correct decision may affect social standing among fellow golfers; so might shopping for clothes since buying the right dress, shirt or trainers may affect the buyer's acceptance within a social group.

4 *Hedonistic influences*: when the purchase is capable of providing a high degree of pleasure, involvement is usually high. The choice of restaurant when on holiday can be highly involving since the difference between making the right or wrong choice can severely affect the amount of pleasure associated with the experience.

Marketers can help in this buying situation by providing information-rich communications—for example, press advertisements and websites are particularly suited to information-rich content, supported by a well-trained salesforce where appropriate. Table 4.2 shows how the consumer decision-making process changes between high- and low-involvement purchases.

Salespeople should be trained to adopt a problem–solution approach to selling. This involves identifying customer needs and acting as an information provider to help the customer evaluate alternatives. This approach will be discussed in Chapter 14 on personal selling.

Limited problem-solving

Many consumer purchases fall into the limited problem-solving category. The consumer has some experience with the product in question so that an information search may be mainly internal, through memory. However, a certain amount of external search and evaluation may

The consumer decision-making process and level of purchase involvement		TABLE 4.2
Stage	**Low involvement**	**High involvement**
Need recognition/ problem awareness	Minor	Major, *personally* important
Information search	*Limited* search	*Extensive* search
Evaluation of alternatives and the purchase	Few *alternatives* evaluated on few choice criteria	Many *alternatives* evaluated on many choice criteria
Post-purchase evaluation of the decision	*Limited* evaluation	Extensive evaluation including media search

take place (e.g. checking prices) before purchase is made. This situation provides marketers with some opportunity to affect purchase by stimulating the need to conduct search (e.g. advertising) and reducing the risk of brand switching (e.g. warranties).

Habitual problem-solving

Habitual problem-solving occurs when a consumer repeat-buys the same product with little or no evaluation of alternatives—for example, buying the same breakfast cereal on a weekly shopping trip. The consumer may recall the satisfaction gained by purchasing a brand and automatically buy it again. Advertising may be effective in keeping the brand name in the consumer's mind and reinforcing already favourable attitudes towards it.

Personal influences

There are six personal influences on consumer behaviour: information processing, motivation, beliefs and attitudes, personality, lifestyle, and life cycle.

Information processing

Information processing refers to the process by which a stimulus is received, interpreted, stored in memory and later retrieved.[45] It is therefore the link between external influences, including marketing activities and the consumer's decision-making process. Two key aspects of information processing are perception and learning.

Perception is the complex process by which people select, organize and interpret sensory stimulation into a meaningful picture of the world.[46] Three processes may be used to sort out the masses of stimuli that could be perceived into a manageable amount. These are selective attention, selective distortion and selective retention. **Selective attention** is the process by which we screen out those stimuli that are neither meaningful to us nor consistent with our experiences and beliefs. On entering a supermarket there are thousands of potential stimuli (brands, point-of-sale displays, prices, etc.) to which we could pay attention. To do so would be unrealistic in terms of time and effort. Consequently we are selective in attending to these messages. Selective attention has obvious implications for advertising considering that studies have shown that consumers consciously attend to only 5–25 per cent of the advertisements to which they are exposed.[47]

4.1 Pause for Thought

Return to a newspaper or magazine you have read in the last week. Examine all the advertisements in it and calculate the percentage you remember seeing. It will probably be less than a quarter.

A number of factors influence attention. We pay more attention to stimuli that contrast with their background than to stimuli that blend with it. The name Apple is regarded as an attention-getting brand name because it contrasts with the technologically orientated names usually associated with computers. The size, colour and movement of a stimulus also affect attention. Position is critical too. Objects placed near the centre of the visual range are more likely to be noticed than those on the periphery. This is why there is intense competition to obtain eye-level positions on supermarket shelves. We are also more likely to notice those messages that relate to our needs (benefits sought)[48] and those that provide surprises (for example, large price reductions).

Selective distortion occurs when consumers distort the information they receive according to their existing beliefs and attitudes. We may distort information that is not in accord with our existing views. Methods of doing this include thinking that we misheard the message, and discounting the message source. Consequently it is very important to present messages clearly without the possibility of ambiguity and to use a highly credible source. In a classic experiment a class of students was presented with a lecturer who was introduced as an expert in the area. To another comparable group of students the same lecturer was presented without such an introduction. The ratings of the same lecture were significantly higher in the former group. Another important implication of selective distortion is always to present evidence of a sales message whenever possible. This again reduces the scope for selective distortion of the message on the part of the recipient.

Distortion can occur because people interpret the same information differently. Interpretation is a process whereby messages are placed into existing categories of meaning. A cheaper price, for example, may be categorized not only as providing better value for money but also as implying lower quality. **Information framing** can affect interpretation. Framing refers to ways in which information is presented to people. Levin and Gaeth asked people to taste minced beef after telling half the sample that it was 70 per cent lean and the other half that it was 30 per cent fat.[49] Despite the fact that the two statements are equivalent, the sample that had the information framed positively (70 per cent lean) recorded higher levels of taste satisfaction.

Information framing has obvious implications for advertising and sales messages. The weight of evidence suggests that messages should be positively framed.

Colour is another important influence on interpretation. Blue and green are viewed as cool, and evoke feelings of security. Red and yellow are regarded as warm and cheerful. Black is seen as an indication of strength. By using the appropriate colour in pack design it is possible to affect the consumer's feelings about the product. The complete branding concept may also be based on colour. For example, mobile phone company Orange has achieved success with the 'colour as brand' approach. The colour orange is distinctive in its sector and conveys feelings of energy and warmth.[50]

Smell can be used to influence interpretation. Part of Singapore Airlines' appeal is the aroma created by the infusion of Stefan Floridian Waters cologne into its hot towels and cabins. It receives consistently positive feedback from passengers and is described as exotic and feminine. Singapore Airlines was the first airline to market itself as a sensory experience appealing to the emotions as opposed to the approach of its competitors, which emphasized price, food and comfort.[51]

Selective retention refers to the fact that only a selection of messages may be retained in memory. We tend to remember messages that are in line with existing beliefs and attitudes. In another experiment, 12 statements were given to a group of Labour and Conservative supporters. Six of the statements were favourable to Labour and six to the Conservatives. The group members were asked to remember the statements and to return after seven days. The result was that Labour supporters remembered the statements that were favourable to Labour and Conservative supporters remembered the pro-Conservative statements. Selective retention has a role to play in reducing cognitive dissonance: when reading reviews of a recently purchased car, positive messages are more likely to be remembered than negative ones.

Learning is any change in the content or organization of long-term memory, and is the result of information processing.[52] There are numerous ways in which learning can take place. These include *conditioning* and *cognitive learning*. **Classical conditioning** is the process of using an established relationship between a stimulus and response to cause the learning of the same response to a different stimulus. Thus, in advertising, humour, which is known to elicit a pleasurable response, may be used in the belief that these favourable feelings will carry over to the product. Red Bull is a brand that benefits from such associations. The humour in its advertising conveys a fun image, and the promotion of Red Bull on the body of racing cars projects the feeling of excitement for the brand by association.

Operant conditioning differs from classical conditioning by way of the role and timing of the reinforcement. In this case, reinforcement results from rewards: the more rewarding the response, the stronger the likelihood of the purchase being repeated. Operant conditioning occurs as a result of product trial. The use of free samples is based on the principles of operant conditioning. For example, free samples of a new shampoo are distributed to a large number of households. Because the use of the shampoo is costless, it is used (desired response), and because it has desirable properties it is liked (reinforcement) and the likelihood of it being bought is increased. Thus the sequence of events is different between classical and operant conditioning. In the former, by association, liking precedes trial; in the latter, trial precedes liking. A series of rewards (reinforcements) may be used over time to encourage repeat buying of a product. Thus the free sample may be accompanied by a coupon to buy the shampoo at a discounted rate (reinforcement). On the pack may be another discount coupon to encourage repeat buying. Only after this purchase does the shampoo rely on its own intrinsic reward— product performance—to encourage purchase. This process is known as *shaping*. Repeat purchase behaviour will have been shaped by the application of repeated reinforcers so that the consumer will have learned that buying the shampoo is associated with pleasurable experiences.

Cognitive learning involves the learning of knowledge and development of beliefs and attitudes without direct reinforcement. **Rote learning** involves the learning of two or more concepts without conditioning. Having seen the headline 'Lemsip is for 'flu attacks' the consumer may remember that Lemsip is a remedy for 'flu attacks without the kinds of conditioning and reinforcement previously discussed.

Vicarious learning involves learning from others without direct experience or reward. It is the promise of the reward that motivates. Thus we may learn the type of clothes that attract potential admirers by observing other people. In advertising, the 'admiring glance' can be used to signal approval of the type of clothing being worn. We imagine that the same may happen to us if we dress in a similar way.

Reasoning is a more complex form of cognitive learning and is usually associated with high-involvement situations. For example, some advertising messages rely on the recipient to draw their own conclusions, through reasoning. An anti-Richard Nixon ad campaign in the USA used a photograph of Nixon under the tag-line 'Would You Buy a Used Car From This Man?' to dissuade people from voting for him in the presidential election.

Whichever type of learning has taken place, the result of the learning process is the creation of *product positioning*. The market objective is to create a clear and favourable position in the mind of the consumer.[53]

One technique that holds great potential for understanding how consumers process information is neuroscience, as Marketing in Action 4.2 discusses.

Motivation

An understanding of **motivation** lies in the relationship between needs, drives and goals.[54] The basic process involves needs (deprivations) that set drives in motion (deprivations with direction) to accomplish goals (anything that alleviates a need and reduces a drive). Motives can be grouped into five categories as proposed by Maslow[55] (see Fig. 4.6).

1 *Physiological*: the fundamentals of survival, e.g. hunger or thirst.
2 *Safety*: protection from the unpredictable happening in life, e.g. accidents, ill-health.
3 *Belongingness and love*: striving to be accepted by those to whom we feel close, and to be an important person to them. The popularity of social network sites such as Facebook is a reflection of the need to belong.
4 *Esteem and status*: striving to achieve a high standing relative to other people; a desire for prestige and a high reputation.
5 *Self-actualization*: the desire for self-fulfilment in achieving what one is capable of for one's own sake.

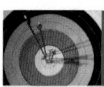
4.2 Marketing in Action

Neuromarketing: New Horizon or False Dawn?

How consumers process information is of great interest to marketers because it sheds light on how they make purchasing choices—for example, what clothes we buy or what music we like to listen to. This is where neuroscience can play a part; it is the study of the brain and nervous system by means of functional magnetic resonance imaging (fMRI) scanning. The brain is made up of networks of neurons. When these cell clusters are stimulated, they use more energy. These active areas light up on fMRI scans, allowing researchers to map emotion and cognition. The scanner produces a colour-coded image of the brain that is helpful in revealing a person's unconscious feelings about a brand, an advertisement or, even, a media channel. For example, the effects of different media channels (e.g. print versus the Internet) on brain stimulation have been found to be useful when making media decisions. This application of the techniques of neuroscience to marketing is called neuromarketing.

Neuromarketing advocates argue that it is an objective tool that scientifically demonstrates and quantifies human reactions and provides new insights into how people process information. The sceptics counter that it has not revealed any huge insights into human behaviour that are not already instinctively known. As applications of neuromarketing develop, the truth about its worth to marketers will be revealed.

Based on: Lovell (2008)[56]

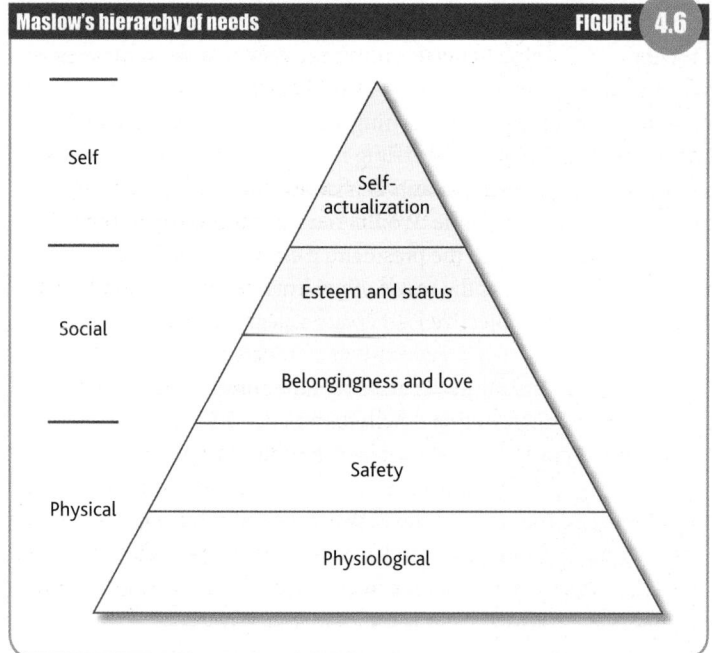

Maslow's hierarchy of needs   **FIGURE 4.6**

It is important to understand the motives that drive consumers because they determine choice criteria. For example, a consumer who is driven by the esteem and status motive may use self-image as a key choice criterion when considering the purchase of a car, clothes, shoes or other visible accessories. Marketers can also tap into motives directly. For example, this advertisement for Rolex watches links the brand to the need to achieve.

Variety-seeking is an important consumer motive. Consumers seek variety to satisfy their need to experiment with different brands, seek new experiences and to explore a product category. Usually, this can be explained by experiential or hedonistic motives rather than by utilitarian aspects of consumption.[57]

Beliefs and attitudes

A *belief* is a thought that a person holds about something. In a marketing context,

Ad insight

Go to the website to see Marmite's TV ad

it is a thought about a product or service on one or more choice criteria. Beliefs about a Volvo car might be that it is safe, reliable and high status. Marketing people are very interested in consumer beliefs because they are related to attitudes. In particular, misconceptions about products can be harmful to brand sales. Duracell batteries were believed by consumers to last three times as long as Ever Ready batteries but in continuous use they lasted over six times as long. This promoted Duracell to launch an advertising campaign to correct this misconception. The promotion for Marmite crisps (see illustration) recognizes that

▲ Rolex watches: a symbol of achievement and its rewards.

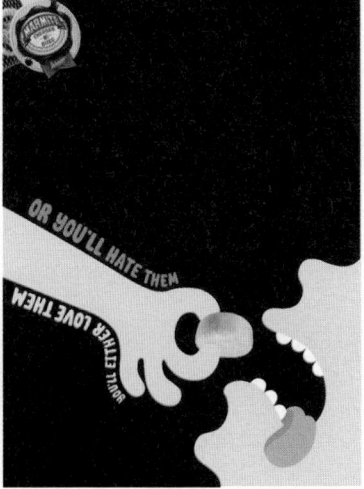

▲ Opposite beliefs are displayed in this advertisement for Marmite-flavoured crisps, inviting the consumer to try the brand.

the beliefs of some consumers will be favourable towards the brand and others negative. By presenting the brand in this way, the advertisement is inviting consumers to try the crisps to discover which group they are in.

An *attitude* is an overall favourable or unfavourable evaluation of a product or service. The consequence of a set of beliefs may be a positive or negative attitude towards the product or service. As we have seen, beliefs and attitudes play an important part in the evaluation of alternatives in the consumer decision-making process. They may be developed as part of the information search activity and/or as a result of product use. As such they play an important role in product design (matching product attributes to beliefs and attitudes), persuasive communications (reinforcing existing positive beliefs and attitudes, correcting misconceptions, and establishing new beliefs—for example, Skoda is a quality car brand) and pricing (matching price with customers' beliefs about what a 'good' product would cost).

Personality

Our everyday dealings with people tell us that they differ enormously in their personalities. **Personality** is the inner psychological characteristics of individuals that lead to consistent responses to their environment.[58] A person may tend to be warm–cold, dominant–subservient, introvert–extrovert, sociable–loner, adaptable–inflexible, competitive–cooperative, etc. If we find from marketing research that our product is being purchased by people with a certain personality profile, then advertising could show people of the same type using the product.

The concept of personality is also relevant to brands. *Brand personality* is their characterization as perceived by consumers. Brands may be characterized as 'for young people' (Tommy Hilfiger), 'for winners' (Nike), or 'intelligent' (Toyota iQ). This is a dimension over and above the physical (e.g. colour) or functional (e.g. taste) attributes of a brand. By creating a brand personality, a marketer may create appeal to people who value that characterization. Research into brand personalities of beers showed that most consumers preferred the brand of beer that matched their own personality.[59]

4.2 Pause for Thought

Think about the brands that you buy, particularly in the clothing and drinks sectors. Do you think that their brand personality matches your own personality to some extent?

Economic circumstances

During periods of economic growth, consumer spending is fuelled by rising income levels and confidence in job security. Products that are the subject of discretionary spending, such as luxury brands, expensive holidays, restaurant meals and top-of-the-range consumer durables, thrive. However, during economic recession, consumer psychology changes. Fears about employment prospects drive many consumers to postpone purchases, become more price sensitive and change their shopping habits. Economic circumstances, therefore, can have a major effect on consumer behaviour, as Marketing in Action 4.3 explains.

4.3 Marketing in Action

How Consumer Behaviour Changes During a Recession

The recent global economic recession has meant hardship for many people, who have responded by changing their purchasing behaviour. The following are some of the ways consumers have reacted to a harsher economic reality.

- *Downsizing*: buying small, fuel-efficient cars rather than large gas-guzzlers. This has meant consumers have moved from SUVs and sports cars to compacts and hybrid (petrol-electric) cars.
- *Discounting*: shopping more at discount supermarkets such as Aldi, Lidl and Netto rather than Marks & Spencer and Waitrose.
- *Eating out less*: visiting restaurants less often, while buying more premium-priced supermarket ready meals and door-delivered foods like Domino's pizzas.
- *Buying low-priced basics*: moving from branded products to lower-priced own-label brands (e.g. Sainsbury's 'Basics' range) for basic items such as frozen peas, bread and rice.
- *De-greening*: being more reluctant to buy environmentally friendly products where cheaper alternatives are available.
- *Inexpensive treating*: looking for inexpensive treats such as eating chocolate.
- *Delaying*: putting off purchases of consumer durables such as cars and household furnishings.

The tendency for many shoppers to place greater emphasis on searching for value has caused markets to respond by launching fighter brands. Rather than drop price across the entire product range, supermarkets like Tesco and Sainsbury's have extended their value ranges, and in the case of Tesco introduced a second-tier 'discounter' range targeted at shoppers who are reluctant to trade down to 'value' items but, nevertheless, wanted to save money from their normal branded products. Another response was to emphasize lifetime costs rather than price. For example, Lexus, the premium-priced car brand, ran advertisements with the tag-line 'Lowest Cost of Ownership', based on its decent fuel economy and high resale value. Finally, money-saving initiatives were launched, such as Sainsbury's 'Feed a Family for a Fiver' (£5) and Marks & Spencer's meal for two and a bottle of wine for £10.

Based on: Alarcon (2008);[60] Finch (2008);[61] Helm (2008)[62]

Lifestyle

Lifestyle patterns have attracted much attention from marketing research practitioners. **Lifestyle** refers to the pattern of living as expressed in a person's activities, interests and opinions. Lifestyle analysis (psychographics) groups consumers according to their beliefs, activities, values, and demographic characteristics such as education and income. For example, the advertising agency Young & Rubicam has identified eight major lifestyle groups that can be found throughout Europe and the USA.

1   *The mainstreamers*: the largest group. Attitudes include conventional, trusting, cautious and family centred. Leisure activities include spectator sports and gardening; purchase behaviour is habitual, brand loyal and in approved stores.

2   *The aspirers*: members of this group tend to be ambitious, suspicious and unhappy. Leisure activities include trendy sports and fashion magazines; they buy fads, are impulse shoppers and engage in conspicuous consumption.

3   *The succeeders*: these people are leaders, industrious, confident and happy. Leisure activities include travel, sports, sailing and dining out. Purchase decisions are based on choice criteria such as quality, status and luxury.

4   *The transitionals*: members of this group are liberal, rebellious, self-expressive and intuitive. They have unconventional tastes in music, travel and movies; and enjoy cooking, and arts and crafts. Shopping behaviour tends to be impulsive and to involve unique products.

5   *The reformers*: these people are self-confident and involved, have broad interests and are issues orientated. They like reading, cultural events, intelligent games and educational TV. They have eclectic tastes, enjoy natural foods, and are concerned about authenticity and ecology.

6   *The struggling poor*: members of this group are unhappy, suspicious and feel left out. Their interests are in sports, music and television; their purchase behaviour tends to be price based, and they are looking for instant gratification.

7   *The resigned poor*: people in this group are unhappy, isolated and insecure. Television is their main leisure activity and their shopping behaviour is price based, although they also look for the reassurance of branded goods.

Lifestyle analysis has implications for marketing since lifestyles have been found to correlate with purchasing behaviour.[63] A company may choose to target a particular lifestyle group (e.g. the succeeders) with a product offering, and use advertising that is in line with the values and beliefs of this group. As information on the readership/viewership habits of lifestyle groups becomes more widely known, so media selection may be influenced by lifestyle research.

An example of how changing lifestyles affect consumer behaviour is the popularity of on-the-go products with people who live very busy lives. On-the-go drinks, such as bottled water and takeaway coffee, and on-the-go food, such as cereal-based breakfast snack bars, have found favour among time-pressured consumers.

4.3 Pause for Thought

Which of the lifestyle categories most closely matches you?

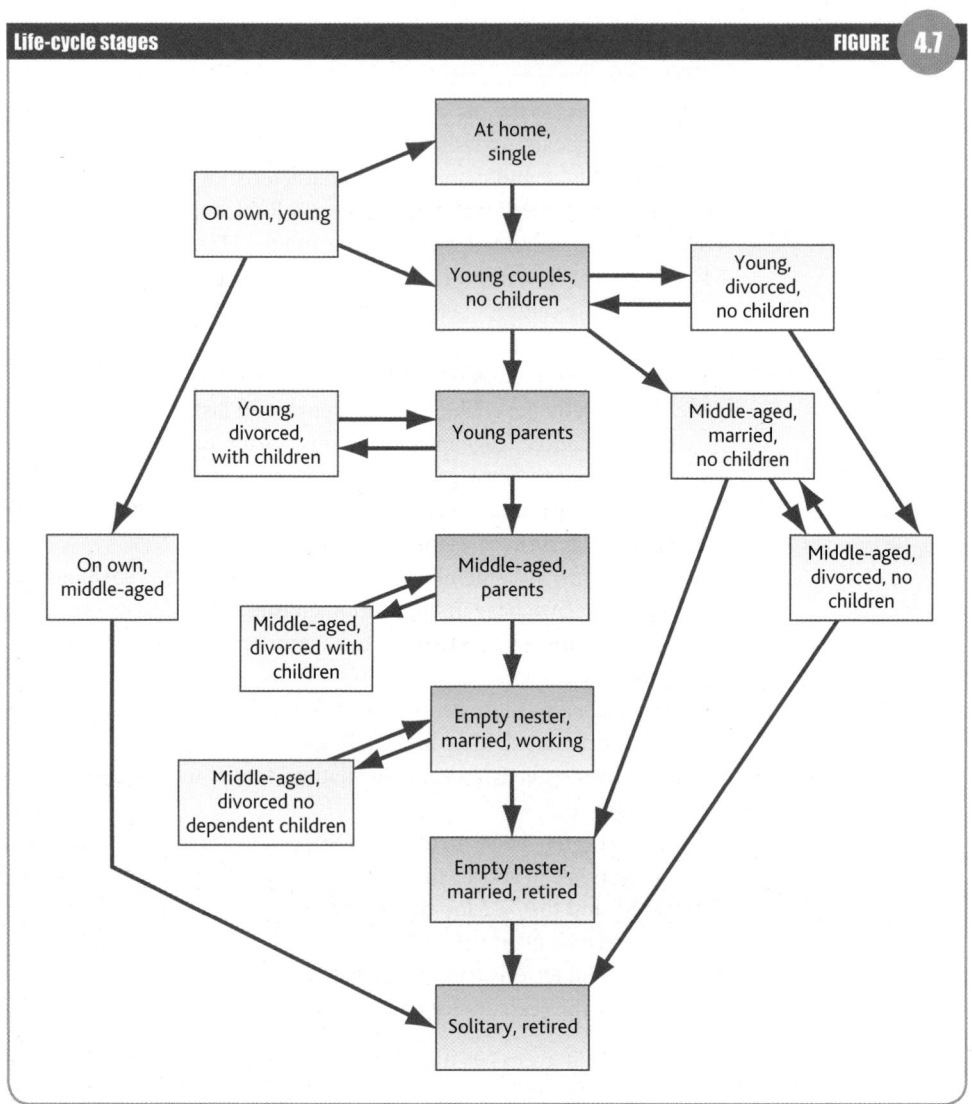

Life-cycle stages   FIGURE 4.7

Life cycle and age

Consumer behaviour may also depend on the stage that people have reached during their life. Of particular relevance is a person's *life-cycle stage* (shown in Fig. 4.7) since disposable income and purchase requirements may vary according to stage. For example, young couples with no children may have high disposable income if both work, and may be heavy purchasers of home furnishings and appliances since they may be setting up home. When they have children, disposable income may fall, particularly if they become a single-income family and the purchase of baby- and child-related products increases. At the empty-nester stage, disposable income may rise due to the absence of dependent children, low mortgage repayments and high personal income. This type of person may be a high-potential target for financial services and holidays. BMW uses life-cycle stage to segment consumers with its 4 × 4 X5 model targeted at young couples with children, and the 4 × 4 X6 model targeted at empty nesters. The X6 is designed for someone who previously owned an X5, or something similar, but now is looking for an SUV that 'doesn't scream "family"'.[64]

It is important to note, however, that not all people follow the classic family life-cycle stages. Figure 4.7 also shows alternative paths that may have consumer behaviour and market segmentation implications.

Age is also an effective discriminator of consumer behaviour. For example, young people have very different tastes in product categories such as clothing, drinks, holidays and television viewing compared to older people. The young have always been a prime target for marketers because of their capacity to spend. Marketing in Action 4.4 describes some characteristics of young consumers.

 ## 4.4 Marketing in Action

Young Consumers

The teenage–early twenty somethings have always been a key target for marketers. Surveys have shown, however, that they are not an easy group to attract. One study of 20- to 22-year-old European consumers found that they are sceptical about conventional aspirational brand advertising. Many reject the dream that 'Nikeworld' is a world of success. They recognize it is a good trainer but then ask about the company's stance on child labour in developing-world countries.

They like their advertising to be entertaining. They deeply dislike sameness, preferring advertising to be quirky, different and relevant.

'European' was not a concept that appealed to them: they preferred to celebrate their national differences. Nor was it something they valued in brands. Even IKEA was only perceived as European through its distribution. As a brand it was praised for its Scandinavian values.

Young consumers were found to be inconsistent between their actions and beliefs, and were comfortable with this. For example, they may not agree with McDonald's but still eat there; they rate a brand like Benetton highly but do not necessarily buy its products.

Young consumers like the Internet. Today's teenagers are the first generation to have grown up with the Internet as part of their everyday lives, and they see it in the same way as previous generations saw television. They often multitask—for example, surfing the net while watching television and listening to music on an iPod. They also use the Internet as a means of social interaction. Sites such as MySpace.com act as social networks allowing people to chat, send information, post photographs and download music. In the USA, teenagers spend on average almost an hour and a half a day social networking on the Internet. European teenagers represent 12 per cent of the European online population and spend long periods online, e-mailing their friends about information they have found on the web. There are clear implications for viral marketing campaigns where brand messages are spread through the target audience by e-mail. Young consumers also treasure mobile phones, another medium for sending SMS messages with the potential for a viral-type spread if the message taps into the values and interests of today's young. They also like to send photographs using sites like Flickr, the web's most popular photo-sharing site, and create and watch videos on YouTube. What they do not like is intrusion by advertisers, making the opportunities created by the enormous success of these sites a key marketing challenge.

Based on: Murphy (2001);[65] *Carter (2002);*[66] *Hempel (2005);*[67] *Wray and Robinson (2008)*[68]

Social influences

There are four social influences on consumer behaviour: culture, social class, geodemographics and reference groups.

Culture

Culture refers to the traditions, taboos, values and basic attitudes of the whole society within which an individual lives. It provides the framework within which individuals and their lifestyles develop. Cultural norms are the rules that govern behaviour, and are based upon values: beliefs about what attitudes and behaviour are desirable. Conformity to norms is created by reward-giving (e.g. smiling) and sanctioning (e.g. criticism). Cultural values affect how business is conducted. In the UK people are expected to arrive on time for a business appointment; in Spain this norm is not so deeply adhered to. In Arabian countries it is not unusual for a salesperson to conduct a sales presentation in the company of a competitor's salesperson. Culture also affects consumption behaviour. In France, for example, chocolate is sometimes eaten between slices of bread.

The spread of global communications technology and greater global mobility has led to a degree of social and cultural convergence. This does not mean that a global culture is replacing the diversity of local and national cultures in the world. Deep-rooted beliefs and values, and religious differences prevent that. However, the emergence of a global consumer, or at least consumers with common preferences across a large part of the world, has created opportunities for global brands (e.g. Chanel, BMW, Apple and IBM), supported by global marketing campaigns with only slight modifications to accommodate national differences.[69]

A comparative study of materialism and life satisfaction in the Netherlands and the USA found that the Dutch displayed higher levels of possessiveness than Americans, but no overall differences in envy, generosity or general materialism were found.[70] The 'possessiveness' of the Dutch is reflected in their reluctance to partake in second-hand markets: car boot sales and flea markets, for example, are virtually non-existent in the Netherlands. Another notable difference was that lower-income Americans were more envious than their Dutch counterparts. The higher level of social welfare spending in the Netherlands may have accounted for this result. The greatest difference, however, was found in the levels of life satisfaction, with the Dutch being significantly more satisfied with life. Thus, even in countries that are very similar in economic development, cultural variations can be seen that have implications for consumption behaviour.

Social class

Social class has long been regarded as an important determinant of consumer behaviour. In the UK it is largely based on occupation, and respondents to marketing research surveys are often classified in this way. Advertising media (e.g. newspapers) usually give readership/viewership figures broken down by social class groupings. Every country has its own method of grouping and, in the UK, the National Statistics Socio-economic Classification system identifies eight categories based on occupation (see Table 4.3). Although consumption patterns are likely to vary within each of the groups (e.g. some people may be more inclined to spend their money on consumer durables, while others may have more hedonistic preferences) two important studies have produced similar conclusions when assessing the discriminatory power of social class compared to other methods such as lifestyle and life-stage analysis.[71]

- Social class provides satisfactory power to discriminate between consumption patterns. For example, within grocery shopping the highest proportion of category 1 and 2 (managerial/professional) shoppers frequent Sainsbury's; Asda attracts a significantly higher share of people in category 5 (lower supervisory and technical occupations); while Tesco's profile mirrors that of society in general.[72]
- No alternative classification provides consistently better discriminatory power.
- No one classification system works best across all product fields.
- Sometimes other classifications discriminate better and often are just as powerful as social class.

Social class categories		TABLE 4.3
Classification	**Descriptors**	**Occupations**
1	Higher managerial and professional occupations	Employers in large organizations; higher managerial and professional
2	Lower managerial and professional occupations	Lower managerial occupations; higher technical and supervisory occupations
3	Intermediate occupations	Intermediate clerical/administrative, sales/service, technical/auxiliary and engineering occupations
4	Small employers and sole traders	Employers in small, non-professional and agricultural organizations, and self-employed sole traders
5	Lower supervisory and technical occupations	Lower supervisory and lower technical craft and process operative occupations
6	Semi-routine occupations	Semi-routine sales, service, technical, operative, agricultural, clerical and childcare occupations
7	Routine occupations	Routine sales/service, production, technical, operative and agricultural occupations
8	Never worked and long-term unemployed	Never worked, long-term unemployed and students

The implication is that social class as a predictive measure of consumption differences is not dead but can usefully be supplemented by other measures such as life stage and lifestyle.

Geodemographics

An alternative method of classifying households is based on their geographic location. This analysis—called **geodemographics**—is based on population census data. Households are grouped into geographic clusters based on information such as type of accommodation, car ownership, age, occupation, number and age of children, and (since 1991) ethnic background. These clusters can be identified by means of their postcodes so that targeting households by mail is easy. There are a number of systems in use in the UK, including PINPOINT and MOSAIC, but the best known is ACORN (A Classification Of Residential Neighbourhoods), which has identified 11 neighbourhood types. These are discussed in more detail in Chapter 8 on market segmentation and positioning, as they form an effective method of segmenting many markets, including financial services and retailing. ACORN has proved to be a powerful discriminator between different lifestyles, purchasing patterns and media exposure.[73]

Reference groups

The term **reference group** is used to indicate a group of people that influences an individual's attitude or behaviour. Where a product is conspicuous—for example, clothing or cars—the brand or model chosen may have been strongly influenced by what buyers perceive as acceptable to their reference group. This group may consist of family members, a group of friends or work colleagues. Some reference groups may be formal (e.g. members of a club or society), while others may be informal (friends with similar interests). Reference groups influence their members by the roles and norms expected of them. For example, students may have to play several roles: to lecturers, the student's role may be that of learner; to other students, their role may vary from peer to social companion. Depending on the role, various behaviours may be expected based upon group norms. To the extent that group norms influence values and attitudes, these reference groups may be seen as an important determinant of behaviour. Sometimes reference group norms can conflict, as when reference to the learning role suggests different patterns of behaviour from that of social companion. In terms of consumption, reference group influence can affect student purchasing of clothing, beverages, social events and textbooks, for example. The more conspicuous the choice is to the reference group, the stronger its influence.

There are two main types of reference group: membership and aspirant groups. *Membership groups* are the groups to which a person already belongs. What is believed to be suitable, acceptable and/or impressive to this group may play a major role in consumption behaviour. What other people think at a party, at work or generally socializing is of great importance. *Aspirant groups* are the groups to which the individual would like to belong. The point of focus could be professional (for example, aspiring to be a member of the board of directors) social (for example, aspiring to be accepted at a golf club) or personal (for example, aspiring to look or feel like someone else). Celebrities often form the basis of aspirant groups. Men want to look/feel like their favourite sport stars and women want to look/feel like famous film stars or models. This motivates the purchase of football shirts with 'Ronaldo' on the back, and the buying of clothing seen to be worn by Angeline Jolie or Kate Moss. ASOS, the online fashion retailer, bases its marketing strategy on aspirant group theory. It copies the style of clothing worn by film stars and models, and sells its clothes to aspirant women who wish to dress like them.

An opinion leader is someone in a reference group from whom other members seek guidance on a particular topic. As such, opinion leaders can exert enormous influence on purchase decisions. In terms of the type of off-road, four-wheel-drive vehicle to buy, the British royal family acts as significant opinion leader. The sight of members of royalty driving Range Rovers on television, and in newspapers and magazines is invaluable publicity, indicating the 'right' model to buy. Celebrities such as David Beckham, Ronaldo, Kate Moss and Angelina Jolie also act as opinion leaders to aspirant group members, influencing their consumption behaviour.

When you have read this chapter

log on to the Online Learning Centre at www.mcgraw-hill.co.uk/textbooks/jobber to explore chapter-by-chapter test questions, links and further online study tools for marketing.

Review ● ● ●

1 **The dimensions of buyer behaviour**
- The dimensions are who is important in the buying decision, how they buy, what their choice criteria are, where they buy and when they buy.

2 **The role of the buying centre (who buys) and its implications**
- Some consumer purchase decisions are made by a group such as a household. A decision may be in the hands of a buying centre with up to five roles: initiator, influencer, decider, buyer and user. It is the interaction of the people playing these roles that determines which purchase will be made.
- The implications are that its identification is helpful in targeting persuasive communications, and provides opportunities to creatively segment markets, allowing the sending of tailored offerings to different family members.

3 **The consumer decision-making process (how people buy)**
- The decision to purchase a consumer product may pass through a number of stages: need recognition/problem awareness, information search, evaluation of alternatives, purchase, and post-purchase evaluation of the decision.

4 **The marketing implications of need recognition, information search, evaluation of alternatives, purchase and post-purchase evaluation stages**
- Need recognition: marketing managers need to be aware of the needs of consumers so that needs can be met and the opportunity of building a competitive advantage is created; aware of need inhibitors so that strategies can be designed to overcome them; and alert to the benefits of stimulating need recognition (for example, through advertisements and the efforts of salespeople) to start the process off.
- Information search: marketing managers need to know where consumers look for information to help solve their decision-making. Communication can then be directed to consumers through those sources. One objective is to ensure that the company's brand appears in the consumer's awareness set.
- Evaluation of alternatives: for decisions where the consumer is highly involved, marketing managers need to provide a lot of information about the positive consequences of buying. The print media may be suitable because these allow detailed and repeated scrutiny of information. Salespeople may also be important in ensuring the consumer is aware of product attributes (features) and benefits. For low-involvement decisions, marketing managers should seek top-of-mind awareness through repetitive advertising, and trial (e.g. through sales promotion). For all consumer decisions, marketing managers must understand the choice criteria used to evaluate brands, including the importance of emotion.
- Post-purchase evaluation of the decision: marketing managers need to dispel cognitive dissonance by using advertisements, direct mail or telephone calls to act as positive reinforcers. However, besides this kind of reassurance, marketing managers need to market products that meet and exceed the needs and expectations of customers so that this stage is associated with high levels of customer satisfaction.

5 **The differences in evaluation of high- versus low-involvement situations**
- High-involvement situations: the consumer is more likely to carry out extensive evaluation and take into account beliefs about the perceived consequences of buying the brand, the extent to which important others believe they should or should not buy the brand, attitudes (which are the degree to which the consumer likes or dislikes the brand overall), and subjective norms (which form an overall evaluation of the degree to which important others approve or disapprove of the purchase). All of this means that a considerable amount of information processing takes place.
- Low-involvement situations: the consumer carries out a simple evaluation and uses simple choice tactics to reduce time and effort. Awareness precedes trial, which, if satisfactory, leads to repeat purchase. The behaviour may become habitual, with little conscious thought or formation of attitudes before purchase.

6 **The nature of choice criteria (what are used) and their implications**

- Choice criteria are the various attributes (and benefits) a consumer uses when evaluating products and services. These may be technical (e.g. reliability), economic (e.g. price), social (e.g. status) or personal (e.g. self-image).
- The implications are that knowledge of the choice criteria used by members of the buying centre aids product design (e.g. are style/looks more important than performance?) and the choice of the appeals to use in advertising and personal selling, which should be linked to the key choice criteria used by those members.

7 **The influences on consumer behaviour—the buying situation, personal and social influences—and their marketing implications**

- Buying situation: the three types are extended problem-solving, limited problem-solving and habitual problem-solving. The marketing implications are that for extended problem-solving marketers should provide information-rich communication and salespeople should adopt the problem–solution approach to selling; for limited problem-solving, marketers should stimulate the need to conduct a search (when their brand is not currently bought) or reduce the risk of brand switching by, for example, giving warranties (when their brand is currently being bought); and for habitual problem-solving, repetitive advertising should be used to create awareness and reinforce already favourable attitudes.
- Personal influences: the six types are information processing, motivation, beliefs and attitudes, personality, lifestyle, and life cycle and age.
- Information processing has two key aspects: perception and learning. Three processes may be used to sort out the masses of stimuli that can be perceived into a manageable amount: (i) selective attention, which implies that advertisements, logos and packaging need to be attention-getting, and explains why there is intense competition to obtain eye-level positions on supermarket shelves; (ii) selective distortion, which implies that messages should be presented clearly, using a credible source and with supporting evidence whenever possible; and (iii) selective retention, which implies that messages that are in line with existing beliefs and attitudes are more likely to be remembered.
- Two ways in which learning takes place are conditioning and cognitive learning. Conditioning suggests that associating a brand with humour (e.g. in advertisements) or excitement (e.g. motor racing sponsorship) will carry over to the brand, and also that the use of free samples and coupons (reinforcers) can encourage sales by inducing trial and repeat buying. Through the reinforcers the consumer will have learnt to associate the brand with pleasurable experiences.
- Cognitive learning suggests that statements in an advertisement may be remembered, the promise of a reward may influence behaviour, as may communications that allow the recipient to draw his/her own conclusions. The result of the learning process is the creation of product positioning.
- Motives influence choice criteria and include physiological, safety, belongingness and love, esteem and status, and self-actualization.
- Beliefs and attitudes are linked in that the consequence of a set of beliefs may be a positive or negative attitude. Marketers attempt to match product attributes to desired beliefs and attitudes, and use communications to influence these and establish new beliefs.
- The personality of the type of person who buys a brand may be reflected in the type of person used in its advertisements. Brand personality is used to appeal to people who identify with that characterization.
- Lifestyles have been shown to be linked to purchase behaviour. Lifestyle groups can be used for market segmentation and targeting purposes.
- Life-cycle stage may affect consumer behaviour as the level of disposable income and purchase requirements (needs) may depend on the stage that people have reached during their life. For similar reasons, age may affect consumer behaviour.
- The four types of social influence are culture, social class, geodemographics and reference groups.
- Culture affects how business is conducted and consumption behaviour. Marketers have to adjust their behaviour and the marketing mix to accommodate different cultures.

- Social class can predict some consumption patterns, and so can be used for market segmentation and targeting purposes.
- Geodemographics classifies consumers according to their location, and is used for market segmentation and targeting purposes.
- Reference groups influence their members by the roles and norms expected of them. Marketers attempt to make their brands acceptable to reference groups, and target opinion leaders to gain brand acceptability.

Key Terms

attitude the degree to which a customer or prospect likes or dislikes a brand

awareness set the set of brands that the consumer is aware may provide a solution to the problem

beliefs descriptive thoughts that a person holds about something

buying centre a group that is involved in the buying decision (also known as a decision-making unit)

choice criteria the various attributes (and benefits) people use when evaluating products and services

classical conditioning the process of using an established relationship between a stimulus and a response to cause the learning of the same response to a different stimulus

cognitive dissonance post-purchase concerns of a consumer arising from uncertainty as to whether a decision to purchase was the correct one

cognitive learning the learning of knowledge, and development of beliefs and attitudes without direct reinforcement

consumer decision-making process the stages a consumer goes through when buying something— namely, problem awareness, information search, evaluation of alternatives, purchase and post-purchase evaluation

evoked set the set of brands that the consumer seriously evaluates before making a purchase

geodemographics the process of grouping households into geographic clusters based on information such as type of accommodation, occupation, number and age of children, and ethnic background

information framing the way in which information is presented to people

information processing the process by which a stimulus is received, interpreted, stored in memory and later retrieved

information search the identification of alternative ways of problem-solving

lifestyle the pattern of living as expressed in a person's activities, interests and opinions

motivation the process involving needs that set drives in motion to accomplish goals

operant conditioning the use of rewards to generate reinforcement of response

perception the process by which people select, organize and interpret sensory stimulation into a meaningful picture of the world

personality the inner psychological characteristics of individuals that lead to consistent responses to their environment

reasoning a more complex form of cognitive learning where conclusions are reached by connected thought

reference group a group of people that influences an individual's attitude or behaviour

rote learning the learning of two or more concepts without conditioning

selective attention the process by which people screen out those stimuli that are neither meaningful to them nor consistent with their experiences and beliefs

selective distortion the distortion of information received by people according to their existing beliefs and attitudes

selective retention the process by which people only retain a selection of messages in memory

vicarious learning learning from others without direct experience or reward

Study Questions

1. Choose a recent purchase that involved not only yourself but other people in making the decision. What role(s) did you play in the buying centre? What roles did these other people play and how did they influence your choice?

2. What decision-making process did you go through? At each stage (need recognition, information search, etc.), try to remember what you were thinking about and what activities took place.

3. What choice criteria did you use? Did they change between drawing up a shortlist and making the final choice?

4. Think of the last time you made an impulse purchase. What stimulated you to buy? Have you bought the brand again? Why or why not? Did your thoughts and actions resemble those suggested by the Ehrenberg and Goodhart model?

5. Can you think of a brand that has used the principles of classical conditioning in its advertising?

6. Are there any brands that you buy (e.g. beer, perfume) that have personalities that match your own?

7. To what kind of lifestyle do you aspire? How does this affect the types of product (particularly visible ones) you buy now and in the future?

8. Are you influenced by any reference groups? How do these groups influence what you buy?

References

1. Leeflang, P. S. H. and W. F. van Raaij (1995) The Changing Consumer in the European Union: A Meta-Analysis, *International Journal of Research in Marketing* 12, 373–87.
2. MacCarthy, C. (2005) Lego Suffers as Children Shun Toys, *Financial Times*, 7 April, 27.
3. Blackwell, R. D., P. W. Miniard and J. F. Engel (2005) *Consumer Behavior*, Orlando, FL: Dryden.
4. Woodside, A. G. and W. H. Mote (1979) Perceptions of Marital Roles in Consumer Processes for Six Products, in Beckwith *et al.* (eds) *American Marketing Association Educator Proceedings*, Chicago: American Marketing Association, 214–19.
5. Donation, S. (1989) Study Boosts Men's Buying Role, *Advertising Age*, 4 December, 48.
6. Anonymous (1990) Business Bulletin, *Wall Street Journal*, 17 May, A1.
7. Weinberg, C. B. and R. S. Winer (1983) Working Wives and Major Family Expenditures: Replication and Extension, *Journal of Consumer Research* 7 (September), 259–63.
8. Bellante, D. and A. C. Foster (1984) Working Wives and Expenditure on Services, *Journal of Consumer Research* 11 (September), 700–7.
9. Swasey, A. (1990) Family Purse Strings Falls into Young Hands, *Wall Street Journal*, 2 February, B1.

10. Blackwell, Miniard and Engel (2005) op. cit.

11. Neal, C., P. Quester and D. I. Hawkins (2007) *Consumer Behavior: Implications for Marketing Strategy*, Boston, Mass: Irwin.

12. O'Shaughnessey, J. (1987) *Why People Buy*, New York: Oxford University Press, 161.

13. Baumgartner, H. and J. Bem Steenkamp (1996) Exploratory Consumer Buying Behaviour: Conceptualisation and Measurement, *International Journal of Research in Marketing* 13, 121–37.

14. Kuusela, H., M. T. Spence and A. J. Kanto (1998) Expertise Effects on Prechoice Decision Processes and Final Outcomes: A Protocol Analysis, *European Journal of Marketing* 32(5/6), 559–76.

15. Creusen, M. E. H. and J. P. L. Schoormans (1997) The Nature of Differences between Similarity and Preference Judgements: A Replication and Extension, *International Journal of Research in Marketing* 14, 81–7.

16. Blackwell, Miniard and Engel (2005) op. cit.

17. Elliott, R. and E. Hamilton (1991) Consumer Choice Tactics and Leisure Activities, *International Journal of Advertising* 10, 325–32.

18. Ajzen, I. and M. Fishbein (1980) *Understanding Attitudes and Predicting Social Behaviour*, Englewood Cliffs, NJ: Prentice-Hall.

19. See e.g. Budd, R. J. and C. P. Spencer (1984) Predicting Undergraduates' Intentions to Drink, *Journal of Studies on Alcohol* 45(2), 179–83; Farley, J., D. Lehman and M. Ryan (1981) Generalizing from 'Imperfect' Replication, *Journal of Business* 54(4), 597–610; Shimp, T. and A. Kavas (1984) The Theory of Reasoned Action Applied to Coupon Usage, *Journal of Consumer Research* 11, 795–809.

20. Ehrenberg, A. S. C. and G. J. Goodhart (1980) *How Advertising Works*, J. Walter Thompson/MRCA.

21. Wright, P. L. (1974) The Choice of a Choice Strategy: Simplifying vs Optimizing, Faculty Working Paper no. 163, Champaign, Ill: Department of Business Administration, University of Illinois.

22. Rothschild, M. L. (1978) Advertising Strategies for High and Low Involvement Situations, *American Marketing Association Educator's Proceedings*, Chicago, 150–62.

23. Rothschild (1978) op. cit.

24. For a discussion of the role of involvement in package labelling see Davies, M. A. P. and L. T. Wright (1994) The Importance of Labelling Examined in Food Marketing, *European Journal of Marketing* 28(2), 57–67.

25. Elliott, R. (1997) Understanding Buyers: Implications for Selling, in D. Jobber (ed.) *The CIM Handbook of Selling and Sales Strategy*, Oxford: Butterworth-Heinemann.

26. See Elliott, R. (1998) A Model of Emotion-Driven Choice, *Journal of Marketing Management* 14, 95–108; Rook, D. (1987) The Buying Impulse, *Journal of Consumer Research* 14(1), 89–99.

27. Neal, Quester and Hawkins (2007) op. cit.

28. Anonymous (2008) Follow the Leader, *Economist*, 14 June, 82–3.

29. Bedell, G. (2003) *The Observer Review*, 19 January, 1–2.

30. See Carrigan, M. and A. Attala (2001) The Myth of the Ethical Consumer—Do Ethics Matter in Purchase Behaviour? *Journal of Consumer Marketing* 18(7) 560–77; and Follows, S. B. and D. Jobber (1999) Environmentally Responsible Behaviour: A Test of a Consumer Model, *European Journal of Marketing* 34(5/6), 723–46.

31. Carrigan and Attala (2001) op. cit.

32. Micheletti, M. (2003) *Political Virtue and Shopping: Individuals, Consumerism, and Collective Action*, Basingstoke: Palgrave Macmillan.

33. Cooper, T. (2005) Slower Consumption: Reflections on Product Life Spans and the 'Throwaway Society', *Journal of Industrial Ecology* 9, 51–67.

34. Connolly, J. and A. Prothero (2008) Green Consumption: Life-Politics, Risk and Contradictions, *Journal of Consumer Culture* 8(1), 117–45.

35. Co-operative Bank (2008) *The Ethical Consumerism Report 2008*, Manchester: Co-operative Bank, retrieved 2 April 2009 from www.ethicalconsumer.org/Portals/0/Downloads/ETHICAL%20CONSUMER%20REPORT.pdf.

36. Mowen, J. C. (1988) Beyond Consumer Decision Making, *Journal of Consumer Research* 5(1), 15–25.

37. Elliot and Hamilton (1991) op. cit.

38. Carter, M. (2002) Ruthlessly Shopping for Comfort, *Financial Times*, 20 May, 12.

39. Smith, L. (2005) Ten Sales a Second: Glastonbury Tickets Go in Record Rush, *Guardian*, 4 April, 7.

40. Gibson, O. (2008) Led Zep Tickets Fetch £7425 as Online 'Touts' Strike Gold in £200m Bonanza, *Guardian*, 8 January, 13.

41. Neal, Quester and Hawkins (2007) op. cit.

42. Blackwell, Miniard and Engel (2005) op. cit.

43. Bettman, J. R. (1982) A Functional Analysis of the Role of Overall Evaluation of Alternatives and Choice Processes, in Mitchell, A. (ed.) *Advances in Consumer Research 8*, Ann Arbor, Michigan: Association for Consumer Research, 87–93.

44. Laurent, G. and J. N. Kapferer (1985) Measuring Consumer Involvement Profiles, *Journal of Marketing Research* 12 (February), 41–53.

45. Blackwell, Miniard and Engel (2005) op. cit.

46. Williams, K. C. (1981) *Behavioural Aspects of Marketing*, London: Heinemann.

47. Neal, Quester and Hawkins (2004) op. cit.

48. Ratneshwar, S., L. Warlop, D. G. Mick and G. Seegar (1997) Benefit Salience and Consumers' Selective Attention to Product Features, *International Journal of Research in Marketing* 14, 245–9.

49. Levin, L. P. and G. J. Gaeth (1988) Framing of Attribute Information Before and After Consuming the Product, *Journal of Consumer Research* 15 (December), 374–78.

50. Key, A. (2000) The Colour-Coded Secrets of Brands, *Marketing*, 6 January, 21.

51. Lindstrom, M. (2005) Sensing the Opportunity, *The Marketeer*, February, 4–17.

52. Neal, Quester and Hawkins (2007) op. cit.

53. Ries, A. and J. Trout (2001) *Positioning: The Battle for Your Mind*, New York: Warner.

54. Luthans, F. (2001) *Organisational Behaviour*, San Francisco: McGraw-Hill.

55. Maslow, A. H. (1954) *Motivation and Personality*, New York: Harper & Row, 80–106.

56. Lovell, C. (2008) Is Neuroscience Making a Difference?, *Campaign*, 3 October, 11.

57. Van Trijp, H. C. M., W. D. Hoyer and J. J. Inman (1996) Why Switch? Product Category-Level Explanations for True Variety-Seeking Behaviour, *Journal of Marketing Research* 33, August, 281–92.

58. Kassarjan, H. H. (1971) Personality and Consumer Behaviour Economics: A Review, *Journal of Marketing Research*, November, 409–18.

59. Ackoff, R. L. and J. R. Emsott (1975) Advertising at Anheuser-Busch, Inc., *Sloan Management Review*, Spring, 1–15.

60. Alarcon, C. (2008) M&S to be Hardest Hit As Consumers Change Food Buying Patterns, *Marketing Week*, 16 October, 6.

61. Finch, J. (2008) Sainsbury's Feels the Difference in Eating Habits, *Guardian*, 19 June, 27.

62. Helm, B. (2008) How to Sell Luxury to Penny-Pinchers, *Business Week*, 10 November, 60.

63. O'Brien, S. and R. Ford (1988) Can We at Last Say Goodbye to Social Class?, *Journal of the Market Research Society* 30(3), 289–332.

64. Smith, G. (2008) On the Road, *Guardian Weekend*, 21 June, 99.

65. Murphy, D. (2001) Connecting with On-line Teenagers, *Marketing*, 27 September, 31–2.

66. Carter, M. (2002) Branding Takes a Road Test, *Financial Times*, 17 April, 14.

67. Hempel, J. (2005) The MySpace Generation, *Business Week*, 12/19 December, 65–72.

68. Wray, R. and B. Robinson (2008) 'I'm Off to Tend My Alpacas'—Flickr Founder's Exit Marks End of a Web Era, *Guardian*, 20 June, 3.

69. Johnson, D. and C. Turner (2006) *European Business*, London: Routledge.

70. Bamossy, G. and S. Dawson (1991) A Comparison of the Culture of Consumption between Two Western Cultures: A Study of Materialism in the Netherlands and United States, *Proceedings of the European Marketing Academy Conference*, Dublin, May, 147–68.

71. See Anonymous (1981) *An Evaluation of Social Grade Validity*, London: Market Research Society; and O'Brien and Ford (1988) op. cit., 309.

72. Anonymous (2005) This Sceptred Aisle, *Economist*, 6 August, 29.

73. Baker, K., J. Germingham and C. Macdonald (1979) The Utility to Market Research of the Classification of Residential Neighbourhoods, Market Research Society Conference, Brighton, March, 206–17.

Cappuccino Wars

The Battle for the High Street

The UK has come a long way from the days when a request for coffee would bring a cup of uniformly grey, unappealing liquid, sometimes served in polystyrene cups, which bore no relation to the rich, flavoursome coffee experienced on trips to continental Europe. The origin of this change was not Europe, however, but the USA, where the coffee bar culture was grounded.

Recent years have seen an explosion of coffee bars on UK high streets, with over 5 million lattés, cappuccinos and espressos served per week. The market is dominated by the US-owned Starbucks, with over 800 coffee bars, Costa Coffee (backed by Whitbread), with over 800, and an independent, Caffè Nero, with around 360 bars. A fourth competitor, Coffee Republic, has closed and sold shops to its rivals in the face of mounting losses. It has repositioned many of its coffee shops to become delicatessens, offering sandwiches and hot food as well as coffee. In total, the UK has over 3000 coffee shops, all charging over £2 for a small coffee. Often three or more bars will be located within 100 yards of each other.

The first US west coast-style coffee shop was opened in the UK in 1995 and was called the Seattle Coffee Company. The owners were Americans who saw an opportunity to serve the British with good-quality coffee in relaxed surroundings just like they experienced in the USA. The concept was a huge success and by 1997 the company had 49 coffee outlets. It was joined by Coffee Republic and Caffè Nero, which also grew rapidly. But in 1997 the coffee market in the UK was to change dramatically with the arrival of the US-based Starbucks coffee bar giant, which bought the Seattle Coffee Company.

Its strategy was to gain market share through fast roll-out. For the first five years, Starbucks opened an average of five shops a month in the UK: in 1999 it had 95 shops, by 2009 this had increased to over 800. Today, Starbucks is in the Fortune Top 500 US companies and has nearly 15,000 coffee shops in more than 40 countries. Its approach is simple: blanket an area completely, even if the shops cannibalize one another's business. A new coffee bar will often capture about 30 per cent of the sales of a nearby Starbucks, but the company considered this was more than offset by lower delivery and management costs (per shop), shorter queues at individual shops and increased foot traffic for all the shops in an area as new shops take custom from competitors too. Twenty million people buy coffee at Starbucks every week, with the average Starbucks customer visiting 18 times a month.

One of its traditional strengths was the quality of its coffee. Starbucks has its own roasting plant, from which the media are banned lest its secrets are revealed. In its coffee shops, coffee is mixed with a lot of milk and offered in hundreds of flavours. Its Frappuccino is positioned as a midday break in advertisements where a narrator explains 'Starbucks Frappuccino coffee drink is a delicious blend of coffee and milk to smooth out your day.' The tag-line is 'Smooth out your day, everyday.'

A key problem is that Starbucks' major competitors—Costa Coffee and Caffè Nero—have also followed a fast roll-out strategy causing rental prices to spiral upwards. For example, Starbucks' Leicester Square coffee shop in London was part of a £1.5 million two-shop rental deal. Many coffee shops are not profitable and, with Starbucks continuing to operate them, it has been accused of unfairly trying to squeeze out the competition. Nevertheless, after sustaining losses in the early years all three major players are now profitable.

The typical consumer at these coffee bars is young, single and a high earner. They are likely to be professionals, and senior or middle managers with company cars. Students also are an important part of the market. Coffee bars are seen as a 'little bit of heaven', a refuge where consumers can lounge on sofas, read broadsheet newspapers and view new age poetry on the walls. They provide an oasis of calm for people between their homes and offices. They are regarded as a sign of social mobility for people who may be moving out of an ordinary café or low-end department store into something more classy. Even the language is important for these consumers, where terms such as latté, cappuccino and espresso allow them to demonstrate connoisseurship.

Coffee bars also cater for the different moods of consumers. For example, Sahar Hashemi, a founding partner of Coffee Republic, explains 'If I'm in my routine, I'll have a tall, skinny latté. But if I'm feeling in a celebratory mood or like spoiling myself, it's a grand vanilla mocha with whip and marshmallows.'

Starbucks has expanded the services it provides by offering a WiFi service that allows laptop and personal digital assistant users to gain high-speed Internet access. In the USA it has introduced an in-store music service in 45 of its shops, which allows customers to listen to a selection from 250,000 tracks. They can then order the tracks they like, have them burnt on to a CD in the shop and buy them when they leave. It has also struck deals to distribute CDs at its stores by artists including Paul McCartney and Joni Mitchell.

While Coffee Republic has made a major move towards becoming a delicatessen, Starbucks, Costa Coffee and Caffè Nero also offer food alongside drinks. Starbucks targets breakfast, lunch and snack times with a limited range of both indulgent and healthy eating options. Costa Coffee has been offering hot foods and salads since 2002. Caffè Nero's food offer is integral to its Italian-style positioning, with most of the ingredients for its meals coming from Italy.

The chains have also embraced the fair trade coffee idea, with Costa Coffee offering Cafédirect products since 2000 and Starbucks introducing fair trade coffee in 2002. Starbucks has also met with considerable success for its low-calorie version of its Frappuccino iced drinks.

The recent recession has hit all the chains, but Starbucks, in particular, has suffered. Declining performance led to the reappointment in 2008 of Howard Schultz as chief executive, the man who grew the firm from just four outlets to nearly 15,000 today. He identified Starbucks' problems as stemming from its outlets losing their 'romance and theatre'. He pointed out that the distinctive aroma of fresh coffee was less evident because of the advent of vacuum-sealed, flavour-locked packaging. Also the use of new automated machines meant that customers could not see their drinks being prepared—eliminating an 'intimate experience' with the barista and impairing the spectacle of coffee making. The result, he concluded, was that some customers found Starbucks coffee shops sterile places that no longer reflected a passion for coffee. The situation was made worse by the smell of sandwiches, which often overpowered the aroma of coffee. Some Starbucks staff were also criticized as being unfriendly.

The problems facing Starbucks were worsened by a strong challenge from McDonald's, which have opened 'McCafes' in some of their outlets where customers can buy similar drinks to Starbucks' at a cheaper price. Starbucks' woes continued with a report from the consumer magazine *Which?*, which showed that Starbucks' coffee was inferior to that sold at Costa Coffee and Caffè Nero, which topped the survey. It was also the most expensive.

Mr Schultz has begun to address some of these problems by introducing new, smaller espresso machines so customers can once again see the baristas making their drink. Coffee is once again being ground by hand, restoring the aroma, and a less potent-smelling cheese is being used in sandwiches. The baristas have all been retrained, not only in the art of making excellent coffee but also in connecting better with customers. The interiors of many of the company's coffee shops are being renovated. Stores in the USA have been closed and expansion of the chain abroad has been slowed as management realize that the market is saturated.

To make the outlets more attractive during the recession, a new instant coffee brand, Via, was launched, which Starbucks claims tastes as good as ground coffee but at a much cheaper price. The company has also introduced a loyalty card, which allows free extras such as a shot of whipped cream, syrup or soy in the coffee.

> **//** *Starbucks' approach is simple: blanket an area completely, even if the shops cannibalize one another's business.* **//**

References

Based on: Anonymous (2001) Coffee Republic Revamps Stores for Social Focus, *Marketing*, 15 March, 4; Hedburg, A. and M. Rowe (2001) UK Goes Coffee House Crazy, *Marketing Week*, 4 January, 28–9; BBC (2003) Cappuccino Kings, *The Money Programme*; Cree, R. (2003) Sahar Hashemi, *The Director*, January, 44–7; Daniels, C. (2003) Mr Coffee, *Fortune*, 14 April, 139–40; Sutter, S. (2003) Staff the Key to Marketing Success, *Marketing*, 19 May, 4; Anonymous (2004) Starbucks to Offer 'Music to Go', *BBC News*, 12 March, http://news.bbc.co.uk; Bainbridge, J. (2005) Off the Boil, *Marketing*, 13 April, 28–9; Anonymous (2008) Coffee Wars, *Economist*, 12 January, 57–8; Clark, A. (2008) Wall St Gets Palpitations Over Caffeine Fuelled Growth, *Guardian*, 7 January, 25; Fernandez, J. (2009) Back to Basics, *Marketing Week*, 26 February, 18–19.

Questions

1. Why have coffee bars been so popular with consumers in the UK?

2. You are considering visiting a coffee bar for the first time. What would influence your choice of coffee bar to visit? Is this likely to be a high- or low-involvement decision?

3. Assess the coffee chains' moves to expand the offerings they provide for their customers.

4. Coffee bars are mainly located in the centres of towns and cities. Are there other locations where they could satisfy customer needs?

This case was written by David Jobber, Professor of Marketing, University of Bradford.

Consumer Behaviour CASE 8

How Do You Decide?

Choose one of the four types of product listed below:

1 mp3 player
2 jeans
3 foreign holiday
4 bar of chocolate.

Questions

1 Who is likely to influence your choice of brand? What buying centre roles do they play?

2 Using the five stages in the consumer decision-making process as a guide, how would you go about purchasing that product? How applicable is this model for purchasing a bar of chocolate?

3 What factors (choice criteria) would you use when evaluating the brands you are considering for purchase?

4 How would you classify this type of buying decision: extended, limited or habitual problem-solving?

This exercise was prepared by David Jobber, Professor of Marketing, University of Bradford.

CHAPTER 5

Understanding organizational buying behaviour

People are people at work or at play.

ANONYMOUS

LEARNING OBJECTIVES

After reading this chapter, you should be able to:

1   discuss the characteristics of organizational buying

2   define the dimensions of organizational buying

3   discuss the nature and marketing implications of who buys, how organizations buy and the choice criteria used to evaluate products

4   explain the influences on organizational buying behaviour—the buy class, product type and purchase importance—and discuss their marketing implications

5   describe the developments in purchasing practice: just-in-time, centralized and online purchasing, reverse marketing and leasing

6   discuss the nature of relationship marketing and how to build customer relationships

7   describe the development of buyer–seller relationships

Organizational buying concerns the purchase of products and services for use in an organization's activities. There are three types of organizational market. First, the *industrial market* concerns those companies that buy products and services to help them produce other goods and services. Industrial goods include raw materials, components and capital goods such as machinery. Second, the *reseller market* comprises organizations that buy products and services to resell. Mail-order companies, retailers and supermarkets are examples of resellers. Manufacturers of consumer goods such as toys, groceries and furniture require an understanding of the reseller market since success depends on persuading resellers to stock their products. Third, the *government market* consists of government agencies that buy products and services to help them carry out their activities. Purchases for local authorities and defence are examples. The activities concerned with marketing to such organizations are sometimes called business-to-business marketing.

An understanding of organizational buying behaviour in all of these markets is a prerequisite for marketing success. One of the fascinating aspects of marketing to organizations is that different players in the buying company may be evaluating suppliers' offerings along totally different choice criteria. The key is to be able to satisfy these diverse requirements in a single offering. A product that gives engineers the performance characteristics they demand, production managers the delivery reliability they need, purchasing managers the value for money they seek and shop floor workers the ease of installation they desire is likely to be highly successful. This complexity of organizational buying makes marketing an extremely interesting task.

This chapter examines some characteristics of organizational buying and marketing before examining the three key elements of buying identified in Chapter 4: who buys, how they buy and what choice criteria they use. For each element, the marketing implications will be addressed. Finally, some developments in purchasing practice—just-in-time purchasing, centralized purchasing, online purchasing and reverse marketing—will be discussed and their implications for marketing explored.

Characteristics of Organizational Buying

Nature and size of customers

Typically the number of customers in organizational markets is small. The Pareto rule often applies, with 80 per cent of output being sold to 20 per cent of customers, who may number fewer than 12. The reseller market is a case in point where, in Europe, most countries have a small number of supermarkets dominating the grocery trade. In the industrial market the same situation is often found. For example, in the games console industry Microsoft, Sony and Nintendo are the dominant global players. Clearly the importance of one customer is paramount. Consequently, when Microsoft decided to move to IBM for the processor that drives the Xbox 360, this was a major blow to Intel, which hitherto had powered almost everything that Microsoft had ever made.[1] The jet aircraft industry is even more concentrated, with only two key players: Airbus and Boeing. The implications are that the importance of a small number of large customers makes it sensible for suppliers to invest heavily in close, long-term relationships with them. Dedicated sales and marketing teams under the title of 'key account management' are usually employed to service such large accounts. Supply is usually direct, dispensing with the services of intermediaries as large order sizes make it economical and customer importance makes it necessary to have face-to-face contact and to supply direct to them.

Complexity of buying

Often, organizational purchases, notably those that involve large sums of money and that are new to the company, involve many people at different levels of the organization. The managing director, product engineers, production managers, purchasing managers and operatives may influence the decision as to which expensive machine to purchase. The sales task may be to influence as many of these people as possible and may involve multilevel selling by means of a sales team, rather than an individual salesperson.[2]

Economic and technical choice criteria

Although organizational buyers, being people, are affected by emotional factors, such as like or dislike of a salesperson, organizational buying decisions are often made on economic and technical criteria. This is because organizational buyers have to justify their decisions to other members of their organization.[3] Also the formalization of the buying function through the establishment of purchasing departments leads to the use of economic rather than emotional choice criteria. As purchasing becomes more sophisticated, economic criteria came to the fore with techniques such as life-cycle cost and value-in-use analysis. Fleet buyers, for example, calculate life-cycle costs including purchase price, running and maintenance costs when considering which company car to buy.

Risks

Industrial markets are sometimes characterized by a contract being agreed before the product is made. Further, the product itself may be highly technical and the seller may be faced with unforeseen problems once work has started. Thus, Scott-Lithgow won an order to build an oil rig for BP, but the price proved uneconomic given the nature of the problems associated with its construction. In the government market, a £12 billion upgrade of the UK's National Health Service IT systems ran over budget, fell behind schedule by four years and saw the departure of two of the programme's four main contractors.[4]

Buying to specific requirements

Because of the large sums of money involved organizational buyers sometimes draw up product specifications and ask suppliers to design their products to meet them. Services, too, are often conducted to specific customer requirements, marketing research and advertising services being examples. This is much less a feature of consumer marketing, where a product offering may be developed to meet a need of a market segment but, beyond that, meeting individual needs would prove uneconomic.

Reciprocal buying

Because an industrial buyer may be in a powerful negotiating position with a seller, it may be possible to demand concessions in return for placing an order. In some situations, buyers may demand that sellers buy some of their products in return for securing the order. For example, in negotiating to buy computers a company like Volvo might persuade a supplier to buy a fleet of Volvo company cars.

Derived demand

The demand for many organizational goods is derived from the demand for consumer goods. If the demand for compact discs increases, the demand for the raw materials and machinery used to make the discs will also expand. Clearly raw material and machinery suppliers would be wise to monitor consumer trends and buying characteristics as well as their immediate organizational customers. A further factor based upon the derived demand issue is the tendency for demand for some industrial goods and services to be more volatile than that for consumer goods and services. For example, a small fall in demand for compact discs may mean the complete cessation of orders for the machinery to make them. Similarly a small increase in demand if manufacturers are working at full capacity may mean a massive increase in demand for machinery as investment to meet the extra demand is made. This is known as the *accelerator principle*.[5]

Negotiations

Because of the existence of professional buyers and sellers, and the size and complexity of organizational buying, negotiation is often important. Thus supermarkets will negotiate with manufacturers about price since their buying power allows them to obtain discounts. Car manufacturers will negotiate attractive prices from tyre manufacturers such as Pirelli and Michelin since the replacement brand may be dependent upon the tyre fitted to the new car. The supplier's list price may be regarded as the starting point for negotiation and the profit margin ultimately achieved will be heavily influenced by the negotiating skills of the seller. The implication is that sales and marketing personnel need to be conversant with negotiating skills and tactics.

The Dimensions of Organizational Buying Behaviour

As with consumer behaviour, the dimensions of organizational buying behaviour cover who buys, how they buy, the choice criteria used, and where and when they buy. We will examine the first three of these issues in detail.

Who buys?

An important point to understand in organizational buying is that the buyer, or purchasing officer, is often not the only person that influences the decision, or actually has the authority to make the ultimate decision. Rather, the decision is in the hands of a **decision-making unit** (DMU), or buying centre as it is sometimes called. This is not necessarily a fixed entity. Members of the DMU may change as the decision-making process continues. Thus a managing director may be involved in the decision that new equipment should be purchased, but not in the decision as to which manufacturer to buy it from. Six roles have been identified in the structure of the DMU, as follows.[6]

1 *Initiators*: those who begin the purchase process, e.g. maintenance contracts.
2 *Users*: those who actually use the product, e.g. welders.
3 *Deciders*: those who have authority to select the supplier/model, e.g. production managers.
4 *Influencers*: those who provide information and add decision criteria throughout the process, e.g. accountants.
5 *Buyers*: those who have authority to execute the contractual arrangements, e.g. purchasing.
6 *Gatekeepers*: those who control the flow of information, e.g. secretaries who may allow or prevent access to a DMU member, or a buyer whose agreement must be sought before a supplier can contact other members of the DMU.

A key point to realize is that the DMU resides within the buying organization. External influences, such as the salespeople of supplying companies, are not therefore part of the DMU: a DMU is customer not supplier based. Consequently a decision-making unit is defined as a group of people within a buying organization who are involved in the buying decision.

For very important decisions the structure of the DMU will be complex, involving numerous people within the buying organization. The marketing task is to identify and reach the key members in order to convince them of the product's worth. Often communicating only to the purchasing officer will be insufficient, as this person may be only a minor influence on supplier choice. Relationship management (discussed later in this chapter) is of key importance in many organizational markets.

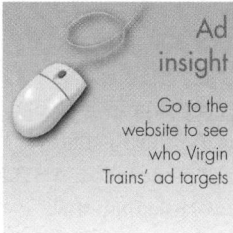

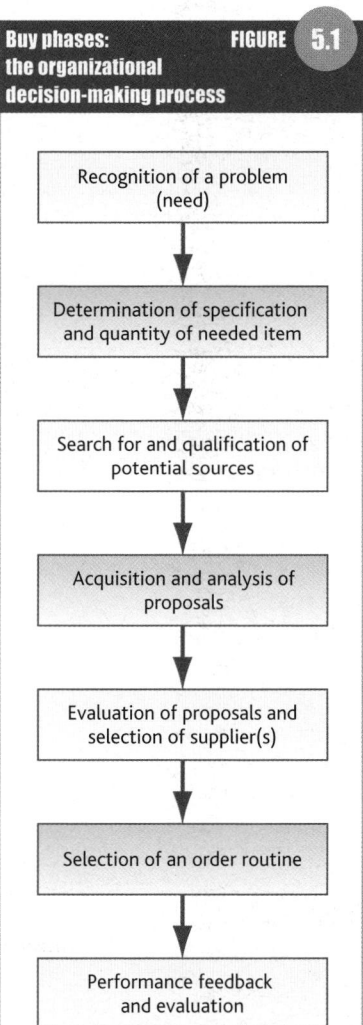

Buy phases: the organizational decision-making process FIGURE 5.1

- Recognition of a problem (need)
- Determination of specification and quantity of needed item
- Search for and qualification of potential sources
- Acquisition and analysis of proposals
- Evaluation of proposals and selection of supplier(s)
- Selection of an order routine
- Performance feedback and evaluation

When the problem to be solved is highly technical, suppliers may work with engineers in the buying organization in order to solve problems and secure the order. One example where this approach was highly successful involved a small company that won a large order from a major car company owing to its ability to work with the car company in solving the technical problems associated with the development of an exhaust gas recirculation valve.[7] In this case, the small company's policy was to work with the major company's engineers and to keep the purchasing department out of the decision until the last possible moment, by which time it alone would be qualified to supply the part.

Often, organizational purchases are made in committees where the salesperson will not be present. The salesperson's task is to identify a person from within the decision-making unit who is a positive advocate and champion of the supplier's product. This person (or 'coach') should be given all the information needed to win the arguments that may take place within the decision-making unit. For example, even though the advocate may be a technical person, he or she should be given the financial information that may be necessary to justify buying the most technologically superior product.

Where DMU members are inaccessible to salespeople, advertising, the Internet or direct marketing tools may be used as alternatives.

The relatively low cost of direct mail and e-mail campaigns makes them tempting alternatives to personal visits or telephone calls. Setting up a website can also be relatively inexpensive once the initial set-up costs have been met. However, wrongly targeted direct mail, a poorly designed website or a badly executed e-mail campaign can cause customer annoyance and tarnish the image of the company and brand. Business-to-business companies are turning to integrated marketing communications as a means of using the strengths of a variety of media to target business customers. Integrated marketing communications is a concept that sees companies coordinate their marketing communications tools to deliver a clear, consistent, credible and competitive message about the organization and its products. Marketing in Action 5.1 describes how Kone successfully used a combination of media to raise awareness of itself in the USA.

How they buy

Figure 5.1 describes the **decision-making process** for an organizational product.[8] The exact nature of the process will depend on the buying situation. In some situations some stages will be omitted. For example, in a routine rebuy situation the purchasing officer is unlikely to pass through the third, fourth and fifth stages (search for suppliers, and analysis and evaluation of their proposals). These stages will be bypassed, as the buyer, recognizing a need—perhaps shortage of stationery—routinely reorders from an existing supplier. In general, the more complex the decision and the more expensive the item, the more likely it is that each stage will be passed through and that the process will take more time.

Recognition of a problem (need)

Needs and problems may be recognized through either *internal or external factors*.[9] An example of an internal factor would be the realization of under-capacity leading to the decision to purchase plant or equipment. Thus, internal recognition leads to active behaviour (internal/active). Some problems that are recognized internally may not be acted upon. This condition may be termed internal/passive. A production manager may realize that there is a problem with a machine but, given more pressing problems, decide to put up with it.

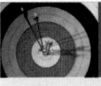

5.1 Marketing in Action

Integrated Marketing Communications at Kone

Although successful in Europe, Kone, the Finnish elevator company, had found the US market to be more challenging. But with its innovative EcoSpace (known as MonoSpace in Europe) elevator, the company believed it had the product to make a significant penetration. A key competitive advantage was its machine-roomless system, which eliminated the need for a space-consuming machine room by putting the hoisting mechanism in the shaft itself. This meant that the space could be used for alternative purposes. The system was also ecologically sound in that it did not use oil, and cut energy bills by up to 60 per cent. The problem was that Kone was not seen to be a major player in the US elevator market.

Using integrated marketing communications Kone targeted architects, as they specify and design elevators into their buildings and so were key decision-makers in the choice of elevators. The campaign began with a booth at the American Institute of Architects trade show and conference, to which 3500 AIA members were invited through a pre-show mailing. The mailer teased Kone's big promotion at the show—the prize of a Ford Escape hybrid car—linking to the EcoSpace's environmentally friendly credentials. The result was 1200 quality leads, which were followed up by Kone salespeople and engineers.

During one evening of the show, Kone hosted an editorial event to help establish relationships with major trade publications. This led to the EcoSpace system being featured in 17 articles following the show.

After the show, direct mail was used to reconnect to the original set of architects, and print advertising in architectural publications was used to convey the system's benefits. Interested readers were directed to www.myecospace.com for more detailed information on specifications, presentations and CAD drawings.

By coordinating direct mail, print advertising, trade show exhibiting, Internet, personal selling and promotion, Kane produced an integrated marketing communications campaign that by the end of the year had resulted in the EcoSpace becoming the basis of elevator design in 9 per cent of the architectural firms where it had qualified leads. As Kane's marketing director said, 'What was so successful was the combination of channels. This generated a tremendous response from architects.'

Based on: Bulik (2005)[10]

Other potential problems may not be recognized internally, and become problems only because of external cues. Production managers may be quite satisfied with their production process until they are made aware of another, more efficient, method.

Clearly, these different problems have important implications for marketing and sales. The internal/passive condition implies that there is an opportunity for a salesperson, having identified the condition, to highlight the problem by careful analysis of cost inefficiencies and other symptoms, so that the problem is perceived to be pressing and in need of solution (internal/active). The internal/active situation requires the supplier to demonstrate a differential advantage of its products over those of the competition. In this situation problem stimulation is unnecessary, but where internal recognition is absent, the marketer can provide the necessary external cues. A fork-lift truck sales representative might stimulate problem recognition by showing how the truck can save the customer money, due to lower maintenance costs, and lead to more efficient use of warehouse space through higher lifting capabilities. Advertising or direct mail could also be used to good effect. The Microsoft illustration shows how advertising was used to create awareness of its videoconferencing and instant messaging capabilities that can keep people on the move in touch.

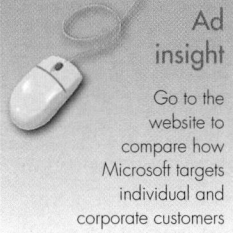

Ad insight

Go to the website to compare how Microsoft targets individual and corporate customers

▲ Microsoft creates awareness of its capability to keep employees in touch with one another.

Determination of specification and quantity of needed item

At this stage of the decision-making process the DMU will draw up a description of what is required. For example, it might decide that five lathes are required to meet certain specifications. The ability of marketers to influence the specification can give their company an advantage at later stages of the process. By persuading the buying company to specify features that only the marketer's own product possesses, the sale may be virtually closed at this stage. This is the process of setting up *lock-out criteria*. Marketing in Action 5.2 explains the powerful effect a lock-out criterion has had on the market for diesel locomotives.

Search for and qualification of potential sources

A great deal of variation in the degree of search takes place in industrial buying. Generally speaking, the cheaper and less important the item, and the more information the buyer possesses, the less search takes place. Marketers can use advertising to ensure that their brands are in the buyers' awareness set and are, therefore, considered when evaluating alternatives.

Acquisition and analysis of proposals

Having found a number of companies that, perhaps through their technical expertise and general reputation, are considered to be qualified to supply the product, proposals will be called for and analysis of them undertaken.

Evaluation of proposals and selection of supplier(s)

Each proposal will be evaluated in the light of the choice criteria deemed to be more important to each DMU member. It is important to realize that various members may use different criteria when judging proposals. Although this may cause problems, the outcome of this procedure is the selection of a supplier or suppliers.

Selection of an order routine

Next, the details of payment and delivery are drawn up. Usually this is conducted by the purchasing officer. In some buying decisions—when delivery is an important consideration in selecting a supplier—this stage is merged into the acquisition and evaluation stages.

Performance feedback and evaluation

This may be formal, where a purchasing department draws up an evaluation form for user departments to complete, or informal through everyday conversations.

The implications of all this are that sales and marketing strategy can affect a sale through influencing need recognition, through the design of product specifications, and by clearly

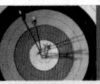

5.2 Marketing in Action

Diesel Lock-Out

The major player in the European diesel locomotive market is Electro-Motive Diesel, a former North American subsidiary of General Motors, which has sold 650 of its Class 66 diesel locomotives to European freight train operators since 1998. In the USA, however, GE is the market leader with about 70 per cent market share. This apparent paradox is explained by GE failing to meet a European lock-out criterion that does not apply in the USA. Until recently GE has not manufactured a locomotive small enough to pass under the low bridges and through the tunnels of the European rail system. EMD's Class 66 is able to fit on networks in nearly all of continental Europe and operates in 10 European countries.

This situation has now changed with the launch of GE's Powerhaul locomotive, which can fit the European system. Now that the lock-out criterion has been overcome, Powerhaul is threatening EMD's market share because, at the 'Evaluation of proposals and selection of supplier(s)' decision-making stage, it possesses competitive advantages on key choice criteria. One is technical (an ability to accelerate freight trains faster than the Class 66) and the other economic (better fuel economy). GE is now winning orders from European operators such as Freightliner, the UK's second-largest freight operator.

This story demonstrates the importance of lock-out criteria and shows how the nature of choice criteria can differ between Stages 2 and 5 of the organizational decision-making process.

Based on: Wright (2008)[11,12]

presenting the advantages of the product or service over that of competition in terms that are relevant to DMU members. By early involvement, a company can benefit through the process of *creeping commitment*, whereby the buying organization becomes increasingly committed to one supplier through its involvement in the process and the technical assistance it provides.

Choice criteria

This aspect of industrial buyer behaviour refers to the criteria used by members of the DMU to evaluate supplier proposals. These criteria are likely to be determined by the performance criteria used to evaluate the members themselves.[13] Thus purchasing managers who are judged by the extent to which they reduce purchase expenditure are likely to be more cost conscious than production engineers, who are evaluated in terms of the technical efficiency of the production process they design.

As with consumers, organizational buying is characterized by *technical, economic, social* (organizational) and *personal criteria*. Key considerations may be, for plant and equipment, return on investment, while for materials and components parts they may be cost savings, together with delivery reliability, quality and technical assistance. Because of the high costs associated with production downtime, a key concern of many purchasing departments is the long-run development of the organization's supply system. Personal factors may also be important, particularly when suppliers' product offerings are essentially similar. In this situation the final decision may rest upon the relative liking for the supplier's salesperson. The Xerox advertisement illustrates the importance of economic (pennies a page), technical (products to fit every need) and personal (rish reduction through the offer of a guarantee) choice criteria.

Customers' choice criteria can change in different regions of the world. For example, Xerox is generally known as a company that provides solutions for creating documents. In the West, when choosing a printer, a consumer considers the print quality and how easy the machine is to network and update. In eastern Europe other choice criteria prevail. Networking and servicing are not issues that are considered very much, rather value for money is the key. The consumer

smart color

Making office color affordable requires new thinking.
Like prints for just pennies a page, products to fit every need,
and a guarantee to ensure total satisfaction.
Xerox Color. It makes business sense.

▲ This Xerox advertisement addresses economic, technical and personal choice criteria.

attitude is: 'I can buy a Xerox, or I can buy a Canon and a car.' The marketing task for Xerox is to reduce the consumer's price sensitivity by stressing its reliability, quality, after-sales service, wide range of suppliers and medium-to long-term value for money.[14]

What are the range of motives that key players in organizations use to compare supplier offerings? Economic considerations play a part because commercial firms have profit objectives and work within budgetary constraints. Emotional factors should not be ignored, however, as decisions are made by people who do not suddenly lose their personalities, personal likes and dislikes and prejudices simply because they are at work. Let us examine a number of important technical and economic motives (quality, price and life-cycle costs, and continuity of supply) and then some organizational and personal factors (perceived risk, office politics, and personal liking/disliking).

Quality

The emergence of **total quality management** as a key aspect of organizational life reflects the important of quality in evaluating suppliers' products and services. Many buying organizations are unwilling to trade quality for price. For example, the success of Intel was not based on price but reliable, ever-faster microprocessors for PCs and servers.[15] In particular, buyers are looking for consistency of product or service quality so that end products (e.g. motor cars) are reliable, inspection costs are reduced and production processes run smoothly. They are installing just-in-time delivery systems, which rely upon incoming supplies being quality guaranteed.

Price and life-cycle costs

For materials and components of similar specification and quality, price becomes a key consideration. For standard items such as ball-bearings, price may be critical to making a sale given that a number of suppliers can meet delivery and specification requirements. The power of large buying organizations also means that they have the power to squeeze suppliers for tighter terms. For example, Marks & Spencer, in its drive to reduce costs, demanded a 10 per cent cut in all suppliers' prices.[16] Tesco, the UK supermarket chain, also demanded price cuts from 12 suppliers including Unilever after it found that they were giving better terms to Hit—a Polish supermarket chain with 12 stores—which Tesco had recently bought. However, it should not be forgotten that price is only one component of cost for many buying organizations. Increasingly buyers take into account **life-cycle costs**, which may include productivity savings, maintenance costs and residual values as well as initial purchase price when evaluating products. Marketers can use life-cycle costs analysis to break into an account. By calculating life-cycle costs with a buyer, new perceptions of value may be achieved.

Continuity of supply

Another major cost to a company is disruption of a production run. Delays of this kind can mean costly machine downtime and even lost sales. Continuity of supply is, therefore, a prime consideration in many purchase situations. Companies that perform badly on this criteria lose out even if the price is competitive because a small percentage price edge does not compare with the costs of unreliable delivery. Supplier companies that can guarantee deliveries and realize their promises can achieve a significant differential advantage in the marketplace. Organizational customers are demanding close relationships with *accredited suppliers* that can guarantee reliable supply, perhaps on a just-in-time basis.

Perceived risk

Perceived risk can come in two forms: *functional risk* such as uncertainty with respect to product or supplier performance, and *psychological risk* such as criticism from work colleagues.[17] This latter risk—fear of upsetting the boss, losing status, being ridiculed by others in the department, or, indeed, losing one's job—can play a determining role in purchase decisions. Buyers often reduce uncertainty by gathering information about competing suppliers, checking the opinions of important others in the buying company, buying only from familiar and/or reputable suppliers and by spreading risk through multiple sourcing. Mercedes reduces perceived risk by communicating its reputation, built over more than 100 years, which results in trucks that can be trusted (see illustration).

Office politics

Political factions within the buying company may also influence the outcome of a purchase decision. Interdepartmental conflict may manifest itself in the formation of competing camps over the purchase of a product or service. Because department X favours supplier 1, department Y automatically favours supplier 2. The outcome not only has purchasing implications but also political implications for the departments and individuals concerned.

▲ Mercedes reduces perceived risk in this advertisement for its trucks.
© Daimler AG. Kindly reproduced with the permission of Mercedes–Benz UK Ltd.

5.1 Pause for Thought

Imagine you are working for a company that is seeking to win a contract from an organization that has never bought from you before. You suspect that it may be reluctant to buy from you because of the risk of changing from its present suppliers to you. What might you do to reduce the perceived risk of change? Some suggestions are given later in this chapter.

Personal liking/disliking

A buyer may personally like one salesperson more than another and this may influence supplier choice, particularly when competing products are very similar. Even when supplier selection is on the basis of competitive bidding, it is known for purchasers to help salespeople they like to be competitive.[18] Obviously perception is important in all organizational purchases as how someone behaves depends upon the perception of the situation. One buyer may perceive a salesperson as being honest, truthful and likeable while another may not. As with consumer behaviour, three selective processes may be at work on buyers.

1 *Selective attention:* only certain information sources may be sought.
2 *Selective distortion:* information from those sources may be distorted.
3 *Selective retention:* only some information may be remembered.

In general, people tend to distort, avoid and forget messages that are substantially different to their existing beliefs and attitudes.

Implications

The implications of understanding the content of the decision are that appeals may need to change when communicating to different DMU members: discussion with a production engineer may centre on the technical superiority of the product offering, while much more emphasis on cost factors may prove effective when talking to the purchasing officer. Orange, the mobile phone operator, recognized the need to change communication when talking to different members of the DMU in business-to-business markets. When talking to information technologists Orange talks technology because that is what they expect. However, for non-technical people, such as accountants and users of the equipment, the message is kept much simpler and focuses on how more effective phone use can boost productivity.[19] Furthermore, the criteria used by buying organizations change over time as circumstances change. Price may be relatively unimportant to a company when trying to solve a highly visible technical problem, and the order will be placed with the supplier that provides the necessary technical assistance. Later, after the problem has been solved and other suppliers become qualified, price may be of crucial significance.

Influences on Organizational Buying Behaviour

Figure 5.2 shows the three factors that influence how organizations buy, who buys and the choice criteria they use: the product type, the buy class and the importance of purchase.[20]

The buy class

Organizational purchases may be distinguished between a new task, a straight rebuy and a modified rebuy.[21] A **new task** occurs when the need for the product has not arisen previously so that there is little or no relevant experience in the company, and a great deal of information is required. A **straight rebuy** occurs where an organization buys previously purchased items from suppliers already judged acceptable. Routine purchasing procedures are set up to

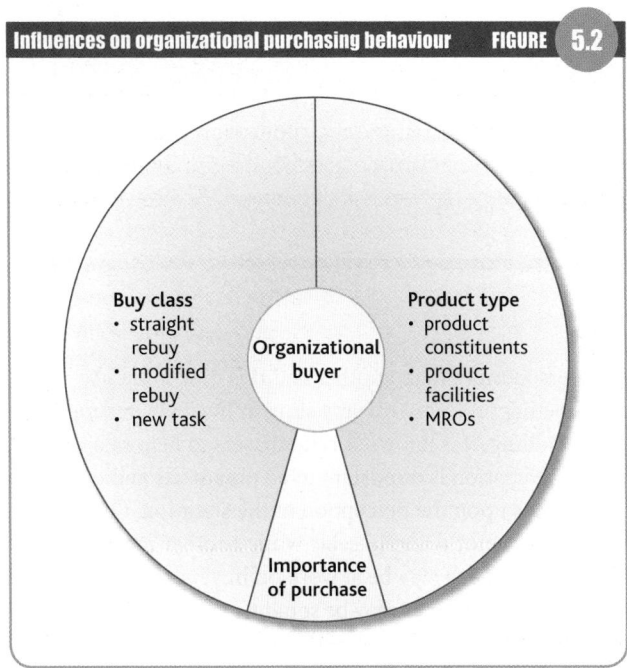

Influences on organizational purchasing behaviour   FIGURE 5.2

Buy class
- straight rebuy
- modified rebuy
- new task

Organizational buyer

Product type
- product constituents
- product facilities
- MROs

Importance of purchase

facilitate straight rebuys. The **modified rebuy** lies between the two extremes. A regular requirement for the type of product exists, and the buying alternatives are known, but sufficient change (e.g. a delivery problem) has occurred to require some alteration to the normal supply procedure.

The buy classes affect organizational buying in the following ways. First, the membership of the DMU changes. For a straight rebuy possibly only the purchasing officer is involved, whereas for a new buy senior management, engineers, production managers and purchasing officers may be involved. Modified rebuys often involve engineers, production managers and purchasing officers, but senior management, except when the purchase is critical to the company, is unlikely to be involved. Second, the decision making process may be much longer as the buy class changes from a straight rebuy to a modified rebuy and to a new task. Third, in terms of influencing DMU members, they are likely to be much more receptive to new task and modified rebuy situations than straight rebuys. In the latter case, the purchasing manager has already solved the purchasing problem and has other problems to deal with. So why make it a problem again?

The first implication of this buy class analysis is that there are big gains to be made if a company can enter the new task at the start of the decision-making process. By providing information and helping with any technical problems that can arise, the company may be able to create goodwill and creeping commitment, which secures the order when the final decision is made. The second implication is that since the decision process is likely to be long, and many people are involved in the new task, supplier companies need to invest heavily in sales personnel for a considerable period of time. Some firms employ missionary sales teams, comprising their best salespeople, to help secure big new-task orders.

Companies in straight rebuy situations must ensure that no change occurs when they are in the position of the supplier. Regular contact to ensure that the customer has no complaints may be necessary, and the buyer may be encouraged to use automatic reordering systems. For the out-supplier (i.e. a new potential supplier) the task can be difficult unless poor service or some other factor has caused the buyer to become dissatisfied with the present supplier. The obvious objective of the out-supplier in this situation is to change the buy class from a straight rebuy to a modified rebuy. Price alone may not be enough since changing supplier represents a large personal risk to the purchasing officer. The new supplier's products might be less reliable, and delivery might be unpredictable. In order to reduce this risk, the company may offer delivery guarantees with penalty clauses and be very willing to accept a small (perhaps uneconomic) order at first in order to gain a foothold. Supplier acquisition of a total quality management (TQM) standard such as EM29000, ISO9000 or BS5750 may also have the effect of reducing perceived buyer risk. Other tactics are the use of testimonials from satisfied customers, and demonstrations. Many straight rebuys are organized on a contract basis, and buyers may be more receptive to listening to non-suppliers prior to contract renewal.

Value analysis and life-cycle cost calculations are other methods of moving purchases from a straight rebuy to a modified rebuy situation. **Value analysis**, which can be conducted by either supplier or buyer, is a method of cost reduction in which components are examined to see if they can be made more cheaply. The items are studied to identify unnecessary costs that do not add to the reliability or functionality of the product. By redesigning, standardizing or manufacturing by less expensive means, a supplier may be able to offer a product of comparable quality at lower cost. Simple redesigns like changing a curved edge to a straight one may have dramatic cost implications.[22] Life-cycle cost analysis seeks to move the cost focus from the initial purchase price to the total cost of owning and using a product. There are three types of life-cycle costs: purchase price, start-up costs and post-purchase costs.[23] Start-up costs would include installation, lost production and training costs. Post-purchase costs include operating (e.g. fuel, operator wages), maintenance, repair and inventory costs. Against these costs would be placed residual values (e.g. trade-in values of cars). Life-cycle cost appeals can be powerful motivators. For example, if the out-supplier can convince the customer organization that its product has significantly lower post-purchase costs than the in-supplier's, despite a slightly higher purchase price, it may win the order. This is because it will be delivering a higher economic value to the customer. This can be a powerful competitive advantage and, at the same time, justify the premium price.

The product type

Products can be classified according to four types: materials, components, plant and equipment, and MROs (maintenance repair and operation), as follows:

1 materials to be used in the production process, e.g. aluminium
2 components to be incorporated in the finished product, e.g. headlights
3 plant and equipment, e.g. bulldozer
4 products and services for maintenance repair and operation (MRO), e.g. spanners, welding equipment and lubricants.

This classification is based upon a customer perspective—how the product is used—and may be employed to identify differences in organizational buyer behaviour. First, the people who take part in the decision-making process tend to change according to product type. For example, senior management tend to get involved in the purchase of plant and equipment or, occasionally, when new materials are purchased if the change is of fundamental importance to company operations, e.g. if a move from aluminium to plastic is being considered. Rarely do they involve themselves in component or MRO supply. Similarly, design engineers tend to be involved in buying components and materials but not normally MRO and plant equipment. Second, the decision-making process tends to be slower and more complex as product type moves from:

MRO → components → materials → plant and equipment

For MRO items, *blanket contracts* rather than periodic purchase orders are increasingly being used. The supplier agrees to resupply the buyer on agreed price terms over a period of time. Stock is held by the seller and orders are automatically printed out by the buyer's computer when stock falls below a minimum level. This has the advantage to the supplying company of effectively blocking the effort of the competitors for long periods of time.

Classification of suppliers' offerings by product type gives clues as to who is likely to be influenced in the purchase decision. The marketing task is then to confirm this in particular situations and attempt to reach those people involved. A company selling MROs is likely to be wasting effort attempting to communicate with design engineers, whereas attempts to reach operating management are likely to prove fruitful.

The importance of purchase

A purchase is likely to be perceived as being important to the buying organization when it involves large sums of money, when the cost of making the wrong decision, e.g. in production downtime, is high and when there is considerable uncertainty about the outcome of alternative offerings. In such situations, many people at different organizational levels are likely to be involved in the decision and the process will be long, with extensive search and analysis of information. Thus extensive marketing effort is likely to be required, but great opportunities present themselves to those sales teams that work with buying organizations to convince them that their offering has the best payoff; this may involve acceptance trials, e.g. private diesel manufacturers supply railway companies with prototypes for testing, engineering support and testimonials from other users. Additionally, guarantees of delivery dates and after-sales service may be necessary when buyer uncertainty regarding these factors is high. An example of the time and effort that may be required to win very important purchases is the order secured by GEC to supply £250 million worth of equipment for China's largest nuclear power station. The contract was won after six years of negotiation, 33 GEC missions to China and 4000 person-days of work.

Developments in Purchasing Practice

Several trends have taken place within the purchasing function that have marketing implications for supplier firms. The advent of just-in-time purchasing and the increased tendency towards centralized, online and systems purchasing, reverse marketing and leasing have all changed the nature of purchasing and altered the way in which suppliers compete.

Just-in-time purchasing

The just-in-time concept aims to minimize stocks by organizing a supply system that provides materials and components as they are required.[24] Stockholding costs are significantly reduced or eliminated, thus profits are increased. Furthermore, since the holding of stocks is a hedge against machine breakdowns, faulty parts and human error they may be seen as a cushion that acts as a disincentive to management to eliminate such inefficiencies.

A number of **just-in-time** (JIT) practices are also associated with improved quality. Suppliers are evaluated on their ability to provide high-quality products. The effect of this is that suppliers may place more emphasis on product quality. Buyers are encouraged to specify only essential product characteristics, which means that suppliers have more discretion in product design and manufacturing methods. Also, the emphasis is on the supplier certifying quality—which means that quality inspection at the buyer company is reduced and overall costs are minimized, since quality control at source is more effective than further down the supply chain.

The total effects of JIT can be enormous. Purchasing, inventory and inspection costs can be reduced, product design can be improved, delivery streamlined, production downtime reduced, and the quality of the finished item enhanced.

However, the implementation of JIT requires integration into both purchasing and production operations. Since the system requires the delivery of the exact amount of materials or components to the production line as they are required, delivery schedules must be very reliable and suppliers must be prepared to make deliveries on a regular basis, perhaps even daily. Lead times for ordering must be short and the number of defects very low. An attraction for suppliers is that it is usual for long-term purchasing agreements to be drawn up. The marketing implication of the JIT concept is that to be competitive in many industrial markets—for example, motor cars—suppliers must be able to meet the requirements of this fast-growing system.

An example of a company that employs just-in-time is the Nissan car assembly plant at Sunderland in the UK. Nissan has adopted what it terms synchronous supply: parts are delivered only minutes before they are needed. For example, carpets are delivered by Sommer Allibert, a French supplier, from its facility close to the Nissan assembly line in sequence for fitting to the correct model. Only 42 minutes elapse between the carpet being ordered and fitted to the car. The stockholding of carpets for the Nissan Micra is now only 10 minutes. Just-in-time practices do carry risks, however, if labour stability cannot be guaranteed. Renault discovered this to its cost when a strike at its engine and gearbox plant caused its entire French and Belgian car production lines to close in only 10 days.

Centralized purchasing

Where several operating units within a company have common requirements, and where there is an opportunity to strengthen a negotiating position by bulk buying, centralized purchasing is an attractive option. Centralization encourages purchasing specialists to concentrate their energies on a small group of products, thus enabling them to develop an extensive knowledge of cost factors and the operation of suppliers.[25] The move from local to centralized buying has important marketing implications. Localized buying tends to focus on short-term cost and profit considerations, whereas centralized purchasing places more emphasis on long-term supply relationships. Outside influences—for example, engineers—play a greater role in supplier choice in local purchasing organizations since less specialized buyers often lack the expertise and status to question the recommendations of technical people. The type of purchasing organization can therefore give clues to suppliers regarding the important people in the decision-making unit and their respective power positions.

Online purchasing

While many people relate the Internet to consumer online shopping, the reality is that business-to-business e-procurement is of a much greater size. Companies not only post their own websites on the Internet but also develop extranets for buyers to send out requests for bids to suppliers. Electronic marketplaces take many forms, as described below.[26]

- Catalogue sites: companies can order items through electronic catalogues.
- Vertical markets: companies buying industrial products such as steel, chemicals or plastic, or buying services such as logistics (distribution) or media can use specialized websites (called e-hubs). For instance, Plastics.com permits thousands of plastics buyers to search for the lowest prices from thousands of plastics sellers.
- Auction sites: suppliers can place industrial products on auction sites where purchasers can bid for them.
- Exchange (or spot) markets: many commodities are sold on electronic exchange markets where prices can change by the minute. CheMatch.com is a spot market for buyers and sellers of bulk chemicals such as benzine.
- Buying alliances: companies in the same market for products join together to gain bigger discounts on higher volumes.

For example, car manufacturers including General Motors, DaimlerChrysler, Ford, Renault-Nissan and Peugeot-Citroën have pooled their individual e-business procurement activities by standardizing the way in which purchases were made. The result is the Covisint online marketplace, which now accounts for between 15 and 25 per cent of all auto-maker purchasing.[27]

The main benefits of online purchasing are reduced buying costs, more rapid supply, the identification of new suppliers, the ability to share information between buyers and sellers, reduced paperwork, and closer working relationships between suppliers and customers. The savings from online purchasing can be huge. For example, United Technologies expected to pay around $25 million for an order for printed circuit boards. Through e-procurement the company attracted 34 bids from suppliers and paid $14 million, a saving of $10 million, or 40 per cent. However, the ability to source large numbers of suppliers and price quotes means that supplier–buyer loyalty may be eroded.

Systems purchasing

Systems purchasing is the desire by buyers to acquire complete systems rather than individual components. As noted in Chapter 1, this means, for example, that to sell door handles to a car company, a supplier must not only be able to sell a door system that includes door handles as well as locking and opening devices, but also have an expert knowledge of door technology and the ability to solve future problems. Some systems purchasing is based on the expectations of benefits a system can provide for a buyer over time, such as an operating chemical plant or telecommunications system.[28]

System sellers may take over responsibility for system provision previously operated by customers, such as inventory control, production control systems, IT and telecommunications networks. Each system sold comprises product and service components. Hardware, or product components, are physical or tangible products that perform a specific function within the system. Software, or service components, are the knowledge or intangible human efforts to solve customers' problems and perform activities needed to design, build, operate and maintain a system (e.g. telecommunications).[29]

System selling requires sellers to create value for customers by cutting costs and/or improving performance by developing innovative solutions that address the needs of business customers. It is widespread in capital goods industries such as IT, telecommunications and trains. For example, Alstom Transport, the train manufacturer, offers solutions for 'train availability', while Thales Training and Simulation, the flight simulator manufacturer, provides military customers with 'flight training solutions'. Such companies offer to design and integrate components into a system and provide services to operate and maintain the system during its life.[30]

Reverse marketing

The traditional view of marketing is that supplier firms will actively seek the requirements of customers and attempt to meet those needs better than the competition. This model places the initiative with the supplier. Purchasers could assume a passive dimension relying on their suppliers' sensitivity to their needs, and on technological capabilities to provide them with solutions to their problems. However, this trusting relationship is at odds with a new corporate purchasing situation that developed during the 1980s and is gaining momentum. Purchasing is taking on a more proactive, aggressive stance in acquiring the products and services needed to compete. This process, whereby the buyer attempts to persuade the supplier to provide exactly what the organization wants, is called **reverse marketing**.[31] ICI, an international supplier of chemicals, uses reverse marketing very effectively to target suppliers with a customized list of requirements concerning delivery times, delivery success rates and how often sales visits should occur. Figure 5.3 shows the difference between the traditional model and this new concept.

The essence of reverse marketing is that the purchaser takes the initiative in approaching new or existing suppliers and persuading them to meet their supply requirements. The implications of reverse marketing are that it may pose serious threats to in-suppliers that are not cooperative but offer major opportunities to responsive in- and out-suppliers. The growth of reverse marketing presents two key benefits to those suppliers willing to listen to the buyer's proposition and carefully consider its merits. First, it provides the opportunity to develop a stronger and longer-lasting relationship with the customer and, second, it may be a source of new product opportunities that may be developed to a broader customer base later on.

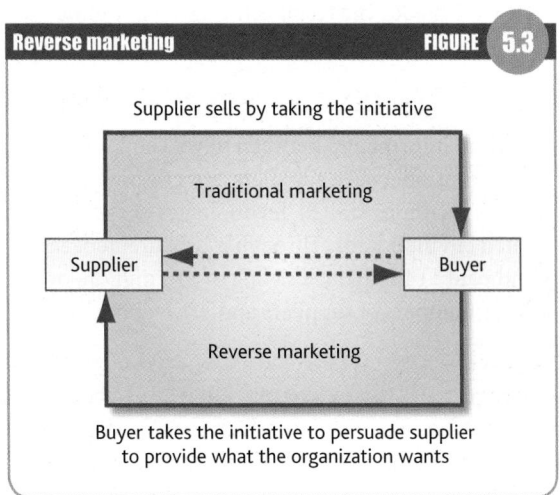

Reverse marketing FIGURE 5.3

Supplier sells by taking the initiative

Traditional marketing

Supplier ⇄ Buyer

Reverse marketing

Buyer takes the initiative to persuade supplier to provide what the organization wants

Leasing

A lease is a contract by which the owner of an asset (e.g. a car) grants the right to another party to use the asset for a period of time in exchange for payment of rent.[32] The benefits to the customer are that a leasing arrangement avoids the need to pay the cash purchase price of the product or service, is a hedge against fast product obsolescence, may have tax advantages, avoids the problem of equipment disposal and, with certain types of leasing contract, avoids some maintenance costs. These benefits need to be weighed against the costs of leasing, which may be higher than outright buying.

There are two main types of leases: financial (or full payment) leases and operating leases (sometimes called rental agreements). A *financial lease* is a longer-term arrangement that is fully amortized over the term of the contract. Lease payments, in total, usually exceed the purchase price of the item. The terms and conditions of the lease vary according to convention and competitive conditions. Sometimes the supplier will agree to pay maintenance costs over the leasing period. This is common when leasing photocopiers, for example. The lessee may also be given the option of buying the equipment at the end of the period. An *operating lease* is for a shorter period of time, is cancellable and is not completely amortized.[33] Operating lease rates are usually higher than financial lease rates since they run for a shorter term. When equipment is required intermittently this form of acquisition can be attractive because it avoids the need to let plant lie idle. Many types of equipment, such as diggers, bulldozers and skips, may be available for short-term hire, as may storage facilities.

Leasing may be advantageous to suppliers because it provides customer benefits that may differentiate product and service offerings. As such it may attract customers who might otherwise find the product unaffordable or uneconomic. The importance of leasing in such industries as cars, photocopiers and data processing has led an increasing number of companies to employ leasing consultants to work with customers on leasing arrangements and benefits. A crucial marketing decision is the setting of leasing rates. These should be set with the following factors in mind:

1   the desired relative attractiveness of leasing vs buying (the supplier may wish to promote/discourage buying compared with leasing)
2   the net present value of lease payments vs outright purchase
3   the tax advantages of leasing vs buying to the customer
4   the rates being charged by competitors
5   the perceived advantages of spreading payments to customers
6   any other perceived customer benefits, e.g. maintenance and insurance costs being assumed by the supplier.

Relationship Management

Four types of relationship have been identified.[34] The first two are market relationships between suppliers and customers. They make up the core of relationship marketing and are externally orientated. The first of these is classic market relationships concerning supplier–customer, supplier–customer–competitor and the physical distribution network. These types of relationship are discussed in this chapter. The second type is special market relationships such as the customer as a member of a loyalty programme and the interaction in the service encounter. These are examined in the direct marketing and marketing services chapters (Chapters 15 and 22).

The third type of relationship is the mega-relationship, and concerns the economy and society in general. Examples of such relationships are mega-marketing (lobbying, public opinion and political power), mega-alliances (the European Union, which forms a stage for marketing) and social relationships (friendships and ethnic bonds). These issues are covered in the marketing environment and consumer behaviour chapters (Chapters 4 and 5). Finally, nano-relationships concern the internal operations of an organization, such as relationships between internal customers, internal markets, divisions and business areas inside organizations. Such relationships are discussed within the managing products (portfolio planning) and marketing implementation organization and control chapters (Chapters 10 and 21).

Managing relationships is a key ingredient in successful organizational marketing. **Relationship marketing** concerns the shifting from activities of attracting customers to activities concerned with current customers and how to retain them. Customer retention is critical since small changes in retention rates have significant effects on future revenues.[35] At its core is the maintenance of relations between a company and its suppliers, channel intermediaries, the public and its customers.

The key idea is to create customer loyalty so that a stable, mutually profitable and long-term relationship is developed.[36] The idea of relationship marketing implies at least two essential conditions. First, a relationship is a mutually rewarding connection between the parties so that they expect to obtain benefits from it. Second, the parties have a commitment to the relationship over time and are, therefore, willing to make adaptations to their own behaviour to maintain its continuity.[37] An absolutely central feature of relationship marketing is the role that trust plays in creating satisfaction between parties in the relationship. Building trust is a very effective way to increase satisfaction and commitment to long-term relationships.[38] It can also help weaker partners in a business relationship to gain power over time in their dealings with more powerful companies.[39]

5.2 Pause for Thought

What might suppliers do in order to build strong relationships with buying organizations?

Applying ethical standards to relationships with business partners can also assist in relationship building and improve the reputation of whole business networks.[40]

The discussion of reverse marketing has given examples of buyers adopting a proactive stance in their dealings with suppliers, and has introduced the importance of buyer–seller relationships in marketing between organizations. The Industrial Marketing and Purchasing Group developed the **interaction approach** to explain the complexity of buyer–seller relationships.[41] This approach views these relationships as taking place between two active parties. Thus reverse marketing is one manifestation of the interaction perspective. Both parties may be involved in adaptations to their own process or product technologies to accommodate each other, and changes in the activities of one party are unlikely without consideration of or consultation with the other party. For example, Airbus consulted FedEx about the design of the A380 cargo plane so that it met the latter's requirement for delivering parcels and other goods.[42]

In such circumstances a key objective of business-to-business markets will be to manage customer relationships. This means considering not only formal organizational arrangements such as the use of distributors, salespeople and sales subsidiaries, but also the informal network consisting of the personal contacts and relationships between supplier and customer staff. Marks & Spencer's senior directors meet the boards of each of its major suppliers twice a year for frank discussions. When Marks & Spencer personnel visit a supplier it is referred to as a 'royal visit'. Factories may be repainted, new uniforms issued and machinery cleaned: this reflects the exacting standards that the company demands from its suppliers and the power it wields in its relationship with them.[43]

The development of technology is facilitating the improvement of buyer–seller relationships. Developments in the use of the Internet to strengthen such relationships are gathering pace. Digital Marketing 5.1 describes one such development. Another example is Cisco, the network router and switches manufacturer, which exploits technology to improve the management of customer relationships. Features of its system include an online customer enquiry and order placement system that handles over 80 per cent of all orders, a website that allows customers to configure and price their router, and an online customer care service.

 **5.1 Digital Marketing**

UPS Widget

UPS's main global business of moving and delivering goods was under attack from existing and new competitors, from the likes of FedEx and DHL to smaller players. This led to a fragmented market where it was difficult for business customers to distinguish between providers.

To counter this lack of advantage, UPS created the UPS widget. Knowing that their core B2B audience was busy dispatch managers, personal assistants and SME owners (segmented as 'Expert Shippers'), UPS was aware that shipping was a dull but important exercise for these people but also one of many other tasks that they had to do.

UPS created the UPS widget to generate some warmth and to increase interaction with the B2B site. It built a microsite and downloadable application (the UPS widget) that allowed direct access to UPS services. Initially launched across western Europe, the widget rehumanized the face of UPS, causing existing and new clients to engage more with the brand. The desktop widget is designed to keep the brand 'top of mind', to encourage exploration of UPS services and, along with the microsite, to act as a barrier to switching to other companies. Overall, the UPS widget was downloaded to nearly 120,000 business computers. UPS now plans to launch the widget across the rest of Europe and parts of South-east Asia.

Useful link: www.widget.ups.com

A key aspect of the work of the IMP group is an understanding of how relationships are established and developed over time. Ford[44] has modelled the development of buyer–seller relationships as a five-stage process (see Fig. 5.4).

Stage 1: the pre-relationship stage

Something has caused the customer to evaluate a potential new supplier. Perhaps a price rise or a decline in service standards of the current supplier has triggered the need to consider a change. The customer will be concerned about the perceived risk of change and the distance that is perceived to exist between itself and the potential supplier. Distance has five dimensions, as follows.

1 *Social distance*: the extent to which both the individuals and organizations in a relationship are unfamiliar with each other's ways of working.
2 *Cultural distance*: the degree to which the norms and values, or working methods, between two companies differ because of their separate national characteristics.
3 *Technological distance*: the differences between the two companies' product and process technologies.
4 *Time distance*: the time that must elapse between establishing contact or placing an order, and the actual transfer of the product or service involved.
5 *Geographical distance*: the physical distance between the two companies.

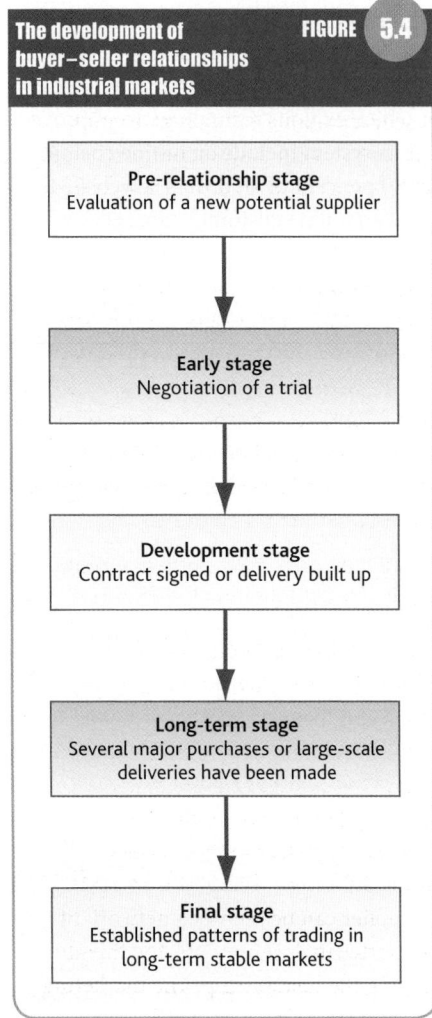

The development of buyer–seller relationships in industrial markets   FIGURE 5.4

Pre-relationship stage
Evaluation of a new potential supplier

Early stage
Negotiation of a trial

Development stage
Contract signed or delivery built up

Long-term stage
Several major purchases or large-scale deliveries have been made

Final stage
Established patterns of trading in long-term stable markets

Stage 2: the early stage

At this stage, potential suppliers are in contact with buyers to negotiate trial deliveries for frequently purchased supplies or components, or to develop a specification for a capital good purchase. Much uncertainty will exist and the supplier will be working to reduce perceived risk of change. The reputation of the potential supplier is likely to be important and the lack of social relationships may mean a lack of trust on the part of both supplier and buyer. The supplier may believe that it is being used as a source of information and that the buyer has no intention of placing an order. The buyer may fear that the supplier is promising things it cannot deliver in order to make a sale. Both companies will have little or no evidence on which to judge their partner's commitment to the relationship.

Stage 3: the development stage

This stage occurs as deliveries of frequently purchased products increase, or after contract signing for major capital purchases. The development stage is marked by increasing experience between the companies of the operations of each other's organizations, and greater knowledge of each other's norms and values. As this occurs, uncertainty and distance reduce. A key element in the evaluation of a supplier or customer at this stage of their relationship depends on perceptions of the degree of commitment to its development. Commitment can be shown by:

- reducing social distance through familiarization with each other's way of working
- making formal adaptations that are contractually agreed methods of meeting the needs of the other company by incurring costs or by management involvement
- making informal adaptations beyond the terms of the contract to cope with particular issues and problems that arise as the relationship develops.

This stage is characterized by an increasing level of business between the companies. Many of the difficulties experienced in the early stages of the relationship are overcome through the processes at work in the development stage.

Stage 4: the long-term stage

By this stage both companies share mutual dependence. It is reached after large-scale deliveries of continuously purchased products have occurred, or after several purchases of major capital products. Experience of the operations of each party and trust are high, with the accompanying low levels of uncertainty and distance. The reduction in uncertainty can cause problems in that routine ways of dealing with the partner may cease to be questioned by this stage. This can happen even though these routines may no longer relate well to either party's needs. This is called 'institutionalization'. For example, the seller may be providing greater product variety (and incurring higher production costs) than the buyer really needs. Since no one questions the arrangements, these inefficiencies continue. Institutionalized practices may make a supplier appear less responsive to a customer or exploit the customer by taking advantage of its lack of awareness of changes in market conditions (for example, by not passing on cost savings) or by accepting annual price rises without question. Strong personal relationships will have developed between individuals in the two companies and mutual problem-solving and informal adaptations will occur. In extreme cases, problems arising from 'side changing' can arise where individuals act in the interests of the other company and against their own on the strength of their personal allegiances.

Extensive formal adaptations resulting from successive contracts and agreements narrow the technological distance between the companies. Close integration of the operations of the companies is motivated by cost reductions and increased control of the other partner. For example, automatic reordering systems based on information technology may act as a barrier to the entry of other supplier companies.

Commitment to the relationship will have been shown by the extensive adaptations that have occurred. However, the supplier has to be aware of two difficulties. First, the need to demonstrate commitment to a customer must be balanced by the danger of becoming too dependent on that customer. The supplier may feel the need to make the customer feel it is important yet does not wield too much power in the relationship. Second, there is a danger that the customer's perception of a supplier's commitment to the relationship is lower than it actually is. This is because the peak of investment of resources has taken place before the long-term stage has been reached. And so, ironically, when a supplier is at its most committed to a long-term and important customer, it may appear less committed than during the development stage.

Stage 5: the final stage

This stage is reached in stable markets over long time periods. The institutionalization process that started during the long-term stage continues to the point where the conduct of business may be based upon industry codes of practice. These may stipulate the 'right way to do business', such as the avoidance of price cutting. Often, attempts to break out of institutionalized patterns of trading will be met by sanctions from other trading partners.

This model of how buyer–seller relationships develop highlights some of the dangers that can occur during the process. Furthermore, suppliers can segment their customers according to the stage of development. Each stage requires differing actions based on the differing requirements of customers. The market for a supplier can be seen as a network of relationships. Each must be assessed according to the opportunity it represents, the threats posed by competitive challenges and the costs of developing the relationship. The marketing task is the establishment, development and maintenance of these relationships. They also need to be managed strategically. Decisions need to be made regarding the relative importance of a portfolio of relationships, and resources allocated to each of them based on their stage of development and likely return.

The reality of organizational marketing is that many suppliers and buying organizations have been conducting business between themselves for many years. Marks & Spencer has trading relationships with suppliers that stretch back almost 100 years. Such long-term relationships can have significant advantages for both buyer and seller. Risk is reduced for buyers as they get to know people in the supplier organization, and know whom to contact when problems arise. Communication is thus improved and joint problem-solving and design management can take place. Sellers gain through closer knowledge of buyer requirements, and by gaining the trust of the buyer an effective barrier to entry for competing firms may be established. New product development can benefit from such close relationships. The development of machine-washable lambs' wool fabrics and easy-iron cotton shirts came about because of Marks & Spencer's close relationship with UK manufacturers.[45]

Closer relationships in organizational markets are inevitable as changing technology, shorter product life cycles and increased foreign competition places marketing and purchasing departments in key strategic roles. Buyers are increasingly treating trusted suppliers as *strategic partners*, sharing information and drawing on their expertise when developing cost-efficient, quality-based new products. The marketing implication is that successful organizational marketing is more than the traditional manipulation of the 4-Ps (product, price, promotion and place). Its foundation rests upon the skilful handling of customer relationships. This had led some companies to appoint customer relationship managers to oversee the partnership and act in a communicational and coordinated role to ensure customer satisfaction. Still more companies have reorganized their salesforces to reflect the importance of managing key customer relationships effectively. This process is called key or national account management. It should be noted, however, that strategic partnerships and key/national account management may not be suitable for all companies. For example, small companies may not be able to afford the resources necessary to make such processes work.[46]

The term 'national account' is generally used to refer to large and important customers that may have centralized purchasing departments that buy or coordinate buying for decentralized, geographically dispersed business units. Selling to such firms involves:

- obtaining acceptance of the company's products at the buyer's headquarters
- negotiating long-term supply contracts
- maintaining favourable buyer–seller relationships at various levels in the buying organization
- establishing first-class customer service.

This depth of selling activity frequently calls for the expertise of a range of personnel in the supplying company in addition to the salesperson. It is for this reason that many companies serving national accounts employ team selling.

Team selling involves the combined efforts of salespeople, product specialists, engineers, sales managers and even directors if the buyer's decision-making unit includes personnel of equivalent rank. Team selling provides a method of responding to the various commercial, technical and psychological requirements of large buying organizations. Such cross-functional selling teams have the ability to increase an organization's competitive advantage, and are employed by such companies as Bayer, Procter & Gamble, Xerox, ABB and Kraft Foods.[47]

Companies are increasingly structuring both external and internal staff on the basis of specific responsibility for accounts. Examples of such companies are those in the electronics industry, where internal desk staff are teamed up with outside staff around key customers. An in-depth understanding of the buyer's decision-making unit is developed by the salesperson being able to develop a relationship with a large number of individual decision-makers. In this way, marketing staff can be kept informed of customer requirements, enabling them to improve products and services, and plan effective communications.

Where companies offer similar high levels of product quality, the quality of an ongoing relationship becomes a means of gaining a competitive advantage. Putting resources into the development and continuation of a relationship with customers is most appropriate where purchases involve a high level of risk, where a stream of product and service benefits is produced and consumed over a period of time or where the costs associated with repeat purchase can be reduced by close relationships.[48] The success of the German machine tool industry is attributable not only to excellent product quality but also its capability and willingness to engage in long-term relationship building through first-rate after-sales service.[49]

How to Build Relationships

A key decision that marketers have to make is the degree of effort to put into relationship building.[50] Some organizations' customers may desire more distant contact because they prefer to buy on price and do not perceive major benefits accruing to closer ties. A supplier that attempts a relationship-building programme may be wasting resources in this situation, However, in most situations there is some potential benefit to be gained from relationship development. Indeed, as Marketing in Action 5.3 describes, there has been a movement towards the establishment of buyer–supplier partnerships and a concomitant reduction in the number of accredited suppliers.

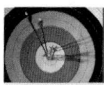

5.3 Marketing in Action

Business-to-Business Relationships

The ability to blend technology with customer requirements is an important success factor for many business-to-business companies, but managing customer relationships is also critical. Increasingly, suppliers have been focusing on improving customer relationships as a method of differentiating themselves from their rivals. To do so they must recognize and take advantage of changes in the environment that have an impact on such relationships. For example, new technology is facilitating electronic business-to-business commerce by allowing much easier and cheaper communications between companies. Web services technology provides a powerful glue that unifies databases and applications across organizations into a single smart information system. Dell Computers Corporation, for example, has saved over £150 million by using web services to improve coordination between its factories and its parts suppliers. Inventories have been significantly reduced and speed of delivery accelerated.

A key trend is the move for buyers to treat trusted suppliers as strategic partners. This can lead to the joint development of products and a lowering of costs and prices, and can act as a strong barrier to entry for competitors. Fiat and the technology-driven car component supplier Bosch not only collaborate on brake systems research but hold joint training courses for employees and engage in common communication campaigns. In the car industry strategic partners jointly develop product—for example, door systems. Process improvements were realized by Honda, which co-located some of its technical experts to the site of a supplier, leading to reduced manufacturing costs for the supplier and lower prices for Honda. When an outside supplier offers lower costs, higher quality or even more advanced technology, companies such as Honda, Toyota and DaimlerChrysler will work with their current strategic partners, giving them the opportunity to match or exceed the offer within a given time frame, which can be as long as 18–24 months.

Chosen suppliers are left in no doubt about the standards expected of them. Toyota, for example, has set up technology help teams to assist suppliers' understanding of what its requirements are and how to meet them. Peugeot and Renault run joint audits to maintain quality with their strategic partners.

The trend towards strategic partnerships is mirrored in the reduction in the number of suppliers. For example, Rank Xerox reduced its number of suppliers from 5000 to 500 when it found that it used nine times more suppliers than Japanese rivals like Canon.

Lean and flexible manufacturing has also meant changes in buyer–seller relationships. The maturing of the market for high-tech products such as video recorders has meant that production and delivery processes can be stabilized, with resultant cost savings. Sony UK, for example, replaced the practice of keeping a month's supply of stock with a 48-hour ordering system, and reduced by two-thirds the time taken to assemble a video recorder. Lean production requires product cycles to be long to allow integration of production processes and coordination among component suppliers, but marketing benefits can accrue. Sony UK had problems in the past when a particular colour television set had sold out. With shorter production times and fast parts supply, however, Sony can now quickly change its production plans to counter such occurrences.

Just-in-time manufacturing was once seen as a Japanese innovation, which gave that country's car manufacturers a competitive edge. Now 'supplier parks'—where component makers are grouped around car plants—are commonplace worldwide, reducing delivery costs and giving the geographical proximity that aids the building of buyer–seller relationships.

Based on: Henke (2000);[51] Hayward (2002);[52] Ploetner and Ehret (2006)[53]

Some features of close partnership relationships are that the parties adapt their processes and products to achieve a better match with each other, and share information and experience, which reduces insecurity and uncertainty. Sharing information and experience demonstrates commitment, leading to trust and a better atmosphere for future business.[54]

Some companies are using the Internet to allow their customers to share information. For example, John Deere, the agricultural machinery manufacturer, has promoted virtual communities among farmers with similar interests.[55]

Effective relationship building is a means to competitive advantage and is especially powerful since it is embedded within the culture of the organization and is therefore difficult for competitors to copy.[56] A relationship-orientated culture is, therefore, necessary for the successful implementation of the following range of customer services, which can be provided by a supplier—at zero or nominal cost to the customer—with the aim of helping the latter to carry out its operations.

Technical support

This can take the form of research and development cooperation, before-sales or after-sales service, and providing training to the customer's staff. The supplier is thus enhancing the customer's know-how and productivity.

Expertise

Suppliers can provide expertise to their customers. Examples include the offer of design and engineering consultancies, and dual selling, where the customer's salesforce is supplemented by the supplier. The customer benefits through acquiring extra skills at low cost.

Resource support

Suppliers can support the resource base of customers by extending credit facilities, giving low-interest loans, agreeing to cooperative promotion and accepting reciprocal buying practices where the supplier agrees to buy goods from the customer. The net effect of all of these activities is a reduced financial burden for the customer.

Service levels

Suppliers can improve their relationships with customers by improving the level of service offered to them. This can involve providing more reliable delivery, fast or just-in-time delivery, setting up computerized reorder systems, offering fast, accurate quotes and reducing defect levels. In so doing the customer gains by lower inventory costs, smoother production runs and lower warranty costs. By creating systems that link the customer to the supplier—for example, through recorder systems or just-in-time delivery—*switching costs* may be built in, making it more expensive to change supplier.[57]

Advances in technology are providing opportunities to improve service levels. The use of electronic data interchange (EDI) and the Internet offers the potential to enhance service provision.

Risk reduction

This may involve free demonstrations, the offer of products for trial at zero or low cost to the customer, product and delivery guarantees, preventative maintenance contracts, swift complaint handling and proactive follow-ups. These activities are designed to provide customers with reassurance.

Online
LearningCentre

When you have read this chapter

log on to the Online Learning Centre at www.mcgraw-hill.co.uk/ textbooks/jobber to explore chapter-by-chapter test questions, links and further online study tools for marketing.

Review

1. **The characteristics of organizational buying**
   - The characteristics are based on the nature and size of customers, the complexity of buying, the use of economic and technical choice criteria, the risky nature of selling and buying, buying to specific requirements, reciprocal buying, derived demand and negotiations.

2. **The dimensions of organizational buying**
   - The dimensions are who buys, how they buy, the choice criteria used, and where and when they buy.

3. **The nature and marketing implications of who buys, how organizations buy and the choice criteria used to evaluate products**
   - Who buys: there are six roles in the decision-making unit—initiators, users, deciders, influencers, buyers and gatekeepers. Marketers need to identify who plays each role, target communication at them and develop products to satisfy their needs.
   - How organizations buy: the decision-making process has up to seven stages—recognition of problem (need), determination of specification and quantity of needed item, search for and qualification of potential sources, acquisition and analysis of proposals, evaluation of proposals and selection of supplier(s), selection of an order routine, and performance feedback and evaluation. Marketers can influence need recognition and gain competitive advantage by entering the process early.
   - Choice criteria can be technical, economic, social (organizational) and personal. Marketers need to understand the choice criteria of the different members of the decision-making unit and target communications accordingly. Other marketing mix decisions such as product design will also depend on an understanding of choice criteria. Choice criteria can change over time necessitating a change in the marketing mix.

4. **The influences on organizational buying behaviour—the buy class, product type and purchase importance—and their marketing implications**
   - The buy class consists of three types: new task, straight rebuy and modified rebuy. For new task, there can be large gains for suppliers entering the decision process early, but heavy investment is usually needed. For straight rebuys, the in-supplier should build a defensible position to keep out new potential suppliers. For out-suppliers, a key task is to reduce the risk of change for the buyers so that a modified rebuy will result.
   - Product types consist of materials, components, plant and equipment, and maintenance items. Marketers need to recognize that the people who take part in the purchase decision usually change according to product type, and channel communications accordingly.
   - The importance of purchase depends on the costs involved and the uncertainty (risk) regarding the decision. For very important decisions, heavy investment is likely to be required on the part of suppliers, and risk-reduction strategies (e.g. guarantees) may be needed to reduce uncertainty.

5. **The developments in purchasing practice: just-in-time and centralized purchasing, reverse marketing and leasing**
   - Just-in-time practices aim to minimize stocks by organizing a supply system that provides materials and components as they are required. Potential gains are reduced purchasing, inventory and inspection costs, improved product design, streamlined delivery, reduced production downtime and improved quality.
   - Centralized purchasing encourages purchasing specialists to concentrate on a small group of products. This often increases the power of the purchasing department and results in a move to long-term relationships with suppliers.
   - Reverse marketing places the initiative with the buyer, who attempts to persuade the supplier to produce exactly what the buyer wants. Suppliers need to be responsive to buyers and provide them with an opportunity to build long-term relationships and develop new products.
   - Leasing may give financial benefits to customers and may attract customers that otherwise could not afford the product.

6   **The nature of relationship marketing and how to build customer relationships**

- Relationship marketing concerns the shift from activities associated with attracting customers to activities concerned with current customers and how to retain them. A key element is the building of trust between buyers and sellers.
- Relationship building can be enhanced by the provision of customer services including giving technical support, expertise, resource support, improving service levels and using risk-reduction strategies.

7   **The development of buyer–seller relationships**

- Relationships are established and developed through a five-stage process: pre-relationship stage, early stage, development stage, long-term stage and final stage.
- The pre-relationship stage is characterized by customer concern about the risk of change and the distance between itself and the potential supplier.
- The early stage is characterized by potential suppliers attempting to reduce risk of change and to build trust.
- The development stage is characterized by the reduction of uncertainty and distance.
- The long-term stage is characterized by shared mutual dependence and high levels of commitment.
- The final stage is characterized by industry codes of practice that stipulate 'the right way to do business'. Processes have become 'institutionalized'.
- Each stage requires different actions by suppliers based on the different requirements of customers.

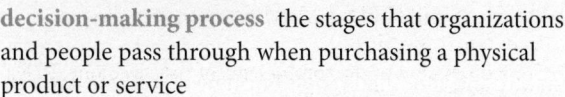

Key Terms

decision-making process the stages that organizations and people pass through when purchasing a physical product or service

decision-making unit (DMU) a group of people within an organization who are involved in the buying decision (also known as the buying centre)

interaction approach an approach to buyer–seller relations that treats the relationships as taking place between two active parties

just-in-time (JIT) this concept aims to minimize stocks by organizing a supply system that provides materials and components as they are required

life-cycle costs all the components of costs associated with buying, owning and using a physical product or service

modified rebuy where a regular requirement for the type of product exists and the buying alternatives are known but sufficient change (e.g. a delivery problem) has occurred to require some alteration to the normal supply procedure

new task refers to the first time purchase of a product or input by an organization

relationship marketing the process of creating, maintaining and enhancing strong relationships with customers and other stakeholders

reverse marketing the process whereby the buyer attempts to persuade the supplier to provide exactly what the organization wants

straight rebuy refers to a purchase by an organization from a previously approved supplier of a previously purchased item

team selling the use of the combined efforts of salespeople, product specialists, engineers, sales managers and even directors to sell products

total quality management the set of programmes designed to constantly improve the quality of physical products, services and processes

value analysis a method of cost reduction in which components are examined to see if they can be made more cheaply

Study Questions

1. What are the six roles that form the decision-making unit (DMU) for the purchase of an organizational purchase? What are the marketing implications of the DMU?

2. Why do the choice criteria used by different members of the DMU often change with the varying roles?

3. What are creeping commitment and lockout criteria? Why are they important factors in the choice of supplier?

4. Explain the difference between a straight rebuy, a modified rebuy and a new task purchasing situation. What implications do these concepts have for the marketing of industrial products?

5. Why is relationship management important in many supplier–customer interactions? How can suppliers build close relationships with organizational customers?

6. Explain the meaning of reverse marketing. What implications does it have for suppliers?

References

1. Naughton, J. (2005) Is Apple Right to Cosy up to the Enemy?, *Observer*, 12 June, 6.
2. Corey, E. R. (1991) *Industrial Marketing: Cases and Concepts*, Englewood Cliffs, NJ: Prentice-Hall.
3. Jobber, D. and G. Lancaster (2009) *Selling and Sales Management*, London: Pitman, 27.
4. Wray, R. (2008) Second Contractor Drops Out of £12bn NHS Computer Upgrade, *Guardian*, 29 May, 26.
5. Bishop, W. S., J. L. Graham and M. H. Jones (1984) Volatility of Derived Demand in Industrial Markets and its Management Implications, *Journal of Marketing*, Fall, 95–103.
6. Webster, F. E. and Y. Wind (1972) *Organizational Buying Behaviour*, Englewood Cliffs, NJ: Prentice-Hall, 78–80. The sixth role of initiator was added by Bonoma, T. V. (1982) Major Sales: Who Really does the Buying, *Harvard Business Review*, May–June, 111–19.
7. Cline, C. E. and B. P. Shapiro (1978) *Cumberland Metal Industries (A): Case Study*, Boston, Mass: Harvard Business School.
8. Robinson, P. J., C. W. Faris and Y. Wind (1967) *Industrial Buying and Creative Marketing*, Boston, Mass: Allyn & Bacon.
9. Jobber and Lancaster (2009) op. cit., 35.
10. Bulik, B. S. (2005) Success Story 3: Kone Corp, B to B Special Report, btobonline.com, 8 August, 32.
11. Wright, R. (2008) GE Challenges EMD Dominance, *Financial Times*, 23 September, 29.
12. Wright, R. (2008) EMD Fighting to Regain Ground, *Financial Times*, Rail Industry Special Report, 23 September, 3.
13. Draper, A. (1994) Organisational Buyers as Workers: The Key to their Behaviour, *European Journal of Marketing* 28(11), 50–62.
14. Parker, D. (1996) The X Files, *Marketing Week*, 8 March, 73–4.
15. Edwards, C. (2006) Inside Intel, *Business Week*, 9 January, 43–8.
16. Walsh, F. (2006) M&S Tightens Screw on Suppliers, *Guardian*, 4 March, 27.
17. For a discussion of the components of risk see Stone, R. N. and K. Gronhaug (1993) Perceived Risk: Further Considerations for the Marketing Discipline, *European Journal of Marketing* 27(3), 39–50.
18. Jobber, D. (1994) What Makes Organisations Buy, in Hart, N. (ed.) *Effective Industrial Marketing*, London: Kogan Page, 100–18.
19. Mazur, L. (2002) Increasing Momentum, *Marketing Business*, June, 16–19.
20. Cardozo, R. N. (1980) Situational Segmentation of Industrial Markets, *European Journal of Marketing* 14(5/6), 264–76.
21. Robinson, Faris and Wind (1967) op. cit.
22. Lee, L. and D. W. Dobler (1977) *Purchasing and Materials Management: Text and Cases*, New York: McGraw-Hill, 265.
23. Forbis, J. L. and N. T. Mehta (1981) Value-Based Strategies for Industrial Products, *Business Horizons*, May–June, 32–42.
24. Hutt, M. D. and T. W. Speh (2006) *Business Marketing Management*, New York: Dryden Press.
25. Brierty, E. G., R. W. Eckles and R. R. Reeder (1998) *Business Marketing*, Englewood Cliffs, NJ: Prentice-Hall, 105.
26. Kotler, P., K. L. Keller, M. Brody and M. Goodman (2009) *Marketing Management*, Harlow: Pearson.
27. Moffat, S. (2003) The Case of Covisint, Working Paper, University of Strathclyde.

28. Davies, A., T. Brady and M. Hobday (2007) Organizing for Solutions: Systems Seller to Systems Integrator, *Industrial Marketing Management* 36, 183–93.

29. Davies, Brady and Hobday (2007) op. cit.

30. Davies, Brady and Hobday (2007) op. cit.

31. Blenkhorn, D. L. and P. M. Banting (1991) How Reverse Marketing Changes Buyer–Seller's Roles, *Industrial Marketing Management* 20, 185–91.

32. Anderson, F. and W. Lazer (1978) Industrial Lease Marketing, *Journal of Marketing* 42 (January), 71–9.

33. Morris, M. H. (1988) *Industrial and Organisation Marketing*, Columbus, OH: Merrill, 323.

34. Gummerson, E. (1996) Relationship Marketing and Imaginary Organisations: A Synthesis, *European Journal of Marketing* 30(2), 33–44.

35. Andreassen, T. W. (1995) Small, High Cost Countries Strategy for Attracting MNC's Global Investments, *International Journal of Public Sector Management* 8(3), 110–18.

36. Ravald, A. and C. Grönroos (1996) The Value Concept and Relationship Marketing, *European Journal of Marketing* 30(2), 19–30.

37. Takala, T. and O. Uusitalo (1996) An Alternative View of Relationship Marketing: A Framework for Ethical Analysis, *European Journal of Marketing* 30(2), 45–60.

38. Geyskens, I., J.-B. E. M. Steenkamp and N. Kumar (1998) Generalizations About Trust in Marketing Channel Relationships Using Meta-Analysis, *International Journal of Research in Marketing* 15, 223–48; Selnes, F. (1998) Antecedents and Consequences of Trust and Satisfaction in Buyer–Seller Relationships, *European Journal of Marketing* 32(3/4), 305–22; and Vlaga, W. and A. Eggert (2006) Relationship Value and Relationship Quality, *European Journal of Marketing* 40(3/4), 311–27.

39. Narayandas, D. and V. K. Rangan (2004) Building and Sustaining Buyer–Seller Relationships in Mature Industrial Markets, *Journal of Marketing*, 68 (July), 63–77.

40. Lindfelt, L.-L. and J.-Å. Törnroos (2006) Ethics and Value Creation in Business Research: Comparing Two Approaches, *European Journal of Marketing* 40(3/4), 328–51.

41. See e.g. Ford, D. (1980) The Development of Buyer–Seller Relationships in Industrial Markets, *European Journal of Marketing* 14(5/6), 339–53; Hakansson, H. (1982) *International Marketing and Purchasing of Industrial Goods: An Interaction Approach*, New York: Wiley; Turnbull, P. W. and M. T. Cunningham (1981) *International Marketing and Purchasing*, London: Macmillan; Turnbull, P. W. and J. P. Valla (1986) *Strategies for Industrial Marketing*, London: Croom-Helm.

42. Foust, D. (2006) Taking Off Like 'A Rocket Ship', *Business Week*, 3 April, 76.

43. Thornhill, J. and A. Rawsthorn (1992) Why Sparks are Flying, *Financial Times*, 8 January, 12.

44. Ford (1980) op. cit.

45. Thornhill and Rawsthorn (1992) op. cit.

46. Sharland, A. (2001) The Negotiation Process as a Predictor of Relationship Outcomes in International Buyer–Seller Arrangements, *Industrial Marketing Management*, 30, 551–9.

47. Arnett, D. B., B. A. Macy and J. B. Wilcox (2005) The Role of Core Selling Teams in Supplier Teams in Supplier–Buyer Relationships, *Journal of Personal Selling and Sales Management* 25(1), 27–42.

48. See Lovelock, C. H. (1983) Classifying Services to Gain Strategic Marketing Insight, *Journal of Marketing* 47, Summer, 9–20; Wray, B., A. Palmer and D. Bejou (1994) Using Neural Network Analysis to Evaluate Buyer–Seller Relationships, *European Journal of Marketing* 28(10), 32–48.

49. See Shaw, V. (1994) The Marketing Strategies of British and German Companies, *European Journal of Marketing* 28(7), 30–43; Meissner, H. G. (1986) A Structural Comparison of Japanese and German Marketing Strategies, *Irish Marketing Review* 1, Spring, 21–31.

50. Jackson, B. B. (1985) Build Customer Relationships that Last, *Harvard Business Review*, Nov–Dec, 120–5.

51. Henke, J. W. Jr (2000) Strategic Selling in the Age of Modules and Systems, *Industrial Marketing Management* 29, 271–84.

52. Hayward, D. (2002) Promise of Big Benefits in the B2B Arena, *Financial Times*, 1 May, 5.

53. Ploetner, O. and M. Ehret (2006) From Relationships to Partnerships—New Forms of Co-operation Between Buyer and Seller, *Industrial Marketing Management* 35, 4–9.

54. Zineldin, M. (1998) Towards an Ecological Collaborative Relationship Management: A 'Co-operative Perspective', *European Journal of Marketing* 32(11/12), 1138–64.

55. London, S. (2002) The Next Core Competence is Getting Personal, *Financial Times*, 13 December, 14.

56. See O'Driscoll, A. (2006) Reflection on Contemporary Issues in Relationship Marketing: Evidence from a Longitudinal Case Study in the Building Materials Industry, *Journal of Marketing Management* 22(1/2), 111–34; and Winklhofer, H., A. Pressey and N. Tzokas (2006) A Cultural Perspective of Relationship Orientation: Using Organisational Culture to Support a Supply Relationship Orientation, *Journal of Marketing Management* 22(1/2), 169–94.

57. Jackson (1985) op. cit., 127.

Jumbo Choices

Buying Aircraft

Buying an aircraft is one of the most difficult, not to mention one of the most expensive, decisions that an airline can take. Choosing the right type, size and priced aircraft to make up an airline's fleet is seen as an important part of competitive strategy. Up to the 1970s fleet decisions were fairly simple and based on technical considerations. Aircraft manufacturers came up with new improved designs and the airlines bought them. Throughout this period the capital cost of aircraft increased substantially and led to two important developments. First, aircraft manufacturers became more involved in making financial arrangements for airlines to purchase aircraft and, second, leasing rather than outright purchasing became a popular choice for airlines. The average price of a commercial aircraft can cost in the hundreds of millions of dollars. It is a multi-billion-dollar industry, with Airbus in 2006 estimating that there were 14,980 100-plus-seater aircraft operated by commercial airlines. Approximately 25–30 per cent of the world's aircraft are leased by airlines. The two largest aircraft leasing companies are International Lease Finance Corporation (ILFC) and GE Commercial Aviation Services (GECAS). GECAS has a fleet of over 1500 owned aircraft with more than 250 airlines in some 78 countries, and it manages over 300 aircraft for others. ILFC leases over 1000 aircraft.

At the end of the 1970s a process of deregulation began in the USA and spread to the EU, which saw a relaxation of rules governing prices, route access, capacity and frequency for airlines. The process of deregulation continued throughout the following decades, culminating in the EU–USA Open Skies Agreement of 2008, which opens up the two markets and removes most of the remaining restrictions. In terms of fleet acquisition, deregulation changed the rules of the game and having the right aircraft became an important element of competition. For example, as a direct result of deregulation, new carriers using cheap older aircraft entered the market and provided stiff competition for the older more established carriers, which had invested heavily in new aircraft. The cost of servicing these acquisitions was a drain on the financial resources of the established airlines. Deregulation also led to increased competition and a greater focus on costs. Aircraft started to play a greater role in determining an airline's market share. Due to all these factors, making the correct purchasing decision became all the more important for airlines.

The aircraft selection process

Airlines are constantly engaged in the fleet planning/aircraft selection process to ensure they have the correct type and mix of aircraft to provide a service. The aircraft selection process typically involves four key steps, as outlined below.

1 *Information gathering*: focusing on the current fleet inventory, corporate and marketing strategy and projections for long-term growth.
2 *Evaluation*: identification of criteria for choosing aircraft.
3 *Selection*: making the choice of aircraft.
4 *Presentation and approval*: agreement from the Board of Directors is required given the scale of financial commitment.

The evaluation and selections stages are the most complex in the entire process. Once the basic information is available, airlines must address a number of early, critically important issues, which will guide them as they move to evaluate and choose particular aircraft types. Airlines are faced with numerous important decisions: whether to buy a new or old

Airbus vs Boeing at a glance		TABLE **C9.1**
Airbus	**Boeing**	
Founded in 1970	Founded in 1916	
Headquarters based in Toulouse, France	Headquarters based in Chicago, USA	
Employs 55,000	Employs 160,000	
The company has received 6300 orders for aircraft and has delivered more than 4100 aircraft Airbus has consistently won market share away from arch-rival Boeing; record number of orders in 2005	World's largest producer of commercial and military aircraft; produces the 7 series of commercial aircraft, weapons systems and satellite launch systems; three-quarters of the world's jets are Boeing aircraft	
Revenue of $22.3 billion	Revenue of $28.3 billion	
Orders in 2008 = 777 new aircraft	Orders in 2008 = 662 new aircraft	
Airbus has 14 different aircraft models, ranging from capacities of 100 seats to 555 seats; its most popular plane is the short-haul A320; the plane is economical and has a moderate flight range; the A330/340 caters for long-haul routes; airlines love Airbus's commonality feature, which reduces training costs	The Boeing 7 series of aircraft caters for an array of different markets The 737 jet is the world's most popular aircraft; reliable, economic, adaptable, it has a moderate range, perfect for short-haul flights; the 767, the 777 and the famous jumbo 747 cater for long-distance markets	
The A380 jet is the world's largest commercial jet ever built; it launched in 2008	The 787 Dreamliner mid-size, long-range jet promises to be super-efficient, using advanced materials, engines and components, which results in a 20% reduction in fuel costs per passenger; over 886 sales orders have already been secured; it is due to launch in 2010	

aircraft; whether to buy a plane outright or use a leasing company; whether to enforce commonality across aircraft purchases by having the same type of aircraft from a single supplier, thereby achieving cost savings; whether the aircraft is suitable for the target market, the proposed routes and frequency of service; and, importantly, the length of the route and the associated costs.

Once these issues have been addressed, the airline can begin to assess the available options. The decision to buy new aircraft will mean the airline has to negotiate with the manufacturer directly, while leasing old or new will necessitate dealing with a lessor company. Fleet commonality is one of the main reasons for purchases of aircraft in large numbers. For example, the Airbus fleet share the same component parts and flight deck instrumentation. Engine choice in large aircraft is also an important factor and is usually based on power plant commonality of the operator's fleet.

The size of the market is an important issue and will largely determine the size of the aircraft chosen. An important moderating factor in this regard is the frequency of use. For example, it is possible to use a large aircraft less often on a route. However, there are dangers associated with this approach, as reduced frequency can erode market share. Frequency can generate traffic due to convenience so this is an important factor. Hub-and-spoke networks require the use of smaller aircraft and have had a profound influence on new aircraft requirements. Long-range aircraft cover point-to-point services, as airlines focus more on non-stop journeys and move away from total dependence on hubbing.

In the case of Ryanair, the European low-cost carrier, the above set of questions are relatively easy to address as it opts to buy new aircraft (737-800) from the manufacturer Boeing. The fact that it operates using one aircraft type—referred to as fleet commonality—makes this element of the selection process relatively easy. Ryanair's strategy of short-haul point-to-point services means that one type of aircraft will work across its entire route network. However, for airlines such as British Airways and Air France, operating short haul

Technical specifications		TABLE C9.2
	Airbus A380	**Boeing 787–9**
Seating	550	250–290
Range (km)	18,000	14,800–15,750
Cabin width	6.58	6.1 m
Length	73 m	63
Height	24.1 m	19.4 m
Wingspan	79.8 m	63 m
Cruise speed	0.84 mach	0.85 mach
Max. take-off weight	560 tonnes	540 tonnes
Sources: Airbus, Boeing		

(300–1000 km), medium haul (1000–1700 km) and long haul (1700+ km), the process is more complex.

Many airlines are faced with making decisions on future requirements for long-haul aircraft and must make decisions in advance to ensure that the aircraft are available when needed. Boeing and Airbus have taken different approaches to providing the next generation of long-haul aircraft, with Airbus designing the A380 and Boeing producing the 787 Dreamliner. The A380 is a double-deck, four-engined, wide-bodied aircraft, with a seating capacity of 525 people in three classes, making it the largest aircraft in the world. It is possible to configure the aircraft in a single economy class with a capacity of 853 passengers. The big question in aviation circles is whether volume in terms of capacity leads to profit for airlines. Some contend that the new super-jumbo could potentially create a viable low-cost, long-haul operation, while others view the market as needing only mid-size, long-range fuel-efficient, twin-engine jets for the global market, moving away from these super-carriers. Consumers want to fly non-stop to destinations rather than through congested hub airports.

The Boeing 787 Dreamliner is a mid-sized, wide-bodied, twin-engine jet airliner. It can carry between 210 and 330 passengers, depending on variant and seating configuration. Boeing has stated that it will be more fuel-efficient than earlier Boeing airliners and will be the first major airliner to use composite materials for most of its construction. There are three variants of the 787 model—we are focusing on the 787–9 as this is the largest of the models and the closest competitor to the A380. This radical plane is made from ground-breaking materials, using lightweight yet super-strong carbon-fibre technology. It is Boeing's first all-new aircraft in over a decade. Rising energy costs for airlines make the fuel efficiency of aircraft a key selling point for the plane. This has led to the Dreamliner becoming a hot seller for Boeing. The jet aims to use 20 per cent less fuel, fewer emissions, and it is quieter.

The technical specifications of both aircraft are shown in Table C9.2.

Both aircraft embody new technology and offer fuel efficiencies over existing aircraft, with reduced environmental impact. They both have the capability of flying long distances with similar ranges. The length, height, wingspan and cruise speeds are quite similar. While the two aircraft have much in common, they differ in size and capacity, and consequently are designed to serve different markets. With a three-class configuration of 550 seats, the A380 has almost double the capacity of the B787. The two have similar seat-kilometre costs, which vary according to the number of seats. Airbus would have a slight advantage in this regard as it has a greater number of seats.

However, in terms of operational costs, the A380 is more expensive, needing more crew on board. Ground handling service costs are higher for the A380 than for the B787. The Airbus also has higher airport charges, especially at those airports where weight-based landing fees are still charged. Dual-level air-bridge access is required for the A380, which once again incurs higher costs. Overall direct operating costs are higher for the

Airbus but, because the costs can be spread over a great number of seats, this differential is reduced when compared to the B787. The average price for the Airbus A380 is $327.4 million and depends on design weights, engine choice and level of customization. The Boeing 787 costs less, at an average of $200 million.

The optimal market size for each aircraft also varies considerably. The market size required for a daily flight by the A380 at 70 per cent load factor with 550 seats is 140,525 passengers. On the other hand, the figure for the B787 with 260 seats at 70 per cent load factor is 66,430 passengers. Therefore, the B787 has more scope to serve city pair markets of medium density. The A380 is more suited to routes such as LA–Sydney and LA–London Heathrow, where the market sizes are 648,205 and 486,941 respectively. If the aircraft is too big for the route and not enough seats are sold then the load factor reduces and losses will occur, or flight frequency will be lost to maintain the load factor and that will impact on yields. If aircraft are too small, flight frequency will increase and direct operating costs will rise, but in competitive markets there is no option to increase price, so yield declines.

Questions

1. Identify and discuss the key choice criteria used in the selection of a commercial aircraft.
2. For an airline serving a medium- to long-haul market with low to medium density, which aircraft is the most appropriate?
3. Discuss ways in which marketing can facilitate the purchase decision process of airlines.

This case was written by Dr Siobhan Tiernan and Conor Carroll, University of Limerick.

Eric Harding worked for CIC, a multinational chemical company in the UK. He had just moved into a new role in the sales department as key account manager in the garden centre sector.

One of Eric's first tasks was to secure distribution for the company's new product, PLANT-ALL. Scheduled for a national launch to the consumer in the spring of the following year, PLANT-ALL was a revolutionary plant compost that was a universal planting medium suitable for use with houseplants and all outdoor planting in pots and containers. The product offered the additional important benefit of water retention. To the consumer this offered the convenience and cost-saving benefits of having to buy only one type of compost, in addition to the need for less frequent watering. PLANT-ALL came in three different pack sizes. To complete the range, the company had produced two plant food concentrates suitable for specific plant groups. These came in easy-to-dispense bottles. The two products were distinguished by different-coloured bottle tops, and the tops from both also served as dosage measures.

Unlike the grocery sector, the garden centre sector in the UK was not dominated by a small number of key players. Instead, it was made up of a large number of independent garden centres. On account of this, wholesalers were key to distribution in the sector. Suppliers would deliver their goods in bulk to wholesalers, who would then deliver the products in the smaller quantities required by the individual garden centres. There were two exceptions to this. These were two multiple retail groups, each of which had garden centre branches located nationwide. The larger of these two retailers, Greenvale, was Eric Harding's biggest key account. Manufacturers routinely delivered direct to the multiple retailers. However, in order to reduce stockholding the multiple retailers also drew their product from dedicated garden trade wholesalers. The key wholesaler for the UK garden centre sector was DB Garden Wholesale, referred to in the trade as DBW. Eric Harding's key account management responsibility included both key multiple accounts and also DBW.

As a key part of the launch strategy for PLANT-ALL, the company had already booked to attend the industry's key trade show, Gardenworld, in September. It was May of the same year and Eric's first challenge in his new role was to secure distribution for PLANT-ALL with the key players in the market prior to the trade show. His clear priorities were Greenvale and DBW. The diary of Eric's selling activity was as follows.

Early June

Eric met with the purchasing manager, Lauren Belles, at Greenvale. The purpose of this meeting was two-fold: to introduce himself as the company's new key account manager, and an exploratory meeting aimed at gaining Greenvale's agreement to stock PLANT-ALL. Eric went to the meeting armed with an impressive collection of product samples and a glossy brochure detailing the product's features and benefits. He was able to impress the purchasing manager with the amount of promotional support being put behind the launch of PLANT-ALL. This included advertising to the consumer in all the key garden magazines, together with bespoke display stands for merchandising the product in garden centres to best effect. The magazine advertisements would also feature money-off coupons to support the national launch.

Lauren Belles was impressed with the product proposition and, based on the manufacturer's proposed recommended retail prices, anticipated that it would meet the company's benchmarks in terms of profit margins. Lauren also liked what she saw in terms of the company's launch plans. However, she did have two key areas of concern. The first related to the need to overcome consumer resistance in-store. Eric explored this issue with Lauren. He learned that the garden centre consumer tended to be a creature of habit and that there would therefore have to be some in-store activity designed to encourage the consumer to try the new compost. Eric asked Lauren what she felt would work best. From long experience, she recommended in-store demonstrations combined with money-off coupons. Her second biggest concern related to distribution. Specifically, for a new product the garden centre would not be able to consider large order quantities and therefore would expect to draw replenishment stock from its wholesaler, DBW.

So, Eric went away from his meeting with two key objectives. The first of these entailed gaining the support of his line manager, Brian Lindrick. The second was the need to secure distribution with DBW. Eric immediately set to work on both. Two days later he had met with his line manager and secured promotional monies to support demonstrator and couponing activity in Greenvale's six biggest garden centres. This sales promotion activity would be timed to coincide with national launch of the product the following spring. These six centres would act as the test centres for the Greenvale group. If the product was successful in these, this could indicate that success would be highly likely not only across all of Greenvale's 20 garden centres but in the sector overall.

Eric then embarked upon trying to secure distribution for PLANT-ALL with DBW. For this, he needed an appointment with Bradley Jons, the company's senior purchasing manager. However, this proved more difficult than he had imagined. As Eric found out, all appointment bookings went through his secretary, Anne Sheffield. When he telephoned for an appointment, the secretary advised him that Mr Jons' diary was full for the next month and that after that Mr Jons was taking three weeks' annual leave. Eric thanked the secretary, put down the telephone and deliberated on his plan of action. He knew that he had a good product and that it would be in the interests of all parties concerned that DBW should stock it.

Following her meeting with Eric Harding, Lauren Belles decided to consult with Fred Elliott, Greenvale's commercial manager. Fred liked the idea that Lauren

> **//** For a new product the garden centre would not be able to consider large order quantities and therefore would expect to draw replenishment stock from its wholesaler. **//**

outlined to him as he could see that it had the potential to contribute to the group's bottom line. However, he would have preferred TV advertising. A few days later Lauren mentioned the PLANT-ALL proposition during a telephone conversation with Margaret Francis, a store manager of one of Greenvale's biggest garden centres. Margaret expressed concern that there would not be enough space to take the additional product and that she had had a bad experience with CIC six months ago over late delivery of another of its products.

Mid-June

Eric again met with Lauren Belles the Greenvale purchasing manager. He outlined the proposals regarding the in-store demonstration and couponing activity in the six largest garden centres, the launch retail price and ongoing margins that he expected the group to achieve based on the expected wholesale price. The plan was to deliver mixed pallets of product direct to the six centres in good time for displays to be built ready for the test. Lauren liked the sound of this, and, in spite of the issues raised by Fred and Margaret, decided that PLANT-ALL was worthy of a trial at six of Greenvale's biggest garden centres. However, she was keen to know if DBW had agreed to stock and distribute replenishment product. Eric explained the difficulty he was experiencing in resolving this problem in time. Lauren was enthusiastic about the concept and as she felt that she had contributed to the design of the launch programme, offered to call Bradley Jons at the first opportunity. She claimed to have a strong working relationship with DBW's senior purchasing manager.

Within a few days of leaving the meeting with Greenvale, Eric received a telephone call direct from Bradley Jons' secretary seeking to set up an urgent meeting.

Late June

Eric met with Bradley Jons. Again, this was a meeting with twin objectives. It was Eric's opportunity to introduce himself to Bradley Jons as the new key account manager, and also his opportunity to sell the features and benefits of his company's new product, PLANT-ALL. Much was made of the planned national launch at the Gardenworld trade show. As the major showcase for all new products in the industry, Eric knew that this would be a key selling point for DBW. At Gardenworld, for example, CIC would consider taking pre-season orders from all garden centres. These would be fulfilled subject to the results of the market test with Greenvale. Eric explained the mechanics of the initial six-centre test. With their agreement, the role of DBW would be to manage all subsequent orders and to replenish stocks in the six test centres. If the test proved successful, DBW would then have the opportunity to supply it nationwide to all garden centres from early spring of the following year. Bradley Jons was clearly impressed with the launch plans and with the potential that he saw. He had only two questions. The first related to unsold stock at the end of the test period. Eric agreed that if the test was unsuccessful and the product withdrawn, unsold stock would be uplifted and DBW reimbursed. Bradley Jons' second question was whether the products would meet their margin expectation. Knowing that the company had provided for adequate shared margin, Eric went on with confidence to outline the deal. Bradley Jons accepted the offer and closed the meeting by wishing CIC a successful product launch.

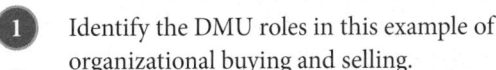

Questions

1. Identify the DMU roles in this example of organizational buying and selling.
2. What are the choice criteria of the DMU roles identified?
3. This was Eric Harding's first major task as a key account manager. For his future attempts to sell new products in this kind of distribution channel, what lessons should he have learned?

This case was written by Belinda Dewsnap, Lecturer in Marketing, Loughborough University.

CHAPTER 6

They said we'd be artistically free
When we signed that bit of paper
They meant let's make a lot of money
And worry about it later.

THE CLASH ('Complete Control')

Understanding marketing ethics and corporate social responsibility

LEARNING OBJECTIVES

After reading this chapter, you should be able to:

1 explain the meaning of ethics, and business and marketing ethics

2 describe ethical issues in marketing

3 discuss business, societal, and legal and regulatory responses to ethical concerns

4 explain the stakeholder theory of the firm

5 discuss the nature of corporate social responsibility

6 describe the dimensions of corporate social responsibility

7 discuss the arguments for and against corporate social responsibility programmes

The storm clouds that have gathered over such companies as BA (price fixing), Siemens (bribery), Enron (financial scandals), Shell (overstating oil reserves), Wal-Mart (allegations of poor employee relations), McDonald's (health concerns), Coca-Cola (Dasani) and Procter & Gamble (Sunny D) bear witness to the importance of business and marketing ethics, not only for their own sake but also for the well-being of organizations. Revelations about unethical behaviour can lead to bad publicity and the unwillingness of consumers to buy from the accused company. Not only should modern organizations consider and define their standards of ethical behaviour, they should also use these standards as the basis for designing corporate social responsibility strategies that take account of how their actions might affect society and the environment. This requires an analysis of how decisions affect the wider community beyond the sole interests of shareholders.

This chapter, then, follows naturally from the discussion in Chapter 3 of the marketing environment where the elements (e.g. social/cultural, ecological/physical and technological) that make up the environment in which organizations operate were discussed. In it we shall discuss the meaning of marketing ethics and specific issues related to this. Then the ways in which companies have responded to ethical issues in marketing will be explored. In particular, organizational responses through corporate social responsibility programmes will be analysed. The nature and dimensions of corporate social responsibility will be examined, together with an analysis of the arguments for and against the establishment of such programmes. Finally, the chapter will conclude with a summary of some of the key issues in marketing ethics and corporate social responsibility.

Marketing Ethics

Underpinning the idea of corporate social responsibility and shaping its implementation is the concept of ethics. **Ethics** are the moral principles and values that govern the actions and decisions of an individual or group.[1] They involve values about right and wrong conduct. **Business ethics** are the moral principles and values that guide a firm's behaviour. Until recently, for many companies, business ethics consisted mainly of compliance-based, legally driven codes and training that outlined in detail what employees could or could not do regarding such areas as conflicts of interest or improper use of company assets. Now, an increasing number of companies are designing values-based ethical programmes that are consistent across global operations. The aim is to provide employees with an in-depth understanding of ethical issues that helps them to make the correct decisions when faced with new ethical situations and challenges.[2] Marketing Ethics and Corporate Social Responsibility in Action 6.1 discusses how Marks & Spencer has embedded ethical standards into its business.

Marketing ethics are the moral principles and values that guide behaviour within the field of marketing, and cover issues such as product safety, truthfulness in marketing communications, honesty in relationships with customers and distributors, pricing issues and the impact of marketing decisions on the environment and society. There can be a distinction between the legality and ethicality of marketing decisions. Ethics concern personal moral principles and values, while laws reflect society's principles and standards that are enforceable in the courts.

Not all unethical practices are illegal. For example, it is not illegal to include genetically modified (GM) ingredients in products sold in supermarkets. However, some organizations, such as Greenpeace, believe it is unethical to sell GM products when their effect on health has not been scientifically proven. Such concerns have led some supermarket chains to withdraw GM ingredients from their own-brand products. Nor was it illegal for Google to launch a

6.1 Marketing Ethics and Corporate Social Responsibility in Action

Ethics Makes Good Business Sense at M&S

Marks & Spencer set the green agenda for retailers when it launched its five-year eco-programme, known as 'Plan A' (because there is no Plan B). By 2012 M&S aims to:

- become carbon neutral
- send no waste to landfill
- extend sustainable sourcing
- help improve the lives of people in its supply chain
- help customers and employees live a healthier lifestyle.

Progress against these objectives is monitored continually. For example, the company has helped 15,000 children in Uganda receive a better education, it is saving 55,000 tonnes of CO_2 per year, it has recycled 48 million clothes hangers, it is tripling sales of organic food and it has converted over 20 million garments to Fairtrade cotton.

Not only is this ethically worthy, it also makes good business sense. M&S market research has found that British consumers fall into four broad segments:

1 the *crusaders* (or *dark greens*) are passionately green and will make every attempt to shop for environmentally friendly goods and services (11 per cent)
2 the *light greens* want green consumption but want it to be easy (27 per cent)
3 the *vaguely concerned* are interested in green issues but do not see how they can make a difference (38 per cent)
4 the *uninterested* do not care about green issues (24 per cent).

In M&S's view these results represent an opportunity: three-quarters of British consumers are interested in green issues to some degree. By taking the lead in green issues, M&S is appealing to the majority of its target market, and benefiting society and the environment: the smart thing to do as well as the right thing to do.

Based on: Anonymous (2008);[3] Bokaie (2008);[4] Franklin (2008)[5]

self-censored search engine that prevents access to 'sensitive' subjects in China, yet the action has been criticized on ethical grounds.[6]

Ethical principles reflect the cultural values and norms of society. Norms guide what ought to be done in a particular situation. For example, being truthful is regarded as good. This societal norm may influence marketing behaviour. Hence—since it is good to be truthful—deceptive, untruthful advertising should be avoided. Often, unethical behaviour may be clear-cut but, in other cases, deciding what is ethical is highly debatable. Ethical dilemmas arise when two principles or values conflict. For example, Ben & Jerry's, the US ice cream firm was a leading member of the Social Venture Network in San Francisco, a group that promotes ethical standards in business. A consortium, Meadowbrook Lane Capital, was part of this group and was formed to raise enough capital to make Ben & Jerry's a private company again. However, its bid was lower than that made by the Anglo-Dutch food multinational Unilever NV. If Ben & Jerry's stayed true to its ethical beliefs it would have accepted the Meadowbrook bid. On the other hand, if the company wished to do the best financially for its shareholders it would accept the Unilever bid. It faced an ethical dilemma because one of its values and preferences inhibited the achievement of the other. Financial considerations won the day: the Unilever bid was accepted.[7]

Many ethical dilemmas derive from the conflict between the desire to increase profits and the wish to make decisions that are ethically justified. For example, the decision by Google to launch a self-censored search engine in China was driven by the need to be competitive in a huge market where it was lagging behind competitors such as Yahoo! and Microsoft, which had already accepted self-censorship.[8] Nevertheless, companies do seek to address such conflicts. For example, companies like Nike and Reebok monitor their overseas production of sports goods to ensure that no child labour is used.

6.1 Pause for Thought

Do you believe companies should act ethically or should they pursue short-term profits regardless of external issues?

Ethical Issues in Marketing

Marketing practices have been subject to criticism from consumers, consumer groups and environmentalists, who have complained that marketing managers have been guilty of harming the interests of consumers, society and the environment. These ethical concerns will be analysed by examining issues specific to the marketing mix; after that, more general societal, environmental and political issues will be explored (see Fig. 6.1).

Ethical issues relating to marketing mix effects on consumers

Ethical concerns relating to specific marketing mix effects on consumers cover all aspects of the mix: product, price, promotion (advertising, personal selling, direct marketing, Internet marketing, and sales promotion and publicity), and place (distribution). Each of the chapters relating to these elements of the marketing mix ends with comprehensive coverage of the main ethical issues. In this chapter, discussion will be limited to one concern per topic, to give a flavour of the range of criticisms levelled at the marketing mix.

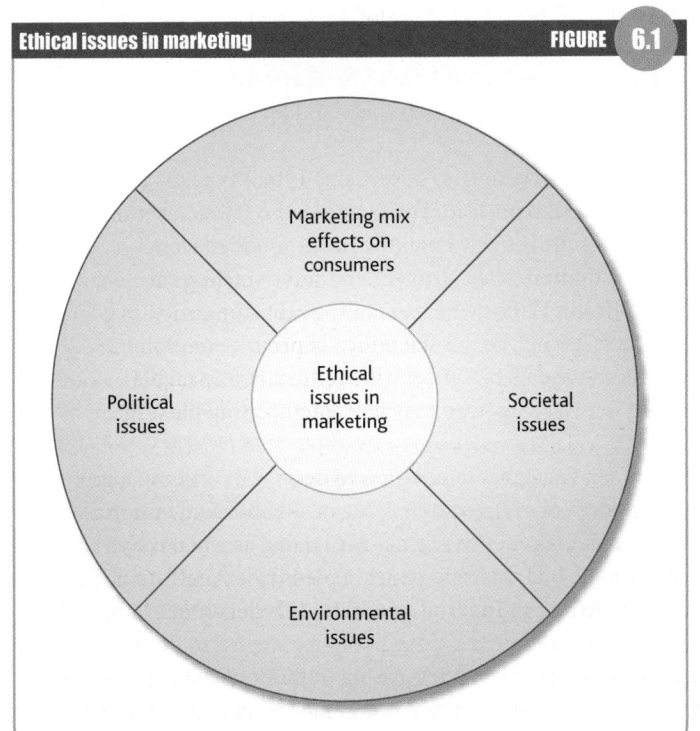

Ethical issues in marketing   FIGURE 6.1

Product: product safety

The tobacco, food and drinks industries have received criticism in recent years regarding the potential harm their products may cause to consumers. Tobacco companies have been criticized for marketing cigarettes, which cause lung cancer. The food industry has been criticized for marketing products that have high levels of fat, which can lead to obesity and, in the drinks industry, concern has been expressed over the marketing to children of sugar-rich fizzy drinks, which cause teeth decay and can also lead to obesity. Concern over Sunny D's high level of sugar forced Procter & Gamble to withdraw the drink's original formulation from the market, and the lack of success of its relaunch persuaded P&G to sell the brand six years after its original launch.[9]

On the other hand, it is also argued that business and government are taking steps to reduce the harmful effects of products, with bans on tobacco promotion escalating across Europe and the creation of bodies such as the Food Standards Agency, the independent food safety body set up to protect public health and consumer interests in relation to food in the UK, and the Portman Group, the industry-sponsored organization that oversees the UK's alcoholic drinks industry. Most European countries have similar organizations, which are also able to provide advice to industry.

Pricing: price fixing

An anti-competitive practice associated with marketing is price fixing, where two or more firms collude to force up the price of products. EU competition policy provides a legal framework that is designed to prevent firms from carrying out this practice. For example, the European Commission has fined three chemical groups (Hoechst, Atofina and Akzo-Nobel) £153 million for fixing the market for monochloroacetic acid, a widely used household and industrial chemical.[10] National laws also ban price fixing as illustrated by BA's £121 million fine from the UK's Office of Fair Trading for fixing long-haul fuel surcharges, and its £148 million fine from the USA's Department of Justice for colluding over cargo and long-haul surcharges.[11] Price fixing is considered unethical because it interferes with the consumer's freedom of choice and artificially raises prices.

Supporters of marketing claim that price fixing is the exception rather than the rule, however, and while it should not be conducted most industries are highly competitive with prices reflecting what consumers are willing to pay.

Promotion

Misleading advertising: this can take the form of exaggerated claims or concealed facts. A claim that a dieting product was capable of one kilogramme weight loss per week when in reality much less was the case is an example of an exaggerated claim. Coca-Cola's launch of Dasani, which concealed the fact that the brand was nothing more than bottled tap water, is an example of misleading advertising through concealed facts. Concealed facts may give a misleading impression to consumers, as when a food brand is advertised as healthy because it contains added vitamins without pointing out its high sugar and fat content. Making such misleading claims is known as 'greenwashing'.

Marketers argue that in most European countries advertising is tightly regulated, minimizing opportunities for advertisers to mislead. For example, the UK's Advertising Standards Authority censured GlaxoSmithKline for making the unfounded claim that drinking Horlicks could make children taller, stronger and more intelligent. EU law states that 'nutritional and health claims which encourage consumers to purchase a product, but are false, misleading, or not scientifically proven are prohibited'.[12] They also point out that high-profile scandals that meet with consumer and media opprobrium are a major deterrent to marketers who may be contemplating making similar mistakes.

Deceptive selling: salespeople can face great temptation to deceive in order to close a sale. The deception may take the form of exaggeration, lying or withholding important information. Occasionally evidence of malpractice reaches the media, as when it was alleged that some financial services salespeople had mis-sold pension plans by exaggerating the expected returns, a scandal that resulted in millions of pounds worth of compensation being awarded to the victims.

Sales managers and marketers point out that an increasing number of companies provide ethical training in personal selling to communicate to salespeople what is and is not acceptable behaviour.

Direct marketing's invasion of privacy: the unethical practice of entering names and addresses onto a database without the consumer's permission has caused concern within the area of direct marketing. Some consumers fear that the act of subscribing to a club or magazine, or buying products by direct mail or over the telephone will result in the inconvenience of receiving streams of unsolicited direct mail.

However, direct marketing is coming under increasing regulation in Europe both through bodies such as the Direct Marketing Association (DMA) in the UK and governments to ensure that consumers are asked for their consent before their names, addresses and telephone numbers are entered into databanks.

Internet privacy: visitors to websites can easily be tracked and online shoppers' purchasing information can be recorded using 'cookies'. These are tiny computer files that marketers can download onto the computer of online shoppers. They allow marketers to provide customized and personalized content for online shoppers. However, many online shoppers do not know that this information is being collected and might object if they did. Such activity can be considered unethical since information about consumers may be held without their permission. While accepting that regulation is required in this area, marketers agree that such information is held only as a code rather than in the form of a name and address.

The use of promotional inducements to the trade: manufacturers like retailers to promote their products rather than those of the competition. They, therefore, sometimes offer inducements to retailers to place special emphasis on their products. So, for example, when a consumer asks to see trainers the salesperson is likely to try to sell the brand of trainers that gives him/her the extra bonus. This may be considered unethical since it may result in the consumer buying a brand that does not best meet his/her needs.

Although marketers concede that this practice has the potential to lead to abuse, they agree that most consumers have a good idea of their needs and the type of product they want. They claim the practice will be most effective in product categories where there are brands from different suppliers that are largely undifferentiated so that the consumer has a number of options that fulfil his/her needs. Critics counter by arguing that if the practice leads to overemphasis on a more expensive alternative to the neglect of a cheaper rival brand, the consumer's interest is still not being upheld.

Place: slotting allowances

A slotting allowance is a fee paid by a manufacturer to a retailer in exchange for an agreement to place a product on the retailer's shelves. The importance of gaining distribution and the growing power of retailers means that slotting allowances are commonplace in the supermarket trade. They may be considered unethical since they distort competition, favouring large suppliers that can afford to pay them over small suppliers who may in reality be producing superior products.

Marketers argue that they are only responding to the realities of the marketplace (i.e. the immense power of some retailers) and claim the blame should rest with the purchasing practices of those retailers that demand payment for display space, rather that the marketing profession who are often powerless to resist such pressures.

General societal, environmental and political issues

Three general societal environmental and political issues relating to marketing are concern that: marketing promotes too much materialism, and that marketing activities place too much emphasis on the short term and too little on the long-term environmental consequences. A political concern is that the power of global companies fuelled by massive marketing budgets works against the interests of consumers and society.

Societal concerns

Two societal concerns are marketing's promotion of materialism and its emphasis on short-term issues.

Materialism: an ethical concern within the realm of society is that marketing promotes materialism—an overemphasis on material possessions. Critics argue that people judge themselves and are judged by others not by who they are but by what they own. Status symbols rule, with consumers desiring expensive houses, cars, second homes, yachts, high-tech gadgets and designer clothing as representations of their success and worth. Such conspicuous consumption is fuelled by the advertising industry, which equates materialism and success with happiness, desirability and social worth. Materialism is not considered natural by the critics but a phenomenon created by business, which benefits by huge sales of mega-margin brands, and driven by huge marketing expenditures designed to create false wants.

Supporters of marketing argue that sociological studies of tribes in Africa, who have never been influenced by marketing's pervasive and persuasive powers, also display signs of materialism. For example, in some tribes people use the number of cows owned as a symbol of status and power. They argue that desire for status is a natural state of mind, with marketing simply promoting the kinds of possessions that may be regarded as indicators of status and success.

Short-termism: marketing is accused of putting the short-term interests of consumers before the consumers' and society's long-term interests. As we have seen when discussing product safety, marketers supply and promote products that can have long-term adverse health repercussions for consumers. Cigarettes may aid short-term relaxation but they have harmful long-term health effects for both smokers and those people forced to breathe in their smoke. Fatty food may be tasty but it may also lead to obesity and heart problems. Too much salt and sugar in food and drinks may enhance the taste but also lead to long-term health problems. Alcohol may remove inhibitions and help to create a convivial atmosphere but may also lead to dependency and liver problems.

Marketers need to act responsibly in response to these issues. For example, Coca-Cola has reduced the sugar levels in some of its fizzy drinks and stopped advertising them in television programmes targeting the under-12s.[13] Marks & Spencer has also moved to reduce salt in its food, including a 15 per cent reduction of salt in its sandwiches.[14] Government and self-regulation is also required to limit individual company's scope for neglecting the longer-term effects of their actions.

Environmental concerns

Marketers' desire to satisfy consumers' wants may also conflict with the interests of the environment. Businesses may want the cheapest ingredients and components in their products, whereas environmentalists favour more expensive materials that are biodegradable or recyclable. Marketers may favour large packaging that gains the attention of consumers in stores, whereas environmentalists favour smaller pack sizes and refill packs. In today's competitive marketplace, businesses may choose to dispose of waste products in the cheapest way even if that means polluting the atmosphere, rivers or the sea. In an attempt to meet consumer demands, marketers may develop and market hardwood furniture originating from the depleted forests of the Amazon.

In an attempt to reconcile business and environmental interests, several governments have introduced car scrappage schemes to cut pollution and stimulate demand for cars, as Marketing Ethics and Corporate Social Responsibility in Action 6.2 discusses.

6.2 Marketing Ethics and Corporate Social Responsibility in Action

Car Scrappage Incentives and the Ailing Automotive Industry

Societal concerns with CO_2 emissions and climate change have meant that petrol-guzzling 4x4 vehicles and private transport in general have been the targets of much criticism in recent years. New European rules demanding that car manufacturers cut the carbon emissions of new vehicles by 18 per cent from 2012 are likely to foster further manufacturing innovation in the automotive industry. However, a call for alternative forms of transport that go beyond fuel-efficient vehicles (i.e. cycling, walking, car-sharing and increased use of public transport) poses a huge threat to the auto industry. Indeed, the economic downturn has shown us the face of a struggling industry, increased unemployment and localized economic collapse. So, the politically and economically desirable option would be to create incentive structures for the advancement of innovation in the area of energy-efficient cars, which could at once reduce emissions and maintain a healthy automotive industry. For example, the French Government has introduced a car scrappage scheme of €1000 for consumers who exchange their old cars for fuel-efficient models, which has improved sales and allowed Renault to relocate the production of one of its models back to France. In Germany, a more generous scrappage scheme of €2500 (£2330) has recently been introduced and has fuelled German consumer demand. In the UK, the government has encourage the scrapping of cars 10 or more years old by offering a £2000 discount on the price of a new car (half paid for from taxes, half from car manufacturers). Members of the European Parliament have called for a consistent European response, backed by the European Investment Bank and other financial bodies.

However, environmentalists have questioned the benefits of such schemes. They have argued that although new cars are technologically greener than old models, efficiency gains tend to be offset by the carbon footprint involved in the manufacture of a new car, and by the fact that consumers insist on buying ever more powerful vehicles. Environmentalists also suggest that such schemes are nothing but yet another attempt to rescue an ailing economy by rewarding business failure and painting it green. Instead, it is argued, the environment would be better off if governments were to invest such budgets towards increasing access to public transport, and improving the efficiency of public vehicles. Such views will prove challenging to an industry that aims to develop new and more fuel-efficient private vehicles.

Based on: Everitt (2009);[15] *Gow (2009);*[16] *Pearce (2009);*[17] *Wood (2009)*[18]

As we shall discuss later, marketers and businesses are developing corporate social responsibility strategies that take account of the external impacts of their decisions so that society's and environmental concerns are addressed. One result of these responses is the development of more fuel-efficient and less polluting cars, as the advertisement for the Honda hybrid.

The politics of globalization

A third issue of ethical concern is the growth of globalization. This is the move by companies to operate in more than one country and is usually a term applied to large multinational corporations that exert considerable power in their host countries. It is the abuse of such power that is of ethical concern. Backed by huge marketing expenditures and global mega-brands, concern is expressed over their influence over consumers, governments and suppliers. Critics argue that their size and huge budgets mean that it is hard for smaller rivals to compete, thus reducing consumer choice. The impact on employment and the economy means that governments vie with each other to attract global organizations to their country. Finally, their purchasing power means that they can negotiate very low prices from suppliers in the developing world.

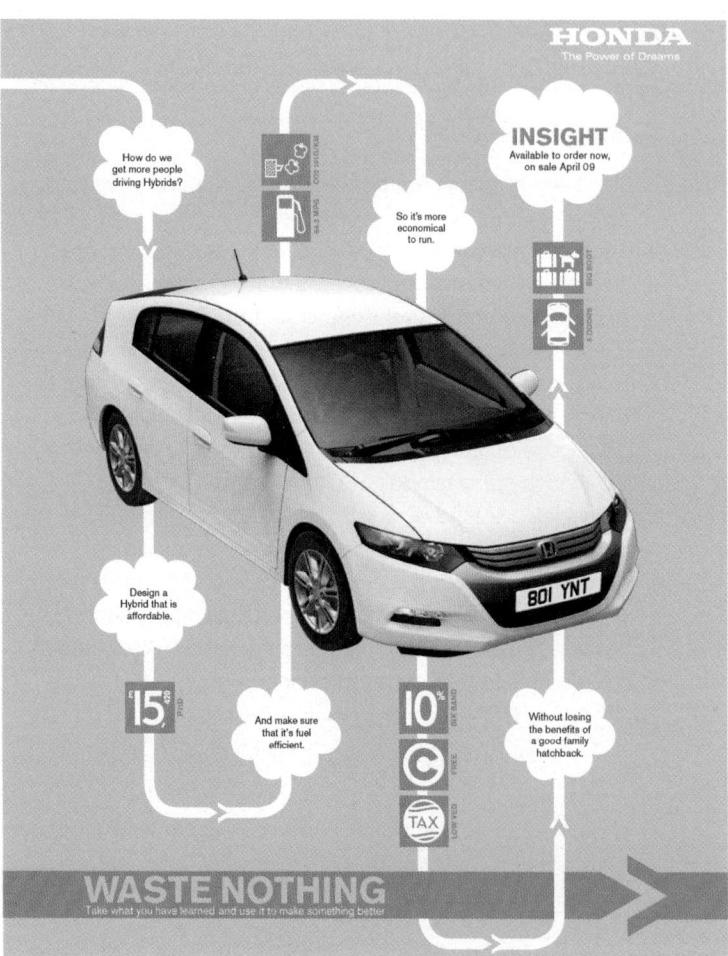

▲ Honda is developing affordable, fuel-efficient and less-polluting hybrid cars.

Supporters of global companies argue that their size and global reach mean that they benefit from economies of scale in production and marketing (making them more efficient and, therefore, in a better position to charge low prices to consumers) and in R&D, enabling them to develop better-quality products and make technological breakthroughs—for example, in the area of healthcare. They further claim that their attraction to governments is evidence of the value they provide to host nations. Regarding their ability to negotiate down prices from developing-world suppliers, global organizations need to recognize their responsibilities to their supplier stakeholders. This is happening as more of them adopt corporate responsibility programmes and global corporations recognize the marketing potential of fair trade products (such as Nestlé, which markets Partners' Blend, a fair trade coffee).

Having discussed the major ethical issues relating to marketing the next section will explore business, societal, and legal and regulatory responses to these concerns (see Fig. 6.2).

Business responses to ethical issues in marketing: corporate social responsibility

Business has taken action to address ethical concerns in marketing and other functional areas by adopting the philosophy of corporate social responsibility (CSR). Over the last 10 years, CSR has blossomed as an idea and commands the attention of executives in Europe and the USA. It would be difficult to find a recent annual report of any large multinational company that does not talk proudly of its efforts to improve society and safeguard the environment.[19] We shall now examine the idea in depth by exploring the nature and dimensions of CSR and assessing the arguments for and against its adoption.

Corporate Social Responsibility

Corporate social irresponsibility can have painful consequences for organizations. The case of Siemens illustrates the negative fallout that can follow. Accused of paying bribes to win lucrative overseas telecoms and power contracts, Siemens was fined £523 million by the US Department of Justice, and £180 million by a court in its home town of Munich. A further £354 million was paid to settle a case in Munich over the failure of its former board to fulfil its supervisory duties. The total cost to Siemens, a symbol of German engineering excellence, was £2.25 billion, including lawyers' and accountants' fees, plus the loss of its reputation and that of former senior executives.[20]

The fallout from this and other cases raises the issue of how harmful corporate social irresponsibility can be to companies and wider society. As a result companies are increasingly

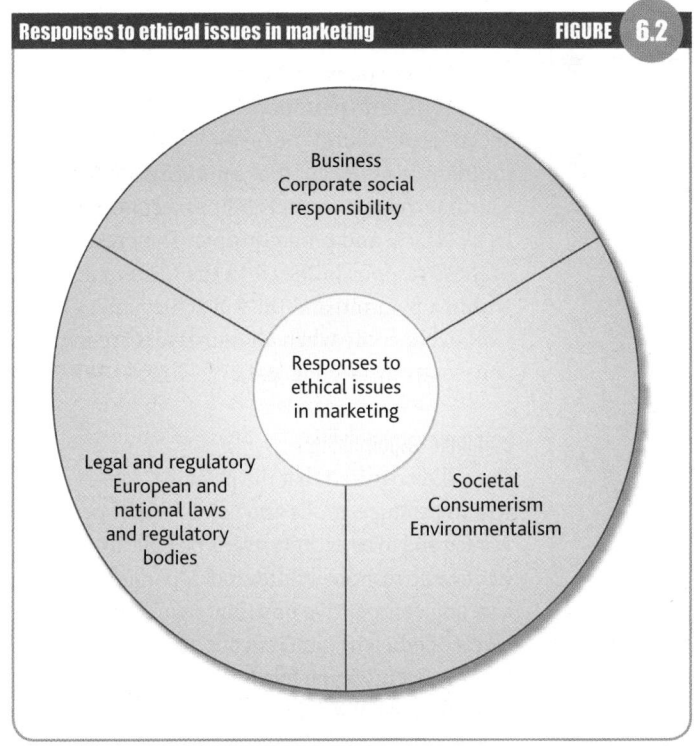

Responses to ethical issues in marketing   FIGURE   6.2

Business
Corporate social
responsibility

Responses to
ethical issues
in marketing

Legal and regulatory
European and
national laws
and regulatory
bodies

Societal
Consumerism
Environmentalism

examining how their actions affect not only their profits but society and the environment. Corporate social responsibility (CSR) refers to the ethical principle that an organization should be accountable for how its behaviour might affect society and the environment.

Commentators have claimed that corporate social responsibility is 'an idea whose time has come'.[21] This is not to say that CSR is new. For many years, companies have been aware of the obligations of being an employer and a consumer of natural resources. For example, the town of Bourneville was created by the founder of Cadbury to house the workers of that company.[22] Nevertheless, there is little doubt that CSR is now higher on the agenda of many companies than it was in the past. Most multinational corporations now have a senior executive, often with a staff at his/her disposal, specifically charged with developing and coordinating the CSR function.[23] Furthermore, most large companies engage in corporate social reporting within their annual financial statements, as separate printed reports and/or on websites. The EMI Group, for example, use a bi-media approach: a short printed summary report allows readers to access the key points, but also acts as a signpost for more detailed information to be found on EMI's website.

The importance of CSR is also reflected in membership organizations, which offer services to members such as providing information, lobbying and promoting the CSR cause. For example, the UK-based Business in the Community (www.bitc.org.uk) has a membership of over 700 companies, and includes in its activities cause-related marketing and the promotion of CSR internationally. Other notable organizations in Europe include Business and Society Belgium, Finnish Business and Society, Business in the Community Ireland, Samenleving and Bedrijf (Netherlands), CSR Europe (Europe-wide) and the European Business Ethics Network (Europe-wide). In the USA, Business for Social Responsibility (www.bsr.org./index.cfm) has grown into a major global organization.[24] These, together with pressure groups such as Greenpeace and ASH (Action on Smoking and Health), highlight the belief that organizations should consider a wider perspective regarding their activities and objectives than a narrow focus on short-term profits.

CSR is based on the **stakeholder theory** of the firm, which contends that companies are not managed purely in the interests of their shareholders alone. Rather, there is a range of groups (stakeholders) that have a legitimate interest in the company as well.[25] Following this theory a **stakeholder** of a company is an individual or group that either:

● is harmed by, or benefits, from the company
  or
● whose rights can be violated, or have to be respected, by the company.[26]

Other groups, besides shareholders who typically would be considered stakeholders, are communities associated with the company, employees, customers of the company's products, and suppliers (see Fig. 6.3). The key point is that stakeholder theory holds that the company has obligations not only to shareholders but to other parties that are affected by its activities. We shall return to the notion of stakeholders when we explore the dimensions of CSR later in this chapter.

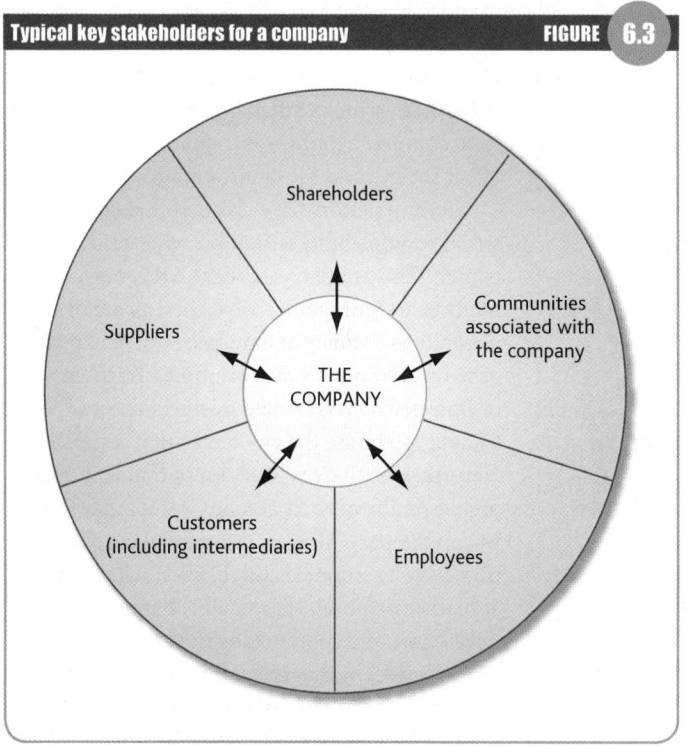

Typical key stakeholders for a company   FIGURE **6.3**

The nature of corporate social responsibility

A useful way of examining the nature of CSR is Carroll's four-part model of corporate social responsibility.[27] Carroll views CSR as a multilayered concept that can be divided into four interrelated responsibilities: economic, legal, ethical and philanthropic. The presentation of these responsibilities is in the form of layers within a pyramid and the full achievement of CSR occurs only when all four layers are met consecutively (see Fig. 6.4).

Economic responsibilities

Carroll recognized that the principal role of a firm was to produce goods and services that people wanted and to be as profitable as possible in so doing. Economic responsibilities include maintaining a strong competitive position, operating at high levels of efficiency and effectiveness, and aiming for consistently high levels of profitability. Without the achievement of economic responsibilities, the other three are redundant since the firm would go out of business. Economic success is the *sine qua non* of CSR.

Legal responsibilities

Companies must pursue their economic responsibilities within the framework of the law. Laws reflect society's principles and standards that are enforceable in the courts. Occasionally, the drive to maximize profits can conflict with the law—as with Microsoft, which has faced heavy financial penalties both in Europe and the USA for anti-competitive behaviour (for example, bundling Media Player into the Windows operating system thereby squeezing out competitors' software). Like economic responsibilities, the meeting of legal responsibilities is a requirement of CSR.

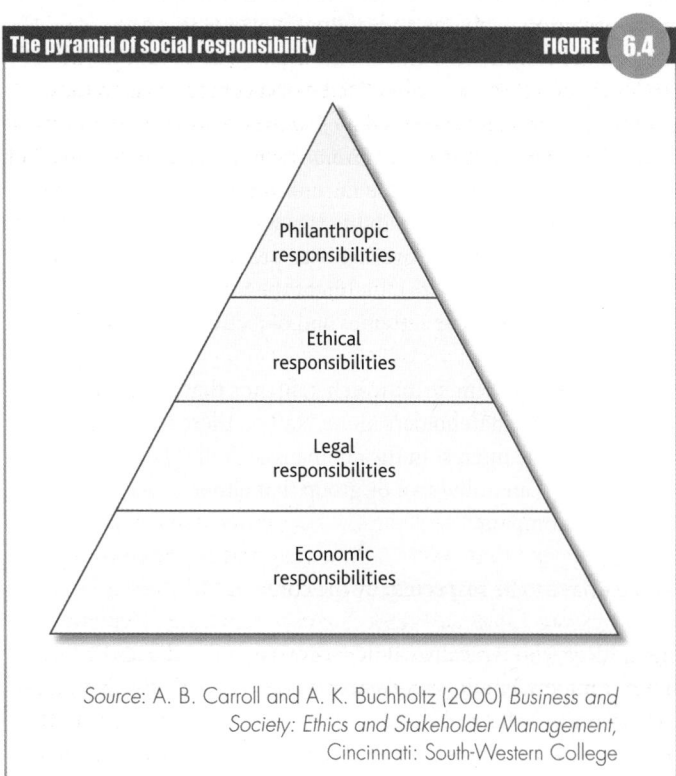

The pyramid of social responsibility   FIGURE **6.4**

Source: A. B. Carroll and A. K. Buchholtz (2000) *Business and Society: Ethics and Stakeholder Management,* Cincinnati: South-Western College

Ethical responsibilities

Although the establishment of laws may be founded on ethical considerations, as we have seen there can be important distinctions, as with the selling of genetically modified (GM) products, which may raise ethical questions and yet be lawful. Ethical responsibilities mean that companies should perform in a manner consistent with the principles and values of society and prevent ethical norms being compromised in order to achieve corporate objectives. Companies such as BP draw up codes of ethical conduct and employ teams to govern legal compliance and business ethics (252 BP employees were dismissed in one year for unethical behaviour in a drive to weed out bribery and corruption).[28] Ethical responsibilities therefore comprise what is expected by society over and above economic and legal requirements.

Philanthropic responsibilities

At the top of the pyramid are the philanthropic responsibilities of firms. These are corporate actions that meet society's expectation that businesses be good corporate citizens. This includes promoting human welfare or goodwill, such as making charitable donations, the building of leisure facilities or even homes for employees and their families, arts and sports sponsorship, and support for local schools.[29] The key difference between philanthropic and ethical responsibilities is that the former is not expected in an ethical sense. Communities may desire companies to contribute to their well-being but do not consider them unethical if they do not. Philanthropic responsibilities are presented at the top of the pyramid as they represent the 'icing on the cake': actions that are desired by society but not expected or required. Bill Gates of Microsoft is noted for his philanthropic gestures. For example, he has donated £500 million towards reducing deaths from tuberculosis, which kills 2 million people a year, most of them in the developing world.[30]

A strength of the four-part model of CSR is its realism in recognizing that, without the fulfilment of economic responsibilities a company would not have the capability to engage in ethical and/or philanthropic activities. However, to gain a deeper understanding of the scope of CSR activities it is necessary to explore its dimensions as well as its responsibilities.

The dimensions of corporate social responsibility

We have seen that CSR has four layers of responsibility: economic, legal, ethical and philanthropic. By examining the dimensions of CSR an insight into where those responsibilities may be discharged can be gained. CSR dimensions are based on four key stakeholders who are the individuals or groups who are affected by a company's activities, plus the physical environment that equally can be affected by its activities such as pollution or usage of scarce natural resources.[31] Table 6.1 outlines the CSR dimensions, lists associated key issues and describes marketing responses for each dimension. An important point to realize is that the key issues relating to each CSR dimension are not all exclusively marketing related. For example, pollution control at a chemical plant is a production-related issue, standard setting for supplies is a procurement-related topic, and the setting of fair pay is a human resources issue. Nevertheless, for most of the issues listed in Table 6.1 marketing practices can affect outcomes. For example, car design can affect pollution levels and the rate at which oil reserves are depleted, and the creation of healthy-eating brands can improve consumers' diets through the reduction in fat, sugar and salt levels.

Physical environment

The key issues in the physical environment, such as the use of environmentally friendly ingredients and components, recycling and non-wasteful packaging and pollution control, are necessarily discussed in Chapter 3, on the marketing environment. Marketers' response can be summarized under the term sustainable marketing. Environmental sustainability means to maintain or prolong the physical environment. It involves action towards the use of renewable rather than finite raw materials, and minimization and eventual elimination of polluting effluents and toxic or hazardous wastes. **Sustainable marketing** contributes to this goal by focusing on environmental issues and reducing environmental damage by creating, producing and delivering sustainable solutions while continuing to satisfy customers and

Dimensions of corporate social responsibility		TABLE 6.1
Dimension	**Key issues**	**Marketing response**
Physical environment	Combating global warming Pollution control Conservation of energy and other scarce resources Use of environmentally friendly ingredients and components Recycling and non-wasteful packaging	Sustainable marketing
Social (community involvement)	Support for the local community Support for the wider community	Societal marketing Cause-related marketing
Consumer	Product safety (including the avoidance of harmful long-term effects) Avoidance of price fixing Honesty in communications Respecting privacy	Societal marketing
Supply chain	Fair trading standard setting for supplies (e.g. human rights, labour standards and environmental responsibility)	Fair trade marketing
Employee relations	Fair pay Equal opportunities Training and motivation Information provision (e.g. on career paths, recruitment policies and training opportunities)	Internal marketing

other stakeholders. As 3M describes it: 'business will need to accept a moral imperative towards planetary ecological problems'.[32]

Since marketing operates at the interface between the organization and its environment it is uniquely positioned to lead the move towards more sustainable products and strategies. Typically, companies will move through several stages (see Fig. 6.5). To facilitate the process, marketing as a function needs to address a range of questions from the strategic to the tactical. Key questions are as follows.[33]

- Have the effects of sustainability issues on company activities been analysed as part of the marketing planning process?
- Has the company conducted marketing research into the probable impacts on the organization of sustainability issues?
- Can the company modify existing products, services or processes to take account of sustainability considerations, or will innovations be required?
- Is the firm developing positive links with environmental groups?
- Do communications strategies accurately emphasize environmental considerations?

Responding positively to environmental issues is important in order to protect and sustain brands. Market-leading brands are always susceptible to attack by media and/or pressure groups following any environmental incident. It is, therefore, sensible to build into brand strategies sustainability issues to nurture and maintain brand trust.

Environmental issues can be a source of threats to organizations, but they can also provide opportunities. Toyota has responded to environmental trends by successfully launching the Toyota Prius hybrid car, which supplements normal fuel with an electric-powered engine. The electric engine starts the car and operates at low speeds using a battery. At higher speeds the Prius automatically switches to a normal engine and fuel. This saves on fuel and is less polluting. The success of the Prius has led many of its rivals, including Honda, to launch similar hybrid cars, and to the development of electric cars powered by lithium-ion batteries.

The production of biofuel has risen dramatically as companies have seized the opportunity to replace petrol. For example, BP has invested £284 million in biofuels. However, opposition from environmentalists may hamper further development. They fear that carbon-absorbing rainforest in countries such as Brazil is being depleted to make way for fuel crops such as soya and palm, and that such crops are displacing land use for food, forcing up prices.[34] Detergent companies like Unilever have also embraced sustainable marketing by producing concentrated soap powder that both helps the environment and improves profitability. Environmental damage is reduced because the product requires less plastic, less water, less space for transportation, less plastic, fewer chemicals and less packaging.[35] Procter & Gamble has also promoted the benefit of low-temperature washing with its award-winning Ariel 'Turn to 30' campaign, which raised awareness of the impact of washing temperatures on emissions.[36]

The giant US corporation GE has also embraced the environment as a source of opportunity, as Marketing Ethics and Corporate Social Responsibility in Action 6.3 describes.

 6.3 Marketing Ethics and Corporate Social Responsibility in Action

A Lean, Green Electric Machine: the Greening of GE

Not hitherto noted for its environmentally green credentials, GE the US-based multinational, has embarked on a project called Ecomagination. This programme is charged with building sales of green technologies (renewable energy, water filtration systems, and cleaner aircraft and locomotive engines) from $10 billion to $20 billion in six years. To achieve this, Jeffrey Immett, GE's chief executive, has pledged to double research spending on clean products from $700 million per year to $1.5 billion. So convinced is he that clean technologies are the future that he has made his new mantra 'green is green', equating the green of the environment with the green of the US dollar.

To qualify for Ecomagination branding, products must 'significantly and measurably' improve customers' environmental and operating performance. Already the company produces the GEnx aero engine, which powers the Airbus 350 and Boeing 787 and is 15 per cent more energy efficient than its predecessors, and the compact florescent light bulb that saves 70–80 per cent of energy compared to ordinary light bulbs.

The Ecomagination programme requires GE to cut its greenhouse gas emissions by 1 per cent by 2012. Given that GE's emissions would have risen by 40 per cent without the programme this represents a mammoth undertaking. In line with this target, managers of its global businesses will be assessed not only on the achievement of the usual financial measures but also held responsible for cutting emissions.

GE has also joined forces with other big companies and NGOs to form the US Climate Action Partnership, to lobby for national legislation in America to cap carbon emissions. GE's actions find favour with environmental groups, which have campaigned against some of its polluting activities in the past.

Based on: Anonymous (2005);[37] Harvey (2005);[38] Caulkin (2006);[39] Anonymous (2008)[40]

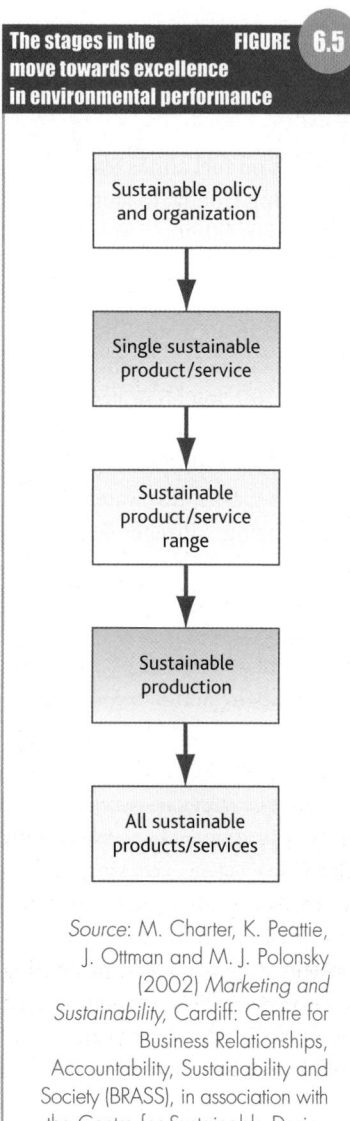

The stages in the move towards excellence in environmental performance   FIGURE 6.5

Sustainable policy and organization

↓

Single sustainable product/service

↓

Sustainable product/service range

↓

Sustainable production

↓

All sustainable products/services

Source: M. Charter, K. Peattie, J. Ottman and M. J. Polonsky (2002) *Marketing and Sustainability*, Cardiff: Centre for Business Relationships, Accountability, Sustainability and Society (BRASS), in association with the Centre for Sustainable Design

Nor should organizations assume that being environmentally sound necessarily means higher costs. For example, energy-efficient measures that help to combat climate change by cutting down on fossil fuel use can save money on energy bills.[41] Nor should it be assumed that ethically based products are inferior. The advertisement for Green & Black's displays its organic credentials, while communicating its taste appeal.

Social and consumer dimensions

Social concerns that business has sought to address are the need to support local and wider communities. Consumer concerns include the effect of business activities on product safety, including the avoidance of harmful long-term effects, the avoidance of price fixing, honesty in communications, and respecting privacy. Although social and consumer dimensions of CSR are distinct as their key issues differ, the two dimensions are analysed together as marketing's major response—societal marketing—embraces both. Whereas sustainable marketing focuses on the physical environment, societal marketing relates to marketing's direct effect on people, both in the form of consumers and society in general.

Societal marketing takes into account consumers' and society's wider interests rather than their short-term consumption. One aim of societal marketing is to consider consumers' needs and long-term welfare and society's long-term welfare as keys to satisfying organization objectives and responsibilities. It aims to rectify potential conflicts between consumers' short-term needs—for example, fast food that may contain high levels of fat, sugar and salt—and their long-term health. In the face of intense media pressure, including the hit film *Super Size Me*, which records a film-maker's descent into serious illness while living on a McDonald's-only diet, the company has introduced healthy-eating options including salads and mineral water (instead of the ubiquitous cola). While cynics may view this as a public relations exercise, the response of McDonald's may be regarded as a move towards implementing societal marketing principles. Kraft is another company responding to consumers' demands for healthier foods by cutting fat in its Philadelphia Lite soft cheese and cutting salt in its Dairylea product line by over 30 per cent.[42] Societal marketing also means that those activities that are not in consumers' or society's short- and long-term interests—such as price fixing, dishonest communications and invasions of privacy—are avoided and training is given to employees to lay out the boundaries of acceptable behaviour.

A further aspect of societal marketing is in providing support for local and wider communities. This may take the form of charitable donations (Wal-Mart, for example, historically has made huge donations to charities), or through partnerships with charities or causes—an activity called **cause-related marketing**. This is a commercial activity by which businesses and charities or causes form a partnership with each other to market an image or product for mutual benefit. As consumers increasingly demand accountability and responsibility from businesses, companies such as Procter & Gamble, Unilever, Tesco, IBM, British Gas and Orange have all incorporated major cause-related marketing programmes. Typical activities include sponsoring events such as Comic Relief (Procter & Gamble and Unilever), raising money and resources for schools (Tesco and IBM) tackling social problems such as fuel poverty (British Gas) and sponsoring the arts (Orange).

A set of cause-related marketing principles has been developed by Business in the Community, as reproduced below.[43]

NEW BAR OPENING

CREAMY MILK

GREEN
&BLACK'S
ORGANIC

Milk Chocolate
smooth and creamy,
it melts in the mouth effortlessly
30% Cocoa
100g ℮

Get in line for the smoothest, creamiest,
most indulgent milk chocolate imaginable.

GREEN
&BLACK'S
ORGANIC

CREATED WITHOUT COMPROMISE

www.greenandblacks.com

▲ Ethical brands can also taste wonderful.

1 Integrity: behaving honestly and ethically.
2 Transparency: misleading information could cast doubt on the equity of the partnership.
3 Sincerity: consumers need to be convinced about the strength and depth of a cause-related marketing partnership.
4 Mutual respect: the partner and its values must be appreciated and respected.
5 Partnership: each partner needs to recognize the opportunities and threats the relationship presents.
6 Mutual benefit: for the relationship to be sustainable, both sides must benefit.

Cause-related marketing works well when the business and charity have a similar target audience. For example, Nambarrie Tea Company, a Northern Ireland winner of the annual Business in the Community award for excellence in cause-related marketing, chose to sponsor the breast cancer agency Action Cancer. The company and the charity targeted women aged 16–60. In a two-month period, Nambarrie released 100,000 specially designed packs promoting its sponsorship of Action Cancer and covered media costs for a TV advertising campaign. This generated income of over £200,000.[44]

Critics of societal marketing view it as a short-term public relations exercise that cynically manipulates a company's stakeholders. Supporters argue that the stakeholder principle suggests that it is in a company's long-term interests to support the long-run concerns of consumers and society, resulting in a win-win situation.

By combining sustainable and societal marketing initiatives, organizations become better prepared to meet the requirements of triple bottom-line reporting, which takes into account not only financial matters but also environmental and social issues.

Supply chain

In her book *No Logo*, Naomi Klein castigated companies that, empowered by global brands, were exploiting the world's poor. Two key concerns were unfair trading and the lack of standard setting for suppliers over such issues as human rights, labour standards and environmental responsibility.[45] One company that came under attack was Nike in relation to the use or exploitation of contract workers in so-called sweatshops in less developed countries. In response to this and other media criticisms, Nike released a 108-page corporate social responsibility report that details the location of all its contract factories, thus facilitating external scrutiny, and provides a critical assessment of its progress towards meeting CSR objectives.[46]

This represented a marked improvement in Nike's handling of its obligations to its supply chain and corporate social responsibilities. IKEA is another company that has made progress towards setting standards for its suppliers by discouraging Indian rug makers from using child labour.

Unfair trading arises when large buyers exert their power on small commodity producers to force prices to very low levels. This can bring severe economic hardship to the producers, who may be situated in countries of the developing world. Many of the growers of such products as coffee, tea and cocoa live in poverty and face hardship in the form of poor working conditions, health problems and prices that fail to provide a living wage. Fair trade seeks to improve the prospects of suppliers through ethical trading, including the guaranteeing of minimum prices.

Fair trade marketing is the development, promotion and selling of fair trade brands and the positioning of organizations on the basis of a fair trade ethos. Companies are increasingly realizing that many consumers care about how suppliers in countries of the developing world are treated, and wish to support them by buying fair trade brands, often at a price premium. For example, Cafédirect, a fair trade company and brand, was launched to protect coffee growers from the volatility in world coffee prices. Minimum prices for coffee beans are paid, which are pegged above market fluctuations, and business support and development programmes are provided. The popularity of fair trade brands has prompted Nestlé to launch its own fair trade coffee, Partners' Blend, and Marks & Spencer has launched a range of fair trade clothing, which benefits Indian cotton farmers through a price that includes a premium that can be invested in their communities.[47] Supermarkets are supporting fair trade products, with the Co-op stocking only own-label fair trade tea, coffee and chocolates, and Sainsbury's selling only fair trade bananas. Coffee bar chains such as Costa Coffee and Pret A Manger offer fair trade varieties. Ben & Jerry's also positions as a fair trade brand with its support for farmers (see illustration).

Ad insight

Go to the website to see how Ben & Jerry's TV ad promotes its fair trade flavour

Fair trade marketing can also be based on the positioning of companies on a fair trade ethos. The Body Shop has for many years operated a 'Trade Not Aid' programme, which assists small-scale, indigenous communities in improving their standard of living through fair prices to suppliers.[48]

The success of fair trade marketing is based upon consumers being willing to try and repeat-buy fair trade brands and organizations developing genuine fair trade programmes. Consumers will not put up with organizations that use such schemes as an ethical veneer, and websites such as Corporate Watch (www.corporatewatch.org) and Greenpeace (www.greenpeace.org) provide examples of dubious practice by companies that consumers can boycott or campaign against in the press.[49]

Employee relations

Poor employee relations can have harmful marketing consequences. For example, Wal-Mart has suffered from years of allegations regarding low pay and sexually discriminatory hiring and employment practices, a situation it is seeking to address.[50] Bad publicity can deter ethically aware consumers from buying from

◄ Ben & Jerry's is a brand supporting farmers by sourcing fair trade sugar, cocoa and vanilla.

companies that suffer such criticism. While most employee relations issues are the province of the human resources function, marketing can play a role through internal marketing programmes. **Internal marketing** is the development, training and motivation of employees designed to enhance their performance in providing customer satisfaction. The idea began in service organizations such as hotels and restaurants where staff are in daily communication with customers, but has spread to all sectors in reflection of the need for all employees who come into contact with customers to be trained in how to deal with such issues as giving help, dealing with complaints and treating customers respectfully. Such training avoids, as far as possible, employee–customer arguments and conflict, which not only improves customer satisfaction but is good for staff morale, reduces stress levels and aids staff retention. Digital Marketing 6.1 describes how such an approach can be applied within a digital environment.

 ## 6.1 Digital Marketing

Happy Employees Win Company Awards

Corporate social responsibility (CSR) has many dimensions, one of which is employee relations; successful staff training programmes can have a significant impact on a company's overall effectiveness. Happy Computers is a company that has an enviable reputation and has won many industry and service excellence awards. The computer training company believes that learning should be fun. The training programmes bring together technical expertise and excellent training skills. The training is based on the following ideas:

- tell me and I will forget
- show me and I will remember
- involve me and I will understand.

Henry Stewart and Cathy Busani founded the company in 1990 in response to their clients asking for help to create *great* workplaces. At Happy, there is a relatively small workforce of 45 employees, which has a unique approach to CSR training. It has won numerous awards for innovative approaches to training, customer service and the quality of the working environment. Cathy is managing director of Happy Ltd and is responsible for Happy employees. She has been rated one of the best bosses in the UK in two separate national awards programmes. She is passionate about valuing people and the role they play in creating truly great places to work. The company achieves its success by applying some straightforward principles:

- transparency is important throughout (e.g. employees at the top or bottom of the scale are all aware of pay information)
- belief in the ability of the individual—members of the Happy team hold a fundamental belief that all people (with no exceptions) are born with enormous intelligence and tremendous eagerness to learn
- celebrate mistakes as part of the culture to engender learning and development—Happy believes that if you do not make mistakes you are not actively learning; it believes that you should enable an employee's natural learning abilities and delight in new possibilities to allow them to come to the fore
- create a feelgood environment as individuals work to their best ability when they feel good about themselves; Happy has created a workplace where people are trusted to make the key decisions about their work
- share information—as Francis Bacon said, 'knowledge is power'; Happy's management team takes the view that information is required to make informed decisions and to enable individuals to take responsibility and full ownership of their jobs.

Applying these principles has enabled Happy to do more than win awards. It has zero recruitment costs. This is due to its employee-focused working environment, high staff morale and demand from potential employees desiring to work for this unique organization.

Based on: www.happy.co.uk

6.2 Pause for Thought

Which corporate social responsibility dimension is particularly relevant to marketing activities or are they all of roughly equal relevance?

Marketing Ethics and Corporate Social Responsibility in Action 6.4 illustrates how some companies are responding to ethical challenges.

6.4 Marketing Ethics and Corporate Social Responsibility in Action

The Feelgood Factor

Companies around the world are taking the corporate social responsibility challenge seriously. Here are some examples.

- TNT, the Dutch logistics firm, has 50 people on standby to intervene anywhere in the world at 48 hours' notice to emergencies. This is part of a partnership with the World Food Programme, the UN agency that fights hunger.
- IBM's philanthropic spending was almost all US-based in the 1990s but is now 60 per cent outside. Part of this involves the assignment of young staff to work on one-month worthy projects in the developing world.
- KPMG, the British accountancy firm, allows staff half a day a month of their paid-for time to work in the community. This now totals 40,000 donated hours a year.
- Novo Nordisk, the Danish manufacturer of insulin, has written the 'triple bottom line' (striving to act in a financially, environmentally and socially responsible way) into its articles of association. It believes that having the ethos anchored so firmly makes the company more alert to both risks and opportunities.
- Orange, the French-owned mobile phone operator, recycles point-of-sale material. For example, metal is recycled into fencing and window grilles, and plastic is sent for the manufacture of pens and garden furniture.

Based on: Franklin (2008);[51] *Jack (2008)*[52]

Arguments for and against corporate social responsibility programmes

Not every observer believes that profit-orientated organizations should undertake CSR programmes. First, the arguments against will be examined.

CSR is misguided

In 1970 the Nobel Prize-winning economist Milton Friedman published a seminal article arguing that it was managers' responsibility to generate profits for their shareholders. To act in any other way was a betrayal of this special responsibility. He saw addressing social problems as being the province of governments not company managers. He did not believe, therefore, that managers should spend other people's money on some perceived social benefit, and thought that to do so was misguided.[53]

CSR is too costly

Spending in the USA on CSR activities is in excess of $3 billion and while Europe does not match this figure spending there is vast too.[54] This brings with it the lost opportunity to spend the money on other priorities, such as research and development.

CSR encourages consumer cynicism

Many consumers regard CSR initiatives as little more than public relations exercises. Corporate brands delegate tasks to 'ethics officers' who in turn outsource the task of delivering the organization's values to consultants.[55] Senior management then takes up the minimum number of initiatives that it believes places the company in an acceptable light among its stakeholders, without really embracing the ideas and ideals associated with those values.

CSR does not improve profitability

Accused of artificially upgrading its oil reserve figures by a fifth to help boost financial bonuses to staff, Shell was fined £84 million by the SEC in the USA and the Financial Services Authority in the UK. The scandal led to the dismissal of its chairman and two other senior executives. More damage to the company's image was done by the FSA's accusation that Shell had engaged in 'unprecedented misconduct', and comments from oil experts that it was a corporate scandal of 'historic proportions'.[56] Critics of CSR point out that, despite the bad publicity and tarnished corporate reputation, Shell's profitability was not harmed since it generated record profits just a few years after the scandal. Further, an academic review of 167 studies over 35 years concluded that although there was a positive association between companies' social and financial performance, the link was weak. It would seem that the companies are not richly rewarded for CSR. However, neither does CSR appear to harm profits, and there is the potential for smarter forms of CSR to produce better returns in the future.[57]

There are also arguments *for* CSR programmes, which help explain their current popularity.

CSR leads to enhanced brand/corporate image and reputation

A strong reputation in environmental and social responsibility can help a company build trust and enhance the image of its brands. For example, BP has also taken steps to reduce harmful emissions, as its advertisement shows. Orange has enhanced its image through sponsorship of the arts. This approach can help when a company is faced with media criticism or regulatory scrutiny. Also if a company is moving to a new area or new market, or opening a new site such as a distribution centre, store or factory, it helps to be seen as trustworthy and a 'good neighbour'.[58]

CSR provides marketing opportunities

Environmental and social responsibility has created new markets for business-to-business and consumer goods and services. For example, GE is expanding its marketing of 'clean' technological goods to companies, and Cafédirect, Green & Black's, innocent drinks and the Body Shop have built their businesses on corporate social responsibility ideals. Market segments have emerged based on 'green' credentials that provide targeting opportunities. One segment—known as ethical hardcores or dark greens—research companies and their practices thoroughly before buying their products. They view ethical consumerism as a way of life, whatever the sacrifice. A second segment—known as ethical lites or light greens—do their bit but do not have the time to research products or companies thoroughly.[59] They are happy to recycle newspapers, plastics and other material from their homes and buy ethical brands, provided there is not too much of a price premium.

CSR can reduce operating costs

Far from increasing operating costs, as is often assumed, better environmental management systems can improve efficiency by reducing waste, increasing energy efficiency and, in some cases, selling recycled materials.[60] For example, DuPont uses 7 per cent less energy than it did in 1990, despite producing 30 per cent more goods, thereby saving $2 billion, including savings of at least $10 million per year by using renewable sources.[61]

CSR increases organizations' ability to attract and retain employees

Many employees are attracted to employers who are active in social issues. For example, membership of Netimpact.org, a network of socially conscious MBA graduates, rose from 4000 in 2002 to over 10,000 in 2009, and some companies, such as salesforce.com (an Internet-based services company), have a policy of good corporate citizenship (staff are encouraged to devote time, at the company's expense, to charitable works) that they believe helps to attract, retain and motivate employees.[62]

CSR is a form of risk management

There are real penalties for companies that are not environmentally or socially responsible. The media criticisms of such companies as Nike (child labour in the developed world), BNFL (toxic discharges in the Irish Sea) and Enron (financial scandals) have shown the harm that can arise from being perceived as irresponsible. CSR, then, can be employed as a form of risk management, which reduces the chances of being the subject of the next corporate scandal to hit the headlines.

CSR improves access to capital

Organizations that are committed to CSR have access to socially responsible investment (SRI), whereby investors take into account considerations such as a company's environmental and socially responsible activities. These can be assessed using indices such as Business in the Community's Corporate Responsibility Index and the FTSE4 Good Index.[63]

Currently the strengths of the arguments for CSR programmes are driving companies increasingly towards the adoption of socially and environmentally responsible strategies.

Societal Responses to Ethical Issues in Marketing

Societal responses to ethical issues in marketing take three forms: consumerism, environmentalism and ethical consumption.

Consumerism

Consumerism takes the form of organized action against business practices that are not in the interests of consumers. Organized action is taken through the **consumer movement**, which is an organized collection of groups and organizations whose objective is to protect the rights of consumers.

The consumer movement seeks to protect consumers' rights, which include the right to expect the product to be safe, for it to perform as expected and for communications for the product to be truthful and not mislead. Pressure from consumer groups in Europe has resulted in prohibitions on tobacco advertising, improvements in car safety, reductions in the levels of fat, sugar and salt in foods, restrictions on advertising alcohol to teenagers and the forcing of financial services companies to display true interest charges (the annual percentage rate, or APR) on advertisements for credit facilities. Further successes include unit pricing (stating the cost per unit of a brand), and ingredient labelling (stating the ingredients that go into a brand).

The consumer movement often takes the form of consumer associations, which campaign for consumers and provide product information on a comparative basis allowing consumers to make informed choices. These have been very successful in establishing themselves as credible and authoritative organizations and are seen as trusted providers of information to help consumer choice. Their actions help to improve consumer power when dealing with organizations.

Environmentalism

While consumerism focuses on improving the balance between consumer and organizational power, and protecting the rights of consumers in consumption decisions, environmentalism is broader in scope with its focus on the physical environment. **Environmentalism** is the organized movement of groups and organizations to protect and improve the physical environment. They are concerned that the production and consumption of products leads to global warming, pollution, the destruction of natural resources such as oil and forests, and non-biodegradable waste. They believe that producers and consumers should take account not only of short-term profits and satisfaction but the cost to the environment of their actions. They wish to maximize environmental quality, which is the satisfaction of individual needs in a manner that will yield the maximum benefits to the individual while minimizing the effects on people and natural resources.[64]

Environmentalists support the concept of environmental sustainability and pressure companies to adopt strategies that promote its objectives. Environmental sustainability means 'to maintain or prolong environmental health'. Pressure groups such as Greenpeace and Friends of the Earth have been successful in persuading organizations to produce 'greener' products such as cadmium-free batteries, ozone-safe aerosols, recycled toilet tissue and packaging, catalytic converters, lead-free petrol, unbleached tea bags and cruelty-free cosmetics. Also environmental groups in individual countries can successfully change company practices. For example, such groups in Finland and Germany, called upon UPM-Kymmene, Finland's largest company and Europe's biggest paper-making firm, to ensure that the replanting of trees matched felling. Major electrical manufactures like Philips and Electrolux incorporate environmental considerations systematically in new product development and this has led to the development of the ISO 14062 guidelines covering the integration of environmental considerations into product design and development.[65]

Environmentalists still have many concerns about how marketing and business actions more generally affect the environment. They will combine to pressure organizations to place more emphasis on controlling emissions that damage the ozone layer and therefore contribute to global warming, reduce harmful pollutants that are released into the air or dumped in rivers or the sea, and use recycled and recyclable materials in products. The aim is to maintain an environment that is not only fit for the current generation but for those in the future.

Ethical consumption

Consumerism and environmentalism are organized movements designed to protect society and the environment from the harmful effects of production and consumption. However, consumers also act in an individual way to protect society and the environment through engaging in ethical consumption. **Ethical consumption** occurs when individual consumers when making purchase decisions take into account not only personal interests but also the interests of society and the environment. Examples include the boycotting of products and companies that have poor records regarding social and environmental concerns, the buying of non-animal-tested products, choosing fair trade or organic products, avoiding products made by sweatshop or child labour and the purchasing of products that are made from recycled materials.[66]

There is considerable evidence that consumers do take ethical considerations into account when making buying decisions. For example, a Europe-wide survey into consumer's attitudes to corporate social responsibility,[67] which questioned 12,000 consumers in 12 countries, revealed that:

- 70 per cent of consumers considered a company's commitment to social responsibility important when buying a product; this was consistent across countries with over half of respondents in all 12 countries stating that CSR was an important factor and was particularly important in Spain (89 per cent) and the Netherlands (81 per cent)
- 20 per cent of consumers said they would be very willing to pay more for products that were environmentally and socially responsible; this proportion was highest in Denmark (56 per cent)
- almost 60 per cent believed businesses did not pay enough attention to their social responsibilities; this was highest in Finland (75 per cent) and the UK (71 per cent), and lowest in the Netherlands (40 per cent), Denmark (44 per cent) and Sweden (46 per cent).

As discussed earlier, ethical consumption can be segmented between ethical hardcores, or dark-green consumers, for whom ethical consumption is a way of life, and ethical lites or light-green consumers, who engage in ethical consumption so long as it does not intrude too much into their busy lifestyles or cost too much in terms of very high prices. The results of such surveys and the existence of ethically based market segments provide opportunities for marketers, and provide motivation for businesses to engage in CSR activities for pure commercial reasons, even when management does not hold ethical standards highly due to an intrinsic belief in moral values.

Legal and Regulatory Responses to Ethical Issues in Marketing

European countries are bound by several layers of laws and regulatory bodies that restrict company actions and encourage the use of ethical practices, as described below.

- **EU competition laws and regulatory bodies that seek to ban anti-competitive practices:** these regulations have teeth and have resulted in fines on such companies as Microsoft (product bundling), AstraZeneca (blocking generic copies of its ulcer drug), and Hoechst, Atofina and Akzo Nobel (price fixing) by the European Commission, a body set up to enforce EU competition and consumer law.
- **EU laws and regulatory bodies that aim to protect the rights of consumers:** consumers' rights are also protected by EU regulatory bodies and regulations. For example, consumers' interests regarding food safety are protected by the European Food Standards Authority, and the right to compensation for air travellers whose flights are overbooked, cancelled or delayed is covered by EU rules.
- **National laws covering consumer rights and protection, and competition regulation supported by government-backed regulatory bodies:** legislation at national level is also designed to prevent marketing and business malpractice. For example, the Financial Services Authority fined Shell £17 million under UK market abuse laws and the Securities and Exchange Commission fined the same company $120 million for breaches of SEC rules and US laws.
- **Voluntary bodies set up by industries to create and enforce codes of practice:** industries often prefer self-regulation to the imposition of laws by government. For example, most European countries are self-regulating with regard to advertising standards through the drawing up and enforcement of codes of practice.

Marketers in Europe have great freedom in which to practise their profession. Business-imposed, societal and legal constraints on their actions not only make good sense from a long-term social and environmental perspective, they make good long-run commercial sense, too.

When you have read this chapter

log on to the Online Learning Centre at www.mcgraw-hill.co.uk/ textbooks/jobber to explore chapter-by-chapter test questions, links and further online study tools for marketing.

Review

1 **The meaning of ethics, and business and marketing ethics**
- Ethics are the moral principles and values that govern the actions and decisions of an individual or group.
- Business ethics are the moral principles and values that guide a firm's behaviour.
- Marketing ethics are the moral principles and values that guide behaviour within the field of marketing.

2 **Ethical issues in marketing**
- Ethical issues in marketing relate to concerns about how the marketing mix is applied to consumers, and more general societal, environmental and political issues.
- Ethical issues relating to how the marketing mix is applied to consumers include product safety, price fixing, misleading advertising, deceptive selling, invasion of privacy through direct and Internet marketing activities, and the use of promotional and slotting allowances.
- Societal concerns focus on materialism and short-termism; environmental concerns focus on the impact of marketing decisions on the environment; and political concerns focus on the power that global companies can exert on consumers, governments and suppliers.

3 **Business, societal, and legal and regulatory responses to ethical concerns**
- The main response from businesses has been the adoption of corporate social responsibility as a philosophy guiding decisions and actions.
- Societal responses take the form of consumerism, environmentalism and ethical consumption.
- Legal and regulatory responses are the enactment of laws at European and national levels to protect the consumer and to outlaw anti-competitive business practices, and the establishment of regulatory bodies to enforce those laws. Many industries have also established organizations to apply self-regulation through the drawing up and enforcement of codes of practice.

4 **The stakeholder theory of the firm**
- Corporate social responsibility is based on the stakeholder theory of the firm, which contends that companies have multiple stakeholders, not just shareholders, to whom they hold a responsibility. These include communities associated with the company, employees, customers (including intermediaries) and suppliers.

5 **The nature of corporate social responsibility**
- Corporate social responsibility refers to the ethical principle that an organization should be accountable for how its behaviour might affect society and the environment.
- It has economic (e.g. the responsibility to aim for high profits), legal (the responsibility not to break the law), ethical (the responsibility to behave in a manner consistent with the principles and values of society) and philanthropic (the responsibility to be a good corporate citizen through, for example, financially supporting good causes) responsibilities.

6   The dimensions of corporate social responsibility

- The responsibilities of corporate social responsibility may be discharged across five dimensions: the physical environment, social, consumer, supply chain, and employee relations.
- Marketing's response to physical environment issues, such as combating global warming, is to apply sustainable marketing that aims to create, produce and deliver sustainable solutions to environmental problems while continuing to satisfy customers and other stakeholders.
- Marketing's response to societal and consumer issues, such as community support and product safety, is to apply societal marketing that seeks to take into account consumers' and society's wider interests rather than just their short-term consumption. Societal welfare is also enhanced by cause-related marketing, which is the commercial activity by which businesses and charities or causes form a partnership to market an image or product for mutual benefit.
- Marketing's response to supply chain issues, such as low prices to producers in the developing world, is to apply fair trade marketing, which is the development, promotion and selling of fair trade brands and the positioning of organizations on the basis of a fair trade ethos.
- Marketing's response to employee relations issues, such as training and motivation, is internal marketing, which is the development, training and motivation of employees designed to enhance their performance in providing customer satisfaction.

7   Arguments for and against corporate social responsibility

- Arguments against are that CSR is misguided and too costly.
- Arguments for are that CSR leads to enhanced brand/corporate image and reputation, provides marketing opportunities, reduces operating costs, increases an organization's ability to attract and retain employees, is a form of risk reduction, and improves access to capital.

Key Terms

business ethics the moral principles and values that guide a firm's behaviour

cause-related marketing a commercial activity by which businesses and charities or causes form a partnership with each other to market an image or product for mutual benefit

consumer movement an organized collection of groups and organizations whose objective it is to protect the rights of consumers

environmentalism the organized movement of groups and organizations to protect and improve the physical environment

ethical consumption the taking of purchase decisions not only on the basis of personal interests but also on the basis of the interests of society and the environment

ethics the moral principles and values that govern the actions and decisions of an individual or group

fair trade marketing the development, promotion and selling of fair trade brands and the positioning of organizations on the basis of a fair trade ethos

internal marketing training, motivating and communicating with staff to cause them to work effectively in providing customer satisfaction; more recently the term has been expanded to include marketing to all staff, with the aim of achieving the acceptance of marketing ideas and plans

marketing ethics the moral principles and values that guide behaviour within the field of marketing

societal marketing focuses on consumers' needs and long-term welfare as keys to satisfying organizational objectives and responsibilities by taking into account consumers' and societies' wider interests rather than just their short-term consumption

stakeholder an individual or group that either (i) is harmed by or benefits from the company, or (ii) whose rights can be violated or have to be respected by the company

stakeholder theory this contends that companies are not managed purely in the interests of their shareholders alone but a broader group including communities

associated with the company, employees, customers and suppliers

sustainable marketing focuses on reducing environmental damage by creating, producing and delivering sustainable solutions while continuing to satisfy customers and other stakeholders

Study Questions

1. 'Every individual necessarily labours to render the annual revenue of the society as great as he can. He generally, indeed, neither intends to promote the public interest, nor knows how much he is promoting it … he intends only his own gain, and he is in this, as in many other cases, led by an invisible hand to promote an end which was no part of his intention. Nor is it always the worse for the society that it was no part of it. By pursuing his own interest he frequently promotes that of the society more effectively than when he really intends to promote it. I have never known much good done by those who affected to trade for the public good.

    It is not from the benevolence of the butcher, the brewer, or the baker, that we expect our dinner, but from their regard to their own interest. We address ourselves, not to their humanity but to their self-love, and never talk to them of our own necessities but of their advantages.'

    (Adam Smith, *Wealth of Nations*)

    To what extent do you believe this viewpoint renders invalid the idea of corporate social responsibility?

2. What is 'marketing ethics'? To what extent do you believe marketing practices to be unethical and how might unethical practices in marketing be restricted?

3. What are the key responsibilities of corporate social responsibility and to what extent do you believe businesses should accept them?

4. Describe the five dimensions of corporate social responsibility. Evaluate marketing's response to the issues underlying each dimension.

5. What is meant by 'consumerism' and 'environmentalism'? To what extent do you believe these movements have achieved their goals of protecting consumers, society and the environment?

6. Evaluate the contention that if ethical consumption was the norm there would be no need to legislate to protect consumers.

References

1. Berkowitz, E. N., R. A. Kerin, S. W. Hartley and W. Rudelius (2004) *Marketing*, Boston, MA: McGraw-Hill.
2. Business for Social Responsibility Issue Briefs (2003) Overview of Business Ethics, www.bsr.org.
3. Anonymous (2008) The Good Consumer, *Economist* Special Report on Corporate Social Responsibility, 19 January, 16.
4. Bokaie, J. (2008) Behind the Ethical Rhetoric, *Marketing*, 21 May, 14.
5. Franklin, D. (2008) Just Good Business, *Economist* Special Report on Corporate Social Responsibility, 19 January, 1.
6. Naughton, J. (2006) Google's Founding Principles Fall at Great Firewall of China, *Observer*, Business and Media, 29 January, 10.
7. Reed, C. (2000) Ethics Frozen Out in the Ben & Jerry Ice Cream War, *Observer*, 13 February, 3; Anonymous (2000) Slipping Slopes, *Economist*, 15 April, 85.
8. Naughton (2006) op. cit.

9. Choveke, M. (2006) Can Anything Rescue Sunny D?, *Marketing Week*, 26 February, 7.

10. Milner, M. (2005) Brussels Inquiry Could Land BT with Huge Tax Bill, *Guardian*, 20 January, 20.

11. Milmo, D. (2007) BA Fined £270m and Now Faces £300m Lawsuit, *Guardian*, 2 August, 1.

12. O'Flaherty, K. (2008) Brands Behaving Badly, *Marketing Week*, 30 October, 20–1.

13. Devaney, P. (2005) Who Cares Wins, But is There a Hidden Agenda?, *Marketing Week*, 28 April, 34–5.

14. Milmo, S. (2006) M&S Boosts Ethical Image With Fairtrade Clothing, *Guardian*, 30 January, 21.

15. Everitt, P. (2009) Car Scrappage Schemes are Not a Motor Industry Green Scam, Guardian.co.uk, 19 March 2009, retrieved 3 April 2009, from www.guardian.co.uk/commentisfree/2009/mar/19/paul-everitt-response.

16. Gow, D. (2009) Germany Extends Car Scrappage Scheme, Guardian.co.uk, 26 March 2009, retrieved 3 April 2009, from www.guardian.co.uk/business/2009/mar/26/germany-car-scrappage-scheme.

17. Pearce, F. (2009) Cash-Back Scheme is Car Crash Logic, Guardian.co.uk, 12 March 2009, retrieved 3 April 2009, from www.guardian.co.uk/environment/2009/mar/12/greenwash-fred-pearce-cash-back-cars.

18. Wood, T. (2009) A British Car Icon Faces Up to Reality, Guardian.co.uk, 22 March 2009, retrieved 3 April 2009, from www.guardian.co.uk/business/2009/mar/22/jaguar-land-rover-automotive-industry.

19. Crook, C. (2005) The Good Company, *Economist*, 22 January, 3–4.

20. Gow, D. (2008) Record US Fine Ends Siemens Bribery Scandal, *Guardian*, 16 December, 24.

21. Moon, J. (2002) Corporate Social Responsibility: An Overview, in *The International Directory of Corporate Philanthropy*, London: Europa Books.

22. Moon (2002) op. cit.

23. Crook (2005) op. cit.

24. Moon (2002) op. cit.

25. Donaldson, T. and L. E. Preston (1995) The Stakeholder Theory of the Corporation: Concepts, Evidence, and Implications, *Academy of Management Review* 20(1), 15–91.

26. Crane, A. and D. Matten (2004) *Business Ethics: A European Perspective*, Oxford: Oxford University Press.

27. See Carroll, A. B. and A. K. Buchholtz (2000) *Business and Society: Ethics and Stakeholder Management*, Cincinnati: South-Western College; and Carroll, A. B. (1991) The Pyramid of Corporate Social Responsibility: Toward the Moral Management of Organizational Stakeholders, *Business Horizons*, July August, 39–48.

28. Boxell, J. and F. Harvey (2005) BP Sacked 252 in Corruption Drive, *Financial Times*, 12 April, 22.

29. Crane and Matten (2004) op. cit.

30. Elliott, L. and S. Boseley (2006) Gates Pledges $900m to Fight Against TB, *Guardian*, 28 January, 19.

31. See Maignan, I. and O. C. Ferrell (2004) Corporate Social Responsibility and Marketing: An Integrated Framework, *Journal of the Academy of Marketing Science* 32(1), 3–19; and Fukukawa, K. and J. Moon (2004) A Japanese Model of Corporate Social Responsibility: A Study of Online Reporting, *Journal of Corporate Citizenship* 16, Winter, 45–59.

32. Charter, M., K. Peattie, J. Ottman and M. J. Polonsky (2002) *Marketing and Sustainability*, Cardiff: Centre for Business Relationships, Accountability, Sustainability and Society (BRASS) in association with the Centre for Sustainable Design.

33. Charter, Peattie, Ottman and Polonsky (2002) op. cit.

34. Macalister, T. (2008) Undercut and Under Fire: UK Biofuel Feels Heat From All Sides, *Guardian*, 1 April, 28.

35. Skapinker, M. (2008) Taking a Hard Line On Soft Soap, *Financial Times*, 7 July, 16.

36. Murphy, C. (2008) Green Gold, *The Marketer*, September, 30–3.

37. Anonymous (2005) A Lean, Clean Electric Machine, *Economist*, 10 December, 79–81.

38. Harvey, F. (2005) GE Looks Out For a Cleaner Profit, *Financial Times*, 1 July, 13.

39. Caulkin, S. (2006) GE Decides it's Best to Look After the Greenhouse, *Observer*, 8 January, 8.

40. Anonymous (2008) A Change in Climate, *Economist* Special Report on Corporate Social Responsibility, 19 January, 14–18.

41. Harvey, F. (2005) How to Reap Profits and Save the Earth Too, *Financial Times*, 7 November, 9.

42. Clarke, B. (2008) Good Marketing Beats Regulation, *The Marketer*, March, 15.

43. Anderson, P. (1999) Give and Take, *Marketing Week*, 26 August, 39–41.

44. Anderson (1999) op. cit.

45. Klein, N. (2000) *No Logo*, London: Flamingo Publishing.

46. Devaney, P. (2005) Who Cares Wins, But is There a Hidden Agenda?, *Marketing Week*, 28 April, 34–5.

47. Milmo (2006) op. cit.

48. Crane and Matten (2004) op. cit.

49. CIM Insight Team (2005) Fair Trade?, *The Marketer*, January, 6–8.

50. Devaney (2005) op. cit.

51. Franklin (2008) op. cit., 4.

52. Jack, L. (2008) Turning Green into Gold, *Marketing Week*, 6 November, 29–35.

53. Friedman, M. (1970) The Social Responsibility of Business is to Increase the Profits, *New York Times Magazine*, 13 September, 8.

54. Grow, B., S. Hamm and L. Lee (2005) The Rebate Over Doing Good, *Economist*, 5/12 September, 78–80.

55. Plender, J. and A. Persaud (2005) Good Ethics Means More Than Ticking Boxes, *Financial Times*, 23 August, 10.

56. Milner, M. (2004) Shell Fined £84m Over Reserves Scandal, *Guardian*, 30 July, 16.

57. The results of the study were reported in Franklin (2008) op. cit., 10.

58. Sclater, I. (2005) Thank Goodness for Success, *The Marketer*, January, 11–13.

59. Parkinson, C. (2005) Make the Most of Your Ethics, *Marketing Week*, 9 June, 30–1.

60. Sclater (2005) op. cit.

61. Aston, A. and B. Helm (2005) The Race Against Climate Change, *Business Week*, 12/19 December, 85–93.

62. See Grow, Hamm and Lee (2005) op. cit. and Anonymous (2005) A Union of Concerned Executives, *Economist*, 22 January, 7–12.

63. Sclater (2005) op. cit.

64. Charter, Peattie, Ottman and Polonsky (2002) op. cit.

65. Charter, Peattie, Ottman and Polonsky (2002) op. cit.

66. Crane and Matten (2004) op. cit.

67. See MORI (2000) at www.csreurope.org, reported in Crane and Matten (2004) op. cit.

Microsoft

Bully or Benefactor?

Choice in marketing is sacrosanct, and increasingly the outcomes of the consumer society are built around the concept that choice is a fundamental right. Choice has long been associated with freedom, but freedom has a relative aspect to it, in that without adequate conditions for the use of freedom, it has little value. Within this view lies an important issue in relation to the nature of choice, freedom and coercion, and one that has been hotly debated between the European Commission and the computer giant Microsoft over the past few years. It is assumed that consumer well-being is synonymous with freedom to choose, rather than being forced to accept certain combinations; from an economic perspective a larger set of alternatives is seen as beneficial for consumers. The ongoing furore surrounding Microsoft hinges on those very issues of choice or, rather, lack of it, within the global computer software market.

Choice and ethics

Several years ago, Craig Smith developed the Consumer Sovereignty Test as a measure of ethical marketing practice. Essentially he identified three key elements that constituted consumer sovereignty: capability, information and choice. Smith argued that, for the marketing manager who wishes to pursue ethical marketing, consumer sovereignty should be the goal. Capability refers to how vulnerable the consumer is in terms of his or her decision-making ability; this might involve age, education or particular situational contexts, such as economic disadvantage. Information implies that information given by the marketer to the consumer should not be misleading or deceptive. Finally, choice is considered in terms of the availability of alternatives, and includes an understanding that a supplier should not aim to monopolize a market and thus reduce the possible alternatives. The central tenet of Smith's ethical concept of choice is whether a consumer can switch to another supplier; this ability depends fundamentally upon what other suppliers are available, and any barriers that might exist should not be put in the way of those consumers who wish to try another supplier.

Choice, ethics and Microsoft

Bill Gates, billionaire boss of Microsoft, has a reputation for philanthropy. His pledges of money to fight many of the world's diseases grab the headlines—not surprising since the Bill and Melinda Gates Foundation has given $20.1 billion since it was set up. In 2005 Bill Gates gave £145 million to fight malaria, and in 2006 he pledged £507 million to cut deaths from tuberculosis. Yet corporate and personal philanthropy have done little to avert the negative headlines about Microsoft's questionable business practices. Since 1999 Microsoft has been at the centre of a number of legal disputes, initially with the US Government, and latterly with the European Commission. At the heart of the disagreements have been accusations that Microsoft has been exploiting its monopoly power in order to reduce competition, and consequently choice, in the marketplace.

Background

Marc Andreeson launched the first commercial web browser in 1995. His company, Netscape, was valued at $2.7 billion, based on the potential that its pioneer Navigator browser made it easy to access the World Wide Web. The software itself didn't generate profits; in fact, it was given away free to computer users. Profits were made by charging companies who run websites for its Netscape 'server' software. (The server is the platform for providing online services to web users.) The strategy was so successful that, by 1996, Netscape had claimed 85 per cent market share and the company rose in value to $6 billion. However the horizon was clouded by a strong rival called Microsoft, set to challenge Netscape's dominance. The company marketed its own package, but this was inferior to the market leader and Microsoft was seen as market laggard. Microsoft boss Bill Gates invested hundreds of millions of dollars and thousands of staff to resolve the problem, and as a result Internet Explorer 3.0 was launched, matching the performance of its rivals. Given the financial clout of Microsoft, it was able to supply the browser software free of charge; in the meantime, Netscape, facing economic pressures, began to charge $49 for its Navigator software. Key to the Microsoft strategy was its domination of PC software, meaning that Internet Explorer would be supplied as part of the Windows 95 package to 46 million users in 1997.

By the time Internet Explorer 4.0 (IE4) was launched in late 1997, Microsoft held 36 per cent market share in the USA and 47 per cent of the UK browser market. However, Microsoft suddenly found itself embroiled in an anti-trust lawsuit brought by the US Government, accusing the company of exploiting its monopoly power in order to reduce competition. Part of the action threatened the practice of integrating its Internet Explorer software with its Windows operating system, which resulted in the shutting out of its main competitors. As it transpired, the US Department of Justice gave up its claim that this was illegal and Microsoft continued to 'bundle' its software; the latest version is now bundled with Windows Vista. Even with the entry of rivals on the scene, Microsoft's Internet Explorer still holds over 65 per cent of the browser market compared to Firefox (22 per cent) and Safari (8 per cent). Netscape, unable to survive alone, has been sold to America Online (AOL). It would seem that the market power and resources held by Microsoft proved too much for its rival.

Trouble brewing on a different front

The bundling of technology, and the ensuing reduction of free choice is an issue that the European Commission has been monitoring within the software industry. Market leader Microsoft was in its sights, and in March 2004 the EU competition commissioner Mario Monti imposed a fine of £330 million ($497m) for the infraction of bundling Media Player into the Windows operating system, and thus breaking the law by using its 'near monopoly' in operating systems to squeeze out rivals in other kinds of software. This was the largest anti-trust fine ever imposed by the EU. The money itself only made a small dent in Microsoft's $53 billion cash resources; however, the real damage lies in the fear that the European market would no longer be so friendly to Microsoft in the future. The ruling was a major inconvenience, requiring Microsoft to deliver two different products: the full Microsoft software with the Windows Media Player, and another with other vendors' software in it. Microsoft was angered, not least because of the uncertainty as to whether a stripped-down version of Windows, without Media Player, would be more popular than one with it, for the same price. More importantly, the long-term worry for Microsoft was the precedent set by the EC ruling, which would force it to unbundle Windows in its next generation of operating systems. Microsoft is looking at ways to wire all different consumer gadgets together and put the PC at the centre. Its vision has the PC, the TV, DVD players, video games machines, portable devices such as smart mobile phones, and gadgets such as the iPod all linking together.

Meanwhile Microsoft is facing other difficulties in Asia where the free Linux operating system may have a better chance of establishing dominance, particularly in the Chinese and Indian markets because Windows is too expensive. Currently Windows holds 88 per cent of the operating systems market, Mac 10 per cent and Linux 1 per cent. In emerging markets the cost-effectiveness of adopting Vista may be even less attractive because it requires new hardware systems to run it, and a newer version, Windows 7, will be out by 2010 to replace it. Institutional buyers are also taking heed; Hewlett-Packard announced worldwide rollout of PCs installed with Linux, and Munich city officials have recently switched from Windows to Linux. John Naughton (2004) of the *Observer* newspaper highlighted Microsoft's dilemma thus:

> Microsoft is a very successful company, but its success does not stem from technological innovation but from buying in innovative ideas, rebadging them and then bundling them with its operating system. In the process it creates a monopoly that wipes out potential markets for innovative newcomers.

Microsoft continued to challenge the EC ruling but, again in December 2004, a senior European judge upheld the decision, making it more difficult for Microsoft to add new functions and programs to its Windows operating system. As part of the March decision, not only was Microsoft ordered to pay the hefty fine and unbundle Media Player from Windows, but also to license information to rivals, making it easier for them to design servers that inter-operate with

// The Microsoft dispute takes place within an industry that is notably volatile and risky. Competitors come and go; dominance waxes and wanes. //

Windows-driven PCs. Microsoft responded by posting on a special website some of its secret protocols to enable rival operators to build server programs that are inter-operable with Windows. One commentator stated that the ruling 'sent a clear signal that Microsoft is not above the law and cannot continue abusing its monopoly power to the detriment of consumers and competitors'.

The software industry

The Microsoft dispute takes place within an industry that is notably volatile and risky. Competitors come and go; dominance waxes and wanes: 2004 was the year of Google and open source; the Apple iPod superseded the Sony Walkman, IBM exited the PC business, WiFi became a mainstream consumer product and demand for broadband in the UK exceeded all expectations. Microsoft found itself up against an institutional obstacle that it could 'neither intimidate nor buy'. It was also the year that open source software finally broke through on the desktop; Mozilla's Firefox, a web browser that outperforms Internet Explorer, led the assault. As a result, Internet Explorer has started to lose market share for the first time in years, and at an increasing rate.

One media commentator likened Microsoft's reaction to all of this as the behaviour of an unruly child: it spent a lot of time whining about imaginary dangers when confronted by the regulators, and argued that its trade secrets were under threat. In the past Sun Microsystems complained that Microsoft had improperly withheld information from rivals in order to ensure that its software for servers that work with desktop PCs was inferior to Microsoft's own; now Microsoft was being forced to license its protocols—the language used by one server to communicate with others—on fair and non-discriminatory terms. However, another dispute was about to ensue; by June 2005 arguments had broken out over the price Microsoft could charge rivals to access portions of software code that are needed so that products can inter-operate smoothly. Microsoft argues that this is intellectual property, and that it should be allowed to decide how to license; rivals say its terms are expensive, they block open source products and that—as the code is simply a matter of translating technical parameters—the intellectual property is nil.

Questions were also raised about the impact of the Commission's ruling about the new stripped-down version of Windows without Media Player software. Several of the world's largest personal computer makers said they had no plans to sell PCs loaded with the new version of Windows, unless European consumers

showed an interest in the pared-down version. Dell and Hewlett-Packard, as well as Gateway, said they were under no obligation to sell computers loaded with Windows 'N' (dubbed the 'N version' for 'not including Media Player'). Some consumers do buy the Windows operating system in retail outlets, but Microsoft sells most of its flagship product directly to the computer makers, who pre-install Windows along with other software. To overcome concerns already surfacing that the N version would be an inferior product, the European Commission ordered Microsoft to remove warnings in manuals and packaging claiming that certain applications would not work on the stripped-down version of Windows, a ruse believed to be aimed at instilling consumer doubts.

The future for Microsoft

While fending off anti-trust actions, Microsoft has continued to develop its portfolio. In May 2005 it unveiled the upcoming version of the Xbox gaming console direct to consumers via MTV, rather than—as had traditionally been the case—at an industry conference. Microsoft's gaming business—selling consoles and developing games—may be losing billions of dollars, but it represents much of the firm's future. Now 30 years old, Microsoft has gained a reputation as a bit of dinosaur in the fast-moving software industry; a company that had famously been 'lean, mean and agile, has become sluggish', It has been getting harder to persuade consumers to upgrade from older versions of Office and Windows to new, updated releases. Internet Explorer continues to lose market share to Firefox, and Microsoft is finding it harder to recruit world-class engineering talent, the best of which is now allegedly heading to the likes of Google, which is hogging the limelight as the most innovative company in the new business of delivering software-based services over the Internet. To further exacerbate matters, the next generation of Windows, Vista, was two years behind schedule, and attracted criticism for its more restrictive licensing terms, lack of compatibility with some pre-Vista hardware and software, and other user glitches. One analyst suggests that 'It isn't that they aren't innovating, but they aren't getting new ideas out fast enough into products.'

Some believe that the problems stem from Microsoft's scale and ambition, as well as a broader corporate strategy that revolves around two big products: Windows and the Office suite of software applications. Microsoft may well have compounded the problem by the scale of its ambition and a corporate strategy that relies on bundling as much as it can into the operating system; a machine that was accustomed to turning out bigger and ever more complex versions of the system finally hit a wall. The obvious response, according to software experts, is to 'unbundle' Windows into a series of separate software components, each linked by standard interfaces. That way, each part can be built independently and bolted together at a later stage, offering more flexibility and greater choice. At the moment, everything is intertwined, and trying to disentangle the 'spaghetti' is problematic.

Packing more features into the Windows code base has been at the heart of the company's strategy. It has been used to justify the regular upgrades that customers make to their PC operating systems. It has also been used as a defence against anti-trust regulators, who have challenged whether Microsoft needs to subsume so many other software categories into its operating system. By redesigning the system as a looser collection of components, there is a risk that Microsoft will find it harder to maintain its familiar argument that each is an integral part that cannot be removed without detriment to the overall system.

Meanwhile, rumblings about whether Microsoft is truly committed to ensuring inter-operability between its Windows operating system and those of rival companies prompted the appointment in 2005 of Professor Neil Barrett as an independent monitor to oversee the European Commission's enforcement of its ruling against Microsoft. Microsoft was still dragging its heels on action to comply with the EC ruling, arguing that the benefits to consumers of having an integrated product outweigh the anti-competitive effects of tying. By January 2006, under threat of further EC fines of £1.4 million ($2 million) per day, Microsoft reluctantly agreed to give rival software companies access to parts of its Windows source code, claiming it was putting its 'most valuable intellectual property on the table'. However, the EC argued it was vital this information be shared to allow rival companies to develop software that works smoothly with Windows-driven computers and servers. Even so, rivals were still unhappy, claiming that Microsoft has effectively dumped vast amounts of data without the 'roadmap' that tells them how to use it.

Consequently, in February 2006 IBM, Oracle, Sun Microsystems, Nokia and other technology groups,

// Some believe Microsoft's problems stem from its scale and ambition, as well as a broader corporate strategy that revolves around two big products. //

known as the 'European Committee for Interoperable Systems', filed a new anti-trust complaint against Microsoft. Issues remained the same: companies feared they would be unable to make software that operates with Microsoft's new Vista operating system; Microsoft was seeking to create an environment where a growing number of web-based applications functioned only with computers and servers driven by Windows; and that Microsoft continued to abuse its dominant position in the market for products and applications, such as Windows Word, Excel and PowerPoint.

By July 2006, the EU had decided to fine Microsoft an additional 280.5 million euros (US$448.58 million), and threatened to increase the fine to 3 million euros (US$4.80 million) per day if Microsoft did not comply. On 17 September 2007, Microsoft lost its appeal against the European Commission's case. The 497 million euro fine was upheld, as were the requirements regarding server interoperability information and bundling of Media Player. In addition, Microsoft had to pay 80 per cent of the legal costs of the Commission. While Microsoft announced that it would comply, and not appeal the EU decision, by February 2008 the EU was fining Microsoft an additional 899 million euros (US$1.44 billion) for failing to comply with the 2004 anti-trust decision. This was the largest penalty ever imposed in 50 years of EU competition policy, intended to punish Microsoft for abusing its dominant market position and, as EU Competition commissioner Neelie Kroes stated, 'to give consumers more choice in software markets'.

One would think that this might mark the end of the EU–Microsoft battle, but not so. At the beginning of 2008 the European Commission opened yet another two new anti-trust investigations of Microsoft's activities. The first case was in response to further complaints about the interoperability of Windows with other software; the second accused Microsoft of preventing other browsers from competing because of the bundling of Internet Explorer with the Windows operating system (violating anti-trust laws). Microsoft's response has been to argue against the EU, suggesting that such a move would strengthen its rival Google's dominance in the global search advertising market. Even individual countries are getting tougher. Germany fined Microsoft 9 million euros (US$11.9 million) for illegally pressing a retailer to sell its Office productivity software for a certain price.

It hasn't all been bad news for Microsoft, though. In 2005, Real Networks dropped its legal action instituted against Microsoft in return for $460 million; the suit had alleged that Microsoft had held back technical information about its Windows operating system that prevented Real Networks from developing compatible software. Microsoft is now working with Real Networks, providing promotional and marketing support for Real Networks' digital music subscription service, Rhapsody, on its MSN websites, and offering Real Networks' digital games through MSN Games and its online games portal, Xbox Live Arcade, for its Xbox 360 console. In a further move, Microsoft announced a deal with Yahoo!, the major Internet portal, to link up the two firms' instant messaging systems. While at one point Yahoo! rejected the deal, which offered $47.5 billion for the Internet business, there are still discussions ongoing about the two companies collaborating on search functions.

Evidently, cooperating with, rather than battling with old foes to compete against new ones is the future objective—and one that can't come too soon, as Microsoft's profits dived 32 per cent and 5000 job losses were announced in January 2009.

References

Ahmed, M. (2009) Microsoft Reopens Door to Deal with Yahoo!, Times Online, 9 March.

Alexander, G. (1999) Alliances Form in Battle to Dominate Mobile Computing, *Sunday Times*, 14 February, 7.

Anonymous (2000) After the Verdict, *Economist*, 8 April, 81–2.

Anonymous (2001) Not Off the Hook, *Economist*, 15 September, 68–9.

Anonymous (2005) Schizophrenia, *Economist*, 4 June, 76.

Barksdale, J. (1996) Microsoft Would Like to Squash Me Like A Bug, *Financial Times*, Special Report on IT, 2 October, 2.

Buck, T. (2004) Microsoft Loses EU Appeal, *Financial Times*, 23 December, 1.

Buck, T. (2005a) Microsoft Moves on EU Demands, *Financial Times*, 5 April, 30.

Buck, T. (2005b) Lawyers Pick over Microsoft Ruling, *Financial Times*, 23 December, 26.

Buck, T. (2006) Microsoft Faces New Antitrust Complaint, *Financial Times*, 23 February, 1.

Buck, T. (2006) Microsoft Offers Rivals Source Code, *Financial Times*, 26 January, 1.

Gapper, J. (2005) Microsoft's Inner Child Finally Gets it Right, *Financial Times*, 5 May, 17.

Garrett, A. (1997) Wrestling for the Soul of the Internet, *Observer*, 5 October, 7.

Gow, D. (2004) EU Upholds Microsoft Anti-Trust Ruling, *Guardian*, 24 December, 16.

Gow, D. (2005) Microsoft Closer to Meeting EU Anti-Trust Ruling, *Guardian*, 6 October, 22.

Gow, D. (2006) Microsoft Offers Codes to Avert EC Fines, *Guardian*, 26 January, 24.

Gow, D. (2007) Microsoft Gives Up Three Year Battle to Keep Windows Closed to Rivals, *Guardian*, 23 October.

Helmore, E. (2004) Do Not Pass Go Say EC, *Observer*, 28 March, 3.

Jobber, D. (2004) *Principles and Practice of Marketing*, London: McGraw-Hill.

Marsh, H. (1998) Microsoft's Real Trial is Trust, *Marketing*, 3 December, 16–17.

Naughton, J. (2005) Microsoft Foiled. Who Said There's No Santa Claus, *Observer*, 2 January, 3.

Smith, N.C. (1995) Marketing Strategies for the Ethics Era, *Sloan Management Review* 36(4), 85–98.

Spiegel, P. and P. Abrahams (2001) Microsoft rivals criticise legal deal, *Financial Times*, 2 November, 21.

Szmigin, I. and M. Carrigan (2004) The Tyranny of Choice: Revisiting the Consumer Sovereignty Test, *Academy of World Business, Marketing and Management Development Conference*, 13–16 July, Gold Coast International Hotel, Queensland, Australia.

Teather, D. and R. Wray (2005) Real Deal Ends Microsoft's US Legal Battle, *Guardian*, 12 October, 26.

Waters, R. (2005) Microsoft's Struggle With Scale, *Financial Times*, 19 September, 12.

Questions

1 To what extent do you believe consumers have a choice when it comes to software? What factors impact upon a consumer's ability to choose computer software and hardware?

2 What evidence is there to suggest that Microsoft is unfairly monopolizing the market? Do you consider its behaviour to be unethical? Justify your answer.

3 Bill Gates is a well-known philanthropist, yet his company appears to have a reputation for questionable business practices. In your opinion, how important is it to stakeholders that the ethics of the CEO match those of the organization? Explain your answer.

4 What do you consider to be the main challenges facing Microsoft in the future? Do you think it is capable of meeting those challenges?

This case was written by Marylyn Carrigan, Senior Lecturer in Marketing, Open University.

Fairtrade Coffee

Grounds for a Fresh Look at Ethical Consumption?

Catrin stood in front of the supermarket shelf labelled 'Coffees' and hesitated. The question 'When customers buy fair trade coffee, what do they really think they're buying into?' went through her mind. It was the question that had rounded off the documentary on fair trade that she had watched the previous night. She hadn't really planned to watch it, but an initial lack of motivation to get up and turn off the TV had given way to real interest in the story that had unfolded. By the end she had resolved to become a 'better shopper', and this was the first test of her resolve.

Before coming to university she had been only vaguely aware of fair trade, and thought (like many other people it seemed) that it was something to do with companies being 'ethical'. Once she had arrived at university, she had learnt more, since the students' union had fair trade coffees and other products, and she now knew it was about giving producers in poorer countries a better deal and a larger share of the purchase price.

The trouble was, as a student, she was what her marketing textbook would describe as a 'price-sensitive consumer', and the fair trade brands were a bit more expensive than the conventional ones. That thought, however, made her feel a little guilty. The documentary had shown how the crisis in coffee production had unfolded during the 1990s. At the beginning of the decade, the global coffee market was worth around $30 billion, of which the farmers received about $12 billion. Ten years later the world was drinking around $55 billion worth of coffee, but the farmers were receiving only about $7 billion. The collapse in global commodity prices had left many millions of farmers and their families in poorer countries struggling to survive at around, or below, subsistence levels. When studying marketing at university, it was easy to assume that 'consumers' were the same the world over, and it came as something of a shock to realize that four-fifths of the global population had no discretionary spending power, and therefore lived outside the world of consumer choice that her books described. She looked again at the various labels and the prices on the shelves in front of her and sighed. How could buying a jar of coffee, one of the mainstays of student life, be so complicated?

Fortunately, there was only a handful from among the hundreds of fair trade coffee brands now on offer in Europe in front of her. Even then, it wasn't as though fair trade was the only 'ethical' choice on offer. There was organically grown and 'rainforest friendly' coffee on the shelf too. Were these comparable? Was it more important how the product was produced, or how it was traded and sold, from an ethical point of view? It wasn't even as if all fair trade products were equal. The documentary had claimed that some of the retailer own-brand fair trade coffees paid farmers only just enough to earn the label, and then pocketed much of the premium price for themselves. She briefly considered going home via her local Co-op to pick up her coffee, since she knew that it was a strong and genuine promoter of fair trade products, and that it carried a range of fair trade own brands. However, that was a little out of her way and she was pressed for time, so she scanned the jars in front of her and told herself to choose.

Catrin tried to picture where all this fitted within the models of consumer behaviour that she had written an assignment on only the week before. The models all seemed to involve very clear-cut decision processes in which everything belonged in its own neat little box, and the whole process flowed along nicely, following the arrows from left to right to arrive at 'purchase'.

▲ The Fairtrade Foundation oversees the award of the fair-trade mark to a growing range of products.

Her purchase decision didn't seem to be flowing at all, but instead seemed to be stuck in a circular eddy. She remembered that some products and brands were described in the textbook as having an 'ethical augmentation'. Surely, though, for fair trade coffee, being fair trade was more than a mere augmentation—it was the whole point of the product in the first place!

Part of the problem was that coffee is not quite like most other groceries. It is something you offer to other people, and because of this it says something about you. If you bought fair trade sugar or pasta sauce, no one would be likely to notice unless you made a big thing about it. A jar of coffee with 'Catrin' written on it would say something to her housemates and everyone who came to visit. So who was she? Saviour of the planet? Defender of the poor? Creature of habit? Gourmet? Cheapskate? Or was she really just someone wasting time and energy over making what was only likely to be a token gesture anyway? She knew she wouldn't be applying this amount of thought and effort to the rest of her shopping, and that if she hadn't seen that documentary last night she would just be reaching for a jar of Nescafé as she usually did.

While thinking about token gestures and Nescafé, her eye came to rest on a jar of Nescafé's Partners' Blend fair trade coffee on the shelf. It was with the introduction of Nestlé into the documentary last night that the story had become both more interesting and a little ironic. The irony came from the fact that, since the early days of fair trade coffee, when it generally needed a strong stomach and a strong sense of social solidarity to enjoy, people had said that to really make a difference to the world, fair trade needed to be embraced by the mainstream brands, not just those in an ethical niche. Even though demand for fair trade coffee had increased

dramatically (with annual growth rates sometimes reaching as high as 50 per cent), still only about half of the coffee grown as fair trade was sold as such. The rest was simply sold as a standard commodity at the standard global market price, which had slipped to under half the fair trade price by 2002. Overall, fair trade coffee still accounted for only about a quarter of 1 per cent of total global production, even though that represented 60 per cent of all fair trade products sold. Now the biggest global coffee company [with a turnover of £38 billion] had moved into fair trade, but instead of being welcomed as a positive development, many people in the fair trade movement seemed to be treating it as a setback.

The Nestlé spokesperson had said that the company was moving into fair trade as a fundamental, serious commitment to improving the conditions of small farmers in Africa and Latin America, and to helping the fair trade market as a whole to grow. The Director of the Fairtrade Foundation, the organization that oversees the award of the Fairtrade mark, had described it as a step in the right direction, and a good example of customers demanding fair trade products and a big company then responding to meet their needs.

Others saw the move less charitably. A spokesperson for Oxfam, one of the charities that founded the fair trade movement, pointed out that it was big coffee companies like Nestlé that had driven down global market prices, which in turn had created so much of the poverty among the farmers, while making a fortune at their expense. A spokesperson for the American fair trade group Equal Exchange had claimed that estimates put Partners' Blend at under one-tenth of 1 per cent of all Nestlé's coffee imports. He claimed that this was one of many token gestures by such large companies, which look good and offer inexpensive marketing and PR opportunities for them, but ultimately forestall real change for impoverished small farmers. If Nestlé is serious about fair trade, he concluded, why isn't it applying it to the other 99 per cent of coffee beans that it buys, or to the vast amounts of cocoa, sugar, dairy products and dozens of other commodities that it also trades in?

This, Catrin had thought, was a good point. If Nestlé's strategy was values led, then shouldn't it be about the whole business rather than one product line? If it was to generate competitive advantage, didn't that suggest a strategy to pre-empt, capture and contain the growing market for fair trade coffee? It was certainly ironic that Nestlé had launched Partners' Blend at the end of 2005, the same year it had been voted the world's 'least responsible company'. A fair trade brand might do wonders for Nestlé's image and credibility, but what would association with Nestlé do for the image and credibility of fair trade?

Catrin picked up a jar of Cafédirect's Classics Medium Roast. She remembered it from the documentary as a major success story of the fair trade market. It had been the first UK coffee brand to carry the Fairtrade mark and had grown to become the sixth biggest UK coffee brand. Its sales growth the previous year had been 14 per cent and, as well as paying a premium price for its coffee, it had invested 86 per cent of its operating profit back into growers' organizations to help them develop their businesses and communities. Cafédirect had managed to rapidly build its brand by focusing on the quality of the coffee, more than by focusing on the fair trade message. As a spokesperson for the brand had said:

> We want people to buy it because it's good quality and once people start buying it because it's a very good product, then people will start getting the fair trade message … It is not that we wanted to do it that way, it just came out in all the different studies that [consumers] were more concerned about the quality of the product than the fair trade element. So we had to respond to that if we want to carry on in the market.

The jar certainly drove home the quality taste message, using the strap-line 'Smooth with a hint of nutty caramel'. The description of the product was also interesting: 'This deliciously smooth coffee brings together expertly blended Arabica and Robusta beans. Being Fairtrade means that growers always get a fair price for their coffee. And that, of course, leaves a better taste in the month'. This struck Catrin as rather a clever way of putting it. The back of the jar also had a picture of one of the coffee growers on it, alongside an endorsement from him. Catrin supposed that this helped to personalize the issue of the producers' welfare, and prevented concepts of trade and commodities just seeming like abstract marketing concepts. It was rather different, mused Catrin, to be marketing a product by stressing the benefits to the producer rather than to the consumer, and by explaining the benefits of a higher price rather than a lower one. Quite an interesting marketing challenge all in all, she thought.

One interesting side-effect of the entry of Nestlé into the fair trade market was the way that it seemed to have impacted the positioning strategies of the other brands. The new ad campaign for Cafédirect, which Catrin had spotted while browsing in the magazine aisle, was very strongly geared to highlighting the ethical difference between its brand and the mainstream.

'So,' thought Catrin to herself, 'what are consumers buying into when they buy a jar of fair trade coffee? I guess ultimately into the idea of a fairer world.' She looked again at the jar in her hand. It was undoubtedly ethical, it wasn't too expensive, the quality was supposed to be good, and it even had rather a nice picture on the front of the jar. 'Fair enough,' she thought, popping the jar into her basket and moving off towards the meat section, trying very hard not to start thinking about animal welfare.

Further reading

Anonymous (2004) Fair Trade: A Cooperative Revolution, *Cooperatives UK Magazine* 3, available at www.caledonia.org.uk/papers/Fair_Trade.doc.

Brinkman, J. and K. Peattie (2006) Integrating Consumer and Marketing Ethics: A Review of an Emerging Research Field, *BRASS Working Paper No. 33*, available at http://www.brass.cf.ac.uk/brassresources/02BRASS_Working_Papers.html.

Cafédirect (n.d.) http://www.cafedirect.co.uk/pressoffice/release.builder/00044.html.

Carter, M. (2005) Big Business Pitches Itself on Fair Trade Territory, *Financial Times*, 25 October, 13.

Golding, K. and K. Peattie (2005) In Search of a Golden Blend: Perspectives on the Marketing of Fair Trade Coffee, *Sustainable Development* 13(3), 154–65.

Questions

1. Is the entry of Nestlé into the fair trade market a step forwards or backwards for the fair trade movement?

2. How would you describe Catrin's behaviour as a consumer, and how well do conventional models of consumer behaviour help to explain it?

3. Is Cafédirect right to shift its strategy to re-emphasizing the ethical strengths of its brand in the light of Nestlé's entry into the market? How do you think it can best build its brand in the long term?

This case was written by Ken Peattie, Professor of Marketing and Strategy, and Director, ESRC Centre for Business Relationships, Accountability, Sustainability and Society, Cardiff University.

CHAPTER 7

Marketing research and information systems

Knowledge is power.

MACHIAVELLI

LEARNING OBJECTIVES

After reading this chapter, you should be able to:

1 discuss the nature and purpose of marketing information systems, and the role of marketing research within such systems

2 identify the types of marketing research

3 describe the approaches to conducting marketing research

4 describe the stages in the marketing research process

5 explain how to prepare a research brief and proposal

6 discuss the nature and role of exploratory research

7 discuss quantitative research design decisions: sampling, survey method and questionnaire design issues

8 explain how to analyse and interpret data

9 explain how to write reports and make presentations

10 distinguish between qualitative and quantitative research

11 describe the factors that affect the usage of marketing information systems and marketing research reports

12 discuss the ethical issues that arise in marketing research

What kinds of people buy my products? What do they value? Where do they buy? What kinds of new products would they like to see on the market? These and other related questions are the key to informed marketing decision-making. As we have seen, a prerequisite for the adoption of a marketing orientation is knowledge about customers and other aspects of the marketing environment that affect company operations. Managers obtain this information by informal and formal means. Casual discussions with customers at exhibitions or through sales calls can provide valuable informal information about their requirements, competitor activities and future happenings in the industry. Some companies, particularly those who have few customers, rely on this type of information gathering to keep abreast of market changes.

As the customer base grows, such methods may be inadequate to provide the necessary in-depth market knowledge to compete effectively. A more formal approach is needed to supply information systematically to managers. This chapter focuses on this formal method of information provision. First, we will describe the nature of a marketing information system and its relationship to marketing research. Then we look at the process of marketing research and its uses in more detail. Next, the essential differences between qualitative and quantitative research are explored. Finally, we will examine the influences on information system and marketing research use. Marketing information system design is important since the quality of a marketing information system has been shown to have an impact on the effectiveness of decision-making.[1]

Marketing Information Systems

A marketing information system has been defined as:[2]

A system in which marketing information is formally gathered, stored, analysed and distributed to managers in accord with their informational needs on a regular planned basis.

The system is built on an understanding of the information needs of marketing management, and supplies that information when, where and how the manager requires it. Data are derived from the marketing environment and transferred into information that marketing managers can use in their decision-making. The difference between data and information is as follows.

- **Data** is the most basic form of knowledge, e.g. the brand of butter sold to a particular customer in a certain town; this statistic is of little worth in itself but may become meaningful when combined with other data.
- **Information** is a combination of data that provide decision-relevant knowledge, e.g. the brand preferences of customers in a certain age category in a particular geographic region.

An insight into the nature of marketing information systems (MkIS) is given in Figure 7.1. The MkIS comprises four elements: internal continuous data, internal ad hoc data, environmental scanning, and marketing research.

Internal continuous data

Companies possess an enormous amount of marketing and financial data that may never be used for marketing decision-making unless organized by means of an MkIS. One advantage of setting up an MkIS is the conversion of financial data into a form usable by marketing management. Traditionally, profitability figures have been calculated for accounting and

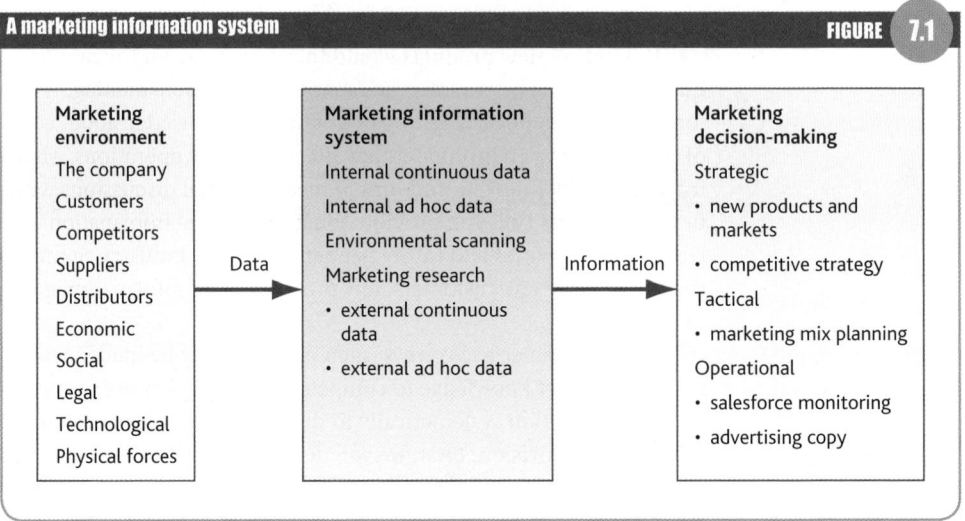

A marketing information system FIGURE 7.1

financial reporting purposes. This has led to two problems. First, the figures may be too aggregated (e.g. profitability by division (SBU)) to be of much use for marketing decisions at a product level, and, second, arbitrary allocations of marketing expenditures to products may obscure their real profitability.

The setting up of an MkIS may stimulate the provision of information that marketing managers can use, e.g. profitability of a particular product, customer or distribution channel, or even the profitability of a particular product to an individual customer.

Another application of the MkIS concept to internal continuous data is within the area of salesforce management. As part of the sales management function, many salesforces are monitored by means of recording sales achieved, number of calls made, size of orders, number of new accounts opened, etc. This can be recorded in total or broken down by product or customer/customer type. The establishment of an MkIS where these data are stored and analysed over time can provide information on salesforce effectiveness. For example, a fall-off in performance of a salesperson can quickly be identified and remedial action taken.

Internal ad hoc data

Company data can also be used for a specific (ad hoc) purpose. For example, management may look at how sales have reacted to a price increase or a change in advertising copy. Although this could be part of a continuous monitoring programme, specific one-off analyses are inevitably required from time to time. Capturing the data on the MkIS allows specific analyses to be conducted when needed.

Environmental scanning

The environmental scanning procedures discussed in Chapter 3 also form part of the MkIS. Although often amorphous in nature, environmental analysis—whereby the economic, social, political, legal, technological and ecological/physical forces are monitored—should be considered part of the MkIS. These are the forces that shape the context within which suppliers, the company, distributors and the competition do business. As such, environmental scanning provides an early warning system for the forces that may impact a company's products and markets in the future.[3] In this way, scanning enables an organization to act on, rather than react to, opportunities and threats. The focus is on the longer-term perspective, allowing a company to be in the position to plan ahead. It provides a major input into such strategic decisions as which future products to develop and market to enter, and the formulation of competitive strategy (e.g. to attack or defend against competition).

Marketing research

Whereas environmental scanning focuses on the longer term, **marketing research** considers the more immediate situation. It is primarily concerned with the provision of information about markets and the reaction of these to various product, price, distribution and promotion decisions.[4] As such, it is a key part of the MkIS because it makes a major contribution to marketing mix planning.

Two types of marketing research can be distinguished: external continuous data and external ad hoc data. This does not mean that internal data are never used by marketing researchers, but usually the emphasis is on external data sources. *External continuous data sources* include television audience monitoring and consumer panels where household purchases are recorded over time. Loyalty cards are also a source of continuous data, providing information on customer purchasing patterns and responses to promotions. The growth of e-commerce has led to new forms of continuous data collection—for example, the measurement of visits to websites ('hits'). *External ad hoc data* are often gathered by means of surveys into specific marketing issues, including usage and attitude studies, advertising and product testing, and corporate image research. For example, Nationwide, a UK building society, surveyed customers to discover what frustrated them about how they were treated by financial institutions. Its findings led it to stop offering lower mortgage loan rates to new customers and charging customers for using their credit cards abroad.[5] The rest of this chapter will examine the process of marketing research and the factors that affect the use of research information.

The Importance of Marketing Research

The importance of marketing research was highlighted in a study of the factors that were significant in the selection of an industrial goods supplier.[6] The company, as part of its marketing audit (see Chapter 2), wanted to know what were the main considerations its customers took into account when deciding to do business with it or its competitors. Before conducting marketing research, it asked its marketing staff; they said that the two main factors were price and product quality. Next the sales staff were asked the same question and their response was that customers mainly considered company reputation and quick response to customer needs (see Table 7.1). When marketing research was carried out, however, the results were very different. Customers explained that, to them, the key issues were technical support services and prompt delivery. Clearly the viewpoints within and outside the company were at odds with each other. The lesson is that it is dangerous to rely solely on the internal views of managers. Only when this company really understood what its customers wanted could it put into action marketing initiatives that improved technical and delivery services. The result was improved customer satisfaction, which led to increased sales and profits.

Marketing research is used by political parties as well as commercial organizations. In the 1996 US presidential election, the winner Bill Clinton was reported to be awash with marketing research findings.[7] The pollsters told him to be a father figure with a powerful red tie, and suggested how he should spend his holidays. 'Can I golf?' asked Clinton sarcastically, 'Maybe if I wear a baseball cap?' 'No sir,' came the reply, 'go rafting.'

Marketing research findings are also used in advertising, as the advertisement on the next page for UK supermarket Waitrose shows.

Ad insight

Go to the website to compare the use of market research in Waitrose's print ad and Nestlé's TV ad

Factors in the selection of a manufacturer*			TABLE 7.1
Factor	Users	Salespeople	Marketing
Reputation	5	1	4
Credit	9	11	9
Sales reps	8	5	7
Technical support services	1	3	6
Literature	11	10	11
Prompt delivery	2	4	5
Quick response to customer needs	3	2	3
Price	6	6	1
Personal relationships	10	7	8
Complete product line	7	9	10
Product quality	4	8	2

*Factors are rated in order of importance from 1 to 11. First and second positions are circled for ease of reference.

Source: Kotler, P., W. McGregor and W. Rodgers (1977) The Marketing Audit Comes of Age, *Sloan Management Review*, Winter, 30. Reprinted with permission. Copyright © 1977 by the Sloan Management Review Association. All rights reserved.

Approaches to Conducting Marketing Research

Depending on the situation facing a company, particularly the resources allocated to marketing research, there are four ways of carrying out marketing research, described below.

In-house—personally

Where a company has marketing staff but a low or non-existent marketing research budget, the only option may be for marketing staff to carry out the marketing research task themselves. This is particularly feasible when the study is small scale, perhaps involving data-gathering from libraries. Where sample sizes are small—for example, in some industrial marketing research studies involving interviews with a small number of organizational customers—this option may also be feasible. Training in research techniques may be necessary. Fortunately there are many good courses available from professional organizations such as the Market Research Society. A disadvantage of doing research in-house is the possibility that responses will be biased through respondents' awareness of who is asking the questions. An organization conducting its own research must make that fact known, in order to comply with market research ethics codes.[8]

In-house—using a market research department

By hiring a marketing research executive, a company would benefit from professional specialist skills. It could be possible for the executive to design, implement and

We are delighted to announce that
Waitrose is the High Street Retailer of the Year,
as awarded by Which? Magazine.

Our highest quality produce comes from trusted suppliers and well cared for animals. And our friendly service
makes for the happiest customers, so smiles all round really. Why not come and see for yourself?

Waitrose
Everyone deserves quality food

waitrose.com

▲ Survey results on behalf of *Which?* Magazine are used here to position Waitrose as the UK's favourite supermarket.

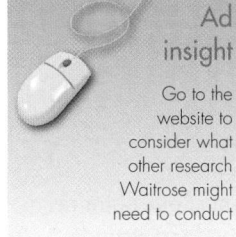

Ad insight

Go to the website to consider what other research Waitrose might need to conduct

present marketing research surveys to marketing management. If the outside services of a marketing research agency are used, the executive would act as the link between company and agency.

In-house—using a market research department

Where the design of the study can be done in-company but interviewing by internal staff is not possible, the fieldwork could be conducted by a marketing research agency. These organizations provide a wide range of services, which include fieldwork services; indeed, some specialize in fieldwork only. One possibility would be for the survey design, questionnaire design and analysis of results to be done in-company but the administration of the questionnaire to be handled by fieldwork staff employed by the marketing research agency.

Using the full services of a marketing research agency

Where resources permit, a company (client) could use the full range of skills offered by marketing research agencies. The company would brief the agency about its marketing research requirements and the agency would conduct the research. A complete service would mean that the agency would:

- prepare a research proposal stating the survey design and costs
- conduct exploratory research
- design the questionnaire
- select the sample
- choose the survey method (telephone, postal or face to face)
- conduct the interviewing
- analyse and interpret the results
- prepare a report
- make a presentation.

An example of a company using this approach is Nestlé, which employs 25 marketing researchers across its 10 divisions; these are closely involved in brand development since they are part of the brand teams. They brief marketing research agencies, help in interpreting their findings and make recommendations to the brand teams.[9]

A key to successful marketing research is close, effective relationships between client and agency. Marketing in Action 7.1 discusses how these can be achieved.

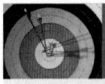

7.1 Marketing in Action

Achieving Close Client–Agency Relationships

Two companies that have worked closely together to produce effective marketing research are British Telecom and the NOP Research Group. Crispin Beale, head of customer satisfaction and competitor intelligence, BT, and Phyllis MacFarlane, client executive officer, NOP, explain how their relationship works.

'I've noticed that I talk to the team at NOP almost as much as I talk to my own team here at BT,' says Beale. 'Today our key agencies are receiving a briefing about what we're doing on broadband. They know as much about what we're doing in certain areas as we do and will be able to make suggestions. We have encouraged NOP to develop a "can do" attitude, whereby they find solutions rather than problems. This involves an investment of time up-front—to create service-level agreements and manage expectations. Yet only by setting up such processes can both parties deliver actionable and insightful intelligence to the business on a timely basis.'

'Our relationship with BT began more than 20 years ago,' explains MacFarlane. 'We've been working together on a wide and growing range of research projects ever since. Now our relationship has evolved into a real partnership. We work closely with BT people across the business and at the highest levels of BT management. We strive to keep ourselves informed so that we can identify opportunities for insight.'

So what are the essentials for making a relationship last?

- Issue a clear brief based on what the marketing problem is and how the research will be used, and agree objectives, outputs and costs.
- Remove any ambiguity—this means personal contact rather than relying on e-mail alone.
- Ensure regular exchange of information.
- Communicate any changes that might affect the research project.
- Encourage honest, open, two-way constructive communication.
- Work as a team—the agency should be empowered to make decisions.
- Work with agencies that adopt a 'can do' attitude and are not afraid to challenge preconceptions.
- Encourage agency presenters of market research findings to make recommendations for marketing action to clients.

Based on: Miles (2002);[10] Clegg (2006);[11] Bainbridge (2008)[12]

Types of Marketing Research

A major distinction is between **ad hoc research** and **continuous research**.

Ad hoc research

An *ad hoc study* focuses on a specific marketing problem and collects data at one point in time from one sample of respondents. Examples of ad hoc studies are usage and attitude surveys, product and concept tests, advertising development and evaluation studies, corporate image surveys, and customer satisfaction surveys. Ad hoc surveys are either custom-designed or omnibus studies.

Custom-designed studies

Custom-designed studies are based on the specific needs of the client. The research design is based on the research brief given to the marketing research agency or internal marketing researcher. Because they are tailor-made, such surveys can be expensive.

Omnibus studies

The alternative is to use an **omnibus survey** in which space is bought on questionnaires for face-to-face or telephone interviews. The interview may cover many topics as the questionnaire space is bought by a number of clients who benefit from cost sharing. Usually the type of information sought is relatively simple (e.g. awareness levels and ownership data). Often the survey will be based on demographically balanced samples of 1000–2000 adults. However, more specialist surveys covering the markets for children, young adults, mothers and babies, the 'grey' market and motorists exist. An example is the CAPIBUS-Europe weekly omnibus developed by Ipsos UK, which covers Britain, France, Germany, Italy and Spain.

Continuous research

Continuous research gathers information from external sources on an ongoing basis. Major types of continuous research are consumer panels, retail audits, television viewership panels, marketing databases, customer relationship management systems and website analysis.

Consumer panels

Consumer panels are formed by recruiting large numbers of households, which provide information on their purchases over time. For example, a grocery panel would record the brands, pack sizes, prices and stores used for a wide range of supermarket brands. The most usual method of data collection is the use of diaries, which panel members fill in with details of purchases and return to the survey organization on a weekly basis. However, an innovation is in the use of data terminals and barcode readers, which allow panel members to scan their purchases at home allowing the data to be sent electronically.[13] By using the same households over a period of time, measures of brand loyalty and switching can be achieved, together with a demographic profile of the type of person who buys particular brands. An example is the Taylor Nelson Sofres Superpanel, which comprises 25,000 households, which are equipped with electronic scanners that record price, place of purchase and selected brand.

Retail audits

Retail audits are a second type of continuous research. By gaining the cooperation of retail outlets (e.g. supermarkets) sales of brands can be measured by means of laser scans of barcodes on packaging, which are read at the checkout. Although brand loyalty and switching cannot be measured, retail audits can provide accurate assessment of sales achieved by store. A major provider of retail audit data is the ACNielsen Corp. Its reports are based on in-store scanning on a weekly or four-weekly basis. This information comprises purchases, sales promotions, stocks, pricing, and sales of products sold through supermarkets, confectioners, tobacconists, newsagents, pharmacies and electrical wholesalers.[14]

Television viewership panels

Television viewership panels measure audience sizes minute by minute. Commercial breaks can be allocated *ratings points* (the proportion of the target audience watching), which are the currency by which television advertising is bought and judged. Viewership information is recorded on online meters capable of monitoring both television and video cassette recorder (VCR) activity. The meter records whether the TV set is on/off, which channel is being watched and, by means of a hand console, who is watching. It also is capable of identifying programmes played back by the VCR following in-home recording. Consequently, reports on programme viewing now give consolidated audience figures of 'live' viewing plus VCR playback audiences. The meter automatically sends the data to the survey organization on a daily basis.[15]

Marketing databases

Companies collect data on customers on an ongoing basis. The data are stored on marketing databases, which contain each customer's name, address, telephone number, past transactions and, sometimes, demographic and lifestyle data. Information on the types of purchase, frequency of purchase, purchase value and responsiveness to promotional offers may be held.

Retailers are encouraging the collection of such data by introducing loyalty card schemes such as the Nectar card, which allows customers to collect points that can be redeemed for cashback or gifts at a group of retailers including Sainsbury's, the Body Shop and Sony stores. The card, which is swiped through the cash machine at the checkout, contains information about the cardholder, such as name and address, so that purchasing data including expenditure per visit, types of brands purchased, how often the customer shops and when, and at which branch, can be linked to individuals.

Customer relationship management systems

A potential problem with the growth of marketing databases is that separate ones are created in different departments of the company. For example, the sales department may have an account management database containing information on customers, while call centre staff may use a different database created at a different time also containing information on customers. This fragmented approach can lead to problems when, for example, a customer transaction is recorded on one but not the other database.

Issues like this have led to the development of customer relationship management systems, where a single database is created from customer information to inform all staff who deal with customers. Customer relationship management is a term for the methodologies, technologies and e-commerce capabilities used by companies to manage customer relationships.[16]

Data is collected, stored, analysed and used in a way that provides information to customer-contact staff in a way that conforms to the way they work and the way customers want to access the company (e.g. via the salesforce, telephone, e-mail or websites).

Website analysis

Continuous data can also be provided by analysing consumers' use of websites. Measurements of the areas of the site most frequently visited, how long each visitor spends seeking out information, which products are purchased and the payment method used can be made. Other measurements include how well the site loads on browsers, how well it downloads, whether it ranks within the top three pages on major search engines and the number of sites to which it is linked.

Website analysis can allow the assessment of current performance of a site and identify key areas for improvement. For example, marketing managers can summarize the actions of visitors to their own websites by analysing their web server logs using either online services or applications software such as WebTrends (www.webtrends.com). For seeing how competitors' sites are performing or what a company's visitors are looking at when not on their site, services such as Alexa (www.alexa.com) and Netcraft (www.netcraft.com) can assist. They both provide an enormous amount of information about the visitors to different websites. For example, Alexa displays such information as page loading times, page rankings based on the Google search engine (www.google.com), data on the other sites visited by people who view a company's site, and the top 500 sites across various industry sectors. Netcraft provides similar information, as well as details of the provider of web services for the site and the type of server used to present the web pages.

Using MarketLeap (www.marketleap.com), and in particular the key word verification tool, a site can again be tested on whether it ranks within the top three pages on major search engines. If the site does not rank within the top few pages of returns, then over 90 per cent of potential customers will not look any further. In addition, using the link popularity tool, it is possible to tell the number of sites on the Internet on which the website address appears as a link; the more sites it can be found on, the more popular it is and the greater the marketing effect. These online tools provide the base level of online marketing research that any online organization should attempt to conduct and act on.

Online retailers can get valuable information through website analysis. For example, an online camera store can track sales by time of day, or they can be related to promotional campaigns or even sporting events. The retailer can analyse a customer's behaviour to build a profile of their habits. For example, if a shopper visits the website but does not buy, a promotional voucher discount might be sent to persuade them to try again.[17]

Stages in the Marketing Research Process

Each ad hoc marketing research project may be different in order to fit the particular requirements and resources of various clients. For example, one study may focus on **qualitative research** using small numbers of respondents while another may be largely quantitative, involving interviewing hundreds or thousands of consumers. Nevertheless, a useful framework for understanding the steps involved in the marketing research process is provided in Figure 7.2. This provides a 'road map' of what is involved in a major marketing research study covering both qualitative and quantitative research. It is used by marketing research practitioners and can form the structure for a student marketing research project. Each of the stages in this process will now be discussed.

The marketing research process FIGURE 7.2

Research planning
• initial contact
• research brief
• research proposal

Exploratory research
• secondary research
• qualitative research
• consultation with experts
• observation

Main quantitative data collection
• descriptive research
• experimental research
• the sampling process
• the survey method
• questionnaire design

Data analysis and interpretation

Report writing and presentation

Research planning

Considerable thought needs to go into a marketing research project before data is gathered. Decisions made at the research planning stage will fundamentally affect what is done later. A commercial marketing research project is likely to involve marketing management at the client company, internal marketing research staff and, usually, research staff at an outside marketing research agency. The following discussion assumes this is the situation. Student projects are usually conducted in small groups. In this case the module leader or tutor takes on the role of the client, and the group becomes the research team responsible for drawing up a research proposal that meets the requirements of the research project brief and for conducting the research.

Initial contact

The start of the process is usually the realization that a marketing problem (e.g. a new product or advertising decision) requires information to help its solution. Marketing management may contact internal marketing research staff or an outside agency. Let us assume that the research requires the assistance of a marketing research agency. A meeting will be arranged to discuss the nature of the problem and the client's research needs. If the client and its markets are new to the agency, some rudimentary exploratory research (e.g. a quick library search for information about the client and its markets) may be conducted prior to the meeting.

Research brief

At the meeting, the client will explain the marketing problem and outline the research objectives. The marketing problem might be to attract new customers to a product line, and the research objectives could be to identify groups of customers (market segments) that might have a use for the product, and the characteristics of the product that appeal to them most.[18] The key point is that clients should not only tell research agencies what they want to understand but what the research will be used for.[19]

Other information that should be provided for the research agency includes the following.[20]

1 *Background information*: the product's history and the competitive situation.

2 *Sources of information*: the client may have a list of industries that might be potential users of the product. This helps the researchers to define the scope of the research.

3 *The scale of the project*: is the client looking for a 'cheap and cheerful' job or a major study? This has implications for the research design and survey costs.

4 *The timetable*: when is the information required?

The client should produce a specific written **research brief**. This may be given to the research agency prior to the meeting and perhaps modified as a result of it, but, without fail, should be in the hands of the agency before it produces its *research proposal*. The research brief should state the client's requirements and should be in written form so that misunderstandings are minimized. In the event of a dispute later in the process, the research brief (and proposal) form the benchmarks against which it can be settled.

Commissioning good research is similar to buying any other product or service. If marketing management can agree on why the research is needed, what it will be used for, when it is needed and how much they are willing to pay for it, they are likely to make a good buy. Four suggestions for buying good research are as follows.

1 Define terms clearly. For example, if market share information is required, the term 'market' should clearly be defined. The car manufacturer TVR has a very small share of the car market but a much higher share of the specialist, exclusive segment in which it markets.

2 Beware of researchers who bend research problems so that they can use their favourite technique. They may be specialists in a particular research-gathering method (e.g. group discussion) or statistical technique (e.g. factor or cluster analysis) and look for ways of using these methods no matter what research problem they face. This can lead to irrelevant information and unnecessary expense.

3 Do not be put off by researchers who ask what appear to be naive questions, particularly if they are new to the client's industry.

4 Brief two or three agencies. The extra time involved is usually rewarded with the benefits of more than one viewpoint on the research problem and design, and a keener quote.

Research proposal

The **research proposal** defines what the marketing research agency promises to do for its client, and how much it will cost. Like the research brief, the proposal should be written to avoid misunderstandings. A client should expect the following to be included.

1 *A statement of objectives*: to demonstrate an understanding of the client's marketing and research problems.

2 *What will be done*: an unambiguous description of the research design, including the survey method, the type of sample, the sample size and how the fieldwork will be controlled.

3 *Timetable*: if and when a report will be produced.

4 *Costs*: how much the research will cost and what, specifically, is/is not being included in those costs.

When assessing proposals a client might usefully check the following points.

1 *Beware of vagueness*: if the proposal is vague, assume that the report is also likely to be vague. If the agency does not state what is going to be done, why, who is doing it and when, assume that it is not clear in its own mind about these important issues.

2 *Beware of jargon*: there is no excuse for jargon-ridden proposals. Marketing research terminology can be explained in non-expert language, so it is the responsibility of the agency to make the proposal understandable to the client.

3 *Beware of omissions*: assume that anything not specified will not be provided. For example, if no mention of a presentation is made in the proposal, assume it will not take place. If in doubt, ask the agency.

Exploratory research

Exploratory research involves the preliminary exploration of a research area prior to the main quantitative data-collection stage. It usually occurs between acceptance of the research proposal and the main data-collection stage, but can also take place prior to the client–agency briefing meeting (as we have seen) and before submission of the research proposal, as an aid to its construction. The discussion that follows assumes that the proposal has been accepted and that exploratory research is being used as the basis for survey design.

A major purpose of exploratory research is to guard against the sins of omission and admission.[21]

- *Sin of omission*: not researching a topic in enough detail, or failing to provide sufficient respondents in a group to allow meaningful analysis.
- *Sin of admission*: collecting data that are irrelevant to the marketing problem, or using too many groups for analysis purposes and thereby unnecessarily increasing the sample size.

Exploratory research techniques allow the researcher to understand the people who are to be interviewed in the main data-collection stage, and the market that is being researched. The main survey stage can thus be designed with this knowledge in mind rather than being based on the researcher's ill-informed prejudices and guesswork.

Figure 7.3 displays the four exploratory research activities. An individual research project may involve all or some of them.

Secondary research

Secondary research is so called because the data come to the researcher 'second-hand' (other people have compiled the data). When the researcher actively collects new data—for example, by interviewing respondents—this is called primary research.

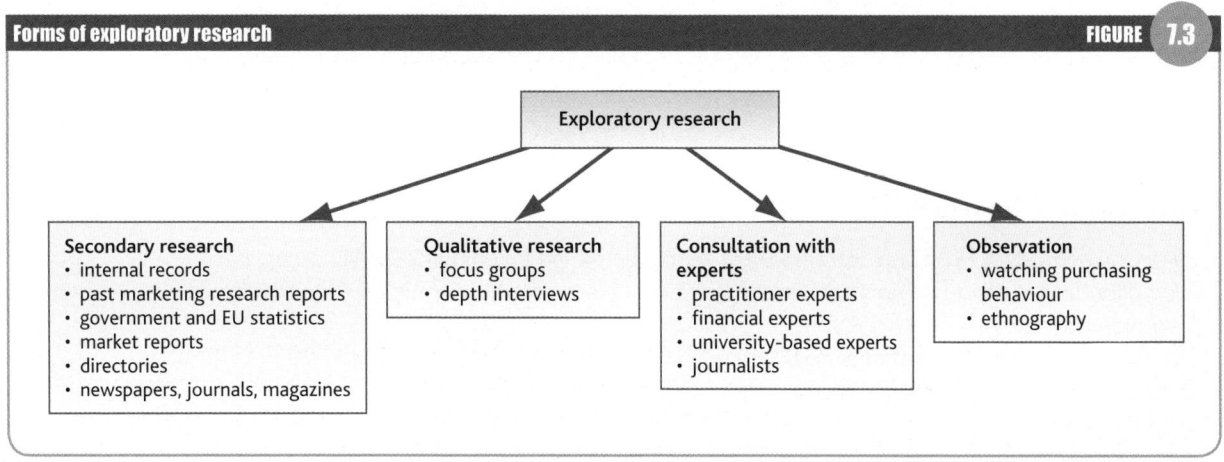

Forms of exploratory research   FIGURE 7.3

Exploratory research

Secondary research
- internal records
- past marketing research reports
- government and EU statistics
- market reports
- directories
- newspapers, journals, magazines

Qualitative research
- focus groups
- depth interviews

Consultation with experts
- practitioner experts
- financial experts
- university-based experts
- journalists

Observation
- watching purchasing behaviour
- ethnography

Secondary data can be found by examination of internal records and reports of research previously carried out for the company. External sources include government and European Union statistics; publishers of reports and directories on markets, countries and industries; trade associations; banks; and newspapers, magazines and journals. The development of search engines, for example, means that secondary information searches on newspapers and journals can be quickly and simply accomplished. By typing in the appropriate keywords the computer searches the relevant publications and can provide a printout of the article. There are also websites, like Trendwatching (www.trendwatching.com), that specialize in identifying emerging global consumer and marketing trends. In addition, all major research companies, like IDC and Gartner, have an Internet presence and although many are fee based, most provide some information, often in the form of newsletters, free of charge. Many traditional sources of information such as newspapers or magazines are readily available on the Internet, either free of charge, as with the *Guardian* (www.guardian.co.uk), or on a subscription basis, such as the *Financial Times* (www.ft.com). Companies that specialize in providing secondary information also provide electronic content either by subscription or selling individual reports. For example, a visit to Mintel (www.mintel.com) can provide hundreds of industry specific reports such as Do-It-Yourself Retailing, Home Shopping and Cereal Bars in a range of European countries and the USA. The European Union is well blessed with secondary sources of data, and Marketing in Action 7.2 lists some of the major sources of marketing information classified by research questions.

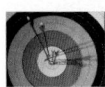 **7.2 Marketing in Action**

Sources of Marketing Information

Is there a survey of the industry?

Global Market Information Database (GMID) has in-depth analysis and current market information in the key areas of country data, consumer lifestyles, market sizes, forecasts, brand and company information, business information sources and marketing profiles.

Business Insight Reports are full text reports available online in the sectors of healthcare, financial services, consumer goods, energy, and e-commerce and technology.

Key Note Reports cover size of market, economic trends, prospects and company performance.

Snapshots The 'Snapshots' database is a complete library of market research reports, providing coverage of consumer, business-to-business and industrial markets. Containing 2000 market reports, this series provides incisive data and analysis on over 8000 market segments for the UK, Europe and the United States.

Marketline Business Information Centre offers a concise overview of over 10,000 company profiles and 3000 industry profiles in over 50 countries, as well as 100 country profiles.

How large is the market?

European Marketing Data and Statistics Now available on the Euromonitor GMID database.
International Marketing Data and Statistics Now available on the Euromonitor GMID database.
European Marketing Pocket Book
The Asia Pacific Marketing Pocket Book
The Americas Marketing Pocket Book
Mintel Reports

Where is the market?

Regional Trends gives the main economic and social statistics for UK regions.
UK Consumer Marketplace Pocket Book

Who are the competitors?

British companies can be identified using any of the following:
  Kompass (most European countries have their own edition)
  Key British Enterprises
  Quarterly Review—KPMG

For more detailed company information consult:
  Companies Annual Reports Collection
  Carol (Company Annual Reports Online) at www.carol.co.uk
  Fame
  Business Ratio Reports
  Northcote at www.northcote.co.uk

Overseas companies' sources include:
  Asia's 7500 Largest Companies
  D&B Europa
  Europe's 15,000 Largest Companies
  Major Companies of Europe, The Arab World, Scandinavia, South West Asia, Latin America, The Far East and Australia
  Million Dollar Directory (US)

What are the trends?

Possible sources to consider are:
  Consumer Europe Now available on the Euromonitor GMID database.
  Economic Trends
  Family Expenditure Survey
  Social Trends
  The Book of European Forecasts Now available on the Euromonitor GMID database.
  World Drink Trends
  Marketing Pocket Book
  Asia Pacific Marketing Pocket Book
  Americas Marketing Pocket Book

EU statistical and information sources

Eurostat is a series of publications that provide a detailed picture of the EU. They can be obtained by visiting European Documentation Centres (often in university libraries) in all EU countries. Themes include general statistics, economy and finance, and population/social conditions.

European Report is a twice-weekly news publication from Brussels on industrial, economic and political issues.

Guides to marketing information

World Directory of Marketing Information Sources

Abstracts and indices

ABI/INFORM on Proquest Direct
Science Direct via Scirus (Elsevier)
Emerald
Web of Knowledge
Wiley Interscience and Boldideas
Zetoc (electronic table of contents)

Statistics

Guide to Official Statistics
Sources of Non-Official UK Statistics
Annual Abstract of Statistics
Key Data
World Directory of Non-Official Statistical Sources Also available on the Euromonitor GMID database.

Other sources

BIZ/ED (http://www.bized.co.uk) provides a range of resources for students of business and economics. Materials include study skills, advice, glossaries, notes and databases of resources.

World Directory of Business Information Websites provides details of a wealth of business information sources that are available on the net. Coverage includes nearly 1400 websites providing access to statistics, market and company information. Also available on the Euromonitor GMID database.

Business Information on the Internet (compiled by Karen Blakeman) is a useful portal for business information on the web, with links to sites covering company and market information, country and news sources and much more: http://www.rba.co.uk/sources/

Mintel market research reports: http://reports.mintel.com
Euromonitor market reports: www.euromonitor.com
Department for Business Enterprise and Regulatory Reform: www.berr.gov.uk
Competition Commission reports: www.competition-commission.org.uk
Company information on companies in 30 European countries: www.europager.com
Company financial information in the UK: http://fame.bvdep.com
Key Note summary reports: www.keynote.co.uk
CIM marketing research reports (members only): cim.co.uk/Knowledge Hub/Market Reports/
    Market Reports.aspx

Note: some of these sites require passwords, which can be obtained from libraries.

Source: the author thanks Reshma Khan and Neil Jukes of Bradford University School of Management Library
for their help in compiling this list.

Secondary research should be carried out before primary research. Without the former, an expensive primary research survey might be commissioned to provide information that is already available from secondary sources. Furthermore, directories such as *Kompass* can be invaluable when selecting a sample in a business-to-business marketing research project.

Qualitative research

The main forms of qualitative research are group discussions and **depth interviews**. Qualitative research aims to establish customers' attitudes, values, behaviour and beliefs. It attempts to understand consumers in a way that traditional methods of interviewing people using questionnaires cannot. Qualitative research seeks to understand the 'why' and 'how' of consumer behaviour.[22] The key differences between qualitative and quantitative research are explored later in this chapter.

Focus groups involve unstructured or semi-structured discussions between a *moderator*, or group leader, who is often a psychologist, and a group of consumers. The moderator has a list of areas to cover within the topic but allows the group considerable freedom to discuss the issues that are important to them. The topic might be coffee drinking, do-it-yourself car mechanics or holiday pursuits. By arranging groups of 6–12 people to discuss their beliefs, attitudes, motivation, behaviour and preferences a good deal of knowledge may be gained about the consumer. This can be helpful when planning questionnaires, which can then be designed to focus on what is important to the respondent (as opposed to the researcher) and worded in language that the respondent uses and understands.

A further advantage of the focus group is that the findings in themselves may provide rich insights into consumer motivations and behaviour because of the group dynamics where group members 'feed off' each other and reveal ideas that would not have arisen on a one-to-one basis. Such findings may be used as food for thought for marketers, without the need for quantitative follow-up. Also, the use of two-way mirrors allows marketers and other people from the client organization to view the focus group session without themselves being viewed, and video taping allows several people to listen to and interpret the data.

The weaknesses of the focus group are that interpretation of the results is highly subjective, the quality of the results depends heavily on the skills of the moderator, sample size is usually small, making generalization to wider populations difficult, and there exists the danger that the results might be biased by the presence of 'research groupies', who enjoy taking part in focus groups and return again and again. Such people sometimes even take on different identities, skewing survey results, and have led the Association of Qualitative Research Practitioners to introduce a rule which says that focus group participants have to provide proof of identity each time they attend a group.[23]

The traditional focus group takes place face to face, but the rise of the Internet has led to the use of online focus groups. The Internet offers 'communities of interests', which can take the form of chat rooms or websites dedicated to specific interests or issues. These are useful forums for conducting focus groups, or at least identifying suitable participants. Questions can be posed to participants who are not under time pressure to respond. This can lead to richer insights since they can think deeply about questions put to them online. Another advantage is that they can comprise people located all over the world at minimal cost. Furthermore, technological developments mean it is possible for clients to communicate secretly online with the moderator while the focus group is in session. The client can ask the moderator certain questions as a result of hearing earlier responses. Clearly, a disadvantage of online focus groups compared with the traditional form is that the body language and interaction between focus group members are missing.[24]

Depth interviews involve the interviewing of consumers individually for perhaps one or two hours about a topic. The aims are broadly similar to those of group discussion but are used when the presence of other people could inhibit honest answers and viewpoints, when the topic requires individual treatment, as when discussing an individual's decision-making process, and where the organization of a group is not feasible (for example, it might prove impossible to arrange for six busy purchasing managers to come together for a group discussion).

Care has to be taken when interpreting the results of qualitative research in that the findings are usually based on small sample sizes, and the more interesting or surprising viewpoints may be disproportionately reported. This is particularly significant when qualitative research is not followed by a quantitative study.

Qualitative research accounts for 12 per cent of all European expenditure on marketing research, of which approximately 77 per cent is spent on group discussions, 19 per cent is spent on in-depth interviews and 4 per cent on other qualitative techniques.[25]

Consultation with experts

Qualitative research is based on discussions and interviews with actual and potential buyers of a brand or service. However, consultation with experts involves interviewing people who may not form part of the target market but who, nevertheless, can provide important marketing-related insights. Many industries have their experts in universities, financial institutions and the press, who may be willing to share their knowledge. They can provide invaluable background information, and can be useful for predicting future trends and developments.

Observation

Observation can also help in exploratory research when the product field is unfamiliar. Watching people buy wine in a supermarket or paint in a DIY store may provide useful background knowledge when planning a survey in these markets, for example. Another form of observational research that focuses on employee performance is *mystery shopping*. The 'shopper' acts like any other customer in visiting a store, but is trained to ask particular questions, and to assess performance on such criteria as service time, friendliness and product knowledge. The objective is to identify service weaknesses and strengths, and to provide input into staff training.

A form of observation that involves detailed and prolonged observation of consumers is called ethnography. Its origins are in social anthropology, where researchers live in a studied society for months or years. Consumer researchers usually make their observations more quickly and use a range of methods, including direct observations, interviews and video and audio recordings.[26] Marketing in Action 7.3 illustrates its use in marketing research.

The objective of exploratory research, then, is not to collect quantitative data and form conclusions but to get better acquainted with the market and its customers. This allows the researcher to base the quantitative survey on *informed assumptions* rather than guesswork.

The main quantitative data-collection stage

Following careful exploratory research, the design of the main quantitative data-collection procedures will be made. Two alternative approaches are descriptive and experimental research.

Assuming the main data-collection stage requires interviewing, the research design will be based on the following factors:

7.3 Marketing in Action

Understanding Consumers through Ethnographic Research

The growing demand for getting closer to consumers and understanding their behaviour has given rise to the increasing use of ethnographic research. Such research investigates ways in which people behave in their own environment and how they interact with the world around them. Unlike focus groups, where consumers are brought to the researcher, ethnography takes the researcher to the consumer. Advocates of this form of research argue that focus groups only provide part of the story and do not yield the kinds of 'consumer insights' that ethnography can.

One company that has embraced ethnographic research is Procter & Gamble. Twenty families in the UK and a further 20 in Italy were chosen to take part in a study that involved the recording of their daily household behaviour by video camera. The idea was that by studying people who buy P&G products—such as Max Factor cosmetics, Ariel washing powder and Pampers nappies—the company could gain valuable insights into people's consumer habits. The findings have had implications for its approach to product design, packaging and promotion. For example, it was ethnographic research which revealed that the nappy was not as important as P&G had previously thought. New mothers were more interested in information and knowledge than nappies. Based on these consumer insights P&G launched Pampers.com, an online community for mothers that attracts over 650,000 users across Europe. P&G has also used ethnographic research in China. It observed low-income consumers doing their washing and found that they were prepared to do the extra hand washing needed to compensate for water hardness. P&G's response was to launch a cut-price version of its China Tide detergent without water softener.[27] A P&G spokesman pointed out that ethnography will not replace other forms of research and that ethical issues concerning privacy are dealt with by getting full permission beforehand and giving the families complete editorial control over what is eventually shown to the marketing team.

Kenco's marketing team also used ethnography to help them dig deeper into how people used their product. They videoed people to understand what was most important in a coffee shop experience. Kenco found that while its own focus was on the coffee beans, a range of other things were just as important to consumers, including the crockery in which the coffee was served. The video project had the added advantage of being much more interesting when presenting the findings to management. Watching consumers talk was much more vivid than watching a PowerPoint presentation.[28]

The objective of ethnographic research is to bridge the gap between what people say they do and what they actually do. Its usefulness is reflected in the fact that companies such as Nokia, Toyota, Land Rover, Intel, Van den Berghs, Adidas and Nike have used this genre of research. It has been used in the technology field to understand how electronic products are really used. The findings showed that people will use technology in ways its inventors never imagined. For example, one family used broadband technology to pipe sound from the local mosque into their home. Another had two Sony PlayStations: one to play games on, the other for only playing CDs. Of 10 families studied, two left their televisions on all day even when they went out—something they were unlikely to admit to in a focus group.

Based on: Earnshaw (2001);[29] Gofton (2001);[30] Singh (2001);[31] James (2002);[32] Ritson (2002);[33] Grant (2005)[34]

- who and how many people to interview (the sampling process)
- how to interview them (the survey method)
- what questions to ask (questionnaire design).

Figure 7.4 displays the two types and three research design methods associated with the main quantitative data-collection stage. These research approaches and methods will now be examined.

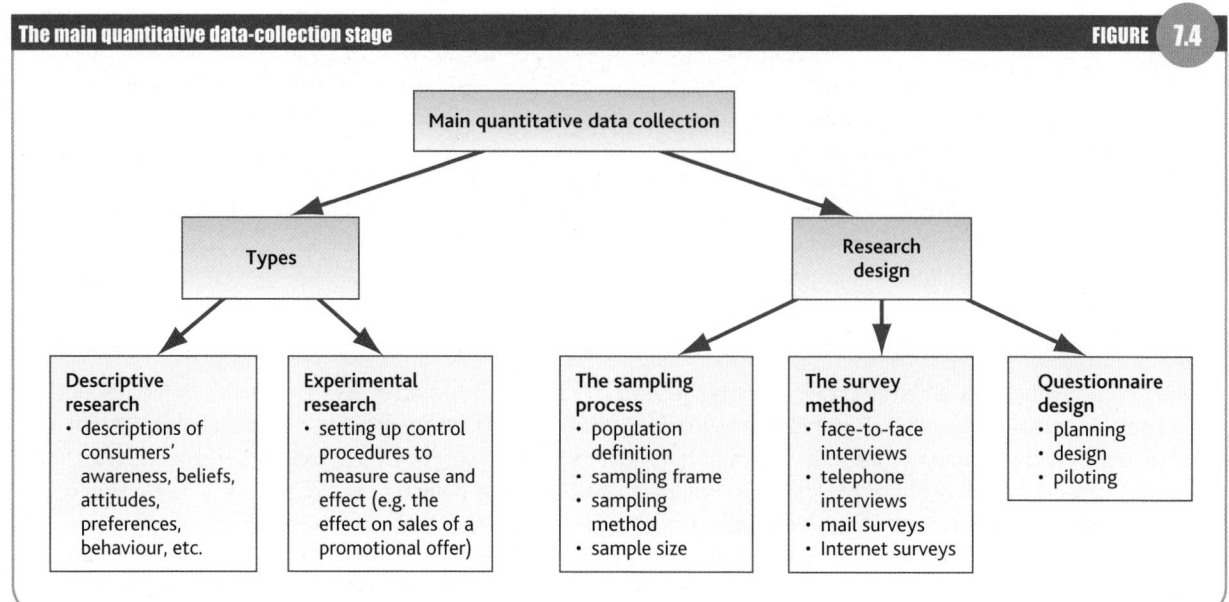

The main quantitative data-collection stage   FIGURE **7.4**

Main quantitative data collection

Types

Research design

Descriptive research
• descriptions of consumers' awareness, beliefs, attitudes, preferences, behaviour, etc.

Experimental research
• setting up control procedures to measure cause and effect (e.g. the effect on sales of a promotional offer)

The sampling process
• population definition
• sampling frame
• sampling method
• sample size

The survey method
• face-to-face interviews
• telephone interviews
• mail surveys
• Internet surveys

Questionnaire design
• planning
• design
• piloting

Descriptive research

Descriptive research may be undertaken to describe consumers' beliefs, attitudes, preferences, behaviour, etc. For example, a survey into advertising effectiveness might measure awareness of the brand, recall of the advertisement and knowledge about its content.

Experimental research

The aim of experimental research is to establish cause and effect. **Experimental research** involves the setting up of control procedures to isolate the impact of a factor (e.g. a money-off sales promotion) on a dependent variable (e.g. sales). The key to successful experimental design is the elimination of other explanations of changes in the dependent variable. One way of doing this is to use random sampling. For example, the sales promotion might be applied in a random selection of stores with the remaining stores selling the brand without the money-off offer. Statistical significance testing can be used to test whether differences in sales are likely to be caused by the sales promotion or are simply random variations. The effects of other influences on sales are assumed to impact randomly on both the sales promotion and the no promotion alternatives.

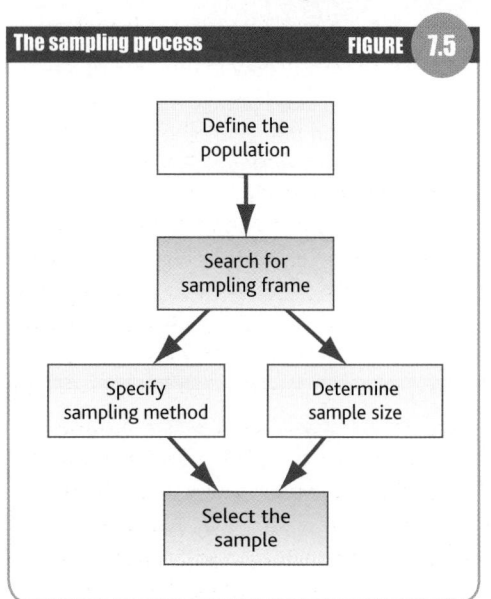

The sampling process   FIGURE **7.5**

Define the population

↓

Search for sampling frame

↓

Specify sampling method

Determine sample size

↓

Select the sample

The sampling process

Figure 7.5 outlines the **sampling process**. It begins by *defining the population*—that is, the group that forms the subject of study in a particular survey. The survey objective will be to provide results that are representative of this group. Sampling planners, for example, must ask questions like: 'Do we interview all people over the age of 18 or restrict it to those of the population aged 18–60?', 'Do we interview purchasing managers in all textile companies or only those that employ more than 200 people?'

Once the population has been defined, the next step is to search for a *sampling frame*—that is, a list or other record of the chosen population from which a sample can be selected. Examples include a register of electors, or the *Kompass* directory of companies. The result determines whether a random or non-random sample can be chosen. A random sample requires an accurate sampling frame; without one, the researcher is restricted to non-random methods.

Three major *sampling methods* are simple random sampling, stratified random sampling and quota sampling. It is also important to determine *sample size*.

- With simple random sampling, each individual (or company) in the sampling frame is given a number, and numbers are drawn at random (by chance) until the sample is complete. The sample is random because everyone on the list has an equal chance of selection.

- With stratified random sampling, the population is broken down into groups (e.g. by company size or industry) and a random sample is drawn (as above) for each group. This ensures that each group is represented in the sample.

- With quota sampling, a sampling frame does not exist but the percentage of the population that falls in various groupings (e.g. gender, social class, age) is known. The sample is constructed by asking interviewers to select individuals on the basis of these percentages, e.g. roughly 50:50 females to males. This is a non-random method since not everyone has an equal chance of selection, but it is much less expensive than random methods when the population is widely dispersed.

- Sample size is a further key consideration when attempting to generate a representative sample. Clearly, the larger the sample size the more likely it will represent the population. Statistical theory allows the calculation of sampling error (i.e. the error caused by not interviewing everyone in the population) for various sample sizes. In practice, the number of people interviewed is based on a balance between sampling error and cost considerations. Fortunately sample sizes of around 1000 (or fewer) can provide measurements that have tolerable error levels when representing populations counted in their millions.

The survey method

There are four options when choosing a *survey method*: face-to-face interviews, telephone interviews, mail surveys or Internet surveys. Each method has its own strengths and limitations; Table 7.2 gives an overview of these.

A major advantage of *face-to-face interviews* is that response rates are generally higher than for telephone interviews or mail surveys.[35] Seemingly the personal element in the contact makes refusal less likely. This is an important factor when considering how representative of the population the sample is and when using experimental designs. Testing the effectiveness of a stimulus would normally be conducted by face-to-face interview rather than a mail survey where high non-response rates and the lack of control over who completes the questionnaire would invalidate the results. Face-to-face interviews are more versatile than telephone and mail surveys.

The use of many open-ended questions on a mail survey would lower response rates,[36] and time restrictions for a telephone interview limit their use. Probing is easier with face-to-face interviews. Two types of probes are *clarifying probes* (e.g. 'Can you explain what you mean by …?'), which help the interviewer understand exactly what the interviewee is saying, and *exploratory probes*, which stimulate the interviewee to give a full answer (e.g. 'Are there any other reasons why …?'). A certain degree of probing can be achieved with a telephone interview, but time pressure and the less personalized situation will inevitably limit its use.

A comparison of face-to-face, telephone, mail and Internet surveys				TABLE 7.2
	Face to face	**Telephone**	**Mail**	**Internet**
Questionnaire				
Use of open-ended questions	High	Medium	Low	Low
Ability to probe	High	Medium	Low	Low
Use of visual aids	High	Poor	High	High
Sensitive questions	Medium	Low	High	Low
Resources				
Cost	High	Medium	Low	Low
Sampling				
Widely dispersed populations	Low	Medium	High	High
Response rates	High	Medium	Low	Low
Experimental control	High	Medium	Low	Low
Interviewing				
Control of who completes questionnaire	High	High	Low	Low/high
Interviewer bias	Possible	Possible	Low	Low

Visual aids (e.g. a drawing of a new product concept) can be used where clearly they cannot with a telephone interview.

However, face-to-face interviews have their drawbacks. They are more expensive than telephone and mail questionnaires. Telephone and mail surveys are cheaper because the cost of contacting respondents is much less expensive, unless the population is very concentrated (face-to-face interviewing of students on a business studies course, for instance, would be relatively inexpensive). The presence of an interviewer can cause bias (e.g. socially desirable answers) and lead to the misreporting of sensitive information. For example, O'Dell found that only 17 per cent of respondents admitted borrowing money from a bank in a face-to-face interview compared to 42 per cent in a comparable mail survey.[37]

In some ways *telephone interviews* are a halfway house between face-to-face and mail surveys. They generally have a higher response rate than mail questionnaires but lower than face-to-face interviews; their cost is usually less than face-to-face but higher than for mail surveys; and they allow a degree of flexibility when interviewing. However, the use of visual aids is not possible and there are limits to the number of questions that can be asked before respondents either terminate the interview or give quick (invalid) answers to speed up the process. The use of computer-aided telephone interviewing (CATI) is common. Centrally located interviewers read questions from a computer monitor and input answers via the

Methods of improving mail survey response rates	TABLE 7.3
Activity	**Effect on response rate**
Prior notification by mail	Increase in consumer research, but not for commercial populations
Prior notification by telephone	Increased response rate
Monetary and non-monetary incentives	Increased response rate
Type of postage	Higher response rates for stamped return envelopes
Personalization	The effect varies: it cannot be assumed that personalization always increases response
Granting anonymity to respondents	Higher response rate when issue is sensitive
Coloured questionnaire	No effect on response rate
Deadline	No effect on response rate
Types of question	Closed-ended questions get higher response than open-ended
Follow-ups	Follow-up telephone calls and mailing increase response rates

keyboard. *Routing* through the questionnaire is computer-controlled, helping the process of interviewing.

Mail surveys, given a reasonable response rate, are normally the least expensive of the first three options. A low research budget, combined with a widely dispersed population, may mean that there is no alternative to the mail survey. However, the major problem is the potential of low response rates and the accompanying danger of an unrepresentative sample. Much research has focused on ways of improving response rates to mail surveys and Table 7.3 gives a summary of the results.[38]

Mail questionnaires must be fully structured, so there is no opportunity to probe further. Control over who completes the questionnaire is low; for example, a marketing manager may pass the questionnaire to a subordinate for completion. However, visual aids can be supplied with the questionnaire and because of self-completion, interviewer bias is low although there may still be a source effect (e.g. whether the questionnaire was sent from a commercial or non-commercial source).

Using the Internet as a survey tool

The Internet is a growing medium for conducting survey research. With *Internet surveys*, the questionnaire is usually administered by e-mail, or signals its presence on a website by registering key words, or appears in banner advertising on search engines such as Yahoo! or Google, which drive people to the questionnaire. Although Internet surveys are a relatively recent development, their popularity has grown to such an extent that they now account for a quarter of all the qualitative data collected in Europe and for 30 per cent of the customized research market in the USA, where research forms provide information tailored to clients' needs.[39]

The major advantage of the Internet as a marketing research vehicle is its low cost, since printing and postal costs are eliminated, making it even cheaper than mail surveys. In other ways its characteristics are similar to those of mail surveys: the use of open-ended questions is limited (as these will reduce response rates) and its impersonal nature limits the ability to probe further on some questions. Visual aids such as video and graphics can be used, as well as audio input. For example, when concept testing new products, images of alternatives can be shown. However, response rates are likely to be lower than for face-to-face and telephone interviews. Experimental control is low since there is not complete control over who responds to the questionnaire, but interviewer bias is likely to be lower than for face-to-face and telephone interviews because of the impersonal administration of the questionnaire. A strength of the Internet survey is its ability to cover global populations at low cost, although sampling problems can arise because of the skewed nature of Internet users. These tend to be from the younger and more affluent groups in society. However, as Internet access has grown this has become less of a problem.

Another key advantage of Internet surveys is speed of data collection compared to mail surveys. A meta-analysis of response time for e-mail versus mail surveys showed that the average response time for the former was 6 days compared to 12 days for the latter.[40] A comparison of face-to-face and telephone is difficult as their response time is dependent on the resources devoted to their execution. For web-based surveys, the researcher controls the response time, which depends on the length of time the survey is posted on the web. The rule of thumb is for the web-based survey to run for between one and two weeks to allow enough time for visitors to the site to participate in the survey.[41] This, again, is quicker than mail surveys where response cut-off dates are usually around three weeks for single-wave surveys and five weeks for surveys using follow-ups. Another factor reducing the time to produce Internet survey reports is that responses can be directly loaded onto data analysis software, saving the time (and resources) associated with the data entry process.[42]

When response is by e-mail the identity of the respondent will automatically be sent to the survey company. This lack of anonymity may restrict the respondent's willingness to answer sensitive questions honestly. However, for e-mail surveys, control over who completes the questionnaire is fairly high, although for Internet surveys that invite anyone to complete the questionnaire, using registration or banner advertising with search engines, control is low.

A problem when using e-mail to survey populations is the absence of accurate lists. Even when lists can be found researchers need to tread very carefully as 'spamming'—sending junk mail—is seen as very offensive by most e-mail users.

When using the Internet to administer questionnaires a key decision is whether to use an e-mail or web-based survey, or a combination of the two. E-mail has the advantage of generating a higher response rate than surveys on the web. This has been verified by empirical research. The researcher also has better control over the sample of respondents since questionnaires are sent out to named people, respondents' identities are known through their e-mail address and the problem of multiple responses from the same person is avoided. In one web-based survey, which offered a prize as an incentive, it was found that one respondent had completed the pop-up questionnaire 750 times in order to increase their chances of winning the prize![43] However, web-based surveys are often better displayed, more interactive and sometimes easier to fill in when they are displayed in a browser than in an e-mail letter. Combining the two approaches by establishing contact through personalized e-mail and providing the questionnaire in HTML format (or sending the website URL) utilizes the advantages of each and, therefore, can be an effective way of collecting data.[44]

Another approach is to recruit a panel of respondents from which members can be selected to take part in a particular survey. This panel-based approach has been popular in the USA for several years and is growing in popularity in Europe.[45]

An online panel is a group of consumers that have been recruited to respond to surveys in return for small financial incentives. Such online panels enable immediate access to thousands of opted-in consumers, while allowing specific targeting of groups, such as fast-food chain users or do-it-yourself enthusiasts, according to member profiles. Two problems of online panels are the possible inclusion of 'professional' respondents—web-savvy individuals who can cause response bias—and high drop-out rates. However, these potential problems are minimized by specialist online research agencies such as YouGov and Toluna, which possess considerable expertise in this area. A variant on this approach is the creation by brand owners of online communities that can be used for research purposes, as Digital Marketing 7.1 explains.

 7.1 Digital Marketing

Online Research Communities

The online world is providing fertile territory for market research. The fondness of Internet users for forming groups when their interests coincide makes the web an ideal environment to cultivate research communities. For example, Del Monte in the USA set up an online panel of 9000 pet owners to research their needs and concerns. One study focused on dog owners. Del Monte had toyed with the idea of launching a breakfast-specific dog snack. The community established that there was an opening in the market for such a product, with members bemoaning the lack of occasion-specific dog food, such as breakfast, lunch and dinner snacks. The community also contributed by refining the product's appearance and ingredients. Based on this online research, Snausages Breakfast Bites was successfully launched, an addition to the Snausages range.

Other companies that have benefited from creating online research communities are Lego, whose tightly knit user panel helped develop its Mindstorms range, and Unilever, which has created Headbox, its young consumer feedback site. Unilever's panel has produced new product ideas and speeded up the process of developing those ideas to launch. BA, Philips and O_2 have also launched their own community websites to engage consumers, and test their reactions to new product concepts and advertisements.

Based on: Benady (2008);[46] Dye (2008)[47,48]

Surveys of consumer discussions on the web are also taking place. For example, Audi commissioned research that monitors consumer discussions across a range of over 20 websites. It receives a stream of information: 500 to 800 individual messages a week. This information is analysed so that the company can see who has been saying what about which model and dealership.[49]

Questionnaire design

Three conditions are necessary to get a true response to a question. First, respondents must *understand* the question; second, respondents must be *able to provide* the information; and,

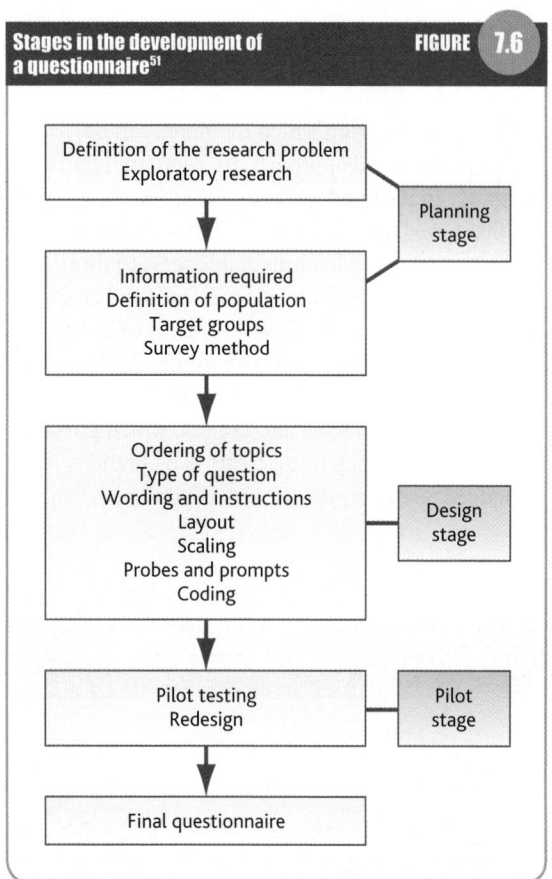

Stages in the development of a questionnaire[51] FIGURE **7.6**

- Definition of the research problem
  Exploratory research

- Information required
  Definition of population
  Target groups
  Survey method

Planning stage

- Ordering of topics
  Type of question
  Wording and instructions
  Layout
  Scaling
  Probes and prompts
  Coding

Design stage

- Pilot testing
  Redesign

Pilot stage

- Final questionnaire

third, they must be *willing* to provide it. Researchers must remember these conditions when designing questionnaires. Questions need to be phrased in language the respondent understands. This can prove problematical with some types of respondents, however. A psychological survey of footballers called upon club managers to pass on questionnaires to their players.[50] One manager replied, 'Please feel free to send your questionnaires to me. I shall be happy to distribute them to the two or three players who can read or write, and have an attention span of longer than two minutes.'

Equally, researchers must not ask about issues that respondents cannot remember or that are outside their experience. For example, it would be invalid to ask about attitudes towards a brand of which the respondent is unaware. Finally, researchers need to consider the best way to elicit sensitive or personal information. As we have already seen, willingness to provide such information depends on the survey method employed.

Figure 7.6 shows the three stages in the development of the questionnaire: planning, design and pilot.

The *planning stage* involves the types of decision discussed so far in this chapter. It provides a firm foundation for designing a questionnaire that provides relevant information for the marketing problem that is being addressed.

The *design stage* involves a number of interrelated issues, as described below.

1 *Ordering of topics*: an effective questionnaire has a logical flow. It is sensible to start with easy-to-answer questions. This helps to build the confidence of respondents and allows them to relax. Respondents are often anxious at the beginning of an interview, concerned that they might show their ignorance. Other rules of thumb are simply common sense: for example, it would be logical to ask awareness questions before attitude measurement questions, and not vice versa. Unaided awareness questions must be asked before aided ones. Classificatory questions that ask for personal information such as age and occupation are usually asked last.

2 *Types of question*: *closed-ended questions* specify the range of answers that will be recorded. If there are only two possible answers (e.g. 'Did you visit a cinema within the last seven days?' YES/NO) the question is *dichotomous* (either/or). If there are more than two possible answers, then the question is *multiple choice* (e.g. 'Which, if any, of the following cinemas have you visited within the last seven days?' ODEON, SHOWCASE, CINEWORLD, NONE). *Open-ended questions* allow respondents to answer the question in their own words (e.g. 'Please tell me what you liked about the cinema you visited?'). The interviewer then writes the answer in a space on the questionnaire.

3 *Wording and instructions*: great care needs to be taken in the wording of questions. Questionnaire designers need to guard against ambiguity, leading questions, asking two-questions-in-one and using unfamiliar words. Table 7.4 gives some examples of poorly worded questions and suggests remedies. Instructions should be printed in capital letters or underlined so that they are easily distinguishable from questions.

Poorly worded questions and how to avoid them	TABLE 7.4
Question	**Problem and solution**
What type of wine do you prefer?	'Type' is ambiguous; respondents; could say 'French', 'red', 'claret', depending on their interpretation. Showing the respondent a list and asking 'from this list ...' would avoid the problem
Do you think that prices are cheaper at Asda than at Aldi?	Leading question favouring Asda; a better question would be 'Do you think that prices at Asda are higher, lower or about the same as at Aldi?' Names should be reversed for half of the sample
Which is more powerful and kind to your hands: Ariel or Bold?	Two questions in one: Ariel may be more powerful but Bold may be kinder to the hands. Ask the two questions separately
Do you find it paradoxical that X lasts longer and yet is cheaper than Y?	Unfamiliar word: a study has shown that less than a quarter of the population understand such words as paradoxical, chronological or facility. Test understanding before use

4 *Layout*: the questionnaire should not appear cluttered. If possible, answers and codes should each form a column so that they are easy to identify. In mail questionnaires, it is a mistake to squeeze too many questions on to one page so that the questionnaire length (in pages) is shortened. Response is more likely to be lower if the questionnaire appears heavy than if its page length is extended.[52]

5 *Scaling*: careful exploratory research may allow attitudes and beliefs to be measured by means of scales. Respondents are given lists of statements (e.g. 'My company's marketing information system allows me to make better decisions') followed by a choice of five positions on a scale ranging from 'strongly agree' to 'strongly disagree'. Exploratory research identifies statements, and a structured questionnaire is used to provide quantification. Computer advances are enabling the measurement of emotions using avatars (pictorial representations of people), as Digital Marketing 7.2 explains.

6 *Probes and prompts*: probes seek to explore or clarify what a respondent has said. Following a question about awareness of brand names, the *exploratory probe* 'Any others?' would seek to identify further names. Sometimes respondents use vague words or phrases like 'I like going on holiday because it is nice.' A *clarifying probe* such as, 'In what way is it nice?' would seek a more meaningful response. *Prompts*, on the other hand, aid responses to a question. For example, in an aided-recall question, a list of brand names would be provided for the respondent.

7 *Coding*: by using closed questions the interviewer merely has to ring the code number next to the respondent's choice of answer. In computer-assisted telephone interviewing and with the increasing use of laptop computers for face-to-face interviewing, the appropriate code number can be keyed directly into the computer's memory. Such questionnaires are *pre-coded*, making the process of interviewing and data analysis much simpler. Open-ended questions, however, require the interviewer to write down the answer verbatim. This necessitates *post-coding*, whereby answers are categorized after the interview. This can be a time-consuming and laborious task.

7.2 Digital Marketing

Emotional Measurement Using Metaphorix

Traditional scaling techniques have been found to be wanting when it comes to measuring emotions. However, better computer graphics are allowing pictorial representation of data. For example, Conquest, a London-based market research agency, has developed Metaphorix, a tool that uses avatars (pictorial representations of themselves) to test consumers' reactions to brands and advertising. Respondents can express warmth, excitement, empathy, proximity and happiness by moving their avatar around. For instance, consumers can express happiness by manipulating the avatar to jump in the air, or emotional proximity by cuddling up on a sofa or maintaining maximum distance (see illustration).

By using an avatar to project their feelings about a brand, respondents can get beyond the limitations of traditional scaling and questioning. This has been found to be particularly useful among groups such as young men, who find it hard to express their emotions.

To illustrate its use the agency tested the highly successful Cadbury gorilla commercial, once with conventional advertising testing (word-based) and again with avatars. In the standard tests, the advertisement did well, but not exceptionally well. In the avatar-based tests it performed outstandingly. Conquest argues that, often, consumers cannot put into words how they feel. By taking words out of the equation, avatars make it easier for people to express extremes of emotion spontaneously.

Based on: Clegg (2008);[53] *Cowlett (2008)*[54]

Once the preliminary questionnaire has been designed, it should be piloted with a representative sub-sample, to test for faults. The *pilot stage* is not the same as exploratory research. Exploratory research helps to decide upon the research design; piloting tests the questionnaire design and helps to estimate costs. Face-to-face piloting, where respondents are asked to answer questions and comment on any problems concerning a questionnaire read out by an interviewer, is preferable to impersonal piloting, where the questionnaire is given to respondents for self-completion and they are asked to write down any problems found.[55] If desired, several kinds of question on the same topic can be asked in order to assess the effects of the wording on respondents.[56] Once the pilot work proves satisfactory the final questionnaire can be administered to the chosen sample.

Data analysis and interpretation

Quantitative analysis of questionnaire data will invariably be carried out by computer. Basic marketing analyses can be carried out using such software-analysis packages as SNAP or MARQUIS on a personal computer. More sophisticated analyses can be conducted using a package such as SPSS-PC.

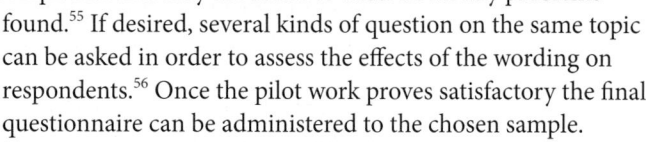

◀ Using Metaphorix, respondents can express their feelings about brands by moving the avatar on the left of the sofa in relation to the one on the right (the brand).

▲ A computer-generated histogram displaying marketing research information.

Basic analysis may be at the descriptive level (e.g. means, standard deviations and frequency tables) or on a comparative basis (e.g. cross tabulations and t-tests). The illustration shows a computer-generated histogram. More sophisticated analysis may search for relationships (e.g. regression analysis), group respondents (e.g. cluster analysis) or establish cause and effect (e.g. analysis of variance techniques used on experimental data). Computer-aided analysis of marketing research data is not limited to quantitative data. The analysis of vast volumes of qualitative data can be aided by the use of a software package called NUD.IST, where data can be filed, accessed and organized in more sophisticated ways than manual analysis.

Great care is required when interpreting marketing research results. One common failing is to infer cause and effect when only association has been established. For example, establishing a relationship that sales rise when advertising levels increase does not necessarily mean that raising advertising expenditure will lead to an increase in sales. Other marketing variables—for example, salesforce effect—may have increased at the same time as the increase in advertising, or the advertising budget may have been dependent on sales levels. Either explanation would invalidate the claim that advertising causes sales to rise.

A second cautionary note concerns the interpretation of means and percentages. Given that a sample has been taken, any mean or percentage is an estimate subject to *sampling error*—that is, the error in an estimate due to taking a sample rather than interviewing the entire population. A market research survey which estimates that 50 per cent of males but only 45 per cent of females smoke does not necessarily suggest that smoking is more prevalent among males. Given the sampling error associated with each estimate, the true conclusion might be that there is no difference between males and females. Statistical hypothesis testing allows sample differences to be evaluated in the light of sampling error to establish whether they are likely to be real differences (statistically significant) or likely to be a result of taking a sample (rather than interviewing the entire population).

Report writing and presentation

Crouch suggests that the key elements in a research report are as follows:[57]

1 title page
2 list of contents
3 preface (outline of agreed brief, statement of objectives, scope and methods of research)
4 summary of conclusions and recommendations
5 previous related research (how previous research has had a bearing on this research)
6 research method
7 research findings
8 conclusions
9 appendices.

Sections 1–4 provide a concise description of the nature and outcomes of the research for busy managers. Sections 5–9 provide the level of detail necessary if any particular issue (e.g. the basis of a finding, or the analytical technique used) needs checking. The report should be written in language the reader will understand; jargon should be avoided.

Software packages such as PowerPoint considerably ease the production of pie charts, histograms, graphs, and so on, for use in the report or for presentational purposes (such as the production of acetates for overhead projection). Clients are increasingly asking for live discussions in which ideas are thought about and the implications for marketing decisions discussed. Some agencies recommend the use of workshops, following the presentation of results, to encourage this kind of discussion.[58]

The Essential Differences Between Qualitative and Quantitative Research

An important distinction in marketing research is that between qualitative and quantitative research. Earlier in this chapter we discussed qualitative and quantitative research as elements in the marketing research process. Qualitative research usually precedes quantitative research and forms the basis for an understanding of consumers that can aid planning questionnaires, which can then be designed to focus on what is important to the consumer, and worded in language that consumers use and understand. However, when the objectives of the research are to gain rich, in-depth insights into consumer motivations, attitudes and behaviour the study may be based on qualitative research alone without the quantitative follow-up. Whichever approach is taken there are a number of essential differences between these two key primary data-gathering methods that mean the skills required vary. Indeed many market research practitioners specialize in one or the other approach. These differences relate to focus, research purpose and outcome, research means and operation, data capture, sampling, analysis and reporting.

Focus

The focus for qualitative research is on verbal data based on statements made by respondents—for example, 'The thing I most like about the iPod is the convenience that comes from being able to store thousands of songs on a small, portable music player.' By contrast, quantitative research focuses on numerical data (e.g. whether the respondent owns or does not own an iPod).

Research purpose and outcome

The purpose of qualitative research is to provide rich, in-depth insights into consumer behaviour, particularly how consumers behave and why they do so. Through focus groups and depth interviews a greater degree of insight may be achieved than asking questions using a structured questionnaire since the former is more flexible and allows a longer period of time to be spent exploring a given issue. The purpose of quantitative research is to provide information that can be generalized across the study population. While, at times, quantitative research results may be more superficial, the researcher can be more confident that the results are applicable to a broad section of consumers.

Research means and operation

The two major means by which qualitative data are gathered are the focus group and the depth interview, whereas quantitative data is gathered using a structured questionnaire. Typically a qualitative interviewer will have a list of topics to discuss but will have the freedom to vary the precise questions asked and the length of time devoted to a particular topic, depending on the circumstances that arise during the discussion or interview. For example, if a respondent makes an interesting or novel comment, the interviewer may decide to ask a series of probing questions to investigate the issue in more depth. The questions asked in a qualitative study may, therefore, depend on the answers given by a respondent to some degree. In quantitative research there is much less flexibility. Although a structured questionnaire can provide the means for varying questions through the use of filter questions (for example, 'If the answer to question 6 is yes, go to question 7, if no go to question 10'), there is much less flexibility to vary the questions at the discretion of the interviewer.

Data capture

In qualitative research the data are usually audio recorded (and occasionally video recorded), whereas in quantitative research the data are captured on a structured questionnaire typically by means of pre-coded response categories (e.g. Yes or No). Audio recording in qualitative research means that the data require post-coding, either manually or with the assistance of a software package such as NUD.IST (see the section on 'Data analysis and interpretation', above).

Sampling

The higher cost per respondent and the focus on insight rather than statistical precision mean that qualitative studies are associated with smaller samples than quantitative research. A typical study using focus groups might involve six groups of eight people per group, or one using depth interviews might be based on 15 people. Quantitative studies involve hundreds or thousands of people. For example, studies of voting intentions use samples in excess of 1000 respondents.

Analysis

Qualitative research is based on content analysis of respondent statements taken from audio recordings, whereas quantitative studies are statistical analyses of pre-coded responses from structured questionnaires. Content analysis of vast amounts of verbal data gathered by means of qualitative techniques may be enabled using computer packages such as NUD.IST (again, see above). Statistical analysis of quantitative data is invariably carried out using a computer.

Reporting

A qualitative report looks very different to one based on quantitative research. The former is verbal, typically using quotes from respondents to provide evidence to support underlying themes. Summary statements (for example 'most respondents stated …', or 'some respondents thought …') are used rather than precise statistical estimates. Such reporting is sometimes considered more vivid than quantitative research reports that rely on statistical reporting (for example, using percentages, tables, graphs, statistical inferences and estimates, etc.). In both cases, careful interpretation of the information is required.

Table 7.5 provides a summary of the key differences between qualitative and quantitative research.

The Use of Marketing Information Systems and Marketing Research

A key issue is an understanding of the factors that affect the use of marketing information systems and marketing research. Systems and marketing research reports that remain unused are valueless in decision-making. So what factors are likely to bring about increased usage? Two studies of MkIS have examined the factors that affect usage. Systems are used more when:

- the system is sophisticated and confers prestige to its users
- other departments view the system as a threat
- there is pressure from top management to use the system
- users are more involved in automation.

The system takes more of the marketing executive's time when:

- it provides information indiscriminately
- it provides less assistance
- it is changed without consultation.

These results have implications for the design of MkIS. Sophisticated systems should be designed to provide information on a selective basis (for example, by means of a direct,

The essential differences between qualitative and quantitative research		TABLE 7.5
	Qualitative research	**Quantitative research**
Focus	Verbal data	Numerical data
Research purpose and outcome	Rich, in-depth insights	Broad generalizations
Research means	Focus groups or depth interviews	Structured questionnaires
Operation	High flexibility in data collection	Low flexibility in data collection
Data capture	Audio recording requiring post-coding	Pre-coded response categories on structured questionnaire
Sampling	Small samples	Large samples
Analysis	Content analysis of respondent statements from audio recording	Statistical analysis of pre-coded responses from a structured questionnaire
Reporting	Underlying themes illustrated by quotes from respondents; summary statements ('most respondents stated ...'; 'some thought ...')	Statistical, e.g. percentages, tables, graphs, statistical inferences and estimates

interactive capability).[59] Senior management should conspicuously support use of the system. These recommendations are in line with Ackoff's view that a prime task of an information system is to eliminate irrelevant information by tailoring information flows to individual manager's needs.[60] It also supports the prescription of Piercy and Evans that the system should be seen to have top management support.[61]

Research into the use of marketing research has shown that use is higher if:[62]

- results conform to the client's prior beliefs
- the research is technically competent
- the presentation of results is clear
- the findings are politically acceptable
- the status quo is not challenged.

These findings suggest that marketing researchers need to appreciate not only the technical aspects of research and the need for clarity in report presentation but also the political dimension of information provision: it is unlikely that marketing research reports will be used in decision-making if the results threaten the status quo or are likely to have adverse political repercussions. As Machiavelli said, 'Knowledge is power.' The sad fact is that perfectly valid and useful information may be ignored in decision-making for reasons that are outside the technical competence of the research.

Ethical Issues in Marketing Research

The intention of marketing research is to benefit both the sponsoring company and its consumers. The company learns about the needs and buyer behaviour of consumers with the objective of better satisfying their needs. Despite these good intentions there are four ethical concerns about marketing research. These are intrusions on privacy, the misuse of marketing research findings, competitive information gathering, and the use of marketing research surveys as a guise for selling.

Intrusions on privacy

While many consumers recognize the positive role marketing research plays in the provision of goods and services, some resent the intrusive nature of some marketing research surveys. Most consumer surveys ask for classificatory data such as age, occupation and income. While most surveys ask respondents to indicate an age and income band rather than request specifics, some people feel that this is an intrusion on privacy. Other people object to receiving unsolicited telephone calls or mail surveys, and dislike being stopped in the street to be asked to complete a face-to-face survey. As the use of the Internet as a marketing research tool grows, ethical issues regarding the unsolicited receipt of e-mail questionnaires may arise. The right of individuals to privacy is incorporated in the guidelines of many research associations. For example, a code of conduct of the European Society for Opinion and Marketing Research (ESOMAR) states that 'no information which could be used to identify informants, either directly or indirectly, shall be revealed other than to research personnel within the researchers' own organization who require this knowledge for the administration and checking of interviews and data processing'.[63] Under no circumstances should the information from a survey combined with the address/telephone number of the respondent be supplied to a salesperson. The whole view of the collection and storage of personal information is contentious, as Marketing Ethics and Corporate Social Responsibility in Action 7.1 explains.

7.1 Marketing Ethics and Corporate Social Responsibility in Action

Big Brother is Watching You!

Proposals for the monitoring of mobile calls, e-mails and Internet usage in general have recently been implemented in the UK; this is in line with a European Union directive that aims to track criminal activity facilitated by communication technologies. Although the content of e-mails and phone calls will not be stored, a new database is supposed to keep details such as IP addresses, browsing histories, e-mail traffic, date, time and telephone numbers. A legal duty to retain private information for an entire year has been placed on Internet and telephone companies, but the government has offered to pay for costs related to data retention. While government officials feel that this is a positive step forward in protecting national security and public safety, MPs and campaigners have been quick to voice their concerns. Such a database will mean that law-abiding citizens will have their private lives, relationships and tastes scrutinized unwarrantedly.

Although social networking websites are not currently covered by the directive, plans to monitor Facebook, Bebo, MySpace and Twitter have already been announced. Such websites are generally used by millions of people across the globe and about half of the UK population, and tend to contain very sensitive data on people's religious beliefs, political views and sexual orientation, as well as consumer preferences. Information on vulnerable populations such as teenagers would also be kept, as they are the main users of Bebo, for example. This begs the question of whether our private data will be kept safe, and whether it will be used solely for the purposes of crime prevention. History tells us otherwise. Indeed the UK Government has already misplaced data on persistent offenders, and corporations have been known to use our data for commercial purposes without prior consent simply because our online footprints are readily available and easy to explore.

One example of the misuse of online data concerns Phorm and its behaviour-targeted advertising technology. The technology enables Internet service providers to analyse, profile and therefore target users based on their online interests and behaviours. BT admitted to having tested the technology without customers' informed consent. This, in turn, prompted campaigners, individuals and MPs to protest and ask the European Commission for help in ensuring tighter controls with regard to data protection and privacy. Thus, the European Commission has required the UK Government to strengthen its laws regarding the interception of Internet communications by Internet service providers. It is hoped that this will ensure better protection of our right to privacy.

Based on: Morris (2009);[64] Verkaik (2009);[65] Wray (2009)[66]

Misuse of marketing research findings

Where the findings of marketing research are to be used in an advertising campaign or as part of a sales pitch there can be a temptation to bias the results in favour of the desired outcome. Respondents could be chosen who are more likely to give a favourable response. For example, a study comparing a domestic versus foreign brand of car could be biased by only choosing people that own domestic-made cars. Another source of bias would be using leading questions—for example, 'In a world that is becoming increasingly environmentally aware, would you prefer more or less recyclable packaging?'

Another potential source of bias in the use of marketing research findings is where the client explicitly or implicitly communicates to the researcher the preferred research result. For example, a product champion for a new product may have a vested interest in the product being launched. For it to be ditched at the later stages of the new product development process may represent a political defeat for the product champion, who may have spent the last six months pushing it through a series of internal committees. In such circumstances, there is the potential for the most favoured outcome to be communicated to the research agency. Where the product champion is influential in the choice of agency, the latter may recognize that giving bad news to the client may sour their relationship and jeopardize future business. While most marketing researchers accept the need for objective studies where there is room for more than one interpretation of study findings, for example, the temptation to present the more favourable representation could be overpowering.

Competitive information gathering

The modern marketing concept stresses the need to understand both customers and competitors in order to build a competitive advantage. However, the methods that may be required to gather competitor intelligence can raise ethical questions. Questionable practices include using student projects to gather information without the student revealing the sponsor of the research, pretending to be a potential supplier who is conducting a telephone survey to understand the market, posing as a potential customer at an exhibition, bribing a competitor's employee to pass on proprietary information, and covert surveillance such as through the use of hidden cameras. Procter & Gamble was embarrassed by a scandal that arose when it emerged that the company had hired 'corporate intelligence agents', who searched through bins outside Unilever's Chicago new product development headquarters in an attempt to spy on the company's plans for the haircare market.[67] Thankfully, competitive information gathering does not exclusively depend on such methods since much useful information can be gathered by reading trade journals and newspapers, searching the Internet, analysing databases and acquiring financial statements.

Selling under the guise of marketing research

This practice, commonly known as 'sugging', is a real danger to the reputation of marketing research. Despite the fact that it is not usually practised by bona fide marketing research agencies but unscrupulous selling companies who use marketing research as a means of gaining compliance to their requests to ask people questions, it is the marketing research industry that suffers from its aftermath. Usually, the questions begin innocently enough but move towards the real purpose of the exercise. Often this is to qualify prospects and ask whether they would be interested in buying the product or have a salesperson call.

In Europe, ESOMAR encourages research agencies to adopt codes of practice to prevent this, and national bodies such as the Market Research Society in the UK draw up strict guidelines. However, the problem remains that the organizations that practise sugging are unlikely to be members of such bodies. The ultimate deterrent is the realization on the part of 'suggers' that the method is no longer effective.

Review

1 **The nature and purpose of marketing information systems, and the role of marketing research within such systems**

- A marketing information system provides the information required for marketing decision-making and comprises internal continuous data, internal ad hoc data and environmental scanning.
- Marketing research is one component of a marketing information system and is primarily concerned with the provision of information about markets and the reaction of these to various product, price, distribution and promotion decisions.

2 **The types of marketing research**

- There are two types of marketing research, which are ad hoc research (custom-designed and omnibus studies) and continuous research (consumer panels, retail audits, television viewership panels, marketing databases, customer relationship management systems and website analysis).

3 **The approaches to conducting marketing research**

- The options are to do it yourself personally, do it yourself using a marketing research department, do it yourself using a fieldwork agency, or use the full services of a marketing research agency.

4 **The stages in the marketing research process**

- The stages in the marketing research process are research planning (research brief and proposal), exploratory research (secondary research, qualitative research, consultation with experts, and observation), the main (quantitative) data-collection stage (descriptive and experimental research, sampling, survey method, questionnaire design), data analysis and interpretation, and report writing and presentation.

5 **How to prepare a research brief and proposal**

- A research brief should explain the marketing problem and outline the research objectives. Other useful information would be background information, possible sources of information, the proposed scale of the project and a timetable.
- A research proposal should provide a statement of objectives, what will be done (research design), a timetable and costs.

6 **The nature and role of exploratory research**

- Exploratory research involves the preliminary exploration of a research area prior to the quantitative data-collection stage. Its major purpose is to avoid the sins of omission and admission. By providing an understanding of the people who are to be interviewed later, the quantitative survey is more likely to collect valid and reliable information.
- It comprises secondary research, qualitative research, consultation with experts and observation.

7 **Quantitative research design decisions: sampling, survey method and questionnaire design issues**

- Sampling decisions cover who and how many people to interview. The stages are population definition, sampling frame search, sampling method specification, sample size determination and sample selection.

- Survey method decisions relate to how to interview people. The options are face to face, telephone, mail and the Internet.
- Questionnaire design decisions cover what questions to ask. Questionnaires should be planned, designed and piloted before administering to the main sample.

8   Analysis and interpretation of data

- Qualitative data analysis can be facilitated by software packages such as NUD.IST.
- Quantitative data analysis is conducted by software packages such as SPSS.
- Care should be taken when interpreting marketing research results. One common failing is inferring cause and effect when only association has been established.

9   Report writing and presentation

- The contents of a marketing research report should be title page, list of contents, preface, summary, previous related research, research method, research findings, conclusions and appendices.
- Software packages such as PowerPoint can be used to make professional presentations.

10   The distinguishing features between qualitative and quantitative research
   (Qualitative research features precede those of quantitative research in the following list)

- Focus: verbal data vs numerical data.
- Research purpose and outcome: rich, in-depth insights vs broad generalizations.
- Research means: focus groups or depth interviews vs structured questionnaires.
- Operation: high flexibility in data collection vs low flexibility in data collection.
- Data capture: audio recording requiring post-coding vs pre-coded response categories on structured questionnaire.
- Sampling: small samples vs large samples.
- Analysis: content analysis of respondent statements from audio recording vs statistical analysis of pre-coded responses from a structured questionnaire.
- Reporting: underlying themes illustrated by quotes from respondents and summary statements vs statistical.

11   The factors that affect the usage of marketing information systems and marketing research reports

- Usage of marketing information systems has been shown to be higher when the system is sophisticated and confers prestige to its users, other departments view it as a threat, there is pressure from top management to use the system and users are more involved.
- Usage of marketing research is higher if results conform to the client's prior beliefs, the research is technically competent, the presentation of results is clear, the findings are politically acceptable and the status quo is not challenged.

12   Ethical issues in marketing research

- These are potential problems relating to intrusions on privacy, misuse of marketing research findings, competitive information gathering, and selling under the guise of marketing research.

Key Terms

ad hoc research a research project that focuses on a specific problem, collecting data at one point in time with one sample of respondents

consumer panel household consumers who provide information on their purchases over time

continuous research repeated interviewing of the same sample of people

data the most basic form of knowledge, the result of observations

depth interviews the interviewing of consumers individually for perhaps one or two hours, with the aim of understanding their attitudes, values, behaviour and/or beliefs

descriptive research research undertaken to describe customers' beliefs, attitudes, preferences and behaviour

experimental research research undertaken in order to establish cause and effect

exploratory research the preliminary exploration of a research area prior to the main data-collection stage

focus group a group normally of six to twelve consumers brought together for a discussion focusing on an aspect of a company's marketing

information combinations of data that provide decision-relevant knowledge

marketing information system a system in which marketing information is formally gathered, stored, analysed and distributed to managers in accordance with their informational needs on a regular, planned basis

marketing research the gathering of data and information on the market

omnibus survey a regular survey, usually operated by a marketing research specialist company, which asks

questions of respondents for several clients on the same questionnaire

qualitative research exploratory research that aims to understand consumers' attitudes, values, behaviour and beliefs

research brief a written document stating the client's requirements

research proposal a document defining what the marketing research agency promises to do for its client and how much it will cost

retail audit a type of continuous research tracking the sales of products through retail outlets

sampling process a term used in research to denote the selection of a sub-set of the total population in order to interview them

secondary research data that has already been collected by another researcher for another purpose

Study Questions

1. What are the essential differences between a marketing information system and marketing research?

2. What are secondary and primary data? Why should secondary data be collected before primary data?

3. What is the difference between a research brief and proposal? What advice would you give a marketing research agency when making a research proposal?

4. Mail surveys should be used only as a last resort. Do you agree?

5. Discuss the problems of conducting a multi-country marketing research survey in the EU. How can these problems be minimized?

6. Why are marketing research reports more likely to be used if they conform to the prior beliefs of the client? Does this raise any ethical questions regarding the interpretation and presentation of findings?

7. What are the strengths and limitations of using the Internet as a data-collection instrument?

References

1. Van Bruggen, A., A. Smidts and B. Wierenga (1996) The Impact of the Quality of a Marketing Decision Support System: An Experimental Study, *International Journal of Research in Marketing* 13, 331–43.

2. Jobber, D. and C. Rainbow (1977) A Study of the Development and Implementation of Marketing Information Systems in British Industry, *Journal of the Marketing Research Society* 19(3), 104–11.

3. Jain, S. C. and G. T. Haley (2009) *Marketing Planning and Strategy*, South Western Publishing.

4. Moutinho, L. and M. Evans (1992) *Applied Marketing Research*, Colorado Springs, CO: Wokingham: Addison-Wesley, 5.

5. Bainbridge, J. (2008) How to Conduct Effective Research, *The Marketer*, May, 33–6.

6. Kotler, P., W. Gregor and W. Rodgers (1977) The Marketing Audit Comes of Age, *Sloan Management Review*, Winter, 25–42.

7. Fletcher, W. (1997) Why Researchers are so Jittery, *Financial Times*, 3 March, 16.

8. Bainbridge (2008) op. cit.

9. Benady, D. (2005) Blinded by Science, *Marketing Week*, 3 February, 37–8.

10. Miles, L. (2002) Making a Research Relationship Work, *Marketing*, 10 October, 29–30.

11. Clegg, A. (2006) Dispel the Cinderella Myth, *Marketing Week*, 2 February, 39–40.

12. Bainbridge (2008) op. cit.

13. Chisnall, P. (2005) *Marketing Research*, Maidenhead: McGraw-Hill.

14. Chisnall (2005) op. cit.

15. Chisnall (2005) op. cit.

16. Foss, B. and M. Stone (2001) *Successful Customer Relationship Marketing*, London: Kogan Page.

17. Pritchard, S. (2003) Clicking the Habits, *Financial Times IT Review*, 5 February, 4.

18. Crouch, S. and M. Housden (2003) *Marketing Research for Managers*, Oxford: Butterworth-Heinemann, 253.

19. Dye, P. (2008) Share The Knowledge, *Marketing*, 19 March, 33–4.

20. Crouch and Housden (2003) op. cit., 260.

21. Wright, L. T., and M. Crimp (2003) *The Marketing Research Process*, London: Prentice-Hall.

22. Clegg, A. (2001) Policy and Opinion, *Marketing Week*, 27 September, 63–5.

23. Flack, J. (2002) Not So Honest Joe, *Marketing Week*, 26 September, 43.

24. Gray, R. (1999) Tracking the Online Audience, *Marketing*, 18 February, 41–3.

25. ESOMAR (2005) op. cit.

26. Peter, J. P., J. C. Olson, and K. G. Grunert (1999) *Consumer Behaviour and Marketing Strategy*, Maidenhead: McGraw-Hill.

27. ESOMAR (2005) op. cit.

28. Taylor, D. (2008) New Year, New Insight, *The Marketer*, February, 13.

29. Earnshaw, D. (2001) Big Brother is Getting on a Bit, *Marketing Week*, 14 June, 36.

30. Gofton, K. (2001) The Search for the Holy Grail, *Campaign*, 15 June, 26–7.

31. Singh, S. (2001) Big Brother Keeps an Eye on Buying Habits, *Marketing Week*, 31 May, 22.

32. James, M. (2002) Big Brother is Watching You, *Marketing Business*, November/December, 26–7.

33. Ritson, M. (2002) The Best Research Comes from Living the Life of Your Customer, *Marketing*, 18 July, 16.

34. Grant, J. (2005) The Switch to the Lower-income Consumer, *Financial Times*, 15 November, 13.

35. Yu, J. and H. Cooper (1983) A Quantitative Review of Research Design Effects on Response Rates to Questionnaires, *Journal of Marketing Research* 20 February, 156–64.

36. Falthzik, A. and S. J. Carroll (1971) Rate of Return for Close v Open-ended Questions in a Mail Survey of Industrial Organisations, *Psychological Reports* 29, 1121–2.

37. O'Dell, W. F. (1962) Personal Interviews or Mail Panels, *Journal of Marketing* 26, 34–9.

38. See Kanuk, L. and C. Berenson (1975) Mail Surveys and Response Rates: A Literature Review, *Journal of Marketing Research* 12 (November), 440–53; Jobber, D. (1986) Improving Response Rates to Industrial Mail Surveys, *Industrial Marketing Management* 15, 183–95; Jobber, D. and D. O'Reilly (1998) Industrial Mail Surveys: A Methodological Update, *Industrial Marketing Management* 27, 95–107.

39. See D. Milmo (2006) Internet Forces Taylor Nelson Shift Towards Advisory Work, *Guardian*, 7 March, 27; and A. Clegg (2005) Let's See How We Click, *Marketing Week*, 18 August, 39.

40. Ilieva, J., S. Baron and N. M. Healey (2002) Online Surveys in Marketing Research: Pros and Cons, *International Journal of Market Research* 44(3), 361–77.

41. Virtual Surveys Ltd (2001) Virtual Surveys: Website Research Experts (www.virtualsurveys.com/services/vsurveys).

42. Ilieva, Baron and Healey (2002) op. cit.

43. Virtual Surveys Ltd (2001) op. cit.

44. Ilieva, Baron and Healey (2002) op. cit.

45. Murphy (2002) Questions and Answers, *Marketing Business*, April, 37.

46. Benady D. (2008) In Search of an Honest Opinion, *Marketing Week*, 3 April, 15–16.

47. Dye, P. (2008) Listen and Learn, *Marketing*, 16 January, 33–4.

48. Dye, P. (2008) A Little More Conversation, *Marketing*, 19 March, 36.

49. Anonymous (2002) Audi Shifts Customer Research up a Gear, *Marketing Week*, 21 March, 37.

50. Price, R. (1992) Soccer Diary, *Guardian*, 19 December, 16.

51. See Kotler *et al.* (1977) op. cit.

52. Jobber, D. (1985) Questionnaire Design and Mail Survey Response Rates, *European Research* 13(3), 124–9.

53. Clegg, A. (2008) Virtual Worlds are the Reality, *Marketing Week*, 3 July, 27–31.

54. Cowlett, M. (2008) Market Research Leagues, *Marketing*, 3 September, 30–9.

55. Reynolds, N. and A. Diamantopoulos (1998) The Effect of Pretest Method on Error Detection Rates: Experimental Evidence, *European Journal of Marketing* 32(5/6), 480–98.

56. Sigman, A. (2001) The Lie Detectors, *Campaign*, 15 June, 29.

57. Crouch and Housden (2003) op. cit.

58. Dye, P. (2008) Share the Knowledge, *Marketing*, 19 March, 33.

59. Jobber, D. and M. Watts (1986) Behavioural Aspects of Marketing Information Systems, *Omega* 14(1), 69–79; Wierenga, B. and P. A. M. Oude Ophis (1997) Marketing Decision Support Systems: Adoption, Use and Satisfaction, *International Journal of Research in Marketing* 14, 275–90.

60. Ackoff, R. L. (1967) Management Misinformation Systems, *Management Science* 14(4), 147–56.

61. Piercy, N. and M. Evans (1983) *Managing Marketing Information*, Beckenham: Croom Helm.

62. See Deshpande, R. and S. Jeffries (1981) Attitude Affecting the Use of Marketing Research in Decision-Making: An Empirical Investigation, in *Educators' Conference Proceedings*, Chicago: American Marketing Association, 1–4; Lee, H., F. Acito and R. L. Day (1987) Evaluation and Use of Marketing Research by Decision Makers: A Behavioural Simulation, *Journal of Marketing Research* 14(May), 187–96.

63. Schlegelmilch, B. (1998) *Marketing Ethics: An International Perspective*, London: International Thomson Business Press.

64. Morris, N. (2009) Now 'Big Brother' Targets Facebook, *Independent*, 25 March 2009, www.independent.co.uk/news/uk/politics/now-big-brother-targets-facebook-1653407.html (retrieved 14 April 2009).

65. Verkaik, R. (2009) Personal Web Data to be Stored for a Year, *Independent*, 4 April 2009, www.facebook.com/ext/share.php?sid=155827145706&h=n0Fjg&u=2lKvw&ref=nf (retrieved 14 April 2009).

66. Wray, R. (2009) Phorm: UK Faces Court for Failing to Enforce EU Privacy Laws, Guardian.co.uk, www.guardian.co.uk/business/2009/apr/14/phorm-privacy-data-protection-eu (retrieved 14 April 2009).

67. Benady, D. (2001) Burst Bubbles, *Marketing Week*, 22 November, 25–6.

iPod

Researching Consumers' Perceptions

Apple's mp3 players hardly need an introduction. The full version of the iPod (the classic) has the capacity to store thousands of music tracks due to its large memory (120 GB), and a well-designed navigation system that allows individual tracks to be accessed with ease. The iPod shuffle, in contrast, has less memory (4 GB) and limited features, but is the smallest and cheapest of Apple's mp3 players. In between, Apple offers the iPod nano, with the navigation system of its big brother, but more limited storage capacity (8 or 16 GB). Critically, though, Apple has squeezed the iPod nano into a business card-sized package. A more recent addition to the range is the iPod touch, with a multi-touch display (8, 16 or 32 GB). The iPod 'package' also allows consumer access to Apple's iTunes with a huge range of easily downloaded tracks. This site alone accounts for 70–80 per cent of legal music downloads. The elegant design of the iPod hardware and its navigation system, and access to iTunes has resulted in a US market share of 74 per cent for Apple in this product category, and a Japanese market share of 45 per cent.

A multitude of accessories increase the spending associated with the iPod. Some of these accessories protect the basic product (insurance and protective cases), some are aimed at increasing convenience to the consumer (worldwide chargers, cables that reduce music download times); others extend where the iPod can be used (car and home stereo connectors, volume booster); while yet others are aimed at increasing either the quality of the basic equipment (headphone upgrades) or the functionality of the iPod (digital camera connectors, equipment allowing dictation to be taken). Toys that dance when music is played are also available.

The iPod is not just important because of the revenue it generates for Apple, it is also important to Apple in other ways as 10–20 per cent of PC users who have an iPod go on to buy a Mac. This 'halo' effect has been noted by shareholders and has boosted Apple's share price. Yet despite its current success, Apple cannot afford to count on the iPod's current phenomenal performance in the market. Consumers have questioned the value for money of the iPod shuffle, and the quality of the iPod nano's screen. Competitors are encroaching on iTunes by setting up alternative music download sites with extensive playlists. They also fear increased competition from mobile handset manufacturers.

Consequently, Apple is interested in learning more about how consumers view the iPod. In particular, it wants to know about three areas.

1 What are the ownership and usage patterns of the different iPod models? Do consumers own multiple models and use them on different occasions, or do they just have one? Which is bought first?
2 Which features do consumers find most useful? Do different age groups use different features? How are accessories used and when do consumers buy them?
3 What are consumers' attitudes towards the iPod? Do they see it as a style/image icon, or do they look at it as a functional product?

An initial draft of the questions to be included on a questionnaire has been written with these objectives in mind (see below). Apple is considering two different ways to collect data. The first idea is to sample from its customer database. After dividing the database into owners of the iPod classic, the iPod nano, the iPod shuffle and the iPod touch, Apple would mail 500 questionnaires at a time to each group. When the responses were returned, it would look at who responded from each group, and then select more customers from each group to mail the questionnaires to. This process would be repeated until it managed to get 1000 responses from each group that reflected the demographic characteristics of owners of the iPod classic, nano, shuffle and touch.

The second way Apple is considering collecting data is to set up an online questionnaire on the iTunes website. This would appear to every 25th visitor to the site, inviting them to contribute. The questionnaire would remain available until 3000 responses had been achieved.

Proposed questions

1 Which of the following Apple products do you own? (tick all that apply)
   - iPod ☐
   - iPod nano ☐
   - iPod shuffle ☐
   - iPod touch ☐

2 When do you use your iPod? (tick all that apply)
   - When commuting/travelling ☐
   - When working/studying ☐
   - When shopping ☐
   - When at the gym ☐
   - When jogging ☐

3 Which accessories for the iPod do you own? (tick all that apply)
   - Protective case ☐
   - Insurance cover ☐
   - Worldwide charger ☐
   - Upgraded headphones ☐
   - Car stereo adaptor ☐
   - Digital camera connector ☐
   - Toy ☐

Please indicate the extent to which you agree/disagree with each of the following statements.

4 The iPod's design is ahead of its time.
   - Strongly agree ☐
   - Agree ☐
   - Neither agree nor disagree ☐
   - Disagree ☐
   - Strongly disagree ☐

5 The technical features of the iPod are miles ahead of other companies' MP3 players.
   - Strongly agree ☐
   - Agree ☐
   - Neither agree nor disagree ☐
   - Disagree ☐
   - Strongly disagree ☐

6 iTunes makes it easy for me to find music I like.
   - Strongly agree ☐
   - Agree ☐
   - Neither agree nor disagree ☐
   - Disagree ☐
   - Strongly disagree ☐

7 I show off my iPod whenever I get the opportunity.
   - Strongly agree ☐
   - Agree ☐
   - Neither agree nor disagree ☐
   - Disagree ☐
   - Strongly disagree ☐

8 Music is a very important part of my life.
   - Strongly agree ☐
   - Agree ☐
   - Neither agree nor disagree ☐
   - Disagree ☐
   - Strongly disagree ☐

9 It is easy to find the track I want on my iPod.
   - Strongly agree ☐
   - Agree ☐
   - Neither agree nor disagree ☐
   - Disagree ☐
   - Strongly disagree ☐

10 I am able to find new artists I like using iTunes.
   - Strongly agree ☐
   - Agree ☐
   - Neither agree nor disagree ☐
   - Disagree ☐
   - Strongly disagree ☐

11 I talk about my iPod to anyone who will listen.
   - Strongly agree ☐
   - Agree ☐
   - Neither agree nor disagree ☐
   - Disagree ☐
   - Strongly disagree ☐

12 Having an iPod impresses people I meet.
   - Strongly agree ☐
   - Agree ☐
   - Neither agree nor disagree ☐
   - Disagree ☐
   - Strongly disagree ☐

13 I enjoy watching films a great deal.
   - Strongly agree ☐
   - Agree ☐
   - Neither agree nor disagree ☐
   - Disagree ☐
   - Strongly disagree ☐

14 The iPod has better memory than other MP3 players.
   - Strongly agree ☐
   - Agree ☐
   - Neither agree nor disagree ☐
   - Disagree ☐
   - Strongly disagree ☐

15 What is your income? _____

16 What is your occupation? _____

17 Gender (please circle) Male/Female

Questions

1. Will the proposed questions in the questionnaire answer Apple's questions? Outline any problems and suggest solutions.

2. Assess the expertise required, and costs associated with, the two proposed survey methods. Which design would you recommend and why?

3. Assess the strengths and weaknesses of the two proposed sampling methods. Which would you recommend and why?

This case was written by Nina Reynolds, Professor of Marketing, Bradford University, and Sheena MacArthur, Senior Lecturer in Marketing, Glasgow Caledonian University.

Airport Catering

Consumer Satisfaction at Gulf International Airport

Background

Ashish Narayan has recently been promoted to the job of catering manager, responsible for his company's five catering outlets at Gulf International Airport (GIA). Competition to get these concessionary facilities is intense. Operators who succeed in getting the concessionary outlets then face severe competition from other catering concessionaires at the airport, as GIA believes in keeping all of the catering providers on their toes.

Narayan reports to the commercial director of Air Catering Enterprises (ACE), a company with airline and airport catering operations throughout the Gulf area. When he took on the job, his boss said to him, 'We need to hold on to our outlets at GIA and, if possible, expand them in the next concession review by displacing some of our competitors.' The difficulty of doing this was brought home to Narayan shortly after he started. There was no information available to indicate how ACE outlets performed relative to customer expectations or relative to the competition.

He decided to do a customer survey in order to gather some insight into customer satisfaction. Having studied competitor examples, he developed a questionnaire (see Table C14.1 overleaf) and arranged for it to be given by the counter staff to customers when they purchased their food and beverages.

The outlets

The following is a brief description of the five ACE outlets at Gulf International Airport.

Hi-Flite Restaurant

This food service outlet is very busy, catering to transit passengers. On average, 650 customers eat at this outlet every day, generating an average daily total revenue of US$5200.

Airport Staff Bar

This food service outlet caters to staff at all levels working at GIA. On average, about 400 customers eat at this outlet every day, yielding an average daily total revenue of US$520.

Airlines Training Café

As the name implies, this outlet serves the catering needs of all categories of staff attending GIA's International Training Facility, which is used by a number of different airlines. On average, 250 customers eat at this outlet, with an average daily total revenue of US$750.

Departure Snack Bar

This outlet caters for passengers departing on all international flights. On average, about 2000 customers eat here every day, generating an average total daily revenue of US$8000 per day.

Technical Workers' Canteen

This food service outlet caters to the technical staff working in the airline hangars and workshops. On an average 500 customers dine at this outlet every day with an average daily total revenue of $750.

Survey results

Altogether over 750 questionnaires were completed, and Narayan analysed the results, curious to find out for the first time what the customers thought of ACE's catering outlets. Table C14.2 overleaf shows a summary of the average scores for all five outlets.

Questions

1. In Narayan's position, what questions should he be asking himself about this data?
2. What management action should he take as a result of this survey?
3. Comment on the method used to develop the questionnaire.

This case was written by Ravi Chandran, Operations Manager at a major airline, and Daragh O'Reilly, Lecturer in Marketing, University of Sheffield.

Customer Satisfaction Survey | **Table C14.1**

PLEASE RATE THE PERFORMANCE BY PUTTING A × FOR EACH OF THE FOLLOWING QUESTIONS.

	Very good	Good	Average	Poor	Very poor
1. FOOD					
How do we rate for:					
1.1 Taste of food?	◯	◯	◯	◯	◯
1.2 Quantity of food?	◯	◯	◯	◯	◯
1.3 Overall quality of food?	◯	◯	◯	◯	◯
2. MENU					
How do we rate for:					
2.1 Range and variety of food?	◯	◯	◯	◯	◯
2.2 Range and variety of drinks?	◯	◯	◯	◯	◯
3. SERVICE					
How satisfied were you with:					
3.1 Being able to order quickly?	◯	◯	◯	◯	◯
3.2 Our speed of service?	◯	◯	◯	◯	◯
3.3 Overall quality of service?	◯	◯	◯	◯	◯
4. PERSONNEL					
How satisfied were you with our staff:					
4.1 Being friendly smiling and courteous?	◯	◯	◯	◯	◯
4.2 Suggesting to buy our food and drinks?	◯	◯	◯	◯	◯
5. CLEANLINESS					
How satisfied were you with:					
5.1 Cleanliness inside the restaurant?	◯	◯	◯	◯	◯
5.2 Cleanliness outside the restaurant?	◯	◯	◯	◯	◯
HOW DO YOU RATE YOUR VISIT TO THIS FOOD SERVICE OUTLET OVERALL?	◯	◯	◯	◯	◯

SUGGESTIONS/COMMENTS

> What do you think we should be concentrating on most to improve our operation?
> Further comments:
> Name: Nationality:

Age: Occupation: Date: Time:
Your favourite food: Your favourite drink:
Thank you very much for your help.

Summary of the average scores for ACE's five food service outlets | **TABLE C14.2**

Category	Hi-Flite Restaurant	Airport Staff Bar	Airlines Training Café	Departure Snack Bar	Technical
Food	4.21	3.23	4.25	4.08	3.45
Menu	3.90	2.97	4.20	3.86	3.07
Service	4.52	4.07	4.09	3.52	3.87
Staff	4.59	3.90	4.16	4.24	3.94
Cleanliness	3.82	3.23	4.34	4.22	3.33
Comparison of mean scores among five catering outlets (n = 752) (maximum score = 5)					

CHAPTER 8

Market segmentation and positioning

// Finding the most revealing way to segment a market is more an art than a science. ... Any useful segmentation scheme will be based around the needs of customers and should be effective in revealing new business opportunities. //

PETER DOYLE,
Value-Based Marketing

LEARNING OBJECTIVES

After reading this chapter, you should be able to:

1 define the concepts of market segmentation and target marketing, and discuss their use in developing marketing strategy

2 discuss the methods of segmenting consumer and organizational markets

3 identify the factors that can be used to evaluate market segments

4 distinguish between the four target marketing strategies—undifferentiated, differentiated, focused and customized marketing

5 define the concept of positioning and discuss the keys to successful positioning

6 discuss positioning and repositioning strategies

Very few products or services can satisfy all customers in a market. Not all customers want or are prepared to pay for the same things. For example, airlines such as British Airways, KLM and SAS recognize that business and pleasure travellers are different in terms of their price sensitivity and the level of service required. In the watch market, the type of person that buys a Swatch is very different from the type of person that buys a Rolex: their reasons for purchase are different (fashion vs status) and the type of watch they want is different in terms of appearance and materials. Therefore to implement the marketing concept and successfully satisfy customer needs, different product and service offerings must be made to the diverse customer groups that typically comprise a market.

The technique that is used by marketers to get to grips with the diverse nature of markets is called **market segmentation**. Market segmentation may be defined as 'the identification of individuals or organizations with similar characteristics that have significant implications for the determination of marketing strategy'.

Market segmentation, then, consists of dividing a diverse market into a number of smaller, more similar, sub-markets. The objective is to identify groups of customers with similar requirements so that they can be served effectively while being of a sufficient size for the product or service to be supplied efficiently. Usually, particularly in consumer markets, it is not possible to create a marketing mix that satisfies every individual's particular requirements exactly. Market segmentation, by grouping together customers with *similar* needs, provides a commercially viable method of serving these customers. It is therefore at the heart of strategic marketing since it forms the basis by which marketers understand their markets and develop strategies for serving their chosen customers better than the competition.

For the process of market segmentation and targeting to be implemented successfully all relevant people in the organization should be made aware of the reasons for segmentation and its importance, and be involved in the process as much as is practicable. By gaining involvement, staff will be more committed to the results, leading to better implementation in the later stages.

Why Bother to Segment Markets?

Why go to the trouble of segmenting markets? What are the gains to be made? Figure 8.1 identifies four benefits, which will now be discussed.

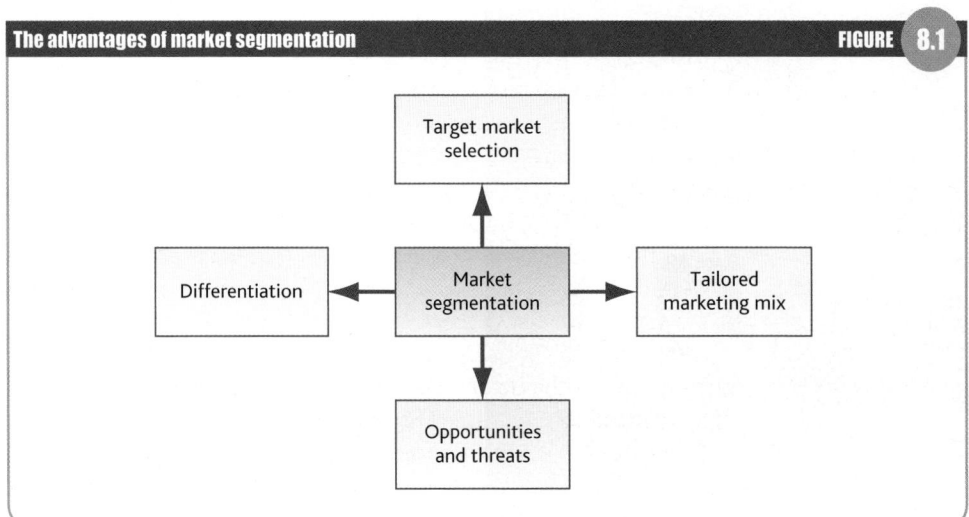

The advantages of market segmentation   FIGURE 8.1

Target market selection

Market segmentation provides the basis for the *selection of target markets*. A *target market* is a chosen segment of market that a company has decided to serve. As customers in the target market segment have similar characteristics, a single marketing mix strategy can be developed to match those requirements. Creative segmentation may result in the identification of new segments that have not been served adequately hitherto and may form attractive target markets to attack. For example, the success of Carphone Warehouse, which supplies mobile phones, was originally based on the founder Charles Dunstone's realization that a key market segment—self-employed tradesmen, such as builders, plumbers and roofers—was not being catered for. The main suppliers were targeting large corporate clients. His vision was to be the first to allow customers to visit a shop and see what mobile phones were available. His staff were trained to help customers decide which combination of rental and call charges best met their needs.[1] Later in this chapter we will explore methods of segmenting markets so that new insight may be gained.

Tailored marketing mix

Market segmentation allows the grouping of customers based upon similarities (e.g. benefits sought) that are important when designing marketing strategies. Consequently this allows marketers to understand in-depth the requirements of a segment and *tailor a marketing mix package* that meets their needs. For example, the BMW 300 series saloon car that targets middle managers is a completely different design to the BMW X5 4x4, which is targeted at well-off couples with children. This is a fundamental step in the implementation of the marketing concept: segmentation promotes the notion of customer satisfaction by viewing markets as diverse sets of needs that must be understood and met by suppliers.

Differentiation

Market segmentation allows the development of **differential marketing strategies**. By breaking a market into its constituent sub-segments a company may differentiate its offerings between segments (if it chooses to target more than one segment), and within each segment it can differentiate its offering from the competition. By creating a differential advantage over the competition, a company is giving the customer a reason to buy from it rather than the competition. For example, the BlackBerry Pearl targets the consumer segment of the smartphone market, while the more expensive BlackBerry 8800 aims at the business segment.

Opportunities and threats

Market segmentation is useful when attempting to spot *opportunities and threats*. Markets are rarely static. As customers become more affluent, seek new experiences and develop new values, new segments emerge. The company that first spots a new under-served market segment and meets its needs better than the competition can find itself on a sales and profit growth trajectory. The success of Next, the UK clothing retailer, was founded on its identification of a new market segment: working women who wanted smart fashionable clothing at affordable prices. Similarly the neglect of a market segment can pose a threat if competition use it as a gateway to market entry. The Japanese manufacturers exploited British companies' lack of interest in the low-powered motorcycle segment, and the reluctance of US motor car producers to make small cars allowed Japanese companies to form a beachhead from which they swiftly achieved market-wide penetration. The lesson is that market segments may need to be targeted by established competitors, even though in short-term commercial terms they do not appear attractive, if there is a threat that they might be used by new entrants to establish a foothold in the market.

The Process of Market Segmentation and Target Marketing

The selection of a target market or markets is a three-step process, as shown in Figure 8.2. First, the requirements and characteristics of the individuals and/or organizations that comprise the market are understood. Marketing research has an important role to play here. Second, customers are grouped according to these requirements and characteristics into segments that have implications for developing marketing strategies. Note that a given market can be segmented in various ways depending on the choice of criteria at this stage. For example, the market for motor cars could be broken down according to type of buyer (individual or organizational), by major benefit sought in a car (e.g. functionality or status) or by family size (empty nester vs family with children). The choice of the most appropriate basis for segmenting a market is a creative act. There are no rules that lay down how a market should be segmented. Using a new criterion, or using a combination of well-known criteria in a novel way, may give fresh insights into a market. Marketing personnel should be alert to the necessity of visualizing markets from fresh perspectives. In this way they may locate attractive, under-exploited market segments, and be the first to serve their needs. For example, Apple was the first to recognize that young consumers not only wanted mobile music, but also access to thousands of songs (via iTunes) that they could download to their mobile music player.

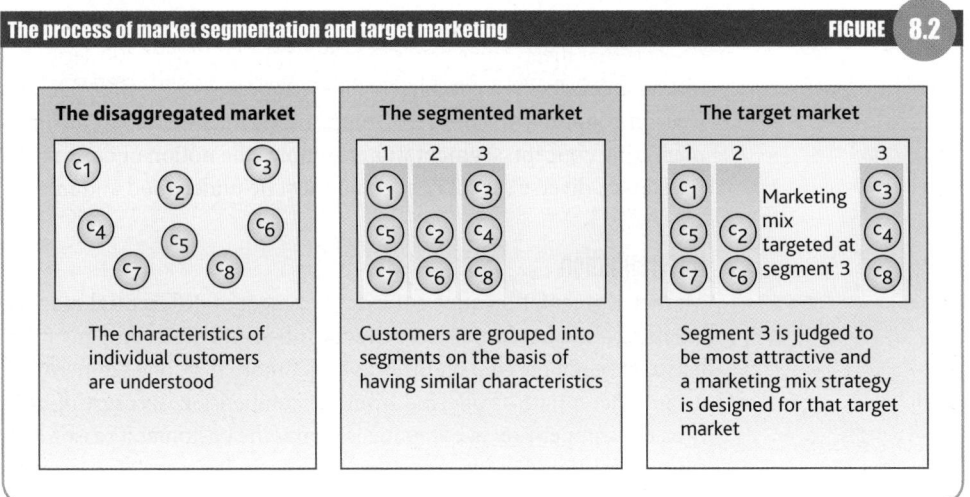

The process of market segmentation and target marketing — **FIGURE 8.2**

The disaggregated market

The characteristics of individual customers are understood

The segmented market

Customers are grouped into segments on the basis of having similar characteristics

The target market

Marketing mix targeted at segment 3

Segment 3 is judged to be most attractive and a marketing mix strategy is designed for that target market

Finally, one or more market segments are chosen for targeting. A marketing mix is developed, founded on a deep understanding of what target-market customers value. The aim is to design a mix that is distinctive from competitors' offerings. This theme of creating a *differential advantage* will be discussed in more detail when we examine how to position a product in the marketplace.

Segmenting Consumer Markets

As we have noted, markets can be segmented in many ways. Segmentation variables are the criteria that are used for dividing a market into segments. When examining criteria, the marketer is trying to identify good predictors of differences in buyer behaviour. There is an array of options and no single, prescribed way of segmenting a market.[2] Here, we shall examine the possible ways of segmenting consumer markets; in the next section we shall look at segmentation of organizational markets.

There are three broad groups of consumer segmentation criteria: *behavioural*, *psychographic* and *profile* variables. Since the purpose of segmentation is to identify differences in behaviour that have implications for marketing decisions, *behavioural variables* such as benefits sought from the product and buying patterns may be considered the ultimate bases for segmentation. Psychographic variables are used when researchers believe that purchasing behaviour is correlated with the personality or lifestyle of consumers: consumers with different personalities or lifestyles have varying product or service preferences and may respond differently to marketing mix offerings. Having found these differences, the marketer needs to describe the people who exhibit them, and this is where profile variables such as socio-economic group or geographic location are valuable.[3] For example, a marketer may see whether there are groups of people who value low calories in soft drinks and then attempt to profile them in terms of their age, socio-economic groupings, and so on.

In practice, however, segmentation may not follow this logical sequence. Often, profile variables will be identified first and then the segments so described will be examined to see if they show different behavioural responses. For example, differing age or income groups may be examined to see if they show different attitudes and requirements towards cars. Figure 8.3 shows the major segmentation variables used in consumer markets and Table 8.1 describes each of these variables in greater detail.

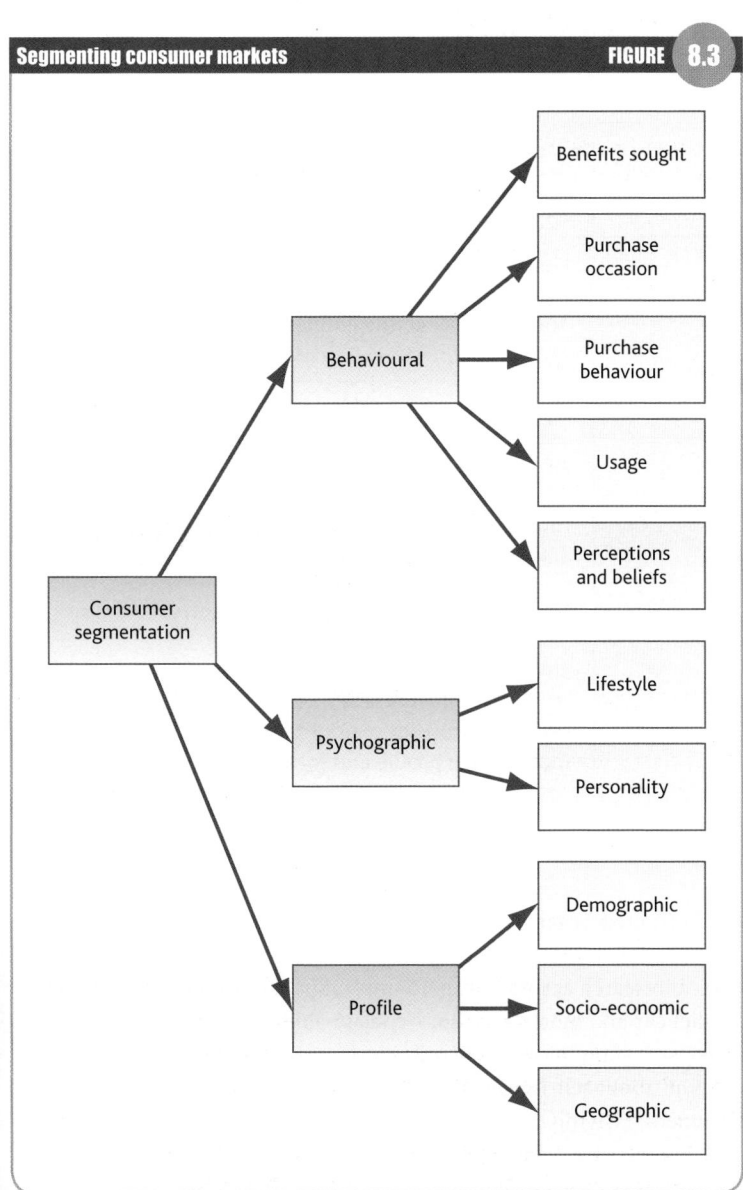

Segmenting consumer markets   FIGURE 8.3

Behavioural segmentation

The key behavioural bases for segmenting consumer markets are benefits sought; purchase occasion; purchase behaviour; usage; and perceptions, beliefs and values. Each will now be discussed.

Benefits sought

This segmentation criterion can be applied when the people in a market seek different benefits from a product. For example, the fruit drink market could be segmented by benefits sought. Table 8.2 shows such a breakdown with examples of the brands targeting each segment. **Benefit segmentation** provides an understanding of why people buy in a market and can aid the identification of opportunities. For example, the highly successful launch of Classic FM, a UK media station, was based on an understanding of the benefits a market segment for classical music sought. This segment wanted 'accessible' classical music with pleasant, down-to-earth presenters. They found the existing classical music radio station, BBC Radio 3, too intimidating, with long pieces of highbrow classical music presented by stuffy presenters. Classic FM chose to target the new segment with short pieces of more familiar classics introduced by

Consumer segmentation methods	TABLE 8.1
Variable	**Examples**
Behavioural	
Benefits sought	Convenience, status, performance, price
Purchase occasion	Self-buy, gift, special occasions, eating occasions
Purchase behaviour	Solus buying, brand switching, innovators
Usage	Heavy, light
Perceptions, beliefs and values	Favourable, unfavourable
Psychographic	
Lifestyle	Trendsetter, conservatives, sophisticates
Personality	Extroverts, introverts, aggressive, submissive
Profile	
Age	Under 12, 12–18, 19–25, 26–35, 36–49, 50–64, 65+
Gender	Female, male
Life cycle	Young single, young couples, young parents, middle-aged empty nesters, retired
Social class	Upper middle, middle, skilled working, unwaged
Terminal education age	16, 18, 21 years
Income	Income breakdown according to study objectives and income levels per country
Geographic	North vs south, urban vs rural, country
Geodemographic	Upwardly mobile young families living in larger owner-occupied houses; older people living in small houses; European regions based on language, income, age profile and location

popular presenters. Some consumers regard ice cream as an indulgence. This segment is targeted by Häagen-Dazs ice cream smoothies (see illustration).

Based upon psychological research across Europe, Sampson has shown how the benefits sought from a car can predict car and motor accessory/consumables buying.[4]

- *Pleasure seekers*: driving is all about pleasure (freedom, enjoyment and well-being).
- *Image seekers*: driving is all about self-image. The car provides feelings of power, prestige, status and self-enhancement. Driving is important too, but secondary.
- *Functionality seekers*: driving is only a means of getting from A to B. They enjoy the convenience afforded by the car rather than the act of driving.

Benefit segmentation in the fruit drink market	TABLE 8.2
Benefits sought	**Products favoured**
Extra energy	Robinson's Barley Water
Vitamins	Ribena
Natural	Pure orange juice
Low calories	'Diet' squash
Low cost	Supermarket own-label

▲ Häagen-Dazs ice cream smoothies target the 'indulgence' segment of the ice cream market.

Many markets are segmented on the basis of price sensitivity. Often a market will be characterized by a segment of customers who value the benefit of low price and another that values high quality or service and is prepared to pay more for that benefit. In the grocery market, the UK market leader, Tesco, has developed two product ranges, Tesco Value and Tesco Finest, to cater for both market segments. Also, in the tyre market, Michelin uses its own brand to target the quality (higher mileage) segment, while marketing its BF Goodrich and Kleber brands to price-sensitive buyers.

It was the failure of established airlines to cater for the price-sensitive market segment that allowed the so-called no-frills airlines easyJet and Ryanair to grow so rapidly.

Intel also used benefit segmentation to define segments in the desktop computer market. It identified three segments of end user: 'basic PC users', who required limited power but were price sensitive; 'mainstream performance seekers', who wanted more power and were prepared to pay more for it; and 'enthusiasts', for whom computing power was vital and who were prepared to pay premium prices for it. Intel developed a range of microprocessors, each with differing price levels to target each of the three segments.[5] In the laptop market it identified two segments: the value segment, which was price sensitive, was served with the Celeron microprocessor; the quality segment, which was much less price sensitive, was targeted with the more expensive Centrino mobile technology brand, which delivered enhanced performance, extended battery life, integrated wireless technology and thinner, lighter designs.[6]

Benefit segmentation is a fundamental method of segmentation because the objective of marketing is to provide customers with benefits they value. Knowing the various benefits people value is therefore a basic prerequisite of understanding markets. Benefit segmentation provides the framework for classifying individuals based upon this knowledge. Profile analyses can then be performed to identify the type of people (e.g. by age, gender, socio-economic grouping) in each benefit segment so that targeting can take place.

Purchase occasion

Customers can be distinguished according to the occasions when they purchase a product. For example, a product (e.g. tyres) or service (e.g. plumbing) may be purchased as a result of an emergency or as a routine unpressurized buy. Price sensitivity, for example, is likely to be much lower in the former case than the latter. Some products (e.g. electric shavers) may be bought as gifts or as self-purchases. These differing occasions can have implications for marketing mix and targeting decisions. If it is found that the gift market is concentrated at Christmas, advertising budgets will be concentrated in the pre-Christmas period. Package design may differ for the gift vs personal-buy segment also. Some brands, such as Black Magic chocolates, are targeted at the gift segment of the confectionery market.

Segmentation by purchase occasion is also relevant in the grocery market. Tesco, the UK's leading supermarket, has provided three store formats according to the occasions when consumers purchase groceries. For the weekly shop there are Tesco Superstores offering a wide range of food (and non-food) items; for convenience purchases, a more restricted range of food products are offered by Tesco Metros in central urban locations and Tesco Express shops next to petrol stations.

Often, special occasions such as Easter and Christmas are associated with higher prices. For example, the prices of chocolate Easter eggs fall dramatically after Easter Sunday. Also marketers have to be aware that the price of a gift can be too low to make it acceptable as a present. Gift occasions, then, pose very interesting marketing problems and opportunities. Eating occasions also provide targeting opportunities. For example, in the UK, KFC outlets have begun to offer breakfast meals in addition to their normal lunchtime and evening food.

Purchase behaviour

Differences in purchase behaviour can be based on the time of purchase relative to the launch of the product or on patterns of purchase. When a new product is launched, a key task is to identify the innovator segment of the market. These people (or organizations) may have distinct characteristics that allow communication to be targeted specifically at them (e.g. young, middle class). Innovators are more likely to be willing to buy the product soon after launch. Other segments of the market may need more time to assess the benefits, and delay purchase until after the innovators have taken the early risks of purchase. An example is the highly successful launch of Boddingtons draught beer. To build the credentials of the brand, Campaign for Real Ale (CamRA) members and beer connoisseurs were initially targeted to gain acceptance first. Only when the credential had been established among these 'innovators' was the brand moved to a wider target audience.

The degree of *brand loyalty* in a market may also be a useful basis for segmenting customers. Solus buyers are totally brand loyal, buying only one brand in the product group. For example, a person might buy Ariel washing powder invariably. Most customers brand-switch, however. Some may have a tendency to buy Ariel but also buy two or three other brands; others might show no loyalty to any individual brand but switch brands on the basis of special offers (e.g. money-off) or because they are variety seekers who look to buy a different brand each time. By profiling the characteristics of each group, a company can target each segment accordingly. By knowing the type of person (e.g. by age, socio-economic group, media habits) who is brand loyal, a company can channel persuasive communications to defend this segment. By knowing the characteristics and shopping habits of the offer seekers, sales promotions can be targeted correctly.

In the consumer durables market, brand loyalty can be used as a segment variable to good purpose. For example, Volkswagen has divided its customers into first-time buyers, replacement buyers (model-loyal replacers and company-loyal replacers) and switch replacers. These segments are used to measure performance and market trends, and for forecasting purposes.[7]

In services, too, brand loyalty has been used to segment and target customers. For example, British Airways identified a new segment that it wanted to target: 'weakly loyals'. These were people who flew BA but would also use any other airline. Using the BA customer database, the 'weakly loyals' were identified and contacted to ask questions about their media habits. This research revealed that they were light and selective television viewers. This led to an advertising campaign using channels such as Channel 4, Eurosport and Sky One, which were popular among this segment. The result was a 15 per cent increase in revenue.[8]

A recent trend in retailing has been towards biographics. This is the linking of actual purchase behaviour to individuals. The growth in loyalty schemes in supermarkets has provided the mechanism for gathering this information. Customers are given cards that are swiped through an electronic machine at the checkout so that points can be accumulated towards discounts and vouchers. The more loyal the shopper, the higher the number of points gained. The supermarket also benefits by knowing what a named individual purchases and where. Such biographic data can be used to segment and target customers very precisely. For example, it would be easy to identify a group of customers that are 'ground coffee' purchasers and target them through direct mail. Analysis of the data allows supermarkets to stock products in each of their stores that are most relevant to their customers' age, lifestyle and expenditure.

Usage

Customers can also be segmented on the basis of heavy users, light users and non-users of a product category. The profiling of heavy users allows this group to receive most marketing attention (particularly promotion efforts) on the assumption that creating brand loyalty among these people will pay heavy dividends. Sometimes the 80:20 rule applies, where about 80 per cent of a product's sales come from 20 per cent of its customers. Beer is a market where this rule often applies.[9] Brands are sometimes developed to target heavy users. For example, Orange has designed its Premier brand specifically with heavy mobile phone users in mind, with extra services such as access to a specialist customer services team.[10]

However, attacking the heavy user segment can have drawbacks if all of the competition are following this strategy. Analysing the light (and non-user) category may provide insights that permit the development of appeals that are not being mimicked by the competition.

The identity of heavy, light and non-user categories, and their accompanying profiles for many consumer goods can be accomplished by using survey information provided by the Target Group Index (TGI). This is a large-scale annual survey of buying and media habits in the UK.

Use occasion can also provide insights into new opportunities. For example, Walkers carried out extensive research of the consumption of snacks. It identified in-home evening snacking as an under-exploited occasion. Further qualitative research identified a 'chill-out' position for a snack that could be shared with friends or partners. Walkers' response was to launch the successful Doritos Dippas snack.[11]

Segmenting by use highlights an important issue in market segmentation. Some observers of markets have noted that an individual may buy product offerings that appear to appeal to different people in the market.[12] For example, the same person may buy shredded wheat and cornflakes, cheap wine and chateau-bottled wine, and an economy-class and a business-class air ticket. These critics argue that markets are not made up of segments with different requirements because buyers of one brand buy other brands as well. However, the fact that an individual may purchase two completely different product offerings does not in itself imply the absence of meaningful segments.[13] The purchases may reflect different use occasions, purchases for different family members or for variety. For example, the purchase of shredded wheat and cornflakes may reflect variety-seeking behaviour or purchases for different family members. Cheap wine may be bought as a family drink and chateau-bottled wine for a dinner party with friends. Finally, someone may purchase an economy-class air ticket when going on holiday and a business-class ticket when on a business trip. Both the wine and air-ticket examples reflect purchasing behaviour that is dependent on use occasion.

The key issue to remember is that market segmentation concerns the grouping of individuals or organizations with similar characteristics that have implications for the determination of marketing strategy. The fact that an individual may have differing requirements at different points in time (e.g. use occasions) does not mean that segmentation is not warranted. For example, it is still worthwhile targeting businesspeople through the media they read to sell business-class tickets, and charging a higher price, and the leisure traveller through different media with a lower price to sell economy flights. The fact that there will be some overlap on an individual basis does not deny the sense in formulating a different marketing strategy for each of the two segments.

Perceptions, beliefs and values

The final behavioural base for segmenting consumer markets is by studying perceptions, beliefs and values. This is classified as a behaviour variable because perceptions, beliefs and values are often strongly linked to behaviour. Consumers are grouped by identifying those people who view the products in a market in a similar way (perceptual segmentation) and have similar beliefs (belief segmentation). These kinds of segmentation analyses provide an understanding of how groups of customers view the marketplace. To the extent that their perceptions and beliefs are different, opportunities to target specific groups more effectively may arise. Marketing in Action 8.1 discusses how differing beliefs regarding beauty products have resulted in L'Oréal and Dove targeting different market segments.

8.1 Marketing in Action

Beauty is More Than Skin Deep

The women's beauty market consists of segments that provide opportunities for brands to be targeted at specific groups. L'Oréal, for example, with its 'Because you're worth it' tag-line, appeals to women who believe that they are entitled to a bit of self-indulgence and pampering. Such clear targeting has built the brand into one of the leading players in the market.

When Unilever decided to enter this market it chose not to compete with L'Oréal directly. Instead, it identified a different belief segment characterized by women who rebel against beauty stereotypes. With its 'Campaign for Real Beauty', Dove promotes its products with images of women who do not fit into the 'tall, thin and young' category. Its advertising is supported by other activities, including a forum for women to debate definitions of beauty, workshops to help young girls with body-related low self-esteem, a touring photography exhibition to showcase diverse images of beauty, a website that advocates a more 'democratic view of beauty', and an Internet television channel designed to be a trusted source of information, education and inspiration for consumers interested in the brand.

Dove has successfully identified a market segment based on beliefs. It has chosen to target a segment that is not well served by competitors, thus avoiding direct competition. It has implemented this strategy by using an integrated marketing communications campaign where each element reinforces the others.

Based on: Bruce (2005);[14] Charles (2008)[15]

Car manufacturers also use belief segmentation to segment the market and target specific groups. For example, Mazda targets car buyers who believe their car is their friend, with which they can have fun and enjoy new experiences. The Toyota Avensis is targeted—using the tag-line 'Quality speaks for itself'—at people who believe their choice of car provides evidence of their understated self-confidence.[16]

Values-based segmentation is based on the principles and standards that people use to judge what is important in life. Values are relatively consistent and underpin behaviour. Values form the basis of attitudes and lifestyles, which in turn manifest as behaviour. One research company has developed seven value groups: self-explorers, experimentalists, conspicuous consumers, belongers, social resisters, survivors, and the aimless.[17] Marketers have recognized the importance of identifying the values that trigger purchase for many years, but now it is possible to link value groups to profiling systems that make targeting feasible (see the section below on 'Combining segmentation variables').

Psychographic segmentation

Psychographic segmentation involves grouping people according to their lifestyle and personality characteristics.

Lifestyle

This form of segmentation attempts to group people according to their way of living, as reflected in their activities, interests and opinions. As we saw in Chapter 4, marketing researchers attempt to identify groups of people with similar patterns of living. The question that arises with lifestyle segmentation is the extent to which general lifestyle patterns are predictive of purchasing behaviour in specific markets.[18] Nevertheless, **lifestyle segmentation** has proved popular among advertising agencies, which have attempted to relate brands (e.g. Hugo Boss) to a particular lifestyle (e.g. aspirational). In television, Sky has used lifestyle segmentation to target special interest groups including sports enthusiasts (Sky Sports), film lovers (Sky Movies) and news followers (Sky News).

Personality

The idea that brand choice may be related to personality is intuitively appealing. Indeed, as we saw in Chapter 4, there is a relationship between the brand personality of beers and the personality of the buyer.[19] However, the usefulness of personality as a segmentation variable is likely to depend on the product category. Buyer and brand personalities are likely to match where brand choice is a direct manifestation of personal values but for most fast-moving consumer goods (e.g. detergents, tea, cereals), the reality is that people buy a repertoire of brands.[20] Personality (and lifestyle) segmentation is more likely to work when brand choice is a reflection of self-expression; the brand becomes a *badge* that makes public an aspect of personality: 'I choose this brand to say this about me and this is how I would like you to see me.' It is not surprising, then, that successful personality segmentation has been found in the areas of cosmetics, alcoholic drinks and cigarettes.[21]

Profile segmentation

Profile segmentation variables allow consumer groups to be classified in such a way that they can be reached by the communications media (e.g. advertising, direct mail). Even if behaviour and/or psychographic segmentation have successfully distinguished between buyer preferences, there is often a need to analyse the resulting segments in terms of profile variables such as age and socio-economic group to communicate to them. The reason is that readership and viewership profiles of newspapers, magazines and television programmes tend to be expressed in that way.

We shall now examine a number of demographic, socio-economic and geographic segmentation variables.

Demographic variables

The demographic variables we shall look at are age, gender and life cycle.

- *Age* has been used to segment many consumer markets.[22] For example, children receive their own television programmes; cereals, computer games, and confectionery are other examples of markets where products are formulated with children in mind. The sweeter tooth of children is reflected in sugared cereal brands targeted at children (e.g. Kellogg's Frosties). L'Oréal targets the over-50s with its Age Perfect and Age Plenitude brands, and Nintendo targets older consumers with its *Brain Training* game, which it claims aids memory. Another example of age segmentation is Vodafone's marketing of an easy-to-use, no-frills mobile phone targeting 35–55 year olds in line with the uncomplicated functionality that many in that age group value.[23]

8.1 Digital Marketing

Understanding Generation @

Today's young people have experienced very different technologies to their parents. Whereas older people may be described as the television generation, the current crop of young people have grown up with VCRs, DVDs, cable, satellite and digital TV choices. They will have learnt from an early age how to use computers, the Internet and games consoles. But they are not just observers of the media explosion, they are learning how to control that media. They are growing up wise to marketing and media messages. For example, research into men's style magazines shows that boys use them almost as cultural catalogues.

For many young people the Internet is a source of social connection. The existence of social networking sites such as MySpace.com, Facebook.com and Bebo.com means that they create home pages, share information, post photographs and download music. For millions of young people being online has become a way of life, with sites such as MySpace.com acting as virtual community centres—a place to go and interact with others. So popular is the site that it is common for over 20 million people to click on MySpace each month. Its importance is reflected in its acquisition by News Corp, which wants to be part of this new social landscape, for $580 million. Companies such as Coca-Cola, Sony Pictures Digital and Apple have used the site to connect to its members, while acts such as Arctic Monkeys and Lily Allen have used the site to build a fanbase.

Young people also connect through YouTube, where videos are shared, Flickr, the web's most popular photo-sharing site, and Twitter, which lets individuals exchange short (140-character) messages via computer or mobile phone with groups of followers. All these sites offer opportunities for communication with young consumers. Since MySpace's acquisition by NewsCorp, YouTube has been bought by Google, Flickr by Yahoo!, Bebo by AOL and Facebook is part-owned by Microsoft, demonstrating their potential as marketing communications vehicles. For example, Facebook Ads offers targeted advertising based on keywords in user profiles. Nevertheless, advertising on sites whose existence is based on person-to-person, not business-to-consumer, interaction presents challenges.

Research into the youth market does not always take the form of standard questionnaire or focus-group approaches. In order to understand their customers, the marketing executives for Unilever's Lynx (known as Axe outside the UK) deodorant for males, and Impulse body spray for females hang out once a month in the coolest clubs and check out the hottest bands. The company has formed a 'youth board' to get closer to the consumers for whom the two products are part of teenage rites of passage. Made up of brand and marketing managers, advertising executives and PR people, it operates through all-day immersion events away from head office. A day's programme might include examining in detail youth brands such as Sony's PlayStation or the energy drink Red Bull to see how they promote themselves through channels such as the Internet or dance clubs. One outcome was the realization that advertising executions (versions of the advert) needed to be changed very frequently. They observed that PlayStation had 19 different advertising executions in one year because Sony knew young people get bored quickly. Their response was to raise the number of Lynx executions from three to 10 a year.

One thing that is known about those in the youth market is that they spend a lot of time out and about. This has led to the use of posters to reach them. Research has shown that 15 to 24 years olds are 35 per cent more likely to notice bus shelter advertising and posters at the sides of roads than other age groups. Based on this knowledge, Coca-Cola launched a new drink, Fanta Icy Lemon, using 3000 Adshel bus shelter panels to target 15 to 24 year olds. The campaign reached 40 per cent of them, with unprompted awareness rising from 17 per cent to 40 per cent. Levi's also used bus shelter advertising as part of its campaign to target young consumers for its Engineered Jeans and Type 1 brands. Posters are also used on university campuses to reach the student population.

Based on: Bosworth (2002);[24] Ray (2002);[25] Hempel (2005);[26] Fernandez (2008);[27] Gibson (2008)[28]

Age is also an important segmentation variable in services. The holiday market is heavily age segmented with offerings targeted at the under-30s and the over-60s segments, for example. This reflects the differing requirements of these age groups when on holiday. As noted in Chapter 3, age distribution changes within the European Union are having profound effects on the attractiveness of various age segments. Many companies covet the youth segment, who are major purchasers of items such as clothing, consumer electronics, drinks, personal care products and magazines. Digital Marketing 8.1 explores some of the issues relating to understanding this key market segment.

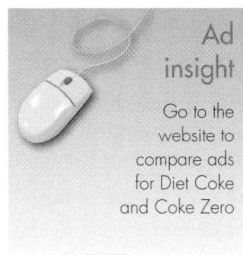

- Differing tastes and customs between men and women are reflected in specialist products aimed at these market segments. Magazines, clothing, hairdressing and cosmetics are product categories that have used segmentation based on *gender*. More recently, the car market has segmented by gender: the Corsa range of cars from General Motors, the Ford Ka and the Renault Clio in Europe are specifically targeted at women. The advertisement for Vaseline is clearly aimed at men.

- The classic family *life cycle* stages were described in Chapter 4. To briefly recap, disposable income and purchase requirements may vary according to life-cycle stage (e.g. young single vs married with two children). Consumer durable purchases may be dependent on life-cycle stage, with young couples without children being a prime target market for furnishings and appliances as they set up home. The use of life-cycle analysis may give better precision than age in segmenting markets because family responsibilities and the presence of children may have a greater bearing than age on what people buy. The consumption pattern of a single 28 year old is likely to be very different from that of a married 28 year old with three children.

Based upon population census data, People UK is arranged in eight life stages—starting out, young with toddlers, young families, singles/couples/no kids, middle-aged families, empty nesters, retired couples, and older singles. Produced by CACI, the system is particularly useful for targeted mailing because it can be applied to everyone on the UK electoral roll. People are classified according to the neighbourhood in which they live.[29] The methodology is described a little later in this section, when we discuss the ACORN geodemographic system.

Socio-economic variables

Socio-economic variables include social class, terminal education age and income. Here we shall look at social class as a predictor of buyer behaviour. *Social class* is measured in varying ways across Europe; in the UK occupation is used, whereas in other European centres a combination of variables is used. Like the demographic variables discussed earlier, social class has the advantage of being fairly easy to measure, and is used for media readership and viewership profiles. The extent to which social class is a predictor of buyer behaviour, however, has been open to question. Clearly many people who hold similar occupations have very dissimilar lifestyles, values and purchasing patterns. Nevertheless, social class has proved useful in discriminating between owning a dishwasher, having central heating, and privatization share ownership, for example, and therefore should not be discounted as a segmentation variable.[30]

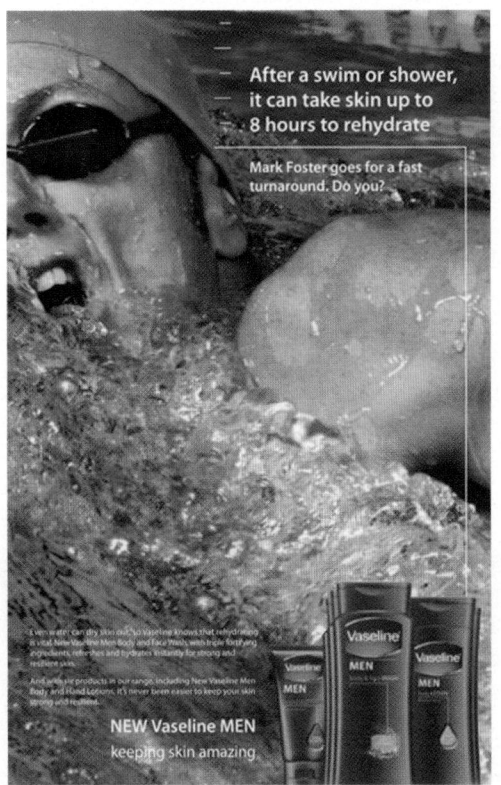

◀ Gender segmentation: Vaseline Men brand targets men in this advertisement.
Printed with the kind permission of Unilever.

Geographic variables

The final set of segmentation variables is based on geographic differences. A marketer can use pure geographic segmentation or a hybrid of geographic and demographic variables called geodemographics.

The *geographic* segmentation method is useful where there are geographic locational differences in consumption patterns and preferences. For example, in the UK beer drinkers in the north of England prefer a frothy head on their beer, whereas in some parts of the south, local taste dictates that beer should not have a head. In Germany, local tastes for beer are reflected in numerous local brewers. In Europe, differences between countries may form geographic segments. For example, variations in food preferences may form the basis of geographic segments: France, Spain and Italy are oil-based cooking markets, while Germany and the UK are margarine and butter orientated.[31] Differences in national advertising expectations may also form geographic segments for communicational purposes. Germans expect a great deal of factual information in their advertisements, to an extent that would bore French or British audiences. France, with its more relaxed attitudes to nudity, broadcasts commercials that would be banned in the UK. In the highly competitive Asian car market both Honda and Toyota have launched their first 'Asia-specific' cars, designed and marketed solely for Asian consumers.

Geodemographic: in countries that produce population census data the potential for classifying consumers on the combined basis of location and certain demographic (and socio-economic) information exists. Households are classified into groups according to a wide range of factors, depending on what is asked for on census returns. In the UK variables such as age, social status, family size, ethnic background, joint income, type of housing and car ownership are used to group small geographic areas (known as enumeration districts) into segments that share similar characteristics. The two best-known geodemographic systems in the UK are ACORN and MOSAIC. Both use census data (and in MOSAIC's case Experian's consumer segmentation database) and classify postcodes (15 addresses) into one of their categories so that households can be targeted by direct mail.

ACORN segments households into five categories: wealthy achievers, urban prosperity, comfortably off, moderate means and hard pressed. Each is subdivided into types. For example, 'wealthy achievers' are broken down into wealthy executives, affluent greys and flourishing families.

MOSAIC groups households into 11 categories: symbols of success, happy families, suburban comfort, ties of community, urban intelligence, welfare borderline, municipal dependency, blue-collar enterprise, twilight subsistence, grey perspectives and rural isolation. Like ACORN, MOSAIC subdivides each category into types. For example, 'symbols of success' are broken down into global connections, cultural leadership, corporate chieftains, golden empty nesters, provincial privilege, high technologists and semi-rural seclusion.

On an international level, MOSAIC Global is available in 18 countries, including most of western Europe. Based on the assumption that the world's cities share common patterns of residential segregation, it uses 14 distinct types of residential neighbourhood, each with a characteristic set of values, motivations and consumer preferences.[32]

Such information has been used to select recipients of direct mail campaigns, to identify the best locations for stores and to find the best poster sites. This is possible because consumers in each group can be identified by means of their postcodes. Another area where census data are employed is in buying advertising spots on television. Agencies depend upon information from viewership panels, which record their viewing habits so that advertisers have an insight into who watches what. Census analyses are combined with viewership data via the postcodes of panellists.[33] This means that advertisers who wish to reach a particular geodemographic group can discover the type of programme they prefer to watch and buy television spots accordingly.

A major strength of geodemographics is to link buyer behaviour to customer groups. Buying habits can be determined by large-scale syndicated surveys (for example, the TGI and MORI Financial Services) or from panel data (for example, the grocery and toiletries markets are covered by the TNS Superpanel). By 'geocoding' respondents, those ACORN groups most likely to purchase a product or brand can be determined. This can be useful for branch location since many service providers use a country-wide branch network and need to match the market segments to which they most appeal to the type of customer in their catchment area. Merchandise mix decisions of retailers can also be affected by customer profile data. Media selections can be made more precise by linking buying habits to geodemographic data.[34]

Combining segmentation variables

We have seen that there is a wide range of variables that can be used to segment consumer markets. Often a combination of variables will be used to identify groups of consumers that respond in the same way to marketing mix strategies. For example, Research Services Ltd, a UK marketing research company, has developed SAGACITY, a market segmentation scheme based on a combination of life cycle, occupation and income; 12 distinct consumer groupings are formed with differing aspirations and behaviour patterns.

Research companies are also combining lifestyle and values-based segmentation schemes with geodemographic data. For example, CACI's Census Lifestyle system classifies segments using lifestyle and geodemographic data. Also, CCN has produced Consumer Surveys, which combines social value groups with geodemographic data. In both cases the link to geodemographic data, which contains household address information, means that targeting of people with similar lifestyles or values is feasible.

Flexibility and creativity are the hallmarks of effective segmentation analyses; for example, one study of Europeans used a combination of demographic, psychographic and socio-economic variables to identify those segments that appeared to be ready for a pan-European marketing approach.[35] Segment 1 comprised young people across Europe who had more unified tastes in music, sports and cultural activities than was the case in previous generations. Trendsetters (intelligent pleasure seekers longing for a rich and full life) and social climbers formed the second segment. The third segment was Europe's businesspeople, totalling over 6 million people (mostly male) who regularly travel abroad and have a taste for luxury goods.

8.1 Pause For Thought

Think of a consumer market with which you are familiar. Consider the brands on offer and the kinds of people who buy them. What do you think are the ways in which that market is segmented?

Segmenting Organizational Markets

While the consumer goods marketer is interested in grouping individuals into marketing-relevant segments, the business-to-business marketer profiles organizations and organizational buyers. The organizational market can be segmented on several factors broadly classified into two major categories: macrosegmentation and microsegmentation.[36]

Macrosegmentation focuses on the characteristics of the buying organization such as size, industry and geographic location. **Microsegmentation** requires a more detailed level of market knowledge as it concerns the characteristics of decision-making within each

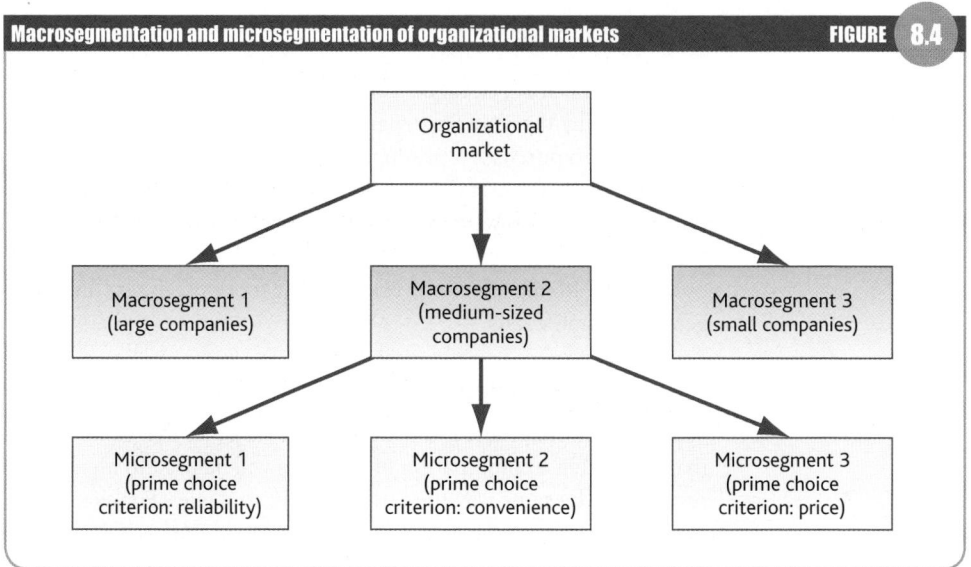

Macrosegmentation and microsegmentation of organizational markets　　FIGURE 8.4

macrosegment, based on such factors as choice criteria, decision-making unit structure, decision-making process, buy class, purchasing organization and organizational innovativeness. Often, organizational markets are first grouped on a macrosegment basis and then finer sub-segments are identified through microsegmentation.[37]

Figure 8.4 shows how this two-stage process works. The choice of the appropriate macrosegmentation and microsegmentation criteria is based on the marketer's evaluation of which criteria are most useful in predicting buyer behaviour differences that have implications for developing marketing strategies. Figure 8.5 shows the criteria that can be used.

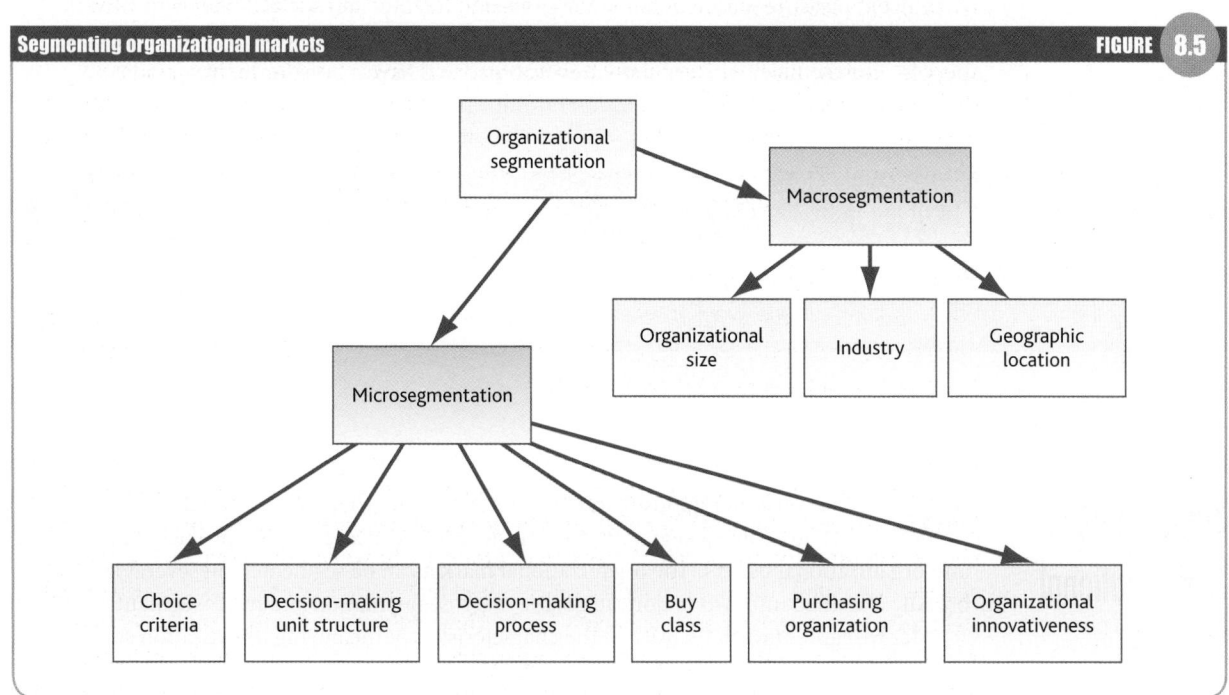

Segmenting organizational markets　　FIGURE 8.5

Macrosegmentation

The key macrosegmentation criteria of organizational size, industry and geographic location will now be discussed.

Organizational size

The size of buying organizations may be used to segment markets. Large organizations differ from medium-sized and small organizations in having greater order potential, more formalized buying and management processes, increased specialization of function, and special needs (e.g. quantity discounts). The result is that they may form important target market segments and require tailored marketing mix strategies. For example, the salesforce may need to be organized on a key account basis, where a dedicated sales team is used to service important industrial accounts. List pricing of products and services may need to take into account the inevitable demand for volume discounts from large purchasers, and the salesforce team will need to be well versed in the art of negotiation.

Industry

Another common macrosegmentation variable is industry sector. Different industries may have unique requirements from products. For example, software application suppliers like Oracle and SAP can market their products to various sectors such as banking, manufacturing, healthcare and education, each of which has unique needs in terms of software programs, servicing, price and purchasing practice. By understanding each industry's needs in depth, a more effective marketing mix can be designed. In some instances further segmentation may be required. For example, the education sector may be further divided into primary, secondary and further education as their product and service requirements may differ.

Geographic location

Regional variations in purchasing practice and needs may imply the use of geographic location as a basis for differentiating marketing strategies. The purchasing practices and expectations of companies in central and eastern Europe are likely to differ markedly from those in western Europe. Their more bureaucratic structures may imply a fundamentally different approach to doing business that needs to be recognized by companies attempting to enter these emerging industrial markets. In Chapter 3, we saw how different cultural factors affect the purchasing practices in European countries. These differences, in effect, imply regional segments since marketing needs to reflect these variations.

Microsegmentation

Marketers may find it useful to divide each macrosegment into smaller microsegments on the basis of the buyer's choice criteria, decision-making unit structure, decision-making process, buy class, purchasing organization, and organizational innovativeness.

Choice criteria

This factor segments the organizational market on the basis of the key choice criteria used by buyers when evaluating supplier offering. One group of customers may rate price as the key choice criterion, another segment may favour productivity, while a third segment may be service-orientated. These varying preferences mean that marketing and sales strategies need to be adapted to cater for each segment's needs. Three different marketing mixes would be needed to cover the three segments, and salespeople would have to stress different benefits when talking to customers in each segment. Variations in key choice criteria can be powerful

MICHELIN Energy™ Saver.
The tyre that saves fuel* mile after mile.

1/2

Did you know that tyres have an impact on fuel consumption?

In 1992, Michelin proved its commitment to the environment by launching the first generation of 'green tyres' designed to reduce fuel consumption through lower rolling resistance. Now this technology has been developed further with the MICHELIN Energy™ Saver. This latest generation of MICHELIN 'green tyres' provides even lower rolling resistance, helping you save money on your fuel bill* and reduce CO$_2$ emissions without compromising on safety. Just look for the 'GREEN X' symbol on the tyre sidewall.

Choosing MICHELIN Energy™ Saver is definitely a better way forward!

*Compared to the average of its principal European competitors. Based on fuel consumption and rolling resistance tests carried out in 2008 by TÜV SÜD Automotive on tyre sizes 195/65 R 15H and 205/55 R 16V and by DEKRA in 2009 on tyre size 195/65 R 15H.

To find out more, visit www.michelin.co.uk

MICHELIN
A better way forward

▲ This advertisement explains how Michelin tyres offer better economic value to the customer than its main competitor.

predictors of buyer behaviour. For example, Moriarty found differences in choice criteria in the computer market.[38] One segment used software support and breadth of product line as key criteria and bought IBM equipment. Another segment was more concerned with price and the willingness of suppliers to negotiate lower prices; these buyers favoured non-IBM machines. An important choice criterion for business customers is economic value to the customer, which takes into account not only price, but other costs. The advertisement for Michelin HydroEdge tyres targets business people, explaining that when longevity and fuel efficiency are taken into account, Michelin tyres are better value than the competition.

Decision-making unit structure

Another way of segmenting organizational markets is based on decision-making unit (DMU) composition: members of the DMU and its size may vary between buying organizations. As discussed in Chapter 5, the DMU consists of all those people in a buying organization who have an effect on supplier choice. One segment might be characterized by the influence of top management on the decision; another by the role played by engineers; and a third segment might comprise organizations where the purchasing manager plays the key role. DMU size can also vary considerably: one segment might feature large, complex units, while another might comprise single-member DMUs.

Decision-making process

As we saw in Chapter 5, the decision-making process can take a long time or be relatively short in duration. The length of time is often correlated with DMU composition. Long processes are associated with large DMUs. Where the decision time is long, high levels of marketing expenditure may be needed, with considerable effort placed on personal selling. Much less effort is needed when the buy process is relatively short and where, perhaps, only the purchasing manager is involved.

Buy class

Organizational purchases can be categorized into straight rebuy, modified rebuy and new task. As we discussed in Chapter 4, the buy class affects the length of the decision-making process, the complexity of the DMU and the number of choice criteria that are used in supplier selection. It can therefore be used as a predictor of different forms of buyer behaviour, and hence is useful as a segmentation variable.

Purchasing organization

Decentralized versus centralized purchasing is another microsegmentation variable because of its influence on the purchase decision.[39] Centralized purchasing is associated with purchasing specialists who become experts in buying a range of products. Specialization means that they become more familiar with cost factors, and the strengths and weaknesses of suppliers than decentralized generalists. Furthermore, the opportunity for volume buying means that their power base to demand price concessions from suppliers is enhanced. They have also been found to have greater power within the DMU vis-à-vis technical people, like engineers, than decentralized buyers, who often lack the specialist expertise and status to challenge their preferences. For these reasons, the purchasing organization provides a good base for distinguishing between buyer behaviour and can have implications for marketing activities. For example, the centralized purchasing segment could be served by a national account salesforce, whereas the decentralized purchasing segment might be covered by territory representatives.

Organizational innovativeness

A key segmentation variable when launching new products is the degree of innovativeness of potential buyers. In Chapter 10 we will discuss some general characteristics of innovator firms but marketers need to identify the specific characteristics of the innovator segment since these are the companies that should be targeted first when new products are launched. Follower firms may be willing to buy the product but only after the innovators have approved it. Although categorized here as a microsegmentation variable it should be borne in mind that organizational size (a macrosegmentation variable) may be a predictor of innovativeness too.

Table 8.3 summarizes the methods of segmenting organizational markets, and provides examples of how each variable can be used to form segments.

Organizational segmentation methods	TABLE 8.3
Variable	**Examples**
Macrosegmentation	
Organizational size	Large, medium, small
Industry	Engineering, textiles, banking
Geographic location	Local, national, European, global
Microsegmentation	
Choice criteria	Economic value, delivery, price, service
Decision-making unit structure	Complex, simple
Decision-making process	Long, short
Buy class	Straight rebuy, modified rebuy, new task
Purchasing organization	Centralized, decentralized
Organizational innovativeness	Innovator, follower, laggard

Target Marketing

Market segmentation is a means to an end: *target marketing*. This is the choice of specific segments to serve and is a key element in marketing strategy. A firm needs to evaluate the segments and decide which ones to serve. For example, CNN targets its news programmes to what are known as 'influentials'. This is why CNN has, globally, focused so much of its distribution effort into gaining access to hotel rooms. Businesspeople know that wherever they are in the world they can see international news on CNN in their hotel. Its sports programming is also targeted, with plenty of coverage of upmarket sports such as golf and tennis. Another example is Samsung Electronics, which targets the 'high-life seeker' segment of the market—consumers who adopt technology early and are willing to pay a high price for it.[40] Nintendo outflanked Microsoft and Sony by targeting market segments not normally associated with games consoles, including older people (see illustration).

We shall first examine how to evaluate market segments, and then how to make a balanced choice about which ones to serve.

Evaluating market segments

When evaluating market segments, a company should examine two broad issues: market attractiveness and the company's capability to compete in the segment. Market attractiveness can be assessed by looking at market factors, competitive factors, and political, social and environmental factors.[41] Figures 8.6 and 8.7 illustrate the factors that need to be examined when evaluating market segments.

Market factors

Segment size: generally, large-sized segments are more attractive than small ones since sales potential is greater, and the chance of achieving economies of scale is improved. However, large segments are often highly competitive since other companies are realizing their attraction, too. Furthermore, smaller companies may not have the resources to compete in large segments, and so may find smaller segments more attractive.

Segment growth rate: growing segments are usually regarded as more attractive than stagnant or declining segments, as new business opportunities will be greater. However, growth markets are often associated with heavy competition (e.g. the personal computer market during the late 1980s). Therefore an analysis of growth rate should always be accompanied by an examination of the state of competition.

Segment profitability: the potential to make profits is an important factor in market attractiveness.

Price sensitivity: in segments where customers are price sensitive there is a danger of profit margins being eroded by price competition. Low price-sensitive segments are usually more attractive since margins can be maintained. Competition may be based more on quality and other non-price factors.

Bargaining power of customers: both end and intermediate customers (e.g. distributors) can reduce the attraction of a market segment if they can exert high bargaining pressure on suppliers. The result is usually a reduction in profit margins as customers (e.g. supermarket chains) negotiate lower prices in return for placing large orders.

◀ Nintendo were the first games console company to target older people for their products.

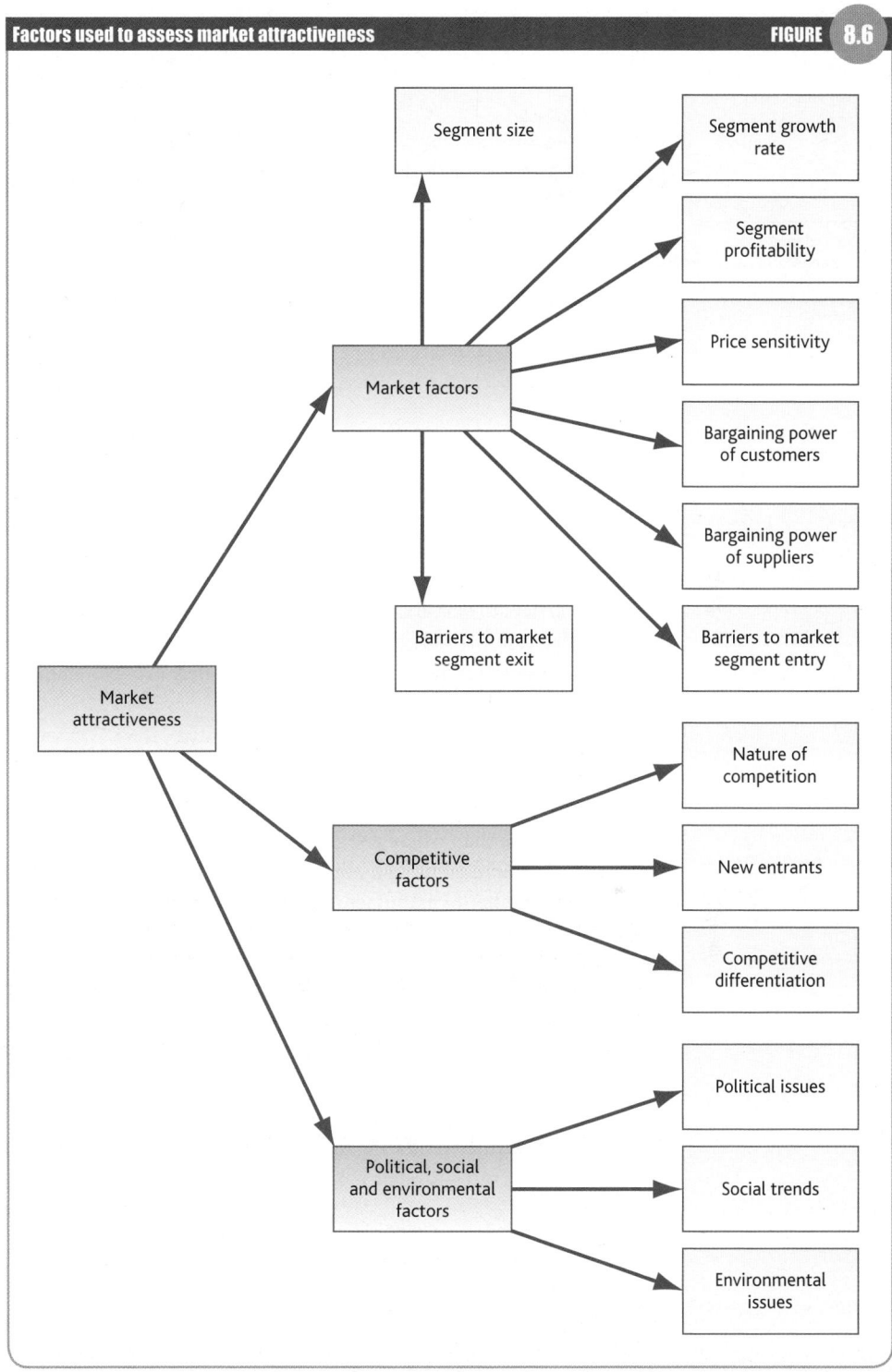

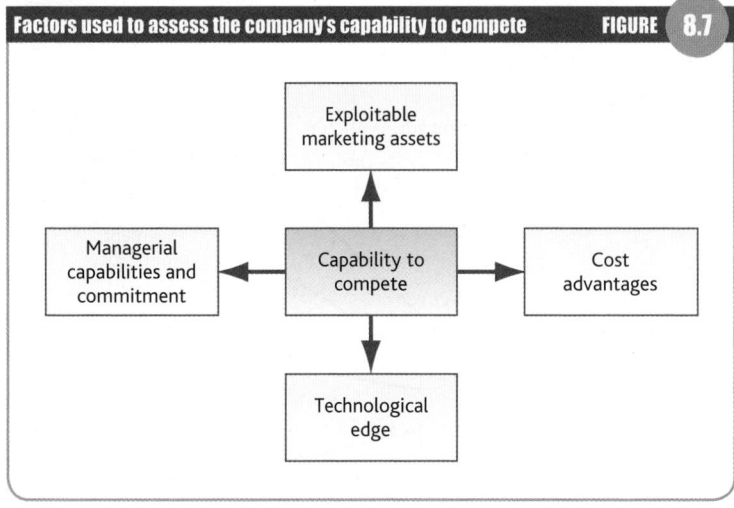

Factors used to assess the company's capability to compete — **FIGURE 8.7**

Bargaining power of suppliers: a company must assess not only the negotiating muscle of its customers but also its potential suppliers in the new segment. Where supply is in the hands of a few dominant companies, the segment will be less attractive than when served by a large number of competing suppliers.

Barriers to market segment entry: for companies considering entering a new segment there may be substantial entry barriers that reduce its attractiveness. Barriers can take the form of the high marketing expenditures necessary to compete, patents, or high switching costs for customers. However, if a company judges that it can afford or overcome barriers to entry, their existence may raise segment attractiveness if the company judges that the barriers will deter new rivals from entering.

Barriers to market segment exit: a segment may be regarded as less attractive if there are high barriers to exit. Exit barriers may take the form of specialized production facilities that cannot easily be liquidated, or agreements to provide spare parts to customers. Their presence may make exit extremely expensive and therefore segment entry more risky.

Competitive factors

Nature of competition: segments that are characterized by strong aggressive competition are less attractive than where competition is weak. The weakness of European and North American car manufacturers made the Japanese entry into a seemingly highly competitive (in terms of number of manufacturers) market segment relatively easy. The quality of the competition is far more significant than the number of companies operating in a market segment.

New entrants: a segment may seem superficially attractive because of the lack of current competition, but care must be taken to assess the dynamics of the market. A judgement must be made regarding the likelihood of new entrants, possibly with new technology, which might change the rules of the competitive game.

Competitive differentiation: segments will be more attractive if there is a real probability of creating a differentiated offering that customers value. This judgement is dependent on identifying unserved customer requirements, and the capability of the company to meet them.

Political, social and environmental factors

Political issues: political forces can open up new market segments (e.g. the deregulation of telecommunications in the UK paved the way for private companies to enter consumer and organizational segments of that market). Alternatively the attraction of entering new geographic segments may be reduced if political instability exists or is forecast.

Social trends: changes in society need to be assessed to measure their likely impact on the market segment. Changes in society can give rise to latent market segments, under-served by current products and services. Big gains can be made by first entrants, as Next discovered in fashion retailing.

Environmental issues: the trend towards more environmentally friendly products has affected market attractiveness both positively and negatively. The Body Shop took the opportunity afforded by the movement against animal testing of cosmetics and toiletries; conversely the market for CFCs has declined in the face of scientific evidence linking their emission with depletion of the ozone layer.

In organizational markets, individual customers may be evaluated on such criteria as sales volume, profitability, growth potential, financial strength and their fit with market and product strategy. Their allocation to a segment will be based on these factors.

Capability

Against the market attractiveness factors must be placed the firm's *capability to serve the market segment*. The market segment may be attractive but outside the resources of the company. Capability may be assessed by analysing exploitable marketing assets, cost advantages, technological edge, and managerial capabilities and commitment.

Exploitable marketing assets: does the market segment allow the firm to exploit its current marketing strengths? For example, is segment entry consonant with the image of its brands, or does it provide distribution synergies? However, where new segment entry is inconsistent with image, a new brand name may be created. For example, Toyota developed the Lexus model name when entering the upper-middle executive car segment.

Cost advantages: companies that can exploit cheaper material, labour or technological cost advantages to achieve a low cost position compared to the competition may be in a strong position, particularly if the segment is price sensitive.

Technological edge: strength may also be derived by superior technology, which is the source of differential advantage in the market segment. Patent protection (e.g. in pharmaceuticals) can form the basis of a strong defensible position, leading to high profitability. For some companies, segment entry may be deferred if they do not possess the resources to invest in technological leadership.

Managerial capabilities and commitment: a segment may look attractive but a realistic assessment of managerial capabilities and skills may lead to rejection of entry. The technical and judgemental skills of management may be insufficient to compete against strong competitors. Furthermore, the segment needs to be assessed from the viewpoint of managerial objectives. Successful marketing depends on implementation. Without the commitment of management, segment entry will fail on the altar of neglect.

Target marketing strategies

The purpose of evaluating market segments is to choose one or more segments to enter. Target market selection is the choice of which and how many market segments in which to compete. There are four generic **target marketing** strategies from which to choose: undifferentiated marketing, differentiated marketing, focused marketing, and customized marketing (see Fig. 8.8). Each option will now be examined.

Undifferentiated marketing

Occasionally, a market analysis will show no strong differences in customer characteristics that have implications for marketing strategy. Alternatively, the cost in developing a separate market mix for separate segments may outweigh the potential gains of meeting customer needs more exactly. Under these circumstances a company may decide to develop a single marketing mix for the whole market. This absence of segmentation is called **undifferentiated marketing**. Unfortunately this strategy can occur by default. For example, companies that lack a marketing orientation may practise undifferentiated marketing through lack of customer knowledge. Furthermore, undifferentiated marketing is more convenient for managers since they have to develop only a single product. Finding out that customers have diverse needs that can be met only by products with different characteristics means that

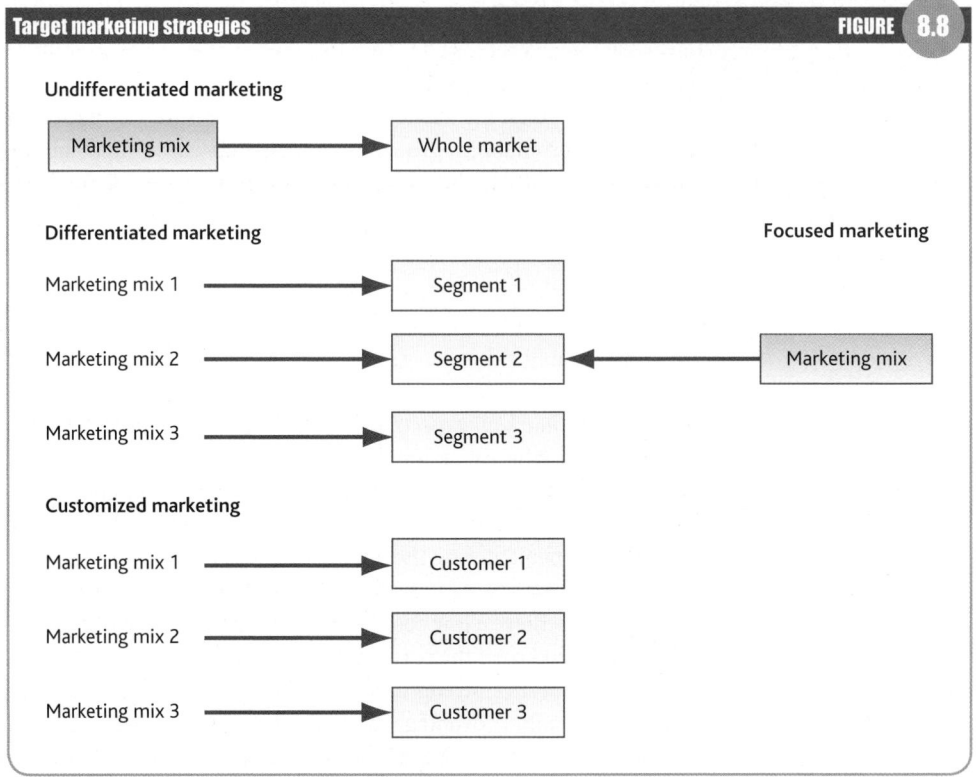

Target marketing strategies   FIGURE **8.8**

Undifferentiated marketing

Marketing mix → Whole market

Differentiated marketing   Focused marketing

Marketing mix 1 → Segment 1

Marketing mix 2 → Segment 2 ← Marketing mix

Marketing mix 3 → Segment 3

Customized marketing

Marketing mix 1 → Customer 1

Marketing mix 2 → Customer 2

Marketing mix 3 → Customer 3

managers have to go to the trouble and expense of developing new products, designing new promotional campaigns, training the salesforce to sell the new products and developing new distribution channels. Moving into new segments also means that salespeople have to start prospecting for new customers. This is not such a pleasant activity as calling on existing customers who are well known and liked.

The process of market segmentation, then, is normally the motivator to move such companies from practising undifferentiated marketing to one of the next three target marketing strategies.

Differentiated marketing

When market segmentation reveals several potential targets, specific marketing mixes can be developed to appeal to all or some of the segments. This is called **differentiated marketing**. For example, airlines design different marketing mixes for first-class and economy passengers, including varying prices, service levels, quality of food, in-cabin comfort and waiting areas at airports. A differentiated target marketing strategy exploits the differences between marketing segments by designing a specific marketing mix for each segment. Marketing in Action 8.2 describes how BMW, Colgate, Marks & Spencer and Sky have designed different products to cater for the segments that exist in their markets.

One potential disadvantage of a differentiated compared to an undifferentiated marketing strategy is the loss of cost economies. However, the use of flexible manufacturing systems can minimize such problems.

Focused marketing

The identification of several segments in a market does not imply that a company should serve all of them. Some may be unattractive or out of line with business strengths. Perhaps the

8.2 Marketing in Action

How Companies Differentiate

Market segmentation is a creative act that relies upon a clear understanding of the groups of consumers that make up a market. The actual basis of segmentation that is followed will vary by market and will depend on market insight and the creativity of the marketing team. For multi-product firms this allows the tailoring of different products to meet the specific needs of consumers—individuals, households and businesses. Here is a selection of the ways in which BMW, Colgate, Marks & Spencer and Sky have differentiated some of their product offerings to target specific segments.

BMW

1 series	→	entry-level models targeting consumers who wish to enjoy the BMW experience for the first time
3 series	→	targets middle managers
5 series	→	targets senior managers
7 series	→	targets top managers
Z4 sports car	→	targets well-off, young and young-minded singles and couples
X5	→	targets well-off couples with children
X6	→	targets well-off empty-nesters

Colgate

Sensodyne	→	targets consumers with sensitive teeth
Aquafresh	→	targets families who want 'three in one' protection
Macleans	→	targets consumers who desire social confidence

Marks & Spencer

Per Una	→	targets young and young-minded fashion-conscious consumers
Autograph	→	targets stylish and sophisticated consumers

Sky

Sky Sports	→	targets sports enthusiasts
Sky Movies	→	targets film lovers
Sky News	→	targets news followers

All of these companies—whether they be consumer durable, toiletry, retail or broadcast orientated—have recognized that market segmentation can lead to higher satisfaction of consumer needs than producing a single offering and hoping it will meet the diverse expectations of a market.

Based on: Rose (2008);[42] *Smith (2008);*[43] *Jack (2009)*[44]

most sensible route would be to serve just one of the market segments. When a company develops a single marketing mix aimed at one target market (*niche*) it is practising **focused marketing**. This strategy is particularly appropriate for companies with limited resources. Small companies may stretch their resources too far by competing in more than one segment. Focused marketing allows research and development expenditure to be concentrated on meeting the needs of one set of customers, and managerial activities can be devoted to understanding and catering for their needs. Large organizations may not be interested in serving the needs of this one segment, or their energies may be so dissipated across the whole market that they pay insufficient attention to their requirements.

Another example of focused marketing in the consumer market is given by Bang & Olufsen, the Danish audio electronics firm. It targets upmarket consumers who value self-development, pleasure and open-mindedness, with its stylish television and music systems.

B&O describes its positioning as 'high quality but we are not Rolls-Royce—more BMW'. The company places emphasis on distinctive design, good quality and simplicity of use. Focused targeting means that B&O defies the conventional wisdom that a small manufacturer could not make profits marketing consumer electronics in Denmark.[45]

Another form of focused marketing is to target a particular age group. For example, Saga targets the over-50s. Originally a specialist holiday company, it has broadened its range of products marketed to this age group to include financial services such as an award-winning share-dealing service.[46]

One form of focused marketing is to concentrate efforts on the relatively small percentage of customers that account for a disproportionately large share of sales of a product (the heavy buyers). For example, in some markets 20 per cent of customers account for 80 per cent of sales. Some companies aim at such a segment because it is so superficially attractive. Unfortunately, they may be committing the *majority fallacy*.[47] The majority fallacy is the name given to the blind pursuit of the largest, most easily identified, market segment. It is a fallacy because that segment is the one that everyone in the past has recognized as the best segment and, therefore, it attracts the most intense competition. The result is likely to be high marketing expenditures, price cutting and low profitability. A more sensible strategy may be to target a small, seemingly less attractive, segment rather than choose the same customers that everyone else is after.

Customized marketing

In some markets the requirements of individual customers are unique and their purchasing power sufficient to make designing a separate marketing mix for each customer viable. Segmentation at this disaggregated level leads to the use of **customized marketing**. Many service providers, such as advertising and marketing research agencies, architects and solicitors, vary their offerings on a customer-to-customer basis. They will discuss face to face with each customer their requirements and tailor their services accordingly. Customized marketing is also found within organizational markets because of the high value of orders and the special needs of customers. Locomotive manufacturers will design and build products to specifications given to them by individual rail transport providers. Customized marketing is often associated with close relationships between supplier and customer in these circumstances because the value of the order justifies large marketing and sales efforts being focused on each buyer.

A fascinating development in marketing in recent years has been the introduction of *mass customization* in consumer markets. This is the marketing of highly individual products on a mass scale. Car companies such as Audi, BMW, Mercedes and Renault have the capacity to build to order where cars are manufactured only when there is an order specification from a customer. Dell Computers will also build customized products, often ordered on the Internet. Such flexible manufacturing processes allow customers to specify their own individual products from an extensive range of optional equipment.[48] For example, promotional material for the BMW Mini claims that there is only a 1 in 10,000 chance that any two Minis are the same. Even trainers can be customized, with both Nike and Adidas offering this service.[49]

Customized marketing is also possible on the Internet, with customers being treated differently on an individual basis.

Positioning

So far our discussion has taken us through market segmentation and on to target market selection. The next step in developing an effective marketing strategy is to clearly position

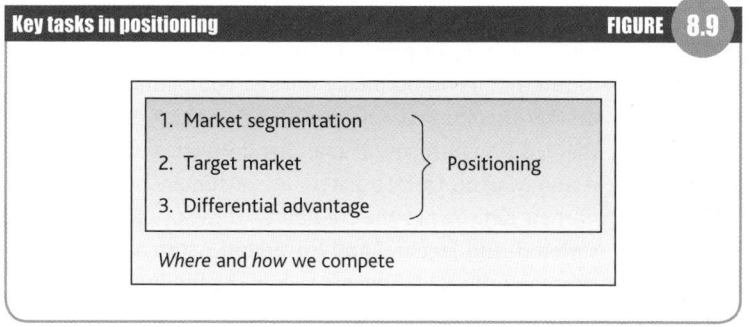

Key tasks in positioning   FIGURE 8.9

1. Market segmentation
2. Target market   } Positioning
3. Differential advantage

Where and *how* we compete

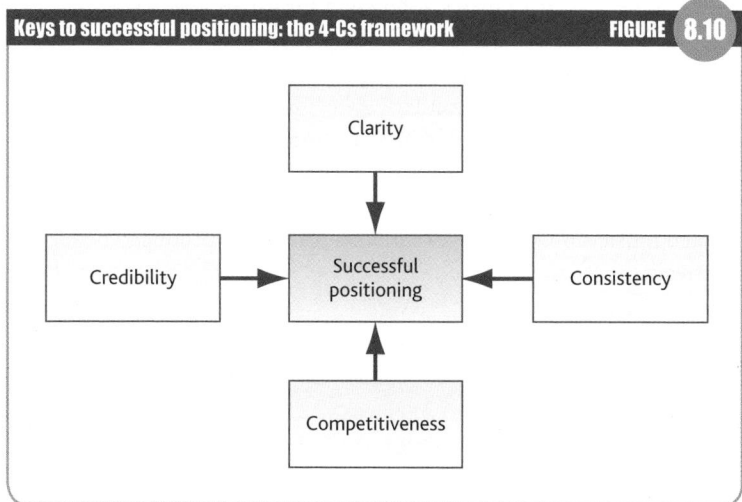

Keys to successful positioning: the 4-Cs framework   FIGURE 8.10

Clarity

Credibility → Successful positioning ← Consistency

Competitiveness

a product or service offering in the marketplace. Figure 8.9 summarizes the key tasks involved, and shows where **positioning** fits into the process.

Positioning is the choice of:

- *target market—where* we want to compete
- *differential advantage—how* we wish to compete.

The objective is to create and maintain a distinctive place in the market for a company and/or its products.

Target market selection, then, has accomplished part of the positioning job already. But to compete successfully in a target market involves providing the customer with a differential advantage. This involves giving the target customer something better than the competition is offering. Creating a differential advantage will be discussed in detail in Chapter 19. Briefly, it involves using the marketing mix to create something special for the customer. Product differentiation may result from added features that give customers benefits that rivals cannot match. Promotional differentiation may stem from unique, valued images created by advertising, or superior service provided by salespeople. Distribution differentiation may arise through making the buy situation more convenient for customers. Finally, price differentiation may involve giving superior value for money through lower prices.

A landmark book by Ries and Trout suggested that marketers are involved in a battle for the minds of target customers.[50] Successful positioning is often associated with products possessing favourable connotations in the minds of customers. For example, Samsung is associated with high-technology, reliable and fashionable mobile phones. These add up to a differential advantage in the minds of its target customers whether they be in London, Amsterdam or Moscow. Similarly, the success of Cilit Bang has been based on its positioning as the most powerful and versatile household cleaner on the market. Such positioning is hard won and relies on four factors, as shown in Figure 8.10.

1   *Clarity*: the positioning idea must be clear in terms of both target market and differential advantage. Complicated positioning statements are unlikely to be remembered. Simple messages such as 'BMW: the ultimate driving machine', Wal-Mart's 'Low prices, always' and Stella Artois' 'Reassuringly expensive' are clear and memorable.

2   *Consistency*: people are bombarded with messages daily. To break through this noise a consistent message is required. Confusion will arise if this year we position on 'quality of service', then next year we change it to 'superior product performance'. Two examples of brands that have benefited from a consistent message being communicated to their target customers are Gillette ('The best a man can get') and L'Oréal ('Because you're worth it'). Both receive high recall when consumers are researched because of the consistent use of a simple message over many years. The Land Rover Defender is clearly positioned as a rugged off-road vehicle (see illustration).

▲ This award-winning advertisement for the Land Rover Defender clearly positions the brand as a rugged off-roader: you cannot get more off-road than the margins of an angry sea.

3   *Credibility*: the differential advantage that is chosen must be credible in the minds of the target customer. Ford found that its brand image was not compatible with the marketing of upmarket cars. It was this lack of credibility that led it to purchase Jaguar, Land Rover, Volvo and Aston Martin. Unfortunately, as consumers became aware of their new owner the credibility of the original brands suffered, and Jaguar, Land Rover and Aston Martin were subsequently sold. Toyota's lack of credibility as an upmarket brand caused it to use 'Lexus' rather than 'Toyota Lexus' as the brand name for its top-of-the-range cars. Honda has followed a similar strategy using the Acura brand name for its luxury models. These examples clearly show the importance of credibility when positioning brands.

4   *Competitiveness*: the differential advantage should have a competitive edge. It should offer something of value to the customer that the competition is failing to supply. For example, the success of the iPod was based on the differential advantage of seamless downloading of music from a dedicated music store, iTunes, to a mobile player that produced better sound quality than its rivals.

8.2 Pause for Thought

Think of a brand that you buy regularly, or a consumer durable such as a car. Using the 4-Cs framework assess how well it has been positioned in the marketplace.

Marketing in Action 8.3 describes how Michelin has used positioning to become the market leader in tyres.

8.3 Marketing in Action

Taking the High Road

Michelin is a company that has used the 4-Cs framework to achieve market leadership in the tyre market. It has achieved *clarity* by sending a single message—'higher mileage from a brand you can trust'—to justify its premium prices. The brand is supported by the 'Michelin Man' logo, which is instantly recognizable and memorable. *Consistency* is achieved by maintaining the same positioning for decades. The positioning is *credible* because drivers do notice the extra miles: independent tests show that Michelin tyres last 20 to 25 per cent longer than their competitors.

This adds up to a differential advantage because drivers value the extra mileage, which means overall costs are no higher than buying a rival's tyre and the inconvenience of changing tyres is less. Trust is vital because of the safety implications of tyres. Michelin is therefore highly *competitive* in its consumer and business target markets, which has meant that it is both the highest-priced product on the market and has the highest market share.

Based on: Rudloff (2008)[51]

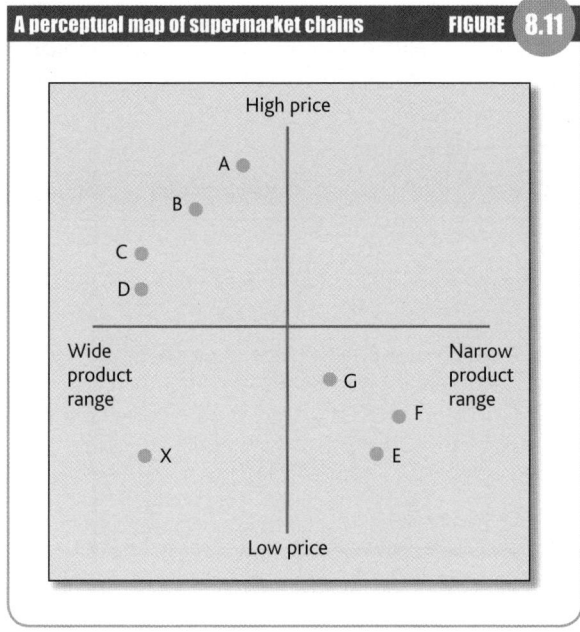

A perceptual map of supermarket chains FIGURE **8.11**

High price

A●

B ●

C ●
D●

Wide
product
range

● G
● F

● X   ● E

Low price

Narrow
product
range

Perceptual mapping

A useful tool for determining the position of a brand in the marketplace is the *perceptual map*. This is a visual representation of consumer perceptions of the brand and its competitors using attributes (dimensions) that are important to consumers. The key steps in developing a perceptual map are as follows.

1 Identify a set of competing brands.
2 Identify important attributes that consumers use when choosing between brands using qualitative research (e.g. group discussions).
3 Conduct quantitative marketing research where consumers score each brand on all key attributes.
4 Plot brands on a two-dimensional map(s).

Figure 8.11 shows a perceptual map for seven supermarket chains. Qualitative marketing research has shown that consumers evaluate supermarkets on two key dimensions: price and width of product range. Quantitative marketing research is then carried out using scales that measure consumers' perception of each supermarket on these dimensions. Average scores are then plotted on a perceptual map.

The results show that the supermarkets are grouped into two clusters: the high price, wide product range group; and the low price, narrow price range group. These are indicative of two market segments and show that supermarkets C and D are close rivals, as measured by consumers' perceptions, and have very distinct perceptual positions in the marketplace compared with E, F and G. Perceptual maps are useful in considering strategic moves. For example, an opportunity may exist to create a differential advantage based on a combination of wide product range and low prices (as shown by the theoretical position at X).

Perceptual maps can also be valuable in identifying the strengths and weaknesses of brands as perceived by consumers. Such findings can be very revealing to managers, whose own perceptions may be very different from those of consumers. Consumers can also be asked to score their ideal position on each of the attributes so that actual and ideal positions can be compared.

Spidergram analysis

An alternative approach to perceptual mapping for the purpose of understanding the position of a brand in the marketplace is spidergram analysis.[52] Like perceptual mapping it provides a visual representation of consumer perceptions of the brand and its competitors using attributes (dimensions) that are important to consumers when evaluating those brands. However, spidergram analysis also asks consumers to rate the importance of the attributes, and their relative importance is represented visually by the length of the spoke on the spidergram. The key steps are as follows.

1 Identify a set of competing brands.
2 Identify important attributes that consumers use when choosing between brands using qualitative research (e.g. group discussions).
3 Conduct quantitative marketing research where consumers:
   (i) rate the importance of each attribute in their choice between brands on a 10-point scale
   (ii) score each brand on all key attributes on a 10-point scale.
4 Plot brands on a spidergram.

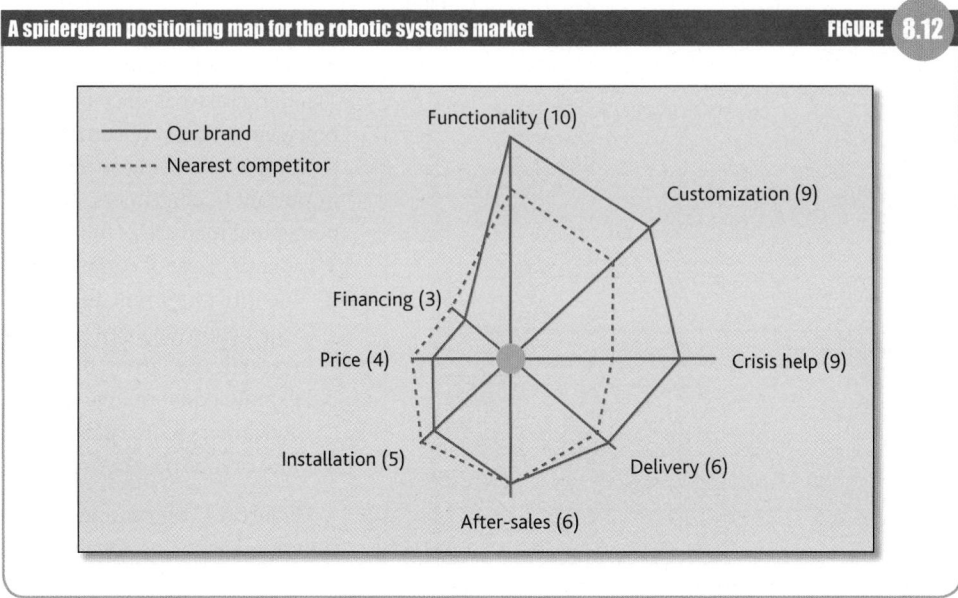

A spidergram positioning map for the robotic systems market FIGURE 8.12

Figure 8.12 shows a spidergram positioning map for the robotic systems market. The length of each spoke is proportional to the importance ratings of each attribute. Functionality is considered an essential attribute and has received a score of 10; the least important attribute is financing, scoring only 3. Each spoke is divided into 10 sections and each brand's score is plotted on each attribute. Our brand has received higher perceptual scores than its nearest competitor for functionality, customization, crisis help and delivery. Our brand and its nearest competitor are similarly rated for after-sales service; but, for installation, price and financing, our nearest competitor is rated more highly. Since our company is rated more highly on those attributes that are more important to consumers it is likely that our brand has a larger market share than its nearest competitor.

Like perceptual maps, spidergram analysis is valuable in identifying how consumers (as opposed to managers) perceive the strengths and weaknesses of competing brands. It provides a visual portrayal of the positions of brands along multiple dimensions. Spidergram software is available from the Aliah Corporation, USA, which permits the simultaneous analysis of up to six brands.

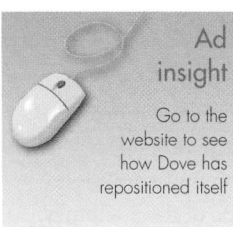

Ad insight

Go to the website to see how Dove has repositioned itself

Repositioning

Occasionally a product or service will need to be repositioned because of changing customer tastes or poor sales performance. **Repositioning** involves changing the target markets, the differential advantage, or both. A useful framework for analysing repositioning options is given in Figure 8.13. Using product differentiation and target market as the key variables, four generic repositioning strategies are shown.

Image repositioning

The first option is to keep product and target market the same but to change the image of the product. In markets where products act as a form of self-expression, the product may be acceptable in functional terms but fail because it lacks the required image.

Product repositioning

With this strategy the product is changed while the target market remains the same. For example, IBM has used product repositioning very successfully by moving away from the manufacture of computers (IBM sold its PC division to Lenovo) to the provision of software

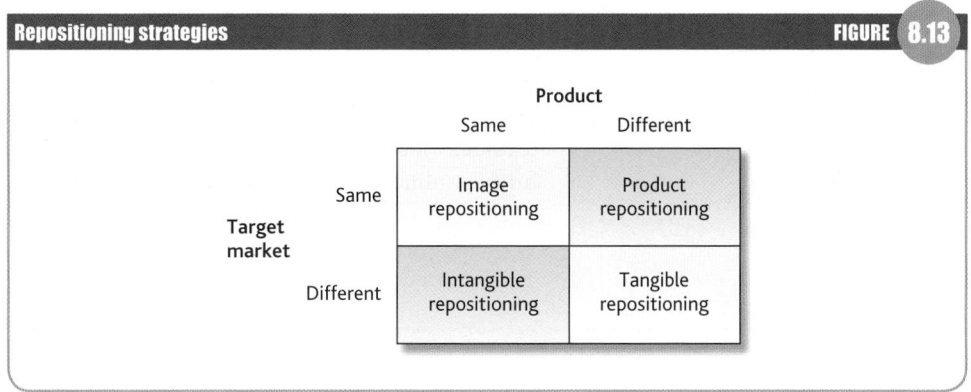

Repositioning strategies   FIGURE 8.13

and services to essentially the same type of business customers. An example of product repositioning in services is the successful rebranding of Talk Radio, a generalist speech-based radio station, as talkSPORT. The target market of 25–44-year-old males remains the same but the product has changed its focus to sport.[53]

Intangible repositioning

This strategy involves targeting a different market segment with the same product. Lucozade, a carbonated drink, was initially targeted by Beecham's Foods at sick children. Marketing research found that mothers were drinking it as a midday pick-me-up and the brand was consequently repositioned to aim at this new segment. Subsequently the energy-giving attributes of Lucozade were used to appeal to a wider target market—young adults—by means of advertisements featuring well-known athletes and footballers. The history of Lucozade shows how a combination of repositioning strategies over time has been necessary for successful brand building.

Pharmaceutical companies practise intangible repositioning when patents on their prescription drugs expire. Rather than fight against generic competition by price-cutting in the prescription segment they often switch to the over-the-counter (OTC) sector where they can fight by investing in brand equity. Market leaders benefit by being able to claim 'the product most often prescribed by doctors'. An example is Tagamet, SmithKline Beecham's indigestion drug, which by switching to the OTC sector was able to transfer to the new segment the value the consumer associated with the brand name developed through doctors' prescriptions.[54]

An example of intangible repositioning in international markets is given by Wagner, a German supplier of paint guns. In Europe, such guns are bought by professional painters, but in the USA the same products are targeted at the consumer market as people use them to paint the interiors of their own homes and outside surfaces such as fences.[55]

Tangible repositioning

When both product and target market are changed, a company is practising tangible repositioning. For example, a company may decide to move up- or downmarket by introducing a new range of products to meet the needs of the new target customers. Highly successful tangible repositioning was undertaken by Samsung Electronics, which was once an unfocused manufacturer of cheap undifferentiated televisions and microwaves selling to all age groups and is now a premium-priced flat-screen television and mobile handset brand focused on, as we have seen, the 'high-life seeker' segment of the market—consumers who are willing to adopt technology early and pay a high price for it.[56]

Mercedes-Benz found it necessary to use tangible and product repositioning in the face of Japanese competition. Tangible repositioning took the form of developing new products (e.g. a city car) to appeal to new target customers. Product repositioning was also required in its current market segments to bring down the cost of development and manufacture in the face of lower-priced rivals such as Toyota's Lexus.

When you have read this chapter

log on to the Online Learning Centre at www.mcgraw-hill.co.uk/textbooks/jobber to explore chapter-by-chapter test questions, links and further online study tools for marketing.

Review

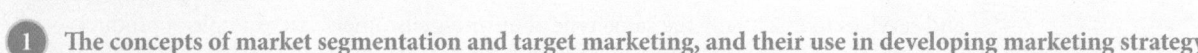

1   The concepts of market segmentation and target marketing, and their use in developing marketing strategy

- Market segmentation is the identification of individuals or organizations with similar characteristics that have significant implications for the determination of marketing strategy.
- Its use aids target market selection, the ability to design a tailored marketing mix, the development of differential marketing strategies, and the identification of opportunities and threats.
- Target marketing is the choice of specific segment(s) to serve. It concerns the decision where to compete.
- Its use is focusing company resources on those segments it is best able to serve in terms of company resources and segment attractiveness. Once chosen, a tailored marketing mix that creates a differential advantage can be designed based on an in-depth understanding of target customers.

2   The methods of segmenting consumer and organizational markets

- Consumer markets can be segmented by behavioural (benefits sought, purchase occasion, purchase behaviour, usage, and perceptions and beliefs), psychographic (lifestyle and personality), and profile (demographic, socio-economic and geographic) methods.
- Organizational markets can be segmented by macrosegmentation (organizational size, industry and geographic location) and microsegmentation (choice criteria, decision-making unit structure, decision-making process, buy class, purchasing organization, and organizational effectiveness) methods.

3   The factors that can be used to evaluate market segments

- Two broad issues should be used: market attractiveness and the company's capability to compete.
- Market attractiveness can be assessed by examining market factors (segment size, segment growth rate, price sensitivity, bargaining power of customers, bargaining power of suppliers, barriers to market segment entry and barriers to market segment exit), competitive factors (nature of competition, the likelihood of new entrants, and competitive differentiation), and political, social and environmental factors (political issues, social trends, and environmental issues).
- Capability to compete can be assessed by analysing exploitable marketing assets, cost advantages, technological edge, and managerial capabilities and commitments.

4   Four target market strategies: undifferentiated, differentiated, focused and customized marketing

- Undifferentiated marketing occurs where a company does not segment but applies a single marketing mix to the whole market.
- Differentiated marketing occurs where a company segments the market and applies separate marketing mixes to appeal to all or some of the segments (target markets).
- Focused marketing occurs where a company segments the market and develops one specific marketing mix to one segment (target market).
- Customized marketing occurs where a company designs a separate marketing mix for each customer.

5   The concept of positioning and the keys to successful positioning

- There are two aspects of positioning: the choice of target market (where to compete) and the creation of a differential advantage (how to compete).

- The objective is to create and maintain a distinctive place in the market for a company and/or its products.
- The four keys to successful positioning are: clarity, consistency, credibility and competitiveness.

6 Positioning and repositioning strategies

- A useful tool for determining the position of a brand in the marketplace is the perceptual map.
- Positioning strategy should be based on a clear choice of target market based on market segment attractiveness and company capability, and the creation of a differential advantage (based on an understanding of the attributes—choice criteria—that consumers use when choosing between brands).
- Repositioning strategies can be based on changes to the product and/or target market. Four strategies are image repositioning, product repositioning, intangible repositioning and tangible repositioning.

Key Terms

benefit segmentation the grouping of people based on the different benefits they seek from a product

customized marketing the market coverage strategy where a company decides to target individual customers and develops separate marketing mixes for each

differentiated marketing a market coverage strategy where a company decides to target several market segments and develops separate marketing mixes for each

differential marketing strategies market coverage strategies where a company decides to target several market segments and develops separate marketing mixes for each

focused marketing a market coverage strategy where a company decides to target one market segment with a single marketing mix

lifestyle segmentation the grouping of people according to their pattern of living as expressed in their activities, interests and opinions

macrosegmentation the segmentation of organizational markets by size, industry and location

market segmentation the process of identifying individuals or organizations with similar characteristics that have significant implications for the determination of marketing strategy

microsegmentation segmentation according to choice criteria, DMU structure, decision-making process, buy class, purchasing structure and organizational innovativeness

positioning the choice of target market (where the company wishes to compete) and differential advantage (how the company wishes to compete)

profile segmentation the grouping of people in terms of profile variables, such as age and socio-economic group, so that marketers can communicate to them

psychographic segmentation the grouping of people according to their lifestyle and personality characteristics

repositioning changing the target market or differential advantage, or both

target marketing the choice of which market segment(s) to serve with a tailored marketing mix

undifferentiated marketing a market coverage strategy where a company decides to ignore market segment differences and develops a single marketing mix for the whole market

Study Questions

1. What are the advantages of market segmentation? Can you see any advantages of mass marketing, i.e. treating a market as homogeneous and marketing to the whole market with one marketing mix?

2. Choose a market you are familiar with and use benefit segmentation to identify market segments. What are the likely profiles of the resulting segments?

3. In what kind of markets is psychographic segmentation likely to prove useful? Why?

4. How might segmentation be of use when marketing in Europe?

5. One way of segmenting organizational markets is to begin with macrosegmentation variables and then develop sub-segments using microsegmentation criteria. Does this seem sensible to you? Are there any circumstances where the process should be reversed?

6. Why is *buy class* a potentially useful method of segmenting organizational markets? (Use both this chapter and Chapter 5 when answering this question.)

7. What is the majority fallacy? Why should it be taken into account when evaluating market segments?

8. What is the difference between positioning and repositioning? Choose three products and services and describe how they are positioned in the marketplace, i.e. what is their target market and differential advantage?

References

1. Steiner, R. (1999) How Mobile Phones Came to the Masses, *Sunday Times*, 31 October, 6.
2. Wind, Y. (1978) Issues and Advances in Segmentation Research, *Journal of Marketing Research*, August, 317–37.
3. Van Raaij, W. F. and T. M. M. Verhallen (1994) Domain-specific Market Segmentation, *European Journal of Marketing* 28(10), 49–66.
4. Sampson, P. (1992) People are People the World Over: The Case for Psychological Market Segmentation, *Marketing and Research Today*, November, 236–44.
5. Fifield, P. (2005) The People Puzzle, *The Marketer*, 12 April, 6–9.
6. Aaker, D. (2004) *Brand Portfolio Strategy*, New York: The Free Press.
7. Hooley, G. J., J. Saunders, N. Piercy and B. Nicoulaud (2007) *Marketing Strategy and Competitive Positioning: The Key to Market Success*, Hemel Hempstead: Prentice-Hall, 148.
8. Anonymous (2002) Best Use of Research Award, Campaign Media Awards, 29 November, 25.
9. Cook, V. J. Jr and W. A. Mindak (1984) A Search for Constants: The 'Heavy-User' Revisited!, *Journal of Consumer Marketing* 1(4), 79–81.
10. Bainbridge, J. (2005) Third Dimension, *Marketing*, 8 June, 36.
11. Anonymous (2002) Examples of Excellence, *Marketing*, 2 May, 15.
12. O'Shaughnessy, J. (1995) *Competitive Marketing: A Strategic Approach*, London: Routledge.
13. Ehrenberg, A. S. C. and G. J. Goodhardt (1978) *Market Segmentation*, New York: J. Walter Thompson.
14. Bruce, L. (2005) On the Mark, *The Marketer*, 12 April, 27–9.
15. Charles, G. (2008) Dove to Introduce 'Real Beauty' Web TV Channel, *Marketing*, 16 April, 3.
16. Bruce (2005) op. cit.
17. Reed, D. (1995) Knowledge is Power, *Marketing Week*, 9 December, 46–7.
18. Sampson (1992) op. cit.
19. Ackoff, R. L. and J. R. Emshoff (1975) Advertising at Anheuser-Busch, Inc., *Sloan Management Review*, Spring, 1–15.
20. Lannon, J. (1991) Developing Brand Strategies across Borders, *Marketing and Research Today*, August, 160–8.
21. Young, S. (1972) The Dynamics of Measuring Unchange, in Haley, R. I. (ed.) *Attitude Research in Transition*, Chicago: American Marketing Association, 61–82.
22. Tynan, A. C. and J. Drayton (1987) Market Segmentation, *Journal of Marketing Management* 2(3), 301–35.
23. Simms, J. (2005) Strategising Simplicity, *Marketing*, 25 May, 15.
24. Bosworth, C. (2002) Playing Hard to Get, *Marketing Business*, Nov./Dec., 24.
25. Ray, A. (2002) Using Outdoor to Target the Young, *Marketing*, 31 January, 25.
26. Hempel, J. (2005) The MySpace Generation, *Business Week*, 12/19 December, 65–72.

27. Fernandez, J. (2008) Balancing the Book, *Marketing Week*, 4 September, 23.

28. Gibson, O. (2008) 200 Million Friends and Counting, *Guardian*, 23 June, 5.

29. Chisnall, P. (2005) *Marketing Research*, Maidenhead: McGraw-Hill.

30. O'Brien, S. and R. Ford (1988) Can We at Last Say Goodbye to Social Class?, *Journal of the Market Research Society* 30(3), 289–332.

31. Kossoff, J. (1988) Europe: Up for Sale, *New Statesman and Society*, 7 October, 43–4.

32. Chisnall (2005) op. cit.

33. Garrett, A. (1992) Stats, Lies and Stereotypes, *Observer*, 13 December, 26.

34. Mitchell, V.-W. and P. J. McGoldrick (1994) The Role of Geodemographics in Segmenting and Targeting Consumer Markets: A Delphi Study, *European Journal of Marketing* 28(5), 54–72.

35. Kossoff (1988) op. cit.

36. See Wind, Y. and R. N. Cardozo (1974) Industrial Market Segmentation, *Industrial Marketing Management*, 3, 153–66; R. E. Plank (1985) A Critical Review of Industrial Market Segmentation, *Industrial Marketing Management* 14, 79–91.

37. Wind and Cardozo (1974) op. cit.

38. Moriarty, R. T. (1983) *Industrial Buying Behaviour*, Lexington, Mass: Lexington Books.

39. Corey, R. (1978) *The Organisational Context of Industrial Buying Behaviour*, Cambridge, MA: Marketing Science Institute, 6–12.

40. Pesola, M. (2005) Samsung Plays to the Young Generation, *Financial Times*, 29 March, 11.

41. See Abell, D. F. and J. S. Hammond (1979) *Strategic Market Planning: Problems and Analytical Approaches*, Hemel Hempstead: Prentice-Hall; G. S. Day (1986) *Analysis for Strategic Market Decisions*, New York: West; Hooley, Saunders, Piercy and Nicoulaud (2007) op. cit.

42. Rose, S. (2008) There Are Plenty of Reasons Why Britain Still Loves M&S, *Guardian*, 25 January, 41.

43. Smith, G. (2008) On The Road, *Guardian Weekend*, 21 June, 99.

44. Jack, L. (2009) Cleaning Up Its Act, *Marketing Week*, 12 February, 21.

45. Gapper, J. (2005) When High Fidelity Becomes High Fashion, *Financial Times*, 20 December, 11.

46. Anonymous (2000) Saga, Dealing in Satisfaction, *Observer*, 19 March, 29.

47. Zikmund, W. G. and M. D'Amico (1999) *Marketing*, St Paul, MN: West, 249.

48. Anonymous (2001) A Long March, *Economist*, 14 July, 79–82.

49. Benady, D. (2003) King Customer, *Marketing Week,* 8 May, 24–7.

50. Ries, A. and J. Trout (2001) *Positioning: The Battle for your Mind*, New York: Warner.

51. Rudloff, T. (2008) On The Road, *The Marketer*, April, 24.

52. The author is indebted to Professor David Shipley, Trinity College, University of Dublin, for material used in this description of spidergram analysis.

53. Brech, P. (2000) MacKenzie Plans Sports Revolution, *Marketing*, 20 January, 9.

54. Platford, R. (1997) Fast Track to Approval, *Financial Times*, 24 April, 27.

55. Bolfo, B. (2005) The Art of Selling One Product in Two Markets, *Financial Times*, 10 August, 11.

56. Pesola (2005) op. cit.

Dell Hell

Strategic Change for a Fallen Market Leader

Early years

Michael Dell founded his company while still a student at the University of Texas in Austin. He decided not to follow the established practices in the industry, which were to manufacture products, then find distributors and attempt to sell the products in the marketplace. Rapid innovations in PC components meant that unsold stock contained out-of-date parts, meaning that such computers had to be heavily discounted in order to sell them. Dell came up with the clever idea of making computers to order. Customers selected from a list of options on hardware and software, and telephoned their orders. An advantage of this approach was that Dell was paid in advance, which by improving cash flow was an enormous benefit to a young, growing company. Business and home buyers then received a machine that was customized to their requirements and the make-to-order model allowed the use of the very latest components, if desired. And so was born one of the most revolutionary business models of the twentieth century.

Dell also worked hard on streamlining manufacturing and coordinating the supply chain. Whereas there were 130 'touches', or interventions, by staff on a standard PC assembly line, Dell reduced this to just 60. He also introduced 'just-in-time' delivery of components and finished products, which resulted in major savings in terms of inventory and storage costs.

The advent of the Internet was a boost to the business in terms of both demand and supply. The company's extensive experience of computer direct marketing meant that it became a 'first mover' in exploiting the Internet as part of its marketing strategy and it became the major sales channel for the company. Further, the virtual integration of the supply chain reduced coordination and communication costs, and decreased order processing time. When a customer placed an order with Dell, it automatically went to Dell suppliers so that product components could immediately be sent to a Dell assembly plant. Customers who visited the Dell website were offered assistance in selecting the type of technology most suited to their needs. Customers were then guided through the process of choosing the most appropriate specification from a range of options. Once a decision was made, the

customer received an instant price quote and the date of delivery. Prices were low, based on Dell's cost structure, which was the lowest in the industry. Dell kept prices low by eliminating distributors, doing very little R&D and keeping overheads lower than 10 per cent of sales.

For large business customers the service was enhanced by offering Premier Pages. The service was dedicated to a particular corporate customer and only accessible by that customer. It could be used for two-way communication and holds records of all previous interactions. It provided additional services including fast response product support, order status, service information and details of special offers available exclusively to them.

Dell's main rivals were using a different strategy. Hewlett-Packard and IBM sold through computer stores and had invested in large salesforces to push stock into their distribution channels. This meant higher costs and hence higher prices than Dell.

The strategy was so successful that Dell's early growth was phenomenal and it became market leader in the PC market. Although thought of as a consumer brand, Dell's major successes were in the large business and educational market segments. Its share price was the top-performing big company stock of the 1990s, rising by a staggering 29,600 per cent between 1990 and 1998 (from 23 cents to $68). Michael Dell became super-rich.

The changing environment

By 2005 the marketing environment facing Dell and its rivals had changed. PCs had become commodities and IBM had sold its PC division to Lenovo, a Chinese company wishing to gain a global presence. Hewlett-Packard had bought Compaq computers several years earlier in an unsuccessful attempt to gain the scale it believed was necessary to compete with Dell.

Dell's situation had also changed. Customers had started complaining about the poor service they were receiving from Dell, which was of increasing importance because some of its computers were failing (at one point, its computers suffered from exploding batteries). The following comments posted on the Internet reflected some of Dell's problems:

> Dell computers are terrible. Aside from their cheap looking design, they are not reliable machines. My friends owned them at law school, and this was enough for me never to buy one. No one I knew was satisfied, but since we were broke law students, people had to get one. If you can afford a better computer, don't go with Dell.

> Their supply chain is horrible. It takes sometimes 2–3 months to get your laptop and good luck trying to cancel and getting your money back. The customer service is horrible and after three bad experiences, I'm scared to order anything from them again.

Dell was regarded as making dull, cheap, entry-level computers. Further, it lost its competitive edge by putting features into its products that that customers did not value enough to pay for. Hewlett-Packard, however, was rejuvenated, launching new computers with innovative features and attractive designs, such as the first touchscreen all-in-one desktop aimed at families with children. Also, its cost-cutting programme meant that it could charge prices that were competitive against Dell. Buyers were regarding their PCs as extensions of themselves, wanting to look 'cool' when seen using their laptop at universities, in coffee shops, on trains, and so on.

Hewlett Packard also hit Dell's corporate business, which at one point was 85 per cent of its total sales revenue. Large companies were increasingly buying computers as part of a package that included IT consultancy services, which added value by offering solutions to particular business problems. Also, as IT systems became more complex, corporate customers were looking to their suppliers to manage the systems for them. HP's IT Solutions for Large Enterprises division placed it in a better position than Dell to meet their needs. By late 2006, Dell had lost its lead in the PC business to Hewlett-Packard.

Competition also intensified with the emergence of Acer, a Taiwanese-based multinational electronics manufacturer, which moved faster than Dell and Hewlett-Packard to become the market leader in inexpensive portable computers, known as netbooks. Its strategy is to use its lowest cost position to become extremely aggressive on price. Lenovo has also emerged as a serious competitor using the IBM-designed 'Think' brand to target large companies, and its Lenovo 3000 brand to target small and medium-sized businesses. The consumer segment was targeted with attractively designed innovative machines such as the IdeaPad U110, a laptop with a bright-red top and an 11-inch screen, and the Y710, which had a keyboard with special controls for video games.

Dell's response

The company's first response was to bring back Michael Dell (who had taken over the role of chairman) as chief executive. He has implemented a number of new initiatives, as outlined below.

- His view was that Dell should stop selling dull grey/black boxes, and aim for products that build 'brand lust', as he called it. In line with this strategy, Dell launched a series of laptops that customers could customize by mixing from an array of colours, patterns and textures for an extra £29. Customers could also choose artistic designs from Nigerian painter Joseph Amedokopo, South African graphic artist Siobhan Gunning, and Canadian designer Bruce Mau, for £69 (see illustration).

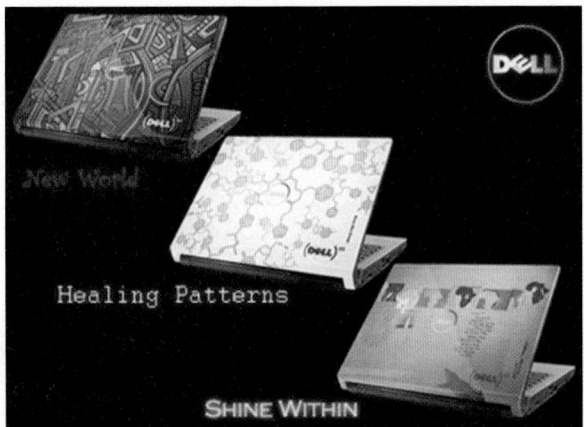

▲ Customers can choose artistic designs for a premium price. These designs were created by artists Joseph Amedokopo, Bruce Mau and Siobhan Gunning as part of the (Product)^Red series, for which the price included a donation to an AIDS charity.

- The company has also cut back on the production of 'utilitarian' computers in favour of premium-priced computers such as the Adamo range of super-thin notebooks, to challenge Apple's MacBook Air.
- A series of computers has been designed for small businesses in fast-growing emerging markets such as China and India, which are the source of most PC growth. Mr Dell has spent a lot of time visiting emerging markets.
- Dell has made massive investments in improving its service capability.
- Its distribution strategy has also changed. Alongside its direct marketing operation, Dell has struck deals to sell its computers through large retailers, including Wal-Mart, on a global scale, with many of them in emerging markets.
- It has moved to work with so-called resellers— outside companies that design and install computer systems for small, medium-sized and large businesses.
- The purchase of several firms to strengthen its consultancy services to large companies.
- Marketing communications has been overhauled. Dell has hired WPP, a multinational marcoms agency, in a \$4.5 billion deal to revitalize its image. It has also set up a corporate blog and website, called Ideastorm, which lets customers make suggestions on how Dell can improve its products and service.
- There has been cost cutting to the tune of \$3 billion. As part of this exercise, Dell's plant at Limerick, Ireland, has closed, with production moving to Poland.

References

Based on: Fernandez, J. (2009) Dell's Long Hard Road, *Marketing Week*, 22 January, 16–17; Allinson, K. (2008) Analysts Assess Dell's New Strategic Thinking, *Financial Times*, 7 April, 26; Anonymous (2009) Dell's Adamo: Good Looks, Bad Timing, *Business Week*, 11 May, 71; Jana, R. (2008) Taking the Dull Out of Dell, *Business Week*, 10 November, 52–3; Fortt, J. (2007) Will the Holy Grail of Marketing Revive Dell?, *Fortune*, 5 December 23–5; Anonymous (2008) Take Two, *Economist*, 3 May, 84; Allison, K. (2008) Dell's Long View Irks Investors, *Financial Times*, 1 September, 20.

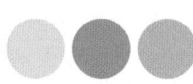

Questions

1. At the height of its success, how was Dell positioned in the marketplace?
2. Using the 4-Cs framework, explain why Dell's fortunes declined.
3. What are the significant changes to Dell's positioning that have taken place since Michael Dell's return as chief executive? Why has Dell made these strategic moves and what are the risks?

This case was written by David Jobber, Professor of Marketing, University of Bradford.

McDonald's
Repositioning the Golden Arches

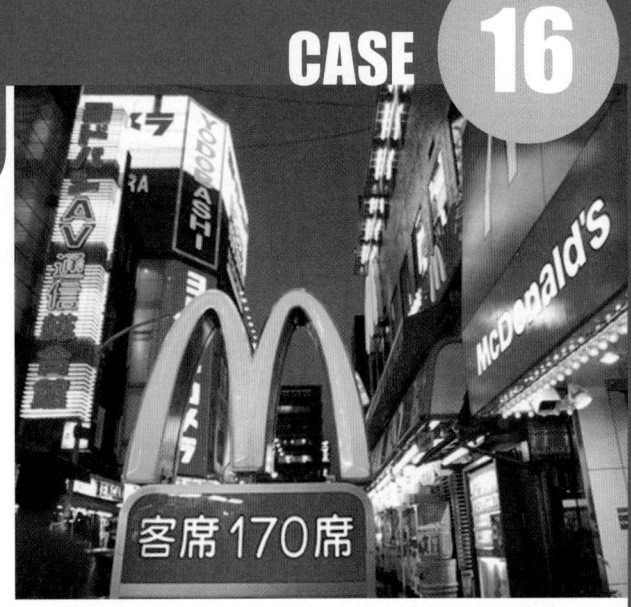

With its head office in Oak Brook, Illinois, USA, fast-food giant McDonald's has ridden the wave of the global trends towards eating out and fast food since it took its modern form in the early 1950s. Outside the USA, customers of the global chain were not, however, only eating hamburgers—they were 'eating and drinking America'.[1] In societies that have never had enough meat, the rapid emergence of fast-food chains was linked to the availability at reasonable prices of hot beef and chicken.

By the 1970s and 1980s, McDonald's and its golden arches logo had become a global phenomenon. By 1996 McDonald's operated in 100 countries and was finally earning more revenue from McDonald's International than from McDonald's America. Indeed the Big Mac had become so globally recognizable that it was adopted as a measure of purchasing power across different markets.

While the golden arches logo and McDonald's brand have achieved global recognition and changed the eating habits of generations of children, McDonald's has packaged itself as a multi-local company, which has a high level of local ownership through a network of franchise outlets. The product offer is also tailored just enough for local cultures; for example, beer is sold in McDonald's Czech Republic, and a different chicken sandwich in England compared to Germany. Sourcing of products is also global in some cases (sesame seeds come from Mexico) but local in others. When McDonald's Canada became partner in a joint venture operation in Moscow, it built its only supply plant and grew its own potatoes in Russia, but produced standardized products and imported Dutch seed potatoes to ensure that the French fries were of regulation size.

Yet despite its global dominance, McDonald's began to see a slowing of its growth in the late 1990s. By 1996 it was beginning to report a decline in its sales in the USA. In part McDonald's had become a victim of its own success. With almost 20,000 restaurants in the USA, each new restaurant was beginning to take business from other restaurants rather than growing the overall market. McDonald's was also affected by the ageing of the customer base that drove sales growth in the 1970s and 1980s. Sales growth was increasingly from opening outlets in more exotic locations, but by the turn of the century McDonald's was also beginning to see a slowdown in sales in some of its more established international markets, such as the UK, Germany and Japan. Attempts were made to win back the baby boomers with more sophisticated adult burgers, but sales remained flat. Analysts commented that McDonald's seemed to be stuck in a 'strategic no-man's land with no easy route back to financial safety'.[2]

While McDonald's has hit rocky patches in the past and recovered—sometimes by cutting prices—the company now seemed to be facing a major marketing challenge to the continued development of its global brand. McDonald's was not helped in this by a growth in protests against the company and what it stands for. This has come, variously, from environmentalists, health chiefs and middle-class commentators.

Yet the last few years have seen a major reversal in the fortunes of McDonald's. The multi-year turnaround in its fortunes is cited by many as 'one of the most successful in food service history'.[3]

This case explores the reasons behind the downturn that faced McDonald's and the way in which the restaurant chain orchestrated the revitalization of its brand.

Changing times

Perhaps the pressures that faced McDonald's were not too surprising but were simply a sign of the maturity of the market for eating outside the home. Competition to fast-food chains such as McDonald's was raised by new entrants into the restaurant market. The arrival of sandwich bars such as Subway, Pret A Manger and Benjys, coffee shops like Starbucks and Costa Coffee and a broader variety of fast-food options placed more pressure on McDonald's to defend its market share.

Combined with this greater competitive intensity, the trend towards healthy eating put increasing pressure on McDonald's. Fast-food outlets that focus on healthy alternatives and the transparency of ingredients—such as Quiet Revolution, Eat and Love Juice—gained ground in response to a new awareness of healthy eating.

A number of factors have fuelled this trend in recent years. In the UK, public awareness of healthy eating was raised by a series of health scares, from the BSE crisis in 1996, which affected confidence in British beef, through a possible bird flu pandemic that challenged consumer confidence in the safety of eating chicken, to the more recent swine flu pandemic. Second, awareness has been focused on the rise in levels of childhood obesity. US figures showed 15 per cent of children between the ages of 6 and 19 to be obese in 2005, a level three times that seen in the 1970s.[4] Indeed McDonald's faced a lawsuit in the USA claiming that the company was liable for the obesity and subsequent heart problems of two teenagers who had eaten its food.

The widespread airing of the documentary film *Super Size Me*, in which the health implications of a fast-food diet were shown, has been followed in the UK by high-profile initiatives such as TV chef Jamie Oliver's campaign to improve the health value of school meals, which appear to have changed UK attitudes towards fast food more rapidly than in Europe. In 2006, a survey showed that the number of 13–15 years olds naming McDonald's as their favourite meal had declined by 7 per cent to just 1 per cent compared with the year before.[5]

Consequently, McDonald's saw a decline in profit margins across Europe, from 15.6 per cent to 14.9 per cent in 2005. The McDonald's Corporation admitted at the time to 'weak sales results' in the UK.[6] While, in 2002, McDonald's was opening four stores a day across its global market, its fortunes dipped such that it revealed an intention to close 25 UK restaurants and had no plans to open any new restaurants. McDonald's European head, Denis Hennequin, admitted, 'The UK has been negative territory for a couple of years now … The brand 15 years ago was very trendy and modern. It is now tired.'[7]

McDonald's marketing and strategy chiefs had to move to revitalize the global brand that was so integral to their global fortunes.

Repositioning the McDonald's brand

The initial response of McDonald's was to revise its menus. Following the BSE crisis, it put more emphasis on white meat such as chicken rather than beef. It experimented with a range of Quorn-based vegetarian meals, with limited success—11 items were axed from the Salads Plus and Breakfast menus after less than 18 months.[8] A McDonald's spokesperson also indicated to a national newspaper that the chain might take chicken off the menu if bird flu became a health concern.

Initially, it seemed that this healthy eating approach had mixed success. McDonald's' revenue grew by 30 per cent in the USA, but sales in Britain remained flat, even when the healthier menu was introduced in 2002.[9]

In parallel, McDonald's launched a global advertising campaign using the strap-line 'It's what I eat and what I do … I'm lovin' it', aimed at educating consumers towards living healthy lives. Chief executive Jim Skinner claimed in 2005, 'We will use our size and strength to set an example.' Global chief marketing officer, Larry Light, explains: 'We lost relevance. The world had changed, and McDonald's stood still. The whole character and personality of our offering was frozen in time.'[10]

The idea for the 'I'm lovin' it' campaign came from Germany. Heye & Partners, a branch of DUB, worked off the McDonald's agency, DDB's, global strategy that McDonald's was a fun place to be. They created the line 'Ich liebe es', which translates as 'I love it', and this became 'I'm lovin' it' in English-speaking markets. The strap-line was also linked to a simple five-note jingle (ba ba ba ba ba, I'm lovin' it), which is easy for people to remember.

Certainly, this campaign seems to have triggered a McDonald's revival. In the second quarter of 2004, it posted its fourth successive quarter of double-digit profit gains in the USA, eclipsing market expectations. Sales for the quarter jumped to $4.7 billion, a 9 per cent rise. Other US burger chains—Wendy's, Burger King and Triarc Co's Arby's—saw slower sales growth during the same period and blamed this on the resurgence of McDonald's.[11] A spokesperson from the Arby's roast beef chain said, 'We don't have the money to spend and McDonald's got their act together.' McDonald's is estimated to have spent $45 million on advertising in the UK alone.[12]

McDonald's went on to introduce fruit bags and portions of vegetables as healthier menu options for children, and a range of smoothies, energy drinks and speciality coffees. In 2008, McDonald's commented that it expected the latter, once rolled out across its whole chain, to add more than $1 billion to its sales in the USA.

McDonald's wants to be seen as a 'modern, relevant progressive burger company'. Its revival is not restricted to the USA. In the UK, despite the recession—or perhaps because of it—McDonald's expects to come out of the economic slump with more customers than it had going in. Overall, McDonald's' sales were up 8.5 per cent in Europe in 2008. This was based on expansion of sales in existing restaurants, not on opening large numbers of new restaurants. In the UK, 70 per cent of the population (80 per cent of all families) report going to McDonald's restaurants.[13] The company has also invested heavily in new-look restaurants.

The increased sales are attributed to fixing the basics: the nutritional content of the food, such as reduced salt and sugar, and using only white chicken breast and free range eggs. Indeed, chicken has been identified as a key area for growth in Europe, a move that aims to break the dominance of KFC (Kentucky Fried Chicken) in the European market.[14] McDonald's also introduced Rainforest Alliance coffee beans and now sells 10 million more cups of coffee in UK alone—an increase of 20 per cent. The company has also launched a range of premium products into its restaurants. These are intended to attract diners who have traded down during the credit crunch, to eating in McDonald's but may pay more for these limited-edition offerings.[15]

McDonald's' new product range is also having a direct impact on the fortunes of its competitors. An analyst from JP Morgan commented that, if just 10 per cent of McDonald's' increased traffic came from customers who would previously have gone to Starbucks, then the latter could suffer a significant profit fall. Certainly Starbucks posted its first ever quarterly loss in 2008. Moreover, analysts suggest that the current economic downturn has made it more difficult for the chain to orchestrate a McDonald's-style revitalization of its brand.[16] Burger King is also launching a product called 'apple fries', intended to challenge the fruit bags offered by McDonald's.[17] Burger King was first to enter the premium end of the burger market, with the launch of the Aberdeen Angus beef burger, which is now challenged by the deluxe beef and chicken burgers served in ciabatta bread at McDonald's.

The company has also increased its focus on emerging markets, where it believes it can cater for customers by devising menus that are adapted to local preferences, while maintaining its iconic American appeal. So some countries have burgers based on lamb products rather than beef, where religion and cultural preferences dictate this. The company also varies its menus in other respects, offering root beer in the USA, beer in the Czech Republic, and making other variations that work for particular markets under the umbrella of the global McDonald's brand. This appears to be McDonald's using expertise in multi-local marketing strategies. There were 800 McDonald's restaurants in China by the end of

2007, and it opened a further 500 in 2008.[18] Taiwan accounted for 6 per cent of sales growth in 2005, and the company extended its concept into Hong Kong, Singapore, the Philippines and Malaysia in 2006.[19]

Notes

1 Anonymous (1997) Coke and Big Mac Aren't the Real Thing, *Guardian*, 4 January.
2 Anonymous (1996) Wall Street Loses its Taste for McDonald's, *The Times*, 14.
3 Anonymous (2008) *Nation's Restaurant News*, 11 August.
4 Anonymous (2005) Who Cares Wins, But is There a Hidden Agenda?, *Marketing Week*, 28 April.
5 Anonymous (2006) I'm Lovin' It, *Guardian*, 4 March.
6 Anonymous (2006) Cracks Begin to Show in McDonald's Golden Arches, *Marketing Week*, 9 March.
7 Ibid.
8 Ibid.
9 Anonymous (2006) World Cup Burger is a Monster, *Mirror*, 22 May.
10 Anonymous (2004) Inside McDonald's, *Adweek*, 8 November.
11 Anonymous (2004) Rivals Not Lovin' McDonald's Comeback, *Advertising Age* 75(30).
12 Anonymous (2009) McDonald's Opened Dialogue to Turn Itself Around, *CMO Strategy*, 23 February.
13 Ibid.
14 Anonymous (2007) McDonald's Puts Focus on Chicken, *Marketing*, 24 October.
15 Anonymous (2008) McDonald's Eyes Range to Draw 'Casual Diners', *Marketing*, 7 September.
16 Anonymous (2008) *Nation's Restaurant News*, 11 August.
17 Anonymous (2008) Burger King Health Launch, *Marketing*, 9 March.
18 Anonymous (2009) Food Market Watch, *Datamonitor*, April.
19 Anonymous (2006) Golden Arches Bridge Local Tastes, *Financial Times*, 9 February.

Questions

1 What environmental trends have challenged McDonald's?
2 Assess the attempt by McDonald's to reposition its brand.
3 To what extent are the actions of McDonald's likely to have an impact on its competitors?
4 What are the challenges facing McDonald's as it expands into emerging markets?

This case was written by Susan Bridgewater, Lecturer in Marketing and Strategy, Warwick University, UK.

Marketing Mix Decisions

Product

Price

Promotion

Place

Spanning the marketing mix

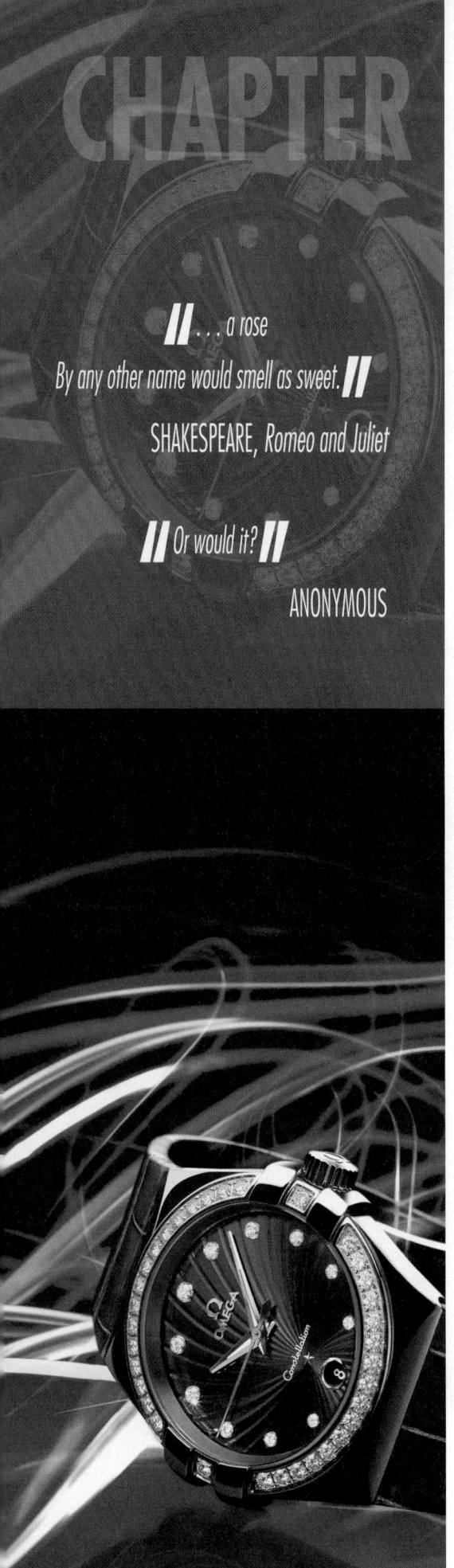

CHAPTER 9

...a rose
By any other name would smell as sweet.

SHAKESPEARE, *Romeo and Juliet*

Or would it?

ANONYMOUS

Managing products: brand and corporate identity management

LEARNING OBJECTIVES

After reading this chapter, you should be able to:

1 define the concepts of product, brand, product line and product mix

2 distinguish between manufacturer and own-label brands

3 distinguish between a core and augmented product (the brand)

4 explain why strong brands are important

5 define brand equity, the components of customer-based and proprietary-based brand equity and brand valuation

6 explain how to build strong brands

7 distinguish between family, individual and combined brand names, and discuss the characteristics of an effective brand name

8 discuss why companies rebrand and explain how to manage the process

9 discuss the concepts of brand extension and stretching, and their uses and limitations

10 describe the two major forms of co-branding, and their advantages and risks

11 discuss the arguments for and against global and pan-European branding, and the strategic options for building such brands

12 define and discuss the dimensions of corporate identity

13 describe how to manage corporate identity programmes

14 discuss ethical issues concerning products

The core element in the marketing mix is the company's product because this provides the functional requirements sought by customers. For example, a watch that does not tell the time or a car that does not start in the morning will rapidly be rejected by consumers. Marketing managers develop their products into brands that help to create a unique position (see Chapter 8) in the minds of customers. Brand superiority leads to high sales, the ability to charge price premiums and the power to resist distributor power. Firms attempt to retain their current customers through brand loyalty. Loyal customers are typically less price sensitive, and the presence of a loyal customer base provides the firm with valuable time to respond to competitive actions.[1] The management of products and brands is therefore a key factor in marketing success.

This chapter will explore the nature of products and brands, and the importance of strong brands. Given that importance, the ways in which successful brands are built and how brand equity is created will be revealed. Then a series of key branding decisions will be examined: brand name strategies and choices, rebranding, brand extension and stretching, and co-branding. Next, the special issues relating to global and pan-European branding will be analysed. Finally, corporate identity management, an area that is gaining increasing attention among corporate brand managers, is discussed.

Products and Brands

A product is anything that is capable of satisfying customer needs. In everyday speech we often distinguish between products and services, with products being tangible (e.g. a car) and services mainly intangible (e.g. a medical examination). However, when we look at what the customer is buying, it is essentially a service whether the means is tangible or intangible. For example, a car provides the service of transportation; a medical examination provides the service of a health check. Consequently, it is logical to include services within the definition of the product. Hence, there are *physical products* such as a watch, car or gas turbine, or *service products* such as medical services, insurance or banking. All of these products satisfy customer needs—for example, a gas turbine provides power and insurance reduces financial risk. The principles discussed in this chapter apply equally to physical and service products. However, because there are special considerations associated with service products (e.g. intangibility), and as service industries (e.g. fast-food restaurants, tourism and the public sector) form an important and growing sector in most developed countries, Chapter 22 is dedicated to examining services marketing in detail.

Branding is the process by which companies distinguish their product offerings from the competition. By developing a distinctive name, packaging and design, a **brand** is created. Some brands are supported by logos—for example, the Nike 'swoosh' and the prancing horse of Ferrari. By developing an individual identity, branding permits customers to develop associations with the brand (e.g. prestige, economy) and eases the purchase decision.[2] The marketing task is to ensure that the associations made are positive and in line with the chosen positioning objectives (see Chapter 8).

Branding affects perceptions since it is well known that in blind product testing consumers often fail to distinguish between brands in each product category, hence the questioning of Shakespeare's famous statement at the start of this chapter.

The word 'brand' is derived from the Old Norse word 'brandr', which means 'to burn' as brands were and still are the means by which livestock owners mark their animals to identify ownership.[3]

The Product Line and Product Mix

Brands are not often developed in isolation. They normally fall within a company's product line and mix. A **product line** is a group of brands that are closely related in terms of their functions and the benefits they provide (e.g. Dell's range of personal computers or Philips Consumer Electronics line of television sets). The *depth* of the product line depends upon the pattern of customer requirements (e.g. the number of segments to be found in the market), the product depth being offered by competitors, and company resources. For example, although customers may require wide product variations, a small company may decide to focus on a narrow product line serving only sub-segments of the market.

A **product mix** is the total set of brands marketed in a company. It is the sum of the product lines offered. Thus, the *width* of the product mix can be gauged by the number of product lines an organization offers. Philips, for example, offers a wide product mix comprising the brands found within its product lines of television, audio equipment, DVD players, digital cameras, and so on. Other companies have a much narrower product mix comprising just one product line, such as TVR, which produces high-performance cars.

The management of brands and product lines is a key element of product strategy. First, we shall examine the major decisions involved in managing brands—namely the type of brand to market (manufacturer vs own-label), how to build brands, brand name strategies, brand extension and stretching, and the brand acquisition decision. Then we shall look at how to manage brands and product lines over time using the product life cycle concept. Finally, managing brand and product line portfolios will be discussed.

Brand Types

The two alternatives regarding brand type are manufacturer and own-label brands. **Manufacturer brands** are created by producers and bear their own chosen brand name. The responsibility for marketing the brand lies in the hands of the producer. Examples include Kellogg's Cornflakes, Gillette Sensor razors and Microsoft Vista software. The value of the brand lies with the producer and, by building major brands, producers can gain distribution and customer loyalty.

A fundamental distinction that needs to be made is between category, brands and variants (see Fig. 9.1). A category (or product field) is divided into brands, which in turn may be divided into variants based on flavour, formulation or other feature.[4] For example, Heinz Tomato Soup is the tomato variant of the Heinz brand of the category 'soup'.

Own-label brands (sometimes called distributor brands) are created and owned by distributors. Own-label branding, if associated with tight quality control of suppliers, can

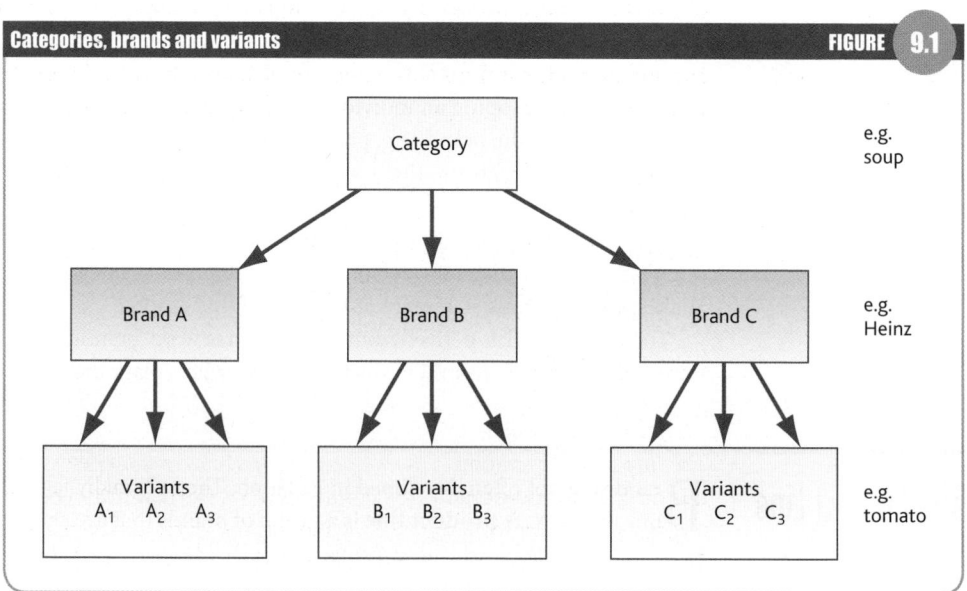

Categories, brands and variants   FIGURE 9.1

e.g. soup

Category

e.g. Heinz

Brand A   Brand B   Brand C

e.g. tomato

Variants
A_1 A_2 A_3

Variants
B_1 B_2 B_3

Variants
C_1 C_2 C_3

provide consistent high value for customers, and be a source of retail power as suppliers vie to fill excess productive capacity with manufacturing products for own-label branding. The power of low-price supermarket own-label brands has focused many producers of manufacturer brands to introduce so-called **fighter brands** (i.e. their own low-price alternative). For example, Unilever has expanded its range of value brands to include ice cream and bouillon, and has sold its frozen foods division, where own-label brands are very strong.[5] Not all own-label brands come with a low price tag, however. An example is Tesco Finest, a premium-priced own-label brand that has overtaken Kellogg's to become the UK's biggest grocery brand.[6]

A major decision that producers have to face is whether to agree to supply own-label products for distributors. The danger is that, should customers find out, they may believe that there is no difference between the manufacturer brand and its own-label equivalent. This led some companies, such as Kellogg's, to refuse to supply own-label products for many years. For other producers, supplying own-label goods may be a means of filling excess capacity and generating extra income from the high sales volumes contracted with distributors.

Why Strong Brands are Important

Strong brands, typically product category leaders, are important to both companies and consumers. Companies benefit because strong brands add value to companies, positively affect consumer perceptions of brands, act as a barrier to competition, improve profits and provide a base for brand extensions. Consumers gain because strong brands act as a form of quality certification and create trust. We shall now look at each of these factors in turn.

Company value

The financial value of companies can be greatly enhanced by the possession of strong brands. For example, Nestlé paid £2.5 billion for Rowntree, a UK confectionery manufacturer, a sum that was six times its balance sheet value. Nestlé was not so much interested in Rowntree's manufacturing base as its brands—such as KitKat, Quality Street, After Eight and Polo—which were major brands with brand-building potential. More recently, Procter & Gamble paid £31 billion for Gillette. Again Gillette's brands were valued at a far higher level than its physical assets. While Gillette's balance sheet mentioned only physical, tangible assets of £4 billion, its brands were worth £10 billion: Gillette £4 billion; Duracell £2.5 billion; Oral B £2 billion; Braun £1.5 billion. The balance consisted of the value of Gillette's distributor and supplier relationships (£10 billion) and its patents (£7 billion).[7] Coca-Cola attributes only 7 per cent of its value to its plants and machinery—its real value lies in its brands.[8]

Consumer perceptions and preferences

Strong brand names can have positive effects on consumer perceptions and preferences. Marketing in Action 9.1 describes evidence from the soft drinks and car markets, which shows how strong brands can influence perception and preference. Clearly, the strength of Diet Coke and Toyota as powerful brand names influenced perception and preference in both markets.

Barrier to competition

The impact of the strong, positive perceptions held by consumers about top brands means it is difficult for new brands to compete. Even if the new brand performs well on blind taste testing, as we have seen, this may be insufficient to knock the market leader off the top spot. This is one of the reasons Virgin Coke failed to dent Coca-Cola's domination of the cola market. The reputation of strong brands, then, may be a powerful barrier to competition.

9.1 Marketing in Action

Strong Brand Names Affect Consumer Perceptions and Preferences

Two matched samples of consumers were asked to taste Diet Coke, the market leader in diet colas, and Diet Pepsi. The first group tasted the drinks 'blind' (i.e. the brand identities were concealed) and were asked to state a preference. The procedure was repeated for the second group, except that the test was 'open' (i.e. the brand identities were shown). The results are presented below.

	Blind	Open
	%	%
Prefer Diet Pepsi	51	23
Prefer Diet Coke	44	65
Equal/can't say	5	12

This test clearly shows the power of strong brand names in influencing perceptions and preferences towards Diet Coke. Advances in neuroscience may go some way to explaining the results. A re-creation of the test produced identical results, but this time the tasters were wired to a brain scanner. When the consumers tasted the drinks blind there was a flurry of activity in the part of the brain that is stimulated by taste. However, when the consumers were told which brand they were drinking, it was the part of the brain associated with higher thinking that was activated during tasting.

A second example comes from the car industry. A joint venture between Toyota and General Motors (GM) resulted in two virtually identical cars being produced from the same manufacturing plant in the USA. One was branded the Toyota Corolla, and the other GM's Chevrolet Prizm. Although the production costs were the same, the Toyota was priced higher than the Chevrolet Prizm. Despite the price difference, the Toyota achieved twice the market share of its near identical twin. The reason was that the Toyota brand enjoyed an excellent reputation for reliable cars whereas GM's reputation had been tarnished by a succession of unreliable cars. Despite the fact that the cars were virtually the same, consumers' perceptions and preferences were strongly affected by the brand names attached to each model.

Based on: De Chernatony and McDonald (2003);[9] Doyle and Stern (2006);[10] Valantine (2009)[11]

High profits

Strong, market-leading brands are rarely the cheapest. Brands such as Heinz, Kellogg's, Coca-Cola, Mercedes, Nokia, Michelin and Microsoft are all associated with premium prices. This is because their superior brand equity means that consumers receive added value over their less powerful rivals. Strong brands also achieve distribution more readily, economies of scale, and are in a better position to resist retailer demands for price discounts. These forces feed through to profitability. A major study of the factors that lead to high profitability (the Profit Impact of Marketing Strategy project) shows that return on investment is related to a brand's share of the market: bigger brands yield higher returns than smaller brands.[12] For example, brands with a market share of 40 per cent generate, on average, three times the return on investment of brands with only 10 per cent market share. These findings are supported by research into net profit margins for US food brands. The category leader's average return was 18 per cent, number two achieved 6 per cent, number three returned 1 per cent, while the number four position was associated with a −6 per cent net profit margin.[13] Another study of

▲ The strong Lego brand provided a foundation for its Bionicle toys.

hand tool manufacturers in the USA produced similar results with the market leader achieving 24 per cent, number two 4 per cent, number three 0.1 per cent and number four −4 per cent net profit margins.[14]

Base for brand extensions

A strong brand provides the foundation for leveraging positive perceptions and goodwill from the core brand to brand extensions. Examples include Diet Coke, Pepsi Max, Lucozade Sport, Smirnoff Ice and Lego Bionicle (see illustration). The new brand benefits from the added value that the brand equity of the core brand bestows on the extension. There is a full discussion of brand extensions later in this chapter.

Quality certification

Strong brands also benefit consumers in that they provide quality certification, which can aid decision-making. The following example illustrates the lengths consumers will go to when using strong brands as a form of quality certification. In former Soviet Russia all television sets were made in two manufacturing plants. The sets were apparently unbranded and were made to the same design. The problem was that some of these sets were unreliable, causing a lot of customer annoyance. Consumers learnt that the problems were arising from television sets made by one of the plants, while the other made reliable sets. The question was how to tell whether a particular set was made by the reliable or unreliable manufacturer. Although they looked the same, consumers discovered that each set had a code printed on the back that identified its source. In effect the code was acting as a brand identifier and consumers were using it as a form of quality certification.

Trust

Consumers tend to trust strong brands. The Henley Forecasting Centre found that consumers are increasingly turning to 'trusted guides' to manage choice. A key 'trusted guide' is the brand name and its perceptual associations. When consumers stop trusting a brand, the fallout can be catastrophic as when the once strong Marks & Spencer brand lost the trust of many of its customers. Happily, the brand is regaining that trust under new management. The lesson is never to do anything that might compromise the trust held by consumers towards a brand. Europe's most trusted brands in 10 product categories are shown in Table 9.1.

Brand Equity

Strong brands are rich in a property called brand equity. **Brand equity** is a measure of the strength of a brand in the marketplace by adding tangible value to a company through the resulting sales and profits. There are two types of brand equity: customer-based and proprietary-based brand equity. Customer-based brand equity resides in the minds of consumers and consists of brand awareness and brand image. Proprietary-based brand equity is based on assets that are attributable to the company, and consists of patents and channel relationships.

Europe's most trusted brands	TABLE 9.1
Product category	**Brands*** **(winners in three or more countries)**
Breakfast cereal	Kellogg's, Nestlé
Camera	Canon
Car	Mercedes, Toyota, VW
Cosmetics	Avon, Nivea, Yves Rocher
Credit card	Visa
Haircare	Pantene
Kitchen appliances	Miele
Mobile phone	Nokia
Personal computer	HP, Dell
Soap powder	Ariel, Persil

*Respondents across 16 European countries were asked to name their most trusted brand in each product category.

Source: based on *Reader's Digest* Trusted Brands 2009 report

Customer-based brand equity

Marketing in Action 9.1 discussed how the strength of the Diet Coke brand name reversed consumer preferences when compared to Diet Pepsi, and how the strong reputation of Toyota meant that it could charge a higher price and still sell more than an identical car carrying GM's Chevrolet badge. This is explained by Diet Coke possessing higher brand equity than Diet Pepsi, and the Toyota brand holding more brand equity than the Chevrolet marque. This type of brand equity resides in the minds of consumers who hold more favourable perceptions and associations towards Diet Coke and Toyota than their rivals, and is called customer-based brand equity.

Customer-based brand equity is defined as the differential effect that brand knowledge has on consumer response to the marketing of that brand.[15] A brand has positive customer-based brand equity when consumers react more favourably to a product when the brand is identified than when it is not (e.g. the Diet Coke vs Diet Pepsi product test). Positive customer-based brand equity is likely to result in high customer loyalty, low price sensitivity, a high willingness for customers to visit more than one outlet in order to purchase the brand and a strong base for brand extensions. On the other hand, negative customer-based brand equity occurs when consumers react less favourably towards the brand when it is identified than when it is not.

There are two sources of customer-based brand equity: brand awareness and brand image (see Fig. 9.2).

Brand awareness

Brand awareness is related to brand equity in two ways. First, by raising brand awareness, the likelihood that the brand will enter a consumer's evoked set (those brands that a consumer

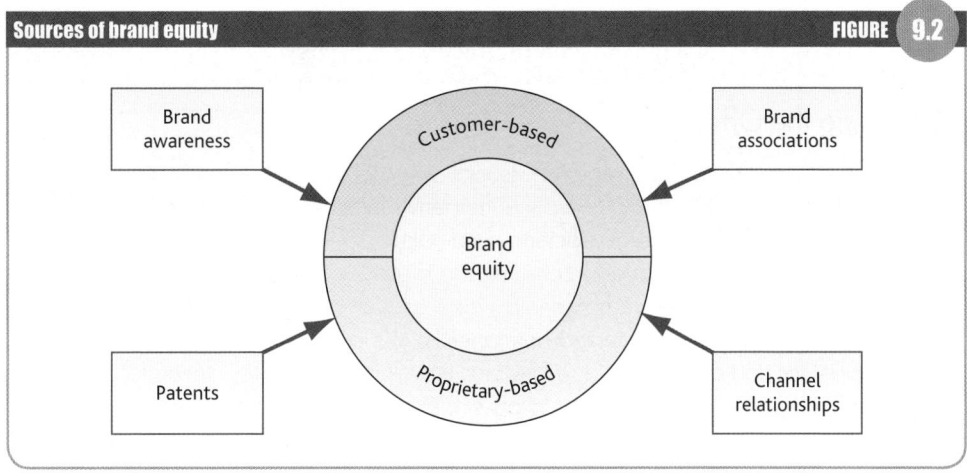

FIGURE 9.2 Sources of brand equity

seriously considers before making a purchase) is increased since awareness is a pre-condition of evaluation of a brand. Second, in low-involvement situations, as we saw in Chapter 4 on understanding consumer behaviour, a purchase may follow awareness of a brand with little information processing since the purchase is of low importance or low price. In both these cases, increasing brand awareness can lead to higher sales and profits and hence increased brand equity. The global brand awareness of brands like Coca-Cola, Canon, Microsoft and Nokia is a major contributor to their brand equity.

Brand image

Brand equity can also be increased by creating a strong brand image. A positive brand image is formed by generating strong, favourable and unique associations to the brand in the memory.[16] A brand image is created through the use of all elements of the marketing mix. The brand image of a car, for example, is influenced by product quality (associating it with perceptions of comfort, reliability, durability, and so on), promotion (an integrated marketing communications campaign may imbue the car with high-status connotations), price (a competitive price may confer associations with value for money), and place (a smart modern dealership may associate the car with efficient after-sales service). Advertising is often employed to create a brand image. A positive brand image, then, increases the likelihood of purchase and hence brand equity. The brands listed in Table 9.1 gain brand equity through their image of being trustworthy.

As we have seen, the value attributable to the customer-based brand equity associated with the Gillette brands (Gillette, Duracell, Oral B and Braun) when acquired by Procter & Gamble was £10 billion.[17]

In an attempt to maintain their brand image, some companies are embarking on offset schemes where, for example, air passengers are offered the option of offsetting their air miles with a fee that is invested in forest regeneration. However, the merits of such schemes need to be scrutinized carefully, as Marketing Ethics and Corporate Social Responsibility in Action 9.1 explains.

Proprietary-based brand equity

Proprietary-based brand equity is derived from company attributes that deliver value to the brand. These can be found in many aspects of corporate activity but the two main sources are patents and channel relationships.

9.1 Marketing Ethics and Corporate Social Responsibility in Action

Offsetting the Offsets

In an attempt to maintain positive brand associations, and to cope with new and stricter environmental regulations, corporations are currently trying to reduce their environmental footprint through the implementation of initiatives such as carbon offsetting, energy efficiency and 'take-back' schemes. For example, Tesco has recently introduced a system, on a trial basis, that asks consumers to dispose of excessive packaging near the till. The regional trial aims to help consumers reduce household waste as well as examine what types of packaging consumers are ready to give up. If implemented permanently, this will mean that Tesco, rather than consumers, will take responsibility for part of the recyclable and non-recyclable waste they generate. Likewise, most airline companies now give their passengers the option to offset their air miles when booking a ticket, for an additional fee. The money collected is then invested in carbon-offsetting projects such as those concerned with forest regeneration.

However, other schemes are less laudable and very contradictory. Tesco itself has recently introduced a 'flights for lights' promotion, which offers air miles to consumers who purchase energy-efficient light bulbs! In this way, all the energy a consumer economizes by using such light bulbs is then offset by the carbon emitted by air travel. Also, although automotive technology has improved dramatically over the years, bigger, faster and increased numbers of cars have offset the gains in energy efficiency. Similarly, after being accused of using far too much water in India and other parts of the world where potable water is scarce, Coca-Cola decided to improve the efficiency of its operations. The company has reduced the amount of water used to make a litre of its drinks by 20 per cent in five years. However, such improvements are offset by the fact that Coca-Cola manufactures more products year on year, so its overall water usage is almost the same. The company is aspiring to be 'water neutral'. Of course, Coca-Cola will never achieve this, as water is the main ingredient in its drinks. These are the types of rhetorical measures that generate much scepticism against prominent brands.

Based on: Pearce (2008);[18] Gillespie (2009);[19] Smithers (2009)[20]

Patents

As we shall see later when discussing brand valuation, a common method is to calculate the value of a brand by taking into account future profits and discounting them to the present day. Patents give greater certainty to future revenue streams by protecting a brand from competitive threat over the lifetime of the patent. Brand equity, therefore, falls towards the end of this period. For example, the value of many pharmaceutical brands falls as their patents expire because of the launch of low-priced generic competitors. As we have seen, the value of Gillette's patents when the company was acquired by P&G was estimated at £7 billion.[21]

Channel relationships

Experience, knowledge and close relationships with distributors and suppliers can enhance the value of company brands. For example, one of the attractions of Gillette to Procter & Gamble was its complementary global distribution strengths. Gillette has strengths in India and Brazil, whereas P&G is strong in China, Russia, Japan and Turkey. This allows Gillette to push P&G brands in India and Brazil, and P&G to use its existing strong channel relationships in China, Russia, Japan and Turkey to distribute Gillette brands.[22] It is reported that the value of Gillette's channel relationships to P&G was estimated at £10 billion.[23]

Brand valuation is a difficult task. It is the process of estimating the financial value of an individual or corporate brand. A widely cited list of the top 100 global brands by financial value is produced by the Interbrand Corporation; part of this is reproduced later in this chapter.

Interbrand bases its calculations on the present value of a brand after discounting future profits, rather like the way financial analysts value other assets. Its procedure is as follows.[24]

1   An estimate is made of the percentage of a company's revenue that can be credited to a brand. For some companies, the brand may be the entire company, as with McDonald's, or just a part, as with Nescafé.

2   A five-year projection of the brand's profits is made. Management consultants and banks help with these calculations.

3   The risk associated with the profit projections is assessed, taking into account such factors as market leadership, stability and global reach (the ability to cross both geographic and cultural borders).

4   A discount rate is calculated based on risk (high risk equals high discount rate), which is used to discount brand profits to arrive at a net present value.

Although Interbrand's approach does not give estimates of the value of brands in the future (something that would be useful to investors), it does provide a picture of the value of brands in any one year. Calculating the value of brand equity is an important task since it indicates the rewards that can be reaped from marketing investments.

Brand Building

The importance of strong brands means that brand building is an essential marketing activity. Successful brand building can reap benefits in terms of premium prices, achieving distribution more readily, and sustaining high and stable sales and profits through brand loyalty.[25]

A brand is created by augmenting a **core product** with distinctive values that distinguish it from the competition. To understand the notion of brand values we first need to understand the difference between features and benefits. A feature is an aspect of a brand that may or may not confer a customer benefit. For example, adding fluoride (*feature*) to a toothpaste confers the customer *benefits* of added protection against tooth decay and decreased dental charges. Not all features necessarily confer benefits: a camera *(feature)* in a mobile phone confers no *benefit* to people not interested in photography, for example.

Core benefits derive from the core product (see Fig. 9.3). Toothpaste, for example, cleans teeth and therefore protects against tooth decay. But all toothpastes achieve that. Branding allows marketers to create added values that distinguish one brand from another. Successful brands are those that create a set of brand values that are superior to other rival brands. So brand building involves a deep understanding of both the functional (e.g. ease of use) and emotional (e.g. confidence) values that customers use when choosing between brands, and the ability to combine them in a unique way to create an augmented *product* that customers prefer. This unique, **augmented product** is what marketers call the *brand*. The success of the Swatch brand was founded on the recognition that watches could be marketed as fashion items to younger age groups. By using colour and design, Swatch successfully augmented a basic product—a watch—to create appeal for its target market. Swatch combined functional and emotional values to create a successful brand. Focusing on functional values alone is rarely sufficient, as Ford discovered with its Mondeo model. Its engineers concentrated on functional attributes such as build and ride quality, fuel economy and luggage space. Exterior body design was dull, however (leading to it being referred to as the 'Blandeo'), and resulted in the car lacking the (emotional) excitement necessary to compete effectively.[26]

Figure 9.3 shows how products can be augmented. Singapore Airlines has augmented its brand by providing superior *service*. The Times provides superior service to its readers by being the only UK newspaper to employ an ocean correspondent (see illustration overleaf). Kia has differentiated its cars by offering seven-year *guarantees* (warrantees) when most of its competitors offer only three. Nivea was the first to differentiate its sun-block brand by the use

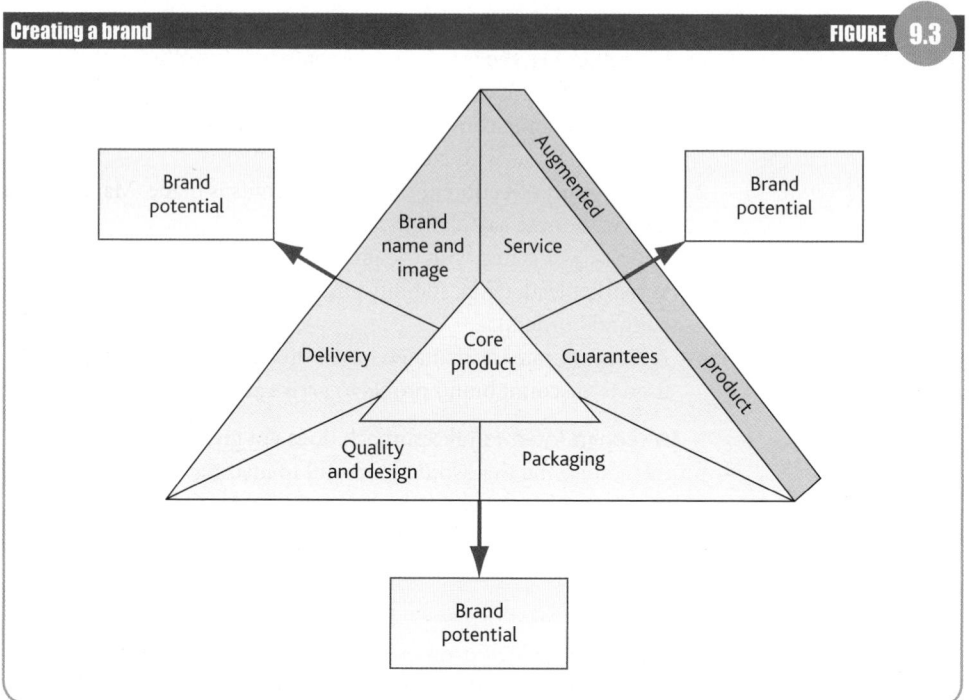

of innovative *packaging* that allowed it to be sprayed on to the body. Bang & Olufsen has differentiated its brand using quality and design. Panasonic augments its televisions through enhanced picture quality. The iPod has created a differential advantage by augmenting its brand through *delivery* by creating a highly efficient means of downloading music from Apple's iTunes music store. Apple has followed this success by creating its apps (applications) store for its iPhone, which allows anyone to create and sell an application, providing efficient *delivery* of extra *services* to customers. Finally, BMW has augmented its brand by its *image*, embodied in its 'The ultimate driving machine' strap-line, which differentiates it from the competition.

▲ *The Times* newspaper is augmented by providing a superior service to readers who care about the environment.

9.1 Pause For Thought

Think of a brand with which you are familiar. Using the elements shown in Figure 9.3, describe how that brand is augmented to distinguish it from the core product.

Managing brands involves a constant search for ways of achieving the full brand potential. To do so usually means the creation of major global brands. Leading brands such as Coca-Cola, Microsoft, IBM, General Electric and BMW have achieved this. But how are successful brands built? A combination of some or all of seven factors can be important.[27] These are shown in Figure 9.4 and described below.

Quality

It is vital to build quality into the core product: a major reason for brand failure is the inability to get the basics right. Marketing a computer that overheats, a car that refuses to start or a garden fork that breaks is courting disaster. The core product must achieve the basic functional requirements expected of it. A major study of factors that affect success has shown statistically that higher-quality brands achieve greater market share and higher profitability than their inferior rivals.[28] Total quality management techniques (see Chapter 5) are increasingly being employed to raise quality standards. Product quality improvements have been shown to mainly be driven by market pull (changing customer tastes and expectations), organizational push (changes in the technical potential and resources of a company) and competitor actions.[29]

Top companies such as Canon, BMW, Nokia, Intel, Toyota and Google understand the importance of quality in the brand-building process. Their success has been based on high-quality foundations. Once a brand is associated with quality, it forms a formidable barrier for competitors to overcome.

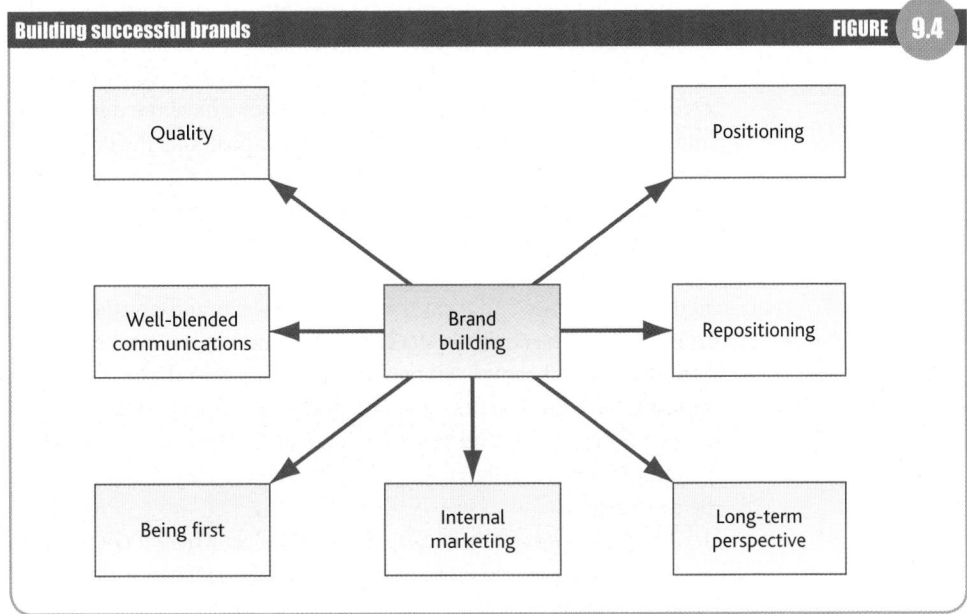

Building successful brands   FIGURE 9.4

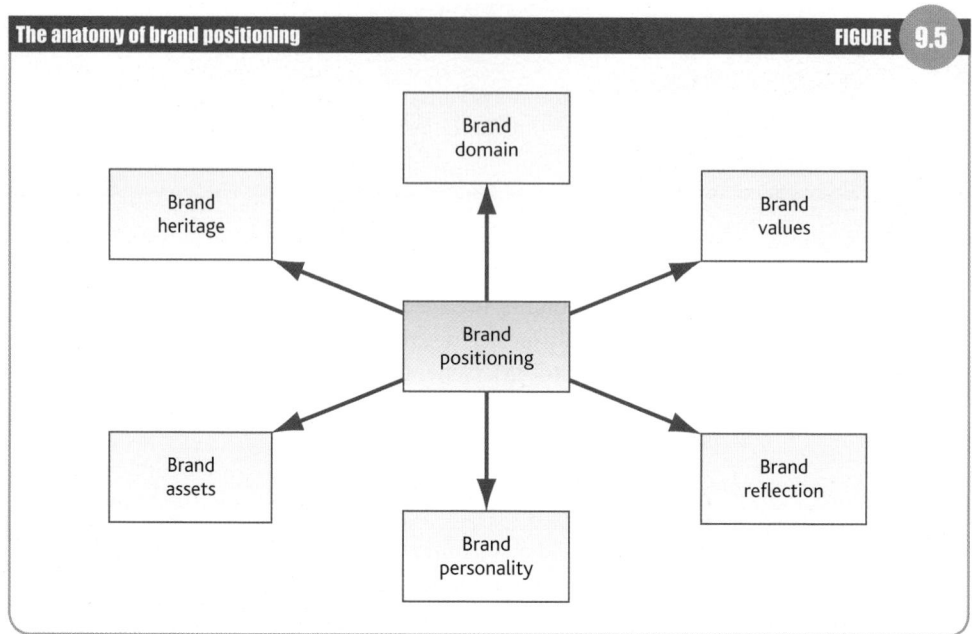

The anatomy of brand positioning   FIGURE 9.5

Positioning

Creating a unique position in the marketplace involves a careful choice of target market and establishing a clear differential advantage in the minds of those people. This can be achieved through brand names and image, service, design, guarantees, packaging and delivery. In today's highly competitive global marketplace, unique positioning will normally rely on combinations of these factors. For example, the success of BMW is founded on a quality, well-designed product, targeted at distinct customer segments and supported by a carefully nurtured exclusive brand name and image. No matter which factors are given highest priority, positioning should be founded on the 4-Cs framework discussed in Chapter 8, on market segmentation and positioning. These are clarity, consistency, credibility and competitiveness. For example, BMW's positioning statement, 'The ultimate driving machine', is clear, has been used consistently over many years, is credible because independent motoring reviews have rated its cars as excellent on handling and performance, and is competitive since it positions the brand as superior to its rivals. Viewing markets in novel ways can create unique positioning concepts. For example, Swatch, as mentioned earlier, was built on the realization that watches could be marketed as fashion items to younger age groups.

An analytical framework that can be used to dissect the current position of a brand in the marketplace and form the basis of a new brand positioning strategy is given in Figure 9.5. The strength of a brand's position in the marketplace is built on six elements: **brand domain**, **brand heritage**, **brand values**, **brand assets**, **brand personality** and **brand reflection**. The first element, brand domain, corresponds to the choice of target market (where the brand competes); the other five elements provide avenues for creating a clear differential advantage with these target consumers. Each will now be explained.

1   *Brand domain*: the brand's target market, i.e. where it competes in the marketplace. For example, the brand domain for the BlackBerry Pearl is the consumer market, while that for the more expensive BlackBerry 8800 is the business market.

For a century, the nation's mums have been relying on us to help them with the washing. They know that no one is better at removing even the toughest stains from the whitest of white dresses than Persil. And no one is gentler on the delicate skin of the little girls wearing them.

PERSIL *Tough but gentle for 100 years*

▲ Heritage can be used in advertisements to position brands in the marketplace, as this illustration featuring Persil shows.

▲ Consumers use brands to reflect their self-identity and project it to other people.

2   *Brand heritage*: the background to the brand and its culture. How it has achieved success (and failure) over its life. Brand heritage can form an extremely useful platform to build on. For example, Rose Marie Bravo built on the upmarket heritage of the Burberry brand and by modernizing its image created a powerful brand that saw the fortunes of the company escalate. The advertisement for Persil uses the brand's '100 years' heritage to support its reliability, toughness and gentleness.

3   *Brand values*: the core *values* and characteristics of the brand. For example, the brand values of Berghaus are high-performance outdoor clothing and the spirit of adventure, for Lycra they are comfort and fit, for Absolut Vodka purity and fun, and for Audi sophistication and progression. Ethical values for brands and companies are important. For example, Ecover, innocent smoothies, Green & Black's chocolate and Cafédirect coffee all combine strong brand values with ethical credentials.

4   *Brand assets*: what makes the brand distinctive from other competing brands, such as symbols, features, images and relationships. For example, the Nike 'swoosh' is a symbol that distinguishes it from other brands; the Dyson yellow bagless vacuum cleaner is a feature that distinguishes it from traditional vacuum cleaners, the image of BMW captured in its 'The ultimate driving machine' strap-line is distinctive, and the close relationship with customers developed by IBM over many years is a major brand asset for the company.

5   *Brand personality*: the character of the brand described in terms of other entities, such as people, animals or objects. Marketing researchers ask consumers to describe brands in these terms. For example, they might be asked 'If brand X were a person what kind of person would it be?', 'If brand X were an animal what kind of animal would it be?' or 'If brand X were a car what kind of car would it be?'

6   *Brand reflection*: how the brand relates to self-identity; how the customer perceives him/herself as a result of buying/using the brand. The branding illustration visualizes how people use brands to reflect and project their self-identity. The importance of brand reflection is apparent in the demand for aspirational brands such as Gucci handbags, Cartier or Rolex watches, and BMW cars.

By analysing each element, brand managers can form an accurate portrait of how brands are positioned in the marketplace. From there, thought can be given to whether and how the brand can be repositioned to improve performance. Nostalgia is increasingly being used as a positioning concept, as Marketing in Action 9.2 discusses.

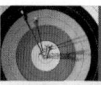

9.2 Marketing in Action

Retro Chic

In recent years, there has been a spate of marketing activity intended to tap in to consumer fondness for a bygone age. This can take the form of retro styling in such product categories as coffee makers, radios, refrigerators, telephones and cars. The car industry, in particular, has mixed nostalgia with progress through the successful launches of the updated Mini, VW Beetle, Fiat 500 and the 1950s-designed Chrysler PT Cruiser.

In confectionery, too, companies have attempted to link in to consumers' desire to connect with the past, with the relaunch of the Cadbury Wispa bar (see illustration), Orangina returning in its iconic glass bottle and Nestlé bringing back the Drifter bar.

The number of car brands launching models in white has snowballed to meet the rise in consumer demand for the retro colour, last popular in the 1980s. The biggest-selling white car is the Mini, encouraging other manufacturers like BMW, Nissan, Toyota, Honda, Seat and Citroën to offer models in the same colour.

Using nostalgia as a positioning concept makes sense as brands attempt to evoke feelings of comfort, authenticity and sanctuary in a world rapt by economic and security concerns.

Based on: Brownsell (2008);[30] Gray (2008);[31] Nettleton and Lovell (2008)[32]

▲ Cadbury connects with the past with the relaunch of its Wispa bar.

Repositioning

As markets change and opportunities arise, repositioning may be needed to build brands from their initial base. Skoda was repositioned from a downmarket car brand of dubious quality to a mid-market brand whose quality has led to several awards, and significant sales and profit growth. Samsung successfully repositioned from being perceived as a producer of cheap televisions and microwave ovens to being regarded as a 'cool' youth brand producing mobile phones and flat-screen televisions for the 'techno savvy'. Nokia also built its brand by repositioning from being a paper manufacturer to market leader in mobile phones.

Well-blended communications

Brand positioning is based on customer perception. To create a clear position in the minds of a target audience requires considerable thought and effort regarding advertising, selling and other promotional activities. Awareness needs to be built, the brand personality projected and favourable attitudes reinforced. Integrated marketing communications, combining the strengths of traditional and digital media, is often used to promote such successful brands as:

- Audi—Vorsprung durch Technik
- Nokia—Connecting People
- HSBC—The World's Local Bank.

These themes need to be reinforced by salespeople, public relations and sales promotion campaigns.

Marketers can make their brands more noticeable through attractive display or package design, and also through generating customer familiarity with brand names, brand logos and a brand's visual appearance. A well-blended communications strategy is necessary to achieve these objectives.[33]

Being first

Research has shown that pioneer brands are more likely to be successful than follower brands.[34] Being first gives a brand the opportunity to create a clear position in the minds of target customers before the competition enters the market. It also gives the pioneer the opportunity to build customer and distributor loyalty. Nevertheless, being first into a market with a unique marketing proposition does not guarantee success; it requires sustained marketing effort and the strength to withstand competitor attacks. Being first into a niche market, as achieved by the Body Shop and Tie Rack, usually guarantees short-term profits but the acid test arrives when competitors (sometimes with greater resources) enter with similar products. Another problem arises when pioneer brands have a competitive disadvantage compared with those using earlier technology. For example, the pioneers of 3G mobile phone handset technology failed to achieve success because the handsets were bulkier and less reliable than those built on 2G technology.[35]

Being first into a market can also bring the potential advantages of technological leadership, cost advantages through the experience curve effect, the acquisition and control of scarce resources and the creation of switching costs to later entrants (for example, the costs of switching from one computer system to another may be considerable).[36] Late entry can be costly: one study showed that a delay of one year in launching the Sierra after GM's Cavalier cost Ford $1 billion in lost profits over five years.[37]

Companies are, therefore, speeding up their new product development (NPD) processes, even if it means being over budget.[38] A McKinsey & Co study showed that being 50 per cent over NPD budget and on time can lead to a 4 per cent reduction in profits. However, being on budget and six months late to launch can lead to a 33 per cent reduction in profits.[39]

Being first does not necessarily mean pioneering the technology. Bigger returns may come to those who are first to enter the mass market. For example, America's Ampex pioneered video recorder technology in the mid-1950s but its machines sold for $50,000. It made little effort to cut costs and expand its market. It was left to Sony, JVC and Matsushita, who had the vision to see the potential for mass-market sales. They embarked on a research and development programme to make a video recorder that could be sold for $500—a goal that took them 20 years to achieve.[40]

Long-term perspective

Brand building is a long-term activity. There are many demands on people's attention. Consequently, generating awareness, communicating brand values and building customer loyalty usually takes many years. Management must be prepared to provide a consistently high level of brand investment to establish and maintain the position of a brand in the marketplace. Unfortunately, it can be tempting to cut back on expenditure in the short term. Cutting advertising spend by £0.5 million immediately cuts costs and increases profits. Conversely, for a well-established brand, sales are unlikely to fall substantially in the short term because of the effects of past advertising. The result is higher short-term profits. This may be an attractive proposition for brand managers who are often in charge of a brand for less than two years. One way of overcoming this danger is to measure brand manager (and brand) performance by measuring brand equity in terms of awareness levels, brand associations, intentions to buy, and so on, and being vigilant in resisting short-term actions that may harm it. To underline the importance of consistent brand investment Sir Adrian Cadbury (then chairman of Cadbury Schweppes) wrote:

For brands to endure they have to be maintained properly and imaginatively. Brands are extremely valuable properties and, like other forms of property, they need to be kept in good repair, renewed from time to time and defended against squatters.[41]

Companies also need to be prepared to suffer losses when marketing brands in entirely new markets. For example, Coca-Cola withstood losses in Japan for 15 years before building the market to become one of its most profitable today. BSkyB was also prepared to incur losses while building its Sky satellite television brand for several years before recording its current high profits.

Internal marketing

Many brands are corporate in the sense that the marketing focus is on building the company brand.[42] This is particularly the case in services, with banks, supermarkets, insurance companies, airlines and restaurant chains attempting to build awareness and loyalty to the services they offer. A key feature in the success of such efforts is internal marketing—that is, training and communicating with internal staff. Training of staff is crucial because service companies rely on face-to-face contact between service provider (e.g. waiter) and service user (e.g. diner). Also, brand strategies must be communicated to staff so that they understand the company ethos on which the company brand is built. Investment in staff training is required to achieve the service levels required for the brand strategy. Top service companies like Federal Express, IBM and Singapore Airlines make training a central element of their company brand-building plans.

Besides incorporating the above factors into brand-building plans, it can be useful to examine the reasons for brand failure so that they can be avoided. Marking in Action 9.3 discusses some of the reasons for failure.

 **9.3 Marketing in Action**

Here Today, Gone Tomorrow: Some Reasons for Brand Failure

Brands live in an unforgiving, harsh environment. Their survival depends on many factors, and their demise can be swift when they are not met. Here are some reasons that explain why brands have disappeared from the marketplace.

- *Failure to live up to the taste test*: Mars' Banjo artificial chocolate and its low-fat chocolate bar Flyte, Jordans' cereal bar, and Nabisco's Snackwell's low-fat, low-sugar biscuits and cakes failed the taste test. The lesson is that healthy snacks need to taste delicious too.
- *Outgunned by a more powerful rival*: KP's Brannigans crisps were popular until PepsiCo acquired Walkers and decided to invest heavily in technical and product innovation, raw materials and, especially, marketing. The result was that Brannigans floundered while Walkers became brand leader.
- *Unsustainable novelty value*: Pot Noodle, Space Dust and alcopops all found life difficult after their initial novelty value wore off.
- *Manufacturer neglect or impatience*: Cadbury's Fuse bar, Biarritz chocolates and Unilever's Radion clothing detergent suffered because of neglect. Although the Fuse bar did well in research and on launch, Cadbury failed to invest in advertising and promotion, and eventually discontinued the line.
- *Changes in consumer motivations*: Sunny Delight was initially very successful, but as consumers became more health conscious its high sugar content brought about its demise.
- *Losing the war*: technology battles often have only one winner. For example, Sony's Betamax video format was beaten by JVC's VHS, and Sony's Blu-Ray DVD killed off the Toshiba-backed HD DVD format, largely because the former gained the support of most of the Hollywood film studios.

Based on: Simms (2008)[43]

Key Branding Decisions

Besides the branding decisions so far discussed, marketers face four further key branding decisions: brand name strategies and choices, rebranding, brand extension and stretching, and co-branding.

Brand name strategies and choices

Another key decision area is the choice of brand name. Three brand name strategies can be identified: family, individual and combination.

Family brand names

A **family brand name** is used for all products (e.g. Philips, Microsoft, Heinz, Motorola). The goodwill attached to the family brand name benefits all brands, and the use of the name in advertising helps the promotion of all of the brands carrying the family name. The risk is that if one of the brands receives unfavourable publicity or is unsuccessful, the reputation of the whole range of brands can be tarnished. This is also called umbrella branding. Some companies create umbrella brands for part of their brand portfolios to give coherence to their range of products. For example, Lego created the umbrella brand of Duplo for its range of bricks and toys targeting small children.

Individual brand names

An **individual brand name** does not identify a brand with a particular company (e.g. Procter & Gamble does not use the company name on brands such as Ariel, Fairy Liquid, Daz and Pampers). This may be necessary when it is believed that each brand requires a separate, unrelated identity. In some instances, the use of a family brand name when moving into a new market segment may harm the image of the new product line. An example was the decision to use the Levi's family brand name on a new product line—Levi's Tailored Classics—despite marketing research information which showed that target customers associated the name Levi's with casual clothes, which was incompatible with the smart suits it was launching. This mistake was not repeated by Toyota, which abandoned its family brand name when it launched its upmarket executive car, which was simply called the Lexus. BMW also chose not to attach its family brand name to the Mini since it would have detracted from the car's sense of 'Britishness'.

Combination brand names

A *combination brand name* combines family and individual brand names to capitalize on the reputation of the company, while allowing the individual brands to be distinguished and identified (e.g. Levi's 501, Volkswagen Golf, Microsoft Windows 7).

Criteria for choosing brand names

The choice of brand name should be carefully thought out since names convey images. For example, Renault chose the brand name Safrane for one of its executive saloons because research showed that the brand name conveyed the image of luxury, exotica, high technology and style. The brand name Pepsi Max was chosen for Pepsi's diet cola targeted at men as it conveyed a masculine image in a product category that was associated with women. So one criterion for deciding on a good brand name is that it evokes *positive associations*.

A second criterion is that the brand name should be easy to *pronounce and remember*. Short names such as Esso, Shell, Daz, Ariel, Orange and Mini fall into this category. There are exceptions to this general rule, as in the case of Häagen-Dazs, which was designed to sound European in the USA where it was first launched. A brand name may suggest *product benefits*, such as Right Guard (deodorant), Head & Shoulders (anti-dandruff shampoo), MacBook Air

Brand name considerations	TABLE 9.2
A good brand name should:	
1. evoke positive associations	
2. be easy to pronounce and remember	
3. suggest product benefits	
4. be distinctive	
5. use numerals or alphanumerics when emphasizing technology	
6. be transferable	
7. not infringe on an existing registered brand name	

(light computer), or express what the brand is offering in a *distinctive way* such as Toys 'Я' Us. Technological products may benefit from *numerical* brand naming (e.g. Airbus 380, Porsche 911) or *alphanumeric* brand names (e.g. Audi A4, Samsung F400). This also overcomes the need to change brand names when marketing in different countries.

The question of brand *transferability* is another brand name consideration. With the growth of global brands, names increasingly need to be able to cross geographical boundaries. Companies that do not check the meaning of a brand name in other languages can be caught out, as when General Motors launched its Nova car in Spain only to discover later that the word meant 'it does not go' in Spanish. The lesson is that brand names must be researched for cultural meaning before being introduced into a new geographic market. One advantage of non-meaningful names such as Diageo and Exxon is that they transfer well across national boundaries.

Specialist companies have established themselves as brand name consultants. Market research is used to test associations, memorability, pronunciation and preferences. Legal advice is important so that a brand name *does not infringe an existing brand name*. Table 9.2 summarizes the issues that are important when choosing a brand name.

Brand names can also be categorized, as shown in Table 9.3.

Rebranding

The act of changing a brand name is called **rebranding**. It can occur at the product level (e.g. Treets to M&M's) and the corporate level (e.g. One2One to T-Mobile). Table 9.4 gives some examples of name changes. Rebranding is risky and the decision should not be taken lightly. The abandonment of a well-known and, for some, favourite brand runs the risk of customer confusion and resentment, and loss of market share. When Coca-Cola was rebranded (and reformulated) as New Coke, negative customer reaction forced the company

Brand name categories	TABLE 9.3
People	Cadbury, Mars, Heinz, Marriott, Bang & Olufsen, Louis Vuitton
Places	Singapore Airlines, Deutsche Bank, Air France
Descriptive	T-Mobile, Body Shop, Federal Express, Airbus, Weetabix
Abstract	KitKat, Kodak, Prozac, IKEA
Evocative	iPod, Orange, Apple, Häagen-Dazs, Dove
Brand extensions	Diet Coke, Pepsi Max, Lucozade Sport
Foreign meanings	Lego (from 'play well' in Danish)
Source: updated from Miller (1999)[44]	

Brand name changes			TABLE 9.4
Product level		**Corporate level**	
Old name	**New name**	**Old name**	**New name**
Treets/Bonitos	M&M's	One2One	T-Mobile
Marathon	Snickers	BT Wireless	O_2
Jif/Cif/Vif/Vim	Cif	Grand Metropolitan/Guinness	Diageo
Raider	Twix	Post Office	Royal Mail Group
Virgin One	The One Account	Airtours	MyTravel
Wanadoo	Orange	Ciba-Geigy/Sandoz	Novartis
ntl	Virgin	Andersen Consulting	Accenture
		Norwich Union	Aviva

to withdraw the new brand and reinstate the original brand.[45] Similarly, the move to rebrand the Post Office as Consignia was met with objections from consumers, employees and the media. The result was a reversal of the decision, with the Royal Mail Group corporate name chosen instead.

Why rebrand?

Despite such well-publicized problems, rebranding is a common activity. The reasons are as follows.[46]

Merger or acquisition

When a merger or acquisition takes place a new name may be chosen to identify the new company. Sometimes a combination of the original corporate names may be chosen (e.g. when Glaxo Wellcome and SmithKline Beecham formed GlaxoSmithKline), a completely new name may be preferred (e.g. when Grand Metropolitan and Guinness became Diageo) or the stronger corporate brand name may be chosen (e.g. when Nestlé acquired Rowntree Mackintosh).

Desire to create a new image/position in the marketplace

Some brand names are associated with negative or old-fashioned images. The move by BT Wireless to drop its corporate brand name was because it had acquired an old fashioned, bureaucratic image. The new brand name O_2 was chosen because it sounded scientific and modern, and because focus groups saw their mobile phones as an essential part of their lives (like oxygen).[47] The negative image of the cable television company ntl, caused by poor service, was part of the reason for buying Virgin Mobile, which allows it to use under licence the Virgin brand across its consumer businesses.[48] Similar motivations were behind the rebranding of Andersen Consulting to Accenture. Image considerations were also prominent when, after the acquisition of Orange, France Telecom decided to drop its Wanadoo brand in favour of Orange. Also the negative association of the word 'fried' in Kentucky Fried Chicken stimulated the move to change the name to KFC.

Digital Marketing 9.1 discusses how video blogging can be used to help position a brand in the marketplace.

9.1 Digital Marketing

Fresh as the Mountain Dew: Video Blogging

Many companies are using digital technologies and the web to update and reposition their brands. Increasingly, multimedia applications such as video blogs are providing a communication channel, which is thought to hit the mark—especially with teenage audiences. Notably, Gordon Brown, the UK Prime Minister, who reportedly has a 'dour image' uses such technology widely as a mechanism to communicate with younger target audiences. Indeed, via YouTube, he invites us to 'ask the PM'.

PepsiCo is a global brand that appears to be making use of video blogs as part of its campaign to stimulate sales and develop some of its markets for its core soft drinks brands. For example, Mountain Dew has suffered declining sales faster than Diet and Classic Coke Cola in the overall slowdown in the soft drinks market in North America. In October 2008, PepsiCo announced that Mountain Dew would have new logos and branding in order to reposition the brand in the hearts and minds of target audiences, who in the USA are typically 12–30-year-old males. Voltage is the brand extension, which is a central part of the campaign. Additionally, it was announced that Mountain Dew (Mtn Dew and a new logo), would be coming to the UK. The drink was available in the late 1990s in the UK market but was withdrawn due to poor sales. In the USA, the brand positioning aims to connect with young males by making associations with extreme sports and the video game culture. It seems that PepsiCo is benefiting from video blogging sites, which are stimulating discussion and interest in the brand in the UK through the use of sites such as YouTube. Hoax recipes have appeared, which demonstrate how to make 'the mountain dew glow' a green light, which is produced by mixing baking soda and Mountain Dew. Fans of the 'Dew' have also created a website to campaign for the reintroduction of Mountain Dew to the UK.

Based on: Sicher (2008);[49] www.hodgson.trelader.btinternet.co.uk/index.htm; www.youtube.com/watch?v=u3gusfHO_vY

The sale or acquisition of parts of a business

The sale of the agricultural equipment operations of the farm equipment maker International Harvester prompted the need to change its name to Navistar. The acquisition of the Virgin One financial services brand by the Royal Bank of Scotland from the Virgin Group necessitated the dropping of the Virgin name. The new brand is called The One Account.

Corporate strategy changes

When a company diversifies out of its original product category, the original corporate brand name may be considered too limiting. This is why Esso (Standard Oil) changed its name to Exxon as its product portfolio extended beyond oil. Also British Steel has become Corus (now owned by Tata Steel) as the company widens its products beyond steel.

Brand familiarity

Sometimes the name of a major product brand owned by a company becomes so familiar to customers that it supersedes the corporate brand. In these circumstances the company may decide to discard the unfamiliar name in favour of the familiar. That is why Consolidated Foods became Sara Lee and BSN became Danone.

International marketing considerations

A major driver for rebranding is the desire to harmonize a brand name across national boundaries in order to create a global brand. This was the motivation for the change of the Marathon chocolate bar name in the UK to Snickers, which was used in continental Europe, the dropping of the Treets and Bonitos names in favour of M&M's, the move from Raider to Twix chocolate bars, the consolidation of the Unilever cleaning agent Jif/Cif/Vif/Vim to Cif, Norwich Union to Aviva, and the One2One brand in the UK to T-Mobile, which is used by its parent company Deutsche Telecom in Germany. Companies may also change brand names to discourage parallel importing. When sales of a premium-priced brand in some countries are threatened by re-imports of the same brand from countries where the brand is sold at lower prices, rebranding may be used to differentiate the product. This is why the Italian cleaning agent Viakal was rebranded in some European countries as Antikal.

Legal problems

A brand name may contravene an existing legal restriction on its use. For example, the Yves St Laurent perfume brand Champagne required a name change because the brand name was protected for use only with the sparkling wine from the Champagne region of France.

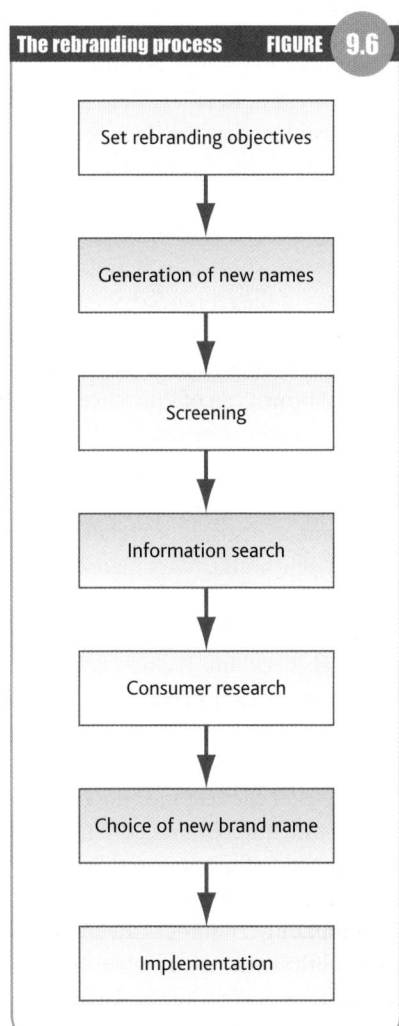

The rebranding process FIGURE 9.6

Set rebranding objectives → Generation of new names → Screening → Information search → Consumer research → Choice of new brand name → Implementation

Managing the rebranding process

Rebranding is usually an expensive, time-consuming and risky activity, and should only be undertaken when there is a clear marketing and financial case in its favour and a strong marketing plan in place to support its implementation.[50] Management should recognize that a rebranding exercise cannot of itself rectify more deep-seated marketing problems.

Once the decision to rebrand has been made, two key decisions remain: choosing the new name and implementing the name change.

Choosing the new brand name

The issues discussed earlier in this chapter regarding choosing brand names are relevant when changing an existing name. These are that the new brand name should evoke positive associations, be easy to pronounce and remember, suggest positive benefits, be distinctive, be transferable, not infringe an existing registered brand name, and consideration should be given to the use of numerals when emphasizing technology. These issues should form the basis of the first step, setting the rebranding objectives (see Fig. 9.6). For example, a key objective of the new name might be that it should be easily remembered, evoke positive associations and be transferable across national boundaries.

The second step is to generate as many brand names as possible. Potential sources of names include consumers, employees, distributors, specialist brand name consultants and advertising agencies.

The third step is to screen the names to remove any with obvious flaws, such as those that are difficult to pronounce, too close to an existing name, have adverse double meanings and do not fit with the rebranding objectives. The objective is to reduce the names to a shortlist of around 6–12. The fourth step, an information search is carried out to check that each name does not infringe on an existing registered brand name in each country where the brand is, or may be, marketed.

The fifth step is to test the remaining names through consumer research. The key criteria, such as memorability, associations and distinctiveness, chosen in step one (rebranding objectives) will be used to assess the performance of the new names. Finally, management will assess the virtues of each of the shortlisted brand names and come to a conclusion about which one should be chosen and registered.

Implementing the name change

Name changes can meet considerable resistance from consumers, employees and distributors. All three groups can feel that their loyalty to a brand has been betrayed. Attention also has to be paid to the media and financial institutions, particularly for corporate name changes. It was such resistance that blocked the mooted renaming of the Post Office as Consignia. Careful thought needs to be given to how the name change should be implemented so that all interested parties understand the logic behind the change and support it. Implementation requires attention to five key issues, as described below.[51]

1 *Coordination*: the delicacy of the name change requires harmonious working between the company departments and those groups most involved—marketing, production, the salesforce, logistics and general management. All must work together to avoid problems and solve any that may arise.

2 *Communication*: consumers, employees and distributors need to be targeted with communications that notify them early and with a full explanation. When the chocolate bar known as Raider in continental Europe changed its name to Twix, which was the name used everywhere else, consumers in Europe were informed by a massive advertising campaign (two years' advertising budget was spent in three weeks). Retailers were told of the name change well in advance by a salesforce whose top priority was the Twix brand. Trial was encouraged by promotional activities at retail outlets. The result was a highly successful name change and the creation of a global brand.

3 *Understanding what the consumer identifies with the brand*: consumer research is required to fully understand what consumers identify as the key characteristics of the brand. Shell made the mistake of failing to include the new colour (yellow) of the rebranded Shell Helix Standard in its advertising, which stressed only the name change from Puissance 7 in France. Unfortunately customers, when looking for their favourite brand of oil, paid most attention to the colour of the can. When they could not find their usual brown can of Puissance 7 they did not realize it had been changed to a yellow can with a name they were not familiar with. The lesson is that advertising for a rebrand should have shown consumers that the colour of the can had changed as well as focusing on the name change from Puissance to Helix.

4 *Providing assistance to distributors/retailers*: to avoid confusion at distributors/retailers, manufacturers should avoid double-stocking of the old and new brand. Mars management took great care to ensure that on the day of the transfer from Raider to Twix, no stocks of Raider would be found in the shops, even if this meant buying back stock. The barcode should be kept the same so that no problems occur at optical checkouts. If a new code is used there is the chance it might not be registered correctly in the store's computer system.

5 *Speed of change*: consideration should be given to whether the change should be immediate (as with Twix) or subject to a transitional phase where, for example, the old name is retained (perhaps in small letters) on the packaging after the rebrand (the Philips name was retained on all Whirlpool household appliances, which were branded Philips Whirlpool in Europe for seven years after the companies joined to form the world's largest household appliance group). Old names are retained during a transitional period when the old name has high awareness and positive associations among consumers. Retaining an old brand name following a takeover may be wise for political reasons, as when Nestlé retained the Rowntree name on its brands for a few years after its takeover of the UK confectionery company.

Brand Extension and Stretching

A brand extension is the use of an established brand name on a new brand within the same broad market or product category. For example, the Anadin brand name has been extended to related brands: Anadin Extra, Maximum Strength, Soluble, Paracetamol and Ibuprofen. The Lucozade brand has undergone a very successful brand extension with the introduction of Lucozade Sport, with isotonic properties that help to rehydrate people more quickly than other drinks, and replace the minerals lost through perspiration. Lucozade Sport has itself been extended, as the advertisement shows. Unilever has successfully expanded its Dove soap brand into deodorants, shower gel, liquid soap and body-wash.[52] Coca-Cola has extended its Coke brand into Diet Coke, which is shown here in its variant form: Diet Coke with cherry. Google has also extended its core brand by launching Froogle, Google Groups, Google Answers, Google Catalogues, Google Calendar, Google Maps, Google Street View, Google Gears and Google Book Search. These are examples of *line* extensions. An extreme form of brand extension is known as brand stretching. **Brand stretching** is when an established brand name is used for brands in unrelated markets or product categories, such as the use of the Yamaha pianos brand name on hi-fi equipment, skis and motorcycles. The Tommy Hilfiger brand has also been extended from clothing to fragrances, footwear and home furnishings.[53] Table 9.5 gives some examples of brand extensions and stretching.

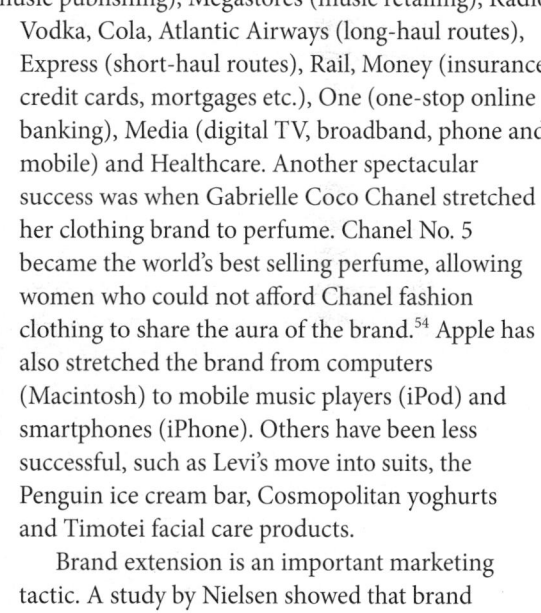

Some companies have used brand extensions and stretching very successfully. Richard Branson's Virgin company is a classic example. Beginning in 1970 as Virgin Records the company grew through Virgin Music (music publishing), Megastores (music retailing), Radio, Vodka, Cola, Atlantic Airways (long-haul routes), Express (short-haul routes), Rail, Money (insurance, credit cards, mortgages etc.), One (one-stop online banking), Media (digital TV, broadband, phone and mobile) and Healthcare. Another spectacular success was when Gabrielle Coco Chanel stretched her clothing brand to perfume. Chanel No. 5 became the world's best selling perfume, allowing women who could not afford Chanel fashion clothing to share the aura of the brand.[54] Apple has also stretched the brand from computers (Macintosh) to mobile music players (iPod) and smartphones (iPhone). Others have been less successful, such as Levi's move into suits, the Penguin ice cream bar, Cosmopolitan yoghurts and Timotei facial care products.

Brand extension is an important marketing tactic. A study by Nielsen showed that brand extensions account for approximately 40 per cent of new grocery launches.[55] Two key advantages of brand extension in releasing new products are that it reduces risk and is less costly than alternative launch strategies.[56] Both distributors and consumers may perceive less risk if the new brand comes with an established brand name. Distributors may be reassured about the 'saleability' of the new

◀ This advertisement illustrates how the Lucozade Sport brand has evolved and been extended over the years. The extensions mean that the brand can meet the diverse needs of consumers.

Brand extensions and stretching		TABLE 9.5
Brand (line) extensions	**Brand stretching**	
Anadin brand name used for Anadin Extra, Maximum Strength, Soluble, Paracetamol and Ibuprofen	Cadbury (confectionery) launched Cadbury's Cream Liqueur	
Guinness launched Guinness draught beer in a can and Guinness Extra Cold	Yamaha (pianos) brand name used on motor cycles, hi-fi, skis, pianos and summerhouses	
Lucozade extends to Lucozade Sport, Energy, Hydroactive and Carbo Gel	Pierre Cardin (clothing) brand name used on toiletries, cosmetics, etc.	
United Distillers used Johnnie Walker brand name for liqueur	Bic (disposable pens) brand name used on lighters, razors and perfumes	
Unilever used Dove brand name for deodorants, shower gel, liquid soap and body wash	Tommy Hilfiger brand name used on fragrances, footwear and home furnishings	
Diageo used Smirnoff brand name for the premium packaged spirit sector (Smirnoff Ice and Black Ice)	Harley-Davidson brand name used on toys and clothing ranges	

brand and therefore be more willing to stock it. Consumers appear to attribute the quality associations they have of the original brand to the new one.[57] An established name enhances consumer interest and willingness to try the new brand.[58] Consumer attitudes towards brand extensions are more favourable when the perceived quality of the parent brand is high.[59]

Launch costs can also be reduced by using brand extension. Since the established brand name is already well known, the task of building awareness of the new brand is eased. Consequently, advertising, selling and promotional costs are reduced. Furthermore, there is the likelihood of achieving advertising economies of scale since advertisements for the original brand and its extensions reinforce each other.[60]

A further advantage of brand extensions is that the introduction of the extension can benefit the core brand because of the effects of the accompanying marketing expenditure. Sales of the core brand can rise due to the enhancement of consumers' perception of brand values and image through increased communication.[61]

However, these arguments can be taken too far. Brand extensions that offer no functional, psychological or price advantage over rival brands often fail.[62] Consumers shop around, and brand extensions that fail to meet expectations will be rejected. There is also the danger that marketing management under-funds the launch believing that the spin-off effects from the original brand name will compensate. This can lead to low awareness and trial. *Cannibalization,* which refers to a situation where the new brand gains sales at the expense of the established brand, can also occur. For example, additional flavour extensions of the Absolut Vodka brand were found to cannibalize sales of existing ones, leading to a refocus on the original brand.[63] Further, brand extension has been criticized as leading to a managerial focus on minor modifications, packaging changes and advertising rather than the development of real innovations.[64] There is also the danger that bad publicity for one brand

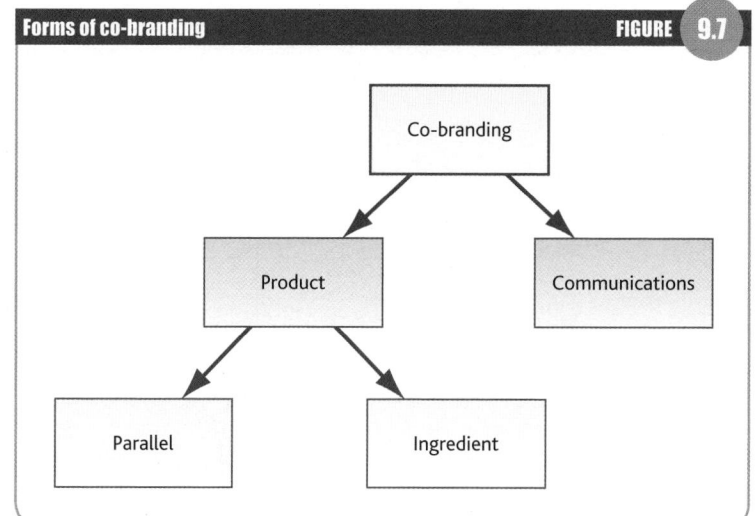

Forms of co-branding   FIGURE **9.7**

```
                    ┌──────────────┐
                    │  Co-branding │
                    └──────────────┘
                       ╱        ╲
              ┌──────────┐   ┌───────────────┐
              │ Product  │   │ Communications│
              └──────────┘   └───────────────┘
                ╱      ╲
        ┌──────────┐  ┌──────────┐
        │ Parallel │  │Ingredient│
        └──────────┘  └──────────┘
```

affects the reputation of other brands under the same name. The Virgin brand name was in danger of being tarnished at one time due to poor punctuality of its trains under the Virgin Trains brand. Massive investment in new locomotives and rolling stock has cured the problem.[65] A related difficulty is the danger of the new brand failing or generating connotations that damage the reputation of the core brand. Both of these risks were faced by Guinness, whose core brand is stout, when it launched its canned beer under the Guinness brand name, and Mars when it extended the Mars brand name into ice cream.

However, research has shown that the danger of the brand extension damaging the reputation of the core brand is much greater when the brand is extended within its original line (as in the Anadin example), than when the brand is stretched into new product categories. For example, if Tag Heuer's mobile phone (the Meridiist) is unsuccessful, the damage to Tag Heuer's brand equity in its original category of watches is far less than if it produced a new line of watches that kept bad time.[66]

A major test of any brand extension opportunity is to ask if the new brand concept is compatible with the values inherent in the core brand. Mention has already been made of the failure to extend the Levi's brand name to suits in the USA partly as a result of consumers refusing to accept the casual, denim image of Levi's as being suitable for smart, exclusive clothing. Another example is Bic's attempt to stretch the brand into perfume. Bic misunderstood the choice criteria that drive perfume sales and how these clashed with its own brand image of being a cheap and disposable pen.[67] Other questionable brand extensions are a Harley-Davidson cake-decorating kit and a Ferrari-branded Segway (two-wheeled personal transporter).

Brand extensions, therefore, are not viable when a new brand is being developed for a target group that holds different values and aspirations from those in the original market segment. When this occurs the use of the brand extension tactic would detract from the new brand. The answer is to develop a separate brand name, as did Toyota with the Lexus, and Seiko with its Pulsar brand name developed for the lower-priced mass market for watches.

Finally, management needs to guard against the loss of credibility if a brand name is extended too far. This is particularly relevant when brand stretching. The use of the Pierre Cardin name for such disparate products as clothing, toiletries and cosmetics has diluted the brand name's credibility.[68]

Brand extensions are likely to be successful if they make sense to the consumer. If the values and aspirations of the new target segment(s) match those of the original segment, and the qualities of the brand name are likewise highly prized, then success is likely. The prime example is Marks & Spencer, which successfully extended from clothing to food based on its core values of quality and reliability.

Co-Branding

There are two major forms of co-branding: **product-based co-branding** and **communications-based co-branding** (see Fig. 9.7).

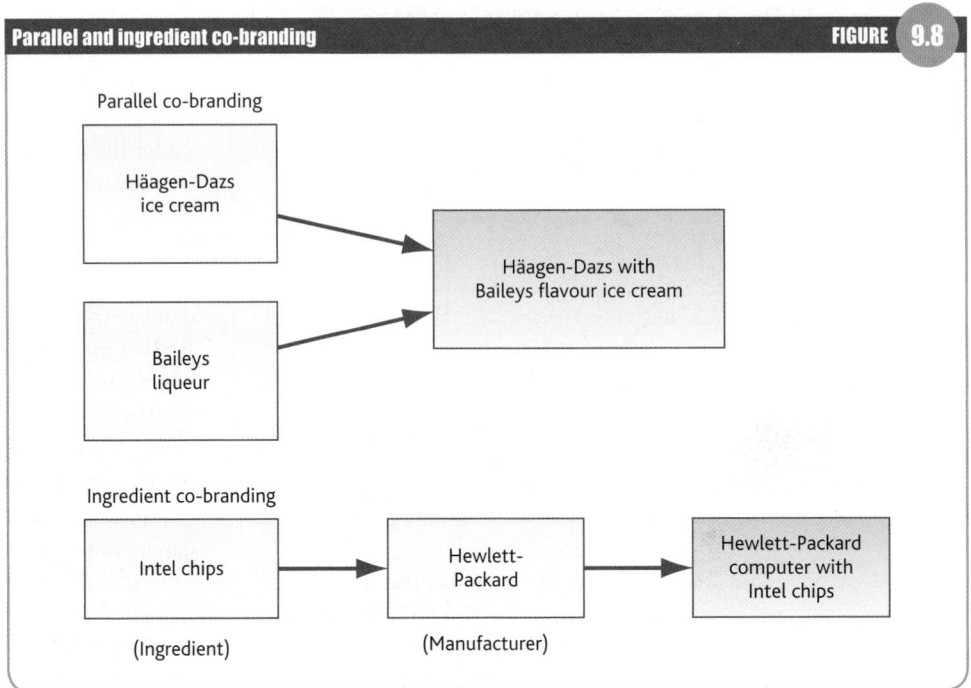

Parallel and ingredient co-branding FIGURE 9.8

Parallel co-branding

Häagen-Dazs ice cream

Baileys liqueur

Häagen-Dazs with Baileys flavour ice cream

Ingredient co-branding

Intel chips

Hewlett-Packard

Hewlett-Packard computer with Intel chips

(Ingredient)   (Manufacturer)

Product-based co-branding

Product-based co-branding involves the linking of two or more existing brands from different companies or business units to form a product in which the brand names are visible to consumers. There are two variants: parallel and ingredient co-branding. **Parallel co-branding** occurs when two or more independent brands join forces to produce a combined brand. An example is Häagen-Dazs ice cream and Baileys liqueur combining to form Häagen-Dazs with Baileys flavour ice cream. Two other examples are Siemens and Porsche Design, which produce a range of kettles, toasters and coffee machines under the Siemens Porsche co-brand, and Senseo Douwe Egberts coffee pods, created for use in the Philips Senseo coffee machine.[69]

Ingredient co-branding is found when one supplier explicitly chooses to position its brand as an ingredient of a product. Intel is an ingredient brand. It markets itself as a key component (ingredient) of computers. The ingredient co-brand is formed by the combination of the ingredient brand and the manufacturer brand—for example, Hewlett-Packard or Sony (as in the illustration). Usually the names and logos of both brands appear on the computer. Although Baileys liqueur may at first sight seem to be an ingredient brand it is not since its main market positioning is as an independent brand (a liqueur) not as an ingredient of ice cream.[70] Figure 9.8 shows the distinction between parallel and ingredient co-branding.

The advantages of product-based co-branding are as follows.

Added value and differentiation

The co-branding alliance of two or more brands can capture multiple sources of brand equity, and therefore add value and provide a point of differentiation. For example, the aforementioned combination of Häagen-Dazs ice cream with Baileys liqueur flavour creates a brand that adds value through the distinctive flavouring and differentiates the brand from competitive offerings. Another example is the alliance between Nike and Lego's 'Bionicle' action heroes to form 'Bionicle by Nike' trainers. The Bionicle brand adds value and differentiates the co-brand from other trainers.[71] The impact of product-based co-branding has been researched by Kodak, which showed that for a fictional entertainment product

SONY

Sony recommends Windows® XP Professional.

I'm a PC   I'm a Mac   I'M a Vaio

VAIO C series proves that performance doesn't have to come at the expense of style. The C15's got enough specs to impress the guy on the left – Intel® Centrino® Duo Mobile Technology with Intel® Core™2 Duo processors, built in LAN 802.11 wireless connectivity, a DVD+/-/RAM Writer and S-Video out to connect straight to your TV. What's more, it runs a stack of programs that aren't designed for the guy in the middle. With looks to kill, 5 cool colours and matching accessories, the VAIO C15 is available for just $1,999 RRP. Why be boring? **sony.com.au/iamvaio**

the non-pc pc

like.no.other   C series   VAIO

▲ The advertisement depicts Intel as an ingredient brand linked to the Sony Vaio laptop.

20 per cent of respondents said they would buy under the Kodak name and 20 per cent would buy under the Sony name. However, 80 per cent claimed they would buy if the product carried both names. Clearly the co-brand carried brand equity that was greater than the sum of its parts.[72] It was this synergistic effect that was the motivation for the Siemens Porsche co-brand.

Positioning

A co-brand can position a product for a particular target market. This was the reason Ford formed an alliance with *Elle* magazine to create the Ford Focus Elle, targeting women. The

Elle-branded Focus has features such as heated leather seats, metallic livery and special wheels in order to appeal to women who choose cars on the basis of look and style. A five-page advertorial appeared in *Elle*, where the brand was positioned as a stylish fashion accessory.[73] Positioning was a key factor in the Senseo Douwe Egberts co-brand since the co-brand name clearly positions the coffee pods as being targeted at owners of the Philips Senseo coffee machine.

Reduction of cost of product introduction

Co-branding can reduce the cost of product introduction since two well-known brands are combined, accelerating awareness, acceptance and adoption.[74]

There are also risks involved in product-based co-branding, as described below.

Loss of control

Given that the co-brand is managed by two different companies (or at the very least different strategic business units of the same company) each company loses a degree of control over decision-making. There is potential for disagreement, misunderstanding and conflict.

Brand equity loss

Poor performance of the co-brand could have negative effects on the original brands. In particular, each or either of the original brands' image could be tarnished.

Communications-based co-branding

Communications-based co-branding involves the linking of two or more existing brands from different companies or business units for the purposes of joint communication. This type of co-branding can take the form of recommendation. For example, Ariel and Whirlpool launched a co-branded advertising campaign where Ariel was endorsed by Whirlpool.[75] In a separate co-branding campaign Whirlpool endorsed Finish Powerball dishwasher tablets. A second variant is when an alliance is formed to stimulate awareness and interest, and to provide promotional opportunities. A deal between McDonald's and Disney gave McDonald's exclusive global rights to display and promote material relating to new Disney movies in its stores. Disney gained from the awareness and interest that such promotional material provides, and McDonald's benefited from the in-store interest and the promotional opportunities, such as competitions and free gifts (e.g. plastic replicas of film characters), the alliance provides. Communications-based co-branding can also result from sponsorship, where the sponsor's brand name appears on the product being sponsored. An example is Shell's sponsorship of the Ferrari Formula One motor racing team. As part of the deal the Shell brand name appears on Ferrari cars.

The advantages of communications-based co-branding are as follows.

Endorsement opportunities

As we have seen, Whirlpool and Ariel engaged in mutual endorsement in their advertising campaign. Endorsement may also be one-way: Shell gains by being associated with the highly successful international motor racing brand, Ferrari.

Cost benefits

One of the parties in the co-brand may provide resources to the other. Shell's deal with Ferrari demands that Shell pays huge sums of money, which helps Ferrari support the costs of motor racing. Also, joint advertising alliances mean that costs can be shared.

Awareness and interest gains

The McDonald's/Disney alliance meant that new Disney movies are promoted in McDonald's outlets, enhancing awareness and interest.

Promotional opportunities

As we have discussed, McDonald's gained by the in-store promotional opportunities afforded by its co-branding alliance with Disney.

The risks involved in communications-based co-branding are similar to those of product-based co-branding.

Loss of control

Each party to the co-branding activity loses some of its control to the partner. For example, in joint advertising there could be conflicts arising from differences of opinion regarding creative content and the emphasis given to each brand in the advertising.

Brand equity loss

No one wants to be associated with failure. The poor performance of one brand could tarnish the image of the other. For example, an unsuccessful Disney movie prominently promoted in McDonald's outlets could rebound on the latter. Conversely, bad publicity for McDonald's might harm the Disney brand by association. Indeed, the Disney/McDonald's partnership was terminated by Disney, amid rumours that it did not want to be associated with a brand that had received unfavourable publicity about unhealthy eating.[76]

Some examples of product and communications-based co-brands are given in Table 9.6.

Co-branding examples	TABLE 9.6
Parallel co-brands	
Häagen-Dazs and Baileys Cream Liqueur form Häagen-Dazs with Baileys flavour ice cream	
Ford Focus and *Elle* women's magazine form Ford Focus Elle car	
Nike and Lego Bionicle form 'Bionicle by Nike' trainers	
Siemens and Porsche Design form Siemens Porsche toasters, kettles and coffee machines	
Phillip Senseo and Douwe Egbert form Senseo Douwe Egbert coffee pods	
Ingredient co-brands	
Intel as component in Hewlett-Packard computers	
Nutrasweet as ingredient in Diet Coke	
Scotchgard as stain protector in fabrics	
Communications-based co-brands	
Ariel and Whirlpool: joint advertising campaign	
Shell and Ferrari: sponsorship	

Global and Pan-European Branding

Global branding is the achievement of brand penetration worldwide. Table 9.7 lists the brands that have achieved this to become top global brands. The USA is the clear market leader in achieving global brand success. The top brand in several European countries is also included.

Levitt is a champion of global branding, arguing that intensified competition and technological developments will force companies to operate globally, ignoring superficial

Some of the top global brands		TABLE 9.7
Brand	**Brand value ($ millions)**	**Country of ownership**
1. Coca-Cola	66,667	USA
2. IBM	59,031	USA
3. Microsoft	59,007	USA
4. GE	53,086	USA
5. Nokia	35,942	Finland
6. Toyota	34,050	Japan
7. Intel	31,261	USA
8. McDonald's	31,049	USA
9. Disney	29,251	USA
10. Google	25,590	USA
11. Mercedes-Benz	25,577	Germany
13. BMW	23,298	Germany
16. Louis Vuitton	21,602	France
17. H&M	13,840	Sweden
27. HSBC	13,143	UK
28. Nescafé	13,055	Switzerland
31. SAP	12,228	Germany
35. IKEA	10,913	Sweden
43. Philips	8,325	Netherlands
44. Gucci	8,254	Italy
48. Siemens	7,943	Germany

Source: based on Business Week/Interbrand Report (2008) Top Global Brands, *Business Week*, 29 September, 52–60

national differences.[77] A *global village* is emerging, where consumers seek reliable, quality products at a low price and the marketing task is to offer the same products and services in the same way, thereby achieving enormous global economies of scale. Levitt's position is that the new commercial reality is the emergence of global markets for standardized products and services on a previously unimagined scale. The engine behind this trend is the twin forces of customer convergence of tastes and needs, and the prospect of global efficiencies in production, procurement, marketing, and research and development. Japanese companies have been successful in achieving these kinds of economies to produce high-quality, competitively priced global brands (e.g. Toyota, Sony, Nikon and Fuji).

The creation of global brands also speeds up a brand's time to market by reducing time-consuming local modifications. The perception that a brand is global has also been found to affect positively consumers' belief that the brand is prestigious and of high quality.[78]

In Europe, the promise of pan-European branding has caused leading manufacturers to seek to extend their market coverage and to build their portfolio of brands. Nestlé has widened its brand portfolio by the acquisition of such companies as Rowntree (confectionery) and Buitoni-Perugina (pasta and chocolate), and has formed a joint venture (Cereal Partners) with the US giant General Mills to challenge Kellogg's in the European breakfast cereal market. Mars has replaced its Treets and Bonitos brands with M&M's, and changed the name of its third largest UK brand, Marathon, to the Snickers name used in the rest of Europe.

The counter-argument to global branding is that it is the exception rather than the rule. It has undoubtedly occurred with high-tech, rapid roll-out products such as audio equipment, cameras, video recorders and camcorders. Furthermore, some global successes, such as Coca-Cola, BMW, Gucci and McDonald's, can be noted, but national varieties in taste and consumption patterns will ensure that such achievements in the future will be limited. For example, the fact that the French eat four times more yoghurt than the British, and the British buy eight times more chocolate than the Italians reflects the kinds of national differences that will affect the marketing strategies of manufacturers.[79] Indeed, many so-called global brands are not standardized, claim the 'local' marketers. For example, Coca-Cola in Scandinavia tastes different from that in Greece.

9.2 Pause for Thought

Think of a global brand with which you are familiar. Why do you think it has been successful in the global marketplace?

The last example gives a clue to answering the dilemma facing companies that are considering building global brands. The question is not whether brands can be built on a global scale (clearly they can) but which parts of the brand can be standardized and which must be varied across countries. A useful way of looking at this decision is to separate out the elements that comprise the brand, as shown in Figure 9.9. Can brand name and image, advertising, service, guarantees, packaging, quality and design, and delivery be standardized or not?

Gillette's global success with its Sensor, Fusion and Mach 3 razors was based on a highly standardized approach: the product, brand name, the message 'The best a man can get', advertising visuals and packaging were standardized; only the voice-overs in the advertisement were changed to cater for 26 languages across Europe, the USA and Japan.

Lever Brothers found that, for detergent products, brand image and packaging could be standardized but the brand name, communications execution and brand formulation needed to vary across countries.[80] For example, its fabric conditioner used a cuddly teddy bear across

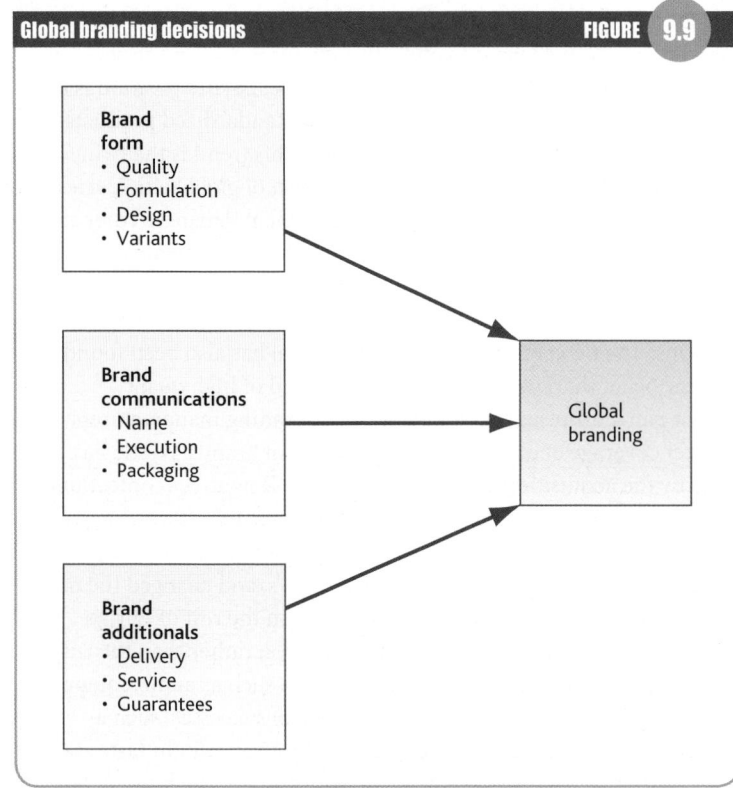

Global branding decisions FIGURE **9.9**

Brand form
- Quality
- Formulation
- Design
- Variants

Brand communications
- Name
- Execution
- Packaging

Brand additionals
- Delivery
- Service
- Guarantees

Global branding

countries but was named differently in Germany (Kuschelweich), France (Cajoline), Italy (Coccolini), Spain (Mimosin), the USA (Snuggle) and Japan (Fa-Fa). Brand image and packaging were the same but the name and formulation (fragrance, phosphate levels and additives) differed between countries.

In other circumstances, the brand form and additions may remain the same (or very similar) across countries but the brand communications may need to be modified. For example, a BMW car may be positioned as having an exclusive image but what Dutch and Italian car buyers consider are the qualities that amount to exclusiveness are very different.[81] Consequently, differing advertising appeals would be needed to communicate the concept of exclusiveness in these countries.

Much activity has taken place over recent years to achieve global and pan-European brand positions. There are three major ways of doing this, as outlined below.[82]

1 *Geographic extension*: taking present brands into the geographic markets.
2 *Brand acquisition*: purchasing brands.
3 *Brand alliance*: joint venture or partnerships to market brands in national or cross-national markets.

Developing global and pan-European brands FIGURE **9.10**

		Criteria for evaluation		
		Speed	Control	Investment
Strategy	Geographic expansion	Slow	High	Medium
	Brand acquisition	Fast	Medium	High
	Brand alliance	Moderate	Low	Low

Source: Barwise, P. and T. Robertson (1992) Brand Portfolios, *European Management Journal* 10(3), 279. Copyright © 1992 with kind permission from Elsevier Science Ltd.

Managers need to evaluate the strengths and weaknesses of each option, and Figure 9.10 summarizes these using as criteria speed of market penetration, control of operations and the level of investment required. Brand acquisition gives the fastest method of developing global brands. For example, Unilever's acquisition of Fabergé, Elizabeth Arden and Calvin Klein immediately made it a major player in fragrances, cosmetics and skincare. Brand alliance usually gives moderate speed. For example, the use of the Nestlé name for the Cereal Partners (General Mills and Nestlé) alliance's breakfast cereals (e.g. Cheerios, Shreddies and Shredded Wheat) in Europe helped retailer and consumer acceptance. Geographic extension is likely to be the slowest unless the company is already a major global player with massive resources, as brand building from scratch is a time-consuming process.

However, geographic extension provides a high degree of control since companies can choose which brands to globalize, and plan their global extensions. Brand acquisition gives a moderate degree of control although many may prove hard to integrate with in-house brands. Brand alliance fosters the lowest degree of control, as strategy and resource allocation will need to be negotiated with the partner.

Finally, brand acquisitions are likely to incur the highest level of investment. For example, Nestlé paid £2.5 billion for Rowntree, a figure that was over five times its net asset value and P&G paid £10 billion for brands owned by Gillette (Gillette, Duracell, Oral B and Braun). Geographic extension is likely to be more expensive than brand alliance since, in the latter case, costs are shared, and one partner may benefit from the expertise and distribution capabilities of the other. For example, in the Cereal Partners' alliance, General Mills gained access to Nestlé's expertise and distribution system in Europe. Although the specifics of each situation need to be carefully analysed, Figure 9.10 provides a framework for assessing the strategic alternatives when developing global and pan-European brands.

Corporate Identity Management

Managers also need to be aware of the importance of the corporate brand as represented by its corporate identity. **Corporate identity** represents the ethos, aims and values of an organization, presenting a sense of its individuality, which helps to differentiate it from its competitors. A key ingredient is visual cohesion, which is necessary to ensure that all corporate communications are consistent with each other and result in a corporate image in line with the organization's defining values and character. The objective is to establish a favourable reputation with an organization's stakeholders, which it is hoped will be translated into a greater likelihood of purchasing the organization's goods and services, and working for and investing in the organization.[83]

Corporate identity management has emerged as a key activity of senior marketing and corporate management because of the following developments.[84]

- Mergers, acquisitions and alliances have led to many new or significantly changed companies that require new identities (e.g. Diageo).
- Some existing companies have undertaken 're-imaging' by changing the reality of their activities and/or via their communications to make their activities/image more technology orientated (e.g. O_2).
- The emergence of dotcom and new media companies created many new company identities (e.g. Lastminute.com).

Corporate identity management is concerned with the conception, development and communication of an organization's ethos, aims (mission) and values. Its orientation is strategic and is based on a company's culture and behaviour. It differs from traditional brand marketing directed towards consumers or organizational purchases since it is concerned with all of an organization's stakeholders and the wide-ranging way in which an organization communicates. If managed well it can affect organizational performance by attracting and retaining customers, increasing the likelihood of creating beneficial strategic alliances, recruiting high-quality staff, being well positioned in financial markets, maintaining strong media relations and strengthening staff identification with the company.[85]

An example of the successful use of corporate identity management is Arcadis, an infrastructural engineering company with its headquarters in the Netherlands but with operations all over the world. A strong corporate identity was particularly important to give a sense of unity to a company that had grown largely through acquisition. The company believes that its identity, which brings with it a set of specific values, has produced benefits both for internal staff and external customers.[86]

Not all corporate identity activities are successful, however. An example is the repainting of British Airways' tail fins. Originally, all BA tail fins were the colour of the Union Jack, symbolizing its British heritage. In an attempt at global repositioning, most of them were repainted using the colours of the national emblems of many overseas countries. The move

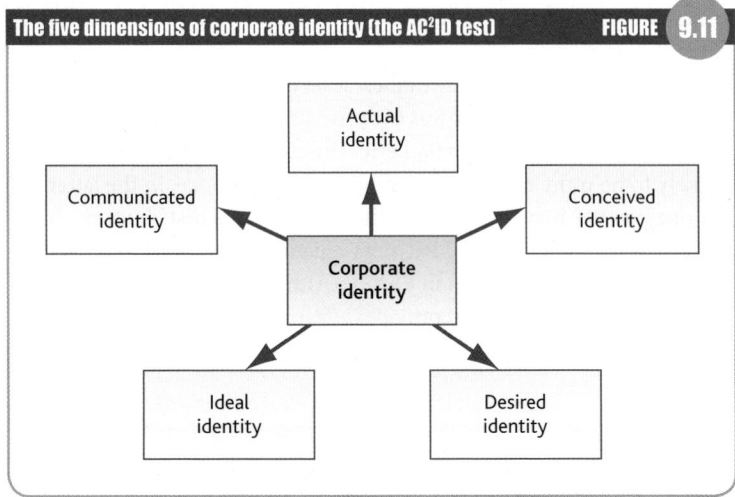

The five dimensions of corporate identity (the AC²ID test)   FIGURE 9.11

allegedly backfired as passengers, especially businesspeople, disliked the excessive variety in tail-fin design.[87] A second failure in corporate identity management was the ill-fated change in name from the Post Office to Consignia, discussed earlier in this chapter. The new name was designed to reflect a wider range of services (mail delivery, retail outlets and the delivery of packages) than the original name, the Post Office, suggested, and to facilitate entry into global markets under an international identity that could work well across national borders. However, implementation of the corporate identity change was not well managed, with consumers (and the media) believing that the name was to be used on Post Office retail outlets across the country. Furthermore, research showed that the brand values associated with one part of the Post Office, the Royal Mail, were very high. With the appointment of a new chairman, Allan Leighton and widespread derision of the Consignia name among the public, staff and media, the decision was taken to rename the company, the Royal Mail Group.[88]

Dimensions of corporate identity

A corporate identity can be broken down into five dimensions or identity types, namely actual identity, communicated identity, conceived identity, ideal identity and desired identity. This framework is called the AC²ID test and is shown in Figure 9.11. By analysing each dimension a company can test the effectiveness of its corporate identity.[89]

Each of these five dimensions will now be explained.

Actual identity

This represents the reality of the organization and describes what the organization is. It includes the type and quality of the products offered by the organization, the values and behaviour of staff, and the performance of the company. It is influenced by the nature of the corporate ownership, the leadership style of management, organization structure and management policies, and the structure of the industry.

Communicated identity

This is the identity the organization reveals through its 'controllable' corporate communication programme. Typically, communicational tools such as advertising, public relations, sponsorship and visual symbols (corporate names, logos, signs, letterheads, use of colour and design, and word font) are used to present an identity to stakeholders.

In addition, communicated identity may derive from 'non-controllable' communications such as word of mouth, media coverage and pressure groups such as Greenpeace. Figure 9.12 illustrates the elements of communicated identity.

Conceived identity

This refers to the perceptions of the organization held by relevant stakeholders such as customers, suppliers, distributors, shareholders, government, employees and the local community where the company operates. It reflects the corporate image and reputation held by these groups.

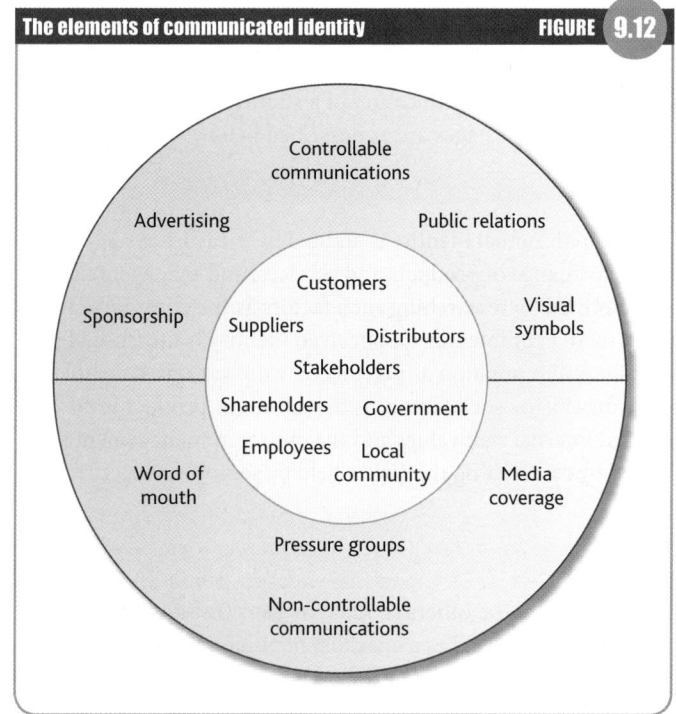

The elements of communicated identity FIGURE **9.12**

Ideal identity

This represents the optimum (best) positioning of the organization in its market or markets. It is normally based on a strategic analysis of the organization's capabilities and prospects in the light of its macro- and microenvironment.

Desired identity

This lives in the hearts and minds of corporate leaders. It is their vision for the organization. This can differ from the ideal identity, which is based on research and analysis. Desired identity is likely to be based on a chief executive's vision, which is influenced more by personality and ego than rational assessment of the organization's strategic position in the marketplace.

Companies, therefore, have multiple identities, and a lack of fit between any two or more of the identities can cause problems that may weaken the company. For example, corporate communications (communicated identity) may be at odds with reality (actual identity); corporate performance and behaviour (actual identity) may fall short of the expectations of key stakeholders (conceived identity); and what is communicated to stakeholders (communicated identity) may differ from what stakeholders perceive (conceived identity). Marketing in Action 9.4 examines a communicated–conceived identity gap at Hilton hotels.

9.4 Marketing in Action

Corporate Identity Misalignment at Hilton Hotels

An example of a gap between communicated and conceived identities is related to the Hilton hotel chain. In the face of financial difficulties, the US-based company sold off most of its non-American operations including the rights to the Hilton brand name internationally. The non-American operations and rights were acquired by the UK entertainment group Ladbrokes, resulting in the Hilton brand name being used by both the US-based Hilton and Ladbrokes. The two companies increasingly employed different communications strategies to support the Hilton brand in their markets.

This caused confusion among consumers and businesspeople who stayed at Hilton hotels in both markets. In corporate identity terms there was a gap between the widely held perception of Hilton as a single entity (conceived identity) and the two communicated identities. Eventually the two companies realized that this misalignment was weakening both corporate brands, and entered into a formal marketing and brand alliance, including visual identity, marketing programmes, technology and reservation systems.

Based on: Balmer and Greyser (2003)[90]

The AC²ID test, then, is a useful framework for assisting companies in researching, analysing and managing corporate identities. The next section explains how it can be used to do this.

Managing corporate identity programmes

Using the AC^2ID test to conduct a corporate identity audit has five stages, known as the $REDS^2$ AC^2ID Test Process.[91] This results in the identification of a strategy to resolve any gaps between the five identity dimensions. The stages are as described below.

Reveal the five identities

Each of the five identity types are audited. Actual identity is audited by measuring such elements as internal staff values, performance of products and services, and management style. Communicated identity is examined by researching such factors as the communications sent out from the organization and media commentary. Conceived identity is measured by such elements as the corporate image and reputation as perceived by the various stakeholder groups. Ideal identity is audited by measuring such factors as the optimum product features and performance, the optimum set of internal staff values and the optimum management style. Finally, desired identity is examined by researching the vision held by senior management, especially the chief executive.

Examine the 10 identity interfaces

Each identity dimension is then compared to the others so that any gaps (misalignments) can be identified. The 10 identity interfaces can be used as a checklist of potential problem areas. To illustrate this stage, Figure 9.13 shows five interfaces and the kinds of questions that should be asked.

Diagnose the situation

The questions posed at the previous stage form the foundation for diagnosing the situation. This involves providing answers to the following questions.
- What are the problems?
- What are their nature?
- What are the implications?

Select the interfaces for attention

Which interfaces should be brought into alignment? Account should be taken of the priorities and the feasibility of the required action.

Strategic choice

What kind of strategies are required to create the corporate identity change needed to bring the interfaces into alignment. Options include reality change (including culture change), modifications to communications strategies, strategic repositioning (including moving into new technologies) and changes in corporation vision and mission.

The $REDS^2$ AC^2ID Test Process, then, encourages management to address the following five questions.[92]

1 What is our current corporate identity?
2 What image is communicated by formal and informal communications?
3 What would be the ideal identity for the organization to acquire in the light of the organization's capabilities and in the light of its micro- and macroenvironment?
4 What corporate identity would senior managers wish their organization to have?
5 How can this required corporate identity be achieved?

As such it provides a practical framework for corporate identity management. It is simple, memorable, logical and operational and, therefore, is a useful tool for managers responsible for corporate branding, corporate communications and corporate identity.[93]

Examining corporate identity interfaces   FIGURE **9.13**

Source: adapted from Balmer, J. M. T. and G. B. Soenen (1999) The Acid Test of Corporate Identity Management, Journal of Marketing Management 15, 69–92

Ethical Issues Concerning Products

There are three major issues regarding ethical issues with products: product safety, planned obsolescence and deceptive packaging.

Product safety

A major concern about product safety has been the issue of the safety of genetically modified products. Vociferous pressure groups such as Greenpeace have spoken out about the dangers of genetic modification. This process allows scientists to manipulate the genetic code of plants to create new characteristics never seen in nature. They are able to isolate any one gene in an organism and insert it into a completely unrelated species. For example, scientists can inject a gene from a bacterium into a grape to make it resistant to viruses; they can engineer maize to make it drought resistant or create potato strains that resist pests.

People are sharply divided as to whether this can be safe. Although plant breeders have for thousands of years been tampering with the genes of plants through traditional cross-pollination of plants of the same species, genetic modification goes one step further as it allows scientists to cross the species barrier. This, its critics claim, is fundamentally unnatural.

Furthermore, they state, no scientist can be sure that all of this genetic manipulation can be safe. Such concerns, and the attendant publicity have led some supermarket chains to ban such produce from their shelves.

Supporters state that many new products are introduced with a certain degree of risk being acceptable. For example, a new pharmaceutical product may harm a tiny percentage of users but the utilitarianist principle of 'the greatest good for the greatest number' would support its launch. The World Trade Organization (WTO) and the US Government support GM technology, stating that it is not only safe but enables farmers to cut their production costs considerably. However, the EU remains sceptical, particularly when GM crops are grown next to traditional produce where strains can cross-pollinate, and GM food is absent from European supermarkets.[94]

It is the reality of modern-day business that new products, such as cars, pharmaceuticals and foods, undergo extensive safety testing before launch. Anything less would violate the consumer's 'right to safety'.

Concerns about product safety relate to tobacco (lung cancer), the levels of fat, sugar and salt in foods (obesity and heart problems), and sugar in soft drinks (obesity and tooth decay). Such issues have led to bans on tobacco advertising, the setting up of independent bodies to protect consumers' interests in the food and drinks industries, and reductions in the levels of fat, sugar and salt in many food and drink brands, particularly the level of sugar in food and soft drinks consumed by children. For example, Nestlé has reduced the level of sugar in its cereals targeted at children and reformulated its Rowntree range of children's sweets to make them free of artificial flavours and colours.[95]

Planned obsolescence

Many products are not designed to last a long time. From the producer's point of view this is sensible as it creates a repeat purchase situation. Hence, cars rust, clothes wear out and fashion items are replaced by the latest styles. Consumers accept that nothing lasts for ever, but the issue concerns what is an acceptable length of time before replacement is necessary. One driving force is competition. To quell the Japanese invasion, car manufacturers such as Ford and Volkswagen have made the body shells of their cars much more rust-resistant than before. Furthermore, it has to be recognized that many consumers welcome the chance to buy new clothes, new appliances with the latest features and the latest model of car. Critics argue that planned obsolescence reduces consumers' 'right to choose' since some consumers may be quite content to drive an old car so long as its body shell is free from rust and the car functions well. As we have noted, the forces of competition may act to deter the excesses of planned obsolescence.

Deceptive packaging

This can occur when a product appears in an oversized package to create the impression that the consumer is buying more than is the case. This is known as 'slack' packaging[96] and has the potential to deceive when the packaging is opaque. Products such as soap powders and breakfast cereals have the potential to suffer from 'slack' packaging. A second area where packaging may be deceptive is through misleading labelling. This may take the form of the sin of omission—for example, the failure of a package to state that the product contains genetically modified soya beans. This relates to the consumer's 'right to be informed', and can include the stating of ingredients (including flavouring and colourants), nutritional contents and country of origin on labels. Nevertheless, labelling can be misleading. For example, in the UK, 'country of origin' is only the last country where the product was 'significantly changed'. So oil pressed from Greek olives in France can be labelled 'French' and foreign imports that are packed in the UK can be labelled 'produce of the UK'. Consumers should be wary of loose terminology. For example, smoked bacon may well have received its 'smoked flavour' from a synthetic liquid solution, 'farm fresh eggs' are likely to be un-date-marked eggs of indeterminate age laid by battery hens, and 'farmhouse cheese' may not come from farmhouses but from industrial factories.[97]

The use of loose language and meaningless terms in the UK food and drink industry has been criticized by the Food Standards Agency (FSA). A list of offending words has been drawn up, which includes fresh, natural, pure, traditional and original. Recommendations regarding when it is reasonable to use certain words have been drawn up. For example, 'authentic' should only be used to emphasize the geographic origin of a product and 'home-made' should be restricted to the preparation of the recipe on the premises and must involve 'some degree of fundamental culinary preparation'. The FSA has also expressed concern about the use of meaningless phrases such as 'natural goodness' and 'country-style' and recommended that they should not be used.[98]

Branding and developing economies

Critics of branding accuse the practice of concentrating power and wealth in the hands of companies and economies that are already rich and powerful, whereas poor countries have to compete on price. A vociferous critic of branding is Naomi Klein,[99] who claims that branding concentrates power in the hands of the already rich and powerful, who exploit the labour force of developing countries by supporting the paying of low wages while charging high prices for their products.[100] Supporters of branding claim that it is not branding's fault that poor countries suffer from low wages and that by sourcing from those countries their economies benefit. They also point out that the companies accused of being the worst offenders, such as Nike and Gap, have taken steps to introduce ethical sourcing policies that apply when dealing with the developing world.

Online LearningCentre

When you have read this chapter

log on to the Online Learning Centre at www.mcgraw-hill.co.uk/textbooks/jobber to explore chapter-by-chapter test questions, links and further online study tools for marketing.

Review

1   The concept of a product, brand, product line and product mix
   • A product is anything that is capable of satisfying customer needs.
   • A brand is a distinctive product offering created by the use of a name, symbol, design, packaging, or some combination of these intended to differentiate it from its competitors.
   • A product line is a group of brands that are closely related in terms of the functions and benefits they provide.
   • A product mix is the total set of products marketed by a company.

2   The difference between manufacturer and own-label brands
   • Manufacturer brands are created by producers and bear their chosen brand name, whereas own-label brands are created and owned by distributors (e.g. supermarkets).

3 **The difference between a core and an augmented product (the brand)**

- A core product is anything that provides the central benefits required by customers (e.g. toothpaste cleans teeth). The augmented product is produced by adding extra functional and/or emotional values to the core product, and combining them in a unique way to form a brand.

4 **Why strong brands are important**

Strong brands are important because they:

- enhance company value
- positively affect consumer perceptions and preferences
- act as a barrier to competition because of their impact on consumer perceptions and preferences
- produce high profits through premium prices and high market share
- provide the foundation for brand extensions
- act as a form of quality certification, which aids consumers' decision-making process
- build trust among consumers.

5 **Brand equity, its components and the concept of brand valuation**

- Brand equity is a measure of the strength of a brand in the marketplace by adding tangible value to a company through the resulting sales and profits.
- It is composed of customer-based brand equity, which is the differential effect that brand knowledge has on consumer response to the marketing of that brand, and proprietary-based brand equity, which is derived from company attributes that deliver value to the brand.
- Sources of customer-based brand equity are brand awareness and brand image.
- Sources of proprietary-based brand equity are patents and channel relationships.
- Brand valuation is the process of estimating the financial value of an individual or corporate brand.

6 **How to build strong brands**

Strong brands can be built by:

- building quality into the core product
- creating a unique position in the marketplace based on an analysis of brand domain, brand heritage, brand values, brand assets, brand personality and brand reflection
- repositioning to take advantage of new opportunities
- using well-blended communications to create a clear position in the minds of the target audience
- being first into the market with a unique marketing proposition
- taking a long-term perspective
- using internal marketing to train staff in essential skills and to communicate brand strategies so that they understand the company ethos on which the company brand is built.

7 **The differences between family, individual and combined brand names, and the characteristics of an effective brand name**

- A family brand name is one that is used for all products in a range (e.g. Nescafé); an individual brand name does not identify a brand with a particular company (e.g. Procter & Gamble does not appear with Daz); a *combination brand name* combines family and individual brand names (e.g. Microsoft Windows).
- The characteristics of an effective brand name are that it should evoke positive associations, be easy to pronounce and remember, suggest product benefits, be distinctive, use numerics or alphanumerics when emphasizing technology, be transferable and not infringe on existing registered brand names.

8 **Why companies rebrand, and how to manage the process**

- Companies rebrand to create a new identity after merger or acquisition, to create a new image/position in the marketplace, following the sale or acquisition of parts of a business where the old name is no longer appropriate, following corporate strategy changes where the old name is considered too limiting, to reflect the fact that a major product brand is more familiar to consumers than the old corporate brand, for international marketing reasons (e.g. name harmonization across national borders), consolidation of brands within a national boundary, and in response to legal problems (e.g. restrictions on its use).

- Managing the rebranding process involves choosing the new brand name and implementing the name change.
- Choosing the new brand name has six stages: setting rebranding objectives, generation of new names, screening to remove any with obvious flaws, information search to identify any infringements of existing brand names, consumer research, and choice of new brand name.
- Implementing the name change requires attention to five key issues: coordination among departments and groups; communication to consumers, employees and distributors; discovering what consumers identify with the brand so that communications can incorporate all relevant aspects of the brand; provision of assistance to distributors/retailers so that the change takes place smoothly; and care over the speed of changeover.

9 The concepts of brand extension and stretching, their uses and limitations
- A brand extension is the use of an established brand name on a new brand within the same broad market or product category; brand stretching occurs when an established brand is used for brands in unrelated markets or product categories.
- Their advantages are that they reduce perceived risk of purchase on the part of distributors and consumers, the use of the established brand name raises consumers' willingness to try the new brand, the positive associations of the core brand should rub off on to the brand extension, the awareness of the core brand lowers advertising and other marketing costs, and the introduction of the extension can raise sales of the core brand due to the enhancement of consumers' perception of brand values and image through increased communication.
- The limitations are that poor performance of the brand extension could rebound on the core brand, the brand may lose credibility if stretched too far, sales of the extension may cannibalize sales of the core brand and the use of a brand extension strategy may encourage a focus on minor brand modifications rather than true innovation.

10 The two major forms of co-branding, and their advantages and risks
- The two major forms are product-based (parallel and ingredient) co-branding and communications-based co-branding.
- The advantages of product-based co-branding are added value and differentiation, the enhanced ability to position a brand for a particular target market, and the reduction of the cost of product introduction.
- The risks of product-based co-branding are loss of control and potential brand equity loss if poor performance of the co-brand rebounds on the original brands.
- The advantages of communications-based co-branding are endorsement opportunities, cost benefits, awareness and interest gains, and promotional opportunities.
- The risks of communications-based co-branding are loss of control, and potential brand equity loss.

11 The arguments for and against global and pan-European branding, and the strategic options for building such brands
- The arguments 'for' are that intensified global competition and technological developments, customer convergence of tastes and needs, and the prospect of global efficiencies of scale will encourage companies to create global brands.
- The arguments 'against' are that national varieties in taste and consumption patterns will limit the development of global brands.
- The strategic options are geographic extension, brand acquisition and brand alliances.

12 The dimensions of corporate identity
There are five dimensions (the AC^2ID test):
- actual identity represents the reality of the organization and describes what the organization is
- communicated identity is what is revealed through the organization's 'controllable' corporate communications programme and through 'non-controllable' communication such as word of mouth
- conceived identity refers to the perceptions of the organization held by relevant stakeholders
- ideal identity represents the organization's best positioning in its market(s)
- desired identity is what lives in the hearts and minds of corporate leaders, in particular the chief executive's vision.

13 The management of corporate identity programmes
This involves conducting an audit based on the REDS[2] AC[2]ID Test Process to:
- reveal the five identities
- examine the 10 identity interfaces
- diagnose the situation
- select the interfaces for attention
- address strategic choice.

14 Ethical issues concerning products
- These are product safety, planned obsolescence, deceptive packaging, and branding and developing economies.

Key Terms

augmented product the core product plus extra functional and/or emotional values combined in a unique way to form a brand

brand a distinctive product offering created by the use of a name, symbol, design, packaging, or some combination of these intended to differentiate it from its competitors

brand assets the distinctive features of a brand

brand domain the brand's target market

brand equity a measure of the strength of a brand in the marketplace by adding tangible value to a company through the resulting sales and profits

brand extension the use of an established brand name on a new brand within the same broad market or product category

brand heritage the background to the brand and its culture

brand personality the character of a brand described in terms of other entities such as people, animals and objects

brand reflection the relationship of the brand to self-identity

brand stretching the use of an established brand name for brands in unrelated markets or product categories

brand valuation the process of estimating the financial value of an individual or corporate brand

brand values the core values and characteristics of a brand

combination brand name a combination of family and individual brand names

communications-based co-branding the linking of two or more existing brands from different companies or business units for the purposes of joint communication

core product anything that provides the central benefits required by customers

corporate identity the ethos, aims and values of an organization, presenting a sense of its individuality, which helps to differentiate it from its competitors

customer-based brand equity the differential effect that brand knowledge has on consumer response to the marketing of that brand

family brand name a brand name used for all products in a range

fighter brands low-cost manufacturers' brands introduced to combat own-label brands

global branding achievement of brand penetration worldwide

individual brand name a brand name that does not identify a brand with a particular company

ingredient co-branding the explicit positioning of a supplier's brand as an ingredient of a product

manufacturer brands brands that are created by producers and bear their chosen brand name

own-label brands brands created and owned by distributors or retailers

parallel co-branding the joining of two or more independent brands to produce a combined brand

product-based co-branding the linking of two or more existing brands from different companies or business units to form a product in which the brand names are visible to consumers

product line a group of brands that are closely related in terms of the functions and benefits they provide

product mix the total set of products marketed by a company

proprietary-based brand equity is derived from company attributes that deliver value to the brand

rebranding the changing of a brand or corporate name

Study Questions

1. Why do companies develop core products into brands?

2. Suppose you were the marketing director of a medium-sized bank. How would you tackle the job of building the company brand?

3. Think of five brand names. To what extent do they meet the criteria of good brand naming as laid out in Table 9.2? Do any of the names legitimately break these guidelines?

4. Do you think that there will be a large increase in the number of pan-European brands over the next 10 years or not? Justify your answer.

5. What are the strategic options for pan-European brand building? What are the advantages and disadvantages of each option?

6. Why do companies rebrand product and corporate names? What is necessary for successful implementation of the rebranding process?

7. What are the two main forms of co-branding? What are their advantages and risks?

8. Describe the five dimensions of corporate identity. How can an analysis of these dimensions and their interfaces aid the management of corporate identity?

9. Discuss the major ethical concerns relating to products.

References

1. DeKimpe, M. C., J.-B. E. M. Steenkamp, M. Mellens and P. Vanden Abeele (1997) Decline and Variability in Brand Loyalty, *International Journal of Research in Marketing* 14, 405–20.
2. De Chernatony, L. (1991) Formulating Brand Strategy, *European Management Journal* 9(2), 194–200.
3. Keller, K. L. (2003) *Strategic Brand Management*, New Jersey: Pearson.
4. East, R. (1997) *Consumer Behaviour*, Hemel Hempstead: Prentice-Hall Europe.
5. Wiggins, J. (2006) Unilever Set to Take on Own-Brand Competition, *Financial Times*, 10 February, 20.
6. Bokaie, J. (2007) Too Much of a Good Thing, *Marketing*, 30 April, 15.
7. Fisk, P. (2005) Proving Marketing's Worth, *Marketing*, 31 March, 27.
8. Simms, J. (2001) The Value of Disclosure, *Marketing*, 2 August, 26–7.
9. De Chernatony, L. and M. H. B. McDonald (2003) *Creating Powerful Brands*, Oxford: Butterworth-Heinemann.
10. Doyle, P. and P. Stern (2006) *Marketing Management and Strategy*, Hemel Hempstead: Prentice-Hall.
11. Valantine, M. (2009) It's All in the Mind, *Marketing Week*, 2 April, 29.
12. Buzzell, R. and B. Gale (1987) *The PIMS Principles*, London: Collier Macmillan.
13. Reyner, M. (1996) Is Advertising the Answer?, *Admap*, September, 23–6.

14. Shipley, D. (2004) private papers.
15. Keller, K. L. (2007) *Strategic Brand Management*, New Jersey: Pearson.
16. Keller (2007) op. cit.
17. Fisk (2005) op. cit.
18. Pearce, F. (2008) Greenwash: Are Coke's Green Claims The Real Thing?, Guardian.co.uk, 4 December 2008 (retrieved 21 April 2009, from www.guardian.co.uk/environment/2008/dec/04/coca-cola-coke-water-neutral).
19. Gillespie, E. (2009) Tesco's 'Flights for Lights' Promotion—Every Little Hurts, Guardian.co.uk, 6 April 2009 (retrieved 21 April 2009, from http://www.guardian.co.uk/environment/ethicallivingblog/2009/apr/06/tesco-advert-energy-saving-bulbs-flights-greenwash).
20. Smithers, R. (2009) Tesco Tells Shoppers: Too Much Packaging? Leave it With Us, e Guardian, 1 April 2009 (retrieved 21 April 2009, from www.guardian.co.uk/business/2009/apr/01/tesco-packaging-waste-trial).
21. Fisk (2005) op. cit.
22. Mitchell, A. (2005) P&G Scales Up Global Ambitions, *Marketing Week*, 3 February, 24–7.
23. Fisk (2005) op. cit.
24. Berner, R. and D. Kiley (2005) Global Brands, *Business Week*, 5/12 September, 54–61.
25. Ehrenberg, A. S. C., G. J. Goodhardt and T. P. Barwise (1990) Double Jeopardy Revisited, *Journal of Marketing* 54 (July), 82–91.
26. MacIntosh, J. (2005) Ford Takes its Image Problem to the Garage, *Financial Times*, 27 September, 17.
27. See S. King (1991) Brand Building in the 1990s, *Journal of Marketing Management* 7(1), 3–14; and P. Doyle (1989) Building Successful Brands: The Strategic Options, *Journal of Marketing Management* 5(1), 77–95.
28. Buzzell and Gale (1987) op. cit.
29. Lemmink, J. and H. Kaspar (1994) Competitive Reactions to Product Quality Improvements in Industrial Markets, *European Journal of Marketing* 28(12), 50–68.
30. Brownsell, A. (2008) Marques Tap into White-Car Orders, *Marketing*, 3 September, 8.
31. Gray, R. (2008) The Good Old Days, *The Marketer*, July/August, 28–31.
32. Nettleton, K. and C. Lovell (2008) Why are Nostalgia Brands Returning?, *Campaign*, 30 May, 10.
33. Pieters, R. and L. Warlop (1999) Visual Attention During Brand Choice: The Impact of Time Pressure and Task Motivation, *International Journal of Research in Marketing* 16, 1–16.
34. For example, Urban, G. L., T. Carter, S. Gaskin and Z. Mucha (1986) Market Share Rewards to Pioneering Brands: An Empirical Analysis and Strategic Implications, *Management Science* 32 (June), 645–59, showed that for frequently purchased consumer goods the second firm in the market could expect only 71 per cent of the market share of the pioneer and the third only 58 per cent of the pioneer's share. Also Lambkin, M. (1992) Pioneering New Markets: A Comparison of Market Share Winners and Losers, *International Journal of Research in Marketing*

9(1), 5–22, found that those pioneers that invest heavily from the start in building large production scale, in securing wide distribution and in promoting their products achieve the strongest competitive position and earn the highest long-term returns. For a useful summary and further evidence see Denstaulli, J. M., R. Lines and K. Grønhaug (2005) First Mover Advantage in the Discount Grocery Industry, *European Journal of Marketing* 39(7/8), 872–84.
35. Lester, R. (2005) 3 Sets Sights on Big Four, *Marketing Week*, 27 October, 26–7.
36. Leibernan, M. B. and D. B. Montgomery (1988) First Mover Advantage, *Strategic Management Journal* 9, 41–56.
37. Nayak, P. R. (1991) *Managing Rapid Technological Development*, London: A. D. Little.
38. Oakley, P. (1996) High-tech NPD Success through Faster Overseas Launch, *European Journal of Marketing* 30(8), 75–81.
39. Reinertsen, R. G. (1983) Whodunit? The Search for the New Product Killers, *Electronic Business*, 9 July, 62–6.
40. Tellis, G. and P. Golder (1995) First to Market, First to Fail? Real Causes of Enduring Market Leadership, *Sloan Management Review* 37(2), 65–76.
41. Cadbury, A. (1988) *Annual Report of Cadbury Schweppes*, Bourneville.
42. King (1991) op. cit.
43. Simms, J. (2008) Here Today, Gone Tomorrow, *Marketing*, 19 March, 17.
44. Miller, R. (1999) Science Joins Art in Brand Naming, *Marketing*, 27 May, 31–2.
45. Benady, D. (2002) The Trouble with Facelifts, *Marketing Week*, 6 June, 21–3.
46. See Keller, K. L. (2007) *Strategic Brand Management*, New Jersey: Pearson Education; Riezebos, R. (2003) *Brand Management*, Harlow: Pearson Education.
47. Thurtle, G. (2002) Papering Over the Cracks, *Marketing Week*, 7 March, 25–7.
48. Wray, R. (2006) ntl Buys Virgin Mobile and Prepares to Battle with BSkyB, *Guardian*, 5 April, 23.
49. Sicher, J. (2008) Top 10 CSD Results for 2007, *Beverage Digest* 52(5), March, Bedford Hills, NY.
50. Keller (2002) op. cit.
51. Kapferer, J.-N. (2008) *The New Strategic Brand Management*, London: Kogan Page.
52. Pandya, N. (1999) Soft Selling Soap Brings Hard Profit, *Guardian*, 2 October, 28.
53. Beale, C. (1999) Tommy Hilfiger Kicks Off £8m Media Review, *Campaign*, 15 October, 5.
54. BBC4 (2009) *Reputations: The Life of Gabrielle Coco Chanel*, 29 January.
55. Sullivan, M. W. (1990) Measuring Image Spillovers in Umbrella-branded Products, *Journal of Business*, July, 309–29.
56. Sharp, B. M. (1990) The Marketing Value of Brand Extension, *Marketing Intelligence and Planning* 9(7), 9–13.

57. Aaker, D. A. and K. L. Keller (1990) Consumer Evaluation of Brand Extensions, *Journal of Marketing* 54 (January), 27–41.

58. Aaker, D. A. (1990) Brand Extensions: The Good, the Bad and the Ugly, *Sloan Management Review*, Summer, 47–56.

59. Bottomley, P. A. and J. R. Doyle (1996) The Formation of Attitudes towards Brand Extensions: Testing and Generalising Aaker and Keller's Model, *International Journal of Research in Marketing* 13, 365–77.

60. Roberts, C. J. and G. M. McDonald (1989) Alternative Naming Strategies: Family versus Individual Brand Names, *Management Decision* 27(6), 31–7.

61. Grime, I., A. Diamantopoulos and G. Smith (2002) Consumer Evaluations of Extensions and their Effects on the Core Brand: Key Issues and Research Propositions, *European Journal of Marketing* 36(11/12), 1415–38.

62. Saunders, J. (1990) Brands and Valuations, *International Journal of Advertising* 9, 95–110.

63. Bokaie, J. (2008) Absolut Scales Back Flavoured Roll-Outs, *Marketing*, 13 August, 8.

64. Bennett, R. C. and R. G. Cooper (1981) The Misuse of the Marketing Concept: An American Tragedy, *Business Horizons*, Nov.–Dec., 51–61.

65. Sharp (1990) op. cit.

66. See Ritson, M. (2008) Build an Extension Outside Home Turf, *Marketing*, 25 June, 21; K. Keller and S. Sood (2003) Brand Equity Dilution, *Sloan Management Review* 45(1), 12–15.

67. Prickett, R. (2003) Listen . . . Selectively, *Marketing Week*, 23 January, 43.

68. Aaker (1990) op. cit.

69. Tomkins, R. (2005) A Desire for Pairings Leads Brands on a Wild Goose Chase, *Financial Times*, 29 November, 13.

70. Riezebos, R. (2003) *Brand Management*, Harlow: Pearson Education.

71. Chandiramani, R. (2002) Lego Strikes Deal with Nike for Kid's 'Bionicle' Trainers, *Marketing*, 7 November, 1.

72. Aaker, D. A. (2009) *Brand Leadership*, New York: Free Press.

73. Brech, P. (2002) Ford Focus Targets Women with *Elle* Tie, *Marketing*, 8 August, 7.

74. Keller, K. L. (2002) op. cit.

75. Kapferer, J.-N. (2004) op. cit.

76. Hickman, M. (2006) Disney Drops McDonald's Amid Health Fears, *Independent*, 10 May, 24.

77. Levitt, T. (1983) The Globalisation of Marketing, *Harvard Business Review*, May–June, 92–102.

78. Steenkamp, J.-B. E. M., R. Batra and D. L. Alden (2003) How Perceived Brand Globalness Creates Brand Value, *Journal of International Business Studies* 34(1), 53–65.

79. Barwise, P. and T. Robertson (1992) Brand Portfolios, *European Management Journal* 10(3), 277–85.

80. Halliburton, C. and R. Hünerberg (1993) Pan-European Marketing-Myth or Reality, *Proceedings of the European Marketing Academy Conference*, Barcelona, May, 490–518.

81. Kern, H., H. Wagner and R. Hassis (1990) European Aspects of a Global Brand: The BMW Case, *Marketing and Research Today*, February, 47–57.

82. Barwise and Robertson (1992) op. cit.

83. Riel, C. B. M. and J. M. T. Balmer (1997) Corporate Identity: The Concept, its Measurement and Management, *European Journal of Marketing* 31(5/6), 340–55.

84. Balmer, J. M. T. and S. A. Greyser (2002) Managing the Multiple Identities of the Corporation, *California Management Review* 44(3), 72–86.

85. Balmer, J. M. T. and S. A. Greyser (2003) *Revealing the Corporation*, London: Routledge.

86. Gander, P. (2000) Image Bank, *Marketing Week*, 16 March, 43–4.

87. Martin, M. and I. Heath (1989) BA Redesign was Global Failure, *Marketing*, 2 December, 21.

88. See Benady, D. (2002) The Trouble with Facelifts, *Marketing Week*, 6 June, 20–3; Cozens, C. (2002) Don't Blame Me for Consignia, *Guardian*, 8 May, 8–9; Thurtle, G. (2002) Papering Over the Cracks, *Marketing Week*, 7 March, 25–7.

89. Balmer and Greyser (2010) op. cit. (The term 'AC²ID test' was trademarked by J. M. T. Balmer in 1999.)

90. Balmer and Greyser (2010) op. cit.

91. See Balmer, J. M. T. and G. B. Soenen (1999) The ACID Test of Corporate Identity Management, *Journal of Marketing Management* 15, 69–92; Balmer and Greyser (2003) op. cit. The REDS² Acid Test Process was trademarked by J. M. T. Balmer in 1999.

92. Balmer and Soenen (1999) op. cit.

93. Davies, G. with R. Chun, R. V. Da Silva and S. Roper (2003) *Corporate Reputation and Competitiveness*, London: Routledge. This study provides empirical evidence of a link between corporate identity/image, customer and employee satisfaction, and financial performance.

94. Grant, J. and R. Minder (2006) Crop Resistance: Why a Transatlantic Split Persists Over Genetically Modified Food, *Financial Times*, 1 February, 17.

95. Sweenier, M. (2005) Nestlé Takes 'Healthier' Line in Rowntree Revamp, *Marketing*, 21 March, 1.

96. Smith, N. C. (1995) Marketing Strategies for the Ethics Era, *Sloan Management Review*, Summer, 85–97. See also T. W. Dunfee, N. C. Smith and W. T. Ross Jr (1999) Social Contracts and Marketing Ethics, *Journal of Marketing* 63 (July), 14–32.

97. Young, R. (1999) First Read the Label, Then Add a Pinch of Salt, *The Times*, 30 November, 2–4.

98. Anonymous (2001) An End to the Packet Racket, *Marketing Week*, 2 August, 3; and Benady, D. (2001) Will They Eat Their Words, *Marketing Week*, 2 August, 24–6.

99. Klein, N. (2000) *No Logo. Taking Aim at the Brand Bullies*. London: HarperCollins.

100. Klein (2000) op. cit.

iPhone

Is the Apple Smartphone a World-Beater?

Background: design is everything

Apple is a company that is good at creating markets. The iPod revolutionized popular youth culture and turned out to be the biggest trend in music markets since the launch of the Sony Walkman. In addition to changing the way we listen to music, the iPod rescued Apple's fortunes. Steve Jobs, chief executive of Apple, is the visionary leader who is responsible for identifying and developing products like the iPod and the iMac. Reportedly, his guiding mantra for success is being able to *focus* and say 'no' to a product unless he feels it has world-beating qualities.

Arguably, design is fundamental to the success of Apple products, and the iPod's phenomenal success was no exception (it is, for example, sleek and has been said to be the antidote to our overly complicated modern lifestyle). The design enabled the iPod to become highly differentiated from other high-tech consumer products that have a tendency to be overloaded with buttons, switches and a multitude of functions that only a few dedicated users ever manage to understand and, ultimately, use. Steve Jobs has been quoted as saying 'most people make the mistake of thinking design is just a veneer', but at Apple designers are interested in how a design works for the user as well as what a product looks and feels like. In his quest for the next world-beating product, Steve turned to another mobile high-tech product: the cell phone.

The launch of the iPhone

In 2007, at the Macworld Expo, Steve Jobs launched the iPhone, which is a similar size to the iPod, runs the Apple operating system OS X, and at the time of its launch was unlike any other smartphone on the market. In terms of design, the iPhone is different to mp3 players and traditional mobile phones as there are no buttons for dialling phone numbers, or scroll wheels to select music, videos or pictures. The iPhone is operated solely through its 3.5-inch 480 × 320 touchscreen, and supports wireless technology. It can be synchronized with the Apple Mac address book, includes Apple's Safari browser and has all the functionality of a video iPod. Additional innovations include a soft keyboard and the ability to change the screen content. At its launch, the phone was sold at a premium price: US$499 for the 4-gigabit (GB) version and US$599 for the 8GB. By July 2007, the iPhone had captured 1.8 per cent of the US mobile phone market, which was nearly double the sales goal set for the period, and was reported to be the best-selling mobile model on the market.

World-beating qualities?

Like its predecessor, the iPod, the iPhone has some unique features, which give it world-beating potential. The touchscreen is a breakthrough in the mobile phone industry as it is 'virtually a blank slate, and the ability to write mobile software free from constraints' has created excitement in the world of mobile phone software development. Indeed, the iPhone is being heralded as the next platform for software development after the personal computer and the World Wide Web. The iPhone enables its users to be connected to the Internet wherever they are: 'Peer over the shoulder of that person fiddling with an iPhone. Chances are they're doing something other than making a phone call; they may be playing a game or trading stocks.'

Smartphone competition

However, Apple has competitors . . .

The BlackBerry, which is produced by Research In Motion (RIM), the Canadian handset manufacturer, is a device that offers a range of functions, and recently the company has produced full touchscreen models in an attempt to rival the iPhone. The Storm is a similar size to the iPhone, and offers better screen resolution, GPS and turn-by-turn navigation software, which is a feature missing from the iPhone. The BlackBerry is particularly popular with business users, perhaps due to its capacity for sending e-mails in a user-friendly manner.

Nokia's 5800XpressMusic touchscreen handset has been produced in direct response to the iPhone. The launch of the phone was timed to coincide with the Christmas market and, at a price of £129.95, it is aimed at parents who are concerned about their children downloading illegal music files. The phone comes with a package that allows unlimited access to 5 million music tracks from large and independent music companies.

T-Mobile's G1 smartphone, powered by Google's open source operating system Android, was launched in autumn 2008. The handset has a small slide-out keyboard. In comparison with the iPhone, this offering lacks aesthetic design features, but the mini-keyboard does have potential appeal to users who need to send e-mails and text messages while on the move, even though its small size makes it difficult to use.

ZTE, the Chinese telecoms equipment manufacturer, is producing low-cost handsets, which are enabling it to take market share from all the major players. The VF 1231 model, ZTE's latest mobile, developed especially for Vodafone, is a smartphone based on the Windows Mobile platform. ZTE is entering the market just as the smartphone is no longer being viewed as a luxury item. The phone has an attractive design that offers a range of features at very low prices, and is based on the latest operating systems. ZTE has made a significant investment in the development of smartphones in recent years.

Apple's response to the competition

This influx of imitators of the iPhone has driven down the price of smartphones and streamlined the functionality of handsets. Apple has responded by changing its original business model of selling at relatively high retail prices. In the US market, the iPhone 3G sold for $199 with a two-year AT&T service contract, which is half the price of the original iPhone.

The iPhone 3G offers software upgrades to owners of the original iPhone, and the introduction of an App Store enables owners to download free programs for every aspect of daily life (e.g. Apps for going out, Apps for around the house, Apps for managing money).

Since the launch of the iPhone, there have also been many changes in mobile markets and the operating software available for mobile handsets. Apple has been quick to respond to these changes, and has developed an upgrade to the iPhone, which is designed to wreak havoc on the competition. In terms of features, the iPhone 3G S has a better camera—3-megapixel auto focus—which also has the capacity to make video recordings. The phone has a faster processor, greater storage capacity and better battery life (when using WiFi networks), all of which significantly improved the phone's performance. The 3G S also has effective voice-dial and speech control. New software enables users to cut and paste text in any application, manipulate the on-screen keyboard to suit the user's preferences, and there is a range of other add-ons (e.g. games and e-books), which can be purchased through the App Store.

> **//** The influx of iPhone imitators has driven down the price of smartphones and streamlined the functionality of handsets. **//**

Convergence and the blurring of boundaries

Competition is making this new generation of mobile phones accessible to more consumers and business customers. Remember, high-tech markets are highly dynamic and the next big thing is always just around the corner. So where is Steve Jobs heading for next with the iPhone? According to Furness (2009), as media (video and audio) content becomes increasingly networked, available over a range of different platforms, there will be increasing demand for high-speed connectivity. Widespread adoption of the Internet and broadband connectivity has made the 365-day, 24×7 culture a reality, and users globally have come to expect instantaneous access to everything, from their e-mails to their favourite television programmes. In Europe, widespread technology adoption by many companies in the media industry is laying the foundations for the launch of mobile TV; however, in the USA, adoption lags behind, although alternative methods of mobile television delivery systems are being developed.

Apple has made significant inroads into the video distribution and online aggregation arena, through the iTunes online store. Users are encouraged to choose from a library of TV shows for use on its iPod. While the service is attractive, it is unlikely in its current from to challenge tradition methods of television viewing. However, Apple TV is allowing the company to move into the traditional television marketplace, and recent partnerships between Google's YouTube and Apple show how quickly the competitive landscape can change. If Apple continues to invest in developing strong content partnerships it could potentially create an alternative method for accessing television and other broadcast content through mobile devices.

Apple has its eye on other markets, too; the iPhone can be used as a navigation device, and can be coupled with a driving kit for easy use in a vehicle. Apple's developers are working hard to create totally innovative uses for the iPhone—for example, real-time remote monitoring of intensive-care patients, and many other, less serious, entertainment applications. It seems that, for the time being at least, Apple's focus on producing well-designed and innovative products with world-beating qualities will enable the company not only to lead the smartphone market but will also help the company create new markets for the future.

References

Based on: Allison, K. (2008) Apple Unveils iPhone Grand Plan, *Financial Times*, 10 March, 23; Wray, R. (2008) Nokia Challenges iPhone with Touch Screen and Unlimited Music, *Guardian*, 3 October, 31; Burrows, P. (2009) The Real Potential of Apple's iPhone, A *Business Week*, 26 January, 74–6; Furness, V. (2009) Emerging IPTV and Mobile TV Models: Marketing Opportunities, Challenges and Key Vendors (report), Business Insights Limited, Mortimer House, 37–41, Mortimer Street, London, United Kingdom; Reuters (2009) http://www.reuters.com/article/pressRelease/idUS167622+10-Feb-2009+PRN20090210; Wildstrom, S. (2009) The 3G S iPhone: Apple's Force to be Reckoned With, *Business Week, Technology & You*, 17 June, available at www.businessweek.com/technology/content/jun2009/tc20090617_040512.htm (accessed July 2009).

Questions

1. Make a list of the range of features offered by a smartphone and then consider how many different devices you might use to achieve the same level of functionality in your daily life.
2. How do the new features of the 3G S iPhone provide superior customer benefits compared to the earlier model?
3. Explain how smartphones are changing our daily lives and business activities.
4. Discuss how convergence might influence the development of future models of the iPhone.

This case was written by Fiona Ellis-Chadwick, Senior Lecturer in Retail Management, Open University.

Burberry
Reinventing the Brand

It is called 'doing a Gucci' after Domenico De Sole and Tom Ford's stunning success at turning nearly bankrupt Gucci Group into a £7 billion (market capitalization) fashion powerhouse. Since 1997 when she took over, Rose Marie Bravo's makeover of the 143-year-old Burberry brand has followed the same path.

The Burberry story began in 1856 when Thomas Burberry opened his first gentlemen's outfitters. By the First World War, business was booming as Burberry won the contract to supply trenchcoats to the British army. Its reputation grew when it proved its contribution to the national cause. The Burberry check was introduced in the 1920s and became fashionable among the British middle to upper classes. Later, when it was worn by Humphrey Bogart in *Casablanca* and Audrey Hepburn in *Breakfast at Tiffany's*, the Burberry trenchcoat gained widespread appeal.

Bought by Great Universal Stores in 1955, the brand's huge popularity from the 1940s to the 1970s had waned by the 1980s. A less deferential society no longer yearned to dress like the upper classes and the Burberry brand's cachet fell in the UK. This was partially offset by a surge in sales to the newly rich Japanese and other Asians after they discovered its famous (and trademarked) tan, black/red and white check pattern. By the mid-1990s, the Far East accounted for an unbalanced 75 per cent of Burberry sales. British and American consumers began to regard it as an Asian brand and rather staid. Furthermore, distribution was focused on small shops with few big fashion chains and upmarket stores like Harrods stocking the brand. In the USA, stores like Barney's, Neiman Marcus and Saks only sold Burberry raincoats, not the higher profit margin accessories (e.g. handbags, belts, scarves and wraps).

Change of strategy

These problems resulted in profit falls in the 1990s culminating in a £37 million drop in profits to £25 million in 1997. This prompted some serious managerial rethinking and the recruitment of American Rose Marie Bravo as a new chief executive. Responsible for the turnaround of the US store chain Saks Fifth Avenue, she had the necessary experience to make the radical changes required at Burberry.

One of her first moves was to appoint young designer Roberto Menichetti to overhaul the clothes range. His challenge was to redesign Burberry's raincoats and other traditional products to keep them fresh and attractive to new generations of younger consumers. Furthermore, he sought to extend the Burberry image to a new range of products. The Burberry brand name began to appear on such products as children's clothes, personal products, watches, blue jeans, bikinis, homewares and shoes in order to attract new customers and broaden the company's sales base. Commenting on Menichetti, Bravo said, 'Coming in, I had studied Hermes and Gucci and other great brands, and it struck me that even during the periods when they had dipped a bit, they never lost the essence of whatever made those brands sing. And I thought, "This man will retain what's good and move us forward."'

Design was further strengthened in 2001 with the appointment of Christopher Bailey (from Gucci) as Burberry's creative director. He created Burberry 'classics with a twist' (for example, recasting the classic trenchcoat in hot pink). Bailey's job was to design clothes that met Bravo's vision of heritage and classic, but young, modern, hip and fashionable.

A second element of her strategy was to bring in advertising agency Baron & Baron and celebrity photographer Mario Testino to shoot ads featuring models Kate Moss and Stella Tennant. Other celebrities, such as the Beckhams, Callum Best, Elizabeth Jagger, Nicole Appleton and Jarvis Cocker, have also featured in Burberry advertising. The focus was to emphasize the new credentials of the Burberry brand without casting off its classic roots. Getting key celebrities to don the Burberry check in its advertising was highly important in achieving this. Bravo once remarked that the famous picture of Kate Moss in a Burberry check bra cut the average age of its customers by 30 years.

A third strand in Bravo's strategy was to sort out distribution. Unprofitable shops were closed and an emphasis placed on flagship stores in cosmopolitan cities. Prestige UK retailers including Harvey Nichols were selected to stock exclusive ranges. Bravo commented, 'We were selling in 20 small shops in Knightsbridge alone, but we weren't in Harrods.' Also, stores that were selling only raincoats were persuaded to stock high-margin accessories as well. Burberry accessories have increased from 20 per cent to 25 per cent of turnover. This was part of a wider focus on gifts —the more affordable side of luxury that can drive heavy footfall through the stores. As Bravo said, 'Burberry has to be thought of as a gift store. Customers have to feel they can go into Burberry and buy gifts at various price points.'

International expansion was also high on Bravo's priority list. A succession of new stores were opened, including flagship stores in London, New York and Barcelona. The New York store on 57th Street was the realization of a personal dream for Bravo, whose vision was to replace the store the company had been running in Manhattan for almost 25 years with one that was bigger, better and far more profitable. It is the biggest Burberry store worldwide and has a number of Burberry 'firsts': a lavish gift department, a large area for accessories, private shopping and an in-store Mad Hatters tea room. It also offers a service called Art of the Trench where customers can get made-to-measure trenchcoats customized by allowing them to pick their own lining, collar, checks and tartan. The Barcelona store was regarded as vital in helping to reposition the Burberry brand in Spain. Prior to its opening the brand was slightly less fashionable and sold at slightly lower prices than in the UK. The opening of the Barcelona store saw the London product being displayed for the first time as Burberry moved towards one global offering. Besides the USA and Spain, Burberry's third priority country was Japan since it was an enormous market for the company already.

The results of this activity were astonishing. Profits soared to £162 million by 2005, a six-fold increase since she took over, and in 2002 Great Universal Stores floated one-third of Burberry, its subsidiary, on the stock market, raising £275 million. Then in December 2005 it demerged Burberry completely, allocating Burberry stores to GUS shareholders in proportion to their holdings in a deal worth £1.4 billion.

Burberry did face problems, however. One was the weeding out of grey-market goods, which were offered cheaply in Asia only to be diverted back to western markets at discounts. Not only were sales affected but brand image could be tarnished. Like Dior before it, Burberry was willing to spend the necessary money to try to eliminate this activity. Another problem was that of copycats, which infringed its trademark. Burberry claim to spend about £2 million a year fighting counterfeits, running advertisements in trade publications and sending letters to trade groups, textile manufacturers and retailers reminding them about its trademark rights. It uses an Internet-monitoring service to help pick up online discussion about counterfeits. It also works with Customs officials and local police forces to seize fakes and sue infringers.

The fondness with which so-called 'chavs' regard the Burberry check was a third problem. One observer defined a chav as a young, white, under-educated underclass obsessed with brands and unsuitable jewellery. One product with which chavs have become particularly associated is the Burberry baseball cap. They are also associated with violence, particularly at football matches. The sight of football hooligans appearing in the media adorned in beige and black check was not one appreciated at Burberry HQ. In response, the company has stopped producing the infamous cap and has shifted emphasis to other non-check lines, including its Prorsum line of luxury clothing designed by Christopher Bailey.

A fourth problem arose in 2005 with the announcement that Bravo had decided to step down as chief executive. The woman who had built Burberry into an ultra-fashionable £2 billion global brand would need to be replaced. Her successor is Angela Ahrendts, who was recruited from the US clothing company Liz Claiborne, which owns such brands as DKNY jeans and Juicy Couture. After a period of working together, Ahrendts took the helm in July 2006 with Bravo taking the newly created role of vice-chairperson, a part-time executive position.

Ms Ahrendts has made changes to the Burberry product line by making the check more subtle, and using it mainly in linings and discreet areas of garments.

> **// Burberry claim to spend about £2 million a year fighting counterfeits. //**

She has also placed greater emphasis on higher-margin accessories, such as handbags and perfumes, and top-of-the-range fashion. Burberry has also opened stores in emerging markets such as China, India, Russia, the Middle East and eastern Europe. In 2008, Burberry's first standalone children's wear store in Hong Kong was opened. It has also built up its presence in the USA, with the opening of its new headquarters in New York and further store openings.

She has also improved efficiency by installing new IT systems and replacing 21 scattered distribution centres with three regional hubs in the USA. Her attention has also been focused on better sourcing, in an effort to improve margins.

These activities meant that Burberry proved remarkably resilient in the early months of the economic downturn, particularly helped by demand from the middle classes in emerging markets. However, as the recession progressed, Burberry, like other luxury goods businesses, saw profits plummet as it was forced to discount some products to maintain sales, incur the costs of new offices in London and New York, and restructure its underperforming Spanish operations. Despite the profit downfall, Burberry sales in 2008/9 were up 21 per cent at £1.2 billion, exceeding £1 billion for the first time.

References

Based on: Heller, R. (2000) A British Gucci, *Forbes*, 3 April, 84–6; Anonymous (2002) Burberry, *Marketing*, 1 August, 17; Voyle, S. (2002) Looking Beyond the Traditional Trenchcoat, *Financial Times*, 12 November, 12; Anonymous (2003) Retail Brief: Burberry Group plc, *Wall Street Journal*, 23 May, 6; White, E. (2003) Protecting the Real Plaid from a Lineup of Fakes, *Wall Street Journal*, 7 May; Barton, B. and N. Pratley (2004) The Two Faces of Burberry, *Guardian* G2, 15 April, 2–3; Barns, E. (2005) Are Advertisers Wise to Chase the Chav Pound?, *Campaign*, 24 March, 18; Callan, E. (2006) Burberry Seeks to Offer Luxury in US Midwest, *Financial Times*, 7 July, 1; Walsh, F. (2006) Burberry Chief Turns on Charm with 19 per cent Growth in Retail Sales, *Guardian*, 13 July, 28; Gumbel, P. (2008) The Luxury Market Loses its Lustre, *Fortune*, 22 August, 27; Kollewe, J. and G. Wearden (2008) Burberry Sees Profits Rise While Laura Ashley Suffers, *Guardian*, 29 May, 26; Wardell, J. (2009) Burberry Makes Loss For Year, *Business Week*, 19 May, 64.

Questions

1. How were the clothes bearing the Burberry name augmented to create a brand before the 1980s?

2. What elements of the brand-building factors discussed in this chapter have been used by Rose Marie Bravo since 1997 to rebuild the Burberry brand?

3. What problems might arise in trying to build Burberry into a global brand?

4. What are the dangers inherent in Burberry's strategy since 1997?

This case was written by David Jobber, Professor of Marketing, University of Bradford.

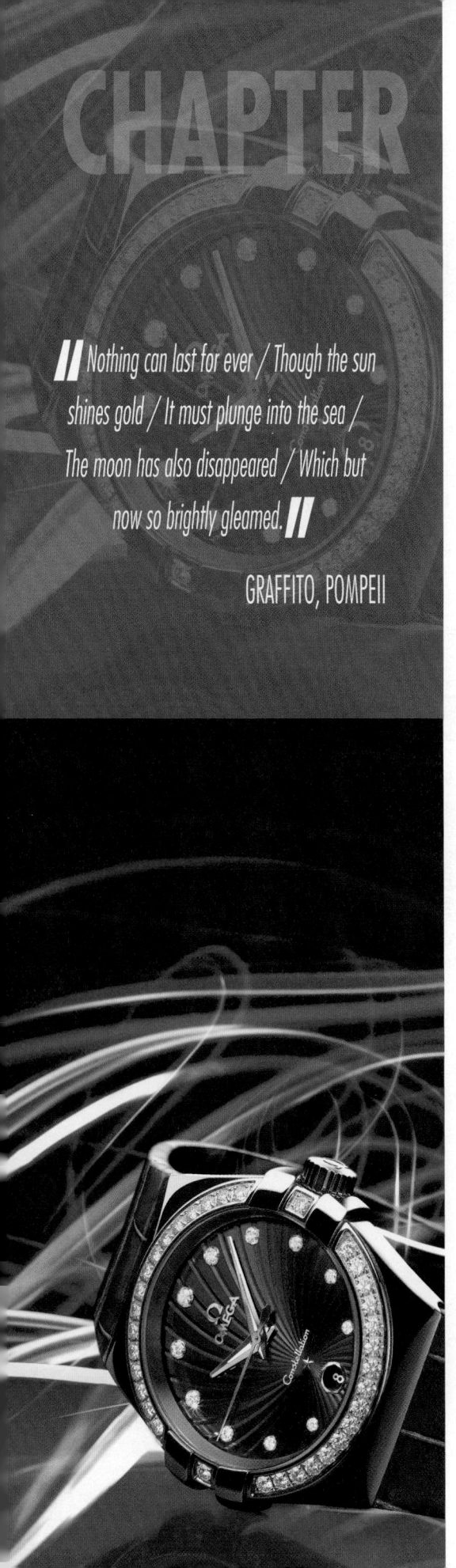

CHAPTER 10

Managing products: product life cycle, portfolio planning and product growth strategies

Nothing can last for ever / Though the sun shines gold / It must plunge into the sea / The moon has also disappeared / Which but now so brightly gleamed.

GRAFFITO, POMPEII

LEARNING OBJECTIVES

After reading this chapter, you should be able to:

1 describe the concept of the product life cycle

2 discuss the uses and limitations of the product life cycle

3 describe the concept of product portfolio planning

4 explain the Boston Consulting Group Growth-Share Matrix, its uses and the criticisms of it

5 explain the General Electric Market Attractiveness— Competitive Position Model, its uses and the criticisms of it

6 discuss the contribution of product portfolio management

7 discuss product strategies for growth

This chapter examines the application of a number of tools that can be used in the area of strategic product planning. Product lines and brands need to be managed over time. The product life cycle will be discussed as a tool for helping managers with this task. Its uses and limitations will be explored.

Marketing managers also need to manage brand and product line portfolios. Many companies are multi-product, serving multiple markets and segments. Managers need to address the question of where to place investment for product growth and where to withdraw resources. These and other questions will be dealt with in the second part of this chapter, which examines portfolio planning. The uses and criticisms of the Boston Consulting Group Growth-Share Matrix and the General Electric Market Attractiveness–Competitive Position Model will be explored.

Finally, this chapter discusses the Ansoff Matrix as a tool for analysing product strategies for growth. Whereas product portfolio planning focuses on existing sets of products, the Ansoff Matrix also considers new products and new markets as a means to achieve future growth.

Managing Product Lines and Brands Over Time: the Product Life Cycle

No matter how wide the product mix, both product lines and individual brands need to be managed over time. A useful tool for conceptualizing the changes that may take place during the time that a product is on the market is called the **product life cycle**. It is quite flexible and can be applied to both brands and product lines.[1] For simplicity, in the rest of this chapter, brands and product lines will be referred to as products. We shall now look at the product life cycle, before discussing its uses and limitations.

The classic product life cycle has four stages (see Fig. 10.1): introduction, growth, maturity and decline.

Introduction

When first introduced on to the market a product's sales growth is typically low, and losses are incurred because of heavy development and promotional costs. Companies will be monitoring the speed of product adoption and, if this is disappointing, may terminate the product at this stage.

All leading companies, such as Canon, IBM, Mercedes, Intel and Apple, invest heavily in new product development to create products that confer new features and benefits for

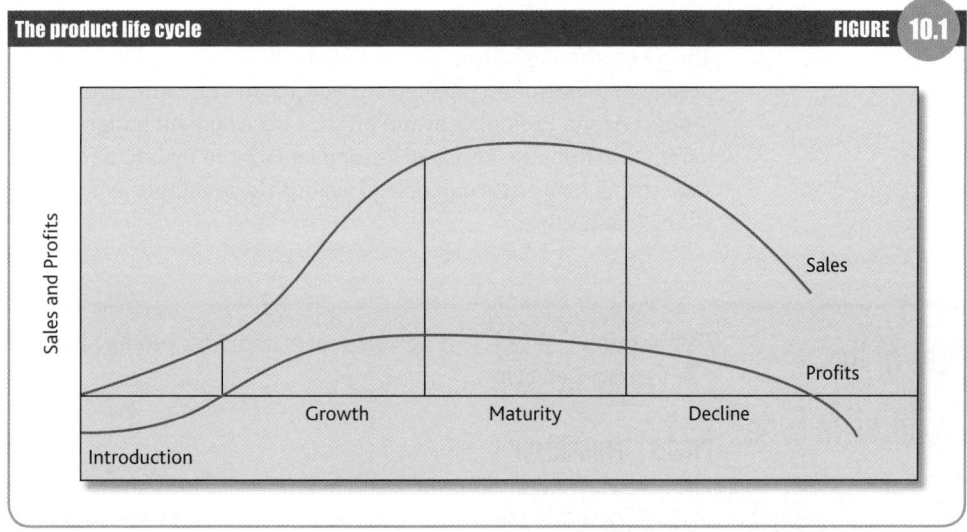

The product life cycle | FIGURE 10.1

▲ Cadbury's Caramel has been marketed for many years, but still receives advertising support to stimulate sales in a mature market.

consumers. Because of this heavy investment, high promotional expenditures and low sales, losses are often suffered during product introduction.

Growth

This stage is characterized by a period of faster sales and profit growth. Sales growth is fuelled by rapid market acceptance and, for many products, repeat purchasing. Profits may begin to decline towards the latter stages of growth as new rivals enter the market, attracted by the twin magnets of fast sales growth and high profit potential. The personal computer market was an example of this during the 1980s, when sales growth was mirrored by a vast increase in competitors, and mobile phones experienced fast growth in the 1990s, with an accompanying increase in the number of competitors. The end of the growth period is often associated with *competitive shakeout*, whereby weaker suppliers cease production.

Smaller, also-ran companies are particularly vulnerable during a shakeout. They need to find profitable niche market segments and/or form strategic alliances to increase their buying and market power.[2]

Maturity

Eventually sales peak and flatten as saturation occurs, hastening competitive shakeout. The survivors battle for market share by employing product improvements, advertising and sales promotional offers, dealer discount and price cutting; the result is strain on profit margins particularly for follower brands. The need for effective brand building is acutely recognized during maturity as brand leaders are in the strongest position to resist the pressure on profit margins.[3] The advertisement for Cadbury's Caramel is an example of a long-standing brand using advertising to stimulate sales in a mature market.

Decline

Sales and profits fall during the decline stage as new technology or changes in consumer tastes work to reduce demand for the product. For example, Sony lost out when the market for cathode-ray TVs went into decline following the development of flat-screen TVs. The new technological advance resulted in Samsung and Panasonic overtaking Sony in sales of televisions.[4] Suppliers may decide to cease production completely or reduce product depth. Promotional and product development budgets may be slashed and marginal distributors dropped as suppliers seek to maintain (or increase) profit margins. Advertising may be used to defend against rivals and prevent the sales of a brand from falling into decline.

Uses of the Product Life Cycle

The product life cycle (PLC) concept is useful for product management in several ways, as described below.

Product termination

First, the PLC emphasizes the fact that nothing lasts for ever. There is a danger that management may fall in love with certain products. Maybe a company was founded on

Marketing objectives and strategies over the product life cycle				TABLE 10.1
	Introduction	**Growth**	**Maturity**	**Decline**
Strategic marketing objective	Build	Build	Hold	Harvest/manage for cash/divest
Strategic focus	Expand market	Penetration	Protect share/innovation	Productivity
Brand objective	Product awareness/trial	Brand preference	Brand loyalty	Brand exploitation
Products	Basic	Differentiated	Differentiated	Rationalized
Promotion	Creating awareness/trial	Creating awareness/trial/repeat purchase	Maintaining awareness/repeat purchase	Cut/eliminated
Price	High	Lower	Lowest	Rising
Distribution	Patchy	Wider	Intensive	Selective

the success of a particular product; perhaps the product champion of a past success is now the chief executive. Under such circumstances there can be emotional ties with the product that can transcend normal commercial considerations. The PLC underlines the fact that companies have to face the fact that products need to be terminated and new products developed to replace them. Without this sequence a company may find itself with a group of products all in the decline stage of their PLC.

Growth projections

The second use of the PLC concept is to warn against the dangers of assuming that growth will continue for ever. Swept along by growing order books, management can fall into the trap of believing that the heady days of rising sales and profits will continue for ever. The PLC reminds managers that growth will end, and suggests a need for caution when planning investment in new production facilities.

Marketing objectives and strategies over the PLC

The PLC emphasizes the need to review marketing objectives and strategies as products pass through the various stages. Changes in market and competitive conditions between the PLC stages suggests that marketing strategies should be adapted to meet them. Table 10.1 shows a set of stylized marketing responses to each stage. Note that these are broad generalizations rather than exact prescriptions but they do serve to emphasize the need to review marketing objectives and strategies in the light of environmental change.

Introduction

The strategic marketing objective is to build sales by expanding the market for the product. The brand objective will be to create product (as well as brand) awareness so that customers will become familiar with generic product benefits.

The marketing task facing pioneer video recorder producers was to gain awareness of the general benefits of the video recorder (e.g. convenient viewing through time-switching, viewing programmes that are broadcast when out of the house) so that the market for video recorders in general would expand. The product is likely to be fairly basic, with an emphasis on reliability and functionality rather than special features to appeal to different customer groups. Promotion will support the brand objectives by gaining awareness for the brand and product type, and stimulating trial. Advertising has been found to be more effective in the beginning of the life of a product than in later stages.[5] Typically price will be high because of the heavy development costs and the low level of competition. Distribution will be patchy as some dealers are wary of stocking the new product until it has proved to be successful in the marketplace.

Growth

The strategic marketing objective during the growth phase is to build sales and market share. The strategic focus will be to penetrate the market by building brand preference. To accomplish this task the product will be redesigned to create differentiation, and promotion will stress the functional and/or psychological benefits that accrue from the differentiation. Awareness and trial to acquire new customers are still important but promotion will begin to focus on repeat purchasers. As development costs are defrayed and competition increases, prices will fall. Rising consumer demand and increased salesforce effort will widen distribution.

Maturity

As sales peak and stabilize the strategic marketing objective will be to hold on to profits and sales by protecting market share rather than embark on costly competitive challenges. Since sales gains can only be at the expense of competition, strong challenges are likely to be resisted and lead to costly promotional or price wars. Brand objectives now focus on maintaining brand loyalty and customer retention, and promotion will defend the brand, stimulating repeat purchase by maintaining brand awareness and values. For all but the brand leader, competition may erode prices and profit margins, while distribution will peak in line with sales.

A key focus will be innovation to extend the maturity stage or, preferably, inject growth. This may take the form of innovative promotional campaigns, product improvements, and extensions and technological innovation. Ways of increasing usage and reducing repeat purchase periods of the product will also be sought. Digital Marketing 10.1 shows how mobile phone manufacturers and operators are seeking to revitalize sales in a mature market.

Decline

The conventional advice to companies managing products in the decline stage of the product life cycle is to harvest or divest. A harvest strategy would result in the raising of prices while slashing marketing expenditures in an effort to boost profit margins. The strategic focus, therefore, is to improve marketing productivity rather than holding or building sales. The brand loyalty that has been built up over the years is in effect being exploited to create profits that can be used

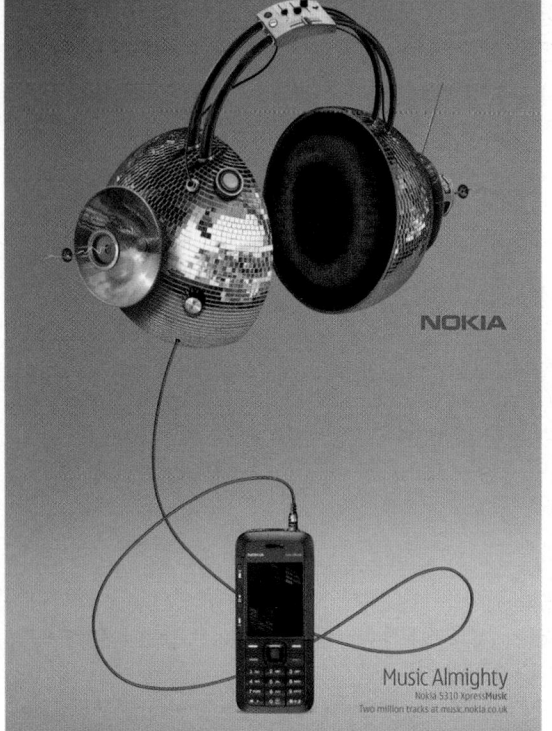

◀ The Nokia 5310 XpressMusic includes a music player and FM radio.

10.1 Digital Marketing

Mobile Marketing in a Mature Market

The mobile phone market in western Europe has reached saturation. For example, ownership has reached 87 per cent in Germany, 83 per cent in the UK and 74 per cent in France. This means that mobile phone companies now operate in a mature market. No longer can profits be fuelled by explosive growth; instead attention has turned to competing for a relatively fixed market of consumers. In classic product life-cycle style, this has meant a move from customer acquisition to retention, attempts to increase usage rates and lower repeat purchase periods, and heavy investment in innovation. It has also resulted in a period of falling prices and rationalization as all players—including Nokia, the market leader—have significantly reduced costs.

Increased usage of mobile phones has been stimulated by SMS (short message service). This allows users to send short text messages at relatively low cost. Usage has also been increased by adding on additional services such as cameras, video recording, and the ability to download and play music (see the ad for the Nokia 5310).

Nokia was the leader in reducing repeat purchase periods: it made mobile phones a fashion item by introducing new, modified models with desirable design and colour features. Its crown was tarnished, temporarily, however, by its slow adoption of the clamshell design, which allowed Motorola and Samsung to gain market share. Motorola's share has since declined because of its failure to successfully replace its Razr mobile phone.

Technological innovations at the maturity stage of the product life cycle can inject growth. This has happened in the mobile phone market with the launch of the BlackBerry and iPhone smartphones. These handsets extend the services available, most notably by allowing fast access to the Internet and e-mails.

The name 'maturity' may conjure up images of tranquillity, but for incumbent companies, competitive and economic forces mean that they face a demanding and volatile marketplace.

Based on: Deere and Kilby (2005);[6] Lester (2005);[7] Odell (2006);[8] Wray (2006)[9]

elsewhere in the company (e.g. new products). Product development will cease, the product line cut to the bare minimum of brands and the promotional expenditure cut, possibly to zero. Distribution costs will be analysed with a view to selecting only the most profitable outlets. The Internet will be examined to explore its potential as a low-cost promotional and distribution vehicle.

Divestment may take the form of selling products to other companies, or, if there are no willing buyers, product elimination. The strategy is to extract any residual value in the products where possible, and to free up managerial time and resources to be redirected at more attractive products and opportunities. Occasionally, products are harvested and then divested. For example, Beecham harvested and then sold Brylcreem to the Health and Personal Care division of Sara Lee at a time when it was unfashionable for males to use hair cream. It proved a fortunate purchase as hair gel became fashionable and Sara Lee had the marketing expertise to reposition the brand in that market.

There are, however, two other strategies that can be applied at the decline stage: industry revitalization and the pursuit of a profitable survivor strategy.

Industry revitalization: some products go into decline not because they are inherently unpopular but because of lack of investment. In fact the application of conventional wisdom for strategy application in the decline stage could be the cause of accelerated sales and profit decline. Such was the case with the cinema market. Years of under-investment saw cinemas become drab affairs offering a very limited choice of films as cinema owners applied a classic harvest strategy. However, one company saw this scenario as a marketing opportunity. Showcase Cinemas was launched, offering a choice of around 12 films in modern purpose-built premises near large conurbations. This completely changed the experience of going to the cinema, resulting in revitalization of the industry and growth in cinema attendances and profits. Thus the classic PLC prescription of harvesting in the decline stage was rejected by a company that was willing to invest in order to reposition cinemas as an attractive means of offering evening entertainment.

Profitable survivor strategy: another alternative to harvesting or divestment is called the profitable survivor strategy.[10] This involves deciding to become the sole survivor in a declining market. This may involve being willing to incur losses while competitors drop out, or if it is thought that this process is likely to be lengthy and slow, to accelerate it by:

- further reducing the attractiveness of the market by such actions as price cuts or increases in promotional expenditures
- buying competitors (which may be offered at a low price due to the unattractive markets they operate in) or their product lines that compete in the same market
- agreeing to take over competitors' contracts (e.g. supplying spare parts or service contracts) in exchange for their agreement to drop out of the market.

Once in the position of sole supplier, the survivor can reap the rewards of a monopolist by raising prices and resuming profitable operations.

Product planning

The PLC emphasizes the need for *product planning*. We have already discussed the need to replace old products with new. The PLC also stresses the need to analyse the balance of products that a company markets from the point of view of the PLC stages. A company with all of its products in the mature stage may be generating profits today, but as it enters the decline stage, profits may fall and the company become unprofitable. A nicely balanced product array would see the company marketing some products in the mature stage of the PLC, a number in the growth stage, with the prospect of new product launches in the near future. The growth products would replace the mature products as the latter enter decline, and the new product successes would eventually become the growth products of the future. The PLC is, then, a stimulus to thinking about products as an interrelated set of profit-bearing assets that need to be managed as a group. We shall return to this theme when discussing product portfolio analysis later in this chapter.

The dangers of overpowering

The PLC concept highlights the dangers of overpowering. A company that introduces a new-to-the-world product may find itself in a very powerful position early in its PLC. Assuming that the new product confers unique benefits to customers there is an opportunity to charge a very high price during this period of monopoly supply. However, unless the product is patent-protected this strategy can turn sour when competition enters during the growth phase (as predicted by the PLC concept). This situation arose for the small components manufacturer that was the first to solve the technical problems associated with developing a seal in an exhaust recirculation valve used to reduce pollution in car emissions. The company took advantage of its monopoly supply position to charge very high prices to Ford. The strategy rebounded when competition entered and Ford discovered it had been overcharged.[11] Had the small manufacturer been aware of the predictions of the PLC concept it may have anticipated competitive entry during the growth phase, and charged a lower price during introduction and early growth. This would have enabled it to begin a relationship-building exercise with Ford, possibly leading to greater returns in the long run.

Limitations of the Product Life Cycle

The product life cycle is an aid to thinking about marketing decisions, but it needs to be handled with care. Management needs to be aware of the limitations of the PLC so that it is not misled by its prescriptions.

Fads and classics

Not all products follow the classic S-shaped curve. The sales of some products 'rise like a rocket then fall like a stick'. This is normal for *fad* products such as skateboards, which saw phenomenal sales growth followed by a rapid sales collapse as the youth market moved on to another craze.

Other products (and brands) appear to defy entering the decline stage. For example, classic confectionery products and brands such as Mars bars, Cadbury's Milk Tray and Toblerone have survived for decades in the mature stage of the PLC. Nevertheless, research has shown that the classic S-shaped curve does apply to a wide range of products, including grocery food products, pharmaceuticals and cigarettes.[12]

Marketing effects

The PLC is the *result* of marketing activities not the cause. One school of thought argues that the PLC is not simply a fact of life—unlike living organisms—but is simply a pattern of sales that reflects marketing activity.[13] Clearly, sales of a product may flatten or fall simply because it has not received enough marketing attention, or has had insufficient product redesign or promotional support. Using the PLC, argue the critics, may lead to inappropriate action (e.g. harvesting or dropping the product) when the correct response should be increased marketing support (e.g. product replacement, positioning reinforcement or repositioning).

Unpredictability

The duration of the PLC stages is unpredictable. The PLC outlines the four stages that a product passes through without defining their duration. Clearly this limits its use as a forecasting tool since it is not possible to predict when maturity or decline will begin. The exception to this problem is when it is possible to identify a comparator product that serves as a template for predicting the length of each stage. Two sources of comparator products exist: first, countries where the same product has already been on the market for some time; second, where similar products are in the mature or decline stages of their life cycle but are thought to resemble the new product in terms of consumer acceptance. In practice, the use of comparator products is fraught with problems. For example, the economic and social conditions of countries may be so different that simplistic exploitation of the PLC from one country to another may be invalid; the use of similar products may offer inaccurate predictions in the face of ever-shortening product life cycles.

Misleading objective and strategy prescriptions

The stylized marketing objectives and strategy prescriptions may be misleading. Even if a product could accurately be classified as being in a PLC stage, and sales are not simply a result of marketing activities, the critics argue that the stylized marketing objectives and strategy prescriptions can be misleading. For example, there can be circumstances where the appropriate marketing objective in the growth stage is to harvest (e.g. in the face of intense competition), in the mature stage to build (e.g. when a distinct, defensive differential advantage can be developed), and in the decline stage to build (e.g. when there is an opportunity to dominate).

As was discussed earlier, the classic PLC advice concerning strategy in the decline stage is to harvest or divest, but other strategies—industry revitalization or the profitable survivor strategy—can be employed if the right conditions apply.

10.1 Pause for Thought

On balance, how useful do you think the product life cycle is to strategic marketing thinking?

A summary of the usefulness of the product life-cycle concept

Like many marketing tools, the product life cycle should not be viewed as a panacea to marketing thinking and decision-making but as an aid to managerial judgement. By emphasizing the changes that are likely to occur as a product is marketed over time, the concept is a valuable stimulus to strategic thinking. Yet as a prescriptive tool it is blunt. Marketing management must monitor the real-life changes that are happening in the marketplace before setting precise objectives and strategies.

Managing Brand and Product Line Portfolios

So far in this chapter we have treated the management of products as separate, distinct and independent entities. However, many companies are multi-product, serving multiple markets and segments. Some of these products will be strong, others weak. Some will require investment to finance their growth, others will generate more cash than they need. Somehow companies must decide how to distribute their limited resources among the competing needs of products so as to achieve the best performance for the company as a whole. Specifically within a product line, management needs to decide which brands to invest in or hold, or from which to withdraw support. Similarly within the product mix, decisions regarding which product lines to build or hold, or from which to withdraw support need to be taken. Canon, for example, took the strategic decision to focus on its profitable products—mainly copiers, printers and cameras—while divesting personal computers, typewriters and liquid crystal displays.[14] Managers that focus on individual products often miss the bigger picture that helps ensure the company's entire portfolio of products fits together coherently rather than being a loose confederation of offerings that has emerged out of a series of uncoordinated historical decisions.[15] Philips found itself in this position, marketing a sprawling set of products, namely semiconductors, consumer electronics, medical equipment, lighting and small electrical appliances.[16] In an attempt to bring coherence to its product lines, Philips has responded by selling its semiconductor business to focus on consumer lifestyle (consumer electronics and domestic appliances), healthcare and lighting.

Clearly, these are strategic decisions since they shape where and with what brands/product lines a company competes and how its resources should be deployed. Furthermore these decisions are complex because many factors (e.g. current and future sales and profit potential, cash flow) can affect the outcome. The process of managing groups of brands and product lines is called **portfolio planning**.

Key decisions regarding portfolio planning involve decisions regarding the choice of which brands/product lines to build, hold, harvest or divest. Marketing in Action 10.1 discusses several companies' approaches to portfolio planning.

In order to get to grips with the complexities of decision-making, two methods have received wide publicity. These are the Boston Consulting Group Growth-Share Matrix and the General Electric Market Attractiveness–Competitive Position portfolio evaluation models. Like the product life cycle these are very flexible tools and can be used at both the brand and product line levels. Indeed, corporate planners can also use them when making resource allocation decisions at the strategic business unit level.

10.1 Marketing in Action

Portfolio Planning to the Core

The composition of a company's product portfolio is a vital strategic issue for marketers. Few companies have the luxury of starting with a clean sheet and creating a well-balanced set of products. An assessment of the strengths and weaknesses of the current portfolio is, therefore, necessary before taking the strategic decisions of which ones to build, hold, harvest or divest.

Major multinationals, like Nestlé, Cadbury Schweppes, Procter & Gamble, GE, IBM and Unilever, constantly review their product portfolios to achieve their strategic objectives. The trend has been to focus on core brands and product categories, and to divest minor, peripheral brands.

Nestlé, for example, has sold Crosse & Blackwell, whose portfolio of brands includes Branston Pickle, Gale's Honey and Sun-Pat Peanut Butter, to Premier International Foods as it focuses on key product categories where it can establish and maintain leadership. The focus is on the core categories of beverages, confectionery, chilled dairy, milks and nutrition. In line with this strategy Nestlé has acquired the Ski and Munch Bunch dairy brands from Northern Foods, propelling it into the number-two position behind Müller in the chilled dairy market.

Cadbury Schweppes is also concentrating on its core brands with the sale of its European soft drinks business, which includes brands such as Orangina, Oasis and Schweppes mixers, to an Anglo-American private equity consortium, and its Australian beverage business to Asahi Breweries. The sale allows the company to concentrate on its higher-growth and more profitable confectionery business, and its regional drinks business in the USA. In line with this strategy, Cadbury Schweppes acquired Green & Black's, the organic chocolate maker, which operates under the fair trade banner.

This trend is not confined to the grocery business, however. For example, Adidas sold its ski and surf equipment firm Salomon to Amer Sports Corporation so that it could focus on its core strength in the athletic footwear and apparel market as well as the growing golf category. IBM sold its PC division to Lenovo to concentrate on software and services.

Philips has also rationalized its product portfolio, selling its semiconductor business to focus on consumer lifestyle, healthcare and lighting. Its mission is to centre on health and well-being, and it has invested in healthcare, moving away from its medical imaging business and into patient monitoring and home healthcare. One example is its acquisition of Respironics, a medical equipment maker specialising in sleep therapy. It sees healthcare as a growth market as people live longer.

One advantage of this strategy is to enable maximum firepower to be put behind core brands. This is the reason Carlsberg-Tetley has dropped minor brands to concentrate its marketing budget on Carlsberg, Carlsberg Export and Tetley Beer.

Based on: Mason (2002);[17] Tomlinson (2005);[18] Milner (2006);[19] Steen (2008)[20]

The Boston Consulting Group Growth-Share Matrix

A leading management consultancy, the Boston Consulting Group (BCG), developed the well-known BCG Growth-Share Matrix (see Fig. 10.2). The matrix allows portfolios of products to be depicted in a 2 × 2 box, the axes of which are based on market growth rate and relative market share. The analysis is based upon cash flow (rather than profits) and its key assumptions are:

- market growth has an adverse affect on cash flow because of the investment in such assets as manufacturing facilities, equipment and marketing needed to finance growth
- market share has a positive affect on cash flow as profits are related to market share.

The following discussion will be based on an analysis at the product line level.

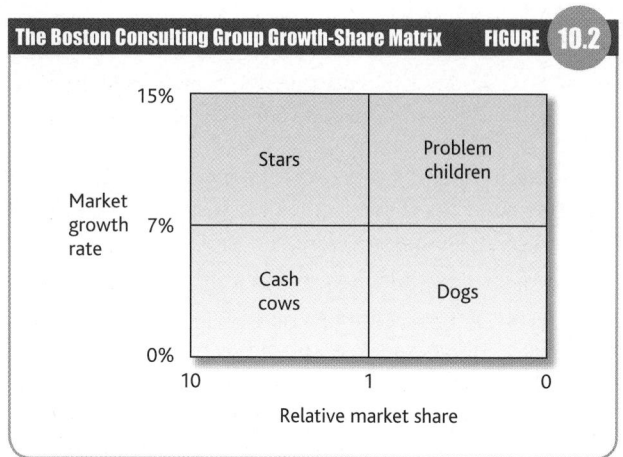

The Boston Consulting Group Growth-Share Matrix   FIGURE 10.2

Market growth rate forms the vertical axis and indicates the annual growth rate of the market in which each product line operates. In Figure 10.2 it is shown as 0–15 per cent although a different range could be used, depending on economic conditions, for example. In this example the dividing line between high and low growth rates is considered to be 7 per cent. Market growth rate is used as a proxy for market attractiveness.

Relative market share is shown on the horizontal axis and refers to the market share of each product relative to its largest competitor. It acts as a proxy for competitive strength. The division between high and low market share is 1. Above this figure a product line has a market share greater than its largest competitor. For example, if our product had a market share of 40 per cent and our largest competitor's share was 30 per cent this would be indicated as 1.33 on the horizontal axis. Below 1 we have a share less than the largest competitor. For example, if our share was 20 per cent and the largest competitor had a share of 40 per cent our score would be 0.5.

The Boston Consulting Group argued that cash flow is dependent on the box in which a product falls. Note that cash flow is not the same as profitability. Profits add to cash flow but heavy investment in such assets as manufacturing facilities, equipment and marketing expenditure can mean that a company can make profits and yet have a negative cash flow.

Stars are likely to be profitable because they are market leaders but require substantial investment to finance growth (e.g. new production facilities) and to meet competitive challenges. Overall cash flow is therefore likely to be roughly in balance. *Problem children* are products in high-growth markets, which cause a drain on cash flow, but these are low-share products; consequently they are unlikely to be profitable. Overall, then, they are big cash users. *Cash cows* are market leaders in mature (low-growth) markets. High market share leads to high profitability and low market growth means that investment in new production facilities is minimal. This leads to a large positive cash flow. *Dogs* also operate in low-growth markets but have low market share. Except for some products near the dividing line between cash cows and dogs (sometimes called *cash dogs*) most dogs produce low or negative cash flows. Relating to their position in the product life cycle, they are the also-rans in mature or declining markets.

What are the strategic implications of the BCG analysis? It can be used for setting strategic objectives and for maintaining a balanced product portfolio.

Guidelines for setting strategic objectives

Having plotted the position of each product on the matrix, a company can begin to think about setting the appropriate strategic objective for each line. As you may recall from Chapter 2, there are four possible strategic objectives: build, hold, harvest and divest. Figure 10.3 shows how each relates to the star, problem children, cash cow and dog categories. However, it should be emphasized that the BCG matrix provides guidelines for strategic thinking and should not be seen as a replacement for managerial judgement.

- *Stars*: these are the market leaders in high-growth markets. They are already successful and the prospects for further growth are good. As we have seen when discussing brand building, market leaders tend to have the highest profitability so the appropriate strategic objective is to build sales and/or market share. Resources should be invested to maintain/increase the leadership position. Competitive challenges should be repelled. These are the cash cows of the future and need to be protected.

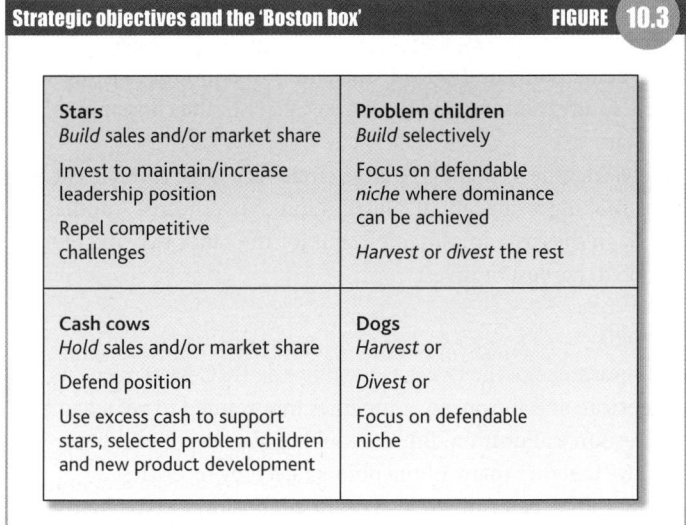

Strategic objectives and the 'Boston box' FIGURE 10.3

Stars	Problem children
Build sales and/or market share	*Build* selectively
Invest to maintain/increase leadership position	Focus on defendable *niche* where dominance can be achieved
Repel competitive challenges	*Harvest* or *divest* the rest
Cash cows	**Dogs**
Hold sales and/or market share	*Harvest* or
Defend position	*Divest* or
Use excess cash to support stars, selected problem children and new product development	Focus on defendable niche

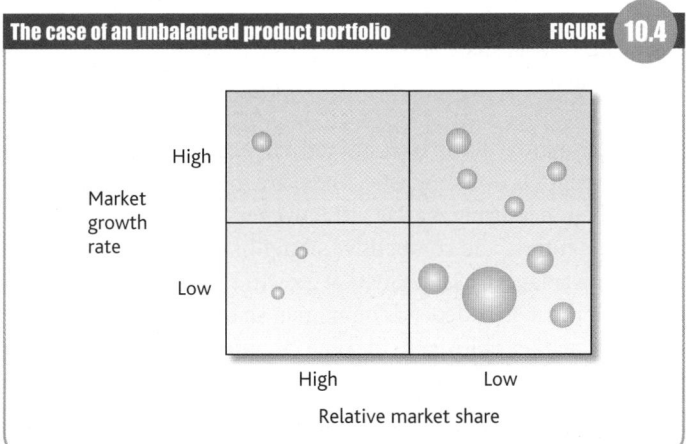

The case of an unbalanced product portfolio FIGURE 10.4

Market growth rate — High / Low

Relative market share — High / Low

- *Problem children*: as we have seen these are cash drains because they have low profitability and need investment to keep up with market growth. They are called problem children because management has to consider whether it is sensible to continue the required investment. The company faces a fundamental choice: to increase investment (*build*) to attempt to turn the problem child into a star, or to withdraw support by either *harvesting* (raising price while lowering marketing expenditure) or *divesting* (dropping or selling it). In a few cases, a third option may be viable: to find a small market segment (*niche*) where dominance can be achieved. Unilever, for example, identified its speciality chemicals business as a problem child. It realized that it had to invest heavily or exit. Its decision was to sell and invest the billions raised in predicted future winners such as personal care, dental products and fragrances.[21]
- *Cash cows*: the high profitability and low investment associated with high market share in low-growth markets mean that cash cows should be defended. Consequently the appropriate strategic objective is to *hold* sales and market share. The excess cash that is generated should be used to fund stars, problem children that are being built, and research and development for new products.
- *Dogs*: dogs are weak products that compete in low-growth markets. They are the also-rans that have failed to achieve market dominance during the growth phase and are floundering in maturity. For those products that achieve second or third position in the marketplace (*cash dogs*) a small positive cash flow may result, and for a few others it may be possible to reposition the product into a defendable *niche*. (The problem with using the niche strategy is lack of economies of scale compared with bigger rivals, as MG Rover found.) But for the bulk of dogs the appropriate strategic objective is to *harvest* to generate a positive cash flow for a time, or to *divest*, which allows resources and managerial time to be focused elsewhere.

Maintaining a balanced product portfolio

Once all of the company's products have been plotted, it is easy to see how many stars, problem children, cash cows and dogs are in the portfolio. Figure 10.4 shows a product portfolio that is unbalanced. The company possesses only one star and the small circle indicates that sales revenue generated from the star is small. Similarly the two cash cows are also low revenue earners. In contrast the company owns four dogs and four problem children. The portfolio is unbalanced because there are too many problem children and dogs, and not enough stars and cash cows. What many companies in this situation do is to spread what little surplus cash is available equally between the products in the growth markets.[22] To do so would leave each with barely enough money to maintain market share, leading to a vicious circle of decline.

The BCG remedy would be to conduct a detailed competitive assessment of the four problem children and select one or two for investment. The rest should be harvested (and the cash channelled to those that are being built) or divested. The aim is to build the existing star (which will be the cash cow of the future) and to build the market share of the chosen problem children so that they attain star status.

The dogs also need to be analysed. One of them (the large circle) is a large revenue earner, which despite low profits may be making a substantial contribution to overheads. Another product (on the left) appears to be in the cash dog situation. But for the other two, the most sensible strategic objective may be to harvest or divest.

Criticisms of the BCG Growth-Share Matrix

The simplicity, ease of use and importance of the issues tackled by the BCG Matrix saw its adoption by a host of North American and European companies that wanted to get a handle on the complexities of strategic resource allocation. But the tool has also attracted a litany of criticism.[23] The following list draws together many of the points raised by its critics.

1   The assumption that cash flow will be determined by a product's position in the matrix is weak. For example, some stars will show a healthy positive cash flow (e.g. IBM PCs during the growth phase of the PC market) as will some dogs in markets where competitive activity is low.

2   The preoccupation of focusing on market share and market growth rates distracts managerial attention from the fundamental principle in marketing: attaining a sustainable competitive advantage.

3   Treating the market growth rate as a proxy for market attractiveness, and market share as an indicator of competitive strength is oversimplistic. There are many other factors that have to be taken into account when measuring market attractiveness (e.g. market size, strengths and weaknesses of competitors) and competitive strengths (e.g. exploitable marketing assets, potential cost advantages), besides market growth rates and market share.

4   Since the position of a product in the matrix depends on market share, this can lead to an unhealthy preoccupation with market share gain. In some circumstances this objective makes sense (for example, brand building) but when competitive retaliation is likely the costs of share building may outweigh the gains.

5   The matrix ignores interdependencies between products. For example, a dog may need to be marketed because it complements a star or a cash cow. For example, the dog may be a spare part for a star or a cash cow. Alternatively, customers and distributors may value dealing with a company that supplies a full product line. For these reasons, dropping products because they fall into a particular box may be naive.

6   The classic BCG Matrix prescription is to build stars because they will become the cash cows of the future. However, some products have a very short product life cycle, in which case the appropriate strategy should be to maximize profits and cash flow while in the star category (e.g. fashion goods).

7   Marketing objectives and strategy are heavily dependent on an assessment of what competitors are likely to do. How will they react if we lower or raise prices when implementing a build or harvest strategy, for example? This is not considered in the matrix.

8   The matrix assumes that products are self-funding. For example, selected problem children are built using cash generated by cash cows. But this ignores capital markets, which may mean that a wider range of projects can be undertaken so long as they have positive net present values of their future cash flows.

9   The matrix is vague regarding the definition of 'market'. Should we take the whole market (e.g. for confectionery) or just the market segment that we operate in (e.g. expensive boxed chocolates)? The matrix is also vague when defining the dividing line between high- and low-growth markets. A chemical company that tends to generate in lower-growth markets

might use 3 per cent, whereas a leisure goods company whose markets on average experience much higher rates of growth might use 10 per cent. Also, over what period do we define market growth? These issues question the theoretical soundness of the underlying concepts, and allow managers to manipulate the figures so that their products fall in the right boxes.

10 The matrix was based on cash flow but perhaps profitability (e.g. return on investment) is a better criterion for allocating resources.

11 The matrix lacks precision in identifying which problem children to build, harvest or drop.

General Electric Market Attractiveness–Competitive Position model

As we have already noted, the BCG Matrix enjoyed tremendous success as management grappled with the complex issue of strategic resource allocation. Stimulated by this success and some of the weaknesses of the model (particularly the criticism of its oversimplicity) McKinsey & Co developed a more wide-ranging Market Attractiveness–Competitive Position (MA–CP) model in conjunction with General Electric (GE) in the USA.

Market attractiveness criteria

Instead of market growth alone, a range of market attractiveness criteria were used, such as:

- market size
- market growth rate
- beatable rivals
- market entry barriers
- social, political and legal factors.

Competitive strength criteria

Similarly, instead of using only market share as a measure of competitive strength, a number of factors were used, such as:

- market share
- reputation
- distribution capability
- market knowledge
- service quality
- innovation capability
- cost advantages.

Assessing market attractiveness and competitive strength

Management is allowed to decide which criteria are applicable for their products. This gives the MA–CP model flexibility. Having decided the criteria, management's next task is to agree upon a weighting system for each set of criteria, with those factors that are more important having a higher weighting. Table 10.2 shows a set of weights for market attractiveness. Management has decided that the key factors that should be used to assess market attractiveness are market size, market growth rate, beatable rivals and market entry barriers. Ten points are then shared between these four factors depending on their relative importance in assessing market attractiveness. Market size (weighting = 4.0) is considered the most important factor and market entry barriers (1.5) the least important of the four factors.

Next, management assesses the particular market for the product under examination on each of the four factors on a scale of 1 to 10. The market is rated very highly on size (rating = 9.0), it possesses beatable rivals (8.0), its growth rate is also rated highly (7.0) and there are some market barriers, although they are not particularly high (6.0). By multiplying each weighting by its corresponding rating, and then summing, a total score indicating the overall

An example of market attractiveness assessment			TABLE 10.2
Market factors	**Relative importance weightings (10 points shared)**	**Factor ratings (scale 1–10)**	**Factor scores (weightings × ratings)**
Market size	4.0	9.0	36
Market growth rate	2.0	7.0	14
Beatable rivals	2.5	8.0	20
Market entry barriers	1.5	6.0	9
			79%

An example of competitive strength assessment			TABLE 10.3
Strengths needed for success	**Relative importance weightings (10 points shared)**	**Factor ratings (scale 1–10)**	**Factor scores (weightings × ratings)**
Market share	2.5	8.0	20
Distribution capability	1.0	7.0	7
Service quality	2.0	5.0	10
Innovation capability	3.0	9.0	27
Cost advantages	1.5	8.0	12
			76%

attractiveness of the particular market for the product under examination is obtained. In this case, the market attractiveness for the product achieves an overall score of 79 per cent.

Competitive strength assessment begins by selecting the strengths that are needed to compete in the market. Table 10.3 shows that market share, distribution capability, service quality, innovation capability, and cost advantages were the factors considered to be needed for success. Management then assigns a weight by sharing 10 points between each of these strengths according to their relative importance in achieving success. Innovation capability (weighting = 3.0) is regarded as the most important strength required to compete effectively. Distribution capability (1.0) is considered the least important of the five factors. The company's capabilities on each of the required strengths are rated on a scale of 1 to 10. Company capabilities are rated very highly on innovative capability (rating = 9.0), market share (8.0) and cost advantages (8.0), highly on distribution capability (7.0) but service quality (5.0) is mediocre. By multiplying each weighting by its corresponding rating, and then summing, a total score indicating the overall competitive strength of the company is obtained. In this example, the competitive strength of the company achieves an overall score of 76 per cent.

The market attractiveness and competitive strength scores for the product under appraisal can now be plotted on the MA–CP matrix (see Fig. 10.5). The process is repeated for each product under investigation so that their relative positions on the MA–CP matrix can be established. Each product position is given by a circle, the size of which is in proportion to its sales.

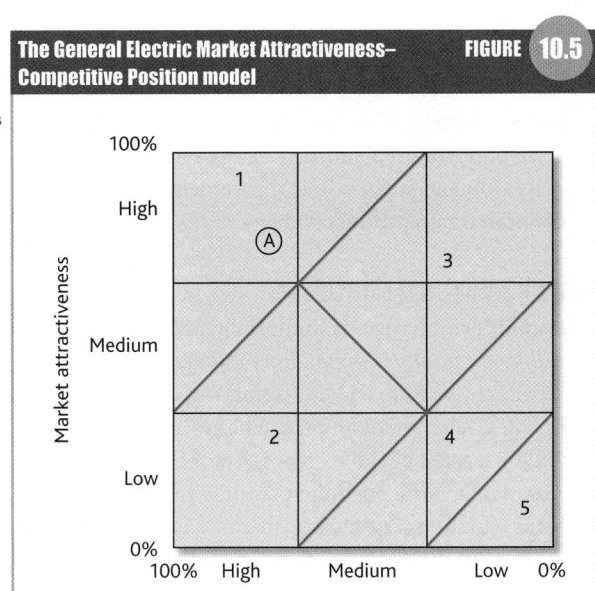

FIGURE 10.5

The General Electric Market Attractiveness–Competitive Position model

Setting strategic objectives

The model is shown in Figure 10.5. Like the BCG Matrix the recommendations for setting strategic objectives are dependent on the product's position on the grid. Five zones are shown in Figure 10.5. The strategic objectives associated with each zone are as follows.[24]

- *Zone 1*: build—manage for sales and market share growth as the market is attractive and competitive strengths are high (equivalent to star products).
- *Zone 2*: hold—manage for profits consistent with maintaining market share as the market is not particularly attractive but competitive strengths are high (equivalent to cash cows).
- *Zone 3*: build/hold/harvest—this is the question-mark zone. Where competitors are weak or passive, a build strategy will be used. In the face of strong competitors a hold strategy may be appropriate, or harvesting where commitment to the product/market is lower. (Similar to problem children.)
- *Zone 4*: harvest—manage for cash as both market attractiveness and competitive strengths are fairly low.
- *Zone 5*: divest—improve short-term cash yield by dropping or selling the product (equivalent to dog products).

In the example shown in Figure 10.5, the circle labelled A indicates the position of the product, which shows that it falls within zone 1 as it operates in an attractive market and its competitive strengths are high. This would suggest a build strategy that probably involves investing in raising service quality levels, which were found to be relatively weak.

Criticisms of the GE portfolio model

The proponents of the GE portfolio model argue that the analysis is much richer than BCG analysis—due to more factors being taken into account—and flexible. These are substantial advantages and the model is widely used, with companies such as BP, IBM, Honda, Nissan, Philips, Centrica, Mitsubishi and GE employing it to aid their strategic thinking. Critics argue, however, that it is harder to use than the BCG Matrix since it requires managerial agreement on which factors to use, their weightings and scoring. Furthermore, its flexibility provides a lot of opportunity for managerial bias to enter the analysis whereby product managers argue for factors and weightings that show their products in a good light (zone 1). This last point suggests that the analysis should be conducted at a managerial level higher than that being assessed. For example, decisions on which product lines to be built, held, and so on, should be taken at the strategic business unit level, and allocations of resources to brands should be decided at the group product manager level.

10.2 Pause for Thought

On balance, how useful do you think the GE portfolio model is to strategic marketing thinking?

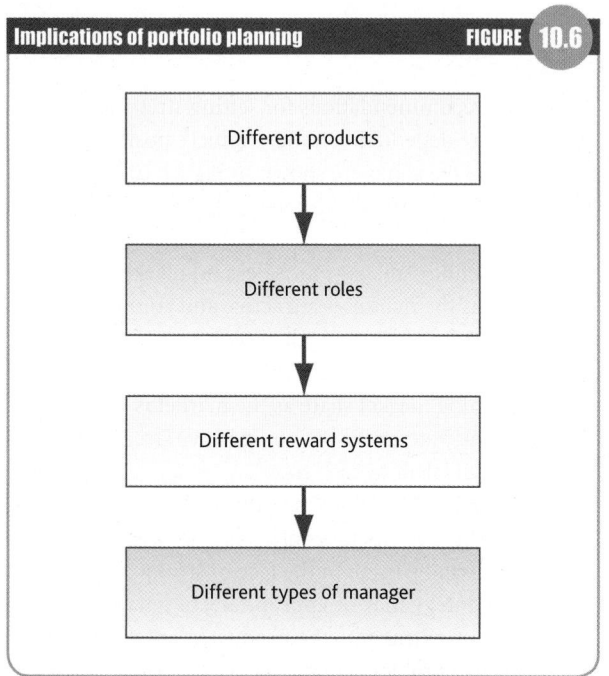

Implications of portfolio planning   FIGURE **10.6**

The contribution of product portfolio planning

Despite the limitations of the BCG and the GE portfolio evaluation models, both have made a contribution to the practice of portfolio planning. We shall now discuss this contribution and suggest how the models can usefully be incorporated into product strategy.

Different products and different roles

The models emphasize the important strategic point that *different products should have different roles* in the product portfolio. Hedley points out that some companies believe that all product lines and brands should be treated equally—that is, set the same profit requirements.[25] The portfolio planning models stress that this should not necessarily be the case, and may be harmful in many situations. For example, to ask for a 20 per cent return on investment (ROI) for a star may result in under-investment in an attempt to meet the profit requirement. On the other hand, 20 per cent ROI for a cash cow or a harvested product may be too low. The implication is that products should be set profitability objectives in line with the strategic objective decisions.

Different reward systems and types of manager

By stressing the need to set different strategic objectives for different products, the models, by implication, support the notion that *different reward systems and types of manager* should be linked to them. For example, managers of products being built should be marketing led, and rewarded for improving sales and market share. Conversely, managers of harvested (and to some extent cash cow) products should be more cost orientated, and rewarded by profit and cash flow achievement (see Fig. 10.6).

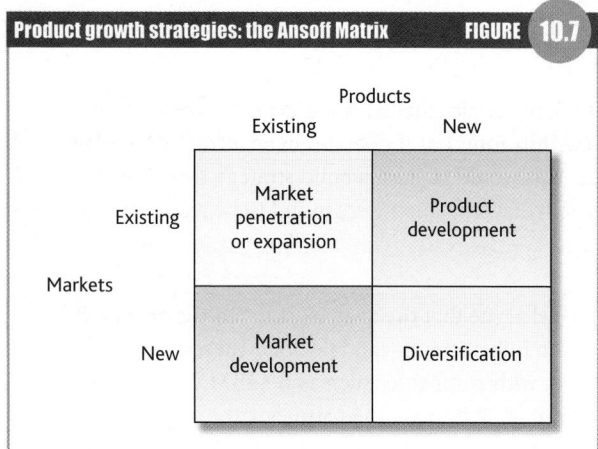

Product growth strategies: the Ansoff Matrix   FIGURE **10.7**

Aid to managerial judgement

Managers may find it useful to plot their products on both the BCG and GE portfolio grids as an initial step in pulling together the complex issues involved in product portfolio planning. This can help them get a handle on the situation and issues to be resolved. The models can then act as an *aid to managerial judgement* without in any way supplanting that judgement. Managers should feel free to bring into the discussion any other factors they feel are not adequately covered by the models. The models can therefore be seen as an aid to strategic thinking in multi-product, multi-market companies.

Product Strategies for Growth

The emphasis in product portfolio analysis is on managing an *existing* set of products in such a way as to maximize their strengths, but companies also need to look to new products and markets for future growth. The Dyson DC08 vacuum cleaner is an example of a new product that is an addition to an existing line.

A useful way of looking at growth opportunities is the Ansoff Matrix, as shown in Figure 10.7.[26] By combining present and new products, and present and new markets into a 2 × 2 matrix, four product strategies for growth are revealed. Although the Ansoff Matrix does not prescribe when each strategy should be employed, it is a useful framework for thinking about the ways in which growth can be achieved through product strategy.

Figure 10.8 shows how the Ansoff Matrix can be used to implement a growth strategy. The most basic method of gaining **market penetration** in existing markets with current products is by *winning competitors' customers*. This may be achieved by more effective use of promotion or distribution, or by cutting prices. The launch of the 3G iPhone is an example of Apple using price to achieve market penetration. The price of $199 was considerably cheaper

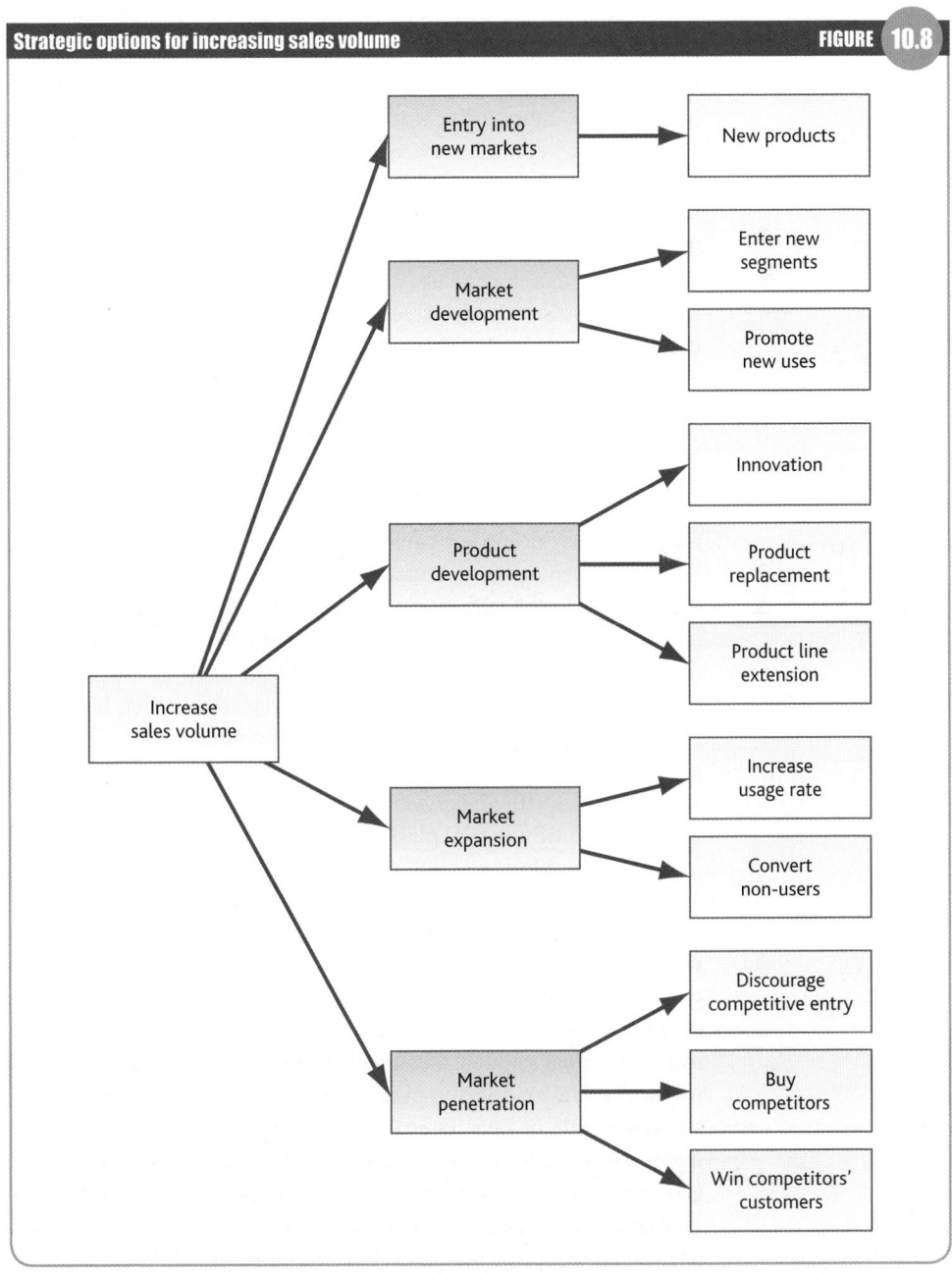

Strategic options for increasing sales volume   FIGURE 10.8

than that of the original 2G iPhone, which was priced at $399, and yet offered considerably more benefits including faster mobile Internet access.[27] Increasing promotional expenditure is another method of winning competitors' customers, as Cadbury Schweppes did by increasing expenditure by 87 per cent over a four-year period.[28] Another way of gaining market penetration is to *buy competitors*. An example is the Morrisons supermarket chain, which bought Safeway, a competitor, in order to gain market penetration. This achieves an immediate increase in market share and sales volume. To protect the penetration already gained in a market, a business may consider methods of *discouraging competitive entry*. *Barriers* can be created by cost advantages (lower labour costs, access to raw materials, economies of scale), highly differentiated products, high switching costs (the costs of changing from existing supplier to a new supplier, for example), high marketing expenditures and displaying aggressive tendencies to retaliate.

A company may attempt **market expansion** in a market that it already serves by converting *non-users to users* of its product. This can be an attractive option in new markets when non-users form a sizeable segment and may be willing to try the product given suitable inducements. Thus when Carnation entered the powdered coffee whitening market with Coffeemate, a key success factor was its ability to persuade hitherto non-users of powdered whiteners to switch from milk. Lapsed users can also be targeted. Kellogg's has targeted lapsed breakfast cereal users (fathers) who rediscover the pleasure of eating cornflakes when feeding their children. Market expansion can also be achieved by *increasing usage rate*. Colman's attempted to increase the use of mustard by showing new combinations of mustard and food. Kellogg's has also tried to increase the usage (eating) rate of its cornflakes by promoting eating in the evening as well as at breakfast.

The **product development** option involves the development of new products for existing markets.[29] One variant is to *extend existing product lines* to give current customers greater choice. For example, the original iPod has been followed by the launches of the iPod nano, shuffle and touch, giving its target market of young music lovers greater choice in terms of size, capacity and price. When new features are added (with an accompanying price rise) trading up may occur, with customers buying the enhanced-value product on repurchase. However, when the new products are cheaper than the original (as is the case with the iPod) the danger is cannibalization of sales of the core product. *Product replacement* activities involve the replacement of old brands/models with new ones. This is common in the car market and often involves an upgrading of the old model with a new (more expensive) replacement. For Skoda and Fiat, product replacement has been essential to their survival, as Marketing in Action 10.2 describes. A final option is the replacement of an old product with a fundamentally different one, often based on technology change. The business thus replaces an old product with an *innovation* (although both may be marketed side by side for a time). The development of DVD players and recorders is an example.

Market development entails the promotion of *new uses of existing products to new customers*, or the marketing of *existing products (and their current uses) to new market segments*. The promotion of new uses accounted for the growth in sales of nylon, which was first marketed as a replacement for silk in parachutes but expanded into shirts, carpets, tyres, etc. Tesco, the UK supermarket chain, practised market development by marketing existing grocery products, which were sold in large out-of-town supermarkets and superstores, to a new market segment—convenience shoppers—by opening smaller grocery shops in town centres and next to petrol stations. Market development through entering new segments could involve the search for overseas opportunities. Andy Thornton Ltd, an interior design business, successfully increased sales by entering Scandinavia and Germany, two geographic segments that provided new expansion opportunities for its services. The growth of overseas markets in China, India, Russia and eastern Europe is providing major market development opportunities for companies such as BP, Vodafone, Wal-Mart, Carrefour and

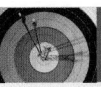

10.2 Marketing in Action

Product Development at Skoda and Fiat

Once decried for its poor design, quality and performance, Skoda has successfully repositioned itself in the car market through investment in product development. The brand's astonishing renaissance is reflected in its position as a top-five car brand for 12 consecutive years in the JD Power Survey of Customer Satisfaction.

Hoping to emulate Skoda's turnaround is Fiat. For many years, the Fiat brand performed poorly in the same survey because of poor reliability. Further hampered by its tendency to make ugly cars, the company became one of Europe's worst-performing car companies. This has begun to change with the appointment of Sergio Marchionne, who told his designers and engineers to make cars that people would want to be seen driving. All the designers were put under one roof and told to give up the wilful eccentricity that had led to some notably ugly cars. Development was speeded up by going further with virtual engineering than any other car maker. This allowed the elimination of the 'prototype' stage of new car development, and cut the time from design to production to 18 months, providing a vital speed advantage over competitors.

The result has been a succession of stylish new models like the Fiat Bravo and 500, which have restored Fiat's fortunes. By implementing an effective product replacement strategy, Mr Marchionne has revived a sleeping giant of the European car industry.

Based on: Anonymous (2008);[30] *Love (2008)*[31]

Nokia.[32] When Wagner, the German manufacturer of spray guns for painting, expanded to the USA in search of market development it found that it had to refocus on an entirely different market segment. In Europe it sells its products to professional painters but in the USA its products are bought by people who use spray guns in their own homes to paint interiors and outside surfaces such as fences.[33]

The **entry into new markets (diversification)** option concerns the development of *new products for new markets*. This is the most risky option, especially when the entry strategy is not based on the *core competences* of the business. However, it can also be the most rewarding, as exemplified by Honda's move from motorcycles to cars (based on its core competences in engines), Sony's move into 8 mm camcorders (based on its core competences in miniaturization and video technology)[34] and Apple Computer's launch of the iPod mobile music player, which can download music via a computer (based on its core competences in computer electronics). This was followed by its highly successful diversification into smartphones (the iPhone) based on its new-found competences in mobile communication. It is the lure of such rewards that has tempted the Internet networking equipment maker Cisco to venture into consumer electronics, and Intel, which manufactures microprocessors that power personal computers, to diversify into platforms combining silicon and software, which has led to new devices and technologies in consumer electronics, wireless communications and healthcare.[35]

Online LearningCentre

When you have read this chapter

log on to the Online Learning Centre at www.mcgraw-hill.co.uk/textbooks/jobber to explore chapter-by-chapter test questions, links and further online study tools for marketing.

Review

1   The concept of the product life cycle

- A four-stage cycle in the life of a product illustrated as sales and profit curves; the four stages being introduction, growth, maturity and decline. It is quite flexible and can be applied to both brands and product lines.

2   The uses and limitations of the product life cycle

- Its uses are that it emphasizes the need to terminate old and develop new products, warns against the danger of assuming growth will last for ever, stresses the need to review marketing objectives and strategies as products pass through the four stages, emphasizes the need to maintain a balanced set of products across the four stages, and warns against the damages of overpowering (setting too high prices early in the cycle when competition is low).
- The limitations are that it is wrong to assume that all products follow the classic S-shaped curve and it is misleading to believe that the product life cycle sales curve is a fact of life; it depends on marketing activity. The duration of the stages are unpredictable, limiting its use as a forecasting tool, and the stylized marketing objectives and strategy prescriptions associated with each stage may be misleading in particular cases.
- Overall it is a valuable stimulus to strategic thinking but as a prescriptive tool it is blunt.

3   The concept of product portfolio planning

- This is the process of managing products as groups (portfolios) rather than separate, distinct and independent entities.
- The emphasis is on deciding which products to build, hold, harvest and divest (i.e. resource allocation).

4   The Boston Consulting Group Growth-Share Matrix, its uses and associated criticisms

- The matrix allows portfolios of products to be depicted in a 2 × 2 box, the axes of which are based on market growth rate (proxy for market attractiveness) and relative market share (proxy for competitive strength).
- Cash flow from a product is assumed to depend on the box in which a product falls.
- Stars are likely to have cash flow balance; problem children cause a drain on cash flow; cash cows generate large positive cash flow; and dogs usually produce low or negative cash flow.
- Its uses are that the matrix provides guidelines for setting strategic objectives (for example, stars should be built; problem children built selectively, harvested or divested; cash cows held; and dogs harvested or divested), and emphasizes the need to maintain a balanced portfolio with the cash generated by the cash cows being used to fund those being built.
- The criticisms are: the assumption that cash flow is determined by a product's position in the matrix is weak; it distracts management from focusing on sustainable competitive advantage; treating market growth rate and market share as proxies for market attractiveness and competitive strength is oversimplistic; it can lead to an unhealthy preoccupation with market share; it ignores interdependencies between products; building stars may be inappropriate; competitor reactions are ignored; the assumption that products are self-funding ignores capital markets; the theoretical soundness of some of the underlying concepts (e.g. market definition) is questionable; cash flow may not be the best criteria for allocating resources; and the matrix lacks precision in identifying which problem children to build, harvest or divest.

5   The General Electric Market Attractiveness–Competitive Position model, its uses and associated criticisms

- The model is based on market attractiveness (e.g. market size, market growth rate, strength of competition) and competitive strength (e.g. market share, potential to develop a differential advantage, cost advantages). By weighting the criteria and scoring products, these can be positioned on a matrix.

- Its advantages over the 'Boston Box' are that more criteria than just market growth rate and market share are used to determine the position of products in the matrix, and it is more flexible.
- Its uses are that the matrix provides guidelines for setting strategic objectives based upon a product's position in the matrix, and that the analysis is much richer than that of the Boston Box because more factors are being taken into account, leading to better resource allocation decisions.
- The criticisms are that it is harder to use than the Boston Box, and its flexibility can provide an opportunity for managerial bias.

6 The contribution of portfolio planning

- The models emphasize the important strategic point that different products should have different roles in a product portfolio, and different reward systems and managers should be linked to them.
- The models can be useful as an aid to managerial judgement and strategic thinking, but should not supplant that judgement and thinking.

7 Product strategies for growth

- A useful way of looking at growth opportunities is offered by the Ansoff Matrix as it is a practical framework for thinking about how growth can be achieved through product strategy.
- It comprises four general approaches to sales growth: market penetration/expansion, product development, market development and diversification.
- Market penetration and expansion are strategies relating to growing existing products in existing markets. Market penetration depends on winning competitors' customers or buying competitors (thereby increasing market share). Defence of increased penetration may be through discouraging competitive entry. Market expansion may be through converting non-users to users or increasing usage rate. Although market share may not increase, sales growth is achieved through increasing market size.
- Product development is a strategy for developing new products for existing markets. It has three variants: extending existing product lines (brand extensions) to give current customers greater choice; product replacement (updates of old products); and innovation (developing fundamentally different products).
- Market development is a strategy for taking existing products and marketing them in new markets. This may be through the promotion of new uses of existing products to new customers, or the marketing of existing products to new market segments (e.g. overseas markets).
- Diversification (entry into new markets) is a strategy for developing new products for new markets. It is the most risky of the four growth strategies but also potentially the most rewarding.

Key Terms

entry into new markets (diversification) the entry into new markets by new products

market development to take current products and market them in new markets

market expansion the attempt to increase the size of a market by converting non-users to users of the product and by increasing usage rates

market penetration to continue to grow sales by marketing an existing product in an existing market

portfolio planning managing groups of brands and product lines

product development increasing sales by improving present products or developing new products for current markets

product life cycle a four-stage cycle in the life of a product illustrated as sales and profits curves, the four stages being introduction, growth, maturity and decline

Study Questions

1. The product life cycle is more likely to mislead marketing management than provide useful insights. Discuss.

2. Evaluate the usefulness of the BCG Matrix. Do you believe that it has a role to play in portfolio planning?

3. What is the difference between product and market development in the Ansoff Matrix? Give examples of each form of product growth strategy.

4. How does the GE Matrix differ from the BCG Matrix? What are the strengths and weaknesses of the GE Matrix?

5. Evaluate the contribution of product portfolio planning models to product strategy.

References

1. Polli, R. and V. Cook (1969) Validity of the Product Life Cycle, *Journal of Business*, October, 385–400.
2. Day, G. (1997) Strategies for Surviving a Shakeout, *Harvard Business Review*, March–April, 92–104.
3. Doyle, P. (1989) Building Successful Brands: The Strategic Options, *Journal of Marketing Management* 5(1), 77–95.
4. Gapper, J. (2006) Sony is Scoring Low at its Close Game, *Financial Times*, 6 November, 17.
5. Vakratsas, D. and T. Ambler (1999) How Advertising Works: What Do We Really Know? *Journal of Marketing* 63, January, 26–43.
6. Deere, G. and N. Kilby (2005) White Heat or Lukewarm, *Marketing Week*, 18 August, 34–5.
7. Lester, R. (2005) 3 Sets Sights on Big Four, *Marketing Week*, 27 October, 26–7.
8. Odell, M. (2006) Mobile Television May Be the Answer, *FT Digital Business*, 13 February, 1.
9. Wray, R. (2006) Falling Prices Bring Nokia Handsets Below £70, *Guardian*, 27 January, 22.
10. Aaker, D. (2007) *Strategic Marketing Management*, New York: Wiley.
11. Cline, C. E. and B. P. Shapiro (1979) *Cumberland Metal Industries (A): Case Study*, Cambridge, Mass: Harvard Business School.
12. Polli and Cook (1969) op. cit.
13. Dhalia, N. K. and S. Yuspeh (1976) Forget the Product Life Cycle Concept, *Harvard Business Review*, Jan.–Feb., 102–12.
14. Rowley, I. and H. Tashiro (2005) Can Canon Keep Printing Money, *Business Week*, 5/12 September, 18–20.
15. Shah, R. (2002) Managing a Portfolio to Unlock Real Potential, *Financial Times*, 21 August, 13.
16. Marsh, P. and I. Bickerton (2005) Stewardship of a Sprawling Empire, *Financial Times*, 18 November, 13.
17. Mason, T. (2002) Nestlé Sells Big Brands in Core Strategy Focus, *Marketing*, 7 February, 5.
18. Tomlinson, H. (2005) Adidas Sells Ski and Surf Group for £329 m, *Guardian*, 3 May, 5.
19. Milner, M. (2006) £1.2bn Sale of Schweppes' European Drinks Business Agreed, *Guardian*, 22 November, 26.
20. Steen, M. (2008) Reinventing the Philips Brand, *Financial Times*, 27 March, 18.
21. Brierley, D. (1997) Spring-Cleaning a Statistical Wonderland, *European*, 20–26 February, 28.
22. Hedley, B. (1977) Boston Consulting Group Approach to the Business Portfolio, *Long Range Planning*, February, 9–15.
23. See e.g. Day, G. S. and R. Wensley (1983) Marketing Theory with a Strategic Orientation, *Journal of Marketing*, Fall, 79–89; Haspslagh, P. (1982) Portfolio Planning: Uses and Limits, *Harvard Business Review*, Jan.–Feb., 58–73; Wensley, R. (1981) Strategic Marketing: Betas, Boxes and Basics, *Journal of Marketing*, Summer, 173–83.
24. Hofer, C. and D. Schendel (1978) *Strategy Formulation: Analytical Concepts*, St Paul, MN: West.
25. Hedley (1977) op. cit.
26. Ansoff, H. L. (1957) Strategies for Diversification, *Harvard Business Review*, Sept.–Oct., 114.
27. Webb, T. (2008) Apple's Guru Calls a New Tune, *Observer*, 15 June, 6.
28. Mitchell, A. (2003) A Plea From the Top for a Marketing Revolution, *Marketing Week*, 20 March, 34–5.
29. Ansoff, I. (1957) Strategies for Diversification, *Harvard Business Review*, Sept.–Oct., 113–24.
30. Anonymous (2008) Rebirth of a Carmaker, *Economist*, 26 April, 91–93.
31. Love, M. (2008) Promise to Do My Best, *Observer Magazine*, 25 May, 75.
32. Anonymous (2008) Face Value, *Economist*, 31 May, 86.
33. Bolfo, B. (2005) The Art of Selling One Product to Two Markets, *Financial Times*, 10 August, 11.
34. Prahalad, C. K. and G. Hamel (1990) The Core Competence of the Corporation, *Harvard Business Review*, May–June, 79–91
35. See Palmer, M. (2006) Cisco Lays Plans to Expand into Home Electronics, *Financial Times*, 16 January, 21; and Edwards, C. (2006) Inside Intel, *Business Week*, 9 January, 43.

Unilever's Quest

Growth by Shedding Brands

In February 2000, when Niall FitzGerald, chairman of Unilever, rose in front of his shareholders to reveal his plans for the most comprehensive restructuring and strategy review to hit the company in over 100 years, there was a sharp intake of breath. His four-year 'Path to Growth' strategy was to see 1200 of its 1600 consumer brands axed to concentrate marketing muscle behind 400 high-growth brands. All brands that were not among the top two sellers in their market segment would be dropped, either immediately or over a period of time.

Buyers would be sought for those that were to be divested immediately, the rest would be harvested (milked) and the cash generated ploughed into support for the 400 big brands. This would mean £450 million of extra marketing expenditure put behind such global brands as Magnum ice cream, Dove soap, Knorr soup and Lipton's tea. Local successes, such as Persil washing powder and Colman's mustard in the UK, would also be supported heavily. The promise was to increase profit margins from 11 to 16 per cent, and to achieve target annual growth rates of between 4.5 and 5 per cent from its 400 top brands. Brands scheduled to be harvested or divested included Timotei shampoo, Brut deodorant, Radion washing powder, Harmony hairspray, Pear's soap and Jif lemon.

The analysis that Unilever had done revealed that only a quarter of its brands provided 90 per cent of its turnover and that disposing of the other three-quarters would lead to a more efficient supply chain and reduced costs of £1 billion over three years. As FitzGerald explained, 'We were doing too many things. We had too many brands in too many places. Many were just not big enough to move the needle so we had to focus and simplify. That simplification would allow us to take cost out of the business.'

Not everyone was convinced. There were £3.5 billion of restructuring costs (bigger than most companies' market capitalizations) and the prospect of 25,000 jobs going. The exercise would require a highly effective internal communications programme to obtain buy-in from Unilever staff.

By the end of 2002, FitzGerald could claim considerable achievements. Cost savings of over £450 million had already been banked and margins had moved from 11 to 15 per cent. The top 400 leading brands accounted for 88 per cent of sales and achieved an average growth rate of 4.5 per cent. Three businesses had also been bought. Bestfoods, the US foods giant, brought the Hellman's mayonnaise, Knorr soups and Skippy peanut butter brands into the Unilever portfolio; the acquisition of Ben & Jerry's gave the company one of two major brands in the premium ice cream sector; and Slimfast provided major penetration of the diet food market.

Unilever was also busy dropping or selling off Elizabeth Arden, Batchelor's soups, Oxo, Knight's Castille soap, Frish toilet cleaner and Stergene hand-washing liquid. Some of Unilever's unwanted brands have been bought by small companies. For example, Buck UK bought Unilever's Sqezy—the washing-up liquid formerly marketed as 'easy, peasy, lemon Sqezy'. Also, Unilever sold its Harmony hairspray and Stergene fabric conditioner brands to Lornamead. Others, such as Oxo and Batchelor's, sold to larger companies, in this case Campbell Grocery Products.

A number of brand extensions were also planned in 2002, most notably in the Bertolli olive oil, Dove soap, Knorr soup, Lynx (Axe) male grooming and Slimfast diet food brands. The Lynx (Axe) men's deodorant was launched in the USA, and three new flavours of Hellman's mayonnaise and an Asian side dishes range were introduced.

The result of all this activity was that Unilever posted a 16 per cent increase in 2002 profits, that is £1.5 billion compared to £1.3 billion in 2001. Sales of its top 400 brands grew 5.4 per cent above the company's target of 4.5 and 5 per cent. The company invested £5.1 billion in

▲ Unilever owns many different ice cream brands across Europe. It has retained the national name of each brand, but replaced their individual logos with its internationally-recognised symbol.

advertising and promotion, up 8.5 per cent on the 2001 level.

During 2003, Unilever earmarked an additional 20 per cent of marketing investment in its global ice cream portfolio over the next three years. The ice cream group has a remarkable global brand portfolio. For example, in the UK, Unilever owns Walls; in France, it bought Miko; in Portugal it owns Ola; and in Sweden it owns GB Glace. Over Europe as a whole, Unilever owns and operates more than 12 different ice cream brands, each with its own strong heritage and relationships with customers. Unilever has retained the names of its national brands while replacing original brand symbols with a single heart-shaped logo.

Unfortunately, the successes of the early years were followed by two years of performance below expectations, leading to the departure of Mr FitzGerald in May 2004. Poor sales and profit performance was blamed on poor organizational structure, lack of innovation and poor advertising. Poor structure stemmed from Unilever's Anglo-Dutch heritage, which resulted in joint chairmen—one for the Dutch arm and one for the UK—and no chief executive. The company was run by two boards and separate headquarters in London and Rotterdam. Consequently, decision-making was cumbersome and slow, with the ever-present threat of conflict between the two groups compounding the

problems. The group was also divided into divisions: health and personal products, food, and frozen foods. These were regarded as fiefdoms under which separate management teams managed their products separately in each country.

Following Mr FitzGerald's departure, Unilever carried out a strategic review under its joint chairmen, Patrick Cescau in the UK and Antony Burgmans in the Netherlands. Mr Cescau, the driving force behind the review, became Unilever's chief executive with Mr Burgmans becoming non-executive chairman. The board was unified and headquarters were centralized in London. These changes gave Mr Cescau the autonomy to push through the reform needed to get Unilever back on track. Under the slogan 'One Unilever', he dismantled the fiefdoms, which were merged to form one executive team covering all divisions and nationalities, resulting in the loss of almost a fifth of senior management. A cull of about 30,000 jobs took place and some loss-making factories were closed to cut costs.

Mr Cescau also changed focus from Path to Growth's fixation on profit margins to boosting market share. This meant price reductions and the introduction of cheaper product ranges to complement the company's premium-priced brands. Its Magnum ice cream brand was complemented in this way, for example.

He also sold Unilever's cosmetics and fragrances arm, Unilever Cosmetics International to Coty International, for £438 million, in a move that allowed it to focus on its core categories of food, cleaning and personal care brands such as Ben & Jerry's ice cream, Knorr soups, Flora margarine, Cif cleaning products, Persil detergents, Dove personal care products, Sunsilk shampoos and Lynx (Axe) men's deodorants. This was quickly followed by the sale of its frozen food division (Bird's Eye) to Permira, a venture capitalist, for £1.2 billion. At the time of the sale, Bird's Eye was the number one food brand in the UK, with a turnover of £500 million a year and profits of around £50 million. It was also the UK's second-biggest supermarket brand after Walkers crisps. Unilever also sold its North American detergents business in 2008, to a private equity firm.

A greater emphasis was placed on emerging markets such as China, India, Brazil, Russia, Africa, and central and eastern Europe. Advertising budgets in western Europe were tightened to fund extra investment in these growth markets. In line with this strategy, Inmarko, Russia's largest ice cream brand, was acquired in 2008. By 2009, emerging markets accounted for around 50 per cent of Unilever's sales revenue.

Another change in strategy was to adopt a more standardized approach to global marketing. The company moved from autonomous localized initiatives to the roll-out of innovation and marketing programmes on a global basis. Power was taken away from country managers and given to global marketing teams to oversee the development and marketing of new products. Brand marketing was split into two divisions: the brand development team and brand building. The brand development team devised a global strategy for each brand, including innovation. A package of recommendations is then created, usually in conjunction with two key countries. This is then sent to brand-building teams in each country and they 'make it happen' within local markets.

Mr Cescau has also invested in 'healthy living' brands to capitalize on the trend towards health and well-being. For example, a number of 'healthy' sauces and soups under the Knorr brand were launched, with no artificial flavours or colourings, reflecting Unilever's 'vitality' positioning.

In 2008, he stepped down as chief executive after achieving what most commentators regard as a fairly successful period at the helm, transforming the company from a lumbering, regionally driven bureaucracy into a more streamlined, globally managed business. However, Unilever's performance did not match that of Reckitt Benckiser, maker of the Cillit Bang cleaner, whose strategy was to launch brands such as stain removers targeting niche markets that avoided direct head-to-head competition with Procter & Gamble and Unilever.

His successor was Paul Polman, an ex P&G and Nestlé man, breaking with an 80-year-old tradition of appointing insiders. Faced with a recession, Mr Polman embarked on a cost-cutting programme, including a freeze on management salaries, and travel budget cuts of 30 per cent (replacing travel with teleconferencing), designed to achieve £45 million savings. A job-cutting and factory-closure programme that began in 2007 was accelerated, and a global procurement officer was recruited to seek savings by using the company's vast scale to obtain better prices. Acquisitions were also made, including the purchase of the Toni & Guy haircare brands, and emphasis on emerging markets continued to be a central plank of Unilever's strategy.

References

Based on: Arnold, M. (2002) Unilever Names Brands for Growth, *Marketing*, 21 February 17; Mason, T. (2002) Unilever Puts its Cash into Ideas, *Marketing*, 10 October, 17; Rogers, D. (2002) Unilever Sells Off Fragrance Brands, *Marketing*, 15 August, 4; Ritson, M. (2003) Unilever Goes with its 'Heart' to Make Global Brand of Local Ices, *Marketing*, 1 May, 18; Stechler Haes, N. and D. Ball (2003) Unilever's Net Profit Rises 16 per cent on Reorganization Successes, *Wall Street Journal*, 14 February, 5; Kilby, N. (2005) Coty Scents Growth Potential in Unilever Cosmetics, *Marketing Week*, 26 May, 11; Cannon, H. (2006) New Hand at Unilever Tries to Pull it Together, *Observer*, 12 June, 7; Kilby, N. (2006) Permira Aims to Make Bird's Eye Cooler than Chilled, *Marketing Week*, 7 September, 10; Wiggins, J. (2008) Unilever Buys Russia's Inmarko Ice Cream, *Financial Times*, 5 February, 21; Wiggins, J. (2008) Unilever Hangs on to European Laundry List, *Financial Times*, 29 July, 18; Jack, L. (2009) The Soaps, the Glory and the Universal Truths in Marketing, *Marketing Week*, 23 April, 20–4; Mortished, C. (2009) Unilever Chief Paul Polman Ditches Pay Rises and Targets, *The Times*, 6 February, 18; Wiggins, J. (2009) Unilever Looks to the Silver Lining, *Financial Times*, 6 February, 19.

Questions

1. What were the advantages to Unilever of reducing the size of its brand portfolio? What were the risks?
2. To what extent does it appear that Unilever followed (i) the BCG Growth-Share Matrix, and (ii) the General Electric Market Attractiveness–Competitive Position model approaches to portfolio planning during the FitzGerald era?
3. What are the attractions to small companies of buying marginal Unilever brands? What are the dangers of doing so?
4. Comment on Unilever's approach to the global marketing of its brands.
5. Why did the sale of Bird's Eye and its North American detergent business make strategic sense for Unilever?

This case was prepared by David Jobber, Professor of Marketing, University of Bradford.

Intel Inside Out
The Search for Growth

Intel is one of the most famous business-to-business brand names in the world, with a value of over $85 billion. With sales of over $30 billion, profit margins of 55 per cent and 80 per cent share of the market for microprocessors that power PCs, it is also one of the most successful. The foundation for its success was the development and marketing of microprocessors for PCs and servers. By investing billions in ever faster processors, Intel has become the dominant force in this industry, with efficient plants that can produce more processors in a day than some rivals can in a year. The combination of low-cost production and ever faster chips was a powerful concoction that none of its rivals could match.

Much of the credit for Intel's success goes to Andy Grove, its former chief executive, who took the decision to leave the unprofitable memory chip business to focus on microprocessors for the fast-growing personal computer market, a move that enabled Intel to bury the competition. Intel's products were supported by powerful branding using the Pentium brand name and 'Intel inside' strap-line, bringing consumer awareness of a product hidden from sight in the heart of a computer. Intel's strategy was to work with Microsoft to appeal to PC industry giants such as Dell, HP, IBM and Compaq to be the first choice for microprocessors.

Under Grove, engineers dominated and the culture at Intel was summarized by his motto: 'Only the paranoid survive.' Managers often engaged in 'constructive confrontation', otherwise known as shouting at each other. Under Grove's successor, Craig R. Barrett, the company continued its successful path to ever greater sales and profits.

Times they are a' changin'

By 2005 the market for microprocessors was changing. Growth in PC demand was slowing as markets became saturated. No longer could Intel rely on double-digit market growth to fuel its sales and profit trajectory. Another change was occurring within Intel itself. A new chief executive, Paul Otellini, was at the helm. A non-engineer, Otellini joined Intel in 1974 straight out of business school at the University of California at Berkeley. A close working associate of Grove, who continued as chairman until 2005 after his departure as CEO in 1998, Otellini has a marketing background. Among his successes was the Centrino brand. When Otellini was head of product planning, he decided, against the wishes of Intel engineers, that rather than launch yet another fast processor, he would bundle it with a relatively new wireless Internet technology called WiFi. The combination enabled consumers to connect from their laptop to the Internet from such places as airport lounges and coffee shops. Supported by a $300 million marketing campaign, Centrino laptops caught on, revitalizing the PC market while encouraging consumers to purchase higher-margin products. Since launch, over $6 billion worth of Centrino chips have been sold.

Intel was also faced with an energetic competitor, Advanced Micro Devices, which had slowly been gaining ground in the battle of the microchip. A major competitive weapon of AMD was price, which prompted Intel to develop the low-priced Celeron microprocessor. AMD stole a march on Intel by being the first to launch a 64-bit chip, which held the competitive advantages of having greater power and lower power consumption. By 2005 AMD had increased its market share to 15 per cent of the PC microprocessor market and held 26 per cent of the market for the microprocessors that drive servers where lower power consumption was highly valued. Even more impressive was its 48 per cent share of the growing multi-core processor market, where two or more chips are put on to a single sliver of silicon. Such products consume less power, enabling laptops to run longer before recharge, and enhance performance without generating more heat, which was a problem with single chips. Using less power is especially important for business-to-business customers. For example, Google claimed that it cost more to run its computers than to buy them. A landmark came in 2005 when Dell, hitherto an Intel stronghold, moved to AMD chips for its servers. Its decision was influenced by the competitive advantage its rivals HP, Toshiba and Gateway were getting by using the more powerful AMD chips in their consumer and business systems, particularly servers.

A change of strategy

The promotion of Otellini to chief executive heralded a change in strategic direction for Intel. The changing technological, competitive and market landscape was reflected in his desire to move the company away from its dependence on single microprocessor chips for the PC market. First, Intel developed new dual-core chips for laptops (using the Core brand name), which place two microprocessors on one sliver of silicon. This allows laptops to run for five to 10 hours rather than three to four, which was typical before. They also power Apple iMacs, allowing them to run at over twice the speed of the models (based on an IBM chip) they replaced without generating additional heat.

Second, Intel is focusing on 'complete technology platforms' rather than individual microprocessors. Platformization, as Intel calls it, means bundling a range of chips and the software needed to tie them all together, offering different features such as security, video, audio and wireless capabilities in a combination to suit a particular target market. This is recognition of the fact that computer manufacturers value the opportunity to buy a complete package of chips from one manufacturer rather than assemble components from several suppliers. It also means that Intel sells more components, and so takes a larger slice of the selling price of each PC. Whereas Intel can handle the process in-house, AMD requires partners to develop platforms.

Otellini also announced plans to broaden Intel's target markets. Rather than focus only on PC manufacturers, Intel intends to be a major technological player in home entertainment, wireless communications and healthcare. In home entertainment, Otellini's vision is for the PC to be the central connection to individual entertainment devices. The company has developed the Viiv multicore chip, which allows PCs to connect to

▲ The ultra-small Atom chip allow Intel to compete in the market for netbooks and other mobile Internet devices.

DVD players, TVs, stereo systems, and so on, so that consumers can move digital content around the home. This means that Viiv computers can act as an all-in-one DVD player, games console, CD player and television, and enable downloads of movies, music and games, which can then be moved around the home. Already Viiv has been chosen as the chip to power Windows Media Centre PCs.

> // The type of person Intel hires has changed too. They include ethnographers, sociologists and software developers. //

In targeting wireless communications, Intel is hoping to make a breakthrough in an area where it has traditionally been weak. Hitherto, Intel's focus on PC microprocessors meant that investment in chips for mobile communications was considered secondary. Intel is supporting WiMax, a 4G wireless broadband technology that could bring fast and cheap wireless computing to both mobile devices and PCs, and, in 2008, launched the Atom, an ultra-small energy-efficient chip. The Atom allowed Intel to compete in the market for mobile Internet devices (MIDs, bigger than smartphones), netbooks (very small laptops) and nettops (cheap, stripped-down desktop PCs). By 2009, the Atom chip was found at the heart of most netbooks. A major deal was sealed in 2009 with the announcement that Intel and Nokia were embarking on technological collaboration to deliver new mobile computing products.

Otellini is also hoping for breakthrough innovations in healthcare. His vision is for digital technology to help healthcare professionals. Ethnographers are employed to understand the problems of the elderly and people with specific diseases such as Alzheimer's. Currently, Intel is developing sensors that can communicate with computer networks, enabling care givers to monitor the health of the elderly remotely. One benefit of this would be to allow elderly people to remain in their own homes.

In line with his strategy, Otellini reorganized Intel into platform-specific divisions: digital home (for consumer PCs and home entertainment), corporate (business PCs and servers), mobility (laptops and mobile devices) and healthcare, and scattered the processor engineers among them. New product development was also reorganized. In the past engineers worked on ever faster chips and marketers were asked to sell them. Now new products are developed by teams of people: chip engineers, software developers and marketers all work together to design attractive new products. The type of person Intel hires has changed too. They include ethnographers, sociologists and software developers. Ethnographers, for example, are researching how people in emerging markets like China and India use technology.

Eric Kim, chief marketing officer, was recruited from Samsung and was widely credited with raising its brand awareness and image as a leading consumer electronics company. Among recent marketing initiatives is the rebranding of the Core family of microprocessors to simplify a range that had become too unwieldy and confusing. The new names—the Core i3, Core i5 and Core i7—describe the basic, mid-range and high-end features of the Core line, respectively. Intel has also become corporate technological partner with BMW, which sees its chips powering operations across BMW dealerships, the company and its cars. The partnership also makes Intel a major sponsor of BMW's Sauber Formula One motor racing team. The male-dominated F1 audience, with its keen interest in technology, is a core target market for Intel.

Not everyone at Intel was happy about the reorganization and the increased emphasis on marketing, however. Before Otellini's elevation to CEO anyone not working for the core PC business was considered a second-class citizen, and many high-level engineers working on PC products feel they have lost their star status. Some regard marketing as little more than gloss and glitz, and others have left to join rivals

such as AMD. The competition is also critical of Intel's practice of offering volume-based rebates to computer manufacturers, which they claim acts as a barrier to entry. This has led to a record £950 million fine imposed by the European Commission for anti-competitive behaviour.

References

Based on: Anonymous (2005) Intel's Right-hand Turn, *Economist*, 14 May, 67–9; Durman, P. (2005) Intel Attacked for Stifling Competition, *Sunday Times*, 20 March, 10; Nuttall, C. (2005) Intel Ventures Beyond PCs, *Financial Times*, 12 November, 3; Edwards, C. (2006) AMD: Chipping Away at Intel's Lead, *Business Week*, 12 June, 72–3; Edwards, C. (2006) Inside Intel, *Business Week*, 9 January; Kilby, N. (2006) Intel's Power Drive, *Marketing Week*, 5 January, 21; Anonymous (2008) Battlechips, *Economist*, 7 June, 76–7; Baldwin, C. (2009) Intel, AMD Take Battle to New Ultra-Thin Laptops, reuters.com, 19 June; Chipperfield, E. (2009) A Pocket Laptop to be Reckoned With, *The Times*, 7 June, 28; Edwards, C. (2009) Intel Tries to Invest its Way Out of a Rut, *Business Week*, 27 April, 44–6; Shiels, M. (2009) Intel and Nokia Band Together, http://news.bbc.co.uk/.

Questions

1 Interpret Intel's move from its reliance on microprocessors for PCs into home entertainment, healthcare and mobile communications using (i) the product life cycle, (ii) the BCG, and (iii) the General Electric Market Attractiveness–Competitive Position models.

2 Locate each of Intel's moves (products and markets) since Otellini became CEO in the Ansoff product growth matrix. Justify your answer.

3 How has the corporate culture changed since Otellini became CEO? Support your answer with examples.

4 What challenges does Intel face as it moves into home entertainment, healthcare and mobile communications?

This case was prepared by David Jobber, Professor of Marketing, University of Bradford.

CHAPTER 11

Developing new products

> *I met R&D people who never left the lab … and who were so snobbish about the sales force that they wouldn't know a customer if they tripped over one. I saw financial controllers whose projections sounded exciting but who didn't have a clue about how to make a company grow with new products.*

DON FREY, *Learning the Ropes: My Life as a Product Champion*

> *You learn more from failure… but the key is to fail early, fail cheaply, and not to make the same mistake twice.*

A. G. LAFLEY, CEO, PROCTER & GAMBLE

LEARNING OBJECTIVES

After reading this chapter, you should be able to:

1 define the different types of new products that can be launched

2 describe how to create and nurture an innovative culture

3 discuss the organizational options that apply to new product development

4 identify the methods of reducing time to market

5 explain how marketing and R&D staff can work together effectively

6 describe the stages in the new product development process

7 explain how to stimulate the corporate imagination

8 discuss the six key principles of managing product teams

9 describe the innovation categories and their marketing implications

10 discuss the key ingredients in commercializing technology quickly and effectively

The life-blood of corporate success is bringing new products to the marketplace. Changing customer tastes, technological advances and competitive pressures mean that companies cannot afford to rely on past product success. Instead they have to work on new product development programmes and nurture an innovation climate to lay the foundations for new product success. The 3M company, for example, places a heavy reliance on new product introduction. Each of its divisions is expected to achieve a quarter of its revenue from products that have been on the market for under six years.

The reality of new product development is that it is a risky activity: most new products fail. But, as we shall see, new product development should not be judged in terms of the percentage of failures. To do so could stifle the spirit of innovation. The acid test is the number of successes. Failure has to be tolerated; it is endemic in the whole process of developing new products.

To fully understand new product development, we need to distinguish between invention and innovation. **Invention** is the discovery of new ideas and methods. **Innovation** occurs when an invention is commercialized by bringing it to market. Not all countries that are good at invention have the capability to innovate successfully. For example, the UK has an excellent record of invention; among major UK inventions and discoveries are the steam engine, the steamboat, the locomotive, the steam turbine, the electric heater, the hydraulic press, cement, the telegraph, the stethoscope, rubber tyres, the bicycle, television, the computer, the radio valve, radar, celluloid, the hovercraft and the jet engine. In terms of innovation, however, the British fall far short of the Japanese, who have the ability to successfully market products by constantly seeking to improve and develop—a process called Kaizen (sometimes Kaisan).[1] The classic example is the Sony Walkman, which was not an invention in the sense that it was fundamentally new; rather its success (over 75 million have been sold worldwide) was based on the innovative marketing of existing technologies.

Scandinavian countries have many businesses built on a local invention. For example, Tetra Pak was founded by a person who conceived of 'pouring milk into a paper bag'. Lego bricks have revolutionized toys and Gambro invented a machine that can take the place of kidneys. In all these cases, the key was not just the invention but the capability to innovate by bringing the product successfully to market.[2]

The USA is a major source of innovation. The Internet is dominated by US companies such as Amazon, Google, eBay and, as Table 11.1 shows, US companies occupy six out of the top 10 places in a survey of the world's most innovative companies.[3]

A key point to remember is that the focus of innovation should be on providing new solutions that better meet customer needs. Innovative solutions often do not require major breakthroughs in technology. For example, the growth of Starbucks was not fuelled by technological breakthroughs but by redefining what city-centre coffee drinking meant, and Ryanair has built its success by creating a different consumer appeal from traditional airlines based on low prices and strict cost control. The Body Shop's success was based on the modern woman's concern for the environment, and Dell became the most profitable computer company by becoming the first to market computers directly to its customers.[4] Because many innovations fail, it is important to understand the key success factors. A study of 60 innovations launched by 34 companies and the PIMS database to determine the key success factors in innovation revealed the following major findings.[5]

- *Innovation success is related to the creation and delivery of added consumer value.* Innovations that produce large improvements in consumer value perform much better than those that fail to show any change in consumer value. Unsurprisingly, radical innovation has greater potential for enhancing performance than small, incremental innovations. Incremental innovations, though, can be very successful provided they meet the first test: the creation and delivery of added consumer value.

The world's most innovative companies		TABLE 11.1
Company	**Reason**	
Apple	Apple's Mac and iPod continue to expand share and success in a mature mobile phone market with the iPhone (supported by its App Store)—proof of the company's innovatory zeal	
Google	The search giant keeps launching new services, such as Google Voice and a way to target ads based on web-browsing behaviour	
Toyota	Toyota continues to innovate in the 'green' car market with a roomier Prius, which has solar-powered AC to keep the car cool when parked outside	
Microsoft	Microsoft continues to innovate with the launch of 'cloud' offerings that allow Windows operating system users to meld their PCs more easily with the Internet	
Nintendo	Has broadened video games' appeal to a wide age range and makes them easy to play	
IBM	IBM is focusing on the 'Smart Planet'—how sensors, data analysis, computers and networks can be joined to improve the performance of everything from transport systems to electrical grids	
Hewlett-Packard	H-P has brought focus to its R&D spending with printer, PC and service units, getting more to launch practical advances like touchscreens	
Research in Motion	RIM continues its wireless e-mail success with its BlackBerry models, and has launched its own app store to compete against Apple	
Nokia	Nokia's success in the mobile phone market has been boosted by its line of touchscreen products	
Wal-Mart	Supply chain innovation has helped Wal-Mart to lower prices, and it is using technology to pioneer digital health-record systems and energy-efficient stores	

Source: a 2009 survey of 2700 senior executives by the Boston Consulting Group, reported in *Business Week* by Jana (2009).[6]

- *Speed to market counts.* The most successful new products tend to be those that are launched within one year of the conception of the new idea. There are two reasons for this. First, delay increases the risk of others getting to market first; second, consumer priorities may change.
- *A product's inferior perceived value cannot be compensated for with high communications spending.* High expenditures on advertising and promotion only have a significant effect on performance where the product is already perceived to have high consumer value. High expenditures for inferior products actually worsen the performance: advertising makes bad products fail quicker.

In this chapter we shall ask the question 'What is a new product?' and examine three key issues in new product development, namely organization, developing an innovation culture and the new product development process. Then we shall examine the strategies involved in product replacement, the most common form of new product development. Finally, we shall look at the consumer adoption process, which is how people learn about new products, try them, and adopt or reject them. Throughout this chapter reference will be made to research that highlights the success factors in new product development.

What is a New Product?

Some new products are so fundamentally different from products that already exist that they reshape markets and competition. For example, the pocket calculator created a new market and made the slide rule obsolete. At the other extreme, a shampoo that is different from existing products only by means of its brand name, fragrance, packaging and colour is also a new product. In fact, four broad categories of new product exist.[7]

1 *Product replacements*: these account for about 45 per cent of all new product launches, and include revisions and improvements to existing products (e.g. Sony PlayStation 3 replacing PlayStation 2), repositioning (existing products such as Lucozade being targeted at new market segments) and cost reductions (existing products being reformulated or redesigned to cost less to produce). An example of a product replacement based on cost reduction is the reformulation of Bell's whisky, which replaced its 'aged eight years' positioning with the less specific Bell's Original tap.[8] The illustration featuring Dyson is an example of a product replacement based on an improvement to an existing product.

2 *Additions to existing lines*: these account for about 25 per cent of new product launches and take the form of new products that add to a company's existing product lines. This produces greater product depth. An example is the launch by Weetabix of a brand extension, Oatibix, to compete with other oat-based cereals. Another example is the addition to the Crest toothpaste brand of Crest Whitestrips, a tooth-whitening product, and the Crest Spinbrush line of inexpensive battery-powered toothbrushes.[9]

**We reduced the size.
We didn't reduce the cleaning performance.**

Making a small vacuum is easy if you are willing to reduce its cleaning performance along with its size. Dyson isn't. Instead, Dyson engineers have had to painstakingly miniaturize all the important components to make a small machine perform like a big one. Housing the technology in a ball has helped them do this. And it comes with a 5 year warranty.

dyson The vacuum that doesn't lose suction.

www.dyson.com

Dyson proves no loss of suction using the IEC 60312 CI 2.9 test standard

▲ This new product replacement from Dyson is an improvement on an existing product.

3 *New product lines*: these total around 20 per cent of new product launches, and represent a move into a new market. For example, in Europe, Mars has launched a number of ice cream brands, which was a new product line for this company. This strategy widens a company's product mix.

4 *New-to-the-world products*: these total around 10 per cent of new product launches, and create entirely new markets. For example, the video games console, the mp3 player, camcorder and the Internet have created new markets because of the highly valued customer benefits they provide.

Clearly the degree of risk and reward varies according to the new product category. New-to-the-world products normally carry the highest risk since it is often very difficult to predict consumer reaction. Often, market research will be unreliable in predicting demand as people do not really understand the full benefits of the product until it is on the market and they get the chance to experience them. Furthermore, it may take time for the products to be accepted. For example, the Sony Walkman was initially rejected by marketing research since the concept of being seen in a public place wearing earphones was alien to most people. After launch, however, this behaviour was gradually accepted by younger age groups, who valued the benefit of listening to music when on a train or bus, walking down the street, and so on. At the other extreme, adding a brand variation to an existing product line lacks significant risk but is also unlikely to proffer significant returns.

Effective new product development is based on creating and nurturing an innovative culture, organizing effectively for new product development and managing the new product development process. We shall now examine these three issues.

Creating and Nurturing an Innovative Culture

The foundation for successful new product development is the creation of a corporate culture that promotes and rewards innovation. Unfortunately many marketing managers regard their company's corporate culture as a key constraint to innovation.[10] Managers, therefore, need to pay more attention to creating a culture that encourages innovation. Figure 11.1 shows the kinds of attitudes and actions that can foster an innovation culture. People in

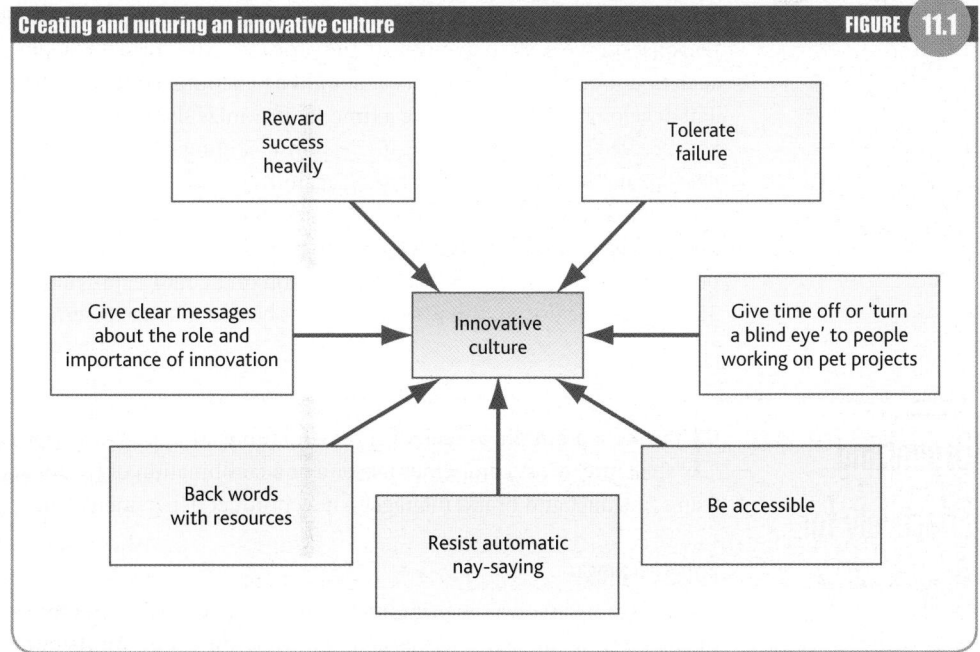

Creating and nuturing an innovative culture FIGURE 11.1

organizations observe those actions that are likely to lead to success or punishment. The surest way to kill innovative spirit is to conspicuously punish those people who are prepared to create and champion new product ideas through to communication when things go wrong, and to reward those people who are content to manage the status quo. Such actions will breed the attitude 'Why should I take the risk of failing when by carrying on as before I will probably be rewarded?' Research has shown that those companies that have supportive attitudes to rewards and risk, and a tolerant attitude towards failure, are more likely to innovate successfully.[11] This was recognized as early as 1941 in 3M when the former president William McKnight said 'Management that is destructively critical when mistakes are made kills initiative, and it is essential that we have people with initiative if we continue to grow.'[12]

An innovation culture can also be nurtured by senior management visibly supporting new product development in general, and high-profile projects in particular.[13] British Rail's attempt to develop the ill-fated Advanced Passenger Train (APT), which involved new technology, was hampered by the lack of this kind of support. Consequently, individual managers took a subjective view on whether they were for or against the project. Beside sending clear messages about the role and importance of new product development, senior management should reinforce their words by allowing time off from their usual duties to people who wish to develop their own ideas, make available funds and resources for projects, and make themselves accessible when difficult decisions need to be taken.[14]

One company that displays its commitment to innovation is 3M. It invests around 7 per cent of its global sales of around £10 billion in research and development and places a high value on staff input. This is formalized by allowing staff to spend 15 per cent of their work time on their own projects. By motivating staff to dedicate time to new product development, 3M generates 30 per cent of sales from products that are less than four years old.[15] Google also supports new product development, allowing employees 20 per cent of their work time to spend on individual projects. Gmail and Google News are two products that have resulted.[16]

Finally, management at all levels should resist the temptation of automatic 'nay-saying'. Whenever a new idea is suggested the tendency of the listener is to think of the negatives. For example, suppose you were listening to the first ever proposal that someone at Nokia made concerning a move into mobile phones. Your response might have been: 'We know nothing about that business', 'We are not strong enough to compete against the Americans and Japanese' and 'If we succeed they will undercut us on price.' All these perfectly natural responses serve only to demotivate the proposer. The correct response is to resist expressing such doubts. Instead, the proposer should be encouraged to take the idea further, to research and develop it. There will come a time to scrutinize the proposal but only after the proposer has received an initial encouraging response. Stifling new ideas at conception serves only to demotivate the proposer from trying again.

Creative leadership is required to release the passions, imaginations and energy needed for outstanding innovation. Such leadership encourages staff to reject the status quo and operate in a productive discomfort zone, has a clear vision of the future, provides support for exploration (as 3M and Google do), and shows in its actions how to tolerate uncertainty and live with paradox.[17]

Organizing Effectively for New Product Development

The second building block of successful innovation is an appropriate organization structure. Most companies use one or a combination of the following methods: project teams, product and brand managers, new product departments and new product committees.

Project teams

Project teams involve the bringing together of staff from such areas as R&D, engineering, manufacturing, finance and marketing to work on a new product development project. Research has shown that assigning the responsibility of new product development to such cross-functional teams has a positive effect on new product performance.[18] Specialized skills are combined to form an effective team to develop the new product concept. This organization form is in line with Kanter's belief that to compete in today's global marketplace, companies must move from rigid functional organizational structures to highly integrated ones.[19] People are assigned to the venture team as a major undertaking and the team is linked directly to top management to avoid having to communicate and get approval from several layers of management before progressing a course of action. This form of organization was used by IBM to successfully develop its first personal computer, and Unilever has also established a venture unit that focuses on developing new business targeted at areas not currently addressed by existing brands.[20] Its advantages include the fostering of a group identity and common purpose, fast decision-making, and the lowering of bureaucratic barriers.

A similar organizational change, which has reduced the product development cycle time, is the bringing together of design and manufacturing engineers to work as a team. Traditionally, design engineers would work on product design and then the blueprint would be passed on to production engineers. By working together each group can understand the problems of the other and effectively reduce the time it takes to develop a new product. The process—simultaneous engineering—was pioneered in Japan but is being adopted by European companies. For example, Ford of Europe brings together design and production engineers, purchasing engineers, finance and quality control specialists, and support staff to work as teams to develop future Ford cars in long-term collaboration with component suppliers.[21] Being faster has been shown to result in better new product performance in terms of higher profits and market share.[22]

Product and brand managers

Product and brand management entails the assignment of product managers to product lines (or groups of brands within a product line) and/or brand managers to individual brands. These managers are then responsible for their success and have the task of coordinating functional areas (e.g. production, sales, advertising and marketing research). They are also often responsible for new product development, including the creation of new product ideas, improving existing products and brand extensions. They may be supported by a team of assistant brand managers and a dedicated marketing researcher. In some companies a new product development manager may help product and brand managers in the task of generating and testing new product concepts. This form of organization is common in the grocery, toiletries and drinks industries.

New product departments and committees

The review of new product projects is normally in the hands of high-ranking functional managers, who listen to progress reports and decide whether further funds should be assigned to a project. They may also be charged with deciding new product strategies and priorities. No matter whether the underlying structure is venture team, product and brand management or new product department, a new products committee often oversees the process and services to give projects a high corporate profile through the stature of its membership.

The importance of teamwork

Whichever method (or combination of methods) is used, effective cross-functional teamwork is crucial for success.[23] In particular, as the quotation by Frey at the beginning of this chapter implies, there has to be effective communication and teamwork between R&D and marketing.[24] Although all functional relationships are important during new product development, the cultural differences between R&D and marketing are potentially the most harmful and difficult to resolve. The challenge is to prevent technical people developing only things that interest them professionally, and to get them to understand the realities of the marketplace.

The role of marketing directors

A study by Gupta and Wileman asked marketing directors of technology-based companies what they believed they could do to improve their relationship with R&D and achieve greater integration of effort.[25] Six major suggestions were made by the marketing directors.

1 *Encourage teamwork*: marketing should work with R&D to establish clear, mutually agreed project priorities to reduce the incidence of pet projects. Marketing, R&D and senior management should hold regular joint project review meetings.

2 *Improve the provision of marketing information to R&D*: one of the major causes of R&D rejecting input from marketing was the lack of quality and timely information. Many marketing directors admitted that they could do a better job of providing such information to R&D. They also believed that the use of information would be enhanced if R&D personnel were made part of the marketing research team so that the questions on their minds could be incorporated into studies. They also felt that such a move would improve the credibility and trust between marketing and R&D.

3 *Take R&D people out of the lab*: marketing should encourage R&D staff to be more customer aware by inviting them to attend trade shows, take part in customer visits and prepare customer materials.

4 *Develop informal relationships with R&D*: they noted that there were often important personality and value differences between the two groups, which could cause conflict as well as being a stimulus to creativity. More effort could be made to break down these barriers by greater socializing, going to lunch together, and sitting with each other at seminars and presentations.

5 *Learn about technology*: the marketing directors believed that improving their 'technological savvy' would help them communicate more effectively with R&D people, understand various product design trade-offs, and comprehend the capabilities and limits of technology to create competitive advantages and provide solutions to customer problems.

6 *Formalize the product development process*: they noted that marketing people were often preoccupied with present products to the neglect of new products, and that the new product development process was far too unstructured. They advocated a more formal process, including formal new project initiation, status reports and review procedures, and a formal requirement that involvement in the process was an important part of marketing personnel's jobs.

The role of senior management

The study also focused on marketing directors' opinions of what senior management could do to help improve the marketing/R&D relationship. We have already noted, when discussing how to create an innovative culture, the crucial role that senior management staff play in creating the conditions for a thriving new product programme. Marketing directors mentioned six major ways in which senior management could play a part in fostering better relations.

1 *Make organizational design changes*: senior management should locate marketing and R&D near to each other to encourage communication and the development of informal relationships. They should clarify the roles of marketing and R&D in developing new products and reduce the number of approvals required for small changes in a project, which would give both R&D and marketing greater authority and responsibility.

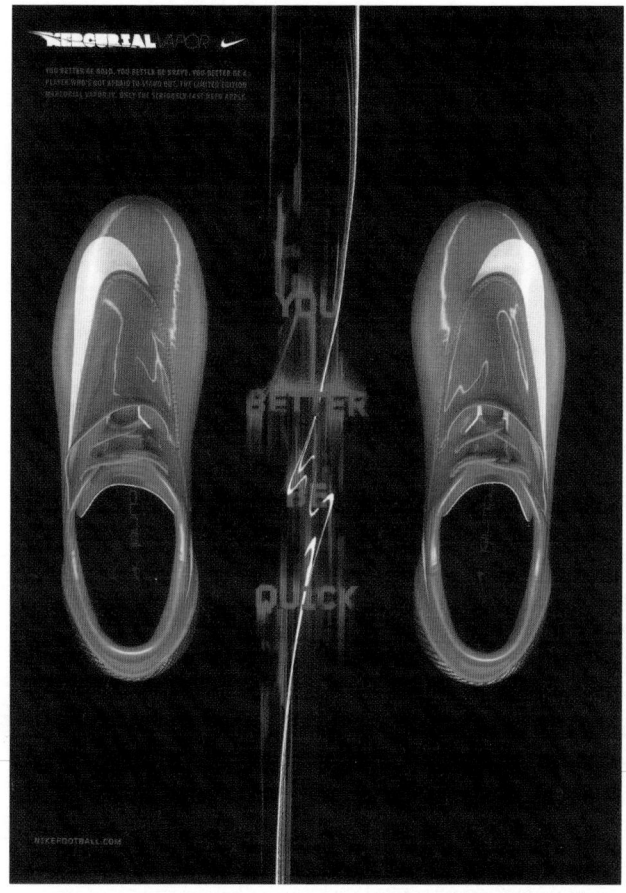

▲ Nike continues to be at the forefront of the specialist shoe market.

2 *Show a personal interest in new product development*: organizational design changes should be backed up by more overt commitment and interest in innovation through early involvement in the product development process, attending product planning and review meetings, and helping to coordinate product development plans.

3 *Provide strategic direction*: many marketing directors felt that senior management could provide more strategic vision regarding new product/market priorities. They also needed to be more long term with their strategic thinking.

4 *Encourage teamwork*: senior management should encourage, or even demand, teamwork between marketing and R&D. Specifically, they should require joint R&D/marketing discussions, joint planning and budgeting, joint marketing research and joint reporting to them.

5 *Increase resources*: *some* marketing directors pointed to the need to increase resources to foster product development activities. The alternative was to reduce the number of projects. Resources should also be provided for seminars, workshops and training programmes for R&D and marketing people. The objective of these programmes would be to develop a better understanding of the roles, constraints and pressures of each group.

6 *Understand marketing's importance*: marketing directors complained of senior management's lack of understanding of marketing's role in new product development and the value of marketing in general. They felt that senior management should insist that marketing becomes involved with R&D in product development much earlier in the process so that the needs of customers are more prominent.

This research has provided valuable insights into how companies should manage the marketing/R&D relationship. It is important that companies organize themselves effectively since cross-functional teamwork and communication has proved to be a significant predictor of successful innovation in a number of studies.[26]

Managing the New Product Development Process

There are three inescapable facts about new product development: it is expensive, risky, and time-consuming. For example, Gillette spent an excess of £100 million over more than 10 years developing its Sensor razor brand. The new product concept was to develop a non-disposable shaver that would use new technology to produce a shaver that would follow the contours of a man's face, giving an excellent shave (through two spring-mounted platinum-hardened chromium blades) with fewer cuts. This made commercial sense since shaving systems are more profitable than disposable razors and allow more opportunity for creating a differential advantage. Had the brand failed, Gillette's position in the shaving market could have been damaged irreparably. Nike is another company that invests heavily in new product development to maintain its lead in the specialist sports shoe market (see illustration).

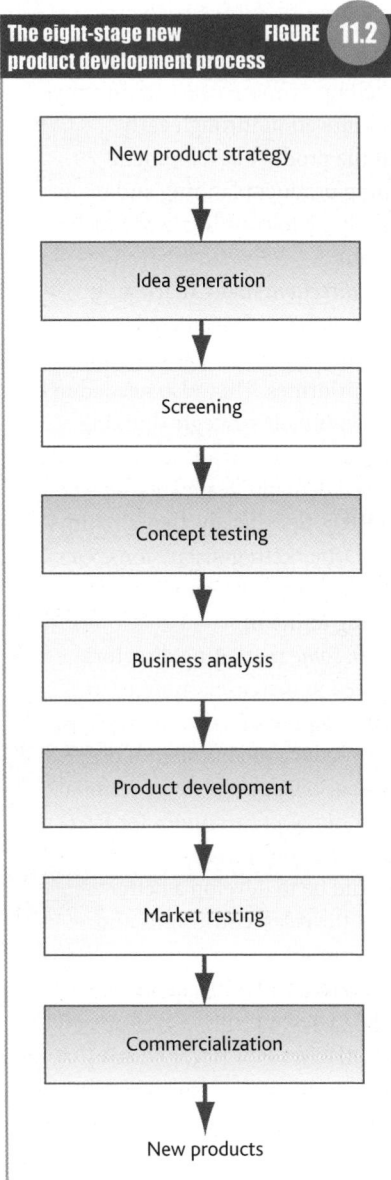

The eight-stage new product development process FIGURE **11.2**

- New product strategy
- Idea generation
- Screening
- Concept testing
- Business analysis
- Product development
- Market testing
- Commercialization
- New products

Managing the process of new product development is an important factor in reducing cost, time and risk. Studies have shown that having a formal process with review points, clear new product goals and a strong marketing orientation underlying the process leads to greater success whether the product is a physical good or a service.[27]

An eight-step new product development process to provide these characteristics is shown in Figure 11.2 and consists of setting new product strategy, idea generation, screening, concept testing, business analysis, product development, market testing and commercialization. Although the reality of new product development may resemble organizational chaos, the discipline imposed by the activities carried out at each stage leads to a greater likelihood of developing a product that not only works, but also confers customer benefits. We should note, however, that new products pass through each stage at varying speeds: some may dwell at a stage for a long period while others may pass through very quickly.[28]

New product strategy

As we have already seen, marketing directors value strategic guidance from senior management about their vision and priorities for new product development. By providing clear guidelines about which products/markets the company is interested in serving, senior management staff can provide a focus for the areas in which idea generation should take place. Also by outlining their objectives (e.g. market share gain, profitability, technological leadership) for new products they can provide indicators for the screening criteria that should be used to evaluate those ideas. An example of a company with a clearly developed new product strategy is Mars, which developed ice cream products that capitalized on the brand equity of its confectionery brand names, such as Twix, Mars and Milky Way.

A key issue in new product strategy is where to allocate resources. A company may have several divisions and a multitude of product lines. Where should funds be invested? Marketing in Action 11.1 discusses how Hewlett-Packard tackles this question.

Idea generation

One of the benefits of developing an innovative corporate culture is that it sparks the imagination. The objective is to motivate the search for ideas so that salespeople, engineers, top management, marketers and other employees are all alert to new opportunities. Interestingly, questioning Nobel Prize winners about the time and circumstances when they had the important germ of an idea that led them to great scientific discovery revealed that it can occur at the most unexpected time: just before going to sleep, on waking up in the morning and at church were some of the occasions mentioned. The common factor seems to be a period of quite contemplation, uninterrupted by the bustle of everyday life and work.

Successful new product ideas are not necessarily based on technological innovation. Often, they are based on novel applications of existing technology (e.g. Velcro poppers on disposable nappies) or new visions of markets (e.g. Levi Strauss's vision of repositioning jeans, which were originally used as working clothes, as a fashion statement through its 501 brand).

The sources of new product ideas can be internal to the company: scientists, engineers, marketers, salespeople and designers, for example. Some companies use **brainstorming** as a technique to stimulate the creation of ideas, and use financial incentives to persuade people to

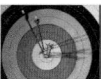

11.1 Marking in Action

Investing in New Product Development the Hewlett-Packard Way

For many years business leaders have tried to grapple with the question of how much money to invest in R&D when the payoff could take 10 years. Even more vexing is the problem of where to allocate scarce funds. Many expert observers believe that Hewlett-Packard has produced the gold standard for resource allocation.

HP's method is simplicity itself. It uses a metric called 'R&D productivity'. It measures R&D spending as a percentage of gross margin for each product line. A standard desktop computer with low margins would normally get a low allocation of funds, perhaps leading to one or two innovative features. A high-end laptop with fat margins would get a high allocation, leading to enough innovative features to differentiate it from its rivals.

To determine the appropriate R&D level, HP calculates three-year projections of expected gross margins. Where it sees an opportunity to raise margins, investment funds follow. For example, HP saw an opportunity for a premium-priced desktop computer with touchscreen technology. It believed that such a feature would make a desktop easier for families with children to use. The result was R&D investment that led to the first touchscreen, all-in-one desktop. The TouchSmart PC, which is sold in the USA for $2000, has helped boost HP's profits and sales.

HP allocates a bigger percentage of its overall budget to game-changing types of technologies—such as multi-touch technology and gesture-based controls, which allow users to point at their computers to launch a music or photo program—that create differentiation and lead to high gross profit margins. By linking R&D expenditure to current and projected gross margins, HP has developed one of the most quantitative approaches to new product development budget allocation in the world.

Based on: Edwards (2008);[29] Edwards (2009)[30]

put forward the ideas they have had. The 3M Post-it adhesive-backed notepaper was a successful product that was thought of by an employee who initially saw it as a means of preventing paper falling from his hymn book as he marked the hymns that were being sung. Because of the innovative culture within 3M, he bothered to think of commercial applications and acted as a product champion within the company to see the project through to become the commercial and global success it is today. In a survey of Dutch industrial goods, over 60 per cent of companies claimed to use brainstorming to generate new product ideas.[31]

11.1 Pause for Thought

Try to think of a new product idea. The best time is during a period of quiet contemplation such as before going to sleep or after waking up. The idea does not have to be 'new to the world'. You could focus on a product that you use/consume regularly. What are its weaknesses? How could it be improved? Many new products are 'incremental' in the sense that they are small or medium-sized improvements on existing products.

Hamel and Prahalad argue that global competitive battles will be won by those companies that have the corporate imagination to build and dominate fundamentally new markets.[32] Introducing such products as speech-activated appliances, artificial bones and automatic language translators would effectively create new and largely uncontested competitive space.

Often, fundamentally new products/markets are created by small businesses that are willing to invent new business models or radically redesign existing models. Sources of new product ideas can also be external to the company. Examining competitors' products may provide clues to product improvements. Competitors' new product plans can be gleaned by training the salesforce to ask distributors about new activities. Distributors can also be a source of new product ideas directly, since they deal with customers and have an interest in selling improved products.

Another source of externally generated new product ideas is the millions of scientists, engineers and other companies globally. By collaborating with them, a firm can gain access to innovative solutions. Procter & Gamble leads the way by using online networks to get in touch with thousands of experts, as Marketing in Action 11.2 explains.

11.2 Marketing in Action

Procter & Gamble Practises Open Innovation

Internal staff are excellent sources of innovation, but why limit the flow of ideas to them? Outside the company there are millions of scientists, engineers, universities, government laboratories and other companies that may have the know-how and technical expertise to contribute to new product development.

Procter & Gamble taps in to this vast well of expertise through its Connect+ Develop programme. It practises open innovation, which is a means of accessing externally developed intellectual property, while allowing its internally developed assets and know-how to be used by others. This two-way process has led to innovation in such areas as technology, engineering, marketing, packaging, design and business services.

Through Connect+ Develop, P&G actively seeks collaboration with external partners to generate and develop new product ideas. As Nabil Sakkab, global leader of its fabric and homecare research and development, commented, 'I pay 7000 scientists to work for me at P&G but there are 1.5 million scientists out there who do not work for P&G. I want to make my R&D department 1,507,000 strong.' This attempt to 'un-source' ideas is working: 45 per cent of the new ideas he is working on have come from outside the company. Across P&G as a whole external collaboration plays a key role in nearly 50 per cent of its products.

An example is the launch of Pringle Prints in North America. The product is a line of potato crisps printed with entertaining pictures and words, and was developed in record time and at a fraction of the usual cost. Instead of looking internally for solutions to the problem of how to print images on crisps, P&G searched its global networks of individuals and institutions. It discovered a small bakery in Italy, owned by a university professor who had invented an ink-jet method of printing edible images on cakes and biscuits. P&G adapted the method for crisps and the result was double-digit growth for its North American Pringles business.

Based on: Huston and Sakkab (2006);[33] Mitchell (2005)[34]

A major source of good ideas is consumers themselves. Their needs may not be satisfied by existing products and they may be genuinely interested in providing ideas that lead to product improvement. Sometimes, traditional marketing research techniques such as focus groups can be useful. For example, marketing research revealed that young drinkers wanted great-tasting portable alcoholic drinks. A new product category—premium bottled spirits—was created as traditional spirits did not possess the portability factor. A prime example is Bacardi Breezer, which is a fruit-flavoured spirit in a small bottle.[35]

Researching blogs and online social community sites can reveal ideas for new products, and insights into the strengths and weaknesses of existing products, which can lead to improved product replacements.

Other companies require a less traditional approach. Procter & Gamble, for example, has used ethnographic research to observe consumers using its products, in order to develop new and improved products. Philips employs anthropologists and cognitive psychologists to gather insights into the needs and expectations of consumers around the world. It conducts 'culture scan' research into shorter-term social, cultural and aesthetic trends, and 'strategic futures' research into trends over a five- to seven-year period. The findings play a major role in which products should be brought to market and how they should be designed.[36]

In organizational markets, keeping in close contact with customers who are innovators and market leaders in their own marketplaces is likely to be a fruitful source of new product ideas.[37] These *lead customers* are likely to recognize required improvements ahead of other customers as they have advanced needs and are likely to face problems before other product users. For example, GE's healthcare division researches 'luminaries', who tend to be well-published doctors and research scientists from leading medical institutions. Up to 25 luminaries are brought together at regular medical advisory board sessions to discuss developments in GE's technology. GE then shares some of its advanced technology with a subset of these people. The result is a stream of new products that emerge from collaboration with these groups. Marketing research can play a role in providing feedback when the product line is familiar to customers. For example, the original idea for Hewlett-Packard's successful launch of its Desk-Jet printer came from marketing research, which revealed that personal computer users would value a relatively slow-speed printer that approached the quality of a laser printer but sold at less than half the price.[38] However, for radically new products customers may be unable to articulate their requirements and so conventional marketing research may be ineffective as a source of ideas. In this situation, as can be seen in Marketing in Action 11.3, companies need to be proactive in their search for new markets rather than rely on customer suggestions.[39]

Screening

Having developed new product ideas, they need to be screened to evaluate their commercial worth. Some companies use formal checklists to help them judge whether the product idea should be rejected or accepted for further evaluation. This ensures that no important criterion is overlooked. Criteria may be used that measure the attractiveness of the market for the proposed product, the fit between the product and company objectives, and the capability of the company to produce and market the product. Texas Instruments focused on financial and market-based criteria when screening new semiconductor products. To pass its screen, a new product idea had to have the potential to sustain a 15 per cent compound sales growth rate, give 25 per cent return on assets, and be of a unique design that lowered costs or gave a performance advantage. Other companies may use a less systematic approach, preferring more flexible open discussion among members of the new product development committee to gauge likely success.

Concept testing

Once the product idea has been accepted as worthy of further investigation, it can be framed into a specific concept for testing with potential customers. In many instances the basic product idea will be expanded into several product concepts, each of which can be compared by testing with target customers. For example, a study into the acceptability of a new service—a proposed audit of software development procedures that would lead to the award of a quality assurance certificate—was expressed in eight service concepts depending on which parts of the development procedure would be audited (e.g. understanding customer needs, documentation, benchmarking, and so on). Each concept was evaluated by potential buyers of the software to gauge which were the most important aspects of software

11.3 Marketing in Action

Creating Radical Innovation

Many new products are incremental, such as Diet Coke from Coca-Cola or Persil detergent tables from Unilever; others fundamentally change the nature of a market and may be based on technological breakthroughs such as the development of mobile phones or the invention of new business models such as Dell selling customized computers direct to consumers or Starbucks' reinvention of city-centre coffee drinking. Radical innovation is risky but can bring huge rewards. The focus is on making the competition irrelevant by creating a leap in value for customers, and entry into new and uncontested market space.

Avoiding an incremental approach to new product development involves a sharpening of the corporate imagination to become more alive to new market opportunities. Five factors can aid this development.

1 *Escaping the tyranny of served markets*: looking outside markets that are currently served can be assisted by defining core competences and looking at products/markets that lie between existing business units. For example, Motorola's core competences in wireless technology led it to look beyond current products/ markets (e.g. mobile phones) and towards global positioning satellite receivers. Looking for white space between business units led Kodak to envisage a market for storing and viewing photographs.

2 *Searching for innovative product concepts*: this can be aided by viewing markets as a set of customer needs and product functionalities. This has led to adding an important function to an existing product (e.g. Yamaha's electronic piano), creating a new way to deliver an existing function (e.g. electronic notepads), or creating a new functionality (e.g. the Internet).

3 *Weakening traditional price–performance assumptions*: traditional price–performance assumptions should be questioned. For example, it was Sony and JVC that questioned the price tag of £25,000 on early video recorders. They gave their engineers the freedom and the technology to design a video recorder that cost less than £500.

4 *Leading customers*: a problem with developing truly innovative products is that customers rarely ask for them. Successful innovating companies lead customers by imagining unarticulated needs rather than simply following them. They gain insights into incipient needs by talking in-depth to and observing closely a market's most sophisticated and demanding customers. For example, Yamaha set up a facility in London where Europe's most talented musicians could experiment with state-of-the-art musical hardware. The objective was not only to understand the customer but also to convey to the customer what might be possible technologically.

5 *Building a radical innovation hub*: a hub is a group of people who encourage and oversee innovation. It includes idea hunters, idea gatherers, internal venture capitalists, members of project evaluation committees, members of overseeing boards and experienced entrepreneurs. The hub's prime function is to nurture hunters and gatherers from all over the company to foster a stream of innovative ideas. At the centre of each project is a product champion who takes risks, breaks the rules, energizes and rescues, and re-energizes the project.

The attitudes and practices within innovative firms are also important and help create a culture that assists in driving radical innovation. Attitudes include a tolerance for risk-taking and a future market focus that encourages managers to seek customer needs through strategic futures research. Key practices are the empowerment of product champions, which encourages them (supported by resources) to explore research and build on promising, but uncertain, future technologies, and the use of generous financial and non-financial (e.g. recognition and autonomy) rewards for innovative employees.

Based on: Hamel and Prahalad (1991);[40] Hamel (1999);[41] Leifer et al. (2001);[42] Hunt (2002);[43] Bartram (2004);[44] Tellis et al. (2009)[45]

ALCOHOL-FREE
WITH NO
COMPROMISE
ON TASTE.

BECK'S. DIFFERENT BY CHOICE.

www.drinkaware.co.uk www.becks.co.uk

▲ New concepts like the introduction of Beck's alcohol-free larger will be tested before development and launch.

development that should be audited.[46] **Concept testing** thus allows the views of customers to enter the new product development process at an early stage. For example, the idea of introducing an alcohol-free version of Beck's larger will be concept tested to research consumer attitudes before development and launch (see illustration).

Group discussion can also be used to develop and test product concepts. For example, a major financial services company decided it should launch an interest-bearing transaction account (product idea) because its major competition had done so.[47] Group discussions were carried out to develop the product idea into a specific product concept (a chequebook feature was rejected in favour of a cash card) with a defined target market (the under-25s). This concept was then developed further using group discussions to refine the product features (a telephone banking service was added) and to select the lifestyle image that should be used to position the new product. The concept may be described verbally or pictorially so that the major features are understood. Potential customers can then state whether they perceive any benefits accruing from the features. A questionnaire is used to ascertain the extent of liking/disliking what is liked/disliked, the kind of person/organization that might buy the product, how/where/when/how often the product would be used, its price acceptability, and how likely they would be to buy the product.

Online marketing research is being used increasingly to test concepts, partly because of its relatively low cost. Companies such as Lego, BA, Philips, O_2 and P&G have set up their own community websites where they can test consumers' reactions to new product concepts. Online images as well as words can be used to describe the new concepts. Firms without their own community sites use research agencies such as YouGov and Toluna, which specialize in conducting online research and have access to panels that can be used to test new concepts.[48]

Considerable ingenuity is needed to research new concepts. For example, research into a new tea shop/tea bar concept avoided the mistake of asking people about it 'cold' (unprepared). This would have resulted in consumers saying negative things like 'only grannies like tea shops' or 'tea isn't fashionable like coffee is'. Instead, in order to establish the tea bar concept as contemporary in feel, a cuttings file of 'articles' about it in fashionable areas such as Soho and Brighton was produced and shown to participants before the market research session took place. Because they felt that the tea bar chain was already up and running and that it was contemporary, the participants became very enthusiastic about it. The research had successfully conveyed the correct concept to the participants and, therefore, their responses were more valid than if they had been asked about their reaction to the concept without the associated image.[49]

This example illustrates the use of a scenario to help the participant in the research visualize the new product concept. The scenario method is of particular use when researching radical innovation concepts that, if launched, produce new-to-the-world products. Traditional marketing research methods rely on asking target consumers what they want, or asking them to rate the attractiveness of new product concepts. This can lead to less radical innovations being favoured because of the concept of *functional fixedness*, which is the tendency for people to evaluate new products in terms of what they already know. New products are evaluated by consumers in terms of already existing products and technologies rather than considering their needs in future situations. This can lead consumers to favour conventional new product concepts that are most likely the ones they already know.

The scenario method overcomes this problem by describing the new product in the context of a future technological and market setting. Usually a short story is told in which a potential consumer uses the new product in a future setting. The scenario can also be accompanied by visual material that shows various design features of the product and its future environment. By portraying the new product concept in a new environment, scenarios help consumers to evaluate new products outside the usage situations that are familiar to them, and encourage them to imagine what it would be like to use the product portrayed. The result is that judgements of radical innovations are less likely to suffer from the consumer's normal frame of reference, on the basis of which more conservative options are usually favoured.[50]

Often the last question (buying intentions) is a key factor in judging whether any of the concepts are worth pursuing further. In the grocery and toiletries industries, for example, companies (and their marketing research agencies) often use *action standards* (e.g. more than 70 per cent of respondents must say they intend to buy) based on past experience to judge new product concepts. Concept testing allows a relatively inexpensive judgement to be made by customers before embarking on a costly product development programme. Although not foolproof, obvious non-starters can be eliminated early on in the process.

Business analysis

Based on the results of the concept test and considerable managerial judgement, estimates of sales, costs and profits will be made. This is the **business analysis** stage. In order to produce sensible figures a marketing analysis will need to be undertaken. This will identify the target market, its size and projected product acceptance over a number of years. Consideration will be given to various prices and the implications for sales revenue (and profits) discussed. By setting a tentative price this analysis will provide sales revenue estimates.

Costs will also need to be estimated. If the new product is similar to existing products (e.g. a brand extension) it should be fairly easy to produce accurate cost estimates. For radical product concepts, costings may be nothing more than informal 'guesstimates'.

Break-even analysis, where the quantity needed to be sold to cover costs is calculated, may be used to establish whether the project is financially feasible. *Sensitivity analysis*, in which variations from given assumptions about price, cost and customer acceptance, for example, are checked to see how they impact on sales revenue and profits, can also prove useful at this stage. Optimistic, most likely and pessimistic scenarios can be drawn up to estimate the degree of risk attached to the project.

If the product concept appears commercially feasible, this process will result in marketing and product development budgets being established based on what appears to be necessary to gain customer awareness and trial, and the work required to turn the concept into a marketable product.

Product development

At this stage the new product concept is developed into a physical product. As we have seen, the trend is to move from a situation where this is the sole responsibility of the R&D and/or engineering department. Multi-disciplinary project teams are established with the task of bringing the product to the marketplace. A study by Wheelwright and Clark lays out six key principles for the effective management of such teams.[51]

1 *Mission*: senior management must agree to a clear mission through a project charter that lays out broad objectives.
2 *Organization*: the appointment of a heavyweight project leader and a core team consisting of one member from each primary function in the company. Core members should not occupy a similar position on another team.

3 *Project plan*: creation by the project leader and core team of a contract book, which includes a work plan, resource requirements and objectives against which it is willing to be evaluated.

4 *Project leadership*: heavyweight leaders not only lead, manage and evaluate other members of the core team, they also act as product champions. They spend time talking to project contributors inside and outside the company, as well as customers and distributors, so that the team keeps in touch with the market.

5 *Responsibilities*: all core members share responsibility for the overall success of the project as well as their own functional responsibilities.

6 *Executive sponsorship*: an executive sponsor in senior management is required to act as a channel for communication with top management and to act as coach and mentor for the project and its leader.

The aim is to integrate the skills of designers, engineers, production, finance and marketing specialists so that product development is quicker, less costly and results in a high-quality product that delights customers. For example, the practice of **simultaneous engineering** means that designers and production engineers work together rather than passing the project from one stage of development to another once the first department's work is finished. Costs are controlled by a method called *target costing*. Target costs are worked out on the basis of target prices in the marketplace, and given as engineering/design and production targets.

Cutting time to market by reducing the length of the product development stage is a key marketing factor in many industries. Allied to simultaneous engineering, companies are using computer-aided design and manufacturing equipment and software (CAD-CAM) to cut time and improve quality. In particular, the use of 3D solid modelling, which completely defines an object in three dimensions on a computer screen and has the ability to compute masses, is very effective in shortening the product development stage.[52] This process, known as *virtual engineering*, has been used by Fiat, which, when designing its Bravo and 500, chose to rely solely on computer simulations rather than take the traditional route of making prototypes. This cut design-to-production time from 26 to 18 months.[53] In addition, three-dimensional CAD system designs can be shared with suppliers and customers. For example, Boeing engages customers such as British Airways and United Airlines in an online design process that allows them to engage in debates over alternative cabin layouts.

There are two reasons why product development is being accelerated. First, markets such as personal computers, video cameras and cars change so fast that to be slow means running the risk of being out of date before the product is launched. Second, cutting time to market can lead to competitive advantage. This may be short-lived but is still valuable while it lasts. For example, Rolls-Royce gained an 18-month window of opportunity by cutting lead times on its successful Trent 800 aero-engine.[54] For Zara, being consistently the fastest to market gives it a competitive advantage in the fashion industry.

Marketing has an important role to play in the product development stage. R&D and engineering may focus on the functional aspects of the product, whereas seemingly trivial factors may have an important bearing on customer choice. For example, the foam that appears when washing up liquid is added to water has no functional value: a washing-up liquid could be produced that cleans just as effectively but does not produce bubbles. However, the customer sees the foam as a visual cue that indicates the power of the washing-up liquid. Therefore, to market a brand that did not produce bubbles would be suicidal. Marketing needs to keep the project team aware of such psychological factors when developing the new product. Marketing staff need to make sure that the project team members understand and communicate the important attributes that customers are looking for in the product.

In the grocery market, marketing will usually brief R&D staff on the product concept, and the latter will be charged with the job of turning the concept into reality. For example, Yoplait, the French market leader in fruit yoghurts, found through marketing research that a yoghurt concept based on the following attributes could be a winner:

- top-of-the-range dessert
- position on a health–leisure scale at the far end of the pleasure range—the ultimate taste sensation
- a fruit yoghurt that is extremely thick and creamy.

This was the brief given to the Yoplait research and development team that had the task of coming up with recipes for the new yoghurt and the best way of manufacturing it. Its job was to experiment with different cream/fruit combinations to produce the right product—one that matched the product concept—and to do it quickly. Time to market was crucial in this fast-moving industry. To help them, Yoplait employed a panel of expert tasters to try out the new recipes and evaluate them in terms of texture, sweetness, acidity, colour, smell, consistency and size of the fruit.

Product testing focuses on the functional aspects of the product and on consumer acceptance. Functional tests are carried out in the laboratory and out in the field to check such aspects as safety, performance and shelf life. For example, a car's braking system must be efficient, a jet engine must be capable of generating a certain level of thrust and a food package must be capable of keeping its contents fresh. Product testing of software products by users is crucially important in removing any 'bugs' that have not been picked up by internal testers. For example, Google releases new products as 'betas' (unfinished versions) so that users can check for problems and suggest improvements.[55]

Besides conforming to these basic functional standards, products need to be tested with consumers to check acceptability in use. For consumer goods this often takes the form of in-house product placement. *Paired companion tests* are used when a new product is used alongside a rival, so that respondents have a benchmark against which to judge the new offering. Alternatively two (or more) new product variants may be tested alongside one another. A questionnaire is administered at the end of the test, which gathers overall preference information as well as comparisons on specific attributes. For example, two soups might be compared on taste, colour, smell and richness. In *monadic placement tests* only the new product is given to users for trial. Although no specific rival is used in the test, in practice users may make comparisons with previously bought products, market leaders or competitive products that are quickly making an impact on the market.

Another way of providing customer input into development is through *product clinics*. For example, prototype cars and trucks are regularly researched by inviting prospective drivers to such clinics where they can sit in the vehicle, and comment on its design, comfort and proposed features. For example, an idea to provide a hook for a woman's handbag in the Ford Mondeo was firmly rejected when researched in this way, and the feature discarded.

Experts can also be used when product testing. For example, the former world champion racing driver Jackie Stewart was used in the development work that led to the launch of the Ford Mondeo. Although there is a danger that expert views may be unrepresentative of the target market, it was found with the Mondeo that Stewart's opinion carried the necessary political clout to force changes in the design of the car that may not have been made without his input.

Information technology is assisting the product development process by allowing various combinations of product features to be displayed on a laptop so that customer preferences can be identified. For example, for a new mobile phone, various combinations of size, colour, screen display, keyboard layout and special facilities can be shown to consumers via a laptop, which enables them to construct their ideal product.

In organizational markets, products may be placed with customers free of charge or at below cost to check out the performance characteristics. A research survey contrasted the attitudes of West German machine tool manufacturers with their less successful British competitors towards product development.[56] The West German companies sought partnerships with customers, and developed and tested prototypes jointly with them. British attitudes were vastly different: marketing research was seen as a way of delaying product development, and customers were rarely involved for fear that they would stop buying existing products.

Market testing

So far in the development process, potential customers have been asked if they intend to buy the product but have never been placed in the position of having to pay for it. **Market testing** takes measurement of customer acceptance one crucial step further than product testing by forcing consumers to 'put their money where their mouth is'. The basic idea is to launch the new product in a limited way so that consumer response in the marketplace can be assessed. Two major methods are used: the simulated market test and test marketing.

The *simulated market test* can take a number of forms, but the principle is to set up a realistic market situation in which a sample of consumers chooses to buy goods from a range provided by the organizing company, usually a marketing research company. For example, a sample of consumers may be recruited to buy their groceries from a mobile supermarket that visits them once a week. They are provided with a magazine in which advertisements and sales promotions for the new product can appear. This method allows measurement of key success indicators such as *penetration* (the proportion of consumers that buy the new product at least once) and *repeat purchase* (the rate at which purchasers buy again) to be made. If penetration is high but repeat purchase low, buyers can be asked why they rejected the product after trial. Simulated market tests are therefore useful as a preliminary to test marketing by spotting problems, such as in packaging and product formulation, that can be rectified before test market launch. They can also be useful in eliminating new products that perform so badly compared to competition in the marketplace that test marketing is not justified. Indeed, as techniques associated with simulated market tests become more sophisticated and distributors increasingly refuse to cooperate in test marketing, they have become an attractive alternative to a full test market.[57]

Test marketing involves the launch of the new product in one or a few geographical areas chosen to be representative of its intended market. Towns or television areas are chosen in which the new product is sold into distribution outlets so that performance can be gauged face to face with rival products. Test marketing is the acid test of new product development since the product is being promoted as it would during a national launch, and consumers are being asked to choose it against competitor products as they would if the new product went national. It is a more realistic test than the simulated market test and therefore gives more accurate sales penetration and repeat purchasing estimates. By projecting test marketing results to the full market, an assessment of the new product's likely success can be made.

Test marketing does have a number of potential problems. Test towns and areas may not be representative of the national market, and thus sales projections may be inaccurate. Competitors may invalidate the test market by giving distributors incentives to stock their product, thereby denying the new product shelf space. Also, test marketing needs to run over a long enough period to measure the repeat purchase rate for the product, since this is a crucial indicator of success for many products (e.g. groceries and toiletries). This can mean a delay in national launch stretching to many months or even years. In the meantime, more aggressive competitors can launch a rival product nationally and therefore gain market pioneer advantages. A final practical problem is gaining the cooperation of distributors. In some instances, supermarket chains refuse to take part in test marketing activities or charge a hefty fee for the service.

The advantages of test marketing are that the information it provides facilitates the 'go/no go' national launch decision, and the effectiveness of the marketing mix elements—price, product formulation/packaging, promotion and distribution—can be checked for effectiveness. Sometimes a number of test areas are used with different marketing mix combinations to predict the most successful launch strategy. Its purpose therefore is to reduce the risk of a costly and embarrassing national launch mistake.

Although commonly associated with fast-moving consumer goods, service companies use test marketing to check new service offerings. Indeed, when they control the supply chain, as is the case with banks and restaurants, they are in an ideal situation to do so. Companies selling to organizations can also benefit from test marketing when their products have short repeat purchase periods (e.g. adhesives and abrasives). For very expensive equipment, however, test marketing is usually impractical, although as we have seen product development with lead users is to be recommended.

On a global scale, many international companies roll out products (e.g. cars and consumer electronics) from one country to another. In so doing they are gaining some of the benefits of test marketing in that lessons learned early on can be applied to later launches.

11.2 Pause for Thought

Why is market testing important in the new product development process? Is it practicable for all new products?

Commercialization

In this section we shall examine four issues: a general approach to developing a commercialization strategy for a new product, specific options for product replacement strategies, success factors when commercializing technology, and reacting to competitors' new product introductions.

Developing a commercialization strategy for a new product

An effective commercialization strategy relies upon marketing management making clear choices regarding the target market (where it wishes to compete), and the development of a marketing strategy that provides a differential advantage (how it wishes to compete). These two factors define the new product positioning strategy, as discussed in Chapter 8.

A useful starting point for choosing a target market is an understanding of the **diffusion of innovation process**.[58] This explains how a new product spreads throughout a market over time. Particularly important is the notion that not all people or organizations who make up the market will be in the same state of readiness to buy the new product when it is launched. In other words, different actors in the market will have varying degrees of innovativeness—that is, their willingness to try something new. Figure 11.3 shows the diffusion *of innovation* curve which categorizes people or organizations according to how soon they are willing to adopt the innovation.

The curve shows that those actors (*innovators* and *early adopters*) who were willing to buy the new product soon after launch are likely to form a minor part of the total number of

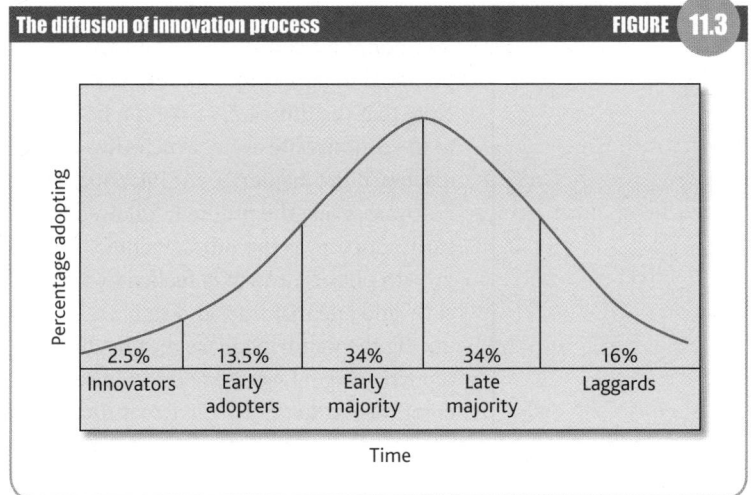

The diffusion of innovation process　　　FIGURE **11.3**

2.5%	13.5%	34%	34%	16%
Innovators	Early adopters	Early majority	Late majority	Laggards

Percentage adopting

Time

actors who will eventually be willing to buy it. As the new product is accepted and approved by these customers, and the decision to buy the new product therefore becomes less risky, so the people that make up the bulk of the market, comprising the *early and late majority*, begin to try the product themselves. Finally, after the product has gained full market acceptance, a group suitably described as the *laggards* adopt the product. By the time the laggards have begun buying the product, the innovators and early adopters have probably moved on to something new.

These diffusion of innovation categories have a crucial role to play in the choice of target market. The key is to understand the characteristics of the innovator and early adopter categories and target them at launch. Simply thinking about the kinds of people or organizations that are more likely to buy a new product early after launch may suffice. If not, marketing research can help. To stimulate the thinking process, Rogers suggests the following broad characteristics for each category.[59]

- *Innovators*: these are often venturesome and like to be different; they are willing to take a chance with an untried product. In consumer markets they tend to be younger, better educated, more confident and more financially affluent, and consequently can afford to take a chance on buying something new. In organizational markets, they tend to be larger and more profitable companies if the innovation is costly, and have more progressive, better-educated management. They may themselves have a good track record in bringing out new products and may have been the first to adopt innovations in the past. As such they may be easy to identify.

- *Early adopters*: these are not quite so venturesome; they need the comfort of knowing someone else has taken the early risk. But they soon follow their lead. They still tend to have similar characteristics to the innovator group, since they need affluence and self-confidence to buy a product that has not yet gained market acceptance. They, together with the innovators, can be seen as opinion leaders who strongly influence other people's views on the product. As such, they have a major bearing on the success of the product. One way of looking at the early adopters is that they filter the products accepted by the innovator group and popularize them, leading to acceptance by the majority of buyers in the market.[60]

- *Early and late majorities*: these form the bulk of the customers in the market. The early majority are usually deliberate and cautious in their approach to buying products. They like to see products prove themselves on the market before they are willing to part with cash for them. The late majority are even more cautious, and possibly sceptical of new products. They are willing to adopt only after the majority of people or organizations have tried the products. Social pressure may be the driving force moving them to purchase.

- *Laggards*: these are tradition-bound people. The innovation needs to be perceived almost as a traditional product before they will consider buying it. In consumer markets they are often the older and less well-educated members of the population.

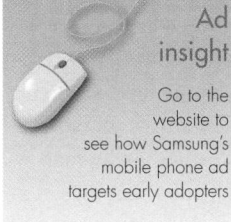

Ad insight

Go to the website to see how Samsung's mobile phone ad targets early adopters

These categories, then, can provide a basis for segmenting the market for an innovative product (see Chapter 8) and for target market selection.[61] For example, Samsung Electronics directs much of its marketing effort towards the innovator/early adopter segments by targeting

*because needing an MRI is scary enough.

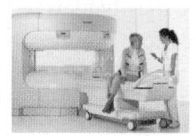

Philips Open MRI scanning produces a high quality image without having to put anyone into a narrow tunnel. By investing time in understanding people's needs, our innovations have been enhancing the quality of care for people for over 100 years. There's more where that came from at www.philips.com/because

PHILIPS

sense and simplicity

▲ Philips enhances patient care through its innovative MRI scanner, which does not require putting anyone into a narrow tunnel.

what it calls 'high-life seekers'—consumers who adopt technology early and are prepared to pay a premium price for it.[62] Note that the diffusion curve can be linked to the product life cycle, which was discussed in Chapter 10. At introduction, innovators buy the product, followed by early adopters as the product enters the growth phase. Growth is fuelled by the early and late majority, and stable sales during the maturity phase may be due to repurchasing by these groups. Laggards may enter the market during late maturity or even decline. Thus promotion designed to stimulate trial may need to be modified as the nature of new buyers changes over time.

The second key decision for commercialization is the choice of marketing strategy to establish a differential advantage. Understanding the requirements of customers (in particular, the innovator and early adopter groups) is crucial to this process and should have taken place earlier in the new product development process. The design of the marketing mix will depend on this understanding and the rate of adoption will be affected by such decisions. For example, advertising, promotion and sales efforts can generate awareness and reduce the customer's search costs, sales promotional incentives can encourage trial, and educating users in product benefits and applications has been found to speed the adoption process.[63] The innovative Philips MRI scanner is an example of a company tapping in to the needs of customers in an attempt to create a differential advantage (see illustration).

As we have seen, the characteristics of customers affect the rate of adoption of an innovation, and marketing's job is to identify and target those with a high willingness to adopt upon launch. The characteristics of the product being launched also affect the diffusion rate and have marketing strategy implications (see Fig. 11.4).

First, its differential advantage compared to existing products affects the speed of adoption. The more added customer benefits a product gives to a customer the more customers will be willing to buy. The high differential advantage of a fax machine over sending telegrams (e.g. convenience) or letters (e.g. speed) meant fast adoption. In turn, the convenience of e-mail over fax has meant rapid adoption. The differential advantage can be psychological, as when the handheld electronic personal organizer ousted the leather Filofax as a status symbol for the business elite.[64] More recently, the adoption of the BlackBerry can be explained by high functional (mobile e-mail and Internet access) and psychological (status symbol among businesspeople) benefits. Digital Marketing 11.1 explains how Kodak is seeking to create a differential advantage for a new product based on lower costs.

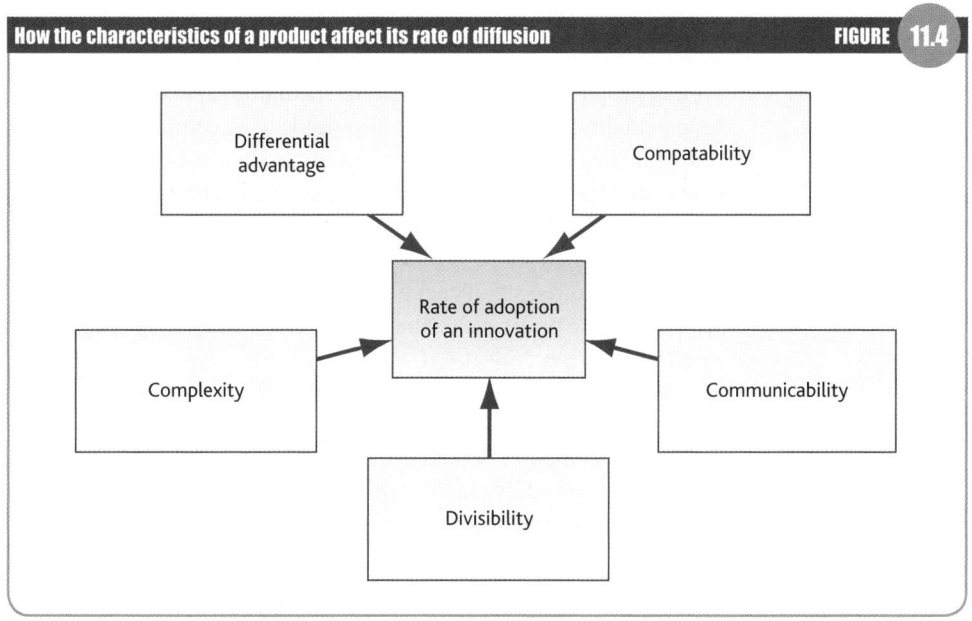

How the characteristics of a product affect its rate of diffusion   FIGURE 11.4

11.1 Digital Marketing

Capture the Moment

For many years the brand name Kodak has been inextricably linked with photographic film and the opportunities to capture magic times and events. Indeed the 'Kodak moment' has become synonymous with great photography around the globe. The Eastman Kodak company was formed in 1892, and Kodak is now the largest supplier of photographic film in the world. During its long history, the company has adopted an innovative approach towards new product development and, in doing so, adds improved and new products to its portfolio that are designed to attract customers who are *innovators* and *early adopters*.

Digital technology had significantly changed the photography market and, in response, the Kodak company is refocusing on two major markets: digital photography and digital printing. Photographic film sales have slowed significantly with the shift towards the use of digital cameras. Kodak's response is to launch the global 'Print and Prosper' campaign using an aggressive commercialization strategy to launch its new printing products. According to research, the greatest obstacle to printing photographs at home is the cost of ink and paper, and obtaining supplies. Kodak's printer is designed to address these problems, and provide consumers and businesses with a means of low-cost printing.

The main challenge for Kodak was how to position the new products to create differential advantage. The creative campaign began by emphasizing the cost of printing; in the UK, television adverts highlight that £600 million are spent on printer jet ink each year. It then asked the question 'Fed up with expensive ink? See how much you can save with Kodak.' The tag-line for the advert promoting the all-in-one inkjet printers is 'The world's most expensive liquid is not found in the Middle East, it's found in your ink cartridges!' This call-to-action aims to encourage consumers to visit a web link at www.kodak.com/printandprosper, where potential customers can use an interactive tool to calculate ink savings using the Kodak all-in-one printer versus the average ink costs of comparable inkjet printers.

Kodak believes that it is revolutionizing the inkjet printer market by saving consumers up to 50 per cent with everything they print, and the Print and Prosper campaign is central to the commercialization strategy that is encouraging consumers and businesspeople to switch to the new product.

Based on: Dewitz (2009)[65]

Second, there is the innovation's *compatibility* with consumers' values, experiences, lifestyles and behaviours. The congruence between mobile phones and the lifestyles of many young people helped their diffusion. The iPod's rapid diffusion was also aided by such compatibility. The new product also needs to be compatible with consumers' behaviour. If its adoption depends on significant behaviour change, failure or prolonged diffusion may result. For example, the unsuccessful Dvorak typing keyboard was supposed to modestly increase typing speed, but at the behavioural cost of having to 'unlearn' the QWERTY keyboard. Although the telephone is now part of our everyday lives, diffusion was slow because its adoption required significant behaviour change.[66] The diffusion of e-books has also been slow, partly because people value the tactility and aesthetics of books rather than reading from an electronic screen.

A third factor affecting diffusion rate is the innovation's *complexity*. Products that are difficult to understand or use may take longer to be adopted. For example, Apple launched its Macintosh computer backed by the proposition that existing computers were too complex to gain widespread adoption. By making its model more user friendly, it gained fast adoption among the large segment of the population that was repelled by the complexity of using computers.

Fourth, an innovation's *divisibility* also affects its speed of diffusion. Divisibility refers to the degree to which the product can be tried on a limited basis. Inexpensive products can be tried without risk of heavy financial loss. The rapid diffusion of Google was aided by the fact that its functionality could be accessed free of charge.

The final product characteristic that affects the rate of diffusion of an innovation is its *communicability*. Adoption is likely to be faster if the benefits and applications of the innovation can be readily observed or described to target customers. If product benefits are long term or difficult to quantify, then diffusion may take longer. For example, Skoda's attempt to produce more reliable cars took time to communicate, as buyers' acceptance of this claim depended on their long-term experience of driving the cars. In service industries, marketing innovations like providing more staff to improve the quality of service are hard to quantify in financial terms (i.e. extra revenue generated) and therefore have a low adoption rate by the management of some companies. The marketing implications are that marketing management must not assume that what is obvious to them will be clear to customers. They need to devise a communications strategy that allows potential customers to become aware of the innovation, and understand and be convinced of its benefits.

 11.3 Pause for Thought

Explain the rapid diffusion of the iPod in terms of the characteristics of the product.

Product replacement strategies

As we found at the start of this chapter, product replacement is the most common form of new product introduction. A study of the marketing strategies used to position *product replacements* in the marketplace found eight approaches based on a combination of product change and other marketing modifications (i.e. marketing mix and target market changes).[67] Figure 11.5 shows the eight replacement strategies used by companies.

1   *Facelift*: minor product change with little or no change to the rest of the marketing mix or target market. Cars are often given facelifts midway through their life cycle by undergoing minor styling alterations, for example. Japanese companies constantly facelift current electronic products such as cameras, DVD players and camcorders by changing product features, a process known as **product churning**.

Product replacement strategies   FIGURE 11.5

	No change	Product modified	Technology change
No change	No change	Facelift	Inconspicuous technological substitution
Remix	Remerchandising	Relaunch	Conspicuous technological substitution
New market/ segment	Intangible repositioning	Tangible repositioning	Neo-innovation

(Marketing)

Source: Saunders, J. and D. Jobber (1994) Strategies for Product Launch and Deletion, in Saunders, J. (ed.) *The Marketing Initiative*, Hemel Hempstead: Prentice-Hall, 227

2 *Inconspicuous technological substitution*: a major technological change with little or no alteration of the other elements of the marketing mix. The technological change is not brought to the consumer's attention. For example, brand loyalty to instant mashed potatoes was retained through major technological process and product changes (powder to granules to flakes) with little attempt to highlight these changes through advertising.

3 *Remerchandising*: a modification of name, promotion, price, packaging and/or distribution, while maintaining the basic product. For example, an unsuccessful deodorant for men was successfully remerchandised with repackaging, heavier advertising, a higher price and new brand name: Brut.

4 *Relaunch*: both the product and other marketing mix elements are changed. Relaunches are common in the car industry where, every four to five years, a model is replaced with an upgraded version. The replacement of the Vauxhall (Opel) Vectra with the Insignia is one example, and Marks & Spencer's relaunch of its food and soft drinks range with the removal of all hydrogenated fats, artificial colours and flavourings is another.[68] The advertisement for Alibi advertises the relaunch of UKTV Drama as a crime drama channel.

5 *Conspicuous technological substitution*: a major technological change is accompanied by heavy promotional (and other mix changes) to stimulate awareness and trial. An example is the replacement of the Rover Mini with the BMW Mini, which, despite remaining faithful to the character of the original, is technologically a fundamentally different car.

6 *Intangible repositioning*: the basic product is retained but other mix elements and target customers change. Lucozade is an example of a product that kept its original formulation but was targeted at different customer segments over time.

7 *Tangible repositioning*: both the product and target market change. Skoda is an example of the product being significantly improved to appeal to a more upmarket, wealthier target market.

8 *Neo-innovation*: a fundamental technology change accompanied by target market and mix changes. For example, Nokia practised neo-innovation when it moved from a conglomerate operating in such industries as paper, chemicals and rubber to being a marketer of mobile phones.

Companies, therefore, face an array of replacement options with varying degrees of risk. Figure 11.5 categorizes these options and provides an aid to strategic thinking when considering how to replace products in the marketplace.

Commercializing technology

Superior commercialization of technology has been, and will continue to be, a key success factor in many industries. Some companies, such as Canon, Sony, and Philips, already have the capability to bring sophisticated high-tech products to market faster than other

▲ Alibi, a crime drama channel, replaced UKTV Drama.
Reproduced with kind permission of UKTV.

companies that treat the commercialization process in a less disciplined manner. For example, Canon spends heavily on R&D (8 per cent of sales revenues) to maintain its leadership in the laser printer market by fast introduction of innovations such as colour improvements and to develop new products such as SED TVs, which can produce the wide viewing angle and deep colours of a cathode-ray TV but are as thin as a liquid-crystal or plasma screen.[69] Consistently beating the competition has been found to rest on four capabilities: being faster to market, supplying a wider range of markets, executing a larger number of product launches, and using a wider breadth of technologies.[70]

Many major market innovations appear in practice to be technologically driven: a technology seeking a market application rather than a market opportunity seeking a technology.[71] Marketing's input in such situations is to provide the insight as to how the technology may provide customer benefits within a prescribed target market. For example, an X-ray brain scanner was developed from a system used to X-ray metal. It was marketing insight that led to its application in medical diagnosis. As we have already discussed, traditional marketing research techniques have only a limited role to play when using technology to create new markets: people find it difficult to articulate their views on subjects that are unfamiliar, and acceptance may come only over time (the diffusion of innovation). Indeed, the price the customer will be asked to pay is usually unclear during the early stage of technological development. A combination of these factors may have been responsible for the first-ever forecast for computers, which predicted worldwide sales of 10 units.

The marketing of technological innovations, therefore, calls for a blend of technology and marketing. The basic marketing question, 'What potential benefits over existing products is this product likely to provide?', needs to be asked constantly during product development.

Furthermore the following lessons from the diffusion of innovation curve need to be remembered.

- The innovator/early adopter segments need to be identified and targeted initially.
- Initial sales are likely to be low: these groups are relatively small.
- Patience is required as the diffusion of an innovation takes time as people/organizations originally resistant to it learn of its benefits and begin to adopt it.
- The target group and message will need to be modified over time as new categories of customer enter the market.

Competitive Reaction to New Product Introductions

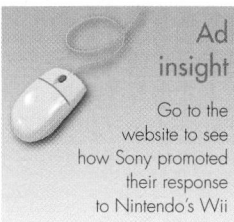

Ad insight

Go to the website to see how Sony promoted their response to Nintendo's Wii

New product launches may be in response to new product entries by competitors. Research suggests that when confronted with a new product entry by a competitor, incumbent firms should respond quickly with a limited set of marketing mix elements. Managers should rapidly decide which ones (product, promotion, price and place) are likely to have the most impact, and concentrate their efforts on them.[72]

Competitors' reaction times to the introduction of a new product have been found to depend on four factors.[73] First, response is faster in high-growth markets. Given the importance of such markets, competitors will feel the need to take action speedily in response to a new entrant. Second, response is dependent on the market shares held by the introducing firm and its competitors. Response time is slower when the introducing firm has higher market share and faster for those competitors who have higher market share. Third, response time is faster in markets characterized by frequent product changes. Finally, it is not surprising to find that response time is related to the time needed to develop the new product.

When you have read this chapter

log on to the Online Learning Centre at www.mcgraw-hill.co.uk/textbooks/jobber to explore chapter-by-chapter test questions, links and further online study tools for marketing.

Review

1 **The different types of new product that can be launched**

- There are four types of new product that can be launched: product replacements, additions to existing lines, new product lines and new-to-the-world products.

2 **How to create and nurture an innovative culture**

- Creating and nurturing an innovative culture can be achieved by rewarding success heavily, tolerating a certain degree of failure, senior management sending clear messages about the role and importance of innovation, their words being supported by allowing staff time off to develop their own ideas, making available resources and being accessible when difficult decisions need to be taken, and resisting automatic nay-saying.

3 **The organizational options applying to new product development**

- The options are project teams, product and brand managers, and new product departments and committees. Whichever method is used, effective cross-functional teamwork is essential for success.

4 **Methods of reducing time to market**

- A key method of reducing time to market is the process of simultaneous engineering. Design and production engineers, together with other staff, work together as a team rather than sequentially.
- Consumer goods companies are bringing together teams of brand and marketing managers, external design, advertising and research agency staff to develop simultaneously the brand and launch strategies.

5 **How marketing and R&D staff can work together effectively**

- A study by Gupta and Wileman suggests that marketing and R&D can better work together when teamwork is encouraged, there is an improvement in the provision of marketing information to R&D, R&D people are encouraged to be more customer aware, informal relationships between marketing and R&D are developed, marketing is encouraged to learn about technology, and a formal process of product development is implemented. Senior management staff have an important role to play by locating marketing and R&D close to each other, showing a personal interest in new product development, providing strategic direction, encouraging teamwork, increasing the resources devoted to new product development and enhancing their understanding of the importance of marketing in new product development.

6 **The stages in the new product development process**

- A formal process with review points, clear new product goals and a strong marketing orientation underlying the process leads to greater success.
- The stages are new product strategy (senior management should set objectives and priorities), idea generation (sources include customers, competitors, distributors, salespeople, engineers and marketers), screening (to evaluate their commercial worth), concept testing (to allow the views of target customers to enter the process early), product development (where the concept is developed into a physical product for testing), market testing (where the new product is tested in the marketplace) and commercialization (where the new product is launched).

7 **How to stimulate the corporate imagination**

- Four ways of stimulating the corporate imagination are: to encourage management to escape the tyranny of served markets by exploring how core competences can be exploited in new markets; to search for innovative product concepts—for example, by creating a new way to deliver an existing function (e.g. the electronic notepad); questioning traditional price–performance assumptions and giving engineers the resources to develop cheaper new products; and gaining insights by observing closely the market's most sophisticated and demanding customers.

8 **The six key principles of managing product teams**

- These are the agreement of the mission, effective organization, development of a project plan, strong leadership, shared responsibilities, and the establishment of an executive sponsor in senior management.

9 **The diffusion of innovation categories and their marketing implications**
- The categories are innovators, early adopters, early and late majorities, and laggards.
- The marketing implications are that the categories can be used as a basis for segmentation and targeting (initially the innovator/early adopters should be targeted). As the product is bought by different categories, so the marketing mix may need to change.
- The speed of adoption can be affected by marketing activities—for example, advertising to create awareness, sales promotion to stimulate trial, and educating users in product benefits and applications.
- The nature of the innovation itself can also affect adoption—that is, the strength of its differential advantage, its compatibility with people's values, experiences, lifestyles and behaviours, its complexity, its divisibility and its communicability.

10 **The key ingredients in commercializing technology quickly and effectively**
- The key ingredients are the ability of technologists and marketing people to work together effectively, simultaneous engineering, constantly asking the question 'What benefits over existing products is this new product likely to provide?', and remembering lessons from the diffusion of innovation curve (i.e. target the innovator/early adopter segments first).

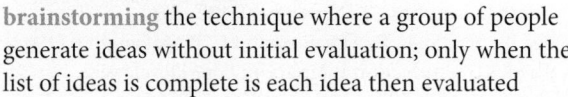

Key Terms

brainstorming the technique where a group of people generate ideas without initial evaluation; only when the list of ideas is complete is each idea then evaluated

business analysis a review of the projected sales, costs and profits for a new product to establish whether these factors satisfy company objectives

concept testing testing new product ideas with potential customers

diffusion of innovation process the process by which a new product spreads throughout a market over time

innovation the commercialization of an invention by bringing it to market

invention the discovery of new methods and ideas

market testing the limited launch of a new product to test sales potential

product churning a continuous and rapid spiral of new product introductions

project teams the bringing together of staff from such areas as R&D, engineering, manufacturing, finance, and marketing to work on a project such as new product development

simultaneous engineering the involvement of manufacturing and product development engineers in the same development team in an effort to reduce development time

test marketing the launch of a new product in one or a few geographic areas chosen to be representative of the intended market

Study Questions

1. Try to think of an unsatisfied need that you feel could be solved by the introduction of a new product. How would you set about testing your idea to examine its commercial potential?

2. The Sinclair C5 was soon withdrawn from market in the UK. The three-wheeled vehicle was designed to provide electric-powered transport over short distances. If you can remember the vehicle, try to think of reasons why the product was a failure. On the other hand, video recorders and fax machines have been huge successes. Why?

3 Why is it difficult for a service company such as a bank to develop new products that have lasting success?

4 You are the marketing manager for a fast-food restaurant chain. A colleague returns from France with an idea for a new dish that she thinks will be a winner.

5 How would you go about evaluating the idea?

6 What are the advantages and disadvantages of test marketing? In what circumstances should you be reluctant to use test marketing?

7 Your company has developed a new range of spicy-flavoured soups. They are intended to compete against the market leader in curry-flavoured soups. How would you conduct product tests for your new line?

8 What are the particular problems associated with commercializing technology? What are the key factors for success?

9 Discuss how marketing and R&D can form effective teams to develop new products.

References

1. Pearson, D. (1993) Invent, Innovate and Improve, *Marketing*, 8 April, 15.
2. Richard, H. (1996) Why Competitiveness is a Dirty Word in Scandinavia, *European*, 6–12 June, 24.
3. McGregor, J. (2006) The World's Most Innovative Companies, *Business Week*, 24 April, 63–76.
4. Doyle, P. (1997) From the Top, *Guardian*, 2 August, 17.
5. A study conducted by Kashami, K. and T. Clayton, reported in Murphy, D. (2000) Innovate or Die, *Marketing Business*, May, 16–18.
6. Jana, R. (2009) Do Ideas Cost Too Much?, *Business Week*, 20 April, 46–8
7. Booz, Allen and Hamilton (1982) *New Product Management for the 1980s*, New York: Booz, Allen and Hamilton, Inc.
8. Gray, R. (2008) The Good Old Days, *The Marketer*, July/August, 28–31.
9. London, S. (2005) Floodgates Open Up to a Sea of Ideas, *Financial Times*, Special Report on Innovation, 8 June, 2.
10. Matthews, V. (2002) Caution Versus Creativity, *Financial Times*, 17 June, 12.
11. See Gupta, A. K. and D. Wileman (1990) Improving R&D/Marketing Relations: R&D Perspective, *R&D Management* 20(4), 277–90; Koshler, R. (1991) Produkt—Innovation as management als Erfolgsfaktor, in Mueller-Boehling, D. *et al.* (eds) *Innovations—und Technologiemanagement*, Stuttgart: C. E. Poeschel Verlagi; Shrivastava, P. and W. E. Souder (1987) The Strategic Management of Technological Innovation: A Review and a Model, *Journal of Management Studies* 24(1), 24–41.
12. Aceland, H. (1999) Harnessing Internal Innovation, *Marketing*, 22 July, 27–8.
13. See Booz, Allen and Hamilton (1982) op. cit.; Maidique, M. A. and B. J. Zirger (1984) A Study of Success and Failure in Product Innovation: The Case of the US Electronics Industry, *IEEE Transactions in Engineering Management*, EM-31 (November), 192–203.
14. See Bergen, S. A., R. Miyajima and C. P. McLaughlin (1988) The R&D/Production Interface in Four Developed Countries, *R&D Management* 18(3), 201–16; Hegarty, W. H. and R. C. Hoffman (1990) Product/Market Innovations: A Study of Top Management Involvement among Four Cultures, *Journal of Product Innovation Management* 7, 186–99; Cooper, R. G. (1979) The Dimensions of Industrial New Product Success and Failure, *Journal of Marketing* 43 (Summer), 93–103; Johne, A. and P. Snelson (1988) Auditing Product Innovation Activities in Manufacturing Firms, *R&D Management* 18(3), 227–33.
15. Aceland, H. (1999) op. cit.
16. Anonymous (2008) Marketing Greats, *The Marketers*, May, 7.
17. Francis, T. (2000) Divine Intervention, *Marketing Business*, May, 20–2.
18. Joshi, A. W. and S. Sharma (2004) Customer Knowledge Development: Antecedents and Impact on New Product Performance, *Journal of Marketing*, 68 (October), 47–9.
19. Kanter, R. M. (1983) *The Change Masters*, New York: Simon & Schuster.
20. Mitchell, A. (2003) The Tyranny of the Brand, *Marketing Business*, January, 17.
21. Done, K. (1992) From Design Studio to New Car Showroom, *Financial Times*, 11 May, 10.
22. Carbonell, P. and A. I. Rodriguez (2006) The Impact of Market Characteristics and Innovation Speed on Perceptions of Positional Advantage and New Product Performance, *International Journal of Research in Marketing*, 23, 1–12.
23. See Hise, R. T., L. O'Neal, A. Parasuraman and J. U. NcNeal (1990) Marketing/R&D Interaction in New Product Development: Implications for New Product Success Rates,

Journal of Product Innovation Management 7, 142–55; Johne and Snelson (1988) op. cit.; Walsh, W. J. (1990) Get the Whole Organisation Behind New Product Development, *Research in Technological Management*, Nov.–Dec., 32–6.

24. Frey, D. (1991) Learning the Ropes: My Life as a Product Champion, *Harvard Business Review*, Sept.–Oct., 46–56.

25. Gupta, A. K. and D. Wileman (1991) Improving R&D/Marketing Relations in Technology Based Companies: Marketing's Perspective, *Journal of Marketing Management* 7(1), 25–46.

26. See Dwyer, L. M. (1990) Factors Affecting the Proficient Management of Product Innovation, *International Journal of Technological Management* 5(6), 721–30; Gupta and Wileman (1990) op. cit.; Adler, P. S., H. E. Riggs and S. C. Wheelwright (1989) Product Development Know-How, *Sloan Management Review* 4, 7–17.

27. Brentani, U. de (1991) Success Factors in Developing New Business Services, *European Journal of Marketing* 15(2), 33–59; Johne, A. and C. Storey (1998) New Source Development: A Review of the Literature and Annotated Bibliography, *European Journal of Marketing* 32(3/4), 184–251.

28. Cooper, R. G. and E. J. Kleinschmidt (1986) An Investigation into the New Product Process: Steps, Deficiencies and Impact, *Journal of Product Innovation Management*, June, 71–85.

29. Edwards, C. (2008) How HP Got the Wow! Back, *Business Week*, 22 December, 60–1.

30. Edwards, C. (2009) The Return on Research, *Business Week*, 23/30 March, 45.

31. Nijssen, E. J. and K. F. M. Lieshout (1995) Awareness, Use and Effectiveness of Models and Methods for New Product Development, *European Journal of Marketing* 29(10), 27–44.

32. Hamel, G. and C. K. Prahalad (1991) Corporate Imagination and Expeditionary Marketing, *Harvard Business Review*, July–August, 81–92.

33. Huston, L. and N. Sakkab (2006) Connect and Develop: Inside Procter & Gamble's New Model for Innovation, *Harvard Business Review* 84(3), 58–72.

34. Mitchell, A. (2005) After Some Innovation? Perhaps You Just Need to Ask Around, *Marketing Week*, 16 June, 28–9.

35. Bower, F. (2000) Latin Spirit, *Marketing Business*, October, 24–5.

36. Tomkins, R. (2005) Products that Aim Straight for Your Heart, *Financial Times*, 29 April, 13.

37. Parkinson, S. T. (1982) The Role of the User in Successful New Product Development, *R&D Management* 12, 123–31.

38. Nevens, T. M., G. L. Summe, and B. Uttal (1990) Commercializing Technology: What the Best Companies Do, *Harvard Business Review*, May–June, 154–63.

39. Johne, A. (1992) Don't Let Your Customers Lead You Astray in Developing New Products, *European Management Journal* 10(1), 80–4.

40. Hamel, G. and C. K. Prahalad (1991) Corporate Imagination and Expeditionary Marketing, *Harvard Business Review*, July–August, 81–92.

41. Hamel, G. (1999) Bringing Silicon Valley Inside, *Harvard Business Review*, Sept.–Oct., 71–84.

42. Leifer, R. G., C. O'Connor and M. Rice (2001) Implementing Radical Innovation in Mature Firms: The Role of Hubs, *Academy of Management Executives* 15(3) 61–70.

43. Hunt, J. W. (2002) Crucibles of Innovation, *Financial Times*, 18 January, 18.

44. Bartram, P. (2004) Why the Competition Doesn't Matter, *The Marketer*, April, 18–21.

45. Tellis, G., J. C. Prabhu and R. K. Chandy (2009) Radical Innovation Across Nations: The Preeminence of Corporate Culture, *Journal of Marketing* 73(1), 3–23.

46. Jobber, D., J. Saunders, G. Hooley, B. Gilding and J. Hatton-Smooker (1989) Assessing the Value of a Quality Assurance Certificate for Software: An Exploratory Investigation, *MIS Quarterly*, March, 19–31.

47. Edgett, S. and S. Jones (1991) New Product Development in the Financial Services Industry: A Case Study, *Journal of Marketing Management* 7(3), 271–84.

48. Valentine, M. (2009) Research Extends Beyond the Lab, *Marketing Week*, 5 March, 27–8.

49. Matthews, V. (2002) Caution Versus Creativity, *Financial Times*, 17 June, 12.

50. The author is indebted to Dr Dirk Snelders of Delft University, Netherlands, for supplying material on the scenario method. For further reading see Burt, G. and K. van der Heijden (2003) First Steps: Towards Purposeful Activities in Scenario Thinking and Future Studies, *Futures*, 35, 1011–26; Carroll, J. M. (2000) Scenario-based Design: A Brief History and Rationale in Eastman C., M. McCracken and W. Newsletter (eds), *Knowing and Learning to Design: Cognitive Perspectives in Design Education*. Amsterdam: Elsevier; Tauber, E. M. (1974) How Marketing Research Discourages Major Innovation, *Business Horizons*, 17 (June), 22–6; and Ulwick, A. W. (2002) Turn Customer Input Into Innovation, *Harvard Business Review*, (January), 91–7.

51. Wheelwright, S. and K. Clark (1992) *Revolutionizing Product Development*, New York: Free Press.

52. Baxter, A. (1992) Shifting to High Gear, *Financial Times*, 14 May, 15.

53. Anonymous (2008) Rebirth of a Carmaker, *Economist*, 26 April, 91–3.

54. Pullin, J. (1997) Time is Money on the Way to Market, *Guardian*, 5 April, 99.

55. Jarvis, J. (2009) The Foresight of Google, *Media Guardian*, 9 February, 8.

56. Parkinson (1982) op. cit.

57. Chisnall, P. (2005) *Marketing Research*, Maidenhead: McGraw-Hill.

58. Rogers, E. M. (2003) *Diffusion of Innovations*, New York: Free Press.

59. Rogers (2003) op. cit.

60. Zinkmund, W. G. and M. D'Amico (1999) *Marketing*, St Paul, MN: West.

61. Easingwood, C. and C. Beard (1989) High Technology Launch Strategies in the UK, Industrial *Marketing Management* 18, 125–38.

62. Pesola, M. (2005) Samsung Plays to the Young Generation, *Financial Times*, 29 March, 11.

63. See Mahajan, V., E. Muller and R. Kerin (1987) Introduction Strategy for New Product with Positive and Negative Word-of-Mouth, *Management Science* 30, 1389–404; Robertson, T. S. and H. Gatignon (1986) Competitive Effects on Technology Diffusion, *Journal of Marketing* 50 (July), 1–12; Tzokas, N. and M. Saren (1992) Innovation Diffusion: The Emerging Role of Suppliers Versus the Traditional Dominance of Buyers, *Journal of Marketing Management* 8(1), 69–80.

64. Daniel, C. (2001) Psion Quits Handheld Organiser Market, *Financial Times*, 12 July, 1.

65. Dewitz, A. (2009) Walking the Talk (retrieved from http://printceo.com/2009/04/walking-the-talk).

66. Gourville, J. (2006) The Curse of Innovation: Why Innovative Products Fail, MSI Report No. 05-117.

67. Saunders, J. and D. Jobber (1994) Product Replacement Strategies: Occurrence and Concurrence, *Journal of Product Innovation Management* (November).

68. Dixon, A. (2009) M&S Success Built on Food Lines Innovation, *Marketing Week*, 15 February, 15.

69. Harding, R. (2008) Canon to Launch Radical TV, *Financial Times*, 2 December, 25.

70. Nevens, Summe and Uttal (1990) op. cit.

71. Brown, R. (1991) Managing the 'S' Curves of Innovation, *Journal of Marketing Management* 7(2), 189–202.

72. Gatignon, H., T. S. Robertson and A. J. Fein (1997) Incumbent Defence Strategies Against New Product Entry, *International Journal of Research in Marketing* 14, 163–76.

73. Bowman, D. and H. Gatignon (1995) Determinants of Competitor Response Time to a New Product Introduction, *Journal of Marketing Research* 33, February, 42–53.

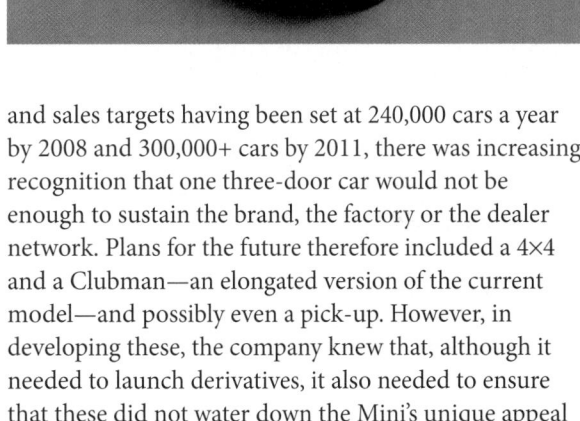

Launched in 1959, the original Mini proved to be one of the longest-lasting fashion and motoring icons of the twentieth century, with production of the car finally coming to a halt almost 40 years later in 1998. The announcement in 2000 by BMW, owner of the Mini brand, that it was to invest £200 million in the development and launch of the new Mini was therefore received, both by the press and the public, with enormous enthusiasm. In the event, the car proved to be enormously successful. Not only did sales prove to be much higher than anticipated, but discounts and other sales incentives have been among the lowest of any brand. It was therefore against this background that the company's announcement in 2008 of the launch of an all-electric version of the car was made, something that led Angus MacKenzie, editor of *Motor Trend*, to suggest that 'the electric version will help to polish the brand'.

The small car market

The global car market is intensely competitive, with one of the most crowded parts of this market, particularly in Europe, being the so-called 'supermini' segment. With the sector being dominated by some of the mass-market players such as Renault, Volkswagen, Nissan, Peugeot, Citroën, Ford and Toyota, but also featuring some of the luxury brands, such as the Mercedes A-Class, competition for the Mini was expected to be particularly tough from the outset. However, the attraction of the sector for BMW, Mini's parent, stemmed from the way in which global demand for small city cars was forecast to grow faster than the overall market and far faster than any other sector of the car market. In the event, the initial sales targets set for the Mini, both in Europe and the United States, were achieved easily and led to the Mini being labelled 'the most successful car launch of the decade'.

The Mini Mark II

In 2006, the company announced that it would launch the Mini Mark II the following year. Within the company, there was the belief that the company was now firmly established as a brand its own right and that it was no longer seen as 'a baby BMW', as its critics had suggested in the early days. With the company having increased its investment commitment by £200 million

and sales targets having been set at 240,000 cars a year by 2008 and 300,000+ cars by 2011, there was increasing recognition that one three-door car would not be enough to sustain the brand, the factory or the dealer network. Plans for the future therefore included a 4×4 and a Clubman—an elongated version of the current model—and possibly even a pick-up. However, in developing these, the company knew that, although it needed to launch derivatives, it also needed to ensure that these did not water down the Mini's unique appeal and the classic Mini values of self-confidence, energy, cheekiness, beauty, charm, reliability and classlessness.

The emergence of new market dynamics and the search for new technologies

Although the Mini has proved to be enormously successful, the global market for cars has changed considerably since the product's initial launch in 2001. Among the most significant and far-reaching of the pressures faced by the industry are:

- a seemingly ever more powerful environmental lobby, which has led to the development of far more demanding legislation designed to reduce CO_2 emissions from cars
- significant fluctuations in the price of oil, with the price of a barrel of crude oil reaching an all-time high of $147 in mid-2008 before falling back to $35, but then rising again over the next few years, and
- a significant global economic downturn, which led to a collapse in car sales and precipitated a crisis throughout the industry; hardest hit were the North American car giants Chrysler and General Motors (GM), both of which were forced to go to the American Government for financial support; then,

in the case of GM, the downturn led in mid-2009 to the company filing for Chapter 11 bankruptcy.

At the same time, the car manufacturers had begun to recognize a series of longer-term social concerns about overcrowding on roads, the problems of pollution (according to a study by the UK's Department of Transport, about 22 per cent of carbon emissions come from transport, with 13 per cent coming from private cars), and the need to conserve scarce resources such as oil.

Faced therefore with what was becoming an increasingly different type of market, both the industry and the government began to pursue a series of new strategies. Throughout the early part of the twenty-first century, governments throughout the world had begun placing ever more stringent demands on the car manufacturers to reduce emission levels from cars and to increase fuel economy. The car companies responded by investing heavily in new, green technologies. For a number of companies, such as Volkswagen, this led to a focus on the development of ever more efficient petrol and diesel engines. Some, such as Toyota with its Prius, pursued a hybrid approach with a combination of petrol-electric technologies. Others—including Mini—chose to focus on the all-electric car.

The launch of the Mini E

For many potential buyers of electric cars, BMW's entry to the market with the Mini E represented a new phase in that it brought speed and style to what had previously been seen to be a somewhat earnest eco-niche.

The result was unveiled at the 2008 Los Angeles Auto Show when BMW revealed an all-electric version of the Mini. Labelled the Mini E and powered by a lithium-ion battery, giving it the equivalent of around 200 horsepower and having a life of 100,000 miles, the approach taken by the company was deliberately cautious and involved it leasing the car for $850 per month to 500 people in California and New York, and then, a few months later, to 50 people in Berlin and 40 in London.

The leasing programme developed by the company was designed to last initially for just 12 months, so that the company could test both the technology in real-world driving conditions and the consumer response. In the event, the initial reactions proved to be very positive. In part, this was seen to be due to the way in which all-electric cars are very quiet, but also because of the speed and smoothness of response when driving (unlike petrol, diesel and hybrid engines, electric motors are capable of delivering maximum power almost instantly).

There were, however, several downsides to the car in that, unlike the conventional Mini and with batteries taking up the rear seat, the Mini E had space for just two people. There was also consumers' fear of being stranded with a flat battery. Electric cars typically have only a limited range. The Mini E's claimed range of 150 miles, for example, often proved to be optimistic, with some users during the test finding that it was more likely to be just 100 miles or so. Finally, there was the issue of cost. At the time of the Mini E's launch, the cost of the car was rumoured to be in the region of $100,000. This compares with $20,000 for the standard model. However, for BMW, this was not the issue. Instead, the company saw the car as part of a pilot programme and the precursor of what was seen to be the potential for explosive growth in the market for relatively affordable electric cars in the near future. The evidence for this was seen in the way in which General Motors had begun talking about the potential launch of its electric Volt saloon, Ford's plan to retool one of its plants to make electric versions of its Focus, Nissan's proposed launch of its sub-$33,000 electric car and Mitsubishi's plans to sell its own electric vehicle in Japan.

> **❚❚** BMW saw the Mini E as part of a pilot programme and the precursor of what was seen to be potential for explosive growth in the market. **❚❚**

But the design and manufacturing of the all-electric car is just one part of a complex and expensive equation. Unlike hybrids, whose batteries can be recharged while the car is moving, electric cars are recharged by plugging in to a 240-volt electricity outlet, an exercise that often takes place overnight and typically costs about £1.50. In the United States, however, where 110-volt systems are more common, recharging can take a full day. To cope with this, BMW provided those leasing their cars with a high-amperage unit that was fitted in their garage.

Other manufacturers, recognizing these problems, have taken a different approach. Determined to establish an early lead in the mass market for electric cars, Renault and Nissan decided that the charging solution could best be addressed by separating the batteries from the cars themselves. In practice, this means that the buyers purchase the cars at about the same price as a conventional model, but then lease the batteries from a third-party energy supplier for a monthly fee that is broadly the same as the fuel costs for an economic petrol or diesel car. These would then be supported by a network of charging stations where batteries can be 80 per cent recharged in 20 minutes, or depleted battery packs could simply be swapped for fully charged ones. GM's approach is different still, with the car also having a small petrol engine that starts automatically when it senses that the batteries are running low and recharges the battery. Others, such as Toyota with its Prius and Honda with its Insight, have opted for hybrids where the battery powers the car at low speeds and a petrol engine then kicks in at higher speed and helps to recharge the battery. With a variety of technologies available, what is clear is that until there is agreement on a standard approach, the heavy investment needed for the development of widely available recharging stations is unlikely to take place.

The government response

In order to help with the development both of the technology and the supporting infrastructure that is needed for fast charging and recharging both at home and on the road, the Obama administration in the USA announced at the beginning of 2009 a $2.4 billion support package. At the same time, the British Government provided a £250 million package to accelerate the development and deployment of low-carbon vehicles across the UK. Moves such as these were welcomed by environmental campaigners, with Friends of the Earth suggesting that electric cars have the potential to play a significant part in cutting carbon emissions. They did, however, also point to something that many people forget: the electricity for recharging the batteries typically comes from conventional sources and that there was therefore the need to think not just about the cars, but also about the ways in which electricity could come from renewable energy sources.

Consumers' concerns

Although the potential attractions to consumers of electric technology—such as cheap to run, offering low or zero carbon emissions and quiet—have been well rehearsed and are understood, many potential buyers have proved to have significant reservations. If the product is to be successful, it needs to appeal not just to a small group of urban innovators and early adopters, but also, and more importantly, to the mass market (the early and then, ultimately, the late majority). These

parts of the market will be likely to buy only if they are convinced by the technology's reliability over several years of charging and recharging, and that they will not need to change their lifestyles to any great degree.

In many ways, it is this that can be seen to be the biggest marketing challenge not just for the Mini E, but for all the other manufacturers looking at the technology—something that was neatly summed up by Ray Hutton of *The Sunday Times*, who said:

> Electric cars need a boost. Cheap to run but expensive to buy, they offer the prospect of low or zero carbon emissions, but manufacturers won't sell them unless motorists want to buy them—and motorists won't buy them unless the price is right and there are enough places to charge the batteries.

References

Based on: Anonymous (2008) Another Mini Adventure, But This Time With Sound Off. And No Back Seat, *Guardian*, 3 December, 3; Anonymous (2008) BMW Takes an Electric Mini for a Spin, *Business Week*, 1 December, 17; Anonymous (2008) The Brightest Spark in Town, *The Sunday Times*, 7 December, 4–5; Hutton, R. (2009) Slow Start for Charge of the Electric Cars, *The Sunday Times*, 19 April 2009, 10.

Questions

1. Identify in detail the possible concerns that the early and late majority of the market might have about all-electric car technology, and suggest how the Mini E marketing team might most effectively address these concerns.

2. What lessons might the Mini E marketing team learn from other companies that have developed and successfully launched new technologies?

3. With several different types of electric technology being developed, what are the implications for Mini of focusing on the one that ultimately proves not to be the industry standard?

This case was written by Colin Gilligan, Emeritus Professor of Marketing, Sheffield Hallam University, and Visiting Professor of Marketing, Newcastle Business School.

A New Heritage

Shannon Heritage Develops New Tourist Experiences

Shannon Heritage provides tourism experiences in some of Ireland's oldest historic sites. Looking after a collection of medieval castles and selected archaeological sites, its role is to develop these historic sites into tourism attractions that entice both foreign and domestic tourists to stay in the mid-west of Ireland. Tourism products have constantly evolved so as to keep abreast of market changes and the heightened expectations of visitors. In order, to ensure that Ireland's unique heritage is preserved, the government-owned subsidiary has the dual mandate of conservation of these pristine historic sites and the generation of tourism revenue for the region. The company contributes an estimated €20 million annually to the local economy in spin-off revenue. Furthermore it employs a total of 300 people in peak season, and indirectly supports many more jobs in the wider region, supporting hotels, restaurants, retail and transport providers. The company has produced a heady mix of history, culture and entertainment to enliven the Irish tourism product.

As one of the first heritage tourism companies in Ireland, Shannon Heritage was developed to keep visitors in the Shannon region. When it was established in 1963 the business was based on just one product, the Bunratty Castle Medieval Banquet. In the intervening years its portfolio has developed significantly to now include a number of day visitor experiences and evening entertainments, which attract audiences from all over the world. The core of the business focuses on preserving the culture, heritage, traditions, customs, castles and historic sites for future generations to enjoy. Its attractions were developed to bring visitors into the magic and mystery of the Prehistoric, Celtic, Viking, Anglo-Norman and native Irish communities starting 5000 years ago. Products were originally designed for tourists but, in recent years, the significance of the domestic customer has prompted Shannon Heritage to design a range of seasonal products targeted at day visitors and in particular families. Although it controls the major tourist attractions in the mid-west region, Shannon Heritage competes with all other forms of entertainment, leisure and recreation activities for its customers.

In recent years, Shannon Heritage has had to adapt its vision and explore customers other than those

provided by the American market. It has evolved from being a one-product company focusing on one market to continually adding value to its core product. It also developed additional products to widen its product range and win a wider audience, thus spreading its market risk and providing a product range that is of continual interest to its customers. From a marketing perspective, this has three implications for Shannon Heritage; first, its products must appear complementary to all of its customers; second, its marketing intelligence must be accurate and instant, so as to customize products for its current customer segments in current market and political conditions; and, third, it must excel in the delivery of an excellent customer experience.

Shannon Heritage's products can be divided into two categories: day and evening entertainment. Since 1963, when the first Medieval Banquet was held, almost 4.5 million people have enjoyed evenings in four distinct and unique evening entertainment venues: Bunratty Castle, Knappogue Castle, Dunguaire Castle, and the

Irish Night at Bunratty Folk Park. The company leverages on the concept that 'Nowhere else can you experience the fun of what the Irish do best—enjoy themselves!' Here tourists would enjoy a spectacular banquet in a foreboding medieval castle where servers would be dressed in authentic traditional attire, drink from goblets, have a feast of food, be entertained by the famous Bunratty choral singers, and all under flickering candlelight. This experience is extremely popular with tour parties. Shannon Heritage caters for quite distinct consumer segments: schools for educational visits, domestic tourists, families, tour parties, day trippers and the important foreign tourist market.

The day visitor attractions are divided into two categories: permanent exhibitions, and seasonal or day events. The permanent features include the world-famous Bunratty Castle and Folk Park (featuring the acclaimed fifteenth-century Bunratty Castle and nineteenth-century Bunratty Folk Park), which has been developed around the original core product: the Bunratty Castle Medieval Banquet. The park is set in 26 acres adjacent to one of the main tourist routes in Ireland. The Castle is the most complete and authentic medieval fortress in Ireland. The Folk Park features over 30 buildings, including a school, post office, doctor's house, hardware shop, printers and pub. These buildings form a 'living' village in a rural setting where nineteenth-century Ireland is recreated with the help of typical street characters and animals of the time, such as the farmer, the blacksmith, the policeman and schoolteacher, who mingle with hens, donkeys, Irish wolfhounds and the like. This type of product very much relies on the cultural stereotypes that foreign tourists hold about traditional Ireland, popularized by films such as *The Quiet Man*. The success of this product has led to the development of additional heritage products, each appealing to different markets: King John's Castle, (featuring the Living Past Experience Museum), Knappogue Castle (featuring a walled garden and banquet experience), Dunguaire Castle (featuring a banquet experience), Lough Gur Stone Age Centre and Brian Boru Heritage Centre.

Seasonal events complement the permanent day exhibitions, bringing traditional Irish customs alive at certain times of the year, such as Christmas and Easter.

// Products were originally designed for tourists, but the significance of the domestic customers prompted Shannon Heritage to design a range of seasonal products targeted at day visitors. //

For example, during the lead-up to Christmas, Santa Claus, Mrs Claus, a troupe of elves and a host of other Christmas characters can be visited in a magical, festive atmosphere in the unique and traditional village street decked with holly and fairy lights. This family event features the Folk Park storyteller, a puppet show and Christmas themed shops. At Easter, visitors are invited to participate in a more contemporary celebration of Easter featuring an Easter egg hunt, a Mad Hatter's tea party, Captain Hook's Corner, story time with Snow White, face painters, stilt walkers and jugglers.

In addition to seasonal events, the park also hosts one-off events such as the restaging of Ireland's largest ever Viking invasion, where over 100 Viking warriors from all over Europe invaded the popular tourist attraction for a weekend Viking festival. During this festival the re-enactors lived in the grounds of Bunratty Castle and Folk Park, working, cooking, eating, fighting and sleeping on site. In addition, a Viking tented village was constructed to house craft displays including bone carving, leatherwork, children's games, weapons display, armour display, chain mail making, shield making, bronze casting, coin making, finger braiding and woodwork.

The success of these new products is based on new product development, and continual product monitoring and refinement, so that Shannon Heritage can develop new business and to optimize its existing products. It focuses on the implementation of new ideas through enhancing existing products, and increasing its product offering to various markets in response to customer and market demands. These ideas can take three formats: first, new product ideas such as the introduction of a Christmas theme with Santa Claus and his helpers in residence for two months of the year; second, new technologies have been introduced to facilitate web-based bookings, ticket sales and production efficiencies for each of its venues; third, additional services such as food and beverages or retail outlets have been introduced at all venues.

Each of these developments has been introduced to attract and retain customers. Traditionally, most of Shannon Heritage's business would have come from tour operators and agents, which made it easy to communicate with its customers. However, in the past few years there has been a rapid decline in the visitor numbers from these traditional sources, and a significant increase in the number of individual bookings by small groups. Shannon Heritage closely monitors its marketing mix and has adapted to meet its new customers' needs, noting their price ranges, promotion channels and product preferences.

In looking to the overall visitor numbers for the region, Shannon Heritage has identified the profitability of its venture as being dependent on the access to and availability of flights, accommodation, and external economic and political forces. To compete in this environment Shannon Heritage must provide a continually updated product that is carefully researched each season, searching for possible product enhancements. However, there is quite often a time lag between the identification of desired product enhancements and their implementation. This can be attributed to the profit assessment mechanism within Shannon Heritage, as careful forecasting and evaluation takes place before any new product suggestions or modifications are operationalized.

In the face of a harsh operating climate, with declining foreign visitor numbers due to worldwide recession, the strength of the euro and tough competition, Shannon Heritage faces numerous marketing challenges. Should the company revitalize its product offering and adapt to the changing marketing environment? And, most importantly, how can it balance its conservation and historical education agenda with making a profit from tourism?

Questions

1. What are the key success factors in launching a new heritage product?
2. Analyse the differences between developing new products for service and manufacturing industries.
3. Recommend possible marketing strategies for new rather than mature products within the Shannon Heritage product family.

This case was written by Dr Michele O'Dwyer, Lecturer in Entrepreneurship, and Conor Carroll, Lecturer in Marketing, University of Limerick.

CHAPTER

12 Pricing strategy

▌▌ *Everything is worth what its purchasers will pay for it.* **▌▌**

SYRUS

▌▌ *There are two fools in every market. One charges too little; the other charges too much.* **▌▌**

RUSSIAN PROVERB

LEARNING OBJECTIVES

After reading this chapter, you should be able to:

1 explain the economist's approach to price determination

2 distinguish between full cost and direct cost pricing

3 discuss your understanding of going-rate pricing and competitive bidding

4 explain the advantages of marketing-orientated pricing over cost and competitor-orientated pricing

5 discuss the factors that affect price setting when using a marketing-orientated approach

6 identify when and how to initiate price increases and cuts

7 identify when and when not to follow competitor-initiated price increases and cuts; when to follow quickly and when to follow slowly

8 discuss ethical issues in pricing

Price is the odd-one-out of the marketing mix, because it is the revenue earner. The price of a product is what the company gets back in return for all the effort that is put into producing and marketing the product. The other three elements of the marketing mix—product, promotion and place—are costs. Therefore, no matter how good the product, how creative the promotion or how efficient the distribution, unless price covers costs the company will make a loss. It is therefore essential that managers understand how to set prices, because both undercharging (lost margin) and overcharging (lost sales) can have dramatic effects on profitability.

One of the key factors that marketing managers need to remember is that price is just one element of the marketing mix. Price should not be set in isolation; it should be blended with product, promotion and place to form a coherent mix that provides superior customer value. The sales of many products, particularly those that are a form of self-expression—such as drinks, cars, perfume and clothing—could suffer from prices that are too low. As we shall see, price is an important part of positioning strategy since it often sends quality cues to customers.

Understanding how to set prices is an important aspect of marketing decision-making, not least because of changes in the competitive arena that many believe will act to drive down prices in many countries. Since price is a major determinant of profitability, developing a coherent pricing strategy assumes major significance.

Many people's introduction to the issue of pricing is a course in economics. We will now consider, very briefly, some of the ideas discussed by economists when considering price.

Economists' Approach to Pricing

Although a full discussion of the approach taken by economists to pricing is beyond the scope of this chapter, the following gives a flavour of some of the important concepts relating to price. The discussion will focus on demand since this is of fundamental importance in pricing. Economists talk of the *demand curve* to conceptualize the relationship between the quantity demanded and different price levels. Figure 12.1 shows a typical demand curve. At a price of P_1, demand is Q_1. As price drops so demand rises. Thus at P_2 demand increases to Q_2. For some products, a given fall in price leads to a large increase in demand. The demand for such products is said to be *price elastic*. For other products, a given fall in price leads to only a small increase in demand. The demand for these products is described as *price inelastic*. Clearly it is useful to know the price elasticity of demand. When faced with elastic demand, marketers know that a price drop may stimulate much greater demand for their products. Conversely, when faced with inelastic demand, marketers know that a price drop will not increase demand appreciably.

An obvious practical problem facing marketers who wish to use demand curve analysis is plotting demand curves accurately. There is no one demand curve that relates price to demand in real life. Each demand curve is based on a set of assumptions regarding other factors such as advertising expenditure, salesforce effectiveness, distribution intensity and the price of competing products, which also affect demand. For the purposes of Figure 12.1, these have been held constant at a particular level so that one unique curve can be plotted. A second problem regarding the demand curve relates to the estimation of the

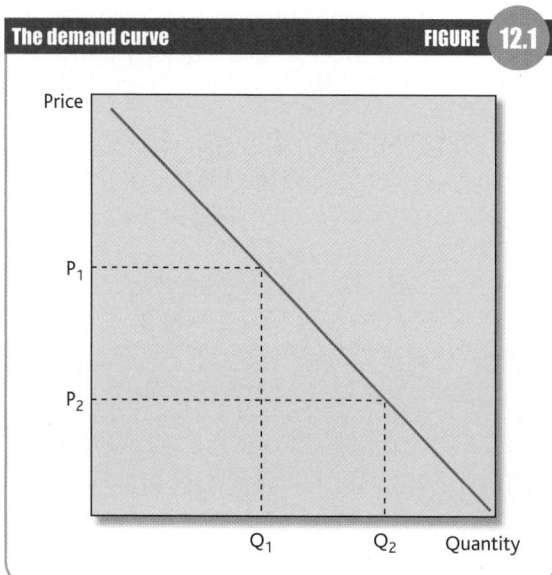

The demand curve   FIGURE **12.1**

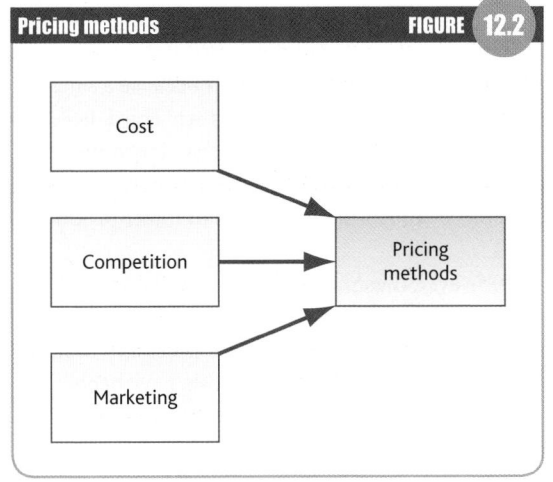

Pricing methods   FIGURE 12.2

Cost

Competition

Marketing

Pricing methods

position of the curve even when other influences are held constant. Some companies conduct experiments to estimate likely demand at various price levels. However, it is not always feasible to do so since they may rely on the cooperation of retailers who may refuse or demand unrealistically high fees. Second, it is very difficult to implement a fully controlled field experiment. Where different regions of the country are involved, differences in income levels, variations in local tastes and preferences, and differences in the level of competitor activities may confound the results. The reality is that while the demand curve is a useful conceptual tool for thinking about pricing issues, in practice its application is limited. In truth, traditional economic theory was not developed as a management tool but as an explanation of market behaviour. Managers therefore turn to other methods of setting prices and it is these methods we shall discuss in this chapter.

Shapiro and Jackson identified three methods used by managers to set prices (see Fig. 12.2).[1] The first reflects a strong internal orientation and is based on costs. The second is to use competitor-orientated pricing where the major emphasis is on competitor activities. The final approach is called marketing-orientated pricing as it focuses on the value that customers place on a product in the marketplace and its marketing strategy. In this chapter we shall examine each of these approaches and draw out their strengths and limitations. We shall also discuss how to initiate and respond to price changes.

Cost-Orientated Pricing

Companies often use cost-orientated methods when setting prices.[2] Two methods are normally used: full cost pricing and direct (or marginal) cost pricing.

Full cost pricing

Full cost pricing can best be explained by using a simple example (see Table 12.1). Imagine that you are given the task of pricing a new product (a widget) and the cost figures given in Table 12.1 apply. Direct costs such as labour and materials work out at £10 per unit. As output increases, more people and materials will be needed and so total costs increase. Fixed costs (or overheads) per year are calculated at £1,000,000. These costs (such as office and manufacturing facilities) do not change as output increases. They have to be paid whether 1 or 200,000 widgets are produced.

Having calculated the relevant costs, the next step is to estimate how many widgets we are likely to sell. We believe that we produce a good-quality widget and therefore sales should be 100,000 in the first year. Therefore total (full) cost per unit is £20 and using the company's traditional 10 per cent mark-up, a price of £22 is set.

In order to appreciate the problem of using full cost pricing, let us assume that the sales estimate of 100,000 is not reached by the end of the year. Because of poor economic conditions or as a result of setting the price too high, only 50,000 units are sold. The company believes that this level of sales is likely to be achieved next year. What happens to price? Table 12.1 gives the answer: it is raised because cost per unit goes up. This is because fixed costs (£1,000,000) are divided by a smaller expected sales volume (50,000). The result is a price rise in response to poor sales figures. This is clearly nonsense and yet can happen if full cost pricing is followed blindly. A major UK engineering company priced one of its main product lines in this way, and suffered a downward spiral of sales as prices were raised each year with disastrous consequences.

Full cost pricing	TABLE 12.1
YEAR 1	
Direct costs (per unit)	= £10
Fixed costs	= £1,000,000
Expected sales	= 100,000
Cost per unit	
Direct costs	= £10
Fixed costs (1,000,000 ÷ 100,000)	= £10
Full costs	= £20
Mark-up (10%)	= £2
Price (cost plus mark-up)	= £22
YEAR 2	
Expected sales	= 50,000
Cost per unit	
Direct costs	= £10
Fixed costs (1,000,000 ÷ 50,000)	= £20
Full costs	= £30
Mark-up (10%)	= £3
Price (cost plus mark-up)	= £33

The first problem with full cost pricing, then, is that it leads to an increase in price as sales fall. Second, the procedure is illogical because a sales estimate is made *before* a price is set. Third, it focuses on internal costs rather than customers' willingness to pay. Finally, there may be a technical problem in allocating overheads in multi-product firms.[3]

However, inasmuch as the method forces managers to calculate costs, it does give an indication of the minimum price necessary to make a profit. Once direct and fixed costs have been measured *break-even analysis* can be used to estimate the sales volume needed to balance revenue and costs at different price levels. Therefore the procedure of calculating full costs is useful when other pricing methods are used since full costs may act as a constraint. If they cannot be covered then it may not be worthwhile launching the product.

Direct cost pricing

In certain circumstances, companies may use **direct cost pricing** (sometimes called marginal cost pricing). This involves the calculation of only those costs that are likely to rise as output increases. In the example shown in Table 12.1 direct cost per unit is £10. As output increases, so total costs will increase by £10 per unit. Like full cost pricing, direct cost pricing includes a mark-up (in this case 10 per cent) giving a price of £11.

The obvious problem is that this price does not cover full costs and so the company would be making a loss selling a product at this low price. However, there are situations where selling at a price above direct costs but below full cost makes sense. Suppose a company is operating at below capacity and the sales director receives a call from a buyer who is willing to place an order for 50,000 widgets but will pay only £11 per unit. If, in management's judgement, to refuse the order will mean machinery lying idle, a strong case for accepting the order can be made since the £1 per unit (£50,000) over direct costs is making a contribution to fixed costs that would not be made if the order was turned down. The decision is not without risk, however. The danger is that customers who are paying a higher price become aware of the £11 price and demand a similar deal.

Direct cost pricing is useful for services marketing—for example, where seats in aircraft or rooms in hotels cannot be stored; if they are unused at any time the revenue is lost. In such situations, pricing to cover direct costs plus a contribution to overheads can make sense. As with the previous example, the risk is that customers who have paid the higher price find out and complain.

Direct costs, then, indicate the lowest price at which it is sensible to take business if the alternative is to let machinery (or seats or rooms) lie idle. Also, direct cost pricing does not suffer from the 'price up as demand down' problem that was found with full cost pricing, as it does not take account of fixed costs in the price calculation. Finally, it avoids the problem of allocating overhead charges found with full cost pricing for the same reason. However, when business is buoyant it gives no indication of the correct price because it does not take into account customers' willingness to pay. Nor can it be used in the long term as, at some point, fixed costs must be covered to make a profit. Nevertheless, as a short-term expedient or tactical device, direct cost pricing does have a role to play in reducing the impact of excess capacity.

12.1 Pause for Thought

What is your overall assessment of cost-orientated pricing methods?

Competitor-Orientated Pricing

A second approach to pricing is to focus on competitors rather than costs when setting prices. This can take two forms: **going-rate pricing** and **competitive bidding**.

Going-rate pricing

In situations where there is no product differentiation—for example, a certain grade of coffee bean—a producer may have to take the going rate for the product. This accords most directly to the economist's notion of perfect competition. To the marketing manager it is anathema. A fundamental marketing principle is the creation of a differential advantage, which enables companies to build monopoly positions around their products. This allows a degree of price discretion dependent upon how much customers value the differential advantage. Even for what appear to be commodity markets, creative thinking can lead to the formation of a differential advantage on which a premium price can be built. A case in point was Austin-Trumans, a steel stockholder, which stocked the same kind of basic steels held by many other stockholders. Faced with a commodity product, Austin-Trumans attempted to differentiate on delivery. It guaranteed that it would deliver on time or pay back 10 per cent of the price to the buyer. So important was delivery to buyers (and so unreliable were many of Austin-Trumans' rivals) that buyers were willing to pay a 5 per cent price premium for this guarantee. The result was that Austin-Trumans were consistently the most profitable company in its sector for a number of years. This example shows how companies can use the creation of a differential advantage to move away from going-rate pricing.

Competitive bidding

Many contracts are won or lost on the basis of competitive bidding. The most usual process is the drawing up of detailed specifications for a product and putting the contract out to tender. Potential suppliers quote a price that is confidential to themselves and the buyer (sealed bids). All other things being equal, the buyer will select the supplier that quotes the lowest price. A major focus for suppliers, therefore, is the likely bid prices of competitors.

Statistical models have been developed by management scientists to add a little science to the art of competitive bidding.[4] Most use the concept of *expected profit* where:

Expected profit = Profit × Probability of winning

It is clearly a notional figure based on actual profit (bid price − costs) and the probability of the bid price being successful. Table 12.2 gives a simple example of how such a competitive

Competitive bidding using the expected profit criterion			TABLE 12.2
Bid price (£)	Profit	Probability	Expected profit
2000	0	0.99	0
2100	100	0.90	90
2200	200	0.80	160*
2300	300	0.40	120
2400	400	0.20	80
2500	500	0.10	50
*Based on the expected profit criterion, recommended bid price is £2200			

bidding model might be used. Based on past experience the bidder believes that the successful bid will fall in the range of £2000–£2500. As price is increased so profits will rise (full costs = £2000) and the probability of winning will fall. The bidder uses past experience to estimate the probability of each price level being successful. In this example the probability ranges from 0.10 to 0.99. By multiplying profit and probability an expected profit figure can be calculated for each bid price. Expected profit peaks at £160, which corresponds to a bid price of £2200. Consequently this is the price at which the bid will be made.

Unfortunately this simple model suffers from a number of limitations. First, it may be difficult, if not impossible, for managers to express their views on the likelihood of a price being successful in precise statistical probability terms. Note that if the probability of the £2200 bid was recorded as 0.70 rather than 0.80, and likewise the £2300 bid was recorded as 0.50 rather than 0.40, the recommended bid price would move from £2200 (expected profit £140) to £2300 (expected profit £150). Clearly the outcome of the analysis can be dependent on small changes in the probability figures. Second, use of the expected profit criterion is limited to situations where the bidder can play the percentage game over the medium to long term. In circumstances where companies are desperate to win an order, they may decide to trade off profit for an improved chance of winning. In the extreme case of a company fighting for survival, a more sensible bid strategy might be to price at below full cost (£2000) and simply make a contribution to fixed costs, as we discussed above under direct cost pricing.

Clearly the use of competitive bidding models is restricted in practice. However, successful bidding depends on having an efficient competitor information system. One Scandinavian ball-bearing manufacturer, which relied heavily on effective bid pricing, installed a system that was dependent on salespeople feeding into its computer-based information system details of past successful and unsuccessful bids. The salespeople were trained to elicit successful bid prices from buyers, and then to enter them into a customer database that recorded order specifications, quantities and the successful bid price.

Because not all buyers were reliable when giving their salespeople information (sometimes it was in their interest to quote a lower successful bid price than actually occurred), competitors' successful bid prices were graded as category A (totally reliable—the salesperson had seen documentation supporting the bid price or it came from a totally trustworthy source), category B (probably reliable—no documentary evidence but the source was normally reliable) or category C (slightly dubious—the source may be reporting a lower than actual price to persuade us to bid very low next time). Although not as scientific as the competitive bidding model, this system, built up over time, provides a very effective database that salespeople can use as a starting point when they are next asked to bid by a customer.

Marketing-Orientated Pricing

Marketing-orientated pricing is more difficult than cost-orientated or competitor-orientated pricing because it takes a much wider range of factors into account. In all, 10 factors need to be considered when adopting a marketing-orientated approach—these are shown in Figure 12.3.

Marketing strategy

The price of a product should be set in line with *marketing strategy*. The danger is that price is viewed in isolation (as with full cost pricing) with no reference to other marketing decisions such as positioning, strategic objectives, promotion, distribution and product benefits. The result is an inconsistent mess that makes no sense in the marketplace and causes customer confusion.

The way around this problem is to recognize that the pricing decision is dependent on other earlier decisions in the marketing planning process (see Chapter 2). For new products, price will depend on positioning strategy, and for existing products price will be affected by strategic objectives. First, we shall examine the setting of prices for new products. Second, we shall consider the pricing of existing products.

Pricing new products

In this section we shall explore the way in which positioning strategy affects price, launch strategies based upon skimming and penetration pricing, and the factors that affect the decision to charge a high or low price.

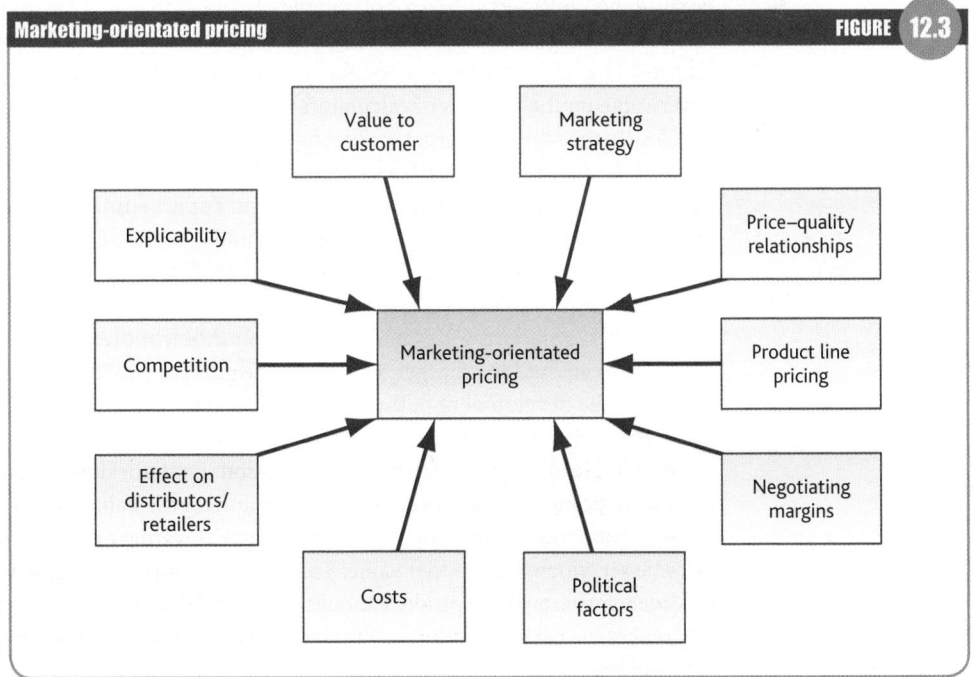

Marketing-orientated pricing FIGURE 12.3

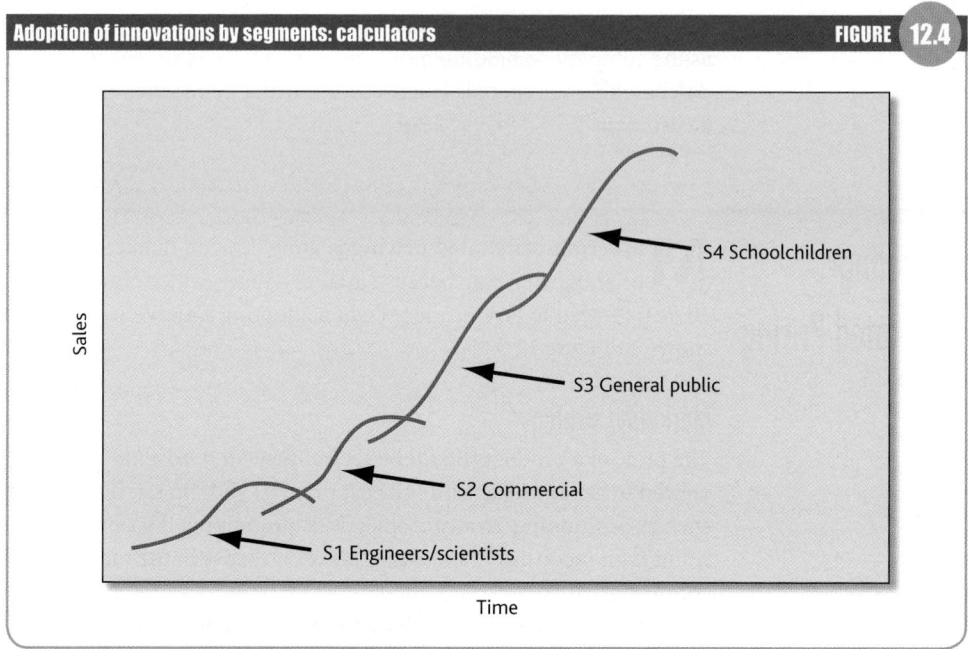

Adoption of innovations by segments: calculators   FIGURE **12.4**

S4 Schoolchildren

S3 General public

S2 Commercial

S1 Engineers/scientists

Sales

Time

Positioning strategy: a key decision that marketing management faces when launching new products is **positioning strategy**. This in turn will have a major influence on price. As discussed in Chapter 8, product positioning involves the choice of target market and the creation of a differential advantage. Each of these factors can have an enormous impact on price.

When strategy is being set for a new product, marketing management is often faced with an array of potential target markets. In each, the product's differential advantage (value) may differ. For example, when calculators were commercially developed for the first time, three distinct segments existed: S1 (engineers and scientists who placed a high value on calculators because their jobs involved a lot of complex calculations); S2 (accountants and bankers who also placed a high value on a calculator because of the nature of their jobs, although not as high as S1); and S3 (the general public, who made up the largest segment but placed a much lower value on the benefits of calculators).[5]

Clearly the choice of target market had a massive impact on the price that could be charged. If engineers/scientists were targeted, a high price could be set, reflecting the large differential advantage of the calculator to them. For accountants/bankers the price would have to be slightly lower, and for the general public a much lower price would be needed. In the event, the S1 segment was chosen and the price set high (around £250/€360). Over time, price was reduced to draw into the market segments S2 and S3 (and a further segment, S4, when exam regulations were changed to allow schoolchildren to use calculators). Much later, when Casio entered the market, it targeted the general public with calculators priced at less than £10. The development of the market for calculators, based upon targeting increasingly price-sensitive market segments, is shown in Figure 12.4.

Two implications follow from this discussion. First, for new products, marketing management must decide on a target market and on the value that people in that segment place on the product (the extent of its differential advantage): only then can a market-based price be set which reflects that value. Second, where multiple segments appear attractive, modified versions of the product should be designed and priced differently, not according to differences in costs, but in line with the respective values that each target market places on the product.

Launch strategies: price should also be blended with other elements of the marketing mix. Figure 12.5 shows four marketing strategies based on combinations of price and promotion. Similar matrices could also be developed for product and distribution, but for illustrative purposes promotion will be used here.

A combination of high price and high promotion expenditure is called a *rapid skimming strategy*. The high price provides high margin returns on investment and the heavy promotion creates high levels of product awareness and knowledge. Nike usually employs a rapid skimming strategy when it launches new ranges of trainers. BMW and Coca-Cola also employ rapid skimming strategies. A *slow skimming strategy* combines high price with low levels of promotional expenditure. High prices mean big profit margins, but high levels of promotion are believed to be unnecessary, perhaps because word of mouth is more important and the product is already well known (e.g. Rolls-Royce) or because heavy promotion is thought to be incompatible with product image, as with cult products. A company that uses a skimming pricing policy effectively is Bosch, the German car components supplier; it has applied an extremely profitable skimming strategy, supported by patents, to its launch of fuel injection and anti-lock braking systems.[6]

Companies that combine low prices with heavy promotional expenditure are practising a *rapid penetration strategy*. The aim is to gain market share rapidly, perhaps at the expense of a rapid skimmer. For example, no-frills airlines such as easyJet and Ryanair have successfully attacked British Airways by adopting a rapid penetration strategy. Direct Line is an example of a company that challenged traditional UK insurance companies with great success by using heavy promotion and a low charge for its insurance policies. Tesco, the supermarket chain, also uses a rapid penetration strategy with low prices heavily promoted using the strap-line 'Every little helps'. Travelodge is marketed using a rapid penetration strategy, with advertising used to communicate that its prices are lower than those of rivals (see illustration).

Finally, a *slow penetration strategy* combines a low price with low promotional expenditure. Own-label brands use this strategy: promotion is not necessary to gain distribution, and low promotional expenditure helps to maintain high profit margins for these brands. The supermarket chains Netto and Aldi adopt a slow penetration strategy. The low promotional expenditures help to promote the low cost base necessary to support their low prices. This price/promotion framework is useful in thinking about marketing strategies at launch.

A major question remains, however: when is it sensible to use a *high price (skimming) strategy* and when should

New product launch strategies   FIGURE **12.5**

	Promotion	
	High	Low
Price — High	Rapid skimming	Slow skimming
Price — Low	Rapid penetration	Slow penetration

◀ Travelodge compares the price of its rooms with that of Comfort Inn.

Characteristics of high-price market segments   TABLE 12.3
1   Product provides high value
2   Customers have high ability to pay
3   Consumer and bill payer are different
4   Lack of competition
5   Excess demand
6   High pressure to buy
7   Switching costs

a *low price* (*penetration*) strategy be used? To answer this question we need to understand the characteristics of market segments that can bear a high price. These characteristics are shown in Table 12.3. The more that each of these characteristics is present, the more likely that a high price can be charged.[7]

The first characteristic is that the market segment should place a *high value on the product,* based on the customer benefits it provides. Calculators provided high functional value to engineers and scientists, other products (for example, perfumes and clothing) may rely more on psychological value where brand image is crucial (for example, Chanel perfume or Gucci shoes). Second, high prices are more likely to be viable where *customers have a high ability to pay.* *Cash rich segments* in organizational markets often correlate with profitability. For example, the financial services sector and the textile industry in Europe may place similar values on marketing consultancy skills but in general the former has more ability to pay.

In certain markets the *consumer of the product is different from the bill payer.* This distinction may form the basis of a high-price market segment. Airlines, for example, charge more for a given flight when the journey is for less than seven days and does not include a Saturday night. This is because that type of air traveller is more likely to be a businessperson, whereas the more price-sensitive leisure travellers who pay for themselves and tend to stay at least a week can travel at a lower fare. Rail travel is often segmented by price sensitivity too. Early morning long-distance trips are more expensive than midday journeys since the former are usually made by businesspeople.

The fourth characteristic of high-price segments is *lack of competition* among supplying companies. The extreme case is a monopoly where customers have only one supplier from which to buy. When customers have no, or very little, choice of supply, the power to determine price is largely in the hands of suppliers. This means that high prices can be charged if suppliers so wish.

The fifth characteristic of high price segments is *excess demand*. When demand exceeds supply there is the potential to charge high prices. For example, when the demand for diamonds exceeds supply the price of diamonds usually rises.

The next situation where customers are likely to be less price sensitive is where there is *high pressure to buy*. For example, in an emergency situation where a vital part is required to repair a machine that is needed to fulfil a major order, the customer may be willing to pay a high price if a supplier can guarantee quick delivery.

The final situation where high prices can be charged is where there are high *switching costs*. Buyers may have made investments in dealing with a supplier that they would have to make again if they switched suppliers. Production, logistical or marketing operations may be geared to using the equipment of a particular supplier (e.g. computer systems). Customers may have invested heavily in product-specific training that would have to be repeated if they chose to switch. These factors are likely to make customers less sensitive to the price charged by existing suppliers in such circumstances.

The task of the marketing manager is to evaluate the chosen target market for a new product using the checklist provided in Table 12.3. It is unlikely that all seven conditions will apply and so judgement is still required. But the more these characteristics are found in the target market, the greater the chances that a high price can be charged.

Table 12.4 lists the conditions when a *low price* (*penetration*) *strategy* should be used. The first situation is when an analysis of the market segment using the previous checklist reveals that a low price is the *only feasible alternative*. For example, a product that has no differential

Conditions for charging a low price	TABLE 12.4
1 Only feasible alternative	
2 Market penetration *or* domination	
3 Experience curve effect/low costs	
4 Make money later	
5 Make money elsewhere	
6 Barrier to entry	
7 Predation	

advantage launched on to a market where customers are not cash rich, pay for themselves, have little pressure to buy and have many suppliers to choose from has no basis for charging a price premium. At best it could take the going-rate price but, more likely, would be launched using a penetration (low-price) strategy, otherwise there would be no incentive for consumers to switch from their usual brand. The power of consumers to force down prices is nowhere greater than on the Internet. Digital Marketing 12.1 discusses the tools available on the Internet to enable consumers to find low prices.

There are, however, more positive reasons for using a low price strategy. A company may wish to gain *market penetration* or *domination* by pricing its products aggressively. This requires a market containing at least one segment of price-sensitive consumers. Direct Line priced its insurance policies aggressively to challenge traditional

12.1 Digital Marketing

Driving a Hard Bargain on the Internet

The Internet is seen as the place to get a bargain as competitive pressures and the lowering of communicational and transactional costs mean that prices are driven down. The availability of search engines and price comparison websites such as PriceRunner (www.pricerunner.com) and Kelkoo (www.kelkoo.com) have ensured greater price transparency between different operators in the market. These sites increase pressure on suppliers to update prices more frequently, giving a better deal for consumers. The global reach of the Internet also allows sites such as Play (www.play.com) to offer low prices due to the legislation benefits of operating in Jersey, which means that they do not have to pass on the normal cost of VAT at 17.5 per cent.

Consumers are also able to get bargains from dynamic pricing websites like eBay (www.ebay.com) and lastminute.com (www.lastminute.com), which find the market value for a product by letting customers set the price. Using online auctions, customers bid for desired products, with the highest bid received within a given time period resulting in the purchase. These sites are some of the most successful on the Internet.

In some cases, however, a bargain may be harder to find. For example, some suppliers, such as Sony, charge Internet-only organizations up to 15 per cent higher than traditional bricks-and-mortar retailers, which are rewarded for displaying and demonstrating products to the end consumer. The higher charge protects the supplier from suffering from prices that may be considered so low that they undermine the brand's positioning; and, in the case of Sony, the practice also protects the position of its franchised Sony Centre retail operation.

Helping consumers get a bargain is Quidco (www.quidco.com), a website that allows them to collect cash back while spending online. It is a cash back cooperative and the idea of the site is that it earns commission on users' online purchases, and passes that commission back to users in the form of rebate.

Quidco has created a community of over half a million subscribers and claims that, collectively, it will save them over £25 million. For an administration fee of £5 a year members of the community benefit from Quidco's novel approach, which earns money for consumers every time they spend with a registered merchant (e.g. retailers like Tesco, Argos and PC World). The Quidco system works by tracking members' spending with merchants and depositing affiliate commissions into the consumer's pocket.

Based on: Kinney (2000);[8] Ancarani (2002);[9] Business.timesonline.co.uk;[10] www.quidco.co.uk

insurance companies and is now market leader for home and motor insurance in the UK. Tesco, the UK supermarket chain, has also become the market leader through charging low prices for good-quality products. The importance of having a sizeable segment of price-sensitive customers is illustrated in Marketing in Action 12.1.

 12.1 Marketing in Action

The New Henry Ford?

Henry Ford famously used a low price penetration strategy to bring affordable cars to the general public in the USA, employing the now legendary strap-line 'You can have any colour of car you want, so long as it is black.' Now another car-making entrepreneur seems to be following a similar strategy.

Tata Motors of India launched a cheap, small 'people's car' priced at £1450. The car is the dream of company chairman Ratan Tata, whose idea is to market a vehicle that would bridge the gap between cars and motor scooters for 3 million people a year in India. 'Families who presently all ride through the heat and dust on a two-wheeler will have an alternative in the form of a car for the first time,' said Ravi Kant, managing director of Tata Motors.

The new model's price is kept low by employing a small-capacity engine, keeping its size small, using more plastic than steel, and swapping high-tech glue for traditional welding. At £1450 it is less than half the price of the next cheapest car in India. With an enormous market segment of people on low incomes, Mr Tata's penetration pricing policy makes sense if the other features of the car, such as reliability and safety, are satisfactory.

Based on: Ramesh (2006);[11] Hutton (2008)[12]

Penetration pricing for market presence is sometimes followed by price increases once market share has reached a satisfactory level. Mercedes followed this strategy in the US car market by pricing close to the market average in 1967, but had moved to over double the market average price by 1982.[13] The Lexus, Toyota's luxury model, appears to be following a similar strategy. Ratners, a jewellery chain (now renamed Signet), achieved market domination using price as its major competitive weapon although indiscreet comments by its chairman regarding the quality of its merchandise dampened sales.

Low prices may also be charged to increase output and so bring down costs through the *experience curve effect*. Research has shown that, for many products, costs decline by around 20 per cent when production doubles.[14] Cost economies are achieved by learning how to produce the product more effectively through better production processes and improvements in skill levels. Economies of scale through, for example, the use of more cost-effective machines at higher output levels also act to lower costs as production rises. Marketing costs per unit of output may also fall as production rises. For example, an advertising expenditure of £1 million represents 1 per cent of revenue when sales are £100 million, but rises to 10 per cent of revenue when sales are only £10 million. Therefore a company may choose to price aggressively to become the largest producer and therefore, if the experience curve holds, the lowest-cost supplier. Intel has taken full advantage of the cost economies that come with being the dominant market leader in the microprocessor market, with over 80 per cent share and the investment of billions of dollars in hyperproductive plants that can produce more processors in a day than some of its rivals can produce in a year.[15] This has given it the option of achieving higher profit margins than its competitors or charging low prices, as it did with its top-performing Pentium 4 chip, the price of which was dropped by 57 per cent in a six-week period in a move designed to hurt its major rival AMD.[16] Indeed, *low costs* through

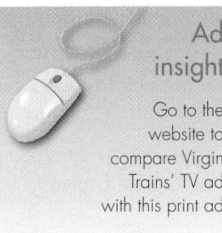

ruthless cost-cutting may be necessary to achieve profits using low price strategies. For example, the German supermarket chain Lidl keeps costs low by displaying products in the cardboard boxes in which they are delivered, stacked on top of wooden crates, and by keeping advertising and promotional expenditure to a minimum in the UK. Interestingly, its strategy is different in Germany, where it has much greater market penetration. Its scale economies allow it to maintain low costs even though its advertising expenditure is much higher. Internet bookings are another way of reducing costs and, thereby, prices. The advertisement for Virgin Trains illustrates how early bookings using its website can mean low prices.

▲ Cutting costs means that consumers can be offered lower prices.

A low price strategy can also make sense when the objective is to *make money later*. Two circumstances can provoke this action. First, the sale of the basic product may be followed by profitable after-sales service and/or spare parts. For example, the sale of an aero-engine at cost may be worthwhile if substantial profits can be made on the later sale of spare parts.

Two companies that have successfully applied this strategy are Hewlett-Packard and Gillette. Hewlett-Packard printers are sold at a low price to consumers but replacement ink cartridges are expensive, which is where it makes large profits. Gillette follows a similar strategy, pricing its razors competitively but charging a high price for replacement blades. Its razors account for 5 per cent of the razor division's profits, while blades account for 95 per cent.[17] Sony and Microsoft have also sold their games consoles at a loss, making money on the subsequent sales of games.

Second, the price sensitivity of customers may change over time: initially customers may be price sensitive, implying the need for a low price, but as circumstances change they may become much less sensitive to price. For example, a publisher of management journals based its pricing strategy on this change. A key customer group was librarians who, faced by budget constraints, were price sensitive to new journals. Consequently these were priced low to encourage adoption. Once established in the library their use by students and staff meant that there would be considerable resistance to them being delisted. The strategy, therefore, was to keep price low until target penetration was achieved. Then price was raised consistently above inflation in response to the fall in price sensitivity.

Marketers also charge low prices to *make money elsewhere*. For example, retailers often use loss leaders, which are advertised in an attempt to attract customers into their stores and to create a low-cost image. Supermarkets, much to the annoyance of traditional petrol retailers, use petrol as a loss leader to attract motorists to their stores.[18] Manufacturers selling a range of products to organizations may accept low prices on some goods in order to be perceived by customers as a full-range supplier. In both cases, sales of other higher-priced and more profitable products benefit.

Low prices can also act as a *barrier to entry*. A company may weigh the longer-term benefits of deterring competition by accepting low margins to be greater than the short-term advantages of a high-price, high-margin strategy, which may attract rivals into its market.

Finally, low prices may be charged in an attempt to put other companies out of business; this is known as *predation*. For example, Microsoft has been accused of predatory pricing by bundling free software such as its Internet browser and Media Player with its best-selling Windows operating system.

An alternative strategy to charging permanently low prices is to run sales promotions (e.g. temporary price cuts or bulk-buy offers). Some advantages of using a permanently low price strategy (sometimes known as 'everyday low prices') are:

- price is perceived as honest, as consumers see consistently low prices, which suggests a fair profit margin; using a promotion may imply that the original price was high—big enough for temporary price reductions
- there is no need for expensive promotional advertising to gain awareness of promotional offers
- the danger of getting into costly promotional battles with rivals is reduced.

Some advantages of varying price levels by the use of sales promotions (sometimes known as 'hi-lo pricing') are:

- sales events and promotions create excitement that can generate extra store traffic
- sales promotions attract 'promotion junkies' who form a segment of consumers that have high price awareness and respond to promotions
- sales promotions have a proven record of increasing short-term sales.

Pricing existing products

The pricing of existing products should also be set within the context of strategy. Specifically, the *strategic objective* for each product will have a major bearing on pricing strategy. As with new products, price should not be set in isolation, but should be consistent with strategic objectives. Four strategic objectives are relevant to pricing: build, hold, harvest and reposition.

- *Build objective*: for price-sensitive markets, a build objective for a product implies a *price lower than the competition*. If the competition raises its prices we would be slow to match it. For price-insensitive markets, the best pricing strategy becomes less clear-cut. Price in these circumstances will be dependent on the overall positioning strategy thought appropriate for the product.
- *Hold objective*: where the strategic objective is to hold sales and/or market share, the appropriate pricing strategy is to *maintain or match price* relative to the competition. This has implications for price changes: if competition reduces prices then our prices would match this price fall.
- *Harvest objective*: a harvest objective implies the maintenance or raising of profit margins even though sales and/or market share are falling. The implication for pricing strategy would be to set *premium prices*. For products that are being harvested, there would be much greater reluctance to match price cuts than for products that were being built or held. On the other hand, price increases would swiftly be matched.

- *Reposition objective*: changing market circumstances and product fortunes may necessitate the repositioning of an existing product. This may involve a *price change*, the direction and magnitude of which will be dependent on the new positioning strategy for the production. As discussed under 'product replacement strategies' (Chapter 10), Skoda's repositioning involved better quality and a higher price.

The above examples show how developing clear strategic objectives helps the setting of price and clarifies appropriate reaction to competitive price changes. Price setting, then, is much more sophisticated than simply asking 'How much can I get for this product?' The process starts by asking more fundamental questions like 'How is this product going to be positioned in the marketplace?' and 'What is the appropriate strategic objective for this product?' Only after these questions have been answered can price sensibly be determined.

Value to the customer

A second marketing consideration when setting prices is estimating a product's value to the customer. Already when discussing marketing strategy its importance has been outlined: price should be accurately keyed to the value to the customer. In brief, the more value a product gives compared to that of the competition, the higher the price that can be charged. In this section we shall explore a number of ways of estimating value to the customer. This is critical because of the close relationship between value and price. Three methods of estimating value will now be discussed: trade-off analysis, experimentation and economic value to the customer analysis.

Trade-off analysis

Trade-off analysis (otherwise known as conjoint analysis) measures the trade-off between price and other product features so that their effects on product preference can be established.[19] Respondents are not asked direct questions about price; instead product profiles consisting of product features and price are described and respondents are asked to name their preferred profile. From their answers, the effect of price and other product features can be measured using a computer model. The following is a brief description of the procedure.

The first step is to identify the most important product features (attributes) and benefits that are expected to be gained as a result of buying the product. Product profiles are then built using these attributes (including price) and respondents are asked to choose which product they would buy from pairs of product profiles. Statistical analysis allows the computation of *preference contributions* that permit the preference for attributes to be compared. For example, if the analysis was for a business-to-business product, trade-off analysis might show that increasing delivery time from one week to one day is worth a price increase of 5 per cent. In addition, the relative importance of each of the product attributes, including price, can be calculated. By translating these results into market share and profit figures for the proposed new product the optimal price can be found.

This technique has been used to price a wide range of industrial and consumer products and services, and can be used to answer such questions as the following.[20]

1 What is the value of a product feature including improving service levels in price terms?
2 What happens to market share if price changes?
3 What is the value of a brand name in terms of price?
4 What is the effect on our market share of competitive price changes?
5 How do these effects vary across European countries?

Marketing in Action 12.2 shows how trade-off analysis was used to price a new German car. By developing product profiles based on four key product attributes—the brand, maximum speed, petrol consumption and price—and interviewing target customers, an optimal price could be set.

12.2 Marketing in Action

Pricing a German Car using Trade-Off Analysis

A German car company used conjoint measurement to set the price for its new Tiger model (name disguised). The managers involved in the decision raised questions like the following: What is the 'price value' of our brand? How much is the customer willing to pay for a higher maximum speed? (There is no speed limit in Germany.) How does petrol consumption relate to price acceptance?

The managers proceeded through the following steps. First, they determined that the most relevant product attributes were brand, maximum speed, petrol consumption and price.

Second, they chose characteristics for each attribute. They would test three brands: one German, one Japanese and their own; three maximum speeds: 200, 220 and 240 kilometres per hour; three levels of petrol consumption: 12, 14 and 16 litres per 100 kilometres; and three prices: €25,000, €30,000 and €35,000.

Third, they designed a questionnaire and collected data. The attributes and characteristics yielded 81 possible product profiles, but the company needed only nine profiles to answer its questions. Researchers developed the nine profiles and presented them to target group respondents in pairs, as shown below. Respondents, interviewed by computer, indicated whether they would buy A or B; 32 such comparisons were presented.

Attribute	Profile A	Profile B
Brand	Tiger	Japanese
Maximum speed	200	240
Petrol consumption	12	16
Price	€30,000	€35,000

From the data, the company calculated preference contributions, numerical values that allow the preference for attributes to be compared. Preference contributions allow you to discover that, say, increasing car speed by 20 kilometres per hour generates the same increase in preference for the car as would decreasing the price by €5000. Adding up the preference contributions results in an overall preference index.

The greater the difference between the lowest and the highest preference contribution within one attribute (that is, the greater the disparity between preference for, say, the most popular brand and the least popular brand), the more important is this attribute. These differences can be translated into percentage importance weights that add up to 100 per cent. In this case:

Brand	35%
Maximum speed	30%
Price	20%
Petrol consumption	15%

Thus customers in this target group were very interested in brand and maximum speed but less sensitive to price and petrol consumption.

Taking the known attribute levels for the Tiger model, the managers could calculate market share and profits for alternative prices. They found that the optimal price was at the upper end of the price range; they set it slightly below €35,000.

Based on: Simon (1992)[21]

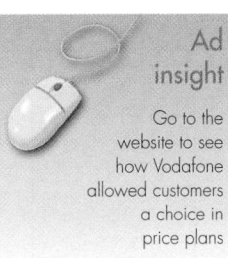

Experimentation

A limitation of trade-off analysis is that respondents are not asked to back up their preferences with cash expenditure. Consequently, what they say they prefer may not be reflected in actual purchase when they are asked to part with their money. *Experimental pricing research* attempts to overcome this drawback by placing a product on sale at different locations with varying prices.

The major alternatives are to use a controlled store experiment or test marketing. In a *controlled store experiment* a number of stores are paid to vary the price levels of the product under test. Suppose 100 supermarkets are being used to test two price levels of a brand of coffee; 50 stores would be chosen at random (perhaps after controlling for region and size) and allocated the lower price, the rest would use the higher price. By comparing sales levels and profit contributions between the two groups of stores the most profitable price would be established. A variant of this procedure would test price differences between the test brand and major rival brands. For example, in half the stores a price differential of 2p may be compared with 4p. In practice, considerable sums need to be paid to supermarkets to obtain approval to run such tests, and the implementation of the price levels needs to be monitored carefully to ensure that the stores do sell at the specified prices.

Test marketing can be used to compare the effectiveness of varying prices so long as more than one area is chosen. For example, the same product could be sold in two areas using an identical promotional campaign but with different prices between areas. A more sophisticated design could measure the four combinations of high/low price and high/low promotional expenditure if four areas were chosen. Obviously, the areas would need to be matched (or differences allowed for) in terms of target customer profile so that the result would be comparable. The test needs to be long enough so that trial and repeat purchase at each price can be measured. This is likely to be between 6 and 12 months for products whose purchase cycle lasts more than a few weeks.

A potential problem of using test marketing to measure price effects is competitor activity designed to invalidate the test results. For example, competitors could run special promotions in the test areas to make sales levels atypical if they discovered the purpose and location of the test marketing activities. Alternatively, they may decide not to react at all. If they know that a pricing experiment is taking place and that syndicated consumer panel data are being used to measure the results they may simply monitor the results since competitors will be receiving the same data as the testing company.[22] By estimating how successful each price has been, they are in a good position to know how to react when a price is set nationally.

Economic value to the customer analysis

Experimentation is more usual when pricing consumer products. However, industrial markets have a powerful tool at their disposal when setting the price of their products: **economic value to the customer (EVC)** analysis. Many organizational purchases are motivated by economic value considerations since reducing costs and increasing revenue are prime objectives of many companies. If a company can produce an offering that has a high EVC, it can set a high price and yet still offer superior value compared to the competition. A high EVC may be because the product generates more revenue for the buyer than competition or because its operating costs (such as maintenance, operation or start-up costs) are lower over its lifetime. The Lexus was marketed using the latter approach, with the tag-line 'Lowest Cost of Ownership' based on its decent fuel economy, durability and resale value. Lexus salespeople were trained to provide the financial evidence to justify the claim.[23] Microsoft also used EVC analysis to defend its Windows platform against the threat from the lower-cost Linux operating system. Microsoft commissioned independent tests that showed how the total lifetime cost of open-source operating systems could exceed the costs of Windows despite their lower purchase

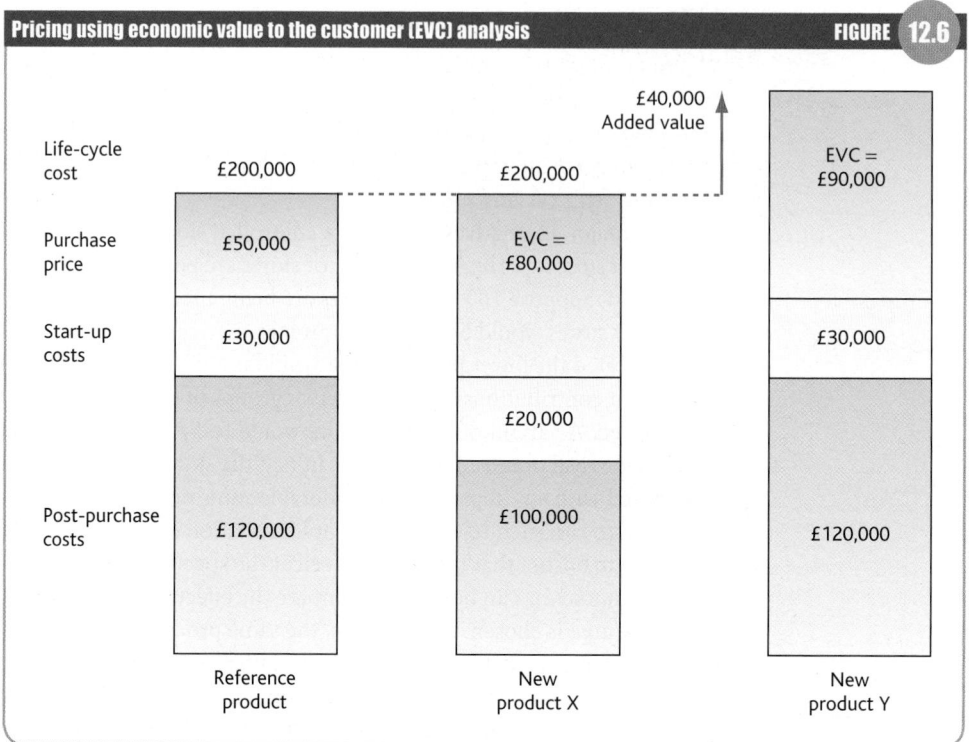

Pricing using economic value to the customer (EVC) analysis   FIGURE 12.6

price.[24] EVC analysis is usually particularly revealing when applied to products whose purchase price represents a small proportion of the lifetime costs to the customer.[25]

Figure 12.6 illustrates the calculation of EVC and how it can be used in price setting. A reference product is chosen (often the market leader) with which to compare costs. In the example, the market leader is selling a machine tool for £50,000. However this is only part of a customer's life-cycle costs. In addition, £30,000 start-up costs (installation, lost production and operator training) and £120,000 post-purchase costs (operator, power and maintenance) are incurred. The total life-cycle costs are, therefore, £200,000.

Our new machine tool (product X) has a different customer cost profile. Technological advances have reduced start-up costs to £20,000 and post-purchase costs to £100,000. Therefore total costs are reduced by £30,000 and the EVC our new product offers is £80,000 (£200,000 − £120,000). Thus the EVC figure is the amount a customer would have to pay to make the total life-cycle costs of the new and reference products the same. If the new machine tool was priced at £80,000 this would be the case. Below this price there would be an economic incentive for customers to buy the new machine tool.

EVC analysis is clearly a powerful tool for price setting since it establishes the upper economic limit for price. Management then has to use judgement regarding how much incentive to give the customer to buy the new product and how much of a price premium to charge. A price of £60,000 would give customers a £20,000 lifetime cost saving incentive while establishing a £10,000 price premium over the reference product. In general, the more entrenched the market leader, the more loyal its customer base and the less well known the newcomer, the higher the cost saving incentive needs to be.

In the second example shown in Figure 12.6 the new machine tool (product Y) does not affect costs but raises the customer's revenues. For example, faster operation may result in more output, or greater precision may enhance product quality leading to higher prices. This product is estimated to give £40,000 extra profit contribution over the reference product because of higher revenues. Its EVC is, therefore, £90,000 indicating the highest price the

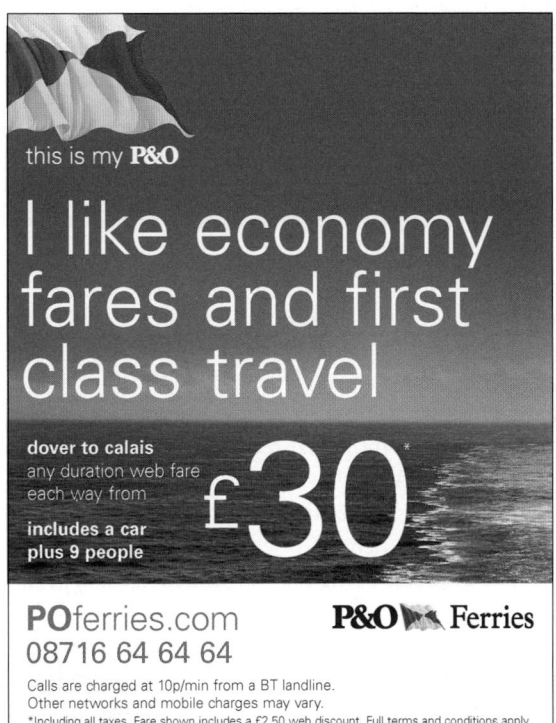

this is my **P&O**

I like economy fares and first class travel

dover to calais
any duration web fare
each way from

£30*

**includes a car
plus 9 people**

POferries.com
08716 64 64 64

Calls are charged at 10p/min from a BT landline.
Other networks and mobile charges may vary.
*Including all taxes. Fare shown includes a £2.50 web discount. Full terms and conditions apply.

P&O 🚢 **Ferries**

▲ P&O avoids low price/
low quality associations.

customer should be willing to pay. Once more, marketing management has to decide how much incentive to give to customers and how much of a price premium to charge.

EVC analysis can be useful in target market selection since different customers may have varying EVC levels. A decision may be made to target the market segment that has the highest EVC figure since for these customers the product has the greatest differential advantage. The implementation of an EVC-based pricing strategy relies on a well-trained salesforce, which is capable of explaining sophisticated economic value calculations to customers, and field-based evidence that the estimates of cost savings and revenue increases will occur in practice.

Price–quality relationships

A third consideration when adopting a marketing-orientated approach to pricing is the relationship between price and perceived quality. Many people use price as an indicator of quality. This is particularly the case for products where objective measurement of quality is not possible, such as drinks and perfume. But the effect is also to be found with consumer durables and industrial products. A study of price and quality perceptions of cars, for example, found that higher-priced cars were perceived to possess (unjustified) high quality.[26] Also sales of a branded agricultural fertilizer rose after the price was raised above that of its generic competitors despite the fact that it was the same compound. Interviews with farmers revealed that they believed the fertilizer to improve crop yield compared with rival products. Clearly price had influenced quality perceptions.

Marketing in Action 12.3 discusses some interesting results of experiments conducted to investigate the influence of price on quality perceptions. A potential problem, therefore, is that, by charging a low price, brand image may be tarnished. In an effort to avoid such associations, P&O Ferries emphasizes that low fares can come with first-class travel (see illustration).

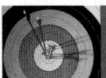 **12.3 Marketing in Action**

Does Price Really Influence Perceptions of Quality?

The question of the influence of price on quality perceptions has interested marketing managers for decades. Two experiments have investigated this issue. The first was a study into the effect of the price of placebos (dummy pills) on the killing of pain. Both pills were identical (a sugar compound) but patients that took the $2.50 placebo judged it better at killing pain than those that took one costing only 10 cents.

In the second experiment, 20 occasional red wine drinkers were asked to taste a Cabernet Sauvignon marked with a $5 price tag and one with a $45 price label. However, both came from the same $5 bottle. The higher-priced wine was selected as tasting superior by most of the drinkers. To explain the results, neuroscience was called upon. In a second experiment, the drinkers were asked to drink again while wired up to a brain scanner. When they drank the 'more expensive' wine, the part of the brain associated with pleasure became more active than when the 'less expensive' wine was drunk. Clearly, the higher price caused the drinkers to experience more pleasure, even if the product itself was no different.

Based on: Anonymous (2008);[27] Rangel, O'Doherty and Shiv (2008);[28] Ritson (2008)[29]

12.2 Pause for Thought

Think of three brands that you consider are high quality. How does their price compare to others in the product category? Usually, their price will be higher than average. The high price supports the high perceived quality positioning in the minds of consumers.

Product line pricing

Marketing-orientated companies also need to take account of where the price of a new product fits into its existing product line. For example, when Apple developed the iPod nano it had to carefully price-position the device against the original iPod mobile music player. Given that some potential buyers of the original iPod might now buy the nano, pricing it too cheaply could have resulted in lower overall profits for Apple.

Some companies prefer to extend their product lines rather than reduce the price of existing brands in the face of price competition. They launch cut-price fighter brands to compete with the low-price rivals. This has the advantage of maintaining the image and profit margins of existing brands (see Marketing in Action 12.4).

12.4 Marketing in Action

Fighter Branding

Successful brands sometimes find that they are attacked by low-priced rivals. One option is to reduce price in order to improve the benefit–cost to buy ratio. This may defend sales volume but at the cost of lowering margins. It also means that consumers who are still prepared to pay the higher price are purchasing the brand at a discount. A better alternative may be to maintain the price of the existing brand and compete by launching a lower-priced fighter brand. This means that the image and profit margins of the original brand are maintained and the new brand may raise overall sales revenue by attracting price-sensitive consumers. The danger is that the fighter brand may cannibalize sales of the original brand.

Apple found itself being attacked by low-priced competitors in the mobile music player and desktop computer markets. The company has chosen the fighter brand strategy in both cases. The iPod Shuffle, originally retailing at £49 compared to £219 for the iPod, was launched to compete with low-price mp3 players, and the Mac mini computer was introduced to compete against cheaper PCs entering the market from companies like China's Lenovo.

Bosch also found itself at a disadvantage compared to low-price white goods competitors. Fearing that the brand would lose its premium positioning if it price discounted, the company has launched Viva, aimed at price-conscious consumers who are looking for no-frills white goods. This means that the Bosch brand can maintain its upmarket image and price, while the company can compete on price using the Viva range of white goods.

The launch of the Celeron microchip by Intel is another example of successful fighter branding. Instead of cutting the price of its flagship Pentium chip, Intel responded to cheap rival chips by creating the Celeron chip, which involved no additional design or tooling costs as it was based on the Pentium design (some co-processor capabilities were simply turned off) and so could be sold at a low price, targeting home and small business computers.

Some supermarkets use fighter branding to minimize the impact of heavy discounters like Netto, Aldi and Lidl. For example, Tesco created its Value brand for this purpose, and Sainsbury's has its Basics range of groceries.

Based on: Parry (2005);[30] Nagle and Hogan (2006);[31] Ritson (2008);[32] Jobber and Fahy (2009)[33]

By producing a range of brands at different price points, companies can cover the varying price sensitivities of customers and encourage them to trade up to the more expensive, higher-margin brands.

Explicability

The capability of salespeople to explain a high price to customers may constrain price flexibility. In markets where customers demand economic justification of prices, the inability to produce cost and/or revenue arguments may mean that high prices cannot be set. In other circumstances the customer may reject a price that does not seem to reflect the cost of producing the product. For example, sales of an industrial chemical compound that repaired grooves in drive-shafts suffered because many customers believed that the price of £500 did not reflect the cost of producing the compound. Only when the salesforce explained that the premium price was needed to cover high research and development expenditure did customers accept that the price was not exploitative.

Competition

Competition factors are important determinants of price. At the very least, competitive prices should be taken into account; yet it is a fact of commercial life that many companies do not know what the competition is charging for its products.

Care has to be taken when defining competition. When asked to name competitors, many marketing managers list companies that supply technically similar products. For example, a paint manufacturer will name other paint manufacturers. However, as Figure 12.7 illustrates, this is only one layer of competition. A second layer consists of dissimilar products solving the same problem in a similar way. Polyurethane varnish manufacturers would fall into this category. A third level of competition would come from products solving the problem (or eliminating it) in a dissimilar way. Since window frames are often painted, PVC double glazing manufacturers would form competition at this level.

This analysis is not simply academic, as the effects of price changes can be misleading if these three layers of competition are not taken into consideration. For example, if all paint manufacturers raised their prices simultaneously they might believe that overall sales would not be dramatically affected if they mistakenly defined competition as technically similar products. The reality is, however, that such price collusion would make polyurethane varnish and, over a longer period, PVC double glazing more attractive to customers. The implication is that companies must take into account all three levels of competition when setting and changing prices.

In Europe a potential competitive threat is the development of **parallel importing**, which is the practice of importing goods from low-priced markets into high-priced

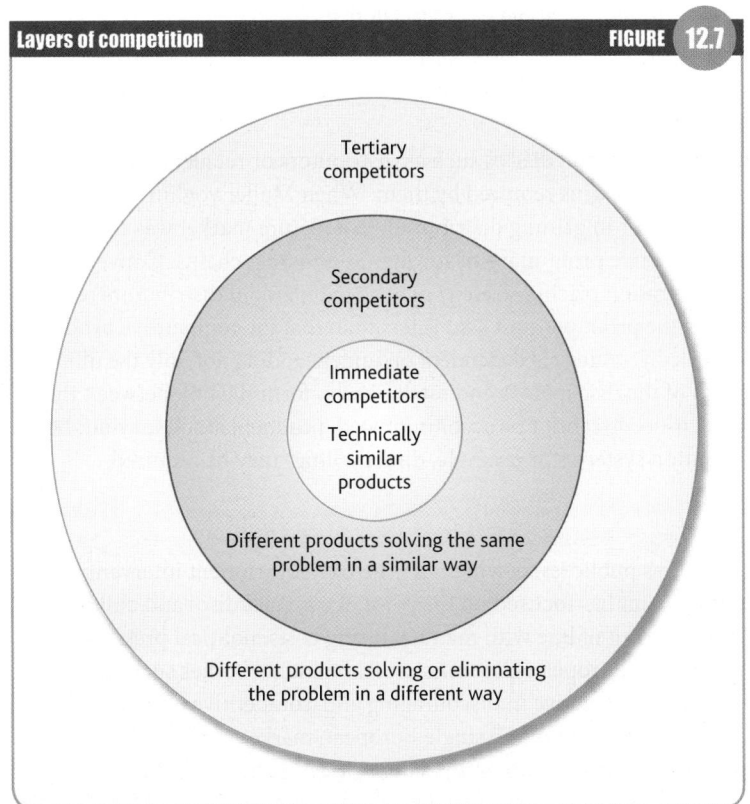

Layers of competition FIGURE 12.7

- Tertiary competitors
- Secondary competitors
- Immediate competitors
- Technically similar products
- Different products solving the same problem in a similar way
- Different products solving or eliminating the problem in a different way

ones by distributors. This produces the novel effect of a brand competing with itself (on price). For example, a pharmaceutical company might sell its drugs in a developing country at a low price only to discover that its discounted drugs have been purchased by distributors in another country where it is in direct competition with the same product sold for higher prices by the same firm. Manufacturers can lose out on this activity. First, it lowers average selling prices and, therefore, reduces profit margins. Second, manufacturers lose control over where and to whom their products are sold. This can damage brand image (compounded by the price drop) as the product range is sold in retail outlets that are incompatible with the brand's position in the marketplace. Finally, the relationship between manufacturers and their traditional distributors can be damaged as the latter see their sales decline in favour of their price-cutting rivals.[34] Levi Strauss sought to prevent the parallel importing of cut-price Levi 501 jeans by Tesco, a UK supermarket chain. Tesco had been selling 501s, purchased cheaply in the USA, for £27.99, compared to £50 in Levi's authorized shops. Levi Strauss won the case, which was heard at the European Court of Justice, arguing that its premium brand reputation was in danger of being damaged by this activity.[35]

Negotiating margins

In some markets, customers expect a price reduction. Price paid is therefore very different from list price. In the car market, for example, customers expect to pay less than the asking price in return for a cash sale. For organizational customers, Marn and Rosiello describe the difference between list price and realized or transaction price as the **price waterfall**.[36] The difference can be accounted for by order-size discounts, competitive discounts (a discretionary discount negotiated before the order is taken), a fast payment discount, an annual volume bonus and promotional allowances.

Managing this price waterfall is a key element in achieving a satisfactory transaction price. Marketing-orientated companies recognize that such discounting may be a fact of commercial life and build in *negotiating margins* that allow prices to fall from list price levels but still permit profitable transaction prices to be achieved.

Effect on distributors/retailers

When products are sold through intermediaries such as distributors or retailers, the list price to the customer must reflect the margins required by them. When Müller yoghurt was first launched in the UK, a major factor in gaining distribution in a mature market was the fact that its high price allowed attractive profit margins for the supermarket chains. Conversely, the implementation of a penetration pricing strategy may be hampered if distributors refuse to stock the product because the profit per unit sold is less than that for competitive products.

The implication is that pricing strategy is dependent on understanding not only the ultimate customer but also the needs of the distributors and retailers who form the link between them and the manufacturer. If their needs cannot be accommodated, product launch may not be viable or a different distribution system (for example, direct selling) may be required.

Political factors

High prices can be a contentious public issue, which may invoke government intervention. In recent years, public opprobrium has focused on the price of compact discs and children's computer games. Where price is out of line with manufacturing costs, political pressure may act to force down prices. The European Commission and national bodies such as the Competition Commission have been active in discouraging anti-competitive practices such as price-fixing. Indeed, the establishment of the single European market was a result of the desire to raise competitive pressures and thereby reduce prices throughout the European Union.

Companies need to take great care that their pricing strategies are not seen to be against the public interest. For example, the UK telecommunications regulator, Ofcom, ordered BT, which controls the nation's telephone network, to cut the prices it can charge rivals such as Orange and AOL for using it. The action was designed to allow them easier access to the residential telephony market with innovative products.[37] Exploitation of a monopoly position may bring short-term profits but incur the backlash of a public inquiry into pricing practices.

Costs

The final consideration that should be borne in mind when setting prices is costs. This may seem in contradiction to the outward-looking marketing-orientated approach but, in reality, costs do enter the pricing equation. The secret is to consider costs alongside all of the other considerations discussed under marketing-orientated price setting rather than in isolation. In this way costs act as a constraint: if the market will not bear the full cost of producing and marketing the product it should not be launched.

What should be avoided is the blind reference to costs when setting prices. Simply because one product costs less to make than another does not imply that its price should be less. Fiat once produced the Uno and Tipo. Because the Tipo was manufactured in a more modern plant than the Uno it cost less to produce; it was priced higher than the Uno, however, because it was a larger car conferring more customer benefits.

12.3 Pause for Thought

How do you rate marketing-orientated pricing compared to cost and competitor-orientated methods?

Initiating Price Changes

Our discussion of pricing strategy so far has looked at the factors that affect it. By taking into account the 10 marketing-orientated factors, managers can judge the correct level at which to set prices. But in a highly competitive world, pricing is dynamic: managers need to know when and how to raise or lower prices, and whether or not to react to competitors' price moves. First, we shall discuss initiating price changes, before analysing how to react to competitors' price changes.

Three key issues associated with initiating price changes are the *circumstances* that may lead a company to raise or lower prices, the *tactics* that can be used, and *estimating competitor reaction*. Table 12.5 illustrates the major points relevant to each of these considerations.

Circumstances

A price increase may be justified as a result of marketing research (for example, trade-off analysis or experimentation) which reveals that customers place a higher *value* on the product than is reflected in its price. *Rising costs*, and hence reduced profit margins, may also stimulate price rises. Another factor that leads to price increases is *excess demand*. A company that cannot supply the demand created by its customers may choose to raise prices in an effort to balance demand and supply. This can be an attractive option as profit margins are automatically widened. The final circumstance when companies may decide to raise prices is when embarking on a *harvest objective*. Prices are raised to increase margins even though sales may fall.

Correspondingly, price cuts may be provoked by the discovery that price is high compared to the *value* that customers place on the product, *falling costs* (and the desire to bring down

Initiating price changes		TABLE 12.5
	Increases	Cuts
Circumstances	Value greater than price Rising costs Excess demand Harvest objective	Value less than price Excess supply Build objective Price war unlikely
Tactics	Price jump Staged price increases Escalator clauses Price unbundling Lower discounts	Price fall Staged price reductions Fighter brands Price bundling Higher discounts
Estimating competitor reaction	Strategic objectives Self-interest Competitive situation Past experience Statements of intent	

costs further through the experience curve effect), and where there is *excess supply* leading to excess capacity. A further circumstance that may lead to price falls is the adoption of a *build objective*. When customers are thought to be price sensitive, price cutting may be used to build sales and market share. A damper on this tactic would be when a *price war* might be provoked, as happened when Reemtsma Cigarettenfabriken cut the price of its West brand from DM3.80 to DM3.30 in West Germany.[38] This was the first price-cutting move of this severity since the 1940s and led to competitor retaliation that saw the collapse of cigarette prices and margins.

The final circumstance that might lead to price cuts is the desire to *pre-empt competitive entry* into a market. Proactive price cuts—before the new competitor enters—are painful to implement because they incur short-term profit sacrifices but immediately reduce the attractiveness of the market to the potential entrant and reduce the risk of customer annoyance if prices are reduced only after competitive entry.[39] This was the tactic used by Cummins Engines, which slashed the prices of its small diesels by 30 per cent to prevent the entry of Japanese companies in its market.[40]

Tactics

Price increases and cuts can be implemented in many ways. The most direct is the *price jump or fall*, which increases or decreases the price by the full amount at one go. A price jump avoids prolonging the pain of a price increase over a long period but may raise the visibility of the price increase to customers. Using *staged price increases* might make the price rise more palatable but runs the risk of a company being charged with 'always raising its prices'. A *one-stage price fall* can have a high-impact dramatic effect that can be heavily promoted, but also has an immediate impact on profit margins. *Staged price reductions* have a less dramatic effect but may be used when a price cut is believed to be necessary but the amount necessary to stimulate sales is unclear. Small cuts may be initiated as a learning process that proceeds until the desired effect on sales has been achieved.

Price can also be raised by using *escalator clauses*. The contracts for some organizational purchases are drawn up before the product has been made. Constructing the product—for example, a new defence system or motorway—may take a number of years. An escalator clause in the contract allows the supplier to stipulate price increases in line with a specified index—for example, increases in industry wage rates or the cost of living.

Price unbundling is another tactic that effectively raises prices. Many product offerings actually consist of a set of products for which an overall price is set (for example, computer hardware and software). Price unbundling allows each element in the offering to be priced separately in such a way that the total price is raised. A variant on this process is charging for services that were previously included in the product's price. For example, manufacturers of mainframe computers have the option of unbundling installation and training services, and charging for them separately.

A final tactic is to maintain the list price but *lower discounts* to customers. In periods of heavy demand for new cars, dealers lower the cash discount given to customers, for example. Quantity discounts can also be manipulated to raise the transaction price to customers. The percentage discount per quantity can be lowered, or the quantity that qualifies for a particular percentage discount can be raised.

Companies that are contemplating a price cut have three options besides a direct price fall. A company defending a premium-priced brand that is under attack from a cut-price competitor may choose to maintain its price while introducing a *fighter brand*. The established brand keeps its premium-price position while the fighter brand competes with the rival for price-sensitive customers. Where a number of products and services that tend to be bought together are priced separately, *price bundling* can be used to effectively lower price. For example, televisions can be offered with 'free three-year repair warranties' or cars offered with 'free labour at first service'. Finally, *discount terms* can be made more attractive by increasing the percentage or lowering the qualifying levels. However, giving higher discounts over too long a period of time can be risky, as General Motors found to disastrous effect. By pursuing a four-year price discounting strategy in the USA in the face of poor sales, it provoked a price war with Ford and Chrysler, caused consumers to focus on price rather than value offered by the product, and has reduced profits.[41]

Estimating competitor reaction

A key factor in the price change decision is the extent of competitor reaction. A price rise that no competitor follows may turn customers away, while a price cut that is met by the competition may reduce industry profitability. Four factors affect the extent of competitor reaction: their strategic objectives, what is in their self-interest, the competitive situation at the time of the price change, and past experience.

Companies should try to gauge their *competitors' strategic objectives* for their products. By observing pricing and promotional behaviour, talking to distributors and even hiring their personnel, estimates of whether competitor products are being built, held or harvested can be made. This is crucial information: the competitors' response to our price increase or cut will depend upon it. They are more likely to follow our price increase if their strategic objective is to hold or harvest. If they are intent on building market share, they are more likely to resist following our price increase. Conversely, they are more likely to follow our price cuts if they are building or holding, and more likely to ignore our price cuts if they are harvesting.

Self-interest is also important when estimating competitor reactions. Managers initiating price changes should try to place themselves in the position of their competitors. What reaction is in their best interests? This may depend on the circumstances of the price change. For example, if price is raised in response to a general rise in cost inflation, the competition is more likely to follow than if price is raised because of the implementation of a harvest objective. Price may also depend upon the *competitive situation*. For example, if the competition has excess capacity, a price cut is more likely to be matched than if this is not the case. Similarly, a price rise is more likely to be followed if the competition is faced with excess demand.

Competitor reaction can also be judged by looking at their reactions to previous price changes. While *past experience* is not always a reliable guide, it may provide insights into the way in which competitors view price changes and the likely responses they might make. Past experience may be supplemented by *statements of intent*. For example, when T-Mobile dropped the price of its Flext brand, Vodafone immediately responded to prevent T-Mobile gaining market share, and its chief executive stated publicly, 'If anyone thinks that just by dropping prices they will take share from us, I will respond. I will compete, so they won't be getting an advantage on pure price.' Such declarations leave competitors in no doubt about Vodafone's reaction to further price falls.[42]

Reacting to Competitors' Price Changes

When competitors initiate price changes, companies need to analyse their appropriate reactions. Three issues are relevant here: when to follow, when to ignore, and the tactics required if the price change is to be followed. Table 12.6 summarizes the main considerations.

When to follow

Competitive price increases are more likely to be followed when they are due to general *rising cost* levels, or industry-wide *excess demand*. In these circumstances the initial pressure to raise prices is the same on all parties. Following a price rise is also more likely when customers are relatively *price insensitive*, which means that the follower will not gain much advantage by resisting the price increase. Where *brand image is consistent* with high prices, a company is more likely to follow a competitor's price rise as to do so would be consistent with the brand's positioning strategy. Finally, a price rise is more likely to be followed when a company is pursuing a *harvest or hold objective* because, in both cases, the emphasis is more on profit margin than sales/market share gain.

Price cuts are likely to be followed when they are stimulated by general *falling costs* or *excess supply*. Falling costs allow all companies to cut prices while maintaining margins, and excess supply means that a company is unlikely to allow a rival to make sales gains at its expense. Price cuts will also be followed in *price-sensitive markets* since allowing one company

Reacting to competitors' price changes		TABLE 12.6
	Increases	Cuts
When to follow	Rising costs Excess demand Price-insensitive customers Price rise compatible with brand image Harvest or hold objective	Falling costs Excess supply Price-sensitive customers Price fall compatible with brand image Build or hold objective
When to ignore	Stable or falling costs Excess supply Price-sensitive customers Price rise incompatible with brand image Build objective	Rising costs Excess demand Price-insensitive customers Price fall incompatible with brand image Harvest objective
Tactics: – quick response – slow response	Margin improvement urgent Gains to be made by being customer's friend	Offset competitive threat High customer loyalty

to cut price without retaliation would mean large sales gains for the price cutter. The image of the company can also affect reaction to price cuts. Some companies position themselves as low-price manufacturers or retail outlets. In such circumstances they would be less likely to allow a price reduction by a competitor to go unchallenged for to do so would be *incompatible with their brand image*. Finally, price cuts are likely to be followed when the company has a *build* or *hold strategic objective*. In such circumstances an aggressive price move by a competitor would be followed to prevent sales/market share loss. In the case of a build objective, response may be more dramatic with a price fall exceeding the initial competitive move.

When to ignore

The circumstances associated with companies not reacting to a competitive price move are in most cases simply the opposite of the above. Price increases are likely to be ignored when *costs are stable or falling*, which means that there are no cost pressures forcing a general price rise. In the situation of *excess supply* companies may view a price rise as making the initiator less competitive, and therefore allow the price rise to take place unchallenged, particularly when customers are *price sensitive*. Companies occupying low-price positions may regard a price rise in response to a price increase from a rival to be *incompatible with their brand image*. Finally, companies pursuing a *build objective* may allow a competitor's price rise to go unmatched in order to gain sales and market share.

Price cuts are likely to be ignored in conditions of *rising costs*, *excess demand* and when servicing *price-insensitive customers*. Premium price positioners may be reluctant to follow competitors' price cuts for to do so would be *incompatible with brand image*. Lastly, price cuts may be resisted by companies using a *harvest objective*.

Tactics

When a company decides to follow a price change it can do so quickly or slowly. A *quick price reaction* is likely when there is an urgent need to *improve profit margins*. Here the competitor's price increase will be welcomed as an opportunity to achieve this objective.

Conversely, a *slow reaction* may be desirable when an *image of being the customer's friend* is being sought. The first company to announce a price increase is often seen as the high-price supplier. Some companies have mastered the art of playing the low-cost supplier by never initiating price increases and following competitors' increases slowly.[43] The key to this tactic is timing the response: too quickly and customers do not notice; too slowly and profit is foregone. The optimum period can be found only by experience but, during it, salespeople should be told to stress to customers that the company is doing everything it can to hold prices for as long as possible.

A *quick response* to a competitor's price fall will happen to ward off a *competitive threat*. In the face of undesirable sales/market share erosion, fast action is needed to nullify potential competitor gains. However, reaction will be slow when a company has a *loyal customer base* willing to accept higher prices for a period so long as they can rely on price parity over the longer term.

Ethical Issues in Pricing

Key issues regarding ethical issues in pricing are price fixing, predatory pricing, deceptive pricing, penetration pricing and obesity, price discrimination and product dumping.

Price fixing

One of the driving forces towards lower prices is competition. Therefore, it can be in the interests of producers to agree among themselves not to compete on price. This is an act of collusion and is banned in many countries and regions, including the EU. Article 83 of the Treaty of Rome is designed to ban practices preventing, restricting or distorting competition, except where these contribute to efficiency without inhibiting consumers' fair share of the benefit. Groups of companies that collude are said to be acting as a cartel and these are by no means easy to uncover. However, the European Commission has had considerable success in this area, as Marketing Ethics and Corporate Social Responsibility in Action 12.1 explains.

12.1 Marketing Ethics and Corporate Social Responsibility in Action

Combating Price Fixing

Cartels push up prices and are outlawed by the European Commission. It has had several notable successes in unearthing and heavily fining price-fixing cartels. One of its most famous success stories is the uncovering of the illicit cartel among 33 of Europe's top chemical companies from the UK, France, Germany, Belgium, Italy, Spain, the Netherlands, Finland, Norway and Austria. Through collusion, they were able to sustain levels of profitability for low-density polyethylene and PVC in the face of severe overcapacity. Quotas were set to limit companies' attempts to gain market share through price competition. Prices were fixed to harmonize the differences between countries to discourage customers from shopping around for the cheapest deals.

In another assault on price fixing in the chemical industry, the European Commission fined three chemical groups £153 million for fixing the market for monochloroacetic acid, a widely used household and industrial chemical. Hoechst, Atofina, Akzo Nobel and Clariant controlled over 90 per cent of the European market for the chemical. The Swiss firm Clariant was given immunity for revealing the practice of allocating volumes and customers, and setting agreed prices.

The European Commission also fined four glass manufacturers (Saint-Gobain, Pilkington, Asahi Glass and Soliver) over £1000 million for illegally fixing the price of glass used in the car industry.

Based on: Mercado et al. (2000);[44] Milner (2005);[45] Tait and Hollinger (2008)[46]

Opponents of price fixing claim that it is unethical because it restrains the consumer's freedom of choice and interferes with each firm's interest in offering high-quality products at the best price. Proponents argue that under harsh economic conditions price fixing is necessary to ensure a fair profit for the industry and to avoid price wars that might lead to bankruptcies and unemployment.

Predatory pricing

This refers to the situation where a firm cuts its prices with the aim of driving out the competition. The firm is content to incur losses with the intent that high profits will be generated through higher prices once the competition is eliminated. Microsoft has been accused of predatory activities by bundling new software such as its Media Player and Internet browser with its best-selling Windows operating system. These products were effectively given to customers free of charge, resulting in massive barriers to entry and elimination of competitors such as Netscape.[47]

Deceptive pricing

This occurs when consumers are misled by the price deals offered by companies. Two examples are misleading price comparisons and 'bait and switch'. Misleading price comparisons occur when a store sets artificially high prices for a short time so that much lower 'sale' prices can be claimed later. The purpose is to deceive the customer into believing they are being offered bargains. Some countries, such as the UK and Germany, have laws that state the minimum period over which the regular price should be charged before it can be used as a reference price in a sale. Bait and switch is the practice of advertising a very low price on a product (the bait) to attract customers to a retail outlet. Once in the store the salesperson persuades the customer to buy a higher-priced product (the switch). The customer may be told that the lower-priced product is no longer in stock or that it is of inferior quality.

Penetration pricing and obesity

A controversial issue is the question of the ethics of charging low prices for fatty food targeting young people. Critics claim that, by doing so, fast-food companies encourage obesity. Others claim that such companies cannot be blamed when consumers are made well aware by the media of the consequences of eating fatty foods.

Price discrimination

This occurs when a supplier offers a better price for the same product to one buyer and not to another, resulting in an unfair competitive advantage. Price discrimination can be justified when the costs of supplying different customers varies, where the price differences reflect differences in the level of competition and where different volumes are purchased. Price discrimination can take place at a regional level. For example, according to the European Commission, UK car prices were 35 per cent higher than elsewhere in Europe before tax.[48] This led to some buyers travelling to mainland Europe to buy new cars and to some dealers planning to import cars for private buyers.[49]

Product dumping

This involves the export of products at much lower prices than charged in the domestic market, sometimes below the cost of production. Products are 'dumped' for a variety of reasons. First, unsold stocks may be exported at a low price rather than risk lowering prices in the home market. Second, products may be manufactured for sale overseas at low prices to fill otherwise unused production capacity. Finally, products that are regarded as unsafe at home may be dumped in countries that do not have such stringent safety rules.

For example, the US Consumer Product Safety Commission ruled that three-wheel cycles were dangerous. Many companies responded by selling their inventories at low prices in other countries.[50]

Online
LearningCentre

When you have read this chapter

log on to the Online Learning Centre at www.mcgraw-hill.co.uk/ textbooks/jobber to explore chapter-by-chapter test questions, links and further online study tools for marketing.

Review ● ● ●

1 **The economist's approach to price determination**
- The economist's approach to pricing was developed as an explanation of market behaviour and focuses on demand and supply. There are limitations in applying this approach in practice, which means that marketers turn to other methods in business.

2 **The differences between full cost and direct cost pricing**
- Full cost pricing takes into account both fixed and direct costs. Direct cost pricing takes into account only direct costs such as labour and materials.
- Both methods suffer from the problem that they are internally orientated methods. Direct cost pricing can be useful when the corporate objective is survival and there is a desperate need to fill capacity.

3 **An understanding of going-rate pricing and competitive bidding**
- Going-rate pricing is setting price levels at the rate generally applicable in the market, focusing on competitors' offerings and prices rather than on company costs. Marketers try to avoid going-rate pricing by creating a differential advantage.
- Competitive bidding involves the drawing up of detailed specifications for a product and putting the contract out to tender. Potential suppliers bid for the order with price an important choice criterion. Competitive bidding models have been developed to help the bidding process but they have severe limitations.

4 **The advantages of marketing-orientated pricing over cost-orientated and competitor-orientated pricing methods**
- Marketing-orientated pricing takes into account a much wider range of factors that are relevant to the setting of prices. Although costs and competition are still taken into account, marketers will take a much more customer-orientated view of pricing, including customers' willingness to pay as reflected in the perceived value of the product. Marketers will also evaluate the target market of the product to establish the price sensitivity of customers. This will be affected by such factors as the degree of competition, the degree of excess demand, and the ability of target customers to pay a high price. A full list of factors that marketers take into account is given in point 5 below.

5 **The factors that affect price setting when using a marketing-orientated approach**
- A marketing-orientated approach involves the analysis of marketing strategy, value to the customer, price–quality relationships, explicability, product line pricing, competition, negotiating margins, effect on distributors/retailers, political factors and costs.

6 **When and how to initiate price increases and cuts**
- Initiating price increases is likely to be carried out when value is greater than price, in the face of rising costs, when there is excess demand and where a harvest objective is being followed.
- Tactics are a price jump, staged price increases, escalator clauses, price unbundling and lower discounts.
- Initiating price cuts is likely to be carried out when value is less than price, when there is excess supply, where a build objective is being followed, where a price war is unlikely and when there is a desire to pre-empt competitive entry.
- Tactics are a price fall, staged price reductions, the use of fighter brands, price bundling and higher discounts.

7 **When and when not to follow competitor-initiated price increases and cuts; when to follow quickly and when to follow slowly**
- Competitor-initiated price increases should be followed when there are rising costs, excess demand, price-insensitive customers, where the price rise is compatible with brand image and where a harvest or hold objective is being followed.
- Competitor-initiated price increases should not be followed when costs are stable or falling, with excess supply, with price-sensitive customers, where the price rise is incompatible with brand image and where a build objective is being followed.

- The price increase should be followed quickly when the need for margin improvement is urgent, and slowly when there are gains to be made by being seen to be the customer's friend.
- Competitor-initiated price cuts should be followed when there are falling costs, excess supply, price-sensitive customers, where the price cut is compatible with brand image, and where a build or hold objective is being followed.
- Competitor-initiated price cuts should not be followed when there are rising costs, excess demand, price-insensitive customers, where the price fall is incompatible with brand image and where a harvest objective is being followed.
- The price cut should be followed quickly when there is a need to offset a competitive threat, and slowly where there is high customer loyalty.

8 **Ethical issues in pricing**
- There are potential problems relating to price fixing, predatory pricing, deceptive pricing, price discrimination and product dumping.

Key Terms

competitive bidding drawing up detailed specifications for a product and putting the contract out to tender

direct cost pricing the calculation of only those costs that are likely to rise as output increases

economic value to the customer (EVC) the amount a customer would have to pay to make the total life-cycle costs of a new and a reference product the same

full cost pricing pricing so as to include all costs and based on certain sales volume assumptions

going-rate pricing pricing at the rate generally applicable in the market, focusing on competitors' offerings rather than on company costs

marketing-orientated pricing an approach to pricing that takes a range of marketing factors into account when setting prices

parallel importing when importers buy products from distributors in one country and sell them in another to distributors who are not part of the manufacturer's normal distribution; caused by big price differences for the same product between different countries

positioning strategy the choice of target market (*where* the company wishes to compete) and differential advantage (*how* the company wishes to compete)

price unbundling pricing each element in the offering so that the price of the total product package is raised

price waterfall the difference between list price and realized or transaction price

trade-off analysis a measure of the trade-off customers make between price and other product features so that their effects on product preference can be established

Study Questions

1 Accountants are always interested in profit margins; sales managers want low prices to help push sales; and marketing managers are interested in high prices to establish premium positions in the marketplace. To what extent do you agree with this statement in relation to the setting of prices?

2 You are the marketing manager of a company that is about to launch the first voice-activated language translator. The owner talks into the device, the machine electronically translates into the relevant language and speaks to the listener. What factors should you take into consideration when pricing this product?

3 Why is value to the customer a more logical approach to setting prices than cost of production? What role can costs play in the setting of prices?

4 Discuss the advantages and disadvantages of experimentation in assessing customers' willingness to pay.

5 What is economic value to the customer analysis? Under what conditions can it play an important role in price setting?

6 Under intense cost-inflationary pressure you are considering a price increase. What other considerations would you take into account before initiating the price rise?

7 You are the marketing manager of a premium-priced industrial chemical. A competitor has launched a cut-price alternative that possesses 90 per cent of the effectiveness of your product. If you do not react, you estimate that you will lose 30 per cent of sales. What are your strategic pricing options? What would you do?

8 The only reason that companies set low prices is that their products are undifferentiated. Discuss.

9 By far the most criticized ethical issue in marketing is the practice of price fixing. Discuss.

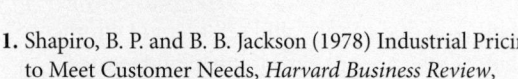

References

1. Shapiro, B. P. and B. B. Jackson (1978) Industrial Pricing to Meet Customer Needs, *Harvard Business Review*, Nov.–Dec., 119–27.
2. See Shipley, D. (1981) Pricing Objectives in British Manufacturing Industry, *Journal of Industrial Economics* 29 (June), 429–43; Jobber, D. and G. J. Hooley (1987) Pricing Behaviour in the UK Manufacturing and Service Industries, *Managerial and Decision Economics* 8, 167–71.
3. Christopher, M. (1982) Value-in-Use Pricing, *European Journal of Marketing* 16(5), 35–46.
4. Edelman, F. (1965) Art and Science of Competitive Bidding, *Harvard Business Review*, July–August, 53–66.
5. Brown, R. (1991) The S-Curves of Innovation, *Journal of Marketing Management* 7(2), 189–202.
6. Simon, H. (1992) Pricing Opportunities—and How to Exploit Them, *Sloan Management Review*, Winter, 55–65.
7. Jobber, D. and D. Shipley (1998) Marketing-Orientated Pricing Strategies, *Journal of General Management* 23(4), 19–34.
8. Kinney, S. (2000) RIP Fixed Pricing: the Internet is on its Way to Marketing Everything, *Business Economics* 35(2), 30–44.
9. Ancarani, F. (2002) Pricing and the Internet: Frictionless Commerce or Pricer's Paradise?, *European Management Journal* 20(6), 680–7.
10. http://business.timesonline.co.uk/article/0,,9558-187254900.html.
11. Ramesh, R. (2006) Indian Motor Maker Gives the Go-Ahead for £1200 'People's Car', *Guardian*, 20 May, 26.
12. Hutton, R. (2008) Tata Takes Lead with Small Cars, *Sunday Times*, 14 December, 6.
13. Simon (1992) op. cit.

14. Abell, D. F. and J. S. Hammond (1979) *Strategic Marketing Planning*, Englewood Cliffs, NJ: Prentice-Hall.
15. Edwards, C. (2006) Inside Intel, *Business Week*, 9 January, 43–8.
16. Popovich, K. (2002) Intel to Cut Chip Pricing by 57 per cent, *eWeek*, 4 January, 16.
17. Nagle, T. T. and J. E. Hogan (2006) *The Strategy and Tactics of Pricing*, New Jersey: Pearson Education.
18. Eastham, J. (2002) Prices Down, Numbers Up, *Marketing Week*, 20 June, 22–5.
19. Kucher, E. and H. Simon (1987) Durchbruch bei der Preisentscheidung: Conjoint-Measurement, eine neue Technik zur Gewinnoptimierung, *Harvard Manager* 3, 36–60.
20. Cattin, P. and D. R. Wittink (1989) Commercial Use of Conjoint Analysis: An Update, *Journal of Marketing*, July, 91–6.
21. Simon, H. (1992) Pricing Opportunities and How to Exploit Them, *Sloan Management Review*, Winter, 62. Copyright © 1992 by the Sloan Management Review Association. Reproduced with permission. All rights reserved.
22. Moutinho, L. and M. Evans (1992) *Applied Marketing Research*, Wokingham: Addison-Wesley, 161.
23. Helm, B. (2008) How to Sell Luxury to Penny-Pinchers, *Business Week*, 10 November, 60.
24. Nagle and Hogan (2006) op. cit.
25. Forbis, J. L. and N. T. Mehta (1979) *Economic Value to the Customer*, McKinsey Staff Paper, Chicago: McKinsey & Co., Inc., February, 1–10.
26. Erickson, G. M. and J. K. Johansson (1985) The Role of Price in Multi-Attribute Product Evaluations, *Journal of Consumer Research*, September, 195–9.
27. Anonymous (2008) In Praise of Placebos, *Guardian*, 5 March, 36.

28. Rangel, A., J. O'Doherty and B. Shiv (2008) *Marketing Actions Can Modulate Neural Representations of Experienced Pleasantness*, Stanford University Working Paper.

29. Ritson, M. (2008) Why Brands Are at a Premium, *Marketing*, 30 April, 19.

30. Parry, C. (2005) A Fridge Too Far for BSH?, *Marketing Week*, 16 June, 31.

31. Nagle and Hogan (2006) op. cit.

32. Ritson, M. (2008) Tesco Take Fight to Aldi, *Marketing*, 29 October, 20.

33. Jobber, D. and J. Fahy (2009) *Foundations of Marketing*, Maidenhead: McGraw-Hill.

34. Ghauri, P. N. and P. R. Cateora (2005) *International Marketing*, Maidenhead: McGraw-Hill.

35. Osborn, A. (2001) Levi's Wins Fight to Halt Tesco Price Cuts, *Guardian*, 21 November, 13.

36. Marn, M. V. and R. L. Rosiello (1992) Managing Price, Gaining Profit, *Harvard Business Review*, Sept.–Oct., 84–94.

37. Wray, R. (2004) BT Told to Cut Costs of Lines to Rivals, *Guardian*, 24 August, 30.

38. Simon (1992) op. cit.

39. Simon (1992) op. cit.

40. Schacht, H. (1988) Leading a Company through Change, *Harvard Business School Seminar*, 11 November.

41. Simon, B. (2005) Detroit Giants Count Cost of Four Year Price War, *Financial Times*, 19 March, 29.

42. Ritson, M. (2008) Mobile Brands Make Poor Call on Value, *Marketing*, 23 January, 21.

43. Ross, E. B. (1984) Making Money with Proactive Pricing, *Harvard Business Review*, Nov.–Dec., 145–55.

44. Mercado, S., R. Welford and K. Prescott (2000) *European Business: An Issue-Based Approach*, Harlow: FT Prentice-Hall.

45. Milner, M. (2005) Brussels Inquiry Could Land BT with Huge Tax Bill, *Guardian*, 20 January, 20.

46. Tait, N. and P. Hollinger (2008) Record Fine for Glass Cartel, *Financial Times*, 13 November, 27.

47. Jobber, D. and J. Fahy (2009) *Foundations of Marketing*, Maidenhead: McGraw-Hill.

48. Mitchell, A. (2000) Why Car Trade is Stalling Over New Pricing Policy, *Marketing Week*, 17 February, 40–1.

49. Griffiths, J. (2000) Dealers Draw up Plan to Import Cheap New Cars, *Financial Times*, 19 January, 1.

50. Schlegelmilch, B. (1998) *Marketing Ethics: An International Perspective*, London: International Thomson Business Press.

The story behind the success of Europe's no-frills airlines began in the USA. Southwest Airlines, a Texas-based carrier, was the first to successfully exploit the deregulation of American skies in 1978. Since then the airline has operated a no-frills, low-fare business model involving no free meals or coffee, only peanuts. The attraction is fares set at about one-fifth of those of the mainstream airlines. Its fleet is made up entirely of one type of aircraft, the Boeing 737, to keep costs down by reducing pilot training and maintenance costs. It flies between secondary airports, which are sometimes over an hour's drive from city centres.

An essential component in the Southwest Airlines approach is fast turnaround times from uncongested airports, which can be as short as 20 minutes with no seat allocation for passengers and cabin crews doing the cleaning. This means that aircraft can be used for 15 hours per day. In comparison, conventional airlines that run a 'hub and spoke' network fly aircraft for only half that length of time, as aircraft must wait to connect with incoming flights. Southwest Airlines has embraced Internet transactions to cut paperwork and administrative costs, and has rejected corporate acquisitions in favour of organic growth. The result has been a continual stream of profits (unlike other American airlines) and a business that attracts nearly 65 million passengers a year.

In Europe, Southwest Airlines' approach and success has been mirrored by easyJet and Ryanair, who have pioneered low-fare, no-frills flying. Growth has been spectacular with both airlines consistently recording annual increases in passenger numbers of 15–20 per cent. What is more, research has shown that three-quarters of those that have travelled with them think that the no-frills airlines are 'great'.

The growth in the low-cost sector has been fuelled by the burgeoning market for short-haul city breaks, the desire of more adventurous holidaymakers to arrange their own vacation packages, and their wish to own holiday homes in warm, sunny climates. These factors, together with the drive by business to trim back on travel costs, have meant growth rates of 30 per cent per year in passenger numbers in recent times.

Marketing strategy at easyJet

A key element in the success of easyJet has been its approach to pricing. The conventional method of selling airline seats was to start selling at a certain price and then lower it if sales were too low. What Stelios Haji-Ioannou, owner of easyJet, pioneered was the opposite: the start was a low headline price that grabbed attention, then it was raised according to demand. Customers are never told how soon or by how much the price will be changed. This system, called yield management, is designed to allow airline seats to be priced according to supply and demand, and achieve high seat occupancy. This reflects the fact that a particular seat on a specific flight cannot be stored for resale: if it is empty, the revenue is lost.

For the customer the result has been fares much lower than those offered by conventional airlines such as BA and Lufthansa. And so, to be profitable, easyJet has needed to control costs strictly. Following the example of Southwest Airlines, it has achieved this through simplicity (using one aircraft type), productivity (fast turnaround times to achieve high aircraft use) and direct distribution (using the Internet for upfront payment and low administrative charges). Also, onboard costs are reduced by not providing free drinks or meals to passengers.

Although easyJet operates out of secondary airports such as Luton in the UK, it is increasingly using mainstream airports such as Gatwick in a direct attempt to take passengers from more conventional rivals such as BA. Its approach is to fly to relatively few destinations but with a higher frequency on each route. This provides a barrier to entry, and the higher frequency attracts high-volume business travellers that prize schedule over price and are, therefore, willing to pay a little more for the service (the average easyJet seat price—£50—is reported to be higher than that of Ryanair—£34). EasyJet also derives revenue from the sale of onboard food and drinks, check-in charges, car hire and hotel bookings.

In 2002, easyJet bought rival Go airlines for £374 million, a price lower than expected by many analysts. For easyJet, the deal is about creating a route network that stretches across Europe. With the exception of domestic routes, the two airlines had few destinations in common. EasyJet's top routes include Amsterdam, Geneva and Paris, while Go took holidaymakers to Faro, Bologna and Bilbao. There was overlap on only a handful of destinations, both flying to Barcelona, Nice, Majorca and Malaga. Furthermore, the UK bases of the two airlines were complementary, with easyJet operating from Luton, Gatwick and Liverpool, while Go operated from Stansted, Bristol and East Midlands airports. The take-over alone gave easyJet scale and increased buying power, a factor that was important when it decided to abandon its policy of using only Boeing 737s by buying a fleet of aircraft from Airbus in 2002 at a knockdown price. The combined companies were about the same size as Ryanair in terms of passenger numbers.

In 2007, easyJet bought GB Airways in a £103 million deal that allowed it to expand its operations at London Gatwick airport and also establish a base at Manchester airport.

Under its entrepreneurial leader, Stelios, the easyJet group moved into other areas, such as car hire, Internet cafés and cruises, using the same low-price model. Another venture was the setting up of easyCinema to challenge the established cinema chains. The motivation was the half-empty cinema auditoriums Stelios saw when visiting conventional cinemas. He could not understand why price was not varied according to demand (by day and by film). Although some cinemas did reduce prices midweek, their pricing policies were not considered flexible enough compared to pricing using yield management. Also, he argued, why pay the same to see a blockbuster as a flop? And

// Ryanair provides cheap point-to-point flying from secondary airports, rather than shadowing and undercutting the major carriers as easyJet increasingly dues. //

why is the price of the blockbuster the same on the opening night as it is six weeks later? What he proposed was an infinite number of prices depending on supply and demand, following his success in the airline business.

The easyCinema formula worked as follows. The pricing structure began at 20 pence (less than €0.30). People logged on to easyCinema.com where they found three options. First, they could select the movie they most wanted to see, the dates when they could see it and at what prices; second, they could select the day on which they wanted to visit the cinema, what films were showing and at what prices; and third they could come to the site with a budget of, say, £1, and find all the movies that could be seen for £1 or less. Bookings could be made up to two weeks in advance. As with aircraft seats, the likelihood was that the earlier the booking was made, the cheaper the seat would be. Also, after examining costs, Stelios decided not to install food and drink stands, saying, 'If ya want popcorn, go to a popcorn vendor. For movies come to easyCinema.' Staff costs were also reduced since there were no tickets. Booking was done through the website and a membership card was printed out that admitted visitors to the cinema via a turnstile. Finally, no advertising for unrelated products (e.g. the local curry house) prior to the movie showing was allowed. The first easyCinema was opened in Milton Keynes with a view to expanding the business across the UK. In 2006, however, three years after its opening, it closed, and the plan to transform the movie business was abandoned in the face of meagre audiences.

In 2002 Mr Haji-Ioannou stood down as chairman to take on the role of non-executive director. He remains the largest shareholder and, in 2008, became embroiled in a dispute with the board, believing that its plans for expansion were too ambitious in the light of a looming recession.

Marketing strategy at Ryanair

Ryanair is run by Michael O'Leary, who is famous for his outspoken views and controversial advertising campaigns. Like easyJet, Ryanair has followed the Southwest Airlines business model but, if anything, has been more ruthless on cost-cutting. It provides cheap point-to-point flying from secondary airports, rather than shadowing and undercutting the major carriers as easyJet increasingly does. Sometimes, the airports can be 60 miles from the real destination: for Frankfurt read Hahn, for Hamburg read Lübeck, for Stockholm read Vesteraas or Skavsta, and for Brussels read Charleroi. Ryanair has kept to its single-aircraft policy, the Boeing 737, which it bought second-hand and cheaply, reducing maintenance, spares and crew training. Its new fleet of 737-800s were purchased at record low prices at the bottom of the market. They offer 45 per cent more seats at lower operating costs and the same number of crew. Ryanair has continued this policy with the purchase of a further 70 Boeings in 2005 at an even lower price. In 2009, it entered negotiations with Boeing and Airbus over the purchase of up to 300 short-haul jets, and announced plans to become a transatlantic carrier.

Turnaround times at airports are fast, to keep more aircraft in the air, and online booking has slashed sales and distribution costs. Ryanair. com has become the largest travel website in Europe, selling more than 1 million seats per month. Ryanair's focus on cost reduction has resulted in profit margins about double those of easyJet despite the latter's higher prices. Some of the cost savings are passed on to the customers in the form of lower fares (the plan is an average fall in fare levels of 5 per cent per year) to make Ryanair even more attractive to its target market: the leisure customer. By contrast, easyJet is increasingly targeting business passengers. Ryanair is the only European airline to record profits for each of the last 16 years. Even during the recession it continued to make a small operating profit despite soaring fuel prices. An important part of its revenue comes from the sale of onboard food and drinks, charges for passengers checking in rather than doing so online and for putting luggage in the hold, and income from car hire and hotel bookings. It plans to reduce the number of toilets from three to one in each of its aircraft, allowing it to put in extra seats.

Ryanair has also been on the acquisition trail by buying Buzz, the budget division of KLM Royal Dutch Airlines, for £15.8 million. Loss-making Buzz was immediately given the Ryanair cost-cutting treatment, including the loss of 440 jobs and new contracts for pilots, which will raise pay but mean longer flying hours. Half of Buzz's routes were axed but Ryanair still

// The stellar growth in low-cost flying has attracted new entrants . . . There are now over 60 no-frills airlines operating in Europe. //

intended to increase passenger load from 2 million to 3 million through lower prices—£31.50 versus £56 previously—and more frequent flying along the retained routes.

Competitive response

The stellar growth in low-cost flying has attracted new entrants such as Flybe, bmibaby and Jet2 in the UK, and Hapag-Lloyd Express, Goodjet and Hallas Jet elsewhere in western Europe. There are now over 60 no-frills airlines operating in Europe. Traditional airlines have also responded. For example, Air France, Lufthansa and BA have cut prices on many of their European flights in an attempt to stem the flow to the low-price carriers.

BA has embarked on an aggressive strategy of slashing prices from Heathrow and Gatwick to almost all its European short-haul destinations. Fares to places such as Berlin, Paris and Barcelona have been cut by up to 50 per cent. Unlike the low-cost carriers, BA still offers its traditional service benefits, including free food and drinks, on all flights and, unlike Ryanair, which charges £5 per bag, there are no charges for checking in luggage. The strategy of competitive fares, in-flight extras and the convenience and flight transfers offered by Heathrow and Gatwick is designed to win large numbers of passengers from no-frills operators. In support of the strategy, BA's chief executive, Willie Walsh, whose nickname—The Slasher—was earned during his time at Aer Lingus, cut 600 managerial jobs and announced a further 1000 job losses at the airline's call centres and travel shops in 2006. BA's regional network, CitiExpress, has also been reorganized to take on the low-cost operators. The network was rebranded as BA Connect and fares from 14 airports, including Manchester, Birmingham and Edinburgh, to European destinations were cut by up to a third, to as little as £25 one way.

Ryanair's reaction was to claim that BA's prices were still more expensive than its own after the cuts, and pointed out that, unlike BA and many other carriers, it had not introduced a fuel surcharge. It also claimed better punctuality—90 per cent flights arriving on time compared to BA's 74 per cent—and a significantly lower missing bags ratio: 0.5 per 1000 passengers against 17.7 for BA.

Customer service

The need to trim costs to the bone has meant that some customers have been dissatisfied with the service provided by both no-frills airlines. For example, the need for fast turnaround times at airports has meant that customers who check in late are usually refused entry. Where lateness is the fault of another travel provider, such as a rail company, customers have been known to complain bitterly about entry refusal. Fast turnaround times also mean that there is little slack should a flight be delayed, with a knock-on effect on other flights.

Another problem is the reluctance of the no-frills airlines to pay compensation. For example, when easyJet cancelled a flight after it admitted it had no crew to fly the aircraft, it offered a refund of the ticket price but no compensation for the other costs, such as the lost hotel deposit and car parking fees incurred by one of its customers. Ryanair, similarly, was reported to have said, 'We never offer compensation, food or hotel vouchers.' Ryanair also experienced teething problems with lost and delayed luggage after switching baggage contractors, and in the past has appeared reluctant to pay compensation with respect to lost luggage.

Questions

1 How do easyJet and Ryanair achieve success using low-price strategies?
2 What are the advantages and risks associated with low-price strategies?
3 To what extent do the conditions for charging low prices discussed in this chapter hold for easyJet and Ryanair?
4 Why did the low-price, no-frills business model fail with easyCinema?

This case was prepared by David Jobber, Professor of Marketing, University of Bradford. It is based on a large number of published sources.

Netto, Lidl, Aldi
The Rise of the Limited Range Discounters

Discounters are powering ahead with their expansion plans throughout Europe and beyond. Their formula of low prices and offering a limited assortment of products on their shelves appears to be a winning pan-European formula for retailing. The retailing concept was pioneered by German hard discounter Aldi, and has now been successfully duplicated by other discounters such as the German Lidl and Danish Netto chains. These 'limited range discounters' (LRDs) believe that success can be achieved through offering good-quality products at low prices, and stocking minimal assortments that match consumers' basic needs, such as staple items that consumers regularly buy. Success is achieved through the generation of high volumes, their ability to communicate to consumers, their price gaps with traditional retailers, and placing costs at the forefront of all their business activities. Their continued success has led to dramatic changes within the retail sector, leaving manufacturers with difficult decisions as to how to supply these LRDs effectively, while not damaging their brands and relations with other retailers. So who are these LRDs, and how do they operate?

Discounters have an estimated 18 per cent market share within European retailing, which is expected to grow even further. Countries like Norway (40 per cent) and Germany (38 per cent) have high levels of discounter activity, whereas countries like the UK (6 per cent) and Ireland (8 per cent) have very low levels. Hard discounters have four central planks in their operating philosophies. First, they stock a very limited product assortment (around 1000 stock-keeping units), whereas a traditional store may have 25,000 different product variants. These are typically fast-moving, high stock rotation items. Usually, a shopper is offered only one type of brand from a category. Second, these stores are very simple in layout, design and operation. They require lean management and very few employees to operate. A hard discounter will typically have longer queues, which people put up with for the greater savings. Third, the retailers have a low-cost and highly efficient supply chain infrastructure, utilizing large regional distribution centres to service their retail outlets. Last, and most important, these stores operate on the principle of EDLP, or 'everyday low prices'.

Competition between discounters is rife. Price wars are common between these retailers. However, if they stock similar products they typically stock different size variants and at different prices, to avoid direct confrontation where possible. Their success has led traditional supermarkets to introduce cheaper brand ranges, such as Tesco Value, in an attempt to deter customers from switching. Some consumers view these discounters as too frugal and downmarket to give them their custom. Also LRDs' decision to locate in socially deprived areas has contributed to this image even further, although this is changing. Open pallets, lack of assortment and lack of extra value added services alienate some shoppers. However, in Germany, where many of these discounters initially emerged, wealthy Mercedes drivers typically frequent these retailers. In some European countries, though, consumers are still in love with their brands rather than extremely low prices.

LRDs: a profile and comparison of Netto, Lidl and Aldi		TABLE C24.1
Netto	Lidl	Aldi
Owned by Dansk Supermarked, part of A. P. Moller–Maersk Group	Owned by Schwarz Group, privately owned	Owned by Theo & Leo Albrecht, privately owned
Stores in the UK: 194	Stores in the UK: 500	Stores in the UK: 430
Stores in Denmark: 400	Stores in Sweden: 151	Stores in Denmark: 244
Stores in Germany: 293	Stores in Germany: 3000	Stores in Germany: 4120
Stores in Sweden: 107	Stores in France: 1350	Stores in USA: 1000
Stores in Poland: 157	Stores in Ireland: 105	Stores in Ireland: 61
Total no. of stores: 1151	Total no. of stores: 6120	Total no. of stores: 8210
Sales not known	Sales of over €21 billion	Sales of over €38 billion
Stocks around 1100 products	Stocks up to 1600 products	Stocks around 1000 products
Stocks favoured brands	A third of products are branded items	Over 90% are private label
Typical store size: 1100 sq metres	Typical store size; 1000 sq metres	Typical store size: 760 sq metres

Netto is operated by Dansk Supermarked which, in turn, is owned by A. P. Moller–Maersk Group. It is Denmark's most successful discounter, having roughly 9 per cent of the Danish grocery retail market. From these origins it has become one of Denmark's most recognized and respected brands. Netto proclaims that it is part of Europe's largest buying groups and passes on these savings to customers. Netto stores resemble large warehouses, with items stocked on pallets. High-quality merchandise presentation is not top of the agenda for Netto—costs are. Stores are run with very few employees and the stores do not accept credit cards so as not to incur any transaction charges. A large proportion of Netto products are well-known retail brands (it stocks brands such as Coca-Cola, Nescafé and Persil) at discount prices. The company takes advantage of large bulk buying and supplier discounts. On the downside, customers may be faced with longer queues, no master butcher is available and favourite brands may not be in stock if no promotion is available that week. In addition, the company stocks Netto own-brand products. This formula made it appealing for many customers, who wanted their favourite brands. The first Netto store opened in 1981 in Denmark. Since then the company has rolled out in other international countries such as Germany in 1990, the UK in 1990 and Sweden in 2002. It successfully entered the Swedish market, through a 50:50 joint venture with leading Swedish retailer ICA, and other markets like Germany through joint ventures. It was created by Dansk Supermarked, Denmark's leading supermarket retailer, as a response to Aldi entering the Danish marketplace.

Aldi is completely privately owned by the secretive Albrecht family. Its owners are now one of Europe's wealthiest families. The name originated from Albrecht Discount. It pioneered the hard discounter market. The Aldi group, from its German base, has two main divisions: Aldi Nord and Aldi Sud. Both operate independently and have clearly defined operating markets and different own-label brands, but both cooperate in terms of pricing and assortment decisions. Aldi Sud is responsible for southern Germany, Austria and English-speaking countries, while Aldi Nord is responsible for all other non-German-speaking European countries. Aldi has saturation coverage within the German market, and possesses limited growth opportunities. Every German is within a 15–20-minute drive to an Aldi outlet. As a result, the chain has grown aggressively abroad.

The emphasis within Aldi is on efficiency and productivity. Each store is responsible for its revenues and cost base. Costs are kept to an absolute minimum. By having a basic store layout and design, low staff numbers, non-expensive in-store storage displays and limited number of products on shelves, it keeps costs to an absolute minimum, which other retailers find hard to compete against. It does not accept credit cards in almost all of its stores. It has built up a reputation among its loyal consumer base on the strength of the quality of its product offering. Products are strenuously tested for quality and are allocated to stores only once they are proven to be fast movers. The company has also moved into selling an organic range of produce. Aldi sources products from leading food manufacturers and sells them under the Aldi own-label brand. Its sheer size enables Aldi to save through bulk buys and strong price negotiation with suppliers. The company now sells products that are specific to a particular country in a bid to attract local customers. Through its scale, it can then source country-specific products suitable for market needs. If it still does not have the necessary scale it will import brands into that country. Aldi utilizes huge regional distribution centres to service up to 50 outlets at a time. Goods are brought into the store on pallets, and are gradually emptied by consumers before being replenished with new pallets. The company is famous for its frugalness and thriftiness at all levels of its operations, utilizing a strong decentralized operation with a focus on simplicity.

The first Lidl discount outlet opened in 1973. It originated as a clone of the successful Aldi format, but has since evolved into having it own strong brand identity. Like Aldi, Lidl has grown rapidly by expanding its international operations. It is privately owned by the Schwarz Group, which is notoriously secretive about its operations. The group owns a suite of different retailing divisions, such as hypermarkets, traditional supermarkets and discounters. The company is still number two in its domestic German market, but has been pursuing a rapid internationalization strategy, hoping to achieve over 70 per cent of its revenues from overseas markets. Its scope of operations is limited to Europe—unlike Aldi, which also owns stores in the USA and Australia. The company utilizes a rapid property acquisition programme and establishes large regional distribution centres to service these new markets. The majority of its stores in international markets are non-unionized; however, in some markets, it has appeased local interests by allowing trades union activity.

One of the biggest weapons in the armoury of discounters is their 'one-off' specials. These promotions typically entail the sale at substantial discount of a non-food item (e.g. a personal computer, gardening or DIY equipment). These specials are promoted on a weekly basis through local press advertising, leaflet drops and e-mails. They act as a major inducement and increase footfall to these stores. These heavily discounted items are allocated to stores, and there are only a handful of

units per store. This creates a weekly sales frenzy at these stores. The biggest problem with 'one-off specials' is that it is very hard to estimate demand, and if a special proves unpopular, the stores are left with unsold stock, which can create logistical difficulties and contributes to costs.

One of the main reasons behind the success of LRDs, and their apparent unstoppable growth, is their store location strategies. Each of these discounter stores is substantially smaller in size than a typical traditional supermarket. In addition, they require smaller property sites, and ancillary works such as car parking and special entry and exit points. This has allowed these LRDs to obtain planning permission at a much faster rate than typical retailers, and with enhanced likelihood of success. In France, Lidl achieved rapid growth rates through store adaptation of its business formula, which overcame strict planning laws through having higher shelves, smaller aisles and smaller product assortments.

The middle tier of supermarkets is under pressure from the discounters as the former's operating philosophy of large assortments places it at a cost disadvantage. The discounters themselves are facing a number of new challenges, with the likes of Tesco testing discount outlets in eastern Europe, and Asda testing discount store concepts. This is a similar strategy to that carried out by continental retailers in response to the threat of discounters. However, in some overseas markets, market share has plateaued after the initial success of the discounters. Shoppers are still drawn to their traditional supermarket retailers because of the attraction of wide choice, one-stop shopping and the availability of low-price product ranges. LRDs are here to stay, though, and leave both retailers and suppliers with difficult decisions to face: how do we compete, and how do we supply?

Questions

 1. Discuss the strengths and weaknesses associated with the limited range discounter format.

2. What are the advantages associated with the EDLP concept versus hi-lo pricing for retailers?

3. How should branded manufacturers respond with their pricing strategies if they want to supply a limited range discounter while simultaneously supplying traditional retailers?

This case was written by Conor Carroll, Lecturer in Marketing, University of Limerick. The material in the case has been drawn from a variety of published sources.

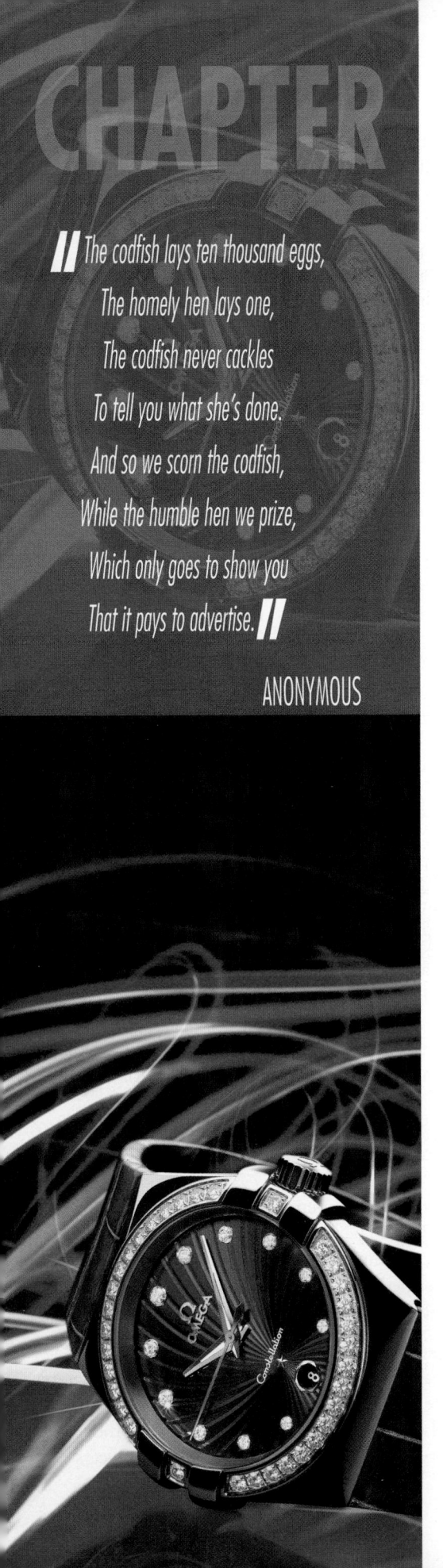

CHAPTER 13

Advertising

The codfish lays ten thousand eggs,
The homely hen lays one,
The codfish never cackles
To tell you what she's done.
And so we scorn the codfish,
While the humble hen we prize,
Which only goes to show you
That it pays to advertise.

ANONYMOUS

LEARNING OBJECTIVES

After reading this chapter, you should be able to:

1 explain the role of advertising in the promotional mix

2 identify the factors that affect the choice of promotional mix

3 discuss the key characteristics of the major promotional tools

4 describe the communication process

5 discuss the nature of integrated marketing communications

6 distinguish between the strong and weak theories of how advertising works

7 explain how to develop advertising strategy—target audience analysis, objective setting, budgeting, message and media decisions, execution and advertising evaluation

8 explain how campaigns are organized, including advertising agency selection and payment systems

9 discuss ethical issues in advertising

To many people advertising epitomizes marketing: it is what they believe marketing to be. Readers of this book will recognize the fallacy in this: marketing concerns much broader issues than simply how to advertise. Nevertheless, advertising is an important element in the *promotional mix*. Six major components of the promotional mix are advertising, personal selling, direct marketing, Internet promotion, sales promotion and publicity.

1 **Advertising**: any paid form of non-personal communication of ideas or products in the prime media, i.e. television, the press, outdoor, cinema and radio.
2 **Personal selling**: oral communication with prospective purchasers with the intention of making a sale.
3 **Direct marketing**: the distribution of products, information and promotional benefits to target consumers through interactive communication in a way that allows response to be measured.
4 **Internet promotion**: the promotion of products to consumers and businesses through electronic media.
5 **Sales promotion**: incentives to consumers or the trade that are designed to stimulate purchase.
6 **Publicity**: the communication of a product or business by placing information about it in the media without paying for the time or space directly.

In addition to these key promotional tools, the marketer can use exhibitions and sponsorship to communicate with target audiences. These, together with sales promotion and publicity, will be discussed in Chapter 16.

A key marketing decision is the choice of promotional blend needed to communicate to the target audience. Each of the five major promotional tools has its own strengths and limitations and these are summarized in Table 13.1. Marketers will carefully weigh these factors against promotional objectives to decide the amount of resources to channel into each tool. Usually, five considerations will have a major impact on the choice of the promotional mix.

1 *Resource availability and the cost of promotional tools*: to conduct a national advertising campaign may require several million pounds. If resources are not available, cheaper tools such as sales promotion or publicity may have to be used.
2 *Market size and concentration*: if a market is small and concentrated then personal selling may be feasible, but for mass markets that are geographically dispersed, selling to the ultimate customer would not be cost effective. In such circumstances advertising, Internet promotion or direct marketing may be the correct choice.
3 *Customer information needs*: if a complex technical argument is required, personal selling may be preferred. If all that is required is the appropriate brand image, advertising may be more sensible.
4 *Product characteristics*: because of the above arguments, business-to-business companies tend to spend more on personal selling than advertising, whereas consumer goods companies tend to do the reverse.
5 *Push versus pull strategies*: a push strategy involves an attempt to sell into channel intermediaries (e.g. retailers) and is dependent on personal selling and trade promotions. A pull strategy bypasses intermediaries to communicate to consumers directly. The resultant consumer demand persuades intermediaries to stock the product. Advertising and consumer promotions are more likely to be used.

Two points need to be stressed. First, marketing communications is not the exclusive province of the promotional mix. All of the marketing mix communicates to target customers. The product itself communicates quality; price may be used by consumers as an indicator of quality, and the choice of distribution channel will affect customer exposure to the product. Second, effective communication is not a one-way producer-to-consumer flow. Producers

Key characteristics of the six key promotional mix tools	TABLE 13.1

Advertising

- Good for awareness building because it can reach a wide audience quickly
- Repetition means that a brand positioning concept can be communicated effectively; TV is particularly strong
- Can be used to aid the sales effort, to legitimize a company and its products
- Impersonal, lacks flexibility and questions cannot be answered
- Limited capability to close the sale

Personal selling

- Interactive: questions can be answered and objectives overcome
- Adaptable: presentations can be changed depending on customer needs
- Complex arguments can be developed
- Relationships can be built because of its personal nature
- Provides the opportunity to close the sale
- Sales calls are costly

Direct marketing

- Individual targeting of consumers most likely to respond to an appeal
- Communication can be personalized
- Short-term effectiveness can easily be measured
- A continuous relationship can be built through periodic contact
- Activities are less visible to competitors
- Response rates are often low
- Poorly targeted direct marketing activities cause consumer annoyance

Internet promotion

- Global reach at relatively low cost
- The number of site visits can be measured
- A dialogue between companies and their customers and suppliers can be established
- Catalogues and prices can be changed quickly and cheaply
- Direct sales possible
- Impersonal and requires consumers to visit a website
- Convenient form of searching for and buying products
- Avoids the necessity of negotiating and arguing with salespeople

Sales promotion

- Incentives provide a quick boost to sales
- Effects may be only short term
- Excessive use of some incentives (e.g. money off) may damage brand image

Publicity

- Highly credible as message comes from a third party
- Higher readership than advertisements in trade and technical publications
- Loss of control: a press release may or may not be used, and its content may be distorted

need to understand the needs and motivation of their target audience before they can talk to them in a meaningful way. For example, marketing research may be used to understand large consumer segments before designing an advertising campaign, and salespeople may ask questions of buyers to unfold their particular circumstances, problems and needs before making a sales presentation.

Advertising decisions should not be taken in isolation. Marketers need to consider the complete communication package, with advertising forming one element of the whole. There is a need to blend the components of the promotional mix so that a clear and consistent message is received by target audiences. This has led to the development of integrated marketing communications, which will now be examined.

Integrated Marketing Communications

An organizational problem many companies face is that the various components of the promotional mix are the responsibility of different departments or agencies. Advertising is controlled by the advertising department in conjunction with an advertising agency. Personal selling strategies are decided by sales management. Publicity is the province of the publicity department and its agency. Other functions are in charge of direct marketing, Internet promotion and sales promotion. The danger is that the messages sent to consumers become blurred at best and conflicting at worst. For example, advertising messages that convey prestige may be discredited by heavy discounting by the sales team, or frequent use of money-off sales promotions. The logos and typefaces used in advertising may differ from those used in direct mail campaigns.

As the array of communications media expands there is a greater need to coordinate the messages and their execution. This has led to the adoption of **integrated marketing communications** by an increasing number of companies. Integrated marketing communications is the concept that companies coordinate their marketing communications tools to deliver a clear, consistent, credible and competitive message about the organization and its products. The objective is to position products and organizations clearly and distinctively in the marketplace. As we discussed in Chapter 8, successful positioning is associated with products possessing favourable connotations in the minds of consumers. Integrated marketing communications facilitates the process by which this is achieved by sending out consistent messages through all of the components of the promotional mix so that they reinforce one another. For example, it means that website visuals are consistent with the images portrayed in advertising and that the messages conveyed in a direct marketing campaign are in line with those developed by the public relations department.

Achieving this consistency can be difficult because of office politics. Some advertising creatives are unwilling to be shackled by an overall branding theme that is inconsistent with their latest 'big idea' for a television commercial. Others may feel threatened when an integrated marketing communications campaign calls for a shift in expenditure from advertising to direct or Internet promotion. Another problem is that the specialist nature of different disciplines can narrow people's minds to such an extent that they fail to understand how some marketing objectives can be better achieved by a different communications technique.[1] However, to be successful, these impediments need to be overcome by the appointment of a high-ranking communications officer to oversee the company's communications activities. Perhaps using the title 'marketing communications director', this person is responsible for deciding the extent to which each of the components of the promotional mix will be used based on communication objectives and the role that each can play in their achievement. The person needs to be a visionary and someone with passion, who has the communication ability to persuade everyone of the benefits of an integrated approach to marketing communications.[2]

Integrated marketing communications can lead to improved consistency and clearer positioning of companies and their brands in the minds of consumers. One company that benefited from this approach was American Express, which found that the messages, images and styles of presentation between its advertising and direct marketing vehicles were inconsistent. Using an integrated marketing communications approach, the team worked to produce the consistency required to achieve a clear position among its target audience.

Some companies, like O_2, turn to an integrated marketing agency to put together the whole execution, while others, such as Sky, prefer to appoint various agencies to work on their behalf. The advantage of using one agency is better communication, but using several agencies leaves clients with more flexibility regarding the choice of the best agencies to handle each media.[3] However, using several agencies can lead to conflict regarding who is paid for what and who takes charge. Suppose an integrated campaign is mainly direct marketing, but includes an online game, created by a digital specialist who also thinks of the main campaign strap-line. Which agency has contributed more to the campaign and which deserves the greater financial reward?[4] Such questions can create conflict between agencies, and problems for clients.

A framework for applying an integrated marketing communications approach is given in Figure 13.1 The starting point is an understanding of the overall marketing strategy for a product. In particular, the product's target market and differential advantage need to be defined. This leads to the creation of a positioning statement. The communications decisions will then depend on this statement. For example, target market definition will lead to an understanding of the target audience that needs to be reached by communications, and the differential advantage will affect message decisions. Once these issues have been decided, communication objectives will be set and promotional options (e.g. advertising, direct marketing and personal selling) will be evaluated to assess their ability to fulfil objectives and reach the desired audience. Care must be taken to achieve consistency across promotional types in the messages communicated.

An aggregation of the resources needed to achieve the communication objectives and reach will lead to an estimation of the size of the promotional budget. This will be evaluated for affordability and political acceptability before approval. The chosen integrated communication strategy will be executed and subsequently evaluated in the light of the set objectives. An example of a successful integrated marketing communications campaign is the Dove campaign 'Real women, real curves'. The campaign used a combination of advertising, public relations and in-store marketing to portray the aspirational image the brand needed.[5] Integrated marketing communications is not restricted to consumer markets. As we saw in Chapter 5, 'Understanding organizational buying behaviour', business-to-business companies such as Kone, the Finnish elevator firm, also use an integrated approach.

The move towards integrated marketing communications has led to the rise of *media-neutral planning*. This is the process of solving communication problems through an unbiased evaluation of all media. The focus is on solving communication problems rather than advertising, direct marketing, public relations problems, and so on.

Successful media-neutral planning depends on setting media planners free to explore a wide range of options. This can be a problem when media agencies are organized into specialist areas such as the press or television, and clients are organized into separate functions such as advertising or direct marketing. Some

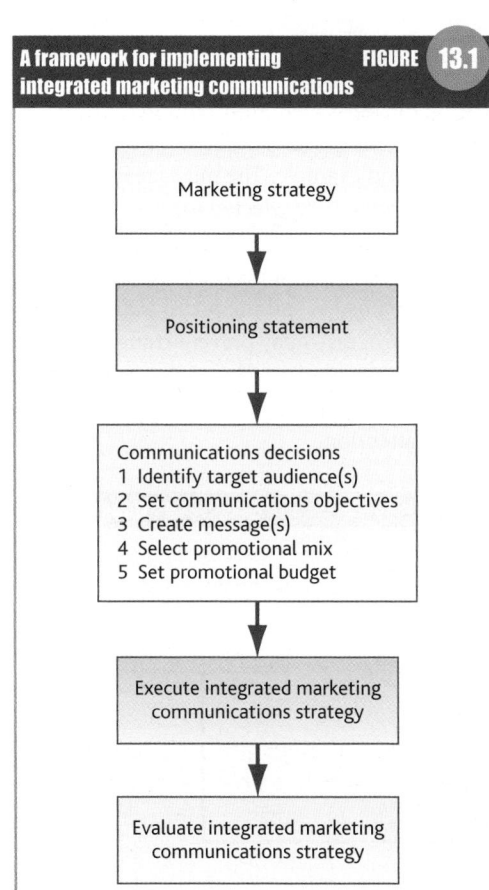

A framework for implementing integrated marketing communications   FIGURE 13.1

- Marketing strategy
- Positioning statement
- Communications decisions
  1 Identify target audience(s)
  2 Set communications objectives
  3 Create message(s)
  4 Select promotional mix
  5 Set promotional budget
- Execute integrated marketing communications strategy
- Evaluate integrated marketing communications strategy

companies are reorganizing in recognition of these issues. For example, Vauxhall, the UK arm of General Motors, has restructured its marketing department with customer relationship management (which oversaw direct marketing, for example) merging with advertising. The department, under one head, is responsible for Vauxhall's advertising, direct mail, online communications, literature and point-of-sale material, as well as all dealer, fleet and after-sales communications. Communication plans are developed by understanding the benefits, costs and synergies of all media opportunities.

Other problems relate to rewards. Media agencies make most of their money through buying in the traditional media, i.e. television, press, cinema, radio and outdoor. Media-neutral planning might suggest an events-based strategy for which there is no clear-cut remuneration. Creative people might also have a vested interest in traditional media-planning approaches. For example, they may be biased towards television because they want to win high-profile awards.

Finally, media-neutral planning can be difficult to implement when clients have pre-set budgets for advertising, public relations, direct marketing, and so on, and still engage with agencies as discrete entities rather than as a whole group. To overcome these problems clients should provide their agency partners with a flexible brief that does not presume the main communication medium and allows the agency to recommend how specific objectives such as perception changes, awareness shifts and stimulating trial should be achieved.

Having placed advertising in its context within the promotional mix, the rest of this chapter will examine the communication process, how advertising works, how to develop advertising strategies, the selection and work of advertising agencies, and ethical issues in advertising.

The Communication Process

A simple model of the *communication process* is shown in Figure 13.2. The *source* (or communicator) *encodes* a message by translating the idea to be communicated into a symbol consisting of words, pictures and numbers. Some advertisements attempt to encode a message using the minimum of words. The iPod is a good example. The message is *transmitted* through media such as television or posters, which are selected for their ability to reach the desired target audience in the desired way. Communication requirements may affect the choice of media. For example, if the encoded message requires the product to be demonstrated, television and cinema may be preferred to posters and the press. *Noise*—distractions and distortions during the communication process—may prevent transmission to some of the target audience. A television advertisement may not reach a member of the household because of conversation or the telephone ringing. Similarly a press advertisement may not be noticed because of editorial competing for attention.

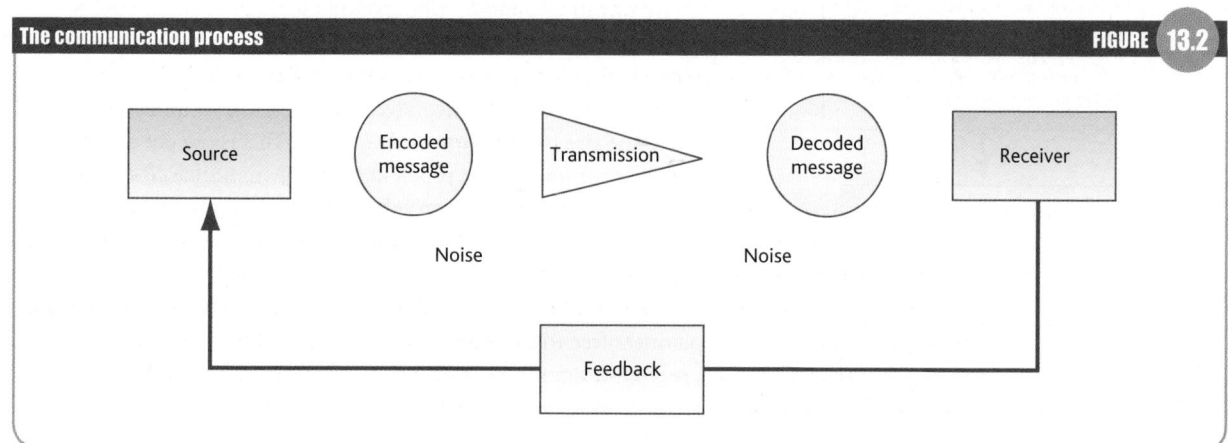

The communication process — FIGURE 13.2

When a *receiver* sees or hears the message, it is *decoded*. This is the process by which the receiver interprets the symbols transmitted by the source. The aim is for the receiver's decoding to coincide with the source's encoding process. The receiver thus interprets the message in the way intended by the source. A Marlboro advertisement may aim to associate the brand name with masculinity. If this is the way the message is decoded then the communications objective has been achieved. However, a non-smoker may interpret the advertisement in an entirely different way, rejecting the association and replacing it with risks to health. Messages that rely on words more than pictures can also be decoded differently. For example, a message such as 'the most advanced washing machine in the world' may be accepted by some receivers but rejected by others. Communicators need to understand their targets before encoding messages so that they are credible. Otherwise the response may be disbelief and rejection. In a personal selling situation, *feedback* from buyer to salesperson may be immediate, as when objections are raised or a sale is concluded. For other types of marketing such as advertising and sales promotion, feedback may rely on marketing research to estimate reactions to commercials, and increases in sales due to incentives.

An important point to recognize in the communication process is the sophistication of receivers. It is just as important to understand what people do with communication (e.g. advertising) as what communication does to them. Uses and gratifications theory suggests that the mass media constitute a resource on which audiences draw to satisfy various needs. Its assumptions are:

- the audience is active and much mass media use is need directed
- the initiative in linking need satisfaction with media choice lies mainly with the individual
- the media compete with other sources of need satisfaction
- the gratifications sought from the media include diversion and entertainment as well as information.[6]

Research suggests that people use advertising for at least seven kinds of satisfaction, namely product information, entertainment, risk reduction, added value, past purchase reassurance, vicarious experience and involvement.[7] Vicarious experience is the opportunity to experience situations or lifestyles to which an individual would not otherwise have access. Involvement refers to the pleasure of participation in the puzzles or jokes contained in some advertisements. Research among a group of young adults aged 18–24 added other uses of advertising including escapism, ego enhancement (demonstrating their intelligence by understanding the advertisement) and checking out the opposite sex.[8]

Strong and Weak Theories of How Advertising Works

For many years there has been considerable debate about how advertising works. The consensus is that there can be no single all-embracing theory that explains how all advertising works because it has varied tasks.[9] For example, advertising that attempts to make an instant sale by incorporating a return coupon that can be used to order a product is very different from corporate image advertising that is designed to reinforce attitudes.

The competing views on how advertising works have been termed the **strong theory of advertising** and the **weak theory of advertising**.[10] The strong theory has its base in the USA and is shown on the left-hand side of Figure 13.3. A person passes through the stages of awareness, interest, desire and action (AIDA). According to this theory, advertising is strong enough to increase people's knowledge and change people's attitudes, and as a consequence is capable of persuading people who had not previously bought a brand to buy it. It is therefore a conversion theory of advertising: non-buyers are converted to become buyers. Advertising is assumed to be a powerful influence on consumers.

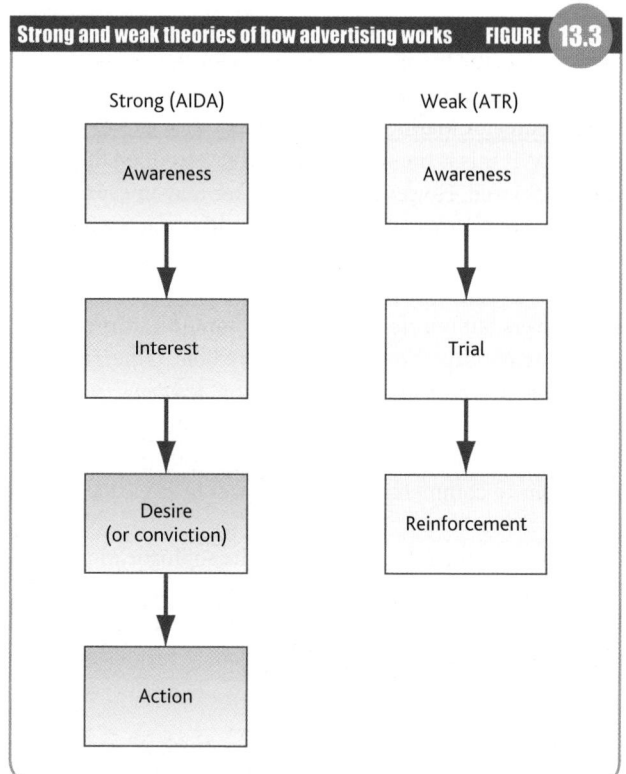

Strong and weak theories of how advertising works FIGURE **13.3**

Strong (AIDA)

Awareness

Interest

Desire
(or conviction)

Action

Weak (ATR)

Awareness

Trial

Reinforcement

This model has been criticized on two grounds.[11] First, for many types of product there is little evidence that consumers experience a strong desire before action (buying the brand). For example, in inexpensive product fields a brand may be bought on a trial basis without any strong conviction that it is superior to competing brands. Second, the model is criticized because it is limited to the conversion of a non-buyer to a buyer. It ignores what happens after action (i.e. first purchase). Yet in most mature markets advertising is designed to affect people who have already bought the brand at least once.

The major alternative to the strong advertising theory is shown on the right-hand side of Figure 13.3. The steps in this model are awareness, trial and reinforcement (ATR). The ATR model, which has received support in Europe, suggests that advertising is a much less powerful influence than the strong theory would suggest. As Ehrenberg explains, 'advertising can first arouse awareness and interest, nudge some customers towards a doubting first trial purchase (with the emphasis on trial, as in "maybe I'll try it") and then provide some reassurance and reinforcement after that first purchase. I see no need for any strong AIDA-like Desire or Conviction before the first purchase is made.'[12]

His work in fast-moving consumer goods (fmcg) markets has shown that loyalty to one brand is rare. Most consumers purchase a repertoire of brands. The proportions of total purchases represented by the different brands show little variation over time, and new brands join the repertoire only in exceptional circumstances. A major objective of advertising in such circumstances is to defend brands. It does not work to increase sales by bringing new buyers to the brand advertised. Its main function is to retain existing buyers, and sometimes to increase the frequency with which they buy the brand.[13] Therefore, the target is existing buyers who presumably are fairly well disposed to the brand (otherwise they would not buy it), and advertising is designed to reinforce these favourable perceptions so they continue to buy it.[14]

As we saw when discussing consumer behaviour, level of involvement has an important role in determining how people make purchasing decisions. Jones suggests that involvement may also explain when the strong and weak theories apply.[15] For high-involvement decisions such as the purchase of expensive consumer durables, mail order or financial services, the decision-making process is studied with many alternatives considered and an extensive information search undertaken. Advertising, therefore, is more likely to follow the strong theory either by creating a strong desire to purchase (as with mail order) or by convincing people that they should find out more about the brand (for example, by visiting a showroom). Since the purchase is expensive it is likely that a strong desire (or conviction) is required before purchase takes place.

However, for low-involvement purchase decisions (such as low-cost packaged goods) people are less likely to consider a wide range of brands thoroughly before purchase and it is here that the weak theory of advertising almost certainly applies. Advertising is mainly intended to keep consumers doing what they already do by providing reassurance and reinforcement. Advertising repetition will be important in maintaining awareness and keeping the brand on the consumer's repertoire of brands from which individual purchases will be chosen.

Developing an Advertising Strategy

The starting point for developing an advertising strategy is a clear definition of marketing strategy. Advertising is one element of the marketing mix and decisions regarding advertising expenditure should not be taken in isolation. In particular, a product's competitive positioning needs to be taken into account: what is the target market and what differential advantage does the product possess? Target market definition allows the **target audience** to be identified in broad terms (e.g. 25–45-year-old men, or purchasing officers in the chemical industry) and recognition of the product's differential advantage points to the features and benefits of the product that should be stressed in its advertising. Figure 13.4 shows the major decisions that need to be taken when developing advertising strategy. Each decision will now be addressed.

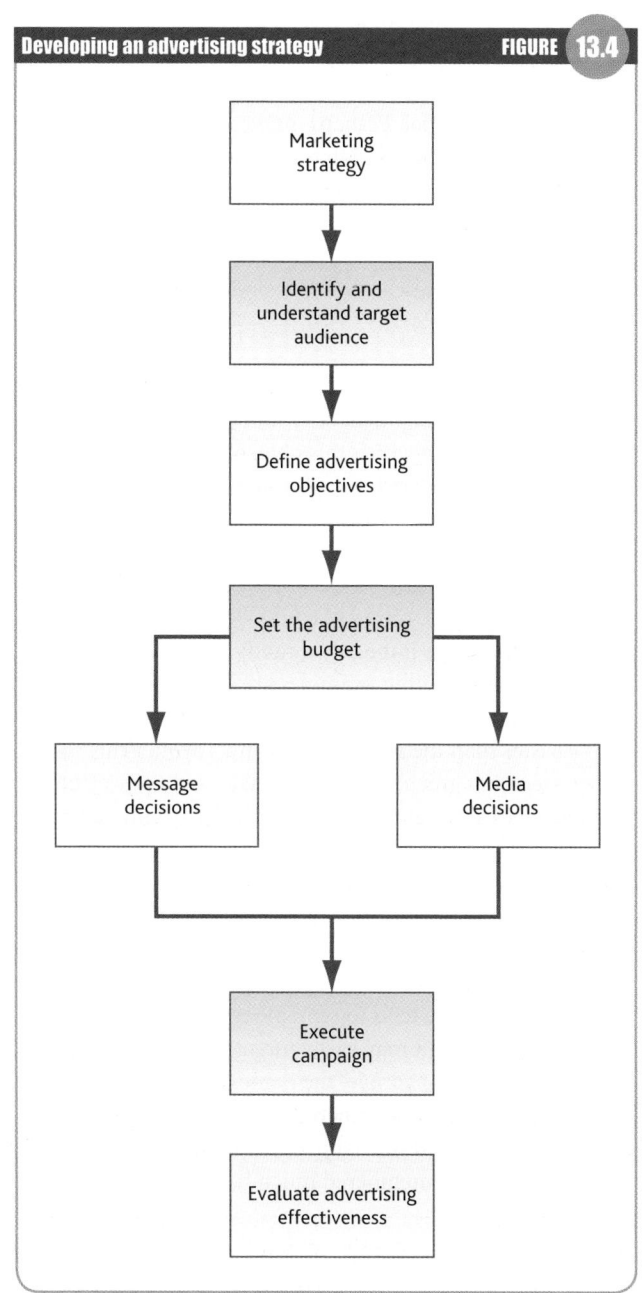

Developing an advertising strategy   FIGURE **13.4**

- Marketing strategy
- Identify and understand target audience
- Define advertising objectives
- Set the advertising budget
- Message decisions
- Media decisions
- Execute campaign
- Evaluate advertising effectiveness

Identify and understand the target audience

The target audience is the group of people at which the advertisement is aimed. In consumer markets, it may be defined in terms of socio-economic group, age, gender, location, buying frequency (e.g. heavy vs light buyers) and/or lifestyle. In organizational markets, it may be defined in terms of role (e.g. purchasing manager, managing director) and industry type.

Once the target audience has been identified, it needs to be understood. Buyer motives and choice criteria need to be analysed. Choice criteria are those factors buyers use to evaluate competing products. Advertising in organizational markets is particularly interesting since different members of the decision-making unit may use different choice criteria to evaluate a given product. For example, a purchasing manager may use cost-related criteria, whereas an engineer may place more emphasis on technical criteria. This understanding is vital: it has fundamental implications for message and media decisions. Where costs allow, two different advertisements may be needed with one stressing cost benefits using media read by purchasing managers and another focusing on technical issues in media read by engineers.

Define advertising objectives

Ultimately, advertising is used to stimulate sales and increase profits, but of more operational value is a clear understanding of its *communication objectives*. Advertising can create awareness, stimulate trial, position products in consumers' minds, correct misconceptions, remind and reinforce, and provide support for the salesforce. Each objective will now be discussed.

Create awareness

Advertising can create awareness of a company, a brand, a website, an event, or a solution to a problem. Creating company awareness helps to legitimize a company, its products and representatives to its customers. Instead of customers saying 'I've never heard of them', their response might be 'They are quite well known, aren't they?' In this way advertising may improve the acceptance of products and salespeople. Brand awareness is an obvious precondition of purchase and can be achieved through advertising. Awareness of websites can also be created through advertising. An example is the rise of lastminute.com, which launched an advertising campaign prior to flotation on the stock market. This raised awareness both of the brand and its website.

Advertising can also be used to create awareness of an event: for example, Comet, the UK electrical retailer, ran an ad with copy that read 'Comet sale now on'. Finally, advertising can be used to make the target audience aware of a solution to a problem. For example, Hewlett-Packard used the following headline in a press advertisement: 'Why can't somebody make a computer that'll get our orders in and out the same day?' 'Somebody does.' The advertisement then explained how Hewlett-Packard did this and contained a coupon that could be used to request further information. In this form of advertising, the problem is described, and this description is followed by an explanation of how a solution may be provided.

Stimulate trial

The sale of some products suffers because of lack of trial. Perhaps marketing research has shown that, once consumers try the product, acceptance is high but for some reason only a small proportion of the target group has tried it. In such circumstances, advertising that focuses on trial may be sensible. For example, the Irish whiskey brand Jameson ran advertisements that claimed 'You'll never know until you've tried it. Jameson, the spirit of Ireland'. Saab encouraged a trial (test drive) of its diesel range in a similar way.

Position products in consumers' minds

Advertising copy and visuals have a major role to play in positioning brands in the minds of the target audience.[16] Creative positioning involves the development or reinforcement of an image or set of associations for a brand. There are seven ways in which this objective can be achieved.[17]

1 *Product characteristics and customer benefits*: this is a common positioning strategy. For example, BMW uses performance with respect to handling and engineering competence as attributes summed up in the statement 'The Ultimate Driving Machine'. Remy Martin advertisements imbue the brandy with status connections. Other examples are Nokia ('Connecting people'), Levi's ('501 Jeans with Anti-fit'), BlackBerry ('Faster than the speed of life') and Toyota Prius ('Mean but green'). Absolut Vodka uses a powerful visual to associate the brand with clarity and purity. The advertisement for the Land Rover Freelander 2TD4e conveys the message that the vehicle comes with an intelligent stop/start system (feature) that improves fuel economy (benefit). A powerful attribute for positioning purposes is being number one. This is because people tend to remember objects that are number one but may easily forget number-two positions. For example, the names of Olympic champions are remembered much better than runners-up, and the name of the highest mountain in a country is remembered much better than the second

◀ Improved fuel economy with the new Land Rover Freelander.

VOTED BRITAIN'S SOFTEST WHITE.
In taste tests of the leading white bread brands.

▲ Hovis claims the number-one position for its Soft White bread.

highest. An example is Sky News, which claims the number one position by its claim to be 'first for breaking news'. Another example is Hovis Soft White, which claims the number one position after being voted the softest white bread (see illustration). Occasionally two attributes are used, as with Aquafresh toothpaste ('Cavity fighting and fresh breath') and Matey ('Cleans your kids and the bath as well').

2 *Price*: this positioning approach focuses on price as a weapon to deliver higher value to consumers. Many airlines, such as easyJet and Ryanair, advertise their low prices. Tesco promotes low price lines branded under the 'Value' name. Price positioning is not always focused on low prices, however. Occasionally a brand is positioned based on its high price, as is the case with Stella Artois ('Reassuringly expensive').

3 *Product use*: another positioning method is to associate the product with a use. An example is 'Lemsip is for flu attacks'. The basic idea is that when people think of flu, they automatically remember the brand. A second example is Cadbury's Roses chocolates ('The chocolates to say "thank you"').

4 *Product user*: another way of positioning is to associate a brand with a user or user type. Celebrity endorsements are often used, such as David Beckham (Adidas, Gillette, Vodafone), Lewis Hamilton (Reebok, Tag Heuer), Beyoncé Knowles (L'Oréal, Pepsi, Wal-Mart) and Tiger Woods (American Express, Nike, Tag Heuer). Positioning by user type has been successfully used by *The Economist* (intelligent, knowledgeable), and the advertisement for Gillette Fusion Power uses no less than three celebrities (see illustration on the following page).

5 *Product class*: some products can benefit by positioning themselves within a product class. For example, Red Mountain coffee positioned itself within the ground coffee class with the tag-line 'Ground coffee taste without the grind' and a margarine called 'I Can't Believe It's Not Butter' was positioned within the butter class by virtue of its name and advertising.

6 *Symbols*: the use of symbols to position brands in the marketplace has been achieved by Michelin (Michelin Man), McDonald's (golden arches) and Apple (a multicoloured apple logo). The use of symbols is particularly effective when the symbol reflects a quality desired in the brand, as with the Andrex puppy (softness) (see illustration on the following pages).

▲ Power endorsements for Gillette.

7 *Competition*: positioning against well-entrenched competitors can be effective since their image in the marketplace can be used as a reference point. For example, Subaru positioned against Volvo by claiming 'Volvo has built a reputation for surviving accidents. Subaru has built a reputation for avoiding them', based on ABS for better braking and four-wheel drive for better traction. Dyson positions against the competition by claiming that, unlike those of its rivals, its vacuum cleaners do not lose suction thanks to Dyson's patented technology. Positioning against competitors can be effective when consumers base their purchase decision on facts. Hence, a well-adjusted statement claiming a factual advantage against a key competitor can be highly successful. However, research has shown that, if used inappropriately, it can tarnish the image of the brand that is using the technique. There is, also, the risk of legal action, as when Ryanair was (unsuccessfully) sued by British Airways over its advertisement headlined 'Expensive ba****ds', which compared the airlines' prices on certain routes.[18]

Correct misconceptions

A fourth objective of advertising can be to correct misconceptions that consumers hold against brands. For example, McCain's, the market leader in the UK for oven chips, ran a successful advertising campaign claiming that oven chips contained 40 per cent less fat than home-cooked chips. However, marketing research showed that consumers still believed that their oven chips contained 30 per cent fat. A new campaign was designed to correct this misconception by stating that they contained only 5 per cent fat. Country Life butter also ran an advertising campaign to connect the misconception that its arch rival, Anchor, is British. The advertisement stated that 39 per cent of people who bought Anchor thought it was British, while it is actually from New Zealand.

Ad insight

Go to the website to see how Country Life Butter's Britishness is emphasised in its ad

Remind and reinforce

Once a clear position in the minds of the target audience has been established, the objective of advertising may be to remind consumers of the brand's existence, and to reinforce its image. For many leading brands in mature markets, such as Coca-Cola and Mars bars, the objective of their advertising is to maintain top-of-mind awareness and favourable associations. Given their strong market position, a major advertising task is to defend against competitive inroads, thus maintaining high sales, market share and profits.

▲ The Andrex puppy is a symbol of the softness of the brand.

Provide support for the salesforce

Advertising can provide invaluable support for the salesforce by identifying warm prospects and communicating with otherwise unreachable members of a decision-making unit. Some business-to-business advertising contains return coupons that potential customers can send to the advertiser indicating a degree of interest in the product. The identification of such warm prospects can enable the salesforce to use its time more efficiently by attempting to call upon them rather than spend time cold calling potential customers who may or may not have an interest in the product.

Given the size and complexity of many organizational decision-making units a salesperson cannot be expected to call on every member. One estimate is that out of 10 decision-making unit members, salespeople manage to talk to three or four on average. Advertising can be used to reach some of the others—for example, the numerous (secretaries) or the inaccessible (managing directors). Advertising can also support salespeople in consumer markets. For example, Avon supports its representatives by advertising new appealing products.

Set the advertising budget

The achievement of communication objectives will depend upon how much is spent on advertising. Four methods of *setting budgets* are the percentage of sales, affordability, matching competition, and the objective and task methods.

Percentage of sales

This method bases advertising expenditure on a specified percentage of current or expected sales revenue. The percentage may be based on company or industry tradition. The method is easy to apply and may discourage costly advertising wars if all competitors keep to their traditional percentage. However, the method encourages a decline in advertising expenditure when sales decline, a move that may encourage a further downward spiral of sales. Furthermore, it ignores market opportunities, which may suggest the need to spend more (or less) on advertising. For example, an opportunity to build market share may suggest raising advertising expenditure and, conversely, a decision to harvest a product would suggest reducing expenditure. Procter & Gamble eschewed the percentage of sales method during the 1930s Great Depression. While its rivals cut back on adspend in the face of falling sales, P&G increased expenditure to dominate share of voice in radio advertising and build market leadership that has lasted to this day. Finally, the method fails to provide a means of determining the correct percentage to use.

Affordability

This method bases advertising expenditure on what executive judgement regards as an amount that can be afforded. While affordability needs to be taken into account when considering any corporate expenditure, its use as the sole criterion for budget setting neglects the communication objectives that are relevant for a company's products and the market opportunities that may exist to grow sales and profits.

Matching competition

Some companies set their advertising budgets based upon matching expenditure to, or using a similar percentage of sales figure as their major competitor. Matching expenditure assumes that the competition has arrived at the correct level of expenditure, and ignores market opportunities and communication objectives. Using a similar percentage of sales ratio likewise lacks strategic vision and can be justified only if it can be shown to prevent costly advertising wars.

Objective and task

This method has the virtue of being logical since the advertising budget depends on communication objectives and the costs of the tasks required to achieve them. It is a popular method in Europe. If the objective is to increase awareness of a brand name from 30 per cent to 40 per cent, the cost of developing the necessary campaign, and using appropriate media (e.g. television, posters) will be calculated. The total cost would represent the advertising budget. In practice, however, the level of effort required to achieve the specified awareness increase may be difficult to estimate. Nevertheless, this method does encourage management to think about objectives, media exposure levels and the resulting costs.

In practice, the advertising budgeting decision is a highly political process.[19] Finance may argue for monetary caution, whereas marketing personnel, who view advertising as a method of long-term brand building, are more likely to support higher advertising spend. The outcome of the debate may depend as much on the political realities within the company as on adherence to any particular budgetary method.

Message decisions

Before a message can be decided, a clear understanding of the **advertising platform** should be acquired. The advertising platform is the foundation on which advertising messages are built. It is the basic selling proposition used in the advertisement (e.g. reliability or convenience). The platform should:
- be important to the target audience
- communicate competitive advantages.

This is why an understanding of the motives and choice criteria of the target audience is essential for effective advertising. Without this knowledge a campaign could be built upon an advertising platform that is irrelevant to its audience.

An **advertising message** translates the platform into words, symbols and illustrations that are attractive and meaningful to the target audience. In the 1980s IBM realized that many customers bought its computers because of the reassurance they felt when dealing with a well-known supplier. It used this knowledge to develop an advertising campaign based on the advertising platform of reassurance/low risk. This platform was translated into the advertising message 'No one ever got the sack for buying IBM.' Marketing in Action 13.1 describes how the 'Keep Walking' advertising message for Johnnie Walker was conceived (see illustration).

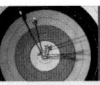

13.1 Marketing in Action

'Keep Walking' to Advertising Success

Although not particularly familiar in the UK, Johnnie Walker whisky is one of the most famous and valuable global brands. It is sold in more than 180 markets and is the world's largest whisky brand. Its fortunes began to fade, however, as years of brand variant-led communications had led to fragmented communications and the lack of a distinctive voice.

The brand's renaissance began with marketing research. Whisky advertising has always been about masculine success, but research showed that success was no longer measured by material wealth or showy displays of status. Instead, it was now more of an internal quality, about having a thirst for self-improvement. A man was judged a success not by where he was, but where he was going. In short, the most powerful expression of masculine success in the twenty-first century was progress.

Early in the history of Johnnie Walker the brand had employed the 'Striding Man' logo, but it had fallen out of the limelight. The logo was chosen as the centrepiece of the new global campaign and would be at the heart of all communications. He was given a more modern visual and was turned around so he strode forwards into the future. The strap-line 'Keep Walking' exhorted consumers to progress too.

The Keep Walking campaign has run globally, with strict controls to ensure that the same creative ran everywhere. The result has been strong sales growth associated with a campaign that won the Grand Prix at the 2008 IPA Effectiveness Awards.

Based on: Mustarde (2008)[20]

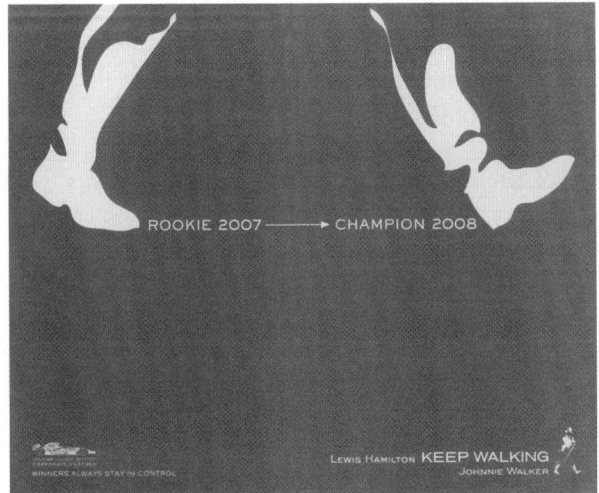

▲ Johnnie Walker strides to success.

Using the right message is important. John Caples, a top direct response copywriter, once wrote:[21]

> I have seen one ad actually sell not twice as much, not three times as much but 19 times as much as another. Both ads occupied the same space. Both were run in the same publication. Both had photographic illustrations. Both had carefully written copy. The difference was that one used the *right* appeal and the other used the *wrong* appeal.

The late David Ogilvy, an extremely successful advertising practitioner, suggested that press advertisements should follow a number of guidelines.[22]

1　The message appeal (benefit) should be important to the target audience.
2　The appeal should be specific; evidence to support it should be provided.
3　The message should be couched in the customers' language, not the language of the advertiser.
4　The advertisement should have a headline that might:
　(a)　promise a benefit
　(b)　deliver news
　(c)　offer a service
　(d)　tell a significant story
　(e)　identify a problem
　(f)　quote a satisfied customer.

5   If body copy (additional copy supporting and flowing from the headline) is to be used:
   (a)   long copy is acceptable if it is relevant to the need of the target audience
   (b)   long paragraphs and sentences should be avoided
   (c)   the copy should be broken up using plenty of white space to avoid it looking heavy to read
   (d)   if the advertiser is after enquiries, use a coupon *and* put the company address and telephone number at the end of the body copy. This is particularly important for industrial advertisements when more than one member of the decision-making unit (perhaps from different departments) may wish to send off for further details. With the address and telephone number appearing outside of the coupon, the second enquirer has the relevant information with which to contact the advertiser even if the coupon has already been used.

Most people who read a press advertisement read the headline but not the body copy. Because of this some advertisers suggest that the company or brand name should appear in the headline, otherwise the reader may not know the source of the advertisement. For example, the headlines 'Levi's 501 Jeans with Anti-fit' and 'Nokia: connecting people' score highly because in one statement they link a customer benefit or attribute with the name of the brand. Even if no more copy is read the advertiser has got one message across by means of a strong headline. The prominence of visuals also makes them important in conveying the message. Simple visuals can be very powerful in creating and reinforcing brand identity. In an age when consumers are being bombarded with advertising verbiage, visual imagery in advertisements is becoming even more important.[23] Humour is a powerful weapon in advertising, associating the brand with a feeling of warmth. In a 1 April press advertisement, BMW claimed to have invented a Canine Repellent Alloy Protection system that delivered electric shocks to any dog trying to relieve itself on the car.

Television messages also need to be built on a strong advertising platform. Because television commercials are usually 30 seconds or less in duration, most communicate only one major selling appeal—sometimes called the *single-minded proposition*—which is the single most motivating and differentiating thing that can be said about the brand.[24]

Television advertising often uses one of three creative approaches.[25] First, the *benefits* approach, where the advertisement suggests a reason for the customer to buy (customer benefit). For example, WeightWatchers advertises the benefits of losing weight, and advertisements for Pantene Ice Shine shampoo promise the benefit of shiny hair. The second approach is more subtle: no overt benefit is mentioned. Instead the intention is to *involve* the viewer. An example of involvement advertising was the commercial for Heinz Spaghetti in which a young couple's son tells them that the tomato on his plate is the sun, the triangles of toast are the mountains, and the Heinz Spaghetti is the sea. When the father enters into the game and asks 'So that's the boat then', the boy responds witheringly 'No, it's a sausage'. The third type of creative approach attempts to register the brand as significant in the market, and is called *salience advertising*. The assumption is that advertising that stands out as being different will cause the brand to stand out as different. An example is the Toshiba 'Tosh' campaign. In that case the significance of Toshiba as a brand was supported by conventional benefit advertising (e.g. 'Stronger components to last longer').

Television advertising is often used to build a brand personality. The *brand personality* is the message that the advertisement seeks to convey.

Lannon suggests that people use brand personalities in different ways.[26] Figure 13.5 shows that brand personality acts as a form of self-expression, reassurance, a communicator of the brand's function and an indicator of trustworthiness. The value of the brand personality to consumers will differ by product category and this will depend on what they use brand

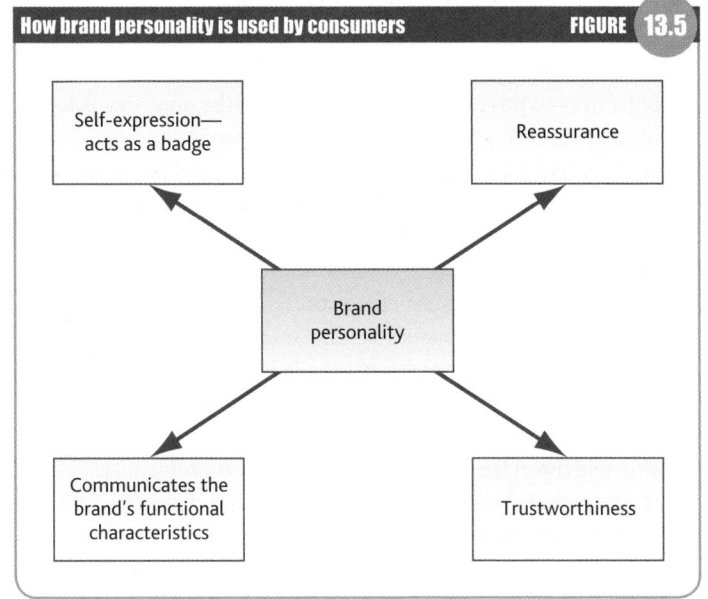

How brand personality is used by consumers   FIGURE **13.5**

- Self-expression—acts as a badge
- Reassurance
- Brand personality
- Communicates the brand's functional characteristics
- Trustworthiness

imagery for. In *self-expressive* product categories such as perfumes, cigarettes, alcoholic drinks and clothing, brands act as *badges* for making public an aspect of personality ('I choose this brand [e.g. Holsten Pils bottled lager] to say this about myself').

Brand personality can also act as *reassurance*. For example, the personality of After Eight Mints is sophistication and 'upper-classness', which does not necessarily correspond to the type of people who buy this mass-market brand. What the imagery is doing is providing reassurance that the brand is socially acceptable. Martini advertising also provides this kind of reassurance.

A third use of brand personality is to *communicate the functional characteristics* of the brand. Absolut Vodka advertising is an emotional representation of its functional characteristics: clarity and purity. Finally, personalities of brands such as Persil and Andrex act to signal *trustworthiness*, a benefit valued by many consumers in their product categories.

Advertisers neglect at their peril the role of *emotion* in consumer decision-making. When choice depends on symbolic meaning helping to define a person's self-concept and sense of identity, and communicate it to other people, decision-making may be largely emotion-driven. Consumers consult their feelings about the decision. For example, a car buyer may ask 'How do I feel about being seen in that car?' If the answer is positive, information search may be confined to providing an objective justification of the choice (for example, the car's reliability, fuel economy, etc.). Television advertising is often used to convey the desired emotional response and the print media to supply objective information. Brands such as Nike with its 'Just do it' attitude, Virgin for its 'us against them' approach and Benetton with its controversial advertising campaigns, including a black stallion mounting a white mare and portraits of American prisoners on death row, have all tried to plug into consumers' emotions.[27] In low-involvement situations, such as with the choice of drinks and convenience foods, humour is sometimes used to create a feeling of warmth about a brand and even regular exposure to a brand name over time can generate the desired feeling of warmth.[28]

Media decisions

There used to be a joke among media people that the client's attitude to their part in advertising was 'Ten minutes to go before lunch. Just enough time to discuss media.'[29] As media costs have risen and brands become more sharply targeted, this attitude has disappeared. Two key media decisions are:

1 the **media class decision** (for example, television versus the press), and
2 the **media vehicle decision** (e.g. a particular newspaper or magazine).

Both decisions will now be examined.

The media class decision

Table 13.2 lists the major media class options (the media mix). The media planner faces the choice of using television, the press, cinema, outdoor, radio, the Internet or some

Media class options	TABLE 13.2
1 Television	

2 Press
    National newspapers
    Regional newspapers
    Trade and technical
    Magazines	

3 Outdoor	
4 Cinema	
5 Radio	
6 The Internet	

combination of media classes. Five considerations will be taken into account. First, *creative factors* may have a major bearing on the decision. The key question that needs to be addressed is 'Does the medium allow the communication objectives to be realized?' For example, if the objective is to position the brand as having a high-status aspirational personality, television would be better than posters. However, if the communication objective is to remind the target audience of a brand's existence, a poster campaign may suffice. Each medium possesses its own set of creative qualities and limitations, as described below.

Television: advertisers can demonstrate the product in action. For example, a lawnmower can be shown to cut grass efficiently, or the ease of application of a paint can be demonstrated. The capability of television to combine colour, movement and sound (unlike the press, posters and radio) means that it is often used when brand image building is required. It is easier to create an atmosphere using television than other media that lack its versatility. Advertisements can be repeated over a short time period but it is a transitory medium (unless the commercial is video recorded) so that consumers cannot refer back to the advertisement once it has been broadcast (unlike the press).

A potential threat to television advertising is the emergence of personal video recorders (PVRs), which can store up to 30 hours of programmes, allowing consumers to play them back at their convenience. It is also possible to record a programme and then start watching it on the PVR shortly after it has started, allowing the ads to be skipped. In the USA, 6 per cent of the population watch 60 per cent of their programmes through PVRs. It is estimated that they skip 92 per cent of ads in the recorded programmes.[30] Although take-up in Europe is slow, as prices fall diffusion may accelerate, bringing a fall in television advertising effectiveness.

Digital television technology means that signals can be compressed, allowing more to be sent to the viewer. The result is the escalation of the number of channels that can be received. The extra 'bandwidth' created by digital technology is likely to reduce costs, enabling small players to broadcast to small target audiences such as small geographical areas and special interest groups (e.g. shoppers). Also, digital technology allows the development of interactive services, promoting the potential for home shopping.[31] During an advertisement, viewers are able to click on the red button on the remote control handset, leading them to an interactive shopping area, the equivalent of an Internet site.[32] This form of advertising is called interactive TV (iTV) and is discussed in more detail in Chapter 18, on digital marketing, and in Digital Marketing 13.1.

Television programmes can now be watched via a computer with the development of such online services as the BBC's iPlayer and iTVPlayer. Also brands such as Audi, Land Rover and Dove have their own dedicated Internet television channels. Audi has found that potential car buyers return 12 times during the decision-making process. Land Rover's web TV channel features six streams of video-on-demand content: sport, adventure, people, culture, places and Land Rover. Dove TV features information on the brand's 'Real Beauty' positioning.[33]

Press: factual information can be presented in a press advertisement (e.g. specific features of a car or computer) and the readers are in control of how long they take to absorb the information. Allied to this advantage is the possibility of re-examination of the advertisement at a later date. But it lacks movement and sound, and advertisements in newspapers and magazines compete with editorial for the reader's attention.

Outdoor: simplicity is required in the creative work associated with outdoor advertising because many people (for example, car drivers) will have the opportunity only to glance at a poster. Like the press it is visual only, and is often used as a support medium (backing

13.1 Digital Marketing

Interactive Television Advertising

Interactive television (iTV) advertising invites viewers to press the red button on the remote control handset to see more information about an advertised product. Viewers may then be asked to request a free sample or brochure, or buy a product, for example. Although in its infancy, iTV is growing, with Sky claiming that around 25 per cent of last-in-break spots on its wholly owned channels carry iTV ads.

One of the key drivers of this growth is iTV's ability to provide measurable results for clients, a characteristic that is shared with direct mail. Advertisers can assess campaign performance by measuring response and, for the first time, attribute a financial value to different channels, times of day and even individual slots. It also allows the targeting of niche audiences through the use of specialist television channels that focus on leisure activities such as sport, music and motoring. A third benefit is the ability to provide more in-depth information than a single television or press ad. For example, a car manufacturer could provide a video of a new model and display its features before asking the viewer to request a brochure, thereby generating a lead.

Interactive television advertising can generate direct sales and encourage home shopping. It also has the benefit of not requiring a call centre, with responses being dealt with electronically rather than requiring the hiring of call centre staff to deal with calls, which is a feature of traditional direct response advertising. It is also more convenient for the viewer, who does not have to rush off to the telephone or computer. Also the red button can be more effective than a telephone call, with one advertiser recording a response rate nine times greater via iTV than via a phone number. Longer commercials are more likely to encourage people to respond, with 40-second and 60-second spots generating up to 25 per cent more response than the standard 30-second ad.

The most active sectors are cars, travel and financial services, where the ability to pass on more information to viewers is most highly valued. For example, Volvo ran a television campaign promoting the S40, accompanied by an eight-minute documentary showcasing the interior and performance of the car. This was made available via web and interactive TV. Around 435,000 people saw the documentary, representing 11 per cent of the Sky Digital viewers who were aware of the ad, and spent an average of six minutes watching it. Grocery brands have been more reluctant to get involved, since they tend to be low-involvement purchases.

A novel form of interactive television advertising took place when, on 28 February 2009 at 21.50 GMT, lastminute.com ran three 60-second advertising slots, which ran in sequence across three different channels: ITV, Channel 4 and five. The campaign message marked the launch of lastminute.com's new brand message, which is 'do more good stuff' by making the most of your free time with new and unexpected ideas. Simon Thompson, European Managing Director at lastminute.com, said 'the simultaneous use of multiple media channels emulates the essence of lastminute.com, the excitement at the heart of our experiences and our constant hunt for innovative, inspiring offerings. We know our customers enjoy new ideas so we felt this interactive platform was the perfect way to assert our TV comeback.'

Lastminute.com has effectively created a new form of interactive television advertising, which gets the audience involved by changing channels to follow the 'Mexican wave'. At the heart of the creative idea for the advert was the 'thumbs up' action, which was shown flowing between friends, family, holidaymakers, crowds of people. Every individual gives the camera the 'thumbs up' as they are enjoying themselves in a variety of situations: on an airline, in a bar, on a ski slope, scuba diving, riding a camel, in the theatre, and more.

Based on: Davies (2002);[34] *Ray (2003);*[35] *Fletcher (2005);*[36] *McCafferty and Christie (2009)*[37]

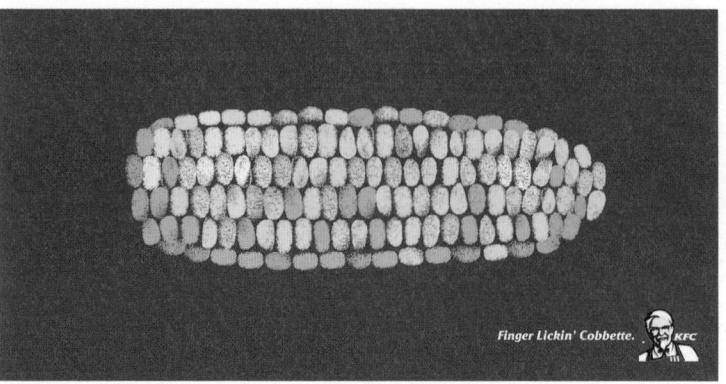

▲ KFC keeps it simple in this award-winning advertisement.

a television or press campaign) because of its creative limitations. It is believed to be effective for reminder advertising. Carlsberg has used posters effectively using the headline 'Carlsberg—Probably the best lager in the world', showing the necessity for simplicity. Often, outdoor advertising sites are sold as a package targeting specific audiences. For example, targeting supermarket shoppers can be realized by buying a retail package where advertisers can buy space on panels in supermarket stores; if businesspeople are the target it is possible to buy a package of sites at major airports.[38]

Technology is helping outdoor advertising gain a bigger share of advertising in the prime media. Backlit and scrolling sites are gradually replacing more traditional glued posters. Digital technology is allowing animated posters, whose content alters during the day, and high-definition-quality moving images. For outdoor advertising the key word is simplicity. An ad has, on average, just six seconds to get a message across, which has led to the golden rule 'no more than seven words on a poster'.[39] KFC applies this principle (see illustration).

Cinema: advertisements can benefit from colour, movement and sound, and exposure is high due to the captive nature of the audience. Repetition may be difficult to achieve given the fact that people visit cinemas intermittently, but the nature of the audience is predictable, usually between 15 and 25 years of age. However, the age range has widened in recent years with the success of family films such as the Harry Potter and Shrek series. This has led companies like Disney to purchase 60-second slots before family feature films. Following the success of the BMW Mini, which used cinema extensively, other car manufacturers such as Volkswagen, Toyota, Citroën and Ford have used cinema to target young audiences.[40]

13.1 Pause for Thought

It is claimed that cinema advertising achieves high recall levels because of the captive nature of the audience. If you have visited the cinema in the last few weeks, can you recall the brands that you saw advertised? Do you agree that it is a powerful advertising medium?

Radio: this is creatively limited to sound and thus may be better suited to communicating factual information (for example, a special price reduction) than attempting to create a brand image. The nature of the audience changes during the day (for example, motorists during rush hours) and so a measure of targeting is possible. Production costs are relatively low. The arrival of digital radio has increased the number of radio stations available, and marginally improved sound quality. Digital radios have screen displays, which allow websites and telephone numbers to be run at the same time as an advertisement is being played.[41] Radio listening may rise with the growth of the Internet as people listen to the radio while surfing and because radio listening through web browsers is fast becoming a reality.[42]

The Internet: this medium allows global reach to be achieved at relatively low cost. The number of website visits, clicks on advertisements and products purchased can be measured. Interactivity between supplier and consumer is possible either by website-based communication or e-mail. Direct sales are possible, which is driving the growth of e-business in such areas as hotels, travel and information technology. Advertising content can be changed quickly and easily. Catalogues and price lists can be amended rapidly, and a dialogue between companies and their customers and suppliers can be established. The fastest form of advertising is the placing of sponsored links to websites on search engines. Google and Yahoo! are the market leaders in so-called 'paid search' or 'pay-per-click' advertising. The basic idea is that advertisers bid in an online auction for the right to have their link displayed next to the results for specific search terms, such as 'used cars' or 'digital cameras', and then pay only when an Internet surfer actually clicks on that link (hence 'pay-per-click'). An advantage to the advertiser is that the consumer has already expressed interest and intent—first by typing in the search term and then by clicking on the advertiser's link—and, therefore, is more likely to make a purchase than someone passively watching an advertisement on television or looking at one in a newspaper.[43]

The disadvantages of Internet advertising are that it is impersonal and requires consumers to visit a website. This may require high expenditure in traditional media or the placing of sponsored links on search engines, which can suffer from 'click fraud' (bogus clicks generated by competitors intent on raising the cost to the online advertiser). Although websites themselves can contain high levels of information content, the creative potential of Internet advertisements is limited by size. Finally, Internet ads (particularly 'pop-ups') can be considered intrusive and an irritant.

The second consideration when making the media class decision is the *size of the advertising budget*. Some media are naturally more expensive than others. For example, £500,000 may be sufficient for a national poster campaign but woefully inadequate for national television. Advertisers with less than £3 million to spend on a national campaign may decide that television advertising is not feasible.

Third, the relative *cost per opportunity to see* is also relevant to the decision: the target audience may be reached much more cheaply using one medium rather than another. However, the calculation of opportunity to see differs according to media class, making comparisons difficult. For example, in the UK, an opportunity to see for the press is defined as 'read or looked at any issue of the publication for at least two minutes', whereas for posters it is 'traffic past site'.

A fourth consideration is *competitive activity*. Two conflicting philosophies are to compete in the same medium and to dominate an alternative medium. The decision to compete in the same medium may be taken because of a belief that the medium chosen by the major competition is the most effective, and that to ignore it would be to hand the competition a massive communication advantage. Domination of an alternative medium may be sensible for third or fourth players in a product market who cannot match the advertising budgets of the big two competitors. Supposing the major players were using television, the third or fourth competitor might choose press or posters, where it could dominate, achieving higher impact than if it followed the competition into television.

Finally, for many consumer-good producers, *the views of the retail trade* (for example, supermarket buyers) may influence the choice of media class. Advertising expenditure is often used by salespeople to convince the retail trade to increase shelf space for existing brands and to stock new brands. Since distribution is a key success factor in these markets, the views of retailers will be important. For example, if it is known that supermarkets favour television advertising in a certain product market, the selling impact on the trade of £3 million spent on television may be viewed as greater than the equivalent spend of 50:50 between television and the press.

Definition of an opportunity to see (OTS)		TABLE 13.3
Television	Presence in room with set switched on at turn of clock minute to relevant channel, provided that presence in room with set on is for at least 15 consecutive seconds	
Press	Read or looked at any issue (for at least two minutes) within the publication period (for example, for weeklies, within the last seven days)	
Posters	Traffic past site (including pedestrians)	
Cinema	Actual cinema admissions	

Sometimes a combination of media classes is used in an advertising campaign to take advantage of their relative strengths and weaknesses. For example, a new car launch might use television to gain awareness and project the desired image, with the press being used to supply more technical information. Later, posters may be used as a support medium to remind and reinforce earlier messages.

The media vehicle decision

The media vehicle decision concerns the choice of the particular newspaper, magazine, television spot, poster site, etc. Although creative considerations still play a part, *cost per thousand calculations* are more dominant. This requires readership and viewership figures. In the UK, readership figures are produced by the National Readership Survey, based on over 36,000 interviews per year. Viewership is measured by the Broadcasters' Audience Research Board (BARB), which produces weekly reports based on a panel of 5100 households equipped with metered television sets. Poster research is conducted by an organization called Postar (Poster Audience Research). It provides information on not only the number of people who pass but also the number of people who are likely to see a particular site.[44] Cinema audiences are monitored by Cinema and Video Industry Audience Research (CAVIAR), and radio audiences are measured by Radio Joint Audience Research (RAJAR). Table 13.3 shows how a viewer or reader is measured in terms of opportunity to see (OTS).

Media buying is a specialized skill and many thousands of pounds can be saved off rate card prices by powerful media buyers. Media buying is accomplished through one of three methods: full service agencies, media specialists or media buying clubs. Full service agencies provide a full range of advertising services for their clients, including media buying. Independent media specialists grew in the early 1990s as clients favoured their focused expertise and negotiating muscle. Media buying clubs were formed by full service agencies joining forces to pool buying power. However, the current trend is back to full service agencies, but with one major difference: today the buying is done by separate profit-making subsidiaries. With very few exceptions, all the world's top media buying operations are now owned by global advertising companies such as Omnicom, WPP and Saatchi & Saatchi.[45]

Today there is more pressure than ever to create critical mass in media buying. With media owners consolidating and advertisers rationalizing, buyers have followed suit to retain buying power. Buying power enables agencies to acquire and retain clients because advertisers believe that the media houses with the biggest budgets buy cheapest. This means that media buyers need to be of a sufficient size to attract global clients.[46]

Execute campaign

Once the advertisements have been produced and the media selected, they are sent to the relevant media for publication or transmission. A key organizational issue is to ensure that the right advertisements reach the right media at the right time. Each media vehicle has its own deadlines after which publication or transmission may not be possible.

Evaluate advertising effectiveness

Three key questions in *advertising research* are what, when and how to evaluate. What should be measured depends on whatever the advertising is trying to achieve. As we have already seen, advertising objectives include gaining awareness, trial, positioning, correcting misconceptions, reminding and providing support for the salesforce (for example, by identifying warm prospects). By setting targets for each objective, advertising research can assess whether objectives have been achieved. For example, a campaign might have the objective of increasing awareness from 10 to 20 per cent, or of raising beliefs that the product is the 'best value brand on the market' from 15 to 25 per cent of the target consumers.

If advertising objectives are couched in sales or market share terms, advertising research would monitor the sales or market share effects of advertising. Finally, if trade objectives are important, distribution and stock levels of wholesalers and/or retailers, and perhaps their awareness and attitudes, should be measured.

Measurement can take place before, during and after campaign execution. *Pre-testing* takes place before the campaign is run and is part of the creative process. In television advertising, *rough* advertisements are created and tested with target consumers. This is usually done with a *focus group*, which is shown perhaps three alternative commercials and asked to discuss its likes, dislikes and understanding of each one.[47] Stills from the proposed commercial are shown on a television screen with a voice-over. This provides an inexpensive but realistic portrayal of what the commercial will be like if it is shot. The results provide important input from target consumers themselves rather than solely relying on advertising agency views. Voice-overs that are disliked, misunderstanding and lack of credibility of messages are examples of problems that can be identified at the pre-testing stage and, therefore, rectified before the cost of shooting a commercial is incurred. Such research is not without its critics, however. They suggest that the impact of a commercial that is repeated many times cannot be captured in a two-hour group discussion. They point to the highly successful Heineken campaign ('Refreshes the parts that other beers cannot reach'), which was rejected by target consumers in pre-testing.[48]

Press advertisements can be pre-tested using the *folder techniques*.[49] Suppose that two advertisements are being compared, two folders are prepared containing a number of advertisements with which the test advertisements will have to compete for attention. The test advertisements are placed in the same position in each folder. Two matched samples of around 50–100 target consumers are each given one of the folders and asked to go through it. Respondents are then asked to state which advertisements they have noticed (*unaided recall*). They are then shown a list of the advertised brands and asked questions such as which one was most liked, which was least liked, and which they intend to buy. Attention is gradually focused on the test advertisement and respondents are asked to recall its content.

Once the campaign has run, *post-testing* can be used to assess its effectiveness. Sometimes formal post-testing is ignored through laziness, fear or lack of funds. However, checking how well an advertising campaign has performed can provide the information necessary to plan future campaigns. In the UK, image/attitude, statistical analysis of sales data and usage surveys (usage rates, changes in usage) were the most popular TV post-testing techniques.[50] The top three measures used in post-test television advertising research mirror the most popular techniques: image/attitude change, actual sales and usage. Image/attitude change was believed to be a sensitive measure that was a good predictor of behavioural change. Some of those agencies favouring the actual sales measure argued that, despite difficulties in establishing cause and effect, sales change was the ultimate objective of advertising and therefore was the only meaningful measure. Recall was also popular (63 per cent used it regularly). Despite the evidence suggesting that recall may not be a valid measure of advertising effectiveness, those favouring recall gave reasons varying from the sweeping 'It usually means good advertising if good recall is present' to the pragmatic 'Because it shows the advertisement is seen and remembered, it is very reassuring to the client'.

Many of the measures used to evaluate television advertising can also be used for press advertisements. For example, spontaneous recall of a brand name could be measured before and after a press campaign. In addition, readers of a periodical in which the advertisement appeared could be asked to recall which advertisements they saw and, if the test advertisement is recalled, its content. In addition, press advertisements that incorporate coupons to promote enquiries or actual sales can be evaluated by totalling the number of enquirers or the value of sales generated.

The key to evaluating advertising is to consult with the target audience, not rely on industry awards as a measure of effectiveness. These can give very different results. For example, a Norwegian charity won an award for an advertising campaign on which it spent NKr3 million (£300,000/€432,000) only to find that it attracted only NKr1.7 million (£170,000/€245,000) in donations.

Organizing for Campaign Development

An advertiser has four options when organizing for campaign development. First, small companies may develop the advertising *in cooperation* with people from the media. For example, advertising copy may be written by someone from the company but the artwork and final layout of the advertisement may be done by the newspaper or magazine. Alternatively, commercial radio stations provide facilities for commercials to be produced. Second, the advertising function may be conducted in-house by creating an *advertising department* staffed with copy-writers, media buyers and production personnel. This form of organization locates total control of the advertising function within the company, but since media buying is on behalf of only one company, buying power is low.

Third, because of the specialist skills that are required for developing an advertising campaign, many advertisers opt to work with an **advertising agency**. Larger agencies offer a full service, comprising creative, media planning and buying, planning and strategy development, market research and production. Figure 13.6 shows the typical structure of a large advertising agency. Key figures in the development of a campaign are account directors and executives, who liaise with client companies and coordinate the work of the other departments on behalf of their clients. Because agencies work for many clients they have a wide range of experience, and can provide an objective outsider's view of what is required, and how problems can be solved.

A fourth alternative is to use in-house staff (or a full service agency) for some advertising functions but to use *specialist agencies* for others. Their attraction, in part, stems from the large volume of business that each specialist controls. This means that they have enormous buying power when negotiating media prices. Alternatively, an advertiser could employ the services of a *creative hot shop* to supplement their own or their full service agency's skills. Saatchi & Saatchi began life as a creative hot shop before developing into a full service agency.

When an advertiser uses an agency, managing the relationship is of critical importance. Marketing in Action 13.2 discusses some of the key issues involved.

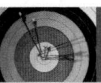

13.2 Marketing in Action

Managing the Client–Agency Relationship

Strong relationships between clients (advertisers) and their agencies can provide the platform for effective advertising. A survey of clients and agencies focused on those issues that were causing problems in achieving this desired state.

Many clients demanded that agencies become more involved in their business, with comments like 'they need to spend more time understanding our challenges and goals' and 'they need to take more notice of the client's view with regard to creative work'. Clearly, clients were looking for agencies to spend more time and attention on understanding their business objectives before beginning the creative process.

The importance of the early stages of the advertising development process was also emphasized by agencies. Some complained about having to deal with junior people at the briefing stage, who had not been trained to write a clear brief. This was critical because unless clients get the briefing stage right things will inevitably go wrong further down the line. This problem was connected to the lack of accessibility of senior marketing staff because they have too much other work to do. This means that briefing is left in the hands of junior staff, who have the power to say 'no' but not 'yes'. This can be very frustrating for agencies. One agency complained about not enough 'ear time' with a senior member of his client's marketing team: 'he is too busy and there is too big an experience gap between him and his team'. Two further consequences of this were insufficient access to business objectives and strategy, and an inability to provide constructive feedback on their proposals.

One issue that can spoil client–agency relationships is client conflict. This occurs when an advertising agency wins a new account from a rival to an existing client, or when an agency is taken over by an agency that holds the account of a rival. Both of these scenarios have happened to Procter & Gamble. Media planning agency Zenith Optimedia won the L'Oréal account, causing potential client conflict with its existing P&G account. P&G was also concerned when its advertising agency Grey Global was acquired by the WPP Group, which counts arch-rival Unilever among its client base. Such situations can end relationships or, as was the case with WPP, the client's fears may be assuaged if it is satisfied that separate agency networks will be working for the two clients.

Three key factors are critical in managing client relationships. First, the agency should be client-centric. This means understanding the client's market and business, and how both are changing. There can be a tendency for such an understanding to dwindle over time. To combat this, agencies should invite clients to talk about their business. Second, agencies should not neglect personal contact. With electronic communication the easy option, it can be tempting to communicate remotely. However, face-to-face contact is critical as it is difficult to build and maintain a business relationship purely through e-mail. Finally, the strength of the relationship needs to be checked regularly. The presumption that everything is fine because nobody has complained is a dangerous path to follow.

Based on: Curtis (2002);[51] Curtis (2002);[52] Singh (2005);[53] Rhind-Tutt (2009)[54]

Agency selection

As with buying any product, agency selection begins by defining requirements clearly. For example, a do-it-yourself or furniture chain may place most emphasis on media selection and buying capabilities so that the lowest cost per thousand can be achieved for its relatively straightforward black and white product information advertisements.[55] On the other hand, a company marketing drinks or perfume may give greater priority to the creative talents of prospective agencies. Smith describes the selection procedure as follows:[56]

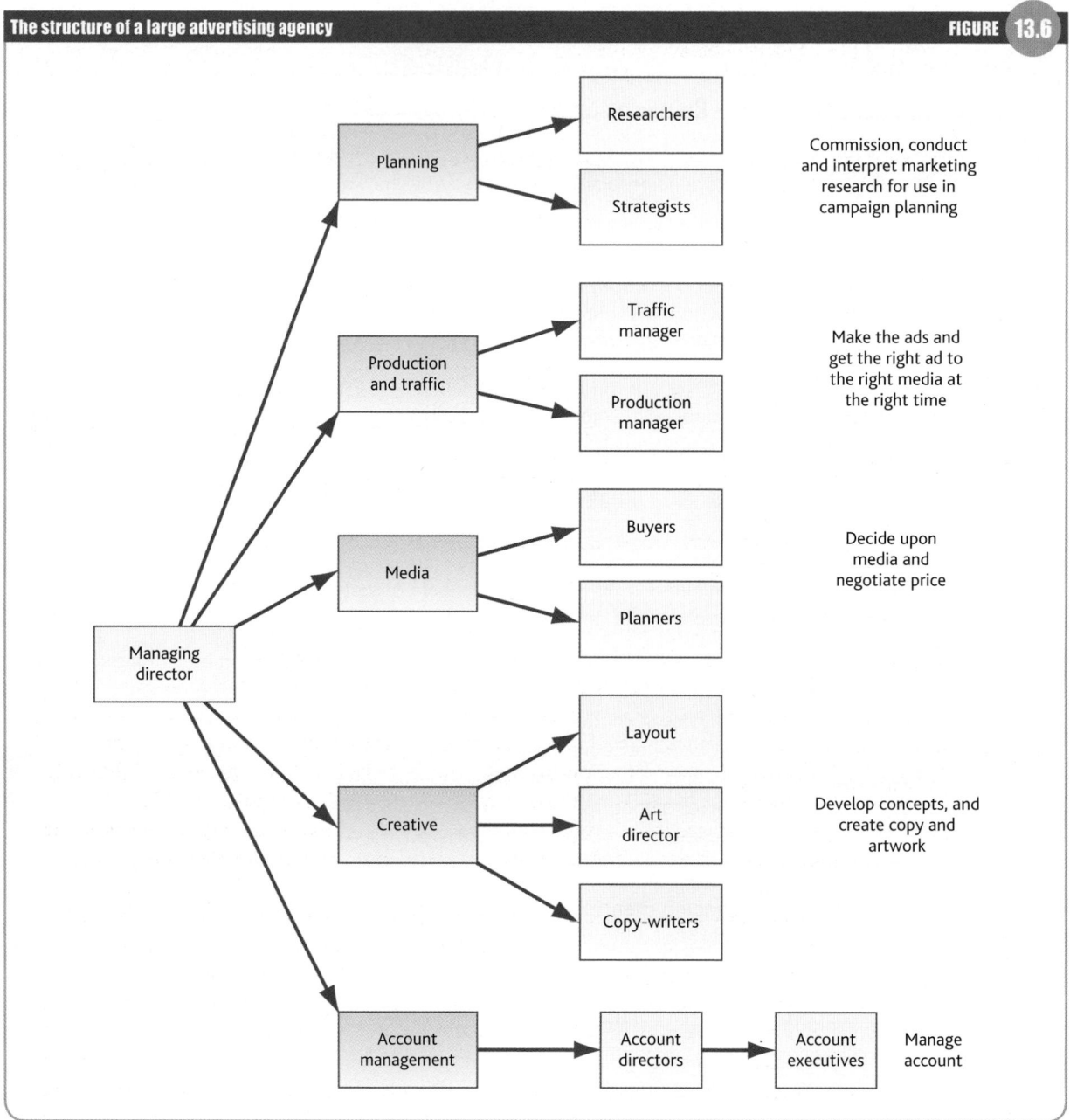

1 define requirements
2 develop a pool list of agencies
3 credentials (e.g. examples of current and previous work, team members, profiles) pitch by agencies
4 issue brief to shortlisted agencies
5 full agency presentation
6 analysis of pitch
7 select winner
8 agree contract details
9 announce winner.

When briefing agencies, the following checklist may be used.
1 *Product history*: e.g. sales, market share, trends, price, past campaigns, competition.
2 *Product features and benefits*: the product's competitive advantages and disadvantages.
3 *Objectives*: the product's marketing and communication objectives.
4 *Target audience*: who they are, their motives and choice criteria.
5 *Timetable*: when the agency presentation is required, when the campaign is planned to commence.
6 *Budget*: how much money is available, which may affect choice of media.

Analysis of the agency presentation will depend on the following six key questions.
1 How good is its creative/media/research work?
2 Does the agency have people you think you can work with?
3 Does your account appear to be important to them?
4 What is their background: who are their clients, how long have they worked with them, is their client list growing or contracting, have they worked in your field before and, if so, why did they lose the account?
5 Are they a full service agency or do they contract out some functions (e.g. media, research)?
6 What do they charge? Do they charge fees as well as commission?

Agency payment systems

The traditional system of agency payment was by *commission* from the media owners. This was because advertising agencies were originally set up on behalf of media owners that wished to provide advertising services to enhance the likelihood of selling advertising space. Hence, it was natural that payment should be from them. Under the commission system, media owners traditionally gave a 15 per cent discount off the rate card (list) price to agencies. For example, a £1 million television advertising campaign would result in a charge to the agency of £1 million minus 15 per cent (£850,000). The agency invoiced the client at the full rate card price (£1 million). The agency commission therefore totalled £150,000.

Large advertisers have the power to demand some of the 15 per cent in the form of a rebate. For example, Unilever announced that it was allowing its advertising agencies 13 per cent commission.[57] Given its worldwide advertising expenditure of £1.5 billion it could probably have demanded a lower figure (possibly 11 per cent) but the company chose not to exercise all of its muscle since it believed that low commission rates ultimately mean poor-quality advertising.

The second method of paying agencies is by *fee*. For smaller clients, commission alone may not be sufficient to cover agency costs. Also, some larger clients are advocating fees rather than commission on the basis that this removes a possible source of agency bias towards media that pay commission rather than a medium like direct mail for which no commission is payable.

The third method of remuneration is through payment by results. This involves measuring the effectiveness of the advertising campaign using marketing research, and basing payment on how well communication objectives have been achieved. For example, payment might be based on how awareness levels have increased, brand image improved or intentions to buy risen. Some agencies are paid by how many sales have been achieved. For example, Holsten Pils pays its agency, TBWA London, by the volume of lager sold; no other payment for its day-to-day work on the client's business is made.[58] Another area where payment by results has been used is media buying. For example, if the normal cost per thousand to reach men in the age range 30–40 is £4.50, and the agency achieves a 10 per cent saving, this might be split 8 per cent to the client and 2 per cent to the agency.[59] Procter & Gamble uses payment by results as the method by which it pays its advertising agencies, which include Publicis, Leo Burnett, Grey Advertising and D'Arcy Masius Benton & Bowles. Remuneration is tied to global brand sales, so aligning their income more closely with the success (or otherwise) of their advertising.[60] Toyota is also following this trend by paying both its creative agency, Saatchi & Saatchi, and its media agency, Zenith Optimedia, in part on the basis of performance. Payment is made on the basis of achievement of communication objectives and sales targets.[61]

Ethical Issues in Advertising

Because it is so visible most people have a view on the value of advertising. Certainly advertising has its critics (and its supporters). Their views will be discussed within the following areas: misleading advertising, advertising's influence on society's values and advertising to children.

Misleading advertising

This can take the form of exaggerated claims and concealed facts. For example, it would be unethical to claim that a car achieved 50 miles to the gallon when in reality it was only 30 miles. Nevertheless, most countries accept a certain amount of puffery, recognizing that consumers are intelligent and interpret the claims in such a way that they are not deceptive. In the UK, the advertising slogan 'Carlsberg: probably the best lager in the world' is acceptable because of this. However, in Europe, advertisers should be aware that a European directive on misleading advertising states that the burden of proof lies with the advertiser should the claims be challenged. Advertising can also deceive by omitting important facts from the message. Such concealed facts may give a misleading impression to the audience. For example, an advertisement that promotes a food product as 'healthy' because it contains added vitamins might be considered misleading if it failed to point out its high sugar and fat content. Many industrialized countries have their own codes of practice that protect the consumer from deceptive advertising. For example, in the UK the Advertising Standards Authority (ASA) administers the British Code of Advertising Practice. It insists that advertising should be 'legal, decent, honest and truthful'.

This means that advertisers need to be very careful about the claims they make. For example, Procter & Gamble was forced to drop its claim 'Pantene Pro-V is the world's best haircare system' after Lever Fabergé complained to the ASA. A recent form of misleading advertising is 'greenwashing', where a brand is falsely attributed with green credentials. For example, the Lexus 'High performance. Low emissions. Zero guilt' press campaign was banned by the ASA for misleading consumers.[62]

Advertising's influence on society's values

Critics argue that advertising images have a profound effect on society. They claim that advertising promotes materialism and takes advantage of human frailties. Advertising is accused of stressing the importance of material possessions, such as the ownership of an expensive car or the latest in consumer electronics. Critics argue that this promotes the wrong values in society. A related criticism is that advertising takes advantage of human frailties such as the need to belong and the desire for status. It promotes the idea that people should be judged on what they possess rather than who they are. For example, advertisements for some cars use status symbol appeals rather than their functional characteristics. Supporters of advertising counter by arguing that these are not human frailties but basic psychological characteristics. They point out that the acquisition of status symbols occurs in societies that are not exposed to advertising messages, such as some African tribes where status is derived from the number of cows a person owns. Marketing Ethics and Corporate Social Responsibility in Action 13.1 gives some examples of how misleading advertising is controlled.

13.1 Marketing Ethics and Corporate Social Responsibility in Action

Pushing the Boundaries of Taste and Decency

Complaints about advertising campaigns are often related to issues of taste and decency. Consumers may find ads offensive, and this is particularly the case when nudity or sexual appeals are used, and when controversial products are advertised. Add sexual appeal to a controversial product, and you have created a moral time bomb. Recently, the UK Durex TV advert for Durex Play, a female pleasure gel, caused much controversy. Not only did the advert portray a collage of women seemly reaching orgasm to Mozart's *The Magic Flute*, but it also ran at 10.05 pm on Channel 4 after receiving a post-11 pm restriction. Such a commercial can be seen as a positive yet controversial celebration of female sexuality and pleasure, which is often a taboo subject in public discourse. The scheduling decision was a conscious attempt to place the commercial alongside a suitable programme, but complaints denounced the ad for being too graphic and offensive. Criticisms were then dismissed, as the ASA stated that the ad was unlikely to cause offence as long as it was scheduled adequately.

However, what is particularly interesting about this case is that relevant debates have been sparked by the current regulatory instability. Advertising rules for abortion and condom usage are currently under review, and proposals suggest such rules should be relaxed. Some stakeholders view this as a positive move towards reducing the rates of teenage pregnancy, and encouraging safe and responsible sexual activity among teenagers and young adults. Others, however, have suggested that pre-watershed condom ads will foster the premature sexualization of young people. The Catholic Church has been particularly critical of the loosening of such rules, and of proposals to have condom usage and pregnancy advice advertised on television. Newly appointed Catholic Archbishop Vincent Nichols is one such voice. He argues that current sex-related commercials are distasteful and degrading, as they represent casual and drunken sex that trivializes the 'appropriate' meaning of human sexuality. In his view, such adverts would be unlikely to reflect the psychological effects that an abortion can have in a woman's life. The Archbishop suggests that such adverts are very likely to commercialize sexual health and family planning, and to oversimplify abortion and its traumatic consequences.

Based on: Bates (2009);[63] Sweeney (2009)[64]

Advertising to children

Advertising to children is a controversial issue. Critics argue that children are especially susceptible to persuasion and that they therefore need special protection from advertising. Others counter by claiming that the children of today are remarkably streetwise and can look after themselves. They are also protected by parents who can counteract advertising influence to some extent. Many European countries have regulations that control advertising to children. For example, in Germany advertising specific types of toys is banned and in the UK alcohol advertising is controlled.[65] In Sweden, advertising to under-12s on terrestrial television stations is banned, and in Belgium and Australia advertising within children's programmes is limited.

Countries like the UK have a code of practice to control advertisements aimed at children. The code is designed to avoid the misleading presentation of products and may require advertisers to disclose product information. For example, when advertising toys, accurate information about their size, price and operation should be included.[66] An example of self-regulation at work was the dropping of an advertisement for a soft drink, which featured a gang of ginger-haired middle-aged men taunting a fat youth. The advertisement was withdrawn after numerous complaints were received contending that it encouraged bullying in schools.[67] Pepsi and McDonald's have also introduced voluntary restrictions on its advertising to children in response to rising levels of obesity in the USA and western Europe.[68]

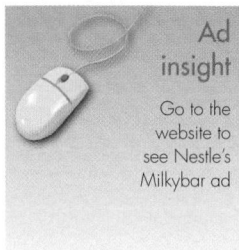

Ad insight

Go to the website to see Nestle's Milkybar ad

Most of the advertising to children is for food (cereals, snacks, sweets and food from fast food outlets), toys, clothes and entertainment products. The emphasis on convenience foods has been criticized for its potential effect on unhealthy eating. This has been countered partially by advertisements that advocate balanced diets and present nutritional information. Nevertheless, the question of whether children understand such information remains unresolved.[69]

Advertisements featuring toys, clothes and entertainment products have been criticized for promoting an acquisitive lifestyle and encouraging 'pester-power', whereby children request their parents to buy them such products, leading to family conflict. However, others point out that advertising may only be one factor in such conflict because some children's products sell well without advertising.[70]

Online LearningCentre

When you have read this chapter

log on to the Online Learning Centre at www.mcgraw-hill.co.uk/textbooks/jobber to explore chapter-by-chapter test questions, links and further online study tools for marketing.

Review

1 The role of advertising in the promotional mix

- Advertising is any paid form of non-personal communication of ideas or products in the prime media, i.e. television, the press, posters, cinema, and radio.
- It possesses strengths and limitations, and should be combined with other promotional tools to form an integrated marketing communications campaign.

2 The factors that affect the choice of the promotional mix

- These are resource availability and the cost of promotional tools, market size and concentration, customer information needs, product characteristics and push versus pull strategies.

3 The key characteristics of the major promotional tools
- Advertising: strong for awareness building, brand positioning, company and brand legitimization, but it is impersonal and inflexible, and has only a limited ability to close a sale.
- Personal selling: strong for interactivity, adaptability, the delivery of complex arguments, relationship building and the closing of the sale, but is costly.
- Direct marketing: strong for individual targeting, personalization, measurement, relationship building through periodic contact, low visibility to competitors, but response rates are often low and can cause annoyance.
- Internet promotion: strong for global reach, measurement, establishing a dialogue, quick changes to catalogues and prices, convenience and avoids arguments with salespeople, but impersonal and requires consumers to visit website.
- Sales promotion: strong on providing immediate incentive to buy but effects may be short term and can damage brand image.
- Publicity: strong on credibility, high readership but loss of control.

4 The communications process
- The communication process begins with the source encoding a message that is transmitted through media to the receiver who decodes. Noise (e.g. distractions) may prevent the message reaching the receiver. Feedback may be direct when talking to a salesperson or through marketing research.

5 The value of integrated marketing communications
- Integrated marketing communications is the concept by which companies coordinate their marketing communications tools to deliver a clear, consistent, credible and competitive message about the organization and its products.
- Its achievement can be hampered by office politics, and a high-ranking communications officer may be needed to see through its successful implementation.
- Its philosophy has led to the rise in media-neutral planning, which is the process of solving communications problems through an unbiased evaluation of all media.

6 The differences between strong and weak theories of how advertising works
- The strong theory of advertising considers advertising to be a powerful influence on consumers, increasing knowledge, changing attitudes, and creating desire and conviction, and as a consequence persuading people to buy brands.
- The weak theory of advertising considers advertising to be a much less powerful influence on consumers. It suggests that advertising may arouse awareness and interest, nudge some consumers towards trial, and then provide some reassurance and reinforcement after the trial.

7 How to develop advertising strategy: target audience analysis, objective setting, budgeting, message and media decisions, execution, and advertising evaluation
- Advertising decisions should not be taken in isolation but should be based on a clear understanding of marketing strategy, in particular positioning. Then the steps are as follows.
- Identify and understand the target audience: the audience needs to be defined and understood in terms of its motives and choice criteria.
- Define advertising objectives: communicational objectives are to create awareness, stimulate trial, position products in consumer's minds, correct misconceptions, remind and reinforce, and provide support for the salesforce.
- Set the advertising budget: options are the percentage of sales, affordability, matching competition, and objective and task methods.
- Message decisions: messages should be important to the target audience and communicate competitive advantages.

- Media decisions: two key decisions are the choice of media (e.g. television versus the press) and media vehicle (a particular newspaper or magazine).
- Execution: care should be taken to meet publication deadlines.
- Evaluation of advertising: three key questions are what, when and how to evaluate.

8 **How campaigns are organized, including advertising agency selection and payment systems**
- An advertiser has four organizational options:
  1 advertising can be developed directly in cooperation with the media
  2 an in-house advertising department can be created
  3 a full service advertising agency can be used
  4 a combination of in-house staff (or the full service agency) can be used for some functions and a specialist agency (media or creative) for others.

- Agency selection should begin with a clear definition of requirements. A shortlist of agencies should be drawn up and each briefed on the product and campaign. Selection will take place after each has made a presentation to the client.
- Agency payment can be by commission, fee or payment by results.

9 **Ethical issues in advertising.**
- There are potential problems relating to misleading advertising, advertising's influence on society's values and advertising to children.

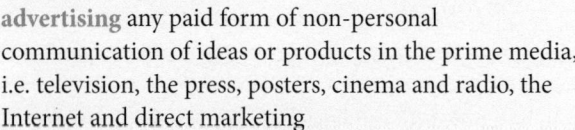

Key Terms

advertising any paid form of non-personal communication of ideas or products in the prime media, i.e. television, the press, posters, cinema and radio, the Internet and direct marketing

advertising agency an organization that specializes in providing services such as media selection, creative work, production and campaign planning to clients

advertising message the use of words, symbols and illustrations to communicate to a target audience using prime media

advertising platform the aspect of the seller's product that is most persuasive and relevant to the target consumer

direct marketing (1) acquiring and retaining customers without the use of an intermediary; (2) the distribution of products, information and promotional benefits to target consumers through interactive communication in a way that allows response to be measured

integrated marketing communications the concept that companies coordinate their marketing communications tools to deliver a clear, consistent, credible and competitive message about the organization and its products

Internet promotion the promotion of products to consumers and businesses through electronic media

media class decision the choice of prime media, i.e. the press, cinema, television, posters, radio, or some combination of these

media vehicle decision the choice of the particular newspaper, magazine, television spot, poster site, etc.

personal selling oral communication with prospective purchasers with the intention of making a sale

publicity the communication of a product or business by placing information about it in the media without paying for time or space directly

sales promotion incentives to customers or the trade that are designed to stimulate purchase

target audience the group of people at which an advertisement or message is aimed

strong theory of advertising the notion that advertising can change people's attitudes sufficiently to persuade people who have not previously bought a brand to buy it; desire and conviction precede purchase

weak theory of advertising the notion that advertising can first arouse awareness and interest, nudge some consumers towards a doubting first trial purchase and then provide some reassurance and reinforcement; desire and conviction do not precede purchase

Study Questions

1. Compare the situations where advertising and personal selling are more likely to feature strongly in the promotional mix.

2. Describe the strong and weak theories of how advertising works. Which theory is more likely to apply to the purchase of a car, and the purchase of a soap powder?

3. Within an advertising context, what is 'positioning in the mind of the consumer'? Using examples, discuss the alternative positioning options available to an advertiser.

4. Advertising has no place in the industrial marketing communications mix. Discuss.

5. Media class decisions should always be based on creative considerations, while media vehicle decisions should be determined solely by cost per thousand calculations. Do you agree?

6. Discuss the contention that advertising should be based on the skills of the creative team, not the statistics of the research department.

7. Describe the structure of a large advertising agency. Why should an advertiser prefer to use an agency rather than set up a full-service internal advertising department?

8. Discuss the advantages and limitations of developing pan-European advertising campaigns.

9. As a highly visible communication tool, advertising has its share of critics. What are their key concerns? How far do you agree or disagree with their arguments?

References

1. Murgatroyd, L. (2004) All Together Now, *Marketing Business*, March, 39.
2. Eagle, L. and P. J. Kitchen (2000) IMC, Brand Communications, and Corporate Cultures, *European Journal of Marketing* 34(5/6), 667–86.
3. Weissberg, T. (2008) One Message, Many Media, *Marketing Week*, 18 September, 31–4.
4. Bidlake, S. (2008) Goodwill to All Agencies, *Campaign*, 5 December, 3.
5. Anonymous (2005) Marketing Communications Awards, *Marketing*, June, 21.
6. Katz, E., M. Gurevitch and H. Haas (1973) On the Use of the Mass Media for Important Things, *American Sociological Review* 38, 164–81.
7. Crosier, K. (1983) Towards a Praxiology of Advertising, *International Journal of Advertising* 2, 215–32.
8. O'Donohoe, S. (1994) Advertising Uses and Gratifications, *European Journal of Marketing* 28(8/9), 52–75.
9. Wright, L. T. and M. Crimp (2003) *The Marketing Research Process*, London: Prentice-Hall, 180.
10. Jones, J. P. (1991) Over-Promise and Under-Delivery, *Marketing and Research Today*, November, 195–203.

11. Ehrenberg, A. S. C. (1992) Comments on How Advertising Works, *Marketing and Research Today*, August, 167–9.

12. Ehrenberg (1992) op. cit.

13. Jones (1991) op. cit.

14. Dall'Olmo Riley, F., A. S. C. Ehrenberg, S. B. Castleberry, T. P. Barwise and N. R. Barnard (1997) The Variability of Attitudinal Repeat-Rates, *International Journal of Research in Marketing* 14, 437–50.

15. Jones (1991) op. cit.

16. Ries, A. and J. Trout (2001) *Positioning: The Battle for your Mind*, New York: McGraw-Hill.

17. Aaker, D. A., R. Batra and J. G. Myers (1996) *Advertising Management*, New York: Prentice-Hall.

18. Grey, R. (2002) Fighting Talk, *Marketing*, 20 September, 26.

19. Piercy, N. (1987) The Marketing Budgeting Process: Marketing Management Implications, *Journal of Marketing* 51(4), 45–59.

20. Mustarde, S. (2008) Johnnie Walker: The Story Behind 'Keep Walking', *Campaign*, 14 November, 12.

21. In Ogilvy, D. (1987) *Ogilvy on Advertising*, London: Pan.

22. Ogilvy (1987) op. cit.

23. Silverman, G. (2005) Image is Everything in the Attention Wars, *Financial Times*, 18 January, 12.

24. Saatchi & Saatchi Compton (1985) *Preparing the Advertising Brief* 9.

25. Hall, M. (1992) Using Advertising Frameworks: Different Research Models for Different Campaigns, *Admap*, March, 17–21.

26. Lannon, J. (1991) Developing Brand Strategies across Borders, *Marketing and Research Today*, August, 160–7.

27. Tomkins, R. (1999) Images with the Power to Shock, *Financial Times*, 18 February, 10.

28. Elliott, R. (1997) Understanding Buyer Behaviour: Implications for Selling, in D. Jobber (ed.) *The CIM Handbook of Selling and Sales Strategy*, Oxford: Butterworth-Heinemann.

29. Syedain, H. (1992) Taking the Expert Approach to Media, *Marketing*, 4 June, 20–1.

30. Shepherd, I. (2005) Views from the Bridge, *Campaign*, 27 May, 4.

31. *Campaign* Report (1997) Global Review of Digital TV, *Campaign*, 30 May, 8–10.

32. See Furber, R. (2000) Early Start, *Marketing Week*, 9 March, 65–6; Reed, D. (2000) Rapid Response, *Marketing Week*, 25 May, 63–5.

33. Lee, J. (2008) Brand Content Faces Quality Test, *Marketing*, 23 April, 21.

34. Davies, O. (2002) Interactive TV is Set to Transform Ads Landscape, *Marketing*, 20 November, 28.

35. Ray, A. (2003) Press the Red Button, *Marketing Business*, April, 28–30.

36. Fletcher, D. (2005) Terms of Engagement, *Campaign*, 27 May, 11.

37. McCafferty, C. and J. Christie (2009) lastminute.com Dominates our Screens on 28th February with a UK Media First, Reuters.com, 17 February 2009 (retrieved 28 April 2009, from www.reuters.com/article/pressRelease/idUS153758+27-Feb-2009+MW20090227).

38. Tomkins, R. (1999) Reaching New Heights of Success, *Financial Times*, 28 May, 16.

39. Fitzsimmonds, C. (2008) Outdoor's Digital Future, *Campaign*, 18 July, 24–5.

40. Donnelly, A. (2008) Big Screen Draw, *Marketing*, 9 July, 19.

41. Hicks, R. (2005) Special Report: Radio, *Campaign*, 4 November, 26.

42. Croft, M. (1999) Listeners Keep Radio On Air, *Marketing Week*, 8 July, 30–1.

43. Anonymous (2005) Pay Per Sale, *Economist*, 1 October, 73.

44. Reid, A. (2005) Should Postar Move Faster?, *Campaign*, 21 October, 8.

45. See Fletcher, W. (1999) Independents May Have Had Their Day, *Financial Times*, 27 August, 15; Anonymous (2000) Star Turn, *Economist*, 11 March, 91.

46. Tomkins, R. (2001) Media Buyers Get Hitched and Attend Critical Mass, *Financial Times Creative Business*, 24 July, 2.

47. Jobber, D. and A. Kilbride (1986) How Major Agencies Evaluate TV Advertising in Britain, *International Journal of Advertising*, 5, 187–95.

48. Bell, E. (1992) Lies, Damned Lies and Research, *Observer*, 28 June, 46.

49. Wright and Crimp (2003) op. cit.

50. Jobber and Kilbride (1986) op. cit.

51. Curtis, J. (2002) Clients Speak Out on Agencies, *Marketing*, 28 March, 22–3.

52. Curtis, J. (2002) Agencies Speak Out on Clients, *Marketing*, 4 April, 20–1.

53. Singh, S. (2005) P&G Reads the Riot Act Over Client Conflict, *Marketing Week*, 4 August, 9.

54. Rhind-Tutt, S. (2009) Put a Positive Spin on Change, *Marketing Week*, 5 February, 14.

55. Smith, P. R. and J. Taylor (2004) *Marketing Communications: An Integrated Approach*, London: Kogan Page, 116.

56. Smith and Taylor (2004) op. cit.

57. Mead, G. (1992) Why the Customer is Always Right, *Financial Times*, 8 October, 17.

58. Dignam, C. (2002) The New Deal, *Financial Times Creative Business*, 13 August, 6.

59. Smith and Taylor (2004) op. cit.

60. See Tomkins, R. (1999) Getting a Bigger Bang for the Advertising Buck, *Financial Times*, 24 September, 17; Waters, R. (1999) P&G Ties Advertising Agency Fees to Sales, *Marketing Week*, 16 September, 1.

61. Stones, J. (2005) Toyota GB to Pay on Performance, *Marketing Week*, 29 April, 11.

62. Hudson, R. (2008) Engineered for Success, *Marketing*, 29 October, 22–3.

63. Bates, S. (2009) Catholic Archbishop Vincent Nichols Attacks Plans for TV Ads for Condoms, Guardian.co.uk, 10 April 2009 (retrieved 14 April 2009, from www.guardian.co.uk/world/2009/apr/10/contraception-ads-archbishop-westminster).

64. Sweeney, M. (2009) It's OK to Orgasm Before 11 pm, Rules Advertising Watchdog, Guardian.co.uk, 8 April 2009 (retrieved 14 April 2009, from www.guardian.co.uk/media/2009/apr/08/durex-ad-asa-11pm).

65. Schlegelmilch, B. (1998) *Marketing Ethics: An International Perspective*, London: International Thomson Business Press.

66. Oates, C., M. Blades and B. Gunter (2003) Marketing to Children, *Journal of Marketing Management* 19(4), 401–10.

67. Anonymous (2000) IPA Chief Denies Tango Ad Own Goal, *Marketing Week*, 9 March, 12.

68. Ward, A. and J. Grant (2005) PepsiCo Admits Curbing Adverts to Children, *Financial Times*, 28 February, 23; J. Simms (2008) From Light Touch to Iron Fist, *Marketing*, 30 July, 30–3.

69. Oates, Blades and Gunter (2003) op. cit.

70. Proctor, J. and M. Richards (2002) Word-of-Mouth Marketing: Beyond Pester Power, *International Journal of Advertising and Marketing to Children* 3(3), 3–11.

A Glass and a Half

Cadbury Gets the Love Back for Dairy Milk

a GLASS and a HALF FULL PRODUCTION

Introduction

The UK is Cadbury's biggest confectionery market. The company leads the chocolate market and holds a share of around 30 per cent of this market, ahead of privately owned Mars and Nestlé. Cadbury Dairy Milk has been around for over a century and is nothing short of a national treasure, enjoyed by young and old alike. Kate Harding, trade communications manager at Cadbury, comments 'Cadbury Dairy Milk has over 100 years of heritage and continues to be the number one chocolate brand in the UK, worth over £370m in retail sales volume'. However, no brand, no matter how popular, comfortable or comforting can afford to stand still. Keen to reinvigorate the brand, Cadbury approached Fallon London, an advertising agency, in March 2007 with a clear, concise brief: 'Get the love back.' According to a Fallon spokesperson, 'The client wanted the brand to be loved. I mean, people knew what Cadbury was about and all that but it needed to win people's hearts.' Cadbury wanted Fallon to create advertisements that would make people smile and offer enjoyment, the same enjoyment that people get from eating a bar of Cadbury Dairy Milk.

The year 2007 saw the birth of 'A Glass and a Half Full Productions' which is described as Cadbury's in-house production company in the UK. 'A Glass and a Half Full Productions' is actually an entire production company-style department within the Fallon advertising agency, devoted to this campaign. In the past few years, this production company has created three entertaining commercials for the Cadbury Dairy Milk brand: 'Gorilla' (launched in 2007), 'Airport Trucks' (aired in 2008) and 'Eyebrows' (launched in 2009). These pieces of entertainment, like Cadbury Dairy Milk, attempt to bring moments of joy and happiness into people's lives. According to Fallon, 'A Glass and a Half Full Productions' strive to create entertainment that is joyful, optimistic, magical, universal (in terms of age and sex), unexpected and deep (i.e. able to bear repeated viewing). This is delivered by producing extraordinary entertainment as well as extraordinary chocolate.

'Gorilla'

In 2007, Cadbury launched its first advertising campaign from the newly established 'A Glass and a Half Full Productions'—a platform created by Cadbury to showcase 'exceptional pieces of entertainment'. The 90-second advertisement, entitled 'Gorilla', was premiered during the season finale of *Big Brother* 2007. With the Phil Collins song 'In the Air Tonight' playing in the background, the advertisement opened with the title 'A Glass and a Half Full Productions presents' and then showed a gorilla's face, before panning out to reveal him sitting at a drum kit. As the music in the advertisement slowly built, the gorilla started to drum in perfect time to the song. As the 1980s song reached a climax, the scene faded out to be replaced by a picture of a Dairy Milk bar—the only reference to chocolate in the whole production.

This advertisement was different from previous Dairy Milk advertisements as there was no chocolate in the ad and there were no people demonstrating their experience of the product. The advertisement related the joy of playing drums to that of eating a Cadbury Dairy Milk chocolate bar. The advertisement represented a real gear shift for the brand, not only in the levels of expenditure, but also in the level of creativity. 'Gorilla' had crossed over from advertising to entertainment. Laurence Green, planning director at Fallon, the ad agency behind the ad, said 'Chocolate is about joy and pleasure. For years Cadbury had told us that it was generous, through the glass and a half strap-line. We thought, don't tell us how generous you are; show us. Don't tell us about joy; show us.

With total spend of about £6.2 million from Cadbury UK, the campaign included the TV advertisement, outdoor and print advertising, a digital campaign, PR and sponsorship. The ad was posted on YouTube on the same night as it first appeared on our TV screens. The campaign lit up YouTube, with nearly 500,000 views in the week after its release, and over 10 million views in total. Speaking about the campaign, Fallon's strategic planner stated, 'It ran as a TV commercial and almost immediately it became the most viewed UK TV commercial on YouTube.' The campaign also put the Phil Collins hit 'In the Air Tonight' back in the UK charts. Cadbury spokesperson Tony Billsborough said 'We have been amazed by the way the advert captured the public's imagination.'

Some excellent spoofs/remixes of the advertisement have appeared online (e.g. 50 Cent remix, ASkillz vs Cadbury Gorilla remix and the Cameo Word Up remix). The 'Gorilla' campaign helped Cadbury's chocolate sales grow by 7 per cent in 2007—30 per cent above the industry average of 5.2 per cent, and Cadbury's highest level of underlying sales growth for well over a decade. 'Gorilla' has won numerous awards, including the Epica d'Or for Film 2007, Gold at the British TV Advertising Awards 2008 and Gold at the Advertising Creative Circle Awards in 2008.

'Airport Trucks'

Keen to build on the success of the 'Gorilla' advertisement, A Glass and a Half Full Productions released its second production on 29 March 2008. This advertisement tells the story of the first ever airport truck race in history, seeing vehicles of all shapes and sizes take to an empty runway for the race of their lives. Each one of the trucks was 'pimped' to show its unique character. With everything from go-faster stripes to customized wheel trims, the trucks lined up on the starting line under a purple sky at dusk and raced to the music of Queen's 'Don't Stop Me Now'. The advertisement was first broadcast on British TV at a time when Heathrow airport chaos was still disrupting the journeys of thousands of passengers, and separating many from their bags. Like the 'Gorilla' ad, it soon became a favourite on YouTube as viewers wanted to view the latest ad from A Glass and a Half Full Productions.

'We've brought the high-speed excitement of a Hollywood car chase to these slow-moving airport trucks,' said Phil Rumbol, marketing director for Cadbury. 'It's a magical piece of film designed to bring a smile to your face.' This Dairy Milk advert shared the esoteric, wacky feel of its predecessor, and also boasted a cult soundtrack. Unfortunately for Cadbury, however, the 'Airport Trucks' ad did not achieve the same viral popularity as the award-winning 'Gorilla' ad.

On 5 September 2008, the 'Gorilla' advert was relaunched with a new soundtrack: Bonnie Tyler's 'Total Eclipse of the Heart'. Similarly, a version of the 'Airport Trucks' ad reappeared, using the Bon Jovi song 'Livin' on a Prayer'. Both remakes premiered once again during the finale of *Big Brother*, 2008.

▲ The 'Airport Trucks' TV advertisement.

▲ The 'Eyebrows' TV advertisement.

'Eyebrows'

In January 2009, Cadbury introduced a new A Glass and a Half Full Productions TV advertisement, entitled 'Eyebrows', which became the third in a trio of videos produced by the production company. The 60-second advertisement brought to life the story of a brother's and sister's moment of madness when backs are turned and they are left to their own devices. The advert opens with two siblings sitting in a traditional photographer's studio, waiting to have their portrait taken. When the photographer is called away by a ringing phone, the children launch into a choreographed eyebrow dance. The children produce a range of eyebrow dance moves to the sound of 'Don't Stop the Rock' by electro-funk superstar, Freestyle.

According to Phil Rumbol, marketing director for Cadbury, 'Over at a Glass and a Half Full Productions, we noticed the wriggly potential of eyebrows and thought we would have a bit of fun with them. Like the other productions, "Eyebrows" is all about losing yourself and embracing the moment of joy.' The 'Eyebrows' campaign was supported by a £3.7 million spend on TV advertising and a further £1 million on cinema advertising. In addition, the 'Eyebrows' campaign was also fully supported by a large digital, PR and point-of-sale campaign. The TV ad was very popular; it was quickly posted on YouTube and became a firm favourite.

Cadbury used the power of the web to support its TV advertising campaign. A Glass and a Half Full Productions hosted some mischievous online events, which Cadbury fans could take part in. As the TV ad was perfect for users to mimic the 'Eyebrows' dance themselves, an online campaign appeared to be the ideal environment for that to take place. On 27 February 2009, Cadbury launched an online campaign called 'JiveBrow '09' to support its Dairy Milk 'Eyebrows' activity, allowing people to record and share their own versions of the ad. For one day, JiveBrow (which was hosted by MSN and www.aglassandahalffullproductions.com) gave the British public a chance to take part in their own 'Eyebrows' production via webcam and have their high-brow facial moves displayed to millions online. JiveBrow '09 was a great success, with over 5500 people taking part in this online campaign. The 'Eyebrows' campaign also included a new digital feature in the campaign, called B-Brow, which acted like any other browser—allowing users to visit a website of their choice—but instead of just letting users view the webpage, it allowed them to draw dancing eyebrows all over it too!

From March 2009, Cadbury used specially created point-of-sale material for retailers, with dump bins that played the music from the ad. The point-of-sale material also displayed mirrors and wobbly eyebrows to create maximum theatre around the campaign in store. Because they carried through the 'Eyebrows' concept to the point-of-sale in-store with mirrors and captions based on the TV ad, this helped reinforce recognition of the brand. The 'Eyebrows' campaign was a huge success. It resulted in an increase in sales of the brand and proved very popular with the general public, and the campaign benefited from huge amounts of free publicity. If imitation is the sincerest form of flattery, Cadbury should be pleased. Various people have re-enacted the Cadbury 'Eyebrows' ad, while others have remixed it. For example, Lily Allen and the comedian Alan Carr took part in a spoof of the ad for the TV programme *The Sunday Night Project*.

Conclusion

Since 2007, Cadbury has adopted a new advertising approach that many view as critical to both the Cadbury Dairy Milk brand and the company. Cadbury decided not to focus on the chocolate in its advertisements, but instead to focus on entertaining the public. This led to the creation of the three memorable advertisements outlined above—'Gorilla', 'Airport Trucks' and 'Eyebrows'. All three advertisements incorporated the Cadbury trademark colour purple into the ads, and displayed the Cadbury Dairy Milk logo and slogan 'A Glass and a Half Full of Joy'. In addition, all three advertisements were supported by the award-winning A Glass and a Half Full Productions interactive website (www.aglassandahalffullproductions.com), where fans could view videos, download ringtones and wallpapers, play games, win prizes and create their own chocolate! All three ads embraced the popularity of viral advertising and used this very much to their advantage. All the ads were a huge hit on YouTube and on social networking sites, and became firm favourites among the online community. However, all three advertisements also had another common thread. They told the public nothing about Dairy Milk. Rather than using the chocolate as the main focal point, Cadbury decided to use emotional appeals to attract the public's attention. Many in the industry viewed this as a huge risk, but it is one that seems to have worked for Cadbury. A Glass and a Half Full Productions was the umbrella concept for all three advertisements. But where to from here? How can Cadbury now top the success of these three very successful advertisements? The public anxiously awaits more from A Glass and a Half Full Productions . . .

References

Based on: Anonymous (2007) Revealed: The Man Behind the Drum-Playing Gorilla Suit in the Cadbury Advertisement', Mailonline, 11 September; Benady, A. (2007) Advertising: Spot the Link Between a Gorilla and Chocolate, *Independent*, 14 May; Anonymous (2008) Cadbury Reveals a Glass and a Half Full Productions Gorilla Adverts Will Make a Return, *Talking Retail*, 6 September; Cadbury (2008) Cadbury Dairy Milk Unveils its Latest Glass and a Half Full Production, 28 March; Anonymous (2009) Cadbury Launches New Dairy Milk Glass and a Half Full, *Talking Retail*, 26 January; Bold, B. (2009) Cadbury Eyebrows Ad Goes Viral to the Tune of 4m Views, *Brand Republic*, 16 February; www.adobomagazine.com; http://www.dandad.org/inspiration/creativityworks/08/; www.photobox.co.uk; http://www.telegraph.co.uk; www.wikipedia.com.

Questions

1. View all three Cadbury Dairy Milk advertisements on YouTube. Describe and evaluate the advertising platform and the advertising objectives of these three ads. How are all three related?

2. Cadbury has relied very heavily on TV advertising for its 'A Glass and a Half Full Productions' advertisements. Comment on the advantages and disadvantages of TV advertising.

3. What role did viral advertising play in these advertising campaigns?

4. All three Cadbury advertisements have nothing to do with chocolate, yet people remember what the advertisements are for. Why is there no actual reference to chocolate in the advertisements? What makes the advertisements so memorable as Cadbury Dairy Milk advertisements?

This case was written by Marie O'Dwyer, Lecturer in Marketing, Waterford Institute of Technology, Ireland. Special thanks to Aideen Murphy, Cadbury Ireland, and Sandie Dilger, Cadbury UK.

White Horse Whisky

Developing a New Advertising Strategy

Market background

United Distillers & Vintners (UDV), the brand owner of Bell's and White Horse, is seeking to recruit a new generation of young drinkers to the whisky market. It has taken the view that this can be achieved by repositioning its White Horse brand so that it shakes free of the old-fashioned imagery currently associated with Scotch whisky. This will involve developing a marketing strategy and advertising campaign that will change the way White Horse is perceived by young people. UDV then intends to promote Bell's in a way that continues to appeal to mainstream, older, established whisky drinkers by continuing to reflect more traditional values.

The Scotch whisky market has been in decline for over 15 years. Drinking patterns generally have moved away from traditional dark spirits (such as rum and whisky) in favour of white spirits (vodka), wine and lagers. Each generation of new drinkers has been attracted to the marketing and promotion of chilled, long, lighter drinks. Brands from exotic countries that combine genuine authenticity with exciting contemporary images have enjoyed persistent growth.

Over time, the profile of whisky drinkers has gradually become older, within a base that is in itself declining (see Tables C26.1 and C26.2). The number of adults drinking whisky at least once a month has declined by around 900,000, and over half the remaining 3.9 million consumers are over 50 years old. The rate of recruitment of people in their twenties and thirties has declined over recent years.

Whisky has always been acknowledged as an 'acquired taste' that was unlikely to appeal to novice drinkers, but rather reflected a more mature palate. However, people are no longer making the transition to traditional dark spirits in anything like the numbers they did historically. Consumers no longer seem motivated to rise to the challenge of drinking traditional dark spirits (although they are still interested in trying new dark spirits as the growth in malt whisky and bourbon has demonstrated).

Blended whisky market (000-litre cases)	TABLE C26.1
2002	10,980
2003	10,090
2004	9,428
2005	9,659
2006	9,540
2007	8,595
2008	8,210

Profile of whisky drinkers			TABLE C26.2
Age	Dec. 1988 %	Dec. 1998 %	Dec. 2008 %
18–24	11	10	9
25–34	19	15	15
35–49	27	24	24
50+	44	50	52
Base 000s	4906	4626	3997

Brand share				TABLE C26.3
	2005 %	2006 %	2007 %	2008 %
Bell's	18.9	17.7	17.7	17.0
Teachers	7.4	7.5	6.9	6.2
Famous Grouse	13.4	12.8	12.4	12.9
White Horse	3.1	2.7	2.9	2.3
Grant's	5.3	5.3	5.1	4.8
Whyte & Mackay	4.4	4.6	4.7	4.1
Own-label	18.3	18.9	19.0	18.9
Cheapest on display	8.7	9.1	10.8	12.8

The leading brand has consistently remained Bell's (see Table C26.3), but the total share of all the brands is consistently being eroded by less expensive and less famous alternatives. So, in addition to operating in a market that is in overall decline, brands are losing their share of that market.

White Horse whisky is available in some off-licences and in supermarkets like Waitrose and Sainsbury's, where it is among a broad competitive set.

The current image of whisky

UDV commissioned qualitative research among 18–25 years olds (typically still experimenting) and 25–30 year olds (usually becoming established in their repertoire) to try and understand what the barriers to drinking whisky are and therefore how it might go about challenging these beliefs through its presentation of White Horse.

This research found that there were both product and image barriers to whisky drinking. It is believed to be a strong and overpowering spirit, with a potent bitter smell and 'rough' or 'fiery' taste that will linger unpleasantly after drinking. It is also universally described as a spirit that is very difficult to mix. Repertoires are usually restricted to 'ordinary' mixes such as ice, water, ginger and lemonade. This makes it more difficult to make whisky accessible in a more dilute form, which is typically how young people learn to acquire a taste for spirits; it is rare to be able to take them neat from the beginning.

For some, these product barriers can be seen as an initiation test, with the reward being the acknowledgement of being a 'real man'.

Current whisky imagery is seen as outdated and largely irrelevant. It elicits tired, safe old images of tartan, hills, heather and glens, lochs, bagpipers, open fires, old men drinking on their own, and so on—which are all considered to have once been targeted at their parents or grandparents. These images are not felt to reflect the more authentic, real-life images of Scotland and its rich heritage. Films such as *Braveheart* and political moves to give Scotland greater independence are all areas of much greater interest, and offer more compelling images of the dignity and depth of Scotland's rich history.

The consumer

This research project also investigated the values of young people generally, not just with respect to whisky. The findings were as follows.

- Today's young people view balance as a necessity to successful life. They are motivated by success in their desired careers, but the focus for them must also be on enjoyment and escapism in their spare time. They are materialistic, but in a less aggressive way than the young people of the Thatcherite 1980s. To some extent, an environmental awareness and the need to treat and respect the world we live in have softened this.

- The 1990s and 2000s also brought a shift towards honesty and authenticity—a move away from the contrived, lifestyle-orientated 1980s. Being true to oneself has been identified as being important. Optimism was also in evidence, as it is with many young people who have not been hardened by the reality of life.

- They appreciate quality, sincerity and unpretentiousness. This reflects a going-back-to-basics mentality. They also consider originality, intelligence and a degree of irreverence (or not taking oneself too seriously) to be particularly important. In sum, 'less is more'.
- Humour is seen to be an important vehicle for facing up to the realities of life. Humour that is self-deprecating, subtle and self-referential is particularly liked. Honesty and insight is also appreciated because it credits the viewer with some intelligence.
- The values associated with young people today are also tinged with a degree of vulnerability. The recent recession has made people recognize that jobs are not for life and that they might underachieve in their lives.

White Horse

White Horse whisky was created in 1890 by Peter Mackie, one of the best-known whisky blenders and distillers of his day. He named it after one of Edinburgh's most famous coaching inns: The White Horse Cellar. Indeed, the brand logo reflects the pub sign design. In its distinctive, modernized, squat bottle, the brand sells for £16.99 per litre, a price below that of Bell's (£18.49) and Teachers (£17.79), but above own-label (e.g. Waitrose at £14.99).

// Current whisky imagery elicits tired, safe old images of tartan, hills, heather and glens, lochs, bagpipers, open fires, old men drinking on their own. //

Yorkshire farmers have always been particularly attached to the brand and created the very smooth and drinkable 'whisky milk'. This consists of a tumbler made up of half old milk and half White Horse whisky. A favourite way to wind down at the end of a hard day. Alternatively, the brand mixes very well with ginger ale or orange juice.

It is many years since the brand had any advertising support, with most of UDV's effort being behind Bell's. However, it is recognized that the successful targeting of a new generation of young consumers is vital to the future of the whisky market. The relaxation of the voluntary code, whereby whisky brands may now be advertised on TV, represents a particular opportunity.

Marketing objective

UDV intends to relaunch White Horse whisky. Its aim is to achieve a brand share of 6 per cent in three years. It is expected that 60 per cent of the brand's consumers should be under 50 years of age by the time of the launch.

The task

Each syndicate must come up with an advertising strategy based on a budget level of £3 million in the first year of advertising. For the purpose of the exercise, in terms of media, you are asked to consider only what your strategy will be (i.e. which target audience should be reached, using which type of media and when), which is the role fulfilled by a media planner, often in conjunction with the creative agency team. You will not be asked to cost out the plan, and will not be given costings for the various media. A simple ratio is included below.

The advertising strategy must answer the following questions.

1 What are the advertising objectives?
2 Who exactly are the people the advertising must affect/reach?
3 What is the main message the advertising must put across and what evidence can be used to support that message?
4 What do we want people to think/feel after seeing the advertising?
5 What should the style of advertising be?
6 Where should the advertising appear (i.e. TV, newspapers, magazines, posters, radio, etc.)? Which would be the primary vehicle and which the secondary support? What percentage of the £3 million would you allocate to which media and why?

Issues to consider when developing your media strategy

Today, most creative agencies use a media agency to plan and buy media. The media agency specializes both in understanding how consumers 'consume' media (and therefore which media are most effective in reaching particular audiences) and in being able to negotiate the best-value schedule from the ever-expanding selection of media opportunities. The average person in Britain today is exposed to around 2500 advertising messages a week, so optimum targeting of the media chosen and cut-through of the message displayed are essential.

Consider what target audience can achieve the advertising objectives you have decided upon; then consider what media that target might 'consume' and when might be the most propitious moment to 'approach' them in that medium. Consider both time of day as well as seasonality, and what their activities might be while viewing the medium as this will impact on their frame of mind when seeing the advertising message. You might feel that one medium is not sufficient and that you need to convey your message using a multi-layered effect (e.g. television with direct response, posters with radio, Internet banners with sales promotion, etc.). Consider where and when they can buy the brand, and how this might affect the media chosen. Most types of media are segmented (e.g. different press titles or TV programmes can reach different audiences), so consider a typical example to clarify your answer.

Think about what sort of message you wish to promote. Do you need to explain your positioning and be able to use a lot of words, or is a simple visual able to convey your message? This will dictate whether press or posters, for example, would be most appropriate.

Allow a notional 10 per cent cost for creative production for each medium that you choose.

Use your own consumption of different media to guide you in your media choice, and then consider whether someone in a different consumer age group would react differently and why.

Note

All figures in the tables in this case are indicative of a real-life situation.

The author of the book is grateful to Ann Murray Chatterton, Director of Training and Development at the Institute of Practitioners in Advertising, for permission to publish this case.

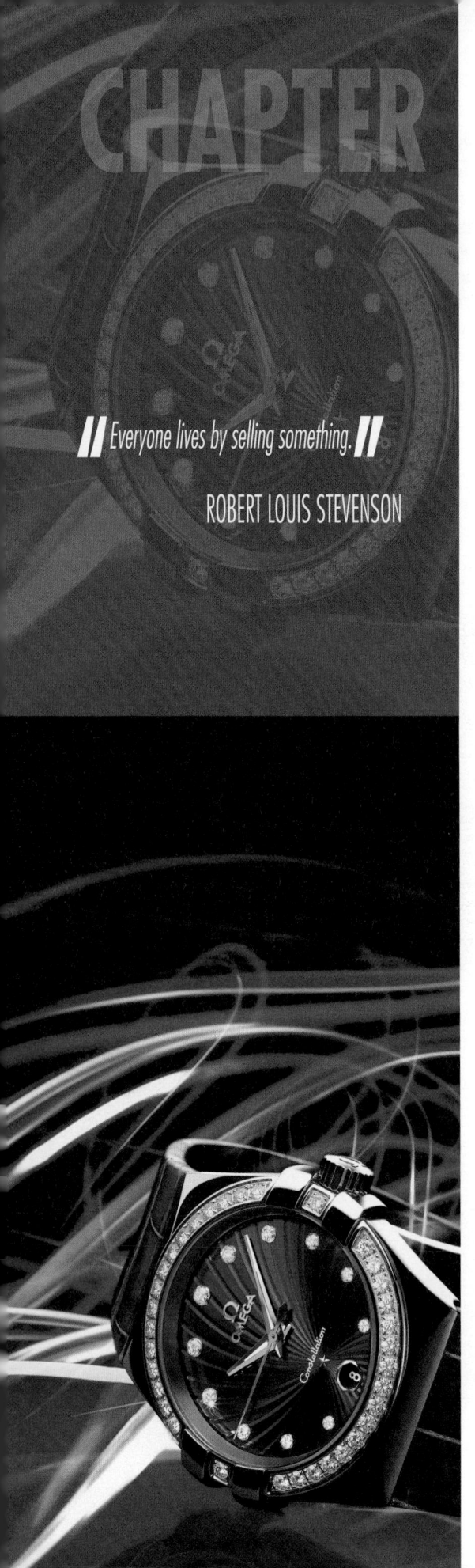

CHAPTER 14

Personal selling and sales management

"Everyone lives by selling something."

ROBERT LOUIS STEVENSON

LEARNING OBJECTIVES

After reading this chapter, you should be able to:

1 describe the environmental and managerial forces affecting sales

2 discuss the characteristics of modern selling

3 explain how to prepare for selling

4 discuss the stages in the selling process

5 describe the tasks of sales management

6 explain how to design a salesforce

7 explain how to manage a salesforce

8 discuss key account management

9 discuss ethical issues in personal selling and sales management

Personal selling is the marketing task that involves face-to-face contact with a customer. Unlike advertising, promotion, sponsorship and other forms of non-personal communication, personal selling permits a direct interaction between buyer and seller. This two-way communication means that the seller can identify the specific needs and problems of the buyer and tailor the sales presentation in the light of this knowledge. The particular concerns of the buyer can also be dealt with on a one-to-one basis.

This flexibility comes only at a cost. The cost of a car, travel expenses and sales office overheads can mean that the total annual bill for a field salesperson is often twice the level of their salary. In business-to-business marketing, over 70 per cent of the marketing budget is usually spent on the salesforce. This is because of the technical nature of the products being sold, and the need to maintain close personal relationships between the selling and buying organizations.

However, the nature of the personal selling function is changing. Organizations are reducing the size of their salesforces in the face of greater buyer concentration, moves towards centralized buying, and recognition of the high costs of maintaining a field sales team. The concentration of buying power into fewer hands has also fuelled the move towards relationship management, often through key account selling. This involves the use of dedicated sales teams that service the accounts of major buyers. As the commercial director of HP Foods said:

> Twenty years ago we had between 70 and 100 salespeople. The change in the retail environment from small retailers to central warehouses and supermarkets has meant a big change in the way we communicate with our customers. Instead of sending salespeople out on the road, we now collect a large proportion of our sales by telephone or computer. We have replaced the traditional salesforce with 12 business development executives, who each have a small number of accounts dealing with customers at both national and regional levels.[1]

Selling and sales management are experiencing a period of rapid change. The next section explores the major forces at work.

Environmental and Managerial Forces Affecting Sales

A number of major behavioural, technological and managerial forces are influencing how selling and sales management is and will be carried out.[2] These are listed in Table 14.1.

Behavioural forces

Just as customers adapt to their changing environment, so the sales function has to adapt to these forces, which are (i) rising customer expectations, (ii) customer avoidance of buyer–seller negotiations, (iii) the expanding power of major buyers, (iv) globalization of markets and (v) fragmentation of markets.

Rising customer expectations

As consumers experience higher standards of product quality and service so their expectations are fuelled to expect even higher levels in the future. This process may be accelerated by experiences abroad, and new entrants to industries (possibly from abroad) that set new standards of excellence. As the executive of the customer satisfaction research firm J. D. Power explained: 'What makes customer satisfaction so difficult to achieve is that you constantly raise the bar and extend the finish line. You never stop. As your customers get better treatment, they demand better treatment.' The implication for salespeople is that they must accept that both consumer and organizational buyer expectations for product quality, customer service and value will continue to rise, and that they must respond to this challenge by advocating and implementing continuous improvements in quality standards.

Forces influencing selling and sales management practices	TABLE **14.1**
Behavioural forces	
Rising customer expectations Customer avoidance of buyer–seller negotiations Expanding power of major buyers Globalization of markets Fragmentation of markets	
Technological forces	
Salesforce automation • Laptop computers and software • Electronic data interchange • Desktop videoconferencing • Global positioning systems (GPSs)	
Virtual sales offices	
Electronic sales channels	
Internet • Television home shopping	
Managerial forces	
Direct marketing • Direct mail	
Telemarketing • Computer salespeople • Customer relationship management (CRM) systems	
Blending of sales and marketing • Intranets	
Qualifications for salespeople and sales managers	
Sources: updated from Anderson, R. (1996) Personal Selling and Sales Management in the New Millennium, *Journal of Personal Selling and Sales Management* 16(4), 17–32; Jones, E., S. P. Brown, A. A. Zoltners and B. A. Weitz (2005) The Changing Environment of Selling and Sales Management, *Journal of Personal Selling & Sales Management* 25(2), 105–11.	

Technological advances have created new, higher customer expectations. The existence of the Internet means that customers expect salespeople calling on them for the first time (and after) to be familiar with their firms, its products and personnel. Improvements in communication through e-mail and the Internet have increased customer expectations regarding response time to their requests and enquiries.[3] Furthermore, customers are increasingly demanding customized solutions to their problems, which often takes the form of buying a system rather than individual components.

As corporate scandals appear in the media, customers are expecting greater transparency in company operations and more ethical practices. Consequently, sales management staff have a responsibility to train their sales teams in ethical selling practices, and salespeople need to be careful about the arguments they use and the inducements they offer when attempting to secure a sale.

Customer avoidance of buyer–seller negotiations

Studies have shown that the purchase of a car is the most anxiety-provoking and least satisfying experience in retail buying.[4] Some car salespeople are trained in the art of negotiation, supported by high-pressure sales tactics. Consequently, customers have taken to viewing the purchase as an ordeal to be tolerated rather than a pleasurable occasion to be savoured. In response, some car companies have moved to a 'fixed price, no pressure and full book value for the trade-in' approach. This was used for the successful launch of the Saturn by General Motors in the USA.

Expanding power of major buyers

The growing dominance of major players in many sectors (notably retailing) is having a profound influence on selling and sales management. Their enormous purchasing power means that they are able to demand and get special services, including special customer status (key account management), just-in-time inventory control, category management and joint funding of promotions. Future success for salespeople will be dependent on their capabilities to respond to the increasing demands of major customers and to coordinate the efforts of selling and technical people in their firm to meet their needs.[5]

Globalization of markets

As domestic markets saturate, companies are expanding abroad to achieve sales and profit growth. Large companies such as Coca-Cola, Colgate-Palmolive and Avon Products now earn the largest proportion of their revenues in foreign markets. The challenges include the correct balance between expatriate and host country sales personnel, adapting to different cultures, lifestyles and languages, competing against world-class brands, and building global relationships with huge customers based in many countries. For example, 3M has a variety of global strategic accounts from industrial high-tech (Motorola, Hewlett-Packard, IBM, Texas Instruments) to original equipment manufacturers in electronics, appliances, automotive, electrical, aerospace, furniture, consumer products and healthcare.[6] A major challenge for such a transnational corporation is the coordination of global sales teams, which sell to the Nortels, Samsungs, Siemens, or P&Gs of this world, where the customer may be located in over 20 countries and requires special terms of sale, technical support, pricing and customization of products. This complexity means that strategic account managers require both enhanced teamwork and coordination skills to ensure that customers receive top-quality service.

As companies expand into new overseas markets, there is a need to understand different cultural expectations and to give thought to various cultural issues (e.g. *Guanxi* networks in China). Ethical differences are also important considerations—what is ethical in one country may be unethical in another.[7]

Fragmentation of markets

Driven by differences in income levels, lifestyles, personalities, experiences and race, markets are fragmenting to form market segments. This means that markets are likely to become smaller, with an increasing range of brands marketed to cater for the diverse requirements (both functional and psychological) of customers. Marketing and sales managers need to be adept at identifying changes in consumer tastes, and developing strategies that satisfy an increasingly varied and multicultural society.

Technological forces

Three major forces are at play: (i) salesforce automation, (ii) virtual sales offices and (iii) electronic sales channels.

Salesforce automation

Salesforce automation includes laptop and palmtop computers, mobile phones, fax machines, e-mail and sophisticated sales-orientated software, which aid such tasks as journey and account planning, recruitment and selection, and evaluation of sales personnel. Wireless technology has proven useful in improving communications between the salesperson and head office. It is typically used in two ways: (i) a salesperson's laptop is synchronized with head office by connecting a mobile phone to the laptop; (ii) a personal digital assistant is used by the salesperson to transmit sales information to, and receive reports from, head office.[8] In addition, electronic data interchange (EDI) and the Internet provide computer links between manufacturers and resellers (retailers, wholesalers and distributors) allowing the exchange of information. For example, purchase orders, invoices, price quotes, delivery dates, reports and promotional information can be exchanged. Technological innovations have also made possible desktop videoconferencing, enabling sales meetings, training and customer interaction to take place without the need for people to leave their offices. Finally, the use of global positioning systems (GPSs) has assisted in the task of finding locations, thus saving time for salespeople.

Virtual sales office

Improved technology has also encouraged the creation of virtual offices, allowing sales personnel to keep in contact with head office, customers and co-workers. The virtual office may be the home or even a car. This can mean large cost and time savings, and enhanced job satisfaction for sales personnel, who are spared some of the many traffic jams that are part of the life of a field salesperson.

Electronic sales channels

The fastest-growing electronic sales channel is undoubtedly the Internet, which is predicted to affect selling and sales management in the following ways.[9]

- *Reduction in salesforce size*: the benefits of the Internet, such as low cost and customized transactions, are expected to reduce the size of salesforces. The formation of e-marketplaces has led to business-to-business purchases, which previously would have been the province of the salesforce, being moved online. For example, the US defence contractor United Technologies bought $450 million worth of metals, motors and other products from an e-marketplace in one year and got prices around 15 per cent lower than previously. Furthermore, companies are moving to the Internet to communicate and sell to smaller accounts.
- *Key account management*: by using the Internet to service small customers and deal with some of the details of key account activities, it can free key account managers to focus on long-term relationship building. For example, the Dell Computer salesforce benefits greatly from the customized information provided to its key account customers through the Premier Page website. By using its customized online Premier Page, Dell's biggest customers can configure PCs, pay for them, track their delivery status, and get access to immediate technical support.
- *Sales processes*: the Internet is smoothing communications between sellers and buyers through the use of e-mail and well-designed company websites. In this way, customers can be made aware of shipping dates, inventory status, and other information traditionally delivered in person by the salesforce. The Internet is also an invaluable tool for the salesperson to use to find information that can be used to support sales presentations.
- *Remote working*: Sales staff can now access their company's internal network through the Internet, using a technology called a Virtual Private Network (VPN). The VPN links remote home computers and laptops into a wider 'virtual' network, using the Internet. This information cannot be viewed by others as the VPN encrypts all data. Field staff have

access to real-time information and can update company files and documents instantaneously (e.g. viewing the latest customer details prior to a sales visit).

ASPs (or application service providers) are services that allow every company worker (with appropriate rights) access to the 'same' application and related information, regardless of where they are in the world. All that is needed is Internet access. Providers like Salesforce.com (www.salesforce.com) rent the use of their application to companies. Company sales staff can update customer records as they make client calls and everyone in the company can then view and use the same central information (stored in salesforce.com databanks in the USA).

VPN and ASPs are gaining wide acceptance in allowing companies to integrate the 'remote worker' more fully into the organization. Mobile technologies, like 3G (third generation mobile phones, first launched in the UK by Hutchison 3G), have yet to gain acceptance but promise even greater benefits through connecting field staff 'on the move'.[10,11,12]

One Internet innovation that is allowing the direct selling of products without the need for a salesforce is the development of 'mini-sites', as Digital Marketing 14.1 discusses.

14.1 Digital Marketing

Selling in Niche Markets: Mini-Sites

Internet marketing gurus are constantly creating innovative online marketing initiatives, which many claim are easy to use, guarantee online sales and quickly make money. One such initiative is 'mini-sites'. These are websites of one to four pages that help build targeted e-mail lists, create and drive traffic to larger websites and generate sales. Creators of mini-sites produce websites with one specific aim: to sell products. This product might be anything from digital books (e-books) to online training courses and audio programmes. The main point is that the originator of the site aims at a highly targeted niche market. The mini-site acts as an order-getter by persuading customers to make a direct purchase in a very structured but innovative manner. Initially, the customer is invited to sign up to receive free information, which could be about any topic from how to survive the credit crunch to how to lose weight permanently. In return for their name and e-mail address, the potential customer receives free information, which could be in the form of handy hints and tips, free articles and links to other websites. The next step is to develop the relationship and, in doing so, move the customer closer to the actual sale. Over a short time period, the potential customer will receive all sorts of free and potentially useful information. The staged delivery of information also helps to build a consumer's trust in the supplier's messages and promises.

The next step in the process is for the mini-site to do the job of selling the product. The final communication will offer potential customers the opportunity to buy the product. In the case of the ebook, it could be a no-nonsense guide to retailing, especially designed to help independent retailers survive the credit crunch. The aim is to ensure that, at this stage in the relationship, the customer has had sufficient information to take them through the evaluation stages of the purchasing process to the point at which they are ready to take action. Mini-sites are being used increasingly to sell business training products as well as products aimed at consumer markets.

Another emerging channel is also worthy of mention, as it will reduce the need for field salesforces. This is television home shopping, where viewers watch cable television presenters promote anything from jewellery to consumer electronics and order by telephone. In effect, the presenter is the salesperson.

Managerial forces

Managers are responding to changes in the environment by developing new strategies to enhance effectiveness. These include: (i) employing direct marketing techniques,

(ii) improving the blend between sales and marketing, and (iii) encouraging salespeople to gain professional qualifications.

Direct marketing techniques

The increasing role of direct marketing is reflected in the growth of direct mail and telemarketing activities. However, a third emerging change is the use of computer stations in US retail outlets to replace traditional salespeople. Although in Europe the use of computer-assisted sales in car showrooms has begun with the employment of kiosks where customers can gather product and price information, the process has moved a stage further in the USA, where several Ford dealerships have installed computer stations that fully replace salespeople. Customers can compare features of competitive models, calculate running costs, compute monthly payments, and use the computer to write up the order and telephone it to the factory—all without the intervention of a salesperson. Finally, customer relationship management (CRM) systems, by means of a common database that all customer-facing personnel can access, permit a unified message and image to be presented to customers. A specific application of CRM systems is in account management, where information such as contact names, telephone numbers, e-mail, type of business, purpose and dates of meetings/telephone calls, status of customer and details of previous orders is stored, permitting easy access by a range of people, including field salespeople and call centre staff. Further, CRM technology allows salespeople to provide company and product information, video material and testimonials, all at the click of a laptop button.

Blending sales and marketing

Although the development of effective relationships between sales and marketing personnel is recognized by all, often, in practice, blending the two functions into an effective whole is hampered by, among other things, poor communication. The establishment of intranets, which are similar to the Internet except that they are proprietary company networks that link employees, suppliers and customers through their PCs, can improve links and information exchange. Intranets are used for such diverse functions as e-mail, team projects and desktop publishing. Clearly, their use can enhance the effectiveness of a field salesforce that requires fast access to rapidly changing information such as product specifications, competitor news and price updates, and allows the sharing of information between sales and marketing.

Professional qualifications

Finally, sales management is responding to the new challenges by recognizing the importance of training and professional qualifications. In the UK, the Chartered Institute of Marketing (CIM) offers the following sales qualifications: the Certificate and Diploma in Professional Sales, the Advanced Certificate in Key Account Management, and the Advanced Certificate in Sales Management. The aim is to enhance salespeople's and sales managers' professionalism, skills and competences.

Next, we shall examine the characteristics of modern selling, and the process and techniques of personal selling.

Characteristics of Modern Selling

In today's competitive environment, a salesforce must have a wide range of skills to compete successfully. Gone are the days when salespeople required simple presentational and closing skills to be successful. The characteristics of the job today (illustrated in Fig. 14.1) require a wide array of skills; these will be identified in the next section. In this part of the

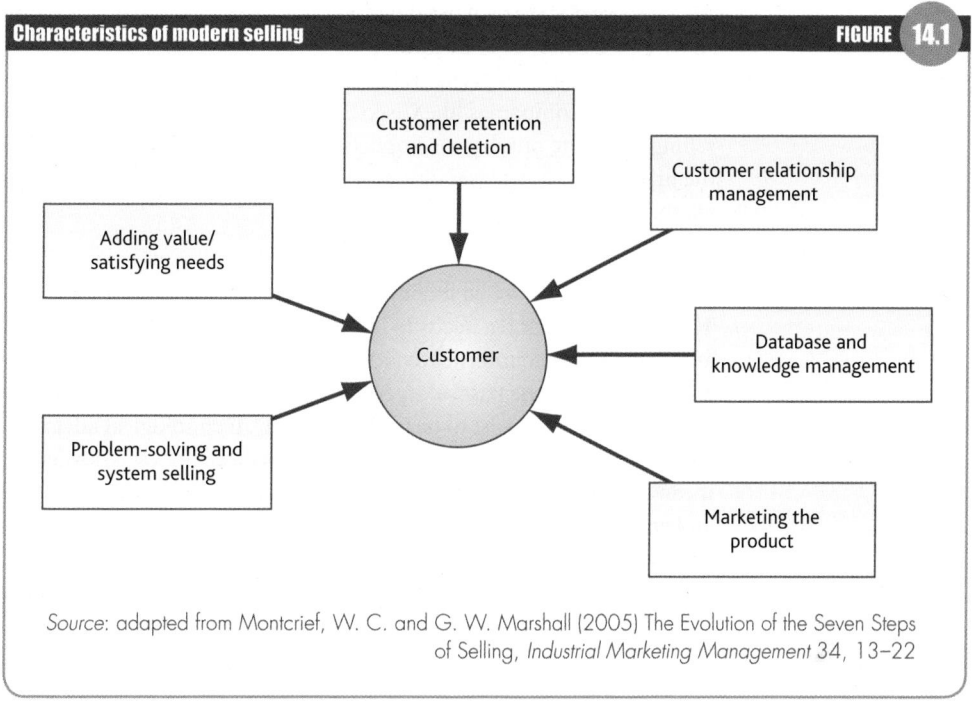

Characteristics of modern selling   FIGURE 14.1

Source: adapted from Montcrief, W. C. and G. W. Marshall (2005) The Evolution of the Seven Steps of Selling, *Industrial Marketing Management* 34, 13–22

book we discuss the characteristics of modern selling. Without such an understanding salespeople will be ill equipped to tackle the job.

Customer retention and deletion

Many companies find that 80 per cent of their sales come from 20 per cent of their customers. This means that it is vital to devote considerable resources to retaining existing high-volume, high-potential and highly profitable customers. Key account management has become an important form of sales organization because it means that a salesperson or sales team can focus their efforts on one or a few major customers.

At the other end of the spectrum, companies are finding that some small customers actually cost the organization money. This is because servicing and distribution products to these customers may push costs beyond the revenue generated. This may mean a change to telemarketing as a means of servicing their requirements and taking orders, or dropping them altogether.

Customer relationship management

The emphasis on customer retention has led to an increasing focus on customer relationship management. Customer relationship management requires that the salesforce focuses on the long term and not simply on closing the next sale.[13] The emphasis should be on creating win/win situations with customers so that both parties to the interaction gain and want to continue the relationship. For major customers, relationship management may involve setting up dedicated teams to service the account and maintain all aspects of the business relationship.

The focus moves from order taking and order making to strategic customer management.[14] The challenge is to reposition sales as a core element of a firm's competitiveness, where the sales organization is closely integrated into marketing strategy and planning.[15] This process places the customer at the centre of the company's focus, with the sales organization charged with taking a strategic view of designing and implementing superior customer relationships.[16] This requires sales management to work towards the total integration of how customer relationships are designed, established, managed and sustained. For example, companies like Cisco Systems have developed sales strategies that use personal selling when the purchase is important and complicated, and the decision uncertain—usually the first sale to a customer or a new application—leaving subsequent purchases to be made via the Internet.[17]

Database and knowledge management

The modern salesforce needs to be trained in the use and creation of customer databases, and how to use the Internet to aid the sales task (e.g. finding customer and competitor information). In the past salespeople recorded customer information on cards and sent in orders through the post to head office. Today, technological advances such as e-mail, mobile phones and videoconferencing have transformed the way knowledge is transferred. Laptops mean that salespeople can store customer and competitor information, make presentations and communicate with head office electronically. Furthermore, information supplied by the company, such as catalogues and price lists, can be held electronically.

Marketing the product

The modern salesperson is involved in a much broader range of activities than simply planning and making a sales presentation. Indeed, face-to-face presentations can now sometimes be substituted by information presented on web pages, and e-mail attachments that can give the customer up-to-date information on many topics quicker, more comprehensively and in a more time-convenient manner than many face-to-face interactions.[18] The role of the salesperson is expanding to participate in marketing activities such as product development, market development and the segmentation of markets, as well as other tasks that support or complement marketing activities, such as database management, provision and analysis of information, and assessing market segments.[19]

Problem-solving and system selling

Much of modern selling, particularly in business-to-business situations, is based upon the salesperson acting as a consultant, who works with the customer to identify problems, determine needs, and propose and implement effective solutions.[20] This approach is fundamentally different from the traditional view of the salesperson as a smooth, fast talker who breezes in to see a customer, persuades them to buy and walks away with an order. Modern selling often involves multiple calls, the use of a team-selling approach and considerable analytical skills. Further, customers are increasingly looking for a systems solution rather than the buying of an individual product. This means, for example, that to sell door handles to a company like Ford a supplier must be able to sell a door *system* that includes door handles, locking and opening devices, as well as having a thorough knowledge of door technology, and the ability to suggest to Ford solutions to problems that may arise.

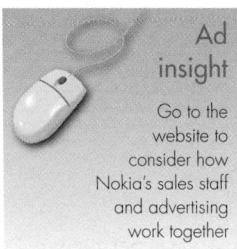

Ad insight

Go to the website to consider how Nokia's sales staff and advertising work together

Satisfying needs and adding value

The modern salesperson must have the ability to identify and satisfy customer needs. Some customers do not recognize that they have a need. It is the salesperson's job in such situations to stimulate need recognition. For example, a customer may not realize that a machine in the production process has low productivity compared to newer, more technologically advanced machines. The salesperson's job will be to make the customer aware of the problem in order to convince him/her that they have a need to modernize the production process. In so doing, the salesperson will have added value to the customer's business by reducing costs, and created a win/win situation for both his/her company and the customer.

14.1 Pause for Thought

Given these characteristics, how well do your skills match the requirements for selling in today's competitive marketplace?

Personal Selling Skills

Many people's perception of a salesperson is of a slick, fast-talking confidence trickster devoted to forcing unwanted products on innocent customers. Personal experience will tell the reader that this is unrealistic in a world of educated consumers and professional buyers. Success in selling comes from implementing the marketing concept when face to face with customers, not denying it at the very point when the seller and buyer come into contact. The sales interview offers an unparalleled opportunity to identify individual customer needs and match behaviour to the specific customer that is encountered.[21] Indeed, research has shown that such customer-orientated selling is associated with higher levels of salesforce performance.[22]

Research has shown that, far from using high-pressure selling tactics, success is associated with:[23]
- asking questions
- providing product information, making comparisons and offering evidence to support claims
- acknowledging the viewpoint of the customer
- agreeing with the customer's perceptions
- supporting the customer
- releasing tension
- having a richer, more detailed knowledge of customers
- increased effort
- confidence in one's own abilities.

All these findings are in accord with the marketing concept.

In order to develop personal selling skills it is useful to distinguish seven phases of the selling process (see Fig. 14.2). These phases need not occur in the order shown. Objections may be raised during the presentation or negotiation, and a trial close may be attempted at any point during the presentation if buyer interest is high. Furthermore, negotiation may or may not take place, or may occur during any of the stages. As Moncrief and Marshall report:[24]

> The evolved selling process assumes that the salesperson typically will perform the various steps of the process in some form, but the steps (phases) do not occur for each sales call. Rather, they occur over time, accomplished by multiple people within the selling firm, and not necessarily in any sequence.

> Each of these phases will now be discussed.

Preparation
Preparation before a sales visit can reap dividends by enhancing confidence and performance when face to face with the customer. Some situations cannot be prepared for—the unexpected

The selling process FIGURE 14.2

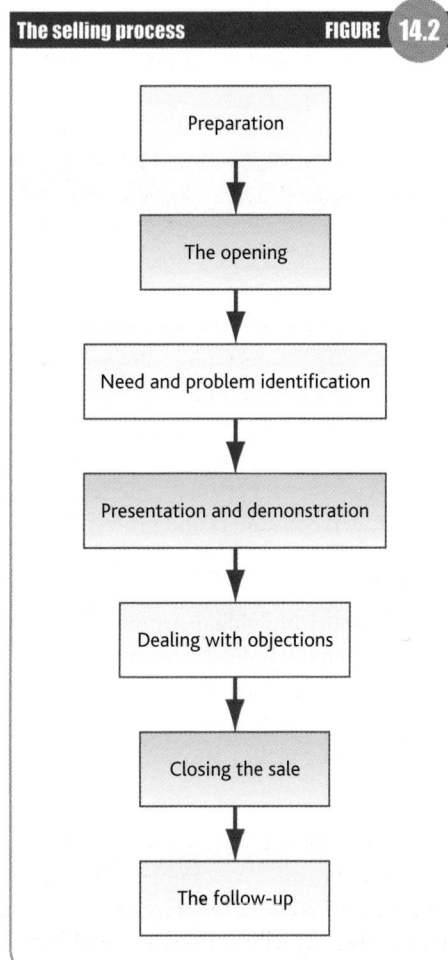

question or unusual objection, for example—but many customers face similar situations, and certain questions and objections will be raised repeatedly. Preparation can help the salesperson respond to these recurring situations.

Salespeople will benefit from gaining knowledge of their own products, competitors' products, sales presentation planning, setting call objectives and understanding buyer behaviour.

Product knowledge

Product knowledge means understanding both product features and the customer benefits that they confer. Understanding product features alone is not enough to convince customers to buy because they buy products for the benefits that the features provide, not the features in themselves. Salespeople need to ask themselves what are the benefits a certain feature provides for customers. For example, a computer mouse (product feature) provides a more convenient way of issuing commands (customer benefit) than using the keyboard. The way to turn features into benefits is to view products from the customer's angle. A by-product of this is the realization that some features may provide no customer benefit whatsoever.

Competitors' products

Knowledge of competitors' products allows their strengths to be offset against their weaknesses. For example, if a buyer claims that a competitor's product has a cost advantage, this may be offset against the superior productivity advantage of the salesperson's product. Similarly, inaccuracies in a buyer's claims can be countered. Finally, competitive knowledge allows salespeople to stress the differential advantage of their products compared to those of the competition.

Sales presentation planning

Preparation here builds confidence, raises the chances that important benefits are not forgotten, allows visual aids and demonstrations to be built into the presentation, and permits the anticipation of objections and the preparation of convincing counter-arguments. Although preparation is vital there should be room left for flexibility in approach since customers have different needs. The salesperson has to be aware that the features and benefits that should be stressed with one customer may have much less emphasis placed on them for another.

Setting call objectives

The key to setting call objectives is to phrase them in terms of what the salesperson wants the customer to do rather than what the salesperson should do. For example:

- for the customer to define what his or her needs are
- for the customer to visit a showroom
- for the customer to try the product, e.g. drive a car
- for the customer to be convinced of the cost saving of 'our' product compared to that of the competition.

This is because the success of the sales interview is customer-dependent. The end is to convince the customer; what the salesperson does is simply a means to that end.

Understanding buyer behaviour

Thought should also be given to understanding *buyer behaviour*. Questions should be asked, such as 'Who are the likely key people to talk to?' 'What are their probable choice criteria?' 'Are there any gatekeepers preventing access to some people, who need to be circumvented?' 'What are the likely opportunities and threats that may arise in the selling situation?' All of the answers to these questions need to be verified when in the actual selling situation but prior consideration can help salespeople to be clear in their own minds about the important issues.

The Internet can provide a wealth of information on the buying organization. The buyer's website, online product catalogues and blogs are useful sources of information. Customer relationship management (CRM) systems allow salespeople to access customer information held by their company via the Internet. For example, Orange, the telecommunications company, enables its field salespeople to access its CRM databases using personal digital assistants (PDAs) equipped with wireless modems.[25]

The opening

Initial impressions often affect later perceptions, and so it is important for salespeople to consider how to create a favourable initial response from customers. The following factors can positively shape first impressions.

- Be businesslike in appearance and behaviour.
- Be friendly but not over-familiar.
- Be attentive to detail, such as holding a briefcase in the hand that is not used for handshaking.
- Observe common courtesies like waiting to be asked to sit down.
- Ask if it is convenient for the customer to see you. This signals an appreciation of their needs (they may be too busy to be seen). It automatically creates a favourable impression from which to develop the sales call, but also a long-term relationship because the salesperson has earned the right to proceed to the next stage in selling: need and problem identification.
- Do not take the sales interview for granted: thank the customer for spending time with you and stress that you believe it will be worthwhile for them.

Using the Internet can help to create favourable first impressions. For example, research using online business databases can make salespeople appear highly knowledgeable about the customer's company and business.

Need and problem identification

People buy products because they have problems that give rise to needs. For example, machine unreliability (problem) causes the need to replace it with a new one (purchase). Therefore the first task is to identify the needs and problems of each customer. Only by doing so can the salesperson connect with each customer's situation. Having done so, the salesperson can select the product that best fits the customer's need and sell the appropriate benefits. It is benefits that link customer needs to product features, as in:

Customer need → Benefit ← Product feature

In the previous example, it would be essential to convince the customer that the salesperson's machine possessed features that guaranteed machine reliability. Knowledge of competitors' products would allow salespeople to show how their machine possessed features that gave added reliability. In this way, salespeople are in an ideal situation to convince customers of a product's differential advantage. Whenever possible, factual evidence of product superiority should be shown to customers. This is much more convincing than mere claims by the salesperson.

Effective needs and problem identification requires the development of questioning and listening skills. The problem is that people are more used to making statements than asking questions. Therefore the art of asking sensible questions that produce a clear understanding of the customer's situation requires training and considerable experience. The hallmark of inexperienced salespeople is that they do all the talking; successful salespeople know how to get the customer to do most of the talking. In this way they gain the information necessary to make a sale.

David Crossland, the entrepreneur who built Airtours (now MyTravel) into one of the UK's biggest travel companies, based his success at selling holidays on his technique of 'just listening' to customers. By asking questions and listening, he picked up clues about what holidays they would prefer from what they said they liked and hated about previous trips.[26]

Presentation and demonstration

The presentation and demonstration provides the opportunity for the salesperson to convince the customer that his or her company can supply the solution to the customer's problem. It should focus on **customer benefits** rather than **product features**. These can be linked using the following phrases:
- which means that
- which results in
- which enables you to.

For example, the machine salesperson might say that the machine possesses proven technology (product feature), *which means that* the reliability of the machine (customer benefit) is guaranteed. Evidence should then be supplied to support this sales argument. Perhaps scientific tests have proved the reliability of the machine (these should be shown to the customer), satisfied customers' testimonials could be produced or a visit to a satisfied customer arranged.

In business-to-business markets, some salespeople are guilty of presenting features and failing to communicate the benefit to the business customer. For example, in telecommunications it is not enough to say how fast the line speed is. The benefit derives from the impact that the extra speed has on the customer. It could be that faster speed means reduced call costs, reduced number of lines or increased customer satisfaction.[27]

The salesperson should continue asking questions during the presentation to ensure that the customer has understood what the salesperson has said and to check that what the salesperson has mentioned really is of importance to the customer. This can be achieved by asking, say, 'Is that the kind of thing you are looking for?'

Technological advances have greatly assisted the presentation. For example, laptops allow the use of online resources such as video material, and the ability to get a response from a sales office during a presentation.[28] Access to company websites permits the carrying of masses of product information, including sound and animation.

Demonstrations allow the customer to see the product in operation. As such, some of the claims made for the product by the salesperson can be verified. Demonstrations allow the customer to be involved in the selling process through participation. They can, therefore, be instrumental in reducing the *perceived risk* of a purchase and moving the customer towards purchase.

Information technology can allow multimedia demonstrations of industrial products in the buyer's office. No longer is it always necessary for buyers to visit the supplier's site or to provide facilities to act as 'video show rooms' for salespeople wishing to demonstrate their product using video projectors.[29]

Dealing with objections

It is unusual for salespeople to close a sale without the need to overcome objections. Objections are any concerns or questions raised by the buyer.[30] While some objections are an expression of confusion, doubt or disagreement with the statements or information presented by the salesperson, objections should not always be viewed negatively since they highlight the issues that are important to the buyer.

The secret of *dealing with objections* is to handle both the substantive and emotional aspects. The substantive part is to do with the objection itself. If the customer objects to the product's price, the salesperson needs to use convincing arguments to show that the price is not too high. But it is a fact of human personality that the argument that is supported by the greater weight of evidence does not always win, since people resent being proved wrong. Therefore, salespeople need to recognize the emotional aspects of objection handling. Under no circumstances should the buyer lose face or be antagonized during this process. Two ways of minimizing this risk are to listen to the objection without interruption, and to employ the agree-and-counter technique.

The Internet can aid the creation of convincing answers to objections. The salesperson can guide buyers to the firm's website, where frequently answered questions and testimonials may be found. Potential customers might also be directed to favourable online reviews at independent websites. This improved dialogue between sellers and buyers can improve the chances of a successful sale.[31]

Listen and do not interrupt

Experienced salespeople know that the impression given to buyers by salespeople that interrupt buyers when they are raising an objection is that the salesperson believes that:

- the objection is obviously wrong
- the objection is trivial
- it is not worth the salesperson's time to let the buyer finish.

Interruption denies buyers the kind of respect they are entitled to receive and may lead to a misunderstanding of the real substance behind the objection.

The correct approach is to listen carefully, attentively and respectfully. The buyer will appreciate the fact that the salesperson is taking the problem seriously, and the salesperson will gain through having a clear and full understanding of what the problem really is.

Agree and counter

The salesperson agrees with the buyer's viewpoint before putting forward an alternative point of view. The objective is to create a climate of agreement rather than conflict, and shows that the salesperson respects the buyer's opinion, thus avoiding loss of face. For example:

> *Buyer*: The problem with your bulldozer is that it costs more than the competition.

> *Salesperson*: You are right, the initial cost is a little higher, but I should like to show you how the full lifetime costs of the bulldozer are much lower than the competition.

Closing the sale

Inexperienced salespeople sometimes think that an effective presentation followed by convincing objection handling should mean that the buyer will ask for the product without the seller needing to close the sale. This does occasionally happen, but more often it is necessary for the salesperson to take the initiative. This is because many buyers still have doubts in their minds that may cause them to wish to delay the decision to purchase.

If the customer puts off buying, the decision may be made when a competitor's salesperson is present, resulting in a lost sale.

Buying signals

The key to closing a sale is to look for **buying signals**. These are statements by buyers that indicate they are interested in buying. For example:

- 'That looks fine.'
- 'I like that one.'
- 'When could the product be delivered?'
- 'I think that product meets my requirements.'

These all indicate a very positive intention to buy without actually asking for the order. They provide excellent opportunities for the salesperson to ask the buyer to make a decision without appearing pushy.

Closing techniques

A variety of closing techniques can be used.

- *Simply ask for the order*: a direct question, such as 'Would you like that one?', may be all that is needed.
- *Summarize and then ask for the order*: with this approach, the salesperson reminds the buyer of the main points of the sales discussion in a manner which implies that the time for decision-making has arrived and that buying is the natural next step: 'Well, Ms Jones, we have agreed that the ZX4 model best meets your requirements of low noise and high productivity at an economical price. Would you like to place an order for this machine?'
- *Concession close*: by keeping a concession back to use in the close, a salesperson may convince an indecisive buyer to place an order: 'I am in a position to offer an extra 10 per cent discount on price if you are willing to place an order now.'
- *Action agreement*: in some situations it is inappropriate to try to close the sale. To do so would annoy the buyer because the sale is not in the hands of one person but a decision-making unit. Many organizational purchasing decisions are of this kind, and the decision may be made in committee without any salesperson being present. Alternatively, the salesperson may be talking to a specifier (such as a doctor or architect) who does not buy directly. In such circumstances, the close may be substituted by an action agreement: instead of closing the sale the salesperson attempts to achieve an action agreement with the customer. For example, in the selling of prescription drugs, either the salesperson or the doctor agree to do something before the next meeting. The salesperson might agree to bring details of a new drug or attempt to get agreement from the doctor to read a leaflet on a drug before the next meeting. This technique has the effect of maintaining the relationship between the parties and can be used as the starting point of the discussion when they next meet.

The follow-up

Once the order is placed there could be a temptation for the salesperson to move on to other customers, neglecting the follow-up visit. However, this can be a great mistake since most companies rely on repeat business. If problems arise, customers have every right to believe that the salesperson was interested only in the order and not their complete satisfaction. By checking that there are no problems with delivery, installation, product use and training (where applicable), the follow-up can show that the salesperson really cares about the customer.

The follow-up can also be used to provide reassurance that the purchase was the right thing to do. As we discussed when analysing consumer behaviour, people often feel tense after deciding to buy an expensive product. Doubts can materialize about the wisdom of spending so much money, or whether the product best meets their needs. This anxiety, known as *cognitive dissonance*, can be minimized by the salesperson reassuring the customer about the purchase during the follow-up phase.

Websites can be helpful following the order, reminding buyers about post-purchase support resources, and salespeople can maintain an open dialogue with buyers through online user newsletters. Companies such as Dell and Xerox allow customers to log in to a secure buyer website to track the status of their orders, order products online or pay invoices.[32]

Salespeople operating in overseas markets need to be aware of the cultural nuances that shape business relationships. For example, in the West, a deadline is acceptable whereas in many Middle Eastern cultures, it would be taken as an insult. In China, salespeople need to acknowledge the importance of personalized and close business relationships, known as *Guanxi. Guanxi* is a set of personal relationships/connections on which a person can draw to secure resources or advantage when doing business. *Guanxi* can lead to preferential treatment in the form of easy access to limited resources, increased accessibility to information and preferential credit terms. For foreigners, this means having as part of their *Guanxi* network an influential person in an organization or government position. Another key issue in Chinese culture is the avoidance of 'loss of face'. Visiting salespeople should avoid creating a situation where a Chinese person might 'lose face' by finding themselves in an embarrassing situation (e.g. by displaying lack of knowledge or understanding).

In the Middle East, selling may involve presentations to kings and high-ranking government officials, as Marketing in Action 14.1 explains.

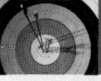

14.1 Marketing in Action

Cisco's Brave New World

Cisco Systems, the networking giant, sees a major part of its future growth coming from massive construction projects in the Middle East. One example is the creation of King Abdullah Economic City (KAEC) in Saudi Arabia. By 2020 the Saudis expect 2 million people to be living in a future metropolis supported by some of the most advanced technology money can buy. All told, King Abdullah plans to build four brand new cities and upgrade the country's infrastructure at a cost of $600 billion over the coming years.

To tap in to this vast potential, Cisco hired a well-connected local person to head the business in the country. He, in turn, hired salespeople and engineers, and got Cisco involved in major government projects. For the KAEC project, senior Cisco executives played host to the King for a demonstration of Cisco technology that allowed a person elsewhere to appear on stage as a holographic image. They realize, though, that Cisco is not just selling technology (a product feature). The real benefit is that it can help countries such as Saudi Arabia modernize their economies and become leaders in the Internet age. The company argues that, by investing in the Internet infrastructure Cisco sells, these governments can better educate their people, improve healthcare and boost national productivity.

To achieve this, Cisco provides consulting services to help government officials work out how best to use the Internet, and pays for training centres to produce the technicians to implement such plans. Cisco is helping the leaders of countries like Saudi Arabia imagine the future, to bring about 'country transformations' and brainstorm big ideas. One example was the call to Cisco to help with a new broadband network for Sudair City, but a Cisco executive saw the potential of the city as a hub for vast computer data centres, based on its cheap electricity rates. The electricity bill is often the biggest expense in running such centres, which are increasingly important to Internet companies such as Google and Amazon. The idea was well received and helped Cisco secure a $280 million contact to create the underlying fibre-optic network for Sudair City.

Based on: Burrows (2008)[33]

Many salespeople make the mistake of using 'self-reference' criteria when selling abroad. They assume that the values and behavioural norms that apply in their own country are equally applicable abroad. To avoid this failing, they need training in the special skills required to sell to people of different cultures.

Sales Management

In many respects, the functions of the sales manager are similar to those of other managers. Sales managers, like their production, marketing and finance counterparts, need to recruit, train, motivate and evaluate their staff. However, there are several peculiarities of the job that make effective sales management difficult and the job considerably demanding.

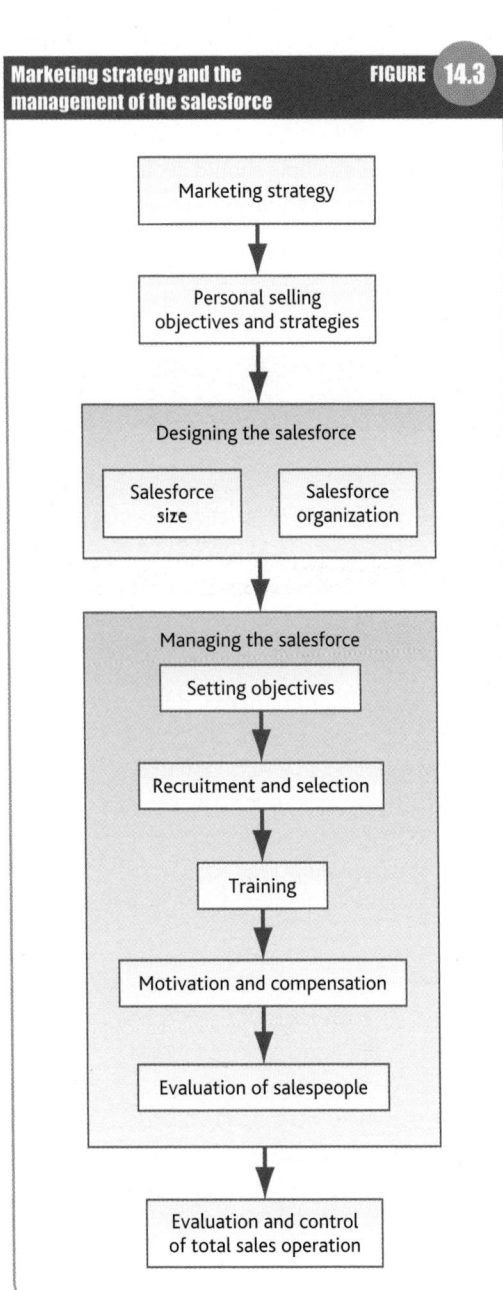

Marketing strategy and the management of the salesforce — FIGURE 14.3

- Marketing strategy
- Personal selling objectives and strategies
- Designing the salesforce
  - Salesforce size
  - Salesforce organization
- Managing the salesforce
  - Setting objectives
  - Recruitment and selection
  - Training
  - Motivation and compensation
  - Evaluation of salespeople
- Evaluation and control of total sales operation

Problems of sales management

Geographic separation

The geographic separation between sales managers and their field salesforce creates problems of motivation, communication and control.

Repeated rejections

Salespeople may suffer repeated rejections when trying to close sales. This may cause attrition of their enthusiasm, attitudes and skills. A major role for sales managers is to provide support and renew motivation in such adverse circumstances.

The salesperson's personality vs the realities of the job

Most people who go into sales are outgoing and gregarious. These are desirable characteristics for people who are selling to customers. However, the reality of the job is that, typically, only 30 per cent of a salesperson's time is spent face to face with customers, with travelling (50 per cent) and administration (20 per cent) contributing the rest.[34] This means that over half of the salesperson's time is spent alone, which can cause frustration in people who enjoy the company of others.

Oversimplification of the task

Some sales managers cope with the difficulties of management by oversimplifying the task. They take the attitude that they are interested only in results. It is their job to reward those who meet sales targets and severely punish those who fail. Such an attitude ignores the contribution that sales management can make to the successful achievement of objectives. Figure 14.3 shows the functions of a sales manager and the relationship between marketing strategy and the personal selling function.

Marketing strategy

As with all parts of the marketing mix, the personal selling function is not a stand-alone element, but one that must be considered in the light of overall marketing strategy. At the product level, two major marketing considerations are choice of target market and the creation of a differential advantage. Both of these decisions affect personal selling.

Target market choice

The definition of the target market has clear implications for sales management because of its relationship to **target accounts**. Once the target market has been defined (e.g. organizations in a particular industry over a certain size), sales management can translate that specification into individual accounts to target. Salesforce resources can, therefore, be deployed to maximum effect.

Differential advantage

The creation of a differential advantage is the starting point of successful marketing strategy, but this needs to be communicated to the salesforce and embedded in a sales plan which ensures that the salesforce is able to articulate it convincingly to customers.

Two common dangers

First, the salesforce undermines the differential advantage by repeatedly giving in to customer demands for price concessions. Second, the features that underlie the differential advantage are communicated but the customer benefits are neglected. Customer benefits need to be communicated in terms that are meaningful to customers. This means, for example, that advantages such as higher productivity may require translation into cash savings or higher revenue for financially minded customers.

Four strategic objectives

Marketing strategy also affects the personal selling function through strategic objectives. Each objective—build, hold, harvest and divest—has implications for *sales objectives* and strategy; these are outlined in Table 14.2. Linking business or product area strategic objectives with

Marketing strategy and sales management		TABLE 14.2
Strategic marketing objective	**Sales objective**	**Sales strategy**
Build	Build sales volume Increase distribution Provide high service levels	High call rates on existing accounts High focus during call Call on new accounts (prospecting)
Hold	Maintain sales volume Maintain distribution Maintain service levels	Continue present call rates on current accounts Medium focus during call Call on new outlets when they appear
Harvest	Reduce selling costs Target profitable accounts Reduce service costs and inventories	Call only on profitable accounts Consider telemarketing or dropping the rest No prospecting
Divest	Clear inventory quickly	Quantity discounts to targeted accounts

Source: adapted from Strahle, W. and R. L. Spiro (1986) Linking Market Share Strategies to Salesforce Objectives, Activities and Compensation Policies, *Journal of Personal Selling & Sales Management*, August, 11–18.

functional area strategies is essential for the efficient allocation of resources, and effective implementation in the marketplace.[35]

Personal selling objectives and strategies

As we have seen, selling objectives and strategies are derived from marketing strategy decisions, and should be consistent with other elements of the marketing mix. Indeed, marketing strategy will determine if there is a need for a salesforce at all, or whether the selling role can be accomplished better by using some other medium, such as direct mail. Objectives define what the selling function is expected to achieve. Objectives are typically defined in terms of:

- sales volume (e.g. 5 per cent growth in sales volume)
- market share (e.g. 1 per cent increase in market share)
- profitability (e.g. maintenance of gross profit margin)
- service levels (e.g. 20 per cent increase in number of customers regarding salesperson assistance as 'good or better' in annual customer survey)
- salesforce costs (e.g. 5 per cent reduction in expenses).

Salesforce strategy defines how those objectives will be achieved. The following may be considered:

- call rates
- percentage of calls on existing vs potential accounts
- discount policy (the extent to which reductions from list prices allowed)
- percentage of resources
    - targeted at new vs existing products
    - targeted at selling vs providing after-sales service
    - targeted at field selling vs telemarketing
    - targeted at different types of customers (e.g. high vs low potential)
- improving customer and market feedback from the salesforce
- improving customer relationships.

Once sales managers have a clear idea of what they hope to achieve, and how best to set about accomplishing these objectives, they can make sensible decisions regarding salesforce design.

Designing the salesforce

Two critical design decisions are those of determining salesforce size and salesforce organization.

Salesforce size

The most practical method for deciding the number of salespeople is called the *workload approach*. It is based on the calculation of the total annual calls required per year divided by the average calls per year that can be expected from one salesperson.[36] The procedure follows seven steps, as outlined below.

1 Customers are grouped into categories according to the value of goods bought and their potential for the future.
2 The call frequency (number of calls per year to an account) is assessed for each category of customer.
3 The total required workload per year is calculated by multiplying the call frequency by the number of customers in each category and then summing for all categories.
4 The average number of calls that can be expected per salesperson per week is estimated.

5 The number of working weeks per year is calculated.
6 The average number of calls a salesperson can make per year is calculated by multiplying (4) and (5).
7 The number of salespeople required is determined by dividing the total annual calls required by the average number of calls one salesperson can make per year.

The formula is:

Number of salespeople = number of customers
× call frequency ÷ average weekly call rate
× number of working weeks per year

An example of how the workload approach can be used will now be given. Steps 1, 2 and 3 may be summarized as shown in Table 14.3.

When **prospecting** forms an important part of the selling job, a separate category (or categories) can be formed with their own call rates to give an estimation of the workload required to cover prospecting. This is then added to the workload estimate based on current accounts to give a total workload figure.

The workload approach: an example — TABLE 14.3

Customer group	No. of accounts	Call frequency	
A (Over £500,000 per year)	20	× 12	= 240
B (£250,000–£500,000 per year)	100	× 9	= 900
C (£100,000–£249,000 per year)	300	× 6	= 1800
D (Less than £100,000 per year)	500	× 3	= 1500
Total annual workload			= 4440
Step 4 gives: Average number of calls per week per salesperson			= 20
Step 5 gives: Number of weeks			= 52
Less: Holidays	4		
Illness	1		
Conferences/meetings	3		
Training	1		= 9
Number of working weeks			= 43
Step 6 gives: Average number of calls per salesperson per year			= 43 × 20 = 860
Step 7 gives: Salesforce size =	$\frac{4440}{860}$		= 6 salespeople

Salesforce organization

There are three basic forms of *salesforce organization*: geographic, product and customer-based structures. The strengths and weakness of each are as follows.

Geographic: the sales area is broken down into territories based on workload and potential, and a salesperson is assigned to each one to sell all of the product range. This provides a simple, unambiguous, definition of each salesperson's sales territory, and proximity to customers encourages the development of personal relationships. It is also a more cost-efficient method of organization than product or customer-based systems. However, when products are technically different and sell in a number of diverse markets, it may be unreasonable to expect a salesperson to be knowledgeable about all products and their applications. Under such circumstances a company is likely to move to a product or customer-based structure.

Product: product specialization is effective where a company has a diverse product range selling to different customers (or at least different people within a given organization). However, if the products sell essentially to the same customers, problems of route duplication (and, consequently, higher travel costs) and multiple calls on the same customer can arise. When applicable, product specialization allows each salesperson to be well informed about a product line, its applications and customer benefits. Hewlett-Packard uses a product-based system because of its wide product range. The salespeople are assigned to one of its three divisions: PCs, laptops and handheld devices; printers and printing; or IT solutions for large enterprises.

Customer-based: the problem of the same customer being served by product divisions of the same supplier, the complexity of buyer behaviour that requires input not only from the sales function but from other functional groups (such as engineering, finance, logistics and marketing), centralization of purchasing, and the immense value of some customers, have led many suppliers to rethink how they organize their salesforces. Companies are increasingly organizing around customers and shifting resources from product or regional divisions to customer-focused business units.[37] Salesforces can be organized along market segment, account size, or new versus existing accounts lines. First, computer firms have traditionally organized their salesforce on the basis of industry served (e.g. banking, retailing and manufacturing) in recognition of their varying needs, problems and potential applications. Specialization by these *market segments* allows salespeople to gain in-depth knowledge of customers and to be able to monitor trends in the industry that may affect demand for their products. In some industries, the applications knowledge of market-based salespeople has led them to be known as *fraternity brothers* by their customers.[38] Second, an increasing trend in many industries is towards **key account management**, which reflects the increasing concentration of buying power into fewer but larger customers. These are serviced by a key account salesforce comprising senior salespeople who develop close personal relationships with customers, can handle sophisticated sales arguments and are skilled in the art of negotiation. Table 14.4 illustrates some important distinctions between traditional (transactional selling) and key account management.

A number of advantages are claimed for a key account structure.

1 *Close working relationships with the customer*: the salesperson knows who makes what decisions and who influences the various players involved in the decision. Technical specialists from the selling organization can call on technical people (e.g. engineers) in the buying organization, and salespeople can call on administrators, buyers and financial people armed with the commercial arguments for buying.

2 *Improved communication and coordination*: the customer knows that a dedicated salesperson or sales team exists so that it is clear who to contact when a problem arises.

Distinctions between transactional selling and key account management		TABLE 14.4
	Transactional selling	**Key account management**
Overall objective	Sales	Preferred supplier status
Sales skills	Asking questions, Handling objections Closing	Building trust Negotiation Providing excellent service
Nature of relationship	Short, intermittent	Long, more intensive interaction
Salesperson goal	Closed sale	Relationship management
Nature of salesforce	One or two salespeople per customer	Many sales people, often involving multifunctional teams

3 *Better follow-up on sales and service*: the extra resources devoted to the key account mean that there is more time to follow up and provide service after a major sale has been made.

4 *More in-depth penetration of the DMU*: there is more time to cultivate relationships within the key account. Salespeople can *pull* the buying decision through the organization from the users, deciders and influencers to the buyer, rather than the more difficult task of pushing it through the buyer into the organization, as is done with more traditional sales approaches.

5 *Higher sales*: most companies that have adopted key account selling claim that sales have risen as a result and research has shown that supplier performance normally improves.[39]

6 *The provision of an opportunity for advancement for career salespeople*: a tiered salesforce system with key (or national) account selling at the top provides promotional opportunities for salespeople who wish to advance within the salesforce rather than enter a traditional sales-management position.

7 *Lower costs*: through joint agreement of optimum production and delivery schedules, and demand forecasting.

8 *Cooperation on research and development*: for new products and joint promotions (for example, within the fast-moving consumer goods/retail sector).

The development and management of a key account can be understood as a process that takes place over time between buyers and sellers. The key account management (KAM) relational development model plots the typical progression of a buyer–seller relationship based on the nature of the customer relationship (transactional–collaborative) and the level of involvement with customers (simple–complex).[40] Figure 14.4 shows five stages: Pre-KAM, Early KAM, Mid-KAM, Partnership-KAM and Synergistic-KAM. A sixth stage (Uncoupling-KAM) represents the breakdown of the relationship, which can happen at any point during the process.

Pre-KAM: this describes preparation for KAM, or 'prospecting'. The task is to identify those with the potential for moving towards key account status and to avoid wasting investment on those accounts that lack potential. Pre-KAM selling strategies involve making products available while attempting to gather information about customers so that their key account potential can be assessed. Where an account is thought to have potential but breaking into the account is proving difficult, patience and persistence are required. A breakthrough may result from the 'in' supplier doing something wrong—for example, refusing to quote for a low-profit order or failing to repair equipment promptly.

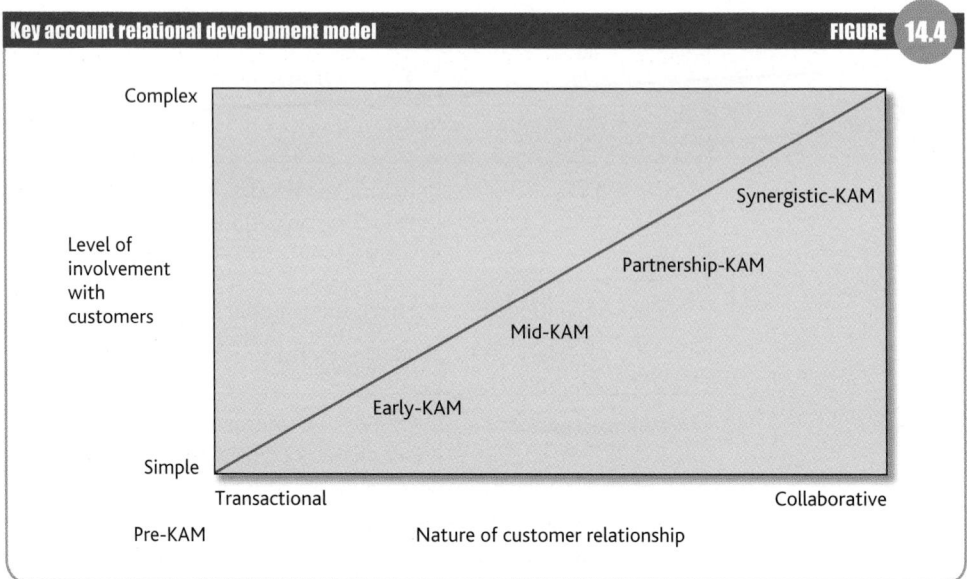

Key account relational development model   FIGURE **14.4**

Early KAM: this involves the exploration of opportunities for closer collaboration by identifying the motives, culture and concerns of the customer. The selling company needs to convince the customer of the benefits of being a 'preferred supplier'. It will seek to understand the customer's decision-making unit and processes, and the problems and opportunities that relate to the value-adding activities. Product adaptations may be made to fit customer needs better. An objective of the sales effort will be to build trust based on consistent performance and open communications. Most communication is channelled through one salesperson (key account manager) and a single contact at the buying organization. This makes for a fragile relationship, particularly as it is likely that the seller is one of many supplying the account. The customer will be monitoring the supplier's performance to assess competence and to identify any problems that might arise. The account manager will be seeking to create a more attractive offering, establish credibility and deepen personal relationships.

Mid-KAM: by now trust has been established and the supplier is one of a small number of preferred sources of the product. The number and range of contacts increase. These may include social events, which help to deepen relationships across the two organizations. The account review process carried out at the selling organization will tend to move upwards to involve senior management because of the importance of the customer and the level of resource allocation. Since the account is not yet exclusive, the activities of competitors will require constant monitoring.

Partnership-KAM: at this stage the buying organization regards the supplier as an important strategic resource. The level of trust will be sufficient for both parties to be willing to share sensitive information. The focus of activities moves to joint problem solving, collaborative product development and mutual training of the other firm's staff. The buying company is now channelling nearly all of its business in the relevant product group(s) to the one supplier. The arrangement is formalized in a partnership agreement of at least three years' duration. Performance will be monitored and contacts between departments of the two organizations are extensive. The buying organization will expect guaranteed continuity of supply, excellent service and top-quality products. A key task of the account manager is to reinforce the high levels of trust to form a barrier against potential competitors.

Synergistic-KAM: this is the ultimate stage of the relational development model. Buyer and seller see one another not as two separate organizations but as part of a larger entity.

Top management commitment manifests itself in joint board meetings. Joint business planning, research and development, and marketing research take place. Costing systems become transparent, unnecessary costs are removed, and process improvements are mutually achieved. For example, a logistics company together with one of its retail key accounts has six cross-boundary teams working on process improvements at any one time.[41]

Uncoupling-KAM: this is when transactions and interaction cease. The causes of uncoupling need to be understood so that it can be avoided. Breakdowns are more often attributable to changes in key personnel and relationship problems than price conflicts. The danger of uncoupling is particularly acute in early KAM when the single point of contact prevails. If, for example, the key account manager leaves to be replaced by someone who, in the buyer's eyes, is less skilled, or there is a personality clash, the relationship may end. A second cause of uncoupling is breach of trust. For example, the breaking of a promise over a delivery deadline, product improvement or equipment repair can weaken or kill a business relationship. The key to handling such problems is to reduce the impact of surprise. The supplier should let the buying organization know immediately a problem becomes apparent. It should also show humility when discussing the problem with a customer. Companies, also, uncouple through neglect. Long-term relationships can foster complacency and customers can perceive themselves as being taken for granted. Cultural mismatches can occur—for example, when the customer stresses price whereas the supplier focuses on life-cycle costs. Difficulties can also occur between bureaucratic and entrepreneurial styles of management. Product or service quality problems can also provoke uncoupling. Any kind of performance problem, or the perception that rivals now offer superior performance can trigger a breakdown in relations. 'In' suppliers must build entry barriers by ensuring that product quality is constantly improved and any problems dealt with speedily and professionally. Not all uncoupling is instigated by the buying company. A key account may be de-rated or terminated because of loss of market share or the onset of financial problems that impair the attractiveness of the account.

Some companies adopt a *three-tier system*, with senior salespeople handling key accounts, sales representatives selling to medium-sized accounts and a telemarketing team dealing with small accounts. Telemarketing is a systematic programme placing outbound sales calls to customers and prospects, and receiving orders and enquiries from them. It is discussed in some detail in Chapter 15.

The importance of key account management on a worldwide scale is reflected in the employment of global account managers by many multinational organizations. *Global account management* (GAM) is the process of coordinating and developing mutually beneficial long-term relationships with a select group of strategically important customers (accounts) operating in globalized industries.[42] Global account managers perform two key roles: (i) managing the internal interface between global and national account management, which is often embedded in a headquarters/subsidiary relationship; (ii) managing the external interface between the supplier and the dispersed activities of its global accounts.[43] Multinational customers are increasingly buying on a centralized or coordinated basis and seek suppliers who are able to provide consistent and seamless service across countries.[44] Consequently, suppliers are developing and implementing GAM and are creating global account managers to manage the interface between seller and buyer on a global basis.

14.2 Pause for Thought

Not all companies are suitable for key account status. Think of three characteristics of buyer organizations that are likely to qualify them as potential key accounts.

A third way of organizing along customer lines is by *new versus existing accounts*. One sales team focuses on the skills of prospecting while another services existing customers. This recognizes the differing skills involved, and the possible neglect of opening new accounts by salespeople who may view their time as being more profitably spent with existing customers.

In practice, a combination of structures may be used to gain the economies of the geographic form with the specialization inherent in the product or customer-based systems. For example, a company using a two-product-line structure may divide into geographically based territories with two salespeople operating in each one.

Managing the salesforce

Besides deciding personal selling objectives and strategies, and designing the salesforce, the company has to manage the salesforce. This requires setting specific salesperson objectives, recruitment and selection, training, motivation and compensation, and evaluation of salespeople. These activities have been shown to improve salesperson performance, indicating the key role sales managers play as facilitators helping salespeople to perform better.[45]

Setting objectives

In order to achieve aggregate sales objectives, individual salespeople need to have their own sales targets to achieve. Usually, targets are set in sales terms (sales quotas) but, increasingly, profit targets are being used, reflecting the need to guard against sales being bought cheaply by excessive discounting. To gain commitment to targets, consultation with individual salespeople is recommended but in the final analysis it is the sales manager's responsibility to set targets. Payment may be linked to their achievement.

Sales management may also wish to set input objectives such as the proportion of time spent developing new accounts, and the time spent introducing new products. They may also specify the number of calls expected per day, and the precise customers who should be called upon.

Recruitment and selection

The importance of recruiting high-calibre salespeople cannot be overestimated. A study into salesforce practice asked sales managers the following question: 'If you were to put your most successful salesperson into the territory of one of your average salespeople, and made no other changes, what increase in sales would you expect after, say, two years?'[46] The most commonly stated increase was 16–20 per cent, and one-fifth of all sales managers said they would expect an increase of over 30 per cent. Clearly the quality of salespeople that sales managers recruit has a substantial effect on performance.

When recruiting salespeople, a commonly held assumption is that money is the most valued attraction. This has been challenged in a study by Galbraith, Kiely and Watkins, which examined the features of the job that were of more interest and value to salespeople.[47] Their findings showed that working methods and independence were more important than earnings as the key attraction to a selling career and that independence was also the most highly valued aspect of doing the selling job. The implication of this study is that sales managers need to discover the reasons why people want to become salespeople in their industry so that they can develop recruitment strategies that reflect those desires.

The recruitment and selection process follows five stages:
1 preparation of the job description and personnel specification
2 identification of sources of recruitment and methods of communication
3 design of the application form and preparation of a shortlist
4 the interview
5 use of supplementary selection aids.

We will now look at each of these in more detail.

Preparation of the job description and personnel specification: a job description will normally include details of job title, duties and responsibilities, and to whom the salesperson will report, the technical requirements (e.g. product knowledge), geographic area to be covered, and the degree of autonomy given to the salesperson.

This job description acts as a blueprint for the personnel specification, which details the type of person the company is seeking. For example, the technical aspects of the job may require a salesperson with an engineering degree or to have worked in a particular industry. The personnel specification will also determine the qualities sought in the recruit. Modern practice is to distinguish between essential and desirable criteria for selection. The criteria will be based on the qualities needed to perform the job and will be used when drawing up the shortlist and deciding on the successful applicant.

Based on extensive research, Mayer and Greenberg reduced the number of qualities believed to be important for effective selling to empathy and ego drive.[48] **Empathy** is the ability to feel as the buyer feels: to be able to understand customer problems and needs. **Ego drive** is the need to make a sale in a personal way, not merely for money. These qualities can be measured using a psychological test, such as the Minnesota Multiphasic Personality Inventory.

Identification of sources of recruitment and methods of communication: sources of recruitment include company personnel, recruitment agencies, education, competitors, other industries, and unemployed people. Advertising is the most common method of communication, with national and local press the most often used media. Recruiters should not attempt to squeeze copy into the smallest possible space since size of advertisement is correlated with impact. The advertisement should contain a headline that attracts the attention of possible applicants.

Design of the application form and preparation of a shortlist: the design of the application form should allow the sales manager to check if the applicant is qualified in the light of the personnel specification. It thus provides a common basis for drawing up a shortlist of candidates, provides a foundation for the interview and is a reference point at the post-interview decision-making stage. Shortlisted candidates must meet all the essential criteria for selection.

The interview: most companies employ a screening interview and a selection interview. The overall objective of the interview is to form a clear and valid impression of the strengths and weaknesses of each candidate in terms of the personnel specification. The following criteria may be used:

- physical requirements (e.g. speech, appearance)
- attainments (e.g. educational attainment, previous sales success)
- qualities (e.g. drive, ability to communicate)
- disposition (e.g. maturity, sense of responsibility)
- interests (e.g. any interests that may have a positive impact on building customer relationships).

The interview should start with a few easy-to-answer questions that allow the candidate to talk freely and relax. Interviewers should be courteous and appear interested in what the candidate says. Open questions (e.g. 'Can you tell me about your experiences selling cosmetics?') should be used during the interview to encourage candidates to express themselves. Probes can be used to prompt further discussion or explanation. For example, the candidate might say 'The one-week introductory sales training course was a waste of my time', to which the interviewer might respond 'That's interesting; why was that?' At the end of the interview the candidate should be told when the decision will be made and how it will be communicated.

Use of supplementary selection aids: some companies use psychological tests as an aid to candidate selection, although their use has been criticized on the grounds that many measure personality traits or interests that do not predict sales success. Consequently, before the use of such tests, validation is necessary to show that test scores are likely to correlate with sales success. A test that may be useful in selecting car salespeople may be useless when filling a vacancy for an aero-engine sales job. However, research has also shown that tests measuring integrity, conscientiousness and optimism perform well at predicting sales success.[49]

Another selection aid is the use of role-playing in order to gauge the potential of applicants. Obviously, previous sales experience has to be allowed for, and the limitations of the exercise need to be recognized. At best, role-playing may be useful in estimating potential in making short-term sales, but is unlikely to provide a reliable guide when the emphasis is on building long-term relationships with customers.

Training

Many sales managers believe that their salespeople can best train themselves by doing the job. This approach ignores the benefits of a training programme that provides a frame of reference in which learning can take place. Its benefits are immense, ranging from enhanced skill levels to improved motivation and greater confidence in the ability to perform well at selling, a factor that has been shown to be related to improved sales performance.[50] Indeed, the importance of training is supported by research, which has found a positive link between training and sales performance.[51] Training should include not only product knowledge but also skills development. Success at selling comes when the skills are performed automatically, without consciously thinking about them, just as a tennis player or footballer succeeds.

A training programme should include knowledge about the company (its objectives, strategies and organization), its products (features and benefits), its competitors and their products, selling procedures and techniques, work organization (including report preparation), and relationship management. Salespeople need to be trained in the management of long-term customer relationships as well as context-specific selling skills.[52] For example, the IBM consultative sales training programme emphasizes working with clients as consultants to build close relationships and to work jointly to solve problems. The core components of the programme involve people and communication skills.[53]

Lectures, films, role-playing and case studies can be used in a classroom situation to give knowledge and understanding and to develop competences. These should be followed up with in-the-field training, where skills can be practised face to face with customers. Sales managers and trainers should provide feedback to encourage on-the-job learning. In particular the sales manager needs to:

- analyse each salesperson's performance
- identify strengths and weaknesses
- communicate strengths
- gain agreement that a weakness exists
- train the salesperson in how to overcome the weakness
- monitor progress.

The heavy time constraints placed on modern salespeople mean that taking days off work to attend a traditional sales training course may not be feasible. Technological advances mean that an alternative method of disseminating information is via the Internet. Using technology to package information is an inexpensive and effective alternative to traditional programmes. This approach means that training can take place over long distances and at a time that fits in with salespeople's work patterns.

Sales managers themselves need training in the considerable range of skills that they require, including analytical, teaching, motivational and communicational skills, and the ability to organize and plan. Some of the skills are not essential to be able to sell (e.g. teaching and motivating others), hence the adage that the best salespeople do not always make the best sales managers.

Motivation and compensation

Effective motivation is based on a deep understanding of salespeople as individuals, their personalities and value systems. In one sense, sales managers do not motivate salespeople—they provide the enabling conditions in which salespeople motivate themselves. Motivation can be understood through the relationship between needs, drives and goals. Luthans stated that, 'the basic process involves needs (deprivations) which set drives in motion (deprivations with direction) to accomplish goals (anything which alleviates a need and reduces a drive)'.[54] For example, the need for more money may result in a drive to work harder in order to receive increased pay. Improving motivation is important to sales success; research has shown that high levels of motivation lead to:[55]

- increased creativity
- working smarter and a more adaptive selling approach
- working harder
- increased use of win/win negotiation tactics
- higher self-esteem
- a more relaxed attitude and a less negative emotional tone
- enhancement of relationships.

Motivation has been the subject of much research over many years. Maslow, Herzberg, Vroom, Adams and Likert, among others, have produced theories that have implications for the motivation of salespeople.[56] Some of their important findings are summarized in the list below.

- Once a need is satisfied it no longer motivates.
- Different people have different needs and values.
- Increasing the level of responsibility/job enrichment, giving recognition of achievement and providing monetary incentives work to increase motivation for some people.
- People tend to be motivated if they believe that effort will bring results, results will be rewarded and the rewards are valued.
- Elimination of disincentives (such as injustices or unfair treatment) raises motivational levels.
- There is a relationship between the performance goals of sales managers and those of the salespeople they lead.

The implication of these findings are that sales managers should:

- get to know what each salesperson values and what each one is striving for (unrealized needs)
- be willing to increase the responsibility given to salespeople in mundane jobs
- realize that training can improve motivation as well as capabilities by strengthening the link between effort and performance
- provide targets that are believed to be attainable yet provide a challenge to salespeople link rewards to the performance they want improved
- recognize that rewards can be both financial and non-financial (e.g. praise).

Churchill, Ford and Walker developed a **salesforce motivation** model that integrated the work of the motivational theorists (in particular Vroom and Herzberg).[57] This model is shown in Figure 14.5, and suggests that there is a cycle of motivation. The higher the salesperson's

The cycle of motivation   FIGURE **14.5**

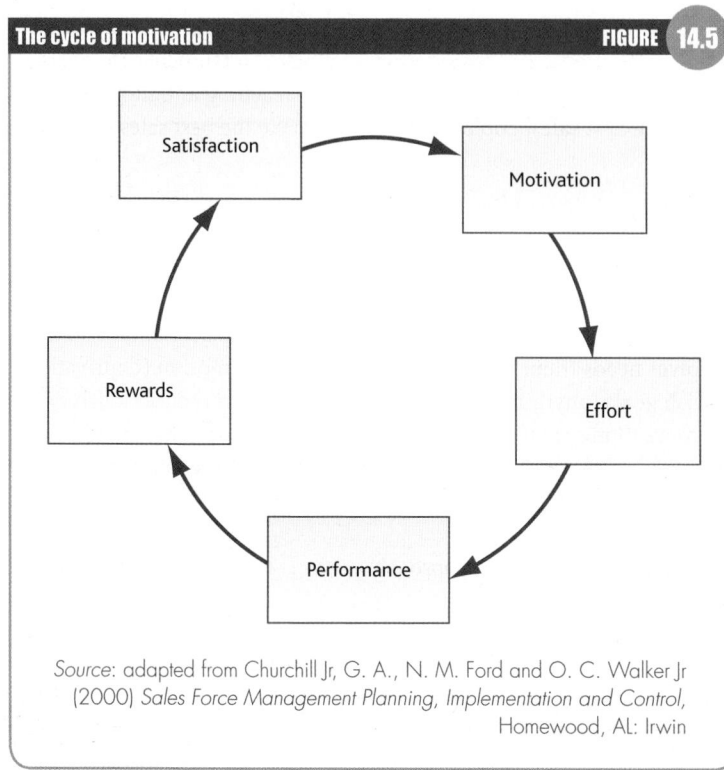

Source: adapted from Churchill Jr, G. A., N. M. Ford and O. C. Walker Jr (2000) *Sales Force Management Planning, Implementation and Control*, Homewood, AL: Irwin

motivation, the greater the effort, resulting in higher performance. Better performance leads to greater rewards and job satisfaction. The cycle is completed through higher satisfaction causing still more motivation.

The implications for sales managers are that they should:

- convince salespeople that they will sell more by working harder or by being trained to work smarter (e.g. more efficient call planning, developing selling skills)
- convince salespeople that the rewards for better performance are worth the extra effort; this implies that the sales manager should give rewards that are valued, and attempt to sell the worth of those rewards to the salesforce (for example, a sales manager might build up the worth of a holiday prize by stating what a good time he or she had personally when there).

Motivation can be affected by the type of compensation plan used by a company. However, as revealed by the research of the motivational theorists, not all people are equally motivated by money. Darmon revealed that there are five types of salespeople, defined by their goal structure.[58]

1 *Creatures of habit*: these salespeople try to maintain their standard of living by earning a predetermined amount of money.
2 *Satisfiers*: these salespeople perform at a level just sufficient to keep their jobs.
3 *Trade-offers*: these salespeople allocate their time based upon a personally determined ratio between work and leisure that is not influenced by the prospect of higher earnings.
4 *Goal-orientated*: these salespeople prefer recognition as achievers by their peers and superiors, and tend to be sales-quota orientated with money mainly serving as recognition of achievement.
5 *Money-orientated*: these salespeople aim to maximize their earnings. Family relationships, leisure and even health may be sacrificed in the pursuit of money.

Consequently, sales managers must categorize their salespeople before deciding their motivational and compensation plan. For example, if a salesforce consists of creatures of habit, satisfiers and trade-offers, increasing commission opportunities is unlikely to be successful. However, where most of the salesforce are goal-orientated or money-orientated, improving commission opportunities is likely to be effective in raising motivation and performance.

Compensation plans are not only determined by motivational considerations. The nature of the selling task, which may determine if the payment of commission is feasible, is another major factor. We shall now examine three types of compensation: fixed salary, commission only and salary plus commission/bonus.

- *Fixed salary*: because payment is not directly tied to sales, salespeople paid by fixed salary are more willing to carry out tasks that do not result in short-term sales, such as providing technical back-up, completing information feedback reports and prospecting, than those paid by commission only. A fixed salary also provides the income security that many salespeople value, although the direct incentive to earn more money by increasing sales is lost. Also the system may lead to perceived injustices if higher-performing salespeople are not being paid more than their lower-achieving colleagues.

- *Commission only*: the lack of a fixed element to income provides a strong incentive to sell, perhaps too strong at times, leading to overbearing salespeople desperate to close sales. Other disadvantages are an unwillingness to take time off from direct selling tasks to attend training courses or fill in reports, and a tendency for there to be high turnover of staff in jobs where commission only is the norm—for example, in insurance selling.
- *Salary plus commission/bonus*: this hybrid system provides some incentive to sell, with an element of security. Usually salary makes up about 70 per cent of income. This system is attractive to ambitious salespeople who wish to combine a base level of income with the opportunity to earn more by greater effort and ability. For these reasons it is the most commonly used method of payment.[59] Bonuses are usually paid on the achievement of some task, such as achieving a sales target or opening a certain number of new accounts.

For many companies their market is the world, which means that they are faced with motivating international sales-forces. Marketing in Action 14.2 discusses some of the problems involved and their solutions.

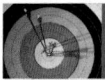

14.2 Marketing in Action

Motivating an International Salesforce

Sales managers should not assume that a motivation and compensation system that works well in their home country will work in overseas markets: the values and expectations of their foreign-based salespeople need to be understood. For example, in Europe financial incentives are often used to motivate salespeople, but in Japan and the Middle East commission is rarely used. Instead, non-financial factors such as increased responsibility or greater job security are more common. An understanding of local customs is essential. In Japan, for example, salary increases are based on seniority. Political factors can also determine the level of fringe benefits provided for employees.

Care needs to be taken over salaries paid to an overseas salesforce when it consists of a mixture of expatriates and local salespeople. Because a salary increase often accompanies an expatriate's overseas move, they may be paid more than local recruits. If this becomes common knowledge, the motivation of locally recruited salespeople may decline.

A common complaint among international salespeople is that their head office does not understand them. They often feel alone or deserted. Their motivation can be boosted through the setting of realistic sales targets, giving them full support and improving communication.

Based on: Cundif and Hilger (1988);[60] Hill et al. (1991);[61] Ghauri and Cateora (2006)[62]

Evaluation of salespeople

Salesforce evaluation provides the information necessary to check if targets are being achieved, and provides the raw information to guide training and motivation. By identifying the strengths and weaknesses of individual salespeople, training can be focused on the areas in need of development, and incentives can be aimed at weak spots such as poor prospecting performance.

Often, performance will be compared to standards of performance such as sales or profit quotas, although other comparisons such as salesperson-to-salesperson or current-to-past sales are also used. Two types of performance measures are used, based on quantitative and qualitative criteria.

Quantitative measures of performance: salespeople can be assessed on input, output and hybrid criteria. Output criteria include:

- sales revenue
- profits generated
- gross profit margin
- sales per active account
- number of new accounts opened.

Input criteria include:

- number of calls
- calls per active account
- calls on new accounts (prospects)
- number of prospects visited.

Hybrid criteria are formed by combining output and input criteria, for example:

- sales revenue per call
- profit per call
- prospecting success ratio = number of new accounts opened ÷ number of prospects visited.

These quantitative measures can be compared against target figures to identify strengths and weaknesses. Many of the measures are diagnostic, pointing to reasons why a target is not being reached. For example, a poor call rate might be a cause of low sales achievement. Some results will merit further investigation. For example, a low prospecting success ratio should prompt an examination of why new accounts are not being opened despite the high number of prospects visited.

Qualitative measures of performance: whereas quantitative criteria will be measured with hard figures, qualitative measures rely on soft data. They are intrinsically more subjective and include assessment of:

- sales skills, e.g. questioning, making presentations
- customer relationships, e.g. how much confidence do customers have in the salesperson, and whether rapport is good
- product knowledge, e.g. how well informed is the salesperson regarding company and competitor products
- self-management, e.g. how well are calls prepared, routes organized
- cooperation and attitudes, e.g. to what extent does the salesperson show initiative, follow instructions?

An increasing number of companies are measuring their salespeople on the basis of the achievement of customer satisfaction. As Richard Harrison, a senior sales manager at IBM states, 'Our sales team is compensated based on how quickly and how efficiently they achieve customer satisfaction.'[63]

The use of quantitative and qualitative measures is interrelated. For example, a poor sales per call ratio will mean a close qualitative assessment of sales skills, customer relationships and product knowledge.

A final form of qualitative assessment does not focus on the salesperson directly but the likelihood of *winning or losing an order*. Particularly for major sales, a sales manager needs to be able to assess the chances of an order being concluded successfully in time to rectify the situation if things seem to be going astray. Unfortunately, asking salespeople directly will rarely result in an accurate answer. This is not because they are trying to deceive but because they may be deluding themselves. The answer is to ask a series of who, when, where, why and

Winning and losing major orders		TABLE 14.5
Question	**Poor (losing answer)**	**Good (winning answer)**
Who will authorize the purchase	The director of MIS	The director of MIS, but it requires an executive director's authorization, and we've talked it over with this person
When will they buy?	Right away. They love the new model	Before the peak processing load at the year end
Where will they be when the decision is made: in the office alone, in their boss's office, in a meeting?	What difference does that make? I think they have already decided	At a board meeting. But don't worry, the in-supplier has no one on its board and we have two good customers on it
Why will they buy from us? Why not their usual supplier?	They and I go way back. They love our new model	The next upgrade from the in-supplier is a big price increase, and ours fits right between its models. They are quite unhappy with the in-supplier about that
How will the purchase be funded?	They've lots of money, haven't they?	The payback period on reduced costs will be about 14 months and we've a leasing company willing to take part of the deal

how questions to probe deeper into the situation. It also means working out acceptable and unacceptable responses. Table 14.5 provides an illustration of how such questions could be employed in connection with a major computer sale.

The losing answers are thin and unconvincing. The salesperson may be convinced that the sale will be achieved but the answers show that this is unlikely. The winning answers are much more assured and credible. The sales manager can be confident that there is no need to take action.

However, with the losing answer the sales manager will need to act and the response will depend on how important the sale and the salesperson are to the company. If they both have high potential, the sales manager should work with the salesperson. He or she should be counselled so that they know why they are being helped and what they will learn from the experience. The aim is to conclude the sale and convince the salesperson that their personal development will be enhanced by the experience.

If the salesperson has high potential but not the sale, only a counselling session is needed. Care should be taken not to offend the salesperson's ego. When only the sale has high potential, the alternatives are not so pleasant. Perhaps the salesperson could be moved to a more suitable post. When neither the salesperson nor the sale has potential, the only question to ask is whether the salesperson is redeployed before or after the sale is lost.

Evaluation and control of the total sales operation

Evaluation of the total personal selling function is necessary to assess its overall contribution to marketing strategy. The results of this assessment may lead to more cost-efficient means of servicing accounts being introduced (e.g. direct mail or telemarketing), the realization that the selling function is under-resourced, or the conclusion that the traditional form of sales organization is in need of reform. One company that suspected its salesforce had become complacent moved every salesperson to a different territory. Despite having to forge new customer relationships, sales increased by a quarter in the following year.

Evaluation of the personal selling function should also include assessing the quality of its relationship with marketing and other organizational units. Salespeople that manage the external relationship with distributors (e.g. retailers) must collaborate internally with their colleagues in marketing to agree joint business objectives and to develop marketing programmes (for example, new products and promotions) that meet the needs of distributors, as well as consumers, so that they are readily adopted by them. This means that close collaboration and good working relations are essential.[64]

Ethical Issues in Personal Selling and Sales Management

Four ethical issues that salespeople may have to face are deception, the hard sell, bribery and reciprocal buying.

Deception

A dilemma that, sooner or later, faces most salespeople is the choice of telling the customer the whole truth and risk losing the sale, or misleading the customer to clinch it. The deception may take the form of exaggeration, lying or withholding important information that significantly reduces the appeal of the product. Such actions should be avoided by influencing salespersons' behaviour by training, by sales management encouraging ethical behaviour by their own actions and words, and by establishing codes of conduct for their salespeople. Nevertheless, from time to time evidence of malpractice in selling reaches the media. For example, in the UK it was alleged that some financial services salespeople mis-sold pensions and endowment mortgages by exaggerating the expected returns. The scandal cost the companies involved millions of pounds in compensation.[65] Lloyds TSB, for example, has paid out over £500 million in compensation to customers as a result of mis-selling endowment mortgages.[66]

Nestlé is a further example of a company that has been criticized for deception. In the 1970s and 1980s, it sold its infant formula (dried milk used to bottle feed babies) in the developing world, using saleswomen dressed to look like nurses. This created the impression, among a vulnerable target group, that the product was endorsed by the medical profession and represented a healthy and desirable alternative to breastfeeding, despite the fact that the medical profession consistently advises that 'breast feeding is best'. Following a major boycott of its products, Nestlé agreed to honour a code drawn up by the World Health Organization, which controls the selling of breast milk substitutes.

Deception can also occur during doorstep selling. Sellers sometimes use misleading claims to sell their products to a particularly vulnerable group, the elderly, or selling can be used as a pretext to carry out a burglary.

The hard sell

Personal selling is also criticized for employing high-pressure sales tactics to close a sale. Some car dealerships have been deemed unethical by using hard-sell tactics to pressure customers into making a quick decision on a complicated purchase that may involve expensive credit facilities. The Internet bank, egg, was found to have instructed its sales staff to use hard-sell techniques to pressurize credit card customers to take out payment protection insurance (PPI) that in most cases they could not claim against or did not need. This resulted in a fine and an instruction to pay compensation.[67]

Bribery

This is the act of giving payment, gifts or other inducements to secure a sale. Bribes are considered unethical because they violate the principle of fairness in commercial negotiations. A major problem is that in some countries bribes are an accepted part of business life: to compete, bribes are necessary. When an organization succumbs, it is usually castigated in its home country if the bribe becomes public knowledge. Yet without the bribe it may have been operating at a major commercial disadvantage. Companies need to decide whether they are going to market in countries where bribery is commonplace. Taking an ethical stance may cause difficulties in the short term but in the long run the positive publicity that can follow may be of greater benefit. Although there are regulations in place to outlaw bribery to foreign individuals, with the 1997 Organization for Economic Cooperation and Development convention on bribery being signed by 36 countries, in practice very few successful prosecutions have resulted.[68] One notable exception is the record fines imposed upon Siemens for paying bribes to win lucrative overseas telecoms and power contracts.[69]

Reciprocal buying

Another practice that might be considered unethical is reciprocal buying. This is where a customer only agrees to buy from a supplier if that supplier agrees to purchase something from the buying organization. This may be considered unfair to other competing suppliers, who may not agree to such an arrangement or may not be in a position to buy from the customer. Supporters of reciprocal buying argue that it is reasonable for a customer to extract the best terms of agreement from a supplier; if this means reaching agreement to sell to the supplier then so be it. Indeed, counter-trade, where goods may be included as part of the payment for supplies has been a feature of international selling for many years and can benefit poorer countries and companies that cannot afford to pay in cash.

When you have read this chapter

log on to the Online Learning Centre at www.mcgraw-hill.co.uk/textbooks/jobber to explore chapter-by-chapter test questions, links and further online study tools for marketing.

Review

1 **Environmental and managerial forces affecting sales**
- The environmental forces are behavioural (rising customer expectations, customer avoidance of buyer–seller negotiations, the expanding power of major buyers, globalization of markets and fragmentation of markets) and technological (salesforce automation, the virtual sales office and electronic channels).
- The managerial forces are the growth in direct marketing techniques, the development of effective relationships between sales and marketing, and recognition of the importance of professional qualifications.

2 Characteristics of modern selling

- The characteristics are customer retention and deletion, customer relationship management, database and knowledge management, marketing the product, problem-solving and system selling, and adding value and satisfying needs.

3 How to prepare for selling

- Salespeople should prepare for selling by gaining knowledge of their own and competitors' products, planning sales presentations, setting call objectives and seeking to understand buyer behaviour.

4 The stages in the selling process

- The stages are preparation, the opening, need and problem identification, presentation and demonstration, dealing with objections, closing the sale and follow-up.

5 The tasks of sales management

- The tasks of a sales manager are to understand marketing strategy, set personal selling objectives and strategies, design the salesforce (salesforce size and organization), manage the salesforce (set salesperson objectives, recruitment and selection, training, motivation and compensation, and evaluation of salespeople), and evaluation and control of the total sales operation.

6 How to design a salesforce

- Designing a salesforce requires determining salesforce size and deciding salesforce organization.
- A useful method of determining salesforce size is the workload method.
- Salesforces can be organized by geographic, product and customer (market segment, account size or new vs existing accounts) structures.

7 How to manage a salesforce

- Managing a salesforce requires setting specific salesperson objectives, recruitment and selection, training, motivation and compensation, and evaluation of salespeople.
- Setting objectives: targets should be set in consultation with salespeople.
- Recruitment and selection: the stages are preparation of the job description and personnel specification, identification of sources of recruitment and methods of communication, design of the application form and preparation of a shortlist, the interview, and the use of supplementary selection aids.
- Training: sales managers need to analyse each salesperson's performance, identify strengths and weaknesses, communicate strengths, gain agreement that a weakness exists, provide training to overcome any weaknesses, and monitor progress.
- Motivation and compensation: sales managers should understand what each salesperson values, be willing to give extra responsibilities and training, provide challenging yet attainable targets, link rewards to performance, and recognize that rewards can be both financial and non-financial (e.g. praise) to improve motivation. Compensation plans can be fixed salary, commission only or salary plus commission/ bonus.
- Evaluation of salespeople: sales managers should use an array of measures, which can be quantitative (input and output) and qualitative (e.g. sales skills and ability to manage customer relationships).

8 Key account management

- Key account management is an approach to selling that focuses resources on major customers and uses a team selling approach.
- Its advantages are close working relationships with customers, improved communication and coordination, better follow-up on sales and service, more in-depth penetration of the decision-making unit, higher sales and the provision of an opportunity for the advancement of career salespeople.
- The stages in the key account management relational development model are Pre-KAM, Early KAM, Partnership-KAM, Synergistic-KAM and Uncoupling-KAM.

9 Ethical issues in personal selling and sales management

- There are potential problems relating to deception, the hard sell, bribery and reciprocal buying.

Key Terms

buying signals statements by a buyer that indicate s/he is interested in buying

customer benefits those things that a customer values in a product; customer benefits derive from product features

ego drive the need to make a sale in a personal way, not merely for money

empathy to be able to feel as the buyer feels, to be able to understand customer problems and needs

key account management an approach to selling that focuses resources on major customers and uses a team selling approach

product features the characteristics of a product that may or may not convey a customer benefit

prospecting searching for and calling on potential customers

salesforce evaluation the measurement of salesperson performance so that strengths and weaknesses can be identified

salesforce motivation the motivation of salespeople by a process that involves needs, which set encouraging drives in motion to accomplish goals

target accounts organizations or individuals whose custom the company wishes to obtain

Study Questions

1. Select a car with which you are familiar. Identify its features and translate them into customer benefits.

2. Imagine you are face to face with a customer for that car. Write down five objections to purchase and prepare convincing responses to them.

3. You are the new sales manager of a company selling abrasives to the motor trade. Your salesforce is paid by fixed salary, and you believe it to be suffering from motivational problems. Discuss how you would handle this.

4. Because of its inherent efficiency the only sensible method of organizing a salesforce is by geographically defined territories. Discuss.

5. Quantitative methods of salesforce organization are superior to qualitative methods because they rely on hard numbers. Evaluate this statement.

6. A company wishes to strengthen its relationships with key customers. How might it approach this task?

7. The key to sales success lies in closing the sale. Discuss.

8. How practical is the workload approach to deciding salesforce size?

9. What are the key stages in the key account relational development model? What implications do they have for marketing to organizational customers?

10. From your own personal experience, do you consider salespeople to be unethical? Can you remember any sales encounters when you have been subject to unethical behaviour?

References

1. Rines, S. (1995) Forcing Change, *Marketing Week*, 1 March, 10–13.

2. See Anderson, R. E. (1996) Personal Selling and Sales Management in the New Millennium, *Journal of Personal Selling and Sales Management* 16(4), 17–52; Magrath, A. J. (1997) A Comment on 'Personal Selling and Sales Management in the New Millennium', *Journal of Personal Selling and Sales Management* 17(1), 45–7.

3. Jones, E., S. P. Brown, A. A. Zoltners and B. A. Weitz (2005) The Changing Environment of Selling and Sales Management, *Journal of Personal Selling & Sales Management* 25(2), 105–11.

4. Anonymous (1996) Revolution in the Showroom, *Business Week*, 19 February, 70–6.

5. Jones, Brown, Zoltners and Weitz (2005) op. cit.

6. Magrath (1997) op. cit.

7. Jones, Brown, Zoltners and Weitz (2005) op. cit.

8. Jobber, D. and G. Lancaster (2009) *Sales and Sales Management*, Harlow: FT Prentice-Hall.

9. See Mandel, M. J. and R. D. Hof (2001) Rethinking the Internet: Down But Hardly Out, *Business Week*, 26 March, 128; Rich, G. A. (2002) The Internet: Boom or Bust to Sales Organizations, *Journal of Marketing Management* 18(3/4), 287–300; and Sharma, A. and N. Tzokas (2002) Personal Selling and Sales Management in the Internet Environment: Lessons Learned, *Journal of Marketing Management* 18(3/4), 249–58.

10. Mandel, M. J. and R. D. Hof (2001) Rethinking the Internet: Down But Hardly Out, *Business Week*, 26 March, 128.

11. Rich, G. A. (2002) The Internet: Boom or Bust to Sales Organizations, *Journal of Marketing Management* 18(3/4), 287–300.

12. Sharma, A. and N. Tzokas (2002) Personal Selling and Sales Management in the Internet Environment: Lessons Learned, *Journal of Marketing Management* 18(3/4), 249–58.

13. Beverage, M. (2001) Contextual Influences and the Adoption and Practice of Relationship Selling in a Business-to-Business Setting: An Exploratory Study, *Journal of Personal Selling and Sales Management* 21, 207–15.

14. Lane, N. and N. Piercy (2004) Strategic Customer Management: Designing a Profitable Future for Your Sales Organization, *European Management Journal* 22(6), 659–68.

15. Stephens, H. (2003) 'CEO' American Marketing Association Summer Educators' Conference, The H. R. Challey Group, August, Chicago.

16. Lane and Piercy (2004) op. cit.

17. Royal, W. (1999) Death of Salesmen, 17 May, 59–60, available at www.industryweek.com.

18. Moncrief, W. and G. W. Marshall (2005) The Evolution of the Seven Stages of Selling, *Industrial Marketing Management* 34, 13–22.

19. Leigh, T. H. and G. W. Marshall (2001) Research Priorities in Sales Strategy and Performance, *Journal of Personal Selling and Sales Management* 21, 83–93.

20. Rackham, N. and J. DeVincentis (1999) *Rethinking the Sales Force: Redefining Selling to Create and Capture Customer Value*, New York: McGraw-Hill.

21. Weitz, B. A. (1981) Effectiveness in Sales Interactions: A Contingency Framework, *Journal of Marketing* 45, 85–103.

22. Román, S., S. Ruiz and J. L. Munuera (2002) The Effects of Sales Training on Salesforce Activity, *European Journal of Marketing* 36(11/12), 1344–66.

23. Schuster, C. P. and J. E. Danes (1986) Asking Questions: Some Characteristics of Successful Sales Encounters, *Journal of Personal Selling and Sales Management*, May, 17–27; Sujan, H., M. Sujan and J. Bettman (1998) Knowledge Structure Differences Between Effective and Less Effective Salespeople, *Journal of Marketing Research* 25, 81–6; Szymanski, D. (1988) Determinants of Selling Effectiveness: the Importance of Declarative Knowledge to the Personal Selling Concept, *Journal of Marketing* 52, 64–77; Weitz, B. A., H. Sujan and M. Sujan (1986) Knowledge, Motivation and Adaptive Behaviour: a Framework for Improving Selling Effectiveness, *Journal of Marketing* 50, 174–91; Krishnan, B. C., R. G. Netemeyer and J. S. Boles (2002) Self-efficacy, Competitiveness, and Effort as Antecedents of Salesperson Performances, *Journal of Personal Selling and Sales Management* 20(4), 285–95.

24. Moncrief, W. C. and G. W. Marshall (2005) The Evolution of the Seven Steps of Selling, *Industrial Marketing Management*, 34, 13–22.

25. Long, M. M., T. Tellefsen and J. D. Lichtenthal (2007) Internet Integration into the Industrial Selling Process: A Step-by-Step Approach, *Industrial Marketing Management* 36, 676–89.

26. Walters, J. (2000) Journey's End For the King of the Costas, *Observer*, 19 November, 9.

27. Brooke, K. (2002) B2B and B2C Marketing is not so Different, *Marketing Business*, July/August, 39.

28. Picaville, L. (2004) Mobile CRM Helps Smith and Nephew Reps Give Hands-On Service, *CRM Magazine* 8(5), 53.

29. Long, Tellefsen and Lichtenthal (2007) op. cit.

30. See Hunt, K. A. and R. Bashaw (1999) A New Classification of Sales Resistance, *Industrial Marketing Management* 28, 109–18.

31. Long, Tellefsen and Lichtenthal (2007) op. cit.

32. Long, Tellefsen and Lichtenthal (2007) op. cit.

33. Burrows, P. (2008) Cisco's Brave New World, *Business Week*, 24 November, 57–68.

34. McDonald, M. H. B. (2002) *Marketing Plans*, London: Heinemann.

35. Strahle, W. and R. L. Spiro (1986) Linking Market Share Strategies to Salesforce Objectives, Activities and Compensation Policies, *Journal of Personal Selling and Sales Management*, August, 11–18.

36. Talley, W. J. (1961) How to Design Sales Territories, *Journal of Marketing* 25(3), 16–28.

37. Homburg, C., J. P. Workman Jr and O. Jensen (2000) Fundamental Changes in Marketing Organization: the Movement Toward a Customer-Focused Organizational Structure, *Journal of the Academy of Marketing Science* 28, 459–78.

38. Magrath, A. J. (1989) To Specialise or Not to Specialise?, *Sales and Marketing Management* 14(7), 62–8.

39. Homburg, C., J. P. Workman Jr and O. Jensen (2002) A Configurational Perspective on Key Account Management, *Journal of Marketing* 66, April, 38–60.

40. Millman, T. and K. Wilson (1995) From Key Account Selling to Key Account Management, *Journal of Marketing Practice* 1(1), 9–21.

41. McDonald, M. and B. Rogers (1998) *Key Account Management*, Oxford: Butterworth-Heinemann.

42. Wilson, K., S. Croom, T. Millman and D. Weilbaker (2000) The SRT-SAMA Global Account Management Study, *Journal of Selling and Major Account Management* 2(3), 63–84.

43. Wilson, K. and T. Millman (2003) The Global Account Manager as Political Entrepreneur, *Industrial Marketing Management* 32, 151–8.

44. Montgomery, G. and P. Yip (1999) Statistical Evidence on Global Account Management Programs, *Fachzeitschrift Für Marketing THEXIS* 16(4), 10–13.

45. Piercy, N., D. W. Cravens and N. A. Morgan (1998) Salesforce Performance and Behaviour Based Management Processes in Business-to-Business Sales Organisations, *European Journal of Marketing* 32(1/2), 79–100.

46. P. A. Consultants (1979) *Salesforce Practice Today: A Basis for Improving Performance*, Cookham: Institute of Marketing.

47. Galbraith, A. J., Kiely and T. Watkins (1991) Salesforce Management: Issues for the 1990s, *Proceedings of the Marketing Education Group Conference*, Cardiff, July, 425–45.

48. Mayer, M. and G. Greenberg (1964) What Makes a Good Salesman, *Harvard Business Review* 42(July–August), 119–25.

49. For a full discussion of modern salesperson selection methods see Cron, W. L., G. Marshall, J. Singh, R. L. Spiro and H. Sujan (2005) Salesperson Selection, Training and Development: Trends, Implications and Research Opportunities, *Journal of Personal Selling & Sales Management* 25(2), 123–36.

50. Krishnan, B. C., R. G. Netemeyer and J. S. Boles (2002) Self-Efficacy, Competitiveness and Effort as Antecedents of Salesperson Performance, *Journal of Personal Selling and Sales Management* 22(4), 285–95.

51. See DeCormier, R. and D. Jobber (1993) The Counsellor Selling Method: Concepts and Constructs, *Journal of Personal Selling and Sales Management* 13(4), 39–60; Román, S., S. Ruiz and J. L. Munuera (2002) The Effects of Sales Training on Salesforce Activity, *European Journal of Marketing* 36(11/12), 1344–66.

52. Wilson, K. (1993) Managing the Industrial Salesforce in the 1990s, *Journal of Marketing Management* 9(2), 123–40.

53. Cron *et al.* (2005) op. cit.

54. Luthans, F. (1997) *Organizational Behaviour*, New York: McGraw-Hill.

55. See Pullins, E. B. (2001) An Exploratory Investigation of the Relationship of Sales Force Compensation and Intrinsic Motivation, *Industrial Marketing Management* 30, 403–13; and Holmes, T. L. and R. Srivastava (2002) Effects of Job Perceptions on Job Behaviours: Implications for Sales Performance, *Industrial Marketing Management* 31, 421–8.

56. See Maslow, A. H. (1954) *Motivation and Personality*, New York: Harper & Row; Herzberg, F. (1966) *Work and the Nature of Man*, Cleveland: W. Collins; Vroom, V. H. (1964) *Work and Motivation*, New York: Wiley; Adams, J. S. (1965) Inequity in Social Exchange, in Berkowitz, L. (ed.) *Advances in Experimental Social Psychology 2*, New York: Academic Press; Likert, R. (1961) *New Patterns of Sales Management*, New York: McGraw-Hill.

57. Churchill Jr, G. A., N. M. Ford and O. C. Walker Jr (2000) *Salesforce Management: Planning, Implementation and Control*, Homewood, AL: Irwin.

58. Darmon, R. Y. (1974) Salesmen's Response to Financial Initiatives: An Empirical Study, *Journal of Marketing Research*, November, 418–26.

59. See Avlonitis, G., C. Manolis and K. Boyle (1985) Sales Management Practices in the UK Manufacturing Industry, *Journal of Sales Management* 2(2), 6–16; Shipley, D. and D. Jobber (1991) Salesforce Motivation, Compensation and Evaluation, *The Services Industries Journal* 11(2), 154–70.

60. Cundiff, E. and M. T. Hilger (1988) *Marketing in the International Environment*, Englewood Cliffs, NJ: Prentice-Hall.

61. Hill, J. S., R. R. Still and U. O. Boya (1991) Managing the International Salesforce, *International Marketing Review* 8(1), 19–31.

62. Ghauri and Cateora (2006) *International Marketing*, Maidenhead: McGraw-Hill.

63. The quotation appears in Jap, S. D. (2001) The Strategic Role of the Salesforce in Developing Customer Satisfaction Across the Relationship Lifecycle, *Journal of Personal Selling and Sales Management* 21(2), 95–108.

64. Dewsnap, B. and D. Jobber (2002) A Social Psychological Model of Relations Between Marketing and Sales, *European Journal of Marketing* 36(7/8), 874–94.

65. Mackintosh, J. (1999) Pensions Mis-Selling Cost May Rise by £1bn, *Financial Times*, 18/19 December, 2.

66. Treanor, J. (2005) Lloyds Pays Customers £150 m for Endowment Mis-Selling, *Guardian*, 13 December, 21.

67. Inman, P. (2008) Bank Fined £721,000 for Misselling Credit Card Insurance, *Guardian*, 11 December, 22.

68. SenGupta, R. (2006) Trouble at Home for Overseas Bribes, *Financial Times*, 2 February, 12.

69. Gow, D. (2008) Record US Fine Ends Siemens Bribery Scandal, *Guardian*, 16 December, 24.

Selling in China

Harnessing the Power of the *Guanxi*

China's economy has been growing at an average of 9 per cent for the past 20 years. The country possesses considerable strengths in mass manufacturing and is currently building large electronics and heavy industrial factories. The country is also investing heavily in education and training, especially in the development of engineers and scientists. While these advances mean that China poses new threats to western companies, the country provides opportunities too. China has a population of over 1.3 billion people, and they are spending their growing incomes on consumer durables such as cars, a market that has reached 3 million, mobile phones, where China has the world's biggest subscriber base of over 500 million, and computers, where over 200 million people browse the Internet on broadband connections. Western companies such as Microsoft, Procter & Gamble, Coca-Cola, BP and Siemens have already seen the Chinese market as an opportunity and entered, usually with the aid of local joint venture partners.

Although the Chinese economy undoubtedly possesses many strengths, it also has several weaknesses. First, it lacks major global brands. When businesspeople around the world were asked to rank Chinese brands, Haier, a white-goods (refrigerators, washing machines, etc.) and home appliance manufacturer, was ranked first, and Lenovo, a computer company, famous for buying IBM's personal computer division, second. Neither company is a major global player in its respective market. Second, China suffers from the risk of social unease, resulting from the widening gap between rich and poor, as well as corruption. Third, the country has paid a heavy ecological price for rapid industrial and population growth, with thousands of deaths attributed to air and water pollution. Fourth, while still a low labour-cost economy, wage levels are rising fast, particularly in skilled areas, reducing its competitive advantage in this area. Finally, bureaucracy can make doing business in China difficult.

Although western companies have made successful entries to the Chinese market, some, such as Whirlpool, a US white-goods manufacturer, and Kraft, the food multinational, have made heavy losses. Overseas companies hoping to sell successfully in China need to understand a number of realities of the market there.

First, the country is very diverse: 1.3 billion people speak 100 dialects, and covering such a large geographic area the climate is very different across regions. For example, parts of the south are humid, while the north is more temperate. Also, income levels vary considerably between less affluent rural districts and richer cities.

Many western companies enter China by means of a joint venture, but they need to be aware of the different business conditions there. In China there is no effective rule of law governing business. Bureaucracy and governmental interference can also bring difficulties. For example, Thames Water pulled out of a 20-year water treatment project in Shanghai after the government ruled that the guaranteed rate of return to investors was illegal.

A key element in Chinese business dealings is the existence of *Guanxi* networks. *Guanxi* is a set of personal connections on which a person can draw to obtain resources or an advantage when doing business. Developing such a network may involve performing favours or the giving of gifts. For example, a businessperson may participate in a public ceremonial function or a profession could send books to a Chinese university. Favours are 'banked', and there is a reciprocal obligation to return a favour.

An important aspect of Chinese culture is the avoidance of 'loss of face'. This can occur when a Chinese person finds him/herself embarrassed by, for example, displaying lack of knowledge or understanding. Chinese people like to gather as much information as possible before revealing their thoughts, to avoid losing face and displaying ignorance. They also value modesty and reasoning, and regard the signing of a contract to be only the beginning of a business relationship.

Questions

1. What are the implications of *Guanxi* networks for selling in China?
2. An important Chinese cultural issue is the avoidance of loss of face. Discuss its implications for selling in China.
3. Explain the concept of self-reference criteria, and its implications for selling in China.

This case was writen by David Jobber, Professor of Marketing, University of Bradford.

Bottling it in Europe CASE 28

Glaztex Sells its Glass Bottling Equipment to Europe

Glaztex plc was a UK-based supplier of bottling plant used in production lines to transport and fill bottles. Two years ago it opened an overseas sales office targeting Scandinavia, Germany, France and the Benelux countries. It estimated that there were over 1000 organizations in those countries that had bottling facilities, and that a major sales push in northern Europe was therefore warranted. Sales so far had been disappointing with only three units having been sold. Expectations had been much higher than this, given the advantages of its product over that produced by its competitors.

Technological breakthroughs at Glaztex meant that its bottling lines had a 10 per cent speed advantage over the nearest competition with equal filling accuracy. A major problem with competitor products was unreliability. Downtime due to a line breakdown was extremely costly to bottlers. Tests by Glaztex engineers at its research and development establishment in the UK had shown its system to be the most reliable on the market. Glaztex's marketing strategy was based around high quality, high price competitive positioning. It believed that the superior performance of its product justified a 10 per cent price premium over its major competitors, which were all priced at around £1 million for a standard production line. Salespeople were told to stress the higher speed and enhanced reliability when talking to customers. The sales organization in northern Europe consisted of a sales manager with four salespeople assigned to Scandinavia, Germany, France and the Benelux countries, respectively. A technical specialist was also available when required. When a sales call required specialist technical assistance, a salesperson would contact the sales office to arrange for the technical specialist to visit the prospect, usually together with the salesperson.

Typically, four groups of people inside buying organizations were involved in the purchase of bottling equipment—namely the production manager, the production engineer, the purchasing officer and, where large sums of money were involved (over £1.5 million), the technical director. Production managers were mainly interested in smooth production flows and cost savings. Production engineers were charged with drawing up specifications for new equipment, and in large firms, they were usually asked to draw up state-of-

the-art specifications. The purchasing officers, who were often quite powerful, were interested in the financial aspects of any purchase, and technical directors, while interested in technical issues, also appreciated the prestige associated with having state-of-the-art technology.

John Goodman was the sales executive covering France. While in the sales office in Paris, he received a call from Dr Leblanc, the technical director of Commercial SA, a large Marseille-based bottling company, which bottled under licence a number of major soft drink brands. It had a reputation for technical excellence and innovation. Goodman made an appointment to see Dr Leblanc on 7 March. He was looking forward to making his first visit to this company. The following extracts are taken from his record of his sales calls.

7 March

Called on Dr Leblanc who told me that Commercial SA had decided to purchase a new bottling line as a result of expansion, and asked for details of what we could provide. I described our system and gave him our sales literature. He told me that three of our competitors had already discussed their system with him. As I was leaving, he suggested that I might like to talk to M. Artois, their production engineer to check specifications.

8 March

Visited M. Artois who showed me the specifications he had drawn up. I was delighted to see that our specifications easily exceeded them but was concerned that his specifications seemed to match those of one of our competitors, Hofstead Gm, almost exactly. I showed M. Artois some of our technical manuals. He did not seem impressed.

11 March

Visited Dr Leblanc who appeared very pleased to see me. He asked me to give him three reasons why they should buy from us. I told him that our system was more technologically advanced than the competition's, was more reliable and had a faster bottling speed. He asked me if I was sure it was the most technologically advanced. I said that there was no doubt about it. He suggested I contact M. Bernard the purchasing manager. I made an appointment to see him in two days' time.

13 March

Called on M. Bernard. I discussed the technical features of the system with him. He asked me about price. I told him I would get back to him on that.

15 March

Visited Dr Leblanc who said a decision was being made within a month. I repeated our operational advantages and he asked me about price. I told him I would give him a quote as soon as possible.

20 March

Saw M. Bernard. I told him our price was £1.1 million. He replied that a major competitor had quoted less than £1 million. I replied that the greater reliability and bottling speed meant that our higher price was more than justified. He remained unimpressed.

21 March

Had a meeting with Mike Bull, my sales manager, to discuss tactics. I told him that there were problems. He suggested that all purchasing managers liked to believe they were saving their company money. He told me to reduce my price by £50,000 to satisfy M. Bernard's ego.

25 March

Told M. Bernard of our new quotation. He said he still did not understand why we could not match the competition on price. I repeated our technical advantages over the competition and told him that our 10 per cent faster speed and higher reliability had been proven by our research and development engineers.

30 March

Visited Dr Leblanc who said a meeting had been arranged for 13 April to make the final decision but that our price of £1.05 million was too high for the likes of M. Bernard.

4 April

Hastily arranged a meeting with Mike Bull to discuss the situation. Told him about Dr Leblanc's concern that M. Bernard thought our price was too high. He said that £1 million was as low as we could go.

5 April

Took our final offer to M. Bernard. He said he would let me know as soon as a decision was made. He stressed that the decision was not his alone; several other people were involved.

16 April

Received a letter from M. Bernard stating that the order had been placed with Hofstead Gm. He thanked me for the work I had put into the bid made by Glaztex.

 Questions

1   Analyse the reasons for the failure to win the order and discuss the lessons to be learnt for key account management.

This case was prepared by David Jobber, Professor of Marketing, University of Bradford.

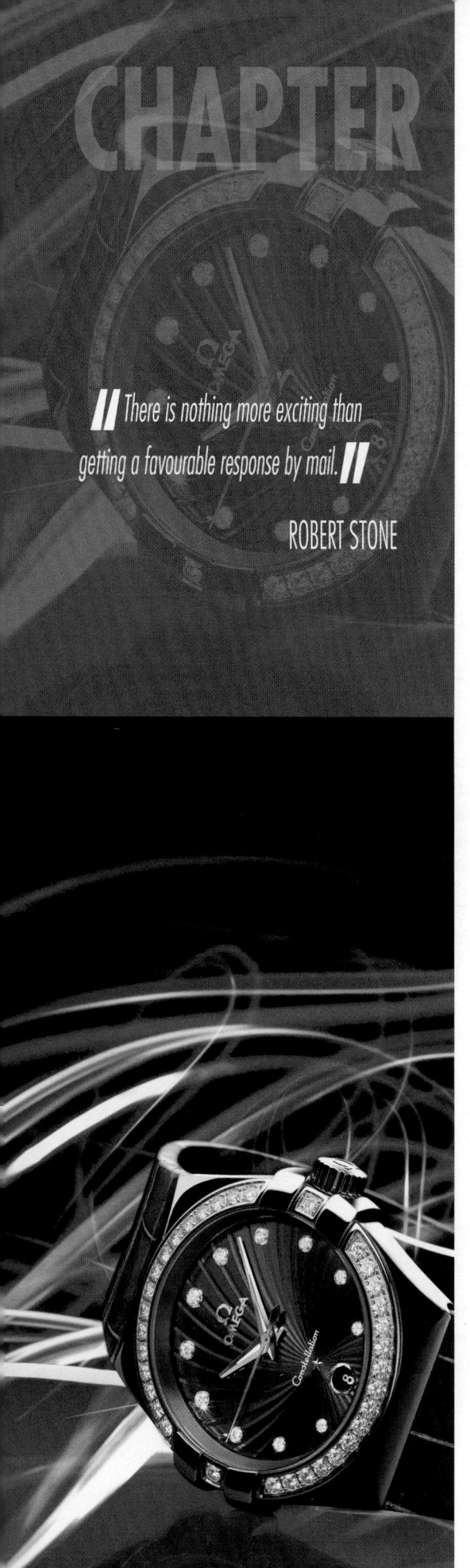

CHAPTER 15

Direct marketing

There is nothing more exciting than getting a favourable response by mail.

ROBERT STONE

LEARNING OBJECTIVES

After reading this chapter, you should be able to:

1 explain the meaning of direct marketing

2 describe the reasons for the growth in direct marketing activity

3 discuss the nature and uses of database marketing

4 discuss the nature of customer relationship management

5 explain how to manage a direct marketing campaign

6 describe the media used in direct marketing

7 discuss the ethical issues in direct marketing

In recent years, direct marketing has established itself as a major component of the promotional mix. Whereas mass advertising reaches a wide spectrum of people, some of whom may not be in the target audience and may only buy at some later unspecified date, direct marketing uses media that can more precisely target consumers and request an immediate direct response. Although the origins of direct marketing lie in direct mail and mail-order catalogues, today's direct marketers use a wide range of media, including telemarketing, direct response advertising, the Internet and online computer shopping to interact with people. No longer is direct marketing synonymous with 'junk mail'—it has grown to be an integral part of the relationship marketing concept, where companies attempt to establish ongoing direct and profitable relationships with customers.

In this chapter, we will examine the types of media that direct marketers use to reach their targets. We will explore the issues relating to database management and customer relationship management. The management of a direct marketing campaign will be analysed, including the need for integrated communications, setting objectives, targeting, achieving customer retention and creating action plans. Finally, a number of ethical issues will be discussed.

First, however, we begin by describing what direct marketing is and the reasons for its growing popularity among marketers.

Defining Direct Marketing

Direct marketing attempts to acquire and retain customers by contacting them without the use of an intermediary. Unlike many other forms of communication, it usually requires an immediate response, which means that the effectiveness of most direct marketing campaigns can be assessed quantitatively.

A definition of direct marketing is:

> The distribution of products, information and promotional benefits to target consumers through interactive communication in a way that allows response to be measured.

Direct marketing campaigns are not necessarily short-term, response-driven activities. More and more companies are using direct marketing to develop ongoing direct relationships with customers. Some marketers believe that the cost of attracting a new customer is five times that of retaining existing customers. Direct marketing activity can be one tool in the armoury of marketers in their attempt to keep current customers satisfied and spending money. Once a customer has been acquired, there is the opportunity to sell that customer other products marketed by the company. Direct Line, a UK insurance company, became market leader in motor insurance by bypassing the insurance broker to reach the consumer directly through direct response television advertisements using a freefone number and financial appeals to encourage car drivers to get in touch. As well as selling motor insurance, their trained telesales people offer substantial discounts on other insurance products, including buildings and contents insurance. In this way, Direct Line has built a major business through using a combination of direct marketing methods.

Direct marketing covers a wide array of methods including:

- direct mail
- telemarketing (both inbound and outbound)
- direct response advertising
- catalogue marketing
- mobile marketing
- electronic media (Internet, e-mail, interactive TV)
- inserts (leaflets in magazines)
- door-to-door leafleting.

The first four of these direct marketing channels will be analysed later in this chapter when discussing media selection for a campaign. Mobile marketing and electronic media will be discussed in Chapter 18, on digital marketing.

Much direct marketing activity is carried out within national boundaries. The number of consumer direct marketers who run large-scale pan-European campaigns are few. These include American Express, Yves Rocher and Mattel. Business-to-business direct marketing activity is more international, with companies such as Xerox, IBM and Hewlett-Packard treating Europe as a single market for many years.

Direct marketing activity, including direct mail, telemarketing and telephone banking, is regulated by a European Commission Directive that came into force at the end of 1994. Its main provisions are that:

- suppliers cannot insist upon pre-payments
- consumers must be told the identity of the supplier, the price, quality of the product and any transport charges, the payment and delivery methods, and the period over which the solicitation remains valid
- orders must be met within 30 days unless otherwise indicated
- a cooling-off period of 30 days is mandatory and cold calling by telephone, fax or electronic mail is restricted unless the receiver has given prior consent.

As with all marketing communications, direct marketing campaigns should be integrated both within themselves and with other communication tools such as advertising, publicity and personal selling. Uncoordinated communication leads to blurred brand images, low impact and customer confusion.

Growth in Direct Marketing Activity

Direct marketing activities have grown over the last 15 years. Smith and Taylor outline five factors that have fuelled this rise.[1]

1 Market and media fragmentation

The trend towards market fragmentation has limited the capability of mass-marketing techniques to reach market segments with highly individualized needs. As markets segment, the importance of direct marketing media to target distinct consumer groups with personalized appeals will grow. One growing segment is women in paid employment who have less time to shop. Direct marketing can satisfy their need for speed and convenience through shopping by telephone or mail using a credit card as a mechanism for payment. Also, specialist interest groups (e.g. bird watchers or personal computer enthusiasts) can be reached directly and efficiently by direct mail and by inserts in direct response advertising in specialist magazines.

The growth of specialist media (media fragmentation) has meant that direct response advertising is more effective since market niches can be tightly targeted. The range of specialist magazines in bookshops these days and the emergence of specialist TV channels such as MTV mean that it is easier to reach a closely defined target segment.

2 Developments in technology

The rise in accessibility of computer technology and the increasing sophistication of software, allowing the generation of personalized letters and telephone scripts, has eased the task of direct marketers. Large databases holding detailed information on individuals can be stored, updated and analysed to enhance targeting. The rise of customer relationship management software has enabled companies to manage one-to-one relationships with huge numbers of consumers. Automated telephone systems make it possible to handle dozens of calls simultaneously, reducing the risk of losing potential customers. Furthermore, developments in technology in telephone, cable and satellite television and the Internet have triggered the rise in home-based electronic shopping.

3 The list explosion

The increased supply of lists and their diversity (e.g. 25,000 Rolls-Royce owners, 20,000 women executives, 100,000 house improvers or 800 brand managers in fmcg and service companies) has provided the raw data for direct marketing activities. List brokers act as an intermediary in the supply of lists of names and addresses from list owners (often either companies who have built lists through transactions with their customers, or organizations that have compiled lists specifically for the purpose of renting them). List brokers thus aid the process of finding a suitable list for targeting purposes. Lists are rented usually on a one-time-use basis. To protect the supplier against multiple use by the client, 'seeds' are planted on the list. These are usually employees of the list broking firm who will receive the mailing so that any multiple mailings from a once-only list will easily be identified.

4 Sophisticated analytical techniques

By using geodemographic analysis, households can be classified into a neighbourhood type—for example, 'modern private housing, young families' or 'private flats, single people'. These, in turn, can be cross-referenced with product usage, media usage and lifestyle statements to create market segments that can be targeted by direct mail (geodemographic information contains the postcode for households).

5 Coordinated marketing systems

The high costs of personal selling have led an increasing number of companies to take advantage of direct marketing techniques such as direct response advertising and telemarketing to make salesforces more cost-effective. For example, a coupon response advertisement or direct mail may generate leads that can be screened by outbound telemarketing. Alternatively, inbound telemarketing can provide the mechanism for accommodating enquiries stimulated by other direct marketing activities.

Database Marketing

At the heart of much direct marketing activity is the marketing database, since direct marketing depends on customer information for its effectiveness. A marketing database is an electronic filing cabinet containing a list of names, addresses, telephone numbers, lifestyle and transactional data. Information such as the types of purchase, frequency of purchase, purchase value and responsiveness to promotional offers may be held.

Database marketing is defined as follows.[2]

An interactive approach to marketing that uses individually addressable marketing media and channels (such as mail, telephone and the salesforce) to:
- provide information to a target audience
- stimulate demand
- stay close to customers by recording and storing an electronic database memory of customers, prospects and all communication and transactional data.

Some key characteristics of database marketing are that, first, it allows direct communication with customers through a variety of media, including direct mail, telemarketing and direct response advertising. Second, it usually requires the customer to respond in a way that allows the company to take action (such as contact by telephone, sending out literature or arranging sales visits). Third, it must be possible to trace the response back to the original communication.[3]

The computer provides the capability of storing and analysing large quantities of data from diverse sources and presenting information in a convenient, accessible and useful format.[4] The creation of a database relies on the collection of information on customers, which can be sourced from:

- company records
- responses to sales promotions
- warranty and guarantee cards
- offering samples that require the consumer to give name, address, telephone number, etc.
- enquiries
- exchanging data with other companies
- salesforce records
- application forms (e.g. to join a credit or loyalty scheme)
- complaints
- responses to previous direct marketing activities
- organized events (e.g. wine tastings).

Collecting information is easiest for companies that have direct contact with their customers such as those in financial services or retailing. However, even for those where the sales contact is indirect, building a database is often possible. For example, Seagram, the drinks company, built up a European database through telephone and written enquiries from consumers, sales promotional returns, tastings in store, visits to company premises, exhibitions, and promotions that encouraged consumers to name like-minded friends or colleagues.[5]

Typical information stored on a database

Figure 15.1 shows typical information that is recorded on a database. This is described in more detail below.[6]

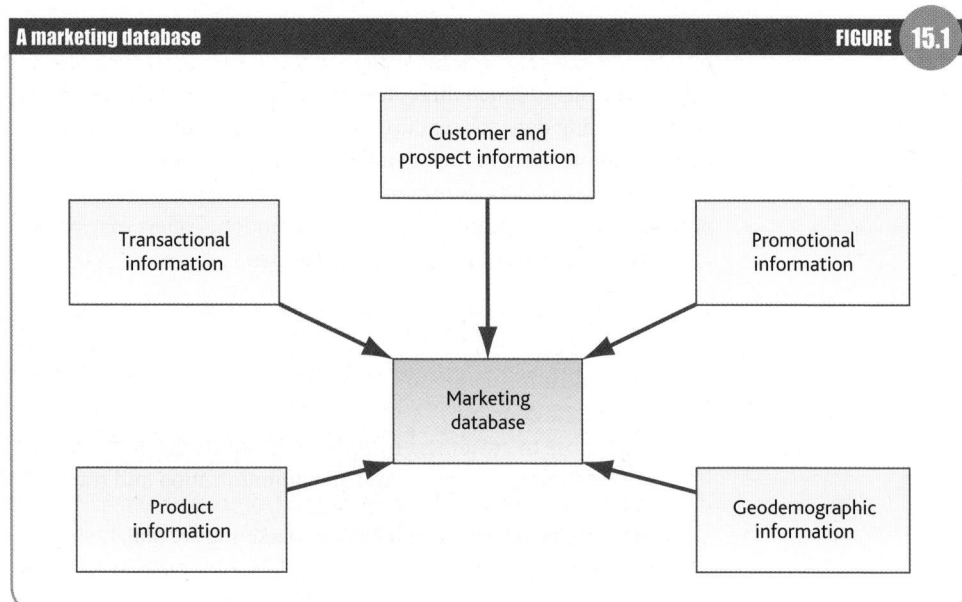

A marketing database   FIGURE **15.1**

Customer and prospect information

This provides the basic data required to access customers and prospects (e.g. name, home and e-mail addresses, telephone number) and contains their general behavioural characteristics (e.g. psychographic and behavioural data). For organizational markets, information on key decision-makers and influencers, and the choice criteria they use would also be stored.

Transactional information

Past transactions are a key indicator of likely future transactions. Transactional data must be sufficiently detailed to allow FRAC (frequency, recency, amount and category) information to be extracted for each customer. *Frequency* refers to how often a customer buys. Both the average frequency and the trend (is the customer tending to buy more or less frequently?) is of use to the direct marketer. *Recency* measures when the customer last bought. If customers are waiting longer before they rebuy (i.e. recency is increasing) the reasons for this (e.g. less attractive offers or service problems) need to be explored. *Amount* measures how much a customer has bought and is usually recorded in value terms. Analysis of this data may reveal that 20 per cent of customers are accounting for 80 per cent of the value of transactions. Finally, *category* defines the type of product being bought. Cross-analysing category data with type of customer (e.g. geodemographics or lifestyle data) can reveal the customer profile most likely to buy a particular product. Also, promotions can be targeted at those individuals known to be interested in buying from a particular product category.

Promotional information

This covers information on what promotional campaigns have been run, who has responded to them and what the overall results were in terms of contacts, sales and profits. The database will contain information on which customers were targeted, and the media and contact strategy employed.

Product information

This information would include which products have been promoted, who responded, when and from where.

Geodemographic information

Information about the geographic areas of customers and prospects, and the social, lifestyle or business category they belong to would be stored. By including postcodes in the address of customers and employing the services of an agency that conducts geodemographic analysis (such as ACORN) a customer profile would be built up. Direct mail could then be targeted at people with similar geodemographic profiles.

An example of the type of data held on a marketing database for a business-to-business company is given in Table 15.1. Both hard (quantitative) and soft (qualitative) data will be held as a basis for direct marketing, salesforce activities and marketing planning applications.

How might a marketing database be used?

One application is to target those people who are more likely to respond to a direct marketing campaign. For example, a special offer on garden tools from a mail-order company could be targeted at those people who have purchased gardening products in the past. Another example would be a car dealer which, by holding a database of customers' names and addresses and dates of car purchase, could use direct mail to promote service offers and new model launches. Telemarketing campaigns can be targeted in a similar way.

A marketing database can also be used to strengthen relationships with customers. For example, Highland Distillers switched all of its promotional budget for its Macallan whisky

A major account information system		TABLE 15.1
	Hard	**Soft**
General	Addresses, telephone, fax and telex numbers, e-mail addresses Customer products sold and markets served (size and growth rates) Sales volume and revenue Profits Capital employed Operating ratios (e.g. return on capital employed, profit margin)	Decision-making unit members Choice criteria Perceptions and attitudes Buying process Assessment of relationships Problems and threats Opportunities Suppliers' strengths and weaknesses Competitors' strengths and weaknesses Environmental changes affecting account now and in the future
Specific	Suppliers' sales to account by product Suppliers' price levels and profitability by product Details of discounts and allowances Competitors' products, price levels and sales Contract expiry dates	

brand from advertising to direct marketing. It built a database of 100,000 of its more frequent drinkers (those who consume at least five bottles a year), mailing them every few months with interesting facts about the brand, whisky memorabilia and offers.[7]

Database marketing can be used strategically to improve customer retention with long-term programmes established to maximize customer lifetime value. This issue will be discussed further when we examine customer retention strategies. Many retailers have created loyalty schemes where customers apply for a card that entitles them to discounts but also enables the retailer to record and store transactional data (e.g. which products are bought, their frequency, value, etc.) on an individual basis. Digital Marketing 15.1 shows how a database could be used by a retailer.

The main applications of database marketing are as follows.

- *Direct mail*: a database can be used to select customers for mailings.
- *Telemarketing*: a database can store telephone numbers so that customers and prospects can be contacted. Also when customers contact the company by telephone, relevant information can be stored, including when the next contact should be made.
- *Distributor management systems*: a database can be the foundation on which information is provided to distributors and their performance monitored.
- *Loyalty marketing*: highly loyal customers can be selected from the database for special treatment as a reward for their loyalty.
- *Target marketing*: other groups of individuals or businesses can be targeted as a result of analysing the database. For example, buyer behaviour information stored by supermarkets can be used to target special promotions to those individuals likely to be receptive to them. For example, a consumer promotion for wine could be sent to wine drinkers exclusively.
- *Campaign planning*: using the database as a foundation for sending consistent and coordinated campaigns and messages to individuals and market segments.
- *Marketing evaluation*: by recording responses to marketing mix inputs (e.g. price promotions, advertising messages and product offers) it is possible to assess how effective different approaches are to varying individuals and market segments.

15.1 Digital Marketing

Using a Marketing Database in Retailing

The potential for using marketing databases is enormous, allowing integrated planning of marketing communications. Suppose a retailer wanted to increase sales and profits using a database. How might this happen? First, the retailer analyses its database to find distinct groups of customers for whom the retailer has the potential to offer superior value. The identification of these target market segments allows tailored products, services and communications to be aimed at them.

The purchasing patterns of individuals are established by means of a loyalty card programme. The scheme's main objective is to improve customer loyalty by rewarding varying shopping behaviours differently. The scheme allows customers to be tracked by frequency of visit, expenditure per visit and expenditure per product category. Retailers can gain an understanding of the types of products that are purchased together. For example, Boots, the UK retailer, uses its Advantage card loyalty scheme (which has 15 million active members) to conduct these kinds of analyses. One useful finding is that there is a link between buying films and photo frames and the purchase of new baby products. Because its products are organized along category lines it never occurred to the retailer to create a special offer linked to picture frames for the baby products buyer, yet these are the kinds of products new parents are likely to want.

Integrated marketing communications is possible using the marketing database, as the system tracks what marketing communications (e.g. direct mail, promotions) customers are exposed to, and measures the cost-effectiveness of each activity via electronic point of sale data and loyalty cards.

The retailer's customers are classified into market segments based on their potential, their degree of loyalty and whether they are predominantly price- or promotion-sensitive. A different marketing strategy is devised for each group. For example, to trade up high-potential, promotionally sensitive, low-loyalty shoppers who do their main shopping elsewhere, high-value manufacturers' coupons for main shopping products are mailed every two months until the consumer is traded up to a different group. Also, high-loyalty customers can be targeted for special treatment such as receiving a customer magazine.

The Tesco Clubcard (which has 15 million members in the UK and 7 million overseas) also gathers a rich stream of information. It is used to define segments—for example, discount-driven 'price sensitives', 'foodies', 'heavy category users', and 'brand loyalists', testing consumer response to promotions, and testing the effects of different prices. Different regional media selection strategies can be tested by monitoring in-store responses. It is also used to communicate more effectively with consumers. Promotions can be targeted more precisely: for example, targeting dog food offers to dog owners, direct mail can be sent out to targeted segments such as 'healthy living' types, and tailored e-mail campaigns developed. Product assortments in stores can also be fine-tuned according to the buying habits of customers. Both schemes have worked hard to tailor the rewards offered to consumers. For example, Boots launched a Health Club and a Parenting Club to offer card holders rewards relevant to their lifestyles and interests.

The success of the Boots Advantage card and the Tesco Clubcard has prompted the launch of the Nectar loyalty card. A key difference is that it is a joint initiative, with the founders (Sainsbury's, BP, Barclaycard and Debenhams) quickly being joined by another 14 members, including Vodafone, the online holiday company ebookers, the restaurant chain Beefeater, and wine and beer retailer Threshers. Within the first six months, 11 million cardholders had been signed up by the original four members. The opportunity to offer attractive rewards to customers, and thereby increase loyalty, as well as the data-gathering opportunities, make Nectar an exciting proposition. Although Barclaycard, Debenhams and Threshers have now withdrawn, other companies, such as Homebase and Thomson Directories, have taken their place.

Based on: Mitchell (2002);[8] James (2003);[9] O'Hara (2003);[10] Barnes (2005);[11] McCawley (2006);[12] Murphy (2008);[13] Finch (2009)[14]

The development of database marketing has taken a step further with the growth of customer relationship management systems that use databases as the foundation for managing customer relationships. The next section discusses these systems.

Customer Relationship Management

Customer relationship management (CRM) is a term for the methodologies, technologies and e-commerce capabilities used by firms to manage customer relationships.[15] In particular, CRM software packages aid the interaction between the customer and the company, enabling the company to coordinate all of the communication effort so that the customer is presented with a unified message and image. CRM companies offer a range of information technology-based services such as call centres, data analysis and website management. The basic principle behind CRM is that company staff have a single-customer point of view of each client.[16] As customers are now using multiple channels more frequently, they may buy one product from a salesperson and another from a website. A website may provide product information, which is used to buy the product from a distributor. Interactions between a customer and a company may take place through the salesforce, call centres, websites, e-mail, fax services or distributors (see Fig. 15.2).

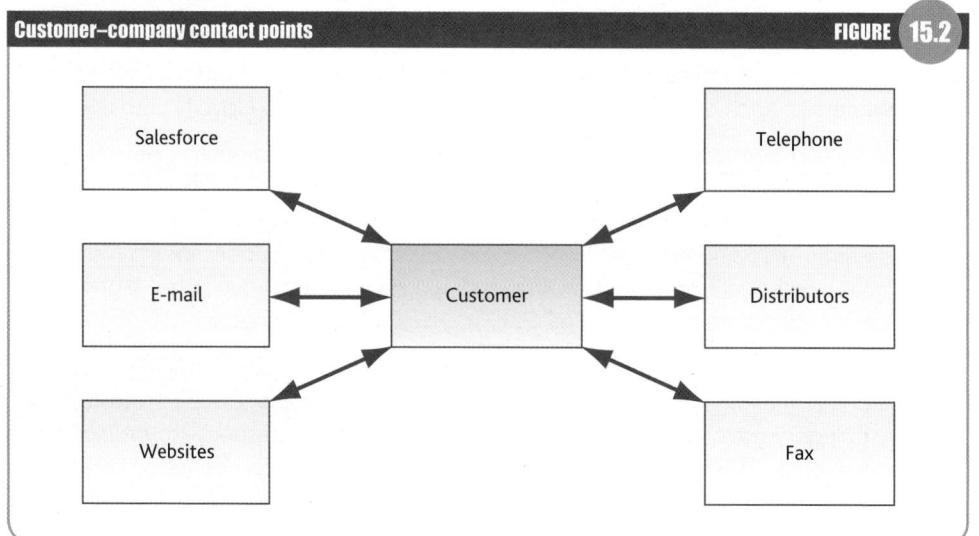

Customer–company contact points   **FIGURE 15.2**

Although the term CRM is relatively new, the ideas and principles behind it are not. Businesses have long practised some form of customer relationship management. What sets present-day CRM apart is that companies now have an increased opportunity to use technology and manage one-to-one relationships with huge numbers of consumers.[17] This is facilitated by companies such as Oracle (www.oracle.com/siebel), SNT (www.snt.com) and Salesforce (www.salesforce.com), which provide specialist consultancy services.

Therefore it is crucial that no matter how a customer contacts a company, frontline staff have instant access to the same data about the customer, such as his/her details and past purchases. This usually means the consolidation of the many databases held by individual departments in a company into one centralized database that can be accessed by all relevant staff on a computer screen.

Customer relationship management is much more than simply the technology, however. A thorough examination of the CRM process is provided by the QCi customer management model (see Fig. 15.3). This model can be used by companies to understand how well they are managing their customers.[18] Each of the elements of the model will now be discussed.

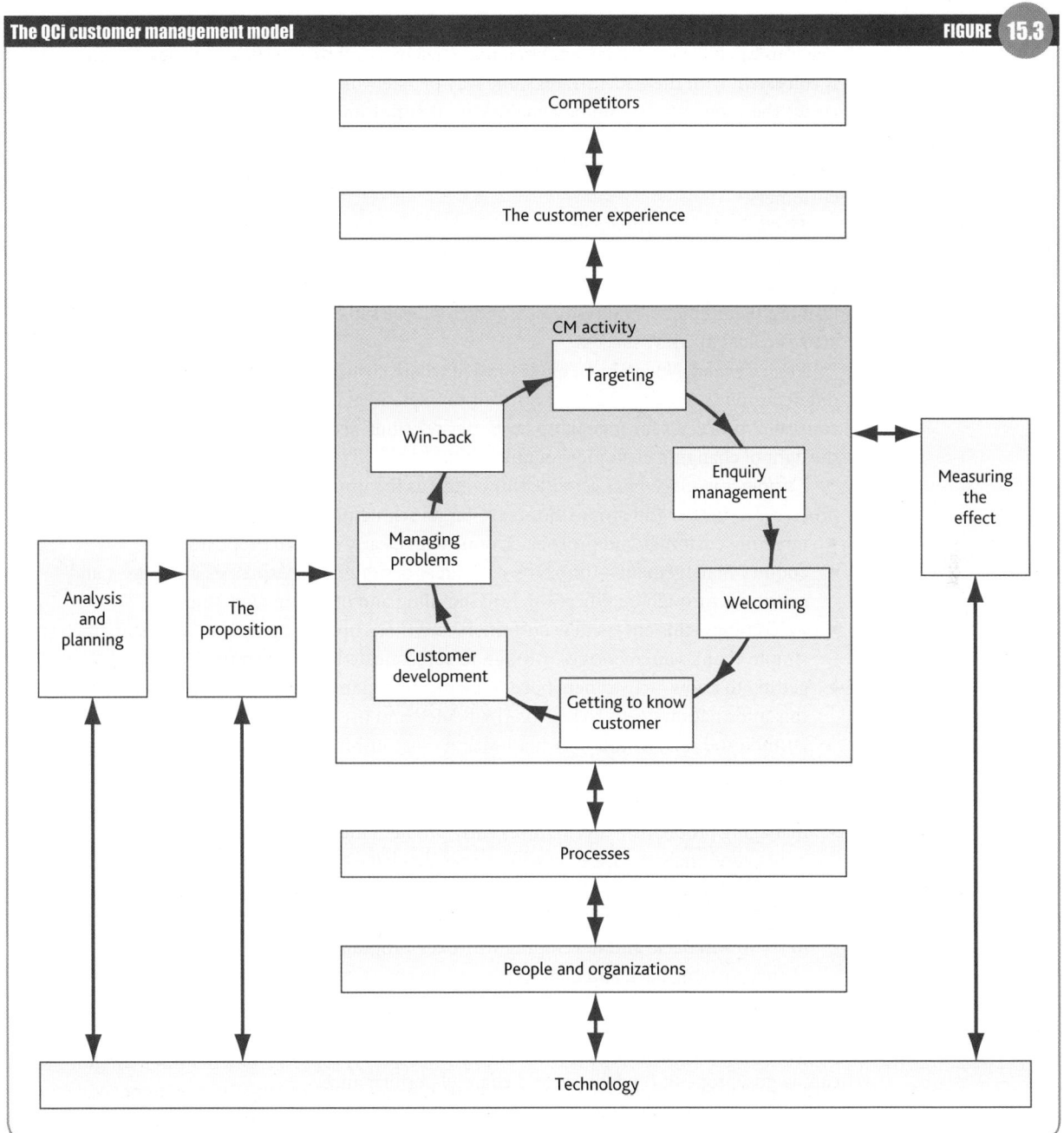

Analysis and planning: effective CRM begins by understanding the value, attitudes and behaviour of various customers and prospects. Once this has been achieved customers and prospects should be segmented so that planning activity can be as effective as possible. The planning will focus on such areas as the cost-effective retention and acquisition of customers.

Proposition: once segments of customers are identified and understood, the proposition to each segment needs to be defined, and appropriate value-based offers planned. The proposition will be defined in terms of such issues as price, brand and service, and should drive the experience the customer can expect when dealing with the organization, its product and its distributors. The proposition must then be communicated to both customers and the people responsible for delivering it.

Information and technology: these provide the foundations for the whole model. Data needs to be collected, stored, analysed and used in a way that provides information that is consistent with the CRM strategy, the way people work and the way customers want to access the company. Technology enables an organization to acquire, analyse and use the vast amounts of data involved in managing customers. It needs to deliver the right information to the relevant people at the right time so that they can achieve their role in managing customers.

People and organization: an organization's frontline staff need to be recruited, trained, developed and motivated to deliver high standards of customer relations. Key elements are an organizational structure that supports effective customer management, role identification, training requirements and resources, and employee satisfaction. It is these 'soft' elements that are so crucial to CRM success.

Process management: in an environment where customer contact can take place at several different points, processes can be difficult to implement and manage. Nevertheless, clear and consistent processes for managing customer relations need to be developed and reviewed in the light of changing customer requirements.

Customer management activity: this concerns the implementation of the plans and processes to deliver the proposition(s) to target segment(s). This involves:

- targeting customer and prospect groups with clearly defined propositions
- enquiry management—this starts as soon as an individual expresses an interest and continues through qualification, lead handling and outcome reporting
- welcoming—this covers new customers and those upgrading their relationship; it covers simple 'thank you' messages through to sophisticated contact strategies
- getting to know—customers need to be persuaded to give information about themselves; this information needs to be stored, updated and used; useful information includes attitude and satisfaction information and relationship 'healthchecks'
- customer development—decisions need to be made regarding which customers to develop through higher levels of relationship management activity, and which to maintain or drop
- managing problems—this involves early problem identification, complaint handling and 'root cause' analysis to spot general issues that have the potential to cause problems for many customers
- win-back—activities include understanding reasons for loss, deciding which customers to try to win back, and developing win-back programmes that offer lost customers the chance to come back and good reason to do so.

Measuring the effect: measuring performance against plan enables the refinement of future plans to continually improve the CRM programme; measurement may cover people, processes, campaigns, proposition delivery and channel performance.

Customer experience: external measurement of customer experiences needs to take place and includes satisfaction tracking, loyalty analysis and mystery shopping.

Competitors: their strengths and weaknesses need to be monitored and the company's performance on the above issues evaluated in the light of the competition.

Success factors in CRM

CRM projects have met with mixed success. Research has revealed that the following factors are associated with success:[19]

- having a customer orientation and organizing the CRM system around customers
- taking a single view of customers across departments, and designing an integrated system so that all customer-facing staff can draw information from a common database
- having the ability to manage cultural change issues that arise as a result of system development and implementation

- involving users in the CRM design process
- designing the system in such a way that it can readily be changed to meet future requirements
- having a board-level champion of the CRM project, and commitment within each of the affected departments to the benefits of taking a single view of the customer and the need for common strategies—for example, prioritizing resources on profitable customers
- creating 'quick wins' to provide positive feedback on the project programmes
- ensuring face-to-face contact (rather than by paper or e-mail) between marketing and IT staff
- piloting the new system before full launch.

Managing a Direct Marketing Campaign

As we shall see, the marketing database is an essential element in creating and managing a direct marketing campaign. However, it is not the starting point for campaign development. As with all promotional campaigns, direct marketing should be fully integrated with all marketing mix elements to provide a coherent *marketing strategy*. Direct marketers need to understand how the product is being *positioned* in the marketplace, which means that its target market and differential advantage must be recognized.

It is crucial that messages sent out as part of a direct marketing campaign do not conflict with those communicated by other channels such as advertising or the salesforce. The integrating mechanism is a clear definition of marketing strategy. Figure 15.4 shows the steps in the management of a direct marketing campaign. Each will now be discussed.

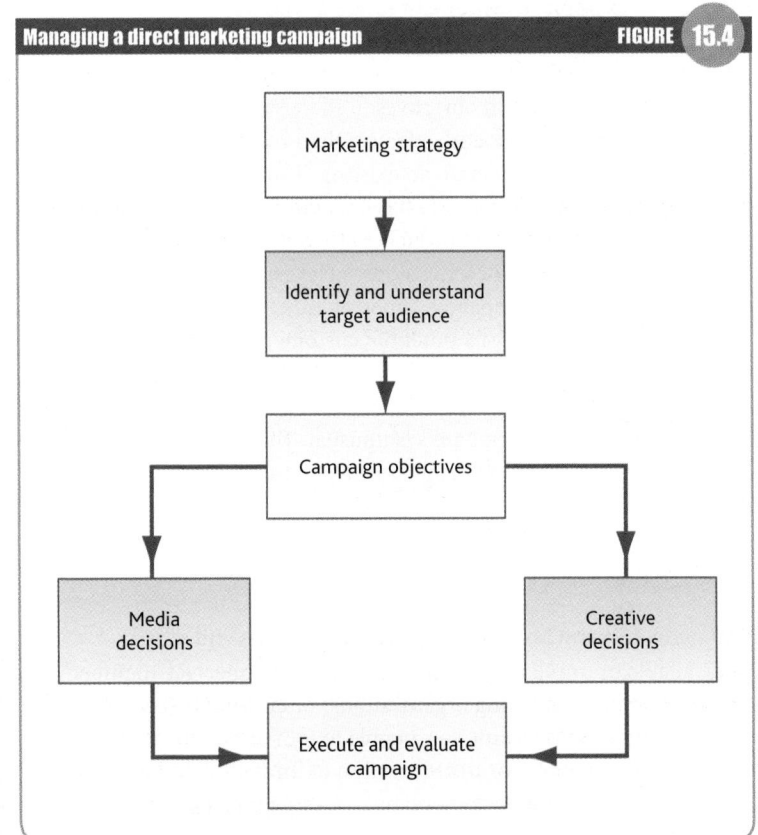

Managing a direct marketing campaign   FIGURE **15.4**

Identify and understand target audience

The late David Ogilvy, the famous advertising guru, once wrote: 'Never sell to a stranger.' The needs and purchasing behaviour of the target audience must be understood from the start.

The target audience is the group of people at which the direct marketing campaign is aimed. The usual ways of segmenting consumer and organizational markets described in Chapter 8 can be applied.

Companies like Experian provide segmentation breakdowns, such as by lifestyle, that can be used for targeting. However, a particularly useful method of segmentation for direct marketing purposes is as follows.

- *Competitors' customers*: all people who buy the types of product our company produces but from our competitors.
- *Prospects*: people who have not bought from our company before but qualify as potential purchasers (e.g. our customers are large companies, therefore other large companies should be targeted).

- *Enquirers*: people who have contacted the organization and shown interest in one or more products but, as yet, have not bought.
- *Lapsed customers*: people who have purchased in the past but appear to have ceased buying.
- *Referrals*: people who have been recommended to the organization as potential customers.
- *Existing customers*: people who are continuing to buy.

Note how an analysis of existing customers can help in identifying prospects. By identifying criteria that describe our customers (e.g. age, location, size of firm) the marketing database can be used to identify other people who may be receptive to a direct marketing campaign.

Having defined the group(s) that are to be targeted, a list is required, which may be obtainable from an in-house database or through an external broker. However, direct marketers need to be aware of possible problems when buying externally. People may have moved address, job or died; duplication of addresses occurs, job titles may be inaccurate, and standard industrial classifications of companies may not accurately describe the type of business the organization is engaged in.

Understanding the buying behaviour of the chosen target groups is important. In particular, understanding the choice criteria of the targeted individuals helps in message development. For example, if a key choice criterion of people buying from competitors rather than our company is technical reputation, we can stress (with evidence) our technical competences when targeting competitors' customers.

Campaign objectives

Campaign objectives can be expressed in financial (for example, sales, profits and return on investment), in marketing (for example, to acquire or retain customers, or to generate enquiries) and/or in communication terms (for example, to create awareness or change beliefs). The first set of objectives is self-apparent and the third set is discussed in Chapter 13. Here we shall focus on acquisition and retention objectives.

Achieving acquisition objectives may be less cost-effective than comparable retention objectives as it is significantly less expensive to retain an existing customer than attract a new one. Furthermore, maintaining customer loyalty has the additional benefit that loyal customers not only repeat-purchase but advocate products to their friends, pay less attention to competitive brands and often buy product line extensions.[20] Nevertheless, in order to grow and offset lost customers, direct marketing campaigns aimed at attracting new customers are inevitable. When measuring the attractiveness of a potential customer, the concept of *lifetime value* is important. This measures the profits that can be expected from customers over their expected life with a company. Banks know, for example, that gaining student accounts has very high lifetime value since switching between banks is unusual. This means that the allowable marketing cost per acquisition (or how much a company can afford to spend to acquire a new customer) can be quite high. If the calculation was based on potential profits while a student, the figure would be much lower. The establishment of a marketing database can, over time, provide valuable information on buying patterns, which aids the calculation of lifetime value.

Where a marketing database does not hold information on prospects and where external lists are either unavailable or unreliable, another option is 'member-get-member' programmes. Existing members (e.g. of motoring organizations) or customers (e.g. of an insurance company) are incentivized to recruit new people to join or buy from the organization. For example, the Royal Society for the Protection of Birds (RSPB) launched a 'Recruit a friend and help yourself to a free pocket organiser' campaign targeted at young ornithologists. New members were offered free gifts as an incentive to join.

Once acquired, the objective is to retain the business of the customer. This is because keeping customers has a direct impact on profitability. A study conducted by Pricewaterhouse showed that a 2 per cent increase in customer retention has the same profit impact as a 10 per cent reduction in overhead costs.[21] Customer loyalty programmes have blossomed as a result, with direct marketing playing a key role. Retention programmes are aimed at maximizing a customer's lifetime value to the company. Maintaining a long-term relationship with a customer provides the opportunity to up-sell, cross-sell and renew business. Up-selling involves the promotion of higher-value products—for example, a more expensive car. Cross-selling entails the switching of customers to other product categories, as when a music club promotes a book collection. Renewal involves the timing of communication to existing customers when they are about to repurchase. For example, car dealers often send direct mail promotional material two years after the purchase of a car, since many people change cars after that period.

Often, the achievement of retention objectives depends on the identification of a company's best customers defined in terms of current and potential profitability. FRAC data (discussed earlier in this chapter), which measure purchasing behaviour in terms of frequency (how often), recency (how recent), amount (of what volume and value) and category (what product type) forms the basis of this analysis. The identity and profile of high-value customers are then drawn up. Profiling enables the identification of similar types of individuals or organizations for the achievement of acquisition programmes. Major international airlines have developed frequent-flyer schemes along these lines. Their best customers (often business travellers) are identified by analysis of their database and rewarded for their loyalty. By collecting and analysing data the airlines identify and profile their frequent flyers, learn how best to develop a relationship with them, and attempt to acquire new customers with similar profiles. Databases can therefore be used to segment customers so that the most attractive groups can be targeted with a tailored direct marketing campaign.

The importance of customer retention has prompted many supermarkets to develop store loyalty cards, which are swiped through a machine at the checkout. The loyalty card contains customer information such as the name and address of the individual, so that purchasing data, such as expenditure per visit, the range of products purchased, the brands purchased, when and how often the customer shops and which branch was used can be linked to individuals. This means that supermarkets such as Tesco and Sainsbury's in the UK know what sort of products and services to offer in different stores and to different customers. One proponent of loyalty schemes claimed, 'Profiling based on spend, frequency and product gives more information about a customer than knowing where someone lives or what their salary is. We won't need demographic information any more.'[22]

15.1 Pause for Thought

Do you have a loyalty card(s)? What benefits does it provide for you? Do you receive any special offers that appear to be based on your previous purchases? What kind of information do you think the sponsor of the loyalty card holds about you?

Direct mail can be used to send targeted promotional offers to people who are known to purchase from a particular product category. For example, a special offer for an Australian red wine could be sent to people who are known to drink red wine. Tesco's Clubcard scheme began in 1995 and has been widely regarded as successful. Customers accumulate points that are electronically added to the card when it is swiped at the checkout. Effectively, points mean money off future purchases at the checkout (plus other promotional offers). Thus the more money a customer spends the greater the points and the higher the discounts on future purchases. This process, it is claimed, generates higher rates of repeat buying and loyalty benefiting the store, as well as providing in-depth purchasing data.

Despite their growth in such industries as petrol retailing, airlines, supermarkets and hotels, loyalty schemes have attracted their critics. Loyalty schemes may simply raise the cost of doing business and, if competitors respond with 'me-toos', the final outcome may be no more than minor tactical advantages.[23] The costs are usually very high when technology, software, staff training, administration, communications and the costs of the rewards are taken into account. Shell, for example, is reported to have spent £20 million on hardware and software alone to support its Smart card, which allows drivers to collect points when purchasing petrol.[24] The danger is that loyalty schemes cost too much when price has become more important in the competitive arena.[25] A second criticism is that the proliferation of loyalty schemes is teaching consumers promiscuity. Evidence from a MORI poll found that 25 per cent of loyalty card holders are ready to switch to a rival scheme if it has better benefits.[26] Far from seeing a loyalty scheme as a reason to stay with a retailer, consumers may be using such schemes as criteria for switching. Third, the basis of loyalty schemes, rewarding loyal customers, is questioned. A company that has a band of loyal customers is presumably already doing something right. Rather than giving them discounts, why not do more of that (e.g. wide product range, better service)? Even if loyal customers spend a little more, do the extra revenues justify the extra costs? Nevertheless, loyalty schemes are seen by many companies as an essential element in doing business. What needs to be questioned by marketing managers is whether exceptional loyalty can be expected from such schemes, what are the true costs and whether focusing on a select group of customers (as with frequent-flyer schemes) leads to the neglect of others.

Media Decisions

Direct marketers have a large number of media which they can use to reach customers and prospects. Each of the major media will now be examined.

Direct mail

Direct mail is material sent through the postal service to the recipient's home or business address with the purpose of promoting a product and/or maintaining an ongoing relationship. Direct mail at its best allows close targeting of individuals in a way not possible using mass advertising media. For example, Heinz employs direct mail to target its customers and prospects. Since it markets 360 products, above-the-line advertising for all of them is impossible. By creating a database based on responses to promotions, lifestyle questionnaires and rented lists, Heinz has built a file of 4.6 million households. Each one now receives the four-times-a-year 'At Home' mailpack, which has been further segmented to reflect loyalty and frequency of purchase. Product and nutritional information is combined with coupons to achieve product trials.[27] Virgin Holidays has also used direct mail successfully (see illustration). The mail pack was lavishly designed and the choices, such as 'I want to have a holiday romance or at least make one up', helped to make it fun.

A major advantage of direct mail is its cost. For example, in business-to-business marketing, it might cost £50 to visit potential customers, £5 to telephone them but less than £1 to send out a mailing.[28]

A key factor in the effectiveness of a direct mail campaign is the quality of the mailing list. Mailing lists are variable in quality. For example, in one year in the UK, 100 million items were sent back marked 'return to sender'.[29] List houses supply lists on a rental or purchase basis. Since lists go out of date quickly, it is usually preferable to rent. *Consumer lists* may be compiled from subscriptions to magazines, catalogues, membership of organizations, etc.

▲ Direct mail can be engaging, as this mailer from Virgin Holidays proves.

Alternatively, consumer lifestyle lists are compiled from questionnaires. The electoral roll can also be useful when combined with geodemographic analysis. For example, if a company wished to target households living in modern private housing with young families, the electoral roll can be used to provide the names and addresses of people living in such areas.

One problem with consumer lists is people moving house and dying. Specialized data-suppression services, such as the 'gone away suppression file' offered by the REaD Group, can reduce this difficulty. It claims to identify over 94 per cent of all home movements and over 80 per cent of deceased people.[30] *Business-to-business lists* may be bought from directory producers such as the *Kompass* or *Key British Enterprises* directories, from trade magazine subscription lists (e.g. *Chemicals Gazette*) or from exhibition lists (e.g. Which? Computer Show). Perhaps the most productive mailing list is that of a company's own customers: the *house list*. This is because of the existing relationship that a company enjoys with its own customers. Also of use would be the names of past buyers who have become inactive, enquirers, and those who have been referred or recommended by present customers of the company. It is not uncommon for a house list to be far more productive than an outside-compiled list. Customer behaviour such as products purchased, recency, frequency and expenditure can also be stored on the database.

The management of direct mail involves asking the following five questions.[31]

1 *Who?* Who is the target market? Who are we trying to influence?
2 *What?* What response is required? A sale, an enquiry?
3 *Why?* Why should they buy or make an enquiry? Is it because our product is faster, cheaper, or whatever?
4 *Where?* Where can they be reached? Can we obtain their home or work address?
5 *When?* When is the best time to reach them? Often this is weekends for consumers, and Tuesday, Wednesday or Thursday for businesspeople (Monday can be dominated by planning meetings and on Friday they may be busy clearing their desks for the weekend).

Other management issues include the organization required for addressing and filling the envelopes; *mailing houses* provide these services, and for large mailings the postal service needs to be notified so that the mailing can be scheduled.

Direct mail allows *specific targeting to named individuals*. For example, by hiring lists of subscribers to gardening catalogues a manufacturer of gardening equipment could target a specific group of people that would be more likely to be interested in a promotional offer than the public in general. *Elaborate personalization* is possible, aided by digital printing that allows different versions of the mailing to be tailored to customers.[32] Since the objective of direct mail is immediate—usually a sale or an enquiry—success can *easily be measured*. Some organizations, such as Reader's Digest, spend money researching alternative creative approaches before embarking on a large-scale mailing. Such factors as type of promotional offer, headlines, visuals and copy can be varied in a systematic manner, and by using code numbers on reply coupons response can be tied to the associated creative approach.

The effectiveness of direct mail relies heavily on the quality of the list. Poor lists raise costs and can contribute to the criticism of *junk mail* since recipients are not interested in the contents of the mailing. *Initial costs* can be much higher than advertising in terms of cost per thousand people reached, and response can be low (an average response rate of 2 per cent is often quoted). Added to these costs is the expense of setting up a database. In these terms direct mail should be viewed as a medium- to long-term tool for generating repeat business from a carefully targeted customer group. An important concept is the *lifetime value of a customer*, which is the profit made on a customer's purchase over the customer's lifetime. Also, with access to broadband becoming available to more people, e-mail campaigns with website links can be less costly than direct mail and can reach a large audience.[33]

15.2 Pause for Thought

As a consumer, what is your view of direct mail? Have you received any recently that you have responded to positively? For example, has it caused you to buy a product or visit a website?

In summary, direct mail can be very cost-effective at targeting specific segments of the population, with easily measurable results, but its critics point to low response rates, the existence of junk mail, the distress that can be caused when letters are sent to people who have died, the fact that personal information can be sold to mailers without the knowledge of the subject, and the fact that some companies persist in sending mail even when they have been asked to stop.[34] Also, direct mail may work out more expensive than e-mail campaigns, which are becoming more attractive as access to broadband expands.

Telemarketing

Telemarketing is a marketing communication system where trained specialists use telecommunications and information technologies to conduct marketing and sales activities.

Inbound telemarketing occurs when a prospect contacts the company by telephone, whereas outbound telemarketing involves the company calling the prospect. Developments in IT have affected both forms. For example, Experian's QAS is a package that enables telemarketing people handling inbound calls to quickly identify the address and account details of the caller with the minimum amount of typing time, and also ensure it is accurate. The caller is asked for their name and postcode (either for the household or company). From this, the correct address will appear on the computer screen. If the caller wishes to purchase (using a credit card, for example) over the telephone, the tedium of giving (and spelling) their address to allow postage is removed. This has gained penetration in such areas as selling football or theatre tickets. Even more sophisticated developments in telecommunications technology allow the caller to be identified even before the agent has answered the call. The caller's telephone number is relayed into the customer database and outlet details appear on the agent's screen before the call is picked up. This service (called *integrated telephony*) has gained penetration in the customer service area.

An integrated telemarketing package would, in response to an incoming call, bring up the customer's file on the computer screen, record the order, check stocks, and provide field salespeople with updated inventory information and estimated delivery times.

A more controversial technological development is the use of interactive voice response (IVR), where the caller talks to a machine rather than a person. IVR is beneficial when the nature of calls is specific such as a brochure request. It can also be used to cover busy periods including the period following a direct response television advertisement. When the majority of callers want the same basic information, IVR permits this to be provided quickly and accurately. It is sometimes used in conjunction with a personalized service when a caller requires it. The main disadvantage of the approach is some callers may dislike dealing with a machine and prefer to talk to a person. Also some queries may not be covered by the automated service.[35]

Badly managed inbound telemarketing can cause customer annoyance when callers are kept on hold too long or are constantly rerouted. This problem can be exacerbated through misguided cost-cutting.[36]

Computerization can also enhance productivity in outbound telemarketing. Large databases can store information that can easily be accessed by telemarketing agents. Call lists can be allocated to agents automatically. Scripts can be created and stored on the computer so that operators have ready and convenient access to them on-screen. Orders can be processed automatically and follow-up actions (such as call-back in one month or send literature) can be recorded and stored. In addition, productivity can be raised by auto-diallers.

A major technological advance is predictive dialling, which makes multiple outbound calls from a call centre. Calls are only delivered to agents when the customer answers, therefore cutting out wasted calls to answer machines, engaged signals, fax machines and unanswered calls. It is claimed to dramatically improve call centre efficiency by providing agents with a constant flow of calls. However, agents get no time to psych themselves up for the call (they are alerted by a bleep and the relevant details appear on a screen). Call centre staff have to work extremely intensively.[37]

Telemarketing automation also allows simple keystroke retrieval of critical information such as customer history, product information or schedules. If the prospect or customer is busy, automated systems can reschedule a call-back and allow the operator to recall the contact on screen at a later date simply by pressing a single key.

The versatility of telemarketing

Telemarketing can be used in a number of roles, and it is this versatility that has seen telemarketing activities grow in recent years. Its major roles are those described below.

Direct selling: when the sales potential of a customer does not justify a face-to-face call from a salesperson, telemarketing can be used to service the account. The telephone call may simply take the form of an enquiry about a re-ordering possibility, and as such does not require complex sales arguments that need face-to-face interaction. Alternatively, an inbound telephone call may be the means of placing an order in response to a direct mail or television advertising campaign. For example, freefone facilities are often used for order placing in conjunction with the advertising of record collections on television.

Supporting the salesforce: customers may find contacting the field salesforce difficult given the nature of their job. A telemarketing operation can provide a communications link to the salesforce, and an enquiry- or order-handling function. In this way customers know that there is someone at the supplier company who they can contact easily if they have a problem, enquiry or wish to place an order.

Generating and screening leads: an outbound telemarketing team can be used to establish contact with prospective customers and attempt to arrange a salesforce visit. Alternatively, it can be used to screen leads that have been generated by direct mail or coupon response to advertising. People who have requested further information can be contacted by telephone to ascertain their potential (qualifying a lead) and, if qualified, to try to arrange a salesforce visit.

Marketing database building and updating: a secondary source of information, such as a directory, can provide a list of companies that partially qualify them for inclusion in a marketing database. However, the telephone may be required to check that they fulfil other conditions. For example, one criterion may be that they are textile companies. A directory such as *Kompass* may be used to identify them; however, a telephone call may be necessary to check that they have a marketing department, which may be a second condition for entry on to the database. The updating (*cleaning*) of lists may require a telephone call, for example, to check that the name of the marketing director on the database is accurate.

Applications of telemarketing

When used professionally, telemarketing can be a most cost-efficient, flexible and accountable medium. The telephone permits two-way dialogue that is instantaneous, personal and flexible, albeit not face to face.

As we have seen, telemarketing is often linked to field selling activities. The link between telemarketing and five field job types was developed by Moncrief.[38] The job types were described in terms of the amount of face-to-face contact required and the complexity of the selling process. The face-to-face contact (horizontal dimension) of Figure 15.5 is particularly useful to illustrate the possible roles of telemarketing in selling strategy.

The missionary seller (making new initial customer contact) and the order-taker job types offer potential opportunities of using telemarketers as the organization's primary salesforce. The role of telemarketing in the institutional seller, trade servicer and trade seller job categories is to supplement field selling efforts. The more routinized the selling process (the vertical dimension of Figure 15.5), the more likely telemarketing is to make an important supplemental contribution to face-to-face selling. An assessment of the need for face-to-face contact indicates whether telemarketing is appropriate in a supporting and/or a primary role in an organization's selling strategy. In some selling situations, both primary and supporting telemarketing strategies may be appropriate.

Telemarketing as a supporting role: the need for this role occurs when face-to-face contact is required, but selected buyer–seller activities can be accomplished by telemarketing personnel. These activities may include taking orders and handling reorders. Successful implementation of a telemarketing support effort requires close coordination of field and telemarketing

Sales job types   FIGURE **15.5**

Source: Moncrief, W. C., S. H. Shipp, C. W. Lamb and D. W. Cravens (1989) Examining the Roles of Telemarketing in Selling Strategy, *Journal of Personal Selling & Sales Management* 9(3), 2. Reproduced with permission

salespeople. Moncrief *et al.* point out that research suggests that the supporting role creates a major organizational design task, and resistance from field personnel will be likely to occur.[39] A carefully formulated plan is essential to assure cooperation of telemarketing and the field salesforce. When face-to-face interaction is needed, telemarketing plays a secondary role in selling strategy.

Primary role: telemarketing can provide a complete sales and customer support effort for selling situations in which face-to-face contact is not required. Conditions that suggest using telemarketing in a primary role include a routinized selling process, low cash value of purchases, a large and widely dispersed customer base, and non-technical products. Regardless of other considerations, a significant factor in deciding not to use face-to-face contact lies in the cost of field sales calls and the margins available to cover these costs.

Combination role: some companies have adopted selling strategies that utilize telemarketing in both supporting and primary roles. Organizations that may benefit from this strategy are those with large and widely dispersed customer bases, whose purchasers range from very small accounts to very large accounts. The accounts signed to the primary telemarketing functions are those that cannot economically be served on a face-to-face basis. Telemarketers often have primary responsibility for smaller customers and provide backup services for other customers when face-to-face salespeople are not available.

No role: importantly, certain selling situations are not appropriate for any type of telemarketing support. Conditions that may require face-to-face customer contact by a field salesperson greatly reduce or eliminate telemarketing's value—for example, where the selling process complexity, contact requirements and importance of the purchase demand face-to-face contact.

Guidelines for telemarketing

An eight-step guide to telephone selling has been published by the Bell Telephone System of America. It runs as follows.[40]

1 Identify yourself and your company.
2 Establish rapport: this should come naturally since you have already researched your potential clients and their business.
3 Make an interesting comment (e.g. to do with cost savings or a special offer).
4 Deliver your sales message: emphasize benefits over features (e.g. your production people will like it because it helps to overcome downtime through waiting for the material to set).
5 Overcome objections: be skilled at objection-handling techniques.
6 Close the sale: when appropriate do not be afraid to ask for the order (e.g. 'Would you like to place an order now?') or fulfil another sales objective (e.g. 'Can I send you a sample?').
7 Action agreement: arrange for a sales call or the next telephone call.
8 Express your thanks.

The advantages of telemarketing

There are a number of reasons why telemarketing has grown in recent years. First, it has lower costs per contact than a face-to-face salesperson visit. Second, it is less time consuming than personal visits. Third, the growth in telephone ownership has increased access to households, and the use of toll-free lines (800 or 0800 numbers) has reduced the cost of responding by telephone. Next, the increasing sophistication of new telecommunications technology has encouraged companies to employ telemarketing techniques. For example, digital networks allow the seamless transfer of calls between organizations. The software company Microsoft and its telemarketing agency can smoothly transfer calls between their respective offices. If the caller then asks for complex technical information it can be transferred back to the relevant Microsoft department.[41] Finally, despite the reduced costs (compared to a personal visit) the telephone retains the advantage of two-way communication.

The disadvantages of telemarketing

Telemarketing is not a panacea since it suffers from a number of disadvantages. First, it lacks the visual impact of a personal visit and it is not possible to assess the mood or reactions of the buyer through observing body language, especially facial expressions. It is easier for a customer to react negatively over the telephone and the number of rejections can be high. Telephone selling can be considered intrusive and some people may object to receiving unsolicited telephone calls. Finally, although cost per contact is cheaper than a personal sales call, it is more expensive than direct mail, media advertising or the Internet. Indeed, the Internet is a threat to telemarketing with e-mail drastically cutting the volume of telephone traffic, airlines encouraging Internet bookings and banks such as ING Direct setting up systems to enable transactions to be carried out on the Internet. Labour costs can be high, although computerized answering can cut the cost of receiving incoming calls.

15.3 Pause for Thought

Do you think a time will come when the Internet totally replaces telemarketing as a direct marketing method?

Direct response advertising

Direct response advertising appears in the prime media, such as television, newspapers and magazines, but differs from standard advertising as it is designed to elicit a direct response such as an order, enquiry or request for a visit. Often a freefone telephone number is included in the advertisement and a website address. This mechanism combines the ability of broadcast

▲ Direct Line offers a price reduction to encourage people to contact them online or by telephone.

media to reach large sections of the population with direct marketing techniques that allow a swift response on behalf of both prospect and company. The advertisement for Direct Line car insurance is an example of direct response advertising designed to encourage consumers to go online or call direct.

Direct response television (or interactive television as it is sometimes called) comes in many formats. The most basic is the standard advertisement with telephone number; 60-, 90- or 120-second advertisements are sometimes used to provide the necessary information to persuade viewers to use the freefone number for ordering. Other variants are 25-minute product demonstrations (generally referred to as infomercials) and live home shopping programmes broadcast by companies such as QVC.

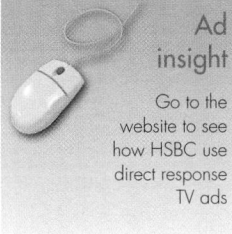

Ad insight

Go to the website to see how HSBC use direct response TV ads

Not all direct response television is focused on immediate sales. As was discussed in Chapter 13, on advertising, the format may be a standard advertisement on a digital channel, which requires the viewer to press the red button on the remote control handset to access further information and/or request a brochure or free sample. Another form is the interactive television advertisement that allows access to the Internet. This relies on digital technology and connection to a telephone line. The advantage is that marketers can get direct response to a mass-market advertisement, but whether viewers will interrupt their programme viewing to surf the web is questionable.[42]

A popular misconception regarding direct response television (DRTV) is that it is suitable only for products such as music compilations and cut-price jewellery. In Europe, a wide range of products is marketed (such as leisure and fitness products, motoring and household goods, books and beauty care products) through pan-European satellite channels such as Eurosport, Super Channel and NBC.

Four circumstances increase the likelihood of DRTV application and success.

1 Goods that benefit from demonstration or a service that needs to be explained.
2 A product that has mass consumer appeal (although specialist products could be placed on a single-interest channel).
3 A good DRTV promotion must make good television to attract and maintain the interest of the audience.
4 DRTV should be supported by an efficient telemarketing operation to handle the response generated by the advertisement.

Catalogue marketing

Catalogue marketing is the sale of products through catalogues distributed to agents and customers, usually by mail or at stores if the catalogue marketer is a store owner. Increasingly, catalogues are also pushed online. Catalogue marketing is popular in Europe, with such organizations as Otto Versand and Quelle Schikedanz (Germany), Great Universal and Next Directory (UK) and Trois Suisse and La Redoute (France). Many of them operate in a number of countries: La Redoute operates in 15 European countries as well as Russia, Lebanon and South Korea (see illustration), and Trois Suisse operates in France, the Netherlands, Belgium, Austria, Germany, Italy, Spain, Portugal and the UK. Catalogue marketing is popular in Austria because legislation restricts retail opening hours.[43] Tchibo also operates in several European countries and has grown into catalogue marketing from selling coffee. Advertising is used by some catalogue marketers to recruit new agents and customers. This is one of the objectives of the Boden advertisement (see illustration overleaf).

A common form of catalogue marketing is mail order, where catalogues are distributed and, traditionally, orders received by mail. This form of marketing suffered from an old-fashioned downmarket image and was based on an agency system where agents passed around the catalogue among friends and relatives, collecting and sending orders to the mail-order company in return for commission. Delivery was slow (up to 28 days) and the range of merchandise usually targeted at lower-status social groups who valued the credit facility of

Unique
chic with
la différence

www.laredoute.co.uk
0500 777 888

LA REDOUTE
La différence

▲ La Redoute uses catalogues to sell its clothes in 15 European countries plus Russia, Lebanon and South Korea.

weekly payment. Some enterprising companies, notably Next and Trois Suisse, saw catalogue marketing as an opportunity to reach a new target market: busy, affluent, middle-class people, who valued the convenience of choosing products at home.

The Next Directory story is an example of how store retailers can use catalogue marketing to reach a wider range of customers. Laura Ashley, Habitat and Marks & Spencer are other examples of companies that publish their catalogues online. Some retailers, notably Argos in the UK, base their entire operation on a catalogue; a wide range of products, including household goods, cameras, jewellery, toys, mobile phones, furniture and gardening equipment, is sold through the Argos catalogue. A customer can select at home, visit a catalogue shop where only a restricted selection of goods is on display and purchase products instantly. Argos's success is based on low prices and an efficient service and inventory system that controls costs and ensures a low out-of-stock situation.

When used effectively, catalogue marketing to consumers provides a convenient way of selecting products at home that allows discussion between family members in a relaxed atmosphere away from crowded shops and streets. Often, credit facilities are available. For remote rural locations it provides a valuable service, obviating the necessity to travel long distances to town shopping centres. For catalogue marketers, the expense of high-street locations is removed and there is the opportunity to display a wider range of products than could feasibly be achieved in a shop. Distribution can be centralized, lowering costs. Nevertheless, catalogues are expensive to produce (hence the need for some retailers to charge for them) and they require regular updating, particularly when selling fashion items. They do not allow goods to be tried (e.g. a vacuum cleaner) or tried on (e.g. clothing) before purchase. Although products can be seen in the catalogue, variations in colour printing can mean that the curtains or suite that are delivered do not have exactly the same colour tones as those that appear on the printed page.

Catalogue marketers have taken full advantage of the potential of database marketing to segment their customers, record purchasing behaviour (types of products bought, when, sizes, etc.) and monitor creditworthiness. Some develop 'scoring systems' to enable them to predict the chances of payment defaults, high merchandise return ratios and low ordering rates, based on an individual's location and personal characteristics.[44]

Catalogues are also important in business-to-business markets. They provide an invaluable aid to the salesperson when calling on customers and, when in their hands, are a perpetual sales aid, acting as a reference book and allowing them to select and order at their convenience (often by telephone). Many companies place their catalogue on their website so that it is readily available to customers.

Business-to-business catalogues often contain an enormous amount of information, such as product specifications and prices. Once in the hands of customers and prospects, direct mail and telemarketing campaigns can be used to persuade them to consult their catalogues. It is hardly surprising, then, that for any supplier of a wide range of products, such as component and office supply companies, the catalogue remains a key marketing tool, whether supplied by hard copy or electronically.

While the Internet was predicted by some to spell the demise of the traditional paper catalogue this has not proven to be the case, as some people prefer the convenience of browsing at leisure without having to stare at a computer screen. Indeed, research has shown that browsing through a catalogue can be the first step before buying online.[45]

Integrated media campaigns

In Chapter 13, on advertising, the need for *integrated marketing communications* was stressed. Communications strategy must be consistent with, and reinforce, other elements of the marketing mix (product, place and price). Within the promotional mix (advertising, personal selling, direct marketing, sales promotion and publicity) the same consistency and reinforcement should apply. Following this logic, messages sent out using various direct marketing media should also form a coherent whole. For example, information disseminated through the Internet should be consistent with that sent out via a direct mail campaign.

In practice, direct marketing does not always use multiple contacts or multiple media. A marketer wishing to attract delegates to a conference might use a single-medium, single-stage

A multiple-medium, multiple-stage campaign   FIGURE **15.6**

Direct response advertising

↓

Inbound telemarketing/direct mail/e-mail

↓

Direct mail

↓   ↓

Outbound telemarketing   Salesforce

campaign—that is, one direct mailing to the target audience. A campaign designed to retain customers (e.g. subscribers to a charity or magazine) might use a single-medium, multiple-stage campaign. Three direct mail letters might be sent to encourage renewal. However, direct marketers have the opportunity to use a combination of media in sequence to achieve their objectives. This is termed a multiple-medium, multiple-stage campaign.

A business-to-business company marketing a new adhesive might place a direct response advertisement in trade magazines to stimulate trial and orders. A response coupon, freefone telephone number and e-mail address would be provided, and prospects invited to choose their most convenient method of contact. An inbound telemarketing team would be trained to receive calls and take either orders or requests for samples for trial. Another team would deal with mail and e-mail correspondence. An outbound telemarketing team would follow up prospects judged to be of small and medium potential and the salesforce targeted at large potential customers and prospects. The sequence would be as shown in Figure 15.6.

In this way, the company has identified prospects, generated an initial sales response, created interest in the new product, begun a dialogue with customers and prospects and, where necessary, arranged demonstrations. Each medium has been used to its best advantage, and salesforce time and effort targeted at prospects and customers who have both the interest and potential to justify a sales call.

Marketing in Action 15.1 describes how the RSPCA used a combination of direct response television, mobile communications and telemarketing to raise funds.

 15.1 Marketing in Action

Integrated Direct Marketing at the RSPCA

The Royal Society for the Prevention of Cruelty to Animals (RSPCA) is the UK's leading animal welfare charity and a highly successful fundraiser. It uses direct response television (DRTV) as a dependable method of fundraising. Potential donors are encouraged to either telephone or visit the RSPCA's website, with the former far more effective because of the call centre's managed human interaction.

However, the organization has found a new way of encouraging donation. Viewers of the RSPCA's DRTV ads were prompted to respond using their mobile phones, by sending an SMS message to a premium-rate text number. The creative 'I'm an animal, help me out' drew on imagery made familiar by reality television shows. Responders were told that they would be charged £3 for their text, which would go to the RSPCA as an immediate donation. A thank you reply was sent, asking them to opt in to or out of further communication.

For those who opted in, telemarketing was used to encourage further donations. The result was highly successful, with large donations from people, who, by their actions, identified themselves to the RSPCA as highly concerned about animal welfare and, therefore, willing to support its work.

Based on: Gray (2008)[46]

Creative decisions

Most direct marketing campaigns have different objectives from those of advertising, Whereas advertising usually attempts to create awareness and position the image of a brand in prospects' minds, the aim of most direct marketing is to make a sale. It is more orientated to immediate action than advertising. Recipients of direct marketing messages (particularly through direct mail) need to see a clear benefit in responding. For example, Direct Line's success in the motor insurance business was built on a clear customer benefit—substantial cost savings from insuring with that company rather than the traditional insurance company—using direct response advertising and a highly efficient telemarketing team. Positioning Direct Line as a telemarketing-based motor insurer was achieved through advertising featuring a red telephone supported on wheels. Its *creative strategy* was consistent with the objectives and message of the campaign.

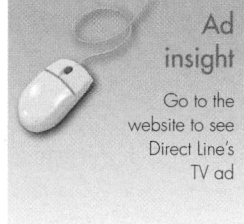

Ad insight

Go to the website to see Direct Line's TV ad

A *creative brief* will include the following elements (see Fig. 15.7).

- *Communication objectives*: what is the campaign hoping to achieve? Common objectives for direct marketing are sales volume and value, number of orders or enquiries, and cost-effectiveness. These will be outlined in more detail when discussing campaign evaluation.
- *Product benefits (and weaknesses)*: the product features will be identified as well as their associated customer benefits. Features can be linked to benefits by the phrases 'which results in' or 'which means that'. Key sources of competitive advantage will be spotlighted, which means that a thorough analysis of competitor products' strengths and weaknesses will have to be made.
- *Target market analysis*: target customers and prospects will be profiled and/or identified individually, and their needs and purchasing behaviour analysed. It is essential that creative people understand the types of people they are communicating with, since messages, to be effective, must be important to the target audience, not simply the 'pet' ideas of the creatives.
- *Development of the offer*: the offer should be valued by the target audience (pre-testing offers through group discussions and/or small-scale tests can measure the attractiveness of alternative offers). Some offers are price related. For example, an offer for a Capital One Visa credit card announced 'Lowest Rate in the UK for Credit Card Purchases 7.9 per cent APR Variable and No Annual Fee'. This message was emblazoned on the envelope and letter, and was supported by financial data showing cost savings compared to the competition. Other offers may take the form of free gifts. Monthly magazines often offer three free copies for a year's subscription. Another example is Legal & General Direct, a financial services company, which offered a free pen to all those who asked for a home insurance quote and a free telephone/radio alarm clock to those who took up insurance with them.
- Communication of the message: as seen in the previous example, the offer or key message can be communicated on the envelope as well as the internal contents. Supporting evidence should be provided wherever possible. Several enclosures in a direct mail shot can be included, each with a different objective, but each should have one clear single-minded purpose. Recipients must be told clearly how to respond. Research has shown that including a freefone number as well as the usual freepost envelope can increase response by 50–125 per cent.47 Today's direct marketers also have the option of including e-mail addresses. Letters should be personalized and the tone of the communication carefully thought out. Should a razzmatazz high-pressure sell or a gentler more subtle approach be used? Pre-testing various approaches can give invaluable information on this issue. Scripts are often used in telemarketing to communicate messages. When combined with powerful

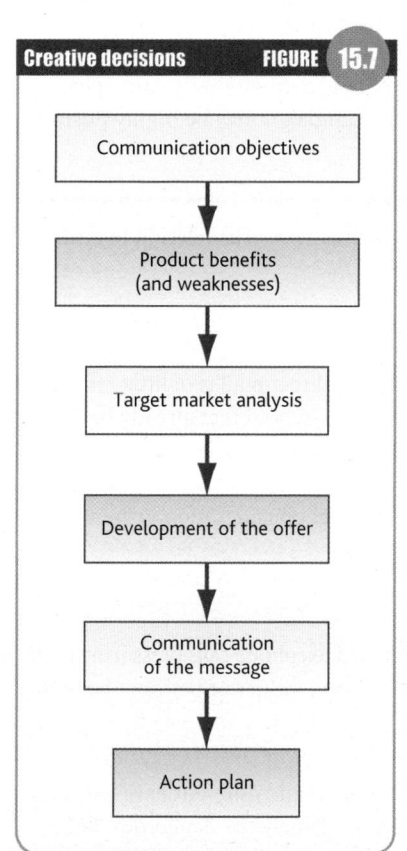

Creative decisions | FIGURE 15.7

- Communication objectives
- Product benefits (and weaknesses)
- Target market analysis
- Development of the offer
- Communication of the message
- Action plan

software and information technology (as discussed earlier, when we looked at telemarketing) they can provide an efficient way of communicating with customers and prospects. Mobile phone text messaging is another option for communicating the message. This is a growing medium, particularly for targeting youth audiences.

- Action plan: decisions regarding when the campaign should be run, how often, and suggestions regarding the most appropriate media to use to communicate the message and achieve the campaign's objectives must be made. For telemarketing campaigns, estimates of the number of operators required and when need to be produced.

Execute and evaluate the campaign

Execution of the campaign may be in-house or through the use of a specialist agency. Direct marketing activity usually has clearly defined short-term objectives against which performance can be measured. Some of the most frequently used measurements are:

- response rate (the proportion of contacts responding)
- total sales (volume and value)
- number of contacts purchasing
- sales rate (percentage of contacts purchasing)
- number of enquiries
- enquiry rate
- cost per contact
- cost per enquiry
- cost per sale
- conversion rate from enquiry to sale
- average order value
- renewal rate
- repeat purchase rate.

Direct marketers should bear in mind the longer-term effects of their activities. A campaign may seemingly be unprofitable in the short term, but when renewals and repeat purchases are taken into account the long-term value of the campaign may be highly positive.

Ethical Issues in Direct Marketing

The use of direct marketing has raised a number of consumer concerns relating to ethics.

The quantity of poorly targeted direct mail

Although designed to foster close targeting of consumers, some direct mail is of little reference to the recipient. The double-glazing promotion received by a household that already has double glazing or the direct mail shot promoting bathroom suites arriving at a new house are clear sources of irritation. Much worse is the distress caused to widows and widowers by mail that continues to arrive for their deceased partner. A further consideration is the waste of natural resources caused by poorly directed mailshots.[48]

The timing and intrusive nature of telemarketing calls

Consumers also complain of the annoyance caused by unsolicited telephone calls pressuring them to buy products at inconvenient times (e.g. in the middle of eating dinner or bathing the baby).

The content of direct mail envelopes

Most direct mail enclosures are harmless, but attempts to be novel and different have led some direct marketers to include devices that have been considered offensive or dangerous. One campaign targeted at marketing managers enclosed a bullet as an attention-getting measure. The response of some recipients was that someone somewhere had them in their sights! The complaints poured in, resulting in a severe reprimand for the culprit. Bullets, scissors and devices that make ticking sounds are all evidence that some direct marketers have paid insufficient attention to the potentially annoying and harmful effects of their actions.

Invasion of privacy

Many consumers fear that every time they subscribe to a club, society or magazine, apply for a credit card, or buy anything by telephone or direct mail, their names, addresses and other information will be entered on to a database that will guarantee a flood of mail from the supplier. Furthermore, where country legislation does not restrict it, their names will be sold, without their knowledge, to other direct marketing organizations, which are free to send further unsolicited mail.

The direct marketing industry and governments are responding to the public concerns noted above. Marketing Ethics and Corporate Social Responsibility 15.1 discusses some developments.

15.1 Marketing Ethics and Corporate Social Responsibility in Action

Consumer Protection in Direct Marketing

Consumer protection in direct marketing is a combination of national laws, Europe-wide directives, the use of suppression files and company actions. National laws, such as the Data Protection Act in the UK, set out principles for the collection and use of personal data. These include the need for transparency where a person should be informed, before his or her personal data are collected, of the purposes for which it will be used, and given the opportunity not to supply the data. Personal data should also be kept secure, which means that staff dealing with personal data need to be trained in how to deal with requests to disclose such data.

In 2003 the European Commission's data protection directive was intended to guarantee people a right to privacy and to create a level playing field for European commerce. However, the result was that the member states' national laws were left largely unaffected meaning that pan-European direct marketing campaigns still need to comply with individual national laws, which can differ substantially in their coverage. One of the toughest is regulated by the Spanish Data Protection Authority, which has fined Reader's Digest and Microsoft €1 million (£675,000) each for holding data longer than they should.

Another method of protection is to provide the opportunity for people who do not wish to receive direct mail or unsolicited telephone calls to enter their details on to a suppression file. This is a list of names, addresses and telephone numbers that direct marketers should check against their own lists and then remove any names appearing on it. In the UK, two suppression lists exist: the Mailing Preference Service and the Telephone Preference Service, with over 300,000 and 7.4 million people registered respectively (which represents 12 per cent of the UK population). Following an EC directive, the latter has been extended to companies in the form of the Corporate Telephone Preference Service.

A major factor in getting these instruments accepted by the direct marketing industry has been the threat of EC directives. If the industry did not regulate itself, the fear was that Europe would impose restrictive legislation on it.

Finally, companies have a responsibility for addressing public concerns. Some companies, like Barclays, a UK bank, are doing so. Barclays has moved into direct marketing for personal loans. A few years ago all current account customers would have received a direct mail shot. Now an in-house team prepares a target list using software that analyses its customer database. Less than 10 per cent of current account customers are chosen as suitable recipients based on analysis of an array of characteristics.

Based on: Fell (2002);[49] Coad (2003);[50] Harrison (2004);[51] Hughes and Rouse (2005)[52]

When you have read this chapter

log on to the Online Learning Centre at www.mcgraw-hill.co.uk/
textbooks/jobber to explore chapter-by-chapter test questions, links
and further online study tools for marketing.

Review

1. **The meaning of direct marketing**
   - Direct marketing is the distribution of products, information and promotional benefits to target customers through interactive communication in a way that allows response to be measured.
   - It includes such methods as direct mail, telemarketing, direct response advertising, catalogue marketing, electronic media, inserts, and door-to-door leafleting.

2. **The reasons for the growth of direct marketing activity**
   - Direct marketing activity has grown because of market and media fragmentation, developments in technology, the list explosion, sophisticated analytical techniques, and coordinated marketing systems.

3. **The nature and uses of database marketing**
   - Database marketing is an interactive approach to marketing that uses individually addressable marketing media and channels to provide information to a target audience, stimulate demand and stay close to customers.
   - It is used in direct mail to provide a database for mailings, in telemarketing to provide a database for telephone contact, in distributor management systems to provide a database for supplying information and monitoring distributors, in loyalty marketing for the selection of highly loyal customers to be given special treatment, in target marketing to target groups of consumers based on their behaviour, in campaign planning to use a database as a foundation to send consistent messages, and in marketing evaluation by using a database to hold responses to marketing mix variables (e.g. price promotions).

4. **The nature of customer relationship management**
   - Customer relationship management (CRM) is the term that describes the methodologies, technologies and e-commerce capabilities used by firms to manage customer relationships.
   - The basic principle behind CRM is that company staff have a single-customer point of view of each client.
   - Companies can assess how well they are managing their customer relationships by examining the following areas: analysis and planning, the proposition made to each customer segment, how well information and technology are being used, how well people are being managed and supported by an effective organizational structure, the efficiency of customer-impinging processes, the effectiveness of the implementation of the customer management activity, the quality of measuring performance against plan and against competitors, and the quality of the customer experience.
   - Success in CRM projects is associated with having a customer orientation, taking a single view of customers across departments, having the ability to manage cultural change, involving users in the design process, having a project champion on the board and a commitment to the benefits of CRM across affected departments, creating 'quick wins', ensuring face-to-face contact between marketing and information technology staff, and piloting the new system before launch.

5. **How to manage a direct marketing campaign**
   - A direct marketing campaign should not be designed in isolation but based on a clear understanding of marketing strategy in particular positioning. Then the steps are as follows.

- Identify and understand the target audience: never sell to a stranger. Who is to be reached, their motives and choice criteria need to be understood.
- Campaign objectives: these can be expressed in financial (e.g. sales), in marketing (e.g. acquire or retain customers) or communication (e.g. change beliefs) terms.
- Media decisions: major media options are direct mail, telemarketing, mobile marketing, direct response advertising, catalogue marketing and the Internet (which is discussed in the next chapter).
- Creative decisions: a creative brief will include a statement of communication objectives, product benefits (and weaknesses), target market analysis, development of the offer, communication of the message, and an action plan.
- Execute and evaluate the campaign: execution of the campaign may be in-house or through the use of a specialist agency. Evaluation should be taken against defined objectives such as total sales, number of enquiries, cost per sale and repeat purchase rate.

6 The media used in direct marketing
- The major media are direct mail, telemarketing, direct response advertising, catalogue marketing and the Internet (which is discussed in the next chapter).
- Direct mail: advantages are that it allows specific targeting to named individuals, elaborate personalization, and measurement; disadvantages are that poor lists give rise to intrusive junk mail, initial costs can be higher than advertising, e-mail campaigns are cheaper and response can be low.
- Telemarketing: advantages are that it is less costly and time consuming than a face-to-face salesperson visit, the growth of telephone ownership means it has wide reach, toll-free lines have reduced the cost of responding, sophisticated software has increased the efficiency of using telemarketing and, compared to advertising and other non-personal promotional methods, it has the advantage of two-way communication; disadvantages are that it lacks visual impact of a personal visit, body language cannot be judged, rejections can be high, unwanted unsolicited telephone calls can cause consumer annoyance, and costs per contact are higher than for direct mail and advertising.
- Direct response advertising: advantages are that the combination of advertising and direct marketing techniques (e.g. telemarketing) allows a swift response, a wide audience can be reached and, when direct response television is used, goods can be demonstrated, services explained, more in-depth information provided, and samples and brochures requested and sent; disadvantages are that not all products are suited to direct response advertising and, for infomercials and home shopping programmes, reach can be low.
- Catalogue marketing: advantages are that product selection can be in the convenience of the home, for people in remote rural locations it removes the need to travel long distances, costs can be reduced by avoiding expensive high-street locations and centralizing distribution, and a wider range of goods can be displayed in a catalogue compared to a shop; disadvantages are that catalogues are expensive to produce and require regular updating, goods cannot be tried or tried on before the order is placed, and colour tones in the catalogue may not match those of the delivered product.

7 Ethical issues in direct marketing
- There are potential problems relating to the quantity of poorly targeted direct mail, the timing and intrusive nature of telemarketing calls, the content of direct mail envelopes and invasion of privacy.

Key Terms

campaign objectives goals set by an organization in terms of, for example, sales, profits, customers won or retained, or awareness creation

catalogue marketing the sale of products through catalogues distributed to agents and customers, usually by mail or at stores

customer relationship management the methodologies, technologies and e-commerce capabilities used by firms to manage customer relationships

database marketing an interactive approach to marketing that uses individually addressable marketing media and channels to provide information to a target audience, stimulate demand and stay close to customers

direct mail material sent through the postal service to the recipient's house or business address

promoting a product and/or maintaining an ongoing relationship

direct response advertising the use of the prime advertising media such as television, newspapers and magazines to elicit an order, enquiry or request for a visit

telemarketing a marketing communications system whereby trained specialists use telecommunications and information technologies to conduct marketing and sales activities

Study Questions

1. Compare the strengths and weaknesses of direct mail and telemarketing.

2. What are the key differences between direct marketing and media advertising?

3. Define direct marketing. What are the seven forms of direct marketing? Give an example of how at least three of them can be integrated into a marketing communications campaign.

4. What is database marketing? Explain the types of information that are recorded on a database.

5. What are the stages of managing a direct marketing campaign? Why is the concept of lifetime value of a customer important when designing a campaign?

6. What are the advantages and disadvantages of loyalty schemes? Why are many companies employing such schemes?

7. What benefits does catalogue marketing provide to consumers and companies? Compare the traditional catalogue marketing approach with its modern equivalent.

8. Discuss the major concerns relating to ethics in direct marketing.

References

1. Smith, P. R. and J. Taylor (2004) *Marketing Communications: An Integrated Approach*, London: Kogan Page.
2. Stone, M., D. Davies and A. Bond (1995) *Direct Hit: Direct Marketing with a Winning Edge*, London: Pitman.
3. Fletcher, K., C. Wheeler and J. Wright (1990) The Role and Status of UK Database Marketing, *Quarterly Review of Marketing*, Autumn, 7–14.
4. Linton, I. (1995) *Database Marketing: Know What Your Customer Wants*, London: Pitman.
5. Nancarrow, C., L. T. Wright and J. Page (1997) Seagram Europe and Africa: The Development of a Consumer Database Marketing Capability, *Proceedings of the Academy of Marketing*, July, Manchester, 1119–30.
6. Stone, Davies and Bond (1995) op. cit.
7. Murphy, C. (2002) Catching up with its Glitzier Cousin, *Financial Times*, 24 July, 13.
8. Mitchell, A. (2002) Consumer Power Is on the Cards in Tesco Plan, *Marketing Week*, 2 May, 30–1.
9. James, M. (2003) The Quest for Fidelity, *Marketing Business*, January, 20–2.
10. O'Hara, M. (2003) Vodafone Joins Loyalty Scheme, *Guardian*, 18 February, 22.
11. Barnes, R. (2005) Nectar Readies B2B Loyalty Card Launch, *Marketing*, 19 January, 14.
12. McCawley, I. (2006) Nectar Loyalty Card Set for Global Roll-out, *Marketing Week*, 19 January, 3.

13. Murphy, C. (2008) No Such Thing as a Freebie, *The Marketer*, May, 28–31.

14. Finch, J. (2009) Tesco Sales Top £1 billion a Week, *Guardian*, 22 April, 22.

15. Foss, B. and M. Stone (2001) *Successful Customer Relationship Marketing*, London: Kogan Page.

16. Dempsey, J. (2001) An Elusive Goal Leads to Confusion, *Financial Times Information Technology Supplement*, 17 October, 4.

17. Payne, A. and P. Frow (2006) Customer Relationship Management: from Strategy to Implementation, *Journal of Marketing Management* 22(1/2), 135–68.

18. See Foss and Stone (2001) op. cit.; Woodcock, N., M. Starkey, J. Stone, P. Weston, and J. Ozimek (2001) *State of the Nation II: 2002, An Ongoing Global Study of how Companies Manage their Customer*, QCi Assessment Ltd, West Byfleet.

19. See Ryals, L., S. Knox and S. Maklan (2002) *Customer Relationship Management: Building the Business Case*, London: FT Prentice Hall; Wilson, H., E. Daniel and M. McDonald (2002) Factors for Success in Customer Relationship Management Systems, *Journal of Marketing Management* 18(1/2), 193–200.

20. Stone, Davies and Bond (1995) op. cit.

21. Murphy, J. (1997) The Art of Satisfaction, *Financial Times*, 23 April, 14.

22. A quotation by G. Harrison in Rines, S. (1995) Blind Data, *Marketing*, 17 November, 26–7.

23. Dowling, G. R. and M. Uncles (1997) Do Loyalty Programs Really Work? *Sloan Management Review* 38(4), 71–82.

24. Burnside, A. (1995) A Never Ending Search for the New, *Marketing*, 25 May, 31–5.

25. East, R. and W. Lomax (1999) Loyalty Value, *Marketing Week*, 2 December, 51–5.

26. Murphy, C. (1999) Addressing the Data Issue, *Marketing*, 28 January, 31.

27. Clegg, A. (2000) Hit or Miss, *Marketing Week*, 13 January, 45–9.

28. Benady, D. (2001) If Undelivered, *Marketing Week*, 20 December, 31–3.

29. Michell, A. (1995) Preaching the Loyalty Message, *Marketing Week*, 1 December, 26–7.

30. Reed, D. (1996) Direct Fight, *Marketing Week*, 1 November, 45–7.

31. Bird, D. (2000) *Commonsense and Digital Direct Marketing*, London: Kogan Page.

32. Bainbridge, J. (2009) How To Wow with Direct Mail and E-Mail, *The Marketer*, December/January, 33–8.

33. Abbot, R. (2008) Pushing the Envelope, *Marketing*, 1 October, 33–7.

34. Benady, D. (2005) DM Puts Boot into Junk, *Marketing Week*, 17 February, 39.

35. Miller, R. (1999) Phone Apparatus, *Campaign*, 18 June, 35–6.

36. Gander, P. (2005) We Don't Talk Anymore, *Marketing Week*, 22 September, 39.

37. Miller (1999) op. cit.

38. Moncrief, W. C. (1986) Selling Activity and Sales Position Taxonomies for Industrial Sales Forces, *Journal of Marketing Research* 23(2), 261–70.

39. Moncrief, W. C., S. H. Shipp, C. W. Lamb and D. W. Cravens (1989) Examining the Roles of Telemarketing in Selling Strategy, *Journal of Personal Selling and Sales Management* 9(3), 1–20.

40. Jobber, D. and G. Lancaster (2009) *Selling and Sales Management*, London: Pitman, 192–3.

41. Stevens, M. (1993) A Telephony Revolution, *Marketing*, 16 September, 38.

42. Murphy, D. (2001) Dare to Be Digital, *Marketing Business*, December/January, 3–5.

43. Mühlbacher, H., M. Botshen and W. Beutelmeyer (1997) The Changing Consumer in Austria, *International Journal of Research in Marketing* 14, 309–19.

44. Stone, Davies and Bond (1995) op. cit.

45. Roche, R. (2005) An Old Medium that's Still Vital in the New Economy, *Marketing Week*, 24 November, 37.

46. Gray, R. (2008) Talking the Lead, *Marketing* Direct Marketing Report, 11 June, 31–5.

47. Roman, E. (1995) *The Cutting Edge Strategy for Synchronizing Advertising, Direct Mail, Telemarketing and Field Sales*, Lincolnwood, IL: NTC Business Books.

48. Reed, D. (2008) Making a Visible Difference, *Marketing Week*, 14 August, 27.

49. Fell, J. (2002) How to Keep it Legal, *FT Creative Business*, 20 May, 12.

50. Coad, T. (2003) Dog's Breakfast, *Marketing Week*, 27 February, 49–50.

51. Harrison, J. (2004) The Final Hang-up for B2B Telemarketing, *Business-to-Business Marketing*, November/December, 18–20.

52. Hughes, M. and S. Rouse (2005) The Death of the Dialler?, *Marketing*, 27 April, 38–46.

Guinness' Rewards

An Award-Winning Relationship Marketing Programme

Introduction

Guinness is one of the world's best-known beer brands, and one of the key drinks in Diageo's global portfolio. Diageo was formed in 1997 through the merger of GrandMet and Guinness. Diageo is the world's leading premium drinks business, with an outstanding collection of beverage alcohol brands, including Guinness, Smirnoff, Baileys, Johnnie Walker and Gordons. Guinness is one of Diageo's priority brands and is the number-one stout in the world. It is brewed in 50 countries to suit local tastes, and sold in more than 150 countries worldwide.[1]

Challenging times

Since the mid-noughties, trends in the Irish alcohol market have been challenging Guinness' market position. Developments in markets along with the price of drinks in pubs increasing, have led to an increase in at-home alcohol consumption.[2] As more consumers were drinking at home, they were switching brands when doing so, opting for lagers and cider brands instead. Guinness always had a presence in the off-licence market, but the above factors encouraged it to look closer at the off-licence sector. Guinness saw the growth in the off-licence market as an opportunity and wanted to develop its presence in this market further. However, the off-licence sales environment was a challenge for Guinness as Guinness was a brand that was strongly associated with the pub scene.

The relationship marketing programme

In 2004, Guinness launched a comprehensive relationship marketing programme, aimed at increasing the loyalty and lifetime value of consumers by strengthening its relationship with publicans. Guinness' parent company, Diageo, invests heavily each year in this programme. According to Diageo, between 8 and 10 per cent of Guinness total advertising budget is dedicated to the relationship marketing programme.[3]

The first goal of the relationship marketing programme was to retain and reward existing loyal consumers and acquire new drinkers to the programme. The idea was to communicate with these drinkers to maintain and deepen their brand commitment and to

Enjoy GUINNESS Sensibly
Visit drinkaware.ie

cross-sell products to them from within the Guinness portfolio (e.g. Guinness draught for at-home consumption). Therefore, the strategy was to maximize the value of the relationship between consumers and their pubs, leveraging that relationship to build further brand loyalty and cross-selling cans of Guinness draught to consumers who change brands when drinking at home.[2]

Initially, the relationship marketing programme encouraged Guinness drinkers to sign up, via their local pub, to receive further information about the brand. The relationship marketing programme was sold to the pubs via sales representatives who provided the pubs with 'The Big Black Book'. This book provided the owners and managers with the information needed to train staff and recruit consumers, including sign-up forms and point-of-sale material for their pub (see illustration). The point-of-sale material allowed consumers to see themselves as 'One of Guinness' Most Wanted', and encouraged them to register. The pubs were allocated a unique code (on all sign-up forms) so that consumers could be mailed personalized vouchers for their local pub. Consumers completed a simple form, which

There's a REWARD out for **Guinness** drinkers

If you're a GUINNESS® drinker, you're a wanted man. Ask at the bar for details.

Enjoy GUINNESS Sensibly
Visit drinkaware.ie

▲ Point-of-sale materials.

The GUINNESS® Relationship Marketing Programme

BAR STAFF GUIDE

Talk to your GUINNESS drinkers
Approach your GUINNESS drinkers and invite them onto the GUINNESS Programme so that the GUINNESS Team and this pub can reward them for their loyalty.

They'll send us the form
GUINNESS drinkers simply fill out the form and return it to us.

We include them on the GUINNESS Programme
Once we receive their form, we check we have all the necessary information and add them to our mailing list. They will hear from us within about 8 weeks.

They get rewarded
GUINNESS drinkers begin receiving mailings with information and offers from the GUINNESS Team, while promoting this pub as the place to go for a pint. A number of times a year we may include a voucher for a free pint in this pub.

REWARD

▲ Guide used to help train bar staff to run the programme.

FREE PINT VOUCHER

enjoy GUINNESS, sensibly

Mr. Frank Sample
Pub: Sample Pub
Addr1, Addr2, Addr3

Valid Mon-Thurs until 30/04/06

00801005008853667119

▲ Pint voucher.

gathered essential information, such as date of birth and signature (which are essential for the responsible marketing of alcohol brands), together with their affinity to the brand and all their contact information.

Shortly after signing up, these participants received a 'Welcome Pack' from Guinness identifying them as a customer of the pub in which they signed up. This was followed by regular mailings throughout the year. Each mailing was personalized and contained information about Guinness. The mailings also included invitations to enter regional competitions (with prizes such as sports tickets or holiday prizes) and vouchers for a free pint at the participant's local pub (see illustration). This allowed Guinness to build up an improved profile of the fans of the Guinness brand.[3]

This campaign won an ECHO Award in 2005. The ECHO awards are prestigious international direct marketing awards, recognizing excellence in strategy, creativity and results. In 2005, the Guinness direct marketing campaign won the top prize out of 2000 entries from 330 agencies in 26 countries. It was the first time an Irish entry had won this award and only the second time an entry from Europe had done so.[4]

The relationship marketing programme update

Since its introduction in 2004, the Guinness relationship marketing programme has evolved and gone from strength to strength. Guinness' most recent relationship marketing programme mailings have focused on leveraging Guinness' sponsorship of Irish rugby. Participants were recruited on to the relationship marketing programme in pubs throughout the Six Nations and Rugby World Cup, and subsequently invited back to sample the product on three separate occasions on these separate days. Participants also received rugby merchandise, memorabilia and behind-the-scenes access to the Irish team.[10]

In addition, there was also a strong emphasis on developing home occasions for Guinness drinkers and increasing at-home Guinness share of consumption. Consumers who signed up for the relationship marketing programme received a customized Guinness poker kit and Guinness vouchers (for different dates mirroring the games) to help promote the trial of Guinness draught cans. Guinness drinkers were then tactically mailed four times a year to encourage a number of 'occasions' for Guinness. The most crucial factor for the programme was personalization through a highly personalized birthday card and

▲ Consumers received a personalized birthday card and voucher for a free pint.

a customized voucher attached for a free pint in his/her local pub.[5] According to RMG Target's Geoff McGrath, up to 20 per cent of these Guinness vouchers are redeemed, which represents a response rate way beyond that of most other programmes of this kind.[5]

'Personalization and the general use of data is what separates this programme from most others,' explains Michael Craig, senior account manager at RMG Target. 'Consumers have a genuine feeling that this is a one-to-one conversation with Guinness and this is a brand that knows and understands them.'[10]

Publicans were also invited to submit names of Guinness enthusiasts who might wish to take part in the relationship marketing programme. Many publicans did so willingly, in an attempt to boost affinity between themselves and their customers, and to potentially encourage incremental business into their pubs.[7] Participants were also asked to name their interests, such as rugby or hurling, so that messages could be targeted at them throughout the year. In this way Guinness could ensure the relevance of its message content to its consumers and ensure that appropriate channels were used for this message.

Each participant was mailed a Guinness calendar and most participants were asked to become involved in what Guinness calls its 'co-creation' projects. One of these projects involves inviting Guinness fans to compose messages that will be featured on a new monument planned for the Guinness Storehouse site in Dublin. Another involved inviting members to provide first-person accounts of their favourite place where they enjoyed a pint of Guinness, including some locations around the world. Responses to these 'co-creation' projects have run into thousands.[5] These projects have encouraged Guinness drinkers to become involved with the brand and have strengthened the relationship. According to Tanya Clarke, Head of Marketing Guinness, 'most relationship marketing is just a monologue between a brand and its customers, but this is really different. People feel they own Guinness anyway, and this is a way for them to be part of it'.[5]

In 2008, Guinness and its Irish agency RMG Target saw their work once again win an international gold ECHO award for direct marketing. This was a record fifth international gold ECHO award for the Guinness relationship marketing programme. Responding to the win, Asta Lund, Digital and Relationship Marketing Manager with Diageo, said 'the programme is a key part of our overall strategy, which has fuelled the brand's turnaround. We are very proud of this achievement. We may be a small market, but our creativity and strategic ability is second to none, having beaten off stiff competition from some of the best marketing brains from around the world'.[6]

In recent years, there has been a growth in integrated direct marketing campaigns—using on- and offline channels. From e-mail to microsites, SMS and other handheld devices, digital media provide opportunities to target increasingly hard-to-get-at audiences. These digital media provide inventive ways to connect with prospects and customers (see illustration). The bulk of the relationship marketing programme is focused around direct mail. However, each year, the elements of the programme evolve. For example, recently, new recruits on the programme have been contacted online. According to Geoff McGrath, RMG Target, 'Guinness's relationship marketing programme continues to demonstrate thought leadership, with an increased shift towards innovative digital and segmentation strategies'.[6]

▲ Use of digital media: two-way dialogue.

Results

The Guinness relationship marketing programme has been a great success, contributing to a 5–15 per cent positive shift in brand equity scores. To date Guinness has signed up about 30 per cent of Irish Guinness drinkers on the Guinness database, 66 per cent of whom have been added in the last four years.[4] In addition, feedback from Guinness drinkers has been very positive. Some Guinness enthusiasts are so committed to their favourite beer, that they send the brewer Christmas cards every year.[4]

The following feedback from customers also illustrates why the relationship marketing programme is so important:

> Most of it's called junk mail for a reason—you just don't open it. But Guinness is not in the same category as everything else. It's something interesting and you will always open it.

> You are not one of their statistics. You feel like a valued customer.

> It's a nice bit of recognition to show you are loyal to the brand.[8]

One big success is that Guinness has grown its home sales in Ireland, despite the fact that the overall Irish beer market is continuing to decline. Sales of Guinness rose by 2.5 per cent in the half year to the end of June 2008, compared to the same period the previous year. For the first time since 2000, sales are growing for the iconic brand, and this upswing is being attributed in large part to marketing spend, which Diageo has increased by 4 per cent globally.[7] According to Oliver Loomes, Diageo's Marketing Director for Ireland, 'It's not just a flash in the pan. We've been working hard for this, we've been trying hard to recruit new drinkers. Our strategy is not by any means only about holding share'.[3] To add to its success, Guinness has found that over 69 per cent of pub drinkers will opt to drink Guinness at home as well as in the pub now. This has grown from 40 per cent. It shows that Guinness has boosted at-home Guinness sales at a time when at-home alcohol consumption is on the increase.

According to Head of Marketing Guinness, Tanya Clarke, 'market share is holding up well at present, despite the market being difficult'. According to Clarke, 'relationship marketing is hard to do right, but it has worked extremely well for Guinness. When it works well, it is enormously rewarding'.[5] In essence, the Guinness relationship marketing programme has been a great success and has created an army of Guinness devotees, who act as walking, talking advertisements for the brand in the places where it counts most—in the pub and at home.[9]

Notes

1 www.diageo.ie/brands/guinness
2 Stone, B. and R. Jacobs (2007) *Successful Direct Marketing Methods* (8th edn.), McGraw-Hill, 138–41.
3 O'Mahoney, C. (2006) 'Stout Relationship with Drinkers', *Sunday Business Post*, 6th November.
4 O'Mahoney, C. (2008) 'Guinness a Stout Performer Again', *Sunday Business Post*, 17th February.
5 O'Mahoney, C. (2008) 'Guinness Marketing Wins Top Award for Fifth Time', *Sunday Business Post*, 16th November.
6 www.anpost.ie
7 Anonymous (2008) 'Guinness Wins Major Award for Marketing', *Business World News*, 18th November.
8 Lund, A. and J. Kiernan (2008) 'Guinness Relationship Marketing Programme – What Makes It Successful?', *An Post Business Breakfast Presentation*, 27th August.
9 www.distrimedia.com.ua
10 Anonymous (2008) 'First Past the Post', *Marketing Age*, 2(3), 44.

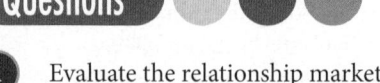

Questions

1 Evaluate the relationship marketing programme used by Guinness in the Irish market. Why do you think this programme has been so successful?

2 Comment on how Guinness has used relationship marketing to build the Guinness brand.

3 Outline the advantages and disadvantages associated with using direct mail to communicate with Guinness customers. How has the role that direct mail plays in the relationship marketing programme changed over the years?

This case was written by Marie O'Dwyer, Lecturer in Marketing, Waterford Institute of Technology, Ireland. Special thanks to Jennifer Kiernan, Guinness Brand Manager and Asta Lund, Digital and Relationship Marketing Manager, Diageo Ireland.

Enjoy GUINNESS Sensibly.
drinkaware.co.uk for the facts

From Understanding to Engaging Customers

Tesco is currently one of the most successful retail organizations in the world. This case study explores how a key element of its strategy since 1995 has been its Clubcard-based loyalty scheme and its development of a strategic CRM (customer relationship management) programme that provides the basis for true customer insight and greater brand engagement.

Background

In 2003, *Management Today* voted Tesco the UK's Most Admired Company and its boss, Sir Terry Leahy, Most Admired Leader. In 2005, the company again picked up the two awards, a feat that had not been achieved since *Management Today*, in conjunction with Mercer Consulting, launched the Most Admired Companies scheme in 1989. In doing this, it also won outright two of the nine criteria used to judge companies: Capacity to Innovate and Use of Corporate Assets. In 2009, the company was ranked by the *Financial Times* as the 106th most valuable company in the world.

The Tesco story, particularly over the past 20 years, is one of sustained growth and financial success. With more than 2300 stores in the UK (4300+ stores worldwide), 85 million square feet of selling space and group sales in 2008–9 of £59.4 billion, it is with more than 300,000 employees in the UK and 470,000+ worldwide, the UK's largest private-sector employer and the world's third-largest grocery retailer. In 2008–9, Tesco made over £3.1 billion in profit (PBT) and accounted for more than £1 in every £8 of UK high-street consumer spending. Its Internet shopping arm, which operates in the UK, Ireland, China and South Korea and has pilot schemes in Slovakia, Poland, Turkey and Thailand, is the world's most successful online retail grocery operation.

The strategy

Founded in 1924, the company for many years pursued a largely price-based strategy. However, in the early 1970s, with customers becoming wealthier and less concerned with price, the company began to rethink its pile-it-high, sell-it-cheap low cost/low price model. Throughout the 1970s and 1980s, the management team restructured and began to focus on superstores of 20,000–50,000 square feet, new store layouts, store

ambience and a far wider product range. During the 1990s, it launched a series of new store formats, including Tesco Express (up to 3000 square feet), Tesco Metro (7000–15,000 square feet) and Tesco Extra (60,000+ square feet), as well as trialling Homeplus stores of 35,000–50,000 square feet dedicated to non-food products (by 2009, non-food sales had reached £12.5 billion). At the same time, it began entering a series of overseas markets including China, Japan, South Korea, Thailand, Malaysia, France, Hungary, Poland, Turkey, Slovakia, the Czech Republic, Ireland, India and the United States. Speaking in 2009, when overseas operations were generating almost £18 billion of sales and more than £700 million in profit, Leahy made the comment that the expectation was that, by 2015, more than half the company's turnover would be generated outside the UK. As part of this, the company's plans for 2009–10 included 500 new stores, 11.5 million square feet of new trading space (75 per cent of this to be outside the UK) and 30,000 additional jobs worldwide.

The success of the company's strategy in the UK was reflected by it overtaking Sainsbury's in 1995 to become the UK grocery market leader. Since then, the company has rapidly reinforced its dominance of the market by expanding both its product range and UK market share, which by mid-2009 had reached 31 per cent. This compared with Wal-Mart Asda's 16.9 per cent, Sainsbury's 16 per cent and Morrisons' 11.4 per cent. Its position in the UK has also been strengthened by its home grocery shopping service, which in 2009 had more than 1 million active customers and sales of almost £2 billion, making the company the largest dotcom grocery business in the world. At the same time, the company was also the groceries market leader in five other countries. Among the other initiatives announced by the company were:

- plans to launch a new own-brand clothing website designed to take on Internet fashion retailers such as ASOS
- the intention to challenge the market leadership of Carphone Warehouse with the opening in 2009–10 of more than 100 in-store phone shops selling mobile and land-line packages, followed by similar shops in all 210 of its Tesco Extra sites within two to three years, and
- a planning application for the development of what was dubbed a 'Tesco Town', which would feature several hundred apartments, a crèche, a health centre, a market square and, of course, a Tesco supermarket.

However, at the beginning of the 1990s, the company's management team had begun to recognize that the key to future success would lie not just in pursuing an aggressive and often very innovative strategy of growth, but must be based on getting ever closer to the customer. It was this that led to the company's development of what has proven to be one of the world's largest and most successful CRM initiatives. Based on the company's statement of its core purpose of creating 'value for customers and *to earn their lifetime loyalty*' (author's emphasis), the CRM programme is seen by many to be a model of best practice.

The CRM initiative

Tesco's move into customer relationship management began in the early 1990s when the company started working with dunnhumby, a marketing services firm, and led in late 1994 to the preliminary test launch of a loyalty card scheme in six stores. The move was driven partly by an awareness of this sort of initiative in other parts of the world, but also by the results of some analysis, which highlighted two significant facts:

1   in many of its stores the top 100 customers were worth as much in terms of sales as the bottom 4000
2   the top 5 per cent of the company's customers accounted for 20 per cent of sales, while the bottom 25 per cent accounted for just 2 per cent.

The scheme, which was underpinned with a major launch to the staff and the distribution of 140,000 educational videos, is based upon the Tesco Clubcard, which rewards customers by giving them one loyalty point for every £1 spent with the company. These points can then be redeemed either for products in store or with a wide range of other organizations, including leisure attractions, hotels, museums, zoos, holiday and travel companies, and restaurants.

However, the Clubcard scheme is far more than a simple customer reward programme. From the outset, the company has focused on capturing, analysing and then, most importantly, *using* the data and information generated by the 10 million-plus transactions made each week. The starting point for this involves each of the transactions being linked to individual customer profiles. Data-mining techniques are then used to pinpoint when and where purchases are made, the amount that customers have spent and the types of products that have been bought. These purchasing habits and behaviour patterns are then used as the basis for segmenting customers on the basis of 5000 need segments.

Armed with this information, segments are targeted with tailor-made campaigns and advertisements, as well as invitations to join Tesco special interest clubs, which include the Wine Club, the Kids Club, the Food Club, the Baby & Toddler Club, and the Healthy Living Club. Customers also receive regular mailings of a mass-customized magazine with 8 million unique coupon variations and a tailored combination of articles, advertisements related to Tesco's offer, and third-party ads.

Internally, the information is used by the company's management teams as the basis for making a series of decisions about:

- management of the product range
- new product development—Tesco's Finest range, for example, was launched when analysis showed that some customers were defecting to Marks & Spencer for high(er)-quality foodstuffs
- pricing strategies that more precisely meet the needs and price sensitivities of different target groups
- merchandising so that the product portfolio is based on *detailed* insights to customer profiles and purchasing patterns
- inventory management
- promotions, with greater rewards being offered to loyal customers
- levels of customer service, with greater attention being paid to the stock levels and promotions on those products bought by loyal customers
- measures of promotional and media effectiveness
- customer acquisition by matching new products, such as the entry to financial services and the launch of Tesco.com, to specific customer types, and
- targeted communications (20 per cent of Tesco's coupons are redeemed against an industry average of 0.5 per cent).

The information is also used by the company as part of the process of identifying and evaluating product development opportunities, promotions, and when dealing with its suppliers.

The changing marketing environment and the Clubcard relaunch

Despite the undoubted success of the Clubcard, in mid-2009 the company announced the relaunch of the scheme. Designed to attract at least one million more customers to the card's existing base of 15 million (one in two UK households were by this time members of the scheme) and underpinned by a £150 million investment, the revised scheme allowed customers to double the value of their Clubcard vouchers against a range of Tesco products both in-store and online. Previously, customers could spend Clubcard vouchers at face value across Tesco's stores or on its websites, or could increase their value by up to four times by trading them with Tesco's partners in the scheme, such as restaurants and theme parks.

But although the relaunch was promoted as stage two of an already enormously successful strategy, a variety of commentators suggested that this was a largely defensive move that had been forced upon the company during a period of significant economic downturn and a response to a series of clever initiatives by others in the sector, including a revitalized Morrisons (Tesco's underlying sales growth in the UK in 2008–9 was 3.4 per cent compared with Morrisons' 7.9 per cent) and the rapidly growing discount retailers such as Aldi, Netto and Lidl. In an additional attempt to compete with the aggressive discounters like Aldi, Tesco introduced a new advertising campaign, calling itself *Britain's biggest discounter*, a move that led to around 30 per cent of customers buying something from the 'Discount Brands at Tesco' range each time they shopped.

However, at the same time, analysts had begun pointing to the disappointing performance of the group's US Fresh & Easy operations. Leahy's stated ambition was to build a chain of 1000 outlets across California, Nevada and Arizona, but by mid-2009 just 60 had been opened, with 200 more planned for the year. However, with losses for the previous 12 months running at £142 million (this compares with predictions of a £100 million loss) and a similar shortfall predicted for the next year, the company announced a three-month halt to store openings in order to refine the concept.

But despite the company's disappointing performance in the States, few would argue that the organization has established a track record of sustained and enviable success, something that is reflected in Millward Brown's brand consultancy BrandZ™ valuing the Tesco brand at $22.9 billion, making it the UK's most valuable retail brand and the twenty-first most valuable global brand. Asda, by contrast, was valued at $5.4 billion.

References

Based on: Mukund, A. (2003) *Tesco: the Customer Relationship Management Champion*, Hyderabad, India: ICFAI Centre for Management Research; Newell, F. (2003) *Why CRM Doesn't Work: How to Win by Letting Customers Manage the Relationship*, Kogan Page; Gwyther, M. and A. Saunders (2005) Another Twin Win for Tesco, *Management Today*, December, 35–43; Anonymous (2009) FT Global 500 2009, *FT Weekend Magazine*, 30/31 May, 31; Anonymous (2009) Off-Colour Tesco is Still World Class, *Daily Mail*, 22 April, 61; Anonymous (2009) Tesco in £150 Million Clubcard Relaunch, www.tescoplc.com, 8 May; Anonymous (2009) Tesco Takes Mobiles War to Carphone, *The Sunday Times*, 19 April, 3; Anonymous (2009) Tesco Town to Set Up Shop With Tower in Earl's Court, *Evening Standard*, 14 May; Anonymous (2009) Tesco Trumpets Strategic Success Overseas, *Financial Times*, 18/19 April, 12; Tesco plc (2009) *Annual Report & Review*.

Questions

1. Evaluate the strategy pursued by Tesco and, in doing this, show how the company has redefined the markets in which it operates and patterns of marketing thinking across the retail sector.

2. The majority of CRM programmes fail to deliver what is promised or expected when they are introduced. Why has the Tesco scheme been so successful when so many others have failed?

3. Identify the lessons that emerge from the Tesco Clubcard and CRM strategy, and the nature of any problems that others might experience in pursuing a similar approach.

This case was written by Colin Gilligan, Emeritus Professor of Marketing, Sheffield Hallam University and Visiting Professor of Marketing, Newcastle Business School.

CHAPTER 16

Other promotional mix methods

Advertising brings the horse to water, sales promotion makes it drink.

JULIAN CUMMINS

Don't tell my mother I'm in public relations, she thinks I play piano in a brothel.

JACQUES SEQUELA

LEARNING OBJECTIVES

After reading this chapter, you should be able to:

1 identify the reasons for the growth in sales promotion activity

2 identify the major sales promotion types

3 discuss the objectives of and how to evaluate sales promotion

4 describe the objectives and targets of public relations

5 discuss the key tasks and characteristics of publicity

6 describe the guidelines to use when writing a press release

7 discuss the objectives and methods of sponsorship

8 explain how to select and evaluate a potential sponsored event or programme

9 discuss the objectives, conduct and evaluation of exhibitions

10 explain the reasons for the growth in product placement and its risks

11 discuss the ethical issues in sales promotion and public relations

In Chapters 13, 14, 15 and 18 we examine the role and use of advertising, personal selling, direct marketing and digital marketing in the promotional mix. This chapter provides an analysis of other methods of promoting products: sales promotion, public relations and publicity, sponsorship, exhibitions and product placement. Traditionally, these were regarded as playing a secondary role compared to advertising and personal selling. In recent years, though, one common factor has linked them all: they are all growth areas in the promotional mix, and marketing people need to know how to manage them effectively. Each method needs to be used as part of a consistent communication programme so that all elements of the promotional mix support and reinforce one another. The message needs to be consistent with the product's positioning strategy.

Sales Promotion

As we saw in Chapter 13, sales promotions are incentives to consumers or the trade that are designed to stimulate purchase. Examples include money off and free gifts (consumer promotions), discounts and salesforce competitions (trade promotions). Incentives to in-company salespeople are sometimes included within the definition of sales promotion but these have been dealt with in Chapter 14, and consequently will not be discussed in this chapter.

A vast amount of money is spent on sales promotion. Peattie and Peattie explain the growth in sales promotion as follows.[1]

- *Increased impulse purchasing*: the retail response to greater consumer impulse purchasing is to demand more sales promotions from manufacturers.
- *Sales promotions are becoming respectable*: through the use of promotions by market leaders and the increasing professionalism of the sales promotion agencies.
- *The rising cost of advertising and advertising clutter*: these factors erode advertising's cost effectiveness.
- *Shortening time horizons*: the attraction of the fast sales boost of a sales promotion is raised by greater rivalry and shortening product life cycles.
- *Competitor activities*: in some markets, sales promotions are used so often that all competitors are forced to follow suit.[2]
- *Measurability*: measuring the impact of sales promotions is easier than for advertising since their effect is more direct and, usually, short term. The use of electronic point-of-sale (EPOS) scanner information makes measurement easier.

The effects of sales promotion

Sales promotion is often used to provide a short, sharp shock to sales. In this sense it may be regarded as a short-term tactical device. Figure 16.1 shows a typical sales pattern. The sales promotion boosts sales during the promotion period because of the incentive effect. This is followed by a small fall in sales to below normal level because some consumers will have stocked up on the product during the promotion. The long-term sales effect of the promotion could be positive, neutral or negative. If the promotion has attracted new buyers, who find that they like the brand, repeat purchases from them may give rise to a positive long-term effect.[3] Alternatively, if the promotion (e.g. money off) has devalued the brand in the eyes of consumers, the effect may be negative.[4] Where the promotion has caused consumers to buy the brand only because of its incentive value, with no effect on underlying preferences, the long-term effect may be neutral.[5] An international study of leading grocery brands has shown that the most likely long-term effect of a price promotion for an existing brand is neutral. Such promotions tend to attract existing buyers of the brand rather than new buyers during the promotional period.[6]

Ad insight

Go to the website to see Tetley's sales promotions on its Redbush tea

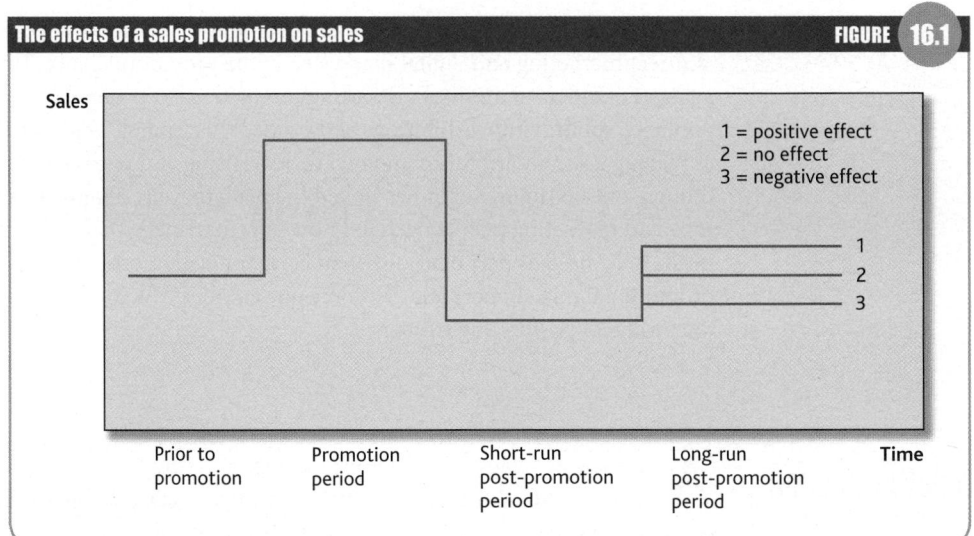

The effects of a sales promotion on sales FIGURE **16.1**

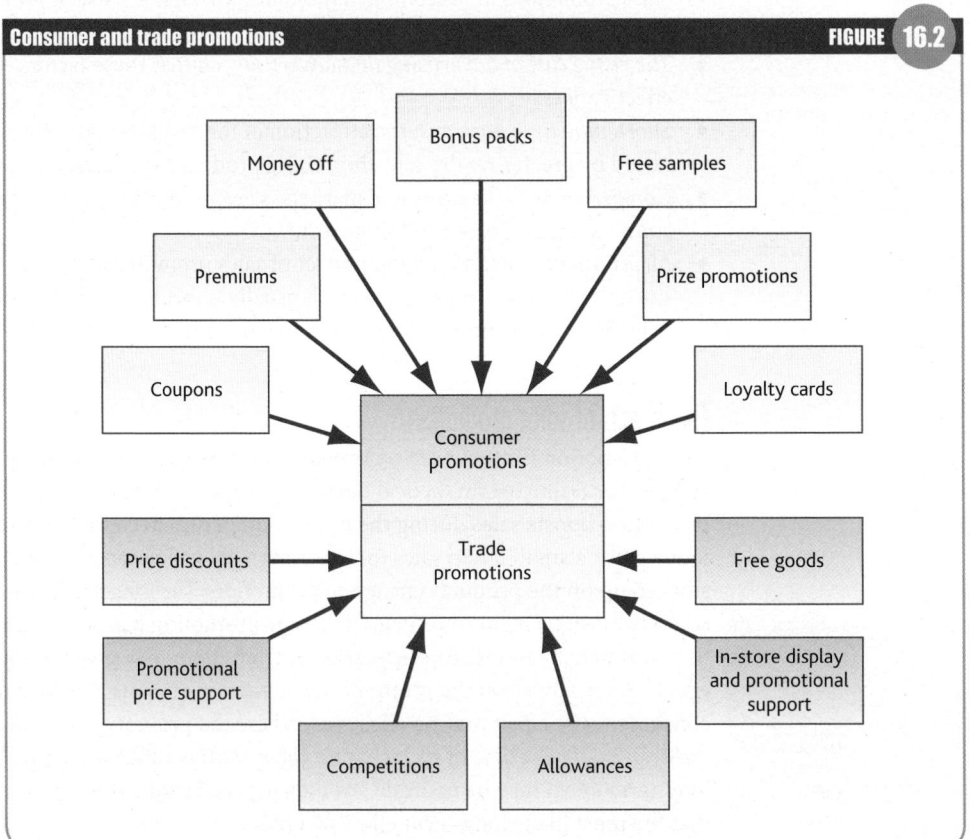

Major sales promotion types

Sales promotion can be directed at the consumer or the trade (see Fig. 16.2). Major consumer sales promotion types are money off, bonus packs, premiums, free samples, coupons, prize promotions and loyalty cards. A sizeable proportion of sales promotions are directed at the trade, including price discounts, free goods, competitions, allowances, promotional price support, and in-store display and promotional support.

Consumer and trade promotions FIGURE **16.2**

The following sections examine the main types of *consumer promotions*.

▲ Ariel washing powder tablets featuring a value pack.

Money off

Money-off promotions provide direct value to the customer, and therefore an unambiguous incentive to purchase. They have a proven track record of stimulating short-term sales increases and encouraging trial.[7] However, price reductions can easily be matched by the competition and if used frequently can devalue brand image. Consumer response may be 'If the brand is that good why do they need to keep reducing the price?' A variant on the normal money-off promotion is the *value pack*. With value packs, the consumer pays a higher price for the larger pack, but the per-unit price (e.g. per gram or per tablet) is less (see the illustration for Ariel washing powder tablets).

Occasionally, companies inadvertently offer money off, as Marketing in Action 16.1 explains.

 16.1 Marketing in Action

Money-Off Promotional Blunders

Some of the world's best-known retail names have been caught up in promotional blunders, including Apple, whose UK website advertised an Olympus digital camera for £98.70 rather than the usual £600; Amazon, where a £287 iPaq handheld computer was mistakenly priced at £7.32; and Kodak, whose 'special offer' on its DX3700 digital cameras advertised on its website was mispriced at £100 instead of £329.

Perhaps the most renowned promotional blunder was Argos's £2.99 television. The UK catalogue retailer's website inadvertently offered Sony Nicam TVs for a rock-bottom £2.99 each instead of £299. As word spread, orders flooded in—including one for 1700 sets! Argos refused to honour the sales. Surprisingly, the retailer repeated the blunder when a £349.99 television appeared on its website for 49p. Again, Argos cancelled the orders, blaming 'an accidental error'.

Based on: Jones (2008)[8]

Bonus packs

These give *added value* by giving consumers extra quantity at no additional cost. **Bonus packs** are often used in the drinks, confectionery and detergent markets. For example, cans of lager may be sold on the basis of '12.5 per cent extra free!'. Because the price is not lowered, this form of promotion runs less risk of devaluing brand image. Extra value is given by raising quantity rather than cutting price. With some product groups, this encourages buyers to consume more. For example, a Mars bar will be eaten or a can of lager drunk whether there is extra quantity or not. The illustration for Sugar Puffs shows a bonus pack promotion.

Premiums

Premiums are any merchandise offered free or at low cost as an incentive to purchase a brand. There are four major forms: free in- or on-pack gifts; free-in-the-mail offers; self-liquidating offers; buy-one-get-one-free offers.

Free in- or on-pack gifts: gifts may be given away free with brands. For example, Twiglets, a snack food, was promoted by enclosing a small can of Appletize, a fizzy apple drink, in its

▲ Sugar Puffs featuring a bonus offer.
© Honey Monster Foods.

pack; PG Tips, a brand of tea, used a plastic dinosaur attached to the outside of its packaging to promote sales.

Occasionally the gift is a free sample of one brand that is banded to another brand (*banded pack offer*). The free sample may be a new variety or flavour that benefits by getting trial. In other cases the brands are linked, as when Nestlé promoted its Cappuccino brand by offering a free KitKat to be eaten while drinking the coffee, and Cadbury ran a similar promotion with a packet of Cadbury's Chocolate Chip Cookies attached to its Cadbury's Chocolate Break, a milk chocolate drink.

When two or more items are banded together the promotion is called a multibuy and can involve a number of items of the same brand being offered together. Multibuys are a very popular form of promotion. They are frequently used to protect market share by encouraging consumers to stock up on a particular brand when two or more items of the same brand are packaged together. However, unlike price reductions, they do not encourage trial because consumers do not bulk buy a brand they have not tried before. When multibuys take the form of two different brands, range trial can be generated. For example, a manufacturer of a branded coffee launching a new brand of tea could band the two brands together, thus leveraging the strength of the coffee brand to gain trial of the new tea brand.[9]

Free-in-the-mail offers: this sort of promotion involves the collection of packet tops or labels, which are sent in the mail as proof of purchase to claim a free gift or money-off voucher: Kellogg's Fruit 'n Fibre has been promoted by such an offer.

Gifts can be quite valuable because redemption rates can be low (less than 10 per cent redemption is not unusual). This is because of *slippage*: consumers collect labels with a view to mailing them but never collect the requisite number.

Self-liquidating offers: these are similar to free-in-the-mail offers except that consumers are asked to pay a sum of money to cover the costs of the merchandise plus administration and postage charges. The consumer benefits by getting the goods at below normal cost because the manufacturer passes on the advantage of bulk buying and prices at cost. The manufacturer benefits by the self-funding nature of the promotion, although there is a danger of being left with surplus stocks of the merchandise. The illustration featuring Weetabix is an example of a self-liquidating offer. Consumers are asked to collect tokens and to pay a small sum of money to cover the cost of the books and administration.

▲ Weetabix featuring a self-liquidating offer where tokens are collected and a small sum of money is paid to cover the cost of the books and administration.

Buy-one-get-one-free offers: sometimes known as BOGOFs, with this type of promotion the consumer is in effect getting two items for the price of one. Wine is sometimes offered as a BOGOF promotion so that the consumer can buy two bottles of a particular brand for the price of one. The danger of running BOGOF promotions for heavily advertised brands is that they lose their premium positioning and are seen as just another brand available in bulk at discount prices.[10]

Free samples

Free samples of a brand may be delivered to the home or given out in a store. The idea is that having tried the sample a proportion of consumers will begin to buy it. For new brands or brand extensions (for example, a new shampoo or fabric conditioner) this form of promotion is an effective if expensive way of gaining consumer trial. However, sampling may be ineffective if the brand has nothing extra to offer the consumer. For existing brands that have a low trial but high purchasing rate, sampling may be effective. As it would appear that many of those who try the brand like it and buy it again, raising the trial rate through free samples could have a beneficial long-term effect.

Coupons

There are three ways of couponing. Coupons can be delivered to the home, appear in magazines or newspapers, or appear on packs. *Home couponing*, after home sampling, is the best way to achieve trial for new brands.[11] *Magazine or newspaper couponing* is much cheaper than home delivery and can be used to stimulate trial, but redemption rates are much lower at around 5 per cent on average. The purpose of *on-pack couponing* is to encourage initial and repeat purchasing of the same brand, or trial of a different brand. A brand carries an on-pack coupon redeemable against the consumer's next purchase, usually for the same brand. Redemption rate is high, averaging around 40 per cent.[12] The coupon can offer a higher face value than the equivalent cost of a money-off pack since the effect of the coupon is on both initial and repeat sales. However, it is usually less effective in raising initial sales than money off because there is no immediate saving and its appeal is almost exclusively to existing consumers.[13]

Prize promotions

There are three main types of *prize promotion*: competitions, draws and games. Unlike other promotions, the cost can be established in advance and does not depend on the number of participants. *Competitions* require participants to exercise a certain degree of skill and judgement. For example, a competition to win free cinema seats might require entrants to name five films based upon stills from each. Entry is usually dependent on at least one purchase. Compared to premiums and money off, competitions offer a less immediate incentive to buy, and one that requires time and effort on the part of entrants. However, they can attract attention and interest in a brand. *Draws* make no demands on skill or judgement: the result depends on chance. For example, a supermarket may run an out-of-the-hat draw, where customers fill in their name and address on an entry card and on a certain day a draw is made. Another example of a draw is when direct mail recipients are asked to return a card on which there is a set of numbers. These are then compared against a set of winning numbers.

An example of a *game promotion* is where a newspaper encloses a series of bingo cards and customers are told that, over a period of time, sets of bingo numbers will be published. If these numbers form a line or full house on a bingo card a prize is won. Such a game encourages repeat purchase of the newspaper.

The national laws governing sales promotions in Europe vary tremendously and local legal advice should be taken before implementing a sales promotion. The UK, Ireland, Spain,

▲ Caffe Nero rewards its loyalty card holders with free coffee.

Portugal, Greece, Russia and the Czech Republic have fairly relaxed laws about what can be done. Germany, Luxembourg, Austria, Norway, Switzerland and Sweden are much more restrictive. For example, in Sweden free mail-ins, free draws and money-off-next-purchase promotions, and in Norway self-liquidating offers, free draws, money-off vouchers and money-off-next-purchase, are not allowed.

Loyalty cards

A major development in retailing is the offering of *loyalty cards* to customers, who gain points every time they spend money at an outlet. An example of a simple and highly successful scheme is Caffe Nero's loyalty card, which offers customers a free coffee after they have purchased nine (see illustration). Other loyalty schemes might involve the accrual of points that can be swapped for money-off vouchers to be used against purchases at the store or for bargain offers on other purchases such as cinema tickets. The intention is to attract customers back to the outlet, but the retailer may gain other advantages. In some schemes, the card contains information on the customer including his or her name and address and, when it is swiped through the checkout machine, detailed information on purchases is recorded. This means that the purchasing behaviour of individual customers is known to the retailer, which can then use this information to, among other things, target tailored direct mail promotions at those who are likely to be responsive since it is known that they purchase within a product category (e.g. wine) or buy certain types of product within a category (e.g. herbal tea).

Loyalty cards are very popular, with over 90 per cent of people in the UK holding at least one loyalty card and, of these, 78 per cent carrying more than one loyalty card. Many loyalty card schemes are specific to an individual company, such as the Tesco Clubcard, but the Nectar card is a joint venture between several companies, such as Sainsbury's, BP, Hertz and Homecare, and boasts over 11 million customers.[14]

16.1 Pause for Thought

Can you remember a recent sales promotion that was associated with a brand you bought? How influential was it in your purchase decision? What kind of objectives do you think the promotion was trying to achieve for the brand?

We will now go on to look at *trade promotions*.

Price discounts

The trade may be offered (or may demand) *discounts* in return for purchase. The concentration of buying into fewer trade outlets has placed increasing power with these organizations. This power is often translated into discounts from manufacturers. The discount may be part of a joint promotion, whereby the retailer agrees to devote extra shelf space, buy larger quantities, engage in a joint competition and/or allow in-store demonstrations. Volume discounts are given to retailers that hit sales targets.[15]

Free goods

An alternative to a price discount is to offer more merchandise at the same price. For example, the *baker's dozen* technique involves offering 13 items (or cases) for the price of 12.

Competitions

This involves a manufacturer offering financial inducements or prizes to distributors' salesforces in return for achieving sales targets for their products. Alternatively, a prize may be given to the salesforce with the best sales figures.

Allowances

A manufacturer may offer an *allowance* (a sum of money) in return for retailers providing promotional facilities in store (*display allowance*). For example, an allowance would be needed to persuade a supermarket to display cards on its shelves indicating that a brand was being sold at a special low price. An *advertising allowance* would be paid by a manufacturer to a retailer for featuring its brands in the retailer's advertising. *Listing allowances* are paid by the manufacturer to have a brand stocked.

Promotional price support

Promotional price support occurs when the manufacturer pays for money-off deals offered by the retailer.

In-store display and promotional support

Another form of trade promotion is when the manufacturer pays for in-store display and promotion. For example, a supplier could pay for a gondola-end display or a 10-second advertisement on the retailer's in-store television network.[16]

Sales promotion objectives

The most basic objective of any sales promotion is to provide extra value that encourages purchase. When targeted at consumers the intention is to stimulate **consumer pull**; when the trade is targeted **distribution push** is the objective. We will now look at specific sales promotion objectives.

Fast sales boost

As we saw when discussing the effects of sales promotion, the usual response is for sales volume to increase. Short-term sales increases may be required for a number of reasons, including the need to reduce inventories or meet budgets prior to the end of the financial year, moving stocks of an old model prior to a replacement, and to increase stockholding by consumers and distributors in advance of the launch of a competitor's product.[17] Promotions that give large immediate benefits, such as money off or bonus packs, have bigger effects on sales volume than more distant promotions such as competitions or self-liquidators. What needs to be realized, however, is that sales promotion should not be used as a means of patching up more fundamental inadequacies such as inferior product performance or poor positioning.

A sales promotion that went seriously wrong was Hoover's attempt to boost sales of its washing machines, vacuum cleaners, refrigerators and tumble driers by offering two free US flight tickets for every Hoover product purchased over £100. The company was the target of much bad publicity as buyers discovered that the offer was wreathed in difficult conditions (found in the promotion's small print) and complained bitterly to Hoover and the media. In an attempt to limit the danger done to its reputation, the company announced that it would honour its offer to its customers, at an estimated cost of £20 million.

Encourage trial

Sales promotions can be highly successful by encouraging trial. If new buyers like the brand, the long-term effect of the promotion may be positive. Home sampling and home couponing are particularly effective methods of inducing trial. Promotions that simply give more product (e.g. bonus packs) are likely to be less successful since consumers will not place much value on the extra quantity until they have decided they like it.

Encourage repeat purchase

Certain promotions, by their nature, encourage repeat purchase of a brand over a period of time. Any offer that requires the collection of packet tops or labels (e.g. free mail-ins and promotions such as bingo games) is attempting to raise repeat purchase during the promotional period. Loyalty cards are designed to offer consumers an incentive to repeat purchase at a store.

Stimulate purchase of larger packs

Promotions that are specifically linked to larger pack sizes may persuade consumers to switch from the less economical smaller packs. For example, Unilever ran a highly successful promotion linked to its jumbo-sized Persil detergent packs, offering vouchers for free rail travel.

Gain distribution and shelf space

Trade promotions are designed to gain distribution and shelf space. These are major promotional objectives since there is a strong relationship between sales and these two factors. Discounts, free gifts and joint promotions are methods used to encourage distributors to stock brands. Also, consumer promotions that provide sizeable extra value may also persuade distributors to stock or give extra shelf space.

2 FOR 1 DESIGNER GLASSES for £125

BOOK AN EYE TEST OR BUY GLASSES ONLINE AT SPECSAVERS.CO.UK

Specsavers

Traditionally, sales promotions have been associated with achieving objectives for supermarket brands. However, their presence has spread to other sectors such as financial services, cars, IT and telecoms. There is a trend towards integrated media campaigns. For example, Fiat used a sales promotion to encourage people to visit its dealers. A direct mailing offered them the chance to compete in a racing game to win free Xbox consoles and DVDs. In the first three weeks, the campaign generated more than 1400 visits and resulted in an extra 203 cars being sold.[18] An example of a sales promotion outside of the supermarket sector is the advertisement for Specsavers.

Evaluating sales promotion

There are two types of research that can be used to evaluate sales promotions: *pre-testing research* is used to select, from a number of alternative promotional concepts, the most effective in achieving objectives; *post-testing research* is carried out to assess whether or not promotional objectives have been achieved.

Pre-testing research

Three major pre-testing methods are group discussions, hall tests and experimentation. **Group discussions** may be used

◄ A two-for-one sales promotion by Specsavers.

with target consumers to test ideas and concepts. They can provide insights into the kinds of promotions that might be valued by them, and allow assessment of several promotional ideas so that some can be tested further and others discounted. Group discussions should be used as a preliminary rather than a conclusive tool.

Hall tests involve bringing a sample of target consumers to a room that has been hired, usually in a town or city location so that alternative promotional ideas can be tested. For example, a bonus pack, a free gift and a free-in-the-mail offer might be tested. The promotions are ranked on the basis of their incentive value. No more than eight alternatives should be tested and the promotions should be of a similar cost to the company.[19] Usually a sample of 100 to 150 is sufficient to separate the winners from the losers.

Experimentation closes the gap between what people say they value and what they actually value by measuring actual purchase behaviour in the marketplace. Usually two panels of stores are used to compare two promotional alternatives, or one promotion against no promotion (control). The two groups of stores must be chosen in such a way that they are comparable (a matched sample) so that the difference in sales is due to the two promotions rather than differences in the stores themselves. Experimentation may be used in a less sophisticated way where one or a small number of stores is used simply as a final check on promotional response before launching a promotion nationally. For service companies, the process may be even easier. Leaflets are produced to communicate the offer and are distributed to a sample of target consumers.[20] Group discussions and hall tests can be used prior to an experiment to narrow the promotional alternatives to a manageable few.

Post-testing research

After the sales promotion has been implemented, the effects must be monitored carefully. Care should be taken to check sales both during *and* after the promotion so that post-promotional sales dips can be taken into account (a *lagged effect*). In certain situations a sales fall can precede a promotion (a *lead effect*). If consumers believe a promotion to be imminent they may hold back purchases until it takes place. Alternatively, if a retail sales promotion of consumer durables (e.g. gas fires, refrigerators, televisions) is accompanied by higher commission rates for salespeople, they may delay sales until the promotional period.[21] If a lead effect is possible, sales prior to the promotion should also be monitored.

Ex-factory sales figures are usually an unreliable guide to consumer uptake at the retail level. Consequently, consumer panels and retail audits are usually employed to measure sales effects. **Consumer panel data** also reveal the types of people who responded to the sales promotion. For example, they would indicate whether any increase in sales was due to heavy buyers stocking up or new buyers trying the brand for the first time.

Retail audit data could be used to establish whether the promotion was associated with retail outlets increasing their stock levels, a rise in the number of outlets handling the brand, as well as measuring sales effects.

An attempt may also be made to assess the long-term impact of a sales promotion. However, in money promotion-prone markets—such as food, drink and toiletries—the pace of promotional activity means that it is impossible to disentangle the long-term effects of one promotion from another.

Public Relations and Publicity

A company is dependent on many groups if it is to be successful. The marketing concept focuses on customers and distributors, but the needs and interests of other groups are also important, such as employees, shareholders, the local community, the media, government and pressure groups. **Public relations** is concerned with all of these groups and may be defined as:

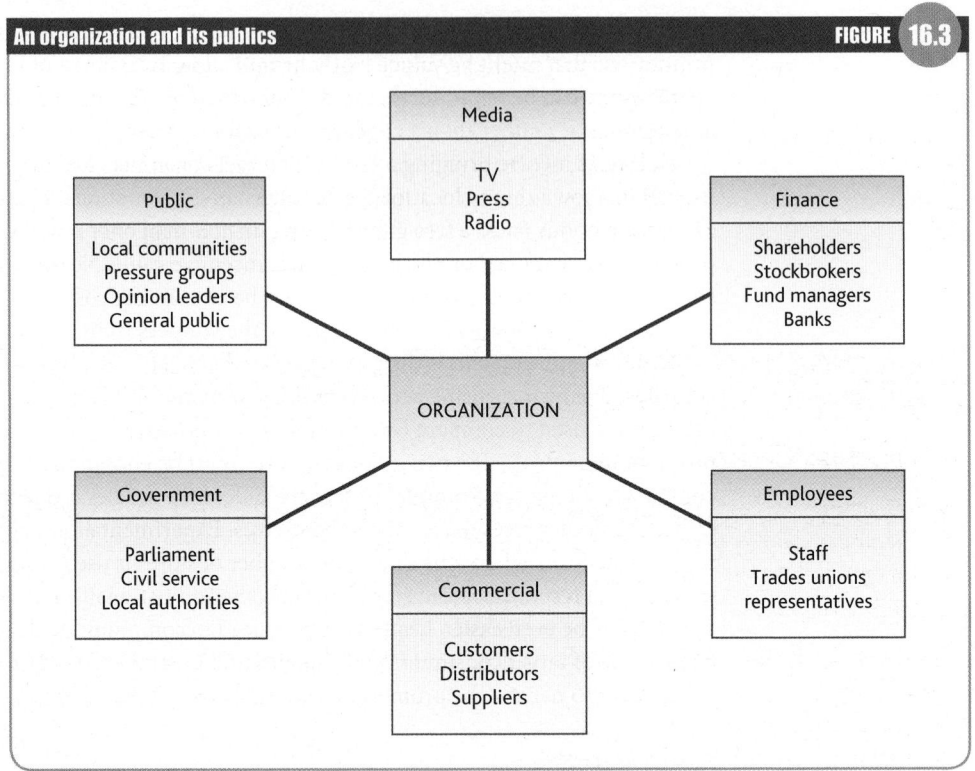

An organization and its publics   FIGURE 16.3

...the management of communications and relationships to establish goodwill and mutual understanding between an organization and its public.

Public relations is therefore more wide ranging than marketing, which focuses on markets, distribution channels and customers. By communicating to other groups, public relations creates an environment in which it is easier to conduct marketing.[22] These publics are shown in Figure 16.3.

Public relations activities include publicity, corporate advertising, seminars, publications, lobbying and charitable donations. It can accomplish many objectives, as outlined below.[23]

1 *Prestige and reputation*: it can foster prestige and reputation, which can help companies to sell products, attract and keep good employees, and promote favourable community and government relations.

2 *Promotion of products*: the desire to buy a product can be helped by the unobtrusive things that people read and see in the press, radio and television. Awareness and interest in products and companies can be generated.

3 *Dealing with issues and opportunities*: the ability to handle social and environmental issues to the mutual benefit of all parties involved.

4 *Goodwill of customers*: ensuring that customers are presented with useful information, are treated well and have their complaints dealt with fairly and speedily.

5 *Goodwill of employees*: promoting the sense of identification and satisfaction of employees with their company. Activities such as internal newsletters, recreation activities, and awards for service and achievement can be used.

6 *Overcoming misconceptions*: managing misconceptions about a company so that unfounded opinions do not damage its operations.

7 *Goodwill of suppliers and distributors*: building a reputation as a good customer (for suppliers) and a reliable supplier (for distributors).

8 *Goodwill of government*: influencing the opinions of public officials and politicians so that they feel the company operates in the public interest.

9 *Dealing with unfavourable publicity*: responding quickly, accurately and effectively to negative publicity such as an oil spill or an air disaster. Unfavourable publicity may be spread by social networking sites, prompting companies to set up rapid response capabilities, as Digital Marketing 16.1 explains.

10 *Attracting and keeping good employees*: creating and maintaining respectability in the eyes of the public so that the best personnel are attracted to work for the company.

 16.1 Digital Marketing

Companies Chatter on Twitter

When unfavourable publicity is spread on social networking sites, companies need to be ready to respond. For example, Twitter, the microblogging service that allows the publication of short messages over the Internet, is sometimes used to spread bad publicity. Companies are opening Twitter accounts so that they are capable of a rapid response.

For example, PepsiCo replied to Twitter users who began posting criticisms of a Pepsi Max advertisement that depicted a cartoon calorie committing suicide. PepsiCo posted a public reply, stating that the creative was inappropriate and would not be run again. Ford also used Twitter to deflect criticism away from the company after it filed a suit against an enthusiast website that was selling unauthorized Ford decals. Fans of the site posted angry messages, but Ford responded by explaining the reasons for its action. In this way, companies are using social networking accounts to try to prevent bad publicity getting out of control.

Based on: Gelles (2008)[24]

A study by Kitchen and Proctor showed that public relations is a growth area in the UK.[25] The three major reasons for this were recognition by marketing teams of the power and value of public relations, increased advertising costs leading to an exploration of more cost-effective communication routes, and improved understanding of the role of public relations.

Communications associated with public relations can take two forms. Asymmetric communications involve an organization communicating with its publics but never, or rarely, taking any action as a result of feedback. For example, consultation about a new building project may take place, but no satisfactory organizational response may result. In contrast, symmetric communications involves two-way communication between an organization and its publics (e.g. through public meetings) and this consultation informs organizational strategic decision-making. For example, public concern about a building project may result in landscaping and the reduction in the number of houses to be built. The second approach is particularly important when seeking to maintain good community relations.

Public relations activity is aided by technological developments, as described below.

• *Video news releases*: coverage of a public relations event is edited to three to four minutes and sent to television and news departments around the world via cassette, vision circuits or by satellite. No commentary is added and the releases can be edited and voice-overs included as news departments see fit. TV is very choosy about which stories it will use. The brand must play only a supporting role in the story as overtly promotional messages are almost always rejected. Birth control pill manufacturer Schering obtained an audience of nearly six million through a VNR for its sponsorship of an exhibition on fertility control.

- *Videoconferencing*: this is two-way communication of both words and pictures via telephone lines. The process can be used to manage pan-European sales and marketing conferences.
- *Satellite conferencing*: this can be used to transmit a message from one location to many sites around Europe. It is gaining in popularity for pan-European product launches, press conferences and conventions.
- *Video magazines*: this medium can be used for disseminating a corporate message to customers and employees. Compared with print magazines it is more personal and can create a sense of involvement for remote subsidiaries.

Publicity

A major element of public relations is publicity. It can be defined as communication about a product or organization by the placing of news about it in the media without paying for the time or space directly. Three key tasks of a publicity department are:[26]

1   responding to requests from the media—although a passive service function, it requires well-organized information and prompt responses to media requests
2   supplying the media with information on events and occurrences relevant to the organization—this requires general internal communication channels and knowledge of the media
3   stimulating the media to carry the information and viewpoint of the organization—this requires creative development of ideas, developing close relationships with media people and understanding their needs and motivations.

The characteristics of publicity

Information dissemination may be through news releases, news conferences, interviews, feature articles, photocalls and public speaking (at conferences and seminars, for example). No matter which method is used to carry the information, publicity has five important characteristics.

1   *The message has high credibility*: the message has higher credibility than advertising because it appears to the reader to have been written independently (by a media person) rather than by an advertiser. Because of this high credibility, it can be argued that it is more persuasive than a similar message used in an advertisement.
2   *No direct media costs*: since space or time in the media is not bought there is no direct media cost. However, this is not to say that it is cost-free. Someone has to write the news release, take part in the interview or organize the news conference. This may be organized internally, by a press officer or publicity department, or externally, by a public relations agency.
3   *Lose control of publication*: unlike advertising, there is no guarantee that the news item will be published. This decision is taken out of the control of the organization and into the hands of an editor. A key factor in this decision is whether the item is judged to be newsworthy. The item must be *distinctive* in the sense of having *news value*. For example, the organization that is first to launch a voice-activated personal computer will receive massive publicity; the second company to do so will barely get any. The topic of the news item must also be judged to be of *interest* to a publication's readers. Table 16.1 lists a number of potentially newsworthy topics.
4   *Lose control of content*: there is no way of ensuring that the viewpoint expressed by the news supplier is reflected in the published article. For example, a news release might point to an increase in capital expenditure to deal with pollution, but this might be used negatively (for example, saying the increase is inadequate).
5   *Lose control of timing*: an advertising campaign can be coordinated to achieve maximum impact. The timing of the publication of news items, however, cannot be controlled. For

Potentially newsworthy topics	TABLE 16.1
Being or doing something first	

Marketing issues
New products
Research breakthroughs: future new products
Large orders/contracts
Sponsorships
Price changes
Service changes
New logos
Export success

Production issues
Productivity achievements
Employment changes
Capital investments

Financial issues
Financial statements
Acquisitions
Sales/profit achievements

Personal issues
Training awards
Winners of company contests
Promotions/new appointments
Success stories
Visits by famous people
Reports of interviews

General issues
Conferences/seminars/exhibitions
Anniversaries of significant events

example, a news item publicizing a forthcoming conference to encourage attendance could appear in a publication after the event has taken place or, at least, too late to have any practical effect on attendance.

Writing news releases

Perhaps the most popular method of disseminating information to the media is through the news release. By following a few simple guidelines (as outlined below), the writer can produce news releases that please editors and therefore stand a greater chance of being used.[27]

- *The headline*: make the headline factual and avoid the use of flamboyant, flowery language that might irritate editors. The headline should briefly introduce the story, e.g. 'A New Alliance to be Formed between Virgin and Lufthansa Airlines'.
- *Opening paragraph*: this should be a brief summary of the whole release. If this is the only part of the news release that is published the writer will have succeeded in getting across the essential message.
- *Organizing the copy*: the less important ideas should be placed towards the end of the news release. The further down the paragraph, the more chance of its being cut by an editor.
- *Copy content*: like headlines, copy should be factual not fanciful. An example of bad copy would be 'We are proud to announce that Virgin Airlines, the world's most innovative airline, will fly an exciting new route to Singapore'. Instead, this should read 'A new route to Singapore will be flown by Virgin Airlines'. Whenever possible, statements should be backed up by facts. For example, a statement claiming 'fuel economy' for a car should be supported by figures.
- *Length*: news releases should be as short as possible. Most are written on one page, some are merely one paragraph. The viewpoint that long releases should be sent to editors so that they can cut out the parts they do not want is a fallacy. Editors' self-interest is that their job should be made as easy as possible; the less work they have to do amending copy the greater the chances of its publication.
- *Layout*: the release should contain short paragraphs with plenty of *white space* to make it appear easy to read. There should be good-sized margins on both sides, and the copy should be double-spaced so that amendments and printing instructions can be inserted by the editor. When a story runs to a second or third page, 'more' should be typed in the bottom right-hand corner and succeeding pages numbered with the headline repeated in the top left-hand corner.

Publicity can be a powerful tool for creating awareness and strengthening the reputation of organizations. For example, it was the inherent newsworthiness of Body Shop, with its emphasis on environmental and animal-friendly products, that provided media coverage, not advertisements. The trick is to motivate everyone in an organization to look for newsworthy stories and events, not simply to rely on the publicity department to initiate them.

Public relations and publicity should be part of an integrated communications strategy so that they reinforce the messages consumers receive from other communication methods. There are three methods of establishing integrated communications. The first is for clients to bring all their specialist agencies around a table and insist on an integrated approach. Another is to use a large international agency that can offer a complete package, such as the Young & Rubicam group, which owns the PR agency Burson-Marsteller. Finally, clients can choose a single integrated agency that includes public relations in its offering. One practical problem is that no matter which option is chosen, the different agencies or sections within agencies may fight for a bigger share of the communications budget. Even using one agency does not prevent this, since each section may operate as a separate profit centre. A problem from the client side is that this may give the strategic thinking role to those representing advertising. The other communication areas are then asked to fall in line, even if it is very difficult to translate the advertising message into public relations, sales promotion or a direct marketing campaign.

Traditionally, public relations agencies are paid on a monthly retainer. This is useful when clients need an ongoing resource, such as a press office service. When PR agencies are used for specific campaigns a different form of payment is increasingly being employed: a project fee sometimes augmented by a bonus if objectives are achieved. This provides the agency with an incentive but may be resisted when it is difficult to work out how much staff time is required for the campaign.[28]

Sponsorship

Sponsorship has been defined by Sleight as:[29]

> … a business relationship between a provider of funds, resources or services and an individual, event or organization which offers in return some rights and association that may be used for commercial advantage.

Potential sponsors have a wide range of entities and activities from which to choose, including sports, arts, community activities, teams, tournaments, individual personalities or events, competitions, fairs and shows. Sports sponsorship is by far the most popular sponsorship medium as it offers high visibility through extensive television press coverage, the ability to attract a broad cross-section of the community and to service specific niches, and the capacity to break down cultural barriers.[30] The illustration features Coca-Cola's Powerade sponsorship of the English Rugby Union team.

▲ Powerade: the official sponsor of the English rugby team.

As we shall see, sponsorship can achieve a number of communicational objectives—but there are also risks, as outlined below.[31]

- Nike entered the golf market with a five-year £90 million sponsorship of Tiger Woods. It came unstuck on the first day when, in a major event, Woods lost his first ball with his first shot using the new Nike driver. He later reverted to his old driver, made by rival Titleist.

- The Festina cycling team was thrown out of the Tour de France following the arrest of the team's masseur. French customs officials had discovered performance-enhancing drugs in his car four days before the start of the race.
- Team Philips' £4 million catamaran broke its hull shortly after the start of The Race, a non-stop around the world yacht race. The sponsor's plight was not helped by having Philips' strap-line 'Let's make things better' emblazoned on the boat. When Zanussi sponsored Real Madrid its sales plummeted in Barcelona.[32]

Companies should be clear about their reasons for spending money on sponsorship. The five principal objectives of sponsorship are to gain publicity, create entertainment opportunities, foster favourable brand and company associations, improve community relations and create promotional opportunities.

Gaining publicity

Sponsorship provides ample opportunities to create publicity in the news media. Worldwide events such as major golf, football and tennis tournaments supply the platform for global media coverage. Sponsorship of such events can provide brand exposure to millions of people. Some events, such as athletics championships, have mass audience appeal, while others such as golf have a more upmarket profile. Dunhill's sponsorship of major golf tournaments allows the brand name to be exposed to its more upmarket customer segment.

The publicity opportunities of sponsorship can produce major *awareness* shifts. For example, Canon's sponsorship of football in the UK raised awareness of the brand name from 40 per cent to 85 per cent among males; and awareness of the name of an insurance company sponsoring a national cricket competition increased from 2 to 16 per cent.

Sponsorship can also be used to position brands in the marketplace. Tag Heuer's sponsorship of the MacLaren motor racing team was designed to position the watch brand as exciting, sporty and international.[33]

Creating entertainment opportunities

A major objective of much sponsorship is to create entertainment opportunities for customers and the trade. Sponsorship of music, the performing arts and sports events can be particularly effective. For example, BMW supported classical concerts in stately homes in the UK to provide dealers with customer entertainment opportunities.[34] Vodafone's sponsorship deal with the England Cricket Team, and Budweiser's sponsorship of the World Cup provide not only wide publicity but also important opportunities to invite key customers to watch matches.[35] Often, sports personalities are invited to join the sponsors' guests. Attendance at sponsored events can also be used to reward successful employees.

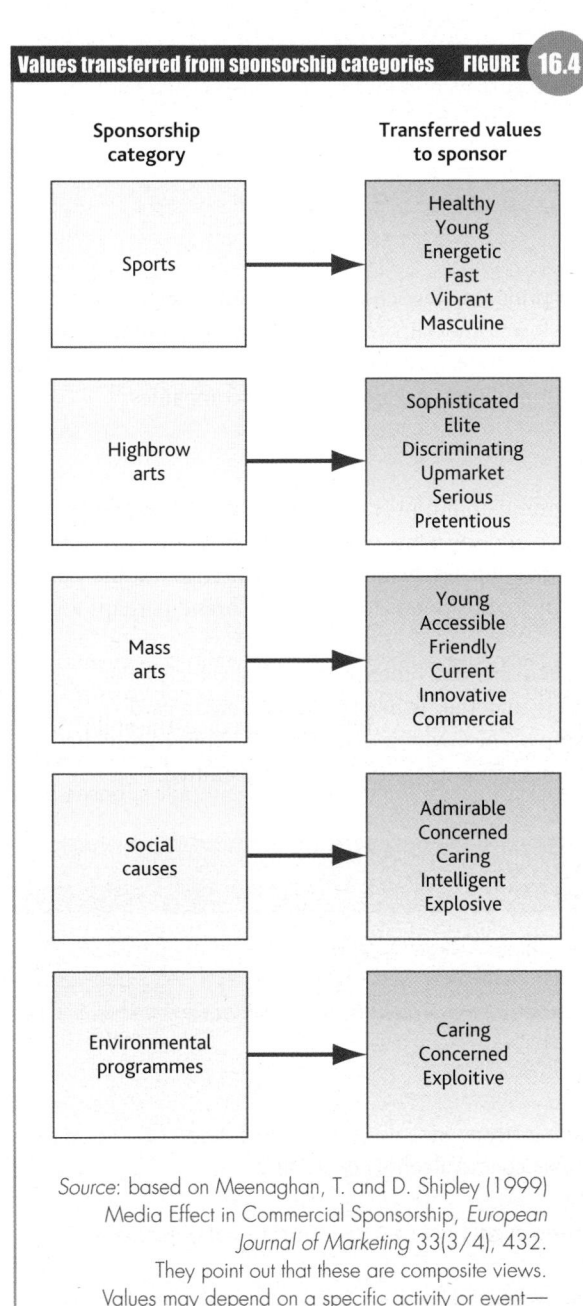

Values transferred from sponsorship categories   FIGURE 16.4

Sponsorship category	Transferred values to sponsor
Sports	Healthy Young Energetic Fast Vibrant Masculine
Highbrow arts	Sophisticated Elite Discriminating Upmarket Serious Pretentious
Mass arts	Young Accessible Friendly Current Innovative Commercial
Social causes	Admirable Concerned Caring Intelligent Explosive
Environmental programmes	Caring Concerned Exploitive

Source: based on Meenaghan, T. and D. Shipley (1999) Media Effect in Commercial Sponsorship, *European Journal of Marketing* 33(3/4), 432. They point out that these are composite views. Values may depend on a specific activity or event— for example, football versus tennis

Fostering favourable brand and company associations

The third objective of sponsorship is to create favourable associations for a brand and company. For example, Red Bull's sponsorship of crazy events such as Flugtag, at which amateur pilots launch handmade flying machines off a 30-foot ramp, reinforces its 'wacky' image, and its sponsorship of UK Athletics reinforced its energy associations.[36] Stella Artois' tennis sponsorship strengthened its association with premium lager. Budweiser's sponsorship of Formula One motor racing and Ford's sponsorship of the UEFA Champions League reinforced their masculine image.

Both the sponsor and the sponsored activity become involved in a relationship with a transfer of values from activity to sponsor. The audience, finding the sponsor's name, logo and other symbols threaded through the event, learns to associate sponsor and activity with one another. The task facing the sponsor is to ensure its presence is clearly associated with the activity and transfer the activity values on to the brand. Support promotions and mainstream advertising can help in this respect. Figure 16.4 shows some broad values conferred on the sponsor from five sponsorship categories.

Improving community relations

Sponsorship of schools—for example, by providing low-cost personal computers—and supporting community programmes can foster a socially responsible, caring reputation for a company. A survey in the Republic of Ireland found that developing community relations was the most usual sponsorship objective for both industrial and consumer companies.[37]

Creating promotional opportunities

Sponsored events provide an ideal opportunity to promote company brands. Sweatshirts, bags, pens, etc., carrying the company logo and the name of the event can be sold to a captive audience. Where the brand can be consumed during the event (e.g. Stella Artois at the Cannes Film Festival) this provides an opportunity for customers to sample the brand perhaps for the first time.

Sponsorship can also improve the effectiveness of other promotional vehicles. For example, responses to the direct marketing materials issued by the Visa credit card organization and featuring its sponsorship of the Olympic Games were 17 per cent higher than for a control group to whom the sponsorship images were not transmitted.[38]

 16.2 Pause for Thought

Think of as many reasons as you can why companies such as Intel, Vodafone, FedEx, Tag Heuer, Red Bull and Virgin sponsor Formula One motor racing.

Expenditure on sponsorship

Six factors account for the growth of sponsorship:

1 restrictive government policies on tobacco and alcohol advertising
2 escalating costs of media advertising
3 increased leisure activities and sporting events
4 the proven record of sponsorship
5 greater media coverage of sponsored events
6 the reduced efficiencies of traditional media advertising (e.g. clutter, and zapping between television programmes).

Although most money is spent on **event sponsorship**, such as a sports or arts event, of increasing importance is **broadcast sponsorship** where a television or radio programme is the focus. An example of event sponsorship is the sponsorship of music designed to target the youth market, as Marketing in Action 16.2 explains.

16.2 Marketing in Action

Music to Their Ears

The clutter to be found in sports sponsorship has meant an increase in sponsorship of events in the arts, education and, particularly, music. Music sponsorship has proven to be very attractive to mobile handset service providers such as Virgin Mobile, O_2, T-Mobile and Orange since music is often downloaded on such devices. Virgin Mobile hosts the V-Festival, while O_2 has its Wireless festivals and has taken over from Carling as partner in the numerous O_2 Academies, which are venues for music gigs around the UK. T-Mobile has been involved in the 'Streets' initiative—secret gigs played exclusively for its customers—while Orange is, also, connected to music sponsorship through its associations with Glastonbury, T in the Park, and the Leeds and Reading Festivals. Sony Ericsson has also gained first-mover advantage among mobile handset producers by sponsoring the Ibiza Rocks event.

The prize is the hearts and minds of the core target market: 18–34 year olds—a notoriously difficult group to reach. Music sponsorship allows marketing communications to take place in a natural setting where this young segment are enjoying themselves. The brands, therefore, benefit by being associated with a key leisure activity enjoyed by these young people.

Based on: Barrand (2005);[39] Stokes (2006);[40] Clark (2008)[41]

Broadcast sponsorship of programmes can extend into the sharing of production costs. This is attractive to broadcasters, who face increasing costs of programming; and sponsors, who gain a greater degree of influence in negotiations with broadcasters, an opportunity to benefit from cheaper advertising, and the rights to exploit the programme, its characters and actors for promotional purposes. A notable example of broadcast sponsorship is the directory service 118 118's sponsorship of *The Simpsons*.

Another growth area is that of **team sponsorship**, such as the sponsorship of a football, cricket or motor racing team. For example, Emirates sponsors Arsenal Football Club, Vodafone sponsors the England Cricket Team and Intel sponsors the Formula One team BMW Sauber. Intel's reasons for motor racing sponsorship are that the sport, like the brand, is global, both are technology driven, and there is fit between F1's audience and Intel's target market, which is predominantly male and interested in technology.[42]

Accompanying the growth of event sponsorship has been the phenomenon of **ambush marketing**. Originally this term referred to the activities of companies that tried to associate themselves with an event (e.g. the Olympics) without paying any fee to the event owner. The activity is legal so long as no attempt is made to use an event symbol, logo or mascot. More recently the term has been broadened to include a range of activities such as sponsoring the television coverage of a major event, sponsoring national teams and the support of individual sportspeople.

Nike has been the supreme ambush marketer, hijacking both the Olympic Games in Atlanta in 1996 and Sydney in 2000. So concerned was the International Olympic Committee that all countries bidding for the 2012 Olympics were asked to secure all outdoor advertising sites situated close to events in order to prevent ambush marketing.[43] Another example involves Heineken, whose Dutch buyers of the beer were given green hats to wear at the Euro 2008 football tournament, much to the annoyance of its rival Carlsberg, who paid $21 million to be an official sponsor.[44]

Selection and evaluation of an event or programme to sponsor
Selection

Selection of an event or programme to sponsor should be undertaken by answering a series of questions.

- *Communications objectives*: What are we trying to achieve? Are we looking for awareness or image, improvement in community relations or entertainment opportunities? Does the personality of the event match the desired brand image?
- *Target market*: Who are we trying to reach? Is it the trade or final customers? How does the profile of our customer base match the likely audience of the sponsored event or programme?
- *Risk*: What are the associated risks? What are the chances that the event or programme might attract adverse publicity (e.g. football hooliganism tainting the image of the sport and, by implication, the sponsor)? To what extent would termination of the sponsorship contract attract bad publicity (e.g. mean the closing of a theatre)?
- *Promotional opportunities*: What are the potential sales promotion and publicity opportunities?
- *Past record*: If the event or programme has been sponsored before, what were the results? Why did the previous sponsor withdraw?
- *Cost*: Does the sponsorship opportunity represent value for money?

Evaluation

This process should lead to a clear idea of why an event or programme is being sponsored. Understanding *sponsorship objectives* is the first step in evaluating sponsorship's success. As we have seen, Canon used football sponsorship to improve awareness levels and market research was carried out as a monitor. Sponsorship of a school by providing personal computers would be monitored by measuring coverage in local newspapers, and on radio stations and possibly television.

For major sponsorship deals, evaluation is likely to be more formal and involve the measurement of *media coverage and name mentions/sightings* using a specialist monitoring agency. For example, Volvo's £2 million sponsorship of tennis resulted in 1.4 billion impressions (number of mentions or sightings, audience size) which it calculated was worth £12 million in media advertising.[45]

Meenaghan[46] recommends the following evaluation procedure designed to measure the effects of the exposure.

1. Determination of the company's brand's present position in terms of pre-sponsorship awareness and image with the target audience, and the setting of objectives.
2. Tracking to detect movements in customer awareness and attitudes towards the company/brand.
3. Post-sponsorship comparison of performance levels against initial objectives.

However, a survey into the evaluation of football sponsorship found that while two-thirds of companies evaluated their sponsorship activities few went beyond the basic measurement of media coverage.[47]

Exhibitions

Exhibitions are unique in that of all the promotional tools available they are the only one that brings buyers, sellers and the competitors together in a commercial setting. In Europe, the Cologne trade exhibitions bring together 28,000 exhibitors from 100 countries with 1.8 million buyers from 150 countries.[48] Overall, the number of exhibitions, exhibitors and visitors is growing. Nevertheless, the perceived value of exhibitions is debatable. The following comments illustrate the wide variation in opinion.

While all elements within the communication program are vital, perhaps only the exhibition will involve all disciplines, and will present the greatest opportunity to present Gould as a total company.[49]

Exhibitions are usually a form of mass hysteria. It is a foregone conclusion that they are very expensive. Even though there may be thousands of visitors, there are also thousands of exhibits.

The retention factor is very debatable … every time we exhibit at a trade show, our conclusion is 'never again'.[50]

Despite these differing views, exhibitions appear to be an important part of the industrial promotion mix. One study into the relative importance of promotional media placed exhibitions as a source of information in the industrial buying process second only to personal selling, and ahead of direct mail and print advertising.[51] Indeed exhibitions have been shown to increase the effectiveness of personal selling activities directly after the show.[52]

Exhibitors sometimes create the unusual to impress visitors. For example, Orange took two stands at the GSM exhibition in Cannes. One was dedicated to products while the other was a relaxation and massage area. This stand had no salespeople, just a team of masseurs offering head and neck massages, comfy chairs and coffee. Many visitors remarked that it was their favourite area of the show.[53]

Exhibition objectives

Exhibitions can achieve a number of objectives, including:

- an opportunity to reach an audience with a distinct interest in the market and the products on display
- create awareness and develop relationships with new prospects
- strengthen existing customer relationships
- provide product demonstrations
- determine and stimulate needs of customers
- gather competitive intelligence
- introduce a new product
- recruit dealers or distributors
- maintain/improve company image
- deal with service and other customer problems
- generate a mailing list
- make a sale.

Bonoma has organized many of these objectives into a matrix depending on whether the objective concerns current or potential customers, and selling versus non-selling objectives (Fig. 16.5).[54] Research into why companies exhibit at trade shows found that the major reasons were:[55]

- to generate leads/enquiries
- to introduce a new product or service
- because competitors are exhibiting
- to recruit dealers or distributors.

Whatever objectives are set, they should be clear and measurable. This enables the exhibitor to identify the real opportunities presented by the event and allows the degree of success of the exhibition to be evaluated.[56]

In no other medium will advertising, publicity, sales promotion, product demonstration, sales staff, key management, present customers and prospects join together in a live event that

Exhibition objectives FIGURE **16.5**

	Selling objectives	Non-selling objectives
Current customers	Maintain relationships Transmit benefits Remedy service problems Stimulate extra sales	Maintain image Demonstrate products Gather competitive intelligence Widen exposure
Potential customers (prospects)	Contact prospects Determine needs Transmit benefits Commit to follow-up or sale	Contact prospects Foster image building Demonstrate products Gather competitive intelligence

Source: adapted from Bonoma, T. V. (1985) Get More Out of Your Trade Shows, in Gumpbert, D. E. (ed.) *The Marketing Renaissance*, New York: Wiley. Copyright © 1985 John Wiley & Sons Inc. Reprinted by permission

offers the opportunity to impress key audience perceptions of the company, its operations and products.[57] It is also an opportunity to gather information about competitors, customers, industry trends and new products.[58]

Planning for an exhibition

Success at an exhibition involves considerable pre-event planning. Clear objectives should be set, selection criteria for evaluating exhibition attendance determined, and design and promotional strategies decided. Pre-show promotions to attract visitors to the stand include direct mail, telephoning, a personal sales call before the event and an advertisement in the trade or technical press.

A high degree of professionalism is required by the staff who attend the exhibition stand. The characteristics of a good exhibitor have been found to be:[59]

- exhibiting a wider range of products, particularly large items that cannot be demonstrated on a sales call
- staff always in attendance at the stand—visitors should never hear that 'the person who covers that product is not here right now'
- well-informed staff
- informative literature available
- seating area or office provided on the stand
- refreshments provided.

Evaluating an exhibition

Post-show evaluation will examine performance against objectives. This is a learning exercise that will help to judge whether the objectives were realistic, how valuable the exhibition appears to have been and how well the company was represented.

Quantitative measures include:

- the number of visitors to the stand
- the number of key influencers/decision-makers who visited the stand
- how many leads/enquiries were generated
- the cost per lead/enquiry
- the number and value of orders
- the cost per order
- the number of new distributorships opened/likely to be opened.

Other more subjective, qualitative criteria include:

- the worth of competitive intelligence
- interest generated in the new products
- the cultivation of new/existing relationships
- the value of customer query and complaint handling
- the promotion of brand values.

Sales and marketing may not always agree on the key evaluation criteria to use. For example, sales may judge the exhibition on the number of leads while marketing may prefer to judge the show on the longer-term issue of the promotion of brand values.[60]

Finally, since a major objective of many exhibitors is to stimulate leads and enquiries, mechanisms must be in place to ensure that these are followed up promptly. Furthermore, the leads generated at an exhibition can be used to build a marketing database for future direct mail campaigns.

Product Placement

Product placement is the deliberate placing of products and/or their logos in movies and television, usually in return for money. The appearance of brands in these media is unlikely to be by accident: usually vast sums of money are paid by brand owners to secure exposure. For example, Steven Spielberg's sci-fi film *Minority Report* featured more than 15 major brands, including Gap, Nokia, Pepsi, Guinness, Lexus and Amex, with their logos appearing on video billboards throughout the film. These product placements earned DreamWorks and 20th Century Fox $25 million, which went some way towards reducing the $102 million production costs for the film.[61] This practice is not new: early records of product placement show film star Joan Crawford drinking Jack Daniel's bourbon whiskey in the 1945 movie *Mildred Pierce* and Katharine Hepburn disposing of Humphrey Bogart's Gordon's gin in the 1951 film *The African Queen*. It is also a welcome source of income for growing film sectors such as the Indian film industry.[62] A notable example of product placement in television is the Coca-Cola logo appearing on the judges' cups in *American Idol*.[63]

The growth in product placement

Product placement is growing for the following reasons.

- *Mass-market reach*: as media fragments (for example, due to the growth of digital television channels), it becomes increasingly hard to reach mass markets. Films can reach hundreds of millions of consumers worldwide, creating rapid brand awareness. Hit television series can also reach mass global audiences, leading to product placement deals like Gabrielle Solis in *Desperate Housewives* driving an Aston Martin, and the Apple brand featuring in *Sex and the City*.[64]
- *Positive associations*: brands can benefit from the positive images in a film or television programme. For example, for James Bond to be seen driving an Aston Martin or Jaguar, or wearing an Omega watch (see illustration) imparts the Bond association of sophistication, masculinity and coolness to the car. Also Samsung's product placement of its mobile phones in the futuristic *Matrix* films enhanced its high-tech image.[65]
- *Credibility*: many consumers do not realize that brands have been product-placed. The brands are seen being used rather than appearing in a paid-for advertisement. This can add to the credibility of the associations sought.
- *Message repetition*: movies are often repeated on television and bought on video or DVD, creating opportunities for brand message repetition.
- *Avoidance of advertising bans*: with bans on advertising certain products, such as cigarettes, in particular media, product placement is an opportunity to reach large audiences.

▲ Omega watches have appeared in James Bond films.

- *Targeting*: by choosing an appropriate movie or television programme, specific market segments can be reached. For example, product placement in 'teen' movies can reach younger age groups.
- *Branding opportunities*: new brands can be launched linked to the film. For example, Philips launched a range of James Bond-branded shaving products to coincide with the launch of *Die Another Day*.[66]
- *Promotional opportunities*: placements in movies can provide promotional opportunities by creating related websites. For example, the *Die Another Day* website provided streamed video clips of Bond using a range of placed products in scenes from the film. Also, a section of the website was devoted to '007 partners' where a gallery of logos was visible and links to the brand partner website provided.[67]
- *Measurement*: market research companies, such as CinemaScore in the USA, conduct viewer exit surveys to measure which brands were noticed during the showing of a movie.[68]

Growth in product placement in Europe has been given a boost by the European Commission, which has issued a directive approving product placement within television programmes. TV audiences must be clearly informed of any product placement at the beginning and end of a broadcast, to prevent 'surreptitious advertising'.[69] However, in 2009 the British Government opposed the introduction of product placement to British-made television programmes.[70]

Risks associated with product placement

Although product placement, as we have seen, has many strong points, there are also certain risks involved.

- *Movie/programme failure*: just as brands can benefit from movie or television successes, failures can tarnish brand image by association.
- *Lack of prominence*: the brand may be overshadowed by action in the film and not be noticed.
- *Audience annoyance*: blatant product placement may cause audience annoyance, tarnishing any brand association.
- *Loss of control*: although brand owners who pay large fees for having their products placed in films and television will be able to exercise some control over how these are portrayed, other people, such as directors and editors, reduce their degree of control compared to standard advertisements.

Ethical Issues in Sales Promotion and Public Relations

Ethical concerns regarding sales promotion and public relations include the use of trade inducements, malredemption of coupons, the use of third-party endorsements and the promotion of anti-social behaviour.

Use of trade inducements

Retailers sometimes accept inducements from manufacturers to encourage their salespeople to push the manufacturers' products. This often takes the form of bonus payments to salespeople. The result is that there is an incentive for salespeople to pay special attention to those product lines that are linked to such bonuses when talking to customers. Customers may, therefore, be subjected to pressure to buy products that do not best meet their needs.

Malredemption of coupons

This ethical issue concerns the behaviour of customers in supermarkets who attempt to redeem reduced-price coupons without buying the associated product. When faced with a large shopping trolley of goods it is easy for supermarket checkout attendants to accept coupons without verification. The key to stopping this practice is thorough training of supermarket employees so that they always check coupons against goods purchased.

Third-party endorsements

Another ethical question is related to the use of third-party endorsements to publicize a product, where a person gives a written, verbal and/or visual recommendation of the product. A well-known, well-respected person is usually chosen but given that payment often accompanies the endorsement the question arises as to its credibility. Supporters of endorsements argue that consumers know that endorsers are usually paid and are capable of making their own judgements regarding their credence.

Promoting anti-social behaviour

The promotion of events that can lead to anti-social behaviour also raises ethical issues. For example, a 'promotion night' in pubs and clubs can lead to excessive drinking. Drunkenness, crime and violence may follow. In the longer term, health problems may arise.

Online LearningCentre

When you have read this chapter

log on to the Online Learning Centre at www.mcgraw-hill.co.uk/ textbooks/jobber to explore chapter-by-chapter test questions, links and further online study tools for marketing.

Review

1. **The growth in sales promotion**
   - The reasons for growth are increased impulse purchasing, the growing respectability of sales promotions, the rising costs of advertising and advertising clutter, shortening time horizons for goal achievement, competitor activities and the fact that their sales impact is easier to measure than that of advertising.

2. **The major sales promotion types**
   - Major consumer promotions are money off, bonus packs, premiums (free in- or on-pack gifts, free-in-the-mail offers, self-liquidating offers and buy-one-get-one-free offers), free samples, coupons, prize promotions (competitions, draws and games), and loyalty cards; major trade promotions are price discounts, free goods, competitions, allowances, promotional price support, and in-store display and promotional support.

3 The objectives and evaluation of sales promotion

- The objectives of sales promotion are to provide a fast sales boost, encourage trial, encourage repeat purchase, stimulate purchase of larger packs, and gain distribution and shelf space.
- Sales promotion can be evaluated using pre-testing research (group discussions, hall tests and experimentation) and post-testing research (consumer panel and retail audit data).

4 The objectives and targets of public relations

- The objectives of public relations are to foster prestige and reputation, promote products, deal with issues and opportunities, enhance the goodwill of customers and employees, correct misconceptions, improve the goodwill of suppliers, distributors and government, deal with unfavourable publicity, and attract and keep good employees.
- The targets of public relations are the general public, the media, the financial community, government, commerce (including customers) and employees.

5 The key tasks and characteristics of publicity

- Three key tasks are: responding to requests from the media; supplying the media with information on events relevant to the organization; stimulating the media to carry the information and the viewpoint of the organization.
- The characteristics of publicity are that the message has higher credibility than advertising, there are no direct media costs and no control over what is published (content), whether the item will be published or when it will be published.

6 The guidelines to use when writing a news release

- The guidelines are: make the headline factual and briefly introduce the story; the opening paragraph should be a summary of the whole release; the copy should be organized by placing the less important messages towards the end; copy should be factual and backed up by evidence; the release should be short; the layout should contain short paragraphs with plenty of white space.

7 The objectives and methods of sponsorship

- The objectives of sponsorship are to gain publicity, create entertainment opportunities, foster favourable brand and company associations, improve community relations and create promotional opportunities.
- The two key methods of sponsorship are event sponsorship (such as a sports or arts event) and broadcast sponsorship (where a television or radio programme is sponsored).

8 How to select and evaluate a potential sponsored event or programme

- Selection should be based on asking what we are trying to achieve (communication objectives), who we are trying to reach (target market), what are the associated risks (e.g. adverse publicity), what are the potential promotional opportunities, what is the past record of sponsorship of the event or programme, and what are the costs.
- Evaluation should be based on measuring results in terms of sponsorship objectives (e.g. changes in awareness and attitudes). Formal evaluation involves measurement of media coverage and name mentions/ sightings using a specialist monitoring agency.

9 The objectives, conduct and evaluation of exhibitions

- Objectives of exhibitions can be classified as selling objectives to current customers (e.g. stimulate extra sales), selling objectives to potential customers (e.g. determine needs and transmit benefits), non-selling objectives to current customers (e.g. maintain image and gather competitive intelligence) and non-selling objectives to potential customers (e.g. foster image building and gather competitive intelligence).
- Staff conduct at an exhibition should ensure that there is always someone in attendance to talk to visitors, staff should be well-informed, provide informative literature, and a seating area/office and refreshments should be provided.
- Evaluation of an exhibition includes number of visitors/key influencers/decision-makers who visit the stand, number of leads/enquiries/orders/new dealerships generated and cost per lead/enquiry/order. Qualitative evaluation includes the worth of competitive intelligence, and interest generated in new products.

10 The reasons for the growth in product placement and its risks
- Product placement activity is growing because of its mass-market reach, ability to confer positive associations to brands, high credibility, message repetition, its ability to avoid advertising bans, its targeting capabilities, the opportunities it provides for new linked brands and promotions, and the ability to measure its impact on audiences.
- Its risks are that the movie or television programme may fail, tarnishing brand image; there is the possibility that the placement may not get noticed or cause annoyance; and there is also the reduction in control, compared to advertisements, concerning how the brand will be portrayed in the movie or television programme.

11 Ethical issues in sales promotion and public relations
- There are potential problems relating to the use of trade inducements, malredemption of coupons, the use of third-party endorsements to publicize a product, and the promotion of anti-social behaviour.

Key Terms

ambush marketing originally referred to the activities of companies that try to associate themselves with an event (e.g. the Olympics) without paying any fee to the event owner; now means the sponsoring of the television coverage of a major event, national teams and the support of individual sportspeople

bonus pack giving a customer extra quantity at no additional cost

broadcast sponsorship a form of sponsorship where a television or radio programme is the focus

consumer panel data a type of continuous research where information is provided by household consumers on their purchases over time

consumer pull the targeting of consumers with communications (e.g. promotions) designed to create demand that will pull the product into the distribution chain

distribution push the targeting of channel intermediaries with communications (e.g. promotions) to push the product into the distribution chain

event sponsorship sponsorship of a sporting or other event

exhibition an event that brings buyers and sellers together in a commercial setting

experimentation the application of stimuli (e.g. two price levels) to different matched groups under controlled conditions for the purpose of measuring their effect on a variable (e.g. sales)

group discussion a group, usually of six to eight consumers, brought together for a discussion focusing on an aspect of a company's marketing

hall tests bringing a sample of target consumers to a room that has been hired so that alternative marketing ideas (e.g. promotions) can be tested

money-off promotions sales promotions that discount the normal price

premiums any merchandise offered free or at low cost as an incentive to purchase

product placement the deliberate placing of products and/or their logos in movies and television, usually in return for money

public relations the management of communications and relationships to establish goodwill and mutual understanding between an organization and its public

retail audit data a type of continuous research tracking the sales of products through retail outlets

sponsorship a business relationship between a provider of funds, resources or services and an individual, event or organization that offers in return some rights and association that may be used for commercial advantage

team sponsorship sponsorship of a team—for example, a football, cricket or motor racing team

Study Questions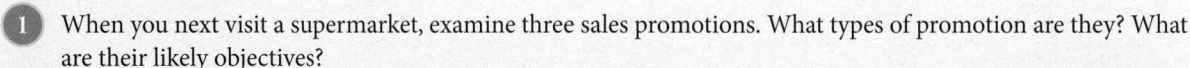

1. When you next visit a supermarket, examine three sales promotions. What types of promotion are they? What are their likely objectives?

2. Why would it be wrong to measure the sales effect of a promotion only during the promotional period? What are the likely long-term effects of a promotion?

3. Distinguish between public relations and publicity. Is it true that publicity can be regarded as free advertising?

4. There is no such thing as bad publicity. Discuss.

5. The major reason for event sponsorship is to indulge senior management in their favourite pastime. Discuss.

6. Exhibitions are less effective than personal selling and more costly than direct mail, so why use them?

References

1. Peattie, K. and S. Peattie (1993) Sales Promotion: Playing to Win?, *Journal of Marketing Management* 9, 255–69.
2. Lal, R. (1990) Manufacturer Trade Deals and Retail Price Promotion, *Journal of Marketing Research* 27(6), 428–44.
3. Rothschild, M. L. and W. C. Gaidis (1981) Behavioural Learning Theory: Its Relevance to Marketing and Promotions, *Journal of Marketing* 45, Spring, 70–8.
4. Tuck, R. T. J. and W. G. B. Harvey (1972) Do Promotions Undermine the Brand?, *Admap*, January, 30–3.
5. Brown, R. G. (1974) Sales Response to Promotions and Advertising, *Journal of Advertising Research* 14(4), 33–9.
6. Ehrenberg, A. S. C., K. Hammond and G. J. Goodhardt (1994) The After-Effects of Price-Related Consumer Promotions, *Journal of Advertising Research* 34(4), 1–10.
7. Wilson, R. (2005) Brands Need Not Pay the Price, *Marketing Week*, 7 July, 39–41.
8. Jones, R. (2008) Don't Count on the Discount, *Guardian Money*, 29 March, 3.
9. Killigran, L. and R. Cook (1999) Multibuy Push May Backfire, *Marketing Week*, 16 September, 44–5.
10. Ritson, M. (2005) Cadbury's Decision to BOGOF is a Strategic Error, *Marketing*, 25 May, 24.
11. Davidson, J. H. (2003) *Offensive Marketing*, Harmondsworth: Penguin, 249–71.
12. Cummins, J. and R. Mullin (2008) *Sales Promotion*, London: Kogan Page, 79.
13. Davidson (2003) op. cit.
14. Dourado, P. (2003) Plastic Population, *Marketing Week*, 24 April, 35–7.
15. Quilter, J. (2005) Aisles of Plenty, *Marketing*, 10 August, 15.
16. Quilter (2005) op. cit.
17. Cummins and Mullin (2008) op. cit.
18. McLukan, R. (2005) Branching Out, *Marketing*, 6 April, 39–40.

19. Collins, M. (1986) Research on 'Below the Line' Expenditure, in Worcester, R. and J. Downham (eds) *Consumer Market Research Handbook*, Amsterdam: North Holland, 537–50.
20. Cummins and Mullin (2008) op. cit.
21. Doyle, P. and J. Saunders (1985) The Lead Effect of Marketing Decisions, *Journal of Marketing Research* 22(1), 54–65.
22. White, J. (1991) *How to Understand and Manage Public Relations*, London: Business Books.
23. Lesly, P. (1998) *The Handbook of Public Relations and Communications*, Maidenhead: McGraw-Hill, 13–19.
24. Gelles, D. (2008) Companies Chatter on Twitter to Pack Public Relations Punch, *Financial Times*, 31 December, 15.
25. Kitchen, P. J. and T. Proctor (1991) The Increasing Importance of Public Relations in Fast Moving Consumer Goods Firms, *Journal of Marketing Management* 7(4), 357–70.
26. Lesly (1998) op. cit.
27. Jefkins, F. (1985) Timing and Handling of Material, in Howard, W. (ed.) *The Practice of Public Relations*, Oxford: Heinemann, 86–104.
27. Gofton, K. (1996) Integrating the Delivery, *Marketing*, 31 October (Special Supplement on Choosing and Using Public Relations), 8–10.
28. Murphy, C. (2009) How to Communicate with PRs, *The Marketer*, March, 33–6.
29. Sleight, S. (1989) *Sponsorship: What It Is and How to Use It*, Maidenhead: McGraw-Hill, 4.
30. Bennett, R. (1999) Sports Sponsorship, Spectator Recall and False Consensus, *European Journal of Marketing* 33(3/4), 291–313.
31. Barrand, D. (2005) When Disaster Strikes, *Marketing*, 9 March, 35–6.
32. Anonymous (2008) Ten Clues for Keen Competition, *The Marketer*, June, 7.

33. De Burton, S. (2004) Fancy a Touch of Star Status?, *Financial Times*, 13/14 November, 7–8.

34. Meenaghan, T. and D. Shipley (1999), Media Effects in Commercial Sponsorship, *European Journal of Marketing* 33(3/4), 328–47.

33. Benady, D. (2005) Be a Super Sponsor, *Marketing Week*, 24 March, 37–8.

36. Clark, N. (2005) Red Bull Eyes Sporting Chance, *Marketing*, 27 July, 14–5.

37. Haywood, R. (1984) *All About PR*, Maidenhead: McGraw-Hill, 186.

38. Crowley, M. G. (1991) Prioritising the Sponsorship Audience, *European Journal of Marketing* 25(11), 11–21.

39. Barrand, D. (2005) Sponsorship Leagues, *Marketing*, 15 June, 37–8.

40. Stokes, B. (2006) Music v Sports Sponsorship, *Marketing Week*, 16 March, 15.

41. Clark, N. (2008) Festival Fever, *Marketing*, 29 October, 27–8.

42. Kilby, N. (2005) Intel in Worldwide BMW and Marketing Tie-up, *Marketing Week*, 15 December, 3.

43. Choueke, M. (2005) When it Pays to Pounce, *Marketing Week*, 7 July, 28–9.

44. Anonymous (2008) Playing the Game, *Economist*, 5 July, 87.

45. Smith, P. R. and J. Taylor (2004) *Marketing Communications: An Integrated Approach*, London: Kogan Page, 240–3.

46. Meenaghan, T. (1991) The Role of Sponsorship in the Marketing Communications Mix, *International Journal of Advertising* 10, 35–47.

47. Thwaites, D. (1995) Professional Football Sponsorship—Profitable or Profligate?, *International Journal of Advertising* 14, 149–64.

48. O'Hara, B., F. Palumbo and P. Herbig (1993) Industrial Trade Shows Abroad, *Industrial Marketing Management* 22, 233–7.

49. Couretas, J. (1984) Trade Shows and the Strategic Mainstream, *Business Marketing* 69, 64–70.

50. Anonymous (1979) Trade Shows are Usually a Form of Mass Hysteria, *Industrial Marketing* 64(4), 6–10.

51. Parasuraman, A. (1981) The Relative Importance of Industrial Promotional Tools, *Industrial Marketing Management* 10, 277–81.

52. Smith, T. M., S. Gopalakrishna and P. M. Smith (2004) The Complementary Effect of Trade Shows on Personal Selling, *International Journal of Research in Marketing* 21(1), 61–76.

53. Prickett, R. (2002) The Key to the Show, *Marketing Week*, 12 September, 49–51.

54. Bonoma, T. V. (1985) Get More Out of Your Trade Shows, in Gumpert, D. E. (ed.) *The Marketing Renaissance*, New York: Wiley.

55. Trade Show Bureau (1983) *The Exhibitor: Their Trade Show Practices*, Research Report No. 19, East Orleans, MA: Trade Show Bureau.

56. Russell, I. (1999) Driving Force, *Marketing Week*, 7 October, 69–73.

57. Couretas (1984) op. cit.

58. Hansen, K. (2004) Measuring Performance at Trade Shows: Scale Development and Validation, *Journal of Business Research* 54, 1–13.

59. Lancaster, G. and H. Baron (1977) Exhibiting for Profit, *Industrial Management*, November, 24–7.

60. Blaskey, J. (1999) Proving Your Worth, *Marketing*, 25 February, 35–6.

61. Anonymous (2002) The Ten Top Product Placements in Features, *Campaign*, 17 December, 36.

62. Barn, S. (2005) Product Placement and Bollywood Movies, *Middlesex University Business School Working Paper No 30*, April, 1–17.

63. Considine, P. (2008) Does Product Placement Really Work?, *Campaign*, 9 May, 10.

64. Grant, J. (2008) Added Value Versus Brazen Branding, *Guardian*, 22 September, 3.

65. Turner, C. (2005) Product Placement Gets EC Go-Ahead, *Marketing Week*, 12 December, 10.

66. Kleinman, M. (2002) Philips to Launch 007 Shaving Range, *Marketing*, 4 April, 3.

67. Wheelright, G. (2003) Bond Encourages Surfers to Buy Another Day, *Financial Times IT Review*, 15 January, 2.

68. Keller, K. L. (2007) Strategic *Brand Management*, New Jersey: Pearson.

69. Sweeney, M. (2007) EU to Allow Product Placement TV, *Guardian*, 30 November, 24.

70. Fernandez, J. (2009) VOD Offers Ideal Home for Product Placement Revenue Stream, *Marketing Week*, 19 March, 8.

Wispa

It's Back!

Introduction

In the same way as the Spice Girls, Boyzone and Take That opted to tap in to nostalgia and relaunch with stadium tours, brands too are jumping on the bandwagon. Recent examples of nostalgia brands making a return include, Nestlé bringing back the Drifter bar, Walkers relaunching Monster Munch and, of course, Cadbury bringing back the Wispa. Many of these products were cast aside by multinational companies that no longer wanted to invest in marketing them as they streamlined their portfolios around global brands. The successful relaunch of the Wispa bar in 2007 has awarded Wispa a place in the brand hall of fame. Not only was it the first brand brought back by consumer demand, and the biggest ever of its kind in the UK and Ireland, it was also the biggest brand launch in Cadbury history.

History of the Wispa bar

The history of the Wispa chocolate bar can be traced back to 1981 when Cadbury launched it as a trial version in north-east England. The Wispa quite quickly became an icon of the 1980s. It was one of the first brands to use high-profile celebrity endorsement for a launch campaign. Wispa sales soared on the back of a celebrated series of adverts featuring Nigel Hawthorne and Paul Eddington from *Yes, Minister*, Victoria Wood, Julie Waters, comedians Mel Smith and Griff Rhys Jones, and Welsh baritone and comedy actor Windsor Davies. As the sales of Wispa increased, new Wispa flavours were introduced to the market, such as Wispa Gold (caramel filling) introduced in 1995, Wispa Bite (caramel and biscuit filling) introduced in 2000, Wispaccino (coffee-flavoured filling) and Wispa mint (mint layer). However, the Wispa bar suffered a decline in popularity and vanished from UK and Irish retailers' shelves in 2003 amid declining sales and production problems. Cadbury claims to have axed the Wispa as part of a move to bring a number of brands under the Dairy Milk umbrella brand.

Social networking sites

Since the discontinuation of the Wispa bar in 2003, several Internet campaigns and online petitions to bring it back slowly gained momentum. It all began when a

student in Britain posted a video plea on YouTube for Cadbury to relaunch the once iconic bar. In Ireland, the campaign was spearheaded by three students at University College Cork: Emily Hughes, Joy Allen and Louise Cremin. The intrepid trio decided to start an online campaign and created a fan page for the bar on Bebo. Fans posted clips from the 1980s advertisements for Wispa on YouTube and thousands of other consumers joined online petitions calling for the return of the bar. At one stage, Cadbury said it had identified 14,000 Wispa fans across 93 user groups on Bebo, MySpace and Facebook, all calling for the return of the Wispa. Die-hard Wispa fans wrote letters to national newspapers, made calls to national radio stations and even took their mission to the Glastonbury Festival in 2007, when two Wispa fans stormed the stage while Iggy Pop was performing, displaying a banner reading 'Bring Back Wispa'! The chocolate company says that it is frequently contacted by consumers asking for old favourites to be reintroduced, but said that the numbers that had joined the Internet campaign to relaunch Wispa were unprecedented.

The relaunch

Confectionery lovers both in Britain and Ireland jumped on the 'Bring Back Wispa' bandwagon to turn it into a juggernaut of consumer pressure that Cadbury couldn't ignore. Taken aback by the strength of the lobbying, and suspecting that it may be no more than a web-generated fad, Cadbury agreed to relaunch the Wispa in Britain and Ireland on 8 October 2007, for an initial limited production of 23 million bars. Cadbury spokesman Tony Bilsborough said 'we have noticed the web interest for some time and the consumer passion has undeniably swayed our opinion to relaunch Wispa. This is the first time that the power of the Internet [has] played such an intrinsic role in the return of the Cadbury brand,' he added. When 23 million bars sold out in Ireland and Britain in the space of seven weeks, Cadbury announced in August 2008 that the Wispa would be relaunched on a permanent basis from 6 October 2008. Tony Bilsborough said 'Wispa is a true icon loved by its fans everywhere. We brought it back temporarily to see if the desire was genuine, but fans are still rallying, so we took the decision to bring it back for good.' The fact that Wispa sold successfully following its relaunch in 2007 probably came as a relief to Cadbury, as it confirmed for the company that the groundswell of public opinion was real, and not just an elaborate hoax by students to test if companies' product policies could be swayed by enough people creating a stir. 'We don't bring back brands every day, so we needed to be sure that this was real,' says Shane Guest, Wispa brand manager for Ireland. 'We also didn't have much time to conduct real market research, so we had to trust the positive noises we heard coming from the retail sector. All that said, we wouldn't be relaunching to the market if we weren't confident that this was for real,' he added.

The role of promotion

All the publicity surrounding the relaunch of the Wispa saved Cadbury from having to shell out a small fortune on a new marketing campaign. However, it is estimated that Cadbury invested £1 million in a marketing campaign to support the relaunch. The main objective of the relaunch was to create hype about the brand. Cadbury approached this in four main ways, as outlined below.

Advertising

Initially, the limited-edition launch was backed by a long-copy press campaign created by Publicis, which aimed to tap in to consumer nostalgia, reminding people of other products and brands that were popular when Wispa was launched in the 1980s (see the Wispa press ad illustration).

The reintroduction of the brand was also supported by billboard advertising. In Ireland, Publicis QMP Dublin came up with a very clever way to talk about a famously quiet brand. With a campaign and a product name that's all about quietness, how do you create a quiet poster? The outdoor advertisement it created was a 48-sheet poster with a small Wispa bar taking centre stage against a white background. Viewers had to get up close to investigate the advertisement's purpose. Outdoor sites were chosen especially so that intrigued viewers could get close enough to see the famous brand. Some viewers wrote messages and drew cartoon drawings of the brand on the advertisement—interacting with the advertisement and the brand! This novel advertisement won two awards at the 46th Kinsale Shark Advertising Festival in 2008. Cadbury also advertised on bus shelters, roadside panels and in some national newspapers to announce the bar's return (see illustration).

▲ Wispa roadside panel advertisement.

From a time when...

Ads looked like this. You had big hair. Phillip Schofield had brown hair. Your mum wore shoulder pads. Your dad wore Speedos. You had to fight for your right to party. Losing meant you got a Blankety-Blank cheque book and pen. It was 01 for London.

You came home from school to Zammo Maguire, Gripper Stebson and Ro-land. You held a chicken in the air and stuck a deckchair up your nose. The Sword of Omens gave you sight beyond sight.

You recorded the top 40 every Sunday, onto a C90 cassette. If you hit 88.8 mph you travelled back in time. Girls just wanted to have fun. Fluorescent colours were the colours to be seen in. Beefy hit the Aussies for six. The Young Ones were young ones.

You drank Slush Puppies in your Hush Puppies. The First Division really was the First Division. You first visited Albert Square, Ramsay Street and Brookside Close. You tried to break dance. You tried to break dance again.

Four TV channels seemed like a lot. You knew never to feed them after midnight and even named your cat after one of them. There was nothing in this game for two in a bed. You couldn't get to sleep without your Glo Worm. Acid rain was a worry. If there was something strange in your neighbourhood, you knew who to call.

You wore leg warmers with everything. Steve Davis made snooker 'interesting'. A crack commando unit was sent to prison by a military court for a crime they didn't commit.

You wondered what would happen if you said 'Beetlejuice' three times. The man from Del Monte, he said "Yes". You wanted to be a Goonie and find One-Eyed Willy's ship. Alex was a steel worker by day, exotic dancer by night. A bunch of bears cared. Kevin Bacon was Footloose.

You practised Ted Rogers' lightning fast 3-2-1 hand gesture in the playground. You were working as a waitress in a cocktail bar. You got, got, got, need, got Panini stickers. Maradona beat England single-handedly. You told the time on your Swatch watch.

A cyborg assassin said he'd be back for the first time. You practised getting in and out of your dad's car through the window, Yee Hah.

Three men struggled to look after one baby. Friendship bracelets were ties that couldn't be broken. You could be his wingman anytime. You tried to catch a fly with chopsticks. Salt and vinegar crisps came in blue packets.

Glenn Close made married men think twice about having an affair. Betamax was cutting edge technology. Michael Knight's best friend was his car. We thought Milli Vanilli were singing. That's not a knife, this is a knife.

You played a word association game where you mustn't pause, hesitate, repeat a word or you'd get a bash on the head like this or like this. Sam Fox was a fox. Tom Hanks fell in love with a mermaid.

Hippos were hungry, hungry. Your Hypercolour T-shirt worked brilliantly until your mum washed it for the first time. You would have gotten away with it if it hadn't been for those meddling kids.

Everyone had a poster of a man holding a baby. Crossroads reached the end of the road. You wanted a day off just like Ferris's. Jessica Fletcher helped police find the 'real' killer. You collected Garbage Pail Kids. Aerobies could travel for miles. Louis Winthorpe III and Billy Ray Valentine traded places.

You completed a Rubik's Cube by peeling the stickers off. Dallas was all a dream. Harry met Sally.

Mobile phones were the size of house bricks. Her name was Rio and she was dancing on the sand. Bats were scared of The Prince of Darkness. Jossy Blair managed The Glipton Giants. Ooh, you could crush a grape. Um Bongo, Um Bongo, you drank it in the Congo. Molly Ringwald, Emilio Estevez, Anthony Michael Hall, Judd Nelson and Ally Sheedy were all members of the same club. Luke and Matt made you want to put bottle tops on your shoes.

You asked Bob for a 'P' please. You knew who the Crafty Cockney was. You were going to live forever, you were going to learn how to fly. Floppy records never worked but made great Frisbees.

A piece of folded paper held in your hands could predict someone's future. You were told to say what you saw. You had to watch out, Beadle was about. Sir Clive thought we'd all be driving battery powered tricycles by now.

A material girl was living in a material world. You switched off your TV set and did something less boring instead. Michael Fish assured us there wasn't a hurricane on the way. A Mannequin came to life.

Nick Kamen did his laundry in his boxer shorts. You wanted to shout, shout, let it all out. Gordon the Gopher lived in a broom cupboard. Zippy, George and Bungle shared a house with Geoffrey.

Rick was never gonna give you up. You wanted to make your very own Kelly LeBrock. Romantic men were new and wore their sisters' make-up. Every car seemed to have a Garfield in its window. Torvill and Dean made you want to go ice-skating.

One story was neverending. Eric the schoolboy ate a banana and an amazing transformation occurred.

There were halfpennies and one pound notes. You were proud of your picture getting in the Gallery. Computer games took half an hour to load.

You knew all the Ninja Turtles' names and colours. Penny sweets actually cost one penny. We were all Rat fans. Chevy Chase was funny. Lenny Henry was funny. Les Dennis was Les Dennis.

Your BMX had Spokey Dokeys. You wanted to go where everybody knew your name. You walked like an Egyptian. You got free milk at break time.

Greed was good. You had Pac-man fever. You got bizzy with the fizzy. You had an E.T. lunchbox. Shops weren't open on a Sunday. You could Rentaghost. 'Ard Wispa first came out.

Cadbury Wispa. Back from the 80s.

▲ Wispa press advertisement.

▲ Wispa pavement advertising.

In addition, Cadbury used novel pavement advertising to promote the Wispa brand. This involved using a template and spraying a dirty pavement with a high-pressure water jet to create the advertising message (see illustration). This was a very novel and unusual method of advertising, and definitely grabbed both the media's and the public's attention.

Point-of-purchase displays

Cadbury decided that point-of-sale marketing would highlight the relaunch of Wispa, which is targeted at the impulse sector. Wispa was merchandised inside dump bins at impulse points throughout stores to drive consumer purchase. Cadbury was also encouraging retailers to create some 'in-store theatre' around the brand to make the most of the opportunity.

Public relations

There was a huge amount of press coverage surrounding the relaunch of the bar. Cadbury generated some PR of its own when the first box of relaunched Wispas was put up for auction on eBay on 24 August 2007. This was accompanied by a press release from Cadbury stating that the auction was real and that the proceeds were going towards the Cadbury charity, Ghana for the Source. As news of the permanent relaunch of the Wispa spread, the Woolworths store in Peckham, London, which was first to receive stock on 22 September 2008, hired security guards to deliver the 'sought-after bars' after news of the launch leaked on several Wispa Facebook sites. Most of the press coverage surrounding the relaunch of Wispa focused on the role

of fans and social network sites in the brand's revival. However, some sources argue that most press coverage doesn't mention that Cadbury employed a PR agency, Borkowski PR, to tell the world about the return of the Wispa. Borkowski PR won the Gold Award for Campaign of the Year and a Digital Innovation Award at the PR Week Awards (2008) for its role in Wispa's relaunch. Spurred on by online fans petitioning for a return of the Wispa bar, Borkowski worked with Cadbury's in-house media team to whip up hype about the brand. In the three months leading up to the relaunch, the team fuelled online rumours of Wispa's return and monitored conversations on the subject so they could break the news once speculation reached fever pitch. It also prepared for the launch by issuing bespoke 'secret dossier' briefing packs to key journalists. It was Borkowski PR that advised Cadbury to announce the return of the Wispa through social networking sites rather than traditional media. The campaign achieved over 332 pieces of press coverage with a PR value of more than £1.4 million. In addition, in the three weeks following the 2007 launch, the number of Facebook groups swelled 60 per cent to 400, with 25,000 members.

Microsite

Fittingly for a 1980s brand that was brought back to life after a grass-roots campaign on social networking sites, Cadbury used a microsite (http://www.wispa.co.uk/) to build interest ahead of Wispa's return. The 1980s-themed website allowed visitors to win great 1980s prizes (including a 1980s-themed day spent cruising in a Ferrari or taking *Dirty Dancing* lessons) and create a personalized viral animation game to share with their friends. The website also included a history of the product and an external link to Flickr, which featured a 1980s 'Hall of Shame' of fashion and hair faux pas. The website also invited enthusiasts to upload photos of themselves and then create a 1980s look to send around to their friends.

The future

Cadbury is hoping to continue the successful return of the Wispa with the relaunch of some of the other Wispa flavours. McDonald's introduced the Wispa McFlurry for a limited time only and a Wispa Easter egg was launched in 2009. It is understood that Cadbury will support seasonal product with press, online and in-store advertising, which is expected to tap in to the retro theme that has been used in the brand's advertising. The relaunch of the Wispa bar has helped Cadbury to achieve an 11 per cent rise in UK sales. It sold 1.2 million Wispa bars in one week alone following its permanent relaunch in September 2008. This may be viewed as a concrete example of the return on investment from monitoring and responding to social media.

References

Based on: Anonymous (2007) Bebo, MySpace Brings Back Choc Fave, *Factfinder*, 21 August; Anonymous (2007) Cadbury's Heralds Wispa Return with Microsite, *Marketing*, 2 October; Anonymous (2007) Web Campaign Prompts Wispa Return, *BBC News*, 18 August; Cadbury (2007) First Wispa Bars Auctioned on eBay, press release, 24 August; Percival, G. (2007) Marketers Tune in to Online Social Networks, *Irish Examiner*, 31 August; Pfanner, E. (2007) Taste of Victory: Online Outcry Revives Chocolate Bar, *New York Times*, 26 August; Power, I. (2007) Chinese Wispas Prompt Choc Comeback, *Irish Examiner*, 29 August; Wainwright, M. (2007) Whisper it Softly … 80s Favourite Revived, *Guardian*, 18 August; Wallop, H. (2007) Cadbury Plans Wispa Revival, *Telegraph*, 18 August; Anonymous (2008) Cadbury Brings Back Wispa Permanently, *Marketing Week*, 10 April; Anonymous (2008) Cadbury Plans Easter Egg Launch and Ad Campaign, *Marketing Week*, 10 July; Anonymous (2008) Campaign of the Year, PR Week Awards; Anonymous (2008) Wispa Back Again, *Forecourt Trader*, 1 September; Anonymous (2008) Woolworths Stages Wispa Launch Publicity Stunt, *Marketing Week*, 22 September; Ananova (2008) Wispa Sweetens Cadbury's Success, www.ananova. com; Nettleton, K. and C. Lovell (2008) Why Are Nostalgia Brands Returning?, *Campaign*, 30 May; Smith, K. (2008) Wispa Campaign Leads to Return of a Chocolate Bubble Bar, *Telegraph*, 3 August; Sturgeon, W. (2008) Why Good PR is Like a Good Referee, *Lewis 360*, 4 August.

Questions

1. Why are nostalgia brands like Wispa making a return?

2. Was it wise for Cadbury to give in to the consumer campaign to relaunch Wispa? Should social networking sites and online campaigns influence product strategy?

3. Evaluate the use of advertising and in-store displays in the relaunch of the Wispa bar. What were the key objectives behind Cadbury's advertising activities?

4. What role did PR play in the relaunch of the Wispa? Do you think public interest in the relaunch of Wispa was genuine or was it really a fake, hyped-up campaign led by Cadbury's PR agency?

This case was written by Marie O'Dwyer, Lecturer in Marketing, Waterford Institute of Technology, Ireland. Special thanks to Shane Guest, Product Group Manager, Cadbury Ireland.

Beckham & Ronaldo

Sports Celebrity Sponsorship

David Beckham is one of the world's most celebrated footballers and is claimed to be worth £125 million. Part of his fortune is based on wages at top football clubs, but the rest has been earned by means of lucrative endorsement contracts. He is a marketing phenomenon, endorsing several products for millions of pounds, ranging from mobile phones to soft drinks to football boots. Nothing could go wrong for the Beckham brand as he was the England captain, had a celebrity wife, a millionaire lifestyle, was a fashion icon and was perceived as a loyal, happy family man—the perfect role model. However, in April 2004, the Sunday tabloid newspaper, the *News of the World* broke the story that shocked the world and became a media sensation. David Beckham, the world's most famous footballer/celebrity/family man, had had an alleged extra-marital affair with his former personal assistant, Rebecca Loos. This news sent shockwaves around the world, especially in the boardrooms of some large multinationals that had invested millions in the Beckham brand, cultivating its image into one of the most lucrative sports marketing properties in the world.

Beckham as a brand has had its fair share of highs and lows. A player can one minute be idolized by a nation for scoring, or vilified for missing two penalties. At a young age the footballer had a prodigious talent. Back in 1995, he entered the public mindset, with probably one of the greatest goals seen in the English football, where he lobbed over a goalkeeper from the halfway line, scoring a wonder goal that will always be remembered. He cemented his position in the Manchester Untied team, scoring spectacular goals and setting up brilliant crosses for the strikers. His profile was on the rise. Having a celebrity wife, former Spice Girl 'Posh Spice', boosted his celebrity status even further. He gained English caps and was regarded as a rising English football superstar. During the 1998 World Cup in France, however, his image took a battering when he was sent off during a crucial match against England's footballing nemesis, Argentina. In a moment of petulance, he kicked out at an opponent and was sent off. Beckham was blamed by an entire nation for losing the match and was vilified in the media for his actions. The Beckham brand had reached its nadir.

Following a slow and steady redemption, he won back the support of fans through his subsequent displays for Manchester Untied and England. His superstardom reached a zenith when he scored a spectacular goal against Greece, in the final seconds of the match, to secure World Cup qualification for England. He was now the nation's hero once again. The Beckham brand was established not only through his footballing prowess, but also through his celebrity lifestyle, the image of being a family man and his model looks. Men saw him as an excellent footballer, while women saw him also as a glamorous celebrity and quiet family man. The world's media had a voracious appetite for all things Beckham, especially with his marriage to Victoria Adams, aka Posh Spice, earning the couple the nickname 'Posh & Becks', which has entered the modern lexicon. Interest in the couple grew from when they began dating. Their plush wedding in an Irish castle earned the couple fame for its extravagance. The couple famously sat in large royal 'thrones' during the event, allowing the media to make inferences that the couple were indeed the new British royalty. Celebrity magazines and tabloid newspapers were filled to the brim with stories relating to the couple and their lifestyle.

Unlike other footballers, David Beckham benefited from huge awareness through the massive levels of exposure he gained in the media by posing for fashion shoots, giving pictorial features in celebrity lifestyle magazines, and so on. Furthermore his fashion choices were always under scrutiny and stirred much public debate. The footballer was famously criticized in the press for wearing a skirt while on holiday. Similarly, his choice of hairstyle, which has gone through numerous incarnations, has been followed religiously by the general public and fashion watchdogs. In his early footballing career, he was known for his gelled hair. Through this, he garnered a lucrative endorsement from Brylcreem, the hair gel company. However, much to his sponsor's annoyance, he chopped all his hair off for one season. Subsequently he grew a 'Mohican' haircut, a mullet, went blond, grew it long, had a ponytail … His hairstyle and hair colour changed much like the seasons, adding to his fame as a style icon.

The Beckham brand has been carefully managed through an array of publicity devices such as appearances at fashion shows, photo specials in celebrity lifestyle magazines, press releases, interviews, and special one-hour television documentaries depicting the couple's glamorous lifestyle and their happy family life. The couple employ public relations advisers who zealously protect their clients' pristine image, controlling the media's access to their famous clients.

The value of the Beckham brand continued to grow and grow, as he had now become one of the world's most well-recognized and photographed soccer players. The player was ripe for celebrity endorsements as he had a well-developed brand persona that companies saw as a perfect fit for their products. Beckham and his wife had entered the cultural psyche, and were well known worldwide. He was seen as a perfect role model and frontman for a variety of products—he was talented, globally well known, successful and had a glamorous wife—the perfect poster boy for any product. Adidas, the sports goods company, signed Beckham at a young age, and he was one of its most successful acquisitions, becoming synonymous with its football-related products. Nike, Adidas's bitter rival, publicly rued its failure to sign Beckham originally as one of its biggest ever sports marketing failures. Beckham has signed numerous personal endorsement deals with leading international companies. He has endorsed such products as boots, phones, shavers, soft drinks, a clothing line and a video game. These deals can be seen in Table C32.1. The range of products that he endorses is vastly larger than other footballers, who typically have

only boot deals with sports clothing companies. It is testament to the brand value and appeal of the Beckham brand that he can successfully be used to promote such a wide array of products—even motor oil!

In the summer of 2003, Beckham was sold to Real Madrid for £18 million. The sale raised many eyebrows in that Manchester Untied were selling one of its biggest marketing and merchandising assets. The Beckham brand had huge appeal in the lucrative Far East markets. Many commentators claimed that the Spanish footballing giant had bought a marketing tool rather than a footballer. His signing in Madrid was greeted with delight. The player's medical examination for the club even became a live pay-per-view television event, which was sponsored by a local private hospital. The signing of Beckham at Real Madrid helped broaden the club's geographic and demographic reach, gaining new overseas supporters. The Spanish club hoped to gain more fans, vying to see their footballing hero, and buying an array of Real Madrid merchandise with Beckham's image and name emblazoned upon it. Real Madrid shirts sales alone rose £14 million when he joined the club.

> **//** Major brands constantly seek out willing celebrities to endorse their products, paying them huge sums of money. **//**

Marketing managers see sponsorship as a highly effective way of reaching their target audiences. Traditional advertising has become increasingly costly. There is increasing media fragmentation, and increased clutter in marketing communications. All these factors have contributed to the rising disillusionment with traditional advertising methods. Marketers are seeking new ways to communicate brand values. Through celebrity endorsements they can break through this clutter to communicate their brands' messages. Having a celebrity like Beckham endorsing a product increases the awareness levels of the message because of his celebrity status; also the product gains from any positive brand associations that may accrue. For example, if you buy Adidas Predator boots perhaps you too can bend the ball like Beckham, or if you buy Police sunglasses you too will become fashionable, and so on. Furthermore, by having a celebrity endorser, the firm may be able to reach a certain target demographic, gain increased media coverage and position the product in a favourable light. The benefits of having a celebrity endorser are immense. Major brands constantly seek out willing celebrities to endorse their products, paying them huge sums of money. LeBron James, then a

The Beckham brand and product endorsements

Current deals

- Motorola — earns £2.5 million a year from mobile phone maker
- Adidas — has sponsored Beckham to the tune of £3 million a year during his career; he is one of its highest-profile celebrity endorsers
- Gillette — the deal with Gillette is reputedly worth over £2.5 million a year; it was, surprisingly, signed after the revelations over Beckham's private life were revealed
- Coty Fragrances — launched a line of David Beckham fragrances, selling at £20 a bottle, under the DVB logo; launched in August 2006
- Walt Disney World and Disneyland — the LA Galaxy deal was crucial here
- Armani — Beckham featured in a series of underwear ads

Past commercial deals

- Coca-Cola — although sponsored by Pepsi at the same time, Coke could still use Beckham's image rights due to his role as England captain, because Coke had a deal with the UK's Football Association; he received a percentage of the overall sponsorship deal, where his image could be used in certain campaigns
- Pepsi — earned £2 million a year; often appeared in ads with other world-class footballers
- Brylcreem — earned close on £1.5 million over three years from the hair gel manufacturer; Beckham, during his early playing career, was associated with hair gel
- Castrol — the oil company paid him £500,000 for promotions in the Far East
- Marks & Spencer — put his name to a range of kids' sports clothes called DB07 until 2005; after his move to Real Madrid, the deal was tarnished as he no longer played in the UK and no longer wore his famous no. 7 shirt; the contract was worth £10 million for its duration
- Vodafone — signed a one-year £6 million deal to front television advertisements
- Police sunglasses — reported to be worth £1.5 million a year
- Rage Software — the video game maker developed the best-selling *David Beckham Soccer* video game for PlayStation; the company went into receivership; paid £1.5 million for the deal
- TBC (Tokyo Beauty Company, a chain of beauty salons) — he is estimated to have received £2 million for his work
- Meiji — a Japanese chocolate biscuit maker
- Tsubasa Systems — a Japanese computer company

(Beckham's sports marketing agents typically earn commission of between 10 and 15 per cent)

19-year-old rising basketball player in the USA, was paid £65 million by Nike to endorse its products.

However, using a celebrity does have its downsides. First, obtaining an endorser is expensive. The endorser may experience a dip in form, lack of success or popularity. For example, the recent dip in form experienced by the golfer Tiger Woods was attributed in the press to a new Nike golf club he was using. Second, the company may be exposed to the risk of a celebrity's possible misbehaviour, which may have ramifications for the endorser. Controversy is never far from the life of a UK soccer star. Countless footballers have been caught in a quagmire of scandals over the past decade. Off-the-pitch scandals concerning drugs, kiss-and-tell stories, gambling and alcoholism have become commonplace. When companies invest in a football player, not only do they have to be concerned about his performance on the pitch, but his behaviour off the pitch as well.

The Beckham brand was thought to be scandal-free and solid. Yet rumours began to circulate in the media that all was not well in the kingdom of Posh & Becks. The tabloids questioned why his wife had not moved with him to Spain, and why the footballer was out late at night, clubbing with a mysterious brunette. The couple had switched their agents to Management 19, owned by Simon Fuller, the ex-manager of the Spice Girls, dumping David Beckham's old sports marketing agency, SFX. Rebecca Loos, the personal assistant of David Beckham in Spain, was fired by SFX after the Beckham account was lost. After that, she went public about her alleged affair with the England captain. The *News of the World* broke the story. The alleged mistress then obtained a whirlwind of publicity surrounding the affair,

Other famous sponsorship controversies	**TABLE C32.2**

- Michelle Smith and Pantene Shampoo — Ireland's four-gold Olympic swimming champion at the Atlanta games was sponsored by the Pantene shampoo brand, only to be found out later as a drugs cheat
- Leicester City Football Club and Alliance & Leicester — Members of first team squad were thrown in a Spanish jail in 2004 over alleged rape claims
- Eric Cantona and his infamous 'kung fu kick' — Nike wasn't too pleased
- Kobe Bryant — the US basketball superstar, who plays for the LA Lakers, was accused of rape in Colorado; had endorsement deals with McDonald's and Sprite; he is one of the world's wealthiest sports stars through his corporate endorsements
- O. J. Simpson — endorsed numerous companies and organizations, such as Hertz, before the infamous Los Angeles murders and freeway chase
- Mike Tyson — the heavyweight boxer was at one time sponsored by Pepsi
- Greek sprinters Kederis and Thanou, and Adidas — the Greek runners were embroiled in drugs controversy during the Athens Olympics; Adidas had to remove its billboards during the games as a result
- Roy Keane and 7UP — when footballer Roy Keane walked out on the Irish football team in the 2002 World Cup, 7UP, who sponsored Keane, had its posters featuring the footballer defaced, as the nation thought he had betrayed his country
- Festina Cycling Team and the Tour de France — the watchmaker sponsored an entire cycling team, which was implicated in a major drugs scandal
- Supermodels Naomi Campbell and Cindy Crawford, and their infamous U-turn on wearing fur — in the 1990s, the supermodels campaigned for PETA, an anti-fur lobbying organization, only to be seen later modelling clothing that used fur
- Wayne Rooney allegedly visited a brothel while engaged to be married

with media organizations entering a bidding war, vying for an interview. Loos then went on to receive £500,000 for an exclusive Sky 1 interview on the subject. Text messages between the couple were published, in an effort to prove the existence of the relationship. Subsequently, another woman emerged, giving details of his infidelity with her only a week later. The Beckhams' marriage and brand was under serious threat. The player, through a press statement, strenuously denied the allegations, stating that the claims were simply ludicrous and he was happily married. The Beckhams put on a show of strength for the cameras by appearing for the paparazzi on holiday riding their quad bikes together and posing for the cameras. The brand that had been meticulously crafted was now under severe scrutiny. Was Beckham still the perfect role model and brand endorser?

Table C32.2 lists some other sponsorship controversies.

In 2006, the Beckham brand faced a renewed threat. After a mediocre performance in the 2006 World Cup, Beckham announced a tearful farewell and resigned as England captain. Although scoring and assisting in setting up crucial goals, Beckham's place in the team came under renewed threat from football analysts. For the Euro 2008 campaign, the new England manager

dropped him from the squad, causing a huge shock. On news that Beckham was being dropped by England, his sponsors circled the wagons around their celebrity endorser, with Gillette saying that 'David Beckham remains an international sports and style icon.'

In an unexpected twist in January 2007, David Beckham announced that he had broken off negotiations with Real Madrid to join LA Galaxy in July 2007. He had accepted a £128 million five-year deal to play in US Major League Soccer. The intention was to improve the standard of and bring credibility to US soccer. The move was greeted by a headline in the *Los Angeles Times*, which ran 'Hello, Brand Beckham!' The move did not meet with the wholehearted approval of Fabio Capello, however, when he became England team manager, as he doubted Beckham's fitness level. Beckham responded by moving on loan to AC Milan, which helped him to return to the England team, and restore the visibility and credibility such a position holds.

While Beckham was building his fortune, another player, Cristiano Ronaldo, was building his own career and reputation at Manchester United, including scoring the winning goal in the 2008 Champions League final. Although earning £7 million a year at United he was reportedly unhappy about Alex Ferguson's reluctance

▲ Cristiano Ronaldo is building his career in brand endorsement, including companies such as Nike.

to encourage his players to exploit their commercial potential, and moved to Real Madrid for £80 million in 2009. As Simon Chadwick, professor of sport business strategy and marketing at Coventry University, commented, 'United have a greater desire for on-field performance, driven by Ferguson. From the people I speak to at Real regularly, there is a much greater sense that Madrid is an entertainment brand rather than a football club.'

At the time of the transfer, Ronaldo was earning £11 million a year from endorsing such brands as Nike, Coca-Cola, Fuji, Xerox and Castrol Oil. Even though he was World Player of the Year this was much less than David Beckham's £26 million a year.

Questions

1 Discuss the factors that should be assessed in making a successful sponsorship property selection.

2 Identify and discuss the risks associated with sponsorship, using this case as an illustration.

3 How can the effectiveness of a sponsorship campaign be measured? Develop a sponsorship evaluation programme, outlining how you would recommend any of Beckham's sponsorships to be evaluated.

4 What are the strategic options available to a sponsor, in the event of the sponsored property receiving negative publicity like that experienced by Adidas during the Beckham/Loos affair? Furthermore, recommend a course of action for a sponsor, giving reasons for your answer.

5 Assess Ronaldo's potential for further sponsorship. What can he learn from David Beckham in order to be attractive to sponsors?

This case was written by Conor Carroll, Lecturer in Marketing, University of Limerick, and David Jobber, Professor of Marketing at the University of Bradford. The material in the case has been drawn from a variety of published sources.

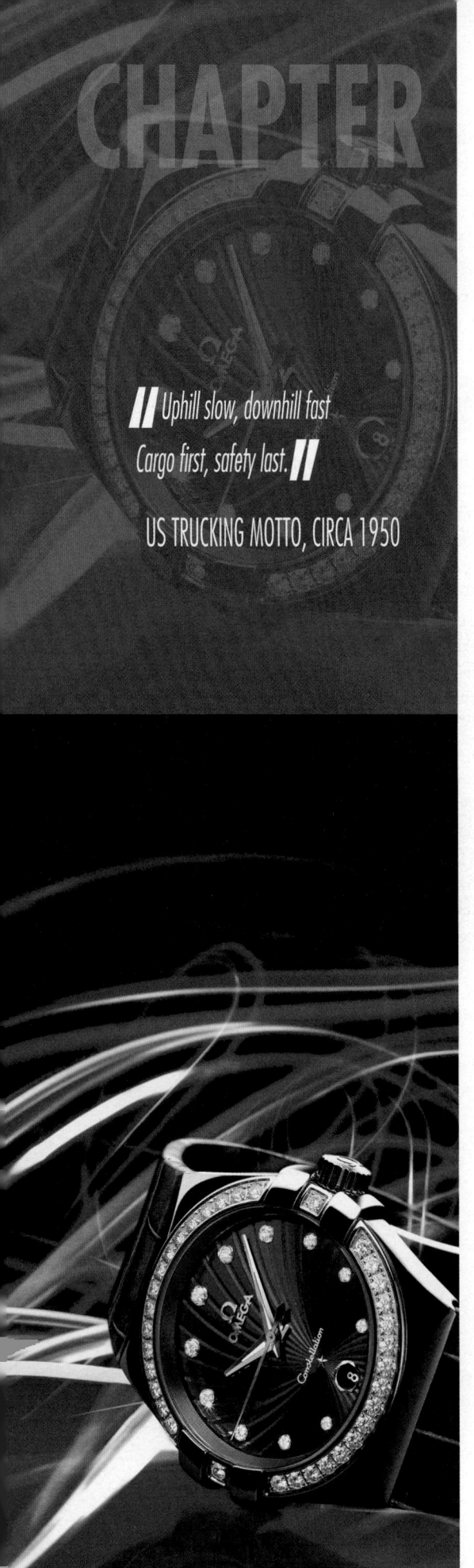

CHAPTER 17

Distribution

> **II** Uphill slow, downhill fast
> Cargo first, safety last. **II**
>
> US TRUCKING MOTTO, CIRCA 1950

LEARNING OBJECTIVES

After reading this chapter, you should be able to:

1 describe the functions and types of channels of distribution

2 explain how to determine channel strategy

3 discuss the three components of channel strategy: channel selection, intensity and integration

4 discuss the five key channel management issues: member selection, motivation, training, evaluation and conflict management

5 explain the cost–service trade-off in physical distribution

6 discuss the components of a physical distribution system: customer service, order processing, inventory control, warehousing, transportation and materials handling

7 explain how to improve customer service standards in physical distribution

8 discuss the ethical issues in distribution

Producing products that customers want, pricing them correctly and developing well-designed promotional plans are necessary but not sufficient conditions for customer satisfaction. The final part of the jigsaw is distribution: the *place* element of the marketing mix. Products need to be available in adequate quantities, in convenient locations and at times when customers want to buy them. In this chapter we shall examine the functions and types of distribution channels, the key decisions that determine channel strategy, how to manage channels and issues relating to the physical flow of goods through distribution channels (physical distribution management).

Producers need to consider not only the needs of their ultimate customer but also the requirement of **channel intermediaries**, those organizations that facilitate the distribution of products to customers. For example, success for Müller yoghurt in the UK was dependent on convincing a powerful retailer group (Tesco) to stock the brand. The high margins the brand supported were a key influence in Tesco's decision. Without retailer support Müller would have found it uneconomic to supply consumers with its brand. Clearly, establishing a supply chain that is efficient and meets customers' needs is vital to marketing success. This supply chain is termed a **channel of distribution**, and is the means by which products are moved from producer to the ultimate customer. Gaining distribution outlets does not come easily. Advertising to channel intermediaries is sometimes used to explain the benefits of the brand to encourage stocking.

The choice of the most effective channel of distribution is an important aspect of marketing strategy. The development of supermarkets effectively shortened the distribution channel between producer and consumer by eliminating the wholesaler. Prior to their introduction the typical distribution channel for products like food, drink, tobacco and toiletries was producer to wholesaler to retailer. The wholesaler would buy in bulk from the producer and sell smaller quantities to the retailer (typically a small grocery shop). By building up buying power, supermarkets could shorten this chain by buying direct from producers. This meant lower costs to the supermarket chain and lower prices to the consumer. The competitive effect was to drastically reduce the numbers of small grocers and wholesalers in this market. By being more efficient and better meeting customers' needs, supermarkets had created a competitive advantage for themselves.

Digital technologies are changing the face of distribution. For example, the Internet has changed the distribution of music and video (downloads), airline booking (electronic ticketing), hotel reservation (electronic booking) and groceries (home shopping). Mobile networks permit the distribution of such products as music, video and ringtones.[1] In business-to-business markets customers can place orders, receive quotes and track deliveries over the Internet.

Next, we shall explore the functions of channel intermediaries and then examine the different types of channels that manufacturers can use to supply their products to customers.

Functions of Channel Intermediaries

The most basic question to ask when deciding channel strategy is whether to sell directly to the ultimate customer or to use channel intermediaries such as retailers and/or wholesalers. To answer this question we need to understand the functions of channel intermediaries—that is, what benefits might producers derive from their use. Their functions are to reconcile the needs of producers and customers, to improve efficiency by reducing the number of transactions or creating bulk, to improve accessibility by lowering location and time gaps between producers and consumers, and to provide specialist services to customers. Each of these functions is now examined in more detail.

Reconciling the needs of producers and consumers

Manufacturers typically produce a large quantity of a limited range of goods, whereas consumers usually want only a limited quantity of a wide range of goods.[2] The role of channel intermediaries is to reconcile these conflicting situations. For example, a manufacturer of tables sells to retailers, each of which buys from a range of manufacturers of furniture and furnishings. The manufacturer can gain economies of scale by producing large quantities of tables, and each retailer provides a wide assortment of products offering its customers considerable choice under one roof.

A related function of channel intermediaries is *breaking bulk*. A wholesaler may buy large quantities from a manufacturer (perhaps a container load) and then sell smaller quantities (such as by the case) to retailers. Alternatively, large retailers such as supermarkets buy large quantities from producers, and break bulk by splitting the order between outlets. In this way, producers can produce large quantities while consumers are offered limited quantities at the point of purchase.

Improving efficiency

Channel intermediaries can improve distribution efficiency by *reducing the number of transactions* and *creating bulk for transportation*. Figure 17.1 shows how the number of transactions between three producers and three customers is reduced by using one intermediary. Direct distribution to customers results in nine transactions, whereas the use of an intermediary cuts the number of transactions to six. Distribution (and selling) costs and effort, therefore, are reduced.

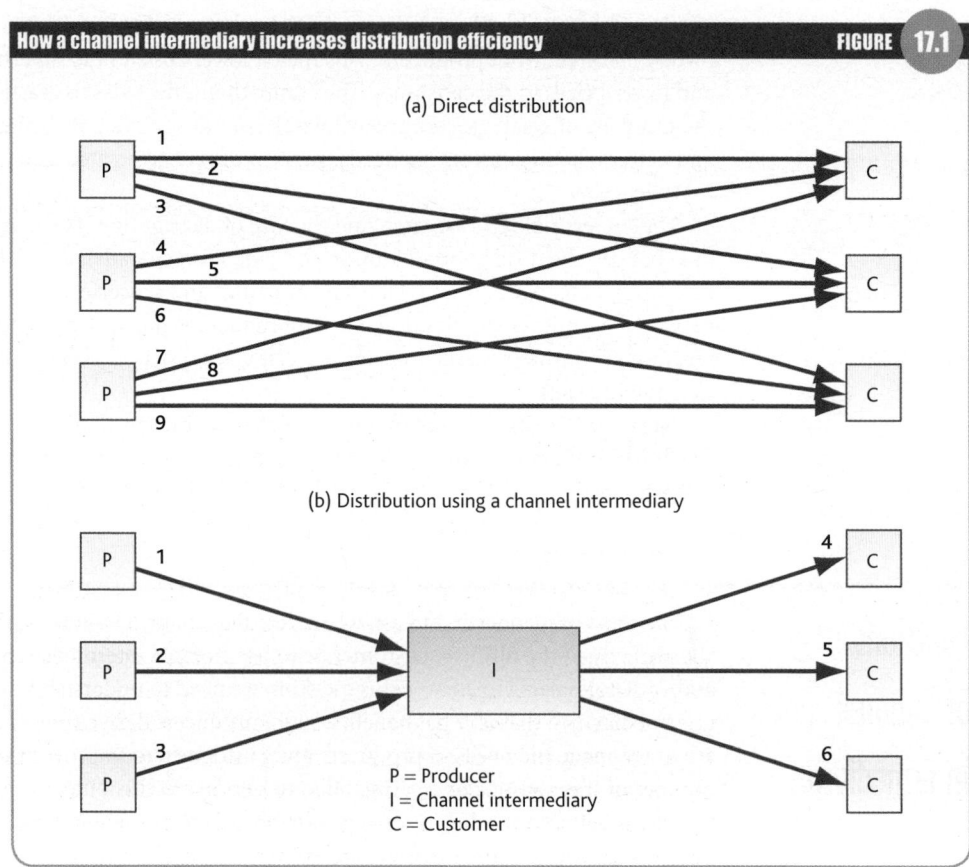

How a channel intermediary increases distribution efficiency   FIGURE 17.1

(a) Direct distribution

(b) Distribution using a channel intermediary

P = Producer
I = Channel intermediary
C = Customer

Small producers can benefit by selling to intermediaries, which then combine a large number of small purchases into bulk for transportation. Without the intermediary it may prove too costly for each small producer to meet transportation costs to the consumer. Agricultural products such as coffee, vegetables and fruit, which are grown by small producers, sometimes benefit from this arrangement.

Improving accessibility

Two major divides that need to be bridged between producers and consumers are the location and time gaps. The *location gap* derives from the geographic separation of producers from the customers they serve. Many of the cars produced in the UK by Nissan and Toyota are exported to Europe. Car dealers in Europe provide customer access to these cars in the form of display and test drive facilities, and the opportunity to purchase locally rather than deal direct with the producer thousands of miles away. The Internet is reducing the location gap, allowing consumers to buy without the need to visit a producer or distributor. Producers can play their part in improving accessibility by making consumers aware of the location of their distributors.

The *time gap* results from discrepancies between when a manufacturer wants to produce goods and when consumers wish to buy. For example, manufacturers of spare parts for cars may wish to produce Monday to Friday but consumers may wish to purchase throughout the week and especially on Saturday and Sunday. By opening at the weekend, car accessory outlets bridge the time gap between production and consumption.

Providing specialist services

Channel intermediaries can perform specialist customer services that manufacturers may feel ill-equipped to provide themselves. Distributors may have long-standing expertise in such areas as selling, servicing and installation to customers. Producers may feel that these functions are better handled by channel intermediaries so that they can specialize in other aspects of manufacturing and marketing activity.

Types of Distribution Channel

All products, whether they be consumer goods, business-to-business goods or services, require a channel of distribution. Business channels tend to be shorter than consumer channels because of the small number of ultimate customers, the greater geographic concentration of customers, and the greater complexity of the products that require close producer–customer liaison. Service channels also tend to be short because of the intangibility of services and the need for personal contact between the service provider and consumer.

Consumer channels

Figure 17.2 shows four alternative consumer channels. Each one is described briefly below.

Producer direct to consumer

Cutting out distributor profit margin may make this option attractive to producers. Direct selling between producer and consumer has been a feature of the marketing of Avon Cosmetics and Dell Computers. As discussed in Chapter 15, direct marketing includes the use of direct mail, telephone selling and direct response advertising.

The Internet is creating new opportunities to supply consumers direct rather than through retailers. Digital Marketing 17.1 discusses the developments in the music industry whereby downloadable music is being offered to consumers via their PCs.

The elimination of a layer of intermediaries from a distribution channel is called *disintermediation*.[3] A major force, as we have seen in the music industry, is the Internet, which

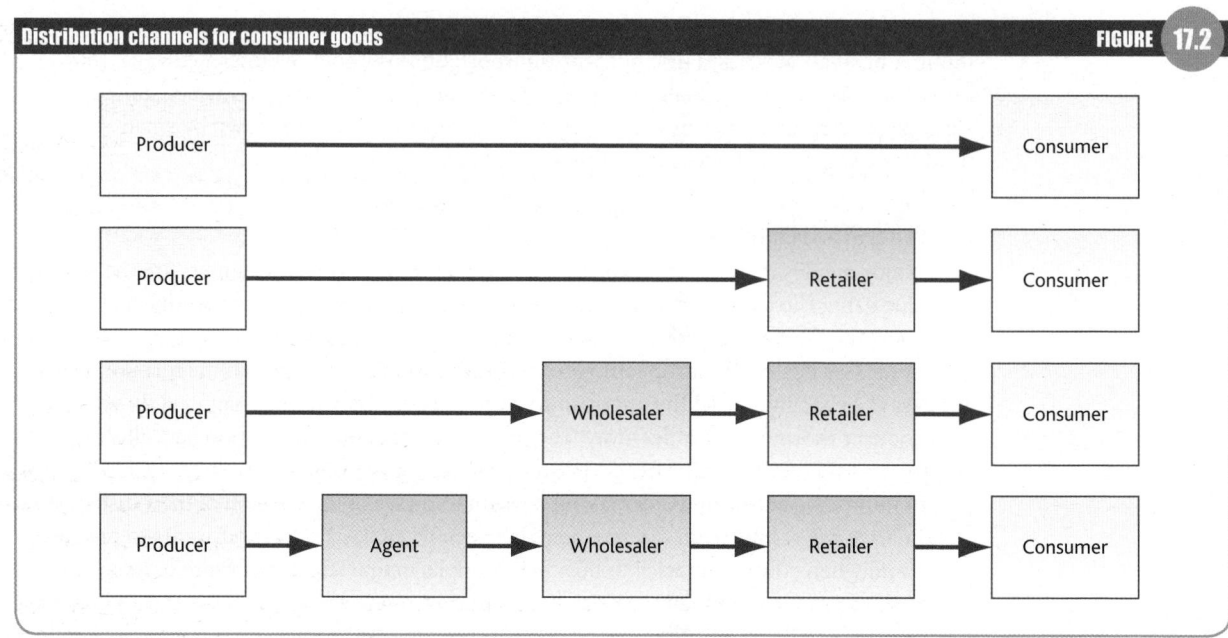

Distribution channels for consumer goods   FIGURE **17.2**

allows direct distribution of music from bands to their fans, bypassing record shops. Airlines such as easyJet and Ryanair have moved towards Internet bookings, eliminating the travel agent. Dell Computers also disintermediated (or eliminated) retailers from the traditional PC distribution channel. A broader definition of disintermediation includes the displacement of traditional channel intermediaries with new forms of distribution. For example, as we saw in the Digital Marketing 17.1, iTunes is displacing record shops in the distribution of music. Disintermediation occurs when a new type of channel intermediary or structure serves customers better than the old channels.

Producer to retailer to consumer

The growth in retailer size has meant that it becomes economic for producers to supply retailers directly rather than through wholesalers. Consumers then have the convenience of viewing and/or testing the product at the retail outlet. Supermarket chains, such as Sainsbury's (see illustration), exercise considerable power over manufacturers because of their enormous buying capabilities. This route to the consumer has changed form, with Internet retailers such as Amazon (books, music, videos, and so on) and expedia (travel and hotel bookings) emerging to compete with traditional retailers. Also, Apple has created its own online retail store, iTunes, to supply music downloads for the iPod, and the App Store to distribute software applications to owners of the iPhone.

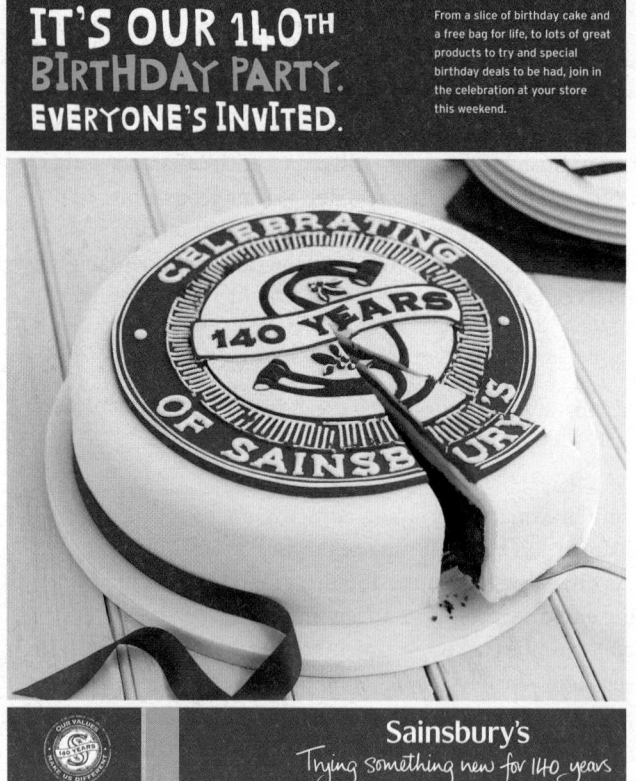

From a slice of birthday cake and a free bag for life, to lots of great products to try and special birthday deals to be had, join in the celebration at your store this weekend.

◀ Sainsbury's has been built into a successful supermarket chain with enormous buying power.

 ## 17.1 Digital Marketing

The Future of Music

Music lovers are no strangers to technological change. Modern generations have already experienced major changes in home entertainment. The rise of the CD to replace vinyl records and the emergence of VHS as a standard for video tapes (now itself superseded by DVD) are some examples. All of these use the same basic delivery platform of a tape or disc inserted into a unit attached to a delivery device (a hi-fi or TV).

In the same way that the Sony Walkman was invented to provide music where and when people wanted it (see the history of the Walkman on www.sony.net/Fun/SH/1-18/h3.html), a new mode of delivery has arrived that was unimaginable even 10 years ago. The rise of the mp3 player (read the history on www.mp3-mac.com/Pages/History_of_MP3.html), with a much greater capacity and improved audio capability, has itself founded a revolution.

The rise of mp3 and later derivatives such as the Apple iPod spawned major changes in the music industry. Following the early years of music file sharing among enthusiasts, typified by the original Napster concept of sharing files at no cost, record companies have improved their service to customers by making legal downloads possible. iTunes (www.apple.com/itunes) is just one example of this. Nokia has also changed the face of music distribution with its Comes with Music service, which offers unlimited music for one year, bundled with a mobile phone, for a one-off fee.

Artists are also breaking ranks to deliver their music direct to their fans. Radiohead offered downloads of their album *In Rainbows* at a price decided by purchasers, including the option to pay nothing. Nine Inch Nails regularly release their music free to download, along with separate tracks of songs for fans to remix. Bands like these now regard albums as promotional devices, with the live gig experience being the real money-maker.

Internet radio stations like Spotify and Last.fm are also challenging the way music is bought, distributed and listened to. Spotify has moved away from the traditional industry formatted playlist and allow users to create their own playlists. Listeners have the choice of paying a subscription, or listening to their self-chosen tracks for free over the Internet while hearing a few advertisements in between.

Clearly, the Internet is now a major music distribution channel, cutting out record shops completely for a large segment of music fans.

Based on: Nettleton (2008);[4] Johnson and Arthur (2009)[5]

 ## 17.1 Pause for Thought

Have you bought a product using the Internet? What were the advantages and disadvantages compared to buying from a traditional retailer?

Producer to wholesaler to retailer to consumer

For small retailers (e.g. small grocery or furniture shops) with limited order quantities, the use of wholesalers makes economic sense. Wholesalers can buy in bulk from producers, and sell smaller quantities to numerous retailers. The danger is that large retailers in the same market have the power to buy directly from producers and thus cut out the wholesaler.

In certain cases, the buying power of large retailers has meant that they can sell products to their customers cheaper than a small retailer can buy from the wholesaler. Longer channels like this tend to occur where retail oligopolies do not dominate the distribution system. In Europe, long channels involving wholesalers are common in France and Italy. In France, for example, the distribution of vehicle spare parts is dominated by small independent wholesalers.[6]

Producer to agent to wholesaler to retailer to consumer

This long channel is sometimes used by companies entering foreign markets. They may delegate the task of selling the product to an agent (who does not take title to the goods). The agent contacts wholesalers (or retailers) and receives commission on sales. Overseas sales of books are sometimes generated in this way.

Some companies use multiple channels to distribute their products. Grocery products, for example, use both producer to wholesaler to retailer (small grocers), and producer to retailer (supermarkets). The advent of the Internet has also encouraged the use of multiple channels. For example, in the tourist industry, package holidays can be booked through travel agencies or via the Internet, and hotels and flights can be booked over the telephone or by using the Internet. Such multi-channel strategies allow companies to differentiate their services to take advantage of the inherent strengths of each channel.[7] For example, the cost savings associated with Internet bookings often mean that lower prices can be offered compared to telephone booking, while booking through travel agencies or by telephone allows queries to be answered and alternatives considered with the help of a member of staff. Multiple channels also provide wide market coverage. For example, mobile handset manufacturers such as Nokia distribute their products through their website, service providers such as Orange, Internet retailers and supermarkets, allowing wide reach of potential customers. Sony also achieves wide distribution coverage by using multiple channels, including its own Sony Centres, electrical goods chain stores such as Comet, catalogue shops such as Argos and online retailers such as Amazon. In Japan, distribution channels to consumers tend to be long and complex, with close relationships between channel members, a fact that has acted as a barrier to entry for foreign companies.

Business-to-business channels

Common business-to-business distribution channels are illustrated in Figure 17.3. Usually a maximum of one channel intermediary is used.

Producer to business customer

Supplying business customers directly is common for expensive industrial products such as gas turbines, diesel locomotives and aero-engines. There needs to be close liaison between supplier and customer to solve technical problems, and the size of the order makes direct selling and distribution economic.

Producer to agent to business customer

Instead of selling to business customers using their own salesforce, a business-to-business goods company could employ the services of an agent who may sell a range of goods from several suppliers (on a commission basis). This spreads selling costs and may be attractive to companies without the reserves to set up their own sales operation. The disadvantage is that there is little control over the agent, who is unlikely to devote the same amount of time selling on products compared with a dedicated sales team.

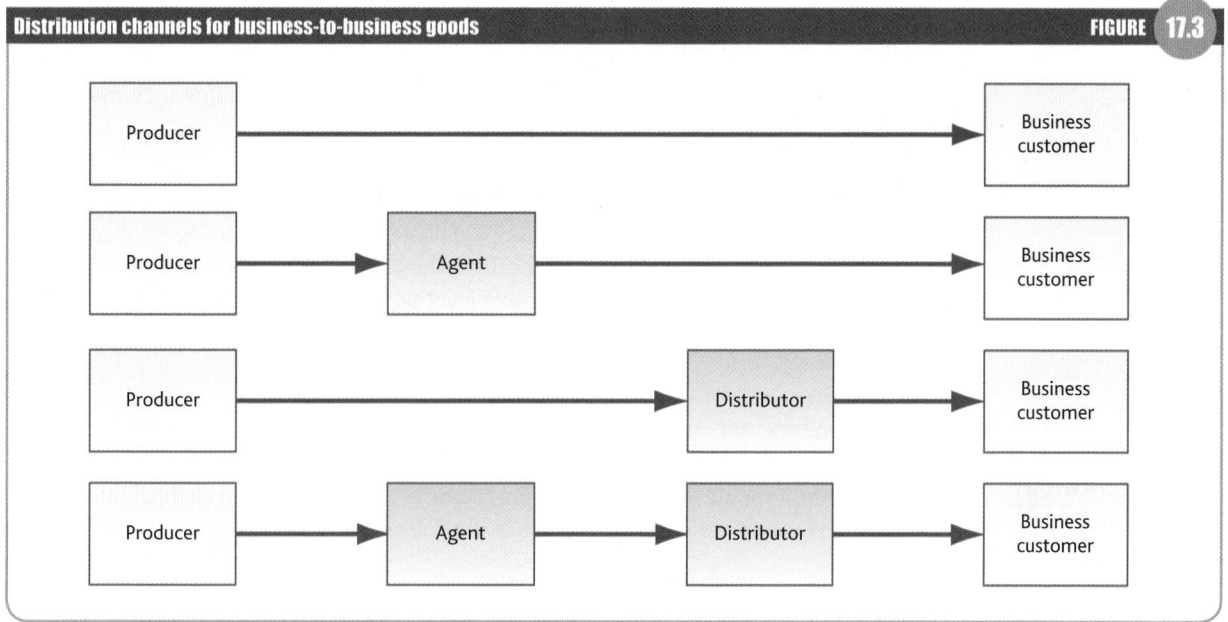

Distribution channels for business-to-business goods   FIGURE 17.3

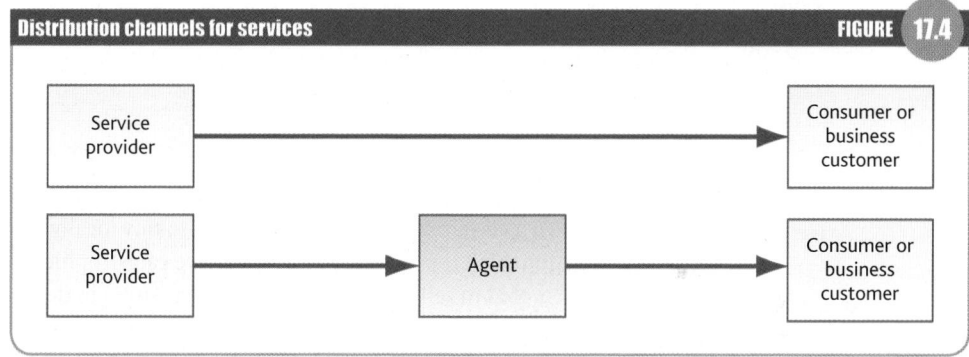

Distribution channels for services   FIGURE 17.4

Producer to distributor to business customer

For less expensive, more frequently bought business-to-business products, distributors are used. These may have both internal and field sales staff.[8] Internal staff deal with customer-generated enquiries and order placing, order follow-up (often using the telephone) and checking inventory levels. Outside sales staff are more proactive: their practical responsibilities are to find new customers, get products specified, distribute catalogues and gather market information. The advantage to customers of using distributors is that they can buy small quantities locally.

Producer to agent to distributor to business customer

Where business customers prefer to call upon distributors, the agent's job will require selling into these intermediaries. The reason why a producer may employ an agent rather than a dedicated salesforce is usually cost based (as previously discussed).

Services channels

Distribution channels for services are usually short: either direct or using an agent. Since stocks are not held, the role of the wholesaler, retailer or industrial distributor does not apply. Figure 17.4 shows the two alternatives whether they be to consumer or industrial customers.

Service provider to consumer or business customer

The close personal relationships between service providers and customers often mean that service supply is direct. Examples include healthcare, office cleaning, accountancy, marketing research and law.

Service provider to agent to consumer or business customer

A channel intermediary for a service company usually takes the form of an agent. Agents are used when the service provider is geographically distant from customers, and where it is not economical for the provider to establish its own local sales team. Examples include insurance, travel, secretarial and theatrical agents.

Channel Strategy

Channel strategy decisions involve the selection of the most effective distribution channel, the most appropriate level of distribution intensity and the degree of channel integration (see Fig. 17.5). Each of these decisions will now be discussed.

Ad insight

Go to the website to see Pilkington's Glass' ad and consider their optimal distribution strategy

Channel selection

Why does Procter & Gamble sell its brands through supermarkets rather than selling direct? Why does General Electric sell its locomotives direct to train operating companies rather than use a distributor? The answers are to be found by examining the following factors that influence *channel selection*. These influences can be grouped under market, producer, product and competitive factors.

Market factors

An important market factor is buyer behaviour: buyer expectations may dictate that the product be sold in a certain way. Buyers may prefer to buy locally and in a particular type of shop. Failure to match these expectations can have catastrophic consequences, as when Levi Strauss attempted to sell a new range of clothing (suits) in department stores, even though marketing research had shown that its target customers preferred to buy suits from independent outlets. The result was that the new range (called Tailored Classics) was withdrawn from the marketplace.

Buyer needs regarding product information, installation and technical assistance also have to be considered. A judgement needs to be made about whether the producer or channel intermediary can best meet these needs in terms of expertise, commitment and cost. For example, products that require facilities for local servicing, such as cars, often use intermediaries to carry out the task. Where the service requirement does not involve large capital investment the producer may carry out the service. For example, suppliers of burglar alarms employ their staff to conduct annual inspection and servicing.

The willingness of channel intermediaries to market a product is also a market-based factor that influences channel decisions. Direct distribution may be the only option if distributors refuse to handle the product. For industrial products, this may mean the recruitment of

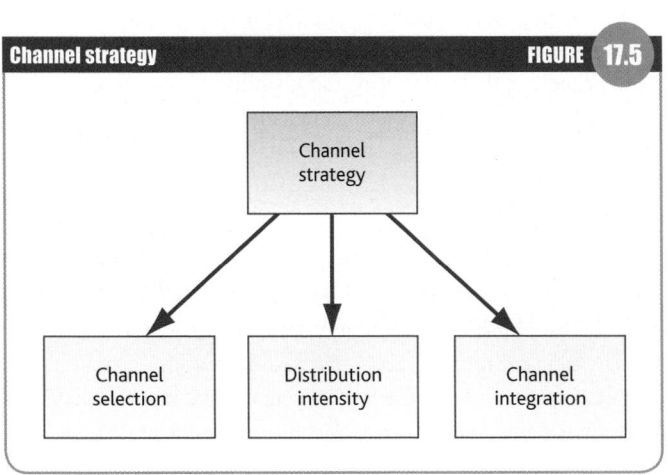

Channel strategy FIGURE 17.5

```
          Channel
          strategy
       /     |     \
      ↓      ↓      ↓
 Channel  Distribution  Channel
selection   intensity  integration
```

salespeople, and for consumer products direct mail may be employed to communicate to and supply customers. The profit margins demanded by wholesalers and retailers, and the commission rates expected by sales agents also affect their attractiveness as channel intermediaries. These costs need to be assessed in comparison with those of a salesforce.

The location and geographical concentration of customers also affects channel selection. The more local and clustered the customer base, the more likely direct distribution is feasible. Direct distribution is also more prevalent when buyers are few in number and buy large quantities. A large number of small customers may mean that using channel intermediaries is the only economical way of reaching them (hence supermarkets).

Producer factors

A constraint on the channel decision is when the producer lacks adequate resources to perform the functions of the channel. Producers may lack the financial and managerial resources to take on channel operations. Lack of financial resources may mean that a salesforce cannot be recruited, and sales agents and/or distributors are used instead. Producers may feel that they do not possess the customer-based skills to distribute their products and prefer to rely on intermediaries.

The product mix offered by a producer may also affect channel strategy. A wide mix of products may make direct distribution (and selling) cost effective. Narrow or single product companies, on the other hand, may find the cost of direct distribution prohibitive unless the product is extremely expensive.

The final product influence is the desired degree of control of channel operations. The use of independent channel intermediaries reduces producer control. For example, by distributing their products through supermarkets, manufacturers lose total control of the price charged to consumers. Furthermore, there is no guarantee that new products will be stocked. Direct distribution gives producers control over such issues.

Product factors

Large complex products are often supplied direct to customers. The need for close personal contact between producer and customer, and the high prices charged, mean that direct distribution and selling is both necessary and feasible. Perishable products such as frozen food, meat and bread require relatively short channels to supply the customer with fresh stock. Finally, bulky or difficult to handle products may require direct distribution because distributors may refuse to carry them if storage or display problems arise.[9]

Competitive factors

If the competition controls traditional channels of distribution—for example, through franchise or exclusive dealing arrangements—an innovative approach to distribution may be required. Two alternatives are to recruit a salesforce to sell direct or to set up a producer-owned distribution network (see the section on vertical marketing systems, under 'Conventional marketing channels', below). Producers should not accept that the channels of distribution used by competitors are the only ways to reach target customers. Direct marketing provides opportunities to supply products in new ways. Increasingly, traditional channels of distribution for personal computers through high-street retailers are being circumvented by direct marketers, who use direct response advertising to reach buyers. The emergence of the more computer-aware and experienced buyer, and the higher reliability of these products as the market reaches maturity has meant that a local source of supply (and advice) is less important.

Distribution intensity

The second channel strategy decision is the choice of *distribution intensity*. The three broad options are intensive, selective and exclusive distribution.

Intensive distribution

Intensive distribution aims to achieve saturation coverage of the market by using all available outlets. With many mass-market products, such as cigarettes, foods, toiletries, beer and newspapers, sales are a direct function of the number of outlets penetrated. This is because consumers have a range of acceptable brands from which they can choose. If a brand is not available in an outlet, an alternative is bought. The convenience aspect of purchase is paramount. New outlets may be sought that hitherto had not stocked the products, such as the sale of confectionery and grocery items at petrol stations.

Selective distribution

Market coverage may also be achieved through **selective distribution**, in which a producer uses a limited number of outlets in a geographical area to sell its products. The advantages to the producer are the opportunity to select only the best outlets to focus its efforts to build close working relationships and to train distributor staff on fewer outlets than with intensive distribution, and, if selling and distribution is direct, to reduce costs. Upmarket aspirational brands are often sold in carefully selected outlets. Retail outlets and industrial distributors like this arrangement since it reduces competition. Selective distribution is more likely to be used when buyers are willing to shop around when choosing products. This means that it is not necessary for a company to have its products available in all outlets. Products such as audio and video equipment, cameras, personal computers and cosmetics may be sold in this way.

Problems can arise when a retailer demands distribution rights but is refused by producers. This happened in the case of Superdrug, a UK discount store chain, which requested the right to sell expensive perfume but was denied by manufacturers who claimed that the store did not have the right ambience for the sale of luxury products. Superdrug maintained that its application was refused because the chain wanted to sell perfumes for less than their recommended prices. A Monopolies and Mergers Commission investigation supported current practice. European rules allow perfume companies to confine distribution to retailers who measure up in terms of décor and staff training. Manufacturers are not permitted to refuse distribution rights on the grounds that the retailer will sell for less than the list price.[10]

Exclusive distribution

This is an extreme form of selective distribution in which only one wholesaler, retailer or industrial distributor is used in a geographic area. Cars are often sold on this basis with only one dealer operating in each town or city. This reduces a purchaser's power to negotiate prices for the same model between dealers since to buy in a neighbouring town may be inconvenient when servicing or repairs are required. It also allows very close cooperation between producer and retailer over servicing, pricing and promotion. Initially, Apple's iPhone was also subject to exclusive distribution in the UK through the mobile phone operator O_2 and retailer the Carphone Warehouse.[11] The right to **exclusive distribution** may be demanded by distributors as a condition for stocking a manufacturer's product line. Similarly, producers may wish for exclusive dealing where the distributor agrees not to stock competing lines. The selection of an exclusive set of distributors can provide the basis for excellent customer service, as Marketing in Action 17.1 explains.

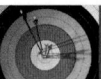

17.1 Marketing in Action

Exclusive Distribution and Service Excellence at Caterpillar

Caterpillar, the tractor manufacturer, is renowned for the quality of its exclusive dealer network. Dealers undergo rigorous selection procedures but, once accepted, are treated royally in order to make them feel part of the Caterpillar family. This is because Caterpillar recognizes the importance of dealer service in backing up its reputation for highly reliable machines. When the inevitable breakdown occurs Caterpillar dealers are quick to move spare parts to anywhere in the USA, no matter how remote, within 24 hours.

Caterpillar dealers regard a breakdown as a potential blight on their family name and will go to any lengths to correct it. Such commitment is well worth the extra cost to Caterpillar of establishing and managing its exclusive distribution network and, together with its product excellence, is the source of the competitive advantage by which its premium prices are justified.

Based on: Nagle and Hogan (2006)[12]

Exclusive dealing can reduce competition in ways that may be considered contrary to consumers' interests. The European Court of Justice rejected an appeal by Unilever over the issue of exclusive outlets in Germany. By supplying freezer cabinets Unilever maintained exclusivity by refusing to allow other competing ice creams into them. Also, Coca-Cola, Schweppes Beverages and Britvic's exclusive ties with the leisure trade (such as sports clubs) were broken by the Office of Fair Trading, making competitive entry easier.[13]

However, the European Court rejected an appeal by the French Leclerc supermarket group over the issue of the selective distribution system used by Yves St Laurent perfumes. The judges found that the use of selective distribution for luxury cosmetic products increased competition and that it was in the consumer's and manufacturer's interest to preserve the image of such luxury products.

Channel integration

Channel integration can range from conventional marketing channels, comprising an independent producer and channel intermediaries, through a franchise operation, to channel ownership by a producer. Producers need to consider the strengths and weaknesses of each system when setting channel strategies.

Conventional marketing channels

The independence of channel intermediaries means that the producer has little or no control over them. Arrangements such as exclusive dealing may provide a degree of control, but separation of ownership means that each party will look after their own interests. Conventional marketing channels are characterized by hard bargaining and, occasionally, conflict. For example, a retailer may believe that cutting the price of a brand is necessary to move stock, even though the producer objects because of brand image considerations.

However, separation of ownership means that each party can specialize in the function in which it has strengths: manufacturers produce, intermediaries distribute. Care needs to be taken by manufacturers to stay in touch with customers and not abdicate this responsibility to retailers.

A manufacturer that dominates a market through its size and strong brands may exercise considerable power over intermediaries even though they are independent. This power may result in an **administered vertical marketing system** where the manufacturer can command considerable cooperation from wholesalers and retailers. Major brand builders such as Procter & Gamble and Lever Brothers had traditionally held great leverage over distribution but, more recently, power has moved towards the large dominant supermarket chains through their purchasing and market power. Marks & Spencer is a clear example of a retailer controlling an administered vertical marketing system. Through its dominant market position it is capable of exerting considerable authority over its suppliers.

Franchising

A **franchise** is a legal contract in which a producer and channel intermediaries agree each member's rights and obligations. Usually, the intermediary receives marketing, managerial, technical and financial services in return for a fee. Franchise organizations such as McDonald's, Benetton, Hertz, the Body Shop and Avis combine the strengths of a large sophisticated marketing-orientated organization with the energy and motivation of a locally owned outlet. Franchising is also commonplace in the car industry, where dealers agree exclusive deals with manufacturers in return for marketing and financial backing. Although a franchise operation gives a degree of producer control there are still areas of potential conflict. For example, the producer may be dissatisfied with the standards of service provided by the outlet, or the franchisee may believe that the franchising organization provides inadequate promotional support. Goal conflict can also arise. For example, some McDonald's franchisees were displeased with the company's rapid expansion programme, which meant that new restaurants opened within a mile of existing outlets. This led to complaints about lower profits and falling franchise resale values.[14] Also, compared with ownership, the franchise organization lacks total control over franchisees. For example, Marriott, which franchises many of its hotels, had to rely on persuasion rather than control when it asked its franchisees to spend more than $1 billion worldwide on new bedding design.[15]

A franchise agreement provides a **contractual vertical marketing system** through the formal coordination and integration of marketing and distribution activities. Some franchise organizations exert a considerable degree of control over marketing operations. For example, Benetton chooses the location of outlets, and determines retail prices, store layout and the colour blocking of the clothes. Some control is also taken over stocking. Some product ranges have to be bought by the franchise and, once purchased, cannot be returned to Benetton. Franchising also shelters the franchiser from some of the financial implications of poor performance. For example, in the USA, 300 of Benetton's shops closed but the company was protected as it did not own any of them.

Three economic explanations of why a producer might choose franchising as a means of distribution have been proposed. Franchising may be a means of overcoming resource constraints, as an efficient system to overcome producer–distributor management problems and as a way of gaining knowledge of new markets.[16] Franchising allows the producer to overcome internal resource constraints by providing access to the franchisee's resources. For example, if the producer has limited financial resources, access to additional finances may come from the franchisee. The second explanation of franchising relates to the problems of managing geographically dispersed operations. In such situations, producers may value the notion of the owner-manager who has a vested interest in the success of the business. Although some control may still be necessary, the franchisee benefits directly from increases in sales and profits and so has a financial incentive to manage the business well. Finally, franchising may be a way for a producer to access the local knowledge of the franchisee. Franchising may therefore be attractive when a producer is expanding into new markets and where potential franchisees have access to information that is important in penetrating such markets.

Franchising can occur at four levels of the distribution chain.

1   *Manufacturer and retailer*: the car industry is dominated by this arrangement. The manufacturer gains retail outlets for its cars and repair facilities without the capital outlay required by ownership.

2   *Manufacturer and wholesaler*: this is commonly used in the soft drinks industry. Manufacturers such as Schweppes, Coca-Cola and Pepsi grant wholesalers the right to make up and bottle their concentrate in line with their instructions, and to distribute the products within a defined geographic area.

3   *Wholesaler and retailer*: this is not as common as other franchising arrangements but is found with car products and hardware stores. It allows wholesalers to secure distribution of their product to consumers.

4   *Retailer and retailer*: an often used method that frequently has its roots in a successful retailing operation seeking to expand geographically by means of a franchise operation, often with great success. Examples include McDonald's, Benetton, Pizza Hut and KFC.

Channel ownership

Total control over distributor activities comes with channel ownership. This establishes a **corporate vertical marketing system**. By purchasing retail outlets, producers control their purchasing, production and marketing activities. In particular, control over purchasing means a captive outlet for the manufacturer's products. For example, the purchase of Pizza Hut and KFC by Pepsi has tied these outlets to the company's soft drinks brands. Channel ownership is common in the clothing industry, with companies such as Zara and H&M owning their own chains of retail outlets.

The advantages of control have to be weighed against the high price of acquisition and the danger that the move into retailing will spread managerial activities too widely. Nevertheless corporate vertical marketing systems have operated successfully for many years in the oil industry where companies such as Shell and BP own not only considerable numbers of petrol stations but also the means of production.

Channel Management

Once the key channel strategy decisions have been made, effective implementation is required. Specifically, a number of channel management issues must be addressed (see Fig. 17.6). These are the selection, motivation, training and evaluation of channel members, and managing conflict between producers and channel members.

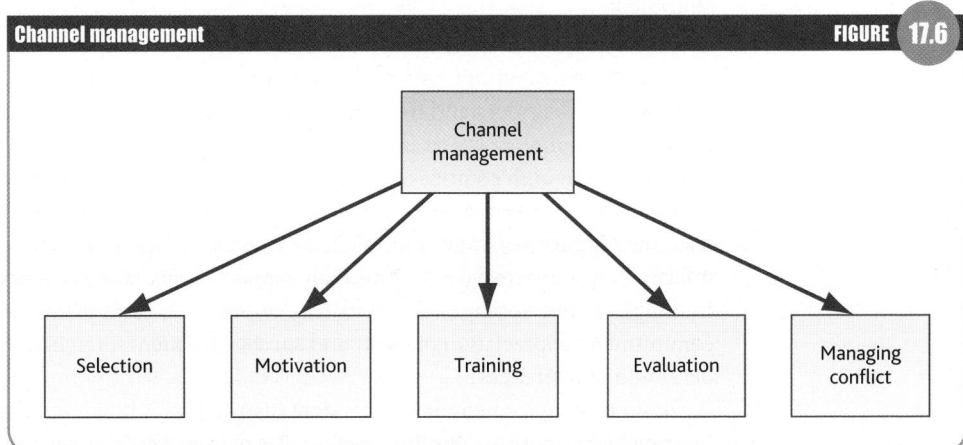

Channel management   FIGURE 17.6

Selection

For some producers (notably small companies) the distribution problem is not so much channel selection as channel acceptance. Their task is to convince key channel intermediaries (especially retailers) to stock their products. However, let us assume that we have a certain amount of discretion in choosing specific channel members to distribute our product. Selection then involves identifying candidates and developing *selection criteria*.

Identifying sources

Sources for identifying candidates include trade sources, reseller enquiries, customers of distributors and the field salesforce.[17] *Trade sources* include trade associations, exhibitions and trade publications. Talking to trade associations can lead to the supply of names of prospective distributors. Other trade publications may be published commercially and the names of possible distributors may be compiled. Exhibitions provide a useful means of meeting and talking to possible distributors. Sometimes channel members may be proactive in contacting a producer to express an interest in handling their products. Such *reseller enquiries* show that the possible distributor is enthusiastic about the possibility of a link. *Customers of distributors* are a useful source since they can comment on their merits and limitations. Finally, if a producer already has a *field salesforce* calling on intermediaries, salespeople are in a good position to seek out possible new distributors in their own territory.

The use of target country-based distributors is a common method of foreign market entry in Europe. A study of the sources of identifying overseas distribution found that the five most common methods were personal visits to search the market, the national trade board, customer and colleagues' recommendations, and trade fairs.[18]

Developing selection criteria

Common selection criteria include market, product and customer knowledge, market coverage, quality and size of the salesforce (if applicable), reputation among customers, financial standing, the extent to which competitive and complementary products are carried, managerial competence and hunger for success, and the degree of enthusiasm for handling the producer's lines. In practice, selection may be complex because large, well-established distributors may carry many competing lines and lack enthusiasm for more. Smaller distributors, on the other hand, may be less financially secure and have a smaller salesforce but be more enthusiastic and hungry for success. The top selection criteria of overseas distributors are market knowledge, enthusiasm for the contract, hunger for success, customer knowledge, and the fact that the distributor does not carry competitors' products.

Motivation

Once selected, channel members need to be motivated to agree to act as a distributor, and allocate adequate commitment and resources to the producer's lines. The key to effective motivation is to understand the needs and problems of distributors since needs and motivators are linked. For example, a distributor that values financial incentives may respond more readily to high commission than one that is more concerned with having an exclusive territory. Possible motivators include financial rewards, territorial exclusivity, providing resource support (e.g. sales training, field sales assistance, provision of marketing research information, advertising and promotion support, financial assistance and management training) and developing *strong work relationships* (e.g. joint planning, assurance of long-term commitment, appreciation of effort and success, frequent interchange of views and arranging distributor conferences).

In short, management of independent distributors is best conducted in the context of informal partnerships.[19] Producers should seek to develop strong relationships with their distributors based on a recognition of their performance and integrated planning and operations. For example, jointly determined sales targets could be used to motivate and evaluate salespeople, who might receive a bonus on achievement. A key element in fostering a spirit of partnership is to provide assurances of a long-term business relationship with the distributor (given satisfactory performance). This is particularly important in managing overseas distributors as many fear that they will be replaced by the producer's own salesforce once the market has been developed. The effort to develop partnerships appears to be worthwhile: a study of Canadian exporters and their British distributors found that success was related to partnership factors like joint decision-making, and close and frequent contact with distributors.[20]

The most popular methods cited by export managers and directors to motivate their overseas distributors were territorial exclusivity, provision of up-to-date product and company information, regular personal contact, appreciation of effort and understanding of the distributors' problems, attractive financial incentives, and provision of salespeople to support the distributors' salesforce.[21] Given overseas distributors' fears that they may be replaced, it was disappointing to note that only 40 per cent of these exporters provided assurances of a long-term business commitment to their distributors as a major motivator.

Mutual commitment between channel members is central to successful relationship marketing. Two types of commitment are affective commitment that expresses the extent to which channel members like to maintain their relationship with their partners, and calculative commitment where channel members need to maintain a relationship. Commitment is highly dependent on interdependence and trust between the parties.[22]

Training

The need to train channel members obviously depends on their internal competences. Large-market supermarket chains, for example, may regard an invitation by a manufacturer to provide marketing training as an insult. However, many smaller distributors have been found to be weak on sales management, marketing, financial management, stock control and personnel management, and may welcome producer initiatives on training.[23] From the producer's perspective, training can provide the necessary technical knowledge about a supplier company and its products, and help to build a spirit of partnership and commitment.

However, the training of overseas distributors by British exporters appears to be the exception rather than the rule.[24] When training is provided, it usually takes the form of product and company knowledge. Nevertheless when such knowledge is given it can help to build strong personal relationships and give distributors the confidence to sell those products.

Evaluation

The evaluation of channel members has an important bearing on distributor retention, training and motivation decisions. Evaluation provides the information necessary to decide which channel members to retain and which to drop. Shortfalls in distributor skills and competences may be identified through evaluation, and appropriate training programmes organized by producers. Where a lack of motivation is recognized as a problem, producers can implement plans designed to deal with the root causes of demotivation (e.g. financial incentives and/or fostering a partnership approach to business).[25]

It needs to be understood, however, that the scope and frequency of evaluation may be limited where power lies with the channel member. If producers have relatively little power because they are more dependent on channel members for distribution than channel members are on individual producers for supply, in-depth evaluation and remedial action will be restricted. Channel members may be reluctant to spend time providing the producers with comprehensive information on which to base evaluation. Remedial action may be limited to tentative suggestions when producers suspect there is room for improvement.

Where manufacturer power is high, through having strong brands and many distributors from which to choose, evaluation may be more frequent and wider in scope. Channel members are more likely to comply with the manufacturer's demands for performance information and agree for their sales and marketing efforts to be monitored by the manufacturer.

Evaluation criteria include sales volume and value, profitability, level of stocks, quality and position of display, new accounts opened, selling and marketing capabilities, quality of service provided to customers, market information feedback, ability and willingness to meet commitments, attitudes and personal capability.

Although the evaluation of overseas distributors and agents is more difficult than that for their domestic counterparts, two studies have shown that over 90 per cent of producers do carry out evaluation, usually at least once a year.[26] For distributors, sales-related criteria were most widely applied, with sales volume, sales value and creating new business three of the top four most commonly applied measures. Channel inputs were also widely used, with provision of market feedback, customer services, selling/marketing inputs and keeping commitments cited frequently. Given the importance of distributors in marketing to Europe, it is important that such evaluation takes place. However, a somewhat disappointing finding was that, with the exception of value of sales, less than half of the exporters used mutually *agreed objectives* to evaluate performance. Such a method is consistent with the partnership approach to channel management, and provides clarity and commitment to objectives since both parties have contributed to setting them. The most common method was to *compare against past performance,* which requires great care to ensure that account is taken of changes in the competitive environment over time.

Managing conflict

When producers and channel members are independent, conflict inevitably occurs from time to time. The intensity of conflict can range from occasional, minor disagreements that are quickly forgotten, to major disputes that fuel continuous bitter relationships.[27]

Sources of channel conflict

The major sources of *channel conflict* are differences in goals, differences in views on the desired product lines carried by channel members, multiple distribution channels, and inadequacies in performance.

- *Differences in goals*: most resellers attempt to maximize their own profit. This can be accomplished by improving profit margin, reducing inventory levels, increasing sales, lowering expenses and receiving greater allowances from suppliers. In contrast, producers might benefit from lower margins, greater channel inventories, higher promotional expenses and fewer allowances given to channel members. These inherent conflicts of interest mean that there are many potential areas of disagreement between producers and their channel members.

- *Differences in desired product line*: resellers that grow by adding product lines may be regarded as disloyal by their original suppliers. For example, WHSmith a UK retailer, originally specialized in books, magazines and newspapers but has grown by adding new product lines such as computer games, DVDs and PC accessories. This can cause resentment among its primary suppliers, who perceive the reseller as devoting too much effort to selling secondary lines. Alternatively, retailers may decide to specialize by reducing their product range. For example, in Europe there has been a growth in the number of speciality shops selling, for example, athletics footwear. A sports outlet that decides to narrow its product range will wish to increase the assortment of the specialized items that make it distinct. This can cause conflict with its original suppliers of these product lines since the addition of competitors' brands makes the retailer appear disloyal.[28]

- *Multiple distribution channels*: in trying to achieve market coverage, a producer may use multiple distribution channels. For example, a producer may decide to sell directly to key accounts because their size warrants a key account salesforce, and use channel intermediaries to give wide market coverage. Conflict can arise when a channel member is denied access to a lucrative order from a key account because it is being serviced directly by the producer. Disagreements can also occur when the producer owns retail outlets that compete with independent retailers that also sell the producer's brands. For example, Clarks, a footwear manufacturer, owns a chain of outlets that compete with other shoe outlets that sell Clarks' shoes.[29]
- *Inadequacies in performance*: an obvious source of conflict is when parties in the supply chain do not perform to expectations. For example, a channel member may underperform in terms of sales, level of inventory carried, customer service, standards of display and salesperson effectiveness. Producers may give poor delivery, inadequate promotional support, low profit margins, poor-quality goods and incomplete shipments. These can all be potential areas of conflict.

Avoiding and resolving conflict

How can producers and channel members avoid and resolve conflict? There are several ways of managing conflict.

- *Developing a partnership approach*: this calls for frequent interaction between producer and resellers to develop a spirit of mutual understanding and cooperation. Producers can help channel members with training, financial help and promotional support. Distributors, in turn, may agree to mutually agreed sales targets and provide extra sales resources. The objective is to build confidence in the manufacturer's products and relationships based on trust. When conflicts arise there is more chance they will be resolved in a spirit of cooperation. Organizing staff exchange programmes can be useful in allowing each party to understand the problems and tensions of the other to avoid giving rise to animosity.
- *Training in conflict handling*: staff who handle disputes need to be trained in negotiation and communication skills. They need to be able to handle high-pressure conflict situations without resorting to emotion and *blaming behaviour*. Instead, they should be able to handle such situations calmly and be able to handle concession analysis, in particular the identification of *win-win situations*. These are situations where both the producer and reseller benefit from an agreement.
- *Market partitioning*: to reduce or eliminate conflict from multiple distribution channels, producers can try to partition markets on some logical basis, such as customer size or type. This can work if channel members accept the basis for the partitioning. Alternatively, different channels can be supplied with different product lines. For example, Hallmark sells its premium greetings cards under its Hallmark brand name to upmarket department stores, and its standard cards under the Ambassador name to discount retailers.[30]
- *Improving performance*: many conflicts occur for genuine reasons. For example, poor delivery by manufacturers or inadequate sales effort by distributors can provoke frustration and anger. Rather than attempt to placate the aggrieved partner, the most effective solution is to improve performance so that the source of conflict disappears. This is the most effective way of dealing with such problems.
- *Channel ownership*: an effective but expensive way of resolving conflicting goals is to buy the other party. Since producer and channel member are under common ownership, the common objective is to maximize joint profits. Conflicts can still occur but the dominant partner is in a position to resolve them quickly. Some producers in Europe have integrated with channel intermediaries successfully. For example, over 40 per cent of household furniture is sold through producer-owned retail outlets in Italy.[31]

- *Coercion*: In some situations, conflict resolution may be dependent on coercion, where one party forces compliance through the use of force. For example, producers can threaten to withdraw supply, deliver late or withdraw financial support; channel members, on the other hand, can threaten to delist the manufacturer's products, promote competitive products and develop own-label brands. In Europe, the increasing concentration of retailing into groups of very large organizations has meant that the balance of power has moved away from the manufacturers. The development of own-label brands has further strengthened the retailers' position, while giving them the double advantage of a high profit margin (because their purchase price is low) and a low price to the customer. Manufacturers' power in the supply chain is increased when they are large with high market share. By having a large and loyal customer base, manufacturers' brands become essential for distributors to stock. This increases manufacturers' negotiating power. Also by dominating a product category (e.g. Unilever and Procter & Gamble in detergents) manufacturers gain power over distributors. By using multiple channels of distribution (e.g. direct as well as through distributors) and using a wide selection of distributors, the power of any one distributor is reduced. Control over distributors can also be gained by franchising and channel ownership (where manufacturers own retail outlets).

Physical Distribution

In the first part of this chapter we examined channel strategy and management decisions, which concern the choice of the correct outlets to provide product availability to customers in a cost-effective manner. Physical distribution decisions focus on the efficient movement of goods from producer to intermediaries and the consumer. Clearly, channel and physical distribution decisions are interrelated, although channel decisions tend to be made earlier.

Physical distribution is defined as a 'set of activities concerned with the physical flows of materials, components and finished goods from producer to channel intermediaries and consumers'.

The aim is to provide intermediaries and customers with the right products, in the right quantities, in the right locations, at the right time. Physical distribution activities have been the subject of managerial attention for some time because of the potential for cost savings and improving customer service levels. Cost savings can be achieved by reducing inventory levels, using cheaper forms of transport and shipping in bulk rather than small quantities. Customer service levels can be improved by fast and reliable delivery, including just-in-time delivery, holding high inventory levels so that customers have a wide choice and the chances of stock-outs are reduced, fast order processing, and ensuring products arrive in the right quantities and quality.

In the clothing industry, fast-changing fashion demands mean that companies such as H&M and Zara use extremely short lead times to create a competitive advantage over their slower, more cumbersome, rivals. The methods used by H&M are discussed in Case 2 (at the end of Chapter 1) and the Zara distribution operation is discussed in Marketing in Action 17.2.

Physical distribution management concerns the balance between cost reduction and meeting customer service requirements. Trade-offs are often necessary. For example, low inventory and slow, cheaper transportation methods reduce costs but lower customer service levels and satisfaction. Determining this balance is a key marketing decision as physical distribution can be a source of competitive advantage. A useful approach is to analyse the market in terms of customer service needs and price sensitivity. The result may be the discovery of two segments:

- segment 1—low service needs, high price sensitivity
- segment 2—high service needs, low price sensitivity.

17.2 Marketing in Action

Managing the Supply Chain the Zara Way

Zara, the Spanish clothing company, has revolutionized the fashion industry. Its key competitive advantage lies in its ability to match fashion trends that change quickly. This relies on an extremely fast and responsive supply chain. While other retailers moved production to the Far East to save money, Zara knew that it could make its best-selling clothes faster in Spain.

Zara uses its stores to find out what consumers want, what styles are selling, what colours are in demand, and which items are hot sellers and which are failures. The data is fed back to Zara headquarters through a sophisticated marketing information system. At the end of each day, Zara sales assistants report to the store manager using wireless headsets to communicate inventory levels. The store managers then inform the Zara design and distribution departments at headquarters about what consumers are buying, asking for and avoiding. Top-selling items are requested and low-selling items are withdrawn from shops within a week. There is a big incentive for the store managers to get it right, as up to 70 per cent of their salary is based on commission.

Garments are made in small production runs to avoid overexposure, and no item stays in the shops for more than four weeks, which encourages Zara shoppers to make repeat visits. Whereas the average high-street store in Spain expects shoppers to visit on average three times a year, Zara shoppers visit up to 17 times.

The company's designers use the feedback from the stores when preparing new designs. The fabrics are cut and dyed at Zara's own highly automated manufacturing facilities, which gives it control over this part of the supply chain. Seamstresses in 350 independently owned workshops in Spain and Portugal stitch about half of the pre-cut pieces into garments; the other half are stitched in-house. Only basic items such as T-shirts are bought from low-cost regions such as eastern Europe, Africa and Asia. Although wages are higher in Spain, Zara saves time and money on shipping.

The finished garments are sent back to Zara's headquarters with its state-of-the-art logistics centre where they are electronically tagged, quality checked and sorted into distribution lots for shipping to their destinations. Although Zara supplies every market from warehouses in Spain, it manages to get new merchandise to European stores within 24 hours, and, by flying goods via commercial airlines, to stores in the Americas and Asia in 48 hours or less.

So efficient are Zara's production and distribution systems that the average turnaround time from design to delivery is 10 to 15 days, with around 12,000 garments being marketed each year. In this way, Zara stays on top of fashion trends rather than being outpaced by the market. And, by producing smaller batches of clothing, it adds an air of exclusivity that encourages customers to shop often. As a result, the chain does not have to slash prices by 50 per cent, as rivals often do, to move mass quantities of out-of-season stock. Since Zara is more in tune with current looks, it can also charge slightly more than, for example, Gap, which it has now overtaken to become the world's largest clothing retailer.

Based on: Anonymous (2002);[32] Roux (2002);[33] BBC (2003);[34] Mitchell (2003);[35] Jobber and Fahy (2006);[36] Capell (2008)[37]

Unipart was first to exploit segment 2 in the do-it-yourself car repair and servicing market. It gave excellent customer service ('The answer's yes. Now what's the question?') but charged a high price. This analysis, therefore, defined the market segment to target and the appropriate marketing mix. Alternatively, both segments could be targeted with different marketing mixes. In business-to-business markets, large companies may possess their own service facilities while smaller firms require producer or distributor service as part of the product offering and are willing to pay a higher price. For example, Norsk Kjem, a Norwegian chemical company, discovered that the market for one of its product lines—wetting agents used in many processes to promote the retention and even distribution of liquids—was segmented in this way.[38] Small firms had less technical expertise and lower price sensitivity, and they ordered smaller quantities than larger companies. This meant that Norsk Kjem required different physical distribution (including service levels) and price structures for the two market segments.

17.2 Pause for Thought

Think of a retail outlet that has given you excellent service. What did it do especially well? Has that encouraged you to use it again? Think of another situation, when a retail outlet has given you poor service. What did it do badly and have you visited it again?

Not only are there trade-offs between physical distribution costs and customer service levels, but there are also possible conflicts between elements of the physical distribution system itself. For example, an inventory manager may favour low stocks to reduce costs, but if this leads to stock-outs this may raise costs elsewhere: the freight manager may have to accept higher costs resulting from fast freight deliveries. Low-cost containers may lower packaging costs but raise the cost of goods damaged in transit. This fact, and the need to coordinate order processing, inventory and transportation decisions, mean that physical distribution needs to be managed as a system with a manager overseeing the whole process. A key role that the physical distribution manager would perform would be to reconcile the conflicts inherent in the system so that total costs are minimized subject to required customer service levels.

The Physical Distribution System

A system is a set of connected parts managed in such a way that overall objectives are achieved. The physical distribution system contains the following parts (see Fig. 17.7).

- *Customer service*: What level of customer service should be provided?
- *Order processing*: How should the orders be handled?
- *Inventory control*: How much inventory should be held?
- *Warehousing*: Where should the inventory be located? How many warehouses should be used?
- *Transportation*: How will the products be transported?
- *Materials handling*: How will the products be handled during transportation?

Companies like DHL provide specialist expertise in these areas. Each of the above questions will now be explored.

Customer service

Customer service standards need to be set. For example, a customer service standard might be that 90 per cent of orders are delivered within 48 hours of receipt and 100 per cent are delivered within 72 hours.

Higher customer service standards normally mean higher costs as inventory levels need to be higher. Since inventory ties up working capital, the higher the inventory level the higher

Components of the physical distribution system   FIGURE 17.7

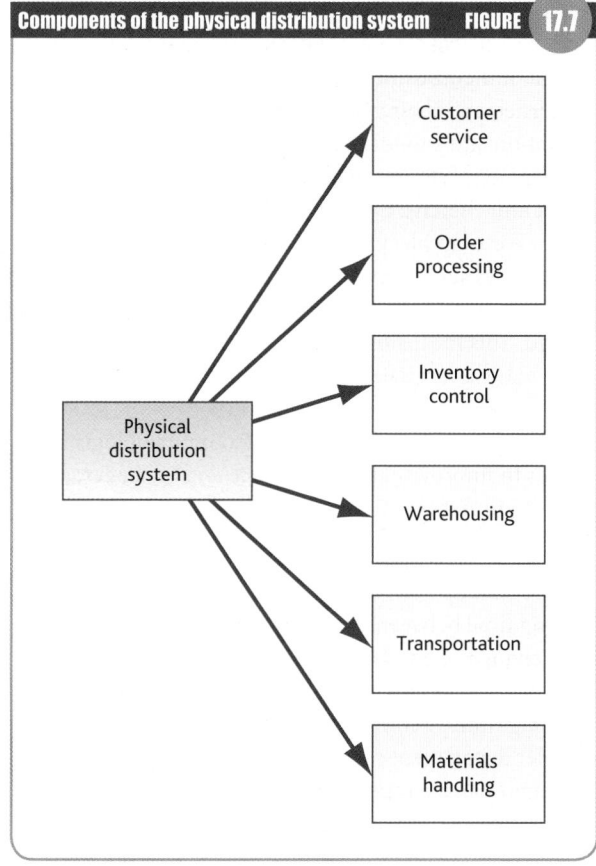

Components of the physical distribution system   FIGURE 17.7

the working capital charge. The physical distribution manager needs to be aware of the costs of fulfilling various customer service standards (e.g. 80, 90 and 100 per cent of orders delivered within 48 hours) and the extra customer satisfaction that results from raising standards.

In some cases customers value consistency in delivery time rather than speed. For example, a customer service standard of guaranteed delivery within five working days may be valued more than that of 60 per cent within two, 80 per cent within five or 100 per cent within seven days. Since the latter standard requires delivery at 60 per cent within two days it may require higher inventory levels than the former. Therefore, by understanding customer requirements, it may be possible to increase satisfaction while lowering costs.

Customer service standards should be given considerable attention because they may be the differentiating factor between suppliers: they may be used as a key customer choice criterion. Methods of improving customer service standards in physical distribution are listed in Table 17.1. By examining ways of improving product availability and order cycle time, and raising information levels and flexibility, considerable goodwill and customer loyalty can be created. The advertisement for UPS explains how it provides excellent service, versatility and a portfolio of shipping solutions.

The Internet is providing the means of improving customer service for some distribution companies. For example, if a customer of Federal Express wants to track a package over the Internet, it simply types 'FedEx' and the package number. On the computer screen will appear where it is, who signed for it and what time it was delivered. Also, since the customer no longer needs to call

Methods of improving customer service standards in physical distribution	TABLE 17.1
Improve product availability Raise in-stock levels Improve accuracy, speed and reliability of deliveries	
Improve order cycle time Shorten time between order and delivery Improve consistency between order and delivery time	
Raise information levels Improve salesperson information on inventory Raise information levels on order status Be proactive in notifying customer of delays	
Raise flexibility Develop contingency plans for urgent orders Ensure fast reaction time to unforeseen problems (e.g. stolen goods, damage in transit)	

ANYTHING, ANYWHERE

UPS is the world's largest express carrier. We have 100 years of service and the widest portfolio of shipping solutions. From international freight to small packages, you can rest assured that we'll allow you to deliver more.

www.ups.com

Deliver more

▲ UPS communicates its excellent service, versatility and portfolio of shipping solutions.

Federal Express, it is saving FedEx $10 million a year.[39] The main logistical companies—FedEx, UPS and DHL—take over half of their business-to-business transactions over the Internet, and their websites provide customer information and support as well as online tracking.

Technology has also enabled logistics to become more efficient and effective through satellite-based distribution systems. For example, Cemex, which makes ready-to-pour concrete, uses such a system to track its trucks. When customers place or change orders, trucks can be re-routed, if needed. This means that customers waste less time waiting and Cemex has become more efficient in supplying them.[40]

Another trend is towards the outsourcing of logistical activities to improve customer service and efficiency, as Marketing in Action 17.3 explains.

Order processing

Reducing time between a customer placing an order and receiving the goods may be achieved through careful analysis of the components that contribute to the order-processing time. A computer link between salesperson and order department may be effective. Electronic data interchange can also speed order-processing time by checking the customer's credit rating, and whether the goods are in stock, issuing an order to the warehouse, invoicing the customer and updating the inventory records. Marketing in Action 17.2, on Zara, discusses some European developments.

Many *order-processing systems* are inefficient because of unnecessary delays. Basic questions can spot areas for improvement, such as what happens when a sales representative receives an order? What happens when it is received in the order department? How long does it take to check inventory? What are the methods for checking inventory? Many companies are moving to computer-based systems to bring efficiency to this area.

Inventory control

Inventory levels can be a source of conflict between finance and marketing management. Since inventory represents costs, financial managers seek stock minimization; marketing management, acutely aware of the customer problems caused by stock-outs, want large inventories. In reality a balance has to be found, particularly as inventory cost rises at an increasing rate as customer service standards near 100 per cent. This means that to always have in stock every conceivable item that a customer might order would normally be prohibitively expensive for companies marketing many items. One solution to this problem is to separate items into those that are in demand and those that are slower-moving. This is sometimes called the 80:20 rule since for many companies 80 per cent of sales are achieved by 20 per cent of products. A high customer service standard is then set for the high-demand 20 per cent (e.g. in stock 95 per cent of the time) but a much lower standard used for those items less in demand (e.g. in stock 70 per cent of the time).

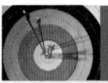

17.3 Marketing in Action

Outsourcing Logistics at Michelin

In an effort to improve efficiency and customer service, Michelin has outsourced its entire distribution system to TNT, a global player in logistics, in North America. TNT runs Michelin's entire network of tyre distribution centres in the United States and Canada. TNT's internal logistics design team redesigned the distribution network and improved material flow, resulting in greater efficiencies and costs savings in outbound distribution to Michelin's retail outlets throughout North America. Three 'super distribution centres' have been established to further improve distribution efficiency.

The benefit of outsourcing is that Michelin gains the specialist expertise of TNT. A possible drawback is that Michelin's control over its distribution network is reduced. Even so, the arrangement appears to be working well, with the distribution centres consistently meeting or exceeding the targets set by Michelin, and the partnership winning an 'outstanding excellence award' from The Outsourcing Center in the USA.

Based on: Grant et al. (2006);[41] www.tntlogistics.com[42]

Two related *inventory decisions* are knowing when and how much to order so that stocks are replenished. As inventory for an item falls, a point is reached when new stock is required. Unless a stock-out is tolerated the *order point* will be before inventory reaches zero. This is because there will be a *lead time* between ordering and receiving inventory. The *just-in-time inventory system* (discussed in Chapter 5) is designed to reduce lead times so that the order point (the stock level at which reordering takes place), and overall inventory levels for production items, are low. The key to the just-in-time system is the maintenance of a fast and reliable lead time so that deliveries of supplies arrive shortly before they are needed.

The order point depends on three factors: the viability of the order lead time, fluctuation in customer demand, and the customer service standard. The more variable the lead time between ordering and receiving stock, and the greater the fluctuation in customer demand, the higher the order point. This is because of the uncertainty caused by the variability, leading to the need for **safety (buffer) stocks** in case lead times are unpredictably long or customer demand unusually high. The higher the customer service standard, the higher the need for safety stocks, and hence the higher the order point. A simple inventory control system is shown in Figure 17.8.

How much to order depends on the cost of holding stock and order-processing costs. Orders can be small and frequent or large and infrequent. Small, frequent orders raise order-processing costs but reduce inventory-carrying costs; large, infrequent orders raise inventory costs but lower order-processing expenditure. Therefore a trade-off between the two costs is required to achieve an **economic order quantity** (EOQ), the point at which total costs are lowest. Its calculation is shown diagrammatically in Figure 17.9. Numerically it can be calculated as follows:

$$EOQ = \sqrt{\frac{2DO}{IC}}$$

where
D = annual demand in units
O = cost of placing an order
I = annual inventory cost as percentage of the cost of one unit
C = cost of one unit of the product

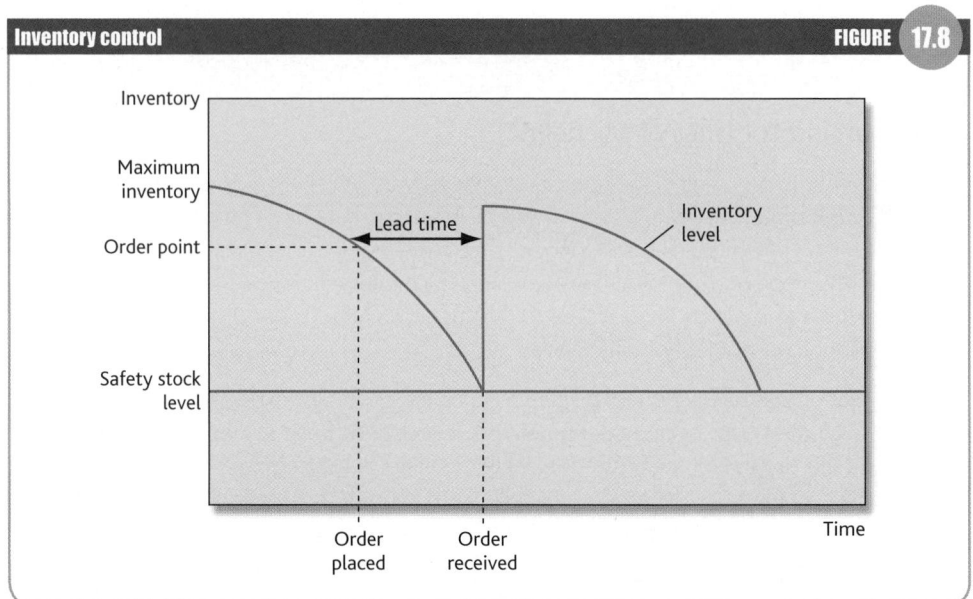

Inventory control   FIGURE 17.8

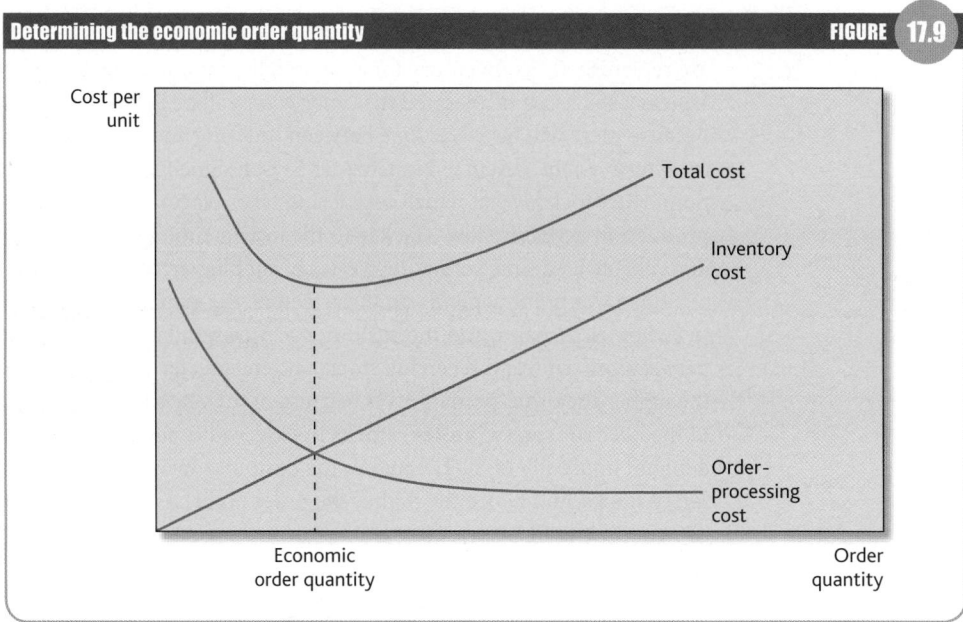

Determining the economic order quantity   FIGURE 17.9

As an example let us assume that:

Annual demand = 4000 units
Cost of placing an order = £4
Per unit annual inventory cost = 20p or 10 per cent of the unit cost (£2)
Cost of one unit = £2

$$\text{EOQ} = \sqrt{\frac{2 \times 4000 \times 4}{0.10 \times 2}} = \sqrt{\frac{32000}{0.20}}$$

$$= \sqrt{160000} = 400 \text{ units per order}$$

Therefore the most economic order size, taking into account inventory and order-processing costs, is 400 units.

Suppliers can build strong relationships with their customers through automated inventory restocking systems, as Marketing in Action 17.2, on Zara, describes.

Warehousing

Warehousing involves all the activities required in the storing of goods between the time they are produced and the time they are transported to the customer. These activities include breaking bulk, making up product assortments for delivery to customers, storage and loading. *Storage warehouses* hold goods for moderate or long time periods whereas *distribution centres* operate as central locations for the fast movement of goods. Retailing organizations use regional distribution centres where suppliers bring products in bulk. These shipments are broken down into loads, which are then quickly transported to retail outlets. Distribution centres are usually highly automated with computer-controlled machinery facilitating the movement of goods. A computer reads orders and controls forklift trucks that gather goods and move them to loading bays.

Warehousing strategy involves the determination of the location and the number of warehouses to be used. At one extreme is one large central warehouse to serve the entire market; at the other is a number of smaller warehouses that are based near to local markets. In Europe, the removal of trade barriers between countries of the EU has reduced transportation time and costs. This change, together with distribution focus being on regional rather than national markets, has fuelled the trend towards fewer, larger warehouses where economies of scale can reduce costs. As with most physical distribution decisions, the optimum number and location of warehouses is a balance between customer service and cost considerations. Usually the more locally based warehouses a company uses, the better the customer service but the higher the cost.

The need for greater efficiency in the supply chain has led to a new generation of warehouse management systems. In traditional warehouse systems, goods are logged in manually and time is wasted chasing paperwork and correcting errors, while stock gets mislaid and pallets mixed up. Warehouse management systems use IT to organize, optimize and, ultimately, replace the labour-intensive tasks of receiving goods and selecting items for orders. In Europe, Lever Fabergé has adopted such systems to virtually eliminate errors and take advantage of such features as paperless picking via radio data terminals, advanced shipping notification and real-time order status checking. Customers can do their own order process checking, if they wish, and receive pre-delivery advice via the Internet.[43]

Transportation

Customer service ultimately depends on the ability of the physical distribution system to transport products on time and without damage. Timely delivery is even more important with the group use of the just-in-time system. Therefore the choice of *transportation mode* is vital to the successful implementation of marketing strategy. The five major transport methods are rail, road, air, water and pipelines. Each has its strengths and limitations.

Rail

Railways are efficient at transporting large, bulky freight on land over large distances. Rail is often used to transport coal, chemicals, oil, aggregates and nuclear flasks. A problem, though, is lack of flexibility. For many companies the use of rail would mean transport by lorry to and from a rail depot. Furthermore for small quantities the use of rail may prove uneconomic. In the UK British Rail withdrew its Speedlink service in which container loads of various goods from different producers were combined into one rail load. However, the building of the Channel Tunnel between Britain and mainland Europe has given a boost to rail transport. British Rail and French railway company SNCF have built freight terminals to encourage rail transport across the Channel.

Rail is more environmentally friendly than road and is ideally suited to freight when it moves 400 kilometres or more in large regular quantities from supplier's siding to customer's siding. Where there is no siding, the journey is usually costlier than road, and more likely to incur theft or damage to goods in transit. Furthermore, distributors of foodstuffs and perishables are obliged by health authorities to transport their products at controlled temperatures. They may be reluctant to rely on freight as it may be difficult to access if delayed.

Road

Motorized transport by road has the advantage of flexibility because of direct access to companies and warehouses. This means that lorries can transport goods from supplier to receiver without unloading en route. Furthermore, the speed of road transport in Europe has increased since the advent of the EU, with the removal of cross-border restrictions.[44] However, the growth of road transport in Europe, and particularly the UK, has received considerable criticism because of increased traffic congestion and the damage done to roads by heavy juggernauts.

Air

The key advantages of air freight are its speed and long-distance capabilities. Its speed means that it is often used to transport perishable goods and emergency deliveries. Furthermore, in a period when companies are seeking to reduce inventories, air freight can be used to supply inventories under just-in-time systems. With the growth in international trade, air freight is predicted to be a growth activity. Its major disadvantages are high cost and the need to transport goods by road to and from air terminals.

Water

Water transportation is slow but inexpensive. Inland transportation is usually associated with bulky, low-value, non-perishable goods such as coal, ore, grain, steel and petroleum. Ocean-going ships carry a wider range of products. When the cost benefits of international sea transportation outweigh the speed advantage of air freight, water shipments may be chosen. A large proportion of long-haul deliveries between Europe and the Pacific Rim is by sea transport. As with air freight, water transport normally needs road transportation of goods to and from docks.

Pipeline

Pipelines are a dependable and low-maintenance form of transportation for liquids and gases. However, their construction is expensive and time consuming. They are usually associated with natural gas, water and crude petroleum. Ownership is in the hands of the companies that use them.

Materials handling

Materials handling involves the activities related to the moving of products in the producer's plant, warehouses and transportation depots. Modern storage facilities tend to be of one storey, allowing a high level of automation. In some cases, robots are used to conduct materials-handling tasks. Lowering the human element in locating inventory and assembling orders has reduced error and increased the speed of these operations.

Two key developments in materials handling are unit handling and containerization. *Unit handling* achieves efficiency by combining multiple packages on to pallets that can be moved by forklift trucks. *Containerization* involves the combining of many quantities of goods (e.g. car components) into a single large container. Once sealed they can easily be transferred from one form of transport to another. For example, a container could be loaded on to a lorry and taken to a rail freight terminal to form part of a train load of containers destined for the docks. There the container can easily be transferred to a ship for transportation to a destination thousands of miles away. Since individual items are not handled, damage in transit is reduced.

An important element in materials handling is the quality of packaging. It is necessary to evaluate not only the appearance and cost of packaging, but also the ability to repackage into larger quantities for transportation. Packages must be sturdy enough to withstand the rigours of physical distribution, such as harsh handling and stacking.

Ethical Issues in Distribution

Five key ethical issues in distribution are the use of slotting allowances, grey markets, exclusive dealing, restrictions on supply, and fair trading.

Slotting allowances
The power shift from manufacturers to retailers in the packaged consumer goods industry has meant that slotting allowances are often demanded to take products. A slotting allowance is a fee paid to a retailer in exchange for an agreement to place a product on the retailer's shelves. Critics argue that they represent an abuse of power and work against small manufacturers who cannot afford to pay the fee. Retailers argue that they are simply charging rent for a valuable, scarce commodity: shelf space.[45]

Grey markets
These occur when a product is sold through an unauthorized distribution channel. When this occurs in international marketing the practice is called parallel importing. Usually a distributor buys goods in one country (where prices are low) and sells them in another (where prices are high) at below the going market price. This causes anger among members of the authorized distribution channel, who see their prices being undercut. Furthermore, the products may well be sold in downmarket outlets that discredit the image of the product, which has been built up by high advertising expenditures. Nevertheless, supporters of grey markets argue that they encourage price competition, increase consumer choice and promote the lowering of price differentials between countries.

Exclusive dealing
This is a restrictive arrangement whereby a manufacturer prohibits distributors that market its products from selling the products of competing suppliers. The act may restrict competition and restrict the entry of new competitors and products into a market. It may be found where a large supplier can exercise power over weaker distributors. The supplier may be genuinely concerned that anything less than an exclusive agreement will mean that insufficient effort will be made to sell its products by a distributor and that unless such an agreement is reached it may be uneconomic to supply the distributor.

Restrictions in supply
A concern of small suppliers is that the power of large manufacturers and retailers will mean that they are squeezed out of the supply chain. In the UK, farmers and small grocery suppliers have joined forces to demand better treatment from large supermarket chains, which are forging exclusive deals with major manufacturers. They claim the problem is made worse by the growth of category management where retailers appoint 'category captains' from their suppliers, who act to improve the standing of the whole product category such as breakfast

cereals or confectionery. The small suppliers believe this forces them out of the category altogether as category captains look after their own interests. They would like to see a system similar to that in France where about 10 per cent of shelf space is by law given to small suppliers.[46]

Fair trading

One problem of free market forces is that when small commodity producers are faced with large powerful buyers the result can be very low prices. This can bring severe economic hardship to the producers, who may be situated in countries of the developing world. In the face of a collapse in world coffee prices, a fair trading brand, Cafédirect, was launched. The company was founded on three principles: to influence positively producers' income security, to act as an example and catalyst for change, and to improve consumer understanding of fair trade values. It pays suppliers a minimum price for coffee beans, pegged above market fluctuations and provides tailor-made business support and development programmes. The fashion industry has been the subject of fair trade criticism over the years, but several new initiatives have now been launched to improve its ethical position, as Marketing Ethics and Corporate Social Responsibility in Action 17.1 discusses.

17.1 Marketing Ethics and Corporate Social Responsibility in Action

Implementing Ethics in the Fashion Industry

The fashion industry has been widely criticized for ethical issues related to inappropriate labour conditions and animal welfare. With the launch of the book *No Logo* in 2000, sweatshop conditions in garment production lines were brought to the fore, and much attention has been devoted to high-street brands' unethical sourcing, manufacturing and supply chain practices ever since. High-profile campaigns have criticized companies such as Gap, Nike, Adidas and, more recently, Primark, for fostering disposable fashion, and due to the precarious working conditions of the people they employ in developing countries. Many corporations targeted by activists have had to improve their labour standards in order to salvage their reputations.

The push for more ethical standards within the fashion industry is now coming from high-fashion designers and the government. London Fashion Week 2009 witnessed the launch of UK Government-backed Estethica, a showcase of ethical fashion designer labels. The aim was to raise the profile of eco-fashion as cutting edge, and each of the 37 designers in the showcase had to comply with at least one of Estethica's organic, fair trade and recycled principles. SCAP, the Sustainable Clothing Action Plan, was also launched. Developed by key names in fashion manufacturing, SCAP sets the blueprint for more sustainable fashion, considering the issues that arise in fashion design, sourcing of materials, manufacture, retailing and disposal. The key objectives of SCAP are to reduce the environmental and social impact of disposable fashion, and to cut down on the tons of clothing that end up in landfill each year. As a result, big retailers, such as Marks & Spencer, Sainsbury's and Tesco, have committed to increase their ranges of clothing made with organic, fairly traded and recyclable fabrics, while the latter also intends to ban the use of cotton from countries that use child labour.

Charities, too, have committed to improving their retail outlets and offerings of second-hand clothing, and the Centre for Sustainable Fashion at the London College of Fashion will receive funding to give practical support to the clothing industry. Such initiatives also seek to show that fashion, luxury, sexiness and style can be harmoniously coupled with ethical supply chain and retail practices. However, will consumers be seduced by the ethical features of their garments?

Based on: Fox (2009);[47] Rosselson (2009)[48]

When you have read this chapter

log on to the Online Learning Centre at www.mcgraw-hill.co.uk/textbooks/jobber to explore chapter-by-chapter test questions, links and further online study tools for marketing.

Review

1 The functions and types of channels of distribution
- The functions are to reconcile the needs of producers and consumers, improving efficiency, improving accessibility and providing specialist services.
- Four types of consumer channel are producer direct to consumer, producer to retailer to consumer, producer to wholesaler to retailer to consumer, and producer to agent to wholesaler to retailer to consumer.
- Four types of industrial channels are producer to industrial customer, producer to agent to industrial customer, producer to distributor to industrial customer, and producer to agent to distributor to industrial customer.
- Two types of service channel are service provider to consumer or industrial customer, and service provider to agent to consumer or industrial customer.

2 How to determine channel strategy
- Channel strategy should be determined by making decisions concerning the selection of the most effective distribution channel, the most appropriate level of distribution intensity and the correct degree of channel integration.

3 The three components of channel strategy: channel selection, intensity and integration
- Channel selection is influenced by market factors (buyer behaviour, ability to meet buyer needs, the willingness of channel intermediaries to market a product, the profit margins required by distributors and agents compared with the costs of direct distribution, and the location and geographic concentration of customers), producer factors (lack of resources, the width and depth of the product mix offered by a producer, and the desired level of control of channel operations), product factors (complexity, perishability, extent of bulkiness and difficulty of handling), and competitive factors (need to choose innovative channels because traditional channels are controlled by the competition or because a competitive advantage is likely to result).
- Channel intensity options are intensive distribution to achieve saturated coverage of the market by using all available outlets, selective distribution, where a limited number of outlets in a geographical area are used, and exclusive distribution, which is an extreme form of selective distribution where only one wholesaler, retailer or industrial distributor is used in a geographic area.
- Channel integration can range from conventional marketing channels (where there is separation of ownership between producer and distributor, although the manufacturer power of channel intermediaries may result in an administered vertical marketing system), franchising (where a legal contract between producers and channel intermediaries defines each party's rights and obligations, leading to a contractual marketing system) and channel ownership (where the manufacturer takes control over distributor activities through ownership, leading to a corporate vertical marketing system).

4 The five key channel management issues: member selection, motivation, training, evaluation and conflict management
- Selection of members involves identifying sources (the trade, reseller enquiries, customers of distributors and the field salesforce) and establishing selection criteria (market coverage, quality and size of the salesforce, reputation, financial standing, extent of competitive and complementary products, managerial competence, hunger for success, and enthusiasm).

- Motivation of distributors involves understanding the needs and problems of distributors, and methods include financial rewards, territorial exclusivity, providing resource support, the development of strong work relationships (possibly in the context of informal partnerships).
- Training may be provided where appropriate. It can provide the necessary technical knowledge about a supplier company and its products, and help to build a spirit of partnership and commitment.
- Evaluation criteria include sales volume and value, profitability, level of stocks, quality and position of display, new accounts opened, selling and marketing capabilities, quality of service, market information feedback, willingness and ability to meet commitments, attitudes and personal capability. Evaluation should be based on mutually agreed objectives.
- Conflict management sources are differences in goals, differences in desired product lines, the use of multiple distribution channels by producers, and inadequacies in performance. Conflict-handling approaches are developing a partnership approach, training in conflict handling, market partitioning, improving performance, channel ownership and coercion.

5 **The cost–customer service trade-off in physical distribution**

- Physical distribution management concerns the balance between cost reduction and meeting customer service requirements. An example of a trade-off is incompatibility between low inventory and slow, cheaper transportation methods that reduce costs, and the lower customer service levels and satisfaction that results.

6 **The components of a physical distribution system: customer service, order processing, inventory control, warehousing, transportation and materials handling**

- The system should be managed so that its components combine to achieve overall objectives. Management needs to answer a series of questions related to each component: customer service (What levels of service should be provided?); order processing (How should orders be handled?); inventory control (How much inventory should be held?); warehousing (Where should the inventory be located and how many warehouses should be used?); transportation (How will the products be transported?); materials handling (How will the products be handled during transportation?).

7 **How to improve customer service standards in physical distribution**

- Customer service standards can be raised by improving product availability (e.g. by increasing inventory levels), improving order cycle time (e.g. faster order processing), raising information levels (e.g. information on order status) and raising flexibility (e.g. fast reaction time to problems).

8 **Ethical issues in distribution**

- There are potential problems relating to slotting allowances, grey markets, exclusive dealing, restrictions on supply, and fair trading.

Key Terms

administered vertical marketing system a channel situation where a manufacturer that dominates a market through its size and strong brands may exercise considerable power over intermediaries even though they are independent

channel integration the way in which the players in the channel are linked

channel intermediaries organizations that facilitate the distribution of products to customers

channel of distribution the means by which products are moved from the producer to the ultimate consumer

channel strategy the selection of the most effective distribution channel, the most appropriate level of distribution intensity and the degree of channel integration

contractual vertical marketing system a franchise arrangement (e.g. a franchise) that ties together producers and resellers

corporate vertical marketing system a channel situation where an organization gains control of distribution through ownership

economic order quantity the quantity of stock to be ordered where total costs are at the lowest

exclusive distribution an extreme form of selective distribution where only one wholesaler, retailer or industrial distributor is used in a geographical area to sell the products of a supplier

franchise a legal contract in which a producer and channel intermediaries agree each other's rights and obligations; usually the intermediary receives marketing, managerial, technical and financial services in return for a fee

intensive distribution the aim of this is to provide saturation coverage of the market by using all available outlets

safety (buffer) stocks stocks or inventory held to cover against uncertainty about resupply lead times

selective distribution the use of a limited number of outlets in a geographical area to sell the products of a supplier

Study Questions

1. What is the difference between channel decisions and physical distribution management? In what ways are they linked?

2. Of what value are channels of distribution? What functions do they perform?

3. The best way of distributing an industrial product is direct from manufacturer to customer. Discuss.

4. Why is channel selection an important decision? What factors influence choice?

5. What is meant by the partnership approach to managing distributors? What can manufacturers do to help build partnerships?

6. Describe situations that can lead to conflict between channel members. What can be done to avoid and resolve conflict?

7. Why is there usually a trade-off between customer service and physical distribution costs? What can be done to improve customer service standards in physical distribution?

8. A distributor wishes to estimate the economic order quantity for a spare part. Annual demand is 5000 units, the cost of placing an order is £5, and the cost of one spare part is £4. The per-unit annual inventory cost is 50p. Calculate the economic order quantity.

9. Unlike advertising, the area of distribution is free from ethical concerns. Discuss.

References

1. Bunwell, S. (2005) One Channel, Many Paths, *The Mobile Channel*, supplement to *Marketing Week*, 7 June, 5.
2. Coughlan, A., E. Anderson, L. W. Stern and A. I. El-Ansany (2005) *Marketing Channels*, Englewood Cliffs, NJ: Prentice-Hall, 6.
3. Mills, J. F. and V. Camek (2004) The Risks, Threats and Opportunities of Disintermediation: A Distributor's View, *International Journal of Physical Distribution and Logistics Management* 34(9), 714–27.
4. Nettleton, K. (2008) Why Radiohead is in Tune with Online Marketing, *Campaign*, 1 August, 9.
5. Johnson, B. and C. Arthur (2009) Is Spotify the Future of Listening to Music? Not if Record Labels Can Help It, *Guardian*, 12 February, 13.

6. Dudley, J. W. (1990) *1992 Strategies for the Single Market*, London: Kogan Page, 327.

7. Wikström, S. (2005) From E-channel to Channel Mix and Channel Integration, *Journal of Marketing Management* 21, 725–53.

8. Narus, J. A. and J. C. Anderson (1986) Industrial Distributor Selling: The Roles of Outside and Inside Sales, *Industrial Marketing Management* 15, 55–62.

9. Rosenbloom, B. (1987) *Marketing Channels: A Management View*, Hinsdale, IL: Dryden, 160.

10. Laurance, B. (1993) MMC in Bad Odour Over Superdrug Ruling, *Guardian*, 12 November, 18.

11. Ritson, M. (2008) iPhone Strategy: No Longer a Grey Area, *Marketing*, 11 June, 21.

12. Nagle, T. T. and J. E. Hogan (2006) *The Strategy and Tactics of Pricing*, Upper Saddle River, NJ: Pearson.

13. Meller, P. (1992) Isostar Enters the Lucozade League, *Marketing*, 2 July, 9.

14. Helmore, E. (1997) Restaurant Kings or Just Silly Burgers, *Observer*, 8 June, 5.

15. Lambert, K. (2005) Marriott Hip? Well, It's Trying, *Business Week*, 26 September, 79.

16. Hopkinson, G. C. and S. Hogarth Scott (1999) Franchise Relationship Quality: Microeconomic Explanations, *European Journal of Marketing* 33(9/10), 827–43.

17. Rosenbloom (1987) op. cit.

18. Shipley, D. D., D. Cook and E. Barnett (1989) Recruitment, Motivation, Training and Evaluation of Overseas Distributors, *European Journal of Marketing* 23(2), 79–93.

19. Shipley, Cook and Barnett (1989) op. cit.

20. Rosson, P. and I. Ford (1982) Manufacturer: Overseas Distributor Relations and Export Performance, *Journal of International Business Studies* 13, Fall, 57–72.

21. Shipley, Cook and Barnett (1989) op. cit.

22. Kumar, N., L. K. Scheer and J.-B. E. M. Steenkamp (1995) The Effects of Perceived Interdependence on Dealer Attitudes, *Journal of Marketing Research* 32 (August), 248–56.

23. See Shipley, D. D. and S. Prinja (1988) The Services and Supplier Choice Influences of Industrial Distributors, *Service Industries Journal* 8(2), 176–87; Webster, F. E. (1976) The Role of the Industrial Distributor in Marketing Strategy, *Journal of Marketing* 40, 10–16.

24. Shipley, Cook and Barnett (1989) op. cit.

25. See Pegram, R. (1965) *Selecting and Evaluating Distributors*, New York: National Industrial Conference Board, 109–25; Shipley, Cook and Barnett (1989) op. cit.

26. Philpot, N. (1975) Managing the Export Function: Policies and Practice in Small and Medium Companies, *Management Survey Report No. 16*, British Institute of Management; Shipley, Cook and Barnett (1989) op. cit.

27. Magrath, A. J. and K. G. Hardy (1989) A Strategic Paradigm for Predicting Manufacturer–Reseller Conflict, *European Journal of Marketing* 23(2), 94–108.

28. Magrath and Hardy (1989) op. cit.

29. Magrath and Hardy (1989) op. cit.

30. Hardy, K. G. and A. J. Magrath (1988) Ten Ways for Manufacturers to Improve Distribution Management, *Business Horizons*, Nov.–Dec., 68.

31. Magrath and Hardy (1989) op. cit.

32. Anonymous (2002) Chain Reaction, *Economist*, 2 February, 1–3.

33. Roux, C. (2002) The Reign of Spain, *Guardian*, 28 October, 6–7.

34. BBC (2003) Store Wars: Fast Fashion, *The Money Programme*, 19 February.

35. Mitchell, A. (2003) When Push Comes to Shove, It's All About Pull, *Marketing Week*, 9 January, 26–7.

36. Jobber, D. and J. Fahy (2009) *Foundations of Marketing*, Maidenhead: McGraw-Hill.

37. Capell, K. (2008) Zara Thrives By Breaking All the Rules, *Business Week*, 20 October, 66.

38. Hardy, K. G. (1985) *Norsk Kjem A/S Case Study*, University of Western Ontario, Canada.

39. Barksdale, J. (1996) Microsoft Would Like to Squash Me Like a Bug, *Financial Times*, Special Report on IT, 2 October, 2.

40. Sawhney, M. (2005) Technology is the Secret of an Agile Advantage, *Financial Times*, 24 August, 10.

41. Grant, D. B., D. M. Lambert, J. R. Stock and L. S. Ellram (2006) *Fundamentals of Logistics Management*, Maidenhead: McGraw-Hill.

42. www.tntlogistics.com/en/press_office/press_releases/archive_2004/20040526-tnt-log.

43. Nairn, G. (2002) More Than Just Boxing Clever, *Financial Times IT Review*, 2 October, 7.

44. Samiee, S. (1990) Strategic Considerations of the EC 1992 Plan for Small Exporters, *Business Horizons*, March–April, 48–56.

45. Schlegelmilch, B. (1998) *Marketing Ethics: An International Perspective*, London: International Thomson Business Press.

46. McCawley, I. (2000) Small Suppliers Seek Broader Shelf Access, *Marketing Week*, 17 February, 20.

47. Fox, I. (2009) London on Parade to Show that Ethical Clothes Can Cut it on the Catwalk, Guardian.co.uk, 21 February 2009 (retrieved 3 April 2009, from www.guardian.co.uk/lifeandstyle/2009/feb/21/london-fashion-week-ethical-fashion/print).

48. Rosselson, R. (2009) Inertia Means We're Failing to Boycott the Least Ethical Clothing Companies, Guardian.co.uk, 16 March 2009 (retrieved 4 April 2009, from www.guardian.co.uk/environment/ethicallivingblog/2009/mar/12/boycott-unethical-fashion).

ASOS

Setting the Pace in Online Fashion

ASOS is the UK's largest online-only fashion retailer. The company has experienced phenomenal growth based on showing young shoppers how to emulate the designer looks of celebrity magazine favourites such as Victoria Beckham, Lindsay Lohan and Jennifer Lopez, at a fraction of the cost.

ASOS was founded in 2000 by Nick Robertson. In 1996 he set up a business called Entertainment Marketing to place products in films and television programmes. By 2000 he was running a website called AsSeenOnScreen, showing and selling brands that were used in films and on TV—from a pair of Oakley sunglasses worn by Tom Cruise in *Mission Impossible* to a pestle and mortar used by Jamie Oliver the TV chef. But it was fashion that proved the biggest success, and Robertson decided to focus on that. ASOS was born.

The company offers 20,000 branded and own-label product lines from dresses to menswear, a much wider range than that offered by other online rivals such as Topshop and New Look. Its key target market is women aged 18–34, with half the online retailer's customers aged under 25—they demand new items to choose from and ASOS provides this. Stock turnover (the speed at which items are replaced) is nine weeks, ensuring that visitors to the site are rewarded with new items on offer.

The company has its own design team and prefers to use suppliers based in Europe rather than the Far East. Between 60 and 70 per cent of its stock is made in Europe. This means that, from spotting a celebrity wearing a new style of dress, ASOS designers and buyers are in a position to have similar ones made and ready to sell in four weeks.

The ASOS website

A major factor in the success of ASOS is its website. Visitors to the site can click on their favourite celebrity or pop star and view clothes they have been seen in. Perhaps a shopper prefers the style of Kate Moss. The cheapest way to emulate this is not to visit ASOS's bricks-and-mortar competitor Topshop but to choose a £6 ASOS Lurex vest 'in the style of' the London supermodel. At any one time on the website there are 400 styles of dresses, plus mountains of tops, trousers, shoes, bags, lingerie, swimwear and jewellery, and an entire men's section, all of which is modelled by people walking on a catwalk. At ASOS headquarters in north London, there are four studios where a pool of 30 models attempt to bring the clothes to life and transmit the excitement of the catwalk to the consumer.

The range of brands has expanded from own-label celebrity lookalike items to include its own luxury brand, together with well-established labels such as Gap, Christian Dior, Ted Baker, Balenciaga and YSL. The website attracts 4.5 million visitors a month, with around 2 million registered users and 1.2 million active customers (those who have bought within the past six months), who place orders worth on average £60. Women's fashion items make up the vast majority of sales. Menswear accounts for 15 per cent of sales, with beauty and cosmetics a further 3 per cent.

One problem with buying online rather than in a traditional retail outlet is that returns are higher. An average catalogue company experiences about 40 per cent returns, but ASOS achieves the much lower figure of 22 per cent.

Customer service

ASOS aims for fast speed of delivery and, when a delay is foreseeable, every effort is made to contact the customer. For example, when snow was forecast e-mails were sent warning customers of probable delays. When it did snow, an apology e-mail was sent, offering a delivery refund and 10 per cent off next orders. The customer care team is available 24 hours a day. They are required to reply to customer enquiries within an hour, and are assessed by the speed and quality of their reply.

Promotion

ASOS's success has provided many opportunities for PR activity in newspapers, including quarterly reports on record profits and sales, and features on the reasons for the company's success. It avoids advertising in traditional media, preferring digital. Search engine optimization and pay-per-click advertising on women's magazine sites such as those of *Look* and *Grazia* help to generate traffic to its site. Social networking also plays a part in raising awareness. ASOS is the second largest UK fan group for any fashion retailer on Facebook (behind H&M).

ASOS's largest marketing expenditure is on a print magazine, which is carefully targeted to reach 500,000 active customers. It showcases well-known brands as well as its own brands, and photos are blended with editorial content to rival the standards of newsstand glossies. This is supplemented by 24-page supplements in magazines such as *Glamour* and *Cosmopolitan*. ASOS achieves 44 per cent awareness among its target market.

New ventures

The company has launched a number of extensions from the core brand.

- ASOS Marketplace: this allows customers to sell their own clothes and accessories on the ASOS site, whether they are recycling their clothes for cash or opening a boutique to sell their own designs. ASOS receives commission on sales.
- Little ASOS: this site caters for babies and children aged two to six years. As well as stocking ranges from high-fashion brands such as Diesel and Tommy Hilfiger, Little ASOS offers a number of boutique and independent labels such as Cath Kidston and No Added Sugar.

- ASOS Outlet: this is the discount arm of ASOS, offering end-of-line and previous-season products at discounts of up to 75 per cent.
- ASOS Life: this allows customers to create their own profiles and communicate through forums, blogs and groups. The site includes a help forum that allows customers to answer each other's questions, and an ideas section that lets customers submit suggestions for site improvements.

References

Based on: ASOS.com http://en.wikipedia.org/w/index; Finch, J. (2008) Nick Robertson: Wannabe Celebs Provide the Silver on Screen, *Guardian*, 18 April, 31; Kollewe, J. (2008) ASOS Defies Shopping Gloom by Reaching Height of Online Fashion, *Guardian*, 18 November, 32; Barda, T. (2009) Winning Looks, *The Marketer*, April, 24–7; Armstrong, L. (2009) ASOS.com: As Seen on the Screens of the Fashion Savvy, *The Times*, 21 January, 26

Questions

1. Discuss the advantages and disadvantages of marketing fashion items online rather than through traditional retail stores.
2. Perform a strengths, weaknesses, opportunities and threats (SWOT) analysis on ASOS.
3. Based on the SWOT analysis, what are your recommendations for ASOS?

This case was written by David Jobber, Professor of Marketing, University of Bradford.

iTunes

Facing the Threat of Nokia

Apple's iTunes (www.itunes.com) has been a remarkable success, thanks in large part to the success of the Apple iPod, the super-cool digital music jukebox. The success of iTunes is altering the very foundations of the entertainment industry and has transformed the fortunes of Apple Computer. Consumers have flocked in their droves to the Internet to download, both legally and illegally, copyrighted music material. The digital music revolution has changed the way people listen to, use and obtain their favourite music.

Apple was seen as a fading star on the technology landscape, whose success was slowly ebbing. The inspired launch of a portable digital music jukebox has turned out to be a stroke of genius and a huge revenue earner for the firm. When launched, it was seen as a nice, complementary product for the Apple Computer product range; now it has become an integral part of the company's future. Now Apple iTunes could represent the future for the company, transforming it from a computer maker to a global online retailer of digital content. Much in the same way Sony became synonymous with the Walkman, so too has Apple with the iPod and iTunes. Now revenues from Apple iPods and iTunes account for over 40 per cent of the company's revenues. The digital music download industry is estimated to be worth $3.7 billion.

The emergence of mp3 players and, in particular, the immensely popular Apple iPod has transformed the music industry. These small, handheld devices allow

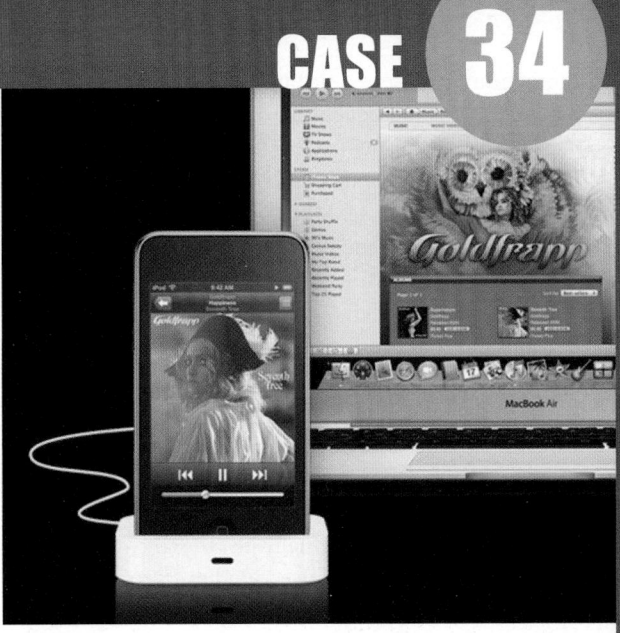

music lovers to download and play huge music libraries, which hold thousands of songs, with ease. Consumers are now downloading songs electronically from the Internet, and storing them on these digital devices or burning them on to rewritable CDs. The Apple iPod transformed the fortunes of the beleaguered computer maker. The iPod is now the best-selling digital music player in the world. Its dominance in the sector is staggering. To put it into perspective, the company made $9.1 billion in 2008 from sales of iPods. Now in its fifth generation, its simplicity, elegance and sheer coolness continue to woo new disciples. Original iPod owners have continued to upgrade to the latest models. Over one million of the latest Apple iPod video models were sold in the first 20 days of their release. It is estimated that Apple has a colossal 80 per cent market share in the digital music device market. Revenue from iTunes has grown exponentially: the company has earned $3.34 billion, growing at a rate of 34 per cent.

In October 2001, Steve Jobs, founder and CEO of Apple Computer, announced the launch of the first generation of iPods at the company's Macworld conference, to self-confessed Apple brand evangelists. The iPod offered people '1000 songs in your pocket'. This was a brilliant, clear and succinct brand promise. Some commentators questioned Apple's strategy and the iPod's high unit price, while others saw the launch as a nice PR exercise for the firm. Neither sceptical analysts nor the firm itself could have envisaged the spectacular ensuing success of the device. Almost instantly these portable digital jukeboxes were highly sought after, and achieved a 'cool' kudos. The iPod became a 'must-have' gadget for any self-respecting technophile. This early sales

Global digital revenue by industry (2008)	TABLE C34.1
	Digital share
Games	35%
Music	20%
Film	4%
Newspaper	4%
Magazines	1%

Source: *PWC Global Entertainment and Media Report* (2008), IFPI.

momentum transferred through to the mainstream audience, with subsequent newer versions, with higher capacities and cheaper prices. Two years later, Apple launched its iTunes music store, creating a digital download powerhouse. Much of the success has been down to the simple and uniform pricing strategy, which has become an industry standard: 99 cents a track. Users could cherry-pick their favourite songs from hundreds of thousands of online albums. Through the success of the iPod, Apple enjoyed a reversal of fortune, with the brand enjoying the benefits of the 'halo effect'. Consumers who were buying the sought-after iPods were now considering other Apple products due to their positive experiences.

Apple iTunes was originally just the software interface program that allowed iPod users to manage their digital jukeboxes with their computers. Through this interface, users could play and organize digital music content on their computer and digital music device. Users could create their favourite music playlists, manage their music library, copy files, edit information and record songs from their record collection on to a digital format. In the fourth version of Apple iTunes, in April 2003, the firm launched its online music store capability. Through this store, users were able to download and access a huge catalogue of legitimate digital copyrighted material that could be played for an unlimited period on their computer and iPod. Greater adoption of high-speed broadband access allowed for an increasing number of Internet users to download their favourite song or album via this mechanism. The killer feature with the iTunes music store format was that a track could be bought for as little as 99 cents—a revolutionary concept for the recording industry. Now users could pick and choose their favourite songs. iTunes was compatible with Windows-based PCs, too, rather than just Apple computers, giving it a wider audience. Not only does the iTunes site cater for music lovers, Internet users can also download audiobooks, TV series, movies, and audio and video podcasts. Podcasts are a method of transmitting digital files through free or paid subscription. For example, a radio station could podcast a popular show on the Internet, which can be downloaded by a surfer and played back at a later time on a digital device. Thousands of podcasts, both professional and amateur, are created daily.

> **//** Although iTunes has near monopoly status, it still faces heavy competition, and large threats continue to loom on the horizon. **//**

Following the initial success, Apple iTunes is now available in 22 different countries including most of the EU, North America, Australia and Japan. All of the different stores are adapted to take into account local music preferences and tastes. For example, the country-specific store would have its own top 100 chart for that particular country and showcase indigenous artists. The US version of iTunes is the standard bearer of the service, offering more advanced features, such as TV episode downloads. Now users can rent movies to download and watch on their electronic devices. The download speed of broadband Internet has broadened the accessibility of different digital entertainment. The catalogue has over 10 million songs, 40,000 TV episodes and 5000 movies to buy, including over 1200 in high-definition video for rent. It has become the largest authorized digital entertainment distributor in the world.

Although iTunes has near monopoly status, it still faces heavy competition, and large threats continue to loom on the horizon. Napster really kick-started the online music revolution. An 18-year-old university dropout named Shawn Fanning created a killer Internet application called Napster. It was basically a file-sharing program allowing music files to be shared over the Internet. This mp3 format became a popular digital music file format. The format reduces the size of song to a tenth of its original size, allowing for it to be transmitted quickly over computer networks. The sound quality is similar to that of a CD. The program allowed users to find their desired music files through the use of a central computer server. The system worked thus: a user would send in a request for a song; the system would check where on the Internet that song was located; then the song was downloaded directly on to the computer of the user that had made the request. Napster never actually held the physical music files, just facilitated the process. At the height of its popularity the service had over 100 million users. In 2002, the company collapsed due to the mounting legal challenges faced by the company over copyright infringement. Bands like the heavy metal group Metallica sued the company directly over what they saw as Napster assisting the piracy of their songs. Internet websites popped up urging Napster to pay Metallica, while others thought that the metal band had sold out to commercialism. Napster as a company lost millions due to litigation,

The major legitimate online music providers		TABLE **C34.2**
Name	**Details**	**Pricing**
Apple iTunes	Multinational presence; downloaded tracks are now playable on other devices, not just the Apple iPod device; market leader	No subscription Downloading 99 cents a track For DRM-free tracks €1.29c For the UK songs are priced at 59p, 79p or 99p each
Napster	5 million songs in its back catalogue; advertising supported; five times listen for free, then charged	£14.95 for downloading subscription Downloading 99p a track
Rhapsody	Owned by Real Networks; has 1.4 million subscribers; available only in USA; has 1.3 million titles in song catalogue; limited previews	Subscription based $9.95 a month Downloading 99 cents a track
Last.fm	Unlimited radio streaming, which is personalized	€3 a month
Spotify	Ad-funded and subscription-based service	Free, ad supported €9.99 premium service, select any song
Sony Ericsson Playnow	1000 preloaded songs with contract, and users can keep songs; to be launched in 2009	Built
Nokia Comes with Music	Large catalogue; users get unlimited downloads for a year and keep the downloads; they are DRM-controlled downloads	Cost of Nokia handset, adds £30 to mobile phone

Note: DRM is digital rights management; it controls which digital devices the content is played on.

despite a late rescue bid from, ironically, one of the 'big four' music groups, whose very existence it threatened.

In the wake of Napster, as both an illegal and its now legal reincarnation, a plethora of other music download sites and software have emerged. A large number of legal download sites have been launched, where surfers can either stream their favourite music or download it for future use in their digital music libraries. The rise in digital music sales, which now account for over 20 per cent of total record sales, has counteracted the continued decline in sales in music discs. Downloading has now overtaken the singles market. À la carte download services and subscription-based services are the two main business models. Highlighting this growing phenomenon of the net as an official channel of distribution, new music charts are now being created, such as the 'Official Download Chart'. A core issue for

the business is that of compatibility. Some digital music players will be able to play only certain music file formats from certain online music retailers.

As of January 2009, users can buy DRM-free songs for an additional 30 per cent extra. The company now has three price points: 69 cents, 99 cents and $1.29 cents for downloads. Music industry executives are alarmed that iTunes has such dominant market share. They wanted a more flexible pricing structure rather than the standard 99 cents a download—for example, charging premium prices for new hits and lower prices for promotions. Apple argues that its pricing structure encourages legal downloading of music: if prices are higher it encourages surfers to illegally download material. Music studios want a greater share of the spoils. Industry sources suggest that, out of a typical 79p UK download, the music label gets 61.5 per cent, royalties account for 8 per cent, and once VAT is paid the online music store is left with just 15 per cent of revenue.

The value of legal digital downloads has grown exponentially since 2004, from $.4 billion to $3.7 billion in 2008. The music industry is hoping that a dominant digital format—an industry standard—emerges. The growth is expected to continue with increased broadband Internet speeds; more digital music devices, including mobile phones, integrated entertainment systems and more digital music download providers. Growth in legal downloading is now exceeding illegal downloading. Record companies are now harnessing the capability of the Internet rather than fearing both it and illegal downloading. There is still a great deal of illegal downloading activity on the Internet through torrent sites, peer-to-peer sharing sites and file hosting sites. One industry commentator estimated that the loss to the UK industry was a conservative £180 million in 2008 alone. The 'free' economy of the Internet has led to interesting pricing models being introduced, like UK group Radiohead offering their latest album free of charge, permitting downloaders to pay what they wished for it (62 per cent did not pay for the content).

In October 2005, iTunes went into further uncharted territory, offering users the opportunity to download video content such as their favourite television shows, movie trailers and music videos. In partnership with several television studios, users could download an entire episode of their favourite programme (such as *Desperate Housewives* and *Lost*) in its entirety, 24 hours after it had been aired on network television. Entire shows can be viewed for $1.99 an episode. This feature is still unavailable in the UK iTunes store as some of the shows have yet to appear on terrestrial television, although, it would appear that it is only a matter of time before this feature becomes available. This represents another viable revenue opportunity for the firm, and should prove an interesting proposition: will users be willing to pay to view television episodes that are free to air on television? The major issues to be overcome are piracy protection and pricing. Movie studios want higher prices, control over release windows and, possibly, subscription charges. Competitors like Sony have seen their market share for portable devices being

eroded, and they now want to reclaim this territory. Sony is a powerful content owner, owning a major Hollywood movie studio and the second-biggest record label in the world. Some other major obstacles lay in wait, too, such as speed of downloading movies and storage capacity restrictions.

Probably the biggest area of concern for iTunes is the growing prominence of music player-enabled mobile phones. Mobile phones have become ubiquitous, with 100 per cent penetration rates in some markets. Much in the same way that they took a portion of the digital camera market, they could also become the dominant players in digital music, rather than stand-alone players like the Apple iPod. More worrying for Apple is that, as technology improves, there will be even greater integration between mobile phones and portable music devices. It is envisaged that consumers will want only one handheld device that will provide telephony, music and camera capabilities. In response to this threat, Apple teamed up with Motorola to launch the Rokr mobile phone, which allowed users to use iTunes to download 100 songs on to their phone.

Other mobile phones have launched competing versions with much larger capacities, holding up to 3000 songs. Despite an aggressive marketing launch, the Rokr was a limited success. Mobile phone operators are already preparing their music retailing divisions: some are offering songs at $2.50 a track, where users get two copies of a song—one suitable for their mobile phone and the other for their PC. The release of the much vaunted Apple iPhone has taken the market by storm, yielding further revenue streams for the company through sales of digital content such as games, applications and music through iTunes. All the major mobile phone makers view music phones as the next key battleground in their industry. For example, Sony Ericsson is launching a range of Walkman-branded mobile phones. Convergence is only a matter of time, as the technology improves. It is intuitively simple that customers will want a single handheld device that will cater for their music needs and their digital content, and be their mobile phone at the same time.

Several wannabes have totally failed in their quest to usurp Apple iTunes—for example, Sony's Connect, Microsoft's Urge, Coca-Cola's mycokemusic.com, Dell and easyGroup. They have all failed despite pouring

> **❚❚** Increasing numbers of people are sourcing their music through the Internet and supermarkets, leaving traditional music retail operations with a severe conundrum: how can they entice shoppers into their stores? **❚❚**

▲ iTunes faces tough competition from Nokia's innovative 'Comes with Music' service, in which one year's music subscription is included in the price of a phone handset.

millions into these services. Why has iTunes' popularity been too hard to beat? Nokia believes it has the answer. The Finnish mobile telephone giant has launched its 'Comes with Music' service, where mobile phone buyers can download from a huge catalogue of music for a year. But the real catch is that people are allowed to keep their downloads after the subscription ends. Nokia has built the price of the music subscription into the price of the Nokia handsets, and charges for them at a premium. This will prove tough competition for Apple in that Nokia is a formidable adversary, and this is an innovative business model in monetizing digital content.

For traditional music retailers, like HMV, the retailing landscape is getting more and more competitive, with multiple channels of distribution emerging due to the Internet and large supermarket chains now selling music CDs. Supermarkets such as Tesco and Asda now sell a selection of the top-selling albums. They view this market as quite lucrative due to the higher margins obtained—more than for typical food items. Also, due to their size and scale, they can obtain large discounts from music publishers. Furthermore, the Internet has given consumers greater choice. They now can buy albums from traditional Internet retailers such as Amazon.com, and also on websites that utilize access to grey markets, such as

cdwow.com, and now through legitimate download retailers. The music industry has truly evolved into a multi-channel world. Increasing numbers of people are going to source their music through the Internet and supermarkets, leaving traditional music retail operations with a severe conundrum: how can they entice more shoppers into their stores? Established retailers like Tesco have now entered the download market, too. Surfers can download tracks through their websites for 79p apiece.

The Internet may emerge as the primary channel of distribution for music and other entertainment content, and these industries are going to have to adapt to these changes. The move towards the online distribution of entertainment content is still in its infancy and more investment into the telecommunications infrastructure—such as greater Internet access, increased access to broadband technology, and changing the way people acquire music and entertainment—will undoubtedly take time. Digital adoption will increasingly occur. Apple, through its iTunes, iPod and iPhone range of products, wants to be at the forefront of this digital technology revolution. iTunes is the platform where all consumers' entertainment content can be accessed through its site. Other competitors have different ideas, and will continue to threaten the long-term sustainability of iTunes, and its possible future success.

Further information

See the resources at www.ifpi.org.

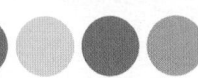
Questions

1. Discuss the how digital technologies are changing music and movie distribution, and how retailers are adapting.
2. Critically appraise Apple iTunes' strategy of now allowing DRM-free downloads to work on Apple iPod devices.
3. Debate whether Apple should respond to the Nokia's 'Comes with Music' service, by launching a similar product for the Apple iPhone. Furthermore, recommend a course of action for Apple, giving reasons for your answer.

This case was written by Conor Carroll, Lecturer in Marketing, University of Limerick.

CHAPTER 18

Digital marketing

// As global competition intensifies, an organization's performance and strategic positioning will become more dependent upon its ability to successfully exploit information technologies. //

DOHERTY AND
ELLIS-CHADWICK[1]

LEARNING OBJECTIVES

After reading this chapter, you should be able to:

1. explain the concept of digital marketing
2. discuss the key elements of the digital age
3. describe the stages of digital marketing planning
4. discuss digital marketing media
5. explore the benefits and limitations of digital technologies
6. discuss ethical issues in digital marketing

Digital technologies are becoming increasingly important in most sectors of economic activity. Due to high levels of interconnectivity, the Internet has been likened to the wheel and the airplane in terms of its ability to affect the future development of business and society. Consequently, the Internet has provided the impetus for many companies to rethink the role of technology, and evidence already indicates the extent of its global impact. Research on major trends in the dispersion of Internet technologies found that approximately 90 per cent of UK businesses have access to the Internet and, in companies with over 50 employees, the percentage is approaching 100 per cent.[2] The situation was found to be very similar in Australia, Canada, France, Germany, Italy, Japan, the Republic of Ireland, South Korea, Sweden and the USA. Interestingly, the report also concluded that the key measure of information and communications technologies (ICT) adoption is no longer just about connectivity and access to the Internet, but rather the degree to which digital technology is being used to deliver real value for businesses. Increasingly, business adoption of technologies focuses on an expanding range of digital devices and platforms (e.g. mobile phones, wireless, and digital TV). Indeed, global system for mobile communications (GMS) has become the fastest-growing communications technology of all time.

The Internet is a major communications channel because of the vast amount of time people spend surfing the web. Research covering 16 countries found that, on average, people spend 29 per cent of their leisure time on the web. Overall, the Chinese spend the largest part of their leisure time online: 44 per cent compared with 28 per cent for British people. Scandinavians spend the least of their leisure time on the Internet, with Danes at 15 per cent, Swedish consumers at 18 per cent and Norwegians at 22 per cent.[3]

The Internet exploded into commercial life in the 1990s. During the same period network technology was also undergoing significant change, switching from analogue to digital circuits, and mobile phone networks and handsets were rapidly developing both in terms of sophistication and number of users. By 2000, further changes had occurred in the world of digital communications infrastructure. Suddenly there were more mobile phone subscribers than fixed-line phone users, Internet traffic exceeded voice traffic on fixed-line telephone networks at night, and wireless technologies began to be developed. Mobile phones have increased facilities for receiving multimedia content, and digital and online television have become available.

For consumers, digital technologies have not only provided the means to search for and buy products while saving time and money, but also to socialize and be entertained. The emergence of social networking sites such as MySpace, Facebook and Bebo has enabled consumers to spend time socializing, and the development of video streaming and music downloads means that they can be entertained as well. A major challenge for marketers is to tap in to the huge youth audiences provided by social networking sites where there is resistance to intrusion from marketing messages.

Digital marketing spans the marketing mix as it provides marketing communications channels and is a means of distribution. Further, as we shall see, digital marketing has implications for all of the elements of the marketing mix and is changing the way marketing is conducted.

This chapter will examine the nature of digital marketing, the key elements of the digital age, how to create a digital marketing plan, the characteristics of the main digital media (the Internet, wireless communications and interactive television), assess the benefits and limitations of digital technologies, and discuss ethical issues in digital marketing.

What is Digital Marketing?

Digital marketing may be defined as:

the application of digital technologies that form channels to market (the Internet, wireless communications and interactive television) to achieve corporate goals through meeting and exceeding customer needs better than the competition.

This definition has evolved during the last decade, spurred by growing commercial adoption of the Internet. Because the web presents a fundamentally different environment for marketing activities than traditional media, conventional marketing activities are being transformed.[4] One of the unique properties of this evolving digital business environment is its capacity to facilitate many-to-many communications. As a result of the advent of this new communication model, the role of the consumer and the importance of interactive digital technologies have increased significantly. There has been a continuing debate as to how to refer to business activities that involve the use of digital technologies. **Internet marketing** is a term that was originally used and is generally considered to mean the achievement of corporate goals through meeting and exceeding customer needs better than the competition through the utilization of Internet technologies. More recently, the term **digital marketing** has become popular due to the inclusion of a wider range of digital and network communication technologies, including mobile phones and digital television, in the pursuit of marketing objectives. The widening application of digital technologies suggests that marketers should extend their thinking beyond the Internet to encompass all the platforms that permit a firm to do business electronically. This wider definition is used for the remainder of this chapter.

E-commerce, e-business and e-marketing

The commercialization of the Internet has generated many terms that are used regularly in the business world. Many of these new terms have the prefix 'e-' and can have different meanings. It is important for organizations to develop a common understanding if they are to develop effective and consistent marketing strategies.[5]

Electronic commerce is often thought to simply refer to buying and selling using the Internet, and as a result people often think of consumer retail purchases from companies such as Amazon and Tesco.com. However, e-commerce involves more than electronically mediated financial transactions between organizations and their customers. It is generally considered to include all electronically mediated transactions between an organization and any third party it deals with, including the exchange of information. An organization might become involved with e-commerce on the *buy-side* as well as the *sell-side*, depending on the type of organization and the markets it serves. *Buy-side e-commerce* refers to transactions to procure resources needed by an organization from its suppliers. *Sell-side e-commerce* refers to transactions involved with selling products to customers.

E-business is a term generally used to refer to both buy-side and sell-side e-commerce, and the internal use of Internet technologies throughout an organization. IBM, originally coined the term:

> e-business—the transformation of key business processes through the use of Internet technologies.

An intranet (internal company network of web browsers and e-mail) is used as part of e-business activities to streamline business processes. A company intranet can facilitate the sharing of ideas, research on a new product development, business decisions and applications. E-business is therefore broader than e-commerce, and may involve the automation of such business processes as the purchase of supplies, production, inventory management, marketing, invoicing and distribution.

E-marketing is a term used to refer to the use of technology (telecommunications and Internet based) to achieve marketing objectives and bring customer and supplier closer together. For instance, a company might use e-mail to manage customer enquiries and also integrate web-based technologies with e-mail and other information systems, such as customer databases, in order to facilitate management of customer and supplier relationships.

From a marketing perspective e-marketing can help identify and anticipate customer needs, and also provide a means to satisfy customers by providing prompt and informed responses quickly.[6]

Key Elements of the Digital Age

Figure 18.1 shows the key elements that underpin the digital revolution. Platforms such as the *Internet*, *wireless* (including mobile communications), and *interactive digital TV* and mobile TV are able to deliver content and enable interactions between individuals and companies around the globe. Each will be discussed in more detail later in the chapter. Since 1982, *digitization* has taken place and there has been a steady increase in the use of digital technologies. Products such as televisions, telephones, watches, cameras and music have changed to digital formats. Computer software also operates in digital format, permitting data storage, operations and applications such as the development of computer games. As digitization spreads, the level of *connectivity* across products and locations increases. For example, digital photographs can be shown on computer screens. The Internet connects billions of people and organizations around the world, allowing fast transfer of information. Intranets connect people within a company, facilitating communications, and extranets connect a company with its trading partners, such as suppliers and distributors.

Convergence is also a key element of the digital age. Convergence means the bringing together into one device of the functions that were previously performed by several products. For example, smartphones perform the functions of telephones, cameras, computers, audio systems and televisions. The key benefit of convergence is the convenience of being able to carry out several tasks using just one product. It is central to the increasing rate of adoption of digital technologies being driven by:

- *platforms* switching from analogue to digital (e.g. television) and also fixed to wireless (e.g. telephones and computers)

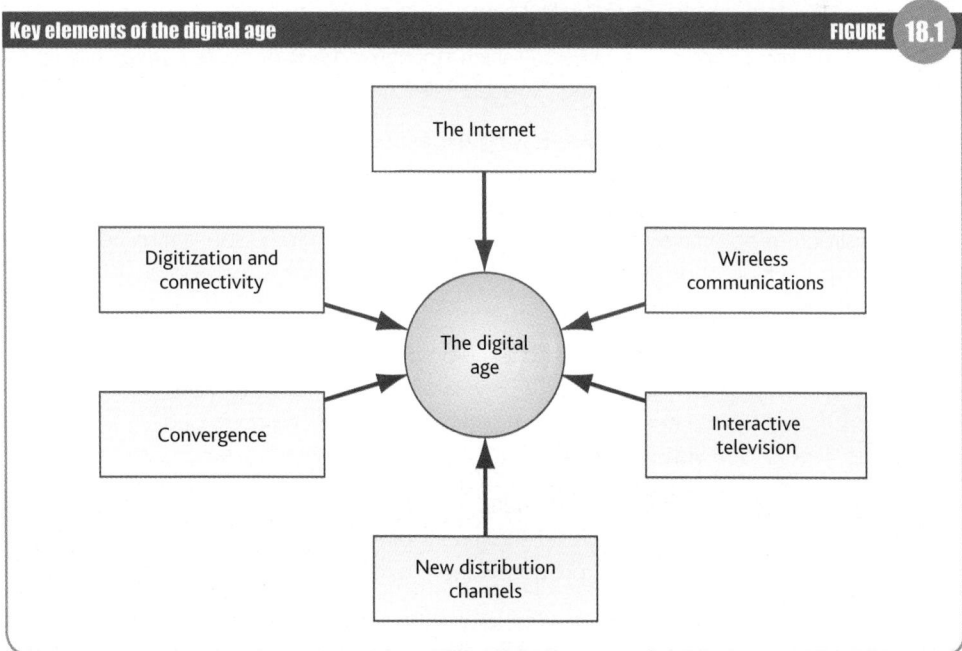

Key elements of the digital age   **FIGURE 18.1**

▲ A screen shot from Rocketboom.com, a web-based video blog.

- *services* increasingly offered over multiple platforms (e.g. online television, see rocketboom.com), TV over broadband (fixed and mobile)
- *devices* becoming increasingly sophisticated (e.g. computers providing voice communications via the Internet, mobile television)
- *industry mergers* and consolidation within and across industry and activity sectors.

Convergence is creating many opportunities for developing new ways to provide access to multimedia content. Rocketboom.com is an example of a web-based video blog (vlog), which presents live newscasts (often with a comedic slant). The daily vlog produces news reports on the unusual and curios, social activities and topical world news (see screen shot). Digital Marketing 18.1 discusses how a shift to mobile television might impact on the media industry.

18.1 Digital Marketing

Digital Television in Your Pocket

In certain areas of daily life, the Internet has transformed the way we live. For example, we are more accustomed to instantaneous consumption, watching television programmes according to our own schedules rather than those of broadcasters. The industry has responded to this trend by introducing new forms of access to television—for example, the Skybox (which stores hundreds of hours of television of the viewer's choice), the BBC iPlayer (which enables viewing of recent television programmes via a computer) and mobile TV.

Mobile TV provides a very different viewing experience. Research into mobile TV viewing habits reveals that it is about 'short snacking rather than the prolonged viewing session of traditional television'. This form of viewing appeals to a very wide mass market but they have high expectations: free services (or very low cost) for mainstream programmes and access to premium content (e.g. sports matches). Content producers are considering the type of programming that might be most suitable for mobile TV. They are also trying to decide whether to stick with traditional models or develop something different for the mobile market.

Nokia is exploring opportunities in mobile TV broadcasting, but Niklas Savander (head of Internet services at Nokia) admitted publicly that mobile TV 'is in a bit of a turmoil'. However, there are some notable areas of success: Orange France has more than a million mobile TV 3G users and, in China, Phoenix TV provides access to 'live TV and video content'.

As a consequence of the increased demand for programmes, ranges of devices providing access, and the number of channels, all content producers, media players, Internet **portals** and traditional television companies are concentrating on how best to provide video playback and how to master the distribution environment.

Based on: Furness (2009)[7]

▲ Nokia invites us to 'point, shoot, and share with N86 8MP', its latest handset, which is optimized for video, still photography and mobile communications.

In addition to content providers and website developers, manufacturers of peripheral devices such as the BlackBerry and iPhone are benefiting from the convergence of digital and analogue platforms. Nokia is making significant investment in developing handsets and support networks, to take advantage of this new digital environment. In its latest advertising, Nokia invites customers to consider what they can do with the latest Nseries, which uses a range of the latest technologies in one device to enable users to work, stay connected to the web, and communicate.

Digital technology convergence has also led to the emergence of *new distribution channels* as suppliers have taken to the Internet to market their products. Consumers not only have the choice of buying from traditional retailers but purchasing from online retailers such as Amazon, eBay and ASOS (the online fashion retailer). Amazon and eBay also provide an online presence for third-party retailers, which can sell their products using the online retailers' sites in return for paying commission.

Forms of E-Commerce

The extent of e-commerce is borne out by the fact that all possible combinations of exchange between consumers and business organizations take place (see Table 18.1). Digital technologies are breaking down barriers in the supply chain, enabling new forms of trading to be established. Buyers and suppliers across all trading markets are exploiting new trading opportunities. The most well-established forms of e-commerce are in business-to-business and business-to-consumer markets. For example, in business-to-business markets, Cisco has, for many years, bought nearly all its purchases on the Internet, and in business-to-consumer markets, established retailers such as Tesco, the UK's leading supermarket chain, have set up online shopping facilities and, in doing so, created an additional channel to market via the Internet. Amazon.com has built a global book-selling operation by using Internet technologies, bringing together consumers, publishers and wholesalers around the globe. Consumer-to-consumer partnerships are developing around the globe through communities and online auctions. Consumer-to-business partnerships are less common, but demonstrate how new trading patterns are creating opportunities. The model of trading partnerships becomes more multidimensional when considered in the context of key industrial markets. Many companies in buyer and seller markets are creating business opportunities through the use of digital technologies—for example, Gist is a leading logistic solutions provider for Marks & Spencer (www.gist-world.com/).

The business world is changing dramatically as digital markets expand; there are many issues and considerations, which can sometimes appear bewildering for marketing managers. In order to succeed, organizations should adopt a structured approach towards developing a digital marketing plan, in order to produce strategies that make the best use of an organization's resources and capabilities, and create competitive advantage through capitalizing on digital market opportunities.[8]

Digital Marketing Planning

This section of the chapter explores the elements and issues that need to be considered when devising a digital marketing plan (see Fig. 18.2).

The formulation of the digital marketing plan is likely to be informed by four significant and interdependent elements.[9]

Trading partnerships: market options		TABLE 18.1
	From business . . .	**From consumer . . .**
. . . to business	b2b Businesses and organizations trading in all three of the leading business markets—industrial, government and reseller—can enter into trading partnerships facilitated by digital technologies. On the web you will find the following: • company websites, e.g. http://www.astrazeneca.com/ • portals, e.g. http://www.constructionplus.com/ (an example of an industry portal) • electronic marketplaces, e.g. http://www.importers.com (helping importers and exporters to conduct trade in a global market)	c2b Digital environments provide fairly equal access to resources for both consumers and businesses. As a result, consumers are better informed and can play a much more active role in the exchange process by influencing the specification of the products they buy and the prices they are prepared to pay. Consumers influence product production, e.g. http://uk.mymuesli.com/ allows German consumers to create their own muesli mix from 70 different ingredients. Online auctions enable consumers to bid for products up to the price they are prepared to pay. eBay has seen a dramatic increase in numbers of SME retailers offering goods via the auction portal, e.g. blue water sports (www.ebay.com)
. . . to consumer	b2c It was the predicted potential of online retailing via the Internet that really started the e-commerce boom in 1998. Now, globally, there are millions of examples of businesses selling to consumers via the Internet and an increasing range of other digital platforms: mobile, iDTV • Web: lastminute.com—holidays, hotels, trips, goods and services • Mobile SMS: Monstermob (www.mob.tv) ringtones, music • Digital TV: bid-up tv (http://www.bid.tv, on Telewest Broadband), an innovative shopping channel that uses web technologies to enable interactive shopping	c2c Digital technologies are enabling individuals to join together to communicate and trade, as outlined below. Digital communities are growing in importance in terms of influence. http://www.MySpace.com is a rapidly growing social network that is not only linking friends and individuals with common interests on a social level, but also affecting business. Arctic Monkeys, a UK band that has risen to fame through downloading, owes much of its success to MySpace.com.[10] Online auctions: consumers sell unwanted goods and services to each other through auction portals like eBay (http://www.ebay.com) and QXL

Source: based on Smith and Chaffey (2008).[11]

1 *Strategic alignment* with corporate, marketing and marketing communication strategies is important as it should ensure development of a potentially successful digital marketing plan. This process should also help define the purpose of the digital marketing activities and the value proposition.

2 The *value proposition* should seek to emphasize the unique advantages created by the use of digital technologies—that is, *choice* (amazon.com offers the world's widest and deepest range of books at very low prices), *convenience* (tesco.com offers round-the-clock shopping), *community* (friendsreunited.com brings together school friends from around the world). The value proposition created by digital technologies should reinforce core brand values and be clearly articulated to target audiences. It will also determine the extent to which organizational change is required.

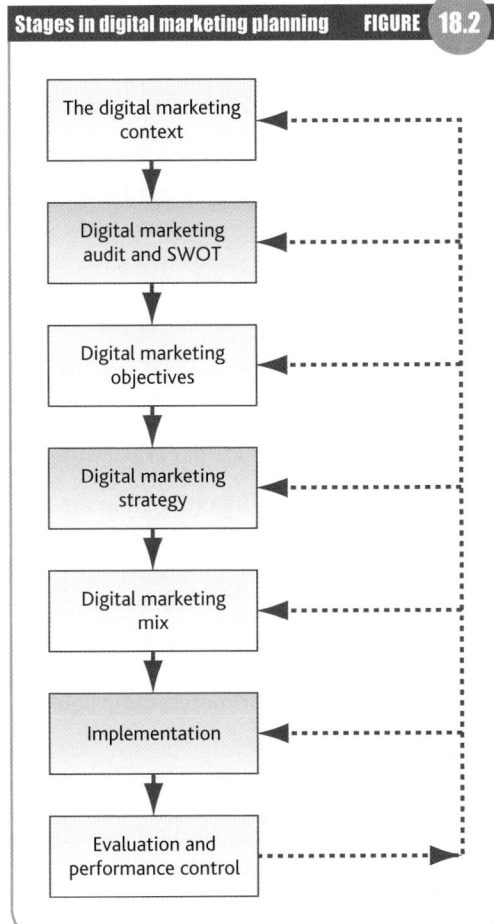

Stages in digital marketing planning   FIGURE 18.2

3 *Organizational change* is likely if the digital marketing plan is to be delivered successfully. A good example to consider is how retailers like Tesco and Sainsbury's have developed unique logistical solutions to support online ordering. E-commerce initiatives can involve applying a wide range of digital technologies: Internet, EDI, e-mail, electronic payment systems, advanced telephone systems, mobile and handheld digital appliances, interactive television, self-service kiosks and smart cards. Consequently, utilizing such technologies may require significant changes to operations and working practices in order to ensure that the right skill sets (capabilities) and resources are available when required.

4 *Implementation* of the plan should be executed in a timely manner. Additionally, the success of the digital marketing plan is likely to be affected by senior management commitment, availability of appropriate resources and the appropriateness of the strategic vision that is guiding the implementation. The significance of the digital marketing plan for a company's overall strategy will also largely be dependent upon levels of technology adoption, investment and integration.

Stages in digital marketing planning
The digital marketing context

Deciding how to plan, resource, integrate, implement and monitor digital marketing activities can be guided by applying established marketing management principles and planning activities. New technologies can be used to meet a range of different business activities. If a company is mainly *selling* via the Internet or other digital platforms then it could be classified as engaging in e-commerce. However, if a company is utilizing digital marketing technology more widely—for example, to restructure the value chain, engage in procurement, stock management, administration, supplier relationship management—this will be classified as engaging in e-business. E-marketing initiatives focus on the development and maintenance of mutually satisfying long-term relationships with customers by using digital technologies.[12] Therefore, the type of activities will determine the significance of the strategic plan and provide an operational context.

Marketing audit and SWOT

For an organization to develop effective and efficient strategies for future business development in the digital age the marketing environment must be clearly understood. This consists of the macroenvironment and microenvironment (see Chapter 2). The marketing audit provides an analysis of these environments, together with an examination of the internal situation facing the company. These analyses will take place in the light of an assessment of the relevance of digital marketing. The following information will be useful.[13]

1 *Customer connectivity*: the proportion of the target markets that has access to relevant technologies.

2 *Customer channel usage*: how often target market participants use online channels and how they use the particular digital channel/platform (e.g. purchase or research?). For instance, for each customer segment and digital channel (e.g. Internet, interactive digital TV or mobile), a company should know the proportion of the target market that:

- *makes use of* and has access to a particular channel
- *browses* and, as a result, is influenced by using the channel for pre-purchase research and evaluation
- *buys* through the particular channel.

An alternative method is to assess media consumption: how many hours each week are spent using the Internet in comparison with traditional media such as watching TV, reading newspapers or magazines, or listening to the radio?

In addition, the marketing audit should consider who are the main competitors. Are they pure online specialists or 'bricks and clicks' rivals? What are their strengths and weaknesses?

Other potential useful information is as follows.

1 *Results generated online:* in this approach, the company determines, say, the percentage of sales that are transacted through a particular platform.
2 *Marketplace impact:* involves assessment of how important the channel is for a particular market, assessed on the number of sales influenced and transacted via digital channels.

Internal analysis will review the digital marketing competences of the organization in the context of whether they represent strengths or weaknesses that might influence future performance. Marketers should ask the following questions.

- What specific strategic resources, capabilities and competences are required for successful digital marketing?
- How well are the expectations of consumers being fulfilled by our digital marketing activities? For example, is our website easy to use? Are our e-mail or mobile campaigns well received or regarded as intrusive?
- What is the number of visitors to our website per month? How many viewers watch our interactive television (iTV) commercials?
- What is the average length of time visitors spend on our site?
- What are the most popular pages and products? What are the least popular?
- Which product categories generate most sales?
- Conversion rates: what is the proportion of visitors who place an order? What is the proportion of recipients of e-mail or mobile campaigns, or iTV viewers who place an order?
- Click-through rates: how many visitors arrive at our site from banner advertisements or web links from other sites?

The SWOT analysis provides a summary of the main findings from the analysis of the internal environment (strengths and weaknesses) and the external marketing environment (opportunities and threats), and will be helpful in defining the key issues that will need to be managed in order to develop an effective digital marketing plan for the future.

Marketing objectives

The degree to which digital marketing objectives will be defined can vary tremendously depending on the extent and time in which digital technologies have been utilized (for example, mobile phone operator Orange may set objectives that focus on customer retention, whereas Internet start-up business, SimplyVital.com, which retails health supplements, is likely to set sales and customer acquisition objectives. Some organizations will merely restrict aims to increasing the effectiveness of their promotional activities. The achievement of marketing objectives is dependent on satisfying customer needs via digital technologies.

Digital marketing objectives fall within some or all of five categories.[14] Marketers must decide whether all or only some are going to drive their marketing plan.

1 *Grow sales:* through cheaper prices, wider distribution or greater product range.
2 *Add value:* through greater convenience (home shopping), improved 24/7 access, and/or more information (e.g. track orders, receive advice, read customer reviews, compare product features and benefits).

3 *Get closer to customers:* inbound by conducting online marketing research, monitoring chatrooms, **blogs** and social network sites, and tracking visits to sites; and outbound by search engine marketing, online public relations and advertising, and e-mail and viral marketing campaigns.

4 *Save costs:* by replacing sales and telemarketing staff with online sales, order confirmation by e-mail rather than post, online purchasing, and replacing hard copy catalogues, manuals and reports with online versions.

5 *Extend the brand online:* by raising awareness, enhance brand image and extend the brand experience.

iTunes has grown music sales by providing an alternative legal distribution method for selling tracks. Many supermarkets have added value by providing a home shopping (via the Internet) and distribution service. Online marketing research is now a common form of data collection, allowing companies to understand their target customers better. Ryanair and easyJet now sell over 80 per cent of their air tickets online, saving themselves millions of pounds in selling and administrative expenses. Many hotels provide virtual tours, enhancing the pre-purchase brand experience of consumers.

Marketing Strategy

A key aspect of strategy development is the creation of a digital marketing competitive advantage.

Creating competitive advantage

Marketers have long accepted that success demands identification of some form of *competitive advantage* capable of distinguishing an organization from other firms operating in the same market sector. The unique properties of digital technologies offer opportunities to establish new forms of competitive advantage. These include highly tailored product assortments and customized products, instant response, uninterrupted trading hours and more informed customer services. The secret of the success of most digital operations is that they have exploited digital market advantages and new technologies, in order to deliver a value proposition superior to that of their non-digital competitors. Perhaps the most critical issue for organizations to consider is how to achieve an effective alignment between web-based IT resources and a variety of complementary resources, skills and capabilities, rather than solely how to apply new technologies.[15]

Potential sources of competitive advantage in digital markets include those described below.

Lower prices

Digital platforms can make direct links between suppliers and customers without using an intermediary. The savings generated by the removal of the intermediary from the transaction can be passed on to the customer in the form of lower prices. An example of this form of competitive advantage is provided by UK airline easyJet. This firm, established some years ago, is now the UK's leading 'no-frills', low-price airline. Further cost savings have been made by creating an automated online flight enquiry, booking service and ticket assurance system, which has replaced all other forms of ticket booking. This has enabled the company to sustain its early competitive advantage.

Lower costs

Large manufacturing companies in traditional industries have reportedly been slow to respond to the opportunities presented by digital technologies. However, a key driver for the adoption of such technologies has been the opportunities for cost reduction, especially within purchasing and administration. For example, Federal Express estimates that it saves between £1 and £3 per customer when it services them online rather than over the telephone, saving the company millions of pounds each year. Similarly, Dell claims to save between £3 and £6 per customer when serving them online.[16]

Improved service quality

In most developed markets it is almost impossible to offer a product proposition that is very different from that of the competition. As a result, one of the few ways of gaining a competitive advantage is through being able to deliver a superior level of customer service. A key influencer of service quality is the speed of information interchange between the supplier and the customer. The information interchange capability facilitated by digital technologies has created opportunities to create competitive advantage. For many years, Federal Express has been a global leader in the application of IT to provide a superior level of customized delivery services to major corporate customers. The firm has enhanced its original customer service software system, COSMOS, by providing major clients with terminals and software that use the Internet to take them into the FedEx logistics management system. In effect, Federal Express now offers customers the ability to create a state-of-the-art distribution system without having to make any investment in self-development of shipping expertise inside their own firms (see www.fedex.com).

Greater product variety

The average high-street retail shop is physically restricted in terms of the amount of space that is available to display goods. Hence its customers, who may have already faced the inconvenience of having to travel to the retailer's location, may encounter the frustration of finding that the shop does not carry the item they wish to purchase. Via digital platforms retailers (pureplays, and so-called 'clicks and bricks' or 'clicks and mortar' companies) can avoid the space restrictions of their 'bricks and mortar' competitors. As a result, they can use their websites to offer a much greater variety of goods to potential customers. Catalogue retailers have also benefited from trading in the digital environment. Empire Stores offers extended ranges of products for sale through its online site—for example, shirts from over 80 different national and international football teams (see illustration).

Product customization

Over the past 20 years, many manufacturers have come to realize that adoption of just-in-time (JIT) production can offer the potential to customize products to meet the

▲ Empire Stores uses the Internet to reach a wider audience.

needs of individual customers. For example, computer giant Dell exploited JIT to assist it in building a product to meet the specific needs of each customer. Furthermore, use of customer data can lead to the development of highly detailed customer profiles. Jeff Bezos (founder of Amazon.com) has used the analogy that the e-commerce retailer can behave like the small-town shopkeeper of yesteryear because of this deep understanding of the customers that visit the online store. Armed with such in-depth knowledge, like the shopkeeper in a village store, the large retailer can personalize service to suit the specific needs of every individual customer across a widely dispersed geographic domain. As with the mass-customization opportunities available to large firms, small companies are also becoming involved in the practice of one-to-one marketing. The outcome is that niche marketers now find it feasible to operate as 'micronichers', customizing products to meet individual customer needs. Acumin, for example, is a web-based vitamin company that blends vitamins, herbs and minerals according to the specific instructions of the customer.

The digital marketing mix

It has been said that utilizing digital technologies to facilitate marketing trading activities affects the whole of the marketing mix, and brings new and unique properties to each element of it. Therefore, careful consideration is required if business goals are to be met through the use of technology. Traditionally, the marketing mix is used strategically to ensure that corporate goals are met, and tactically as a guide for practical actions in various parts of business operations. However, Peppers and Roger[17] went as far as to say that transaction-based marketing and the traditional mix fail to deliver in the digital age, and they subsequently offered the '5-Is' as a replacement framework when companies are working with digital media to develop customer-centric strategies.

The 5-Is are:

1 Identification—customer specifics
2 Individualization—tailored for lifetime purchases
3 Interaction—dialogue to learn about customers' needs
4 Integration—of knowledge of customers throughout the company
5 Integrity—develop trust through non-intrusive marketing such as permission marketing.

However, while on the one hand it is unlikely that such a framework will ever replace the traditional marketing mix as a strategic planning tool, as even after a decade of commercial global trading via the Internet the fundamentals of business have not changed,[18] on the other hand, it highlights the power of new technologies to engender a shift in orientation in (digital) marketing planning, which makes the customer even more significant in trading relationships. Figure 18.3 shows how each of the elements of the traditional marketing mix is potentially reshaped by digital technologies, and the text that follows explores this further.

Product

There are three ways in which digital technologies create opportunities for product enhancement. *Individual requirements* can be met by offering a wide choice. For example, Apple provides a selection of optional accessories for its iPods, allowing consumers to make highly individual product selections. NikeID goes even further by providing the opportunity to design a pair of trainers, by selecting styles, features and colours from a wide range of options. Tesco's online shopping website captures details of shoppers' regular purchase choices and then provides a *customized* list of favourites, allowing faster online shopping. Amazon also produces a customized selection of recommended books based on a customer's previous selection. For example, a customer who bought Antony Beevor's *Stalingrad* would be shown books by the same author, books by others who had bought *Stalingrad* and books on the same subject.[19] The Internet has facilitated the growth and distribution of *digital* (bit-based)

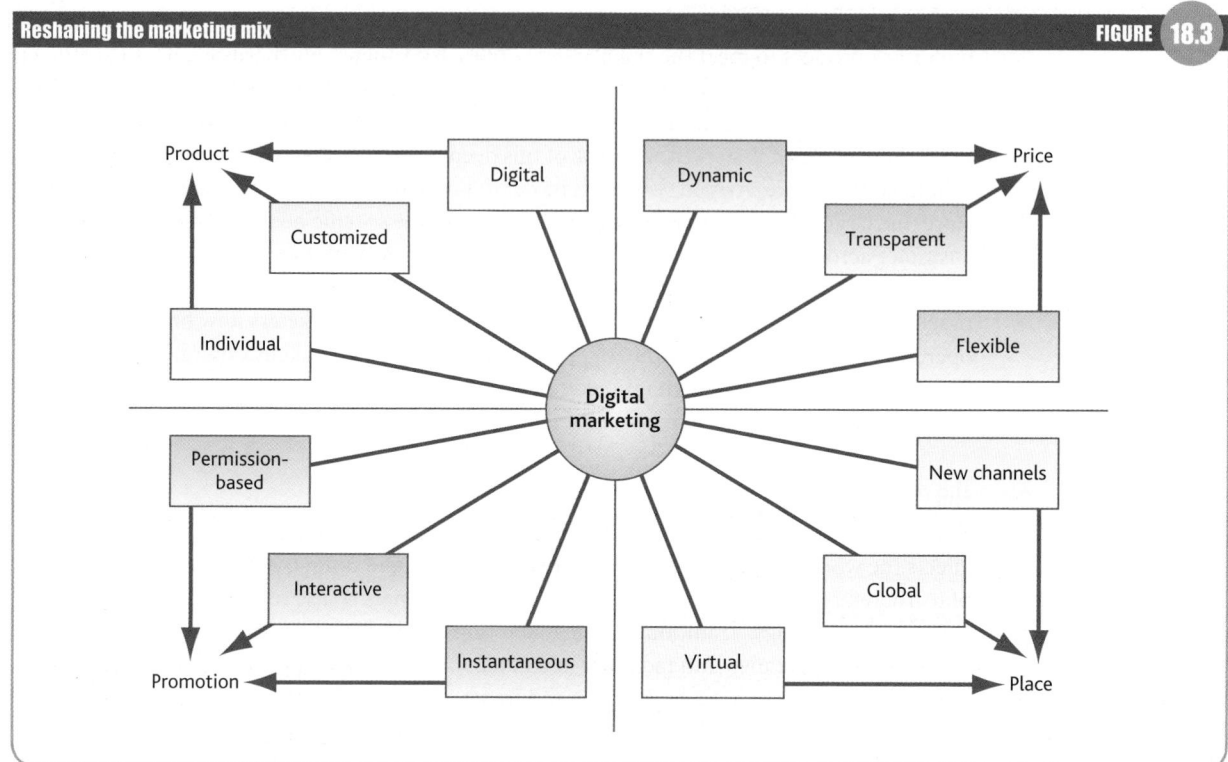

products. These can be delivered directly to the consumer via a digital interface (e.g. music, videos, software upgrades, computer games, flight bookings and hotel reservations). Once the customer has made the payment, products are downloaded regardless of the physical location of the supplier or the buyer.

Price

Prices are more transparent and new dynamic purchasing practices are emerging. A major impact of digital technologies from an economic perspective is the potential to reduce search costs when a buyer is looking for information about new products. The net effect is a reduction in suppliers' power to control, and therefore pricing strategies become more *transparent*. Buyers are increasingly turning to the web for pre-purchase information, which facilitates evaluation of the best offers in terms of both price and quality. Additionally, prices can become *dynamic*, changing almost instantaneously in response to demands experienced by users of online auction sites such as eBay and QXL. Priceline.com demonstrates opportunities for *flexible* pricing strategies as customers can set their own prices for products. Also, Radiohead famously released their album *In Rainbows* online, allowing customers to name their own price.[20]

Promotion

Digital interfaces provide *instantaneous* access to information about products in real time. Traditionally, marketing communications would work by interrupting the receiver of the message in order to capture their attention, as in the case of broadcast and print media advertising. However, via the Internet, web mobile phones and other digital interfaces, a company can send *permission-based* bulletins containing information about, say, the latest product features and any promotional offers that the customer has agreed to accept. Sometimes the strength of traditional and digital media can be combined, as the

For more surprising facts visit
www.newscientist.com/thinksmart

advertisement for the Smart car shows. Furthermore, the digital technologies enable customers to engage in *interactive* dialogues and communication exchanges. Interactive features can be incorporated into online communications in various different forms (e.g. surveys, multimedia advertisements, competitions, call-backs, chat and 'e-mail a friend'). Specific media are discussed in more detail later in this chapter. Digital Marketing 18.2 discusses how Barack Obama used digital technologies to promote his bid for the US presidency.

◀ Advertising in traditional media is sometimes used to direct people to websites where more detailed information can be provided.
© *Daimler AG. Kindly reproduced with the permission of Mercedes-Benz UK Ltd.*

 **18.2 Digital Marketing**

Digital Technology and the US Presidency

Barack Obama, through his adept use of digital technology, has rewritten the textbook on how political campaigns will be conducted in the future. His campaign against Hillary Clinton for the Democrat candidacy was at a disadvantage at first, having less exposure through traditional media. Obama's solution was to go direct, appealing directly to voters, through blogs and podcasts. This meant that his message could not be distorted by traditional media channels. As he wrote, 'it is because the Internet is a neutral platform that I can put out a podcast without having to go through any corporate media middleman'.

Obama also used Flickr and YouTube to reach out to Americans. They responded with 35 per cent watching online political videos in 2008. He also used online platforms in a novel way. When an American signed up to Hillary Clinton's Twitter, they began receiving her tweets (short messages). When someone signed up to Obama's, within minutes he had signed up to theirs. This was good netiquette and, to users of Twitter, showed that he had 'got it'.

Barack Obama also enlisted help from a founding member of Facebook who worked with his campaign team in developing a network of young, energetic campaign staff across America via the Internet. That online network raised money to defeat John McCain, the Republican presidential candidate (who admitted to never using e-mail), to levels never seen before in US politics. The campaign created a database of over 3 million opt-in supporters and raised over $600 million. Obama realized the potential of the Internet to aggregate millions of small donations (90 per cent were less than $200) that enabled him to win the US presidential election in November 2008.

Based on: Adegoke (2008);[21] Walmsley (2008)[22]

Place (distribution)

Trading via digital channels means there are no physical boundaries and an opportunity exists for companies to utilize *new channels* to market. The Internet provides a conduit through which transactions can take place and there is no longer a need for a physical presence, which in turn reduces capital investment in stores, office buildings and warehouses. Through the Internet and an increasing range of mobile and wireless technologies, trading exchanges take place in a *virtual* market space, created by computer networks and layers of application software. Such computer networks stretch around the world, giving companies access to global markets. The survival of many businesses is dependent on such access. For example, dustbag.co.uk, which sells bags for thousands of vacuum cleaner models worldwide, would not stay in business if it were not for the Internet.[23] For companies engaging in digital marketing activities and selling via the Internet there is the need to recognize the following implications of trading in these new channels.

- Distance ceases to be a cost influencer from the buyer's perspective as access to purchasing information is the same no matter where the point of supply is based. However, this can lead to highly complex and costly logistical issues for the seller.
- Business location becomes an irrelevance as buyers and sellers can be based anywhere in the world.
- Technology permits continuous real-time trading, 24 hours a day, 365 days a year.

18.1 Pause for Thought

What are the main ways that digital technology has affected your purchase behaviour?

The digital remix

A key benefit of digital technology is that it allows companies to target very specific markets, even a market of one. This means developing plans to operate as 'micronichers', customizing products and services to meet the needs of an individual: products delivered to personal specifications (e.g. computers, books, music CDs). Broadly speaking, at this highly customized level it is crucial to know which variables are most important for the target customer. A planner should know the key triggers for individual (targeted) customer decisions (best price, best quality, best delivery, best service, best image, best environment) as this will help to determine which aspects of the marketing mix are the most significant. The implications of this are as follows.

- The reach of the traditional marketing mix needs to be reviewed to reflect the opportunities created by digital technologies.
- Customizing the marketing mix and focusing on relationships becomes a central issue in digital marketing planning.

Marketing mix implementation

Once the issues associated with digital marketing mix selection have been resolved, these variables will provide the basis for specifying the technological infrastructure that will be needed to support the planned digital marketing operation. In some cases the firm will decide to manage all of these matters in-house, but in others the firm may outsource a major proportion of its digital operations to specialist subcontractors. An example of where the supplier tends to manage all aspects of the distribution management function is the financial services sector. Online banks usually wish to retain absolute control over both the transaction and delivery processes. The alternative is that all or part of the transaction process is outsourced, but the delivery responsibility is retained (as in the airline industry, for example). Many of the airlines use online service providers such as www.expedia.com to act as retailers of their unsold seat capacity. Regardless of the actual arrangement of the infrastructure solutions, the key concepts to be aware of are integration and interoperability. The greater the extent to which company systems are operationally linked across the full range of business units, the greater the opportunity to satisfy the customer via the Internet and other digital platforms.

An action plan is needed so that all staff receive detailed descriptions of the actions to be taken to manage the digital marketing mix. This plan will include timings and allocations of responsibility.

Evaluation and performance control

Evaluation and control systems need to be created that permit management to rapidly identify variance in actual performance versus forecast for all aspects of the digital marketing mix. Management also requires mechanisms that generate diagnostic guidance on the cause of any variance. To achieve this aim, control systems should focus on the measurement of key variables within the plan, such as targeted market share, customer attitudes, awareness objectives for digital promotions and distribution targets.

Web analytics are the methods used to evaluate the success of digital marketing programmes. Such techniques allow the checking of whether objectives have been achieved by recording website visitor numbers, the most popular pages and products, how long visitors spend on site, which pages they visit (clickstreams), sales, and the individual sites or search terms used by visitors to find a site. Google Analytics is an excellent analytical tool, which is free to use. Omniture and Visual Sciences also provide web analytics systems.[24]

Digital Marketing Media

This section focuses on the main digital marketing media: the Internet, mobile communications, interactive television, and wireless. Although the media tend to focus on organizations and their web-based activities, it is important to understand the potential of all the major digital platforms and how each of the technologies is being integrated into marketing activities.

Internet and web

Globally, the *Internet, web and supporting digital technologies* have revolutionized how organizations communicate, and organizations have begun to explore ways to incorporate these new technologies into promotional campaigns, the focus quite often creating innovative ways of communicating. The nature of communication between not only businesses and consumers, but also the technologies employed is changing. In 1989 the first commercial transactions occurred across the computer networks that form the Internet. Over the next few years the number of computers connected to the Internet increased exponentially, giving connected companies and their customers the opportunity to explore the value of this innovative digital trading environment. By 1992 the World Wide Web (WWW), developed by Tim Berners-Lee, provided millions of technically unqualified users with the opportunity to access the vast online resource of text, graphics and multimedia content. Shortly afterwards, web browsers (such as Microsoft's Internet Explorer and Netscape Navigator) were developed to help guide users around the Internet and the web through an easy-to-use graphical user interface. Globally, tens of thousands of companies (both established and new market entrants) sought to establish ways to exploit this new commercial medium. Many Internet companies have now become successful at using the web as both a channel to market and as a communication medium. Examples of popular global Internet brands are Google, Yahoo!, Amazon and eBay.

The Internet and the web provide innovative options for the digital marketer: communications can be interactive, animated, personalized and instantaneous. But the marketer needs to understand how their target customers will respond if they are to use this media successfully. For instance, sending personalized e-mail marketing messages can help to build customer relationships but the level of personalization should be appropriate to the stage of the relationship. If a company is too familiar too early in the relationship the customer is likely to feel the company is being intrusive.[25]

Many studies have explored the significance of online buyer behaviour and customer relations, and now a great deal is understood about the profile of the consumer and their online experiences. Many variables have been identified to help companies understand who is online, to gain an insight into their needs and wants, and what affects their behaviour in the virtual world.[26]

- *Classification variables*—these include income, education, race and age,[27] lifestyle,[28] and cultural and social influences.
- *Character variables*—these include attributes of consumers' perceptions, beliefs and value sets, but may be modified by the consumer's online buying experiences: attitudes, intentions to shop,[29] privacy and trust,[30] perceived usefulness.[31]
- *Consumer experiences* of Internet and web-based retailing affect their overall assessment of the online shopping process. For instance, the effect of site quality,[32] store layout[33] and offline factors such as delivery.

The Internet allows advertisements to be targeted on an individual basis. *Behavioural targeting* (or personalized Internet advertising) is a method of directing advertisements at consumers based on their previous online behaviour. At its most basic, it is the Amazon 'you've bought this so you might like to buy this' approach. However, more sophisticated behavioural techniques log where Internet users have been surfing online, using 'cookies'. Once this is known, advertisements on other sites appear based on that information. For example, an online user could be browsing cinema listings when a banner advertisement for bargain breaks in Rome appears—something the user had been researching a few days previously.[34] There is some evidence that consumers object to this kind of tracking of their Internet activity, with a survey revealing that 77 per cent objected to behavioural targeting.[35]

18.2 Pause for Thought

What do you consider to be the characteristics of a well-designed website?

Once a company has developed an understanding of the target market it can then begin to decide which digital tools are likely to be most effective. The web-based and Internet options described below can be utilized as virtual promotional tools.

Internet and web-based options

- *Search engine marketing* involves optimization of search listings and keyword searching. For instance, if searching Yahoo!, using key words such as 'jewellery shop' will result in a list of companies offering such services. Yahoo! provides its Keyword Selector to help advertisers choose the best search term. Search engines like Yahoo! and Google generate revenue by charging each time an individual clicks on a sponsored link. The higher up the listing, the higher the price for click-through. Google sells a product called AdWords, and claims:

> AdWords ads connect you with new customers at the precise moment when they're looking for your products or services. With Google AdWords you create your own ads, choose keywords to help us match your ads to your audience and pay only when someone clicks on them.[36]

It has been argued that it is very important for advertisers to appear in the optimum position on the computer screen if they are to attract the greatest number of visitors to their online offering. By paying for a sponsored link, an advertiser gains a prominent position on the search engine's listings. The amount a company pays depends on how much it bids for keywords that Internet users seeking a particular product are likely to enter: the higher the keyword bid compared to rivals, the higher the listing. While the average cost per click is 10–20p, in some competitive industries, such as financial services, it can be as high as £3.[37]

A second method of traffic building to a particular website is known as search engine optimization (SEO). This involves the achievement of the highest position in the natural listings on the search engine results pages after a keyword or phrase has been entered. The position depends on a calculation made by a search engine (e.g. Google) that matches relevant site page content with the keyword (phrase) that is typed in. Unlike sponsored search (pay-per-click) SEO does not involve payment to a search engine to achieve high rankings. What a digital marketer needs is an understanding of how to achieve high natural rankings. Search engines use 'spiders' to identify the titles, links and headings that are employed to assess relevance to keywords and phrases. It is therefore important to ensure that the website includes the keywords (phrases) that a potential visitor might use to search for a particular type of company. For example, Ragdale Hall spa hotel's website includes terms such as 'weekend spa break', 'spa resort' and 'health spa' because they are key phrases used by consumers when searching for that type of hotel. This has achieved high ranking for the hotel on search engine listings.[38]

The second way in which high rankings can be achieved is by generating external links from other websites. This is because positions on listings are partially dependent on the number of links (the number of times a website is mentioned by other websites) from external websites. This occurs naturally, but digital marketers have devised ways of boosting external links. First, potential sites (e.g. trade associations, media sites, distributors and suppliers) should be identified. Second, they should be contacted by e-mail or telephone to encourage them to include the company's web address on their website.

- *Online PR*: comment and commentaries can originate from a variety of different sources, from journalists to individuals. Much of online PR is generated in the form of *blogs* and comments from online communities (see Digital Marketing 18.3).

 **18.3 Digital Marketing**

Technorati Media

Technorati is an authority in the world of blogging. It was founded to help collect, highlight and distribute 'the online global conversation'. It currently tracks over 40 million sites and 2.4 billion links, and provides access to the 'blogosphere' by acting as a real-time search engine. A weblog ('blog' for short) is a personal commentary, a collection of thoughts and comments, which creates a sort of personal diary on the web. Millions of people around the world have created blogs containing ideas and comments, and many Internet users read them regularly. Blogs are search engine friendly as they are indexed, making it easy for like-minded individuals to connect and exchange thoughts.

Company's advertise through Technorati blogs and, potentially, benefit from 'connecting the brand with influential bloggers and consumers'. However, blogs can be quite powerful, as individuals are able to make comments about products, which are permanently recorded online for all to see. According to Immediate Futures, blogs can have a negative impact on corporate image. Its study into blogs shows how individuals who are dissatisfied with a company's level of offering can have quite a powerful effect. In a case study of Dell Computers it was revealed that a customer was totally dissatisfied when he discovered that the extra amount he had paid to have his computer serviced at home by an engineer was money wasted as it was a service no longer offered. The situation escalated when, by searching personal blogs, he was able to find hundreds and then thousands of other customers with complaints about Dell's customer service. Aggrieved customers began communicating and posting comments in weblogs, which were potentially very detrimental to Dell's reputation.

Based on: Immediate Futures (2005);[39] www.technorati.com[40]

- *E-mail marketing*: the Internet is widely used by companies as part of the communication mix. E-mail marketing is often used to extend web-based marketing activities, particularly when companies are aiming to develop online customer relationships and the volume of online sales. The use of e-mail marketing has grown rapidly; for many companies it is widely accessible and a low-cost option. Indeed, it is accessible to everyone with an Internet connection and an e-mail account. As a result, e-mail marketing has become a mainstream business communication tool during the past decade. Retailers in particular have begun to make use of this interactive form of communication to instantaneously deliver messages and information to large numbers of existing and potential customers.

- *Permission-based marketing* is an extension of e-mail marketing and can be used as the principle method of communication when developing online customer relationships. Traditionally, marketing communications interrupt the message receiver but, online, it is possible to seek permission prior to sending marketing messages. The major incentive for individuals to opt in to a firm's e-mailing list is the prospect of receiving relevant material that matches the consumer's interests. Research suggests that individuals attribute higher value to promotional messages they perceive as relevant, and message recipients are subsequently more likely to open, and then read, targeted promotional messages. There is an opportunity for firms to develop close and potentially highly profitable customer relationships by gaining permission to send advertising messages, which may increase the likelihood of messages being effective.[41]

- *Viral marketing* is a further option for e-mail marketers. Many companies are using viral marketing techniques to promote their products to a wider online audience. Viral marketing is not a new concept by any means—it is the electronic version of word of mouth. Viral messages are spread every day (for example, when a joke is received via e-mail and then forwarded on to friends). Hotmail provided one of the first free e-mail services and rapidly expanded its user base by attaching a tag at the end of each message stating 'get your private free e-mail at www.hotmail.com'. The viral effect soon took hold and messages were exchanged between users across the Internet. Hotmail (www.hotmail.com) became the number-one web-based e-mail supplier, with over 14 million users worldwide, most from a message sent to a handful of paid 'e-mail' users. The prospect of free e-mail was hard to resist and it was impossible not to tell others. To be effective, viral campaigns need to provide some incentive for the user to pass on the message, which may be in the form of giveaways.[42] Additionally, companies attempt to harness this viral effect by building messages that are suitably engaging and promote an aspect of their company using content that customers want to read and send on. This requires some creativity and a strong understanding of the customer base. Humour is one way of creating a strong viral (or pass-along) effect. In January 2009, Cadbury launched its 'Eyebrows' campaign using viral and buzz marketing. The video advert was passed around the Internet at great speed and Cadbury claims that it took the Internet by storm.[43] Companies like 5pm.co.uk (www.5pm.co.uk) now send e-mails promoting specific off-peak restaurant deals, redeemable only through unique links noted on the e-mail, with the intention that these will be passed on to 'new' customers. Almost everything has viral marketing potential. Companies that do not have an e-mail signature file are missing a viral marketing opportunity.

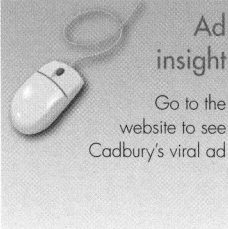

Ad insight

Go to the website to see Cadbury's viral ad

- *Affiliate marketing*: this refers to a relationship between an e-commerce website (known as a merchant) and a network of affiliate websites (or publishers), who operate as a virtual salesforce.[44] The purpose of the affiliate publisher is to drive customers to the merchant's site. Typical affiliates are price comparison sites such as moneysupermarket.co.uk, kelkoo.co.uk, pricerunner.co.uk and cheapflights.co.uk. When a visitor to one of these websites clicks on a link to an external website, the price comparison site may receive commission, or commission may be paid on a sale-only basis. The process is monitored using affiliate tracking software, which ensures that affiliates are properly paid for the leads or sales they provide.

Wireless communications

The convergence of the Internet and wireless technology has revolutionized telecoms services. Technological advances are enabling more and more data and multimedia content to be accessed through mobile phone handsets. Global mobile operators are now accelerating technological transition from 2G to 3G, and the number of users worldwide exceeds 115 million, which is creating opportunities for advertisers. 'Short messaging services' (SMS) has become a new technological buzz-phrase in business-to-consumer markets. Marketing communication messages can be sent directly to mobile telephones, pagers and PDAs. Many companies add text message numbers to their marketing messages to capture the interest of the consumers. This form of advertising is being used to enhance customer relationships, and to carry out direct marketing and promotional activities. The sending of short text messages direct to mobile phones) is extremely successful. Every month billions of chargeable text messages are sent. Marketers have been quick to spot the opportunities of this medium to communicate, particularly to a youth audience. Marketers now send out messages to potential customers via their mobile phones to promote such products as fast food, movies, banks, alcoholic drinks, magazines and books. The advantages of this approach for marketers are as follows.[45]

- *Cost effective*: the cost per message is between 15p and 25p compared with 50p to 75p per direct mail shot, including print production and postage.
- *Personalized*: like direct mail each message is sent to individuals, in contrast to traditional advertising.
- *Targeting*: given that SMS use among 15–25 year olds is 86 per cent, and 87 per cent among 25–34 year olds in the UK, **mobile marketing** has high potential as a youth targeting tool.[46]
- *Interactive*: the receiver can respond to the text message, setting up the opportunity for two-way dialogue.
- *Customer relationship building*: by establishing an ongoing dialogue with consumers it can aid the relationship-building process.
- *Time flexible*: unlike direct mail, mobile marketing can be sent at various times of the day, giving greater flexibility when trying to reach the recipient.
- *Immediate and measurable*: the results of the mobile campaign can be immediate (for example, the number of people taking up an offer) and the results measurable.
- *Database building*: creative use of mobile marketing allows marketers to gather consumer information, which can be stored on a database.

Mobile communications do have certain limitations, though.[47] These are as follows.
- *Short text messages*: the number of words in a text message is limited to 160 characters. Future technological advances may remove this limitation.
- *Visually unexciting*: 2G systems do not permit picture messaging. Although multimedia messaging services and 3G technology allow picture messaging, the extra cost may slow its widespread use.
- *Wear-off*: while mobile marketing is still novel, response rates are good, but sceptics argue that once the novelty has worn off and consumers receive more and more advertising/promotion-related messages the effectiveness of the medium will wane.
- *Poor targeting*: as with poorly targeted direct mail, 'junk' text messages cause customer annoyance and lead to poor response rates. An important consideration as mobile marketing develops is gaining consumer acceptance. A number of key rules should be followed, as outlined below.[48]
- *Permission*: mobile communications are very personal and any unwelcome intrusion runs the risk of consumer rejection. Therefore, permission-based mobile marketing is essential when using mobile phones as communication channels. In the UK, the Mobile Marketing Association (MMA) was set up to ensure that consumers were protected from spamming. Three sets of regulations govern mobile marketing: the Data Protection Act, the MMA

code of conduct and the New Electronic Communications Directive. The Data Protection Act requires companies to indicate how often they will be communicating to people and also what types of message will be sent. All consumers must have a clear and easy way of opting out (e.g. using SMS or the web). The MMA code of conduct states that mobile marketing must be an opt-in system with a clear and free opt-out route. The New Electronic Communications Directive states that mobile marketing must be an opt-in system with a clear and free opt-out route.

- *Targeting*: since mobile phones are extremely personal devices with the brand, fascia colour, size and ringtone reflecting, often, the owner's personality, messages sent to consumers via the phone must be highly relevant and targeted. This can be achieved through direct communication, or by using Mosaic or Prizm lifestyle segmentation data.
- *Value added*: the communication should be of value to the recipient. This can take the form of entertainment or special access to products and information.
- *Interactive*: mobile communications should engage consumers in a two-way dialogue. Today's youth love to talk back, and often demand the right to talk back to the message sender. Rather than developing one-way 'push' campaigns, companies should explore the possibilities of integrating voice and text-based games, images and sounds to take full advantages of this developing medium.

So far, the discussion has focused on simple SMS communications, but broader mobile advertising is likely to take off, as Digital Marketing 18.4 explains.

 ## 18.4 Digital Marketing

Mobile Advertising Lifts Off

Marketers have often claimed that mobile advertising is about to take off, but there is reason to believe that, this time, there will be lift-off. This is because the barriers that have held mobile advertising back are disappearing.

First, surfing the Internet on a mobile has been difficult because screens were too small and the controls too clunky. That has now largely changed with the emergence of smartphones such as Apple's iPhone, Google's G1 and the BlackBerry Storm. They have touchscreens large enough to display web pages properly—and advertisements too. Nokia estimates that 5 billion people globally will have access to an always-on mobile Internet connection by 2015.

Second, faster networks and lower call rates are also speeding the adoption of mobile advertising. Having to wait for an advertisement to download, and be charged for the privilege, caused user annoyance. Now, with faster download speeds and flat-rate data charges, this is less of a problem.

Third, mobile marketers are learning about how best to approach the task of advertising on mobile phones. One method is to offer a free mobile contract in return for the user agreeing to receive a given number of advertisements per day. For example, Blyk, a mobile operator, offers 16–24-year-old subscribers 217 free text messages and 43 minutes of free airtime per month in exchange for an agreement to receive six ads per day. A year after its launch, Blyk had signed up over 200,000 subscribers, double its target. Another mobile company, Amobee, allows clients to advertise using several channels—not just advertisements inserted into text messages and mobile Internet sites, but also into games and other applications that run on handsets.

Advertising on mobile phones offers problems and opportunities. One problem is that it can seem intrusive in a context that is, by its very nature, extremely personal. But the opportunity to target a young audience, who are increasingly difficult to reach using traditional media, means that marketers will continue to seek ways of meeting the challenges of mobile advertising.

Based on: Anonymous (2008);[49] Clark (2008)[50]

Your iPhone gets better with every new app.

Applications for iPhone are like nothing you've ever seen on a mobile phone. Explore some of our favorite apps here and see how they allow iPhone to do even more.

Apps for Everything

Apps for Working Out
8 Featured Apps

Work out with fitness apps that keep you motivated from treadmill to trail. View apps for fitness ▸

Apps for Around the House
7 Featured Apps

Let iPhone lend a hand around the house, at the store, and with family. View apps for the household ▸

Apps for Going Out
8 Featured Apps

Find places to eat, people to see, events to watch, and music to hear. View apps for going out ▸

Apps for Managing Money
9 Featured Apps

Money matters with apps that help you budget, save, and spend smart. View apps for managing money ▸

▲ Apple pushes back the boundaries in wireless communications with the iPhone.

The extension of the use of mobile devices and *wireless* technologies has created an opportunity for further innovation within organizations. In the same way as the Internet and PC provided the foundations for e-business, mobile solutions utilizing wireless devices can create freedom and flexibility that might eventually change the way companies interact with customers, partners and employees. There are different types of wireless device, which provide access to various services. One class of devices is those that have an immediate connection to a network—for example, wireless application protocol (WAP) phones, palmtops, personal digital assistants (PDAs) and BlackBerry-type devices. Mobile devices are improving all the time: the latest smartphones provide larger screen sizes, and better memory and processing capacity, allowing the use of browser-based applications utilizing wireless connectivity (e.g. Apple's iPhone, which pushes back the boundaries in mobile communications, as can be seen in the web-based advertisement for iPhone3G).

A wireless device, such as Apple's iPhone3G, offers a range of services that can facilitate better business communications: personal numbering, Instant Messaging (IM), and automated directory enquiries. A personal communication assistant (PCA) application can give an employee the capability to control access by, for example, forwarding important calls to the most convenient number, screening incoming calls and easily setting up conference calls. The user can manage these advanced self-service features without recourse to technical assistance.

These devices can be used for marketing and communication purposes in both business-to-business and consumer situations. From a mobile phone it is possible to check a bank account, take and send pictures, buy travel and event tickets, have access to selected news and information services, and be informed of real-time promotional offers when shopping in certain locations. On the one hand, wireless devices have grown in popularity due to their flexibility, immediacy, privacy and high levels of interactivity,[51] but on the other hand, it is the evolution of the underlying technology that is driving forward adoption. Global System for Mobile Communications (GSM) technology has developed rapidly and enables mobile phones and wireless services to work globally, providing individual consumers and businesses with opportunities to meet customer needs through a digital and mobile interface. GSM technology is in use by more than one in five of the world's population: by mid-March 2006 there were over 1.7 billion GSM subscribers, representing approximately 77 per cent of the world's cellular market. The growth of GSM continues unabated, with almost 400 million new customers in 2009.[52]

The wireless revolution is facilitating greater freedom in business-to-business markets. Signorini[53] has identified four key areas into which the majority of wireless data applications in companies fall.

1 *Field sales*, including inventory and pricing systems, access to customer account information and real-time ordering.
2 *Mobile office*, including e-mail, personal information management (PIM), access to corporate intranets, and human resources.
3 *Fleet management*, including dispatch applications for courier companies, call scheduling systems for taxi firms, location tracking applications for the management of large fleets, and routing and mapping systems.
4 *Field service*, including work scheduling in the service and repair industry, access to customer records and information while on-site, financial services applications, such as insurance claims handling and assessing, and access to national databases while 'on the road'.

Field sales currently constitutes the biggest single use of wireless technology, accounting for more than a quarter of all applications in large organizations.[54]

Interactive television

Digital technology has enabled the conversion of TV pictures and sounds into a digital signal. Not only does this mean better-quality images and sound, but it also means that the signal can be understood by computers. The convergence of digital technology (as discussed earlier in the chapter) is driving adoption and expansion. According to recent research, 70 per cent of UK households have at least one digital television set. This is set to increase as the government initiates the switching off of the analogue signal, which will take place between 2008 and 2012. Interactive television (iTV) advertising invites viewers to 'press the red button' on the remote control handset to see more information about an advertised product. Viewers may then be asked to request a free sample or brochure, say, or buy a product. Although still in its infancy, iTV is growing, with Sky claiming around 25 per cent of last-in-break spots on its wholly owned channels carrying iTV adverts.

One of the key drivers of this growth is iTV's ability to provide measurable results for clients— a characteristic that is shared with direct mail. Advertisers can assess campaign performance by measuring responses and, for the first time, attribute a financial value to different channels, times of the day and even individual slots. It also allows the targeting of niche audiences through specialist television channels that focus on leisure activities such as sport, music and motoring. A third benefit is the ability to provide more in-depth information than a single television or press advert. For example, a car manufacturer could provide a video of a new model and display its features before asking the viewer to request a brochure, thereby generating a lead.[55]

Interactive television advertising can generate direct sales and encourage home shopping; Thomas Cook TV provides a channel offering showcase holidays that viewers can buy by telephone or via the Internet. It also has the benefit of not requiring a call centre, as responses are dealt with electronically. It is also more convenient for viewers, who do not have to rush off to the telephone or computer to place their order. In addition, the red button can be more effective that a telephone call, with one advertiser recording a response rate nine times greater via iTV than by using a phone number. Longer commercials are more likely to encourage people to respond, with 40-second and 60-second spots generating up to 25 per cent more responses that a standard 30-second ad.[56] One disadvantage is that consumers cannot inspect a product in as much detail as they can when visiting a shop.

The most active sectors are cars, travel and financial services, where the ability to pass on more information to viewers is most highly valued. For example, Volvo ran a television campaign promoting its S40, accompanied by an eight-minute documentary showing the interior and performance of the car. This was made available via the web and iTV. Around 435,000 people saw the documentary, representing 11 per cent of Sky Digital viewers aware of the advert, and spent an average of six minutes watching it.[57]

Benefits and Limitations of Digital Technologies to Consumers and Organizations

Digital technologies offer consumers and organizations considerable benefits. For example, consumers benefit from greater convenience, access to information and lower prices. Organizations benefit through investment reduction, reduced order and selling costs, and wider distribution. There are, however, some limitations. For example, for consumers, inflexible delivery may mean they have to stay at home awaiting delivery, and there may be concerns about security and not receiving paid-for goods. For organizations, the logistical costs of sending goods to individual consumers may be high, as may the set-up costs of moving to an Internet-based procurement systems.

In order to maximize the opportunities created by digital technologies, an organization should assess the benefits and limitations of such technologies and their likely impact on organizational success. By asking questions such as 'Does technology change the target or scope of the market?', 'Does new technology help satisfy customer needs better than existing offers?' and 'To what extent will customers adopt new digital technology over the long term?', a company can begin to plan how it should proceed. Table 18.2 shows some of the key considerations from a consumer perspective, and Table 18.3 from an organizational perspective.

Ethical Issues in Digital Marketing

Increased adoption of digital technologies within marketing has had many beneficial effects, such as increasing customer choice and convenience, and enabling smaller companies to compete in global markets across a range of digital platforms. However, there are some key ethical issues emerging as a result of increased usage of digital technologies.

The digital divide

The historical timeline of the development of Internet technologies reveals that, in the early days, it served highly specialized purposes and was used by expert technologists. Expansion and changes in the development of the World Wide Web have made Internet technology more accessible to a greater number of people, but there remains a virtual divide between the technology's 'haves' and 'have nots'. Hoffman and Novak[58] examined the extent to which the Internet has become indispensable, and found significant differences in usage based on race, and educational attainment. They concluded that educational attainment is crucial if the digital divide is to be closed, and that efforts should be made to improve access for Hispanic and black populations in North America.[59]

Public and private organizations around the globe need to find creative solutions to improve Internet access for all citizens, regardless of their demographic background, as they should not be deprived of Internet access due to financial restrictions, a poor education and/or a lack of computer skills. From a commercial perspective, it is also important to acknowledge that while the networks forming the Internet reach around the globe, access is far from equal and equitable.

However, mobile phones and digital television (DTV) have been more widely adopted and reach into the community. For example, mobile phone ownership is currently nearing 95 per cent of the adult population and DTV reaches 63 per cent of households.[60] The digital

Potential benefits and limitations of digital technologies to consumers	TABLE 18.2

Benefits	Limitations
Convenience in terms of being able to access information and services 24 hours a day, 365 days a year, from wherever they are at the time	*Delivery times* are not quite so flexible. The logistical complexities of getting physical goods the last mile to the customer's home can mean that the customer must stay in and wait until the goods arrive
Access to information: the Internet, mobile phone and a range of other devices enable end users to acquire detailed and real-time information about products, entertainment, flight details, weather reports, sport updates, and much more	*Information overload*: the amount of information that can be accessed via digital platforms by an end user can be overwhelming
Enhanced functionality: using the latest digital technology, customers can gain a better understanding of products and services by examining multimedia content, viewing 3D displays of car interiors or hotel room accommodation	*Access to technology*: the greater the capacity to incorporate multimedia content, the higher the required specifications of the equipment that can receive and download such content. However, some consumers around the globe do not have access to even the most basic means of access
New products and services can be purchased in areas such as online financial services, and there is the ability to mix together audio, music and visual materials to customize the entertainment goods being purchased	*Risk*: many consumers are concerned about using credit and/or debit cards to purchase goods online, for fear that their details will be captured. The 'Y' generation is not adopting secure payment via mobile phones at the rate expected, due to security concerns. Consumers are also concerned about the risk of not receiving goods that they have paid for
Lower prices: it is possible to search for the lowest price available for brands. Specific sites (e.g. Kelkoo) allow consumers to surf the Internet to find the best available price	*Cost implications*: the consumer has to make an initial investment in suitable technology, pay for consumables like printer ink and fund the cost of downloading company information

divide in computing might also be on the point of being bridged, with a £7 laptop being launched in India.[61]

Recent research suggest that there is a new form of digital divide forming.[62] As digital technologies become more widespread it is specific aspects of the technologies that form divisions. For example, Londoners prefer to talk rather than text, whereas in Northern Ireland more texts are sent per week than anywhere else in the UK; rural Internet users are stuck with slow connections in comparison with their urban neighbours; and three hours more television is watched per week in Scotland than anywhere else in the UK.

Social exclusion

Another ethical consideration is the fear of technological exclusion of the poorest members of society who cannot afford a computer, broadband connection, interactive television, digital radio or 3G phone and therefore cannot benefit from the vast array of products and services available, or access to information sources. For example, Prudential, the financial services company, has faced strong criticism for the way Egg, its high-interest savings bank, cut itself off from mainstream customers by offering Internet-only access, thereby creating a system that ensured it attracted only the wealthiest customers. Some utility companies, too, may be

Potential benefits and limitations of digital technologies to organizations	TABLE 18.3
Benefits	**Limitations**
Investment reduction through actions such as replacing retail outlets with an online shopping mall, saving on paper by converting a sales catalogue into an electronic form, connecting with customers via SMS	*Operational costs*: organizations are likely to incur increased logistical costs and, in the case of retailers, the cost of selecting goods for the consumer prior to delivery (a particularly high cost in the case of the grocery retailer). Furthermore, significant investment and expertise is required to achieve interoperability across networks and digital platforms
Reduced order costs: e-procurement systems can significantly reduce the costs associated with handling a purchase order by streamlining order entry systems and reducing administration costs	*Set-up costs*: moving from a paper-based system to a fully integrated e-procurement system, say, can have high cost implications—for example, investment in networked systems to enable multi-platform communications systems to interface with back-office systems, cost of human resources skills
Improved distribution: once information-based products such as magazines, software and images are digitized, a company can achieve global distribution without having to make capital investment in physical premises	*Short-termism*: companies should adopt a strategic focus towards technology adoption and look for opportunities to create long-term economic value rather than the short-term gain achieved through technologically facilitated cost reductions
Opportunity for reduced selling costs: as in certain instances the salesperson as a provider of one-to-one information can be replaced with an interactive website or an SMS message	*High-cost content*: end users have high expectations of the 'up to dateness' of online content. Not only does content have to be updated regularly, but also there are high cost implications for content creation
Relationship building: via a website or mobile phone a firm can acquire data on customers' purchase behaviour that can be used to develop higher levels of customer service	*Connective to transactional relationships*: the focus on price reductions by suppliers as a mechanism to attract customers can undermine the very nature of a relationship. It can become difficult to build a relationship based on anything but price
Customized promotion: unlike traditional media, such as television or print advertising, the firm can develop highly customized communications materials in order to meet the needs of small, specific groups of customers	*Over-specialization*: while it is technically possible to target a segment of one using, say, Internet technologies, an organization should always question the profitability of adopting such a strategy
New market opportunities: digital technology permits firms, whether large or small, to offer their products or services to any market in the world	*Technological deserts*: parts of the world are poorly served by telecommunications and network access providers; as a result some places do not have access to the Internet, television or radio
Marketing research opportunities: e-mail and website-based surveys provide a low-cost method of questioning large samples, although the representativeness of the sample needs to be considered, as does the acquisition of e-mail lists and the potential resentment that unsolicited e-mail questionnaires can cause. The Internet also provides a rich source of secondary information through websites	*Authenticity*: not all Internet users respond to Internet surveys by providing factual data. Potentially false or deliberately incorrect responses can bias research findings and give misleading results

discriminating against low-income groups by offering cut-price energy only over the Internet. Conversely, many other public- and private-sector organizations throughout the European Union are committed to finding ways to support sectors of the community that are currently excluded from the growing knowledge economy. The Abbey National, a UK bank, working in conjunction with the charity Age Concern, has invested in free computer and Internet taster sessions for the over-50s as part of an initiative to encourage use of the Internet.

However, there is also evidence of technology delivering advantages to socially deprived sectors of society. Mobile phones have aided homeless people by allowing them to avoid the embarrassment of not having a permanent address by giving a mobile number on job applications.[63] Additionally, mobile phones are reportedly popular with people who are deaf and hard of hearing, as using the short messaging service (SMS) functions on mobiles helps people with hearing difficulties to communicate freely by sending text messages.[64]

A major issue in some industries, such as music and film, is the illegal downloading of copyrighted material, depriving artists and companies of revenue from the sale of these items. Marketing Ethics and Corporate Social Responsibility in Action 18.1 discusses the important issues for the music industry.

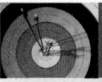

18.1 Marketing Ethics and Corporate Social Responsibility in Action

Fighting Piracy, or Consumer and Artist Empowerment?

Piracy has been a long-standing issue for holders of copyrights across several industries. The music industry, for example, has suffered hugely with increased online file sharing among e-consumers. File sharing has also meant declining CD sales, and in an attempt to combat piracy, the industry has reshaped the way in which it sells its tunes. Music can now be purchased 'per song' at about £0.79 each, and downloaded in one click. But critics argue that the music industry has failed hugely in its attempt to come to grips with the new environment in which it operates. Paid-for music downloads, they suggest, have fallen short of both combating piracy and keeping music fans happy. Fans show dissatisfaction with current download offers, as compressed music files have lower quality than music stored in other media. Current research also suggests that in 2008 only 5 per cent of music downloads were legal, and the biggest consumers of online music are also said to be the people who share music illegally.

As a result, coalitions of music labels have been created in order to exercise tighter controls over copyrighted materials. An example of the success of this industry's exercise of power is Sweden's recent introduction of IPRED, a new law that forces Internet service providers to hand in details about users who share content of copyrighted material to the owners of such rights. After the introduction of this new law, daily Internet traffic in Sweden fell more than 40 per cent. Also, the co-founders of Swedish online file-sharing website Pirate Bay have recently been fined $905,000 each, and sentenced to one year in prison. The conviction reflects the industry's attempt to hold on to a profit-making model that no longer works, in a marketplace that now caters for empowered artists and consumers. Indeed, some consumers share music illegally in a conscious attempt to defy the power of music labels in the market, while research suggests that unknown or less-known music artists enjoy sharing their music for free, and see this as a gift to their fans, and as a way to publicize their work.

Even famous music artists have recently become disheartened with the controls exercised by record labels upon their creations, with bands finding alternative ways to distribute and sell their songs. Radiohead, for example, adopted a 'pay what you like' pricing policy when their *In Rainbows* album was launched, and Coldplay gave free access to some tracks in order to promote a new album. If record labels are to survive at all, they will have to learn to give up some of their control, and work with artists and consumers in a more co-creative and collaborative way.

Based on: Arthur (2009);[65] Bragg and Rowntree (2009);[66] Brown (2009);[67] Kiss (2009);[68] Swash (2009)[69]

Intrusions on privacy

Some Internet users are very wary of online shopping because of the information provided about them by cookies. These are tiny computer files that a marketer can download on to the computer of the online shoppers that visit the marketer's website, to record their visits. Cookies serve many useful functions: they remember users' passwords so individuals do not have to log on each time they revisit a site; they remember users' preferences in order to provide more relevant pages or data; they remember the contents of consumers' shopping baskets from one visit to the next. However, because they can provide a record of users' movements around the web, cookies can give a very detailed picture of people's interests and circumstances. For example, cookies contain information provided by visitors, such as product preferences, personal data and financial information, including credit card numbers. From a marketer's point of view, cookies allow customized and personalized content for online shoppers. However, most Internet users probably do not know that this information is being collected and stored, and would object if they did. (Incidentally, online users can check if their drive contains cookies by opening any file named 'cookies'.) Some people fear that companies will use this information to build psychographic profiles that enable them to influence a customer's behaviour. Others simply object that information about them is being held without their express permission. Although users are identified by a code number rather than a name and address (and this, therefore, does not violate the EU data protection directive), the fear is that direct marketing databases will be combined with information on online shopping behaviour to create a vast new way of peering into people's private lives.

Another form of invasion of privacy is the sending of unsolicited e-mails (spam). Recipients find spam intrusive and annoying. One remedy is for Internet service providers to install protection against spam on behalf of their customers. The EU's Electronic Data Protection Directive states that marketers must not send e-mails to consumers who have not expressly stated their wish to receive them.

> E-mail is an excellent medium, but it is a mistake to use it without prior consent. It is better suited to the later stages of developing a relationship. We believe the best solution is for Internet service providers to install the protection on behalf of their customers, who shouldn't have to worry about it.[70]

Once again, there are also examples of how technologies are enhancing rather than reducing an individual's privacy—for instance, texting medical results to individuals so avoiding anyone else being able to intercept the message.

Marketing to children

Another potential ethical issue is that of using the Internet to market to children. The Internet is a very popular medium with youngsters and there are ethical issues that companies need to keep in mind. For example, websites may contain advertisements. Are children being tricked by merging advertising with other website content? Are children aware that personal information that is being solicited from them may be used for future marketing purposes? Do they realize that every mouse click may be being monitored?

When you have read this chapter

log on to the Online Learning Centre at www.mcgraw-hill.co.uk/textbooks/jobber to explore chapter-by-chapter test questions, links and further online study tools for marketing.

Review ● ● ●

1 **The concept of digital marketing**
- The application of digital technologies that form channels to market (the Internet, mobile, wireless, and digital television) to achieve corporate goals through meeting and exceeding customer needs better than the competition.

2 **The key elements of the digital age**
- These are the Internet, wireless communications (including mobile devices), interactive television, new distribution channels, convergence, and digitization and connectivity.

3 **The stages in digital marketing planning**
- The stages are as follows.
  - The digital context: what type of activities are being considered for digital application.
  - Digital marketing audit and SWOT analysis: analysis of the marketing environment and internal competences to assess strengths, weaknesses, opportunities and threats, and to identify the key issues that will need to be managed in the digital context.
  - Digital marketing objectives and strategy: determination of what is being sought (for example, customer acquisition or retention) and how the objectives are to be achieved. A key decision is the creation of a competitive advantage among target consumers. Sources include lower prices, lower costs, improved service, greater product variety, and product customization.
  - Digital marketing mix: the mix must match target customer needs based upon product (individual, customized, digital), price (dynamic, transparent, flexible), promotion (instantaneous, permission-based, interactive) and place (new channels, virtual, global).
  - Digital marketing implementation: a decision needs to be made regarding whether all the implementation is handled 'in-house' or whether it is partly outsourced. Key issues are integration and interoperability. An action plan must be drawn up.
  - Digital marketing evaluation and performance control: key variables such as targeted market share and attitudes need to be evaluated, and reasons for poor performance analysed.

4 **Digital marketing media**
- The Internet and web: an understanding of users can be achieved by using classification variables (e.g. income), character variables (e.g. perceptions) and consumer experiences (e.g. consumer assessments of their online shopping process). Promotion can be achieved through search engine marketing, online PR, permission-based marketing, e-mails and viral marketing, and affiliate marketing.
- Wireless communications: this includes mobile and smartphones, palmtops and personal digital assistants. In companies, wireless technology applications are to be found in field sales, the mobile office, fleet management and field service. The advantages of mobile communications are its cost effectiveness, ability to target, its interactive nature, the ability to develop customer relationships, its time flexibility, its ability to allow immediate and measurable results, and the capability to create databases. Limitations are that text messages must be short, visuals are usually unexciting, wear-off may become a problem, and there is the possibility that poorly targeted messages could cause annoyance. The key rules are to gain permission, accurately target, add value and encourage two-way dialogue (interaction).
- Interactive television: this form of promotion allows viewers of advertisements to 'press the red button' on a handset to see more information about a product. It facilitates home shopping and measurement of response. Targeting of niche audiences is possible. A disadvantage is that consumers cannot inspect a product in as much detail as when visiting a shop.

5 **Benefits and limitations of digital technologies**
- For consumers the potential benefits are convenience, access to information, enhanced functionality, new products and services, and lower prices.

- For consumers the potential limitations are inflexible delivery times, information overload, lack of access to technology, risk and the cost implications.
- For organizations the potential benefits are investment reduction, reduced order costs, improved distribution, the opportunity for reduced selling costs, relationship building, customized promotion, new market opportunities and marketing research opportunities.
- For organizations the potential limitations are increased logistical costs, high set-up costs, short-termism, high-cost content, the danger of moving to transactional relationships based on price, over-specialization, lack of access in some parts of the world to the Internet, and the possibility that Internet users may provide biased marketing research responses.

6 Ethical issues in digital marketing
- These are the potentially harmful effects of creating a digital divide between those with digital access and those without, of producing the social exclusion of those who cannot afford digital devices, of permitting intrusions on privacy, and of marketing to children.

Key Terms

blog short for weblog; a personal diary/journal on the web; information can easily be uploaded on to a website and is then available for general consumption by web users

digital marketing the application of digital technologies that form channels to market (the Internet, mobile communications, interactive television and wireless) to achieve corporate goals through meeting and exceeding customer needs better than the competition

e-business a term generally used to refer to both buy-side and sell-side e-commerce, and the internal use of Internet, mobile and wireless technologies through an organization

e-marketing a term used to refer to the use of technology (telecommunications and Internet-based) to achieve

marketing objectives and bringing the customer and supplier closer together

electronic commerce involves all electronically mediated transactions between an organization and any third party it deals with, including exchange of information

Internet marketing the achievement of corporate goals through meeting and exceeding customer needs better than the competition, through the utilization of digital Internet technologies

mobile marketing the sending of text messages to mobile phones to promote products and build relationships with consumers

portal a website that serves as an 'entry point' to the World Wide Web; portals usually offer guidance on using the Internet and search engines that permit keyword searches

Study Questions

1. Marketing via digital platforms is on the increase. Explain why this is so and highlight the barriers a company might encounter when expanding its use of digital technology.

2. Discuss the ways that the operations of organizations are likely to need to change as a result of using digital platforms and technologies when expanding their sales operations.

3. What are the benefits of the Internet and e-commerce to customers and organizations? Are there any potential disadvantages and pitfalls of digital marketing?

(4) Explain the potential impact of the convergence of digital and analogue technologies on (a) the consumer and (b) the media industry.

(5) Discuss how digital technologies can be used to create competitive advantage.

(6) How can the marketing mix be extended and utilized to support a digital marketing strategy?

(7) Discuss the key ethical issues likely to be considered when formulating a digital marketing plan.

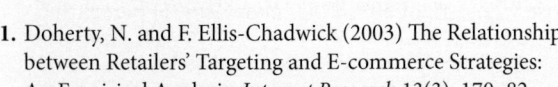

References

1. Doherty, N. and F. Ellis-Chadwick (2003) The Relationship between Retailers' Targeting and E-commerce Strategies: An Empirical Analysis, *Internet Research* 13(3), 170–82.
2. DTI (2004) *Business in the Information Age: The International Benchmarking Study 2004.*
3. Pidd, H. (2009) Web Worldwide: UK Housewives Love It, Chinese Use It Most, Danes Are Least Keen, *Guardian*, 1 January, 3.
4. Hoffman, D. and T. Novak (1997) A New Marketing Paradigm for Electronic Commerce, *The Information Society* 13, 43–54.
5. Chaffey, D., R. Mayer, K. Johnston and F. Ellis-Chadwick (2009) *Internet Marketing: Strategy Implementation and Practice* (4th edn), Harlow: FT/Prentice-Hall.
6. Chaffey, D. and P. R. Smith (2008) *eMarketing Excellence: Planning and Optimizing your Digital Marketing*, Oxford: Butterworth Heinemann.
7. Furness, V. (2009) *Emerging IPTV and Mobile TV Models: Marketing Opportunities, Challenges and Key Vendors,* Report, Business Insights Limited, Mortimer House, 37–41 Mortimer Street, London, United Kingdom.
8. Ellis-Chadwick, F. E. and N. F. Doherty (2009) Exploring the Drivers, Form and Success of E-Commerce Strategies in the UK Retail Sector, *European Journal of Marketing*, forthcoming.
9. Doherty, N. and F. Ellis-Chadwick (2006) Strategic Thinking in the Internet Era, *British Rail Consortium [BRC] Consortium Solutions* 3, February 2004, 59–63.
10. Duffy, J. (2006) The MySpace Age, *BBC News Magazine*, 7 March.
11. Chaffey, D. and P. R. Smith (2005) *eMarketing Excellence: Planning and Optimizing your Digital Marketing*, Oxford: Butterworth Heinemann.
12. Chaffey and Smith (2005) op. cit.; Payne, A. F. T. and P. Frow (2005) A Strategic Framework for Customer Relationship Marketing, *Journal of Marketing* 69(4), 161–76.
13. Chaffey *et al.* (2009) op. cit.
14. Chaffey and Smith (2008) op. cit.
15. Ellis-Chadwick, F. E., N. F. Doherty and L. Anastaskis (2007) E-Strategy in the UK Retail Grocery Sector: A Resource-based Analysis, *Managing Service Quality* 17(6), 702–27.
16. Chaffey and Smith (2008) op. cit.
17. Peppers, D. and M. Rogers (1997) *The One to One Future: Building Relationships One Customer at a Time,* New York: Doubleday.
18. Barwise, P., A. Elberse and K. Hammond (2002) Marketing and the Internet, in Barton, A. and R. Wensley (eds) *The Handbook of Marketing* 69(4), 161–76.
19. Jarvis, G. (2008) How to Track Customer Behaviour, *The Marketer*, July/August, 32–7.
20. Nettleton, K. (2008) Why Radiohead is in Tune with Online Marketing, *Campaign*, 1 August, 9.
21. Adegoke, Y. (2008) Obama's Election Success is a Victory for Digital Marketing, *Marketing Week*, 20 November, 30–1.
22. Walmsley, A. (2008) Campaigning 2.0 Could Swing UK Vote, *Marketing*, 30 July, 14.
23. Simms, J. (2008) SMEs Look to Web Answers, *Marketing*, 29 October, 33–4.
24. Chaffey, D. (2008) How to Exploit Search Engines, *The Marketer*, December/January, 32–7.
25. White, T. B., D. L. Zahay, H. Thorbjørnsen and S. Shavitt (2008) Getting too Personal: Reactance to Highly Personalized Email Solicitations, *Marketing Letters* 19(1), 39–50.
26. Doherty, N. and F. Ellis-Chadwick (2006) New Perspectives in Internet Retailing: A Review and Strategic Critique of the Field, *International Journal of Retail & Distribution Management* 34(4/5), 411–28.
27. Hoffman, D., T. Novak and A. Schlosser (2000) The Evolution of the Digital Divide: How Gaps in Internet Access May Impact on E-Commerce, *Journal of Computer-Mediated Communications* 5(3).
28. Brengman, M., M. Guens, B. Weijters, S. Smith and W. Swinyard (2005) Segmenting Internet Shoppers Based on their Web-Usage-Related Lifestyle: A Cross-Cultural Validation, *Journal of Business Research* 58(1), 79–88.
29. Keen, C., M. Wetzels, K. de Ruyter and R. Feinberg (2004) E-tailers Versus Retailers: Which Factors Determine Consumer Preferences, *Journal of Business Research* 57, 685–95.
30. George, J. (2004) The Theory of Planned Behaviour and Internet Purchasing, *Internet Research* 14(3), 198–211.
31. O'Cass, A. and T. Fenech (2002) Web Retailing Adoption, Exploring the Nature of the Internet User's Web Retailing Behaviour, *Journal of Consumer Services* 10(2), 81–94.

32. Wolfinburger, M. and M. Gilly (2003) eTailQ: Dimensionalizing, Measuring and Predicting Etail Quality, *Journal of Retailing* 79(3), 183–98.

33. Vrechopolus, A., R. O'Keefe, G. Doukidis and G. Siomkos (2004) Virtual Store Layout: An Experimental Comparison in the Context of Retail Grocery, *Journal of Retailing* 8(1), 13–22.

34. Grant, J. (2008) Timesaver or Digital Foot in the Door?, *Guardian*, Special Report on Internet Advertising, 3 November, 4.

35. Murphy, C. (2008) Campaigns Get Smart, *Guardian*, Media Guardian Report on Changing Advertising, 22 September, 1.

36. Google AdWords (2006) https://adwords.google.co.uk/select/Login?sourceid=AWO&subid=UK-ET-ADS&hl-en_GB, accessed 30 April 2006.

37. Chaffey (2008) op. cit.

38. Chaffey (2008) Rise Through the Ranks, *The Marketer*, November, 51–3.

39. Immediate Futures (2005) Measuring the Influence of Bloggers on Corporate Reputation, www.publicrelationsonline.com/files/MeasuringBloggerInfluence61205.pdf.

40. http://www.technorati.com/about/.

41. Postma, O. J. and M. Brokke (2002) Personalization in Practice: The Proven Effects of Personalisation, *Journal of Database Management* 9(2), 137–42.

42. Wilson, R. (2000) The Six Principles of Viral Marketing, *web marketing today* 20, at http://www.crmodyssey.com/Documentation/Documentation_PDF/Principles_viral_marketing.pdf, accessed 2 May 2006.

43. Bold, B. (2009) Cadbury's 'Eyebrow' Ad Goes Viral to Tune of 4m Views, Brandrepublic.com, 16 February 2009 (retrieved from www.brandrepublic.com/News/881308/Cadburys-eyebrow-ad-goes-viral-tune-4m-views).

44. Woods, A. (2008) The Bluffer's Guide to Affiliate Marketing, *Marketing*, 25 June, 36–40.

45. Anonymous (2002) Can SMS Ever Replace Traditional Direct Mail?, *Marketing Week,* 26 September, 37.

46. Middleton, T. (2002) Sending Out the Winning Message, *Marketing Week*, 16 May, 43–5.

47. McCartney, N. (2003) Getting the Message Across, *Financial Times*, 15 January, 3.

48. De Kerckhove, A. (2002) Introduction to Making Mobile Marketing Work, *Campaign*, 1 March, 17.

49. Anonymous (2008) Madison, We Have Lift Off, *Economist*, 29 November, 74.

50. Clark, M. (2008) Mobile Search: All to Play For, *Marketing*, 23 July, 31–3.

51. Carat Interactive (2002) The Future of Wireless Marketing, White Paper, at http://www.bjoconsulting.com/download/Wireless_WhitePaper.pdf.

52. GSM World (2006) http://www.gsmworld.com/technology/index.shtml.

53. Signorini, E. (2001) *The Enterprise Wireless Data Application Opportunity: A Segmentation Analysis*, The Yankee Group, December.

54. Yankee Group (2001) *Wireless Connectivity to the Enterprise: 2001 Survey Analysis,* The Yankee Group, March.

55. Michell, A. (1995) Preaching the Loyalty Message, *Marketing Week*, 1 December, 26–7.

56. Reed, D. (1996) Direct Flight, *Marketing Week*, 1 November, 45–7.

57. Fletcher, D. (2005) Terms of Engagement, *Campaign*, 27 May, 11.

58. Hoffman, D. and T. Novak (1999) *The Growing Digital Divide: Implications for an Open Research Agenda*, eLab Owen Graduate School of Management Vanderbilt University (http://ecommerce.vanderbilt.edu/).

59. Hoffman, D. L., T. P. Novak and A. Venkatesh (2004) Has the Internet Become Indispensable?, *Communications of the ACM* 47(7), July, 37–42.

60. Ofcom (2005) Digital Television UK Household Penetration, at www.ofcom.org.uk/media/news/2005/09/nr_20050915#content.

61. Ramesh, R. (2009) After the World's Cheapest Car, India Launches £7 Laptop, *Guardian*, 3 February, 19.

62. Office of Communications (2005) http://www.ofcom.org.uk/.

63. Office of the Deputy Prime Minister (2005) Digital Solutions to Social Exclusion, at http://egovmonitor.com/node/3362.

64. *BBC News* (2002) Deaf Go Mobile Phone Crazy, at http://news.bbc.co.uk/1/hi/ sci/tech/1808872.stm.

65. Arthur, C. (2009) Swedish Internet Use Plummets After Filesharing Curb Introduced, *Guardian*, 4 April 2009 (retrieved 22 April 2009, from www.guardian.co.uk/technology/2009/apr/04/sweden-pirate-bay-filesharing-internet).

66. Bragg, B. and D. Rowntree (2009) Fair Play in the Music Industry, Guardian.co.uk, 10 March 2009 (retrieved 22 April 2009, from www.guardian.co.uk/commentisfree/2009/mar/10/google-music-prs-youtube).

67. Brown, P. (2009) Streaming Music: Even Better Than The Real Thing?, Guardian.co.uk, 21 January 2009 (retrieved 21 April 2009, from www.guardian.co.uk/technology/2009/jan/22/digitalmusic-drm/print).

68. Kiss, J. (2009) What does the Pirate Bay Verdict Mean for Innovation?, Guardian.co.uk, 17 April 2009 (retrieved 22 April 2009, from www.guardian.co.uk/media/pda/2009/apr/17/pirate-bay-startups).

69. Swash, R. (2009) Online Piracy: 95% of Music Downloads are Illegal, *Guardian*, 17 January 2009 (retrieved 22 April 2009, from www.guardian.co.uk/music/2009/jan/17/music-piracy).

70. Anonymous (2002) UK Consumers Have Had Enough of Spam E-Mail, *Marketing Week*, 31 October, 39.

Google

Staying Ahead of the Game?

Google helps the world to answer questions and solve problems by using its search engine, which originally provided an innovative approach to searching the Internet. Graduate students Larry Page and Sergey Brin began developing the search technology in 1996, and Google.com was launched in September 1998. By 2008, the company had grown rapidly and was valued at $742 billion. Google has become a global success of the digital age. Its rapid rise to being 'the world's biggest and best-loved search engine' can in part be attributed to the smart algorithms (mathematical instructions that computers can understand) devised by Larry and Sergey. But equally important is the value proposition (the benefits to the user) the search engine provides: Google enables its users to find relevant information quickly and easily, and delivers search results in an uncluttered format, which improves usability and increases user enjoyment and satisfaction. This winning combination has enabled Google to become market leader in less than a decade, but also to sustain its competitive advantage.

However, competition is dynamic and intense in high-tech markets, and business commentators have begun to question whether Google can maintain its market position for much longer. In fact, investors have been quoted as saying that they fear 'Google, at the ripe old age of nine, might already be over the hill'.

This case looks at Google, its resources and capabilities, and considers how the company will sustain competitive advantage and its market-leading position in the future.

Resources, capabilities and competitive advantage

According to Barney (1991), by examining the resources and capabilities a company has invested in, it is possible to get a better understanding of its sources of competitive advantage. Google has developed sophisticated IT resources that offer distinctively better functionality and services than its competitors. In the early days, the company adopted a lean and flexible operations strategy. According to Vogelstein (2002), what lies behind Google's success is its network of data centres based around Santa Clara, USA. It uses thousands of computer servers to provide a search capacity much greater than its rivals provide. The company has also gained significant knowledge about web-based markets, which has enabled it to develop superior information system capabilities.

Google's search principle is straightforward: by focusing on page rankings rather than just indexing contents, the search engine is able to provide more relevant search results than its competitors (e.g. Yahoo!, AltaVista, Excite). Search tools crawl the web, checking the content of pages without needing to understand the meaning of the content. As a result, such 'web crawlers' are unable to differentiate between relevant and irrelevant web pages when delivering search results. However, adopting a rank-ordering system, logging pages according to the number of links from other web pages and the structure of these connections, has enabled Google to become a quasi-intelligent search tool. To assist the ranking process, Google also checks font sizes, whether a word appears in the page title, the position on the page in which a word appears, and a range of other page characteristics, in order to give an indication of the significance of the search term within a given page.

By making creative use of information technology resources to enhance the capabilities of its search engine, Google created a search service that was quickly perceived by its users as superior to the competition. The Google brand differentiated itself from the competition by introducing the customer benefit of 'relevance' to online searching. The business continued to grow as consumers and business users increasingly turned to the Internet as a primary source of information (searching is the second most common function of the web).

In addition to its effective and efficient use of technology resources and capabilities, Google's strong market position was supported by its financial success. This was generated by the application of an e-business model that provided free-to-user search services, highly targeted and yet discreet advertising and licensing the search technology to third parties (Google currently provides search services for a number of leading search engines). It should be noted that Google continues to generate the majority of its income from advertising. Advertisers pay per click for referrals to their web pages via the Google interface using AdWords, which are search terms chosen by the advertisers and paid for at a rate determined by the popularity of the term. The cost per click varies according to the level of competition from advertisers for a particular keyword.

Competitive markets

Since it was established, Google has used technology resources creatively and, in so doing, has developed superior technology-based capabilities that have enabled the company to become financially successful and get ahead of the competition. However, competition in the search engine market has intensified: Microsoft launched a new search engine, MSN Search, which promises precise and relevant answers from its billions of web pages and images. Yahoo!, another leading market player, has found a niche in the search market, where it has gained market share by focusing on local searching (see www.local.yahoo.com). Cuil.com was developed by a technology company that claims to have developed 'a pioneering a new approach to search … which combines the biggest Web index with content-based relevance methods, results organized by ideas, and complete user privacy' (source: http://www.cuil.com/info/news_press/, June 2009).

Despite the growing competition, Google maintains a dominant market position (see Table C35.1) and appears to continue to be users' favourite choice when searching online.

Future sources of competitive advantage

Larry and Sergey had a good idea and implemented it in a manner that enabled the company to differentiate itself from the competition, while protecting itself by raising market entry barriers through innovative applications of its resources and capabilities. However, the marketplace is changing as technologies advance and new entrants join the market. Google has responded by diversifying and providing niche search services—news, maps, alerts, blogs, videos for specific target audiences; Scholar (for academics) and Mobile (for remote users)—and the company continues to explore how new technologies can be used to provide innovative search services and products.

More recently, Google has begun to look for ways of entering and dominating new markets:

- web browsers—Chrome, Google's first attempt at developing a web browser, was released in September 2008; the browser is designed to be more robust than Internet Explorer, but is said not to be a threat to its Microsoft rival at the moment
- e-mail—Gmail (Google e-mail), a free e-mail service, became available to the general public in 2007 and has become very popular, with over 100 million users worldwide

Top search engines*			TABLE C35.1
Rank	Name	Domain	%
1	Google	www.google.com	74
2	Yahoo!	search.yahoo.com	16
3	Bing	www.bing.com	5
4	Ask	www.ask.com	3
* Ranked by volume of searches (http://www.hitwise.com/datacenter/main/dashboard-10133.html, June 2009).			
Note: Hitwise measures the number of visits to search engines and then calculates the percentage of total visits to a particular site.			

- mobile Internet—Google's android phone allows owners to call their friends, surf the web and find their way around with the built-in compass as they, say, search for a restaurant or entertainment venue; the Google phone has taken market share from Apple by offering more functionality at more affordable prices.

Investors' fears of Google being 'over the hill' are likely to be unfounded, as it continues to dominate the search market and is gaining ground by diversifying, but the question of sustainability remains open to debate. Google came to the market with a technically superior product but is now heavily reliant on advertising revenue. The company may need to continue to innovate if it is to stay ahead.

References

Based on: Barney, J. B. (1991) From Resources and Sustained Competitive Advantage, *Journal of Management* 17(1), 99–120; Naughton, J. (2002) Web Masters, *Observer*, 15 December, 27; Vogelstein, F. (2002) Looking for a Dotcom Winner? Search no Further, *Fortune* 145(11), 65–8; McHugh, J. (2003) Google vs Evil, *Wired* 11(1), 130–5; Hitwise (2006) http://www.hitwise.com/news/us200508.html (accessed May 2006); Rose, F. (2006) Are You Ready for Googlevision?, *Wired* 14(5), at www.wired.com/wired/archive/14.05/google_pr.html; Brit, B. (2005) Google Moves Beyond Search, *Marketing*, September, 19.

Questions

1. What are Google's resources and capabilities, which have enabled the company to create competitive advantage in the search engine market?

2. How does Google differentiate itself from the competition and, in doing so, create competitive advantage?

3. Google will remain as market leader in the search engine market for the next decade. Debate this statement.

4. Assess Google's attempts to launch new products.

This case was written by Fiona Ellis-Chadwick, Senior Lecturer in Retail Management, Open University Business School.

Giftmaster
Moving Retail Online

With his second Christmas online coming up, Peter McAuley is reflecting on the changes in the business over the last three years and how it has moved from being a classic retail outlet in a busy shopping centre to a purely online retail offering, to what it is currently: a diversified business with both an online and an offline retail presence. This has involved a number of major changes to his business not least of which was the change of name from Special Days (his original offline trading name) to Giftmaster.ie.

Initial situation (1999–2006)

The Special Days retail outlet was created in 1999, and is owned and operated by Peter McAuley. Special Days operated as a tenant of the Liffey Valley Shopping Centre outlet until late 2006. Liffey Valley Shopping Centre (www.liffeyvalley.ie) is one of Ireland's leading shopping destinations and is situated, out of town, to the west of Dublin city. With over 90 tenants and close proximity to major infrastructure, its catchment area reaches well beyond city boundaries.

Peter McAuley has over 20 years' experience in the gift and retail trade. Working in retail in the UK, a decade ago, he identified a market niche on trips home and responded with the creation of the Special Days outlet. The concept of the shop was 'whatever day, your special day, we have something for it'. This included 'quirky gifts', novelty products, children's novelty items and games, house-warming gifts, pottery, greeting cards and decorating accessories. Seasonal products featured prominently for Valentine's Day, Easter, Mother's and Father's Day, Halloween and Christmas. The range was constantly refreshed and updated.

The Liffey Valley outlet was very much a browsing shop—customers were attracted by the displays, the colours and product presentations, and the smell of the Yankee candles that were featured as a key product (http://www.yankeecandle.co.uk/). Many customers browsed but did not purchase; however, once it came to Christmas, they bought a range of items altogether.

The Special Days trade name was registered on its creation in 1999 and the owner has received several offers to purchase it since then. Initially the outlet carried a wide range of board games, which differentiated it from other retailers. However, over time this,

differentiation was eroded by larger centre operators such as Boots, Dunnes Stores and Marks & Spencer, as well as Argos catalogue sales. Promotions such as three products for the price of two, and loyalty card promotions, common particularly with Boots outlets, can be supported by these larger operators based on volume sales achieved, but prove more difficult for independent retailers to deal with.

2006: a time of change

Peter McAuley felt that, effectively the 'writing was on the wall'[1] and the main reason behind the company's change of format from a bricks-and-mortar outlet to alternative channel options was mainly financial. Peter McAuley felt it was too expensive to keep the original store running in the Liffey Valley Shopping Centre due to operating and rental cost escalation. Also the limited floor space constrained his plans for product range expansion. By 2006 the company was paying €330,000 in rental costs p.a. for 2000 square feet of retail space within Liffey Valley, a price that highlights the increasing trend of shopping centres to be dominated by larger chain stores and multiples. This demonstrates that the costs of retailing for independents has 'gone through the stratosphere and it is just not possible' to sustain independent outlets within larger shopping centres.[1]

The Special Days retail outlet was closed in late 2006 and the operation was migrated to the Giftmaster site (www.giftmaster.ie)—which is now the group's parent site—in December 2006, and was a fully transactional site from the beginning. A key concern for the company was the risk of customer confusion and the inability to retain offline traditional shoppers in the move online.

Peter McAuley's original prediction was that the company would probably lose 80 per cent of its traditional shoppers with only 20 per cent of the original shopper base[1] following Special Days online, though it is difficult to measure this given the lack of data on offline retail customers in the absence of a database.

It is difficult for any company to accurately estimate the Return on Investment (ROI) in online channels, but despite this the move online was intuitively appealing for Special Days at this stage. The company envisaged being able to take about 20 per cent off all retail prices with the move to an online sales channel.

The Giftmaster site was positioned as 'Ireland's most comprehensive online gifts web store, selling a unique and extensive range of gifts for all occasions'. The connection with Special Days was leveraged and the site promised 'the best of Special Days and much more at even better value prices'. Surfers searching for Special Days as a specific term were redirected to the Giftmaster homepage.

The company also manages another site in parallel to Giftmaster.ie, the CasinoShop site (www.casinoshop.ie). This is positioned as Ireland's foremost supplier of poker and casino products to homes and clubs, and carries products such as poker sets, chips and tables, playing cards, blackjack and roulette tables, and casino supplies. This site was also established in late 2006. There are plans to host a separate casino site for businesses involved in poker tournaments, which would be password protected, offering business customers price discounts based on volume purchases. A large percentage of poker-related sales are currently to the trade.

Having experimented with various gift promotions in the past to encourage a certain level of euro purchasing on the site, the company has observed that free delivery is the most pertinent promotional tool for potential customers. Though not feasible for all products, the company runs special promotional periods offering free delivery on certain product categories over a specified purchase value; for example, on orders over €59. The busiest day of the week for online orders is usually Thursday.

The Giftmaster.ie site specializes in Yankee candles, toys, games, gifts, party boxes, balloons and chocolates. It aimed to deliver sales in the region of 10,000 in the first month of operation to help to determine the viability of the venture in the longer term. In fact, sales of 22,000 were achieved in the first month of trading in December 2006. Of these, approximately 90 per cent were generated outside Dublin, and approximately 20 per cent originated outside the domestic marketplace for delivery in Ireland. Peter McAuley feels that the company's Google AdWords campaign delivered strong results for this period. The company plans to target countries such as the USA and UK via Google AdWords, to strengthen the international sales pipeline in the future. Approximately 40 per cent of sales for the Giftmaster.ie site are generated by Christmas trade, with other peaks around Valentine's Day in February, Mother's Day in March and Father's Day in June. At present the company delivers only within Ireland (within 48 hours) but has plans to add UK delivery in the near future. Delivery charges average €4.95.

For 2007, Peter McAuley estimated that approximately 55 per cent of traffic was coming from Google. Yahoo!, which previously had been very strong, now represented only 12–13 per cent of site traffic. The company also generates site traffic from discussion boards, such as www.boards.ie, which has a specific poker forum within it. The company involves itself in the forum by sponsoring prizes and giving product advice.

> **//** *Giftmaster envisaged being able to take about 20 per cent off all retail prices with the move to an online sales channel.* **//**

An affiliate marketing campaign was introduced in June 2007. This offers interested parties a commission of 6 per cent of sales net of VAT (value added tax) on referred sales, to be paid at the end of each quarter. This affiliate scheme is promoted on both the Giftmaster.ie site and also the Casinoshop.ie site.

In order to rank highly (in the top 20 or 30 entries) on search engine listings and achieve visibility with target customers, the web stores are indexed with the major search engines, such as Google and Yahoo! Directory listings are also managed with current site links through directories such as www.armchair.ie, www.browseireland.com, www.search.ie and some discussion forums, such as www.boards.ie and www.irishwebmasterforum.ie.

The company also owns a site for Yankee candles, which is a well-recognized brand within this product sector. The site www.yankee.ie redirects to the Giftmaster.ie site. Another domain name owned is www.giftsireland.ie, which also redirects traffic to the Giftmaster site. It also owns www.pokerchips.ie, which redirects to the CasinoShop site. Though consumers may access the products offered through a variety of web stores, the payment software is supported across all the sites and effectively offers the same checkout facility for all sites.

Going multi-channel

Showrooms to display products and warehouse facilities were opened in February 2007 in Athy business park, which is based in County Kildare. The cost was in the region of €14,500 for 5000 square feet, a significant reduction on the costs of operation in Liffey Valley.

In mid-August 2008, the company opened a 2400-square foot retail store in the centre of Carlow town,[2] called Special Days Gift and Gourmet Emporium (www.specialdays.ie). This has enabled the company to offer a far greater range of gifts, along with gourmet food and wine hampers, occasion hampers and an even larger range of Yankee candles. The company has also enhanced its offering with value-adding features, such as product, outlet, contact and company information. The www.Giftsonline.ie webstore opened for business on 19 September 2008 and redirects all traffic from the Giftmaster site to this new homepage.[3] Giftsonline is a trading name of E-StoresRetail Ltd. The company is committed to this online sales channel, as evidenced by the resources devoted to building and maintaining the online channel.

The company has also taken steps to improve the payment process on the site. UseCash, launched in May 2008, is a service aimed at opening up online purchasing to users who are wary of using credit cards over the Internet, or to people who simply don't possess such a card. Eurostat research suggests that one in eight Europeans wouldn't use their credit cards to shop online. UseCash's system works by giving users a barcode when they order a product online; they print out the barcode and then take it in person to a Payzone store, where they pay in cash and the transaction is processed. Once the transaction has been processed, the online retailer is notified and the ordered item sent out. Giftmaster is one of a small number of online retailers that has set up a partnership with UseCash.[4]

Notes

1   Interview with CEO, 2 February 2007.
2   Carlow is a regional town, approximately 90 km south of Dublin, with a large rural hinterland.
3   Interview with CEO, 21 October 2008.
4   IPSO Wants Cheques Out, ElectricNews.net, 18 April 2008.

Questions

1   What attracts people to buy online? What are the likely perceived drawbacks of buying online?

2   Do you think the product categories offered for sale by the company—Special Days, Giftsonline and Casino Shop—are well suited to an online channel? Why or why not?

3   Discuss what is meant by search engine marketing (SEM). Do you feel the company is good at this? Do you have comments or suggestions for improvement?

4   Summarize Special Days' current market position via a SWOT analysis, and identify the key challenges the company may encounter over the next few years in operation.

This case was prepared by Roisin Vize, Doctoral Candidate in Marketing, Aileen Kennedy, Lecturer in Services Marketing, and Dr Joseph Coughlan, Research Fellow, all at the Faculty of Business, Dublin Institute of Technology.

Competition and Marketing

Analysing competitors and creating a competitive advantage

The race is not always to the swift, nor the battle to the strong, but that is the way to bet.

DAMON RUNYON

If you don't have a competitive advantage, don't compete.'

JACK WELCH, FORMER CHIEF EXECUTIVE OF GENERAL ELECTRIC

LEARNING OBJECTIVES

After reading this chapter, you should be able to:

1   describe the determinants of industry attractiveness

2   explain how to analyse competitors

3   distinguish between differentiation and cost leader strategies

4   discuss the sources of competitive advantage

5   discuss the value chain

6   explain how to create and maintain a differential advantage

7   explain how to create and maintain a cost leadership position

Satisfying customers is a central tenet of the marketing concept, but it is not enough to guarantee success. The real question is whether a firm can satisfy customers better than the competition. For example, many car manufacturers market cars that give customer satisfaction in terms of appearance, reliability and performance. They meet the basic requirements necessary to compete. Customer choice, however, will depend on creating a little more value than the competition. This extra value is brought about by establishing a competitive advantage—a topic that will be examined later in this chapter.

Since corporate performance depends on both customer satisfaction and being able to create greater value than the competition, firms need to understand their competitors as well as their customers. By understanding its competitors, a firm can better predict their reaction to any marketing initiative that the firm might make, and exploit any weaknesses they might possess. Competitor analysis is thus crucial to the successful implementation of marketing strategy. The discussion will begin by examining competitive industry structure: rivalry between firms does not take place within a vacuum. For example, the threat of new competitors and the bargaining power of buyers can greatly influence the attractiveness of an industry and the profitability of each competitor.

Analysing Competitive Industry Structure

An **industry** is a group of firms that market products that are close substitutes for each other. In common parlance we refer to the car, oil or computer industry, indicating that the definition of an industry is normally product-based. It is a fact of life that some industries are more profitable than others. For example, the car, steel, coal and textile industries have had poor profitability records for many years, whereas the book publishing, television broadcasting, pharmaceuticals and soft drinks industries have enjoyed high long-run profits. Not all of this difference can be explained by the fact that one industry provides better customer satisfaction than another. There are other determinants of industry attractiveness and long-run profitability that shape the rules of competition. These are the threat of entry of new competitors, the threat of substitutes, the bargaining power of buyers and of suppliers, and the rivalry between the existing competitors.[1] Where these forces are intense, below-average industry performance can be expected; where these forces are mild, superior performance is common. Their influence is shown diagrammatically in Figure 19.1, which is known as the Porter model of competitive industry structure. Each of the 'five forces' in turn comprises a number of elements that, together, combine to determine the strength of each force and its effect on the degree of competition. Each force is discussed below.

The threat of new entrants

New entrants can raise the level of competition in an industry, thereby reducing its attractiveness. For example, in Denmark, foreign entrants such as Sweden's SE-Banken posed a threat to the largest banks, Den Danske Bank and Unibank, and Norway's Finax.[2] The threat of new entrants depends on the barriers to entry. High entry barriers exist in some industries (e.g. pharmaceuticals), whereas other industries are much easier to enter (e.g. restaurants). Key **entry barriers** include:

- economies of scale
- capital requirements
- switching costs
- access to distribution
- expected retaliation.

For present competitors, industry attractiveness can be increased by raising entry barriers. High promotional and R&D expenditures, and clearly communicated retaliatory actions to

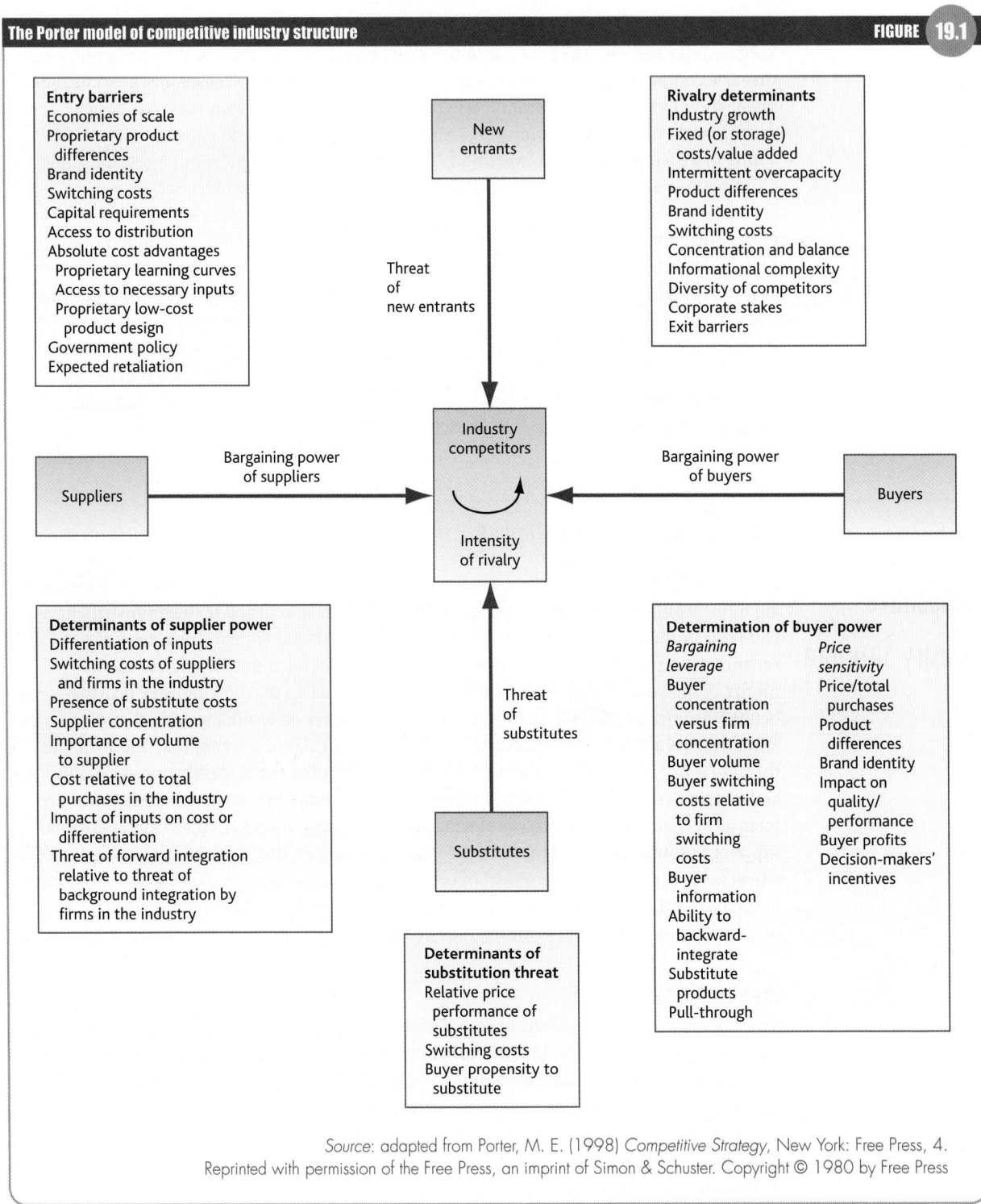

Entry barriers
Economies of scale
Proprietary product
  differences
Brand identity
Switching costs
Capital requirements
Access to distribution
Absolute cost advantages
  Proprietary learning curves
  Access to necessary inputs
  Proprietary low-cost
    product design
Government policy
Expected retaliation

New
entrants

Threat
of
new entrants

Rivalry determinants
Industry growth
Fixed (or storage)
  costs/value added
Intermittent overcapacity
Product differences
Brand identity
Switching costs
Concentration and balance
Informational complexity
Diversity of competitors
Corporate stakes
Exit barriers

Bargaining power
of suppliers

Industry
competitors

Intensity
of rivalry

Bargaining power
of buyers

Suppliers

Buyers

Determinants of supplier power
Differentiation of inputs
Switching costs of suppliers
  and firms in the industry
Presence of substitute costs
Supplier concentration
Importance of volume
  to supplier
Cost relative to total
  purchases in the industry
Impact of inputs on cost or
  differentiation
Threat of forward integration
  relative to threat of
  background integration by
  firms in the industry

Threat
of
substitutes

Substitutes

Determination of buyer power

Bargaining leverage	Price sensitivity
Buyer concentration versus firm concentration	Price/total purchases
Buyer volume	Product differences
Buyer switching costs relative to firm switching costs	Brand identity
	Impact on quality/ performance
Buyer information	Buyer profits
Ability to backward-integrate	Decision-makers' incentives
Substitute products	
Pull-through	

**Determinants of
substitution threat**
Relative price
  performance of
  substitutes
Switching costs
Buyer propensity to
  substitute

Source: adapted from Porter, M. E. (1998) *Competitive Strategy*, New York: Free Press, 4.
Reprinted with permission of the Free Press, an imprint of Simon & Schuster. Copyright © 1980 by Free Press

entry are some methods of raising barriers. One example of a company taking clear retaliatory action is that of Rotaprint, a US manufacturer of printing machines and accessories. The company made it common knowledge that it would retaliate if attacked. Despite this it was attacked by Toshiba in the USA. Rotaprint retaliated by launching an offensive against Toshiba in Japan where it cut its prices by 50 per cent. Toshiba matched the price cuts, only for Rotaprint to further reduce them by another 25 per cent. Shortly afterwards Toshiba left the USA, to be followed by Rotaprint's withdrawal from Japan. Other ways of raising barriers are by taking out patents and tying up suppliers and/or distributors. Some managerial actions can unwittingly lower barriers. For example, new product designs that dramatically lower manufacturing costs can ease entry for newcomers.

The bargaining power of suppliers

The cost of raw materials and components can have a major bearing on a firm's profitability. The higher the bargaining power of suppliers, the higher these costs. The bargaining power of suppliers will be high when:

- there are many buyers and few dominant suppliers
- there are differentiated highly valued products
- suppliers threaten to integrate forward into the industry
- buyers do not threaten to integrate backward into supply
- the industry is not a key customer group to the suppliers.

A firm can reduce the bargaining power of suppliers by seeking new sources of supply, threatening to integrate backward into supply, and designing standardized components so that many suppliers are capable of producing them.

The bargaining power of buyers

The concentration of European retailing has lowered manufacturers' bargaining power. Benetton's use of many suppliers has increased its bargaining power. The bargaining power of buyers is greater when:

- there are few dominant buyers and many sellers
- products are standardized
- buyers threaten to integrate backwards into the industry
- suppliers do not threaten to integrate forwards into the buyer's industry.
- the industry is not a key supplying group for buyers.

Firms in the industry can attempt to lower buyer power by increasing the number of buyers they sell to, threatening to integrate forwards into the buyer's industry and producing highly valued, differentiated products. In supermarket retailing, the brand leader normally achieves the highest profitability partially because being number one means that supermarkets need to stock the brand, thereby reducing buyer power in price negotiations.

Threat of substitutes

The presence of substitute products can lower industry attractiveness and profitability because these put a constraint on price levels. For example, tea and coffee are fairly close substitutes in most European countries. Raising the price of coffee, therefore, would make tea more attractive. The threat of substitute products depends on:

- buyers' willingness to substitute
- the relative price and performance of substitutes
- the costs of switching to substitutes.

The threat of substitute products can be lowered by building up switching costs, which may be psychological—for example, by creating strong distinctive brand personalities—and maintaining a price differential commensurate with perceived customer values. If these tactics fail to deter a rival from launching a substitute product, the incumbent is faced with the following options: copy the substitute; copy but build in a differential advantage; form a strategic alliance with the rival; buy the rival; or move to a new market. An example of the last option is the case of Rockware Glass, which was threatened by the desire of supermarkets to move from glass beer containers to cans. Its response was to move to the production of wine bottles for the French market, where there was no threat of the substitute container.

Industry competitors

The intensity of rivalry between competitors in an industry will depend on the following factors.

- *Structure of the competition*: there is more intense rivalry when there are a large number of small competitors or a few equally balanced competitors, and less rivalry when a clear leader (at least 50 per cent larger than the second) exists with a large cost advantage.
- *Structure of costs*: high fixed costs encourage price-cutting to fill capacity.
- *Degree of differentiation*: commodity products encourage rivalry, while highly differentiated products that are hard to copy are associated with less intense rivalry.
- *Switching costs*: rivalry is reduced when switching costs are high because the product is specialized, the customer has invested a lot of resources in learning how to use the product or has made tailor-made investments that are worthless with other products and suppliers. For example, a product might be customized, production, logistical or marketing operations might be geared to using the equipment of a particular supplier (e.g. computer systems), or retraining may be required as a result of a switch to another supplier.
- *Strategic objectives*: when competitors are pursuing build strategies, competition is likely to be more intense than when playing hold or harvesting strategies.
- *Exit barriers*: when barriers to leaving an industry are high due to such factors as lack of opportunities elsewhere, high vertical integration, emotional barriers or the high cost of closing down plant, rivalry will be more intense than when exit barriers are low.

Firms need to be careful not to spoil a situation of competitive stability. They need to balance their own position against the well-being of the industry as a whole. For example, an intense price or promotional war may gain a few percentage points in market share but lead to an overall fall in long-run industry profitability as competitors respond to these moves. It is sometimes better to protect industry structure than follow short-term self-interest.

A major threat to favourable industry structure is the use of a no-frills, low-price strategy by a minor player seeking positional advantage. For example, the launch of generic products in the pharmaceutical and cigarette industries has lowered overall profitability.

Despite meeting customers' needs with high-quality, good-value products, firms can 'compete away' the rewards. An intensive competitive environment means that the value created by firms in satisfying customer needs is given away to buyers through lower prices, dissipated through costly marketing battles (e.g. advertising wars) or passed on to powerful suppliers through higher prices for raw materials and components.

In Europe the competitive structure of industries was fundamentally changed with the advent of the single European market. The lifting of barriers to trade between countries has radically altered industry structure by affecting its underlying determinants. For example, the threat of new entrants and the growth in buyer/supplier power through acquisition or merger are fundamentally changing the competitive climate of many industries.

Competitor Analysis

The analysis of how industry structure affects long-run profitability has shown the need to understand and monitor competitors. Their actions can spoil an otherwise attractive industry, their weaknesses can be a target for exploitation, and their response to a firm's marketing initiatives can have a major impact on their success. Indeed, firms that focus on competitors' actions have been found to achieve better business performance than those who

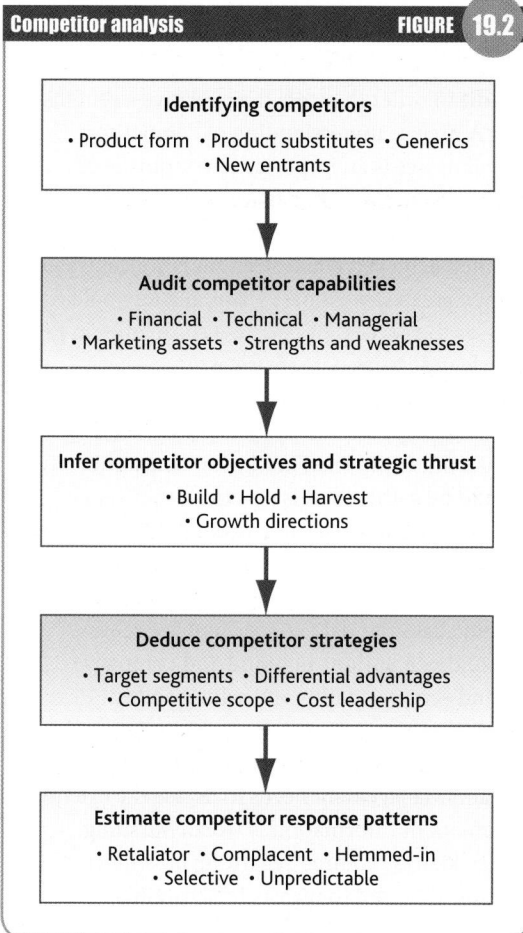

Competitor analysis   FIGURE 19.2

Identifying competitors
• Product form • Product substitutes • Generics
• New entrants

Audit competitor capabilities
• Financial • Technical • Managerial
• Marketing assets • Strengths and weaknesses

Infer competitor objectives and strategic thrust
• Build • Hold • Harvest
• Growth directions

Deduce competitor strategies
• Target segments • Differential advantages
• Competitive scope • Cost leadership

Estimate competitor response patterns
• Retaliator • Complacent • Hemmed-in
• Selective • Unpredictable

pay less attention to their competitors.[3] Competitive information can be obtained from marketing research surveys, recruiting competitors' employees (sometimes interviewing them is sufficient), secondary sources (e.g. trade magazines, newspaper articles), distributors, stripping down competitors' products and gathering competitors' sales literature.

Competitor analysis seeks to answer five key questions.

1 Who are our competitors?
2 What are their strengths and weaknesses?
3 What are their strategic objectives and thrust?
4 What are their strategies?
5 What are their response patterns?

These issues are summarized in Figure 19.2. Each question will now be examined.

Who are our competitors?

The danger when identifying competitors is that competitive myopia prevails. This malady is reflected in a narrow definition of competition resulting in too restricted a view of which companies are in competition. Only those companies that are producing technically similar products are considered to be the competition (e.g. paint companies). This ignores companies purchasing substitute products that perform a similar function (e.g. polyurethane varnish firms) and those that solve a problem or eliminate it in a dissimilar way (e.g. PVC double-glazing companies). The actions of all of these types of competitors can affect the performance of our firm and therefore need to be monitored. Their responses also need to be assessed as they will determine the outcome of any competitive move that our firm may wish to make. For example, we need to ask how likely it would be that polyurethane varnish companies would follow any price move we might wish to make.

Beyond these current competitors the environment needs to be scanned for potential entrants into the industry. These can take two forms: entrants with technically similar products and those invading the market with substitute products. Companies with similar core competences to the present incumbents may pose the threat of entering with technically similar products. For example, Apple's skills in computer electronics provided the springboard for it to become market leader in the portable music player market with its iPod brand. The source of companies entering with substitute products may be more difficult to locate, however. A technological breakthrough may transform an industry by rendering the old product obsolete as when the calculator replaced the slide rule, or when the car replaced the horse-drawn buggy. In such instances it is difficult to locate the source of the substitute product well in advance. Figure 19.3 illustrates this competitive arena.

 19.1 Pause for Thought

Think of an airline with which you are familiar. Who/what are its product form competitors? Can you think of as many product substitute competitors as possible? What are the marketing implications of recognizing that competitors should be identified beyond just those that supply technically similar products.

Competitor identificaton	FIGURE **19.3**

The competitive arena

Product form competitors
• technically similar products

Product substitutes
• technically dissimilar products

Generic competitors
• products that solve the problem or eliminate it in a dissimilar way

Potential new entrants
• with technically similar products
• with technically dissimilar products

What are their strengths and weaknesses?

Having identified our competitors the next stage is to complete a **competitor audit** in order to assess their relative strengths and weaknesses. A precise understanding of competitor strengths and weaknesses is an important prerequisite of developing competitor strategy. In particular, it locates areas of competitive vulnerability. Military strategy suggests that success is most often achieved when strength is concentrated against the enemy's greatest weakness.[4] This analogy holds true for business, as the success of Japanese companies in the car and motorcycle industries demonstrates.

The process of assessing competitors' strengths and weaknesses may take place as part of a marketing audit (see Chapter 2). As much internal, market and customer information should be gathered as is practicable. For example, financial data concerning profitability, profit margins, sales and investment levels, market data relating to price levels, market share and distribution channels used, and customer data concerning awareness of brand names, and perceptions of brand and company image, product and service quality, and selling ability may be relevant.

Not all of this information will be accessible, and some may not be relevant. Management needs to decide the extent to which each element of information is worth pursuing. For example, a decision is required regarding how much expenditure is to be allocated to measuring customer awareness and perceptions through marketing research.

This process of data gathering needs to be managed so that information is available to compare our company with its chief competitors on the *key factors for success* in the industry. A three-stage process can then be used, as follows.

1 Identify key factors for success in the industry

These should be restricted to about six to eight factors otherwise the analysis becomes too diffuse.[5] Their identification is a matter of managerial judgement. Their source may be functional (such as financial strength or flexible production) or generic (for example, the ability to respond quickly to customer needs, innovativeness, or the capability to provide other sales services). Since these factors are critical for success they should be used to compare our company with its competitors.

2 Rate our company and competitors on each key success factor using a rating scale

Each company is given a score on each success factor using a rating device. This may be a scale ranging from 1 (very poor) to 5 (very good); this results in a set of company capability profiles (an example is given in Fig. 19.4). Our company is rated alongside two competitors on six key success factors. Compared with our company, competitor 1 is relatively strong regarding technical assistance to customers and access to international distribution channels, but relatively weak on product quality. Competitor 2 is relatively strong on international distribution channels but relatively weak on innovativeness, financial strength and having a well-qualified workforce.

Company capability profiles   FIGURE **19.4**

Key success factor

	Our company	Competitor 1	Competitor 2
Innovativeness	1 2 3 4 5	1 2 3 4 5	1 2 3 4 5
Financial strength	1 2 3 4 5	1 2 3 4 5	1 2 3 4 5
Technical assistance to customers	1 2 3 4 5	1 2 3 4 5	1 2 3 4 5
Product quality	1 2 3 4 5	1 2 3 4 5	1 2 3 4 5
Well-qualified workforce	1 2 3 4 5	1 2 3 4 5	1 2 3 4 5
Access to international distribution channels	1 2 3 4 5	1 2 3 4 5	1 2 3 4 5

3 Consider the implications for competitive strategy

The competitive profile analysis is then used to identify possible competitive strategies. This analysis would suggest that our company should consider taking steps to improve technical assistance to customers to match or exceed competitor 1's capability on this factor. At the moment, our company enjoys a differential advantage over competitor 1 on product quality. Our strength in innovativeness should be used to maintain this differential advantage and competitor 1's moves to improve product quality should be monitored carefully.

Competitor 2 is weaker overall than competitor 1 and our company. However, it has considerable strengths in having access to international distribution channels. Given our company's weakness in this area, a strategic alliance with or take-over of competitor 2 might be sensible if our company's objective is to expand internationally. Our company's financial strength and competitor 2's financial weakness suggests that a take-over might be feasible.

What are their strategic objectives and thrust?

The third part of competitor analysis is to infer their *strategic objectives*. Companies may decide to build, hold or harvest products and strategic business units (SBUs). To briefly recap, a build objective is concerned with increasing sales and/or market share, a hold objective suggests maintaining sales and/or market share, and a harvest objective is followed when the emphasis is on maximizing short-term cash flow through slashing expenditure and raising prices whenever possible. It is useful to know what strategic objectives are being pursued by competitors because their response pattern may depend upon objectives. Looking at this topic from a product perspective, if we are considering building market share of our product by cutting price, a competitor who is also building is almost certain to follow; one who is content to hold sales and market share is also likely to respond, but a company following a harvest objective for its product is much less likely to reduce price because it is more concerned with profit margin than unit sales.

Conversely, if we are considering a price rise, a competitor pursuing a build strategy is not likely to follow; the price of a product subject to a hold objective is now likely to rise in line with our increase; and a company using a harvest objective will almost certainly take the opportunity to raise its product's price, maybe by more than our increase.

Knowing competitors' strategic objectives is also useful in predicting their likely strategies. For example, a build objective is likely to be accompanied by aggressive price and promotional moves, a hold objective with competitive stability, and a harvest objective with cost- rather than marketing-orientated strategies.

Strategic thrust refers to the future areas of expansion a company might contemplate. Broadly, a company can expand by penetrating existing markets more effectively with current products, launching new products in existing markets or by growing in new markets with existing or new products. Knowing the strategic thrust of competitors can help our strategic decision-making. For example, knowing that our competitors are considering expansion in North America but not Europe will make expansion into Europe a more attractive strategic option for our company.

What are their strategies?

At the product level, competitor analysis will attempt to deduce positioning strategy. This involves assessing a competitor product's target market and differential advantage. The marketing mix strategies (e.g. price levels, media used for promotion, and distribution channels) may indicate target market, and marketing research into customer perceptions can be used to assess relative differential advantages.

Companies and products need to be monitored continuously for changes in positioning strategy. For example, Volvo's traditional positioning strategy, based on safety, has been modified to give more emphasis to performance and style.

Strategies can also be defined in terms of competitive scope. For example, are competitors attempting to service the whole market or a few segments of a particular niche? If a niche player, is it likely that they will be content to stay in that segment or will they use it as a beachhead to move into other segments in the future? Japanese companies are renowned for their use of small niche markets as springboards for market segment expansion (e.g. the small car segments in the USA and Europe).

Competitors may be playing the cost-leadership game, focusing on cost-reducing measures rather than expensive product development and promotional strategies. (Cost leadership will be discussed in more detail later in this chapter.) If competitors are following this strategy it is more likely that they will be focusing research and development expenditure on process rather than product development in a bid to reduce manufacturing costs.

What are their response patterns?

A key consideration in making a strategic or tactical move is the likely response of competitors. As we have discussed, understanding competitor objectives and strategies is helpful in predicting competitor reactions. Indeed, a major objective of competitor analysis is to be able to predict competitor response to market and competitive changes. Competitors' past behaviour is also a guide to what they might do. Market leaders often try to control competitor response by retaliatory action. These are called *retaliatory* competitors because they can be relied on to respond aggressively to competitive challenges. Len Hardy, ex-chairman of Lever Brothers, explained the role of a retaliation as follows:

> A leader must enforce market discipline, must be ruthless in dealing with any competitive challenge. If you make a price move and a competitor undercuts it, then he should be shown that this action has been noticed and will be punished. If he is not punished he will repeat the move—and soon your leadership will be eroded.[6]

Thus by punishing competitor moves, market leaders can condition competitors to behave in predicted ways—for example, by not taking advantage of a price rise by the leader. As we discussed in Chapter 12, Pricing Strategy, Vodafone sought to condition competitor actions and response patterns when it responded aggressively to a cut in price of T-Mobile's Flext brand, and declared that no competitor would be allowed to gain an advantage purely on price.[7]

It is not only market leaders that retaliate aggressively. Where management is known to be assertive, and our move is likely to have a major impact on their performance, a strong response is usual.

The history, traditions and managerial personalities of competitors also have an influence on competitive response. Some markets are characterized by years of competitive stability with little serious strategic challenge to any of the incumbents. This can breed complacency, with predictably slow reaction times to new challenges. For example, innovation that offers superior customer value may be dismissed as a fad and unworthy of serious attention.

Another situation where competitors are unlikely to respond is where their previous strategies have restricted their scope for retaliation. An example of such a *hemmed-in competitor* was a major manufacturer of car number plates that were sold to car dealerships. A new company was started by an ex-employee who focused on one geographical area, supplying the same quality product but with extra discount. The national supplier could not respond since to give discount in that particular region would have meant granting the discount nationwide.

A fourth type of competitor may respond *selectively*. Because of tradition or beliefs about the relative effectiveness of marketing instruments a competitor may respond to some competitive moves but not others. For example, extra sales promotion expenditures may be matched but advertising increases (within certain boundaries) may be ignored. Another reason for selective response is the varying degree of visibility of marketing actions. For example, giving extra price discounts may be highly visible, but providing distributors with extra support (e.g. training, sales literature, loans) may be less discernible.

A final type of competitor is totally *unpredictable* in its response pattern. Sometimes there is a response and, at other times, there is no response. Some moves are countered aggressively; with others reaction is weak. No factors explain these differences adequately; they appear to be at the whim of management.

Some companies use role-play to assess competitor reactions: their most knowledgeable managers act out the roles of key competitors to aid prediction of their response to a proposed marketing initiative.[8] Interestingly, research has shown that managers tend to over-react more frequently than they under-react to competitors' marketing activities.[9]

Competitive Advantage

The key to superior performance is to gain and hold a *competitive advantage*. Firms can gain a competitive advantage through *differentiation* of their product offering, which provides superior customer value, or by managing for *lowest delivered cost*. Evidence for this proposition was provided by Hall, who examined the competitive strategies pursued by the two leading firms (in terms of return on investment) in eight mature industries characterized by slow growth and intense competition.[10] In each industry the two leading firms offered either high product differentiation or the lowest delivered cost. In most cases, an industry's return on investment leader opted for one of the strategies, while the second-placed firm pursued the other.

Competitive strategies

These two means of competitive advantage, when combined with the **competitive scope** of activities (broad vs narrow), result in four generic strategies: differentiation, cost leadership, differentiation focus, and cost focus. The differentiation and cost leadership strategies seek competitive advantage in a broad range of market or industry segments, whereas differentiation focus and cost focus strategies are confined to a narrow segment[11] (see Fig. 19.5).

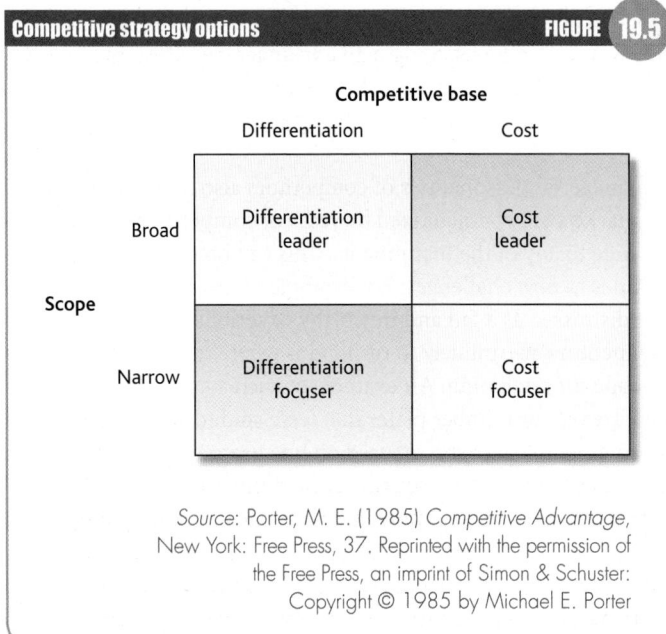

Competitive strategy options

FIGURE 19.5

Competitive base

Source: Porter, M. E. (1985) *Competitive Advantage*, New York: Free Press, 37. Reprinted with the permission of the Free Press, an imprint of Simon & Schuster: Copyright © 1985 by Michael E. Porter

Differentiation

Differentiation strategy involves the selection of one or more choice criteria that are used by many buyers in an industry. The firm then uniquely positions itself to meet these criteria. Differentiation strategies are usually associated with a premium price, and higher than average costs for the industry as the extra value to customers (e.g. higher performance) often raises costs. The aim is to differentiate in a way that leads to a price premium in excess of the cost of differentiating. Differentiation gives customers a reason to prefer one product over another and thus is central to strategic marketing thinking. Here are some examples of brands that have achieved success using a differentiation strategy.

- Nokia became market leader in mobile phones by being the first to realize that they were fashion items and to design stylish phones to differentiate the brand from its rivals.
- Toyota has built its success and reputation by targeting a broad market with highly reliable, high build quality, low running cost and stylish cars, which differentiate the brand from its competitors, such as GM, Ford and Fiat.
- Dyson differentiated its vacuum cleaners by inventing a bagless version, which outperformed its rivals by providing greater suction and convenience, and by eliminating the need to buy and install dust bags. Its vacuum cleaners are also differentiated from other brands by their distinctive colours.
- Google created a differential advantage over its search engine rivals by enabling the most relevant websites to be ranked at the top of listings.

Smaller companies are also creating differential advantages using Internet technologies. Digital Marketing 19.1 discusses how Moo.com is doing that.

Cost leadership

This strategy involves the achievement of the lowest cost position in an industry. Many segments in the industry are served and great importance is attached to minimizing costs on all fronts. So long as the price achievable for its products is around the industry average, cost leadership should result in superior performance. Thus cost leaders often market standard products that are believed to be acceptable to customers. Heinz and United Biscuits are believed to be cost leaders in their industries. They market acceptable products at reasonable prices, which means that their low costs result in above-average profits. Wal-Mart is also a cost leader, which allows the company the option of charging lower prices than its rivals to achieve higher sales and yet achieve comparable profit margins, or to match competitors' prices and attain higher profit margins. Dell has also achieved success using a cost leadership strategy. It outsources manufacturing, sells direct to customers, does little R&D and keeps overheads to less than 10 per cent of sales. This meant that it was able to undercut Hewlett-Packard on price while achieving higher profit margins, and to force IBM out of the PC business. However, the Dell case provides an example of the dangers of a cost focus. Dell took its eye off the customer (e.g. it became the subject of many complaints about poor service) and rapidly lost market share to a rejuvenated Hewlett-Packard.

19.1 Digital Marketing

Customer Satisfaction: Moo.com

Moo.com is an Internet-based digital business that allows customers to upload their own designs and create high-quality business cards and stationery at comparatively low prices. Moo.com considers itself a global business that supplies customers anywhere. What makes Moo.com interesting is that its entire operation is automated (with very few people involved), and that the whole printing business is in fact handled by another organization, 1st Byte.

Moo.com handles satisfaction in shipping by having a single shipping rate irrespective of global destination—an almost unique proposition. When things go wrong, there are humans to help at the end of a phone line, but careful attention to the design of the whole ordering and card design process minimizes interaction. Such is the level of success in developing and maintaining customer satisfaction that many of Moo.com's new orders come from word-of-mouth recommendation by an almost evangelistic group of existing customer advocates, with significant repeat purchasing occurring as well. This happens because Moo.com regularly exceeds their expectations—the first time with the price, the second time with the quality of the product (which often exceeds customers' experiences at regular printers). Finally, the informal, almost 'cutesie', but strong brand voice (evidenced by the automated 'robot' responses (Little Moo) sent out by e-mail) gives customers a feeling of being involved in something special, personalized and unique to them, and provides an experience no other printer can provide.

Based on: www.revolutionmagazine.com[12]

Differentiation focus

With this strategy, a firm aims to differentiate within one or a small number of target market segments. The special needs of the segment mean that there is an opportunity to differentiate the product offering from the competition's, which may be targeting a broader group of customers. For example, some small speciality chemical companies thrive on taking orders that are too small or specialized to be of interest to their larger competitors. Differentiation focusers must be clear that the needs of their target group differ from those of the broader market (otherwise there will be no basis for differentiation) and that existing competitors are underperforming. Examples of differentiation focusers are Burberry, Bang & Olufsen, Mercedes and Ferrari; each of these markets differentiated products to one or a small number of target market segments.

Cost focus

With this strategy a firm seeks a cost advantage with one or a small number of target market segments. By dedicating itself to the segment, the cost focuser can seek economies that may be ignored or missed by broadly targeted competitors. In some instances, the competition, by trying to achieve wide market acceptance, may be over-performing (for example, by providing unwanted services) to one segment of customers. By providing a basic product offering, a cost advantage will be gained that may exceed the price discount necessary to sell it. Examples of cost focusers are easyJet and Ryanair, who focus on short-haul flights with a basic product trimmed to reduce costs. Lidl is also a cost focuser, targeting price-sensitive consumers with a narrow product line (around 300 items in stock) but with large buying power. Travelodge, the no-frills hotel chain, is another example with its focus on one market segment: price-conscious consumers.

Choosing a competitive strategy

The essence of corporate success, then, is to choose a generic strategy and pursue it with gusto. Below-average performance is associated with the failure to achieve any of these generic strategies. The result is no competitive advantage: a *stuck-in-the-middle position* that results in lower performance than that of the cost leaders, differentiators or focusers in any market segment. An example of a company that made the mistake of moving to a stuck-in-the-middle position was General Motors with its Oldsmobile car. The original car (the Oldsmobile Rocket V8) was highly differentiated, with a 6-litre V8 engine, which was virtually indestructible, very fast and highly reliable. In order to cut costs, this engine was replaced by the same engine that went into the 5-litre Chevrolet V8. This had less power and was less reliable. The result was catastrophic: sales plummeted. Two other examples of the dire consequences of being stuck in the middle are Gap and Woolworths, as Marketing in Action 19.1 explains.

19.1 Marketing in Action

Stuck in the Middle with Gap and Woolworths

Two companies that have suffered from stuck-in-the-middle syndrome are Gap and Woolworths. The result for Gap was falling sales and profits, and loss of market leadership to Zara, and for 'Woolies' the demise of the company.

Gap has lost ground by being squeezed by other fashion brands such as Burberry defining themselves as premium designer brands, and volume retailers such as Zara and H&M creating fast fashion. Gap's positioning as a mid-market brand, its slow reaction to competition and its high-end prices have diverted consumers to other more attractive options. These include Abercrombie & Fitch, Uniqlo and River Island, as well as Zara, H&M, Primark and Topshop.

For Woolworths, the result was catastrophe—being squeezed by specialist retailers such as Game for video games and HMV for DVDs and CDs, and cheaper operators such as supermarkets and Poundland (where everything from Toblerones to dog food is priced at £1). Hindered by unsightly pile 'em high aisles and high rents, the stores found no buyers when the company went into administration. Only an online version of Woolworths now exists to continue the name.

Based on: Finch (2008);[13] Venkatraman (2008);[14] Wood (2008)[15]

Firms need to understand the generic basis for their success and resist the temptation to blur strategy by making inconsistent moves. For example, a no-frills cost leader or focuser should beware the pitfalls of moving to a higher cost base (perhaps by adding expensive services). A focus strategy involves limiting sales volume. Once domination of the target segment has been achieved there may be a temptation to move into other segments in order to achieve growth with the same competitive advantage. This can be a mistake if the new segments do not value the firm's competitive advantage in the same way.

In most situations differentiation and cost leadership strategies are incompatible: differentiation is achieved through higher costs. However, there are circumstances when both can be achieved simultaneously. For example, a differentiation strategy may lead to market share domination, which lowers costs through economies of scale and learning effects; or a highly differentiated firm may pioneer a major process innovation that significantly reduces manufacturing costs leading to a cost-leadership position. When differentiation and cost leadership coincide, performance is exceptional since a premium price can be charged for a low-cost product.

Advertisement promotion

Let's go Dutch

Refreshing and packed with flavour – Grolsch is the perfect beer for a sunny afternoon

Since its invention in Holland in 1615, Grolsch has been made using only the finest ingredients. Mostly, these are simply superior versions of those used to make any good lager – spring water, malted barley and yeast. There are, however, a couple of things that make Grolsch an exceptional beer to enjoy in the sun.

The first is the hops used in the Grolsch brewing process. Early on, a carefully selected blend of hops are added to increase the beer's intensity. Later, Hallertau Perle hops are introduced, to create that distinctive Grolsch nose. It is, however, perhaps the final ingredient that is the most important: time. Grolsch is brewed for longer than most beers, which allows its flavour to develop fully. The resultant grassy-fresh aroma and citrus notes are resolved in a long, satisfying finish.

Grolsch's combination of cool refreshment and well-developed flavours make it the perfect beer to enjoy with friends on a sunny afternoon in the garden. After all, people have been doing the same whenever the sun comes out for almost 400 hundred years.

▲ Grolsch's competitive advantage lies in its long history and core competence in the brewing process.

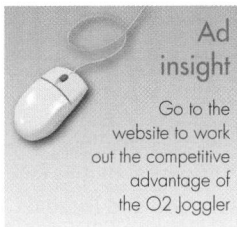

Ad insight

Go to the website to work out the competitive advantage of the O2 Joggler

Sources of competitive advantage

In order to create a differentiated or lowest cost position, a firm needs to understand the nature and location of the potential *sources of competitive advantage*. The nature of these sources are the superior skills and resources of a firm. One key source of competitive advantage for Grolsch is its long-established skills in brewing (see illustration). Management benefits by analysing the superior skills and resources that are contributing, or could contribute, to competitive advantage (i.e. differentiation or lowest cost position). Their location can be aided by value chain analysis. A **value chain** is the discrete activities a firm carries out in order to perform its business.

Superior skills

Superior skills are the distinctive capabilities of key personnel that set them apart from the personnel of competing firms.[16] The benefit of superior skills is the resulting ability to perform functions more effectively than other firms. For example, superior selling skills may result in closer relationships with customers than competing firms achieve. IBM is renowned for its selling skills, based upon its salespeople acting as consultants for clients, resulting in close long-term relationships. Superior quality assurance skills can result in higher and more consistent product quality.

Superior resources

Superior resources are the tangible requirements for advantage that enable a firm to exercise its skills. Superior resources include:

- the number of sales people in a market
- expenditure on advertising and sales promotion
- distribution coverage (the number of retailers who stock the product)
- expenditure on R&D
- scale of and type of production facilities
- financial resources
- brand equity
- knowledge.

The value chain   FIGURE 19.6

Primary activities

Inbound logistics	Operations	Outbound logistics	Marketing and sales	Service

Procurement

Technology development

Human resource management

Firm infrastructure

Margin through value

Support activities

Source: Porter, M. E. (1985) *Competitive Advantage*, New York: Free Press, 37. Reprinted with the permission of the Free Press, an imprint of Simon & Schuster. Copyright © 1985 by Michael E. Porter

Core competences

The distinctive nature of these skills and resources makes up a company's **core competences**. For example, Canon's core competences lie in printer, copier and camera technologies. Canon invests 8 per cent of its sales revenues in these technologies to maintain and extend its competitive advantages in these fields.[17]

Value chain

A useful method for locating superior skills and resources is the value chain.[18] All firms consist of a set of activities that are conducted to design, manufacture, market, distribute and service its products. The value chain categorizes these into primary and support activities (see Fig. 19.6). This enables the sources of costs and differentiation to be understood and located.

Primary activities include inbound physical distribution (e.g. materials handling, warehousing, inventory control), operations (e.g. manufacturing, packaging), outbound physical distribution (e.g. delivery, order processing), marketing (e.g. advertising, selling, channel management) and service (e.g. installation, repair, customer training). A key skill of Wal-Mart is its inbound logistics, which is based on real-time information systems and lets customers decide what appears in its stores. The Internet is used to inform suppliers what was sold the day before. In this way, it buys only what sells. Zara's competitive advantage relies on its marketing skills, which relate product design to fashion trends, and operational and logistical skills that get new clothing designs in stores faster than competitors.

Support activities are found within all of these primary activities, and consist of purchased inputs, technology, human resource management and the firm's infrastructure. These are not defined within a given primary activity because they can be found in all of them. Purchasing can take place within each primary activity, not just in the purchasing department; technology is relevant to all primary activities, as is human resource management; and the firm's infrastructure, which consists of general management, planning, finance, accounting and quality management, supports the entire value chain.

By examining each value-creating activity, management can look for the skills and resources that may form the basis for low cost or differentiated positions.

To the extent that skills and resources exceed (or could be developed to exceed) those of the competition, they form the key sources of competitive advantage. Not only should the skills and resources within value-creating activities be examined, the *linkages* between them should be examined too. For example, greater coordination between operations and inbound

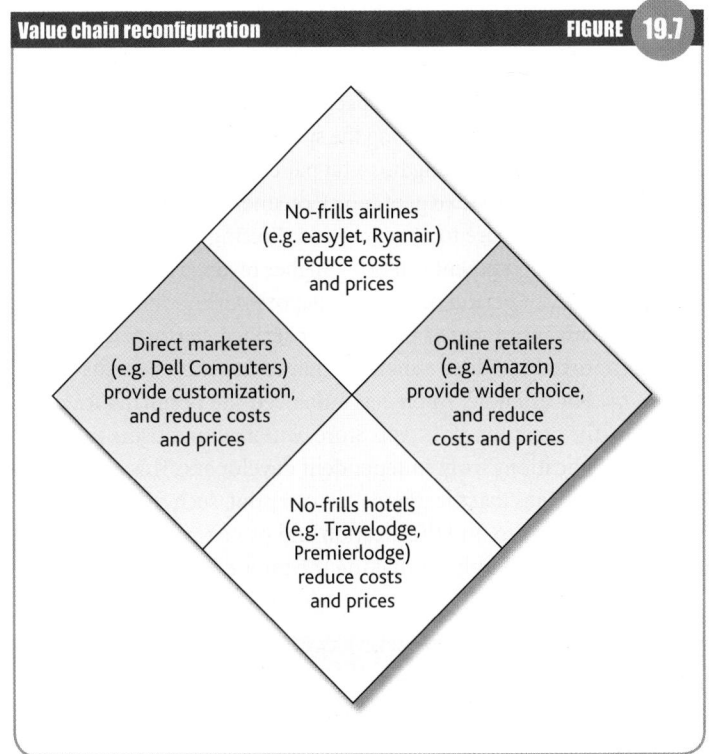

Value chain reconfiguration   FIGURE 19.7

No-frills airlines
(e.g. easyJet, Ryanair)
reduce costs
and prices

Direct marketers
(e.g. Dell Computers)
provide customization,
and reduce costs
and prices

Online retailers
(e.g. Amazon)
provide wider choice,
and reduce
costs and prices

No-frills hotels
(e.g. Travelodge,
Premierlodge)
reduce costs
and prices

physical distribution may give rise to reduced costs through lower inventory levels.

Value chain analysis can extend to the value chains of suppliers and customers. For example, just-in-time supply could lower inventory costs; providing salesforce support to distributors could foster closer relations. Thus, by looking at the linkages between a firm's value chain and those of suppliers and customers, improvements in performance can result that can lower costs or contribute to the creation of a differentiated position.

Overall, the contribution of the value chain is in providing a framework for understanding the nature and location of the skills and resources that provide the basis for competitive advantage. Furthermore, the value chain provides the framework for cost analysis. Assigning operating costs and assets to value activities is the starting point of cost analysis so that improvement can be made, and cost advantages defended. For example, if a firm discovers that its cost advantage is based on superior production facilities, it should be vigilant in upgrading those facilities to maintain its position against competitors. Similarly, by understanding the sources of differentiation, a company can build on these sources and defend against competitive attack. For example, if differentiation is based on skills in product design, then management knows that sufficient investment in maintaining design superiority is required to maintain the firm's differentiated position. Also, the identification of specific sources of advantage can lead to their exploitation in new markets where customers place a similar high value on the resultant outcome. For example, Marks & Spencer's skills in clothing retailing were successfully extended to provide differentiation in food retailing. Finally, analysis of the value chain can lead to its reconfiguration to fundamentally change the way a market is served. Figure 19.7 provides some examples.

Creating a Differential Advantage

Although skills and resources are the sources of competitive advantage, they are translated into a **differential advantage** only when the customer perceives that the firm is providing value above that of the competition.[19] The creation of a differential advantage, then, comes with the marrying of skills and resources with the key attributes (choice criteria) that customers are looking for in a product offering. However, it should be recognized that the distinguishing competing attributes in a market are not always the most important ones. For example, if customers were asked to rank safety, punctuality and onboard service in order of importance when flying, safety would undoubtedly be ranked at the top. Nevertheless, when choosing an airline, safety would rank low because most airlines are assumed to be safe. This is why airlines look to less important ways of differentiating their offerings (e.g. by giving superior onboard service).

A differential advantage can be created with any aspect of the marketing mix. Product, distribution, promotion and price are all capable of creating added customer value (see Fig. 19.8). The key to whether improving an aspect of marketing is worthwhile is to know whether the potential benefit provides value to the customer. Table 19.1 lists ways of creating differential advantages and their potential impact on customer value.

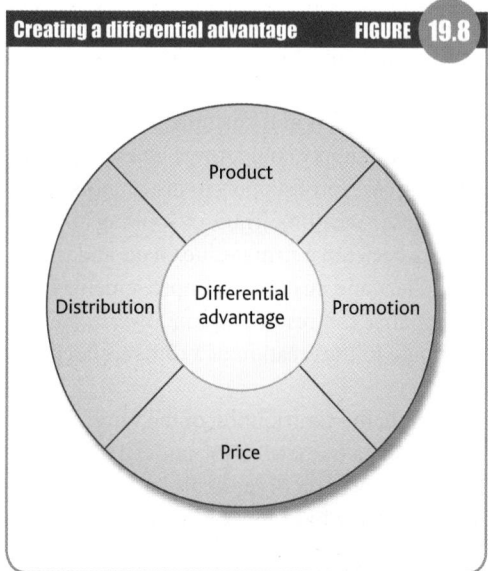

Creating a differential advantage   **FIGURE 19.8**

Product

Product performance can be enhanced by such devices as raising speed, comfort and safety levels, capacity and ease of use, or improving taste or smell. For example, raising the speed of operation of a scanner can lower the cost of treating hospital patients. Improving comfort levels (e.g. of a car), taste (e.g. of food), or smell (e.g. of cosmetics) can give added pleasure to consumption. Raising productivity levels of earth-moving equipment can bring higher revenue if more jobs can be done in a given period of time. Singapore Airlines has created a differential advantage based on superior service. Performance can also be improved by added functions that create extra benefits for customers. For example, Apple has enhanced the performance of its iPhone by the creation of its App Store, which allows users to access software applications from independent developers. This creates additional functions that the iPhone can carry out, such as Urbanspoon, which allows users to find the location and price range of restaurants nearby in London simply by shaking the phone (see illustration).[20]

Creating a differential advantage using the marketing mix   **TABLE 19.1**

Marketing mix	Differential advantage	Value to the customer
Product	Performance	Lower costs; higher revenue; safety; pleasure; status; service; added functions
	Durability	Longer life; lower costs
	Reliability	Lower maintenance and production costs; higher revenue; fewer problems
	Style	Good looks; status
	Upgradability	Lower costs; prestige
	Technical assistance	Better-quality products; closer supplier–buyer relationships
	Installation	Fewer problems
Distribution	Location	Convenience; lower costs
	Quick/reliable delivery	Lower costs; fewer problems
	Distributor support	More effective selling/marketing; close buyer–seller relationships
	Delivery guarantees	Peace of mind
	Computerized reordering	Less work; lower costs
Promotion	Creative/more advertising	Superior brand personality
	Creative/more sales promotion	Direct added value
	Cooperative promotions	Lower costs
	Well-trained salesforce	Superior problem-solving and building close relationships
	Dual selling	Sales assistance; higher sales
	Fast, accurate quotes	Lower costs; fewer problems
	Free demonstrations	Lower risk of purchase
	Free or low-cost trial	Lower risk of purchase
	Fast complaint handling	Fewer problems; lower costs
Price	Lower price	Lower cost of purchase
	Credit facilities	Lower costs; better cash flow
	Low-interest loans	Lower costs; better cash flow
	Higher price	Price–quality match

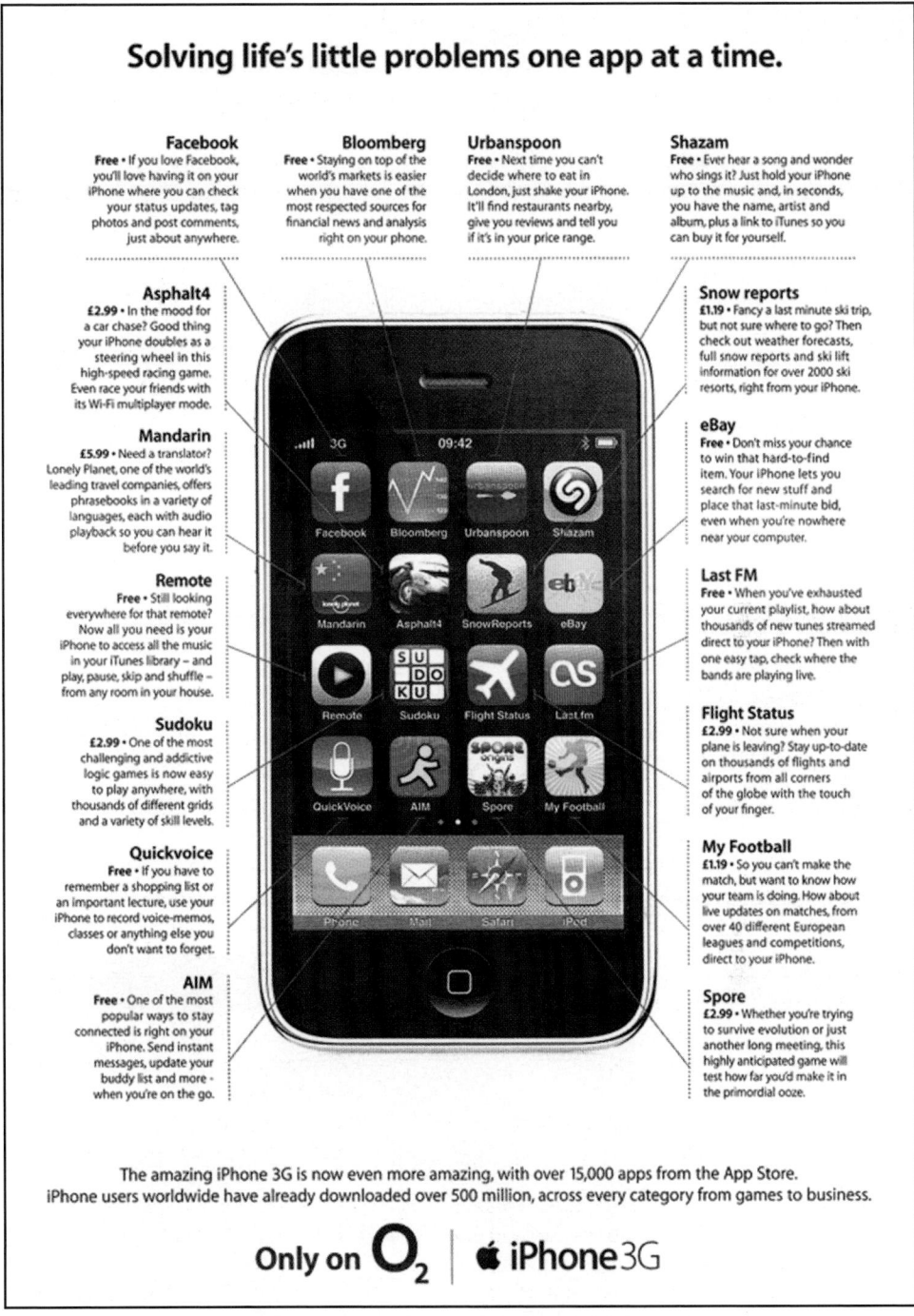

▲ The iPhone differentiates by offering more and better apps.

The *durability* of a product has a bearing on costs since greater durability means a longer operating life. Improving product *reliability* (i.e. lowering malfunctions or defects) can lower maintenance and production costs, raise revenues through lower downtime and reduce the hassle of using the product. Product *styling* can also give customer value through the improved looks that good style brings. This can confer status to the buyer and allow the supplier to charge premium prices, as with Bang & Olufsen hi-fi equipment. Marketing in Action 19.2 discusses how style can be used as a differentiator.

19.2 Marketing in Action

Using Style to Differentiate Products

Two companies that have successfully used style to differentiate their products from those of the competition are Bang & Olufsen and Audi. Bang & Olufsen has long been regarded as the style leader in audio and television equipment, and Audi has become one of the car industry's most successful luxury brands, producing some of the world's most coveted and copied cars.

Bang & Olufsen has built a worldwide reputation for quality and a fanatically loyal customer base. Its sleek, tastefully discrete designs and high standards of production have earned it elite status in the market. For decades, these factors have formed the basis of its advertising and marketing strategy. The company recognizes that style needs to be displayed distinctively in retail outlets. This has led to the creation of 'concept shops' where subtle images are projected on to walls and products displayed in free-standing areas constructed from translucent walls. The company's view is that you cannot sell Bang & Olufsen equipment when it is sandwiched between a washing machine and a shelf of videos. The concept shop gives the right look to make the most of the products. The company exemplifies the importance of style and aesthetics rather than technology or low prices in buying decisions. It trades on ambience as much as sound. Bang & Olufsen's challenge is to keep the brand relevant in a world where media habits (e.g. listening to music via portable devices) are changing, and to maintain its style distinction in the face of the high-end equipment produced by Samsung and Sony.

A major element in Audi's surge in popularity has been based on style. An online survey of 800 car enthusiasts conducted for the *Financial Times* by Britain's *WhatCar* magazine revealed that Audi was the most admired car brand for design, winning 44 per cent of the poll, well ahead of Jaguar, BMW or Mercedes-Benz. Perhaps most famous for its iconic TT sports car, Audi has benefited from the sleek lines of the A4, which has made it a major challenger against the BMW 300 series. Audi's challenge is to continue to produce stylish cars as it expands its range into a number of niches, from sports utility vehicles to tiny eco-cars.

Based on: Gapper (2005);[21] *Brownsell (2008);*[22] *Reed (2008)*[23]

▲ Bang & Olufsen's stylish audio and television equipment.

The capacity to *upgrade* a product (to take advantage of technological advances) or to meet changing needs (e.g. extra storage space in a computer) can lower costs, and confer prestige by maintaining state-of-the-art features. The Apple iMac computer demonstrates how style can be used to create a differential advantage.

Products can be augmented by the provision of *guarantees* that give customers peace of mind and lower costs should the product need repair, as well as giving *technical assistance* to customers, so that they are provided with better-quality products. Both parties benefit from closer relationships and from the provision of product *installation*, which means that customers do not incur problems in properly installing a complex piece of equipment.

Distribution

Wide distribution coverage and/or careful selection of distributor *locations* can provide convenient purchasing for customers. *Quick and/or reliable delivery* can lower buyer costs by reducing production downtime and lowering inventory levels. Reliable delivery, in particular, reduces the frustration of waiting for late delivery. Providing distributors with *support* in the form of training and financial help can bring about more effective selling and marketing, and offers both parties the advantage of closer relationships. FedEx has continued to prosper by giving *delivery guarantees* of critical documents 'down to the hour'.[24] Working with organizational customers to introduce *computerized reordering* systems can lower their costs, reduce their workload and increase the cost for them of switching to other suppliers.

Promotion

A differential advantage can be created by the *creative use of advertising*. For example, Heineken was differentiated by the use of humour and the tag-line 'Heineken refreshes the parts other beers cannot reach' at a time when many other lagers were promoted by showing groups of men in public houses enjoying a drink together. The award-winning Levi's advertisement shows how creativity can be used to differentiate a brand. The creative makes the viewer of the advertisement its subject in a way that both engages and unnerves. *Spending more on advertising* can also aid differentiation by creating a stronger brand personality than competitive brands. Similarly, using *more creative sales promotional methods* or simply *spending more on sales incentives* can give direct added value to customers. By engaging in *cooperative promotions* with distributors, producers can lower their costs and build goodwill.

The salesforce can also offer a means of creating a differential advantage. Particularly when products are similar, a *well-trained salesforce* can provide superior problem-solving skills for their

▲ Wear the wrong jeans at your peril!
Photographer: Joseph Rodriguez.

customers. Part of the success of IBM in penetrating the mainframe computer market in the early 1980s was due to its well-trained salesforce, which acted as problem solver and information consultant for its customers. As IBM has been transformed into a services-orientated company, its salesforce has been retrained to deliver consultancy services and, in so doing, *build close relationships* with its customers. *Dual selling*, whereby a producer provides salesforce assistance to distributors, can lower the latter's costs and increase sales. For example, a chemical company might supply product specialists who support a distributor's salesforce by providing technical expertise when required. Sales responsiveness in the form of *fast, accurate quotes* can lower customer costs by making transactions more efficient, and reduce the hassle associated with ordering supplies. Furthermore, *free demonstrations* and *free (or low cost) trial* arrangements can reduce the risk of purchase for customers. Finally, *superior complaint handling* procedures can lower customer costs by speeding up the process, and reduce the inconvenience that can accompany it.

Price

Using low price as a means of gaining differential advantage can fail unless the firm enjoys a cost advantage and has the resources to fight a price war. For example, Laker Airways challenged British Airways in transatlantic flights on the basis of lower price, but lost the battle when British Airways cut its prices to compete. Without a cost advantage and with fewer resources, Laker Airways could not survive BA's retaliation. The lesson has been learned by the Taiwanese company Acer, which has successfully challenged Dell and Hewlett-Packard in the market for the inexpensive portable computers known as netbooks. Their strategy is to exploit their lowest cost position, allowing them to become extremely aggressive on price.[25] Budget airlines such as Ryanair and easyJet have challenged more traditional airlines by charging low prices based on low costs.

A less obvious means of lowering the effective price to the customer is to offer *credit facilities* or *low-interest loans*. Both serve to lower the cost of purchase and improve cash flow for customers. Finally, a *high price* can be used as part of a premium positioning strategy to support brand image. Where a brand has distinct product, promotional or distributional advantages, a premium price provides consistency within the marketing mix.

This analysis of how the marketing mix can be used to develop a differential advantage has focused on how each action can be translated into value to the customer. It must be remembered, however, that for a differential advantage to be realized, a firm needs to provide not only customer value but also value that is superior to that offered by the competition. If all firms provide distributor support in equal measure, for example, distributors may gain value, but no differential advantage will have been achieved.

Fast reaction times

In addition to using the marketing mix to create a differential advantage, many companies are recognizing the need to create *fast reaction times* to changes in marketing trends. For example, H&M and Zara have developed fast-reaction systems so that new designs can be delivered to stores within three weeks, and top-selling items are requested and poor sellers withdrawn from shops within a week. This is made possible by sophisticated marketing information systems that feed data from stores to headquarters every day.

Scale of operations

Companies can also create a differential advantage when the scale of their operations creates value for their customers. For example, eBay has built a sustainable differential advantage by building a large participant base. As the customer value of an auction site is directly related to the size of the participant base, once eBay gained a large user base advantage it became extremely difficult for any competitor to duplicate the value that it offers.[26]

19.2 Pause for Thought

Consider a market-leading brand that you have bought in the last 12 months. Why did you buy it and why do you think it is so successful? Your answers will identify its differential advantage(s).

Sustaining a differential advantage

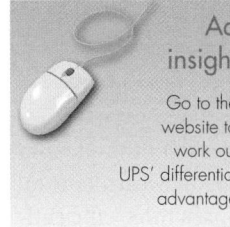

Ad insight

Go to the website to work out UPS' differential advantage

When searching for ways to achieve a differential advantage, management should pay close attention to factors that cannot easily be copied by the competition. The aim is to achieve a *sustainable differential advantage*. Competing on low price can often be copied by the competition, meaning that any advantage is short-lived. Other attempts at creating a differential advantage may also be copied by the competition. For example, when DHL challenged FedEx and UPS in the US postal delivery market, all their attempts at gaining a competitive edge were copied by their rivals. When DHL hired the US Postal Service to carry out its domestic deliveries, a move that was popular with customers, FedEx and UPS followed suit. The result was that DHL could not find a way of creating a differential advantage and was forced to exit the US market.[27] The key to achieving a long-term advantage is to focus on areas that the competition find impossible or, at the very least, very difficult to copy, including:

- patent-protected products
- strong brand personality
- close relationships with customers
- high service levels achieved by well-trained personnel
- innovative product upgrading
- creating high entry barriers (e.g. R&D or promotional expenditures)
- strong and distinctive internal processes that deliver the above and are difficult to copy
- scale (where the scale of operations provides value to the customer, e.g. eBay).[28]

Eroding a differential advantage

However, many advantages are contestable. For example, IBM's stronghold on personal computers was undermined by cheaper clones. Three mechanisms are at work that can erode a differential advantage:[29]

1 technological and environment changes that create opportunities for competitors by eroding the protective barriers (e.g. long-standing television companies are being challenged by satellite television)
2 competitors learn how to imitate the sources of the differential advantage (e.g. competitors engage in a training programme to improve service capabilities)
3 complacency leads to lack of protection of the differential advantage.

Creating Cost Leadership

Creating a cost-leadership position requires an understanding of the factors that affect costs. Porter has identified 10 major *cost drivers* that determine the behaviour of costs in the value chain (see Fig. 19.9).[30]

Economies of scale

Scale economies can arise from the use of more efficient methods of production at higher volumes. For example, United Biscuits benefits from more efficient machinery that can produce biscuits more cheaply than that used by Fox's Biscuits, which operates at much lower

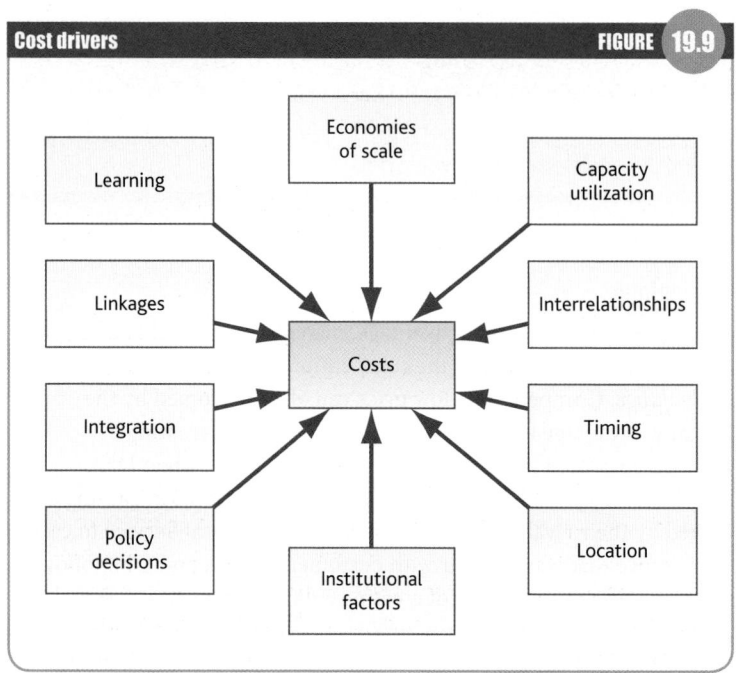

Cost drivers   FIGURE 19.9

volume. Scale economies also arise from the less-than-proportional increase in overheads as production volume increases. For example, a factory with twice the floor area of another factory is less than twice the price to build. A third scale economy results from the capacity to spread the cost of R&D and promotion over a greater sales volume. Such scale economies mean that companies such as Coca-Cola, General Electric, Intel, Microsoft and Wal-Mart have a huge advantage over their competitors. However, economies of scale do not proceed indefinitely. At some point, diseconomies of scale are likely to arise as size gives rise to overcomplexity and, possibly, personnel difficulties.

Learning

Costs can also fall as a result of the effects of learning. For example, people learn how to assemble more quickly, pack more efficiently, design products that are easier to manufacture, lay out warehouses more effectively, cut driving time and reduce inventories. The effect of learning on costs was seen in the manufacture of fighter planes for the Second World War. The time to produce each plane fell over time as learning took place. The combined effect of economies of scale and learning as cumulative output increases has been termed the **experience curve**. The Boston Consulting Group has estimated that costs are reduced by approximately 15–20 per cent on average each time cumulative output doubles. This suggests that firms with greater market share will have a cost advantage through the experience curve effect, assuming all companies are operating on the same curve. However, a move towards a new manufacturing technology can lower the experience curve for adopting companies, allowing them to leap-frog more traditional firms and thereby gain a cost advantage even though cumulative output may be lower.

Capacity utilization

Since fixed costs must be paid whether a plant is manufacturing at full or zero capacity, underutilization incurs costs. The effect is to push up the cost per unit for production. The impact of capacity utilization on profitability was established by the PIMS (profit impact of marketing strategy) studies, which have shown a positive association between utilization and return on investment.[31] Changes in capacity utilization can also raise costs (e.g. through the extra costs of hiring and laying off workers). Careful production planning is required for seasonal products such as ice cream and fireworks, in order to smooth output.

Linkages

These describe how the costs of activities are affected by how other activities are performed. For example, improving quality-assurance activities can reduce after-sales service costs. In the car industry, the reduction in the number of faults on a new car reduces warranty costs. The activities of suppliers and distributors also link to affect the costs of a firm.

For example, the introduction of a just-in-time delivery system by a supplier reduces the inventory costs of a firm. Distributors can influence a firm's physical distribution costs through their warehouse location decision. To exploit such linkages, though, the firm may need considerable bargaining power. In some instances it can pay a firm to increase distributor margins or pay a fee in order to exploit linkages. For example, Seiko paid its US jewellers a fee for accepting its watches for repair and sending them to Seiko; this meant that Seiko did not need local services facilities and its overall costs fell.[32]

Interrelationships

Sharing costs with other business units is another potential cost driver. Sharing the costs of R&D, transportation, marketing and purchasing lower costs. Know-how can also be shared to reduce costs by improving the efficiency of an activity. Car manufacturers share engineering platforms and components to reduce costs. For example, Volkswagen does this across its VW, Skoda, Seat and Audi cars. Care has to be taken that the cars appearing under different brand names do not appear too similar, however, or this may detract from the appeal of the more expensive marques.[33]

Integration

Both integration and de-integration can affect costs. For example, owning the means of physical distribution rather than using outside contractors could lower costs. Ownership may allow a producer to avoid suppliers or customers with sizeable bargaining power. De-integration can lower costs and raise flexibility. For example, by using many small clothing suppliers, Benetton is in a powerful position to keep costs low while maintaining a high degree of production flexibility.

Timing

Both first movers and late entrants have potential opportunities for lowering costs. First movers in a market can gain cost advantages: it is usually cheaper to establish a brand name in the minds of customers if there is no competition. Also, they have prime access to cheap or high-quality raw materials and locations. However, late entrants to a market have the opportunity to buy the latest technology and avoid high market development costs.

Policy decisions

Firms have a wide range of discretionary policy decisions that affect costs. Product width, level of service, channel decisions (e.g. small number of large dealers vs large number of small dealers), salesforce decisions (e.g. in-company salesforce vs sales agents) and wage levels are some of the decision areas that have a direct impact on costs. Southwest Airlines, for example, cuts costs by refusing to waste time assigning seats and does not wait for late arrivals. The overriding concern is to get the aeroplane in and out of the gate quickly so that it is in the air earning money. Southwest flies only one kind of aircraft, which also keeps costs down.[34]

Companies can also collaborate to reduce costs. For example, Vodafone has teamed up with O_2's parent company, Telefónica, to share mobile network infrastructure (e.g. masts, equipment and power supply), following a similar deal between T-Mobile and 3.[35]

As we saw in Digital Marketing 19.1, no-frills airline operators are using the Internet to further reduce costs. Indeed, Ryanair accepts bookings only over the Internet, thus eliminating the need for an inbound telemarketing team and allowing e-ticketing, which cuts postage and paper costs. Other sectors, such as insurance, rail, banking, package holidays and hotels, encourage transactions over the Internet in order to reduce costs. Care must be taken, however, not to reduce costs with regard to activities that have a major bearing on customer value. For example, moving from a company-employed salesforce to sales agents may not only cut costs but also destroy supplier–customer relationships. Even high-technology companies such as Nokia and Ericsson have had to make policy decisions designed to cut costs in the face of intense competition. The problem is that, for undifferentiated companies, cost cutting alone, as General Motors found, is insufficient to ensure success.

Location

The location of plant and warehouses affects costs through different wage, physical distribution and energy costs. Dyson, for example, manufactures its vacuum cleaners in Malaysia to take advantage of low wage costs.[36] Car manufacturers such as VW, Peugeot, Citroën and Fiat have moved production to eastern Europe to take advantage of low costs.[37] Locating near customers can lower outbound distributional costs, while locating near suppliers reduces inbound distributional costs.

Institutional factors

These include government regulations, tariffs and local content rules. For example, regulations regarding the maximum size of lorries affect distribution costs.

Firms employing a cost leadership strategy will be vigilant in pruning costs. This analysis of cost drivers provides a framework for searching out new avenues for cost reduction.

Online
LearningCentre

When you have read this chapter

log on to the Online Learning Centre at www.mcgraw-hill.co.uk/textbooks/jobber to explore chapter-by-chapter test questions, links and further online study tools for marketing.

Review

1 The determinants of industry attractiveness
- Industry attractiveness is determined by the degree of rivalry between competitors, the threat of new entrants, the bargaining power of suppliers and buyers, and the threat of substitute products.

2 How to analyse competitors
- Competitor analysis should identify competitors (product from competitors, product substitutes, generic competitors and potential new entrants); audit their capabilities; analyse their objectives, strategic thrust and strategies; and estimate competitor response patterns.

3 The difference between differentiation and cost leadership strategies
- Differentiation strategy involves the selection of one or more choice criteria used by buyers to select suppliers/brands and uniquely positioning the supplier/brand to meet those criteria better than the competition.
- Cost leadership involves the achievement of the lowest cost position in an industry.

4 The sources of competitive advantage
- Competitive advantage can be achieved by creating a differential advantage or achieving the lowest cost position.
- Its sources are superior skills, superior resources, and core competences. A useful method of locating superior skills and resources is value chain analysis.

5 The value chain
- The value chain categorizes the value-creating activities of a firm. The value chain divides these into primary and support activities. Primary activities are in-bound physical distribution, operations, outbound physical distribution, marketing and service. Support activities are found within all of these primary activities, and consist of purchased inputs, technology, human resource management and the firm's infrastructure.

- By examining each value-creating activity, management can search for the skills and resources (and linkages) that may form the basis for low cost or differentiated positions.

6 **How to create and maintain a differential advantage**
- A differential advantage is created when the customer perceives that the firm is providing value above that of the competition.
- A differential advantage can be created using any element in the marketing mix: superior product, more effective distribution, better promotion and better value for money by lower prices. A differential advantage can also be created by developing fast reaction times to changes in marketing trends.
- A differential advantage can be maintained (sustained) through the use of patent protection, strong brand personality, close relationships with customers, high service levels based on well-trained staff, innovative product upgrading, the creation of high entry barriers (e.g. R&D or promotional expenditures), and strong and distinctive internal processes that deliver the earlier points and are difficult to copy.

7 **How to create and maintain a cost leadership position**
- Cost leadership can be created and maintained by managing cost drivers, which are economies of scale, learning effects, capacity utilization, linkages (e.g. improvements in quality assurance can reduce after-sales service costs), interrelationships (e.g. sharing costs), integration (e.g. owning the means of distribution), timing (both first movers and late entrants can have low costs), policy decisions (e.g. controlling labour costs), location, and institutional factors (e.g. government regulations).

Key Terms

competitive scope the breadth of a company's competitive challenge, e.g. broad or narrow

competitor audit a precise analysis of competitor strengths and weaknesses, objectives and strategies

core competences the principal distinctive capabilities possessed by a company—what it is really good at

differential advantage a clear performance differential over the competition on factors that are important to target customers

differentiation strategy the selection of one or more customer choice criteria and positioning

the offering accordingly to achieve superior customer value

entry barriers barriers that act to prevent new firms from entering a market, e.g. the high level of investment required

experience curve the combined effect of economies of scale and learning as cumulative output increases

industry a group of companies that market products that are close substitutes for each other

value chain the set of a firm's activities that are conducted to design, manufacture, market, distribute, and service its products

Study Questions

1 Using Porter's 'five forces' framework, discuss why profitability in the European textile industry is lower than in book publishing.

2 For any product of your choice identify the competition using the four-layer approach discussed in this chapter.

3 Why is competitor analysis essential in today's turbulent environment? How far is it possible to predict competitor response to marketing actions?

4 Distinguish between differentiation and cost-leadership strategies. Is it possible to achieve both positions simultaneously?

5 Discuss, with examples, ways of achieving a differential advantage.

6 How can value chain analysis lead to superior corporate performance?

7 Using examples, discuss the impact of the advent of the single European market on competitive structure.

8 What are cost drivers? Should marketing management be concerned with them, or is their significance solely the prerogative of the accountant?

References

1. Porter, M. E. (1998) *Competitive Strategy: Techniques for Analysing Industries and Competitors*, New York: Free Press.
2. Graham, G. (1997) Competition is Getting Tougher, *Financial Times*, Special Report on Danish Banking, 9 April, 2.
3. Noble, C. H., R. K. Sinha and A. Kumar (2002) Market Orientation and Alternative Strategic Orientations: A Longitudinal Assessment of Performance Implications, *Journal of Marketing* 66, October, 25–39.
4. Von Clausewitz, C. (1908) *On War*, London: Routledge & Kegan Paul.
5. Macdonald, M. (2007) *Marketing Plans*, Oxford: Butterworth Heinemann.
6. Dudley, J. W. (1990) *1992: Strategies for the Single Market*, London: Kogan Page.
7. Ritson, M. (2008) Mobile Brands Make Poor Call on Value, *Marketing*, 23 January, 21.
8. Ross, E. B. (1984) Making Money with Proactive Pricing, *Harvard Business Review* 62, Nov.–Dec., 145–55.
9. Leeflang, P. H. S. and D. R. Wittink (1996) Competitive Reaction versus Consumer Response: Do Managers Over-react? *International Journal of Research in Marketing* 13, 103–19.
10. Hall, W. K. (1980) Survival Strategies in a Hostile Environment, *Harvard Business Review* 58, Sept.–Oct., 75–85.
11. Porter (1998) op. cit.
12. www.revolutionmagazine.com/news/888768/create-perfect-e-commerce-website
13. Finch, J. (2008) Woolies: Out of Date, Out of Stock—Now Out of Time, *Guardian*, 18 December, 35.
14. Venkatraman, A. (2008) Basic Instinct, *Marketing Week*, 21 August, 27.
15. Wood, Z. (2008) As Woolworths Goes Under, Poundland Rises to Record Profits, *Guardian*, 20 December, 13.
16. Day, G. S. and R. Wensley (1988) Assessing Advantage: A Framework for Diagnosing Competitive Superiority, *Journal of Marketing* 52, April, 1–20.
17. Anonymous (2002) Hard to Copy, *Economist*, 2 November, 79.
18. Porter, M. E. (1998) *Competitive Advantage*, New York: Free Press.

19. For methods of calculating value in organizational markets, see Anderson, J. C. and J. A. Narus (1998) Business Marketing: Understand What Customers Value, *Harvard Business Review*, Nov.–Dec., 53–65.
20. Anonymous (2009) In Praise of Smarter Phones, *Guardian*, 24 February, 20.
21. Gapper (2005) When High Fidelity Becomes High Fashion, *Financial Times*, 20 December, 11.
22. Reed, J. (2008) Designs that Keep on Moving, *Financial Times*, 29 July, 12.
23. Brownsell, A. (2008) Bang & Olufsen, *Marketing*, 28 May, 24.
24. Anonymous (2006) Business Week Top 50 US Companies, *Business Week*, 3 April, 82–100.
25. Einhorn, B. (2009) Acer's Game-Changing PC Offensive, *Business Week*, 20 April, 65.
26. Nagle, T. T. and J. E. Hogan (2006) *The Strategy and Tactics of Pricing*, Upper Saddle River, NJ: Pearson.
27. Anonymous (2008) Failure to Deliver, *Economist*, 15 November, 80.
28. De Chernatony, L., F. Harris and F. Dall'Olmo Riley (2000) Added Value: Its Nature, Roles and Sustainability, *European Journal of Marketing* 34(1/2), 39–56.
29. Day, G. S. (1999) *Market Driven Strategy: Processes for Creating Value*, New York: Free Press.
30. Porter (1998) op. cit.
31. Buzzell, R. D. and B. T. Gale (1987) *The PIMS Principles*, New York: Free Press.
32. Porter (1998) op. cit.
33. MacKintosh, J. (2005) Car Design in a Generalist Market, *Financial Times*, 6 December, 20.
34. McNulty, S. (2001) Short on Frills Big on Morale, *Financial Times*, 31 October, 14.
35. Kollewe, J. (2008) Vodafone Cuts Costs by Sharing Networks with Telefónica, *Guardian*, 24 March, 26.
36. Marsh, P. (2002) Dismay at Job Losses as Dyson Shifts Production to Malaysia, *Financial Times*, 6 February, 3.
37. Milne, R. and H. Williamson (2005) BMW Ignores Signals and Puts its Faith in Germany, *Financial Times*, 13 May, 20.

The Wii Fits Us All!

CASE 37

Nintendo Regains Video Game Supremacy

In a few years, Nintendo has regained supremacy in the video games industry, a position the firm had lost to Sony in the mid-1990s. Indeed 'Big N', as its fans affectionately call it, leads the two parts of the console market: handheld devices (Nintendo's DS, Sony's PSP) and lounge consoles (Sony's PS3, Microsoft's Xbox 360 and Nintendo's Wii). Yet, very few people would have bet on the Wii's success.

Late 2006: a new game begins

In November 2006, two new consoles entered the video games market. Following Microsoft, which had launched the Xbox 360 a year earlier, Sony and Nintendo released, respectively, the PS3 and the Wii on the lounge consoles market (see Figure C37.1). Even though these three consoles were supposed to belong to the same generation, one was very different from the two others: the Wii.

Indeed, the PS3 and the Xbox 360 shared some common characteristics. Both were far more powerful than their predecessors (the PS2 and the Xbox). They displayed the most realistic graphics ever in console video games, and offered a much improved sound experience. These characteristics appealed to hard-core gamers in particular, i.e. those who are very fond of video games and play a lot. Moreover, both could be connected to the Internet, enabling the consoles to download movies or games trailers, browse the Internet, buy videos and music, and of course play online with people all over the world. In truth, Sony and Microsoft wanted to sell actual home entertainment centres, not only consoles. That is even more the case with the PS3, described as delivering 'the next generation of interactive entertainment' (source: PlayStation website), in particular thanks to a high-definition Blu-Ray player, which the X360 does not possess. Finally, both exist in multiple versions, which can easily confuse customers.

Another common trait between the two firms was their pricing strategy. Both consoles were very expensive when they first hit the shelves. The suggested retail price of the X360 was €399, whereas the PS3 was €599. Yet, despite these high prices, neither company was making money with the consoles. In November 2006, iSuppli (a firm specializing in market intelligence) revealed that Microsoft was losing $120 per console sold, whereas Sony was estimated to lose from $240 to $300 on each PS3 it sold. This kind of business model was not new since it has existed in the console sector since the end of the 1970s (mainly with the Atari VC-2600). In fact, money is usually made with games. Indeed, any games editor who wishes to develop and sell a game for a console has to pay for a licence, which generates royalties for consoles manufacturers. Hence their willingness to sell consoles at a loss in order to make money on the resulting games purchases.

However, by 2009, the Xbox 360 had 29.6 per cent of the market, with 29.68 million consoles sold worldwide, while the sales of the PS3 were a mere 21.60 million (i.e. a 21.6 per cent market share). Despite a its one-year-earlier release, the X360 accumulated sales were overtaken by the Wii in September 2007, with the

---

Chronological release of the current generation of lounge consoles

FIGURE C37.1

Xbox 360 (Microsoft)	PlayStation 3 (Sony)	Wii (Nintendo)
22 November 2005 (USA)	11 November 2006 (Japan)	19 November 2006 (USA)
2 December 2005 (Europe)	17 November 2006 (USA)	2 December 2006 (Japan)
10 December 2005 (Japan)	23 March 2007 (Europe)	7, 8, 9 December 2006 (Europe)

PS3 selling the least. Despite the huge reserves of cash supporting its console, Microsoft has failed to become the sector's world leader even though the X360 was released a year earlier than its competitors. This strategy did not even enable the firm to get a foothold in the Japanese market (more than three years after its launch the X360 had barely sold a million units in this market). Furthermore, the X360 encountered some technical problems—in particular, it overheated, which turned its starting button red, a phenomenon labelled RROD (red ring of death)—and relayed by many video games websites, blogs and video-sharing websites (e.g. YouTube).

The situation was even worse for Sony, which had been leader of the market with its PS2 (more than 100 million sold between 2000 and 2006, and more than 120 million by early 2009), and had burnt a lot of cash developing and promoting the PS3. It appears that only a few customers are interested in the high-definition Blu-Ray player. This is all the more disappointing as the Blu-Ray diodes are most expensive and largely accounted for the delayed launch of the PS3 (its release was delayed two or three times, which tarnished Sony's reputation). In addition, only a few very good games are purely exclusive to the console, meaning that they are also available on the X360, or even on the Wii. However, Microsoft has some strong exclusive games (e.g. *Halo 3*), and so has the Wii (see below).

Wii succeeds because Wii can

With 48.95 million units sold, the Wii has 48.8 per cent of the market, and is by far the leader of this generation of consoles. This success has been a total surprise for most of video games analysts and professionals, who had deemed it unable to measure up to its two powerful competitors. For instance, 'We didn't realize the Wii was going to come on so strong,' acknowledged Kaï Huang, co-founder of RedOctane (a video game editor) in April 2009.

Indeed, Nintendo's strategy for this console raised many questions. From a purely technical standpoint, the Wii is far less powerful than the PS3 and the X360: no high-definition graphics and no exceptional sound experience (which made it possible to create a smaller console than the PS3 and the X360). In fact, the quality

of the Wii's graphics is roughly equivalent to the quality of the Gamecube that preceded it. Due to these characteristics, many hard core gamers have looked on the console with disdain. However, it is differentiated by its revolutionary gameplay, thanks to a new kind of controller developed by Nintendo. Called the Wiimote, it has motion-sensing capabilities, which allow the player to interact with and manipulate items on screen by moving. Here, technology in itself is less important than the way it is used. It is interesting to note that Sony had created something similar in 2002. Back then, Sony was selling the Eye Toy, a mini camera that captured gamers' motions to include them in the game. But the firm did not really advance this any further, and missed the opportunity of developing a real new business.

So, unlike players using other consoles, the Wii player is active, and actually makes the moves needed when playing tennis or bowling, for example. This provides more fun and gives video games a social dimension they are usually deprived of. It is reinforced by the possibility offered to gamers to create their own personalized avatar (called 'Mii'), usable in many games. The Wii also provides many web services (weather, news, a 'Virtual Console' service that allows the user to buy and download games from older consoles, and social networking services).

// Nintendo has expanded the games market beyond its traditional frontiers by targeting non-players //

Since it differed greatly from traditional devices, such a cutting-edge technology needed to be heavily promoted so that customers understood its advantages. That's why Nintendo spent more than $200 million in the communications campaign that supported the launch of the Wii (never had 'Big N' invested so much to launch a console!). TV ads showed players having fun with the console, alone or with friends and family, rather than just showing the graphics of the game. In other words, the players themselves were at the heart of TV ads, Internet videos or other promotional support, which was totally unusual in the sector. Nintendo has retained this strategy ever since, and new games for the Wii are still promoted in the same way.

At the same time, Nintendo has worked really hard to make sure that people will try its console. As Satoru Iwata, Nintendo's CEO, said in 2007: 'We want as many people as possible to touch and use a Wiimote', since this is the best way to communicate the console's advantages. This is all the more important as this gameplay enables new ways of playing, and this has attracted people who

Monthly average use of the current generation of lounge consoles (December 2008)			TABLE C37.1
Console	Average usage session (mins)	Average usage (days)	Usage trend (Jan 2008–Jan 2009)
PS3	64	6.8	Downward
Xbox 360	78	7.1	Upward
Wii	58	5.0	Upward

Source: The Nielsen Company – Gameplay Metrics (full report available at http://blog.nielsen.com/nielsenwire/wp-content/uploads/2009/04/stateofvgamer_040609_fnl1.pdf).

initially were not interested in video games at all. Thus, more and more females and elderly people are now equipped with a Wii (or a DS). For example, many retirement homes have announced the purchase of a Wii for their residents, who enjoy it and use it to keep fit. This trend has continued with Nintendo releasing the Wiiboard and Wiifit, on which people can practise many sports at home (gym, fitness, ski simulations . . . even yoga). This has meant that Nintendo has expanded the games market beyond its traditional frontiers by targeting non-players (called 'casual gamers'), which largely explains its tremendous success. Yet, since sales have exceeded Nintendo's most optimistic forecasts, the company has frequently suffered from many stock shortages.

Another advantage of Nintendo over its competitors is that it has developed over the years its own universe, with exclusive characters, and thus exclusive games. *Zelda*, *Mario*, *Pokémon* and *Donkey Kong* are video game legends that can only be played with Nintendo's consoles. This explains why Nintendo is the first developer on its own games, which generates considerable revenues.

Since it does not rely on state-of-the-art technologies, the Wii's production costs are lower than its competitors', and Nintendo has been profitable from the very first Wii. These differences give it two other advantages. First, its price is far lower: in Europe, it costs €249 (£179.99) with one Wiimote and the game *WiiSports*. Second, developing a new PS3 or X360 game costs nearly $20 million versus around $5 million for a Wii game (accordingly, the Wii game's retail price is usually lower as well). Though this should have attracted many developers, only a few of them (e.g. Ubisoft and Sega) believed in the potential of the console and decided to support it from the beginning. However, this situation is changing, and the biggest developers (such

as Electronic Arts) have recently announced many new Wii games.

What's next?

Despite this massive success, dark clouds may be gathering on the horizon for Nintendo. To begin with, the Wii is the least-used console of its generation (see Table C37.1), and is even less used than the PS2 and the first Xbox.

Also, its two competitors have become more aggressive. First, they released cheaper, yet less advanced consoles. Then, thanks to reduced production costs, Microsoft and Sony have dramatically decreased their prices (about €249 for an X360 and €399 for a PS3 in Europe). Further, at the beginning of 2009, Nintendo announced to UK retailers that they would pay £20 more for the Wii, because of the pound sterling's depreciation!

Moreover, by mid-2008, Microsoft had apparently decided to position differently in the market. While still targeting hard-core gamers, the firm also now tries to reach casual gamers. To do so, it heavily promotes such exclusive games as *Lips* or *You're in the Movies*, which emphasize both fun and social interactivity. And there have been recurrent rumours about Microsoft's working on a controller with features similar to that of the Wiimote. This would not be surprising, even though it may reinforce Microsoft's image as a follower rather than a real innovator. As for Sony, the PS3 outsold the Wii in Japan for the very first time in March 2009 (monthly sales), an event Nintendo put into perspective thus: 'It is still the first few months of the year, when sales are low for the industry, so we are not particularly concerned.'

In 2009, Nintendo released a new accessory: the Wii-Motion Plus, which is designed to enhance the accuracy of players' moves. Many games will benefit from this improvement. But will this enable Nintendo to stay one step ahead?

References

Based on: http://www.ft.com/cms/s/0/d5adbcfc-229d-11de-9c99-00144feabdc0.html?nclick_check=1 (retrieved 8 April 2009); http://www.gamalive.com/Date-de-sortie-du-Wii-MotionPlus.html (retrieved 3 April 2009); http://www.gamasutra.com/blogs/DonDaglow/20090323/966/The_Four_Stages_of_Wii.php (retrieved 15 April 2009); http://www.gamasutra.com/php-bin/news_index.php?story=22087 (retrieved 3 April 2009); http://www.gamesindustry.biz/articles/consumers-to-be-hit-by-ii-price-rise (retrieved 15 April 2009); http://www.gamesindustry.biz/articles/third-parties-misjudged-the-wii (retrieved 3 April 2009); http://www.gamesindustry.biz/articles/wii-tops-us-february-hardware-sales (retrieved 3 April 2009); http://www.journaldugamer.com/2006/11/18/la-ps3-coute-cher-pour-sony/ (retrieved 3 April 2009); http://www.journaldugamer.com/tag/isupply/ (retrieved 3 April 2009); http://www.liberation.fr/economie/0101559915-le-raz-de-maree-du-casual-gaming (retrieved 15 April 2009); http://www.liberation.fr/medias/0101310298-ps2-la-replay-station (retrieved 8 April 2009); http://www.

nintendo.com/whatsnew/detail/eMMuRj_N6vntHPDycCJAKWhEO9zBvyPH (retrieved 3 April 2009); Joffre O. and L. Plé (2007) Nintendo: Une DS à laquelle tout le monde dit Wii!, in Joffre O., L. Plé and E. Simon (eds) *Cas en management stratégique: Autour du diagnostic*, Éditions EMS, 46–61; Plé, L. (2009) Sony's PlayStation 3: The Fall of the King?, in Jobber, D. and J. Fahy, *Foundations of Marketing* (3rd edn), McGraw-Hill, 211–14.

Questions

1. Explain how the analysis of its competitors has helped Nintendo to develop the Wii.
2. How would you describe Nintendo's competitive strategy?
3. Based on the marketing mix, identify the sources of Nintendo's competitive advantage in the lounge consoles market.
4. How do you see Nintendo's future in this market?

This case was written by Loïc Plé, Assistant Professor, IÉSEG School of Management, France.

On 1 June 2009, General Motors filed for bankruptcy protection—a historic landmark event. GM was the world's largest automobile maker, and has been leading the automotive business for over 100 years. The company owned several internationally known automotive brands, which it markets around the world. It builds nearly 9 million vehicles a year, making it an industry colossus. It is seen as the heartbeat of the American manufacturing industry. For decades it was viewed as an exemplar in the effective management, strategic thinking and organization of a modern corporation. Yet it is in catastrophic trouble for this once pillar of American industry, and with more problems looming on the horizon. Low-cost competition is eroding its market share. It lost its mantle as the world's largest car manufacturer to Toyota in 2007. Most alarmingly, the company has over $176 billion in liabilities, and lost a staggering $30 billion in 2008. Sales are in trouble within its North American division, with the pickup truck and SUV market plummeting. The company has some fundamental problems, which it needs to address, or it could be in serious trouble, as its strategy is beginning to rust.

General Motors was the iconoclast of the American multinational corporation. The contribution of GM to American industry is gargantuan, spending $50 billion dollars a year on parts, and with a wage bill of $476 million a month. However, it has lost a colossal $88 billion since 2004, an untenable situation. The US Government has now stepped in to restructure the company, bailing it out to a tune of $50 billion, and taking a 60 per cent ownership in the new entity, where it will have to offload several divisions. The company has offloaded several brands so that it can concentrate on core car models, and it will shed thousands of dealerships to make it leaner.

General Motors has a huge product portfolio, where its sells cars in nearly every single market. Under its 10 different car brands it manufactures 89 different car models. The company has a truly international manufacturing presence with 11 assembly plants in Europe, three in Asia, eight in South America and 29 in North America. The company has set up a number of manufacturing centres in low-cost countries such as Mexico, India, South Africa and China. In addition, the company has grown through a series of acquisitions and alliances, which it is hoped will strengthen its brand portfolio even further. In 2000, GM gained 100 per cent control over Swedish luxury car maker Saab. It has several joint ventures, such as with Chinese car maker Shanghai Automotive Industry Corporation to build a family car for the Chinese market. In 2002, it took over troubled South Korean car maker Daewoo. This has proved to be one of GM's remarkable success stories. Now the firm produces low-cost cars under the Chevrolet brand in 140 different international markets, using low-cost manufacturing bases. The company dropped the Daewoo brand in 2004, using the Chevrolet brand, with the aim of turning it into a global brand, moving it away from the firm's over-reliance on the North American market.

It is attempting to strengthen its international presence by focusing on growth areas such as China. However, growth in China is stalling: Buick sales in China fell 16 per cent when the overall market was up 7 per cent. Consumers were obviously thinking twice about buying large-ticket items and status symbols from a beleaguered company that could possibly fail. To get a synopsis of GM's 10 main automotive brands see Table C38.1. The company uses these different brands to target different segments of the market in different countries. In the USA, its uses eight different car brands (Chevrolet, GMC, Pontiac, Buick, Cadillac, Saturn, Saab and Hummer), while in Europe it sells Opel/Vauxhall, Saab and Chevrolet. In Australia it sells under the Holden brand.

One of the biggest difficulties for the GM stable of car brands is the lack of distinction between the various car marques. Car buyers view many of the models

General Motors' main automotive brands				TABLE C38.1
Chevrolet	**Pontiac**	**Saab**	**Opel/Vauxhall**	**GMC**
The Chevrolet brand is the third biggest car brand in the world and GM's most important. Has an offering in nearly every sector of market. Focuses strongly in the SUV sector of the market. GM wants to hold on to the brand	Pontiac is a mid-level brand, aimed typically at a young market. Focuses on projecting an image of performance, sporty and youth. Only available in North America. Sells roadsters, saloons and SUVs. Brand to be phased out or sold	Bought the Swedish luxury car maker to boost its presence in sector. Focuses on premium market with sporty designs. Small niche brand. Sold to Swedish super luxury car maker, with support from the Swedish Government. Sales down 23 per cent in EU	Uses the Vauxhall brand for UK. Wide range of cars and vans in product range. Sells approx. 1 million vehicles a year. Its market share has declined to 14 per cent. To be sold in the face of crippling losses. Lost €1.6 billion in 2008	It focuses on producing SUVs, pickup trucks and a range of commercial vehicles. Formerly known as GMC Truck. Sales are falling sharply, due to high oil prices
Buick	**Cadillac**	**GM Daewoo**	**Hummer**	**Saturn**
A mid-tier brand, with several luxury saloon cars and SUV offerings. Criticized for lacking distinction and rationalizing its current car model portfolio. Focuses on safety, quality and premium interiors at attainable prices. Brand has been successful in China	The luxury car brand in the GM stable. The quintessential luxury American car brand, with an emphasis on luxury, comfort, performance and technology. Aims to hold on to its premium brand	Formerly South Korean Daewoo brand. GM now sells this brand in Asian and European markets under the Chevrolet brand. Focus on small and medium-sized cars, that are value for money. Changed to Chevrolet brand in Jan 2005. Performs well	The former military vehicle jeep has been transformed into a highly popular and ridiculously expensive 4×4 vehicle. Launched in 1999, has earned a cache for cool. Sold for $100 million to Chinese manufacturer	Created Saturn brand in 1990 in response to low-cost Japanese imports in the sub-compact sector, using plastic body styling. Saturn is now repositioning in several different sectors, such as saloons, SUVs, roadsters and minivans. GM sold brand to auto dealership chain

launched by GM as very similar to other cars in its range. Several industry analysts have suggested that GM adopt a 'euthanasia' policy on several of its underperforming brands, in an effort to quell costs and create a stronger brand proposition. They argue that the cars sold under the various brands confuse customers, and that better returns could be yielded by a coordinated branding strategy, which communicates the true brand essence of each of the brands. For example, you can buy a similar saloon car under the Pontiac, Buick, Saturn and Chevrolet brand names with little or no discernable difference. GM suffers from the curse of sameness. Other companies have developed stronger reputations on a smaller repertoire of vehicles. Originally each of the GM brands had a strong distinctive image, with various brands focusing on different tiers of the market. For instance, Chevrolet focused on the value end, while

Cadillac focused on the premium spectrum of the market. Now those clear distinctions are blurred. It has culled its line-up in the past in an effort to rationalize its product portfolio; it scrapped the Oldsmobile brand in 2000. This famous US car brand perennially suffered a decline in its revenue, due to a poor product offering and the brand's lack of differentiation. Now the company is culling the Pontiac, Saab, Saturn and Hummer brands from its portfolio.

To put the malaise into perspective, its eight different brands have eight different slogans in America, such as:

1 GMC—Professional grade
2 Saturn—People first
3 Chevrolet—An American revolution
4 Pontiac—Action
5 Buick—Beyond precision
6 Cadillac—Break through

7   Hummer—Like nothing else
8   Saab—Born from jets.

These slogans really highlight the failings of GM's brand strategy as meaningless.

One of the key challenges for its brand stable is the production of eco-friendly cars, due to rising oil prices and growing environmental concerns. It hopes to launch the Chevrolet Volt, an electric hybrid car, in 2011. However, this is not its first foray into green energy: in 1999 it launched the EV11, an innovative electric car. This car was immortalized in a documentary called *Who Killed the Electric Car?*, which suspected oil companies, car dealers and the car companies themselves of helping to accelerate the project's downfall. This green initiative failed to be capitalized upon by General Motors, whereas Toyota's Prius hybrid car became an instant hit. GM let this innovative technology languish, while driving ahead with its traditional product portfolio. GM focused on hydrogen-powered technology as the future for the car industry. However, this technology is years from providing a viable alternative to oil, leaving GM without any foothold in this sector. Hybrid technology, ethanol and electricity were seen as viable technologies.

Mounting troubles

The company has been prone to difficulties throughout its history. It managed to stave off bankruptcy by 40 minutes in 1992 during a credit crunch. During that turbulent period it bounced back by slashing 21 plants and cutting 70,000 jobs, eliminating corporate bureaucracy, and improving productivity and quality. GM is heavily reliant on the North American market, where most of it problems reside. Excess capacity, diminishing margins, a rigid sales channel structure, confusing brand propositions, falling market share, labour problems and exorbitant legacy costs have all made a serious impact. Over 42 per cent of its sales come from North America, making it very susceptible to market shocks within the US market. In 2008, the Western European car market contracted 8.4 per cent due to the global economic recession, with some car inventories piling up due to lack of demand and consumer confidence. Key markets like Spain collapsed by 28 per cent.

During recent years the firm had focused on churning out gas-guzzling SUVs (large sports utility vehicles) and pickup trucks, diverting its attention from normal saloon cars. These vehicles were much sought after at the time by the market, and yielded higher margins. The company lost sight of developing a solid car range, while foreign competitors developed strong reputations in the sector. In the wake of rising oil prices, demand for these expensive-to-run SUVs has slumped, and consumers have turned to more fuel-efficient cars. With so much of GM's portfolio focused on large cars, it has been particularly susceptible to rising petrol prices. Consumers swapped their gas guzzlers for smaller cars, which collapsed the residual value of second-hand GM cars. This led to losses for the GM finance division as

Global vehicle sales and market share, 2008			TABLE C38.2
GM Global Vehicle Sales and Market Share—2008			
	Industry Sales* Units	GM Sales* Units	GM Market Share* %
North America	16,556,124	3,563,991	21.5
Europe	21,915,787	2,039,360	9.3
Asia-Pacific	21,049,035	1,475,340	7.0
LAAM**	7,478,285	1,246,570	17.1
Total Global	**66,999,231**	**8,355,261**	**12.5**
*Preliminary figures.			
**Latin America, Africa and Middle East.			
Source: GM Europe, Facts & Figures 2009.			

Global vehicle sales and market share, 2008 FIGURE **C38.1**

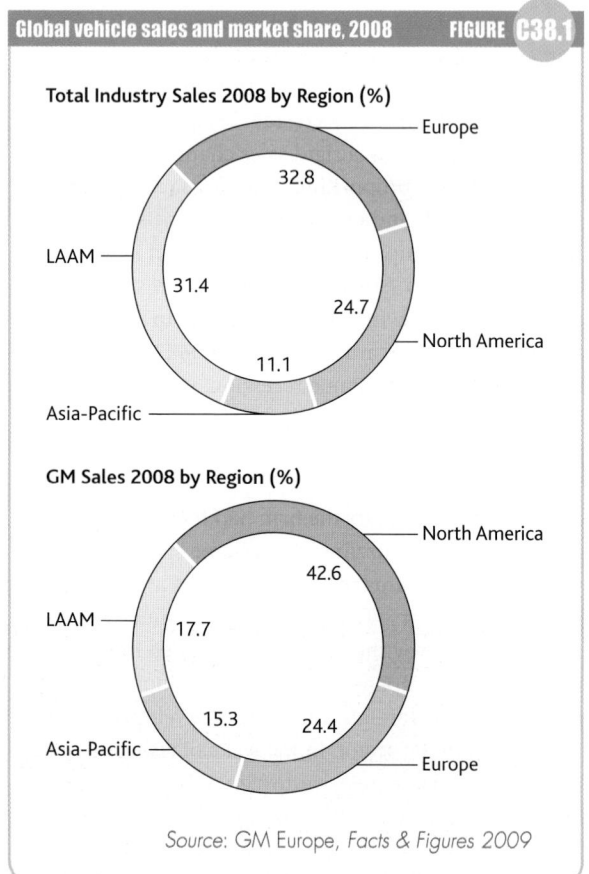

Total Industry Sales 2008 by Region (%)

- Europe 32.8
- North America 24.7
- Asia-Pacific 11.1
- LAAM 31.4

GM Sales 2008 by Region (%)

- North America 42.6
- Europe 24.4
- Asia-Pacific 15.3
- LAAM 17.7

Source: GM Europe, Facts & Figures 2009

General Motors is much derided in the business press as the 'world's biggest healthcare provider', rather than the 'world's biggest car manufacturer'. To put it into perspective, the firm's healthcare costs add nearly $1500 to the cost of each new GM vehicle produced. This is seen as totally untenable for the company. GM is severely curtailed by the legacy costs of former employees. Each GM worker must now produce enough profit to provide for the future healthcare of 2.5 former GM workers. The company has to spend a massive $61.5 billion on healthcare for its past and current employees. This commitment could rise even further, with the spiralling costs associated with the American healthcare system. This legacy of fixed costs has contributed nothing to the future well-being of the company.

Key to its future survival is the efficiency and effectiveness of GM's manufacturing capabilities. GM factories have won several awards for quality processes, however this is not reflected in the market, where consumers have poor quality perceptions towards GM brands. Continued improvement in its manufacturing capabilities is vital, focusing on quality, efficiency and costs. For instance, it takes 34 hours to build a typical GM car, while a Toyota takes 28 hours. The company has only recently focused on harmonizing production, and sharing parts and car platforms. With falling sales, GM has closed several plants, which is incurring the wrath of its unions. Trades unions are worried about the increasing concessions workers have had to make in order to stem the company's losses, including redundancies, reduced compensation and amendments to their healthcare provisions. Strikes potentially loom. Also, its main supplier of automotive parts, Delphi (spun off from GM in 1999), is in severe financial difficulty too, which could have dangerous repercussions for GM's supply chain, albeit that some of it new car models, like Vauxhall's Insignia saloon car, have won 'car of the year' awards.

GM has been criticized for launching numerous new models under different brands, then subsequently ditching them if they are not proven to be a stellar success, creating huge levels of product churn. This is a substantial investment in terms of marketing expenditure, constantly boosting brand recognition for these new brands. Other car makers have several cornerstone car marques, which they frequently update with the latest technology and revamp with subtle stylistic changes. GM has increased the level of new product launches to unprecedented levels, placing an emphasis on getting newer models out to market very

cars returning from a lease were depreciating at a calamitous rate.

Its US market share is continuing to slide: where it once garnered 41 per cent of the market in 1985, it now accounts for only 24.7 per cent. In an effort to stave off the decline, the company has deployed an aggressive price discounting strategy, which has devalued many of its venerable brands. The company on average offers cash rebates of nearly $1500 per vehicle off the ticket price. Some Buick models sell with 20 per cent discounts off the ticket price. It recently offered its cars at 'employee discount for everyone'. Sales drop when a promotion ends as consumers wait for the next rebate or promotional offer. The average price of a GM car is $18,900, a figure that has remained static for several years. The company hopes to shift away from price promotions and focus on building brands through lower advertised prices, more advertising expenditure and extra equipment as standard. One of the biggest problems for GM is the brand, in that similar models of cars sold by Toyota sell for between $3000 and $11,000 more than their GM equivalents.

quickly. In addition, GM is seen as having too many dealers: it has five times more dealers than Toyota. Now it is cutting nearly a half of its dealer network. Dealer margins have slipped to 1.6 per cent. The dealership structure needs to be consolidated and to become more sustainable.

The turnaround strategy

The group has launched several initiatives in order to try to reverse its declining fortunes, namely reducing exorbitant fixed costs, maximizing manufacturing capacity and revitalizing a weak product offering through improved R&D. Manufacturing plants that are not operating at full capacity really hurt the business, especially in high-cost manufacturing countries. Previously the company had allowed autonomous R&D within divisions, but now the firm is seeking to leverage engineering expertise across its global operations. This, it is hoped, will improve design, reduce costs and avoid fruitless duplication of activities. It is spending nearly $8 billion on R&D every year, which equates to approximately 5 per cent of its revenue. It also hopes to eliminate lookalike products from its portfolio.

It partially sold off 51 per cent of its financing division, GMAC. This financing arm provides commercial, residential and automotive finance packages in over 40 countries. The firm has sold equity stakes in several businesses. GM is now attempting to amalgamate several brands into one sales channel. For instance, in the USA, it is creating dealerships where Pontiac, Buick and GMC are sold under the same dealership. Similarly, in Europe, it is selling Vauxhall and Chevrolet (formerly Daewoo) car marques in the same dealer premises, creating strong sales propositions. Continued efforts to alter GM sales channels have been restricted due to franchised dealers' rights under US law. However, bankruptcy enables the company to make radical changes that would normally be impossible. The only way to change a dealership contract is through expensive compensation to the franchise. Also the company hopes to offer lower ticket prices, moving away from the endless stream of price promotions. As a result of the bankruptcy, GM is going to have to face a seismic shift in the way it competes.

Questions

1. Using Porter's 'five forces' framework, discuss the competitiveness of the global automobile market.
2. Identify and discuss the weaknesses associated with General Motors' marketing strategy.
3. What are GM's sources of competitive advantage? Discuss how it could achieve a differential advantage over competitors.

This case was written by Conor Carroll, University of Limerick. The material in the case has been drawn from a variety of published sources and research reports. For further reading to assist in answering these questions, visit www.acea.be.

CHAPTER 20

Competitive marketing strategy

The easiest victories are in those places where there is no enemy.

ANONYMOUS ARMY GENERAL

LEARNING OBJECTIVES

After reading this chapter, you should be able to:

1. discuss the nature of competitive behaviour

2. explain how military analogies can be applied to competitive marketing strategy

3. identify the attractive conditions and strategic focus necessary to achieve the following objectives—build, hold, niche, harvest and divest

4. discuss the nature of frontal, flanking, encirclement, bypass and guerrilla attacks

5. discuss the nature of position, flanking, pre-emptive, counter-offensive and mobile defences, and strategic withdrawal

The strategic triangle FIGURE **20.1**

In many markets, competition is the driving force of change. Without competition companies satisfice: they provide satisfactory levels of service but fail to excel. Where there is a conflict between improving customer satisfaction and costs, the latter often take priority since customers have little choice and cost-cutting produces tangible results. Competition, then, is good for the customer as it means that companies have to try harder or lose their customer base. A case in point is the impact of Eurotunnel on cross-Channel ferry operators. As Barratt commented:[1]

> One thing is certain: Eurotunnel's plans have galvanized the ferry operators and the Dover Harbour Board into making long-overdue changes to their operating procedures. P&O European Ferries announced this month that from next spring it will operate a cross-Channel service every 45 minutes. Check-in time will also be cut from 30 minutes to 20 minutes.

> Dover Harbour Board has met the challenge by drastically streamlining the loading and unloading process. Last month, for the first time, I drove off the ferry at Dover and went straight out of the terminal without stopping—just the briefest pause to wave the passports at the immigration officer.

When developing marketing strategy, companies need to be aware of their own strengths and weaknesses, customer needs, and the competition. This three-pronged approach to strategy development has been termed the 'strategic triangle' and is shown in Figure 20.1. This framework recognizes that to be successful it is no longer sufficient to be good at satisfying customers' needs: companies need to be better than the competition. In Chapter 19 we discussed various ways of creating and sustaining a competitive advantage. In this chapter we shall explore the development of marketing strategies in the face of competitive activity and challenges. First, we shall look at alternative modes of competitive behaviour and then, drawing on military analogy, examine when and how to achieve strategic marketing objectives.

Competitive Behaviour

Rivalry between firms does not always lead to conflict and aggressive marketing battles. **Competitive behaviour** can take five forms: conflict, competition, co-existence, cooperation and collusion.[2]

Conflict

Conflict is characterized by aggressive competition, where the objective is to drive competitors out of the marketplace. British Airways and TWA's successful battle with Laker is an example of competitive conflict where the financial muscle of the established airlines brought down their price-cutting competitor. More recently British Airways' unsuccessful attempt to discredit Virgin Atlantic with its so-called 'dirty tricks' campaign is another manifestation of conflict.

Competition

The objective of competition is not to eliminate competitors from the marketplace but to perform better than them. This may take the form of trying to achieve faster sales and/or profit growth, larger size or higher market share. Competitive behaviour recognizes the limits of aggression. Competitor reaction will be an important consideration when setting strategy. Players will avoid spoiling the underlying industry structure, which is an important influence on overall profitability. For example, price wars will be avoided if competitors believe that their long-term effect will be to reduce industry profitability.

Co-existence

Three types of co-existence can occur. First, co-existence may arise because firms do not recognize their competitors owing to difficulties in defining market boundaries. For example, a manufacturer of fountain pens may ignore competition from jewellery companies since its definition may be product-based rather than market-centred (i.e. the gift market). Second, firms may not recognize other companies they believe are operating in a separate market segment. For example, Waterman is likely to ignore the actions of Bic pens as they are operating in different market segments. Third, firms may choose to acknowledge the territories of their competitors (for example, geography, brand personality, market segment or product technology) in order to avoid harmful head-to-head competition.

Cooperation

This involves the pooling of the skills and resources of two or more firms to overcome problems and take advantage of new opportunities. A growing trend is towards **strategic alliances** where firms join together through a joint venture, licensing agreement, long-term purchasing and supply arrangements, or joint research and development contract to build a long-term competitive advantage. For example, Boeing's cooperation with Rolls-Royce has led to the development of quieter and more efficient jet engines. In today's global marketplace, where size is a key source of advantage, cooperation is a major type of competitive behaviour.

Collusion

The final form of competitive behaviour is collusion, whereby firms come to some arrangement that inhibits competition in a market. For example, vitamin manufacturers from France, Germany, Japan and Switzerland, including Aventis, BASF and Roche, were found guilty of collusion in the areas of price fixing and setting sales quotas by the European Commission.[3] Collusion is more likely where there are a small number of suppliers in each national market, the price of the product is a small proportion of buyer costs, where cross-national trade is restricted by tariff barriers or prohibitive transportation costs, and where buyers are able to pass on high prices to their customers.

Developing Competitive Marketing Strategies

The work of such writers as Ries and Trout, and Kotler and Singh has drawn attention to the relationship between military and marketing 'warfare'.[4,5] Their work has stressed the need to develop strategies that are more than customer based. They placed the emphasis on attacking and defending against the competition, and used military analogies to guide strategic thinking. They saw competition as the enemy and thus recognized the relevance of the principles of military warfare as put forward by such writers as Sun Tzu and von Clausewitz to business.[6,7] As von Clausewitz wrote:

> Military warfare is a clash between major interests that is resolved by bloodshed—that is the only way in which it differs from other conflicts. Rather than comparing it to an art we could more accurately compare it to commerce, which is also a conflict of human interests and activities.

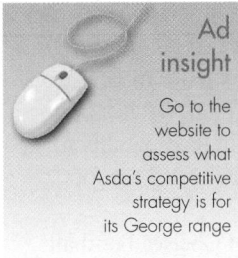

Indeed, military terms have been used in business and marketing for many years. Terms such as *launching a campaign*, *achieving a breakthrough*, *company division* and *strategic business unit* are common in business language. Frequently, sales and service personnel are referred to as *field forces*.[8]

The context in which we shall explore the development of competitive marketing strategy is the achievement of *strategic marketing objectives*. Four of these objectives have already been discussed (to *build, hold, harvest* and *divest*), to which a fifth objective—to *niche*—may be added. The discussion of each objective will focus on the *attractive conditions* that favour its adoption, and the **strategic focus**, which comprises the strategies that can be employed to achieve the objective.*

Build Objectives

Attractive conditions

A *build objective* is suitable in *growth markets*. Because overall market sales are growing, all players can achieve higher sales even if the market share of one competitor is falling. This is in marked contrast to mature (no growth) markets where an increase in the sales of one player has to be at the expense of the competition (zero sum game).

Some writers point out that if competitors' expectations are high in a growth market (for example, because they know that the market is growing) they may retaliate if those expectations are not met.[9] While this is true, their reaction is not likely to be as strong or protracted as in a no-growth situation. For example, if expectations have led to an expansion of plant capacity that is not fully utilized because of competitor activity, the situation is not as serious as when over-capacity exists in a no-growth market. In the former case, market growth will help fill capacity without recourse to aggressive retaliatory action, whereas, in the latter, capacity utilization will improve only at the expense of the competition.

A build objective also makes sense in growth markets because new users are being attracted to the product. Since these new users do not have established brand or supplier loyalty it is logical to invest resources into attracting them to our product offering. Provided the product meets their expectations, trial during the growth phase can lead to the building of goodwill and loyalty as the market matures. One company that has pursued a build objective in growth markets is Cisco Systems. Riding the Internet boom, the company has achieved staggering growth by providing 'routers' that direct traffic around the Internet and corporate intranets. In one 15-year period the company doubled its size every year. It has continued to build through acquisition and move into related emerging areas, including technology to transmit telephone calls over the Internet and security systems. It has also announced plans to diversify into the mainstream consumer electronics market, challenging companies such as Sony and Samsung in the marketing of radios, stereos, phones and home theatre equipment.[10]

A build objective is also attractive in mature (no growth) markets where there are *exploitable competitive weaknesses*. For example, Japanese car producers exploited US and European car manufacturers' weaknesses in reliability and build quality; Starbucks exploited competitive weaknesses in traditional coffee shops to build a global business; easyJet and Ryanair exploited traditional airlines' high prices on short-haul flights; and Virgin Airlines took advantage of long-haul carriers' unexceptional service levels across the Atlantic to build based on service excellence (which now includes massage for business-class passengers).

*The format of this part of Chapter 20 is similar to that of 'Offensive and Defensive Marketing Strategies' in *Market Strategy and Competitive Positioning* by John Saunders, Graham Hooley and Nigel Piercy (London: Prentice-Hall). This is because the approach was developed by the author of the current text and Graham Hooley when they worked together at the University of Bradford School of Management.

▲ M&S celebrates 125 years of producing quality product.

A third attractive condition for building sales and market share is when the company has *exploitable corporate strengths*. For example, Casio built on its core competence in microelectronics to move from calculators to watches. Marks & Spencer's core competence lies in its capability to produce quality products, whether they be clothes or food (see illustration).

The exploitable corporate strengths of Chelsea Football Club were enhanced with the arrival of Roman Abramovich, who has funded the building of the team to challenge the triumvirate of Manchester United, Liverpool and Arsenal.

When taking on a market leader, an attractive, indeed a necessary, condition is *adequate corporate resources*. The financial muscle that usually accompanies market leadership, and the importance of the situation, mean that forceful retaliation can be expected. The iPod's challenge to the Sony Walkman benefited from Apple's resources, derived from its Macintosh range of computers. Occasionally a market challenger can out-resource the market leader based on cash accumulations from other businesses. For example, Microsoft successfully challenged Netscape, not because it marketed a superior browser but because its financial muscle meant that it could supply its browser software free of charge with its Windows package.

Finally, a build objective is attractive when *experience curve effects* are believed to be strong. Some experience curve effects (the combined impact on costs of economies of scale and learning) are related to cumulative output: by building sales faster than the competition, a company can achieve the position of cost leader, as United Biscuits has done in the UK and Wal-Mart has achieved worldwide.

20.1 Pause for Thought

Can you recall a successful brand that has increased sales over the past few years? How many of the attractive conditions for a build strategy apply in this case? Which one is the main reason for the brand's sales growth?

Strategic focus

A build objective can be achieved in four ways: through market expansion, winning market share from the competition, by merger or acquisition, and by forming strategic alliances.

Market expansion

This is brought about by creating new users or uses, or by increasing frequency of purchase. *New users* may be found by expanding internationally, as Tesco has done, or by moving to larger target markets, as with Lucozade, which was initially targeted at ill children but now has mass-market appeal. *New uses* can be promoted, as when Johnson's Baby Lotion was found to be used by women as a facial cleanser. The technique of brand extension can be used in new use situations. The umbrella brand Flash has been extended from a bath cleaner to mops and dusters in this way. *Increasing frequency of use* may rely on persuasive communications—

for example, by persuading people to clean their teeth twice a day rather than only once. Kellogg's attempted to increase the frequency of consumption of its Special K breakfast cereal by suggesting that women should eat it at two meals for two weeks during the summer in an attempt to lose weight before going on holiday.

Winning market share

If a market cannot be expanded, a build strategy implies gaining marketing success at the expense of the competition. Winning market share is an important goal as market share has been found to be related to profitability in many studies (see Chapter 9, 'Managing Products: Brand and Corporate Identity Management'). There are several reasons why this should be so. Market leaders are often high-price brands (examples include Coca-Cola, Kellogg's, Heinz, Nestlé, Nike and Nokia). They are also in a stronger position to resist distributor demands for trade discounts. Because of economies of scale and experience curve effects, their costs are likely to be lower than those of their smaller-volume rivals. Therefore, their profit margins should be greater than those of their competitors. Since they are market leaders by definition the unit sales volume is higher and consequently their overall profits (profit margin × sales volume) should be higher than those of their rivals. It is for this reason that companies such as GE, Unilever, Procter & Gamble and Heinz are willing to compete only in those markets where they can reach number one or two position.

In business, companies seek to win market share through product, distribution, promotional innovation and penetration pricing. Kotler and Singh have identified five competitor confrontation strategies (see Fig. 20.2) designed to win sales and market share.[11]

Frontal attack involves the challenger taking on the defender head on. For example, the number two in the PC market, Hewlett-Packard has successfully challenged the one-time market leader, Dell, using a combination of innovation and price cutting. If the defender is a

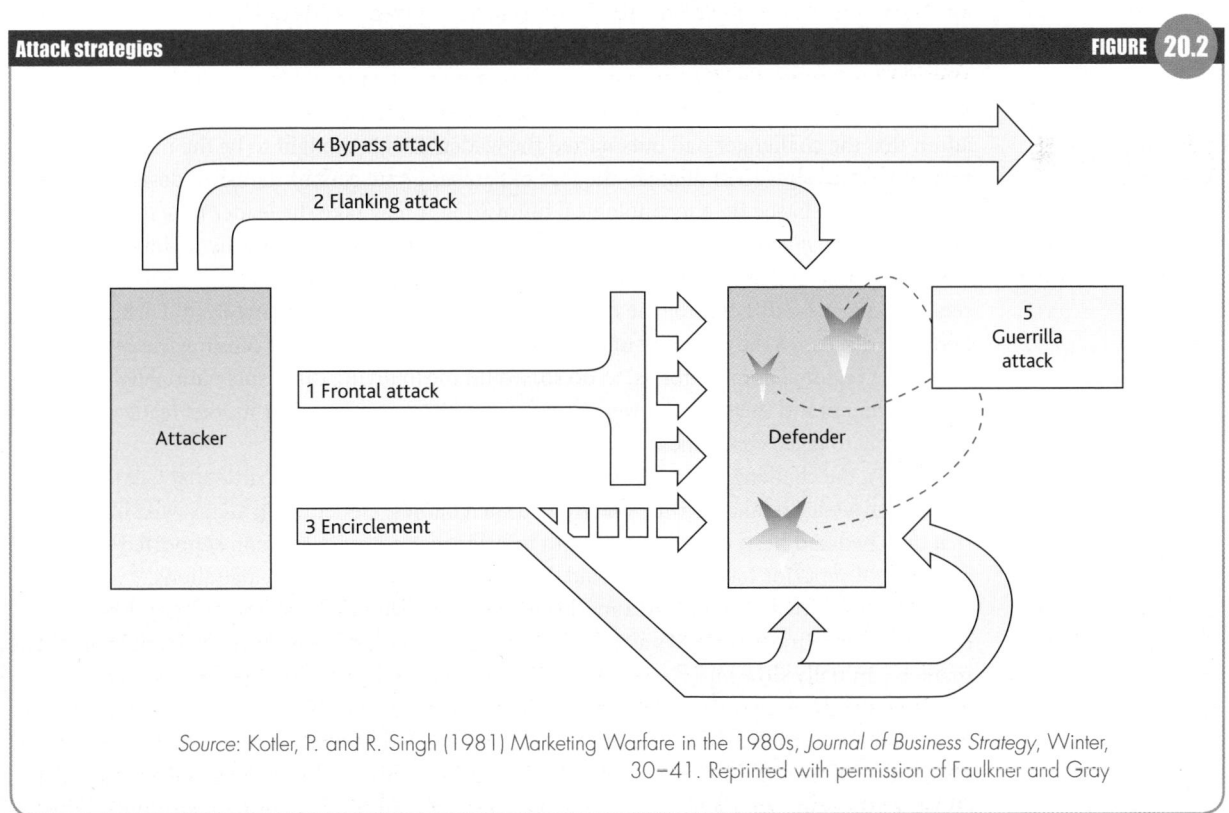

Attack strategies   FIGURE **20.2**

Source: Kotler, P. and R. Singh (1981) Marketing Warfare in the 1980s, *Journal of Business Strategy*, Winter, 30–41. Reprinted with permission of Faulkner and Gray

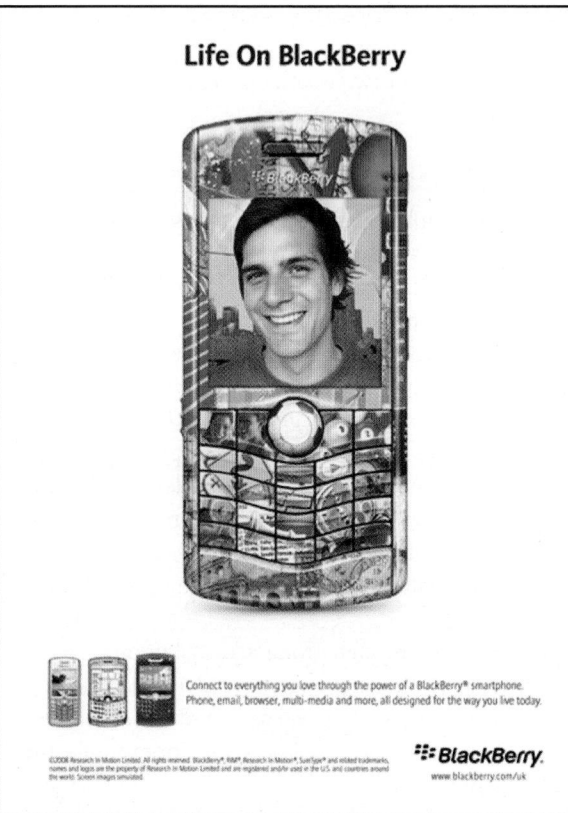

Life On BlackBerry

Connect to everything you love through the power of a BlackBerry® smartphone.
Phone, email, browser, multi-media and more, all designed for the way you live today.

::: BlackBerry.
www.blackberry.com/uk

▲ Market leader in the business market, BlackBerry challenges the iPhone in the consumer market.

market leader, the success of a head-on challenge is likely to depend on four factors.[12] First, the challenger should have a clear and sustainable *competitive advantage*. Virgin Atlantic's challenge to British Airways and American Airlines on transatlantic routes is based upon continuous service innovation. For example, it was the first to introduce in-seat video screens and the 'limo to lounge in 10 minutes' offering, which promises passengers arriving at its Upper Class Wing at Heathrow airport to speed them through check-in.[13] If the advantage is based on cost leadership this will support a low price strategy to fight the market leader. Ryanair is the cost leader in short-haul air travel, allowing it to undercut traditional carriers such as British Airways and Lufthansa on price. A distinct differential advantage provides the basis for superior customer value. Sustainability is necessary to delay the leader's capability to respond. The advertisement for the BlackBerry smartphone is a challenge to the iPhone's position in the consumer market.

Second, the challenger should achieve proximity *in other activities*. In the earth-moving market, John Deere took on Caterpillar with a machine that gave buyers productivity gains; it failed, however, due to its inability to match Caterpillar in after-sales service.

Third, success is more likely if there is some *restriction on the leader's ability to retaliate*. Restrictions include patent protection, pride, technological lead times and the costs of retaliation. Where a differential advantage or cost leadership position is supported by *patent protection*, imitation by the market leader will be very difficult. *Pride* may hamper retaliation; the market leader refused to imitate because to do so would admit that the challenger had outsmarted the leader. This is thought to be the main reason why Nokia was slow to retaliate in the face of Samsung's successful clamshell design. Where the challenge is based on a technological innovation it may take the leader *time to put in place the new technology*. John Deere's challenge to Caterpillar was based on a hydrostatic drive that would take Caterpillar two to three years to install in its own machines. Furthermore, retaliation may be difficult for the market leader because of the *costs* involved. Earlier in the book, we discussed the difficulty of a car number plate market leader offering the discounts given by a regional competitor as, to do so, would mean giving discounts nationally. The risk of damaging brand image and lowering profit margins may also deter market leaders from responding to price challenges.

Finally, the challenger needs *adequate resources* to withstand the battle that will take place should the leader retaliate. After studying 30 such battles, General von Clausewitz observed that only two had been won by a side with inferior manpower. Napoleon supported the principle of superior force when he said, 'God is on the side of the big battalions.'[14]

An example of a challenge to a market leader that succeeded because most of these conditions were met was IBM's attack on Apple, once market leader in the personal computer market.[15] Initially slow into the segment, IBM developed a computer that possessed a competitive advantage over Apple based on a 16-bit processor that was faster and more powerful than Apple's 8-bit machine. IBM also persuaded software houses to develop a wide range of software that would run only on its machines. Buyers would therefore have a wider choice of software from which to choose if they bought an IBM rather than an Apple

Major marketing head to heads	TABLE 20.1
Companies	**Competitive area**
Nike vs Adidas	Footwear
Coca-Cola vs Pepsi	Soft drinks
McDonald's vs Burger King	Fast-food restaurants
Unilever vs Procter & Gamble	Fast-moving consumer goods
Apple (iPhone) vs Research in Motion (BlackBerry)	Smartphones
Nokia vs Samsung	Mobile handsets
Dell vs Hewlett-Packard	Computers
Google vs Yahoo!	Search engines
Intel vs Advanced Micro Devices	Microchips
Boeing vs Airbus	Aircraft
Cadbury (Trident) vs Mars (Wrigley)	Chewing gum
Microsoft (Explorer) vs Google (Chrome)	Internet browsers

computer (a major differential advantage). IBM also managed to achieve proximity to Apple in other activities, particularly in terms of reliability and after-sales service.

Apple refused to follow IBM's route regarding software, preferring to remain distinctive (perhaps pride was a factor here). Instead it retaliated by launching the Macintosh based on an *ease of use* differential advantage. IBM, therefore, still held the software edge.

IBM's massive resources, based on its mainframe computer cash cows, enabled it to launch a powerful promotional campaign aimed at the business market. IBM's ability to create a differential advantage, its ability, initially, to match Apple on other activities, Apple's inability to generate as wide a range of software as IBM, and IBM's superior resources made up the platform that led to IBM overtaking Apple as market leader. However, IBM's inability to sustain its differential advantage with software as IBM clones entered the market with cheaper prices has been a major factor in its recent downturn in sales and profits, and its decision to sell its PC division to Lenovo.

As Table 20.1 illustrates, many markets are characterized by head-to-head competition between the major protagonists. One of those that has been resolved was the conflict between Sony and Toshiba over the future standard for the next generation of DVDs; this is discussed further in Marketing in Action 20.1.

A **flanking attack** involves attacking unguarded or weakly guarded ground. In marketing terms it means attacking geographical areas or market segments where the defender is poorly represented. For example, in the USA as major supermarket chains moved out of town, the 7-11 chain prospered by opening stores that provided the convenience of local availability and longer opening hours.

The growth in ethical consumption has provided opportunities for ethically based brands to issue a flanking attack on traditional suppliers. For example, companies such as Green & Black's (organic chocolate), Cafédirect (fair trade coffee), innocent (smoothie drinks based on natural ingredients), Pret A Manger (sandwiches and salads made from natural ingredients free from chemicals and preservatives) and Ben & Jerry's (an ethically orientated company marketing ice cream) have all been highly successful in growing sales and profits.

20.1 Marketing in Action

Two Tribes Go to War—With Victory to Sony

Sony and Toshiba were locked in a battle over next-generation DVDs. Resembling the video format war between Sony (Betamax) and JVC (VHS), which JVC won, Sony was committed to Blu-Ray technology, while Toshiba backed its HD-DVD format.

Each system offers different benefits to consumers. Blu-Ray discs have more recording capacity, but HD-DVD is much cheaper. The cheapest Blu-Ray player was launched in 2006 at around $1000, whereas the least expensive HD-DVD player was half that price. Unsurprisingly, Sony incorporated a Blu-Ray drive in its PlayStation 3 consoles, while Microsoft offered a version of its Xbox 360 with HD-DVD. Both systems offered more capacity than current DVDs, and better protection against piracy.

Learning from its lack of support for Betamax, which was technically superior to VHS, Sony recruited a formidable list of allies, including Dell, Apple, Philips, Matsushita and four studios—MGM, Fox, Walt Disney and Sony Pictures—which fully supported Blu-Ray. Two other studios, Warner and Paramount, supported both formats. Toshiba was fully supported by IT giants Microsoft and Intel, and one studio, Universal. Sony's superior firepower eventually won, with Warner and Paramount stating that they would no longer back HD-DVD and Wal-Mart announcing that the format would no longer be stocked. But will the victory be short-lived? With a consortium of high-tech big guns like Intel and Hewlett-Packard announcing that they are seeking ways to make film downloads easier, there is the possibility that consumers will bypass Blu-Ray and download films from the Internet.

Based on: Nakamoto (2005);[16] Schofield (2006);[17] Edwards (2008);[18] Sanchanta (2008)[19]

The attack by Japanese companies on the European and US car markets was a flanking attack—on the small car segment—from which they have expanded into other segments including sports cars. The success of Next, the retail clothing chain, was based on spotting an underserved, emerging market segment: working women aged 25–40 who were finding it difficult to buy stylish clothes at reasonable prices.

Another example of a flanking attack was when Mars attacked Unilever's Walls ice cream subsidiary in Europe by launching a range of premium brands such as its ice cream Mars bar and a series of ice cream versions of its chocolate brands, such as Snickers, Galaxy and Bounty. This flanking attack was regarded by Unilever as a major threat to its ice cream business. Its response was to launch a range of premium brands, including Magnum and Gino Ginelli, and to defend vigorously its *shop exclusivity deals*, which prevent competitors from selling its products in shops that sell Walls ice cream, and *freezer exclusivity*, which prohibits competitors from placing their ice cream in Unilever-supplied freezer cabinets.

The advantage of a flanking attack is that it does not provoke the same kind of response as a head-on confrontation. Since the defender is not challenged in its main market segments, there is more chance that it will ignore the challenger's initial successes. If the defender dallies too long, the flank segment can be used as a beachhead from which to attack the defender in its major markets, as Japanese companies have repeatedly done.

An **encirclement attack** involves attacking the defender from all sides. Every market segment is hit with every combination of product features to completely encircle the defender. An example is Seiko, which produces over 2000 different watch designs for the worldwide market. These cover everything the customer might want in terms of fashion and features. A variant on the encirclement-attack approach is to cut off supplies to the defender. This could be achieved by the acquisition of major supply companies.

A **bypass attack** circumvents the defender's position, as the German army did in 1940 when it bypassed the Maginot Line, built by the French to protect themselves from invasion.

In business, a bypass attack changes the rules of the game, usually through technological leap-frogging as Casio did when bypassing Swiss analogue watches with digital technology. Also the BlackBerry and iPod bypassed traditional mobile phone producers like Nokia and Motorola to create a new growth market in smartphones. A bypass attack can also be accomplished through diversification. An attacker can bypass a defender by seeking growth in new markets with new products, as Tesco and Marks & Spencer have done with their move into financial services, and Cisco is doing with its move into consumer electrical goods.[20]

A **guerrilla attack** hurts the defender with pin-pricks rather than blows. Just as the French Resistance used guerrilla tactics against the German forces in the Second World War, not to defeat the enemy but to weaken it, so in business the underdog can make life uncomfortable for its stronger rivals. Unpredictable price discounts, sales promotions or heavy advertising in a few television regions are some of the tactics attackers can use to cause problems for defenders.

Guerrilla tactics may be the only feasible option for a small company facing a larger competitor. Such tactics allow the small company to make its presence felt without the dangers of a full-frontal attack. By being unpredictable, guerrilla activity is difficult to defend against. Nevertheless, such tactics run the risk of incurring the wrath of the defender, who may choose to retaliate with a full-frontal attack if sufficiently provoked.

Merger or acquisition

A third approach to achieving a build objective is to merge with or acquire competitors. By joining forces, costly marketing battles are avoided, and purchasing, production, financial, marketing and R&D synergies may be gained. Further, a merger can give the scale of operation that may be required to operate as an international force in the marketplace. Such potential gains are fuelling merger and acquisition activity. Table 20.2 highlights some recent merger and acquisition activity.

Recent mergers and acquisitions	TABLE 20.2
Companies	**Competitive area**
Cadbury/Green & Black's	Chocolate
WPP/Taylor Nelson Sofres	Marketing research
Google/YouTube	Internet videos
InBev/Anheuser-Busch	Alcoholic drinks
Mars/Wrigley	Chewing gum
Nanjing Automobile/MG Rover	Cars
NewsCorp/MySpace	Social networking
Oracle/Sun	Computing
Pernot Ricaud/Vin & Sprit	Alcoholic drinks
Pfizer/Wyeth	Pharmaceuticals
Tata/Jaguar Land Rover	Cars
Vodafone/Zyb	Wireless Internet
Yahoo/Flickr	Internet photos

Mergers are not without their risks, though, not least when they involve parties from different countries. Differences in culture, language, business practices, and the problems associated with restructuring may cause terminal strains. For example, the problems faced by AOL and Time Warner following their merger were partly attributable to the culture strains of welding a nifty e-culture to a sedate media business.[21] Two European examples of merger failure are Dunlop and Pirelli (rubber) and Hoechst and Hoogovens (steel). Indeed, a study by McKinsey & Co. management consultants into the success or failure of 319 mergers and acquisitions claimed that about half had been successful in terms of post-acquisition return on equity and assets, and whether or not they exceeded the acquirer's cost of capital.[22]

The objectives of most mergers and acquisitions fall within five categories, as described below.[23]

Reduce overcapacity and increase market share and efficiency: the acquiring company aims to eliminate capacity, gain market share and improve efficiency. This type of merger and acquisition is the most difficult to implement as it often occurs between two large companies that have deeply entrenched processes and values.[24]

Also, if the problems facing the acquiring company are deeper than inefficiencies, a merger designed to gain share, lower costs and reduce capacity will fail. For example, Hewlett-Packard's acquisition of Compaq sought these benefits, but failed because it did not address HP's flawed business model of low inventory direct sales to compete with Dell and its traditional high-inventory model used when it distributed through its retail partners. In the former, the company lost out to Dell, which had greater scale and efficiency, and in the latter it failed to complete with IBM, which targeted higher-margin corporate accounts.[25]

Geographic expansion: the merger or acquisition allows both companies to expand geographically. Part of the logic behind P&G's acquisition of Gillette was based on this benefit. The deal allowed P&G to expand in India and Brazil, where Gillette had distribution strengths, and Gillette to take advantage of P&G's strengths in China, Russia, Japan and Turkey. Also, by buying Reebok, Adidas gained a strong presence in the USA, as did BP with its highly successful acquisition of Amoco and Arco. Marketing in Action 20.2 explains that geographic expansion of beer brands was at the heart of InBev's acquisition of Anheuser-Busch.

 20.2 Marketing in Action

InBev Buys Bud

There have to be good reasons to pay $52 billion for a company. InBev, the Brazilian-run, Belgian-located brewer, believed it had them when it bought the US beer company Anheuser-Busch. The acquisition catapulted the combined company to the number-one position in global brewing and to one of the world's top five consumer products companies. Such scale gives it enormous negotiating power when buying hops, barley, glass and aluminium, but the major potential benefits lie in the marketing opportunities that their combined assets present.

First, Anheuser controls almost half of the American beer market, the world's most profitable. InBev's American operations are tiny, but it is big in Europe and Latin America, where A-B is hardly present. The acquisition therefore gives InBev's brands—such as Stella Artois, Skol and Becks—access to A-B's vast distribution network in the US, while InBev's strong distribution channels gives A-B brands such as Budweiser and Bud Light access to Europe and Latin America.

Second, the ownership of such strong international brands is becoming increasingly important to brewers because they are prized by consumers in fast-growing markets such as Russia and China. Also, even in mature western markets, the profit margins on leading global brands are high. For example, Heineken says that profits on its Heineken brand are twice those on its regional brands, such as Amstel, which still form about 80 per cent of sales. By buying the company that owns Budweiser and Bud Light, InBev is buying the world's number-one and number-three brands (second place is taken by China's Snow beer).

Like all mergers, there are risks. First, InBev is better known for cost cutting than brand building. For example, when it acquired Boddingtons, a UK beer brand, it cut advertising support, and its record with Stella Artois in the UK is questionable. Second, Budweiser is seen by Americans to be quintessentially American. US beer drinkers may react negatively to its new Brazilian-Belgian ownership, providing opportunities for A-B's arch-rival SABMiller. Third, the cultures of the two companies differ. InBev is a cost cutter and is stinting with standard industry perks like company cars and free beer. Anheuser-Busch, on the other hand, comes with expensive tastes like helicopters, two free cases of beer each month for employees, and free admission to the company's theme parks.

These issues mean that the merger is full of opportunities but the risks of failure are also present. It will take skilful management to make the merger a success.

Based on: Anonymous (2008);[26] Foust (2008);[27] Ritson (2008);[28] Wiggins (2008)[29]

Product and/or market extension: the objective here is to extend a company's product line and/or its market coverage. For example, L'Oréal's purchase of Body Shop extended its product line into ethically orientated cosmetics, and hence extended its market appeal to ethically conscious consumers. Tata Motors' purchase of Jaguar and Land Rover extended its product line and allowed it to compete in the prestige car market sector.

Research and development benefits: the merger or acquisition is to acquire research and development expertise and output, instead of in-house research, so that market position can be built quickly. Most of Cisco System's acquisitions fall into this category.

Exploitation of industry convergence: the company judges that a new industry is emerging and tries to establish a position by acquiring resources from existing companies. For example, a key reason for eBay's purchase of Skype was to acquire resources to take advantage of the converging market for Internet telephone communications.

Despite these potential gains, studies have shown that 65 per cent of acquisitions and mergers fail to benefit shareholders.[30] There are several reasons for this. First, cultural problems can arise. An extreme example is the merger of the Metal Box Company, based in the UK, with the French company Carnaud: at times the French and British directors refused even to speak to each other. More usually, the problem arises that the cultures of the two companies take so long to meld that new marketplace opportunities are missed. Second, so much emphasis may be placed on the benefits of the merger that potential negative consequences are ignored. For example, when PepsiCo acquired fast-food operators KFC, Pizza Hut and Taco Bell, the benefits of tying these outlets to sell Pepsi rather than Coca-Cola were realized. What was not appreciated was that this gave Coca-Cola an easy entry into its competitors, such as McDonald's.

A third problem is deciding who is in charge. Mergers of equals can be dangerous because it is not always clear who is the boss. This can lead to indecision while more nimble competitors move ahead. Finally, acquisitions and mergers can lead to staff-related problems. Top managers and salespeople become recruitment targets for competitors, and redundancies damage morale.

Clearly, building through merger and acquisition is not an easy option. Before doing so, managers need to ask (i) 'What advantages will the merger bring that competitors will find difficult to match?', and (ii) 'Would the premium that is usually paid to the shareholders of the acquired company be better spent on another strategy that will build sales and market share—for example, by improving customer service levels or expanding internationally?'

Forming strategic alliances

A final option for companies seeking to build is the strategic alliance. The aim is to create a long-term competitive advantage for the partners, often on a global scale. The partners typically collaborate by means of a joint venture (a jointly owned company), licensing agreements, long-term purchasing and supply arrangements, or joint R&D programmes. Strategic alliances maintain a degree of flexibility not apparent with a merger or acquisition. The illustration overleaf featuring Nokia and Orange shows how they have formed an alliance to market the E71 mobile device.

A major motivation for strategic alliances is the sharing of product development costs and risks. For example, the cost of developing and creating manufacturing facilities for a new car targeted at world markets exceeds £2 billion, and developing a new drug can cost over £25 million. Sharing these costs may be the only serviceable economic option for a medium-sized manufacturer in either of these industries.

Marketing benefits can accrue too. For example, access to new markets and distribution channels can be achieved, time to market reduced, product gaps filled and product lines widened.[31] It was to take advantage of marketing opportunities in financial services that Tesco partnered a bank. Virgin Trains also required a partner to improve the service it provided

20.1 Digital Marketing

A Strategic Alliance: Brands Coming Together to Improve Service

Sometimes it's clear that 'sticking to the knitting' (when a company focuses on what it does best rather than diversify into new, unrelated areas of business) is a well-established strategy. Virgin Trains knows that, despite its brand relationship to a number of other Virgin enterprises (including Virgin Mobile and Virgin Media), it needs to focus on the business and marketing of its rail transport business.

In considering ways to add value for travellers using its high-speed Pendolino train network, the creation of a wireless network on board each train seemed like a logical extension of its service, given that the same kind of service was being offered to their passengers by some airlines. In addition, Virgin had to contend with the fact that a competitor service, National Express, offered a service on an alternative route to Scotland—and Virgin Trains had received some considerable criticism for being late in providing a similar service.

Virgin, rather than attempting to branch out into the business of WiFi provision itself, partnered with T-Mobile, which has a core business in the provision of public WiFi subscription services. T-Mobile had previously developed public WiFi services on other transport services and so had a level of expertise in the area.

This approach limited risk for Virgin, because its business had no expertise in this area and provided T-Mobile with an opportunity for additional revenue. WiFi is offered free to first-class passengers, while standard-class passengers pay a charge. In addition, T-Mobile mobile broadband customers are also offered free use of the facility, boosting T-Mobile's attractiveness to its current and potential customers.

Useful link: www.nationalexpresseastcoast.com[32]

NOKIA
Connecting People

Work. Good.
Home. Good.
Balance. Good.
Nokia E71. Two lives. One phone.
nokia.co.uk/E71

E71 Black. Only on Orange.
Visit your local Orange shop.

◀ This strategic alliance is to supply the E71 mobile device.

customers (see Digital Marketing 20.1). Furthermore, a strategic alliance can be the initial stage to a merger or acquisition, allowing each party to assess their abilities to work together effectively. Examples of companies that have successfully formed strategic alliances to build sales, market share and profits are GlaxoSmithKline and Hoffman-La Roche to market Zantac, the anti-ulcer drug, in the USA, the alliance between European aircraft manufacturers to create Airbus, and JVC's successful attempt to establish VHS as the global standard for video recording, which involved a large number of alliances with consumer electronics firms around the world.

A third reason for alliances is because mergers and acquisitions are sometimes not possible because of legal restrictions or national sensitivities. Many airline alliances, such as the multi-airline Star Alliance, led by United Airlines of the USA and Lufthansa of Germany, are formed for this reason.[33] Finally, strategic alliances can provide production benefits. For example, BP's alliance with the Russian oil producer TNK gave BP access to Russian oil fields, while TNK gained BP's extensive resources and oil exploration skills.

Some key strategic alliances	TABLE 20.3
Companies	**Competitive area**
Apple/O_2	Smartphones
British Airways/American Airlines/Iberia	Transatlantic air travel
Best Buy/Carphone Warehouse	Consumer electronics retailing
Ericsson/China Mobile/China Unicom	Telecoms network equipment
Fiat/Chrysler	Cars
Virgin Rail/T-Mobile	Onboard wireless Internet access
Vodafone/China Mobile/Verizon Wireless	Mobile phones and other telecoms equipment
VW/Sanyo	Lithium car batteries

Build objectives	TABLE 20.4
Attractive conditions	
Growth markets Exploitable competitive weaknesses Exploitable corporate strengths Adequate corporate resources	
Strategic focus	
Market expansion • new users • new uses • increasing frequency of use Winning market share • product innovation • distribution innovation • promotional innovation • penetration pricing • competitor confrontation Merger or acquisition Forming strategic alliances	

A key factor in benefiting from strategic alliances is the desire and ability to learn from the alliance partner. Japanese companies have excelled at this, while European and US companies have traditionally lagged. The risk is that the alliance leaks technological and core capabilities to the partner, thereby giving away important competitive information. This one-way transfer of skills should be avoided by building barriers to capability seepage: core competences should be protected at all costs. This is easier when a company has few alliances, when only a limited part of the organization is involved, and when the relationships built up in the alliance are stable.[34]

Strategic alliances can lead to conflict, however. For example, in the TNK–BP alliance, the Russian side demanded greater control of the company, a reduction in the number of BP staff and more overseas investment, even when it meant competing with BP operations. The conflict was settled when BP agreed to an independent chief executive officer, parity between the partners at board level and international expansion.[35]

Table 20.3 lists some of the major strategic alliances of recent years.

A summary of the key attractive conditions and strategic focuses for build objectives is given in Table 20.4.

Hold Objectives

Hold objectives involve defending a company's current position against would-be attackers. The principles of defensive warfare are, therefore, relevant. Perhaps the principle that has the most relevance in business is the recognition that strong competitive moves should always be blocked. This has not been missed by political parties, which, ever since Bill Clinton's successful challenge to George Bush Snr, have recognized the importance of rapid response. Learning from attacks by Republicans on Democratic candidates in earlier presidential elections, Clinton's strategists established a 24-hour-response capability to any Bush attack. As predicted, Bush attempted to position Clinton as a man of high taxes. Clinton was accused in a television advertisement of increasing taxes if elected. The advertisement featured the kinds of people who would suffer as a result of the extra tax they would have to pay.

Within 24 hours Clinton ran his own advertisement quoting the *Washington Post* as stating that the Republican ad was misleading. This fast response capability was believed by the Democrats to be a major factor in Clinton's ability to maintain his opinion poll lead and emerge the victor in the election. Now all major political parties have in place a fast-response capability.

We shall now analyse the conditions that make a hold objective attractive, and the strategic focus necessary to achieve the objective.

Attractive conditions

The classic situation where a hold objective makes strategic sense is a *market leader in a mature or declining market*. This is the standard cash cow position discussed as part of the Boston Consulting Group market share/market growth rate analysis. By holding on to market leadership, a product should generate positive cash flows that can be used elsewhere in the company to build other products and invest in new product development. Holding on to market leadership per se makes sense because brand leaders enjoy the marketing benefits of bargaining power with distribution outlets, and brand image (the number one position), as well as enjoying experience curve effects that reduce costs. Furthermore, in a declining market, maintaining market leadership may result in becoming a virtual monopolist as weaker competitors withdraw.

A second situation where holding is suitable is in *growth markets when the costs of attempting to build sales and market share outweigh the benefits*. This may be the case in the face of aggressive rivals, who will respond strongly if attacked. In such circumstances it may be prudent to be content with the status quo, and avoid actions that are likely to provoke the competition.

Strategic focus

A hold objective may be achieved by monitoring the competition or by confronting the competition.

Monitoring the competition

In a market that is characterized by competitive stability, the required focus is simply to *monitor the competition*. Perhaps everyone is playing the 'good competitor' game, content with what they have, and no one is willing to destabilize the industry structure. Monitoring is necessary to check that there are no significant changes in competitor behaviour but, beyond that, no change in strategy is required.

Confronting the competition

In circumstances where rivalry is more pronounced, strategic action may be required to defend sales and market share from aggressive challenges. The principles of defensive warfare provide a framework for identifying strategic alternatives that can be used in this situation. Figure 20.3 illustrates six methods of defence derived from military strategy.[36]

Position defence involves building a fortification around one's existing territory as the French did with their Maginot Line. Unfortunately, this static defence strategy was unsuccessful because the Germans simply went around it. In marketing, the analogy is to build a fortification around existing products. This reflects the philosophy that the company has good products, and all that is needed is to price them competitively and promote them effectively. This is more likely to work if the products have differential advantages that are not easily copied—for example, through patent protection. Also marketing assets like brand names and reputation may provide a strong defence against aggressors, although it can be a dangerous strategy. For example, Ever Ready's refusal to develop an alkaline battery in the face of an aggressive challenge to its market leadership by Duracell was an example of position defence. Instead it stuck with its zinc-carbon product, which had a shorter life than its alkaline rival, and invested £2 million in promotion. Only later did Ever Ready develop its own alkaline battery.[37]

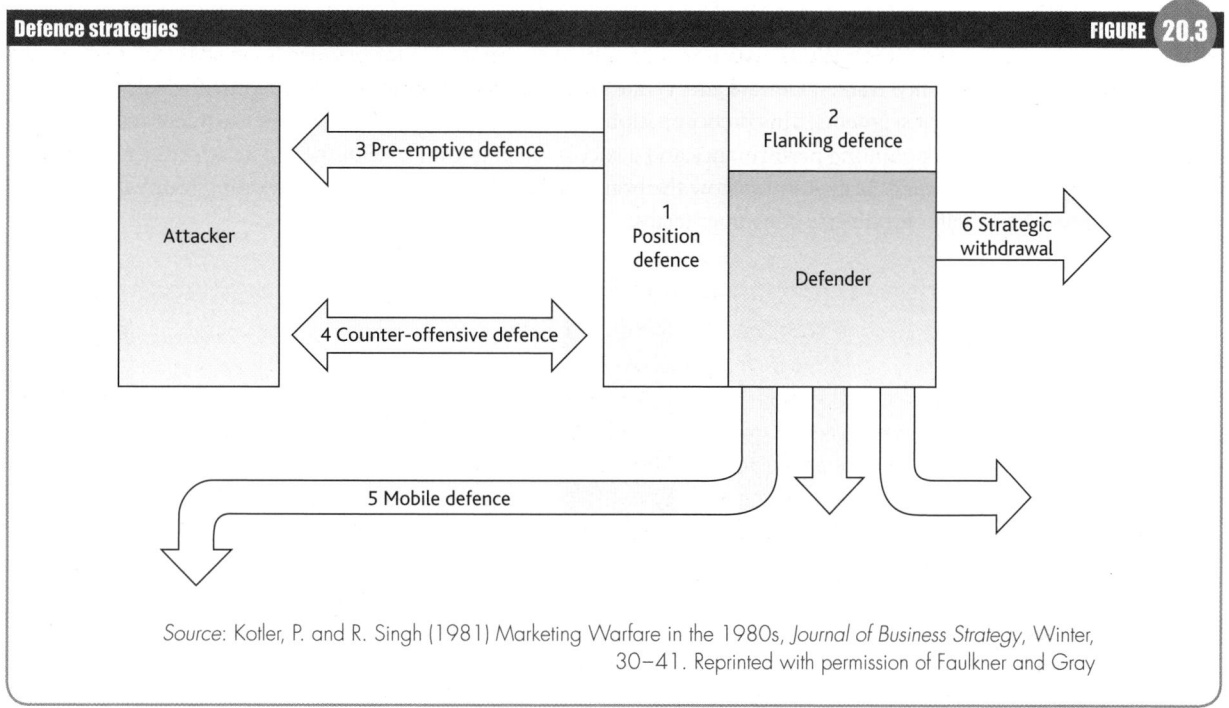

Defence strategies

FIGURE 20.3

Source: Kotler, P. and R. Singh (1981) Marketing Warfare in the 1980s, *Journal of Business Strategy*, Winter, 30–41. Reprinted with permission of Faulkner and Gray

Land Rover and Range Rover provide another instance of an unsuccessful position defence. Based on a belief in their invincibility, they conducted little new product development. This created the opportunity for Subaru to introduce its cheaper, 'fun' four-wheel-drive vehicles. Only belatedly did Land Rover respond by developing the successful Discovery model.

Flanking defence is characterized by the defence of a hitherto unprotected market segment. The danger is that if the segment is left unprotected, it will provide a beachhead for new entrants to gain experience in the market and attack the main market later. This means that if it helps to avoid or slow down competitive inroads, it can make sense for a defender to compete in a segment that, in pure short-term profitability terms, looks unattractive. This danger has prompted Wal-Mart's defence of the small-format grocery market on the west coast of the USA. In retaliation to Tesco's entry with its Fresh & Easy stores, Wal-Mart has opened its own version under the banner 'Marketside', which also has an emphasis on fresh food.[38]

A further problem is that the defence of the segment may be half-hearted as it is not central to the main business. An example is General Motors' and Ford's weak attempts to build a small car to compete with Volkswagen and the Japanese companies. The products—the Vega and Pinto—suffered from poor build quality and unreliability, and proved ineffective in defending the exposed flank. When a flanking defence is required against successful but smaller attackers, acquisition may be an attractive option. For example, many large companies have responded to the attacks by ethically minded rivals by buying them. For example, L'Oréal has bought Body Shop, Cadbury has acquired Green & Black's, and Unilever has purchased Ben & Jerry's.

20.2 Pause for Thought

Can you think of any brands not listed above that have successfully challenged the market leader by focusing on an unprotected market segment?

Failure to defend an emerging market segment can have catastrophic consequences. For example, Distillers, which was dominant in the market for blended Scotch whisky with its Johnny Walker, Dewars and White Horse brands, ignored the growing malt whisky and white spirit segments. This preoccupation with the declining blended whisky segment resulted in disappointing performance and a successful take-over by Guinness. The advertisement for Green & Black's shows how the brand has defended its flanks by marketing four variants to cater for diverse consumer tastes.

▲ Green & Black's defends its position in the organic chocolate market by supplying Milk, Dark 70%, White and Creamy Milk brand varieties.

Pre-emptive defence follows the philosophy that the best form of defence is to attack first. This may involve continuous innovation and new product development, a situation characteristic of the camcorder market. Japanese manufacturers are caught up in a continuous spiral of product introductions (known as product *churning*). Failure to maintain this rate of change would soon lead to product obsolescence and market share collapse.

A pre-emptive defence may also be used to dissuade a would-be attacker. For example, ICI, the market leader in the UK chemical fertilizer market, feared that Norsk Hydro's purchase of Fisons, the number two in the market, would bring a strong offensive from the Norwegian company. ICI's strategy was to launch a pre-emptive defence by severely cutting the price of its fertilizer brands, thereby reducing profitability, which made future plant expansion less attractive to Norsk Hydro. These actions succeeded in discouraging Norsk Hydro from increasing capacity in the UK.[39]

Counter-offensive defence: a defender can choose from three options when considering a counter-offensive defence. It can embark on a head-on counter-attack, hit the attacker's cash cow or encircle the attacker.

With a *head-on counter-attack* a defender matches or exceeds what the attacker has done. This may involve heavy price cutting or promotion expenditure, for example. This can be a costly operation but may be justified to deter a persistent attacker. For example, when Microsoft was challenged by Linux, which began to find favour as the operating system in netbooks, the company cut the price of a version of Windows that normally cost around $70 to $15. The result was that Linux was driven off the majority of netbooks.[40] Tesco also launched a counter-offensive against the growth of discount supermarkets (Netto, Aldi and Lidl) by introducing two cut-price ranges—Tesco Value and Discount—to discourage shoppers from switching.[41]

Alternatively, the counter-attack may be based on innovation, as when Apple counter-attacked IBM's challenge in the personal computer market by launching its successful Macintosh.

Hitting the attacker's cash cow strikes at the attacker's resource supply line. For example, when Xerox attacked IBM in the mainframe computer market, IBM counter-attacked by striking at Xerox's cash cow (the medium-range photocopier) with a limited range of low-priced copiers plus leasing arrangements that were particularly attractive to Xerox's target market (smaller businesses). The result was that Xerox sold its computer business to Honeywell, and concentrated on defending copiers.[42] As we saw in Chapter 19, on analysing competitors and creating a competitive advantage, Rotaprint hit Toshiba's cash cow (the Japanese market) as a counter-offensive defence in retaliation to Toshiba's attack in Rotaprint's home market of the USA. The result was that Toshiba withdrew from the USA.

The third strategic option is to *encircle the attacker*. This strategy was successfully employed by Heublein when its Smirnoff vodka brand was attacked by the cheaper Wolfsmidt brand in the USA. Its response was to maintain the price of Smirnoff while launching two new brands, one at the same price as Wolfsmidt and one at a lower price. This manoeuvre successfully defended Heublein's position as market leader in the vodka market.

When a company's major market is under threat a **mobile defence** may make strategic sense. The two options are diversification and market broadening. A classic example of a company using *diversification* as a form of mobile defence is Imperial Tobacco, which responded to the health threat to its cigarette business by diversifying into food and leisure markets. *Market broadening* involves broadening the business definition, as film companies like Warner Brothers did in the face of declining cinema audiences. By defining its business as entertainment provider rather than film maker, it successfully moved into television, gambling and theme parks.

A **strategic withdrawal**, or contraction defence, requires a company to define its strengths and weaknesses, and then to hold on to its strengths while divesting its weaknesses. This results in the company concentrating on its core business. An example is Diageo, which withdrew from the fast-food business by selling Burger King, and from food by selling Pillsbury to concentrate on premium drinks.[43] Nokia also practised strategic withdrawal, moving initially from a paper, rubber goods and cables group into computers, consumer electronics and telecoms, and then, very successfully, concentrating on mobile handsets, where it is market leader. IBM also practised strategic withdrawal by selling its PC division to Lenovo in a move designed to focus the company more towards high-margin services and software than manufacturing. Strategic withdrawal can also be on a geographic basis. For example, in the face of a worsening financial situation Vodafone has withdrawn from Japan.[44]

A strategic withdrawal allows a company to focus on its core competences and is often required when diversification has resulted in too wide a spread of activities away from what it does really well. Peters and Waterman termed this focus on core skills and competences *sticking to your knitting*.[45]

Table 20.5 summarizes the key points for hold objectives.

Hold objectives	TABLE 20.5
Attractive conditions	
Market leader in a mature or declining market Costs exceed benefits of building	
Strategic focus	
Monitoring the competition Confronting the competition	

Niche Objectives

A company may decide to pursue a market **niche objective** by pursuing a small market segment or even a segment within a segment. In doing so, it may avoid competition with companies that are serving the major market segments. However, niche-orientated companies, if successful, run the risk that larger competitors are attracted into the segment. For example, the initial success of Sock Shop, a niche provider of stylish men's socks, stimulated large department stores such as Marks & Spencer to launch their own competitive ranges.

Also the success of 'boutique' hotels has caused larger chains to copy them. For example, Hilton has launched Denizen Hotels to provide a similar experience.[46] There is also the danger of not having the support of revenue from other segments if demand falls or costs rise in the niche market. This was the case for niche operators Silverjet, Eos and MAXjet, which targeted only business-class passengers and went into liquidation following a fall in demand in the recent recession and a rise in fuel costs.

Attractive conditions

'Nicheing' may be the only feasible objective for companies with a small budget and where strong competitors are dominating the main segments. As such, it may be an attractive option for small companies that lack the resources to compete directly against the major players. But there need to be pockets within the market that provide the opportunity for profitable operations, and in which a competitive advantage can be created. Typical circumstances where these conditions apply are when the major players are under-serving a particular group of customers as they attempt to meet the needs of the majority of customers, and where the market niche is too small to be of interest to them.

Strategic focus

A key strategic tool for a niche-orientated company is *market segmentation*. Management should be vigilant in its search for underserved segments that may provide profitable opportunities. The choice will depend upon the attractiveness of the niche and the capability of the company to serve it. Once selected, effort—particularly research and development expenditure—will be focused on serving customer needs. An example is Tyrrell's, which saw an opportunity to produce a better-quality potato chip than those found in supermarkets. Targeting a segment that would be prepared to pay more, and avoiding direct competition with the market leader, Walkers crisps, its products are sold in top food halls, farm shops, delis and gastropubs.

Focused R&D expenditure gives a small company a chance to make effective use of its limited resources.[47] The emphasis should be on creating and sustaining a *differential advantage* through intimately understanding the needs of the customer group, and focusing attention on satisfying those needs better than the competition. Tyrrell's differentiates by hand cooking its potato chips from home-grown potatoes, and processing them on the farm—hand stirred in small batches.[48] Finally, niche operators should be wary of pursuing growth strategies by broadening their customer base. Often this will lead to a blurring of the differential advantage upon which their success has been built. Indeed, since some niche companies trade on *exclusivity*, to broaden their market base would by definition run the risk of diluting their differential advantage. TVR, which specializes in distinctive, high-performance sports cars, is a company that consistently pursues a niche objective. TVR consciously *thinks small*, eschewing unsustainable growth in favour of profitability. The emphasis is on high margin not high volume. Table 20.6 summarizes this brief discussion of niche objectives.

Niche objectives	TABLE 20.6
Attractive conditions	
Small budget	
Strong competitors dominating major segments	
Pockets existing for profitable operations	
Creating a competitive advantage	
Strategic focus	
Market segmentation	
Focused R&D	
Differentiation	
Thinking small	

Harvest Objectives

A company embarking upon a **harvest objective** attempts to improve unit profit margins even if the result is falling sales. Although sales are falling, the aim is to make the company or product extremely profitable in the short term, generating large positive cash flows that can be used elsewhere in the business (for example, to build stars and selected problem children, or to fund new product development).

Attractive conditions

Also-ran products or companies in *mature or declining markets* (dogs) may be candidates for harvesting, since they are often losing money, and taking up valuable management time and effort.[49] Harvesting actions can move them to a profitable stance, and reduce management attention to a minimum. In *growth markets* harvesting can also make sense where the *costs of building or holding exceed the benefits*. These are problem children companies or products that have little long-term potential. Harvesting is particularly attractive if a *core of loyal customers* exists, which means that sales decline to a stable level. For example, a SmithKline Beecham hair product, Brylcreem, was harvested but sales decline was not terminal as a group of men who used the product in their adolescence continued to buy it in later life. This core of loyal customers meant it was still profitable to market Brylcreem, although R&D and marketing expenditure was minimal. More recently, Brylcreem has been repositioned as a hair gel targeting young men. Cussons Imperial Leather soap and Fry's Turkish Delight chocolate are also examples of brands that are marketed with very little promotional support. Both are long-standing brands that benefit from a core of loyal customers. A final attractive condition is where *future breadwinners exist* in the company or product portfolio to provide future sales and profit growth potential. Obviously harvesting a one-product company is likely to lead to its demise.

Harvest objectives	TABLE 20.7
Attractive conditions	
Market is mature or declining (dog products) In growth markets where the costs of building or holding exceed the benefits (selected problem children) Core of loyal customers Future breadwinners exist	
Strategic focus	
Eliminate R&D expenditure Product reformulation Rationalize product line Cut marketing support Consider increasing price	

Strategic focus

Implementing a harvest objective begins with *eliminating research and development expenditure*. The only product change that will be contemplated is *reformulations* that reduce raw material and/or manufacturing costs. *Rationalization of the product line* to one or a few top sellers cuts costs by eliminating expensive product variants. *Marketing support is reduced* by slashing advertising and promotional budgets, while every opportunity is taken to *increase price*.

Table 20.7 summarizes the attractive conditions and strategic focus for achieving harvest objectives.

Divest Objectives

A company may decide to **divest** itself of a strategic business unit or product. In doing so it may stem the flow of cash to a poorly performing area of its business.

Attractive conditions

Divestment is often associated with *loss-making products or businesses* that are a drain on both financial and managerial resources. An example is Konica Minolta, which pulled out of the manufacture of cameras and photographic film in the face of growing losses.[50] *Low-share products or businesses in declining markets* (dogs) are prime candidates for divestment. Other areas may be considered for divestment when it is judged that the *costs of turnaround exceed the benefits*. As such, also-rans in growth markets may be divested, sometimes after harvesting has run its full course. However, care must be taken to examine interrelationships within the corporate portfolio. For example, if a product is making a loss it would still be worthwhile supporting it if its removal would *adversely affect sales of other products*. In some industrial markets, customers expect a supplier to provide a full range of products.

Consequently, even though some may not be profitable, sales of the whole range may be affected if the loss makers are dropped.

Strategic focus

Because of the drain on profits and cash flow, once a decision to divest has been made, the focus should be to *get out quickly so as to minimize costs.* If a buyer can be found then some return may be realized; if not, the product will be withdrawn or the business terminated.

Table 20.8 summarizes the attractive conditions and strategic focus relating to divestment.

Divest objectives	TABLE 20.8
Attractive conditions	
Loss-making products or businesses: drain on resources Often low share in declining markets Costs of turnaround exceed benefits Removal will not significantly affect sales of other products	
Strategic focus	
Get out quickly; minimize the costs	

When you have read this chapter

log on to the Online Learning Centre at www.mcgraw-hill.co.uk/textbooks/jobber to explore chapter-by-chapter test questions, links and further online study tools for marketing.

Review

1 The nature of competitive behaviour
- Competitive behaviour can take five forms: conflict, competition, co-existence, cooperation and collusion.

2 How military analogies can be applied to competitive marketing strategy
- Military analogies are used to guide strategic thinking because of the need to attack and defend against competition.
- Attack strategies are the frontal attack, the flanking attack, encirclement, the bypass attack and the guerrilla attack.
- Defence strategies are the position defence, the flanking defence, the pre-emptive defence, the counter-offensive defence, the mobile defence, and strategic withdrawal.

3 The attractive conditions and strategic focus necessary to achieve the following objectives: build, hold, niche, harvest and divest
- Build objectives: attractive conditions are growth markets, exploitable competitive weaknesses, exploitable corporate strengths and adequate corporate resources; strategic focus is market expansion, winning market share, merger or acquisition, and forming strategic alliances.
- Hold objectives: attractive conditions are market leader in a mature or declining market, and costs exceed benefits of building; strategic focus is monitoring the competition, and confronting the competition.
- Niche objectives: attractive conditions are small budget, strong competitors dominating major segments, pockets exist for profitable operations, and opportunity to create a competitive advantage; strategic focus is market segmentation, focused R&D, differentiation and thinking small.

- Harvest objectives: attractive conditions are market is mature or declining, growth markets where the cost of building or holding exceeds the benefits, a core of loyal customers and future breadwinners exists; strategic focus is eliminate R&D expenditure, reformulate product, rationalize the product line, cut marketing expenditure and consider increasing price.

4 The nature of frontal, flanking, encirclement, bypass and guerrilla attacks
- Frontal attack: the challenger takes on the defender head on.
- Flanking attack: this involves attacking unguarded or weakly guarded ground (e.g. geographical areas or market segments).
- Encirclement attack: the defender is attacked from all sides (every market segment is hit with every combination of product features).
- Bypass attack: the defender's position is circumvented by, for example, technological leap-frogging or diversification.
- Guerrilla attack: the defender's life is made uncomfortable through, for example, unpredictable price discounts, sales promotions or heavy advertising in a few selected regions.

5 The nature of position, flanking, pre-emptive, counter-offensive and mobile defences, and strategic withdrawal
- Position defence: building a defence around existing products, usually through keen pricing and improved promotion.
- Flanking defence: defending a hitherto unprotected market segment.
- Pre-emptive defence: usually involves continuous innovation and new product development, recognizing that the best form of defence is attack.
- Counter-offensive defence: a counter-attack that takes the form of a head-on counter-attack, an attack on the attacker's cash cow or an encirclement of the attacker.
- Mobile defence: moving position by diversification or broadening the market by redefining the business.
- Strategic withdrawal: holding on to the company's strengths while divesting its weaknesses (e.g. weak strategic business units or product lines), resulting in the company focusing on its core business.

Key Terms

bypass attack circumventing the defender's position, usually through technological leap-frogging or diversification

competitive behaviour the activities of rival companies with respect to each other; this can take five forms—conflict, competition, co-existence, cooperation and collusion

counter-offensive defence a counter-attack that takes the form of a head-on counter-attack, an attack on the attacker's cash cow or an encirclement of the attacker

divest to improve short-term cash yield by dropping or selling off a product

encirclement attack attacking the defender from all sides, i.e. every market segment is hit with every combination of product features

flanking attack attacking geographical areas or market segments where the defender is poorly represented

flanking defence the defence of a hitherto unprotected market segment

frontal attack a competitive strategy where the challenger takes on the defender head on

guerrilla attack making life uncomfortable for stronger rivals through, for example, unpredictable price discounts, sales promotions or heavy advertising in a few selected regions

harvest objective the improvement of profit margins to improve cash flow even if the longer-term result is falling sales

hold objective a strategy of defending a product in order to maintain market share

mobile defence involves diversification or broadening the market by redefining the business

niche objective the strategy of targeting a small market segment

position defence building a fortification around existing products, usually through keen pricing and improved promotion

pre-emptive defence usually involves continuous innovation and new product development, recognizing that attack is the best form of defence

strategic alliance collaboration between two or more organizations through, for example, joint ventures, licensing agreements, long-term purchasing and supply arrangement or a joint R&D contract to build a competitive advantage

strategic focus the strategies that can be employed to achieve an objective

strategic withdrawal holding on to the company's strengths while getting rid of its weaknesses

Study Questions

1. Why do many monopolies provide poor service to their customers?

2. Discuss the likely impact of the single European market on competitive behaviour.

3. Compare and contrast the conditions conducive to building and holding sales/market share.

4. Why is a position defence risky?

5. Why are strategic alliances popular in Europe? How do they differ from mergers?

6. A company should always attempt to harvest a product before considering divestment. Discuss.

7. In defence it is always wise to respond to serious attacks immediately. Do you agree? Explain your answer.

References

1. Barratt, F. (1992) Britain Lets Down the Drawbridge, *Independent*, 19 September, 43.
2. Easton, G. and L. Araujo (1986) Networks, Bonding and Relationships in Industrial Markets, *Industrial Marketing and Purchasing* 1(1), 8–25.
3. Anonymous (2002) Fixing for a Fight, *Economist*, 20 April, 71–2.
4. Ries, A. and J. Trout (2005) *Marketing Warfare*, New York: McGraw-Hill.
5. Kotler, P. and R. Singh (1981) Marketing Warfare in the 1980s, *Journal of Business Strategy*, Winter, 30–41.
6. Sun Tzu (1963) *The Art of War*, London: Oxford University Press.
7. Von Clausewitz, C. (1908) *On War*, London: Routledge & Kegan Paul.
8. Jeannet, J.-P. (1987) *Competitive Marketing Strategies in a European Context*, Lausanne: International Management Development Institute, 101.
9. See Aaker, D. and G. S. Day (1986) The Perils of High-Growth Markets, *Strategic Management Journal* 7, 409–21; Wensley, R. (1982) PIMS and BCG: New Horizons or False Dawn?, *Strategic Management Journal* 3, 147–58.
10. Palmer, M. (2006) Cisco Lays Plans to Expand into Home Electronics, *Financial Times*, 16 January, 21.
11. Kotler and Singh (1981) op. cit.
12. Porter, M. E. (1998) *Competitive Advantage*, New York: Free Press, 514–17.
13. Benady, D. (2008) Trouble in the Air for Virgin, *Marketing Week*, 16 November, 20–1.
14. Von Clausewitz (1908) op. cit.
15. Hooley, G., J. Saunders, N. Piercy and B. Nicoulaud (2007) *Marketing Strategy and Competitive Positioning*, London: Prentice-Hall, 224.
16. Nakamoto, M. (2005) Toshiba and Sony Braced for DVD War, *Financial Times*, 26 August, 17.

17. Schofield, J. (2006) Two Tribes Go to War, *Guardian Technology*, 12 January, 1.

18. Edwards, C. (2008) Blu-Ray: Playing for a Limited Engagement, *Business Week*, 29 September, 70.

19. Sanchanta, M. (2008) Last Showing for Toshiba's DVD Format, *Financial Times*, 18 February, 25.

20. Wildstrom, S. H. (2009) Meet Cisco, the Consumer Company, *Business Week*, 4 May, 73–4.

21. Anonymous (2002) When Something is Rotten, *Economist*, 27 July, 61–2.

22. Mercado, S., R. Welford and K. Prescott (2000) *European Business: An Issue-Based Approach*, Harlow: FT Prentice-Hall.

23. London, S. (2001) Risks of Grasping a Tiger by the Tail, *Financial Times*, 10 September, 15.

24. Research conducted by Professor J. Bowers, Harvard Business School, and reported by London (2001) op. cit.

25. See Elgin, B. (2004) A Licence to Print Money but is the System Overloaded at HP?, *Independent on Sunday*, 15 December, 8–9; Teather, D. (2005) HP to Cut 1000 UK Jobs, *Guardian*, 14 September, 28.

26. Anonymous (2008) A Bid for Bud, *Economist*, 21 June, 91.

27. Foust, D. (2008) Looks Like a Beer Brawl, *Business Week*, 28 July, 52–3.

28. Ritson, M. (2008) InBev May Create Bud Brand Crisis, *Marketing*, 18 June, 23.

29. Wiggins, J. (2008) Thirst to Be First, *Financial Times*, 24 July, 11.

30. Shapinker, M. (2000) Marrying in Haste, *Financial Times*, 12 April, 22.

31. Lorenz, C. (1992) Take your Partner, *Financial Times*, 17 July, 13.

32. http://www.nationalexpresseastcoast.com/On-Board-Our-Trains/In-your-coach/WiFi---Internet-Facilities/.

33. Shapinker, M. (2001) Tips for a Beautiful Relationship, *Financial Times*, 11 July, 14.

34. Lorenz, C. (1992) The Risks of Sleeping with the Enemy, *Financial Times*, 16 July, 11.

35. See Crooks, E. and C. Hoyos (2008) BP Pledges to Stay as Partner with Russians as TNK Dispute Ends, *Financial Times*, 5 September, 17; Macalister, T. (2008) Oligarchs to Sue TNK–BP After Failing to Agree Control of Company, *Guardian*, 12 June, 30.

36. Kotler and Singh (1981) op. cit.

37. Urry, M. (1992) Takeover put Spark into Battery Maker, *Financial Times*, 14 April, 21.

38. Birchall, J. (2008) Wal-Mart Takes on Tesco's US Challenge, *Financial Times*, 14 January, 1.

39. Jeannet (1987) op. cit.

40. Burrows, P. (2009) How Microsoft is Fighting Back (Finally), *Business Week*, 20 April, 63–4.

41. Anonymous (2008) Is Tesco's Latest Discount Brands Range A Step Too Far?, *Marketing*, 5 November, 24.

42. James, B. J. (1984) *Business Wargames*, London: Abacus.

43. Eastham, J. (2002) Thin Times Ahead for Burger King, *Marketing Week*, 1 August, 19–20.

44. Teather, D. (2006) Vodafone Chief Hailed as Victor in Board Battle, *Guardian*, 14 March, 25.

45. Peters, T. J. and R. H. Waterman Jr (1995) *In Search of Excellence: Lessons from America's Best-Run Companies*, New York: Harper & Row.

46. Roberts, J. (2009) Hilton's Boutique Brands, *Marketing Week*, 19 April, 15–16.

47. Hammermesh, R. G., M. J. Anderson and J. E. Harris (1978) Strategies for Low Market Share Businesses, *Harvard Business Review* 50(3), 95–102.

48. Anonymous (2008) *Cool Brands*, Superbrands UK (Ltd), sponsored supplement to the *Observer*, 20.

49. Hedley, B. (1977) Strategy and the Business Portfolio, *Long Range Planning*, February, 9–15.

50. Nakamoto, M. and A. Yee (2006) Minolta to Stop Making Cameras, *Financial Times*, 20 January, 21.

Airbus vs Boeing

The Battle for Air Supremacy

Every day Airbus and Boeing fight an ongoing battle for mastery of the skies. Both these American and European giants of aviation are at loggerheads, fighting for every last dollar of the aircraft market. In 2008, Airbus garnered 777 orders, while Boeing achieved 662, despite a difficult trading environment, and both have huge order backlogs. Airbus celebrated this much-lauded triumph over its long time adversary. However, both are cautious about the future in such a volatile market. Many of the large airline carriers are facing bankruptcy, and the market is very susceptible to environmental shocks such as the credit crunch, September 11th, SARS and any airline crash. The demand is credited to the growth in the low-cost industry, demand in Asian markets, new models being launched and airlines striving to have more fuel-efficient planes in the wake of rising oil prices. The industry is notoriously cyclical as a result. In some years, orders have fallen in the world aviation market to a total of just 250 aircraft for the duopoly, as in 1994.

The battle for dominance has seen many peaks and troughs. Over past few years, Airbus has emerged as the industry leader, supplanting Boeing. European Airbus rose to prominence due to a strong portfolio of jets, a winning formula of 'commonality', efficient manufacturing and an excellent reputation, while Boeing was beginning to languish in the late 1990s. Airbus is the quintessential pan-European company; it is the pride of the European Union, representing possible close integration between member countries. The aircraft wings are made in northern Wales, and shipped by barge and boat to France for assembly. Tailfins are made in Germany, while fuselage sections are flown in from Spain, in super-large transport aircraft. The company's headquarters is based in Toulouse, France, but it has a network of manufacturing centres around Europe, and global supply partners. A company called EADS, an amalgam of several European aerospace and defence manufacturing companies, controls Airbus. The integration of several European aerospace companies was the only way the necessary scale could be achieved to take on the might of the American giant Boeing. The company built up much of its initial success in the mid-size jet market. Developing hit products in this duopoly is tremendously important, as revenues generated can be poured back into the next generation

of products used in future battles. This can create a virtuous circle, leaving competitors at a distinct disadvantage. However, Boeing still dominated the large wide body aircraft market, reaping huge dividends. Airbus wanted a bigger slice of this market and decided to develop the world's first double-decker jumbo jet, capable of carrying 555 passengers.

The big gamble

Developing the new A-380 double-decker superjumbo, the largest, most expensive commercial plane ever built, was a big gamble for Airbus, not only in terms of design, technology and manufacturing, but also in terms of capital resources. With so much capital tied up in the development of a new aircraft, any delays in delivery could cripple a firm. Airbus was extremely successful in the mid-size jet market, but the real profit lay in the wide-body, long-range jet aircraft like Boeing's iconic 747 jumbo and its 777 series. But now at least, Airbus has a competitive offering that will test the dominance of the Boeing 747 in the market. The Boeing 747 has been untouched for over five decades, being conceived back in the 1960s. Development of the A-380 began back in 1994, with €12 billion allocated to a formal budget in 1999. Airbus promises that the A-380 will deliver 15–20 per cent lower operating costs than a 747 jumbo. This news set the aircraft industry abuzz. It announced its first customer in 2001, with Singapore Airlines committing to several orders. Other customers, like Virgin Atlantic, envisaged that the new plane could accommodate bars, a beauty salon and a casino. Its first flight took place to much fanfare in April 2005. Despite all the hype, some industry commentators question whether there is a market for planes with a capacity of 555 passengers.

Airbus vs Boeing at a glance		TABLE C39.1
Airbus	**Boeing**	
Founded in 1970	Founded in 1916	
Headquarters based in Toulouse, France	Headquarters based in Chicago, USA	
Employs 55,000	Employs 160,000	
The company has received 6300 orders for aircraft and has delivered more 4100 aircraft. Airbus has consistently won market share away from archrival Boeing. Record number of orders in 2005	World's largest producer of commercial and military aircraft. Produces the 7 series of commercial aircraft, weapons systems and satellite launch systems. Three-quarters of the world's jets are Boeing aircraft	
Revenue of $22.3 billion	Revenue of $28.3 billion	
Orders in 2008 = 777 new aircraft	Orders in 2008 = 662 new aircraft	
Airbus has 14 different aircraft models, ranging from capacities of 100 seats to 555 seats. Its most popular plane is the short-haul A-320. The plane is economical and has a moderate flight range. The A-330/340 caters for long-haul routes. Airlines love Airbus's commonality feature, which reduces training costs	The Boeing 7 series of aircraft caters for an array of different markets. The 737 jet is the world's most popular aircraft. Reliable, economic, adaptable, has a moderate range, perfect for short haul flights. The 767, the 777 and the famous jumbo 747 cater for long-distance markets	
The A-380 jet is the world's largest commercial jet ever built. The A-380 launched in 2008	The 787 Dreamliner mid-size, long-range jet promises to be super-efficient, using advanced materials, engines and components, which results in a 20% reduction in fuel costs per passenger. Over 886 sales orders have already been secured; launching 2010	

Table C39.2 The colossal superjumbo Airbus A-380 vs the Boeing 747 jumbo		TABLE C39.2
Features	**Airbus A-380**	**Boeing 747 (stretch version)**
Capacity	555	450
Range	15,000 km	15,000 km
Speed	560 mph	567 mph
Purchased by	Singapore Emirates Lufthansa Qantas Virgin Atlantic	Air France British Airways Cathay Pacific Japan Airlines KLM
Cost per plane	$316 million	$275 million

The scale of the project is breathtaking, with specially built ships used for exclusively transporting sections of the plane to final assembly in Toulouse, specially widened roads to transport sections, and new airport terminals/customer delivery centres created in Toulouse to cater for the handover of the aircraft to airline customers. While Airbus garnered an impressive order book for the A-380 initially, sales have slowed. The company now has 198 firm orders for the plane from 17 different customers. The big question in aviation circles is will volume in terms of capacity lead to profit for airlines? Some contend that the new superjumbo could potentially create a viable low-cost, long-haul operation, while others view the market as needing only mid-size, long-range fuel-efficient, twin-engine jets for the global market, moving away from these super-carriers. Consumers want to fly non-stop to destinations rather than through congested hub airports.

The double-decker jumbo will take years to become a core profit centre for the Airbus group. The challenge for Airbus was to build a superjumbo at a reasonable cost, and get enough airlines interested in the project to make it viable. It needs 250 sales orders to break even on the project. Some of the big carriers are sitting on the sidelines waiting to see how things pan out, before taking a gamble. With $12 billion invested, it is huge table stakes poker. It is hoped that it will dominate the sector for the next 20 years, like its predecessor the Boeing 747. Airbus does not want the A-380 to be the next Concorde, which was an unmitigated commercial disaster, albeit a technological marvel. After 15 years in development, the first A380 entered service in 2007 with Singapore Airlines.

Airbus shook the market when it announced that its new superjumbo's launch would be held up for several months due to manufacturing delays. The cause of this was pinpointed to delays caused by the complex wiring needed for the planes' customized entertainment systems for different airlines. Further slippages to the plane's delivery timetable have antagonized airlines, which are losing confidence in Airbus. Huge penalty clauses are invoked if it fails to meet delivery deadlines. The company worked flat out to get the first batch completed. It delivered only one superjumbo in 2007, down from the projected 25 aircraft due to be delivered, and only 12 in 2008. These types of delay could lead to a variety of penalties, customers could cancel orders, jeopardize future orders for the aircraft, and cause untold damage to Airbus's reputation. It is estimated that there is a late delivery charge of €60 million per plane.

Boeing bounces back

After seeing years of decline, problems with production and the company mired in a spate of corporate ethics

> **//** The battles between Airbus and Boeing are worth billions and affect countries' balances of trade. **//**

scandals, Boeing is now boasting a strong order book and claims to have left its troubles behind. The company was beleaguered by corporate woes such as charges of corporate espionage, harassment and political shenanigans surrounding military contracts, which have cost two CEOs their jobs. In 2003, the firm lost its coveted status as the world's number one commercial aircraft manufacturer to Airbus. In an effort to recapture the lead, Boeing is banking on the introduction of its highly innovative 787 Dreamliner jet. This radical plane is made from groundbreaking materials, using lightweight yet super-strong carbon-fibre technology. This is its first all-new aircraft in over a decade. The company is using the technology developed in the Dreamliner project in its other aircraft. Rising energy costs for airlines make the fuel efficiency of aircraft a key selling point. This has led the Dreamliner to be a hot seller for Boeing. Airlines have committed 886 orders, worth billions to Boeing. The jet aims to use 20 per cent less fuel, produce fewer emissions, and it is quieter. The success of Dreamliner led Airbus to launch the A-350, its foray into the long-range mid-sized fuel-efficient market, delivery of which is estimated to be in 2012. Airbus has attracted 493 orders for its competing plane, however. Boeing, for the first time, has outsourced several core aspects of the plane's manufacturing, to cut down on costs and access key technology. Over 80 per cent of the plane's structure is being fabricated by external suppliers, unlike the typical 51 per cent for other Boeing aircraft. Sections of the plane are built in Japan and Italy, and flown into the USA. In the midst of rising energy prices, Boeing is experiencing a rise in demand due to the popularity of its two fuel-efficient long-range jets: the 777 and the 787. With its attention focused on the launch of its superjumbo, Airbus failed to see the same opportunity as Boeing in the market seeking a long-range, mid-sized jet like the Dreamliner. Thanks in large part to the success of the project, it reclaimed the mantle of world's most successful aircraft manufacturer by overtaking Airbus in terms of aircraft orders in 2006 and 2007.

Like Airbus, Boeing is wrestling with production difficulties with its Dreamliner project due to delays in testing its ground-breaking new technology; these glitches have led to missed deadlines, and this has pushed out delivery times. In addition, a 57-day strike exacerbated the problem, costing Boeing $100m a day.

If delivery times are not met, huge penalty clauses are invoked. Over 90 per cent of the plane's value is paid on delivery. In the late 1990s the firm tried to build too many planes, leading to overstretched production lines and inevitable delays, resulting in penalties of $2.5 billion. Its reputation for reliability was irrevocably damaged. Airbus won many subsequent airline orders from new business as a result. Now Boeing is regaining the momentum, with strong sales for its ever popular 737 series from low-cost airlines, new product development and a strong order book for the new Dreamliner. Also, the company recently launched a 'stretch' version of its 747 jumbo jet series to fight Airbus's new superjumbo, proclaiming larger capacities and greater efficiency, although demand for these colossal planes is weak.

Airbus has the ability to build planes for less, even with all the logistical complexities associated with assembly, allowing greater flexibility in setting prices for its aircraft, which were real deal clinchers. Now Boeing has upped its game through excellent product innovation and improvements in its manufacturing operations. Selling aircraft is a long and laborious process, yet the battles between Airbus and Boeing are worth billions and affect countries' balances of trade. Both firms execute bitter contests to pitch to clients, some going down to the wire with last-minute deals being cut, using an array of discounts, financing and leasing options, as well as extra training and service arrangements for clients.

Both companies receive state aid from national governments, which both largely dispute, and giving rise to charges of unfair competition between both parties. This has led to heated debates between the USA and Europe over trade subsidies. Both demand a level playing field, yet both garner lucrative tax breaks, repayable launch aid, indirect research and technological subsidies and a whole array of other state supports, worth billions. The governments of Britain, France, Germany and Spain contribute money to safeguard their aerospace industry in their respective countries, and protect jobs. For instance, the new A-350 cost $4.35 billion to develop, a third of which has been sought in state aid support. The row over subsidies has nearly led to a trade war between the USA and Europe on several occasions. Commercial Aircraft Corporation of China is seen as possibly the next aviation industry rival to emerge, given the country's manufacturing prowess. Airbus has entered a joint venture with the Chinese concern, to manufacture four A320 jets a year; it realizes that there will be technological transfer to the Chinese, however the initiative will lead to enhanced access to the booming Chinese market.

As in any war, the battle ebbs and flows. One thing is for sure, though: the intense rivalry between Airbus and Boeing is good for the industry.

Questions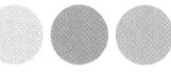

1. Why is the aircraft manufacturing industry dominated by only two companies? Discuss the barriers to entry that exist in the market.
2. Critically appraise Airbus's decision to enter the superjumbo market by launching its double-decker A-380 plane.
3. Develop a competitive marketing strategy for Airbus in the wake of Boeing's success with its new Dreamliner 787 jet.

This case was written by Conor Carroll, Lecturer in Marketing, University of Limerick. The material in the case has been drawn from a variety of published sources.

Displaying Strategy CASE 40

Finding a Competitive Advantage for Data Display

Data Display is a manufacturing company based in County Clare in Ireland, operating from offices in Europe, Australia and North America. Even though it is located on the periphery of Europe, it has established a reputation as one of the world's leading suppliers of electronic information displays to customers such as Siemens, Warner Cinemas and London Underground. To reach this position, Data Display has had to engage in careful market analysis, the results of which have directed its strategy in a highly competitive and dynamic marketplace dominated by multinational companies. This has resulted in the company focusing on developing high-quality, state-of-the-art products and technologies, diversifying into three key industries, building strong relationships with customers who can also be competitors, and building a strong network of strategic alliances to help compete with larger competitors.

Many of Data Display's customers are international blue-chip companies, which compete for multi-million-dollar/pound/euro contracts in three different industry sectors: road, rail and cinema. For example, in the rail industry, the company has won major contracts to supply electronic signs to transport agencies worldwide, including the New York Subway, the London Underground, Seattle's Public Transport System and the Paris Metro. The signs provided by Data Display are only one part of a much bigger bid by a large multinational, and mean that the company must meet the highest international quality standards to produce systems that integrate seamlessly, and operate flawlessly, with every system it bids for.

One of the major strengths of the company is being agile enough to react to whatever the customer wants. One of the biggest advantages for Data Display is that it has an international direct salesforce, which constantly feeds the management team with the latest market trends and pertinent market intelligence. This invaluable feedback mechanism allows the firm to adapt to changing market needs, and adjust and enhance product offerings. Since it was established in 1990, Data Display has used a highly competitive marketing strategy to support its growth, to a point where it now it offers an unrivalled range of technologies, which means that it can provide complete display solutions,

incorporating software and hardware components, that are designed and produced in-house to meet customer requirements.

The company has an interesting relationship with its customers. The nature of the industry means that Data Display is an SME competing against much larger firms, and selling to multinational firms. It needs to close two sales to get one sale. First, it needs to sell to its customers; once it has been selected as the nominated electronic signage partner for its customer, it then becomes part of its customers' sales team and helps them to bid against their competitors for the overall project. This means that the company invests a lot of time and money in travel, meetings, tenders and prototype development, without any guarantee of achieving a sale. For example, a multinational company such as Siemens could be involved in a bid tendering for an upgrade of New York City Subway. In turn, Siemens would then look for tenders from each of its sub-suppliers for each component required in the upgrade. One of these sub-suppliers might be Data Display, which would be asked to tender for the electronic display sign section of the contract. Notably, Data Display could be in competition with Siemens itself in this part of the tender process. However, assuming that Data Display wins the tender it then becomes part of the Siemens sales team in the bid for the overall tender from New York City subway. The overall Siemens bid is

Data display at a glance

TABLE C40.1

Background
Founded by Kevin Neville in 1979
Designs and manufactures customized electronic information displays
Generates nearly €20 million a year in revenue
'Europe's leading supplier of electronic information displays'

Location of Data Display
Data Display headquarters is based in the picturesque town of Ennistymon, Co. Clare. Ennistymon is a small town on Ireland's westerly seaboard; Data Display is the town's largest employer; approximately 263 km from Dublin

Location of Data Display sales offices	Clients include:
• Data Display USA • Data Display UK • Data Display Ireland • Data Display France • Data Display Netherlands • Data Display Portugal • Data Display Sweden (TA Poltech)	• New York Metro • Warner Cinemas • Charles De Gaulle Airport • Heathrow Express • London Underground • Copenhagen Stock Exchange • National Amusements • Seattle Light Rail

Types of product sold	Markets include:
LCD display signs Datalines Data boards TFT displays Reception displays Advertising displays Ticker displays Forecourt petrol displays Large departure boards Large highway signs	Public transport—rail and bus Road Airports Banks Cinemas Call centres Shopping centres Forecourt stations Hotels and conference centres Leisure parks and stadia Municipalities Banks Stock markets

judged on many elements, some of which include the price, reputation, quality and standards of each of its sub-suppliers and their sub-suppliers. Thus quality assurance is crucial for Data Display.

Operating in such a remote, beautiful location has both advantages and notable drawbacks. The company has an intensely loyal and dedicated workforce, who are focused on ensuring Data Display's success, as there are limited job opportunities in a small town such as Ennistymon. The factory itself is one of the company's most powerful selling tools. Potential clients are invited to the factory, a hive of activity showcasing the plant's excellent manufacturing capability. On the downside, coordinating an international sales effort from the periphery of Europe presents unique challenges for the firm. Many commentators within Ireland see the

manufacturing industry in Ireland as unsustainable due to competition from low-cost countries.

The marketplace is constantly evolving due to technology. Markets are being created in new sectors that were previously unviable and not technically feasible. For example, with outdoor advertising, the costs of installing a high-impact display suitable for advertising have fallen dramatically. Now these displays can be powered through low-cost solar energy units, and the content can be managed remotely through 3G mobile technologies. Technology advancements provide both new opportunities and threats for the business.

In order to invest its limited resources widely and not spend too much time chasing sales that won't result in a winning bid, Data Display needs to use marketing intelligence and expertise to maximize every

Two of Data Display's largest markets for display devices are film information in cinemas and traffic information on roads **FIGURE C40.1**

opportunity identified, bearing in mind the investment required to close the sale and the potential profit from the deal. However, once it closes the two sales, the company becomes deeply embedded with its customer and their customer. This is highlighted on its website, where it illustrates that, 'At Data Display, we think long term regarding the relationships we have with our customers, and in relation to the products and services with which we provide them. This is why we design our electronic display solutions with long-term performance and ease of maintenance in mind, and back them up with a comprehensive range of after-sales support options.'

In looking to its positioning within a highly competitive, dynamic market, Data Display has clearly identified that low-cost competition from the Far East makes specialization and customization of its products essential. Mass-produced products from the Far East enjoy economies of scale with which Data Display cannot hope to compete on price; thus it needs to be cost-effective for its customers but also to provide a level of customization that makes it unattractive for its customers to purchase more cost-effective products: 'Everything we do is in a niche because otherwise we'd be up against mass markets, and if we were up against mass markets, then as a small company we can't compete.' This approach is feasible only if Data Display adopts a market-centred approach, focusing on customer needs.

> // The marketplace is constantly evolving due to technology. Markets are being created in new sectors that were previously unviable and not technically feasible. //

To survive in this market Data Display has spread its risk by operating across three industries: cinema, rail and road. In each of these it has competitors, none of which compete in all three markets. Data Display's success in the face of such competition can be attributed to two factors: first, its participation in different markets, each of which has its own economic cycle, so when one market is depressed Data Display concentrates on a more buoyant market; second, it has formed strategic alliances with similar companies in other countries—Australia, Estonia, France, Germany, Ireland, Israel, Italy, the Netherlands, Portugal, Spain, Sweden, the UK and the USA. These alliances mean that Data Display can mimic the business strategies and models of much larger companies; this reassures large customers, which like the reassurance of dealing with a larger rather than small company. Furthermore, having a local presence reassures customers.

Data Display is one of the longest-established manufacturers in a highly competitive market, with new entrants entering and exiting the market on a regular basis. It has survived and grown in this market based on its clear identification of its competitive advantage in a global market as being based on its commitment to customer service, in combination with its flexibility in providing the best dedicated solutions for each customer. It would be wrong to envisage Data Display as a just a simple manufacturing company, producing an array of products for industrial clients. The company is solution-driven, rather than a product company. When a potential client comes to Data Display with a problem, it develops a customized solution to that problem. For example, the firm's R&D section would develop a customized design solution for that particular customer, matching their particular specifications. Customized management software would be developed for the particular client (e.g. a cinema chain required software that would display information over the auditorium, the screens and outdoors). For example, the company has created highly customized products for its client base, with numerous value-added benefits for customers. One of its products has an inbuilt diagnostics system that will identify to a controller problems within the system, down to the exact location of a fault (e.g. one faulty LED on a display array). This type of value-added mechanism allows clients to make repairs quickly and cost effectively, causing minimal disruption. The sale of 10-year maintenance contracts for display systems is a lucrative additional revenue stream. The firm will look after the whole life-cycle cost of a display solution.

Data Display engages in a proactive approach towards its suppliers, customers, products, processes and technologies. This approach is necessary in order for Data Display to identify and successfully engage multinational companies in a highly intuitive sales process. In engaging with such multinational companies Data Display must illustrate its competences, quality benchmarking, change management skills and ability to service a world-class multinational relationship in the face of strong international low-cost competition. Data Display is successful in this domain given its strength of relationships with clients that demand excellence.

Questions

1. What is Data Display's source of competitive advantage?
2. Discuss the merits of Data Display's strategic focus in building its business.
3. Assess Data Display's relationship with its customers.

This case was written by Dr Michele O'Dwyer, Lecturer in Entrepreneurship, and Conor Carroll, Lecturer in Marketing, University of Limerick.

Be Humankind ⚭ **Oxfam**

Be Humankind ♀ Oxfam

Marketing Implementation and Application

CHAPTER 21

Managing marketing implementation, organization and control

LEARNING OBJECTIVES

After reading this chapter, you should be able to:

1 describe the relationship between marketing strategy, implementation and performance

2 identify the stages that people pass through when they experience disruptive change

3 describe the objectives of marketing implementation and change

4 discuss the barriers to the implementation of the marketing concept

5 discuss the forms of resistance to marketing implementation and change

6 explain how to develop effective implementation strategies

7 describe the elements of an internal marketing programme

8 discuss the skills and tactics that can be used to overcome resistance to the implementation of the marketing concept and plan

9 discuss marketing organizational structures

10 explain the nature of a marketing control system

Designing marketing strategies and positioning plans that meet today's and tomorrow's market requirements is a necessary but not a sufficient condition for corporate success. They need to be translated into action through effective implementation. This is the system that makes marketing happen in companies: it is the face of marketing that customers see in the real world. As we shall see, how implementation is managed has a crucial bearing on business outcomes, and its accompanying process—the management of change—must be accomplished with skill and determination if strategies and plans are to become marketing practice.

This chapter examines the relationship between strategy, implementation and performance, how people react to change, and the objectives of implementation. It then explores the kinds of resistance that can surface when implementing the marketing concept and strategic marketing decisions. Finally, a framework for gaining commitment is laid out before looking at the skills and tactics that marketing managers can use to bring about marketing implementation and change. A key factor in implementing a change programme is top management support. Without its clear, visible and consistent backing a major change programme is likely to falter under the inertia created by vested interests.[1]

It is important for companies to monitor change and ensure that systems are in place to gather and disseminate information throughout the organization. For example, Cisco invites groups of key clients three or four times a year for workshops and discussions over several days with all functional areas of the company. The objectives are to analyse how the company is doing and how it should go forward to better serve key customer needs. This allows Cisco not only to gain first-hand knowledge of customer preferences, but also to ensure the entire organization is immediately aware of customers' experiences, demands and how the company should operate in the future.[2]

This chapter also examines how companies organize their marketing activities and establish control procedures to check that objectives have been achieved.

Marketing Strategy, Implementation and Performance

Marketing strategy concerns the issues of *what* should happen and *why* it should happen. Implementation focuses on actions: *who* is responsible for various activities, *how* the strategy should be carried out, *where* things will happen and *when* action will take place. Lou Gerstner, the man admired for reviving IBM's fortunes, once said that the last thing the company needed was another strategy. What he actually meant was that the company's problem was not developing great strategies, but in its willingness and ability to implement them.[3] This chapter looks at how to do just that.

Managers devise marketing strategies to meet new opportunities, counter environmental threats and match core competences. The framework for strategy development was discussed in Chapter 2, which dealt with marketing planning. Although implementation is a consequence of strategy, it also affects strategy and should form part of the strategy development process. The proposition is straightforward: strategy, no matter how well conceived from a customer perspective, will fail if people are incapable of carrying out the necessary tasks to make the strategy work in the marketplace. Implementation capability, then, is an integral part of strategy formulation. The link between strategy and implementation is shown in Figure 21.1. Implementation affects marketing strategy choice. For example, a company that traditionally has been a low-cost, low-price operator may have a culture that finds it difficult to implement a value-added, high-price strategy. Strategy also determines implementation requirements: for example, a value-added, high-price strategy may require the salesforce to refrain from price discounting.

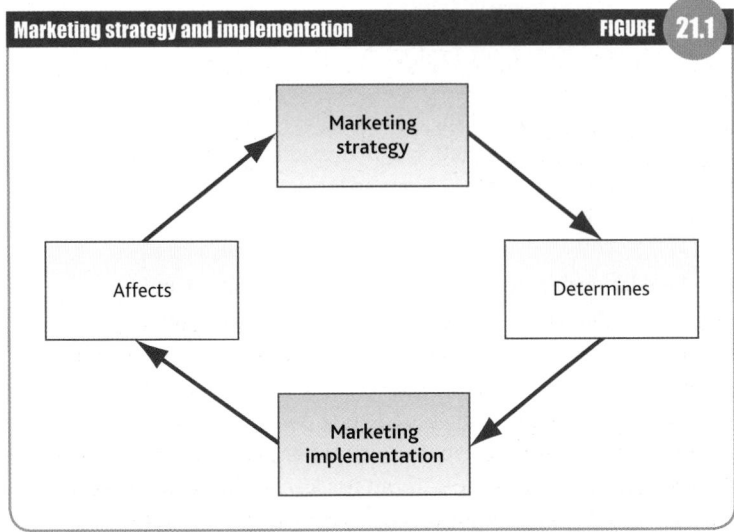

Marketing strategy and implementation   **FIGURE 21.1**

Combining strategies and implementation

Bonoma has argued that combinations of appropriate/inappropriate strategy and good/poor implementation will lead to various business outcomes.[4] Figure 21.2 shows the four-cell matrix, with predicted performances.

Appropriate strategy—good implementation

This is the combination most likely to lead to success. No guarantee of success can be made, however, because of the vagaries of the marketplace, including competitor actions and reactions, new technological breakthroughs and plain bad luck; but with strong implementation backing sound strategy, marketing management has done all it can to build success.

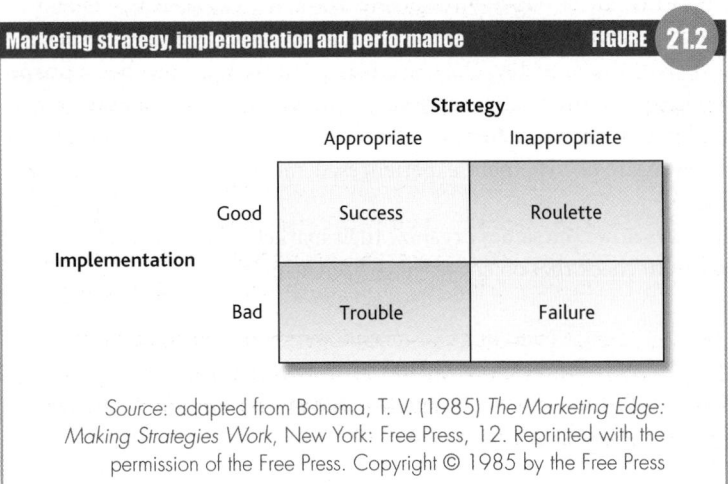

Marketing strategy, implementation and performance   **FIGURE 21.2**

Source: adapted from Bonoma, T. V. (1985) *The Marketing Edge: Making Strategies Work*, New York: Free Press, 12. Reprinted with the permission of the Free Press. Copyright © 1985 by the Free Press

Appropriate strategy—bad implementation

This combination is likely to lead to trouble if sub-standard performance is attributed to poor strategy. Management's tendency to look for strategy change in response to poor results will result in a less appropriate strategy being grafted on to an already wayward implementation system.

Inappropriate strategy—good implementation

Two effects of this combination can be predicted. First, the effective implementation of a poor strategy can hasten failure. For example, very effectively communicating a price rise (which is part of an inappropriate repositioning strategy) to customers may accelerate a fall in sales. Second, if good implementation takes the form of correcting a fault in strategy, then the outcome will be favourable. For example, if strategy implies an increase in sales effort to push a low margin *dog* product to the detriment of a new *star* product in a growing market (perhaps for political reasons), modification at the implementation level may correct the bias. The reality of marketing life is that managers spend many hours supplementing, subverting, overcoming or otherwise correcting shortcomings in strategic plans.

Inappropriate strategy—bad implementation

This obviously leads to failure, which is difficult to correct because so much is wrong. An example might be a situation where a product holds a premium price position without a competitive advantage to support the price differential. The situation is made worse by an advertising campaign that is unbelievable, and a salesforce that makes misleading claims leading to customer annoyance and confusion.

Implications

So what should managers do when faced with poor performance? First, strategic issues should be separated from implementation activities and the problem diagnosed. Second, when in doubt about whether the problem is rooted in strategy or implementation, implementation problems should be addressed first so that strategic adequacy can be assessed more easily.

Implementation and the Management of Change

The implementation of a new strategy may have profound effects on people in organizations. Brand managers that discover their product is to receive fewer resources (harvested) may feel bitter and demoralized; a salesperson that loses as a result of a change in the payment system may feel equally aggrieved. The implementation of a strategy move is usually associated with the need for people to adapt to *change*. The cultivation of change, therefore, is an essential ingredient in effective implementation. Some companies have charismatic leaders, like Virgin and Richard Branson, which can help the cultivation of change (see illustration).

A key ingredient in the management of change is getting the speed of change right. Procter & Gamble suffered by trying to change too quickly. The new chief executive Durk Jaeger's vision was to transform P&G into a global brand powerhouse with Organization 2005, a six-year plan to improve sales and become truly global. But the upheaval left too many loyal managers alienated; costs were slashed but the required growth did not materialize. As Chris Lapuente explains:

▲ Change can be assisted by the presence of a charismatic leader like Richard Branson.

> What we tried to do was change the whole organization back to front, with a promise of record earnings. Virtually everybody changed jobs. And we were excited and inspired by the new vision and direction. It was very intoxicating.
>
> This is a winning culture and everybody signed up for it. The problem was that we didn't get the balance right between speed, stretch, innovation and commitments. We were far, far too impatient.[5]

Another issue is avoiding making change becoming a fetish.[6] The danger is that change becomes an end in itself and managers become preoccupied with managing the process of change rather than serving customers. For example, successful UK governments have 'reformed' the National Health Service on average every six years since its creation in 1948. The danger is that the accompanying bureaucracy of targets, new relationships that have to be reforged, jobs redescribed and reapplied for, and the new IT and office systems that have to be implemented takes precedence over caring for patients and managing hospital beds.

It is helpful to understand the emotional stages that people pass through when confronted with an adverse change. These stages are known as the **transition curve** and are shown in Figure 21.3.[7]

Numbness

The first reaction is usually shock. The enormity of the consequences leads to feelings of being overwhelmed, despair and numbness. The outward symptoms include silence and lack of overt response. The news that a field salesforce is to be replaced by a telemarketing team is likely to provoke numbness in the field salespeople.

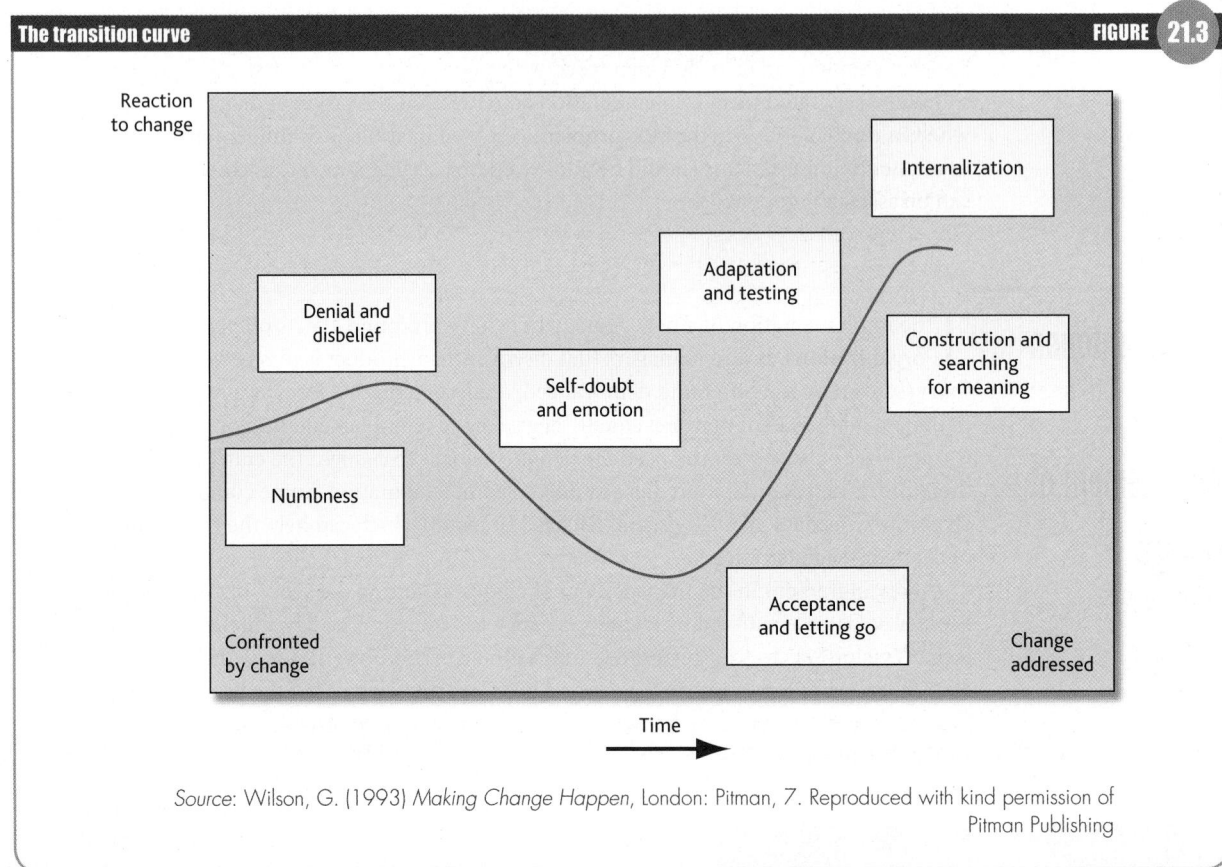

Source: Wilson, G. (1993) *Making Change Happen*, London: Pitman, 7. Reproduced with kind permission of Pitman Publishing

Denial and disbelief

Denial and disbelief may follow numbness, leading to trivializing the news, denying it or joking about it. The aim is to minimize the psychological impact of the change. News of the abandonment of the field salesforce may be met by utter disbelief, and sentiments such as 'They would never do that to us.'

Self-doubt and emotion

As the certainty of the change dawns, so personal feelings of uncertainty may arise. The feeling is one of powerlessness, of being out of control: the situation has taken over the individual. The likely reaction is one of anger: both as individuals and as a group, salesforce staff are likely to vent their anger and frustration on management.

Acceptance and letting go

Acceptance is characterized by tolerating the new reality and letting go of the past. This is likely to occur at an emotional low point but is the beginning of an upward surge as comfortable attitudes and behaviours are severed, and the need to cope with the change is accepted. In the salesforce example, salespeople would become accustomed to the fact that they would no longer be calling upon certain customers and receiving a particular salary.

Adaptation and testing

As people adapt to the changes they become more energetic, and they begin testing new behaviours and approaches to life. Alternatives are explored and evaluated. The classic case is the divorcee who begins dating again. This stage is fraught with personal risk, as in the case of the divorcee who is let down once more, leading to anger and frustration. Salespeople may consider another sales job, becoming part of the telemarketing team or moving out of selling altogether.

Construction and searching for meaning

As people's emotions become much more positive and they feel they have got to grips with the change, they seek a clear understanding of the new. The salespeople may come to the conclusion that there is much more to life than working as a salesperson for their previous company.

Internalization

The final stage is where feelings reach a new high. The change is fully accepted, adaptation is complete and behaviour alters too. Sometimes this is reflected in statements like 'That was the best thing that could have happened to me.'

21.1 Pause for Thought

Try to remember an event in your business or personal life that could be described as an 'adverse change' that has caused you distress. Can you recall passing through some or all of the stages described in the transition curve? What are your feelings now about the event?

Implications

Most people pass through all the above stages, although the movement from one stage to the next is rarely smooth. The implication for managing marketing implementation is that the acceptance of fundamental change such as the reprioritizing of products, jobs or strategic business units will take time for people to accept and come to terms with. The venting of anger and frustration is an accompanying behaviour to this transition from the old to the new, and should be accepted as such. Some people will leave as part of the fifth stage— the testing of new behaviours—but others will see meaning in and internalize the changes that have resulted from strategic redirection.

Objectives of Marketing Implementation and Change

The overriding objective of marketing implementation and change from a strategic standpoint is the successful execution of the marketing plan. This may include:

- gaining the support of key decision-makers in the company for the proposed plan (and overcoming the opposition of others)
- gaining the required resources (e.g. people and money) to be able to implement the plan
- gaining the commitment of individuals and departments in the company who are involved in frontline implementation (e.g. marketing, sales, service and distribution staff)
- gaining the cooperation of other departments needed to implement the plan (e.g. production and R&D).

For some people, the objectives and execution of the plan are consonant with their objectives, interests and viewpoints; gaining support from them is easy. But there are likely to be others who are involved with implementation from whom support is not so readily gained. They are the losers and neutrals. Loss may be in the form of lower status, a harder life or a reduction in salary. Neutrals may be left untouched overall with gains being balanced by

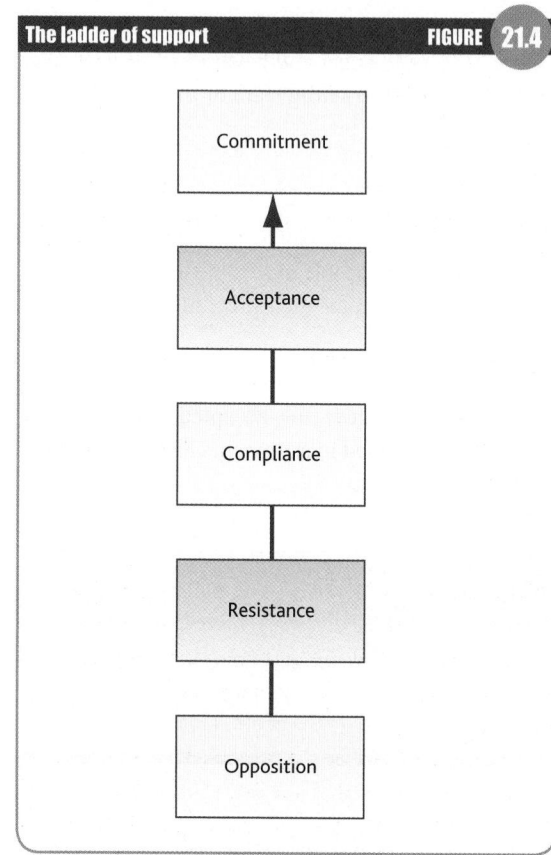

The ladder of support   FIGURE **21.4**

losses. For some losers, support will never be forthcoming, for others they may be responsive to persuasion, whereas neutrals may be more willing to support change.

The ladder of support

What does support mean? Figure 21.4 illustrates the degree of support that may be achieved; this can range from outright opposition to full commitment.

Opposition

The stance of direct opposition is taken by those with much to lose from the implementation of the marketing strategy, and who believe they have the political strength to stop the proposed change. Opposition is overt, direct and forceful.

Resistance

With resistance, opposition is less overt and may take a more passive form such as delaying tactics. Perhaps because of the lack of a strong power base, people are not willing to display open hostility but, nevertheless, their intention is to hamper the implementation process.

Compliance

Compliance means that people act in accordance with the plan but without much enthusiasm or zest. They yield to the need to conform but lack conviction that the plan is the best way to proceed. These reservations limit the lengths to which they are prepared to go to achieve its successful implementation.

Acceptance

A higher level of support is achieved when people accept the worth of the plan and actively seek to realize its goals. Their minds may be won but their hearts are not set on fire, limiting the extent of their motivation.

Commitment

Commitment is the ultimate goal of an effective implementation programme. People not only accept the worth of the plan but also pledge themselves to secure its success. Both hearts and minds are won, leading to strong conviction, enthusiasm and zeal. This can be encouraged by making people feel valued. Halifax Bank, for example, uses members of staff in its television advertising to promote its financial services (see illustration and go to the website to see the television advert).

◀ Staff feel valued when included in key organizational practices/activities. The Halifax Bank uses members of staff when advertising its financial services products.

Barriers to the Implementation of the Marketing Concept

Over the following pages we shall discuss the various forms of opposition and resistance, and examine the skills and tactics necessary to deal with them. This reflects the growing realism that marketing managers need to be adept at managing the internal environment of the company as well as the external. But first we shall examine some of the barriers to the implementation of the marketing concept mentioned in Chapter 1. This is necessary because the acceptance of marketing as a philosophy in a company is a necessary prerequisite for the successful development of marketing strategy and implementation.

The marketing concept states that business success will result from creating greater customer satisfaction than the competition. The concept is both seductive and tautological. It is seductive because it encapsulates the essence of business success, and is tautological because it is necessarily true. So why do so many companies score so badly at marketing effectiveness? The fact is that there are inherent *personal and organizational barriers* that make the achievement of marketing implementation difficult in practice. These are summarized in Figure 21.5.

High-cost solutions

Often giving what the customer wants involves extra costs. In today's heavily competitive environment most companies will meet customers' low-cost solutions. Therefore many marketing recommendations to beat competition will involve higher costs. Travelworld, a travel agency, was founded on giving better service to its customers. The chief executive recognized that the competition often required customers to queue at peak periods when booking a holiday. This he felt was unacceptable when customers were involved in a major transaction: a holiday is one of the highest-expenditure items for families each year. The solution was to hire enough staff at his outlets to ensure that queuing was not a problem. He came from a marketing background and accepted the higher costs involved.

Meeting customer requirements can also conflict with production's desire to gain cost economies of scale, and the finance director's objective of inventory reduction. Customers invariably differ in their requirements—they have different personalities, experiences and lifestyles—and to meet individual requirements is clearly not feasible. A solution to this problem is to group customers into segments that have similar needs and to target one product or service offering to each group. This allows the production manager to reap some economies of scale, and marketing to tailor offerings to the marketplace.

It was the failure of Henry Ford to compromise that almost led to his company's downfall.[8] He continued to make the Model T in the face of competition from General Motors, which was making a range of cars in many colours (including pink) because Americans no longer wanted the drab old Model T and could afford something more glamorous. Ford's predilection with economies of scale lost him number-one position in the ranking of US car companies, a position that Ford has never managed to regain.

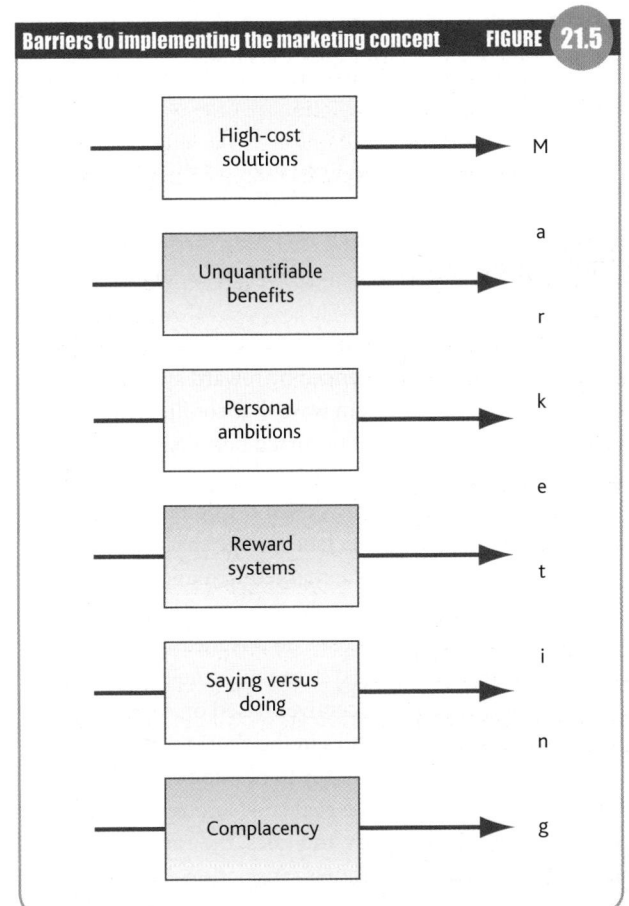

Barriers to implementing the marketing concept — FIGURE 21.5

High-cost solutions

Unquantifiable benefits

Personal ambitions

Reward systems

Saying versus doing

Complacency

Marketing

To a finance director stocks mean working capital tied up and interest charges to be made. To the marketing director stocks mean higher service levels and thus higher customer satisfaction. In the retailing of paint, for example, an out-of-stock situation is likely to mean a lost customer. Once more the marketing approach of giving customers what they want is a high-cost solution. Clearly, a compromise needs to be reached and target market segmentation can provide its basis. Unipart, a supplier of spare parts for cars, recognized that inventory cost control procedures meant that the competition was holding low stocks. This resulted in customer dissatisfaction when an urgently needed part could not be provided when required. Unipart's strategy was to target those motorists (do-it-yourselfers) that valued instant (or very quick) parts provision and were willing to pay a little more for the service. Its tag-line, 'The answer's yes. Now what's the question?', reflected the company's strategy. It identified a *high-price, high-service* segment and chose to serve those customers. In other situations, a *low-price, low-service* segment may be identified, and low stocks and a low price may be the appropriate response.

Unquantifiable benefits

A problem with marketing recommendations is that they are often unquantifiable in the sense that it is difficult to measure the exact increase in revenue (and profits) that will result from their implementation. A case that illustrates this point is that of a business school faced with a customer problem. The student car park was regularly being raided by thieves who stole radios and cars. One marketing solution was to employ at least one security guard. The extra cost could easily be quantified, not so the economic benefits to the business school, however. On a purely commercial basis, it is impossible to say what the marginal revenue would be. On a similar theme, what is likely to be the reduced revenue from removing one platform attendant from a railway station? The cost saving is immediate and quantifiable; the reduced customer satisfaction through not having someone to answer queries is not.

Personal ambitions

Personal ambitions can also hinder the progress of marketing in an organization. The R&D director may enjoy working on challenging, complex technical problems at the cutting edge of scientific knowledge. Customers may simply want products that work. Staff may want an easy life, which means that the customer is neglected.

Reward systems

It is a basic tenet of motivation theory that behaviour is influenced by reward systems.[9] Unfortunately organizations are prone to reward individuals in ways that conflict with marketing-orientated action. An example is the situation that occurred between a supplier of motor oil and a supermarket chain. The supplier delivered 200 litres of motor oil in cans to each supermarket petrol station at a time. The supermarket asked if it would be possible to deliver smaller quantities more often as it did not have sufficient storage space. In return it was willing to pay extra to cover the additional journeys. The marketing manager, anxious to please a major customer, asked the logistics manager to meet this request. The logistics manager refused on the grounds that it would raise delivery costs: he was measured and rewarded on the basis of efficiency. A classic case of a reward system (and efficiency) being in conflict with effectiveness. Sales staff who are rewarded by incentives based on sales revenue may be tempted to give heavy discounts, which secure easy sales in the short term but may ruin positioning strategies and profits. Webster argues that the key to developing a market-driven, customer-orientated business lies in how managers are evaluated and rewarded.[10] If managers are evaluated on the basis of short-term profitability and sales, they are likely to pay heed to these criteria and neglect market factors such as customer satisfaction, which ensure the long-term health of an organization.

Saying versus doing

Another force that blocks the implementation of the marketing concept is the gap between what senior managers say and what they do. Webster suggests that senior management must give clear signals and establish clear values and beliefs about serving the customer.[11] However, Argyris found that senior executives' behaviour often conflicted with what they said—for example, they might say 'Be customer orientated' and then cut back on marketing research funds.[12] This resulted in staff not really believing that management was serious about achieving a customer focus.

For those companies preaching an ethical stance, their words need to be backed up by deeds, as Marketing Ethics and Corporate Social Responsibility in Action 21.1 discusses.

21.1 Marketing Ethics and Corporate Social Responsibility in Action

'Saying' versus 'Doing' in CSR

Corporations are increasingly under the scrutiny of savvy consumers, and, as a result of mounting public pressure, many companies have turned to corporate social responsibility (CSR) as a means to maintain or improve their corporate reputations among internal and external stakeholder groups. For example, GlaxoSmithKline has recently announced a strategy aimed at helping one in every six people currently suffering from neglected tropical diseases such as malaria, leprosy, tuberculosis, trachoma, chagas and leishmaniasis. At the core of its strategy is a price cut of up to 25 per cent on selected drugs in the least-developed countries, the sharing of patents and a reinvestment of 20 per cent of its profits in such countries towards health infrastructure projects. The strategy has been acclaimed by the media and NGOs, as well as employees, and GlaxoSmithKline is certainly capitalizing upon the reputational benefits that this strategy has brought. However, as noted by the *Ethical Corporation Magazine*, the optimism could end if the corporation fails to deliver on its promises.

In fact, responsible and ethical marketing strategies are often the subject of much cynicism. Greenwash, for example, is a term used to describe inflated environmental claims made by corporations. A recent example is HSBC's marketing of its Half-price Green HSBC Plus, an online current account that promises the planting of 'virtual trees' for every new account opened, and guarantees its customers will not receive any paper-based materials such as direct mail. Sceptical consumers see no real benefit in such offerings, in that they would not want to receive 'junk mail' anyway, and although the bank promises to plant a real tree for every 20 virtual trees accumulated, the company has been slow to plant trees, despite the 400,000 virtual trees it has in stock.

HSBC has also faced criticisms with regard to its 'carbon-neutral' claims, which state that the bank has offset carbon emissions linked to its direct business activities. However, its investment portfolios across the globe remain far from having a substantial ethical orientation, which in turn reflects the bank's inconsistent approach to corporate social responsibility. Indeed, organizations that attempt to respond to societal demands by using CSR are faced with many challenges and paradoxes, and they must do so with integrity and consistency if they are to avoid a consumer backlash.

Based on: Crane (2005);[13] Balch (2009);[14] Pearce (2009)[15]

Complacency

A final barrier to the implementation of marketing change is complacency, which can be fuelled by past success. For example, at BMW, whose engineers had been used to success based on building powerful gas-guzzling cars, there was strong resistance to the introduction of a new fuel-efficiency programme called Efficient Dynamics. Their argument was that there was no need for efficient dynamics. Given their past success they believed that dynamics was enough. To drive through the change required to meet new market requirements, BMW's chief executive had to successfully change this mindset.[16]

Implications

The implications are that marketing managers have to face the fact that some people in the organization will have a vested interest in blocking the introduction and growth of marketing in an organization, and will have some ammunition (e.g. the extra costs, unquantifiable benefits) to achieve their aims. Marketing implementation, then, depends on being able to overcome the opposition and resistance that may well surface as a result of developing market-driven plans. The following sections discuss the nature of such resistance, and ways of dealing with it.

Forms of Resistance to Marketing Implementation and Change

Opposition to the acceptance of marketing and the implementation of marketing plans is direct, open and conflict driven. Often, arguments such as the lack of tangible benefits and the extra expense of marketing proposals, will be used to cast doubt on their worth. Equally likely, however, is the more passive type of *resistance*. Kanter and Piercy suggest 10 forms of resistance:[17,18]

1 criticism of specific details of the plan
2 foot-dragging
3 slow response to requests
4 unavailability
5 suggestions that, despite the merits of the plan, resources should be channelled elsewhere
6 arguments that the proposals are too ambitious
7 hassle and aggravation created to wear the proposer down
8 attempts to delay the decision, hoping the proposer will lose interest
9 attacks on the credibility of the proposer with rumour and innuendo
10 deflation of any excitement surrounding the plan by pointing out the risks.

Market research reports supporting marketing action can also be attacked. Johnson describes the reaction of senior managers to the first marketing research report commissioned by a new marketing director.[19]

> As a diagnostic statement the research was full, powerful, prescriptive. The immediate result of this analysis was that the report was rubbished by senior management and directors. The analysis may have been perceived by its initiator as diagnostic but it was received by its audience as a politically threatening statement.

In general, there are 10 ways of blocking a marketing report.[20] These are described in Marketing in Action 21.1.

Ansoff argues that the level of resistance will depend on how much the proposed change is likely to disrupt the culture and power structure of the organization and the speed at which the change is introduced.[21] The latter point is in line with the previous discussion about how people adapt to adverse change, requiring time to come to terms with disruptions. The greatest level of opposition and resistance will come when the proposed change is implemented quickly and is a threat to the culture and politics of the organization; the least opposition and resistance will be found when the change is consonant with the existing culture and political structure, and is introduced over a period of time. Further, Pettigrew states that resistance is likely to be low when a company is faced with a crisis, arguing that

21.1 Marketing in Action

Ten Ways of Blocking a Marketing Report

Reports that present critical conclusions or unpopular recommendations to an audience of managers are likely to meet stiff opposition. There are 10 devices used by managers to block an undesired report.

1 *Straight rejection*: the report and its writer/commissioner are dismissed without further discussion. This approach requires political strength and self-confidence

2 *Bottom drawer*: the report is effectively 'bottom drawered' by praising its contents but taking no action on its recommendations. The writer/commissioner, happy to receive praise, does not press the matter further.

3 *Mobilizing political support*: recognizing there is strength in numbers, the opposer gathers support from other managers who are threatened by the report.

4 *Criticizing the details*: a series of minor technical criticisms are raised to discredit the report, such as poor question wording and unrepresentative samples.

5 *But in the future*: the report is recognized as being accurate for today but does not take into account future events and so should not be implemented.

6 *Working on emotions*: make the writer feel bad by asking 'How can you do this to me?'

7 *Invisible man tactic*: the opposer is never available for comment on the report.

8 *Further study is required*: the report is returned for further work.

9 *The scapegoat*: 'I have no problems with this report but I know the boss/head office, etc. will not approve of it.'

10 *Deflection*: an extension of criticizing the details, where attention is directed at areas where the opposer's knowledge is sufficient to contradict some points made by the writer/commissioner and so discredit the whole report.

Based on: Pettigrew (1974)[22]

a common perception among people that the organization is threatened with extinction also acts to overcome inertia against change.[23]

Developing Implementation Strategies

Faced with the likelihood of resistance from vested interests, a **change master** needs to develop an implementation strategy that can deliver the required change.[24] For example, at Xerox, a well-respected employee, Anne Mulcahy, was appointed to chief executive officer with a brief to act as a change master. She began by talking to customers and employees, to gain an understanding of what was wrong. She ran meetings differently, forcing people to face the tough decisions that were necessary, and used the severity of the crisis at Xerox to gain acceptance for the required changes, which included cutting $1 billion of overheads and closing unprofitable businesses.[25] The workforce was cut by almost 40 per cent, while gaps in Xerox's product portfolio were filled with lower-priced products. This has given the company its largest product portfolio and has made it more competitive when selling to small and medium-sized businesses. Mulcahy was succeeded in 2009 by her trusted lieutenant Ursula Burns, having gained the reputation for pulling Xerox back from the brink of bankruptcy.[26]

A change master is a person who is responsible for driving through change within an organization. This necessitates a structure for thinking about the problems to be tackled and the way to deal with them. Figure 21.6 illustrates such a framework. The process starts with a definition of objectives.

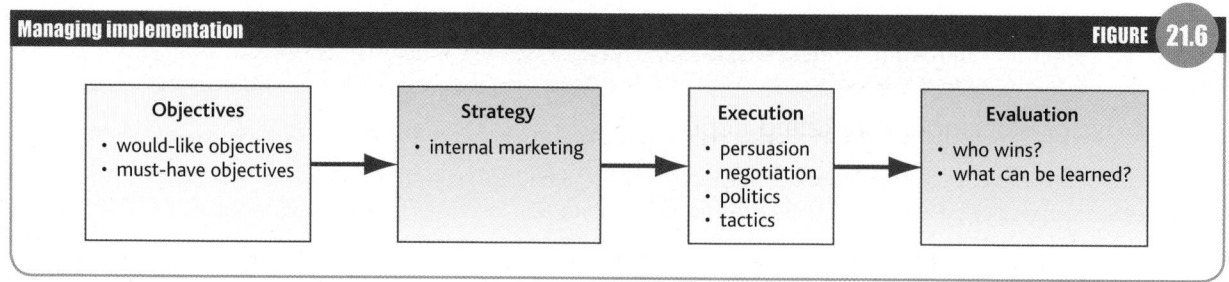

Managing implementation   FIGURE 21.6

Objectives
• would-like objectives
• must-have objectives

→

Strategy
• internal marketing

→

Execution
• persuasion
• negotiation
• politics
• tactics

→

Evaluation
• who wins?
• what can be learned?

Implementation objectives

These are formulated at two levels: what we would like to achieve (*would-like objectives*) and what we must achieve (*must-have objectives*). Framing objectives in this way recognizes that we may not be able to achieve all that we desire. Would-like objectives are our preferred solution: they define the maximum that the implementer can reasonably expect.[27] Must-have objectives define our minimum requirements: if we cannot achieve these then we have lost and the plan or strategy will not succeed. Between the two points there is an area for negotiation, but beyond our must-have objective there is no room for compromise.

By clearly defining these objectives at the start, we know what we would like, the scope for bargaining, and the point where we have to be firm and resist further concessions. For example, suppose our marketing plan calls for a move from a salary-only payment system for salespeople to salary plus commission. This is predicted to lead to strong resistance from salespeople and some sales managers, who favour the security element of fixed salary. Our would-like objective might be a 60:40 split between salary and commission. This would define our starting point in attempting to get this change implemented. But in order to allow room for concessions, our must-have objective would be somewhat lower, perhaps an 80:20 ratio between salary and commission. Beyond this point we refuse to bargain: we either win or lose on the issue. In some situations, however, would-like and must-have objectives coincide: here there is no room for negotiation, and persuasive and political skills are needed to drive through the issue.

Strategy

All worthwhile plans and strategies necessitate substantial human and organizational change inside companies.[28] Marketing managers, therefore, need a practical mechanism for thinking through strategies to drive change. One such framework is known as internal marketing, sometimes called the 'missing half' of the marketing programme.[29]

Originally the idea of internal marketing was developed within the area of services marketing, where it was applied to develop, train, motivate and retain employees at the customer interface in such areas as retailing, catering and financial services.[30] However, the concept can be expanded to include marketing to all employees with the aim of achieving successful marketing implementation. The framework is appealing as it draws an analogy with external marketing structures such as market segmentation, target marketing and the marketing mix. The people inside the organization to whom the plan must be marketed are considered *internal customers*. We need to gain the support, commitment and participation of sufficient of these to achieve acceptance and implementation of the plan. For those people where we fail to do this we need to minimize the effectiveness of their resistance. They become, in effect, our competitors in the internal marketplace.

Internal market segmentation

As with external marketing, analysis of customers begins with market segmentation. One obvious method of grouping internal customers is into three categories.

1 *Supporters*: those who are likely to gain from the change or are committed to it.
2 *Neutrals*: those whose gains and losses are in approximate balance.
3 *Opposers*: those who are likely to lose from the change or are traditional opponents.

These three market segments form distinct *target groups* for which specific *marketing mix* programmes can be developed (see Fig. 21.7).

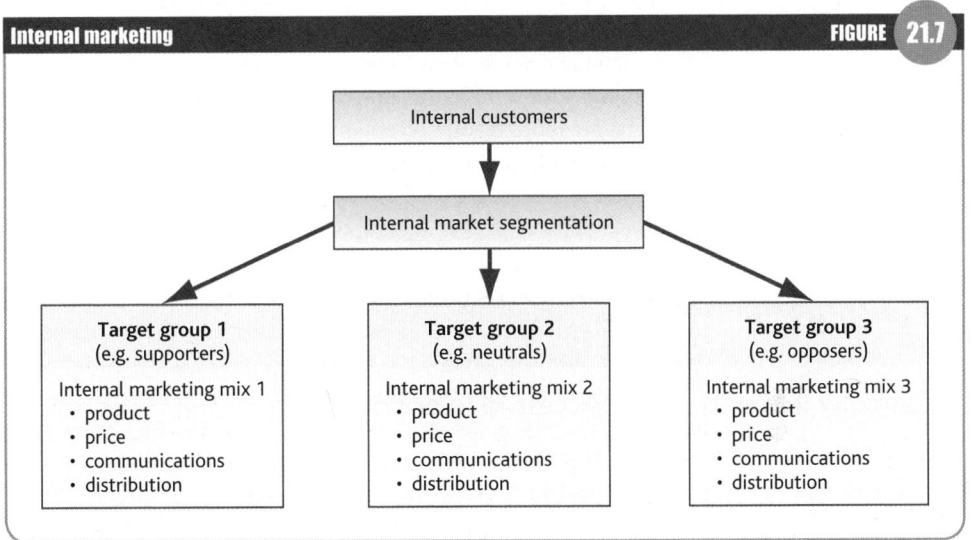

Internal marketing   FIGURE **21.7**

Internal customers

Internal market segmentation

Target group 1 (e.g. supporters)	**Target group 2** (e.g. neutrals)	**Target group 3** (e.g. opposers)
Internal marketing mix 1 • product • price • communications • distribution	Internal marketing mix 2 • product • price • communications • distribution	Internal marketing mix 3 • product • price • communications • distribution

Internal marketing mix programmes

Product is the marketing plan and strategies that are being proposed, together with the values, attitudes and actions that are needed to make the plan successful. Features of the product may include increased marketing budgets, extra staff, different ways of handling customers, different pricing, distribution and advertising, and new product development strategies. The product will reflect our would-like objectives; however, it may have to be modified slightly to gain acceptance from our opponents. Hence the need for must-have objectives.

The *price* element of the marketing mix is what we are asking our internal customers to pay as a result of accepting the marketing plan. The price they pay may be lost resources, lower status, fear of the unknown, harder work and rejection of their pet projects because of lack of funds. Clearly, price sensitivity is a key segmentation variable that differentiates supporters, neutrals and opposers.

Communications is a major element of the internal marketing mix and covers the communications media and messages used to influence the attitudes of key players. A combination of personal (presentations, discussion groups) and non-personal (the full report, executive summaries) can be used to inform and persuade. Communication should be two-way: we should listen as well as inform. We should also be prepared to adapt the product (the plan) if necessary in response to our internal customers' demands. It may also be necessary to fine-tune the language of marketing (e.g. eliminating jargon) to fit the corporate culture and background of the key players.[31] This is analogous to adaptation of a new product in the external marketplace as a result of marketing research. Communication objectives will differ according to the target group, as follows.

- *Supporters*: to reinforce existing positive attitudes and behaviour, mobilize support from key players (e.g. chief executive).

- *Neutrals*: the use of influence strategies to build up perception of rewards and downgrade perceived losses; display key supporters and explain the benefits of joining 'the team'; negotiate to gain commitment.
- *Opposers*: disarm and discredit; anticipate objections and create convincing counterarguments; position them as 'stuck in their old ways'; bypass by gaining support of opinion and political leaders; negotiate to lower resistance.

Opposition to the proposals may stem from a misunderstanding on the part of staff of the meaning of marketing. Some people may equate marketing with advertising and selling rather than the placing of customer satisfaction as central to corporate success. An objective of communications, therefore, may be to clarify the real meaning of marketing, or to use terms that are more readily acceptable such as 'improving service quality'.[32]

Digital Marketing 21.1 discusses how company intranets can aid communication within companies.

21.1 Digital Marketing

Company Intranets: Open Access to Information

Internal communications are important to the success of implementation strategies. Internal customers should be understood in the same way as external customers. In other words, their needs and wants, attitudes and behaviours, all need to be taken into account. Increasingly, companies are using digital technologies as a means of communicating with employees and other internal stakeholders. Company intranets can provide electronic and remote access through virtual private networks across the Internet to large resources of company information, and facilitate collaborative working. Intranets can be used in different ways to communicate with internal stakeholders (e.g. daily news updates, induction and training programmes, and information resources).

The Open University, the world-leading provider of distance learning, has an intranet that provides access to information and support resources to its central academic staff and over 18,000 associate lecturers. But having an intranet, and providing access to vast stores of information, is only part of the story. According to Elizabeth Daniel, Professor of Information Management at the Open University, 'the average knowledge worker spends around 10 per cent of their working time trying to find the information within their organization that they need to do their job'. She has five key recommendations, which can help to maximize the value of a company's information resources:

1 Ownership: all information, should be assigned an owner to ensure effective stewardship.
2 Identification of all documents so they can be classified and retrieved easily.
3 Life cycle: documents become out of date and should be archived when no longer current.
4 Storage: systems should enable relevant staff to access the document they need at the time they need it. The maxim for many organizations is 'store once, use many'.
5 Audit: organizations should regularly review information stored, information requested, and the cost and value of the company's information resources.

Based on: Daniel (2006)[33]

Distribution describes the places where the product and communications are delivered to the internal customers such as meetings, committees, seminars, informal conversations and away-days. Consideration should be given to whether presentations should be direct (proponents to customers) or indirect (using third parties such as consultants). Given the conflicting viewpoints of the three target segments, thought should be given to the advisability of using different distribution channels for each group. For example, a meeting may be arranged with only supporters and neutrals present. If opponents tend to be found in a particular department, judicious selection of which departments to invite may accomplish this aim.

Execution

In order to execute an implementation strategy successfully, certain skills are required, and particular tactics need to be employed. Internal marketing has provided a framework to structure thinking about implementation strategies. Within that framework, the main skills are persuasion, negotiation and politics.

Persuasion

The starting point of persuasion is to try to understand the situation from the internal customer's standpoint. The new plan may have high profit potential, the chance of real sales growth and be popular among external customers, but if it causes grief to certain individuals and departments in the organization, resistance may be expected. As with personal selling, the proponents of the plan must understand the needs, motivations and problems of their customers before they can hope to develop effective messages. For example, appealing to a production manager's sense of customer welfare will fail if that person is interested only in smooth production runs. In such a situation the proponent of the plan needs to show how smooth production will not be affected by the new proposals, or how disruption will be marginal or temporary.

The implementer also needs to understand how the features of the plan (e.g. new payment structure) confer customer benefits (e.g. the opportunity to earn more money). Whenever possible, evidence should be provided to support claims. Objectives should be anticipated and convincing counter-arguments produced. Care should be taken not to bruise egos unnecessarily.

Negotiation

Implementers have to recognize that they may not get all they want during this process. By setting would-like and must-have objectives (see earlier in this chapter) they are clear about what they want and have given themselves negotiating room wherever possible. Two key aspects of negotiation will be considered next: concession analysis and proposal analysis.

The key to **concession analysis** is to value the concessions the implementer might be prepared to make from the viewpoint of the opponent. By doing this it may be possible to identify concessions that cost the implementer very little and yet are highly valued by the opponent. For example, if the must-have objective is to move from a fixed salary to a salary plus commission, a salesperson's compensation plan conceding that the proportions should be 80:20 rather than 70:30 may be trivial to the implementer (an incentive to sell is still there) and yet highly valued by the salesperson as they will gain more income security and value the psychological bonus of winning a concession from management. By trading concessions that are highly valued by the opponent and yet cost the implementer little, painless agreement can be reached.

Proposal analysis: another sensible activity is to try to predict the proposals and demands that opponents are likely to make during the process of implementation. This provides time to prepare a response to them rather than relying on quick decisions during the heat of negotiation. By anticipating the kinds of proposals opponents are likely to make, implementers can plan the types of counter-proposal they are prepared to make.

Politics

Success in managing implementation and change also depends on the understanding and execution of political skills. Understanding the sources of power is the starting point from which an assessment of where power lies and who holds the balance can be made. The five sources are reward, expert, referent, legitimate and coercive power.[34]

Reward power derives from the implementer's ability to provide benefits to members in the organization. The recommendations of the plan may confer natural benefits in the form of increased status or salary for some people. In other cases, the implementer may create rewards for support—for example, promises of reciprocal support when required, or backing for promotion. The implementer needs to assess what each target individual values and whether the natural rewards match those values, or whether created rewards are necessary. A limit on the use of reward power is the danger that people may come to expect rewards in return for support. Created rewards, therefore, should be used sparingly.

Expert power is based on the belief that implementers have special knowledge and expertise that renders their proposals more credible. For example, a plan outlining major change is more likely to be accepted if produced by someone who has a history of success rather than a novice. Implementers should not be reluctant to display their credentials as part of the change process.

Referent power occurs when people identify with and respect the architect of change. That is why charismatic leadership is often thought to be an advantage to those who wish to see change implemented.

Legitimate power is wielded when the implementer insists on an action from a subordinate as a result of their hierarchical relationship and contract. For example, a sales manager may demand compliance with a request for a salesperson to go on a training course or a board of directors may exercise its legitimate right to cut costs.

The strength of **coercive power** lies with the implementer's ability to punish those who resist or oppose the implementation of the plan. Major organizational change is often accompanied by staff losses. This may be a required cost-cutting exercise but it also sends messages to those not directly affected that they may be next if further change is resisted. The problem with using coercive power is that, at best, it results in compliance rather than commitment.

Applications of power

The balance of power will depend on who holds the sources of power and how well they are applied. Implementers should pause to consider any sources of power they hold, and also the sources and degree of power held by supporters, neutrals and opposers. Power held by supporters should be mobilized, those neutrals who wield power should be cultivated, and tactics should be developed to minimize the influence of powerful opposers. The tactics that can be deployed will be discussed shortly, but two applications of power will be discussed first: overt and covert power plays.

Overt power plays are the visible, open kind of power plays that can be used by implementers to push through their proposals. Unconcealed use of the five sources of power is used to influence key players. The use of overt power by localized interests, who battle to secure their own interests in the process of change has been well documented.[35]

Covert power plays are a more disguised form of influence. Their use is more subtle and devious than that of overt power plays. Their application can take many forms including agenda setting, limiting participation in decisions to a few select individuals/ departments, and defining what is and what is not open to decision for others in the organization.[36]

Tactics

The discussion of overt and covert power plays has introduced some of the means by which implementers and change agents can gain acceptance of their proposals and overcome opposition. We shall now examine in more detail the array of tactics that can be used to achieve these ends. The discussion so far has described the kinds of resistance and opposition that may arise when trying to implement the marketing concept and, more specifically, marketing plans and strategies. We have also examined the skills that are needed to win implementation battles. We shall now outline the tactics that can be used to apply those skills in the face of some hostile reaction within the organization. These can be grouped into tactics of persuasion, politics, time and negotiation (see Fig. 21.8), and are based on the work of a number of authorities.[37] They provide a wide-ranging checklist of approaches to mobilizing support and overcoming resistance.

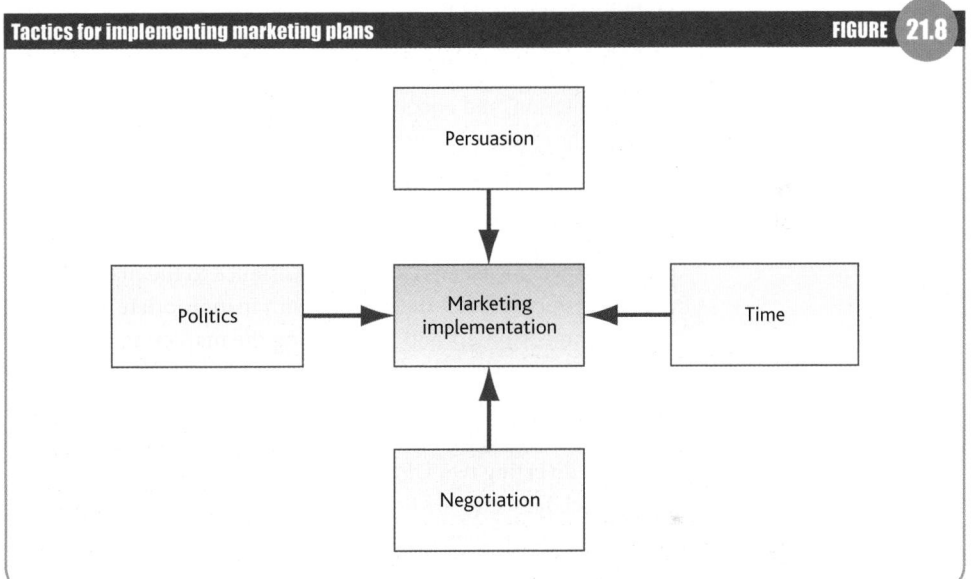

Tactics for implementing marketing plans   FIGURE **21.8**

Persuasion

- *Articulate a shared vision*: the vision—a picture of the destination aspired to and the desired results of the change—needs to be spread to the key players in the organization. For example, if the marketing plan calls for a reduction in staffing levels, the vision that this is required to reposition the company for greater competitiveness needs to be articulated. Without an understanding of the wider picture, people may regard the exercise as 'just another cost drive'.[38] Since most change involves risk and discomfort, a clear vision of its purpose and consequences can make the risk acceptable and the discomfort endurable.
- *Communicate and train*: implementation of the marketing concept or a fundamentally different marketing plan means that many individuals have to reorientate and engage in new activities. To achieve this requires a major commitment to communicating the nature and purpose of the change, as well as to training staff in the new skills to be mastered. Major changes require face-to-face communication at discussion sessions and management education seminars. Formal training programmes are needed to upgrade skills and introduce new procedures.
- *Eliminate misconceptions*: a major part of the communication programme will be designed to eliminate misconceptions about the consequences of the change. Unfounded fears and

anxieties should be allayed. Certain individuals will exaggerate the negative consequences of the proposed changes, and their concerns need to be addressed.

- *Sell the benefits*: the needs of key players have to be identified and the benefits of the change sold to them on that basis. The benefits may be economic (e.g. increased salary) or psychological (e.g. increased status, enhanced power). Whereas shared vision provides evidence of a wider general benefit (e.g. increased competitiveness) personal benefits should also be sold. This recognizes the fact that individuals seek to achieve not only organizational goals but also personal ambitions.

- *Gain acceptance by association*: position the plan against some well-accepted organizational doctrine such as *customer service* or *quality management*. Because the doctrine is heavily backed, the chances of the plan being accepted and implemented are enhanced. Another positioning strategy is to associate the plan with a powerful individual (e.g. the chief executive). The objective is to create the viewpoint that if the boss wants the plan, there is no point in opposing it.

- *Leave room for local control over details*: leaving some local options or local control over details of the plan creates a sense of ownership on the part of those responsible for implementation, and encourages adaptation to different situations. Thought should be given to the extent of uniformity in execution, and the areas where local adoption is both practical and advisable.

- *Support words with action*: when implementation involves the establishment or maintenance of a marketing-orientated culture, it is vital to support fine words with corresponding action. As we saw when discussing resistance to the marketing concept, it is easy for managers to contradict their words with inappropriate actions (e.g. stressing the need to understand customers and then cutting the marketing research budget). An illustrative case of how management actions supported the culture they were trying to create is the story of a regional manager of US company United Parcel Service (UPS), who used his initiative to untangle a misdirected shipment of Christmas presents by hiring an entire train and diverting two UPS-owned 727s from their flight plans.[39] Despite the enormous cost (which far exceeded the value of the business), when senior management learned what he had done they praised and rewarded him: their actions supported and reinforced the culture they wanted to foster. As this story became folklore at UPS, its staff knew that senior management meant business when they said that the customer had to come first.

- *Establish two-way communication*: it is important that the people who are responsible for implementation feel that they can put their viewpoints to senior management, otherwise the feeling of top-down control will spread and resistance will build up through the belief that 'no one ever listens to us'. It is usually well worth listening to people lower down the management hierarchy and especially those who come face to face with customers. One way of implementing this approach is through staff suggestion schemes, but these need to be managed so that staff believe it is worth bothering to take part.

Asda, the UK supermarket chain acquired by Wal-Mart, is well known for its policy of tapping into the collective wisdom of its 85,000 staff. It encourages them to put forward suggestions for improved customer service and the best ideas are presented at an annual meeting called the National Circle. It also invites staff to write directly to its chief executive officer, with the most promising ideas being rewarded with 'star points' that staff can redeem against a catalogue of offers including clothes and holidays.

Politics

- *Build coalitions*: the process of creating allies for the proposed measures is a crucial step in the implementation process. Two groups have special significance: power sources that control the resources needed for implementation such as information (expertise or data), finance and support (legitimacy, opinion leadership and political backing); and stakeholders, who are those people likely to gain or lose from the change.[40] Discussion with potential losers may reveal ways of sharing some rewards with them ('Invite the opposition in'). At the very least, talking to them will reveal their grievances and so allow thought to be given to how these may be handled. Another product of these discussions with both potential allies and foes is that the original proposals may be improved by accepting some of their suggestions.

- *Display support*: having recruited powerful allies these should be asked for a visible demonstration of support. This will confirm any statements that implementers have made about the strength of their backing ('gain acceptance by association'). Allies should be invited to meetings, presentations and seminars so that stakeholders can see the forces behind the change.

- *Invite the opposition in*: thought should be given to creating ways of sharing the rewards of the change with the opposition. This may mean modifying the plan and how it is to be implemented to take account of the needs of key players. So long as the main objectives of the plan remain intact, this may be a necessary step towards removing some opposition.

- *Warn the opposition*: critics of the plan should be left in no doubt as to the adverse consequences of opposition. This has been called *selling the negatives*. However, the tactic should be used with care because statements that are perceived as threats may stiffen rather than dilute resistance, particularly when the source does not have a strong power base.

- *Use of language*: in the political arena the potency of language in endorsing a preferred action and discrediting the opposition has long been apparent. For example, during the first Gulf War the following terminology was used:[41]

We (UN) have:	*They (Iraq) have:*
Army, Navy and Air Force	the war machine
reporting guidelines	censorship
press briefings	propaganda
We:	*They:*
suppress	destroy
eliminate	kill
neutralize	kill
We launch:	*They launch:*
first strikes	sneak missile attacks
pre-emptively	without provocation
Our men are:	*Their men are:*
boys, lads	troops, hordes

Language can be used as a weapon in the implementation battle with critics being labelled 'outdated', 'backward looking' and 'set in their ways'. In meetings, implementers need to avoid the temptation to *overpower* in their use of language. For people without a strong power base (such as young newcomers to a company) using phrases like 'We must take this action' or 'This is the way we have to move' to people in a more senior position (e.g. a board of directors), will provoke psychological resistance even to praiseworthy plans. Phases like 'I suggest' or 'I have a proposal for you to consider' recognize the inevitable desire on the part of more senior management to feel involved in the decision-making rather than being treated like a rubber stamp.

- *Decision control*: this may be achieved by agenda setting (i.e. controlling what is and is not discussed in meetings), limiting participation in decision-making to a small number of allies, controlling which decisions are open for debate in the organization, and timing important meetings when it is known that a key critic is absent (e.g. on holiday, or abroad on business).

- *The either/or alternative*: finally, when an implementation proposal is floundering, a powerful proponent may decide to use the either/or tactic in which the key decision-maker is required to choose between two documents placed on the desk: one asks for approval of the implementation plan, the other tenders the implementer's resignation.

Time

- *Incremental steps*: people need time to adjust to change, therefore consideration should be given to how quickly change is introduced. Where resistance to the full implementation package is likely to be strong, one option is to submit the strategy in incremental steps. A small, less controversial strategy is implemented first. Its success provides the impetus for the next implementation proposals, and so on.
- *Persistence*: this tactic requires the resubmission of the strategy until it is accepted. Modifications to the strategy may be necessary on the way but the objective is to wear down the opposition by resolute and persistent force. The game is a battle of wills, and requires the capability of the implementer to accept rejection without loss of motivation.
- *Leave insufficient time for alternatives*: a different way of using time is to present plans at the last possible minute so that there is insufficient time for anyone to present or implement an alternative. The proposition is basically 'We must move with this plan as there is no alternative'.
- *Wait for the opposition to leave*: for those prepared to play a waiting game, withdrawing proposals until a key opposition member leaves the company or loses power may be feasible. Implementers should be alert to changes in the power structure in these ways as they may present a window of opportunity to resubmit hitherto rejected proposals.

Negotiation

- *Make the opening stance high*: when the implementer suspects that a proposal in the plan is likely to require negotiation, the correct opening stance is to start high but be realistic. There are two strong reasons for this. First, the opponent may accept the proposal without modification; second, it provides room for negotiation. When deciding how high to go, the limiting factor is the need to avoid unnecessary conflict. For example, asking for a move from a fixed salary to a commission-only system with a view to compromising with salary plus commission is likely to be unrealistic and to provoke unnecessary antagonism among the salesforce.
- *Trade concessions*: sometimes it may be possible to grant a concession simply to secure agreement to the basics of the plan. Indeed, if the implementer has created negotiating room, this may be perfectly acceptable. In other circumstances, however, the implementer may be able to trade concession for concession with the opponent. For example, a demand from the salesforce to reduce list price may be met by a counter-proposal to reduce discount levels. A useful way of trading concessions is by means of the *if ... then* technique: 'If you are prepared to reduce your discount levels from 10 to 5 per cent, I am *then* prepared to reduce list price by 5 per cent.'[42] This is a valuable tool in negotiation because it promotes movement towards agreement and yet ensures that concessions given to the opponent are matched by concessions in return. Whenever possible, an attempt to create *win-win* situations should be made where concessions that cost the giver very little are highly valued by the receiver.

Evaluation

Finally, during and after the implementation process, evaluation should be made to consider what has been achieved and what has been learned. Evaluation may be in terms of the degree of support gained from key players, how well the plan and strategy have been implemented in the marketplace (e.g. by the use of customer surveys), the residual goodwill between opposing factions, and any changes in the balance of power between the implementers and other key parties in the company.

Some important lessons for implementing change programmes are identified when contrasting the fortunes of the move from Waterloo to St Pancras stations for the Eurostar cross-channel train service, and the opening of Heathrow airport's Terminal 5 (see Marketing in Action 21.2).

21.2 Marketing in Action

Change at St Pancras and Heathrow

Managers deal with change as a fundamental part of their job, but with varying degrees of success. Within months of each other London played host to two mammoth change programmes: the relocation of the cross-channel train service Eurostar from Waterloo to St Pancras stations, and the opening of Heathrow airport's Terminal 5. Their contrasting outcomes highlight the importance of preparation and communication in change management.

When Eurostar opened for business, it managed 97 per cent punctuality on the first day. The relocation not only meant a massive redesign of St Pancras station but also the move of 1600 employees, including 400 engineering and maintenance staff from south to north London. The keys to success were preparation and communication. Preparations began 18 months earlier and managers appreciated that the move was going to be an enormous event for their employees, both physically and emotionally. Business psychologists from the consultancy Kaisen were employed to advise managers. A huge two-way communication effort with staff was made to win their emotional engagement, as well as training them physically in how to work on the new site.

The Heathrow project was also a success—in terms of the construction of the site, which was completed on budget and on time. But, in spite of British Airways running a three-year change programme called 'Fit for 5', the opening day was a disaster, with over 30 flights cancelled as the baggage-handling operation ground to a halt. The baggage handlers had tried to warn their managers about the problems they could foresee. A key problem was that on the new, huge, site employees, who had not had enough training, simply did not know where they were supposed to go, and not enough time had been allowed to get staff from their locker rooms to the arrival and departure gates. The lockers themselves were too small to hold all the baggage handlers' clothing, and parking space was inadequate. All these problems had been communicated to managers beforehand.

So what lessons can be learned? First, change requires preparation that includes practical training (a BA baggage handler complained that his training resembled guided tours of the terminal rather than hands-on practice). Second, managers need to recognize that employees (internal customers) may have useful things to say about the reality of the work they are doing, and that their insights should be built in to the change management programme.

Based on: Jones (2008);[43] Milmo (2008);[44] Stern (2008)[45]

Marketing Organization

Marketing organization provides the context in which marketing implementation takes place: companies may have no marketing departments; those that do may have functional, product-based market-centred or matrix organizational structures.

No marketing department

As we have seen this is a common situation. Small companies that cannot afford the luxury of managerial specialism, production or financially driven organizations, and companies that eschew marketing because they believe it to be nothing more than glitz, glamour and promotion are unlikely to have a marketing department. In small companies, the owner-manager may carry out some of the functions of marketing, such as developing customer relationships, providing market feedback and product development. In larger companies, which may use the traditional production, finance, personnel and sales functional division, the same task may be undertaken by those departments, especially sales (e.g. customer feedback, sales forecasting). The classic case of a company that has scorned the popular concept of marketing was the Body Shop. Despite being based on many of the essentials of marketing (e.g. a clearly differentiated product range, clear, consistent positioning and effective PR), the Body Shop refused to set up a marketing department. However, the growth of me-too brands led to the need to reappraise the role of marketing through the establishment

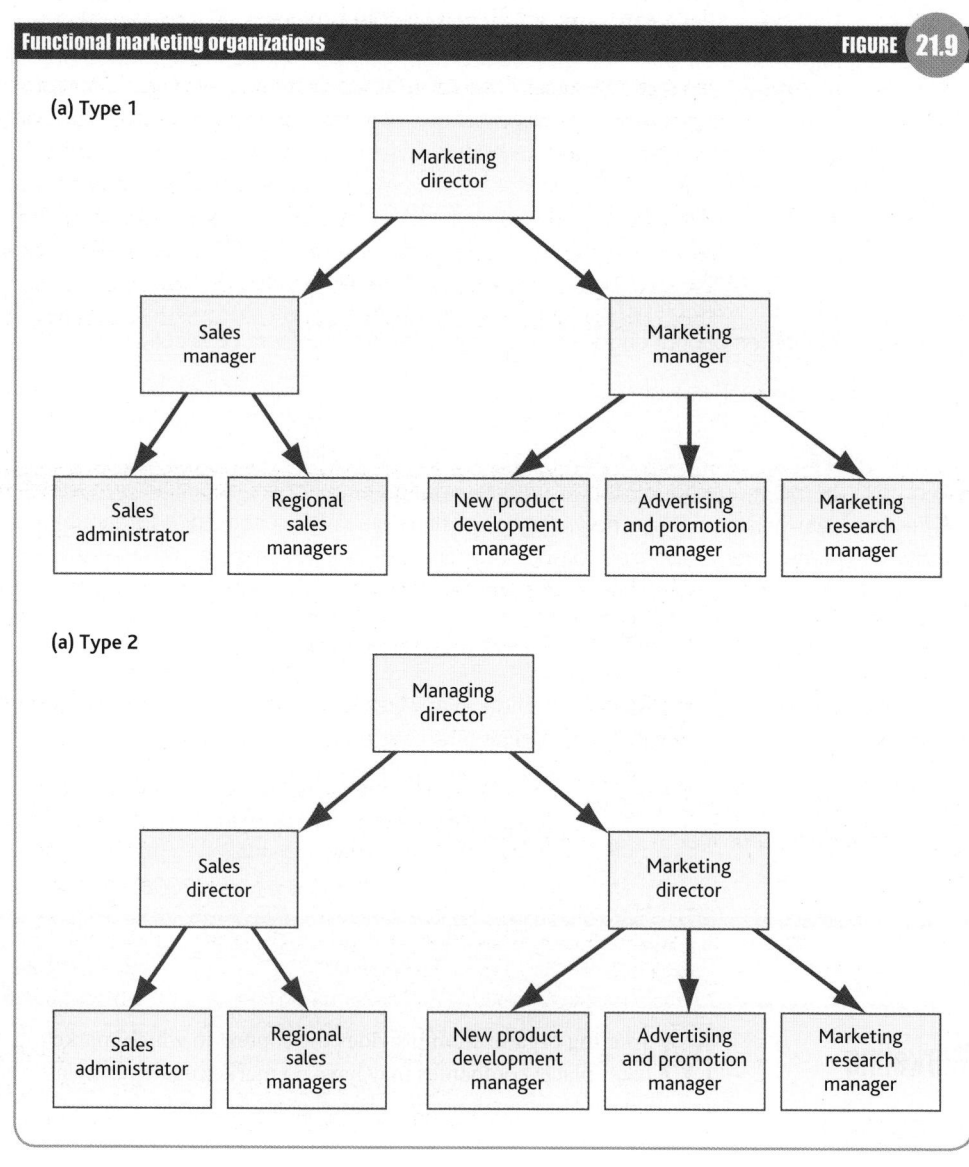

Functional marketing organizations   **FIGURE 21.9**

(a) Type 1

(a) Type 2

of a marketing department in 1994.[46] Marketing is likely to assume greater importance now that the Body Shop is owned by L'Oréal.[47]

It should be noted that not all companies that do not have a marketing department are poor at marketing; nor does the existence of a marketing department guarantee marketing orientation. As we have seen, many marketing departments carry out only a selected range of marketing functions and lack the power to influence key customer-impinging decisions or to drive through a marketing-orientated philosophy within the business. Marketing should be seen as a company-wide phenomenon, not something that should be delegated exclusively to the marketing department.

Functional organization

As small companies grow, the most likely emergence of a formal marketing structure is as a section within the sales department. As the importance of marketing is realized and the company grows, the status of marketing may rise with the appointment of a marketing manager on equivalent status with the sales manager who reports to a marketing director (see Fig. 21.9a). If the marketing director title is held by the previous sales director, little may change in terms of company philosophy: marketing may subsume a sales support role. This is the case in many companies where a more appropriate name for the person given the title 'marketing manager' would be 'communications manager'. An alternative route is to set up a *functional structure* under a sales director and a marketing director (see Fig. 21.9b). Both have equal status and the priorities of each job may lead to conflict[48] (see Table 21.1). A study of Fazer, a Finnish confectionery firm, showed that these conflicts can be heightened by the different backgrounds of marketing people who had business training and salespeople who relied more on personal experience and skills.[49] The preferred solution, then, is to appoint a marketing director who understands and has the power to implement marketing strategies that recognize sales as one (usually a key) element of the marketing mix.

Potential areas of conflict between marketing and sales		TABLE 21.1
Area	**Sales**	**Marketing**
Objectives	Short-term sales	Long-term brand/market building
Focus	Distributors/retail trade	Consumers
Marketing research	Personal experience with customers/trade	Market research reports
Pricing	Low prices to maximize sales volume. Discount structure in the hands of the salesforce	Price set consistent with positioning strategy. Discount structure built in to the marketing implementation plan
Marketing expenditure	Maximize resources channelled to the salesforce	Develop a balanced marketing mix using a variety of communication tools
Promotion	Sales literature, free customer give-aways, samples, business entertainment, sales promotions	Design a well-blended promotional mix including advertising, promotion and public relations

Product-based organization
FIGURE **21.10**

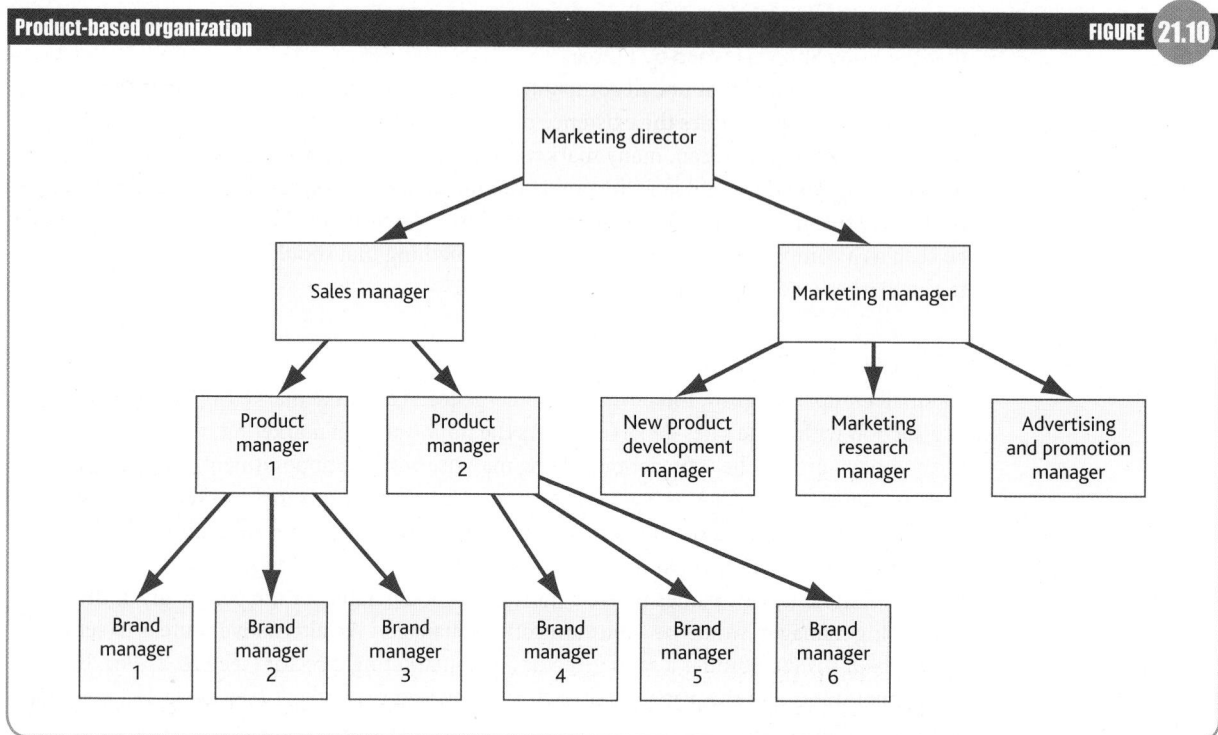

Functionalisms bring the benefit of specialization of task and a clear definition of responsibilities, and is still the most common form of marketing organization.[50] However, as the product range widens and the number of markets served increases, the structure may become unwieldy with insufficient attention being paid to specific products and markets since no one has full responsibility for a particular product or market.

Product-based organization

The need to give sufficient care and attention to individual products has led many companies (particularly in the fast-moving consumer goods field) to move to a product-based structure. For example, Nestlé has moved from a functional to a product management system. A common structure is for a product manager to oversee a group of brands within a product field (e.g. lagers, shampoos) supported by brand managers who manage specific brands (see Fig. 21.10). Their role is to coordinate the business management of their brands. This involves dealing with advertising, promotion and marketing research agencies, and function areas within the firm. Their dilemma stems from the fact that they have responsibility for the commercial success of their brands without the power to force through their decisions as they have no authority over other functional areas such as sales, production and R&D. They act as ambassadors for their brands, attempting to ensure adequate support from the salesforce, and sufficient marketing funds to communicate to customers and the trade through advertising and promotion.

The advantages of a *product-based organization* are that adequate attention is given to developing a coordinated marketing mix for each brand, and assigning specific responsibility means that speed of response to market or technological developments is quicker than relying on a committee of functional specialists. A by-product of the system is that it provides excellent training for young businesspeople as they are required to come into contact with a wide range of business activities.

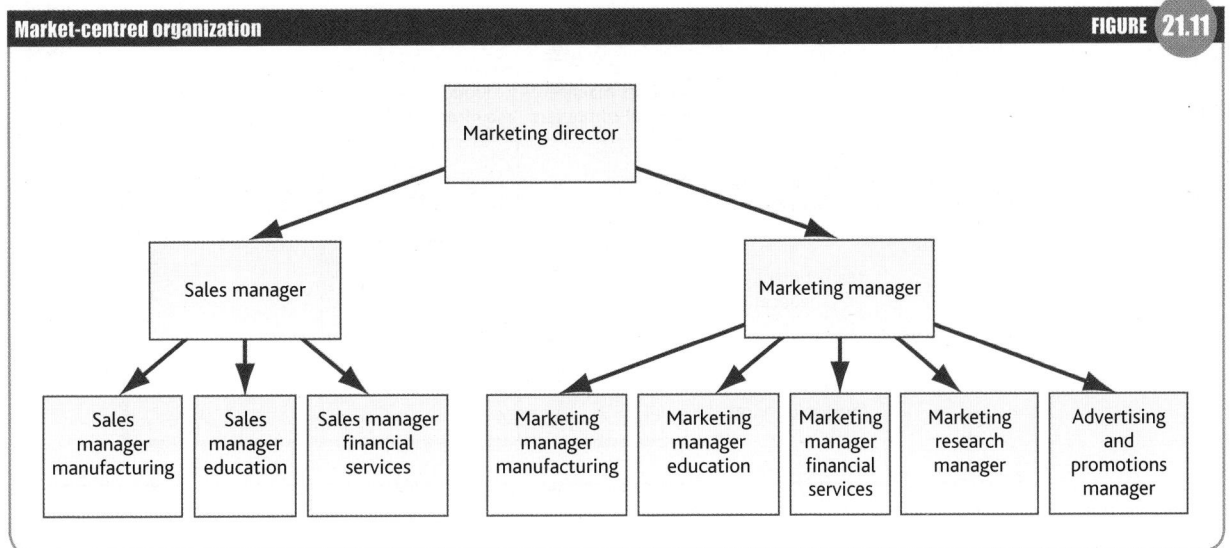

Market-centred organization   FIGURE 21.11

However, there are a number of drawbacks. First, the healthy rivalry between product managers can sometimes spill over into counter-productive competition and conflict. Second, the system can breed new layers of management, which can be costly. For example, brand managers might be supplemented by assistants and as brands are added so new brand managers need to be recruited. Big strides have been taken to reduce inefficiency with brand managers being asked to handle multiple brands.

Also, companies such as Procter & Gamble and Unilever are eliminating layers of management in the face of increasing demands from supermarkets to trim prices (and thus increase efficiency). Procter & Gamble, for example, has eliminated the title of assistant brand manager. Third, brand managers are often criticized for spending too much time coordinating in-company activities and too little time talking to customers. In response to these problems some companies are introducing **category management** to provide a focus on a category of brands. Category management is the management of brands in a group, portfolio or category with specific emphasis on the retail trade's requirements. Suppliers such as Unilever, Heinz and L'Oréal have moved to category management to provide greater clarity in strategy across brands in an age where retailers themselves are managing brands as categories. Usually, a retailer will appoint a leading supplier as 'category captain' who makes recommendations for the category as a whole. If the merchandising, stocking, pricing and promotional proposal make sense, the retailer accepts and implements the plan. If not, the retailer may consult other suppliers within the category before asking the category captain to present a new plan.[51]

Market-centred organization

Where companies sell their products to diverse markets, *market-centred organizations* should be considered. Instead of managers focusing on brands, *market managers* concentrate their energies on understanding and satisfying the needs of particular markets. The salesforce, too, may be similarly focused. For example, Figure 21.11 shows a market-centred organization for a hypothetical computer manufacturer. The specialist needs and computer applications in manufacturing, education and financial services justify a sales and marketing organization based on these market segments.

Occasionally, hybrid product/market-centred organizations based on distribution channels are appropriate. For example, at Philips, old organizational structures based on brands or

Matrix organization   FIGURE 21.12

	Product manager personal computers	Product manager mainframe computers	Product manager printers
Market manager manufacturing			
Market manager education			
Market manager financial services			

products have been downgraded, replacing them with a new focus on distribution channels. Product managers who ensure that product designs fit market requirements still exist. However, under a new combined sales and marketing director the emphasis has moved to markets. Previously, different salespeople would visit retailers selling different products from the Philips range. This has been replaced by dedicated sales teams concentrating on channels such as the multiples, the independents and mail order.[52]

The enormous influence of the trade in many consumer markets has forced other firms, besides Philips, to rethink their marketing organization. This has led to the establishment of **trade marketing** teams, which serve the needs of large retailers.

The advantage of the market-centred approach is the focus it provides on the specific customer requirements of new opportunities, and developing new products that meet their customer needs. By organizing around customers, it embodies the essence of the marketing concept. However, for companies competing in many sectors it can be resource-hungry.

Matrix organization

For companies with a wide product range selling in diverse markets, a *matrix structure* may be necessary. Both product and market managers are employed to give due attention to both facets of marketing activity. The organizational structure resembles a grid, as shown in Figure 21.12, again using a hypothetical computer company. Product managers are responsible for their group of products' sales and profit performance, and monitor technological developments that impact on their products. Market managers focus on the needs of customers in each market segment.

For the system to work effectively, clear lines of decision-making authority need to be drawn up because of the possible areas of conflict. For example, who decides the price of the product? If a market manager requires an addition to the product line to meet the special needs of some customers, who has the authority to decide if the extra costs are justified? How should the salesforce be organized: along product or market lines? Also, it is a resource-hungry method of organization. Nevertheless, the dual specialism does promote the careful analysis of both product and markets so that customer needs are met.

Marketing organization and implementation are inevitably intertwined as the former affects the day-to-day activities of marketing managers. It is important that we understand the organizational world as marketing managers have come to understand it, in particular the activities that constitute their job.[53] Marketing in Action 21.3 describes what marketing managers actually do with their time and how organizational change affects activities.

21.3 Marketing in Action

What Marketing Managers Really Do

Marketing managers fully recognize their crucial role in planning for the future but the realities of the job often mean that the short-term pressures of dealing with administrative tasks leave little time for strategic planning. One survey of 50 brand and marketing managers found that short-term business accounted for 83 per cent of their day, broken down as follows:

- 29 per cent on marketing operations or 'maintenance'
- 23 per cent working with other functions
- 11 per cent preparing and giving presentations
- 8 per cent on administration
- 6 per cent travelling
- 6 per cent training.

This left only 17 per cent of the day available for 'future marketing'.

Organizational structures can influence how much time is spent on various tasks. Virgin, for example, has flattened structures, which gives individuals more responsibility. As a result there are fewer meetings. One executive reported that he had only three meetings a month: one for manufacturing where all the divisions meet, one for marketing (if needed) and one for sales. Since there were few layers of middle management, work was invigorating because 'you spend your time doing what you are meant to be doing'. This contrasted with his experience in an advertising agency where much wasted effort was spent presenting the same information to different groups of colleagues, clients and their colleagues. When the process of preparing contact reports, monthly updates and three-monthly reviews was added, the time left over for strategic thinking was minimal.

One area of the marketing mix where marketing has less influence than it should is pricing. In a survey of marketing directors only 39 per cent said they had a high influence on price. Since price is the revenue-earning element of the marketing mix it is quite disturbing to find that marketing does not play a more prominent role in many companies.

One thing that senior marketing managers do not do is sit on boards. A survey of the top 100 UK companies found that only 14 have main board-level marketers. One reason for this may be that other managers believe that marketing is about communications rather than strategy. Another factor may be the behaviour of senior marketing managers themselves, which is to move organizations regularly, changing jobs on average every 22 months. Their loyalty seems to be more to their profession than their organization—and they tend to move to bigger marketing jobs in terms of size of budget and team, rather than becoming chief executives.

Based on: Leggett (1996);[54] Murphy (2002);[55] Simms (2008)[56]

Marketing Control

Marketing control is an essential element of the marketing planning process because it provides a review of how well marketing objectives have been achieved. A framework for controlling marketing activities is given in Figure 21.13. The process begins by deciding marketing objectives, leading to the setting of performance standards. For example, a marketing objective of 'widening the customer base' might lead to

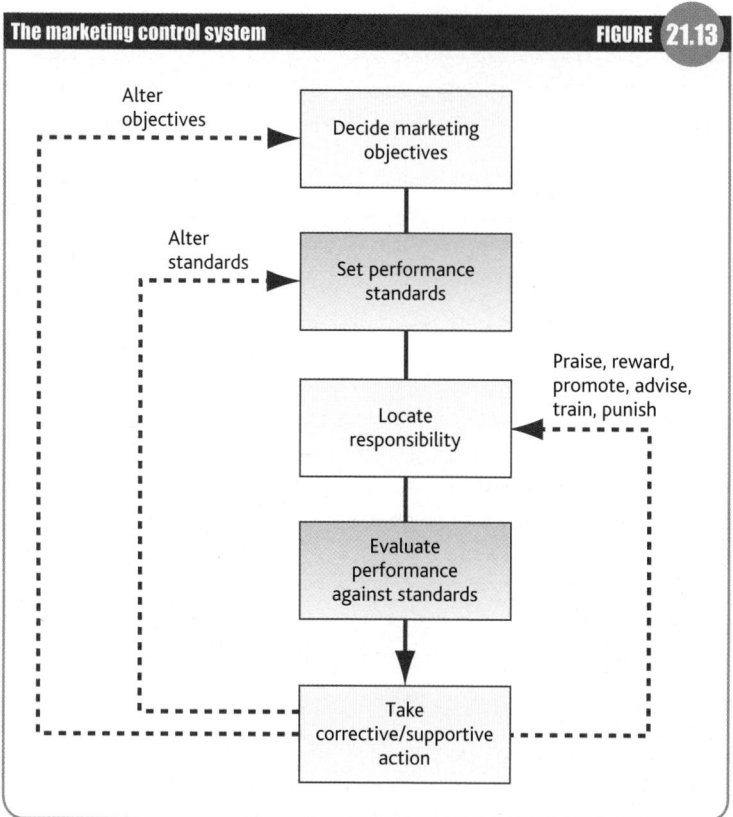

FIGURE 21.13 The marketing control system

the setting of the performance standard of 'generating 20 new accounts within 12 months'. Similarly the marketing objective of 'improving market share' might translate into a performance standard of 'improving market share from 20 per cent to 25 per cent'. Some companies set quantitative marketing objectives, in which case performance standards are automatically derived.

The next step is to locate responsibility. In some cases responsibility ultimately falls on one person (e.g. the brand manager), in others it is shared (e.g. the sales manager and salesforce). It is important to consider this issue since corrective or supportive action may need to focus on those responsible for the success of marketing activity.

Performance is then evaluated against standards, which relies on an efficient information system, and a judgement has to be made about the degree of success and/or failure achieved, and what corrective or supportive action is to be taken. This can take various forms.

- First, failure that is attributed to poor performance of individuals may result in the giving of advice regarding future attitudes and actions, training and/or punishment (e.g. criticism, lower pay, demotion, termination of employment). Success, on the other hand, should be rewarded through praise, promotion and/or higher pay.
- Second, failure that is attributed to unrealistic marketing objectives and performance standards may cause them to be lowered for the subsequent period. Success that is thought to reflect unambitious objectives and standards may cause them to be raised next period.
- Third, the attainment of marketing objectives and standards may also mean modification next period. For example, if the marketing objective and performance standard of opening 20 new accounts is achieved, this may mean the focus for the next period may change. The next objective may focus on customer retention, for instance.
- Finally, the failure of one achieved objective to bring about another may also require corrective action. For example, if a marketing objective of increasing calls to new accounts does not result in extra sales, the original objective may be dropped in favour of another (e.g. improving product awareness through advertising).

Strategic Control

Two types of control system may be used. The first concerns major strategic issues and answers the question 'Are we doing the right thing?' It focuses on company strengths, weaknesses, opportunities and threats, and the process of control is through a marketing audit. This was discussed in depth in Chapter 2 under the heading 'The process of marketing planning' and will not be elaborated upon here.

Operational Control and the Use of Marketing Metrics

The second control system concerns tactical ongoing marketing activities, and is called operational control. An array of measures (often referred to as **marketing metrics**) are available to marketing managers who wish to measure the effectiveness of their activities.[57] However, it is often difficult to determine the exact contribution of marketing efforts because outcomes are usually dependent on several factors. For example, higher sales may be caused by increased (or better) advertising, a more motivated salesforce, weaker competition, more favourable economic conditions, and so on. This makes it difficult to justify, for example, increased advertising expenditure, because it is hard to quantify the past effects of advertising. This contrasts starkly with production, where the effects of the introduction of a new machine can be calculated by measuring output; or finance, where a cost-cutting programme's effect on costs is easily calculated.

Despite these problems, there are now demands on marketing to become accountable for its activities. In order to be accountable, marketing managers are using *marketing metrics*, which are quantitative measures of the outcomes of marketing activities and expenditures. No longer can marketing executives attend budget meetings expecting to spend more money on advertising, promotion, direct marketing and other marketing activities without quantitative justification of these expenditures. The new mantra is **marketing accountability**: the requirement to justify marketing investment by using marketing metrics. Without such justification it is hardly surprising that marketing budgets are often the first to be cut in an economic downturn.

A research study has identified the kinds of marketing metrics being employed by companies, and the 10 most used metrics are shown in Table 21.2, together with an importance measure.[58] Although discussed under operational issues, the information can also usefully be fed into the marketing audit for strategic purposes.

The use of marketing metrics in UK firms		TABLE 21.2	
Rank	Metric	% using measure	% rating it as important
1	Profit/profitability	92	80
2	Sales: value and/or volume	91	71
3	Gross margin	81	66
4	Awareness	78	28
5	Market share (value/volume)	78	37
6	Number of new products	73	18
7	Relative price	70	36
8	Customer dissatisfaction	69	45
9	Customer satisfaction	68	48
10	Distribution/availability	66	18

Source: Ambler, T., F. Kokkinaki and S. Puntoni (2004) Assessing Marketing Reasons for Metric Selection, *Journal of Marketing Management* 20, 475–98.

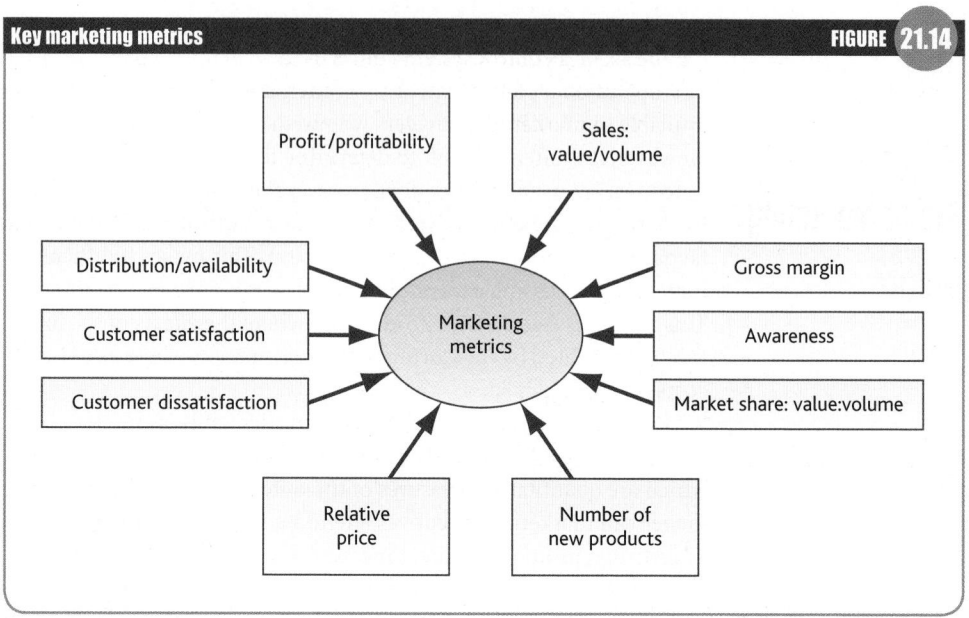

Key marketing metrics   **FIGURE 21.14**

Since profit is the financial objective of most organizations it is unsurprising that it is the most used metric. Similarly, profitability, which measures the profit return on investments such as products or advertising campaigns, is a popular metric since it relates to the financial objectives of companies. It is usually measured as return on investment (ROI) and, increasingly, marketers are attempting to measure return on marketing investment, although, as discussed earlier, accounting for marketing contribution to a sales (and hence profit) increase is sometimes difficult. What is required is a baseline figure (i.e. what would have happened without the marketing expenditure). Apart from direct marketing, where experiments can be conducted to test effects, such baseline figures can be difficult to establish. Also ROI is usually measured over a short time period (e.g. a year) and so such calculations can underestimate the full effects of marketing investments, which, through brand building, often have positive long-term effects.[59]

For operational control, **profitability analysis** can provide useful information on the profit performance of key aspects of marketing, such as products, customers or distribution channels. The example given focuses on products. The hypothetical company sells three types of product: paper products, printers and copiers. The first step is to measure marketing inputs to each of these products. These are shown in Table 21.3. Allocation of sales calls to products is facilitated by separate sales teams for each group.

The text between the figure and the final paragraphs:

Each of these metrics—as shown in Figure 21.14—will now be assessed, and specific measures identified, together with their calculation.

Profit/profitability

Typical metrics	Calculation
Profit	Profit = total revenue − total costs
Return on investment (ROI)	$\text{ROI} = \dfrac{\text{net profit}}{\text{investment}}$

Allocating functional costs to products			TABLE 21.3
Products	Salesforce (number of sales calls per year)	Advertising (number of one-page ads placed)	Order processing (number of orders placed)
Paper products	500	20	1000
Printers	400	20	800
Copiers	250	10	200
Total	1150	50	2000
Total cost	£190,000	£130,000	£80,000
Functional cost per unit	£165 per call	£2600 per ad	£40 per order

Profitability statement for products (£)			TABLE 21.4
	Paper products	Printers	Copiers
Sales	1,000,000	700,000	300,000
Cost of goods sold	500,000	250,000	250,000
Gross margin	500,000	450,000	50,000
Marketing costs			
Salesforce (at £165 per call)	82,500	66,000	41,250
Advertising (at £2600 per advertisement)	52,000	52,000	26,000
Order processing (at £40 per order)	40,000	32,000	8,000
Total cost	174,500	150,000	72,250
Net profit (or loss) before tax	325,500	300,000	(25,250)

If the sales teams were organized on purely geographic lines, an estimate of how much time was devoted to each product, on average, at each call would need to be made. Table 21.3 shows how the costs of an average sales call, advertising insertion and order are calculated. This provides vital information to calculate profitability for each product.

Table 21.4 shows how the net profit before tax is calculated. The results show how copiers are losing money. Before deciding to drop this line the company would have to take into account the extent to which customers expect copiers to be sold alongside paper products and printers, the effect on paper sales of dropping copiers, the possible annoyance caused to customers that already own one of its copiers, the extent to which copiers cover overheads that otherwise would need to be paid for from paper products and printer sales, the scope for pruning costs and increasing sales, and the degree to which the arbitrary nature of some of the cost allocations has unfairly treated copier products.

Sales

Typical metrics*	Calculation
Sales revenue	Sales revenue = unit sales × price
Sales volume	Sales volume = unit sales
Sales revenue against target	Variance = sales revenue − target sales revenue
More sales metrics are given in Chapter 14, Personal Selling and Sales Management.	

Processing sales revenue and sales volume is easy and the metrics are important determinants of marketing investments. Sales increases are normally sought to justify higher marketing expenditures, but without corresponding profit metrics can be misleading. This is because sales can be bought with excessive discounting, leading to higher sales but lower profit. For this reason, rewarding salesforces' for higher sales without also measuring profits can be harmful.

Despite these dangers, **sales analysis** of actual against target sales revenue can be useful for operational control. Negative variance may be due to lower sales volume or lower prices. Product, customer and regional analysis will be carried out to discover where the shortfall arose. A change in the product mix could account for a sales fall, with more lower-priced products being sold. The loss of a major customer may also account for a sales decline. Regional analysis may identify a poorly performing area sales manager or salesperson. These findings would point the direction of further investigations to uncover the reasons for such outcomes.

Gross margin

Typical metrics	Calculation
Gross margin per unit (GMU)	GMU = price − cost of goods sold (material plus labour)
Gross margin percentage (GMP)	$GMP = \dfrac{GMU \times 100}{price}$

The third most popular metric is gross margin. Different industries can achieve widely varying gross margins. For example, high-volume, low-price supermarkets achieve low single-digit margins, while traditional jewellers typically require and achieve 50 per cent or more gross margins because their business is lower volume. Calculated as a percentage, gross margin is an indication of the percentage of the selling price that is a contribution to profit. It is not necessarily actual profit, as other expenses such as sales, marketing, distribution and administrative costs have not been deducted. A problem with using gross margin as a marketing metric is that it can be misleading if these other expenses are high. The answer is to calculate unit margin, where all costs are included.

Awareness

Typical metrics	Calculation
Recall	Survey respondents are asked to name all the brands in a product category that they can think of
Recognition	Survey respondents are shown a list of brands and asked to name those that they have heard of

Awareness is an important metric because it measures whether a marketing communications campaign is entering target consumers' minds. Awareness measures before and after a campaign are particularly useful. However, awareness does not necessarily raise purchase levels if the brand is not liked. It is therefore best used alongside other communications-orientated metrics such as measures of beliefs, liking, willingness to recommend, and purchase intention.

Market share

Typical metrics	Calculation
Market share (value)	$\text{Market share (value)} = \dfrac{\text{sales revenue}}{\text{total market revenue}}$
Market share (unit)	$\text{Market share (unit)} = \dfrac{\text{unit sales}}{\text{total market unit sales}}$
Relative market share	$\text{Relative market share} = \dfrac{\text{brand's market share}}{\text{largest competitor's share}}$

Market share analysis evaluates a company's performance in comparison to that of its competitors. Sales analysis may show a healthy increase in revenues but this may be due to market growth rather than an improved performance over competitors. An accompanying decline in market share would sound warning bells regarding relative performance. This would stimulate further investigation to root out the causes.

It should be recognized that a market share decline is not always a symptom of poor performance. This is why outcomes should always be compared to marketing objectives and performance standards. If the marketing objective was to harvest a product, leading to a performance standard of a 5 per cent increase in profits, its achievement may be accompanied by a market share decline (through the effect of a price rise). This would be a perfectly satisfactory outcome given the desired objective. Conversely, a market share gain may not signal improved performance if it was brought about by price reductions that reduced profits.

The relative market share metric (%) was used when calculating a brand's position on the Boston Consulting Group matrix (see Chapter 10, Managing Products: Product Life Cycle, Portfolio Planning and Product Growth Strategies). When a brand is a market leader, relative market share has a value greater than one.

Number of new products

Typical metrics	Calculation
Number of new products	Number of new products launched per year
Number of successful new products	Number of new products achieving objectives
Proportion of sales attributable to new products (PSANP)	$\text{PSANP} = \dfrac{\text{sales revenue of products on the market for less than } n \text{ years}}{\text{total sales revenue}}$

Because the lifeblood of companies is successful innovation, it is not surprising that an important marketing metric is the number of new products. However, simply counting the number of new products launched per year does not take into account their success rate. Two other metrics can be used to indicate success: the number (and proportion) of successful launches, where success is recognized when objectives are achieved, can be measured; also the proportion of sales revenue (and profits) attributable to new products within a given time period can be used. For example, 3M measures the proportion of sales attributable to new products launched within six years as a check on their innovative capability.

Care needs to be taken when defining what is a new product. As we saw in Chapter 11, Developing New Products, there are many categories of new product, stretching from brand extensions to radical innovation (new-to-the-world products). Therefore it can be sensible to categorize each of the metrics according to type of new product.

Relative price

Typical metrics	Calculation
Ratio of brand A's price to the average price charged in the product category (RPAP)	$RPAP = \dfrac{\text{brand A's price}}{\text{average price in the product category}}$
Ratio of brand A's price to the price of its main competitor (RPPM)	$RPPM = \dfrac{\text{brand A's price}}{\text{price of its main competitor}}$

The relative price metric indicates the extent to which a brand is operating at a price premium or discount in a product category. A benchmark is required, which is usually the average price charged, the price of the brand's main competitor or the market leader. If brand A was priced at £4 and the average price charged was £3, the RPAP would be 1.33, demonstrating that the brand was charging a price premium (over the market average) of 33 per cent. If this metric was supported by market leadership (indicated by using a market share metric), this would suggest a strong differential advantage for the brand: not only does the brand outsell its rivals but it does so with a higher price. Therefore, when used with other metrics, relative price measures can be indicative of the strength of a brand (brand equity).

Customer dissatisfaction

Typical metrics	Calculation
Number of customer complaints	Number of complaints per period
Number of lost customers	Number of lost customers per period
Proportion of lost customers (PLC)	$PLC = \dfrac{\text{number of lost customers per period}}{\text{total number of customers at the start of the period}}$

Companies measure customer dissatisfaction because it is associated with losing customers. Companies monitor customer complaints to assess weaknesses in the product offering, including service levels. The outcomes of customer complaints should also be measured as research has shown that the successful resolution of a complaint can cause customers to feel more positive about the firm than before the service failure.[60] The number and proportion of lost customers are also useful metrics. These can be measured for consumer packaged goods by consumer panels and for business-to-business accounts directly from sales data.

Customer satisfaction

Typical metrics	Calculation
Satisfaction rating scales	Responses to 'Very dissatisfied' to 'Very satisfied' rating scales
Satisfaction compared to expectations	Responses to 'Worse than expected' to 'Better than expected' rating scales
Willingness to recommend	Responses to 'Would you recommend brand X to a friend or colleague?' question

An increasingly common barometer of marketing success is **customer satisfaction measurement**. This is an encouraging sign, as customer satisfaction is at the heart of the marketing concept. Although this measure does not appear directly on a company's profit and loss account, it is a fundamental condition for corporate success. The process involves the setting of customer satisfaction criteria, the design of a questionnaire to measure satisfaction on those criteria, the choice of which customers to interview, and the analysis and interpretation of results. The use of a market research agency is advised, to take advantage of its skills and unbiased viewpoint. A potential problem is that its measurement can lead to harmful behaviour on the part of the employees whose performance is being measured. For example, in one company salespeople gave price concessions to customers simply to build up goodwill that they hoped would improve their scores on a customer satisfaction questionnaire.[61]

One business-to-business marketing research agency advocates interviewing three customer groups to give a valid picture of customer satisfaction and marketing effectiveness:

1   10 current customers
2   10 lapsed customers (who bought from us in the past but do not now)
3   10 non-customers (who are in the market for the product but hitherto have not bought from us).

Invaluable information can be gained concerning customer satisfaction, how effective the salesforce is, why customers have switched to other suppliers, and why some potential customers have never done business with our company.

A powerful question to ask customers is 'Would you recommend brand X to a friend or colleague?' It provides insight into the strength of customer relationships and, therefore, likely future performance. Research by Reichheld into 14 companies in six industries in the USA showed that the answers to this question provided the first or second best predictor of future customer behaviour in 11 out of 14 tests.[62] Responses are given on a scale of 1 to 10, with 9s and 10s being defined as promoters, and 6s and below as detractors. The difference between the two gives the Net Promoter Score (NPS). A major benefit of this is its simplicity, but it has been criticized because a given NPS score can arise from very different sets of responses. For example, an NPS of 40 may arise from 70 per cent promoters and 30 per cent detractors, or one of 40 per cent promoters and zero detractors. Also the method does not allow measurement of satisfaction of particular aspects of the product offering such as product performance, service quality and salesperson satisfaction. In practice, the question is normally followed by the open-ended 'why' question, to tease out these elements. It also tends to be used alongside the normal customer satisfaction rating scales, rather than as a replacement for them.[63]

21.2 Pause for Thought

Does it seem credible to you that a single question can predict future customer behaviour? Think of a brand that you are likely to purchase in the future. Would you answer 'Yes' to the question 'Would you recommend [brand name] to a friend or colleague?'

Distribution/availability

Typical metrics	Calculation
Availability ratio (AR)	$AR = \dfrac{\text{number of outlets stocking brand A}}{\text{total number of outlets}}$
Out of stock ratio (OSR)	$OSR = \dfrac{\text{number of outlets where brand A is listed but unavailable}}{\text{total number of outlets where brand A is listed}}$

The availability of a brand in distribution outlets is an important marketing metric because, if an outlet is out of stock, a consumer may be unwilling to visit another shop, preferring the convenience of buying a rival brand instead. Two important metrics are the availability ratio, which measures the proportion of outlets stocking the brand, and the out-of-stock ratio, which measures the proportion of outlets that normally stock the brand but are out of stock at a particular point in time. Poor scores on these ratios mean that the causes need to be identified and remedial action taken.

Other important metrics appear throughout this book, in the relevant chapters. For example, a brand equity metric is explained in Chapter 9, Managing Products: Brand and Corporate Identity Management; opportunity-to-see metrics are discussed in Chapter 13, Advertising; salesforce effectiveness metrics are outlined in Chapter 14, Personal Selling and Sales Management; and the lifetime value of a customer metric is discussed in Chapter 15, Direct Marketing. Further discussion of this important topic can be found on the website that accompanies this book, under the title 'Marketing Accountability and Metrics'.

In practice, marketing managers need to decide on the set of metrics that are relevant to their business, and seek ways of gathering them, which may mean employing a marketing research agency.

When you have read this chapter

log on to the Online Learning Centre at www.mcgraw-hill.co.uk/textbooks/jobber to explore chapter-by-chapter test questions, links and further online study tools for marketing.

Review

1 **The relationship between marketing strategy, implementation and performance**
- Strategy, no matter how well conceived, will fail if people are incapable of carrying out the necessary tasks (implementation) to make the strategy work in the marketplace.
- Appropriate strategy with good implementation will have the best chance of successful outcomes; appropriate strategy with bad implementation will lead to trouble, especially if the substandard implementation leads to strategy change; inappropriate strategy with good implementation may hasten failure or may lead to actions that correct strategy and therefore produce favourable outcomes; and inappropriate strategy with bad implementation will lead to failure.

2 **The stages that people pass through when they experience disruptive change**
- The stages are numbness, denial and disbelief, self-doubt and emotion, acceptance and letting go, adaptation and testing, construction and meaning, and internalization.

3 **The objectives of marketing implementation and change**
- The overall objective is the successful execution of the marketing plan.
- This may require gaining the support of key decision-makers, gaining the required resources and gaining the commitment of relevant individuals and departments.

4 **The barriers to the implementation of the marketing concept**
- The barriers are the fact that new marketing ideas often mean higher costs, the potential benefits are often unquantifiable, personal ambitions (e.g. the desire of R&D staff to work on leading-edge complex problems) may conflict with the customer's desire to have simple but reliable products, reward systems may reward short-term cost savings, sales and profitability rather than long-term customer satisfaction, and there may be a gap between what managers say (e.g. 'be customer-orientated') and what they do (e.g. cut back on marketing research funds).

5 **The forms of resistance to marketing implementation and change**
- The 10 forms of resistance are criticisms of specific details of the plan; foot-dragging; slow response to requests; unavailability; suggestions that, despite the merits of the plan, resources should be channelled elsewhere; arguments that the proposals are too ambitious; hassle and aggravation created to wear the proposers down; attempts to delay the decision; attacks on the credibility of the proposer; and pointing out the risks of the plan.

6 **How to develop effective implementation strategies**
- A change master is needed to drive through change.
- Managing the implementation process requires the setting of objectives ('would like' and 'must have'), strategy (internal marketing), execution (persuasion, negotiation, politics and tactics) and evaluation (who wins, and what can be learned).

7 **The elements of an internal marketing programme**
- An internal marketing programme mirrors the structures used to market externally such as market segmentation, targeting and the marketing mix.
- The people to whom the plan must be marketed within the organization are known as internal customers. These can be segmented into three groups: supporters, neutrals and opposers. These form distinct target markets that require different internal marketing mixes to be designed to optimize the chances of successful adoption of the plan.

8 The skills and tactics that can be used to overcome resistance to the implementation of the marketing concept and plan

- The skills are persuasion (the needs, motivations and problems of internal customers need to be understood before appealing messages can be developed), negotiation (concession and proposal analysis) and political skills (the understanding of the sources of power, and the use of overt and covert power plays).
- The tactics are persuasion (articulating a shared vision, communicating and training, eliminating misconceptions, selling the benefits, gaining acceptance by association, leaving room for local control over details, supporting words with action, and establishing two-way communication); politics (building coalitions, displaying support, inviting the opposition in to share the rewards, warning the opposition of the consequences of opposition, the use of appropriate language, controlling the decision-making process and the use of the either/or alternative (either accept or I tender my resignation); timing (incremental steps, persistence, leaving insufficient time for alternatives, and waiting for the opposition to leave); and negotiation (starting high and trading concessions).

9 Marketing organizational structures

- The options are no marketing department, functional, product-based, market-centred or matrix organizational structures.

10 The nature of a marketing control system

- There are two types of marketing control: strategic and operational control systems.
- Strategic control systems answer the question 'Are we doing the right things?' and are based on a marketing audit.
- Operational control systems concern tactical ongoing marketing activities. Marketing metrics are used for this purpose and to justify marketing investments. The most commonly used metrics are profit/profitability, sales (value and/or volume), gross margin, awareness, market share, number of new products, relative price, customer dissatisfaction, customer satisfaction, and distribution/availability.

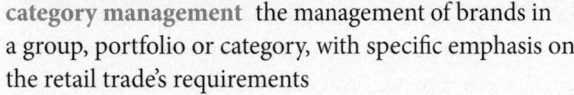

Key Terms

category management the management of brands in a group, portfolio or category, with specific emphasis on the retail trade's requirements

change master a person that develops an implementation strategy to drive through organizational change

coercive power power inherent in the ability to punish

concession analysis the evaluation of things that can be offered to someone in negotiation valued from the viewpoint of the receiver

covert power play the use of disguised forms of power tactics

customer satisfaction measurement a process through which customer satisfaction criteria are set, customers are surveyed and the results interpreted in order to establish the level of customer satisfaction with the organization's product

expert power power that derives from an individual's expertise

legitimate power power based on legitimate authority, such as line management

market share analysis a comparison of company sales with total sales of the product, including sales of competitors

marketing accountability the requirement to justify marketing investment by using marketing metrics

marketing control the stage in the marketing planning process or cycle when performance against plan is monitored so that corrective action, if necessary, can be taken

marketing metrics quantitative measures of the outcomes of marketing activities and expenditures

overt power play the use of visible, open kinds of power tactics

profitability analysis the calculation of sales revenues and costs for the purpose of calculating the profit performance of products, customers and/or distribution channels

proposal analysis the prediction and evaluation of proposals and demands likely to be made by someone with whom one is negotiating

referent power power derived by the reference source, e.g. when people identify with and respect the architect of change

reward power power derived from the ability to provide benefits

sales analysis a comparison of actual with target sales

trade marketing marketing to the retail trade

transition curve the emotional stages that people pass through when confronted with an adverse change

Study Questions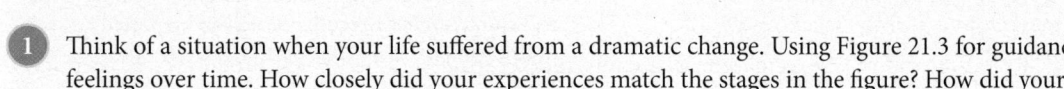

1. Think of a situation when your life suffered from a dramatic change. Using Figure 21.3 for guidance, recall your feelings over time. How closely did your experiences match the stages in the figure? How did your feelings at each stage (e.g. denial and disbelief) manifest themselves?

2. Can good implementation substitute for an inappropriate strategy? Give an example of how good implementation might make the situation worse and an example of how it might improve the situation.

3. What might be the objectives of market implementation and change? Distinguish between gaining compliance, acceptance and commitment.

4. Why do some companies fail to implement the marketing concept?

5. Describe the ways in which people may resist the change that is implied in the implementation of a new marketing plan. Why should they wish to do this?

6. What is internal marketing? To what extent does it parallel external marketing strategy?

7. Describe the skills that are necessary to see a marketing plan through to successful implementation.

8. What tactics of persuasion are at the implementer's disposal? What are the advantages and limitations of each one?

9. Without the use of political manoeuvres, most attempts at marketing implementation will fail. Discuss.

10. Discuss the options available for organizing a marketing department. How well is each form likely to serve customers?

11. Discuss the problems involved in setting up and implementing a marketing control system.

References

1. Johannessen, J.-A., J. Olaisen and A. Havan (1993) The Challenge of Innovation in a Norwegian Shipyard Facing the Russian Market, *European Journal of Marketing* 27(3), 23–38.

2. Calder, M. (2004) Customer Listening, Strategic Customer Management Conference, Warwick Business School, 10 November.

3. Hirst, C. (2008) Time for Less Talk, More Action, *Marketing Week*, 7 June, 23.

4. Bonoma, T. V. (1985) *The Marketing Edge: Making Strategies Work*, New York: Free Press.

5. Mazur, L. (2002) No Pain, No Gain, *Marketing Business*, September, 10–13.

6. Caulkin, S. (2005) Doing the Right Thing for a Change, *Observer*, 16 October, 12.

7. Wilson, G. (1993) *Making Change Happen*, London: Pitman.

8. Abopdaher, D. (1986) *A Biography of Iacocca*, London: Star.

9. Stanton, W. J., R. H. Buskirk and R. Spiro (2002) *Management of a Sales Force*, Boston, Mass: Irwin.

10. Webster, F. E. Jr (1988) Rediscovering the Marketing Concept, *Business Horizons* 31 (May–June), 29–39.

11. Webster (1988) op. cit.

12. Argyris, C. (1966) Interpersonal Barriers to Decision Making, *Harvard Business Review* 44 (March–April), 84–97.

13. Crane, A. (2005) Meeting the Ethical Gaze: Challenges for Orienting to the Ethical Market, in Harrison, R., T. Newholm and D. Shaw (eds) *The Ethical Consumer*, London: Sage, 219–32.

14. Balch, O. (2009) How GSK's Access to Medicine Plans Will Shake Up Big Pharma, Ethical Corporation, 31 March (retrieved 1 April 2009, from http://www.ethicalcorp.com/content.asp?contentid=6408).

15. Pearce, F. (2009) Greenwash: Calling HSBC to Account Over Green Banking Claims, *Guardian Unlimited*, 12 February (retrieved 24 March 2009, from www.guardian.co.uk/environment/2009/feb/12/greenwash-banking-hsbc).

16. Reed, J. and D. Schäfer (2008) BMW's Accelerator of Change, *Financial Times*, 6 October, 18.

17. Kanter, R. M. (1997) *The Change Masters*, London: Allen & Unwin.

18. Piercy, N. (2008) *Marketing-Led Strategic Change*, Oxford: Butterworth-Heinemann.

19. Johnson, G. (1987) *Strategic Change and the Management Process*, Oxford: Basil Blackwell.

20. Pettigrew, A. M. (1974) The Influence Process between Specialists and Executives, *Personnel Review* 3(1), 24–30.

21. Ansoff, I. and E. McDonnell (1990) *Implanting Strategic Management*, Englewood Cliffs, NJ: Prentice-Hall.

22. Pettigrew, A. M. (1974) op. cit.

23. Pettigrew, A. M. (1985) *The Awakening Giant: Continuity and Change in ICI*, Oxford: Basil Blackwell.

24. Kanter (1997) op. cit.

25. London, S. and A. Hill (2002) A Recovery Strategy Worth Copying, *Financial Times*, 16 October, 12.

26. McGregor, J. (2009) An Historic Succession at Xerox, *Business Week*, 8 June, 18–22.

27. Kennedy, G., J. Benson and J. MacMillan (1987) *Managing Negotiations*, London: Business Books.

28. Piercy, N. (1990) Making Marketing Strategies Happen in the Real World, *Marketing Business*, February, 20–1.

29. Piercy, N. and N. Morgan (1991) Internal Marketing: The Missing Half of the Marketing Programme, *Long Range Planning* 24(2), 82–93.

30. See Grönroos, C. (1985) Internal Marketing: Theory and Practice, in Bloch, T. M., G. D. Upah and V. A. Zeithaml (eds) *Services Marketing in a Changing Environment*, Chicago: American Marketing Association; Gummesson, E. (1987) Using Internal Marketing to Develop a New Culture: The Case of Ericsson Quality, *Journal of Business and Industrial Marketing* 2(3), 23–8; Mudie, P. (1987) Internal Marketing: Cause of Concern, *Quarterly Review of Marketing*, Spring–Summer, 21–4.

31. Research conducted by Oxford Strategic Marketing and Hunter Miller Executive Search and reported in Anonymous (2005) 100 Days, *Marketing Business*, June, 15–17.

32. Laing, A. and L. McKee (2001) Willing Volunteers or Unwilling Conscripts? Professionals and Marketing in Service Organizations, *Journal of Marketing Management* 17(5/6), 559–76.

33. Daniel, E. (2006) The World According to Google, Open2.net, January, http://www.open2.net/money/briefs_20060120information.html.

34. French, J. R. P. and B. Raven (1959) The Bases of Social Power, in Cartwright, D. (ed.) *Studies in Social Power*, Ann Arbor: University of Michigan Press, 150–67.

35. See Hickson, D. J., C. R. Hinings, C. A. Lee, R. E. Schneck and J. M. Pennings (1971) A Strategic Contingencies Theory of Intraorganizational Power, *Administrative Science Quarterly* 16(2), 216–29; Hinings, C. R., D. J. Hickson, J. M. Pennings and R. E. Schneck (1974) Structural Conditions of Intraorganizational Power, *Administrative Science Quarterly* 19(1), 22–44.

36. Wilson, D. C. (1992) *A Strategy of Change: Concepts and Controversies in the Management of Change*, London: Routledge.

37. See Kanter, R. M., B. A. Stein and T. D. Jick (1992) *The Challenge of Organizational Change*, New York: Free Press; Kanter (1988) op. cit.; Piercy (2001) op. cit.; Ansoff and McDonnell (1990) op. cit.

38. Kanter, Stein and Jick (1992) op. cit.

39. Bonoma, T. V. (1984) Making your Marketing Strategy Work, *Harvard Business Review* 62 (March–April), 68–76.

40. Kanter, Stein and Jick (1992) op. cit.

41. Wilson (1993) op. cit.

42. Kennedy, Benson and MacMillan (1984) op. cit.

43. Jones, A. (2008) Shambolic But Totally Predictable, *Guardian*, 28 March, 3.

44. Milmo, D. (2008) Passengers Fume in the Chaos of Terminal 5's First Day, *Guardian*, 28 March, 2.

45. Stern, S. (2008) Managers Who Bring About Change We Can Believe In, *Financial Times*, 10 June, 14.

46. Hewitt, M. (1994) Body Shop Opens its Doors to Marketing, *Marketing*, 26 May, 20.

47. Benady, D. (2006) Body Shop, L'Oréal Plot Food Range, *Marketing Week*, 23 March, 3.

48. Dewsnap, B. and D. Jobber (2006) A Social Psychological Study of Marketing and Sales Relationships, *University of Bradford School of Management Working Paper*.

49. Eriksson, P. and K. Räsänen (1998) The Bitter and the Sweet: Evolving Constellations of Product Mix Management in a Confectionery Company, *European Journal of Marketing* 32(3/4), 279–304.

50. Workman J. P. Jr, C. Homburg and K. Gruner (1998) Marketing Organisation: an Integrative Framework of Dimensions and Determinants, *Journal of Marketing* 62, July, 21–41.

51. For further insights into category management see D. Aaker (2009) *Brand Leadership*, New York: Free Press; and T. Ambler (2001) Category Management is Best Deployed for Brand Positioning, *Marketing*, 29 November, 18.

52. Mitchell, A. (1994) Dark Night of Marketing or a New Dawn?, *Marketing*, 17 February, 22–3.

53. Brownlie, D. and M. Saren (1997) Beyond the One-Dimensional Marketing Manager: The Discourse of Theory, Practice and Relevance, *International Journal of Research in Marketing* 14, 147–61.

54. Leggett, D. (1996) Hours Not to Reason Why, *Marketing*, 31 October, 26–7.

55. Murphy, D. (2002) Cause and Effect, *Marketing Business*, October, 22–4.

56. Simms, J. (2008) Marketing 2008—A Discipline in Crisis, *Marketing Week*, 16 January, 27.

57. Faris, P. W., N. T. Bendle, P. E. Pfeifer and D. J. Reibstein (2006) *Key Marketing Metrics*, Harlow: Pearson.

58. Ambler, T., F. Kokkinaki and S. Puntoni (2004) Assessing Marketing Performance: Reasons for Metrics Selection, *Journal of Marketing Management* 20, 475–98.

59. Ambler, T. and J. H. Roberts (2008) Assessing Marketing Performance: Don't Settle For a Silver Metric, *Journal of Marketing Management* 24, 733–50.

60. Maxham III, J. G. and R. G. Netemeyer (2002) A Longitudinal Study of Complaining Customers' Evaluations of Multiple Service Failures and Recovery Efforts, *Journal of Marketing* 66, October, 57–71.

61. Piercy, N. and N. A. Morgan (1995) Customer Satisfaction Measurement and Management: A Processual Analysis, *Journal of Marketing Management* 11, 817–34.

62. Reichheld, F. (2006) *The Ultimate Question*, Boston: Harvard Business School Press.

63. Mitchell, A. (2008) The Only Number You Need to Know Does Not Add Up To Much, *Marketing Week*, 6 March, 15–16.

Internal Marketing

Influencing the Board at Hansen Bathrooms

Hansen Bathrooms has been a producer of baths, washbasins, toilets and bidets for over 50 years. Despite being a market follower rather than leader, a technologist at the company developed a special coating that could be applied to all bathroom items (basins, toilets, washbasins and tiles). The coating contained an agent that dispersed the usual grime and grease that accumulates in baths, washbasins, and so on.

A market research study commissioned by Susan Clements, assistant to Rob Vincent, Hansen's marketing director, showed that people clean their bathroom fittings on average once every two weeks, and generally hate the task. Product trials with a prototype bathroom incorporating the new coating showed that cleaning could easily be extended to once every three months. Respondents in the test were delighted with the reduction in workload. Hansen sought and obtained a patent for the new coating. Rob decided, on Susan's advice, to recommend a premium price for the launch of a new bathroom range using the new coating. Susan argued that the new coating created extra value for consumers and should be reflected in a higher price

Accordingly Rob had recommended to the board a consumer price of £470. This was only £5 and £20 more, respectively, than the prices of the two main competitors. After the usual 25 per cent discount, the price differential would be even less. But the board remained unconvinced.

The first meeting to discuss pricing strategy for the new Hansen bathroom range featuring the new, patent-protected coating had taken place three weeks ago. No conclusion had been arrived at. Consequently, a second meeting had been arranged to thrash out a coherent strategy.

Rob decided to play it tough. At 30 he was considerably younger than the other board members, who were all in their fifties. Rob began: 'I recommended a price of £470 three weeks ago and that recommendation still stands! I hope my arguments have sunk in since our last meeting because quite honestly they are watertight. Let's go through them once again.

'One: the new coating provides tangible customer value—cleaning is extended from once every two weeks to once every three months.

'Two: marketing research has shown that the customer is delighted with this change.

'Three: our bathroom design and quality of fittings match those of the competition.

'Four: our main competitors are priced at £450 and £465. Our price premium reflects the added value that the coating provides.

'Five: the higher price feeds directly into our bottom-line profit figures.'

'Thank you, Rob,' said Karl Hansen, chairman of the board, 'We are well aware of the price impact on profit margins, but at £470 we will sell fewer units than if we enter the market at £440, which gives the consumer two incentives to buy: price and value.'

'I totally agree,' opined Jack Sunderland, the sales director. 'The foundation of this company has been built on volume. We need volume to keep our factories working.'

'But you will get volume,' interrupted Rob, 'the market wants this product. What we need to do is to cash in on a major technological improvement.'

'It certainly is that,' agreed Chris Henderson, the technical director, 'the coating has taken five years to develop and is fully protected by patent. But I thought demand fell as price increased. I tend to agree with Karl and Jack.'

'Not necessarily. In this case I feel a price premium is fully justified. The market research proves it,' continued Rob.

'Could we try out two price levels?' said John France, the finance director, 'We have strong ties with Outram Brothers, a major bathroom retailer. I'm sure Bill Outram would agree to a few trials.'

'Absolutely not!' shouted Rob, 'We must act decisively. Every week we wait is lost profit for us.'

'Yes,' said Hansen, 'but your suggestion is too risky, Rob. We need to follow our tried-and-tested approach. I propose that we launch at £440. If the public like it, we can always raise the price later. Do I have agreement?'

Later that day Rob told Susan about the outcome: 'I can't believe those old guys could reach a decision like that. They refuse to accept the facts. All they like to do is eat a hearty lunch in the executive dining room and sleep it off in the afternoon. If they went jogging like me at lunchtime they might realize that work is about more than food and drink. Do you know, Sue, the only time I've been in that dining room is when old man Hansen took me in there for a drink on my appointment.'

Questions

1. What do you think of Rob Vincent as a manager?

2. How well has he marketed his pricing proposals internally?

3. Can you suggest a better internal marketing approach?

4. Suggest six marketing metrics that Rob and Sue could find useful when evaluating the success of the new product after launch.

This case was prepared by David Jobber, Professor of Marketing, University of Bradford.

Munster Rugby

Implementing Change

Introduction

Munster Rugby is looked on by many of its sporting counterparts with envy, in terms of how it has successfully adapted to the major transitions imposed on it within the sport in the last 15 years. With the conversion of Rugby Union from amateur to professional in 1995, club rugby in Ireland was 'ruthlessly sidelined, with the professional game being concentrated on the national team and the provinces'. Suddenly there were very significant new costs imposed on these teams—in 2006 the Irish Rugby Football Union (IRFU) spent €22 million on player and management costs in Ireland. These costs would have been relatively insignificant in the days of the amateur game. When Munster Rugby branch administrator John Coleman, fondly known as 'Mr Musgrave Park', retired in October 2008 it was noted that he was leaving an organization with over 60 paid employees; when he commenced employment with Munster Rugby in 1995 there was only one other paid member in the organization!

The CEO of Munster Rugby, Garret Fitzgerald, states: 'At the start of professionalism we got pulled up into it. It wasn't as if we set up a structure, as if we knew everything that was going to happen. It happened because of the evolution in world rugby . . . For a number of years there was an awful lot of fire brigade action.'

Munster Rugby, or as it is commonly known Munster, is one of four Irish provincial sides that field professional teams representative of each of the IRFU branches. Despite the transition of its flagship team the governance structure of the Munster Rugby branch remains amateur and voluntary, and revolves firmly around representatives from the clubs. Munster Rugby competes in two competitions: the Magners League and the Heineken Cup.

The change in the late 1990s

Rugby Union's international governing body, the International Rugby Board, made the decision in August 1995 to make the game professional. There was no branch of the Union more opposed to this development than the IRFU, and it was equally ill-prepared to deal with it. A statement issued by the IRFU earlier the same year, on 16 May, illustrated this opposition: 'The IRFU

will oppose the payment of players to play the game and payment of others . . . for taking part in the game, because the game is a leisurely activity played on a voluntary basis.' However, the teams in the northern hemisphere were fast losing ground to the big three of the southern hemisphere—New Zealand, Australia and South Africa—who had already made the move to professionalism.

According to Garret Fitzgerald, there was no noticeable shift until 1997. Until that point the All-Ireland Rugby League, an inter-club league, was proving immensely popular, but now attempts were being made to marginalize it, in order to make way for a provincial side, based on a team picked from the best of these club players. Fitzgerald states: '1997 was when they really went more full-time. There was definitely a shift because the Munster Rugby team of that era was based totally on the successful club players. The shift was you were taking the good players out of what was a successful product and moving them to a higher level . . . There was competition and conflict there . . . Change for the player was made easier because they were getting paid to go to one place and not the other. There was certainly a level of conflict and debate during the early years, however that is normal as any organization develops.'

Munster Rugby's sales and marketing manager, Glyn Billinghurst, speaks of the change felt at club level: 'There is a lot of discussion about the sizes of the crowds that used to turn up for senior clubs and the AIL [All Ireland League] matches, and the clubs feel that was taken away from them by the provincial set-up. The one difference the Munster Rugby set-up has versus the other Irish provinces is that we work very closely with the clubs and schools within the region. The clubs are an integral part of our whole structure and benefited from the professional game; financially they benefited from the professional game, which has helped to fund and develop their own structure. I am not sure they see that as an equal but it is some form of compensation.'

Fitzgerald expands on Billinghurst's comments thus: 'There is no doubt that the real die-hard club people that you get today . . . feel they have been let down. There is no point in saying otherwise. They feel they have been let down by the organization. What they sometimes don't remember or realize is the organization is actually made up of their own people . . . But they feel that way . . . It's vitally important we maintain those people.'

Munster Rugby was fortunate that there were many local people involved in the change from amateurism to professionalism. There wasn't as much opposition from the clubs as there might have been if they had brought in a whole lot of outside commercial people initially. While the move from amateurism to professionalism firmly placed Munster Rugby in the business domain, it did not set about drastically altering its organizational structure to suit. Had it done this, and brought in outside businesspeople and outside players in the early days, then it would have been fighting against a tradition of 100 years, resulting in far more conflict. Instead, the people who brought it through the transition period had been in the old amateur game—many had whole families and generations involved. The players who benefited from the transition to professionalism were very dominantly those who had been competing at local club level, while the support personnel were also largely made up of people already involved in the game. One author writes regarding the Munster Rugby set-up: 'The fan factor was critical because it was so unusual in a high-profile professional sport. Everybody knew a player, or a player's brother or sister, or a player's parents. The supporters felt they had a vested interest; they were shareholders.'

The professional team has led to huge benefits at the grass-roots level, too. According to Fitzgerald, a large portion of the growth has been in the domestic game, in the amateur game, development officers and support staff. Some 30 posts known as youth development officers (YDOs) have been created, who work to develop the game through the clubs and schools. It's a form of partnership between Munster Rugby and the clubs in the locality. Fitzgerald states that, whereas people might

> **❚❚** It wasn't as if we set up a structure, as if we knew everything that was going to happen. It happened because of the evolution in world rugby. **❚❚**

think all the staff is in the professional game, there are, aside from the players, actually more staff in the domestic game. The professional game fuels everything else that happens from a money viewpoint, according to him.

The current commercial structure

Fitzgerald reiterates that, in the early years, Munster Rugby found it hard to keep pace with the changes taking place in the game: 'I'd say we were many years behind many other countries, even countries in Europe. The success pulled people up. There was an awful lot of fire-brigade action early on . . . With a very small staff you just got pulled up into it and you had to reach. The team pulled people up to a level that you were sprinting to catch up.'

After the Heineken Cup success in 2006 Munster Rugby identified the need for the role of someone to assist in developing the commercial potential of its brand, acknowledging that there were a number of things they could have done differently. Speaking on his appointment, Billinghurst stated: 'The new commercial focus will help to generate the funds to ensure continued success on the field. With the continued development of the professional game, a new commercial approach and structure will help accelerate the development of the Munster Rugby brand and maximize the potential that exists.'

Two years into the role and Billinghurst acknowledges the need for proper structures: 'Too much too soon, you have got to be really conscious of. When I came into Munster Rugby I'm sure that a number of people were wondering what's he going to do? What's he doing here? You come in and it's like what are the barriers? There's no point in changing everything. I choose to look and learn—then identify a few things and get them right. And, if it's working, just improve on it. Try and get some structure around it and develop a better way . . . What I'd say: try to do two new things well each season and improve on everything else.'

Billinghurst does not see himself having done anything drastically different; instead he sees himself looking at things a little differently, given his commercial background. He comments: 'What I look to do is I take advice off everybody and then it's about alignment. The hardest thing is implementing it.' However, in terms of getting things done in this organization, he says it is no different from any other business: 'Just like in normal business, if one was to get a project done or signed off, you gain input from people, get their advice and understand their perspectives; then structure your proposal accordingly. In most instances, working with the Munster Rugby branch is an easy process as we have the same goals at the end of the day. It is also aided by the fact that a lot of these individuals run their own businesses, so they too have a business mindset.'

Munster Rugby is implementing a new CRM system to measure fans' match-day experience, to get qualitative feedback from this key customer set. Philip Quinn, the finance manager, has key performance indicators in place already that set targets on attendances, and targets on revenue for each game. Actual figures are benched against these targets so, from a commercial perspective, the business can be reviewed through the season on a game-by-game basis. However, in contrast to such number-crunching exercises, the new CRM system is going to facilitate the gathering of 'softer' feedback. After each game, a number of people from different sections of the stadium will be e-mailed and asked questions on their experience, including with regard to their entry, the stewarding, the bar facilities, and so on. This will enable Munster Rugby to build and develop the match-day experience through the season based on feedback taken after every match.

As a consequence of a comparison of merchandise sales via the club website, against the equivalent of those for a leading UK Guinness Premiership team, Munster Rugby instigated a fundamental redesign of its own retail website (www.munsterrugbystore.com), which led to a doubling of sales via this distribution mechanism in the following 12-month period. Billinghurst takes it up: 'Having information like that is the one thing that will help you move to the next level and help yourself bench against other clubs . . . We felt we're one of the best-supported clubs, so you know you can look at the facts and say you have one of the best in terms of travelling support, but then a top English side's sales through its

website were three times ours at the time. That made us think, what is our retail website doing, so we changed our approach.'

CEO Fitzgerald concludes: 'ultimately the best marketing tool you have is what happens on the pitch . . . and then you kick on from there'.

References

Based on: Anonymous (2007) Marketing Mogul Aims to Maximise Munster Brand, *Irish Examiner*, 3 February; Anonymous (2007) Take the Money and Scrum, *Irish Independent*, 17 March; Fanning, B. (2007) *From There to Here—Irish Rugby in the Professional Era*, Gill and Macmillan Ltd, 25, 121; Urlich, D. (2008) Mr Musgrave Park Calls Time, 9 December, http://www.munsterrugby.ie/8707.php (accessed 30 April 2009); interview with CEO, 27 March 2009; interview with sales and marketing manager, 27 March 2009.

Questions

1. Within the Munster branch of the IRFU, identify the various internal customers that needed to have the benefits of professionalism marketed to them. Discuss whether each group of these internal customers would have been supporters or opposers to the change to professionalism during the late 1990s.

2. What tactics does Billinghurst use in implementing his marketing plans?

3. Evaluate the appropriateness of the operational control systems currently being planned for Munster Rugby. What other marketing metrics might be useful to the club?

This case was written by Conor Kelleher, Lecturer in Marketing, Waterford Institute of Technology, Ireland. Special thanks to Garret Fitzgerald, CEO Munster Rugby, and Glyn Billinghurst, Sales and Marketing Manager Munster Rugby.

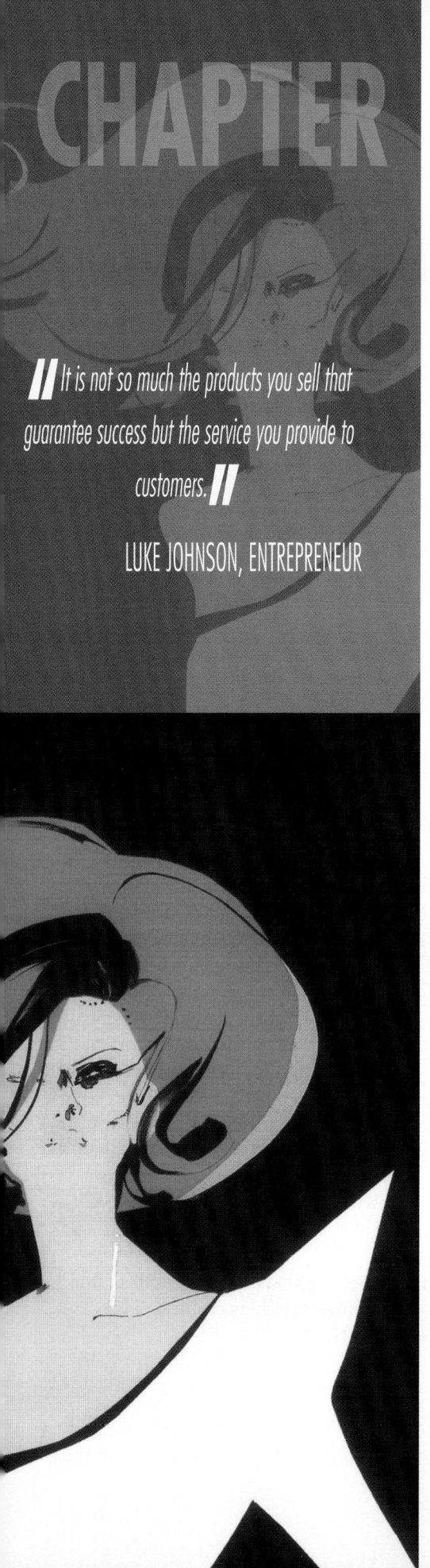

CHAPTER 22

Services marketing

It is not so much the products you sell that guarantee success but the service you provide to customers.

LUKE JOHNSON, ENTREPRENEUR

LEARNING OBJECTIVES

After reading this chapter, you should be able to:

1 describe the nature and special characteristics of services

2 explain how customer relationships should be managed

3 explain how to manage service quality, productivity and staff

4 explain how to position a service organization and brand

5 discuss the services marketing mix

6 describe the major store and non-store retailing types

7 discuss the theories of retail evolution

8 discuss the key retail marketing decisions

9 describe the nature and special characteristics of non-profit marketing

This chapter discusses the special issues concerning the marketing of services. This is not to imply that the principles of marketing covered in earlier chapters of this book do not apply to services; rather it reflects the particular characteristics of services and the importance of service firms to the economy. In most industrialized economies, expenditure on services is growing. There are a number of reasons for this.[1]

- Advances in technology have led to more sophisticated products that require more design, production and maintenance services.
- Growth per capita income has given rise to a greater percentage being spent on luxuries such as restaurant meals, overseas holidays and weekend hotel breaks, all of which are service intensive. Greater discretionary income also fuels the demand for financial services such as investment trusts and personal pensions.
- A trend towards outsourcing means that manufacturers are buying services that are outside the firm's core expertise (such as distribution, warehousing, and catering).
- Deregulation has increased the level of competition in certain service industries (e.g. telecommunications, television, airlines), resulting in expansion.

Retailing is an important element of services. Because of this, some of the special marketing considerations relevant to retailing will be covered later in this chapter. Marketing in the non-profit sector will also be discussed, with hospitals, national television companies, employment services, museums, charities, schools and universities all being service-orientated. First, we shall examine the nature of services.

The Nature of Services

Cowell states that 'what is significant about services is the relative dominance of *intangible attributes* in the make-up of the 'service product'. Services are a special kind of product. They may require special understanding and special marketing efforts.[2] Pure services do not result in ownership, although they may be linked to a physical good. For example a machine (physical good) may be sold with a one-year maintenance contract (service).

Many offerings, however, contain a combination of the tangible and intangible. For example, a marketing research study would provide a report (physical good) that represents the outcome of a number of service activities (discussions with client, designing the research strategy, interviewing respondents and analysing the results). This distinction between physical and service offerings can, therefore, best be understood as a matter of degree rather than in absolute terms. Figure 22.1 shows a physical goods–service continuum, with the position of each offering dependent upon its ratio of tangible/intangible elements. At the pure goods end of the scale is clothing, as the purchase of a skirt or socks is not normally accompanied by a service. Carpet purchases may involve an element of service if they require professional laying. Machinery purchase may involve more service elements in the form of installation and maintenance. Software design is positioned on the service side of the continuum since the value of the product is dependent on design expertise rather than the cost of the physical product (disk). Marketing research is similarly services based, as discussed earlier. Finally, psychotherapy may be regarded as a pure service since the client receives nothing tangible from the transaction.

We have already touched on one characteristic of services that distinguishes them from physical goods: intangibility. There are, in fact, four key distinguishing characteristics: intangibility, inseparability, variability and perishability (see Fig. 22.2).

Intangibility

Pure services cannot be seen, tasted, touched, or smelled before they are bought—that is, they are intangible. Rather a **service** is *a deed*, *performance* or *effort*, not an object, device or thing.[3]

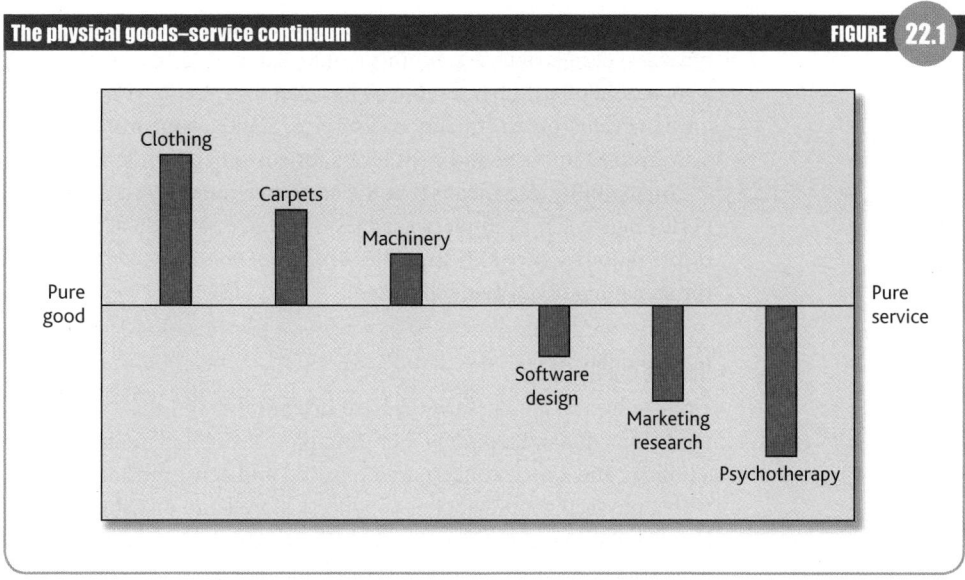

The physical goods–service continuum   FIGURE 22.1

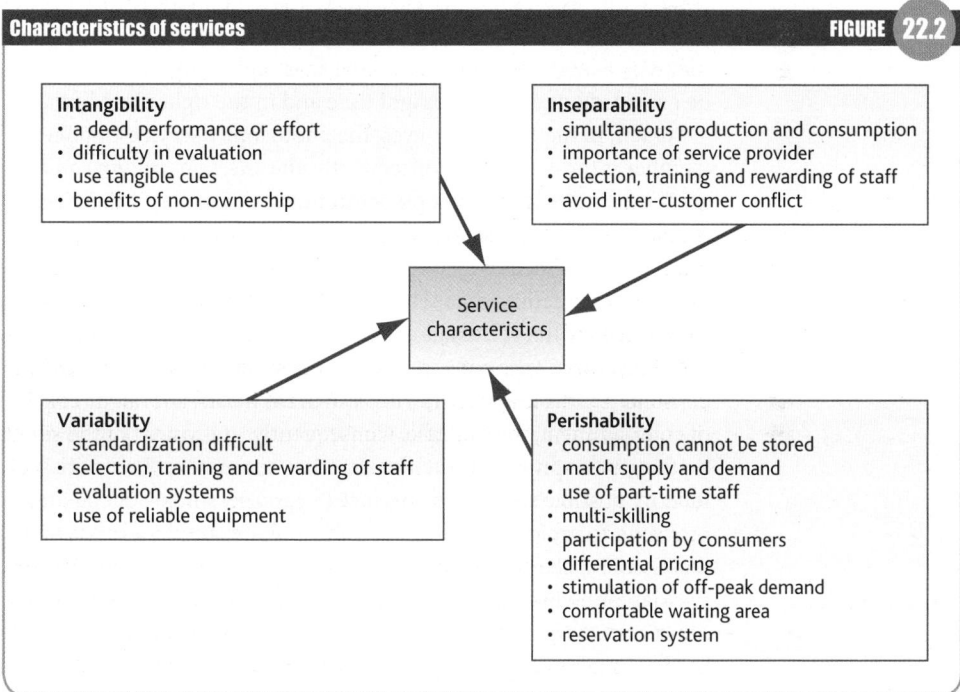

Characteristics of services   FIGURE 22.2

This may mean that a customer finds difficulty in evaluating a service before purchase. For example, it is virtually impossible to judge how enjoyable a holiday will be before taking it because the holiday cannot be shown to a customer before consumption.

For some services, their **intangibility** leads to *difficulty in evaluation* after consumption. For example, it is not easy to judge how thorough a car service has been immediately afterwards: there is no way of telling if everything that should have been checked has been checked.

The challenge for the service provider is to *use tangible cues* to service quality. For example, a holiday firm may show pictures of the holiday destination, display testimonials from satisfied holidaymakers and provide details in a brochure of the kinds of entertainment available. A garage may provide a checklist of items that are required to be carried out in a service, and an indication that they have been.

The task is to provide evidence of service quality. McDonald's does this by controlling the physical settings of its restaurants and by using its 'golden arches' as a branding cue. By having a consistent offering, the company has effectively dealt with the difficulties that consumers have in evaluating the quality of a service. Standard menus and ordering procedures have also ensured uniform and easy access for customers, while allowing quality control.[4]

Intangibility also means that the customer cannot own a service. Payment is for use or performance. For example, a car may be hired or a medical operation performed. Service organizations sometimes stress the *benefits of non-ownership* such as lower capital costs and the spreading of payment charges.

Inseparability

Unlike physical goods, services have **inseparability**—that is, they have *simultaneous production and consumption*. For example, a haircut, a medical operation, psychoanalysis, a holiday and a rock concert are produced and consumed at the same time. This contrasts with a physical good, which is produced, stored and distributed through intermediaries before being bought and consumed. This illustrates the *importance of the service provider*, which is an integral part of the satisfaction gained by the consumer. How service providers conduct themselves may have a crucial bearing on repeat business over and above the technical efficiency of the service task. For example, how courteous and friendly the service provider is may play a large part in the customer's perception of the service experience. The service must be provided not only at the right time and in the right place but also in the right way.[5]

Often, in the customer's eyes, the photocopier service engineer or the airline cabin crew member *is* the company. Consequently, the *selection, training and rewarding of staff* who are the frontline service people are of fundamental importance in the achievement of high standards of service quality. This notion of the inseparability of production and consumption gave rise to the idea of relationship marketing in services. In such circumstances, managing buyer–seller interaction is central to effective marketing and can only be fulfilled in a relationship with the customer.[6]

Furthermore, the consumption of the service may take place in the presence of other consumers. This is apparent with restaurant meals, air, rail or coach travel, and many forms of entertainment, for example. Consequently, enjoyment of the service is dependent not only on the service provided, but also on other consumers. Therefore service providers need to identify possible sources of nuisance (e.g. noise, smoke, queue jumping) and make adequate provision to *avoid inter-customer conflict*. For example, a restaurant layout should provide reasonable space between tables so that the potential for conflict is minimized.

Marketing managers should not underestimate the role played by customers in aiding other customers in their decision-making. A study into service interactions in IKEA stores found that almost all customer–employee exchanges related to customer concerns about 'place' (e.g. 'Can you direct me to the pick-up point?') and 'function' (e.g. 'How does this chair work?'). However, interactions between customers took the form of opinions on the quality of materials used in products, advice on bed sizes and how to move around the in-store restaurant. Many customers appeared to display a degree of product knowledge or expertise bordering on that of contact personnel.[7]

 22.1 Pause for Thought

Can you recall a situation where service staff and/or other consumers have spoilt your experience of a service? What would you do if you worked for that company to ensure that this was not repeated?

Variability

Service quality may be subject to considerable **variability**, which makes standardization difficult. Two restaurants within the same chain may have variable service owing to the capabilities of their respective managers and staff. Two marketing courses at the same university may vary considerably in terms of quality depending on the lecturers. Quality variations among physical products may be subject to tighter controls through centralized production, automation and quality checking before dispatch. Services, however, are often conducted at multiple locations, by people who may vary in their attitudes (and tiredness), and are subject to simultaneous production and consumption. The last characteristic means that a service fault (e.g. rudeness) cannot be quality checked and corrected between production and consumption, unlike a physical product such as misaligned car windscreen wipers.

The potential for variability in service quality emphasizes the need for rigorous selection, training, and rewarding of staff in service organizations. Training should emphasize the standards expected of personnel when dealing with customers. *Evaluation systems* should be developed that allow customers to report on their experiences with staff. Some service organizations, notably the British Airports Authority (BAA), tie reward systems to customer satisfaction surveys, which are based, in part, on the service quality provided by their staff. The telecoms company BT also rewards staff for providing good customer service, and this has proven effective in raising standards.[8]

Service standardization is a related method of tackling the variability problem. For example, a university department could agree to use the same software package when developing overhead transparencies for use in lectures. The *use of reliable equipment* rather than people can also help in standardization—for example, the supply of drinks via vending machines or cash through bank machines. However, great care needs to be taken regarding equipment reliability and efficiency. For example, bank cash machines have been heavily criticized for being unreliable and running out of money at weekends.

Perishability

The fourth characteristic of services is their **perishability** in the sense that *consumption cannot be stored* for the future. A hotel room or an airline seat that is not occupied today represents lost income that cannot be gained tomorrow. If a physical good is not sold, it can be stored for sale later. Therefore it is important to *match supply and demand* for services. For example, if a hotel has high weekday occupancy but is virtually empty at weekends, a key marketing task is to provide incentives for weekend use. This might involve offering weekend discounts, or linking hotel use with leisure activities such as golf, fishing or hiking.

Service providers also have the problem of catering for peak demand when supply may be insufficient. A physical goods provider may build up inventory in slack periods for sale during peak demand. Service providers do not have this option. Consequently, alternative methods need to be considered. For example, supply flexibility can be varied through the *use of part-time staff* during peak periods. *Multi-skilling* means that employees may be trained in many tasks. Supermarket staff can be trained to fill shelves and work at the checkout at peak periods. *Participation by consumers* may be encouraged in production (e.g. self-service breakfasts in hotels) and in avoiding queues (e.g. self-service checkouts in supermarkets). Demand may be smoothed through *differential pricing* to encourage customers to visit during off-peak periods (for example, lower-priced cinema and theatre seats for afternoon performances). *Stimulation of off-peak demand* can be achieved by special events (e.g. golf or history weekends for hotels). If delay is unavoidable then another option is to make it more acceptable—for example, by providing a comfortable waiting area with seating and free refreshments. Finally, a *reservation system*, as commonly used in restaurants, hair salons and theatres, can be used to control peak demand and assist time substitution.

Managing Services

Four key aspects of managing services are managing customer relationships, managing service quality, managing service productivity, managing service staff and positioning services.

Managing customer relationships

Relationship marketing in services has attracted much attention in recent years as organizations focus their efforts on retaining existing customers rather than only attracting new ones. It is not a new concept, however, since the idea of a company earning customer loyalty was well known to the earliest merchants, who had the following saying: 'As a merchant, you'd better have a friend in every town.'[9] Relationship marketing involves the shifting from activities concerned with attracting customers to activities focused on current customers and how to retain them. Although the idea can be applied to many industries it is particularly important in services since there is often direct contact between service provider and consumer—for example, doctor and patient, hotel staff and guests. The quality of the relationship that develops will often determine its length. Not all service encounters have the potential for a long-term relationship, however. For example, a passenger at an international airport who needs road transportation will probably never meet the taxi driver again, and the choice of taxi supplier will be dependent on the passenger's position in the queue rather than free choice. In this case the exchange—cash for journey—is a pure transaction: the driver knows that it is unlikely that there will ever be a repeat purchase.[10] Organizations, therefore, need to decide when the practice of relationship marketing is most applicable. The following conditions suggest potential areas for the use of relationship marketing activities:[11]

- where there is an ongoing or periodic desire for the service by the customer, e.g. insurance or theatre service versus funeral service
- where the customer controls the selection of a service provider, e.g. selecting a hotel versus entering the first taxi in an airport waiting line
- where the customer has alternatives from which to choose, e.g. selecting a restaurant versus buying water from the only utility company service in a community.

Having established the applicability of relationship marketing to services, we will now explore the benefits of relationship marketing to organizations and customers, and the customer retention strategies used to build relationships and tie customers closer to service firms.

Benefits for the organization

There are six benefits to service organizations in developing and maintaining strong customer relationships.[12]

1 *Increased purchases*: a study by Reichheld and Sasser[13] has shown that customers tend to spend more each year with a relationship partner than they did in the preceding period. This is logical as it would be expected that as the relationship develops, trust would develop between the partners, and as the customer becomes more and more satisfied with the quality of services provided by the supplier so it will give a greater proportion of its business to the supplier.

2 *Lower cost*: the start-up costs associated with attracting new customers are likely to be far higher than the cost of retaining existing customers. Start-up costs will include the time of salespeople making repeat calls in an effort to persuade a prospect to open an account, the advertising and promotional costs associated with making prospects aware of the company and its service offering, the operating costs of setting up accounts and systems, and the time costs of establishing bonds between the supplier and customer in the early stages of the relationship. Furthermore, costs associated with solving early teething

problems and queries are likely to fall as the customer becomes accustomed to using the service.

3 *Lifetime value of a customer*: the lifetime value of a customer is the profit made on a customer's purchases over the lifetime of that customer. If a customer spends £80 in a supermarket per week, resulting in £8 profit, uses the supermarket 45 times a year over 30 years, the lifetime value of that customer is £10,800. Thus a bad service experience early on in this relationship, which results in the customer defecting to the competition, would be very expensive to the supermarket, especially when the costs of bad word of mouth are added, as this may deter other customers from using the store.

4 *Sustainable competitive advantage*: the intangible aspects of a relationship are not easily copied by the competition. For example, the friendships and high levels of trust that can develop as the relationship matures can be extremely difficult for competitors to replicate. This means that the extra value to customers that derives from the relationship can be a source of sustainable competitive advantage for suppliers.[14]

5 *Word of mouth*: word of mouth is very important in services due to their intangible nature, which makes them difficult to evaluate prior to purchase. In these circumstances, potential purchasers often look to others who have experienced the service (e.g. a hotel) for personal recommendation. A firm that has a large number of loyal customers is more likely to benefit from word of mouth than another without such a resource.

6 *Employee satisfaction and retention*: satisfied, loyal customers benefit employees in providing a set of mutually beneficial relationships and less hassle. This raises employees' job satisfaction and lowers job turnover. Employees can spend time improving existing relationships rather than desperately seeking new customers. This sets up a virtuous circle of satisfied customers, leading to happy employees that raise customer satisfaction even higher.

The net result of these six benefits of developing customer relationships is high profits. A study has shown across a variety of service industries that profits climb steeply when a firm lowers its customer defection rate.[15] Firms could improve profits from 25 to 85 per cent (depending on the industry) by reducing customer defections by just 5 per cent. The reasons are that loyal customers generate more revenue for more years and the costs of maintaining existing customers are lower than the costs of acquiring new ones. An analysis of a credit card company revealed that improving the defection rate from 10 to 20 years increased the lifetime value of a customer from $135 to $300.

Benefits for the customer

Entering into a long-term relationship can also reap the following four benefits for the customer.

1 *Risk and stress reduction*: since the intangible nature of services makes them difficult to evaluate before purchase, relationship marketing can benefit the customer as well as the firm. This is particularly so for services that are personally important, variable in quality, complex and/or subject to high-involvement buying.[16] Such purchases are potentially high risk in that making the wrong choice has severe negative consequences for the buyer. Banking, insurance, motor servicing and hairstyling are examples of services that exhibit some or all of the characteristics—importance, variability, complexity and high involvement—that would cause many customers to seek an ongoing relationship with a trusted service provider. Such a relationship reduces consumer stress as the relationship becomes predictable, initial problems are solved, special needs are accommodated and the consumer learns what to expect. After a period of time, the consumer begins to trust the service provider, can count on a consistent level of quality service and feels comfortable in the relationship.[17]

2 *Higher-quality service*: experiencing a long-term relationship with a service provider can also result in higher levels of service. This is because the service provider becomes knowledgeable about the customer's requirements. For example, doctors get to know

the medical history of their patients, and hairstylists learn about the preferences of their clients. Knowledge of the customer built up over a series of service encounters facilitates the tailoring or customizing of the service to each customer's special needs.

3 *Avoidance of switching costs*: maintaining a relationship with a service supplier avoids the costs associated with switching to a new provider. Once a service provider knows a customer's preferences and special needs, and has tailored services to suit them, to change would mean educating a new provider and accepting the possibility of mistakes being made until the new provider has learnt to accommodate them. This results in both time and psychological costs to the customer. Bitner suggests that a major cost of relocating to a new geographic location is the need to establish relationships with unfamiliar service providers such as banks, schools, doctors and hairdressers.[18]

4 *Social and status benefits*: customers can also reap social and status benefits from a continuing relationship with a supplier. Since many service encounters are also social encounters, repeated contact can assume personal as well as professional dimensions. In such circumstances, service customers may develop relationships resembling personal friendships. For example, hairdressers often serve as personal confidantes, and restaurant managers may get to know some of their customers personally. Such personal relationships can feed one's ego (status) as when a hotel customer commented, 'When employees remember and recognize you as a regular customer you feel really good.'[19]

Developing customer retention strategies

The benefits of developing long-term relationships with customers mean that it is worthwhile for services organizations to consider designing customer retention strategies. This involves the targeting of customers for retention, bonding, internal marketing, promise fulfilment, building of trust and service recovery (see Fig. 22.3), as described below.

1 *Targeting customers for retention*: not all customers are worthy of relationship building. Some may be habitual brand switchers, perhaps responding to the lowest deal currently on offer; others may not generate sufficient revenue to justify the expense of acquiring them and maintaining the relationship; and, finally, some customers may be so troublesome, and their attitudes and behaviour cause so much disruption to the service provider, that

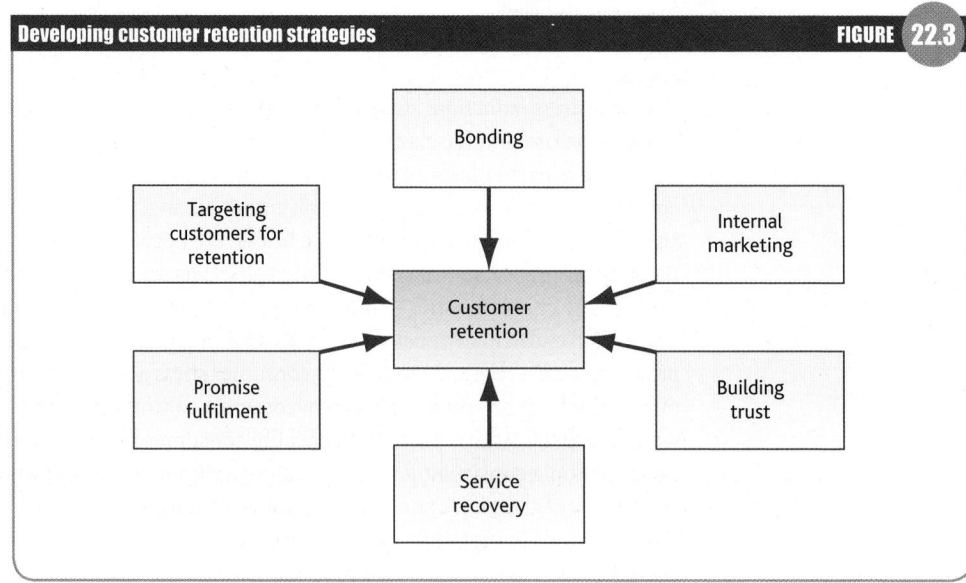

Developing customer retention strategies   **FIGURE 22.3**

the costs of servicing them outweigh the benefits. Firms need, therefore, to identify those customers with whom they wish to engage in a long-term relationship, those for whom a transactional marketing approach is better suited, and those with whom they would prefer not to do business. This is the classical market segmentation and targeting approach discussed in Chapter 8. The characteristics of those customers that are candidates for a relationship marketing approach are high-value, frequent-use, loyalty-prone customers for whom the actual and potential service offerings that can be supplied by the firm have high utility.

Targeting customers for retention involves the analysis of loyalty and defection-prone customers. Service suppliers need to understand why customers stay or leave, what creates value for them, and their profile. Decisions can then be made regarding which types of customer defector they wish to try to save (e.g. price or service defectors) and the nature of the value-adding strategy that meets their needs, while at the same time maintaining bonds with loyalty-prone customers.[20]

2   *Bonding*: retention strategies vary in the degree to which they bond the parties together. One framework that illustrates this idea distinguishes between three levels of retention strategy based on the types of bond used to cement the relationship.[21]

- *Level 1*: at this level the bond is primarily through financial incentives, for example, higher discounts on prices for larger-volume purchases or frequent-flyer or loyalty points resulting in lower future prices. The problem is that the potential for a sustainable competitive advantage is low because price incentives are easy for competitors to copy even if they take the guise of frequent-flyer or loyalty points. Most airlines and supermarkets compete in this way and consumers have learnt to join more than one scheme, thus negating the desired effect. Digital Marketing 22.1 discusses the role of e-mail marketing in communication information about such programmes.

22.1 Digital Marketing

Online Bonding: Customer Retention Strategies

Customer retention strategies vary. At the basic level, financial incentives encourage customers to remain loyal. Sales promotions such as price incentives and competitions are used to encourage customers to make repeat purchases. Accor is a global brand that operates hotels and conference facilities in over 100 countries. Individual brands operated by Accor are Sofitel, Pullman, MGallery, Novotel, Mercure, Suitehotel, Ibis, All Seasons, Etap Hotel, Formule 1 and Motel 6.

Accor's A/Club loyalty scheme offers the opportunity to earn bonus points, which can be used to purchase hotel accommodation (2000 points are equivalent to €40). Membership of A/Club is free and offers various price incentives. There are various tiers of membership, depending on the number of stays a customer makes at the group's participating hotels. Accor also has the A/Club Favourite Guest loyalty programme. Under this scheme, the customer pays over €200 to enjoy additional benefits, such as guaranteed rooms, and advantages—unlimited rewards, worldwide reductions on room rates and other specific member advantages and exclusive benefits. The aim of this programme is to strengthen the level of commitment and build longer-term relationships by giving the customer the opportunity to enjoy more personalized and customized services.

E-mail marketing plays a key role in communication with customers and building longer-term relationships. Accor A/Club uses e-mail marketing newsletters to inform members of A/Club events, and invite them to take part in competitions and benefit from various sales promotion initiatives.

- *Level 2*: this higher level of bonding relies on more than just price incentives, and consequently raises the potential for a sustainable competitive advantage. Level 2 retention strategies build long-term relationships through social as well as financial bonds, capitalizing on the fact that many service encounters are also social encounters. Customers become clients, the relationship becomes personalized and the service customized. Characteristics of this type of relationship include frequent communication with customers, providing community of service through the same person or people employed by the service provider, providing personal treatment like sending cards, and enhancing the core service with educational or entertainment activities such as seminars or visits to sporting events. Some hotels keep records of their guests' personal preferences, such as their favourite newspaper and alcoholic drink. This builds a special bond between the hotel and their customers, who feel they are being treated as individuals.

  Other companies form social relationships with their customers by forming clubs—for example, Harley-Davidson has created the Harley Owners Group, fostering camaraderie among its membership and a strong bond with the motorbike, and Nokia has established a club for its mobile phone customers for similar reasons.

- *Level 3*: this top level of bonding is formed by financial, social and structural bonds. Structural bonds tie service providers to their customers through providing solutions to customers' problems that are designed into the service delivery system. For example, logistics companies often supply their clients with equipment that ties them into their systems. When combined with financial and social bonds, structural bonds can create a formidable barrier against competitor inroads and provide the basis for a sustainable competitive advantage.

3 *Internal marketing*: a fundamental basis for customer retention is high-quality service delivery. This depends on high-quality performance from employees since the service product is a performance and the performers are employees.[22] Internal marketing concerns training, communicating to and motivating internal staff. Staff need to be trained to be technically competent at their job as well as to be able to handle service encounters with customers. To do this well, they must be motivated and understand what is expected of them. Service staff act as 'part-time marketers' since their actions can directly affect customer satisfaction and retention.[23] They are critical in the 'moments of truth' when they and customers come into contact in a service situation.

   A key focus of an internal marketing programme should be employee selection and retention. Service companies that suffer high rates of job turnover are continually employing new, inexperienced staff to handle customer service encounters. Employees that have worked for the company for years know more about the business and have had the opportunity to build relationships with customers. By selecting the right people and managing them in such a way that they stay loyal to the service organization, higher levels of customer retention can be achieved through the build-up of trust and personal knowledge gained through long-term contact with customers.

4 *Promise fulfilment*: the fulfilment of promises is a cornerstone for maintaining service relationships. This implies three key activities: *making* realistic promises initially, and *keeping* those promises during service delivery by *enabling* staff and service systems to deliver on promises made.[24]

   Making promises is done through normal marketing communications channels such as advertising, selling and promotion, as well as the specific service cues that set expectations such as the dress of the service staff, and the design and décor of the establishment. It is important not to over-promise with marketing communications or the result will be disappointment, and consequently customer dissatisfaction and defection. The promise should be credible and realistic. Some companies adhere to the adage 'under-promise and over-deliver'.

A necessary condition for promises to be kept is the enabling of staff and service systems to deliver on the promises made. This means staff must have the skills, competences, tools, systems and enthusiasm to deliver. Some of these issues have been looked at in the earlier discussion of internal marketing, and are dependent on the correct recruitment, training and rewarding of staff, and on providing them with the right equipment and systems to do their jobs.

The final activity associated with promise fulfilment is the keeping of promises. This relies on service staff or technology such as the downloading of software via the Internet. The keeping of promises occurs when the customer and the service provider interact: the 'moment of truth' mentioned earlier. Research has shown that customers judge employees on their ability to deliver the service right the first time, their ability to recover if things go wrong, how well they deal with special requests, and on their spontaneous actions and attitudes.[25] These are clearly key dimensions that must play a part in a training programme and should be borne in mind when selecting and rewarding service staff; not all service encounters are equal in importance, however. Research conducted on behalf of Marriott hotels has shown that events occurring early in a service encounter affect customer loyalty the most. Based on these findings Marriott developed its 'First 10 Minutes' strategy. It is hardly surprising that first impressions are so important since before then the customer has had no direct contact with the service provider and will be uncertain of the outcome.

Finally, we need to recognize that the keeping of promises does not depend solely on service staff and technology. Because service delivery is often in a group setting (e.g. listening to a lecture, watching a film or travelling by air) the quality of the experience can be as dependent on the behaviour of other customers as that of the service provider. Lovelock, Vandermerwe and Lewis label the problem customers 'jaycustomers'.[26] These are people who act in a thoughtless or abusive way, causing problems for the organization, its employees and other customers. One particular kind of jaycustomer is the belligerent person who shouts abuse and threats at service staff because of some service malfunction. Staff need to be trained to develop the self-confidence and assertiveness required to deal with such situations, and to practise this using role-play exercises. If possible, the jaycustomer should be moved away from other customer contact to minimize the discomfort of the latter. Finally, where the service employee does not have the authority to resolve the problem, more senior staff should be approached to settle the dispute.

5 *Building trust*: customer retention relies heavily on building trust. This is particularly so for service firms since the intangibility of services means that they are difficult to evaluate before buying and experiencing them (indeed some, such as car servicing, are hard to evaluate after purchasing them). Purchasing a service for the first time can leave the customer with a feeling of uncertainty and vulnerability, particularly when the service is personally important, variable in quality, complex and subject to high-involvement purchasing. It is not surprising that customers who have developed trust in a supplier in these circumstances are unlikely to switch to a new supplier and undergo the uncomfortable feelings of uncertainty and vulnerability all over again.

22.2 Pause for Thought

How important is trust to you when you buy a service? Think of a situation where you have repeatedly bought a service because you trust the service provider even though there may be cheaper alternatives.

Companies that wish to build up their trustworthiness should keep in touch with their customers by regular two-way communication to develop feelings of closeness and openness, provide guarantees to symbolize the confidence they feel in their service delivery as well as reducing their customers' perceived risk of purchase, and to operate a policy of fairness and high standards of conduct with their customers.[27]

The recent credit crunch and the associated global recession have led to a fall in trust towards many financial institutions, as Marketing Ethics and Corporate Social Responsibility in Action 22.1 explains.

 **22.1 Marketing Ethics and Corporate Social Responsibility in Action**

The Credit Crunch, the Financial Sector and Ethics

The credit crunch has meant that banks worldwide have become very wary of lending money to each other, or to consumers and businesses in need of credit. The financial sector crisis, which led to a global economic downturn, has occurred due to several reasons. These include speculative financial tactics, and irresponsible lending practices. In the UK, several banks have had to appeal for emergency relief from the Bank of England and, as a result, some have become part-nationalized. Although banks have had to restructure and reformulate their business strategies while becoming more conservative in their lending practices, they have been hit hard by ruined reputations and a general crisis in public confidence. This was further accentuated when the media publicized the lavish parties and the huge bonuses that were awarded to the very bankers whose activities had led to widespread unemployment and recession.

The French and American Governments have curbed bankers' rewards, but in the UK regulatory powers seem a little more hesitant and conservative. On the one hand, some argue that payment curbs are usually full of loopholes and drive brilliant professionals away from the sector. Others suggest that regulations would make immoral banking practices more difficult, and remind us that professions such as teaching and medicine are full of excellent practitioners without outrageous rewards.

It seems that renewed confidence in the banking sector will require a lot more than rebranding. Above all, we need a change of thinking to reflect the fact that financial markets and services affect and function within society, and must therefore operate within society's moral frameworks. Indeed, during the 2009 World Economic Forum, founder Klaus Schwab called for a focus on business morality, and suggested that the current crisis reflects structural issues that must be addressed.

Based on: Budworth (2008);[28] Wachman (2008);[29] Elliott and Seager (2009);[30] Sunderland (2009)[31]

6   *Service recovery*: service recovery strategies should be designed to solve the problem and restore the customers' trust in the firm, and to improve the service system so that the problem does not recur in the future.[32] They are crucial because the inability to recover service failures and mistakes loses customers both directly and through their tendency to tell other actual and potential customers about their negative experiences.

The first ingredient in a service recovery strategy is to set up a tracking system to identify system failures. Customers should be encouraged to report service problems since it is those customers that do not complain that are least likely to purchase again. Systems should be established to monitor complaints, follow up on service experiences by telephone calling, and to use suggestion boxes for both service staff and customers.

Second, staff should be trained and empowered to respond to service complaints. This is important because research has shown that the successful resolution of a complaint can cause customers to feel more positive about the firm than before the service failure. If a second problem occurs, though, this effect (called the 'recovery paradox') disappears.[33] The first response from a service provider to a genuine complaint is to apologize. Often this will take the heat out of the situation and lead to a spirit of cooperation rather than recrimination. The next step is to attempt to solve the problem quickly. Marriott hotels facilitates this process by empowering frontline employees to solve customers' problems quickly, even though this may mean expense to the hotel, and without recourse to seeking approval from higher authority. Other key elements in service recovery are to appear pleasant, helpful and attentive, show concern for the customer and be flexible. Regarding problem resolution, service staff should provide information about the problem, take action and should appear to put themselves out to solve the problem.[34]

A common area of criticism is poor service recovery by tour operators when aircraft failure causes long delays at airports. Marketing in Action 22.1 describes how well one such service recovery situation was handled by Thomas Cook.

Finally, a service recovery strategy should encourage learning so that service recovery problems are identified and corrected. Service staff should be motivated to report problems and solutions so that recurrent failures are identified and fixed. In this way, an effective service recovery system can lead to improved customer service, satisfaction and higher customer-retention levels.

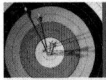 **22.1 Marketing in Action**

Five-Star Service Recovery with Thomas Cook

An example of how to handle the dreaded airport delay can be found in the case of Thomas Cook, the UK travel agency and tour operator. An electrical fault on an aircraft due to leave Madeira for the UK meant that 220 passengers were delayed at Funchal airport for two hours while engineers tried to solve the problem. Towards the end of this period, passengers were directed to the cafeteria to receive a free drink and snack.

When it became clear that the flight would not take place that day, a Thomas Cook representative announced that all passengers would stay the night in a five-star hotel and would receive free dinner with drinks. After 30 minutes the passengers boarded coaches and were seamlessly transferred to the hotel. While at the hotel passengers were kept fully informed of the situation and given the time to meet the following morning. Representatives were on hand to answer queries.

Overnight an engineer and spare parts from the UK were flown to Madeira and the fault rectified. When passengers met to take the early-morning (5 am) trip to the airport, they were served coffee and biscuits. Coaches were waiting outside the hotel ready for departure.

Despite the inconvenience of arriving a day late, passengers appreciated the smoothness of the service recovery operation. Clearly, Thomas Cook, and its airport representative Serviceair, had service processes in place, including prior agreement with a hotel, to accommodate the needs of large numbers of passengers who might find themselves stranded many thousands of miles from home.

Managing service quality

Intuitively, it makes sense to suggest that improving service quality will increase customer satisfaction, leading to higher sales and profits. Indeed, it has been shown that companies that are rated higher on service quality perform better in terms of market share growth and profitability.[35] Yet, for many companies, high standards of service quality remain elusive.

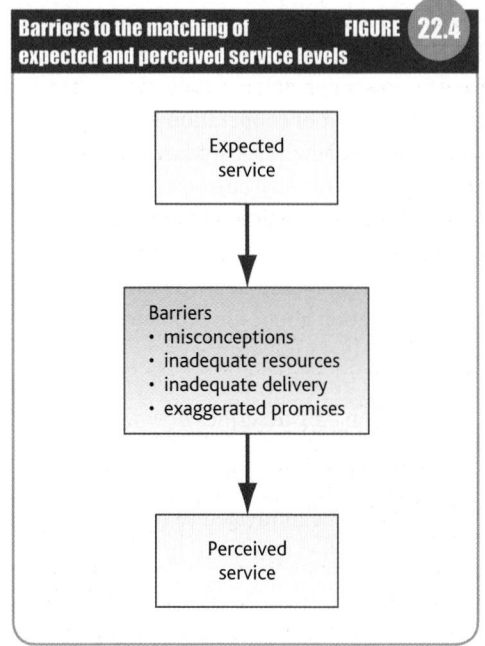

Barriers to the matching of expected and perceived service levels

FIGURE **22.4**

Expected service

↓

Barriers
• misconceptions
• inadequate resources
• inadequate delivery
• exaggerated promises

↓

Perceived service

There are four causes of poor perceived quality (see Fig. 22.4). These are the barriers that separate the perception of service quality from what customers expect.[36]

Barriers to the matching of expected and perceived service levels

Misconception barrier: this arises from management's misunderstanding of what the customer expects. Lack of marketing research may lead managers to misconceive the important service attributes that customers use when evaluating a service, and the way in which customers use attributes in evaluation. For example, a restaurant manager may believe that shortening the gap between courses may improve customer satisfaction, when the customer actually values a pause between eating.

Inadequate resources barrier: managers may understand customer expectations but be unwilling to provide the resources necessary to meet them. This may arise because of a cost reduction or productivity focus, or simply because of the inconvenience it may cause.

Inadequate delivery barrier: managers may understand customer expectations and supply adequate resources but fail to select, train and reward staff adequately, resulting in poor or inconsistent service. This may manifest itself in poor communication skills, inappropriate dress, and unwillingness to solve customer problems.

Exaggerated promises barrier: even when customer understanding, resources and staff management are in place, a gap between customer expectations and perceptions can still arise through exaggerated promises. Advertising and selling messages that build expectations to a pitch that cannot be fulfilled may leave customers disappointed even when receiving good service. For example, a tourist brochure that claims a hotel is 'just a few minutes from the sea' may lead to disappointment if the walk takes 10 minutes.

Meeting customer expectations

A key to providing service quality is the understanding and meeting of *customer expectations*. To do so requires a clear picture of the criteria used to form these expectations, recognizing that consumers of services value not only the *outcome* of the service encounter but also the *experience* of taking part in it. For example, an evaluation of a haircut depends not only on the quality of the cut but also the experience of having a haircut. Clearly, a hairdresser needs not only technical skills but also the ability to communicate in an interesting and polite manner. Meeting and exceeding customers' expectations is even more important as good and bad experiences can easily be shared via blogs, social networking sites and websites. For example, the tripadvisor.com website publishes the experiences of customers when using hotels and airlines around the world.[37] Ten criteria may be used when evaluating the outcome and experience of a service encounter.[38]

1 *Access*: is the service provided at convenient locations and times with little waiting?
2 *Reliability*: is the service consistent and dependable?
3 *Credibility*: can customers trust the service company and its staff?
4 *Security*: can the service be used without risk?
5 *Understanding the customer*: does it appear that the service provider understands customer expectations?
6 *Responsiveness*: how quickly do service staff respond to customer problems, requests and questions?

▲ Tesco targets new mums by meeting their needs and expectations.

7 *Courtesy*: do service staff act in a friendly and polite manner?
8 *Competence*: do service staff have the required skills and knowledge?
9 *Communication*: is the service described clearly and accurately?
10 *Tangibles*: how well managed is the tangible evidence of the service (e.g. staff appearance, décor, layout)?

These criteria form a useful checklist for service providers wishing to understand how their customers judge them. A self-analysis may show areas that need improvement, but the most reliable approach is to check that customers use these criteria and to conduct marketing research to compare performance against competition. Where service quality is dependent on a succession of service encounters (for example, a hotel stay may encompass the check-in, the room itself, the restaurant, breakfast and check-out), each should be measured in terms of their impact on total satisfaction so that corrective actions can be taken.[39] Questionnaires have now been developed that allow the measurement of perceived customer satisfaction at distinct stages of the service-delivery process (for example, the stages encountered while visiting a museum).[40]

The advertisement for Tesco.com is designed to meet the expectations of new mums by offering delivery to the door, as well as a financial incentive.

Measuring service quality

A scale called *SERVQUAL* has been developed to aid the measurement of *service quality*.[41] Based on five criteria—reliability, responsiveness, courtesy, competence and tangibles—it is a multiple-item scale that aims to measure customer perceptions and expectations so that gaps can be identified. The scale is simple to administer with respondents indicating their strength of agreement or disagreement with a series of statements about service quality using a Likert scale. Service quality can also be measured by *mystery shoppers*, who visit retail outlets as normal consumers. Their job is to assess and report the quality of the service they receive.[42]

Managing service productivity

Productivity is a measure of the relationship between an input and an output. For example, if more people can be served (output) using the same number of staff (input), productivity per employee has risen. Clearly there can be conflict between improving service productivity (efficiency) and raising service quality (effectiveness). For example, a doctor who reduces consultation time per patient or a university that increases tutorial group size raise productivity at the risk of lowering service quality. Table 22.1 shows how typical operational goals that seek to minimize costs can cause marketing concerns. Marketers need to understand why operations managers have such goals, and operations managers need to recognize the implications of their actions for customer satisfaction.[43]

Clearly a balance must be struck between productivity and service quality. At some point quality gains become so expensive that they are not worthwhile. However, there are ways of

Marketing and operations' views on operational issues		TABLE 22.1
Operational issues	**Typical operations goals**	**Common marketing concerns**
Productivity improvement	Reduce unit cost of production	Strategies may cause decline in service quality
Standardizaton versus customization	Keep costs low and quality consistent: simplify operations tasks; recruit low-cost employees	Consumers may seek variety, prefer customization to match segmented needs
Batch vs unit processing	Seek economies of scale, consistency, efficient use of capacity	Customers may be forced to wait, feel 'one of a crowd', be turned off by other customers
Facilities layout and design	Control costs; improve efficiency by ensuring proximity of operationally related tasks; enhance safety and security	Customers may be confused, shunted around unnecessarily, find facility unattractive and inconvenient
Job design	Minimize error, waste and fraud; make efficient use of technology; simplify task for standardization	Operationally orientated employees with narrow roles may be unresponsive to customer needs
Management of capacity	Keep costs down by avoiding wasteful under-utilization of resources	Service may be unavailable when needed; quality may be compromised during high-demand periods
Management of queues	Optimize use of available capacity by planning for average throughput; maintain customer order, discipline	Customers may be bored and frustrated during wait, see firm as unresponsive

Source: Lovelock, C. (1992) Seeking Synergy in Service Operations: Seven Things Marketers Need to Know about Service Operations, *European Management Journal* 10(1), 22–9. Reprinted with permission from Elsevier Science Ltd, The Boulevard, Langford Lane, Kidlington OX5 1GB, UK.

improving productivity without compromising quality. Technology, obtaining customer involvement in production of the service, and balancing supply and demand are three methods of achieving this.

Technology

Technology can be used to improve productivity and service quality. For example, airport X-ray surveillance equipment raises the throughput of passengers (productivity) and speeds the process of checking-in (service quality). Automatic cash dispensers in banks increase the number of transactions per period (productivity) while reducing customer waiting time (service quality). Automatic vending machines increase the number of drinks sold per establishment (productivity) while improving accessibility for customers (service quality). Computerization can also raise productivity and service quality. For example, Direct Line, owned by the Royal Bank of Scotland, is based on computer software that produces a motor insurance quote instantaneously. Callers are asked for a few details (such as how old they are, where they live, what car they drive and number of years since their last claim) and this is keyed into the computer, which automatically produces a quotation.[44]

Retailers have benefited from electronic point of sale (EPOS) and electronic data interchange (EDI). Timely and detailed sales information can aid buying decisions and provide retail buyers with a negotiating advantage over suppliers. Other benefits from this technology include better labour scheduling, and stock and distribution systems.

Customer involvement in production

The inseparability between production and consumption provides an opportunity to raise both productivity and service quality. For example, self-service breakfast bars and petrol stations improve productivity per employee and reduce customer waiting time (service quality). The effectiveness of this tactic relies heavily on customer expectations, and on managing transition periods. It should be used when there is a clear advantage to customers in their involvement in production. In other instances, reducing customer service may reduce satisfaction. For example, a hotel that expected its customers to service their own rooms would need a persuasive communications programme to convince customers that the lack of service was reflected in cheaper rates.

Balancing supply and demand

Because services cannot be stored, balancing supply and demand is a key determinant of productivity. Hotels or aircraft that are less than half full incur low productivity. If in the next period, the hotel or airline is faced with excess demand, the unused space in the previous period cannot be used to meet it. The combined result is low productivity and customer dissatisfaction (low service quality). By smoothing demand or increasing the flexibility of supply, both productivity and service quality can be achieved.

Smoothing demand can be achieved through differential pricing and stimulating off-peak demand (e.g. weekend breaks). Increasing supply flexibility may be increased by using part time employees, multi-skilling and encouraging customers to service themselves.

Managing service staff

Many services involve a high degree of contact between service staff and customers. This is true for such service industries as healthcare, banking, catering and education. The quality of the service experience is therefore heavily dependent on staff–customer interpersonal relationships. John Carlzon, the head of Scandinavian Airlines System (SAS), called these meetings *moments of truth*. He explained that SAS faced 65,000 moments of truth per day and that the outcomes determined the success of the company.

Research on customer loyalty in the service industry showed that only 14 per cent of customers who stopped patronizing service businesses did so because they were dissatisfied with the quality of what they had bought. More than two-thirds stopped buying because they found service staff indifferent or unhelpful.[45] Clearly, the way in which service personnel treat their customers is fundamental to success in the service industry.

Also, frontline staff are important sources of customer and competitor information and, if properly motivated, can provide crucial inputs in the development of new service products.[46] For example, discussions with customers may generate ideas for new services that customers would value if available on the market.

In order for service employees to be in the frame of mind to treat customers well, they need to feel that their company is treating them well. In companies where staff have a high regard for the human resources policy, customers also have a positive opinion of the service they receive.

The *selection of suitable people* is the starting point of the process. Personality differences mean that it is not everyone who can fill a service role. The nature of the job needs to be defined and the appropriate personality characteristics needed to perform effectively outlined.

Once selected, training is required to familiarize recruits with the job requirements and the culture of the organization. Orientation is the process by which a company helps new recruits understand the organization and its culture. Folklore is often used to show how employees have made outstanding contributions to the company. Training needs to continue when required, particularly when service staff face change. Inadequate training can be disastrous, as when the opening of Heathrow Terminal 5 descended into chaos, partly through service staff not knowing where they should go.[47] Sales at the electrical retailer Currys suffered partly as a result of poorly trained staff giving customers poor advice, a problem the company is addressing.[48]

Socialization allows the recruit to experience the culture and tasks of the organization. Usually, the aim is creative individualism, whereby the recruit accepts all of the key behavioural norms but is encouraged to display initiative and innovation in dealing with problems. Thus standards of behaviour are internalized, but the creative abilities of the individual are not subjugated to the need to conform.

Service quality may also be affected by the degree to which staff are *empowered*, or given the authority to satisfy customers and deal with their problems. For example, each member of staff of Marriott hotels is allowed to spend up to £1000 on their own initiative to solve customer problems. The company uses some of the situations that have arisen where employees have acted decisively to solve a customer problem in their advertising. The advantage is quicker response times since staff do not have to consult with their supervisors before dealing with a problem.[49] However, empowerment programmes need to recognize the increased responsibility thrust on employees. Not everyone will welcome this, and reward systems need to be thought through (e.g. higher pay or status).

Pret A Manger empowers staff in a different way. Following application and interview, prospective job candidates are paid to work for one day in a Pret store. The people working in that store then make the final decision as to whether the candidate is taken on. This empowers staff and ensures that only staff with the right attitude are employed.[50]

Maintaining a motivated workforce in the face of irate customers, faulty support systems and the boredom that accompanies some service jobs is a demanding task. The motivational factors discussed when examining salesforce management are equally relevant here and include recognition of achievement, role clarity, opportunities for advancement, the interest value of the job, monetary rewards, and setting challenging but achievable targets. Some service companies (e.g. Holiday Inn) give employee-of-the-month awards as recognition of outstanding service. A key factor in avoiding demotivation is to monitor support systems so that staff work with efficient equipment and facilities to help them carry out their job.

Service evaluation is also important in managing staff. Customer feedback is essential to maintaining high standards of service quality. McDonald's continually monitors quality, service, cleanliness and value (QSCV), and if a franchisee fails to meet these standards they are dropped. The results of customer research should be fed back to employees so that they can relate their performance standards to customer satisfaction. Enlightened companies tie financial incentives to the results of such surveys.

Positioning services

Positioning is the process of establishing and keeping a distinctive place in the market for a company and its products. Most successful service firms differentiate themselves from the competition on attributes that their target customers value highly. They develop service concepts that are highly valued, and communicate to target customers so that they accurately perceive the position of the service. For example, Credit Suisse Financial Products positions itself as a specialist in risk management products and services, an area whose image was tarnished during the credit crunch.

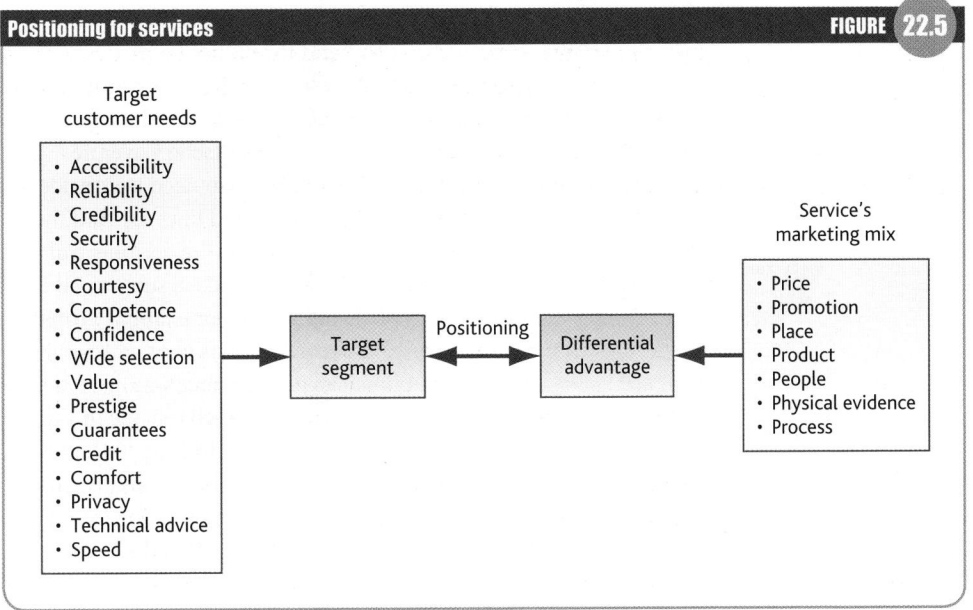

Positioning for services — FIGURE 22.5

Target customer needs

- Accessibility
- Reliability
- Credibility
- Security
- Responsiveness
- Courtesy
- Competence
- Confidence
- Wide selection
- Value
- Prestige
- Guarantees
- Credit
- Comfort
- Privacy
- Technical advice
- Speed

Target segment → Positioning ← Differential advantage

Service's marketing mix

- Price
- Promotion
- Place
- Product
- People
- Physical evidence
- Process

The positioning task entails two decisions:

1 choice of target market (where to compete)
2 creation of a differential advantage (how to compete).

These decisions are common to both physical products and services. Creating a differential advantage is based on understanding the target customers' requirements better than the competition. Figure 22.5 shows the relationship between *target customer needs* and the *services marketing mix*. On the left of the figure is an array of factors (choice criteria) that customers may use to judge a service. How well a service firm satisfies those criteria depends on its marketing mix (on the right of the figure). Marketing research can be useful in identifying important choice criteria but care needs to be taken in such studies. Asking customers which are the most important factors when buying a service may give misleading results. For example, the most important factor when travelling by air may be safety. However, this does not mean that customers use safety as a choice criterion when deciding which airline to use. If all major airlines are perceived as being similar in terms of safety, other less important factors like the quality of in-flight meals and service may be the crucial attributes used in decision-making.

Target marketing

The basis of target marketing is market segmentation. A market is analysed to identify groups of potential customers with similar needs and price sensitivities. The potential of each of these segments is assessed on such factors as size, growth rate, degree of competition, price sensitivity, and the fit between its requirements and the company's capabilities.

Note that the most attractive markets are often not the biggest, however, as these may have been identified earlier and will already have attracted a high level of competition. There may, however, be pockets of customers who are underserved by companies that are compromising their marketing mix by trying to serve too wide a customer base. The identification of such customers is a prime opportunity during segmentation analysis. Target marketing allows service firms to tailor their marketing mix to the specific requirements of groups of customers more effectively than trying to cater for diverse needs. For example, the airline Lufthansa has targeted first-class passengers by opening the world's first dedicated terminal to them

Target and halo customers   FIGURE **22.6**

Halo customers

Target customers

at Frankfurt airport. Help with parking the car is available, a personal assistant is on hand throughout and check-in is swift. Individual offices, rest rooms, and a dining and cigar room are available while executives await their flight. To travel to the aircraft, passengers are chauffeur-driven in a Mercedes S-class or Porsche Cayenne.[51]

Marketing managers also need to consider those potential customers that are not directly targeted but may find the service mix attractive. Those customers that are at the periphery of the target market are called **halo customers** and can make a substantial difference between success and failure (see Fig. 22.6). For example, Topshop, a UK clothing retailer targeting 16–24 year olds, was very successful in attracting this group to its shops but financial performance was marred by the lack of interest from its halo customers: those who fell outside this age bracket but nevertheless may have found Topshop's clothing to their taste. Launching into a new target market may require trials to test the innovation and refine the concept. For example, when KFC was considering moving into the breakfast segment of the fast-food market it ran trials in selected outlets before the full launch.[52]

Differential advantage

Understanding customer needs will be the basis of the design of a new service concept that is different from competitive offerings, is highly valued by target customers, and therefore creates a differential advantage. It will be based on the creative use of marketing-mix elements, resulting in such benefits as more reliable or faster delivery, greater convenience, more comfort, higher-quality work, higher prestige or other issues (listed on the left of Fig. 22.5). Marketing in Action 22.2 describes how small hotel chains have differentiated themselves from larger chains, which themselves are launching new boutique brands to bring a different experience to consumers.

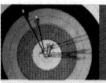

22.2 Marketing in Action

Boutique Hotels: Small is Beautiful

For some travellers, the reassurance of a global hotel chain with many standardized features is highly valued so that they know what to expect. For others, though, such chains are regarded as bland and boring. This segment is looking for a different experience, something that the Eton Collection, a small UK boutique hotel company, provides with individually designed hotels, personalized service and packages with partners like Harvey Nichols, the Tate and the British Museum. Franklin Hotels, a small boutique chain of hotels, also offers a different experience. Its success is built on building the 'wow' factor into service, something that traditionally big corporate chains have found hard to create.

Their success has not gone unnoticed, however. Larger chains have responded by launching their own boutique brands. For example, Hilton has launched Denizen Hotels, a new premium lifestyle brand. Denizen appeals across generations, with a fusion of styles from boutique ideas such as chandeliers to technology spaces and hubs where customers can relax. The concept is to create an engaging personality rather than dull corporate blandishments. The chain is not a simple-minded crib of its smaller rivals: its design is partly based on marketing research exploring the views and opinions of 4500 people. In this way, the chain is hoping to create a differential advantage of its own.

Based on: Roberts (2009)[53]

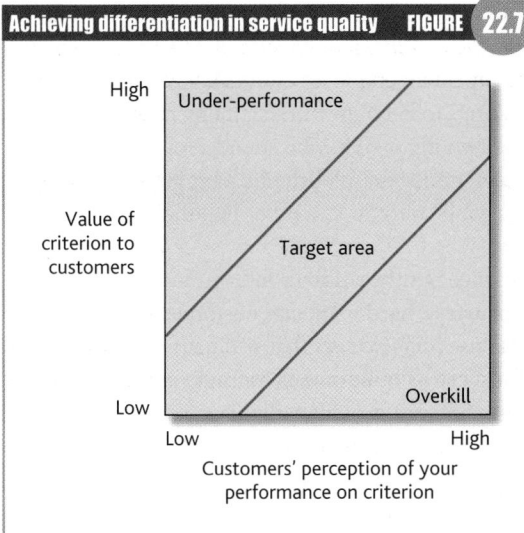

Achieving differentiation in service quality FIGURE 22.7

Source: Christopher, M. and R. Yallop (1990) Audit Your Customer Service Quality, *Focus*, June/July. Reprinted with kind permission of Martin Christopher

Research can indicate which choice criteria are more or less valued by customers, and how customers rate the service provider's performance on each.[54] Figure 22.7 shows three possible outcomes: *underperformance* results from performing poorly on highly valued choice criteria; *overkill* arises when the service provider excels at things of little consequence to customers; and the *target area* is where the supplier performs well on criteria that are of high value to customers and less well on less valued criteria. Differentiation is achieved in those areas that are of most importance, while resources are not wasted improving service quality levels in areas that are unimportant to customers. The result is the achievement of both effectiveness and efficiency in the service operation.

The services marketing mix

The **services marketing mix** is an extension of the 4-Ps framework introduced in Chapter 1. The essential elements of *product*, *promotion*, *price* and *place* remain, but three additional variables—*people*, *physical evidence* and *process*—are included to produce a 7-Ps mix.[55] The need for the extension is due to the high degree of direct contact between the firm and the customer, the highly visible nature of the service assembly process, and the simultaneity of production and consumption. While it is possible to discuss people, physical evidence and process within the original 4-Ps framework (for example, people could be considered part of the product offering) the extension allows a more thorough analysis of the marketing ingredients necessary for successful services marketing. Each element of the marketing mix will now be examined.

Product: physical products can be inspected and tried before buying, but pure services are intangible; you cannot go to a showroom to see a marketing research report or medical operation that you are considering. This means that service customers suffer higher perceived risk in their decision-making and that the three elements of the extended marketing mix—people, physical evidence and process—are crucial in influencing the customer's perception of service quality. These will be discussed later.

The *brand name* of a service can also influence the perception of a service. Four characteristics of successful brand names are as follows.[56]

1 *Distinctiveness*: it immediately identifies the services provider and differentiates it from the competition.
2 *Relevance*: it communicates the nature of the service and the service benefit.
3 *Memorability*: it is easily understood and remembered.
4 *Flexibility*: it not only expresses the service organization's current business but is also broad enough to cover foreseeable new ventures.

Examples of effective brand names are: Visa, which suggests internationality; Travelodge, which implies travel accommodation; and Virgin Atlantic, which associates the airline with flights to and from North America.

Although trial of some services is impossible, for others it can be achieved. For example, some hotels invite key decision-makers of social clubs (for example, social secretaries of pensioner groups) to visit their hotels free of charge to sample the facilities and service. The hotels hope that they will recommend a group visit to their members. Service providers such as hotels are constantly seeking ways of differentiating themselves from their competitors. For example, Marriott has invested heavily in new super-comfortable beds and bedding to gain an advantage over its competitors.

The quality of the physical product is also used as a differentiator by airlines—for example, stainless-steel rather than plastic cutlery, more leg room, personal television screens showing up-to-date movies and, for first-class long-haul passengers, more comfortable beds. Service companies need to reassess their product offerings to keep up with changing consumer tastes. For example, to appeal to a generation of young people who spend a lot of time playing computer games, Disneyland has designed attractions that offer theme park guests the chance to 'get interactive', and is experimenting with mobile phones and other handheld electronic devices to add interactive appeal.[57]

Promotion: the intangible element of a service may be difficult to communicate. For example, it may be difficult to represent courtesy, hard work and customer care in an advertisement. Once again, the answer is to use *tangible cues* that will help customers understand and judge the service. A hotel can show its buildings, swimming pool, friendly staff and happy customers. An investment company can provide tangible evidence of past performance. Testimonials from satisfied customers can also be used to communicate services benefits. Netto, the Danish-based supermarket chain, used testimonials from six customers in its UK advertising to explain the advantages of shopping there.

Ad insight

Go to the website to see how HSBC's ad makes its services tangible

Advertising can be used to communicate and reinforce the image of a service. For example, store image can enhance customer satisfaction and build store loyalty.[58] Advertising can also be used to create awareness of the benefits consumers can expect from the service provider, as the advertisement for HSBC shows. Promotions can be used to provide value-based offerings such as the Marks & Spencer 'Dine in for £10' and Sainsbury's 'Feed a Family for a Fiver' campaigns.

New media can also be used to promote services. For example, some online retailers use targeted e-mail to encourage customers to visit their sites. The travel and leisure retailer Lastminute.com sends more than two million e-mails to customers every week with content tailored to fit the recipient's age and lifestyle.[59] Online retailers Amazon and eBay also use e-mail to send regular messages to their customers about products and special offers. Traditional methods are also used, however. For example, eBay uses direct mail to tell businesses about the benefits of using its site to sell goods.[60]

Personal selling can also be effective in services marketing because of the high perceived risk inherent in many service purchases. For example, a salesperson can explain the details of a personal pension plan or investment opportunity, answer questions and provide reassurance.

Because of the high perceived risk inherent in buying services, salespeople should develop lists of satisfied customers to use in reference selling. Also salespeople need to be trained to ask for referrals. Customers should be asked if they know of other people or organizations that might benefit from the service. The customer can then be used as an entrée and point of reference when approaching and selling to the new prospect.

Word of mouth is critical to success for services because of their experiential nature. For example, talking to people that have visited a resort or hotel is more convincing than reading holiday brochures. Promotion, therefore, must acknowledge the dominant role of personal influence in the choice process and stimulate word of mouth communication. Cowell suggests four approaches, as follows.[61]

1 Persuading satisfied customers to inform others of their satisfaction (e.g. American Express rewards customers that introduce others to its service).
2 Developing materials that customers can pass on to others.
3 Targeting opinion leaders in advertising campaigns.
4 Encouraging potential customers to talk to current customers (e.g. open days at universities).

Viral communications—sometimes called electronic word of mouth—can also be used to promote services. This may take the form of an e-mail sent to a target audience, who are encouraged to spread the word among their friends by passing the message on electronically.

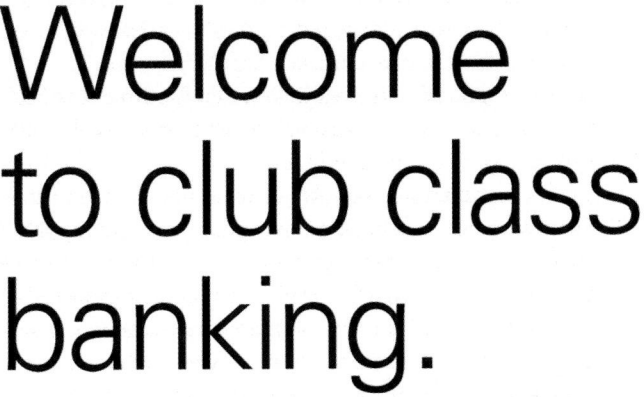

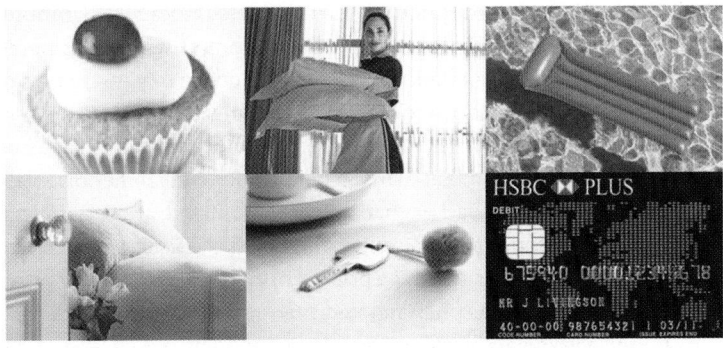

▲ HSBC's Plus account offers customers extra services, such as preferential rates, insurance and discounts on travel and entertainment for a monthly fee.

Communication should also be targeted at employees because of their importance in creating and maintaining service quality. Internal communications can define management expectations of staff, reinforce the need to delight the customer and explain the rewards that follow from giving excellent service. External communications that depict service quality can also influence internal staff if they include employees and show how they take exceptional care of their customers.

Care should be taken not to exaggerate promises in promotional material since this may build up unachievable expectations. For example, Delta Airlines used the advertising slogan 'Delta is ready when you are.' This caused problems because it built up customers' expectations that the airline would always be ready—an impossible task. This led Delta to change its slogan to the more realistic 'We love to fly and it shows.'[62]

The unethical promotion of service products has caused problems in some sectors. A study of senior managers in UK insurance companies revealed an awareness of a range of ethical problems. The design of commission systems which may encourage bias towards products that provide greater returns to the salesperson, and the promotion of inappropriate products were of particular concern.[63]

Price: price is a key marketing tool for three reasons. First, as it is often difficult to evaluate a service before purchase, price may act as an indicator of perceived quality. For example, in a travel brochure the price charged by hotels may be used to indicate their quality. Some companies expect a management consultant to charge high fees, otherwise they cannot be particularly good. Second, price is an important tool in controlling demand: matching demand and supply is critical in services because they cannot be stored. Creative use of pricing can help to smooth demand. Third, a key segmentation variable with services is price sensitivity. Some customers may be willing to pay a much higher price than others. Time is often used to segment price-sensitive and price-insensitive customers. For example, the price of international air travel is often dependent on length of stay. Travellers from Europe to the USA will pay a lot less if they stay a minimum of six nights (including Saturday). Airlines know that customers who stay for less than that are likely to be businesspeople who are willing and able to pay a higher price.

Many companies do not take full advantage of the opportunities to use price creatively in the marketing of their services. For example, in the business-to-business services sector, one study found that firms 'generally lack a customer orientation in pricing; emphasize formula-based approaches that are cost-orientated; are very inflexible in their pricing schemes; do not develop price differentials based on elasticity of different market segments; and rarely attempt to measure customer price sensitivity'.[64] An exception is the budget hotel chain, Travelodge. The company has adopted a demand-led online pricing system similar to that pioneered by easyJet and Ryanair. Rooms are often priced cheaply to begin with, but the price rises as the hotel becomes fully booked.[65]

Some services, such as accounting and management consultancy, charge their customers fees. A strategy needs to be thought out concerning fees. How far can fees be flexible to secure or retain particular customers? How will the fee level compare to that of the competition? Will there be an incentive built in to the fee structure for continuity, forward commitment or the use of the full range of services on offer? Five pricing techniques may be used when setting fee levels.

1 *Offset*: low fee for core service but recouping with add-ons.
2 *Inducement*: low fee to attract new customers or to help retain existing customers.
3 *Diversionary*: low basic fees on selected services to develop the image of value for money across the whole range of services.
4 *Guarantee*: full fee payable on achievement of agreed results.
5 *Predatory*: competition's fees undercut to remove them from the market; high fees charged later.

The Internet is making price transparency a reality. This has caused problems for premium-price service companies such as Avis. In the face of online holiday companies offering cheap holidays and car rental deals, and the ease with which consumers can compare prices, Avis has had to reduce prices, thereby depressing profitability.[66]

Place: distribution channels for services are usually more direct than for many physical goods. Because services are intangible, the services marketer is less concerned with storage, the production and consumption is often simultaneous, and the personal nature of services means that direct contact with the service provider (or at best its agent) is desirable. Agents are used when the individual service provider cannot offer a sufficiently wide selection for customers. Consequently, agents are often used for the marketing of travel, insurance and

▲ Iggy Pop, a rock icon, is used to grasp attention in this advertisement, which claims faster service when you buy online at Swiftcover.com.

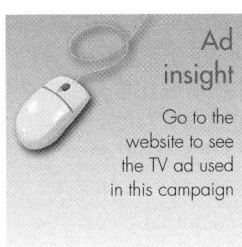

entertainment. However, the advent of the Internet means that direct dealings with the service provider are becoming more frequent.

Growth for many service companies means opening new facilities in new locations. Whereas producers of physical goods can expand production at one site to serve the needs of a geographically spread market, the simultaneous production and consumption of hotel, banking, catering, retailing and accounting services, for example, means that expansion often means following a multi-site strategy. The evaluation of store locations is therefore a critical skill for services marketers. Much of the success of top European supermarket chains has been due to their ability to choose profitable new sites for their retailing operations.

Service companies are also employing multi-channel strategies to make their products widely available. For example, the retailer Next uses bricks-and-mortar stores and the Next Directory mail-order channel, as well as an online business.[67] Consumers are increasingly buying services through the Internet. This can often mean lower prices and, in some cases, faster service. The advertisement for Swiftcover.com promises both.

People: because of the simultaneity of production and consumption in services, the firm's personnel occupy a key position in influencing customer perceptions of product quality.[68] In fact, service quality is inseparable from the quality of the service provider. Without courteous, efficient and motivated staff, service organizations will lose customers. A survey has shown that one in six consumers have been put off making a purchase because of the way they were treated by staff.[69] An important marketing task, then, is to set standards to improve the quality of service provided by employees and monitor their performance. Without training and control, employees tend to be variable in their performance, leading to variable service quality.

Training is crucial so that employees understand the appropriate forms of behaviour. British Airways trains its flight attendants to identify and categorize different personality types of passengers, and to modify their behaviour accordingly. Staff (e.g. waiters) need to know how much discretion they have to talk informally to customers, and to control their own behaviour so that they are not intrusive, noisy or immature. They also need to be trained to adopt a warm and caring attitude to customers. This has been shown to be linked to customers' perceptions of likeability and service perception, as well as loyalty to the service provider.[70] Finally, they need to adopt a customer-first attitude rather than putting their own convenience and enjoyment before that of their customers. This is not to say that staff should not enjoy their work. As Ross Urquhart, managing director of brand experience consultancy RPM, puts it:

> When people enjoy their work it is clear from their body language and the tone of their voice. They give off positive messages about their employer and will go the extra mile for their clients too. The company brand enjoys a very real boost as a result.[71]

Marketing should also examine the role played by customers in the service environment and seek to eliminate harmful interactions. For example, the enjoyment of a restaurant meal or air travel will very much depend on the actions of other customers. At Christmas, restaurants are often in demand by groups of work colleagues for staff parties. These can be rowdy affairs that can detract from the pleasure of regular patrons. This situation needs to be managed, perhaps by segregating the two types of customer in some way.

Physical evidence: this is the environment in which the service is delivered, and any tangible goods that facilitate the performance and communication of the service. Customers look for clues to the likely quality of a service by inspecting the tangible evidence. For example, prospective customers may gaze through a restaurant window to check the appearance of the waiters, the décor and furnishings. The ambience of a retail store is highly dependent on décor, and colour can play an important role in establishing mood because colour has meaning. For example, black signifies strength and power, whereas green suggests mildness. The interior of jet aircraft is pastel-coloured to promote a feeling of calmness, whereas many nightclubs are brightly coloured, with flashing lights to give a sense of excitement.

The layout of a service operation can be a compromise between operations' need for efficiency, and marketing's desire to serve the customer effectively. For example, the temptation to squeeze in an extra table at a restaurant or extra seating in an aircraft may be at the expense of customer comfort.

Process: this is the procedures, mechanisms and flow of activities by which a service is acquired. Process decisions radically affect how a service is delivered to customers. For example, a self-service cafeteria is very different from a restaurant. Marketing managers need to know if self-service is acceptable (or indeed desirable). Queuing may provide an opportunity to create a differential advantage by reduction/elimination, or making the time spent waiting more enjoyable. Certainly waiting for service is a common experience for customers and is a strong determinant of overall satisfaction with the service and customer loyalty. Research has shown that an attractive waiting environment can prevent customers becoming irritated or bored very quickly, even though they may have to wait a long time. Both appraisal of the wait and satisfaction with the service improved when the attractiveness of the waiting environment (measured by atmosphere, cleanliness, spaciousness and climate) was rated higher.[72] Providing a more effective service (shorter queues) may be at odds with operations as the remedy may be to employ more staff.

Reducing delivery time—for example, the time between ordering a meal and receiving it—can also improve service quality. As discussed earlier, this need not necessarily cost more if customers can be persuaded to become involved in the production process, as successfully reflected in the growth of self-service breakfast bars in hotels.

Finally, Berry suggests seven guidelines when implementing a positioning strategy.[73]

1 Ensure that *marketing* happens at all levels, from the marketing department to where the service is provided.
2 Consider introducing *flexibility* in providing the service; when feasible, customize the service to the needs of customers.
3 Recruit *high-quality staff*, treat them well and communicate clearly to them; their attitudes and behaviour are the key to service quality and differentiation.
4 Attempt to market to *existing customers* to increase their use of the service, or to take up new service products.

5 Set up a *quick-response facility* to customer problems and complaints.
6 Employ *new technology* to provide better services at lower cost.
7 Use *branding* to clearly differentiate service offerings from those of the competition in the minds of target customers.

Retailing

Retailing is an important service industry: it is the activity involved in the sale of products to the ultimate consumer. Retailing is a major employer of the European Union's workforce and its international nature is increasing despite laws such as France's Loi Royer, Belgium's Loi Cadenas and Germany's Baunutzungsverordnung, which restrict retail developments above certain sizes.

The purchasing power of retailers has meant that manufacturers have to maintain high service levels and good relations with them. Many are turning to trade marketing teams to provide dedicated resources to service their needs. Trade marketers focus on retailers' needs: what kind of products they want, in which sizes, with which packaging, at what prices and with what kind of promotion. Supermarkets are demanding more tailored promotions. (For example, a large supermarket chain also owned a group of hotels. It demanded from a drinks supplier that the next competition promotion offer holiday breaks in its hotels as prizes—paid for by the manufacturer.) They also feed information on trade requirements back to brand managers, who develop appropriate products. Trade marketers then brief the salesforce on how best to communicate the value of these to retailers. In this way, trade marketing is designed to ensure that the retailer's needs are met, while helping the coordination between brand and key account management.[74]

Consumer decision-making involves not only the choice of product and brand, but also the choice of retail outlet. Most retailing is conducted in stores such as supermarkets, catalogue shops and departmental stores, but non-store retailing such as mail order and automatic vending also accounts for a large amount of sales. Retailing provides an important service to customers, making products available when and where customers want to buy them.

Store choice may be dependent on the buying scenario relevant to consumers in a market. For example, two unique choice situations in Germany are relevant for grocery shopping: shopping for daily household needs (*Normaleinkauf*) and grocery shopping for stocking up for weekly or monthly household needs (*Vorratseinkauf*). The stores chosen for the former activity are largely different to those used for the latter.[75]

Many large retailers exert enormous power in the distribution chain because of the vast quantities of goods they buy from manufacturers.

This power is reflected in their ability to extract 'guarantee of margins' from manufacturers. This is a clause inserted in a contract that ensures a certain profit margin for the retailer irrespective of the retail price being charged to the customer. One manufacturer is played against another and own-label brands are used to extract more profit.[76]

Major store and non-store types
Supermarkets
These are large self-service stores traditionally selling food, drinks and toiletries, but range broadening by some supermarket chains means that such items as non-prescription pharmaceuticals, cosmetics and clothing are also being sold. While one attraction of supermarkets is their lower prices compared with small independent grocery shops, the extent to which price is a key competitive weapon depends on the supermarket's positioning strategy. For example, in the UK Sainsbury's, Waitrose and Marks & Spencer rely less on price than Lidl, Aldi or Netto.

Department stores

So called because related product lines are sold in separate departments, such as men's and women's clothing, jewellery, cosmetics, toys, and home furnishings, in recent years department stores have been under increasing pressure from discount houses, speciality stores and the move to out-of-town shopping. Nevertheless, they are still surviving in this competitive arena.

Speciality shops

These outlets specialize in a narrow product line. For example, many town centres have shops selling confectionery, cigarettes and newspapers in the same outlet. Many speciality outlets sell only one product line, such as Tie Rack and Sock Shop. Specialization allows a deep product line to be sold in restricted shop space. Some speciality shops, such as butchers and greengrocers, focus on quality and personal service.

Discount houses

These sell products at low prices by bulk buying, accepting low margins and selling high volumes. Low prices, sometimes promoted as sale prices, are offered throughout the year. As an executive of Dixons, a UK discounter of electrical goods, commented, 'We only have two sales—each lasting six months.' Many discounters operate from *out-of-town retail warehouses* with the capacity to stock a wide range of merchandise.

Category killers

These are retail outlets with a narrow product focus but, unusually, with a pronounced width and depth to that product range. Category killers emerged in the USA in the early 1980s as a challenge to discount houses. They are distinct from speciality shops in that they are bigger and carry a wider and deeper range of products within their chosen product category, and are distinguished from discount houses in their focus on only one product category. Two examples of the category killer are Toys 'Я' Us and Nevada Bob's Discount Golf Warehouses.[77]

Convenience stores

These stores offer customers the convenience of close location and long opening hours every day of the week. Because they are small they pay higher prices for their merchandise than supermarkets, and therefore have to charge higher prices to their customers. Some of these stores join buying groups such as Spar or Mace to gain some purchasing power and lower prices. But the main customer need they fulfil is for top-up buying—for example, when short of a carton of milk or loaf of bread. Although average purchase value is low, convenience stores prosper because of their higher prices and low staff costs: many are family businesses.

Catalogue stores

These retail outlets promote their products through catalogues that are either posted or are available in the store for customers to take home. Purchase is in city-centre outlets, where customers fill in order forms, pay for the goods and then collect them from a designated place in the store. In the UK, Argos is a successful catalogue retailer selling a wide range of discounted products such as electrical goods, jewellery, gardening tools, furniture, toys, car accessories, sports goods, luggage and cutlery.

Mail order

This non-store form of retailing may also employ catalogues as a promotional vehicle but the purchase transaction is conducted via the mail. Alternatively, outward communication may be by direct mail, television, magazine or newspaper advertising. Increasingly orders are being placed by telephone, a process facilitated by the use of credit cards as a means of payment. Goods are then sent by mail. A growth area is the selling of personal computers by mail order. By eliminating costly intermediaries, products can be offered at low prices. Otto, the German mail-order company, owns Grattan, a UK mail-order retailer, and has leading positions in Austria, Belgium, Italy, the Netherlands and Spain. Its French rival, La Redoute, has expanded into Belgium, Italy and Portugal. Mail order has the prospect of pan-European catalogues, central warehousing and processing of cross-border orders.

Online retailers

Specialist online retailers such as Amazon and eBay sell only online. Amazon has expanded from books to sell an array of products, including consumer electronics, music, DVDs, video, software, computer games and toys. The online auction site eBay allows consumers to sell unwanted goods to the highest bidder, but also allows businesses to operate goods listings and sales within their own stores on eBay. This provides a globally recognizable brand that customers trust to purchase from, and to handle personal details and financial transactions. This is of particular value to small businesses, which may not get the required visits to their own website without eBay's recognition. In return, eBay receives commission fees for the services it provides. Amazon also offers its services to outside retailers that wish to sell goods on its website. This is big business for Amazon, which achieves 30 per cent of its sales from this source. The company has rolled out new services such as help with setting up shop and managing order fulfilment, to attract new retailers to its site.[78]

The second type of online retailer is the traditional outlet that adds a facility to buy online. Many supermarkets, travel operators, hotels and car hire firms operate online, often (in the case of travel) offering price discounts compared to alternative means of purchase, such as booking by telephone.

Automatic vending

Vending machines offer such products as drinks, confectionery, soup and newspapers in convenient locations, 24 hours a day. No sales staff are required although restocking, servicing and repair costs can be high. Cash dispensers at banks have improved customer service by permitting round-the-clock access to savings. However, machine breakdowns and out-of-stock situations can annoy customers.

Theories of retail evolution

Three retailing theories explain the changing fortunes of different retailing types, and how one type is replaced by another. These are the **wheel of retailing**, the **retail accordion** and the **retail life cycle**.

The wheel of retailing

This theory suggests that new forms of retailing begin as cut-price, low-cost and narrow-profit-margin operations. Eventually, the retailer trades up by improving display and location, providing credit, delivery and sales services, and by raising advertising expenditures. The retailer thus matures as a high-cost, high-price conservative operator, making it vulnerable to new, lower-price entrants.[79] The theory has been the subject of much debate, but anecdotal evidence concerning department stores, supermarkets and catalogue stores suggests that many began as low-price operators that subsequently raised costs and prices, creating marketing opportunities for new, low-price competitors, developments that are consistent with the theory.

The retail accordion

This theory focuses on the width of product assortment sold by retail outlets and claims a general—specific—general cycle. The cycle begins with retailers selling a wide assortment of goods, followed by a more focused range; this, in turn, is replaced by retailers expanding their range.[80] The theory was developed with regard to the evolution of the entire retail system and is broadly in accord with experience in the USA where the general store of the nineteenth century was superseded by the specialist retailers of the early twentieth. These then gave way to the post-1940s mass merchandisers.

The retail life cycle

The concept of a retail life cycle is based on the well-known product life cycle, which states that new types of retailing pass through the stages of birth, growth, maturity and decline.[81] A retailing innovation enjoying a competitive advantage over existing forms is rewarded by fast sales growth. During the growth stage, imitators are attracted by its success, and by the end of this phase problems arise through over-ambitious expansion. Maturity is characterized by high competition, and is replaced by decline as new retail innovations take over. Evidence suggests that variety stores and counter-service grocery stores evolved in this manner.[82]

Key retail marketing decisions

The three theories of retailing explain the evolution in retailing methods, but there is nothing inevitable about the demise of a given retailer. The key is to anticipate and adapt to changing environmental circumstances. We shall now explore some of the key retailing decisions necessary to prosper in today's competitive climate.

The basic framework for deciding retail marketing strategy is that described earlier in this chapter, when services were discussed. However, there are a number of specific issues that relate to retailing and are worthy of separate discussion. These are retail positioning, store location, product assortment and services, price and store atmosphere. These call for decisions to be taken against a background of rapid change in information technology. Digital Marketing 22.2 describes some developments and their impact on retail marketing decisions.

Retailing differentiation   FIGURE 22.8

Source: Davies, G. and N. Sanghavi (1993) Is the Category Killer a Significant Innovation?, ESRC Seminar: Strategic Issues in Retailing, Manchester Business School, 1–23

Retail positioning

As with all marketing decisions, **retail positioning** involves the choice of target market and differential advantage. Targeting allows retailers to tailor their marketing mix, which includes product assortment, service levels, store location, prices and promotion, to the needs of their chosen customer segment. Differentiation provides a reason to shop at one store rather than another. A useful framework for creating a differential advantage has been proposed by Davies, who suggests that innovation in retailing can come only from novelty in the process offered to the shopper, or from novelty in the product or product assortment offered to the shopper.[83] Figure 22.8 shows that differentiation can be achieved through *process innovation* or *product innovation*, or a combination of the two (*total innovation*). Online retailers have offered innovation in the process of shopping, whereas Next achieved success through product innovation (stylish clothes at affordable prices). Toys 'Я' Us is an example of both product and process innovation through providing the widest range of toys at one location (production innovation) and thereby offering convenient, one-stop shopping (process innovation). By way of contrast, Woolworths, by not offering differentiation in

22.2 Digital Marketing

Information Technology in Retailing

Retailers are no strangers to information technology developments, with electronic point of sale (EPOS) systems allowing the counting of products sold, money taken and faster service at checkouts. More recent innovations, such as loyalty cards, however, have shifted the focus to understanding the customer. By monitoring individual purchasing patterns, direct mail promotions can be targeted at named individuals and adapted to match their known preferences and likely purchases. In-store product assortments can be matched more closely to purchasing patterns. In the USA, retailers are tailoring in-store promotions and discounts to individuals. One supermarket has a scheme where shoppers swipe their loyalty cards through 'readers' as they enter the shop and a list of money-off vouchers, based on their previous spending patterns, is printed.

A key technological development that is changing the way products are bought is the Internet. Online shopping is growing as more people become accustomed to electronic payment and fears over security subside. Already e-commerce has made inroads in books, information technology, travel and groceries. One success story is Tesco.com, the Internet arm of the UK supermarket chain. It now takes revenues of around £1 million a day. Shoppers can visit Tesco.com's website to order their groceries, which are delivered for a charge of £5 or free on deliveries over £50, as well as a range of consumer durables such as furniture, telephones, and electrical goods. The company uses its loyalty card scheme to target direct mail at those shoppers likely to value this service. For example, shoppers who appear to be price sensitive and, therefore, unlikely to be willing to pay the delivery charge are excluded from the mailing.

With direct mail being used to generate trial interest, e-mail is employed to keep the interest ongoing. But the main driver of success is the fact that the system works. Shoppers go to the site, choose the items they want, pay by credit card and at the prescribed time (within a chosen two-hour range) the Tesco delivery people arrive with the produce. Digital photo-developing kiosks are also being installed in stores, offering hard-copy prints from memory cards or CDs.

Tesco and Sainsbury's also analyse basket-level transactions, which provide insights into the type of household buying. For example, from the array of products in a basket it is easy to identify those households with babies or young children. Using a statistical technique called cluster analysis, such data were analysed to produce lifestyle segments—for example, 'High-spending superstore families'. This allows the tailoring of communications and promotional offers to specific market segments.

Technology is also helping to personalize the face of online retailing. An astonishing 95 per cent of potential customers abandon their basket of goods before completing a transaction. If a customer has a problem in a real store they ask an assistant, but this is difficult—if not impossible—to do in an online environment. However, 'Click to Call' technology is changing this, as it allows the online customer to contact a customer adviser to assist with the purchase. A Click to Call pop-up box can be programmed to appear if the potential buyer pauses for a long time, indicating that there may be a problem. For example, problems often occur at the credit card payment stage, at which point the pop-up would appear. Such technology has the potential to drastically reduce customer abandonment of transactions at the basket stage.

Information technology is also improving links between manufacturers and retailers. Electronic data interchange (EDI) allows them to exchange purchase orders, invoices, delivery notes and money electronically rather than using paper-based systems.

Based on: Reid (2002);[84] Croft (2005);[85] Quilter (2005);[86] Humby, Hunt and Phillips (2008);[87] Cuddleford-Jones (2009);[88] Fisher (2009)[89]

either of these dimensions, lost market share in toys and went out of business on the high street. The customer was offered a limited choice, no price advantage and the risk of having to shop around to be sure of finding a suitable toy. Toys 'Я' Us is now suffering from the impact of online retailers who translate their cost advantage into lower prices. Woolworths has been repositioned as an online retailer with its stores closing.[90]

Store location

Convenience is an important issue for many shoppers, and so store location can have a major bearing on sales performance. Retailers have to decide on regional coverage, the towns and cities to target within regions, and the precise location within a given town or city. Location for Ted Baker, the clothes-to-home-furnishings fashion retailer is absolutely key as the company does not advertise. Ted Baker is at Gatwick and Heathrow airports, Bluewater and Glasgow but also in Miami, Paris and New York's Bloomingdales. Its London store sits opposite Paul Smith, the designer clothes store, in one of the city's trendiest enclaves.[91] Many retailers begin life as regional suppliers, and grow by expanding geographically. In the UK, for example, the Asda supermarket chain expanded from the north of England, while the original base for Sainsbury's was in the south of England.

The choice of town or city will depend on such factors as correspondence with the retailer's chosen target market, the level of disposable income in the catchment area, the availability of suitable sites and the level of competition. The choice of a particular site may depend on the level of existing traffic (pedestrian and/or vehicular) passing the site, parking provision, access to the outlet for delivery vehicles, the presence of competition, planning restrictions and the opportunity to form new retailing centres with other outlets. For example, an agreement between two or more non-competing retailers (e.g. Marks & Spencer and Tesco) to site outlets together out of town means greater drawing power than could be achieved individually. Having made that decision, the partners will look for suitable sites near their chosen towns or cities.

The location of stores can be greatly aided by geographic information systems (GISs), which profile geographical areas according to such variables as disposable income, family size, age and birth rates. We saw in Chapter 8, on market segmentation and positioning, how such systems can be used to segment markets. GISs allow marketers to understand the profiles of people living in specific geographic areas. Asda, the UK supermarket chain uses GIS data as a method of finding new store locations. By understanding the number and profile of consumers living in different geographical areas, it can plan its stores (and product assortment) to be located in the right areas to serve its target market.[92]

Product assortment and services

Retailers have to decide upon the breadth of their product assortment and its depth. A supermarket, for example, may decide to widen its product assortment from food, drink and toiletries to include clothes, electrical goods and toys; this is called *scrambled merchandising*. Within each product line it can choose to stock a deep or shallow product range. Some retailers, like Tie Rack, Sock Shop and Toys 'Я' Us, stock one deep product line, as mentioned above. Department stores, however, offer a much broader range of products including toys, cosmetics, jewellery, clothes, electrical goods and household accessories. Some retailers begin with one product line and gradually broaden their product assortment to maximize revenue per customer. For example, petrol stations broadened their product range to include motor accessories, confectionery, drinks, flowers and newspapers. A by-product of this may be to reduce customers' price sensitivity since selection of petrol station may be based on the ability to buy other products rather than the lowest price.

The choice of product assortment will be dependent on the positioning strategy of the retailer, customer expectations and, ultimately, on the profitability of each product line. Slow-moving unprofitable lines should be dropped unless they are necessary to conform with the range of products expected by customers. For example, customers expect a full range of food products in a supermarket. McDonald's has increased its product assortment to conform to changing customer expectations, adding deli sandwiches, organic milk, fruit bags, bagels and fair trade coffee to its traditional burger product line.[93]

Another product decision concerns own-label branding. Large retailers may decide to sell a range of own-label products to complement national brands. Often the purchasing power of large retail chains means that prices can be lower and yet profit margins higher than for competing national brands. This makes the activity an attractive proposition for many retailers. Consumers also find own-label brands attractive, with many of them in the grocery field being regarded as being at least equal to, if not better than, established manufacturer brands.[94] Supermarkets have moved into this area, as have UK consumer electrical retailers Dixons and Currys, which are part of the same group. They both market televisions under the Matsui brand name. In this case the use of a Japanese-sounding name (even though some of the products were sourced in Europe) was believed to enhance their customer appeal. Marks & Spencer has moved in the opposite direction, adding 140 branded goods, such as Coca-Cola, Budweiser, Fairy Liquid, Shredded Wheat and Tetley tea, to its previously own-brand-only range of grocery products. The aim is to convert some M&S food halls into full supermarkets where shoppers do their entire weekly shop rather than merely for top-up and luxury shopping.[95]

Finally, retailers need to consider the nature and degree of *customer service*. Discount stores traditionally provided little service but, as price differentials have narrowed, some have sought differentiation through service. For example, many electrical goods retailers provide a comprehensive after-sales service package for their customers. Superior customer service may make customers more tolerant of higher prices and even where the product is standardized (as in fast-food restaurants) training employees to give individual attention to each customer can increase loyalty to the outlet.[96]

Price

For some market segments price is a key factor in store choice. Consequently, some retailers major on price as their differential advantage. This requires vigilant cost control and massive buying power. Where price is a key choice criterion, retailers who lose price competitiveness can suffer. For example, Carrefour, the world's second largest retailer after Wal-Mart, lost its reputation for low prices in France because of its focus on profit margins rather than volume. Market share plummeted in the face of intense competition from its domestic rivals, Leclerc and Auchan, and discounters such as Germany's Aldi and Lidl.[97] A recent trend is towards *everyday low prices* favoured by retailers rather than higher prices supplemented by promotions supported by manufacturers. Retailers such as B&Q, the do-it-yourself discounter, Aldi and Asda, maintain that customers prefer predictable low prices rather than occasional money-off deals, three-for-the-price-of two offers and free gifts. Supermarket chains are also pressurizing suppliers to provide consistently low prices rather than temporary promotions. This action is consistent with the desire to position themselves on a low-price platform.

The importance of price competitiveness is reflected in the alliance of European food retailers called Associated Marketing Services. Retailers such as Morrisons (UK), Ahold (the Netherlands), ICA (a federation of Swedish food retailers) and Superquinn (Ireland) have joined forces to foster cooperation in the areas of purchasing and marketing of brands. Its range of activities includes own branding, joint buying, the development of joint brands and services, and the exchange of information and skills. A key aim is to reduce cost price since this accounts for 75 per cent of the sales price to customers.[98]

Some supermarkets sell *no-frills products*. These are basic commodities, such as bread, sugar and soft drinks, sold in rudimentary packaging at low prices. For example, Tesco offers its Value range of own-label products and Aldi sells its 'no-frills' own-label brands at low prices.

Retailers need to be aware of the negative consequences of setting artificial 'sales' prices. The use of retail 'sales' by outlets to promote their merchandise can lead to increasing scepticism as to their integrity, especially those that 'must end soon' but rarely do, and the 'never to be repeated' bargain offers that invariably are.[99]

Store atmosphere

This is created by the design, colour and layout of a store. Both exterior and interior design affect atmosphere. External factors include architectural design, signs, window display and use of colour, which together create an identity for a retailer and attract customers. Retailers aim to create a welcoming rather than an intimidating mood. The image that is projected should be consonant with the ethos of the shop. The Body Shop, for example, projects its environmentally caring image through the green exterior of its shops, and window displays that feature environmental issues.

Interior design also has a major impact on atmosphere. Store lighting, fixtures and fittings, and layout are important considerations. Supermarkets that have narrow aisles that contribute to congestion can project a negative image, and poorly lit showrooms can feel intimidating. Colour, sound and smell can affect mood. As we have discussed earlier in this chapter, colour has meaning and can be used to create the desired atmosphere in a store. Sometimes red-toned lighting is used in areas of impulse purchasing. For example, one stationer uses red tones at the front of its stores for impulse buys such as pens and stationery. Supermarkets often use music to create a relaxed atmosphere, whereas some boutiques use pop music to attract their target customers. Departmental stores often place perfume counters near the entrance, and supermarkets may use the smell of baking bread to attract their customers. Luxury car manufacturers are even said to spray their cars and showrooms with 'essence of leather' to convey the perception of luxury. Marketing in Action 22.3 discusses how music can affect in-store behaviour.

22.3 Marketing in Action

The Sound of Music

Music can be an integral part of retail environments and has been proven to affect behaviour. For example, matching retail products with background music from the same country of origin can increase sales. An experiment showed that French wine significantly outsold German wine in a store when typical French accordion music was played. However, when German bierkeller music was played, the German wine came out top. Studies have also shown that playing songs from a particular target age groups' teenage to early-adult years can be effective, as this gives rise to feelings of comfort and nostalgia.

Music can create the desired atmosphere in a service setting. For example, when the Connaught Hotel, London, was refitted, the Coburg Bar was redesigned to be a quiet, modern and chic place with its own identity. A music playlist was drawn up to create a relaxed atmosphere. The hotel is pleased with the results, as guests linger in the bar and 40 per cent of customer reviews mention the music.

Retailers have known for many years that the right kind of music can encourage consumers to stay in the store longer, but using music is not without its potential problems. A study showed that, while 20 per cent of those surveyed said music encouraged them to linger longer in stores, 40 per cent reported that irritating, annoying or offensive music encouraged them to leave the store earlier.

As with all techniques to influence consumer behaviour, careful research is required to check that music is having the desired effect.

Based on: Goodman (2008);[100] Oakes (2008);[101] Orton-Jones (2009)[102]

The success of Stew Leonard's supermarket in Connecticut, USA, in projecting a fun atmosphere for shoppers has attracted the attention of European retailers. The Quinn's supermarket chain in Ireland has emulated its success, and other chains, such as Asda in the UK, provide a face-painting service for children at holiday times to make grocery shopping more fun.

Marketing in Non-Profit Organizations

Non-profit organizations attempt to achieve some other objective than profit. This does not mean they are uninterested in income as they have to generate cash to survive. However, their primary goal is non-economic—for example, to provide cultural enrichment (an orchestra), to protect birds and animals (Royal Society for the Protection of Birds, Royal Society for the Prevention of Cruelty to Animals), to alleviate hunger (Oxfam), to provide education (schools and universities), to foster community activities (community association), and to supply healthcare (hospitals) and public services (local authorities). Their worth and standing is not dependent on the profits they generate. They are discussed in this chapter as most non-profit organizations operate in the services sector. Indeed, non-profit organizations account for over half of all service provision in most European countries.

Marketing is of growing importance to many non-profit organizations because of the need to generate funds in an increasingly competitive arena. Even organizations that rely on government-sponsored grants need to show how their work is of benefit to society: they must meet the needs of their customers. Many non-profit organizations rely on membership fees or donations, which means that communication to individuals and organizations is required, and they must be persuaded to join or make a donation. This requires marketing skills, which are increasingly being applied. Such is the case with political parties, which use marketing techniques to attract members (and the fees their allegiance brings) and votes at elections.[103]

Advertising is also used by charities such as Oxfam to raise funds and create awareness of their services. The advertisement for Oxfam asks people to buy clothes from its shops (see illustration).

Fashion loved for longer

Beautiful clothes and accessories. From vintage classics to designer one-offs.

Visit Oxfam's London Boutiques:
245 Westbourne Grove | 123a Shawfield St | 190 Chiswick High Road

www.oxfam.org.uk/shop

Be Humankind ⊗ Oxfam

◄ Oxfam urges the public to be 'Humankind' and buy from its clothing shops to raise money for the charity.

Characteristics of non-profit marketing

There are a number of characteristics of *non-profit marketing* that distinguish it from that conducted by profit-orientated marketing organizations.[104]

Education vs meeting current needs

Some non-profit organizations see their role as not only meeting the current needs of their customers but also educating them in terms of new ideas and issues, cultural development and social awareness. These goals may be in conflict with maximizing revenue or audience figures. For example, a public broadcasting organization like the BBC may trade off audience size for some of these objectives, or an orchestra may decide that more esoteric pieces of classical music should be played rather than the more popular pieces.

Multiple publics

Most non-profit organizations serve several groups, or publics. The two broad groups are *donors*, who may be individuals, trusts, companies or government bodies, and *clients*, who include audiences, patients and beneficiaries.[105] The need is to satisfy both donors and clients, complicating the marketing task. For example, a community association may be part-funded by the local authority and partly by the users (clients) of the association's buildings and facilities. To succeed both groups have to be satisfied. The BBC has to satisfy not only its viewers and listeners, but also the government, which decides the size of the licence fee that funds the BBC's activities.

Non-profit organizations need to adopt marketing as a coherent philosophy for managing multiple public relationships.[106]

Measurement of success and conflicting objectives

For profit-orientated organizations success is measured ultimately in terms of profitability. For non-profit organizations measuring success is not so easy. In universities, for example, is success measured in research terms, number of students taught, the range of qualifications or the quality of teaching? The answer is that it is a combination of these factors, which can lead to conflict: more students and a larger range of courses may reduce the time available for research. Decision-making is therefore complex in non-profit-orientated organizations.

Public scrutiny

While all organizations are subject to public scrutiny, public-sector non-profit organizations are never far from the public's attention. The reason is that they are publicly funded from taxes. This gives them extra newsworthiness as all taxpayers are interested in how their money is being spent. They have to be particularly careful that they do not become involved in controversy, which can result in bad publicity.

Marketing procedures for non-profit organizations

Despite these differences, the marketing procedures relevant to profit-orientated companies can also be applied to non-profit organizations. Target marketing, differentiation and marketing-mix decisions need to be made. We shall now discuss these issues with reference to the special characteristics of non-profit organizations.

Target marketing and differentiation

As we have already discussed, non-profit organizations can usefully segment their target publics into donors and clients (customers). Within each group, sub-segments of individuals and organizations need to be identified. These will be the targets for persuasive communications and the development of services. The needs of each group must be understood. For example, donors may judge which charity to give to on the basis of awareness and reputation, the confidence that funds will not be wasted on excessive administration and the perceived worthiness of the cause. The charity needs, therefore, not only to promote itself but also to gain publicity for its cause. Its level of donor funding will depend on both factors. The brand name of the charity is also important. 'Oxfam' suggests the type of work the organization is mainly concerned with—relief of famine—and so is instantly recognizable.

Market segmentation and targeting are key ingredients in the marketing of political parties. Potential voters are segmented according to their propensity to vote (obtainable from electoral registers) and the likelihood that they will vote for a particular party (obtainable from door-to-door canvassing returns). Resources can then be channelled to the segments most likely to switch votes in the forthcoming election, via direct mail and doorstep visits. Focus groups provide a feedback mechanism for testing the attractiveness of alternative policy options and gauging voters' opinions on key policy areas such as health, education and taxation. By keeping in touch with public opinion, political parties have the information to differentiate themselves from their competitors on issues that are important to voters. While such marketing research is unlikely to affect the underlying beliefs and principles on which a political party is based, it is a necessary basis for the policy adaptations required to keep in touch with a changing electorate.[107]

Developing a marketing mix

Many non-profit organizations are skilled at *event marketing*. Events are organized to raise funds, including dinners, dances, coffee mornings, book sales, sponsored walks and theatrical shows. Not all events are designed to raise funds for the sponsoring organization. For example, the BBC hosts the Comic Relief and Children in Need *telethons* to raise money for worthy causes.

The pricing of services provided by non-profit organizations may not follow the guidelines applicable to profit-orientated pricing. For example, the price of a nursery school place organized by a community association may be held low to encourage poor families to take advantage of the opportunity. Some non-profit organizations exist to provide free access to services—for example, the National Health Service in the UK. In other situations, the price of a service provided by a non-profit organization may come from a membership or licence fee. For example, the Royal Society for the Protection of Birds (RSPB) charges an annual membership fee. In return, members receive a quarterly magazine and free entry to RSPB reserves. The BBC receives income from a licence fee that all television owners have to pay. The level of this fee is set by government, as noted above, making relations with political figures an important marketing consideration.

Like most services, distribution systems for many non-profit organizations are short, with production and consumption simultaneous. This is the case for hospital operations, consultations with medical practitioners, education, nursery provision, cultural entertainment and many more services provided by non-profit organizations. Such organizations have to think carefully about how to deliver their services with the convenience that customers require. For example, although the Hallé Orchestra is based in Manchester, over half of its performances are in other towns or cities. Some not-for-profit organizations have their own retail outlets. For example, Oxfam, an organization that seeks to reduce poverty and suffering around the world through fundraising and issue-awareness campaigns, has 750 shops around the UK that sell second-hand clothing, books, music and household items that have been donated to it. It has also formed alliances with online retailers such as abebooks.co.uk to list and sell second-hand books from which Oxfam receives a commission.

Many non-profit organizations are adept at using promotion to further their needs. The print media are popular with organizations seeking donations for worthy causes, such as famine relief in Africa. Direct mail is also used to raise funds. Mailing lists of past donors are useful here, and some organizations use lifestyle geodemographic analyses to identify the type of person that is more likely to respond to a direct mailing. Non-profit organizations also need to be aware of the publicity opportunities that may arise because of their activities. Many editors are sympathetic to such publicity attempts because of their general interest to the public. Sponsorship is also a vital income source for many non-profit organizations and events. For example, Accenture has sponsored the Royal Shakespeare Company since 2003, and Beck's has sponsored the arts for over 20 years. Marketing in Action 22.4 explains how ActionAid and the Association for International Cancer Research use marketing approaches to raise funds.

22.4 Marketing in Action

Charity Marketing

The charity ActionAid needs to maintain a consistent level of committed donors who pledge £15 per month. To do this it uses a variety of media, using fresh creative when a specific channel's impact shows signs of weakening. Direct-response television, inserts in newspapers such as the *Guardian*, press ads, face-to-face fundraising and telephone calls work well, but direct mail is not so effective. One-third of new child sponsors are recruited via ActionAid's website, but will have been encouraged to go there by activity in other media. The charity monitors the effectiveness of different channels, including mobile and Internet communications, to help plan future campaigns.

The Association for International Cancer Research (AICR) derives significant income from its prize-led fundraising activity. More than 200,000 donors who have shown a preference for prize draws and raffles are targeted with opportunities to win prizes such as cars, holidays or up to £10,000. Many donors have indicated that they prefer methods of support that bring them the chance of some personal benefit, such as prizes. AICR has also found that giving donors extra information about research projects that the charity has funded has significantly raised response.

Based on: Rubach (2008);[108] Clews (2009)[109]

Public relations has an important role to play to generate positive word-of-mouth communications and to establish the identity of the non-profit organization (e.g. a charity). Attractive fund-raising settings (e.g. sponsored lunches) can be organized to ensure that the exchange proves to be satisfactory to donors. A key objective of communications efforts should be to produce a positive assessment of the fundraising transaction and to reduce the perceived risk of the donation so that donors develop trust and confidence in the organization, and become committed to the cause.[110]

Online
LearningCentre

When you have read this chapter

log on to the Online Learning Centre at www.mcgraw-hill.co.uk/textbooks/jobber to explore chapter-by-chapter test questions, links and further online study tools for marketing.

Review ●●●

1 **The nature and special characteristics of services**
- Services are a special kind of product that may require special understanding and special marketing efforts because of their special characteristics.
- The key characteristics of pure services are intangibility (they cannot be touched, tasted or smelled); inseparability (production and consumption takes place at the same time, e.g. a haircut); variability (service quality may vary, making standardization difficult); and perishability (consumption cannot be stored, e.g. a hotel room).

2 **Managing customer relationships**
- Relationship marketing involves shifting from activities concerned with attracting new customers to activities focused on retaining existing customers.
- The benefits to the organization are increased purchases, lower costs, maximizing lifetime value of customers, sustainable competitive advantage, gaining word of mouth, and improved employee satisfaction and retention.
- The benefits to the customer are risk and stress reduction, higher-quality service, avoidance of switching costs, and social and status advantages.
- Customer retention strategies are targeting customers worthy of retention, bonding, internal marketing, promise fulfilment, building of trust, and service recovery.

3 **Managing service quality, productivity and staff**
- Two key service quality concepts are customer expectations and perceptions. Customers may be disappointed with service quality if their service perceptions fail to meet their expectations. This may result because of four barriers: the misconception barrier (management's misunderstanding of what the customer expects); the inadequate resources barrier (management provides inadequate resources); inadequate delivery barrier (management fails to select, train and adequately reward staff); and the exaggerated promises barrier (management causes expectations to be too high because of exaggerated promises).
- Service quality can be measured using a scale called SERVQUAL, which is based on five criteria: reliability, responsiveness, courtesy, competence and tangibles (e.g. quality of restaurant décor).
- Service productivity can be improved without reducing service quality by using technology (e.g. automatic cash dispensers); customer involvement in production (e.g. self-service petrol stations); and balancing supply and demand (e.g. differential pricing to smooth demand).
- Staff are critical in service operations because they are often in contact with customers. The starting point is the selection of suitable people, socialization allows the recruit to experience the culture and tasks of the organization, empowerment gives them the authority to solve customer problems, they need to be trained and motivated, and evaluation is required so that staff understand how their performance standards relate to customer satisfaction.

4 **How to position a service organization or brand**
- Positioning involves the choice of target market (where to compete) and the creation of a differential advantage (how to compete). These decisions are common to both physical products and services. However, because of the special characteristics of services, it is useful for the services marketer to consider not only the classical 4-Ps marketing mix but also an additional 3-Ps—people, physical evidence and process—when deciding how to meet customer needs and create a differential advantage.

5 **The services marketing mix**
- The service marketing mix consists of 7-Ps: product, price, place, promotion, people (important because of the high customer contact characteristic of services), physical evidence (important because customers look for cues to the likely quality of a service by inspecting the physical evidence, e.g. décor), and process (because the process of supplying a service affects perceived service quality).

6 **The major store and non-store retailing types**
- These are supermarkets, department stores, speciality shops, category killers (narrow product focus but with a pronounced width and depth to their product range), convenience stores, catalogue stores, mail order and automatic vending.

7 **Theories of retail evolution**
- There are three theories: (i) the wheel of retailing suggests that new forms of retailing begin as cut-price, low-price and narrow-profit-margin operations, but later the retailer trades up by adding on services to become a high-cost, high-price conservative operator; (ii) the retail accordion claims a general, wide assortment, specific/focused, general merchandiser sequence of retail evolution; and (iii) the retailer life cycle states that new types of retailing pass through the stages of birth, growth, maturity and decline.

8 **Key retail marketing decisions**
- Key retailing decisions are retail positioning, store location, product assortment and services, price and store atmosphere.

9 **The nature and special characteristics of non-profit marketing**
- Non-profit organizations attempt to achieve some other objective than profit. For example, an orchestra's primary objective may be cultural enrichment. Non-profit organizations are still interested in income as they have to generate cash to survive.
- Their special characteristics are that they may wish to pursue educational objectives as well as meeting the current needs of customers; they often serve multiple publics—for example, donors (e.g. the government) and clients (e.g. audiences); the difficulty of measuring success given multiple, sometimes conflicting objectives; and the close public scrutiny of public-sector organizations because of their funding from taxes.

Key Terms

exaggerated promises barrier a barrier to the matching of expected and perceived service levels caused by the unwarranted building up of expectations by exaggerated promises

halo customers customers that are not directly targeted but may find the product attractive

inadequate delivery barrier a barrier to the matching of expected and perceived service levels caused by the failure of the service provider to select, train and reward staff adequately, resulting in poor or inconsistent delivery of service

inadequate resources barrier a barrier to the matching of expected and perceived service levels caused by the unwillingness of service providers to provide the necessary resources

inseparability a characteristic of services, namely that their production cannot be separated from their consumption

intangibility a characteristic of services, namely that they cannot be touched, seen, tasted or smelled

misconception barrier a failure by marketers to understand what customers really value about their service

perishability a characteristic of services, namely that the capacity of a service business, such as a hotel room, cannot be stored—if it is not occupied, this is lost income that cannot be recovered

retail accordion a theory of retail evolution that focuses on the cycle of retailers widening and then contracting product ranges

retail life cycle a theory of retailing evolution that is based on the product life cycle, stating that new types of retailing pass through birth, growth, maturity and decline

retail positioning the choice of target market and differential advantage for a retail outlet

service any deed, performance or effort carried out for the customer

services marketing mix product, place, price, promotion, people, process and physical evidence (the '7-Ps')

variability a characteristic of services, namely that, being delivered by people, the standard of their performance is open to variation

wheel of retailing a theory of retailing development which suggests that new forms of retailing begin as low-cost, cut-price and narrow-margin operations and then trade up until they mature as high-price operators, vulnerable to a new influx of low-cost operators

Study Questions

1. The marketing of services is no different to the marketing of physical goods. Discuss.

2. What are the barriers that can separate expected from perceived service? What must service providers do to eliminate these barriers?

3. Discuss the role of service staff in the creation of a quality service. Can you give examples from your own experiences of good and bad service encounters?

4. Use Figure 22.7 to evaluate the service quality provided on your college course. First, identify all criteria that might be used to evaluate your course. Second, score each criterion from 1 to 10, based on its value to you. Third, score each criterion from 1 to 10 based on your perception of how well it is provided. Finally, analyse the results and make recommendations.

5. Of what practical value are the theories of retail evolution?

6. Identify and evaluate how supermarkets can differentiate themselves from their competitors. Choose three supermarkets and evaluate their success at differentiation.

7. Discuss the problems of providing high-quality service in retailing in central and eastern Europe.

8. How does marketing in non-profit organizations differ from that in profit-orientated companies? Choose a non-profit organization and discuss the extent to which marketing principles can be applied.

9. Discuss the benefits to organizations and customers of developing and maintaining strong customer relationships.

References

1. Gross, A. C., P. M. Banting, L. N. Meredith and I. D. Ford (1993) *Business Marketing*, Boston, Mass: Houghton Mifflin, 378.
2. Cowell, D. (1995) *The Marketing of Services*, London: Heinemann, 35.
3. Berry, L. L. (1980) Services Marketing is Different, *Business Horizons*, May–June, 24–9.
4. Edgett, S. and S. Parkinson (1993) Marketing for Services Industries: A Review, *Service Industries Journal* 13(3), 19–39.
5. Berry (1980) op. cit.
6. Aijo, T. S. (1996) The Theoretical and Philosophical Underpinnings of Relationship Marketing, *European Journal of Marketing* 30(2), 8–18; Grönroos, C. (1990) *Services Management and Marketing: Managing the Moments of Truth in Service Competition*, Lexington, MA: Lexington Books.
7. Baron, S., K. Harris and B. J. Davies (1996) Oral Participation in Retail Service Delivery: A Comparison of the Roles of Contact Personnel and Customers, *European Journal of Marketing* 30(9), 75–90.

8. Fernandez, J. (2009) Case Study: BT, *Marketing Week*, 26 March, 20.

9. Grönroos, C. (1994) From Marketing Mix to Relationship Marketing: Towards a Paradigm Shift in Marketing, *Management Decision* 32(2), 4–20.

10. Egan, C. (1997) Relationship Management, in Jobber, D. (ed.) *The CIM Handbook of Selling and Sales Strategy*, Oxford: Butterworth-Heinemann, 55–88. See also Coviello, N. E., R. J. Brodie, P. J. Danaker and W. J. Johnson (2002) How Firms Relate to Their Markets: An Empirical Examination of Contemporary Marketing Practices, *Journal of Marketing* 66, July, 33–46.

11. Berry, L. L. (1995) Relationship Marketing, in Payne, A., M. Christopher, M. Clark and H. Peck (eds) *Relationship Marketing for Competitive Advantage*, Oxford: Butterworth-Heinemann, 65–74.

12. Zeithaml, V. A., M. J. Bitner, and D. D. Gremier (2005) *Services Marketing*, New York: McGraw-Hill, 174–8.

13. Reichheld, F. F. and W. E. Sasser Jr (1990) Zero Defections: Quality Comes to Services, *Harvard Business Review*, Sept.–Oct., 105–11.

14. Roberts, K., S. Varki and R. Brodie (2003) Measuring the Quality of Relationships in Consumer Services: An Empirical Study, *European Journal of Marketing* 37(1/2), 169–96.

15. Reichheld and Sasser Jr (1990) op. cit.

16. Berry, L. L. (1995) Relationship Marketing of Services—Growing Interest, Emerging Perspectives, *Journal of the Academy of Marketing Science* 23(4), 236–45.

17. Bitner, M. J. (1995) Building Service Relationships: It's All About Promises, *Journal of the Academy of Marketing Science* 23(4), 246–51.

18. Bitner (1995) op. cit.

19. Parasuraman, A., L. L. Berry and V. A. Zeithaml (1991) Understanding Customer Expectations of Service, *Sloan Management Review*, Spring, 39–48.

20. Berry (1995) op. cit.

21. Berry, L. L. and A. Parasuraman (1991) *Marketing Services*, New York: Free Press, 136–42.

22. Berry (1995) op. cit.

23. Gummesson, E. (1987) The New Marketing–Developing Long-term Interactive Relationships, *Long Range Planning* 20, 10–20.

24. Bitner (1995) op. cit.

25. See Bitner, M. J., B. H. Booms and M. S. Tetreault (1990) The Service Encounter: Diagnosing Favourable and Unfavourable Incidents, *Journal of Marketing* 43, January, 71–84; Bitner, M. J., B. H. Booms and L. A. Mohr (1994) Critical Service Encounters: The Employee's View, *Journal of Marketing* 58, October, 95–106.

26. Lovelock, C. H., S. Vandermerwe and B. Lewis (1999) *Services Marketing—A European Perspective*, New York: Prentice-Hall, 176.

27. Berry (1995) op. cit.

28. Budworth, D. (2008) The credit crunch explained. Times Online, 14 August 2008, available at www.timesonline.co.

uk/tol/money/reader_guides/article4530072.ece (retrieved 15 November 2008).

29. Wachman, R. (2008) Virgin Claims Rock Brand will Deter Savers, Observer Online, 3 February, available at: http://www.guardian.co.uk/media/2008/feb/03/virginmedia.northernrock (retrieved 18 November 2008).

30. Elliott, L. and Seager, A. (2009) Financiers in the Spotlight as Ethics Takes Centre Stage at Davos, Guardian.co.uk, 27 January 2009 (retrieved 9 April 2009, from www.guardian.co.uk/business/2009/jan/27/world-economic-forum-davos/print).

31. Sunderland, R. (2009) Earth to Overpaid Bankers: You're Working for Us Now, *Observer*, 8 February 2009 (retrieved 9 April 2009, from http://www.guardian.co.uk/business/2009/feb/08/executive-salaries-banks).

32. Kasper, H., P. van Helsdingen and M. Gabbott (2006) *Services Marketing Management*, Chichester: Wiley, 528.

33. Maxham III, J. G. and R. G. Netemeyer (2002) A Longitudinal Study of Complaining Customers' Evaluations of Multiple Service Failures and Recovery Efforts, *Journal of Marketing* 66, October, 57–71.

34. Johnson, R. (1995) Service Failure and Recovery: Impact, Attributes and Process, in Swartz, T. A., D. E. Bowen and S. W. Brown (eds) *Advances in Services Marketing and Management* 4, 52–65.

35. Buzzell, R. D. and B. T. Gale (1987) *The PIMS Principles: Linking Strategy to Performance*, New York: Free Press, 103–34.

36. Parasuraman, A., V. A. Zeithaml and L. L. Berry (1985) A Conceptual Model of Service Quality and its Implications for Future Research, *Journal of Marketing*, Fall, 41–50.

37. Johnson, L. (2008) The Incalculable Appeal of Good Service, *Financial Times*, 26 March, 16.

38. Parasuraman, Zeithaml and Berry (1985) op. cit.

39. Danaher, P. J. and J. Mattson (1994) Customer Satisfaction during the Service Delivery Process, *European Journal of Marketing* 28(5), 5–16.

40. De Ruyter, K., M. Wetzels, J. Lemmink and J. Mattsson (1997) The Dynamics of the Service Delivery Process: A Value-Based Approach, *International Journal of Research in Marketing* 14, 231–43.

41. Zeithaml, V. A., A. Parasuraman and L. L. Berry (1988) SERVQUAL: A Multiple Item Scale for Measuring Consumer Perceptions of Service Quality, *Journal of Retailing* 64(1), 13–37.

42. Sherwood, B. (2008) An Eye For The Next Opportunity, *Financial Times*, 17 September, 16.

43. Lovelock, C. (1992) Seeking Synergy in Service Operations: Seven Things Marketers Need to Know about Service Operations, *European Management Journal* 10(1), 22–9.

44. Mudie, P. and A. Cottam (1997) *The Management and Marketing of Services*, Oxford: Butterworth-Heinemann, 211.

45. Schlesinger, L. A. and J. L. Heskett (1991) The Service-

Driven Service Company, *Harvard Business Review*, Sept.–Oct., 71–81.

46. Lievens, A. and R. K. Moenaert (2000) Communication Flows During Financial Service Innovation, *European Journal of Marketing* 34(9/10), 1078–110.

47. Jones, A. (2008) Shambolic But Totally Predictable, *Guardian*, 28 March, 3.

48. Finch, J. (2008) What's Wrong With Currys?, *Guardian*, 16 May, 9.

49. Bowen, D. E. and L. L. Lawler (1992) Empowerment: Why, What, How and When, *Sloan Management Review*, Spring, 31–9.

50. Hiscock, J. (2002) The Brand Insiders, *Marketing*, 23 May, 24–5.

51. Milne, R. (2004) High Fliers Get a Champagne Check-in, *Financial Times*, 23 November, 12.

52. Charles, G. (2008) KFC Launches Breakfast Menu, *Marketing*, 7 May, 1.

53. Roberts, J. (2009) When the Big Go Boutique, *Marketing Week*, 19 March, 12–16.

54. Christopher, M. and R. Yallop (1990) Audit your Customer Service Quality, *Focus*, June–July, 1–6.

55. Booms, B. H. and M. J. Bitner (1981) Marketing Strategies and Organisation Structures for Service Firms, in Donnelly, J. H. and W. R. George (eds) *Marketing of Services*, Chicago: American Marketing Association, 47–51.

56. Berry, L. L., E. E. Lefkowith and T. Clark (1980) In Services: What's in a Name?, *Harvard Business Review*, Sept.–Oct., 28–30.

57. Garrahan, M. (2005) The Ride of a Lifetime, *Financial Times*, 18 August, 19.

58. Bloemer, J. and K. de Ruyter (1998) On the Relationship Between Store Image, Store Satisfaction and Store Loyalty, *European Journal of Marketing* 32(5/6), 499–513.

59. Cole, G. (2003) Window Shopping, *Financial Times IT Review*, 5 February, 4.

60. Parry, C. (2005) Consumers and E-tail Begin to Click, *Marketing Week*, 14 April 2005.

61. Cowell, D. (1995) op. cit.

62. Sellers, P. (1988) How to Handle Customers' Gripes, *Fortune* 118 (October), 100.

63. Diacon, S. R. and C. T. Ennew (1996) Ethical Issues in Insurance Marketing in the UK, *European Journal of Marketing* 30(5), 67–80.

64. Morris, M. H. and D. Fuller (1989) Pricing an Industrial Service, *Industrial Marketing Management* 18, 139–46.

65. Fernandez, J. (2009) Sparking a Hotel Price War, *Marketing Week*, 12 March, 22–3.

66. Davoudi, S. (2005) From Brand Leader to Struggler in Eight Years, *Financial Times*, 17 June, 24.

67. Jack, L. (2008) Painful Times for the Next Generation, *Marketing Week*, 27 November, 8.

68. Rafiq, M. and P. K. Ahmed (1992) The Marketing Mix Reconsidered, *Proceedings of the Annual Conference of the Marketing Education Group*, Salford, 439–51.

69. Wilkinson, A. (2002) Employees can get the Message Across, *Marketing Week*, 3 October, 20.

70. Lemmink, J. and J. Mattsson (1998) Warmth During Non-Productive Retail Encounters: The Hidden Side of Productivity, *International Journal of Research in Marketing* 15, 505–17.

71. Sumner-Smith, D. (2001) A Winning Strategy, *Marketing Business*, May, 26–8.

72. Pruyn, A. and A. Smidts (1998) Effects of Waiting on the Satisfaction with the Service: Beyond Objective Times Measures, *International Journal of Research in Marketing* 15, 321–34.

73. Berry, L. L. (1987) Big Ideas in Services Marketing, *Journal of Services Marketing*, Fall, 5–9.

74. See Dewsnap, B. and D. Jobber (2000) The Sales–Marketing Interface in Consumer Packaged-goods Companies: a Conceptual Framework, *Journal of Personal Selling and Sales Management* 20(2), 109–19; Nicholas, R. (1999) Thirsty Work, *Marketing Week*, 11 November 79–83; and Dewsnap, B. (1997) Trade Marketing, in D. Jobber (ed.) *The CIM Handbook of Selling and Sales Strategy*, Oxford: Butterworth-Heinemann, 104–25.

75. Thelen, E. M. and A. G. Woodside (1997) What Evokes the Brand or Store? Consumer Research on Accessibility Theory Applied to Modelling Primary Choice, *International Journal of Research in Marketing* 14, 125–45.

76. Krishnan, T. V. and H. Soni (1997) Guaranteed Profit Margins: A Demonstration of Retailer Power, *International Journal of Research in Marketing* 14, 35–56.

77. Davies, G. and N. Sanghavi (1993) Is the Category Killer a Significant Innovation? *ESRC Seminar: Strategic Issues in Retailing*, Manchester Business School, 1–23.

78. McGregor, J. (2009) When Service Means Survival, *Business Week*, 2 March, 26–39.

79. Brown, S. (1990) Innovation and Evolution in UK Retailing: The Retail Warehouse, *European Journal of Marketing* 24(9), 39–54.

80. Hollander, S. C. (1966) Notes on the Retail Accordion, *Journal of Retailing* 42(2), 24.

81. Davidson, W. R., A. D. Bates and S. J. Bass (1976) The Retail Life Cycle, *Harvard Business Review* 54 (Nov.–Dec.), 89–96.

82. Knee, D. and D. Walters (1985) *Strategy in Retailing: Theory and Application*, Oxford: Philip Adam.

83. Davies, G. (1992) Innovation in Retailing, *Creativity and Innovation Management* 1(4), 230.

84. Reid, A. (2002) Tesco.com Leads the Way with Completely Integrated Thinking, *Campaign*, 19 April, 14.

85. Croft, M. (2005) The Science of Compliance, *Marketing Week*, 24 March, 35.

86. Quilter, J. (2005) Aisles of Plenty, *Marketing*, 10 August, 15–17.

87. Humby, C., T. Hunt and T. Phillips (2008) *Scoring Points*, London: Kogan-Page.

88. Cuddleford-Jones, M. (2009) This Time it's Very Personal, *Marketing Week*, 28 May, 26–8.

89. Fisher, L. (2009) The Data is There for the Taking, *Marketing Week*, 16 April, 25–6.

90. Harwood, J. (2008) The Worth of Woolies, *Marketing Week*, 21 August, 20–1.

91. Ryle, S. (2002) How to Get Ahead in Advertising at No Cost, *Observer*, 1 December, 8.

92. Hayward, C. (2002) Who, Where, Win, *Marketing Week*, 12 September, 43.

93. Charles, G. (2008) Big Mac is Back, *Marketing*, 5 March 30–1.

94. Burt, S. (2000) The Strategic Role of Retail Brands in British Grocery Retailing, *European Journal of Marketing* 34(8), 875–90.

95. Finch, J. (2008) From Dog Food to Dentures: M&S Lets in Other Brands to Save its Bottom Line, *Guardian*, July 5, 39.

96. Bloemer, S., K. de Ruyter and M. Wetzels (1999) Linking Perceived Service Quality and Service Loyalty: A Multi-Dimensional Perspective, *European Journal of Marketing* 33(11/12), 1082–106.

97. Anonymous (2005) Carrefour at the Crossroads, *Economist*, 22 October, 79.

98. Elg, U. and U. Johansson (1996) Networking When National Boundaries Dissolve: The Swedish Food Sector, *European Journal of Marketing* 30(2), 61–74.

99. Betts, E. J. and P. J. McGoldrick (1996) Consumer Behaviour with the Retail 'Sales', *European Journal of Marketing* 30(8), 40–58.

100. Goodman, L. (2008) Shoppers Dance to the Retailers' Tune, *Financial Times*, 21 August, 12.

101. Oakes, S. (2008) Music To Set Your Till Ringing, *The Marketer*, September, 15.

102. Orton-Jones, C. (2009) The Perfect Touch, *The Marketer*, February, 28–31.

103. See Lock, A. and P. Harris (1996) Political Marketing— Vive La Difference, *European Journal of Marketing* 30(10/11), 21–31; Butler, P. and N. Collins (1996) Strategic Analysis in Political Markets, *European Journal of Marketing* 30(10/11), 32–44.

104. Bennett, P. D. (1988) *Marketing*, New York: McGraw-Hill, 690–2.

105. Shapiro, B. (1992) Marketing for Non-Profit Organisations, *Harvard Business Review*, Sept.–Oct., 123–32.

106. Balabanis, G., R. E. Stables and H. C. Phillips (1997) Market Orientation in the Top 200 British Charity Organisations and its Impact on their Performance, *European Journal of Marketing* 31(8), 583–603.

107. For an in-depth examination of political marketing, see Butler, P. and N. Collins (1994) Political Marketing: Structure and Process, *European Journal of Marketing* 28(1), 19–34.

108. Rubach, E. (2008) Less Charitable More Cut-Throat, *Marketing*, 6 February, 26–7.

109. Clews, M.-L. (2009) Chugging Through Hard Times, *Marketing Week*, 5 February, 16–17.

110. Hibbert, S. A. (1995) The Market Positioning of British Medical Charities, *European Journal of Marketing* 29(10), 6–26.

Build-A-Bear

A Custom-Made Experience

Build-A-Bear Workshop: a dream come true for everyone

The dream began in October 1997, when Maxine Clark officially opened the first Build-A-Bear Workshop (BBW) store in Saint Louis Galleria. Before that, she had worked in firms where she had developed her expertise in detecting emerging marketing and retailing trends. This proved to be most useful when she founded her own company.

Indeed, nowadays, a lot of people like to participate in the creation of custom-made products and services. The Internet has played a great role in this development, since customers now have online opportunities to design their own T-shirts, sneakers, furniture, and so on. This trend has boomed with the emergence and spread of what has become known as Web 2.0. Well, in a way, 10 years before, Maxine Clark created 'Teddy-Bear Factory 2.0'.

BBW enables its customers to actively participate in the design and production of teddy bears through a specific eight-step process, at the end of which customers go home with their own personalized stuffed friend. From the very beginning, BBW was thought of 'as an interactive retail entertainment experience based on the enduring love and friendship that connects us all to stuffed animals, and especially to our teddy bears'. The concept has been successful from the very beginning, and BBW was recognized in 2001 with an award for most innovative retailer from the National Retail Federation. The firm also won many other awards in the years that followed.

However, the best award of all lies undoubtedly in its customers' (whom BBW calls its 'Guests') satisfaction and loyalty. As a matter of fact, 60 per cent of the firm's business is generated by a returning guest. And 80 per cent of them plan their visit in advance. This is not so surprising, since they consider that BBW delivers 'wow store experience'. In truth, 90 per cent of the guests rate the overall experience they have in a BBW store as the highest or second-highest rating among the largest US toy retailers. This explains why BBW hosted more than 1.4 million children at over 144,000 in-store parties in 2007; unsurprisingly, most of the guests are children— 'From 3 to 103' (so says the firm)! Yet, even though this is a rather wide age range, BBW aims mainly at families with children aged from three to 12: about 70 per cent of its customers are between birth and 12 years old, while the rest are about equally composed of teens and adults (more specifically, these other segments are: grandparents, aunts and uncles shopping for kids; teen girls 13–17 who bring along boyfriends; child-centric organizations; leisure travellers and special interest collectors). The average age of BBW's bear owners is 10 years old; 70 per cent of them are girls and 30 per cent are boys—and about 20 per cent of these bear owners are over 14 years old.

According to analyst Jaison Blair of Rochdale Securities Corp., customers are so satisfied by this customization feature that, just like Harley-Davidson motorcycles or Dell computers, 'it builds fiercely loyal customers'. Accordingly, at the end of 2007, BBW had more than 5 million US members in its Stuff Fur Stuff club loyalty programme, which it considers as its 'key Guest retention program and communication platform'. This exemplifies, once more, how customers are committed to the firm, its products and its services.

Make your own best friend!

Even though BBW has a website where bears can be customized and bought online, the largest part of the firm's business is done in its stores, where customers can choose between more than 30 stuffed animal styles. These stores are very colourful (bright yellow), very attractive, and are decorated and fitted out with original teddy bear fixtures and artwork. All this creates a friendly atmosphere, favourable for fun and

Some BBW Customers' Testimonies	TABLE C43.1

- I love your stores and your employees. Everyone is ALWAYS so friendly!
- I just wanted to send a huge thank you to Kate Lynch who was the party coordinator at my daughter's 9th birthday party. She was absolutely great to work with and the kids loved her and the party.
- My children went to the Build-A-Bear Workshop at Ridgmar Mall to purchase a Labrador retriever and a Westie dog. Devastated when they found out the store was out of these dogs, our children began to cry. The sales representative Catherine was fantastic. Our youngest child was also excited about a bunny rabbit Catherine showed her. And Catherine also satisfied our oldest child showing her we could order her Westie dog on-line. Catherine is a fantastic sales representative for Build-A-Bear Workshop. Thank you very much!
- I understood your concept and how cool it was, so I expected a nice party. What I didn't expect was the exceptionally high standard of customer service provided by EVERYONE at the store. Our party leader was awesome! There are many ways to do her job, but she really put her heart into it. Her big eyes and bright smile conveyed a genuineness that both the kids and the parents bought into. She was patient yet perky and even though she was having fun, I could tell that she was very organized and knew her job. She literally made the party. So chalk me up as one of those gushing moms that can't say enough about Build-A-Bear Workshop. What can I say, the legend is true. You guys take customer service to a new level. Your emphasis on training and commitment to excellence are obvious.
- Build-a-Bear Workshop is not age-biased! When I got a bear the associates treated me with just as much kindness and delight as they did my daughter! I loved that! Thank you.

Source: www.buildabear.com/aboutus/ourcompany/guesttestimonials.aspx.

entertainment, and a place where customers are supposed to have an experience they will remember with their friends and family.

On entering the store, customers are welcomed by 'master bear builder associates', who will share their experience with them. They are reckoned to be kindly, friendly, warm, enthusiastic, patient and helpful, as is illustrated by many customers' testimonies (see Table C43.1). Bear builder associates are trained to offer customers the best possible experience, so that they enjoy their time at BBW and want to come back. The bear builders' behaviour mirrors BBW's culture of openness and communication, sponsored by Maxine Clark herself. She empowers her employees, who are encouraged to propose improvements to enrich the experience or enhance the products sold by the company. Moreover, according to her, it is also important to let them know how much they actually contribute to the firm's progress and growth.

The mission of bear builder associates is to help customers through the bear-making process, as well as lead and enliven birthday parties for kids, where each guest makes their own stuffed animal. The whole bear-making process is divided into eight steps, carried out at 'stations', which the customer may become acquainted with on BBW's website (see illustration). The customer will also find the same information about each step in pictures at the store itself.

First, at the 'Choose Me' station, guests select the furry character they will personalize, from a range of products priced from $10 to $25. Second, guests may choose to place a sound (several available, from $3 to $5), or record their own message ($8), inside their stuffed animal; this is done at the 'Hear Me' station. At 'Stuff Me', the third station, guests are helped by bear builder associates to fill their animal. They also select a small satin heart, which they place inside their furry friend. This 'brings the furry friendship to life'! The fourth station is called 'Stitch Me', since this is where the last seam is pulled shut. This step is very important for the future possessor, as the bear builder associate also inserts a barcode that makes it possible to reunite the owner and its furry friend, in case the latter is ever lost (the Find-A-Bear ID Program). The next stage is labelled 'Fluff Me': the guest brushes his or her animal to ensure it is well groomed and perfectly huggable. The three last steps are 'Name Me', 'Dress Me' and 'Take Me Home'.

During the 'Dress Me' stage, guests choose clothes and accessories for all occasions, with outfits ranging from $5 to $15, and accessories from $1 to $15. Guests may even rely on the opinion of BBW fashion expert mascot, Pawlete Coufur®, 'fashion advisor to the furry famous'. Clothes and accessories are renewed regularly, and seasonal editions are often sold to stay close to kids' changing heroes (e.g. Spider-Man, Hello Kitty). At the 'Name Me' computer station, guests answer several

Choose Me   Hear Me   Stuff Me   Stitch Me   Fluff Me   Name Me   Dress Me   Take Me Home®

▲ The eight steps of the bear-making process.

questions about their new friend, including of course its birth date and name. Using this information, the owner is given a personalized birth certificate, and enters its friend into the aforementioned Find-A-Bear ID Program. Guests conclude their in-store experience of making their bear at the 'Take Me Home' station, where they are delivered their customized birth certificate and a special Stuff Fur Stuff club membership. They leave with their new friend in its own Cub Condo® carrying case, which looks like a handy travel carrier and new home. Once at home, guests can access www.buildabearville.com (available since December 2007), a virtual world where they can bring their furry friends to life free of charge, with exclusive virtual items, to continue their store experience and nurture their relationship with their animal—and the brand!

Next: your best friends everywhere!

Historically, BBW stores are located in malls, where they can reach a large audience. However, the company has recently begun to get out of malls and has opened stores in new places. For instance, BBW has teamed up with Major League Baseball. The firm has opened ballpark stores that offer the same experience and products as at classic stores, at AT&T Park in San Francisco, Busch Stadium in St Louis, Citizens Bank Park in Philadelphia and Great American Ball Park in Cincinnati. It also opened a store at the St Louis Zoo, which offers 10 animals to make. Among other attempts to develop, a Build-A-Dino store has been opened in July 2006 inside the T-Rex Café, located in the Village West district of Kansas City (Kansas). In the same vein, a store was opened in July 2007 inside the Rainforest Café. Guests are supposed to find in each of these new stores the same customer care available at conventional BBW stores.

Even before this, however, BBW had moved out of malls by introducing Build-A-Bear Workshop On Tour, 'a 53-foot tractor trailer that opens into a complete

800 square foot Build-A-Bear Workshop store'. The aim of this 'bright yellow and bear-covered mobile store' is to bring the BBW brand and experience outside the malls.

BBW On Tour is one of the multiple components of BBW's promotional strategy, expenditure on which has amounted to 7.5 per cent of sales since 2007 (i.e. about $35 million). The firm has announced that 65 per cent of this total is dedicated to customer acquisition, whereas the remaining 35 per cent is targeted at customer retention. To achieve this, the firm has announced that it will be relying on:

- 'focused and tailored TV advertising to convert awareness to trial'
- an integrated and multi-channel communication plan (TV, radio and online advertising)
- its Stuff Fur Stuff loyalty club
- its virtual world at www.buildabearville.com.

Finally . . .

BBW has opened 341 company-owned stores in North America, the UK, Ireland and France, as well as 60 franchise stores in 14 countries, and has sold more than 65 million stuffed animals. It also delivered (in 2007) its tenth consecutive year of total revenue growth, with net sales increasing from about $432 million to nearly $468 million. BBW has also become the tenth largest US toy retailer, and has 'the second largest percent increase in sales of any company of the Top 25 Toy Retailers'. Yet . . .

References

Based on: http://library.corporate-ir.net/library/18/182/182478/items/286985/2007_AR_FINAL.pdf (last accessed 28 November 2008); http://library.corporate-ir.net/library/18/182/182478/items/316880/InvestorUpdateFINAL.pdf (last accessed 28 November 2008); http://www.buildabear.com/aboutus/ourcompany/awards.aspx (last accessed November 28 2008); http://www.buildabear.com/aboutus/ourcompany/media/default.aspx (last accessed 28 November 2008); http://www.buildabear.com/aboutus/ourcompany/ourfounder.aspx (last accessed 28 November 2008); http://www.buildabear.com/aboutus/ourcompany/process.aspx (last accessed 28 November 2008); http://www.buildabear.com/babw/us/pages/aboutus/ourcompany/factsheet.pdf (last accessed 28 November 2008); http://www.businessweek.com/magazine/content/05_23/b3936411.htm (last accessed 7 December 2008); http://www.businessweek.com/smallbiz/content/sep2007/sb20070912_785676.htm (last accessed 7 December 2008); http://www.playthings.com/article/CA6500235.html (last accessed 7 December 2008); http://www.sbnonline.com/National/Article/14181/0/The_bear_necessities.aspx?Category=118 (last accessed 28 November 2008); http://www.washingtonpost.com/wp-srv/style/shopping/features/buildabear.htm (last accessed 7 December 2008).

Questions

. . . this success makes some people jealous, and you would really like to become one of its competitors. However, before launching your own business, you want to create a benchmark that allows you to clearly understand the reasons for its extraordinary growth since its creation.

1. Select two service marketing concepts that would help you perform this analysis, and explain them.

2. Following the different concepts you have come up with, explain why BBW has been so successful so far.

This case was written by Loïc Plé, Assistant Professor, IÉSEG School of Management, France.

Services Marketing in a Recession

The Tale of Five Supermarkets

An economic recession is associated with falling output, rising unemployment, lower incomes for many, a fall in consumer demand for products, and lower inflation. Companies need to adjust their marketing strategies to take account of the changing marketing environment—most notably shifts in consumer behaviour. This case study identifies the key changes in marketing strategies used by five UK supermarkets as they battled to compete in the recent economic downturn. The five supermarkets are: Tesco, the market leader; Sainsbury's and Asda, its main rivals; and Lidl and Aldi, two rising stars of the discount sector.

Tesco

A key move by Tesco was to launch 350 discount product lines under the Discount Brands at Tesco banner. The brands included Country Barn cornflakes, Mermaid Buy fish fingers, Gold Sun vitamins, Packers Best tea bags, Daisy washing-up liquid and Shanghai garden sauces. They were price positioned below manufacturer brands and Tesco's premium own-label brand, Tesco Finest, but above its low-price own-label brand, Tesco Value. The supermarket also expanded its Value offerings by, for example, launching a range of cut-price wines. These product line changes were supported with an advertising campaign announcing that Tesco was 'Britain's biggest discounter'.

Sainsbury's

During the recession, Sainsbury's ran a high-profile 'Switch and Save' campaign that encouraged consumers to buy its lower-priced own-label brands. In line with this strategy, the supermarket moved its advertising away from the famous Jamie Oliver advertisements promoting its premium-priced Taste the Difference own-label brands, towards 'Feed Your Family for a Fiver' and 'Love Your Leftovers' campaigns supporting its cut-price Basics range. Jamie Oliver was retained but employed to show how tasty, nutritional meals could be prepared to feed a family for less than £5. Expenditure on sales promotions was also increased.

Asda

Well known for its 'Asda Price' advertising campaigns, the supermarket met the recession with ever sharper prices and promotions. According to Andy Bond, Asda's chief executive, this strategy was founded on being assertive and aggressive with suppliers of global brands. It was supported by high-profile TV advertising showing how Asda achieved lower prices than its arch-rival Tesco, and full-page newspaper ads for 50p bargains—including 400 g of mince, two pints of milk, a white loaf, six eggs and 2 kg of carrots. Further, the supermarket adopted the 'round pound' approach, putting hundreds of products on the shelves for a simple £1 price point. Asda also led other supermarkets by cutting the cost of unleaded petrol and diesel to 99.9p a litre in July 2009 when its rivals were selling them for over £1 per litre (for example, Sainsbury's price was £1.09). Asda's commercial director, David Miles, claimed that there was no justification for any major retailer selling fuel for over £1 given the recent large fall in the price of oil.

Aldi

Aldi might be considered a minnow in the UK, with a grocery market share of around 3 per cent compared with Tesco's 30 per cent but, like other discounters, it expanded its number of stores during the recession, and increased sales and market share. Some of the new store openings were in more middle-class locations than previously. Recognized as being cheaper but having a more limited product range than traditional supermarkets, Aldi placed more emphasis on fresh food and introduced a Specially Selected premium range, including Italian pasta sauce, Colombian ground coffee and West Country Cheddar cheese, during the economic downturn.

Lidl

Like Aldi, Lidl mainly stocks own-label products using a wide variety of exclusive names such as Manor House soup, J. D. Gross dark chocolate and Vitafit apple juice. However, during the recession it increased the number of manufacturer brands, such as Anchor butter and Kingsmill bread, in its stores. The discounter also introduced some organic, free-range and Fairtrade foods as well as more fresh produce. New stores were opened with a greater emphasis on middle-class locations, and in 2008 ten smaller stores ranging from 200 to 500 square metres (compared to the usual 1000 square metres) were opened. Although holding a market share of only around 2.5 per cent of the UK grocery market, Lidl increased sales and market share during the recession.

References

Based on: Butler, S. (2008) Discount Chain Lidl Confident that its Moment has Arrived, *The Times*, 22 December, 24; Finch, J. (2008) Mighty Tesco Feels Bite of the Hamster, *Guardian*, 3 December, 9; Finch, J. and A. Clark (2008) 70,000 Extra Customers a Week Head for Asda, *Guardian*, 15 August, 29; Hawkes, S. (2008) Where Jamie and Del Boy Lead, Aldi Follows, *The Times*, 4 September, 21; Finch, J. and Z. Wood (2009) Back to Basics Lifts Sainsbury's Profits 11%, *Guardian*, 14 May, 24; Wearden, G. and T. Webb (2009) Asda Launches New Petrol Price War, *Guardian*, 10 July, 27.

Questions

1. What characteristics of services are displayed by supermarkets?
2. Explain the marketing strategies employed by the five supermarkets.
3. What lessons are there to be learned about marketing services in a recession?

This case was prepared by David Jobber, Professor of Marketing, University of Bradford.

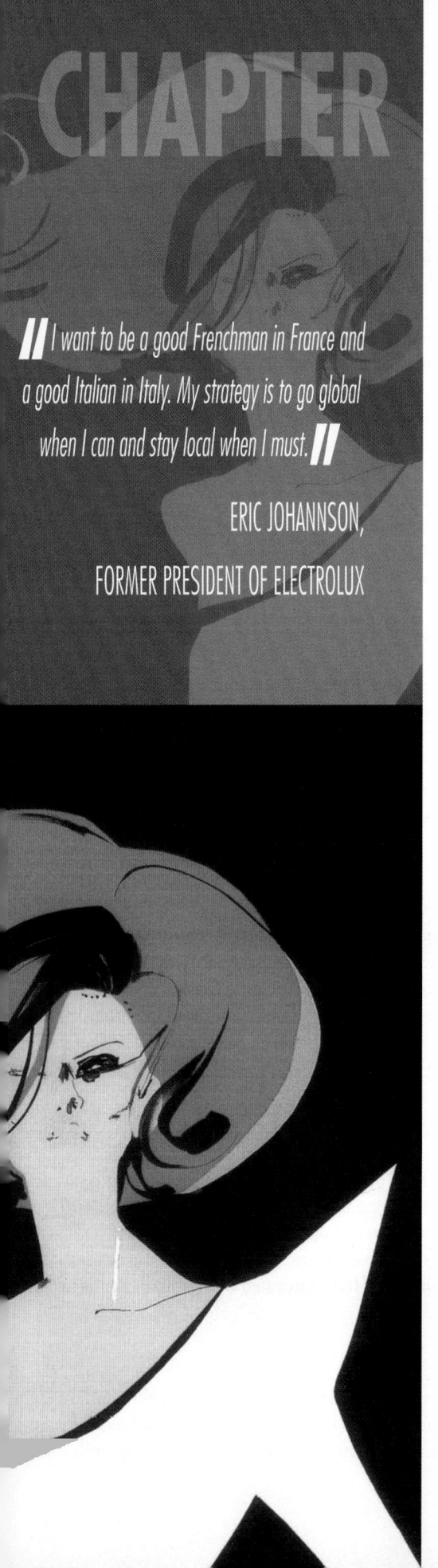

CHAPTER 23

International marketing

I want to be a good Frenchman in France and a good Italian in Italy. My strategy is to go global when I can and stay local when I must.

ERIC JOHANNSON,
FORMER PRESIDENT OF ELECTROLUX

LEARNING OBJECTIVES

After reading this chapter, you should be able to:

1 explain why companies seek foreign markets

2 discuss the factors that influence which foreign market to enter

3 identify and discuss the range of foreign market entry strategies

4 identify the factors influencing foreign market entry strategies

5 discuss the influences on the degree of standardization or adaptation

6 discuss the special considerations involved in designing an international marketing mix

7 explain how to organize for international marketing operations

Today's managers need international marketing skills to be able to compete in an increasingly global marketplace. They require the capabilities to identify and seize opportunities that arise across the world. Failure to do so brings stagnation and decline, not only to individual companies but also to whole regions.

The importance of international marketing is reflected in the support given by governmental bodies set up to encourage and aid export activities. Such organizations often provide help in gathering information on foreign markets, competitors and their products, and barriers to entry. They disseminate such information through libraries, abstract services and publications. Furthermore, they organize business missions to foreign countries, provide exhibition space at international trade fairs and may give incentives to firms to attend such fairs. Often, they employ trade officers in important foreign markets to help exporters gather marketing research information and find prospective customers for their products.[1] The importance of such government-sponsored activities in assisting the exporting performance of firms was supported by the findings of a study of Greek exporters.[2]

The emergence of the international marketplace known as the World Wide Web is transforming international transactions. Suppliers and customers communicate electronically across the world by sending e-mail messages and setting up interactive websites. Small companies can gain access to global markets without the need for expensive salesforces or retail outlets. Transactions are accomplished by giving credit card details and clicking a button. Not all markets will be fundamentally changed by Internet marketing because of delivery considerations and the fact that many customers may prefer to buy such things as clothing and furniture after personal contact and viewing. Nevertheless, established players in mature global markets are harnessing the potential of the Internet to provide opportunities for their businesses.

The purpose of this chapter, then, is to explore four issues in developing international marketing strategies. First, the question of whether to go international or stay domestic is addressed; second, the factors that impact upon the selection of countries in which to market are considered; third, foreign market entry strategies are analysed; finally, the options available for developing international marketing strategies are examined.

Deciding Whether to Go International

Many companies shy away from the prospect of competing internationally. They know their domestic market better, and they would have to come to terms with the customs, language, tariff regulations, transport systems and volatile currencies of foreign countries. On top of that, their products may require significant modifications to meet foreign regulations and different customer preferences. So, why do companies choose to market abroad? There are seven triggers for international expansion (see Fig. 23.1).

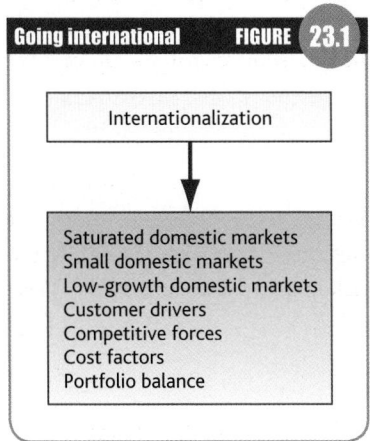

Going international   FIGURE 23.1

Internationalization

Saturated domestic markets
Small domestic markets
Low-growth domestic markets
Customer drivers
Competitive forces
Cost factors
Portfolio balance

Saturated domestic markets

The pressure to raise sales and profits, coupled with few opportunities to expand in current domestic markets, provide one condition for international expansion. This has been a major driving force behind Tesco's moves into the Far East, the USA, and central and eastern Europe.[3] Many of the foreign expansion plans of European supermarket chains were fuelled by the desire to take a proven retailing formula out of their saturated domestic market into new overseas markets.

Small domestic markets

In some industries, survival means broadening scope beyond small national markets to the international arena. For example, Philips, Nokia and Electrolux (electrical goods) could not compete against the strength of global competitors by servicing their small domestic market alone. For them, internationalization was not an option: it was a fundamental condition for survival.

Low-growth domestic markets

Often recession at home provides the spur to seek new marketing opportunities in more buoyant overseas economies. This was the reason for the international moves of Andy Thornton, a small company specializing in the refurbishment of commercial premises. Survival in the severe UK recession of the early 1990s was achieved through winning contracts in countries such as Denmark, Sweden and Germany, and more recently growth has been maintained by entering central and eastern Europe.

Customer drivers

Customer-driven factors may also affect the decision to go international. In some industries customers may expect their suppliers to have an international presence. This is increasingly common in advertising, with clients requiring their agencies to coordinate international campaigns. A second customer-orientated factor is the need to internationalize operations in response to customers expanding abroad.

Competitive forces

There is a substantial body of research which suggests that when several companies in an industry go abroad, others feel obliged to follow suit to maintain their relative size and growth rate.[4] This is particularly true in oligopolistic industries. A second competitive factor may be the desire to attack, in their own home market, an overseas competitor that has entered our domestic market. This may make strategic sense if the competitor is funding its overseas expansion from a relatively attractive home base.

Cost factors

High national labour costs, shortages of skilled workers, and rising energy charges can raise domestic costs to uneconomic levels. These factors may stimulate moves towards foreign direct investment in low-cost areas such as China, Taiwan, Korea, and central and eastern Europe. Expanding into foreign markets can also reduce costs by gaining economies of scale through an enlarged customer base.

Portfolio balance

Marketing in a variety of regions provides the opportunity to achieve portfolio balance as each region may be experiencing different growth rates. At any one time, the USA, Japan, individual European and Far Eastern countries will be enjoying varying growth rates. By marketing in a selection of countries, the problems of recession in some countries can be balanced by the opportunities for growth in others.

Deciding Which Markets to Enter

Having made the commitment to internationalize, marketing managers require the analytical skills necessary to pick those countries and regions that are most attractive for overseas operations. Two sets of factors will govern this decision: macroenvironmental issues and microenvironmental issues. These are shown in Figure 23.2.

Macroenvironmental issues

These consist of *economic*, *socio-cultural* and *political-legal influences* on market choice.

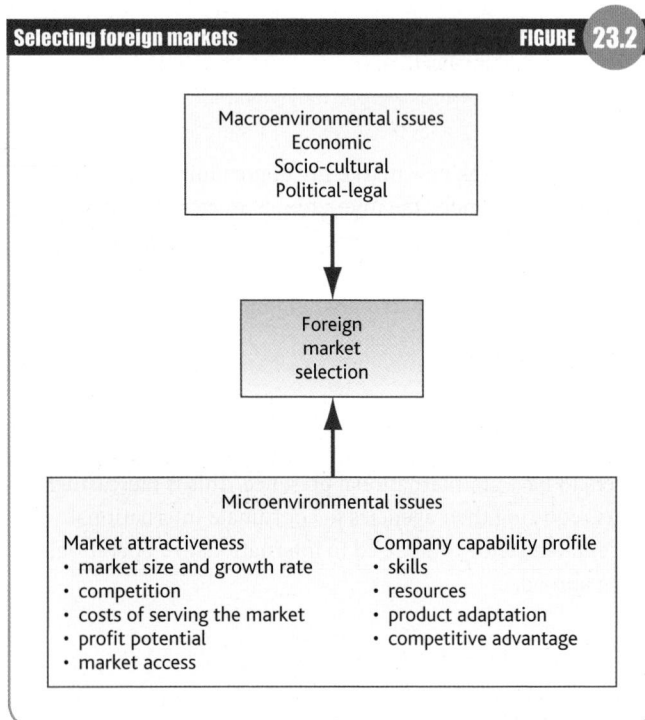

Selecting foreign markets FIGURE 23.2

Macroenvironmental issues
Economic
Socio-cultural
Political-legal

↓

Foreign
market
selection

↑

Microenvironmental issues

Market attractiveness
- market size and growth rate
- competition
- costs of serving the market
- profit potential
- market access

Company capability profile
- skills
- resources
- product adaptation
- competitive advantage

Economic influences

A country's size, per capita income, stage of economic development, infrastructure, and exchange rate stability and conversion affect its attractiveness for international business expansion. Small markets may not justify setting up a distribution and marketing system to supply goods and services. Low per-capita income will affect the type of product that may sell in that country. The market may be very unattractive for car manufacturers but feasible for bicycle producers. Less developed countries, in the early stages of economic development, may demand inexpensive agricultural tools but not computers. Research into the decision to enter a new foreign market found that the issue that had the greatest impact was that the country had a developed economy, emphasizing the importance of economic considerations in this decision.[5]

The economic changes that have taken place in central and eastern Europe have had varying effects on each country's attractiveness. For example, Poland's move from a centrally planned to market-based economy initially caused a rise in unemployment to 400,000 people, and a 40 per cent fall in purchasing power of some households as government subsidies and price controls were abolished.[6] However, these shocks were followed by greater investment on the part of western countries and a fall in inflation from as high as 250 per cent to 3.4 per cent.[7]

Another economic consideration is a nation's infrastructure. This comprises the transportation structures (roads, railways, airports), communication systems (telephone, television, the press, radio) and energy supplies (electricity, gas, nuclear). A poor infrastructure may limit the ability to manufacture, advertise and distribute goods, and provide adequate service back-up. Some central and eastern European countries suffer because of this. In other areas of Europe infrastructure improvements are enhancing communications—for example, the ambitious, if costly, Eurotunnel that links the UK with mainland Europe, and the bridge and tunnel that connect the two main parts of Denmark.

Finally, exchange rate stability and conversion may affect market choice. A country that has an unstable exchange rate or one that is difficult to convert to hard currencies such as the dollar or euro may be considered too risky to enter.

Socio-cultural influences

Differences in socio-cultural factors between countries are often termed *psychic distance*. These are the barriers created by cultural disparities between the home country and the host country, and the problems of communication resulting from differences in social perspectives, attitudes and language.[8] This can have an important effect on selection. International marketers sometimes choose countries that are psychically similar to begin their overseas operations. This has a rationale in that barriers of language, customs and values are lower. It also means that less time and effort is required to develop successful business relationships.[9] Johanson and Vahlne, on the basis of four Swedish manufacturing firms, showed that firms often begin by entering new markets that are psychically close—that is, both culturally and geographically—and gaining experience in these countries before expanding operations abroad into more distant markets.[10] Erramilli states that this is also true of service firms that move from culturally similar foreign markets into less familiar markets as their experience grows.[11] Language, in particular, has caused many well-documented problems for marketing communications in international markets. Marketing in Action 23.1 describes some of the classic mistakes that have been made.

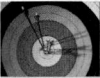 **23.1 Marketing in Action**

Classic Communication Faux Pas

Language differences have caused innumerable problems for international marketers, and can provide a barrier to foreign market entry. The problem is particularly acute in countries like Britain, where one-third of its small and medium-sized companies admit to having communication difficulties abroad. This contrasts with Belgium, where 92 per cent of companies employ foreign language specialists, closely followed by the Netherlands and Luxembourg. It is no excuse to claim that English is a world business language and consequently there is no need to develop foreign language skills. As the former German Chancellor Willy Brandt once exclaimed, 'If I am selling to you I will speak English, but if you are selling to me dann müssen Sie Deutsch sprechen!'

Here are some classic examples of translations that have gone wrong.
- A Thai dry cleaners: 'Drop your trousers here for best results'.
- A sign in Hong Kong tailor: 'Ladies may have a fit upstairs'.
- A Moscow guide to a Russian Orthodox monastery: 'You are welcome to visit the cemetery where famous Russian and Soviet composers, artists, and writers are buried daily, except Thursday'.
- A Portuguese restaurant that offers 'butchers' mess from the oven'.
- A Spanish sports shop called 'The Athlete's Foot'.
- A French dress shop advertising 'Dresses for street walking'.

The world of advertising is not without its humorous errors in translation:
- Come alive with Pepsi: Rise from the grave with Pepsi (German)
- Avoid embarrassment—use Parker pens: Avoid pregnancy—use Parker pens (Spanish).
- Cleans the really dirty parts of your wash—Cleans your private parts (French)
- Body by Fisher: Corpse by Fisher (Flemish)
- Chrysler for power: Chrysler is an aphrodisiac (Spanish)
- Tropicana orange juice: Tropicana Chinese juice (Cuba)
- Tomato paste: Tomato glue (Arabic).

Brand names have also caused problems:
- GM car called Nova which means 'doesn't go' in Spanish
- Mitsubishi had to change the name Pajero in Spanish-speaking countries because it is a slang word meaning masturbator
- Toyota's MR2 is pronounced 'merde' in French which translates to excrement
- Nissan's Moco means mucus in Spanish.

Based on: Halsall (1994);[12] Egan and McKiernan (1994);[13] Bashford (2005);[14] Ghauri and Cateora (2006)[15]

Political-legal influences

Factors that potential international marketers will consider are: the general attitudes of foreign governments to imports and foreign direct investment; political stability;

governmental policies; and trade barriers. Negative attitudes towards foreign firms may also discourage imports and investment because of the threat of protectionism and expropriation of assets. Positive governmental attitudes can be reflected in the willingness to grant subsidies to overseas firms to invest in a country and a willingness to cut through bureaucratic procedures to assist foreign firms and their imports. The willingness of the UK government to grant investment incentives to Japanese firms was a factor in Nissan, Honda and Toyota setting up production facilities there.

Eagerness to promote imports has not always been a feature of Japanese attitudes, however. Until recently, imports of electrical goods were hampered by the fact that each one had to be inspected by government officials. Also their patent laws rule that patents are made public after 18 months but are not granted for four to six years. In many western countries patents remain secret until they are granted. The Japanese system discourages high-technology and other firms that wish to protect their patents from entering Japan. Legal regulations can also act as a barrier. For example, Russian Government regulations classify beer as 'perishable' even though when canned it has a shelf life of up to a year. This forces companies to refrigerate beer when it is transported, pushing up costs.[16]

Countries with a history of political instability may be avoided because of the inevitable uncertainty regarding their future. Countries such as Iraq and Lebanon have undoubtedly suffered because of the political situation.

Government policies can also influence market entry. For example, the Chinese Government's censorship of information has been a barrier to the early entry of Google into that country, although it is now there, competing with such companies as Yahoo! and Microsoft.

Finally, a major consideration when deciding which countries to enter will be the level of tariff barriers. Undoubtedly the threat of tariff barriers to imports to the countries of the EU has encouraged US and Japanese foreign direct investment into Europe. Within the single market the removal of trade barriers is making international trade in Europe more attractive, as not only tariffs fall but, in addition, the need to modify products to cater for national regulations and restrictions is reduced.

Microenvironmental issues

While the macroenvironmental analysis provides indications of how attractive each country is to an international marketer, microenvironmental analysis focuses on the attractiveness of the particular market being considered, and the company capability profile.

Market attractiveness

Market attractiveness can be assessed by determining market size and growth rate, competition, costs of serving the market, profit potential and market access.

- *Market size and growth rate*: large, growing markets (other things being equal) provide attractive conditions for market entry. Research supports the notion that market growth is a more important consideration than market size.[17] It is expectations about future demand rather than existing demand that are important, particularly for foreign direct investment. It is China's enormous market size and growth rate that is attracting the UK's Tesco, France's Carrefour and Louis Vuitton, and Germany's Metro and Tengelmann.[18] Russia's large and growing market is also attracting multinationals like Unilever, PepsiCo, Kellogg's, Kraft, Nestlé, Coca-Cola and Carlsberg, which have made large-scale acquisitions in the country.[19]
- *Competition*: markets that are already served by strong, well-entrenched competitors may dampen enthusiasm for foreign market entry. However, when a competitive weakness is identified a decision to enter may be taken. For example, Tesco, the leading UK supermarket chain, spotted an opportunity on the west coast of the USA, based on Wal-Mart's weakness in the convenience sector. Tesco has entered that market based on a small store format

targeting the 'top-up' shopper.[20] Volatility of competition also appears to reduce the attractiveness of overseas markets. Highly volatile markets, with many competitors entering and leaving the market and where market concentration is high, are particularly unattractive.[21]

- *Costs of serving the market*: two major costs of servicing foreign markets are distribution and control. As geographic distance increases, so these two costs rise. Many countries' major export markets are in neighbouring countries—such as the USA, whose largest market is Canada. Costs are also dependent on the form of market entry. Obviously, foreign direct investment is initially more expensive than using distributors. Some countries may not possess suitable low-cost entry options, making entry less attractive and more risky. Long internal distribution channels (e.g. as in Japan) can also raise costs as middlemen demand their profit margins. If direct investment is being contemplated, labour costs and the supply of skilled labour will also be a consideration. Finally, some markets may prove unattractive because of the high marketing expenditures necessary to compete in them.
- *Profit potential*: some markets may be unattractive because industry structure leaves them with poor profit potential. For example, the existence of powerful buying groups may reduce profit potential through their ability to negotiate low prices.
- *Market access*: some foreign markets may prove difficult to penetrate because of informal ties between existing suppliers and distributors. Without the capability of setting up a new distribution chain, this would mean that market access would effectively be barred. Links between suppliers and customers in organizational markets would also form a barrier. In some countries and markets, national suppliers are given preferential treatment. The German machine tool industry is a case in point, as is defence procurement in many western European countries.

Company capability profile

Company capability to serve a foreign market also needs to be assessed: this depends on skills, resources, product adaptation and competitive advantage.

- *Skills*: does the company have the necessary skills to market abroad? If not, can sales agents or distributors compensate for any shortfalls? Does the company have the necessary skills to understand the requirements of each market?
- *Resources*: different countries may have varying market servicing costs. Does the company have the necessary financial resources to compete effectively in them? Human resources also need to be considered as some markets may demand domestically supplied personnel.
- *Product adaptation*: for some foreign markets, local preferences and regulations may require the product to be modified. Does the company have the motivation and capability to redesign the product?
- *Competitive advantage*: a key consideration in any market is the ability to create a competitive advantage. Each foreign market needs to be studied in the light of the company's current and future ability to create and sustain a competitive advantage.

Deciding How to Enter a Foreign Market

Once a firm has decided to enter a foreign market, it must choose a mode of entry—that is, select an institutional arrangement for organizing and conducting international marketing activities.

The choice of foreign market entry strategy is likely to have a major impact on a company's performance overseas.[22] Each mode of entry has its own associated levels of commitment, risks, control and profit potential. The major options are indirect exporting, direct exporting, licensing, joint ventures, and direct investment either in new facilities or through acquisition (see Fig. 23.3).

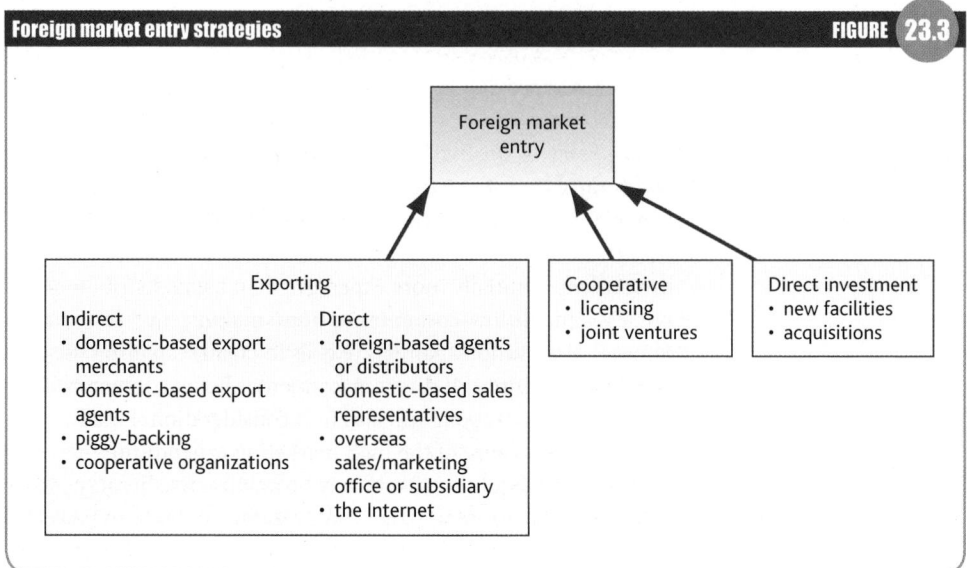

Foreign market entry strategies   FIGURE 23.3

Indirect exporting

Indirect exporting involves the use of independent organizations within the exporter's domestic market; these include the following.

1 *Domestic-based export merchants* who take title to the products and sell them abroad.
2 *Domestic-based export agents* who sell on behalf of the exporter but do not take title to the products; agents are usually paid by commission.
3 *Piggy-backing*, whereby the exporter uses the overseas distribution facilities of another producer.
4 *Cooperative organizations*, which act on behalf of a number of producers and are partly controlled by them; many producers of primary products such as fruit and nuts export through cooperative organizations.

Indirect exporting has three advantages. First, the exporting organization is domestically based, thus communication is easier than using foreign intermediaries. Second, investment and risk are lower than setting up one's own sales and marketing facility. Third, use can be made of the exporting organization's knowledge of selling abroad.

Direct exporting

As exporters grow more confident, they may decide to undertake their own exporting task. This will involve building up overseas contracts, undertaking marketing research, handling documentation and transportation, and designing marketing-mix strategies. **Direct exporting** modes include export through foreign-based agents or distributors (independent middlemen), a domestic-based salesforce, an overseas sales/marketing office or subsidiary, and via the Internet.

Foreign-based agents or distributors

Most companies use agents or distributors in some or all of their exporting abroad. Over 60 per cent of US companies use them for some or all of their export activity, and for European firms the figure rises to over 70 per cent.[23] Agents may be *exclusive*, where the agreement is between the exporter and the agent alone; *semi-exclusive*, where the agent handles the exporter's goods along with other non-competing goods from other companies;

or *non-exclusive*, where the agent handles a variety of goods, including some that may compete with the exporter's products.

Distributors, unlike agents, take title to the goods, and are paid according to the difference between the buying and selling prices rather than commission. Distributors are often appointed when after-sales service is required as they are more likely to possess the necessary resources than agents.

The advantages of both agents and distributors are that they are familiar with the local market, customs and conventions, have existing business contracts and employ foreign nationals. They have a direct incentive to sell through either commission or profit margin, but since their remuneration is tied to sales they may be reluctant to devote much time and effort to developing a market for a new product. Also, the amount of market feedback may be limited as the agent or distributor may see themselves as a purchasing agent for their customers rather than a selling agent for the exporter.

Overall, exporting through independent middlemen is a low-investment method of market entry although significant expenditure in marketing may be necessary. Also it can be difficult and costly to terminate an agreement with them, suggesting that this option should be viewed with care and not seen as an easy method of market entry.

Domestic-based sales representatives

As the sales representative is a company employee, greater control of activities compared to that when using independent middlemen can be expected. Whereas a company has no control over the attention an agent or distributor gives to its products or the amount of market feedback provided, it can insist that various activities be performed by its sales representatives.

Also the use of company employees shows a commitment to the customer that the use of agents or distributors may lack. Consequently they are often used in industrial markets, where there are only a few large customers that require close contact with suppliers, and where the size of orders justifies the expense of foreign travel. This method of market servicing is also found when selling to government buyers and retail chains, for similar reasons.

Overseas sales/marketing office or subsidiary

This option displays even greater customer commitment than using domestic-based sales representatives, although the establishment of a local office requires a greater investment. However, the exporter may be perceived as an indigenous supplier, improving its chances of market success. In some markets, where access to distribution channels is limited, selling direct through an overseas sales office may be the only feasible way of breaking into a new market. The sales office or subsidiary acts as a centre for foreign-based sales representatives, handles sales distribution and promotion, and can act as a customer service centre.

For the company contemplating exporting for the first time, there are many potential pitfalls.[24]

The Internet

The global reach of the Internet means that companies can now engage in exporting activities direct to customers. By creating a website, overseas customers can be made aware of a company's products and ordering can be direct. Products can be supplied straight to the customer without the need for an intermediary. The Internet is not only a channel to market but also a useful research tool. Sites like International Growth (www.internationalgrowth.org) offer skills and resources for specific industries—for example, software and computing services companies. It provides free market research reports, a skills area and information on the main international marketing issues to consider.

23.1 Pause for Thought

Have you purchased a product from a foreign country using the Internet? What were the benefits of using the Internet and did you have any reservations about doing so?

Licensing

Licensing refers to contracts in which a foreign licensor provides a local licensee with access to one or a set of technologies or know-how in exchange for financial compensation.[25] The licensee will normally have exclusive rights to produce and market the product within an agreed area for a specific period of time in return for a *royalty* based on sales volume. A licence may relate to the use of a patent for either a product or process, copyright, trademarks and trade secrets (e.g. designs and software), and know-how (e.g. product and process specifications).

Licensing agreements allow the exporter to enter markets that otherwise may be closed for exports or other forms of market entry, without the need to make substantial capital investments in the host country. However, control of production is lost and the reputation of the licensor is dependent on the performance of the licensee. A grave danger of licensing is the loss of product and process know-how to third parties, which may become competitors once the agreement is at an end.

The need to exploit new technology simultaneously in many markets has stimulated the growth in licensing by small high-tech companies that lack the resources to set up their own sales and market offices, engage in joint ventures or conduct direct investment abroad. Licensing is also popular in R&D-intensive industries such as pharmaceuticals, chemicals and synthetic fibres, where rising research and development costs have encouraged licensing as a form of reciprocal technology exchange.

Sometimes the licensed product has to be adapted to suit local culture. For example, packaging that uses red and yellow, the colours of the Spanish flag, is seen as an offence to Spanish patriotism; in Greece purple should be avoided as it has funereal associations; and the licensing of a movie, TV show or book whose star is a cute little pig will have no prospect of success in Muslim countries, where the pig is considered an unclean animal.[26]

In Europe, licensing is encouraged by the European Union (EU), which sees the mechanism as a way of offering access to new technologies to companies lacking the resources to innovate; this provides a means of technology sharing on a pan-European scale. Licensing activities have been given exemption in EU competition law (which means that companies engaged in licensing cannot be accused of anti-competitive practices), and *tied purchase* agreements whereby licensees must buy components from the licensor have not been ruled anti-competitive since they allow the innovating firm protection from loss of know-how to other component suppliers.

Franchising

Franchising is a form of licensing where a package of services is offered by the franchisor to the franchisee in return for payment. The two types of franchising are *product* and *trade name franchising*, the classic case of which is Coca-Cola selling its syrup together with the right to use its trademark and name to independent bottlers, and *business format franchising* where marketing approaches, operating procedures and quality control are included in the franchise package as well as the product and trade name. Business-format franchising is mainly used in service industries such as restaurants, hotels and retailing, where the franchisor exerts a high level of control in the overseas market since quality-control procedures can be established as part of the agreement. For example, McDonald's specifies precisely who should supply the ingredients for its fast-food products wherever they are sold to ensure consistency of quality in its franchise outlets.

The benefits to the franchisor are that franchising may be a way of overcoming resource constraints, as an efficient system to overcome producer–distributor management problems and as a way of gaining knowledge of new markets.[27] Franchising provides access to the franchisee's resources. For example, if the franchisor has limited financial resources, access to additional finance may be supplied by the franchisee.

Franchising may overcome producer–distributor management problems in managing geographically dispersed operations through the advantages of having owner-managers that have vested interests in the success of the business. Gaining knowledge of new markets by tapping into the franchisee's local knowledge is especially important in international markets where local culture may differ considerably between regions.

There are risks, however. Although the franchisor will attempt to gain some control of operations, the existence of multiple, geographically dispersed owner-managers makes control difficult. Service delivery may be inconsistent because of this. Conflicts can arise through dissatisfaction with the standard of service, lack of promotional support and the opening of new franchises close to existing ones, for example. This can lead to a breakdown of relationships and deteriorating performance. Also, initial financial outlays can be considerable because of expenditures on training, development, promotional and support activities.

The franchisee benefits by gaining access to the resources of the franchisor, its expertise (sometimes global) and buying power. The risks are that it may face conflicts (as discussed above) that render the relationship unviable.

Franchising is also exempt from EU competition law as it is seen as a means of achieving increased competition and efficient distribution without the need for major investment. It promotes standardization, which reaps scale economies with the possibility of some adaptation to local tastes. For example, in India McDonald's uses goat and lamb rather than pork or beef in its burgers, and Benetton allows a degree of freedom to its franchisees to stock products suitable to their particular customers.[28]

Joint ventures

Two types of joint venture are *contractual* and *equity* joint ventures. In **contractual joint ventures** no joint enterprise with a separate personality is formed. Two or more companies form a partnership to share the cost of an investment, the risks and long-term profits. The partnership may be to complete a particular project or for a longer-term cooperative effort.[29] They are found in the oil exploration, aerospace and car industries, and in co-publishing agreements.[30] An **equity joint venture** involves the creation of a new company in which foreign and local investors share ownership and control.

Joint ventures are sometimes set up in response to government conditions for market entry or because the foreign firm lacks the resources to set up production facilities alone. Also the danger of expropriation is less when a company has a national partner than when the foreign firm is the sole owner.[31] Finding a national partner may be the only way to invest in some markets that are too competitive and saturated to leave room for a completely new operation. Many of the Japanese/US joint ventures in the USA were set up for this reason. The foreign investor benefits from the local management talent, and knowledge of local markets and regulations. Also, joint ventures allow partners to specialize in their particular areas of technological expertise in a given project. They may also be the only means of entering a country because of national laws. For example, in India overseas supermarket chains are not allowed to operate as retailers unless they can find a local partner to own and operate the store.[32] For this reason, Marks & Spencer's stores are operated by Indian retailer Planet Retail.

Finally, the host firm benefits by acquiring resources from its foreign partners. For example, in Hungary host firms have gained through the rapid acquisition of marketing resources, which has enabled them to create positions of competitive advantage.[33]

There are potential problems, however. The national partner's interests relate to the local operation, while the foreign firm's concerns relate to the totality of its international operations. Particular areas of conflict can be the use made of profits (pay out vs plough back), product line and market coverage of the joint venture, and transfer pricing.

Equity joint ventures are common between companies from western European and eastern European countries. Western European firms gain from low-cost production and raw materials, while former eastern bloc companies acquire western technology and know-how. Eastern European governments are keen to promote joint ventures rather than wholly owned foreign direct investment in an attempt to prevent the exploitation of low-cost labour by western firms. A joint research project between French car makers and British designers led to the Renault Clio winning European Car of the Year Award.

Direct investment

This method of market entry involves investment in foreign-based assembly or manufacturing facilities. It carries the greatest commitment of capital and managerial effort. Wholly owned **direct investment** can be through the acquisition of a foreign producer (or by buying out a joint venture partner) or by building *new facilities*. Acquisition offers a quicker way into the market and usually means gaining access to a qualified labour force, national management, local knowledge, and contacts with the local market and government. Acquisition also is a means of getting ownership of global brands. This was the motivation behind Lenovo's acquisition of IBM's PC division and Tata Motors' buying of Jaguar and Land Rover.[34] In saturated markets, acquisition may be the only feasible way of establishing a production presence in the host country.[35] However, coordination and styles of management between the foreign investor and the local management team may cause problems. Whirlpool, the US white goods (washing machines, refrigerators, etc.) manufacturer, is an example of a company that has successfully entered new international markets using acquisition. The company has successfully entered European markets through its acquisition of Philips' white goods business and its ability to develop new products that serve cross-national Euro-segments. European companies have also gained access to North American markets through acquisition. For example, ABN-Amro has built up market presence in the USA through a series of acquisitions to become the largest foreign bank in that country.[36] One company that has built a global brand through acquisitions is Vodafone, as Digital Marketing 23.1 explains.

Central and eastern Europe have been the recipients of high levels of direct investment as companies have sought to take advantage of low labour costs. Car companies, in particular, have opened production facilities there, notably VW in the Czech Republic and Slovakia; Renault in Romania, Slovakia and Turkey; and Fiat in Poland.

Wholly owned direct investment offers a greater degree of control than licensing or joint ventures, and maintains the internalization of proprietary information for manufacturers. It accomplishes the circumvention of tariff and non-tariff barriers, and lowers distribution costs compared with domestic production. A local presence means that sensitivity to customers' tastes and preferences is enhanced, and links with distributors and the host nation's government can be forged. Foreign direct investments can act as a powerful catalyst for economic change in the transition from a centrally planned economy. Foreign companies bring technology, management know-how and access to foreign markets.[37] Direct investment is an expensive option, though, and the consequent risks are greater. If the venture fails, more money is lost and there is always the risk of expropriation. Furthermore, closure of plant may mean substantial redundancy payments.

 **23.1 Digital Marketing**

Global Brand Building by Acquisition

Vodafone, the mobile phone operator, has built an enviable reputation of building a global brand by acquisition. Sir Christopher Gent transformed Vodafone from an obscure British company into a global giant through a series of daring acquisitions, most famously the takeover of Mannesmann, a German telecoms company.

Arun Sarin, his successor, was supposed to be a steady hand who would fit the pieces of Vodafone's empire together and focus attention on detail and operational efficiency. While attempting to do this, however, Sarin moved strategy from developed markets where mobile phone usage was saturated to high-growth emerging markets. Acquisitions in the Czech Republic, Romania and Turkey followed this strategy, while Vodafone's ailing Japanese division was sold. His crowning glory, though, was the acquisition of Hutchison Essar, an Indian operator, enabling Vodafone to supply inexpensive handsets to the booming Indian market.

With a strong presence in the US market with its 45 per cent stake in Verizon Wireless, the leading US mobile operator, Vodafone has built a formidable global presence. Vodafone also has a 3 per cent stake in China Mobile, the world's largest mobile operator. Mr Sarin's successor, Vittorio Colao, is continuing the strategy with further acquisitions in Africa and Asia. The company faces challenges, though. It needs to work out how to compete and cooperate with industry giants like Microsoft, Google and Apple as digital technologies converge and the Internet goes mobile. Unless it can do this, Vodafone might find itself selling commodity products in markets that are fast becoming saturated.

Based on: Anonymous (2008);[38] *Gapper (2008)*[39]

Selecting a foreign market entry mode: control, resources and risk			FIGURE 23.4
	Factor		
	Risk of losing proprietary information	Resources	Control
High		Direct investment	Direct investment Exporting (own staff)
Medium	Licensing Joint venture	Joint venture Exporting (own staff)	Joint venture Licensing
Low	Exporting (own staff) Exporting (middlemen) Direct investment	Licensing Exporting (middlemen)	Exporting (middlemen)

Level (applies to High/Medium/Low row labels)

The creation of the single European market allows free movement of capital across the EU, removing restrictions on direct investment using greenfield sites. Foreign direct investment through acquisition, however, may be subject to investigation under EC competition policy. American firms, in particular, sought to acquire European firms prior to 1992 in an attempt to secure a strong position in the face of the threat of 'Fortress Europe'.

The selection of international market entry mode is dependent on the trade-offs between the levels of control, resources and risk of losing proprietary information and technology. Figure 23.4 summarizes the levels associated with exporting using middlemen, exporting using company staff, licensing, joint ventures and direct investment.

Considerable research has gone into trying to understand the factors that have been shown to have an impact on selection of market entry method. Both external (country

Factors affecting choice of market-entry method	TABLE 23.1

External variables

Country environment
- Large market size and market growth encourage direct investment
- Barriers to imports encourage direct investment[40]
- The more the country's characteristics are rated favourable, the greater the propensity for direct investment[41]
- The higher the country's level of economic development, the greater the use of direct investment
- Government incentives encourage direct investment
- The higher the receiving company's technical capabilities, the greater the use of licensing
- Government intervention in foreign trade encourages licensing[42]
- Geocultural distance encourages independent modes, e.g. agents, distributors[43]
- Psychical distance does not favour integrated modes, e.g. own salesforce, overseas sales/marketing offices[44]
- Low market potential does not necessarily preclude direct investment for larger firms[45]

Buyer behaviour
- Piecemeal buying favours independent modes
- Project and protectionist buying encourages cooperative entry, e.g. licensing and joint ventures[46]

Internal variables

Company issues
- Lack of market information, uncertainty and perception of high investment risk lead to the use of agents and distributors[47]
- Large firm size or resources encourage higher level of commitment[48]
- Perception of high investment risk encourages joint ventures[49]
- Small firm size or resources encourage reactive exporting[50]
- Limited experience favours integrated entry modes[51]
- Service firms with little or no experience of foreign markets tend to prefer full control modes, e.g. own staff, overseas sales/marketing offices
- Service firms that expand abroad by following their clients' expansion plans tend to favour integrated modes[52]
- When investment rather than exporting is preferred, lack of market information leads to a preference for cooperative rather than integrated modes[53]

Source: Whitelock, J. and D. Jobber (1994) The Impact of Competitor Environment on Initial Market Entry in a New, Non-Domestic Market, *Proceedings of the Marketing Education Group Conference*, Coleraine, July, 1008–17.

environment and buyer behaviour) and internal (company issues) factors have been shown to influence choice. A summary of these research findings is given in Table 23.1.

Developing International Marketing Strategy

Standardization or adaptation

A fundamental decision that managers have to make regarding their international marketing strategy is the degree to which they standardize or adapt their marketing mix around the world (these are referred to, respectively, as the **adapted marketing mix** and the **standardized marketing mix**). Many writers on the subject discuss standardization and adaptation as two distinct options. Pure standardization means that a company keeps the same marketing mix in all countries to which it markets. Such an approach is in line with Levitt's view that world markets are being driven 'towards a converging commonality'.[54] This

▲ McDonald's: a truly
global brand.

he terms the globalization of markets fuelled by travel, common lifestyles and developments in technology that have universal appeal. The company of the future, according to Levitt, will be a global organization that views the world as one market to which it sells a global product. The commercial reality, however, is that few mixes are totally standardized. The brands that are most often quoted as being standardized are Coca-Cola, McDonald's and Levi Strauss. It is true that many elements of their marketing mixes are identical in a wide range of countries but even here adaptation is found (see the illustration for McDonald's).

First, in Coca-Cola, the sweetness and carbonization vary between countries. For example, sweetness is lowered in Greece and carbonation lowered in eastern Europe. Diet Coke's artificial sweetener and packaging differ between countries.[55] Second, Levi Strauss uses different domestic and international advertising strategies.[56] As Dan Chow Len, Levi's US advertising manager, commented:

The markets are different. In the US, Levi's is both highly functional and fashionable. But in the UK, its strength is as a fashion garment. We've tested UK ads in American markets. Our primary target market at home is 16–20 year olds, and they hate these ads, won't tolerate them, they're too sexy. Believe it or not, American 16–20 year olds don't want to be sexy. . . . When you ask people about Levi's here, it's quality, comfort, style affordability. In Japan, it's the romance of America.[57]

Third, in McDonald's, menus are changed to account for different customer preferences. For example, in France, McDonald's offers 'Croque McDo', its version of the French favourite the croque monsieur. It also works with French companies to offer local products such as yoghurts from Danone and coffee from Carte Noire, and buys 80 per cent of its products from French farmers. The proportion of meat in the hamburgers also varies between countries.

Most global brands adapt to meet local requirements. Even high-tech electronic products have to conform to national technical standards and may be positioned differently in various countries. As Unilever's former chairman Michael Perry has warned, most brands will remain national:

Global brands are simply local brands reproduced many times. Although it may be true that increasingly we address even larger numbers of consumers we do well to remember that we continue to do that one-to-one.[58]

How, then, do marketers tackle the standardization–adaptation issue? A useful rule of thumb was cited at the start of this chapter: go global (standardize) when you can, stay local (adapt) when you must. For example, HSBC recognizes the need to adapt to local requirements.

Figure 23.5 provides a grid for thinking about the areas where standardization may be possible, and where adaptation may be necessary. There are many variations on which element is standardized and which is adapted. For example, IKEA's product offering and stores are largely standardized, but advertising is varied between countries. Seat's car models are standardized but its positioning alters. For example, it is positioned as a more upmarket brand in Spain than in the UK. Also, the Kronenbourg product is standardized, but it is positioned as more of a premium beer in the UK than in Germany. Occasionally the brand name changes for the same product. For example, Unilever's male toiletries brand is marketed as Lynx in the UK and Ireland, because of trademark problems, and as Axe across the rest of

| A grid to aid thinking about standardization and adaptation of the marketing mix | FIGURE 23.5 |

	Full adaptation	Full standardization
Product positioning		
Product formulation		
Product design		
Service offering		
Brand name		
Pack design		
Advertising proposition		
Creating presentation		
Sales promotion		
Personal selling style		
Price		
Discount structure		
Credit terms		
Distribution channels		

the world.[59] Standardization is an attractive option because it can create massive economies of scale.

For example, lower manufacturing, advertising and packaging costs can be realized. Also the logistical benefit of being able to move stock from one country to another to meet low-stock situations should not be underestimated. This has led to the call to focus on similarities rather than differences between consumers across Europe, and the rest of the world. Procter & Gamble, for example, standardizes most of its products across Europe, so Pampers nappies and Pringles crisps are the same in all western European countries, although P&G's detergent Daz does differ.[60] However, there are a number of barriers to developing standardized global brands. These are discussed in Marketing in Action 23.2.

Developing global and regional brands requires commitment from management to a coherent marketing programme. The sensitivities of national managers need to be accounted for as they may perceive a loss of status associated with greater centralized control. One approach is to have mechanisms that ensure the involvement of national managers in planning, and that encourage them to make recommendations. The key is to balance this local involvement with the need to look for similarities rather than differences across markets. It is the essential differences in consumer preferences and buyer behaviour that need to be recognized in marketing mix adaptation, rather than the minor nuances. Managers must also be prepared to invest heavily and over a long time period to achieve brand penetration. Success in international markets does not come cheaply or quickly. Market research should be used to identify the required positioning in each global market segment.[61]

This discussion has outlined the difficulties in achieving a totally standardized marketing mix package. Rather the tried-and-tested approach of market segmentation based on understanding consumer behaviour and identifying international target markets, which allows the benefits of standardization to be combined with the advantages of customization, is recommended. The two contrasting approaches are summarized in Figure 23.6.

23.2 Marketing in Action

Barriers to Developing Standardized Global Brands

The cost of the logistical advantages of developing standardized global marketing approaches has meant that many companies have looked carefully at standardizing their approach to the European market. Mars, for example, changed the name of its chocolate bar Marathon in the UK to conform to its European brand name Snickers. Full standardization of the marketing mix is difficult, however, because of five problems.

1   *Culture and consumption patterns*: different cultures demand different types of product (e.g. beer and cheese). Some countries use butter to cook with rather than to spread on bread; people in different countries wash clothes at different temperatures; UK consumers like their chocolate to be sweeter than people in mainland Europe; and in South America hot chocolate is a revitalizing drink to have at breakfast, whereas in the UK it is a comfort drink to have just before going to bed. In South America there are two female beer drinkers to every three males, while in the USA, one in four women drinks beer. Yet in the UK, only 10 per cent of women drink beer. In China, a fashionable drink is red wine with a dash of Coca-Cola, and in Singapore Guinness is drunk out of shared jugs as though it were Sangria. The failure of KFC in India is believed to be due to its standardized offering of plain fried chicken while McDonald's has succeeded by adapting its offering—for example, the Maharajeh Mac made from chicken and local spices—to the Indian palate. Coca-Cola also had to change its Minute Maid orange juice for the UK market. After spending almost two years trying to understand what the British consumer wanted, Coca-Cola changed its US formulation of concentrate and water to fresh orange juice without concentrate. Consumer electrical products are less affected, though.

2   *Language*: brand names and advertising may have to change because of language differences. For example, the popular French drink PSCHITT would probably require an alteration of its brand name if launched in the UK.

3   *Regulations*: while national regulations are being harmonized in the single market, differences still exist—for example, with colourings and added vitamins in food.

4   *Media availability and promotional preferences*: varying media practices also affect standardization. For example, wine cannot be advertised on television in Denmark, but in the Netherlands this is allowed. Beer cannot be advertised on television in France, but this is allowed in most other European countries. In Italy, levels of nudity in advertising that would be banned in some other countries are accepted. Sales promotions may have to change because of local preferences. For example, French shoppers prefer coupons and twin packs, whereas their British counterparts favour X per cent extra free.

5   *Organizational structure and culture*: the changes necessary for a standardized approach may be difficult to implement where subsidiaries have, historically, enjoyed considerable power. Also where growth had been achieved through acquisition, strong cultural differences may lead to differing views about pan-European brand strategy.

The reality is that full standardization is rarely possible. Even brands that are regarded as global, such as Sony, Nike, Visa, IBM, Disney, Heineken, McDonald's and Pringles, are not as identical globally as they may first appear. For example, Visa uses different logos in some countries, Heineken is positioned as a mainstream beer in some countries but as a premium beer in others, Pringles uses different flavours and advertising executions in different countries, and although McDonald's core food items are consistent across countries some products are customized to local tastes. Setting the objective as being to develop a standardized global brand should not be the priority; instead, global brand leadership—strong brands in all markets backed by effective global brand management—should be the goal.

Based on: De Chernatony (1993);[62] Kirby (2000);[63] Aaker and Joachimsthaler (2002);[64] Luce (2002);[65] Benady (2003);[66] Charles (2008);[67] Lovell (2008)[68]

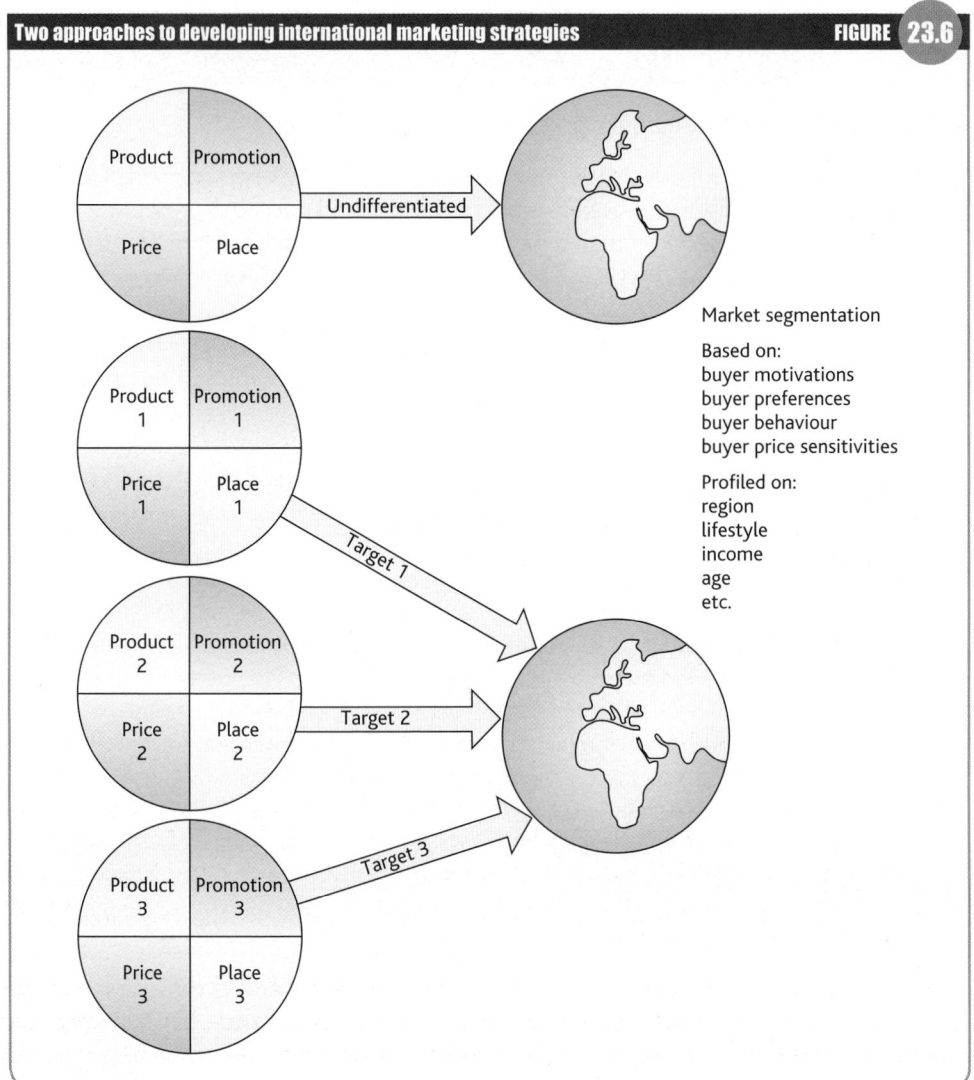

Two approaches to developing international marketing strategies   FIGURE 23.6

Product | Promotion
Price | Place
→ Undifferentiated

Market segmentation

Based on:
buyer motivations
buyer preferences
buyer behaviour
buyer price sensitivities

Profiled on:
region
lifestyle
income
age
etc.

Product 1 | Promotion 1
Price 1 | Place 1
→ Target 1

Product 2 | Promotion 2
Price 2 | Place 2
→ Target 2

Product 3 | Promotion 3
Price 3 | Place 3
→ Target 3

International marketing mix decisions

When developing an international marketing mix, marketers need to avoid falling into the trap of applying national stereotypes to country targets. As with domestic markets, overseas countries contain market segments that need to be understood before a tailored marketing mix can be designed. Marketing in Action 23.3 discusses how companies conduct marketing research to gain such insights.

Once a thorough understanding of the target market has been achieved, marketing managers can then tailor a marketing mix to fit those requirements. We will now explore some of the special considerations associated with developing an effective *international marketing mix*.

Product

Some companies rely on global markets to provide the potential necessary to justify their huge research and development costs. For example, in the pharmaceutical industry, GlaxoSmithKline's Zantac and Zovirax could not have been developed (R&D costs exceeded

23.3 Marketing in Action

Researching Overseas Markets

Before entering an overseas market it is essential for a firm to understand the motivations and behaviour of its target customers. This is to avoid the danger of using self-reference criteria where there is an assumption that the choice criteria, motivations and behaviour that are important to overseas customers are the same as those used by domestic customers.

Although Audi adopts a standardized approach to product design, it still researches overseas customers. For example, it sent members of its design team to California and China for eight weeks each, to live with families and better understand how they live and drive. Its research in the USA persuaded Audi to put cup and bottle holders on its car doors. Also, Chinese drivers' liking of tea led to the installation of a cup holder in its A8 that can be heated or cooled. Rather than incur the expense of changing designs for specific countries, Audi has made these features standard globally. The cup holder used by Chinese drivers for green tea is promoted for use as a baby bottle holder elsewhere. About 98 per cent of its cars are the same globally, with the 2 per cent caused by legal differences (such as Canada's demanding requirements for bumpers), or colour and trim features where tastes differ.

Having spotted a perceived Wal-Mart weakness in the convenience grocery sector, Tesco embarked on an ambitious, if risky, launch of its Fresh & Easy chain of convenience supermarkets on the west coast of the USA. Before launch a team of 20 executives was sent to the States to carry out in-depth research, including visiting every rival. The company also hired a team of anthropologists to live with consumers for two weeks and analyse what they bought and why. Tesco then built a mock store and asked consumers selected as representative of its target market to try it out. It discovered much from this research, such as the fact that US consumers were less bothered about the selection of wines on offer compared to British shoppers, but wanted better-quality meat. Although Tesco is facing stiff competition now that Wal-Mart has launched its own chain of convenience stores, the research has proven invaluable in providing the foundation upon which its stores are designed and the product assortment chosen.

Expanding into overseas markets is notoriously difficult. Marks & Spencer failed in continental Europe, B&Q withdrew from South Korea and Tesco itself pulled out of France. But marketing research can provide dividends, with Tesco's in-depth study of overseas markets being the platform that has led it to build over half of its retailing space overseas, with 670 stores in Europe and over 700 in Asia.

Based on: Jones (2008);[69] Reed (2008)[70]

£30 million in both cases) without a worldwide market. Canon's huge research and development budget is also justified by the potential of global markets. For example, the bubble-jet and laser-beam computer printers it invented formed the basis upon which it has built world market shares of 30 and 65 per cent, respectively.[71] Once developed, the company can offer a standardized product to generate huge positive cash flow as the benefits that these products provide span national boundaries. Many car companies also standardize as much of their car models as possible, particularly those parts that are not visible to drivers, such as the air-conditioning system, suspension and steering column.

A second situation that supports a standardized product is where the brand concept is based on *authentic national heritage* across the globe: Scotch whisky, Belgian chocolate and French wine are relevant examples. Clearly, there are sound marketing reasons for a standard product. A third basis for standardization is where a global market segment of like-minded people can be exploited. This is the basis for the success of such products as Swatch and Rolex watches, Gucci fashion accessories and Chanel perfume. Where brands make statements about people, the *international properties* of the brand add significantly to its appeal.

In other cases, however, products need to be modified. Product adaptations come in two forms: permanent and temporary.[72] A company may make a fairly standard product worldwide, but make adaptations for particular markets. For example, the Barbie doll is a standardized product for most countries but in Japan, based on market research, it had to be redesigned by making it smaller, darkening hair colour and giving it smaller breasts. This was a *permanent adaptation*. However, the change may be only a *temporary adaptation* if the local consumer needs time to adjust gradually to a new product. This often occurs with food products. For example, when McDonald's entered Japan it had to alter the red meat content of its hamburgers because Japanese consumers preferred fat to be mixed with beef. Over time, the red meat content has been increased making it almost as high as it is in the USA. Also when Mister Donut was introduced in Japan the cinnamon content was reduced as market research had shown that the Japanese customers did not like the taste. Over time, the cinnamon content was increased to US levels.[73]

Many products that appear to be the same are modified to suit differing tastes. For example, the ubiquitous Mars bar has different formulations in northern and southern Europe, with northern Europeans favouring a sweeter taste. Also, the movement of large multinational companies to seek global brand winners can provide opportunities for smaller companies to exploit emerging market segments. For example, in the Netherlands, a small company took the initiative to sell environmentally friendly products, and captured one-quarter of the household cleaning market.[74]

Brand names may require modification because of linguistic idiosyncrasies. Many companies are alive to this type of problem now. Mars, for example, changed the name of its Magnum ice cream in Greece to Magic. However, in France McVitie's had problems trying to convince consumers that the word 'digestive' has nothing to do with stomach disorders. Brand name changes also occur in the UK with Brooke Bond PG Tips being called Scottish Blend in Scotland and coming in distinctive Scottish packaging.[75]

Promotion

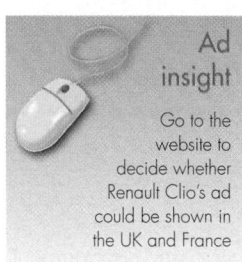

Ad insight

Go to the website to decide whether Renault Clio's ad could be shown in the UK and France

A survey of agency practitioners found that the use of standardized advertising campaigns is set to increase in the future.[76] Standard campaigns can realize cost economies and a cohesive positioning statement in a world of increasing international travel. Standardization allows the multinational corporation to maintain a consistent image identity throughout the world, and minimizes confusion among consumers who travel frequently.[77] As with all standardization–adaptation debates, the real issue is one of degree. Rarely can a campaign be transferred from one country to another without any modifications because of language difference. The clever use of pop music (an international language) in Levi's advertising was one exception, however. Coca-Cola is also close to the full standardization position with its one-sound, one-sight, one-appeal philosophy. Audi has successfully used the strap-line 'Vorsprung durch Technik' globally. Other examples of the same copy being used globally are McDonald's ('I'm Lovin' It'), Johnnie Walker ('Keep Walking') and HSBC ('The World's Local Bank'). Yet research has found that full standardization of advertising is rare.[78]

Other companies find it necessary to adopt different positions in various countries, resulting in the need for advertising adaptation. In Mexico, Nestlé managed to position the drinking of instant coffee as an upmarket activity. It is actually smarter to offer guests a cup of instant coffee than ground coffee. This affects the content of its advertising. When brands are used differently in various countries, the advertising may need to be changed accordingly. For example, Schweppes tonic water is very much a mixer (e.g. drunk with gin) in the UK and

23.4 Marketing in Action

Global Advertising Taboos

Standardized advertising campaigns are hampered by the rules and regulations in various countries around the world. These prevent certain types of advertising from appearing. Here are some examples.

France	ban on alcohol advertising
Eastern Europe	alcohol advertising banned or heavily restricted; for example, in the Czech Republic drink cannot be poured, and ads cannot show people enjoying it; in Bulgaria no bottles, glasses, or any actors drinking can be shown
Sweden	no TV advertising of toys to children under 12
Nordic countries	strict regulations on tobacco advertising
Finland	children may not sing or speak the name of a product
UK	TV tobacco ads banned
Austria	children not allowed to appear in an ad unless accompanied by a parent or comparable adult figure
Lithuania	pet food ads banned before 11 pm
Malaysia	cannot show baseball caps worn back to front (claimed to be indicative of gang influences and the undesirable side of western society); blue jeans cannot appear in ads (other colours are acceptable)
Asia	men with long hair banned from ads
Muslim countries	women can appear only if suitably attired; certain parts of the body (e.g. armpits) are not allowed to be shown for religious reasons
Korea	all models, actors and actresses in ads have to be Korean
Belgium, Luxembourg and Germany	ban on comparative advertising
Kuwait	ban on advertising cigarettes, lighters, pharmaceuticals, alcohol, airlines and chocolates

Based on: Richmond (1994);[79] Cateora et al. (2006)[80]

Ireland, but is drunk on its own in Spain and France. Marketing in Action 23.4 gives examples of regulations on advertising in various countries.

An analysis of the extent of advertising adaptation that is necessary can be assisted by separating the advertising proposition from the creative presentation of that proposition. The advertising platform is the aspect of the seller's product that is most persuasive and relevant to the potential customer: it is the fundamental proposition that is being communicated. The *creative presentation* is the way in which that proposition is translated into visual and verbal statements.[81] Advertising platforms, being broad statements of appeal, are more likely to be transferable than creative presentations. If this is the case, the solution is to keep the platform across markets but change the creative presentation to suit local demands. In other cases both platform and presentation can be used globally, as is the case with the McDonald's 'I'm Lovin' It' campaign.

Advertising can be used to position brands using one of three strategies, as outlined below.[82]

1 **Global consumer culture positioning**: this strategy defines the brand as a symbol of a given global culture. For example, a jeans brand could be positioned as one worn by adult, upper-middle-class men who are globally cosmopolitan. The objective would be to have consumers identify the brand as a sign of membership in a globally cosmopolitan segment. Real-world examples include Sony ('My First Sony'), which positioned one of its brands as appropriate for young people around the world; Philips ('Sense and Simplicity'), whose advertisements featured people from different countries; and Benetton ('The United Colours of Benetton') whose slogan emphasizes the unity of humankind and promotes the idea that people all over the world consume the brand. Brands sponsor Formula One racing to be seen as symbols of a global culture and to tap in to a global reach of 55 million people per race.[83]

▲ Lavazza uses its Italian heritage to position its brand.

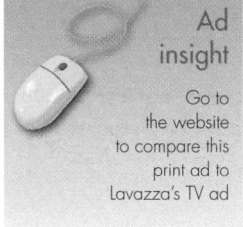

Ad insight

Go to the website to compare this print ad to Lavazza's TV ad

2 **Foreign consumer culture positioning**: with this strategy the brand is associated with a specific foreign culture. It becomes symbolic of that culture so that the brand's personality, use occasion and/or user group are associated with a foreign culture. For example, Gucci in the USA is positioned as a prestigious and fashionable Italian product; Singapore Airlines' use of the 'Singapore Girl' in its global advertising campaign, and the positioning of Louis Vuitton as representing French style and gracious living are two further examples.[84] Lavazza also uses this type of positioning (see illustration).

3 **Local consumer culture positioning**: this involves the association of the brand with local consumer culture. The brand is associated with local cultural meanings, reflects the local culture's norms and identities, is portrayed as consumed by local people in the national culture and/or depicted as locally produced for local people. For example, Dr Pepper soft drink is positioned in the USA as part of the 'American' way of life. In international advertising, it could be used when a good is produced or a service supplied locally.

23.2 Pause for Thought

People often associate countries with certain characteristics. For example, France is often associated with gracious living, style and haute cuisine. This can help (or hinder) the positioning of a brand that is associated with a particular country. When you think of Italy, the USA and Japan, what words come to mind? Think of at least one brand from each of those countries that benefits from the positive associations you have thought of.

Selling styles may also require adaptation because of cultural imperatives. Various cultures have different *time values*: In Latin American cultures, salespeople are often kept waiting a long time for a business appointment and in Spain delay in answering correspondence does not mean the matter has low priority but may reflect the fact that close family relatives take absolute priority and, no matter how important other business is, all other people are kept waiting. In the West, deadlines are common in business but in many Middle Eastern countries a deadline is taken as an insult and may well lose the overseas salesperson business.

The concept of space has different meanings in different cultures too. In the West the size of an executive's office is often taken to indicate status. In the Arab world this is not the case: a managing director may share the same office with clerks. In western cultures business is often conducted at a distance, say six feet or more. In the Middle East and Latin America, business discussions are often carried out in close proximity, involving physical contact to which the western salesperson needs to get accustomed.

The unwritten rules of doing business are often at variance too. In the West business may be discussed over lunch or at dinner in the businessperson's home. In India, this would violate hospitality rules. Western business relies on the law of contract for sales agreements but in Muslim culture a person's word is just as binding. In fact, a written contract may be seen as a challenge to his or her honour.[85] Salespeople need to adapt their behaviour to accommodate the expectations of customers abroad. For example, in Japan, sales presentations should be low key with the use of a moderate, deliberate style reflecting their preferred manner of doing business. Salespeople should not push for a close of sale; instead they should plan to cultivate relationships through sales calls, courtesy visits, the occasional lunch and other social events.

A study by Campbell, Graham, Jolibert and Meissner suggests that sales negotiation outcomes may depend on country factors in the West.[86] In Germany the *hard sell* approach was positively related to negotiation success; in France similarity (in terms of background and personality) was important; in the UK the role of the negotiator had a significant bearing on outcomes with buyers outperforming sellers; and in the USA adopting a problem-solving approach was related to negotiation success.

The Internet is creating opportunities for companies to advertise globally by setting up a website. Using electronic media as a promotional tool may be hampered by the need to set price lists, however. Where prices are currently very different across national borders some companies may decide that the risks of establishing a global Internet presence outweigh the advantages.

Country images may have a role to play in the selection of goods in overseas markets. For example, a negative image of a country may influence a consumer's attitudes towards products originating from that country. Country of origin is sometimes used to promote products abroad when associations are believed to be favourable and the extent to which the national image is considered suitable for the specific type of product being marketed. For example, the product categories most often promoted by means of the Danish image are foodstuffs and dairy produce, design goods and products related to agriculture.[87]

Germany is highly regarded for its engineering excellence, which is a major asset for companies such as Audi, BMW and Volkswagen. So strong is this image that Citroën ran an advertising campaign for its C5 claiming German engineering excellence even though the car is made in France.[88]

A clear instance of the power of country images is the case of the Toyota Corolla, which was built on the same assembly line as the near-identical GM Prism in the USA. However, because of the added value of Japanese origin, the Corolla commanded a 10 per cent price premium.[89]

A trend in organizing global advertising campaigns is for consolidation. Advertisers are either using an agency network where the agency has a global presence, or a holding group that contains many agencies spread worldwide; both routes provide the opportunity for greater coordination than employing different agencies in different countries. This also provides the client with the likelihood of negotiating a reduction in fees because of the large budgets involved. Unilever and Diageo have consolidated their network of agencies, while HSBC has preferred the holding company approach, employing WPP to handle its global account.[90] Not all clients are happy with placing all their global advertising with one agency or holding company. For example, Samsung and Motorola have moved away from this approach, claiming that one organization cannot excel at everything.[91]

Price

Price setting is a key marketing decision because price is the revenue-generating element of the marketing mix. Poor pricing decisions can undermine years of toil on fashioning strategy and pruning costs. As Leszinski states:

> As Europe moves towards a single market, lack of attention to pricing is a serious problem. The stakes are unusually high. . . . On average, a 1 per cent increase results in a 12 per cent improvement in a company's operating margin. This is four times as powerful as a 1 per cent increase in its volume. But the sword cuts both ways. A price decrease of 5 to 10 per cent will eliminate most companies' profits. As the single market develops, decreases of this magnitude can easily happen: the existing price differentials across Europe for some products are in the region of 20 to 40 per cent.[92]

In the face of more intense global competition, international marketers need to consider six issues when considering cross-national pricing decisions:

1 calculating extra costs and making price quotations
2 understanding the competition and customers
3 using pricing tactics to undermine competitor actions
4 parallel importing
5 transfer pricing
6 counter-trade.

Each of these special considerations will now be explored.

Calculating extra costs and making price quotations: the extra costs of doing business in a foreign market must be taken into account if a profit is to be made. *Middlemen and transportation costs* need to be estimated. Distributors may demand different mark-ups and agents may require varying commission levels in different countries. The length of the distribution channel also needs to be understood, as do the margins required at each level before a price to the consumer can be set. These can sometimes almost double the price in an overseas market compared to at home. Overseas transportation may incur the additional costs of insurance, packaging and shipping. *Taxes and tariffs* also vary from country to country. Although there are moves to standardize the level of value added tax in the single market there are still wide variations. Denmark, in particular, is a high-tax economy. A tariff is a fee charged when goods are brought into a country from another country. Although tariff barriers have fallen among the member states of Europe, they can still be formidable between other countries. Companies active in international business need to protect themselves against the costs of *exchange rate fluctuations*. Nestlé, for example, lost $1 million in six months due to adverse exchange rate moves.[93] Companies are increasingly asking that transactions be written in terms of the vendor company's national currency, and *forward hedging* (which effectively allows future payments to be settled at around the exchange rate in question when the deal was made) is commonly practised.

Care should be taken when *quoting a price* to an overseas customer. The contract may include such items as credit, who is responsible for the goods during transit, and who pays insurance and transportation charges (and from what point). As we have seen, the currency in which payment is made can have a dramatic effect on profitability. This must be spelled out. Finally, the quantity and quality of the goods must be defined. For example, the contract should specify whether a 'ton' is a metric 'tonne' or an imperial 'ton'. Quality standards to be used when evaluating shipments should be agreed so that future arguments regarding returned-as-defective products may be minimized. The price charged, then, in a quotation can vary considerably depending on these factors.

Understanding the competition and customers: as with any pricing decision these factors play a major role. The difference is that information is often more difficult to acquire for exporters because of the distances involved. When making pricing moves, companies need to be aware of the present *competitors' strategic degrees of freedom*, how much room they have to react, and the possibility of the price being used as a weapon by companies entering the market from a different industry. Where prices are high and barriers to entry low, incumbent firms are especially vulnerable.

Companies also need to be wary of using **self-reference criteria** when evaluating overseas customer's perceptions. This occurs when an exporter assumes that the choice criteria, motivations and behaviour that are important to overseas customers are the same as those used by domestic customers. The viewpoints of domestic and foreign consumers to the same product can be very different. For example, a small Renault car is viewed as a luxury model in Spain but utilitarian in Germany. This can affect the price position vis-à-vis competitors in overseas markets.

Using pricing tactics to undermine competitor actions: four tactics can be used in the face of competitor activity.[94]

1 *Disguise price reductions*: rather than reduce advertised list price, which is visible to competitors and may lead to a downward price spiral, cuts should be communicated directly to customers via the salesforce or direct mail by such methods as changes in the terms of sale (training included), reduced service charges or revised discount structures.

2 *Abolish printed lists*: quote price directly on a customer-by-customer basis. This creates uncertainty in the market as competitors are less confident of knowing what to quote against.

3 *Build barriers to price switching*: try to build up switching costs. For example, in the mobile phone market, the problems involved for users in changing numbers and acquiring a new handset limit switching between providers and raise their price flexibility.

4 *Respond to competitor attacks decisively*: for example, an electrical components supplier that held market leadership was successfully attacked by a competitor on price. The situation was not helped by the leader's policy of strictly following a printed price list along with predictable discounts for large accounts. A major plank of the leader's response was to target the aggressor's largest account with massive discounts. Although the customer stayed loyal, the aggressor understood the message and refrained from continuing its price attack.

International marketers need to understand how to use such pricing tactics in the face of increasingly fierce global competition.

Parallel importing: a major consideration in international markets is the threat of parallel imports. These occur when importers buy products from distributors in one country and sell them in another to distributors who are not part of the manufacturer's normal distribution system. The motivation for this practice occurs when there are large price differences between countries, and the free movement of goods between member states means that it is likely to grow. Companies protect themselves by:

- lowering price differentials
- offering non-transferable service/product packages
- changing the packaging—for example, a beer producer by offering differently shaped bottles in various countries ensured that the required recyclability of the product was guaranteed only in the intended country of sale.[95]

Another means of parallel importing (or 'grey market' trading as it is sometimes called) is by supermarkets buying products from abroad to sell in their stores at reduced prices. A landmark legal battle was won by Levi Strauss to prevent Tesco, the UK supermarket chain, from selling Levi's jeans imported cheaply from outside Europe.

Transfer pricing: this is the price charged between profit centres (e.g. manufacturing company to foreign subsidiary) of a single company. Transfer prices are sometimes set to take advantage of lower taxation in some countries than others. For example, a low price is charged to a subsidiary in a low-tax country and a high price in one where taxes are high. Similarly, low transfer prices may be set for high-tariff countries. Transfer prices should not be based solely on taxation and tariff considerations, however. For example, transfer pricing rules can cause subsidiaries to sell products at higher prices than the competition even though their true costs of manufacture are no different.

Counter-trade: not all transactions are concluded in cash; goods may be included as part of the asking price. Four major forms of counter-trade are as follows.

1   *Barter*: payment for goods with other goods, with no direct use of money; the vendor then has the problem of selling the goods that have been exchanged.

2   *Compensation deals*: payment using goods and cash. For example, General Motors sold $12 million worth of locomotives and diesel engines to former Yugoslavia and received $8 million in cash plus $4 million worth of cutting tools.[96]

3   *Counter-purchase*: the seller agrees to sell a product to a buyer and receives cash. The deal is dependent on the original seller buying goods from the original buyer for all or part of the original amount.

4   *Buy-backs*: these occur when the initial sale involves production plant, equipment or technology. Part or all of the initial sale is financed by selling back some of the final product. For example, Levi Strauss set up a jeans factory in Hungary that was financed by the supply of jeans back to the company.

A key issue in setting the counter-trade 'price' is valuing the products received in exchange for the original goods, and estimating the cost of selling on the bartered goods. However, according to Shipley and Neale, this forms 20–30 per cent of world trade with yearly value exceeding $100 billion.[97]

Place

A key international market decision is whether to use importers/distributors or the company's own personnel to distribute a product in a foreign market. Initial costs are often lower with the former method, so it is often used as an early method of market entry. For example, Sony and Panasonic entered the US market by using importers. As sales increased they entered into exclusive agreements with distributors, before handling their own distribution arrangements by selling directly to retailers.[98]

International marketers must not assume that overseas distribution systems resemble their own. As we have mentioned, Japan is renowned for its long, complex distribution channels; in Africa, distribution bears little resemblance to that in more developed countries. An important consideration when evaluating a distribution channel is the power of its members. Selling directly to large powerful distributors such as supermarkets may seem attractive logistically but their ability to negotiate low prices needs to be taken into account.

Customer expectations are another factor that has a bearing on the channel decision. For many years, in Spain, yoghurt was sold through pharmacies (as a health product). As customers expected to buy yoghurt in pharmacies, suppliers had to use them as an outlet. Regulations also affect the choice of distribution channel. For example, over-the-counter (OTC) pharmaceuticals are sold only in pharmacies in Belgium, France, Spain and Italy, whereas in Denmark, the UK and Germany, other channels (notably grocery outlets) also sell them.

Nevertheless, there can be opportunities to standardize at least part of the distribution system. For example, BMW standardizes its dealerships so that customers have the same experience when they enter their showrooms around the world.[99]

As with domestic marketing, the marketing mix in a foreign market needs to be blended into a consistent package that provides a clear position for the product in the marketplace. Furthermore, managers need to display high levels of commitment to their overseas activities as this has been shown to be a strong determinant of performance.[100]

Organizing for International Operations

The starting point for organizing for international marketing operations is, for many companies, the establishment of an export department. As sales, the number of international markets and the complexity of activities increase, so the export department may be replaced by a more complex structure. Bartlett and Ghoshal describe four types of structure for managing a worldwide business enterprise: international, global, multinational and transnational organization.[101]

International organization

The philosophy of management is that overseas operations are appendages to a central domestic operation. Subsidiaries form a coordinated federation with many assets, resources, responsibilities and decisions decentralized, but overall control is in the hands of headquarters. Formal management planning and control systems permit fairly tight headquarters–subsidiary links.

Global organization

The management philosophy is that overseas operations should be viewed as 'delivery pipelines' to a unified global market. The key organizational unit is the centralized hub that controls most strategic assets, resources, responsibilities and decisions. The centre enforces tight operational control of decisions, resources and information.

Multinational organization

A multinational mentality is characterized by a regard for overseas operations as a portfolio of independent businesses. Many key assets, responsibilities and decisions are decentralized. Control is through informal headquarters–subsidiary relationships supported by simple financial controls.

Transnational organization

This organizational form may be described as a complex process of coordination and cooperation in an environment of shared decision-making. Organizational units are integrated with large flows of components, products, resources, people and information among interdependent units. The transnational organization attempts to respond to an environment that is characterized by strong simultaneous forces for both global integration and national responsiveness.[102]

Centralization vs Decentralization

A key determinant of the way international operations are organized is the degree to which the environment calls for global integration (centralization) versus regional responsiveness (decentralization). **Centralization** reaps economies of scale and provides an integrated marketing profile to channel intermediaries that, themselves, may be international, and customers that are increasingly geographically mobile. Confusion over product formulations, advertising approaches, packaging design and labelling, and pricing is eliminated by a coordinated approach. (However, too much centralization can lead to the *not invented here syndrome*, where managers in one country are slow to introduce products that have been successful in others, or fail to fully support advertising campaigns that have been conceived elsewhere.)

Decentralization maximizes customization of products to regional tastes and preferences. Since decentralized decision-making is closer to customers, speed of response to new opportunities is quicker than with a centralized organizational structure. Relationships with the trade and government are facilitated by local decision-making.

Many companies feel the pressure of both sets of forces, hence the development of the transnational corporation. European integration has led many companies to review their overseas operations with the objective of realizing global economies wherever possible. European centralized marketing teams carry the responsibility for looking at the longer-term strategic picture alongside national marketing staff who deal less with advertising theme development and brand positioning, and more with handling retailer relationships.[103] The result is loss of responsibility and power for national marketing managers. This is a sensitive issue, and many companies are experimenting with the right blend of centralization and national power.[104] Desire to preserve national identity and resentment of centralized European interference can run deep. One British company, owned by a German parent for more than a decade, still battled to preserve its national identity by holding its own formal board meetings and publishing its own separate annual report.[105] When Pampers was launched across Europe by Procter & Gamble, an employee found that 'as soon as it was known that I was from the European Technical Centre . . . my local support dried up'.[106]

The fact that national marketing managers often lose responsibility and power in moves to a more centralized marketing approach means that simply preaching the virtues of globalization will not gain their commitment. Neither is compelling business logic likely to remove their opposition.

One approach to developing support is through the creation of *taskforces*. A business area is selected where the urgency of need is most clear; and where positive early results can begin a 'ripple effect', creating champions for change within the company. Procter & Gamble, for example, created a taskforce of national product managers to decide upon common brand requirements. A freight company, under intense pressure from international buying groups, set up a pricing taskforce to thrash out a coordinated European pricing strategy. One by-product of the taskforce approach is that it provides top management with a forum for identifying potential Euro-managers.

For some intransigent national managers, removing them from office may be the only effective solution. But there are less blatant methods. One approach is to put responsibility for planning prospective changes in the hands of the individual managers most threatened by them. For example, the roles of national marketing managers could be expanded to include responsibility for developing brands across Europe. Another way forward is to establish an accountability and compensation system for national marketing managers that reflects their new situation. When a centralized approach is needed, they are more willing to give up power in return for what makes them succeed.

Companies such as Coca-Cola, McDonald's, Shell and HSBC employ a global marketing director to coordinate worldwide operations. Such a role is not for the faint-hearted: much of their time is spent travelling and they have to combine an ability to digest reams of consumer research with the talent to persuade, through powerful argument, local marketing executives to adopt a strategy. HSBC's global marketing chief managed to achieve the right balance between the need to create a global positioning statement for its advertising and local demands for a bank by the use of the tag-line 'HSBC—the world's local bank'.

To minimize conflict, some companies are trying to build tiered systems where the marketing decisions that are centrally determined and those that are subject to local control are clearly defined. For example, the brand positioning and advertising theme issues may be determined centrally but the creative interpretation of them is decided locally.

Whichever approach is used, a system that shares insights, methods and best practice should be established. The system should provide a global mechanism to identify first-hand observations of best practice, communicate them to those who would benefit from them, and allow access to a store of best-practice information when required. To do this, companies need to nurture a culture where these ideas are communicated. This can be helped by rewarding the people who contribute. Tracking employees who post insights and examples of best practice, and rewarding them during annual performance reviews is one method. Regular meetings can also aid communication, especially when they include workshops that engage the participants in action-orientated learning. Sometimes the sharing of information at these meetings is less important than the establishment of personal relationships that foster subsequent communications and interactions. Technological developments can also make communication easier and quicker, such as the formation of intranets that allow global communication of best practice news, competitor actions and technological change. Of more lasting use, however, is the sending of teams to see best practice at first hand to facilitate the depth of understanding not usually achieved by descriptive accounts.

When you have read this chapter
log on to the Online Learning Centre at www.mcgraw-hill.co.uk/ textbooks/jobber to explore chapter-by-chapter test questions, links and further online study tools for marketing.

Review

1 **The reasons why companies seek foreign markets**
- The reasons are to find opportunities beyond saturated domestic markets; to seek expansion beyond small, low-growth domestic markets; to meet customer expectations; to respond to competitive forces (e.g. the desire to attack an overseas competitor); to act on cost factors (e.g. to gain economies of scale); and to achieve a portfolio balance where problems of economic recession in some countries can be balanced by growth in others.

2 **The factors that influence which foreign markets to enter**
- The factors are macroenvironmental issues (economic, socio-cultural and political-legal) and microenvironmental issues (market attractiveness, which can be assessed by analysing market size and growth rate, degree of competition, the costs of serving the market, profit potential and market accessibility) and company capability profile (skills, resources, product adaptability and the ability to create a competitive advantage).

3 **The range of foreign market entry strategies**
- Foreign market entry strategies are indirect exporting (using, for example, domestic-based export agents), direct exporting (using, for example, foreign-based distributors); licensing (using, for example, a local licensee with access to a set of technologies or know-how); joint venture (where, for example, two or more companies form a partnership to share the risks, costs and profits) and direct investment (where, for example, a foreign producer is bought or new facilities built).

4 **The factors influencing foreign market entry strategies**
- The factors are the risk of losing proprietary information (for example, direct investment may be used to avoid this risk), resources (for example, when resources are low, exporting using agents or distributors may be favoured) and the desired level of control (for example, when high control is desired direct investment or exporting using the company's staff may be preferred).

5 **The influences on the degree of standardization or adaptation**
- A useful rule of thumb is to go global (standardize) when you can and stay local (adapt) when you must.
- The key influences are cost; the need to meet local regulations, language and needs; the sensitivities of local managers, who may perceive a loss of status associated with greater centralized control; media availability and promotional preferences; and organizational structure and culture (for example, where subsidiaries hold considerable power).

6 **The special considerations involved in designing an international marketing mix**
- The special considerations are huge research and development costs, where a brand concept is based on an authentic national heritage that transcends global boundaries, where a global segment of like-minded people can be exploited, and where a cohesive positioning statement makes sense because of increasing global travel. All of these considerations favour a standardized marketing mix. Where there are strong local differences an adapted marketing mix is required.

7 **How to organize for international marketing operations**
- Many companies begin with an export department but this may be replaced later by more complex structures.
- Four types of structure for managing a worldwide business enterprise are: international (where overseas operations are appendages to a central domestic operation); global (where overseas operations are delivery pipelines to a unified global market); multinational (where overseas operations are managed as a portfolio of independent businesses); and transnational organizations (which are characterized by a complex process of coordination and cooperation in an environment of shared decision-making).

Key Terms

adapted marketing mix an international marketing strategy for changing the marketing mix for each international target market

centralization in international marketing it is the global integration of international operations

contractual joint venture two or more companies form a partnership but no joint enterprise with a separate identity is formed

counter-trade a method of exchange where not all transactions are concluded in cash; goods may be included as part of the asking price

decentralization in international marketing it is the delegation of international operations to individual countries or regions

direct exporting the handling of exporting activities by the exporting organization rather than by a domestically based independent organization

direct investment market entry that involves investment in foreign-based assembly or manufacturing facilities

equity joint venture where two or more companies form a partnership that involves the creation of a new company

foreign consumer culture positioning positioning a brand as associated with a specific foreign culture (e.g. Italian fashion)

franchising a form of licensing where a package of services is offered by the franchisor to the franchisee in return for payment

global consumer culture positioning positioning a brand as a symbol of a given global culture (e.g. young cosmopolitan men)

indirect exporting the use of independent organizations within the exporter's domestic market to facilitate export

licensing a contractual arrangement in which a licensor provides a licensee with certain rights, e.g. to technology access or production rights

local consumer culture positioning positioning a brand as associated with a local culture (e.g. local production and consumption of a good)

self-reference criteria the use of one's own perceptions and choice criteria to judge what is important to consumers. In international markets, the perceptions and choice criteria of domestic consumers may be used to judge what is important to foreign consumers

standardized marketing mix an international marketing strategy for using essentially the same product, promotion, distribution, and pricing in all the company's international markets

transfer pricing the price charged between the profit centres of the same company, sometimes used to take advantage of lower taxes in another country

Study Questions

1. What are the factors that drive companies to enter international markets?

2. Joint ventures are a popular method of entering markets in Europe. Choose an example (many are given in this book) and research its background (and outcomes if any).

3. For a company of your choice, research its reasons for expanding into new foreign markets, and describe the moves that have been made.

4. Using information in this chapter and from Chapter 17, on distribution, describe how you would go about selecting and motivating overseas distributors.

5. Why are so many companies trying to standardize their global marketing mixes? With examples, show the limitations to this approach.

6. What are the factors that influence the choice of market entry strategy?

7. Select a familiar advertising campaign in your country and examine the extent to which it is likely to need adaptation for another country of your choice.

8. Describe the problems of pricing in overseas markets and the skills required to price effectively in the global marketplace.

References

1. Cuyvers, L., P. de Pelsmacker, G. Rayp and I. T. M. Roozen (1995) A Decision Support Model for the Planning and Assessment of Export Promotion Activities by Government Export Promotion Institutions—the Belgian Case, *International Journal of Research in Marketing* 12, 173–86.

2. Katsikeas, C. S., N. F. Piercy and C. Ioannidis (1996) Determinants of Export Performance in a European Context, *European Journal of Marketing* 30(6), 6–35.

3. Glaister, D. (2006) Tesco Thinks Big for its Foray into America's West, *Guardian*, 22 September, 24.

4. See Aharoni (1966) *The Foreign Investment Decision Process*, Boston, Mass: Harvard University Press; Agarwal, S. and S. N. Ramaswami (1992) Choice of Foreign Market Entry Mode: Impact of Ownership, Location and Internalisation Factors, *Journal of International Business Studies*, Spring, 1–27; Knickerbocker, F. T. (1973) *Oligopolistic Reaction and Multinational Enterprise*, Boston, Mass: Harvard University Press.

5. Whitelock, J. and D. Jobber (2004) An Evaluation of External Factors in the Decision of UK Industrial Firms to Enter a New Non-domestic Market: an Exploratory Study, *European Journal of Marketing* 38(1/2), 1437–56.

6. Borrell, J. (1990) Living with Shock Therapy, *Time*, 11 June, 31.

7. Tully, S. (1990) Poland's Gamble Begins to Pay Off, *Fortune*, 27 August, 91–6.

8. Litvak, I. A. and P. M. Banting (1968) A Conceptual Framework for International Business Arrangements, in King, R. L. (ed.) *Marketing and the New Science of Planning*, Chicago: American Marketing Association, 460–7.

9. Conway, T. and J. S. Swift (2000) International Relationship Marketing, *European Journal of Marketing* 34(1/2), 1391–413.

10. Johanson, J. and J.-E. Vahlne (1977) The Internationalisation Process of the Firm: A Model of Knowledge Development and Increasing Foreign Market Commitments, *Journal of International Business Studies* 8(1), 23–32.

11. Erramilli, M. K. (1991) Entry Mode Choice in Service Industries, *International Marketing Review* 7(5), 50–62.

12. Halsall, M. (1994) Nova Means 'Does Not Go' in Spanish: Why British Firms Need to Learn the Language of Customers, *Guardian*, 11 April, 16.

13. Egan, C. and P. McKiernan (1994) *Inside Fortress Europe: Strategies for the Single Market*, Wokingham: Addison-Wesley, 118.

14. Bashford, S. (2005) What's Yours Called?, *Marketing*, 7 September, 36–8.

15. Ghauri, P. and P. Cateora (2006) *International Marketing*, Maidenhead: McGraw-Hill.

16. Wiggins, J. (2008) Brands Make a Dash into Russia, *Financial Times*, 4 September, 12.

17. Knickerbocker (1973) op. cit.

18. Birchall, J. and C. Parkers (2006) Assault on West Coast Market, *Financial Times*, 10 February, 21.

19. Wiggins, J. (2008) Multinationals Eat into the Russian Market, *Financial Times*, 18 June, 22.

20. Watts, J. (2006) Wal-Mart Leads Charge in Race to Grab a Slice of China, *Guardian*, 25 March, 20.

21. Whitelock, J. and D. Jobber (1994) The Impact of Competitor Environment on Initial Market Entry in a New, Non-Domestic Market, *Proceedings of the Marketing Education Group Conference*, Coleraine, July, 1008–17.

22. Young, S., J. Hamill, C. Wheeler and J. R. Davies (1989) *International Market Entry and Development*, Englewood Cliffs, NJ: Prentice-Hall.

23. West, A. (1987) *Marketing Overseas*, London: Pitman.

24. For comprehensive coverage of the problem faced by exporters, see Katsikeas, C. S. and R. E. Morgan (1994) Differences in Perceptions of Exporting Problems Based on Firm Size and Export Market Experience, *European Journal of Marketing* 28(5), 17–35.

25. Young et al. (1989) op. cit.

26. Bloomgarden, K. (2000) Branching Out, *Marketing Business*, April, 12–13.

27. Hopkinson, G. C. and S. Hogarth-Scott (1999) Franchise Relationship Quality: Microeconomic Explanations, *European Journal of Marketing* 33(9/10), 827–43.

28. Welford, R. and K. Prescott (2000) *European Business*, London: Pitman.

29. Wright, R. W. (1981) Evolving International Business Arrangements, in Dhawan, K. C., H. Etemad and R. W. Wright (eds) *International Business: A Canadian Perspective*, Reading, MA: Addison Wesley.

30. Young et al. (1989) op. cit.

31. Terpstra, V. and R. Sarathy (1999) *International Marketing*, Fort Worth, Texas: Dryden.

32. Rigby, E. and J. Leaky (2008) Tesco Finds its Passage to India, *Guardian*, 13 August, 17.

33. Hooley, G., T. Cox, D. Shipley, J. Fahy, J. Beracs and K. Kolos (1996) Foreign Direct Investment in Hungary: Resource Acquisition and Domestic Competitive Advantage, *Journal of International Business Studies* 4, 683–709.

34. Terpstra and Sarathy (1999) op. cit.

35. Anonymous (2008) The Challengers, *Economist*, 12 January, 61–3.

36. Smit, B. (1996) Dutch Bank Moves Deeper into the Mid West, *European*, 28 November–4 December, 25.

37. Ghauri, P. N. and K. Holstius (1996) The Role of Matching in the Foreign Market Entry Process in the Baltic States, *European Journal of Marketing* 30(2), 75–88.

38. Anonymous (2008) Ringing Off, *Economist*, 31 May, 86.

39. Gapper, J. (2008) Global Brands Special Report, *Financial Times*, 21 April, 1–6.

40. Buckley P. J., H. Mirza and J. R. Sparkes (1987) Foreign Direct Investment in Japan as a Means of Market Entry: The Case of European Firms, *Journal of Marketing Management* 2(3), 241–58.

41. Goodnow, J. D. and J. E. Hansz (1972) Environmental Determinants of Overseas Market Entry Strategies, *Journal of International Business Studies* 3(1), 33–50.

42. Contractor, F. J. (1984) Choosing between Direct Investment and Licensing: Theoretical Considerations and Empirical Tests, *Journal of International Business Studies* 15(3), 167–88.

43. Anderson, E. and A. T. Coughlan (1987) International Market Entry and Expansion via Independent or Integrated Channels of Distribution, *Journal of Marketing* 51, January, 71–82.

44. Klein, S. and J. R. Roth (1990) Determinants of Export Channel Structure: The Effects of Experience and Psychic Distance Reconsidered, *International Marketing Review* 7(5), 27–38.

45. See Agarwal and Ramaswami (1992) op. cit.; Knickerbocker (1973) op. cit.

46. Sharma, D. D. (1988) Overseas Market Entry Strategy: The Technical Consultancy Firms, *Journal of Global Marketing* 2(2), 89–110.

47. Johanson and Vahlne (1977) op. cit.

48. Johanson, J. and J.-E. Vahlne (1990) The Mechanisms of Internationalisation, *International Marketing Review* 7(4), 11–24.

49. Buckley *et al.* (1987) op. cit.

50. Sharma (1988) op. cit.

51. Klein and Roth (1990) op. cit.

52. Erramilli (1991) op. cit.

53. Buckley *et al.* (1987) op. cit.

54. Levitt, T. (1983) The Globalization of Markets, *Harvard Business Review*, May/June, 92–102.

55. Quelch, J. A. and E. J. Hoff (1986) Customizing Global Marketing, *Harvard Business Review*, May–June, 59–68.

56. Banerjee, A. (1994) Transnational Advertising Development and Management: An Account Planning Approach and a Process Framework, *International Journal of Advertising* 13, 95–124.

57. Mayer, M. (1991) *Whatever Happened to Madison Avenue? Advertising in the '90s*, Boston, MA: Little, Brown, 186–7.

58. Mitchell, A. (1993) Can Branding Take on Global Proportions? *Marketing*, 29 April, 20–1.

59. Lewis, E. (2006) Going Global, *The Marketer*, June (Issue 25), 7–9.

60. Mazur, L. (2002) No Pain, No Gain, *Marketing Business*, September, 10–13.

61. De Chernatony (1993) op. cit.

62. De Chernatony, L. (1993) Ten Hints for EC-wide Brands, *Marketing*, 11 February, 16.

63. Kirby, K. (2000) Globally Led Locally Driven, *Marketing Business*, May, 26–7.

64. Aaker, D. A. and E. Joachimsthaler (2002) *Brand Leadership*, New York: Free Press, 303–9.

65. Luce, E. (2002) Hard Sell to a Billion Consumers, *Financial Times*, 15 April, 14.

66. Benady, D. (2003) Uncontrolled Immigration, *Marketing Week*, 20 February, 24–7.

67. Charles, C. (2008) Coors Seeks Feminine Touch, *Marketing*, 27 August, 16.

68. Lovell, C. (2008) Universal Truths Cross Booze Borders, *Campaign*, 15 August, 8.

69. Jones, H. (2008) How To . . . Tackle Foreign Markets, *Marketer*, September, 35–8.

70. Reed, J. (2008) Designs that Keep on Moving, *Financial Times*, 29 July, 12.

71. Dawkins, W. (1996) Time to Pull Back the Screen, *Financial Times*, 19 November, 14.

72. Dudley, J. W. (1989) *1992: Strategies for the Single Market*, London: Kogan Page.

73. Ohmae, K. (1985) *Triad Power*, New York: Free Press.

74. Mitchell (1993) op. cit.

75. Harris, P. and F. McDonald (1994) *European Business and Marketing: Strategic Issues*, London: Chapman.

76. Duncan, T. and J. Ramaprasad (1993) Ad Agency Views of Standardised Campaigns for Multinational Clients, Conference of the American Academy of Advertising, Chicago, IL, 17 April.

77. Papavassiliou, N. and V. Stathakopoulos (1997) Standardisation versus Adaptation of International Advertising Strategies: Towards a Framework, *European Journal of Marketing* 31(7), 504–27.

78. Harris, G. and S. Attour (2003) The International Advertising Practices of Multinational Companies: A Content Analysis Study, *European Journal of Marketing* 37(1/2), 154–68.

79. Richmond, S. (1994) Global Taboos, in World Advertising, *Campaign Report*, 13 May, 19–21.

80. Cateora, P. R., J. L. Graham and P. J. Ghauri (2006) *International Marketing*, London: McGraw-Hill, 376.

81. Killough, J. (1978) Improved Pay-offs from Transnational Advertising, *Harvard Business Review*, July–Aug., 58–70.

82. Alden, D. L., J.-B. E. M. Steenkamp and R. Batra (1998) Brand Positioning Through Advertising in Asia, North America, and Europe: The Role of Global Consumer Culture, *Journal of Marketing* 63, January, 75–87.

83. Weeks, R. and M. Stoves (2008) Defensive vs Disillusioned, *Campaign*, 28 November, 11.

84. Wachman, R. (2004) Papa of the Branded Bags, *Observer*, 25 July, 16.

85. Jobber, D. and G. Lancaster (2009) *Selling and Sales Management*, London: Pitman.

86. Campbell, N. C. G., J. L. Graham, A. Jolibert and H. G. Meissner (1988) Marketing Negotiations in France, Germany, the United Kingdom and the United States, *Journal of Marketing* 52, April, 49–62.

87. Niss, N. (1996) Country of Origin Marketing Over the Product Life Cycle: A Danish Case Study, *European Journal of Marketing* 30(3), 6–22.

88. Whitehead, J. (2008) More to Citroën Campaign than Stereotypes, *Guardian*, 22 September, 7.

89. See Powell, C. (2000) Why We Really Must Fly the Flag, *Observer*, Business Section, 25 April, 4 and Yip, G. (2003) *Total Global Strategy*, Englewood Cliffs, NJ: Prentice-Hall, 88.

90. Benady, A. (2004) Global Clients Queue Up at the Agency, *FT Creative Business*, 30 November, 10–11.

91. Benady, D. (2005) The End of the World, *Marketing Week*, 3 November, 26–7.

92. Leszinski, R. (1992) Pricing for the Single Market, *McKinsey Quarterly* 3, 86–94.

93. Cateora *et al.* (2006) op. cit.

94. Garda, R. A. (1992) Tactical Pricing, *McKinsey Quarterly* 3, 75–85.

95. Leszinski (1992) op. cit.

96. Cateora *et al.* (2006) op. cit.

97. Shipley, D. and B. Neale (1988) Countertrade: Reactive or Proactive, *Journal of Business Research*, June, 327–35.

98. Darlin, D. (1989) Myth and Marketing in Japan, *Wall Street Journal*, 6 April, B1.

99. Anonymous (2005) When the World is your Market, *Campaign*, 27 May, 46–7.

100. Chadee, D. D. and J. Mattsson (1998) Do Service and Merchandise Exporters Behave and Perform Differently?, *European Journal of Marketing* 32(9/10), 830–42.

101. Bartlett, C. and S. Ghoshal (2002) *Managing Across Borders: The Transnational Solution*, Cambridge, MA: Harvard Business School Press.

102. Ghoshal, S. and N. Nohria (1993) Horses for Courses: Organizational Forms of Multinational Corporations, *Sloan Management Review*, Winter, 23–35.

103. Mazur, L. (1993) Brands sans Frontières, *Observer*, 28 November, 8.

104. Ohbora, T., A. Parsons and H. Riesenbeck (1992) Alternative Routes to Global Marketing, *McKinsey Quarterly* 3, 52–74.

105. Blackwell, N., J.-P. Bizet, P. Child and D. Hensley (1992) Creating European Organisations that Work, *McKinsey Quarterly* 2, 31–43.

106. Bartlett, C. (1991) *Procter & Gamble Europe*, Cambridge, MA: Harvard Business School Case, No. 9-384-139.

IKEA

Building a Cult Global Brand

IKEA is a state of mind that revolves around contemporary design, low prices, wacky promotions and an enthusiasm that few institutions in or out of business can muster. Perhaps more than any other company in the world, IKEA has become a curator of people's lifestyles, if not their lives. At a time when consumers face so many choices for everything they buy, IKEA provides a one-stop sanctuary for coolness. It is a trusted safe zone that people can enter and immediately be part of a like-minded cost/design/environmentally sensitive global tribe. There are other would-be curators around—Starbucks and Virgin do a good job—but IKEA does it best.

If the Swedish retailer has its way, you too will live in a BoKlok home and sleep in a Leksvik bed under a Brunskära quilt. Beds are named after Norwegian cities; bedding after flowers and plants. One disaster: a child's bed called Gutvik, which sounds like 'good f***' in German. IKEA wants to supply the food in your fridge, it also sells the fridge, and the soap in your shower.

The IKEA concept has plenty of room to run: the retailer accounts for just 5 to 10 per cent of the furniture market in each country in which it operates. It is, however, a global phenomenon. That is because IKEA is far more than a furniture merchant. It sells a lifestyle that consumers around the world embrace as a signal that they've arrived, that they have good taste and recognize value. 'If it wasn't for IKEA,' writes British design magazine *Icon*, 'most people would have no access to affordable contemporary design.' The magazine even voted IKEA founder Ingvar Kamprad the most influential tastemaster in the world today.

As long as consumers from Moscow to Beijing and beyond keep striving to enter the middle class, there will be a need for IKEA. Think about it. What mass-market retailer has had more success globally? Not Wal-Mart Stores Inc., which despite vast strengths has stumbled in Brazil, Germany and Japan. Not France's Carrefour, which has never made it in the USA. IKEA has had its slip-ups, too. But right now its 296 stores, mainly in Europe, Asia, Australia and the USA, are thriving, hosting over 500 million shoppers a year. The emotional response is unparalleled. The promise of store vouchers for the first 50 shoppers drew thousands to an IKEA store in the Saudi Arabian city of Jeddah. In the ensuing melee, two people died and 16 were injured. An opening in London attracted up to 6000 before police were called in.

Why the uproar?

IKEA is the quintessential global cult brand. Just take those stunts. Before an Atlanta opening, IKEA managers invited locals to apply for the post of Ambassador of Kul (Swedish for fun). The five winners wrote an essay on why they deserved $2000 in vouchers. There was one catch. They would have to live in the store for three days before the opening, take part in contests and sleep in the bedding department. 'I got about eight hours of sleep total because of all the drilling and banging going on,' says winner Jordan Leopold, a manager at Costco Wholesale.

Leopold got his bedroom set. And IKEA got to craft another story about itself—a story picked up in the press that drew even more shoppers. More shoppers, more traffic. More traffic, more sales. More sales, more buzz. Such buzz has kept IKEA's sales growing at a healthy clip: for the fiscal year ended 31 August 2009, in the midst of a recession, revenues rose 1.5 per cent to $30 billion. Although privately owned, IKEA guards profit figures as jealously as its recipe for Swedish meatballs; pre-tax operating profits are conservatively estimated at $3 billion. IKEA maintains these profits even while it cuts prices steadily. 'IKEA's operating margins of

IKEA at a glance	TABLE C45.1
Privately owned home products retailer that markets flat-pack furniture, accessories, and bathroom and kitchen items globally	
IKEA is the world's largest furniture manufacturer	
Sales of £30 billion (2009)	
Estimated profits of £3 billion (2009)	
Number of stores at 2009: 296 in 36 countries, mainly in Europe, USA, Canada, Asia and Australia. The largest number of stores are in Germany (44) and the USA (36)	
New store openings: 20 in 2008 and 14 in 2009 (reduced because of the global recession)	

approximately 10 per cent are among the best in home furnishing,' says Mattias Karlkjell of Stockholm's ABG Sundal Collier. They also compare well with margins of 5 per cent at Pier 1 Imports and 7.7 per cent at Target, both competitors of IKEA in the USA.

To keep growing at that pace, IKEA has continued its new store openings around the world, with up to 20 per year (although that number was reduced during the recent recession) at a cost of $66 million per store, on average. IKEA has boosted its profile in three of its fastest-growing markets: the USA, Russia (where IKEA is already a huge hit—today's Russian yuppies are called 'the IKEA generation'—and $4 billion had been invested in 12 stores by 2009) and China (now worth over $150 million in sales). In the USA, the number of stores has grown from 25 in 2005 to 36 in 2009. IKEA is also investing in emerging markets such as Croatia, Slovenia and Ukraine. Investment has slowed in Russia, however, in the face of what IKEA sees as unnecessary bureaucracy. On several occasions the company had to delay openings of its stores as regional authorities raised issues with store construction and design, safety or environmental issues. In the UK, IKEA has built smaller multi-level city stores in Coventry and Southampton in response to restrictions on the building of out-of-town retail establishments.

The key to these roll-outs is to preserve the strong enthusiasm IKEA evokes—an enthusiasm that has inspired endless shopper comment on the Internet. Examples: 'IKEA makes me free to become what I want to be' (from Romania). Or this: 'Half my house is from IKEA—and the nearest store is six hours away' (the USA). Or this: 'Every time, it's trendy for less money' (Germany).

The shopping experience

What enthrals shoppers and scholars alike is the store visit—a similar experience the world over. The blue-and-yellow buildings average 28,000 square metres in size, about equal to five football fields. The sheer number of items—7000, from kitchen cabinets to candlesticks—is a decisive advantage. 'Others offer affordable furniture,' says Bryan Roberts, research manager at Planet Retail, a consultancy in London. 'But there's no one else who offers the whole concept in the big shed.'

The global middle class, which IKEA targets, share buying habits. The $120 Billy bookcase, $13 Lack side table and $190 Ivar storage system are best-sellers worldwide. Even spending per customer is similar. According to IKEA, the figure in Russia is $85 per store visit—exactly the same as in affluent Sweden.

Wherever they are, customers tend to think of the store visit as more of an outing than a chore. That's intentional. IKEA practises a form of 'gentle coercion' to keep you as long as possible. Right at the entrance, for example, you can drop off your kids at the playroom, an amenity that encourages more leisurely shopping.

Then, clutching your dog-eared catalogue (the print run is over 160 million—more than the Bible, IKEA claims), you proceed along a marked path through the warren of showrooms. 'Because the store is designed as a circle, I can see everything as long as I keep walking in one direction,' says Krystyna Gavora, an architect who frequents IKEA in Schaumburg, Illinois. Wide aisles let you inspect merchandise without holding up traffic. The furniture itself is arranged in fully accessorized displays, down to the picture frames on the nightstand, to inspire customers and get them to spend more. The settings are so lifelike that one writer is staging a play at IKEA in Renton, Washington.

Along the way, one touch after another seduces the shopper, from the paper measuring tapes and pencils to strategically placed bins with items like pink plastic watering cans, scented candles and picture frames. These are things you never knew you needed but at less than $2 each you load up on them anyway. You set out to buy a $40 coffee table but end up spending $500 on everything from storage units to glassware. 'They have this way of making you believe nothing is expensive,' says Bertille Faroult, a shopper at IKEA on the outskirts of Paris. The bins and shelves constantly surprise. IKEA replaces a third of its product line every year.

Then there's the stop at the restaurant, usually placed at the centre of the store, to give shoppers a breather and encourage them to keep going. You proceed to the warehouse, where the full genius of founder Kamprad is on display. Nearly all the big items are flat-packed, which not only saves IKEA millions in shipping costs from suppliers but also enables shoppers to haul their own stuff home—another saving. Finally, you have the fun, or agony, of assembling at home, equipped with nothing but an Allen key and those cryptic instructions.

A vocal minority rails at IKEA for its long queues, crowded car parks, exasperating assembly experiences and furniture that's hardly built to last. The running joke is that IKEA is Swedish for particle board. But the converts outnumber the critics. And for every fan who shops at IKEA, there seems to be one working at the store itself. The fanaticism stems from founder Ingvar Kamprad, 79, a figure as important to global retailing as Wal-Mart's Sam Walton. Kamprad started the company in 1943 at the age of 17, selling pens, Christmas cards and seeds from a shed on his family's farm in southern Sweden. In 1951, the first catalogue appeared. Kamprad penned all the text himself until 1963. His credo of creating 'a better life for many' is enshrined in his almost evangelical 1976 tract, *A Furniture Dealer's Testament*. Peppered with folksy titbits—'divide your life into 10-minute units and sacrifice as few as possible in meaningless activity', 'wasting resources is a mortal sin' (that's for sure: employees are the catalogue models) or the more revealing 'it is our duty to expand'—the pamphlet is given to all employees the day they start. Employees at IKEA will never get rich but they do get to enjoy autonomy, very little hierarchy and a family-friendly culture. In return they buy into the culture of frugality and style that drives the whole company.

Kamprad, though officially retired, is still the cheerleader for the practices that define IKEA culture. One is egalitarianism. IKEA regularly stages Antibureaucracy Weeks, during which executives work on the shop floor or tend the checkouts. 'In February,' says CEO Dahlvig, 'I was unloading trucks and selling beds and mattresses.'

Prices and costs

A feature of IKEA is its steely competitiveness. You get a sense of that at one of IKEA's main offices, in Helsingborg, Sweden. At the doorway, a massive bulletin board tracks weekly sales growth, names the best-performing country markets and identifies the best-selling furniture. The other message that comes across loud and clear: cut prices. At the far end of the Helsingborg foyer is a row of best-selling Klippan sofas, displaying models from 1999 to 2006 with their euro price tags. In 1999 the Klippan was $354; by 2009 it was less than $200.

The montage vividly illustrates IKEA's relentless cost-cutting. The retailer aims to lower prices across its entire offering by an average of 2 per cent to 3 per cent each year. It goes deeper when it wants to hit rivals in certain segments. 'We look at the competition, take their price and then slash it in half,' says Mark McCaslin, manager of IKEA Long Island, in Hicksville, NY.

It helps that frugality is as deeply ingrained in the corporate DNA as the obsession with design. Managers fly economy, even top brass. Steen Kanter, who left IKEA in 1994 and now heads his own retail consultancy in Philadelphia, Kanter International, recalls that while flying with founder Ingvar Kamprad once, the boss handed him a coupon for a car rental he had ripped out from an in-flight magazine.

This cost obsession fuses with the design culture. 'Designing beautiful-but-expensive products is easy,' says Josephine Rydberg-Dumont, president of IKEA of Sweden. 'Designing beautiful products that are inexpensive and functional is a huge challenge.'

// The global middle class, which IKEA targets, shares buying habits … Even spending per customer is similar. //

No design—no matter how inspired—finds its way into the showroom if it cannot be made affordable. To achieve that goal, the company's 12 full-time designers at Almhult, Sweden, along with 80 freelances, work hand in hand with in-house production teams to identify the appropriate materials and least costly suppliers, a trial-and-error process that can take as long as three years. Example: for the PS Ellan, a $39.99 dining chair that can rock back on its hind legs without tipping over, designer Chris Martin worked with production staff for a year and a half to adapt a wood-fibre composite, an inexpensive blend of wood chips and plastic resin used in highway noise barriers, for use in furnishings. Martin also had to design the chair to break down into six pieces, so it could be flat-packed and snapped together without screws.

With a network of 1300 suppliers in 53 countries, IKEA works overtime to find the right manufacturer for

▲ In developing its PS line, IKEA challenged designers to reuse discarded materials. This 'Selma' chair has a choice of different cushions a Hached based on materials dating from 1969 to 300 BCE.

the right product. It once contracted with ski makers—experts in bent wood—to manufacture its Poang armchairs, and it has tapped makers of supermarket carts to turn out durable sofas. Simplicity, a tenet of Swedish design, helps keep costs down. The 50¢ Trofé mug comes only in blue and white, the least expensive pigments. IKEA's conservation drive extends naturally from this cost cutting. For its new PS line, it challenged 28 designers to find innovative uses for discarded and unusual materials. The results: a table fashioned from reddish-brown birch heartwood (furniture makers prefer the pale exterior wood) and a storage system made from recycled milk cartons.

Adaptation to local tastes

Adding to the challenge, the suppliers and designers have to customize some IKEA products to make them sell better in local markets. In China, the 250,000 plastic placemats IKEA produced to commemorate the year of the rooster sold out in just three weeks. Julie Desrosiers, the bedroom-line manager at IKEA of Sweden, visited people's houses in the USA and Europe to peek into their closets, learning that 'Americans prefer to store most of their clothes folded, and Italians like to hang.' The result was a wardrobe that features deeper drawers for US customers.

The American market poses special challenges for IKEA because of the huge differences inside the USA. 'It's so easy to forget the reality of how people live,' says IKEA's US interior design director, Mats Nilsson. For example, IKEA realized it might not be reaching California's Hispanics, so its designers visited the homes of Hispanic staff. They soon realized they had set up the store's displays all wrong. Large Hispanic families need dining tables and sofas that fit more than two people, the Swedish norm. They prefer bold colours to the more subdued Scandinavian palette and display tons of pictures in elaborate frames. Nilsson warmed up the showrooms' colours, adding more seating and throwing in numerous picture frames.

IKEA is particularly concerned about the USA since it is key to expansion—and since IKEA came close to blowing it. 'We got our clocks cleaned in the early 1990s because we really didn't listen to the consumer,' says Kanter. Stores weren't big enough to offer the full IKEA experience, and many were in poor locations. Prices were too high. Beds were measured in centimetres, not king, queen and twin. Sofas weren't deep enough, curtains were too short and kitchens didn't fit US-size appliances. 'American customers were buying vases to drink from because the glasses were too small,' recalls Goran Carstedt, the former head of IKEA North America, who helped engineer a turnaround. Parts of the product line were adapted (no more metric measurements), new and bigger store locations chosen, prices slashed and service improved. Now US managers are paying close attention to the tiniest details. 'Americans want more comfortable sofas, higher-quality textiles, bigger glasses, more spacious entertainment units,' says Pernille Spiers-Lopez, head of IKEA North America.

The future

Can the cult keep thriving? IKEA has stumbled badly before. A foray into Japan 30 years ago was a disaster (the Japanese wanted high quality and great materials, not low price and particle board). The company returned to Japan in 2006. IKEA is also seeing more competition than ever. In the USA, Target Corp. recruited top designer Thomas O'Brien to develop a range of low-priced furnishings. An IKEA-like chain called Fly is popular in France. In Japan, Nitori Co. is the major player in low-cost furniture. ILVA is successfully selling upmarket furniture in Denmark and Sweden, although its foray into the UK market was unsuccessful.

Perhaps the bigger issue is what happens inside IKEA. 'The great challenge of any organization as it becomes larger and more diverse is how to keep the core founding values alive,' says Harvard Business School Professor Christopher A. Bartlett. IKEA is still run by managers who were trained and groomed by Kamprad himself—and who are personally devoted to the founder. As the direct links with Kamprad disappear, the culture may start to fade.

For now, the founder's legacy is alive and well. The Klippan sofas are selling briskly. New lines of foods, travel gear and toiletries are due soon. IKEA is gearing up for its Christmas tree promotion—you buy a live tree, then return it for a rebate and end up shopping at IKEA in the slow month of January.

And the fans keep clamouring for more. At least once a year, Jen Segrest, a 36-year-old freelance web designer, and her husband make a 10-hour round-trip from their home in Middletown, Ohio, to IKEA in Schaumburg, Illinois, near Chicago. 'Every piece of furniture in my living room is IKEA—except for an end table, which I hate. And next time I go to IKEA I'll replace it,' says Segrest. To lure the retailer to Ohio, Segrest has even started a blog called OH! IKEA. The banner on the home page reads 'IKEA in Ohio— Because man cannot live on Target alone.'

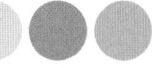

Questions

1. IKEA has chosen to enter new markets by direct investment. What advantages does this form of entry give it? Why doesn't IKEA use franchising like McDonald's and Benetton?
2. How would you categorize IKEA's approach to developing standardization and adaptation?
3. What are the factors that have helped IKEA to build a successful global brand?

This case is an updated version, by Professor David Jobber, of Sains, A., C. Lindblad, A. T. Palmer, J. Bush, D. Roberts and K. Hall (2005) IKEA: How The Swedish Retailer Became a Global Cult Brand, Business Week, *14 November, 45–54.* Updating is based on Wearden, G. (2009) IKEA to Cut More Jobs, *Guardian,* 8 July, 22; Clark, N. (2008) ILVA, *Marketing,* 30 January, 20; IKEA, http://en.wikipedia.org/wiki/IKEA; Boyle, C. (2009) IKEA to Cut More Staff as Demand Falls, http://business.timesonline.co.uk/tol/business/industry; Bush, J. (2009) Why IKEA is Fed Up with Russia, *BusinessWeek,* 2 July, 32.

Made in China

Marketing Tsingtaoo Beer Internationally

China's gross domestic product (GDP) has grown at a rapid rate in the last ten years; the Chinese economy is now the second biggest in the world. The growth has arisen as many overseas investors have been attracted to the country by cheap labour and the government's policies, which have enabled them to outsource manufacturing to China and reduce production costs.

Despite being renowned as a manufacturer, few domestic brands are known outside China. The most famous are probably Haier, which manufactures domestic appliances, Lenovo, which produces personal computers, and Tsingtao the brewers (pronounced 'ching dow'). However, no mainland Chinese brands are ranked in the *Business Week* top 100.

The reasons put forward for this are because the country's industrial emergence is so recent there has not been time for international brands to develop. The drawback of not developing brands is that the country is seen as a low-cost producer and assembler, hence profit margins are low. The country is estimated to produce 75 per cent of the world's toys by volume, but by value the figure is only 20 per cent—a huge imbalance. There is also an image problem, with the 'made in China' label being associated with poor quality, cheap labour and environmental neglect.

The 2008 Beijing Olympics provided opportunities for Chinese companies to showcase their brands alongside multinationals as official sponsors and reach a global audience. Tsingtao took advantage of this, providing beer for the organizers, and had booths set up around the event.

General Administration of Quality Supervision, Inspection and Quarantine (GAQSIQ)

This is a state body that is trying to improve the status of domestic brands and use branding as a way of developing the economic status of the country. It set up the China Promotion Committee to develop a strategy to foster brand development for Chinese companies. 'China Top Brand Strategy Development Report' was published in 2006. The 6000-word report pointed out the significance of developing brands and the importance to the economy of cultivating Chinese companies with strong brands.

It could also be argued that, since this report was published, branding in European markets has become more important with the increase in domestic inflation and the rise in the Chinese RMB against the euro and other European currencies, leading to Chinese products becoming more expensive for European consumers.

The committee aims to identify and help companies with potentially strong brands, certify the quality of those who are already in this category, apply international quality standards and assist in exporting. Most marketing experts tend to agree that, though the country is skilled in manufacture, it lacks expertise and skills in marketing and branding, another reason why few domestic brands are known outside China.

Tsingtao Brewery

Tsingtao was founded in 1903 by German settlers as a German-British brewing company in Qingdao, north China. The ownership passed from German hands into Japanese ownership in 1915, and the company was nationalized in 1949. It was privatized in the early 1990s, merged with three other breweries in 1993 and renamed Tsingtao Brewery Company Limited.

The company is the biggest brewer in China, the tenth largest brewer in the world and the eleventh largest beer brand in the world (see www.tsingtaobeer.com), having nearly 50 breweries throughout the country. In 2007 it opened its first overseas brewery in Bangkok, Thailand. To help meet overseas demand, more overseas production could follow. However, exports currently occupy only 1 per cent of total production.

Tsingtao beer is the major brand that accounts for most of the production. It is a 4.7 per cent alcohol content lager, brewed with all-natural ingredients and no artificial preservatives. It includes rice, domestically grown hops from western China, high-quality barley (imported from Australia, Canada and France) and underground spring water from the mountains of Laoshan. Other products brewed by Tsingtao include: an unpasteurized version sold as Tsingtao draft beer; Tsingtao dark beer (5.2 per cent alcohol); and Tsingtao green beer (4.5 per cent alcohol), a green-coloured beer that it is claimed promotes good health.

For a long time the beer was advertised as being brewed with Laoshan spring water, but this now applies only to beer brewed in Qingdao, not that produced at its other Chinese breweries. Exports to the UK contain Laoshan water. The beer has a light, crisp taste and is viewed as an ideal accompaniment to food.

The beer market in China did not develop until the mid-1980s; the product was sold in Hong Kong and launched in the United States in 1972, becoming the top-selling Chinese beer in the USA. Currently it sells in over 50 counties, accounting for over 50 per cent of China's beer exports and being regarded as the country's top exported consumer product.

As already mentioned Tsingtao acted as an official Olympic Games sponsor at the 2008 Beijing Olympics; the Olympic sailing event took place in the brewer's home city. This, it is believed, has led to increased interest in Chinese brands, and has been recognized as a contributory factor to an increase in both domestic and overseas sales.

The American brewer Anheuser-Busch (AB) currently own 27 per cent of the company. In July 2008, it accepted a takeover bid for the company from the Belgian-based InBev. It is unclear at present what the change of ownership will mean for Tsingtao, but as it is a communist state the Chinese Government exerts some influence on the operation of the company.

AB-InBev

The proposed $52 billion takeover of AB will make the AB-InBev group the world's largest beer maker, producing about a quarter of the world's supply. InBev's major global brands are Beck's, Stella Artois and Brahma; the takeover will add Budweiser to this portfolio. In total, it has over 200 brands throughout the world. These are categorized as global, multi-country or local (see www.inbev.com for a complete list of brands).

Marketing in the United Kingdom

The marketing and distribution of Tsingtao in the UK and Ireland is handled by Halewood International Ltd. It obtained exclusive distribution rights in December 2007 for all product formats in both the on- and off-trade. Global brands terminated their distribution agreement late in 2007, unhappy about the lack of exclusivity and having to share distribution with ethnic foods importer Westmill Foods.

Halewood International

Established in 1978 the company is a producer and supplier of wines, spirits and speciality drinks (see www.halewood-int.com/home/brands for a complete list of brands), with an annual turnover of about £250 million. Tsingtao is currently the only beer it distributes. It markets it as a beer linked to Chinese food, and sold in Chinese restaurants and ethnic grocers. However, it aims to develop brand awareness as part of a strategy to increase distribution and sales in both on- and off-trade channels, making it the number one Asian beer in the UK.

As part of this strategy, various events were sponsored in 2008, including the Legacy of Taste Final to find the best Chinese restaurant in the UK, the London Hong Kong Dragon Boat Festival and the Dunlop Table Tennis Masters.

A major push took place early in 2009 to improve the popularity of the brand outside the Chinese community. There are plans for sponsorship of festivals that celebrate the Chinese New Year, and point-of-sale

European countries with populations of over 100,000 ethnic Chinese	TABLE C46.1
Country	**Population (000s)**
Russia	680
United Kingdom	500*
France	300
Netherlands	145
Italy	112
Spain	100
*Figure for 2008	
Source: New World Encyclopedia, at http://www.newworldencyclopedia.org/entry/Overseas_Chinese.	

material will be supplied to 4000 Chinese restaurants. There are also plans to extend activities into on-trade bars.

To date, product listings have been obtained in supermarkets, with Tesco, Waitrose and Makro (330 ml bottles) and Sainsbury's (640 ml bottles) marketing the brand.

The Chinese diaspora in Europe

There were estimated to be 1.7 million people of Chinese descent resident in Europe in 2006, this figure excludes tourists and students. The European countries listed in Table C46.1 have populations of over 100,000 ethnic Chinese.

References

Based on: Sherman, L. (n.d.) Chinese Brands Go for Global Gold, at www.forbes.com/sportsbusiness; Trout, J. (n.d.) China at the Crossroads, at www.Forbes.com/opinions; Anonymous (2006) Top Brands or Not?, *China Daily*, 23–24 January, 4; Van der Kamp, J. (2006) Export Riches to Follow Products Abroad until Ideas Financed in China, *South China Morning Post*, 6 October, B14; Xie, C. (2006) Branding to Further Boost Economy, *China Daily*, 21 December, 2; Withrington, A. (2007) Tsingtao Gets New UK Distributor, *The Publican*, 12 December; Yang, Z. (2007) This Beer Tastes Really Good, *Chinese Historical Review* 14(1), 29–58; Eley, M. (2008) Chinese New Year Plans for Tsingtao, *The Publican*, 18 December; Li, F. (2008) Brewing Profits, *China Business Weekly*, 20–26 October, 6; Porter, J. (2008) Tsingtao Celebrates Olympic Success, *The Publican*, 18 August.

Questions

1 Explain how GAQSIQ can help Chinese companies in branding, particularly in overcoming the low-cost/quality image associated with many Chinese brands.

2 Justify investment in branding in an attempt to develop the market in the UK.

3 Tsingtao beer is marketed in the UK by Halewood International Ltd. What are the advantages and disadvantages of using a foreign–based distributor as a method of entry into a foreign market?

4 To what extent should Tsingtao promote its German heritage, American links or future Belgian ownership in the UK market?

5 Apply the anatomy of brand positioning framework to Tsingtao in the UK. Are there any areas within the framework where more information is needed?

6 Evaluate the possible development of Tsingtao as a global brand?

This case was written by Adrian Pritchard, Senior Lecturer in Marketing, Coventry University.

Glossary

A

ad hoc research a research project that focuses on a specific problem, collecting data at one point in time with one sample of respondents

adapted marketing mix an international marketing strategy for changing the marketing mix for each international target market

administered vertical marketing system a channel situation where a manufacturer that dominates a market through its size and strong brands may exercise considerable power over intermediaries even though they are independent

advertising any paid form of non-personal communication of ideas or products in the prime media, i.e. television, the press, posters, cinema and radio, the Internet and direct marketing

advertising agency an organization that specializes in providing services such as media selection, creative work, production and campaign planning to clients

advertising message the use of words, symbols and illustrations to communicate to a target audience using prime media

advertising platform the aspect of the seller's product that is most persuasive and relevant to the target consumer

ambush marketing originally referred to the activities of companies that try to associate themselves with an event (e.g. the Olympics) without paying any fee to the event owner; now means the sponsoring of the television coverage of a major event, national teams and the support of individual sportspeople

attitude the degree to which a customer or prospect likes or dislikes a brand

augmented product the core product plus extra functional and/or emotional values combined in a unique way to form a brand

awareness set the set of brands that the consumer is aware may provide a solution to the problem

B

beliefs descriptive thoughts that a person holds about something

benefit segmentation the grouping of people based on the different benefits they seek from a product

blog short for weblog; a personal diary/journal on the web; information can easily be uploaded on to a website and is then available for general consumption by web users

bonus pack giving a customer extra quantity at no additional cost

brainstorming the technique where a group of people generate ideas without initial evaluation; only when the list of ideas is complete is each idea then evaluated

brand a distinctive product offering created by the use of a name, symbol, design, packaging, or some combination of these intended to differentiate it from its competitors

brand assets the distinctive features of a brand

brand domain the brand's target market

brand equity a measure of the strength of a brand in the marketplace by adding tangible value to a company through the resulting sales and profits

brand extension the use of an established brand name on a new brand within the same broad market or product category

brand heritage the background to the brand and its culture

brand personality the character of a brand described in terms of other entities such as people, animals and objects

brand reflection the relationship of the brand to self-identity

brand stretching the use of an established brand name for brands in unrelated markets or product categories

brand valuation the process of estimating the financial value of an individual or corporate brand

brand values the core values and characteristics of a brand

broadcast sponsorship a form of sponsorship where a television or radio programme is the focus

business analysis a review of the projected sales, costs and profits for a new product to establish whether these factors satisfy company objectives

business ethics the moral principles and values that guide a firm's behaviour

business mission the organization's purpose, usually setting out its competitive domain, which distinguishes the business from others of its type

buying centre a group that is involved in the buying decision (also known as a decision-making unit)

buying signals statements by a buyer that indicate s/he is interested in buying

bypass attack circumventing the defender's position, usually through technological leap-frogging or diversification

C

campaign objectives goals set by an organization in terms of, for example, sales, profits, customers won or retained, or awareness creation

catalogue marketing the sale of products through catalogues distributed to agents and customers, usually by mail or at stores

category management the management of brands in a group, portfolio or category, with specific emphasis on the retail trade's requirements

cause-related marketing a commercial activity by which businesses and charities or causes form a partnership with each other to market an image or product for mutual benefit

centralization in international marketing it is the global integration of international operations

change master a person that develops an implementation strategy to drive through organizational change

channel integration the way in which the players in the channel are linked

channel intermediaries organizations that facilitate the distribution of products to customers

channel of distribution the means by which products are moved from the producer to the ultimate consumer

channel strategy the selection of the most effective distribution channel,

the most appropriate level of distribution intensity and the degree of channel integration

choice criteria the various attributes (and benefits) people use when evaluating products and services

classical conditioning the process of using an established relationship between a stimulus and a response to cause the learning of the same response to a different stimulus

coercive power power inherent in the ability to punish

cognitive dissonance post-purchase concerns of a consumer arising from uncertainty as to whether a decision to purchase was the correct one

cognitive learning the learning of knowledge, and development of beliefs and attitudes without direct reinforcement

combination brand name a combination of family and individual brand names

communications-based co-branding the linking of two or more existing brands from different companies or business units for the purposes of joint communication

competitive advantage the achievement of superior performance through differentiation to provide superior customer value or by managing to achieve lowest delivered cost

competitive behaviour the activities of rival companies with respect to each other; this can take five forms—conflict, competition, co-existence, cooperation and collusion

competitive bidding drawing up detailed specifications for a product and putting the contract out to tender

competitive scope the breadth of a company's competitive challenge, e.g. broad or narrow

competitor analysis an examination of the nature of actual and potential competitors, and their objectives and strategies

competitor audit a precise analysis of competitor strengths and weaknesses, objectives and strategies

competitor targets the organizations against which a company chooses to compete directly

concept testing testing new product ideas with potential customers

concession analysis the evaluation of things that can be offered to someone in negotiation valued from the viewpoint of the receiver

consumer decision-making process the stages a consumer goes through when buying something—namely, problem awareness, information search, evaluation of alternatives, purchase and post-purchase evaluation

consumer movement an organized collection of groups and organizations whose objective it is to protect the rights of consumers

consumer panel household consumers who provide information on their purchases over time

consumer panel data a type of continuous research where information is provided by household consumers on their purchases over time

consumer pull the targeting of consumers with communications (e.g. promotions) designed to create demand that will pull the product into the distribution chain

consumerism organized action against business practices that are not in the interests of consumers

continuous research repeated interviewing of the same sample of people

contractual joint venture two or more companies form a partnership but no joint enterprise with a separate identity is formed

contractual vertical marketing system a franchise arrangement (e.g. a franchise) that ties together producers and resellers

control the stage in the marketing planning process or cycle when the performance against plan is monitored so that corrective action, if necessary, can be taken

core competences the principal distinctive capabilities possessed by a company—what it is really good at

core product anything that provides the central benefits required by customers

core strategy the means of achieving marketing objectives, including target markets, competitor targets and competitive advantage

corporate identity the ethos, aims and values of an organization, presenting a sense of its individuality, which helps to differentiate it from its competitors

corporate social responsibility the ethical principle that an organization should be accountable for how its behaviour might affect society and the environment

corporate vertical marketing system a channel situation where an organization gains control of distribution through ownership

counter-offensive defence a counter-attack that takes the form of a head-on counter-attack, an attack on the attacker's cash cow or an encirclement of the attacker

counter-trade a method of exchange where not all transactions are concluded in cash; goods may be included as part of the asking price

covert power play the use of disguised forms of power tactics

culture the traditions, taboos, values and basic attitudes of the whole society in which an individual lives

customer analysis a survey of who the customers are, what choice criteria they use, how they rate

competitive offerings and on what variables they can be segmented

customer-based brand equity the differential effect that brand knowledge has on consumer response to the marketing of that brand

customer benefits those things that a customer values in a product; customer benefits derive from product features

customer relationship management the methodologies, technologies and e-commerce capabilities used by firms to manage customer relationships

customer satisfaction measurement a process through which customer satisfaction criteria are set, customers are surveyed and the results interpreted in order to establish the level of customer satisfaction with the organization's product

customer satisfaction the fulfilment of customers' requirements or needs

customer value perceived benefits minus perceived sacrifice

customized marketing the market coverage strategy where a company decides to target individual customers and develops separate marketing mixes for each

D

data the most basic form of knowledge, the result of observations

database marketing an interactive approach to marketing that uses individually addressable marketing media and channels to provide information to a target audience, stimulate demand and stay close to customers

decentralization in international marketing it is the delegation of international operations to individual countries or regions

decision-making process the stages that organizations and people pass

through when purchasing a physical product or service

decision-making unit (DMU) a group of people within an organization who are involved in the buying decision (also known as the buying centre)

demography changes in the population in terms of its size and characteristics

depth interviews the interviewing of consumers individually for perhaps one or two hours, with the aim of understanding their attitudes, values, behaviour and/or beliefs

descriptive research research undertaken to describe customers' beliefs, attitudes, preferences and behaviour

differential advantage a clear performance differential over the competition on factors that are important to target customers

differential marketing strategies market coverage strategies where a company decides to target several market segments and develops separate marketing mixes for each

differentiated marketing a market coverage strategy where a company decides to target several market segments and develops separate marketing mixes for each

differentiation strategy the selection of one or more customer choice criteria and positioning the offering accordingly to achieve superior customer value

diffusion of innovation process the process by which a new product spreads throughout a market over time

digital marketing the application of digital technologies that form channels to market (the Internet, mobile communications, interactive television and wireless) to achieve corporate goals through meeting and exceeding customer needs better than the competition

direct cost pricing the calculation of only those costs that are likely to rise as output increases

direct exporting the handling of exporting activities by the exporting organization rather than by a domestically based independent organization

direct investment market entry that involves investment in foreign-based assembly or manufacturing facilities

direct mail material sent through the postal service to the recipient's house or business address promoting a product and/or maintaining an ongoing relationship

direct marketing (1) acquiring and retaining customers without the use of an intermediary; (2) the distribution of products, information and promotional benefits to target consumers through interactive communication in a way that allows response to be measured

direct response advertising the use of the prime advertising media such as television, newspapers and magazines to elicit an order, enquiry or request for a visit

distribution analysis an examination of movements in power bases, channel attractiveness, physical distribution and distribution behaviour

distribution push the targeting of channel intermediaries with communications (e.g. promotions) to push the product into the distribution chain

divest to improve short-term cash yield by dropping or selling off a product

E

e-business a term generally used to refer to both buy-side and sell-side e-commerce, and the internal use of Internet, mobile and wireless technologies through an organization

ecology the study of living things within their environment

economic order quantity the quantity of stock to be ordered where total costs are at the lowest

economic value to the customer (EVC) the amount a customer would have to pay to make the total life-cycle costs of a new and a reference product the same

effectiveness doing the right thing, making the correct strategic choice

efficiency a way of managing business processes to a high standard, usually concerned with cost reduction; also called 'doing things right'

ego drive the need to make a sale in a personal way, not merely for money

electronic commerce involves all electronically mediated transactions between an organization and any third party it deals with, including exchange of information

e-marketing a term used to refer to the use of technology (telecommunications and Internet-based) to achieve marketing objectives and bringing the customer and supplier closer together

empathy to be able to feel as the buyer feels, to be able to understand customer problems and needs

encirclement attack attacking the defender from all sides, i.e. every market segment is hit with every combination of product features

entry barriers barriers that act to prevent new firms from entering a market, e.g. the high level of investment required

entry into new markets (diversification) the entry into new markets by new products

environmental scanning the process of monitoring and analysing the marketing environment of a company

environmentalism the organized movement of groups and organizations to protect and improve the physical environment

equity joint venture where two or more companies form a partnership that involves the creation of a new company

ethical consumption the taking of purchase decisions not only on the basis of personal interests but also on the basis of the interests of society and the environment

ethics the moral principles and values that govern the actions and decisions of an individual or group

event sponsorship sponsorship of a sporting or other event

evoked set the set of brands that the consumer seriously evaluates before making a purchase

exaggerated promises barrier a barrier to the matching of expected and perceived service levels caused by the unwarranted building up of expectations by exaggerated promises

exchange the act or process of receiving something from someone by giving something in return

exclusive distribution an extreme form of selective distribution where only one wholesaler, retailer or industrial distributor is used in a geographical area to sell the products of a supplier

exhibition an event that brings buyers and sellers together in a commercial setting

experience curve the combined effect of economies of scale and learning as cumulative output increases

experimental research research undertaken in order to establish cause and effect

experimentation the application of stimuli (e.g. two price levels) to different matched groups under controlled conditions for the purpose of measuring their effect on a variable (e.g. sales)

expert power power that derives from an individual's expertise

exploratory research the preliminary exploration of a research area prior to the main data-collection stage

F

fair trade marketing the development, promotion and selling of fair trade brands and the positioning of organizations on the basis of a fair trade ethos

family brand name a brand name used for all products in a range

fighter brands low-cost manufacturers' brands introduced to combat own-label brands

flanking attack attacking geographical areas or market segments where the defender is poorly represented

flanking defence the defence of a hitherto unprotected market segment

focus group a group normally of six to twelve consumers brought together for a discussion focusing on an aspect of a company's marketing

focused marketing a market coverage strategy where a company decides to target one market segment with a single marketing mix

foreign consumer culture positioning positioning a brand as associated with a specific foreign culture (e.g. Italian fashion)

franchise a legal contract in which a producer and channel intermediaries agree each other's rights and obligations; usually the intermediary receives marketing, managerial, technical and financial services in return for a fee

franchising a form of licensing where a package of services is offered by the franchisor to the franchisee in return for payment

frontal attack a competitive strategy where the challenger takes on the defender head on

full cost pricing pricing so as to include all costs and based on certain sales volume assumptions

G

geodemographics the process of grouping households into geographic clusters based on information such as type of accommodation, occupation, number and age of children, and ethnic background

global branding achievement of brand penetration worldwide

global consumer culture positioning positioning a brand as a symbol of a given global culture (e.g. young cosmopolitan men)

going-rate pricing pricing at the rate generally applicable in the market, focusing on competitors' offerings rather than on company costs

group discussion a group, usually of six to eight consumers, brought together for a discussion focusing on an aspect of a company's marketing

guerrilla attack making life uncomfortable for stronger rivals through, for example, unpredictable price discounts, sales promotions or heavy advertising in a few selected regions

H

hall tests bringing a sample of target consumers to a room that has been hired so that alternative marketing ideas (e.g. promotions) can be tested

halo customers customers that are not directly targeted but may find the product attractive

harvest objective the improvement of profit margins to improve cash flow even if the longer-term result is falling sales

hold objective a strategy of defending a product in order to maintain market share

I

inadequate delivery barrier a barrier to the matching of expected and perceived service levels caused by the failure of the service provider to select, train and reward staff adequately, resulting in poor or inconsistent delivery of service

inadequate resources barrier a barrier to the matching of expected and perceived service levels caused by the unwillingness of service providers to provide the necessary resources

indirect exporting the use of independent organizations within the exporter's domestic market to facilitate export

individual brand name a brand name that does not identify a brand with a particular company

industry a group of companies that market products that are close substitutes for each other

information combinations of data that provide decision-relevant knowledge

information framing the way in which information is presented to people

information processing the process by which a stimulus is received, interpreted, stored in memory and later retrieved

information search the identification of alternative ways of problem-solving

ingredient co-branding the explicit positioning of a supplier's brand as an ingredient of a product

innovation the commercialization of an invention by bringing it to market

inseparability a characteristic of services, namely that their production cannot be separated from their consumption

intangibility a characteristic of services, namely that they cannot be touched, seen, tasted or smelled

integrated marketing communications the concept that companies coordinate their marketing communications tools to deliver a clear, consistent, credible and competitive message about the organization and its products

intensive distribution the aim of this is to provide saturation coverage of the market by using all available outlets

interaction approach an approach to buyer–seller relations that treats the relationships as taking place between two active parties

internal marketing training, motivating and communicating with staff to cause them to work effectively in providing customer satisfaction; more recently the term has been expanded to include marketing to all staff with the aim of achieving the acceptance of marketing ideas and plans

Internet marketing the achievement of corporate goals through meeting and exceeding customer needs better than the competition, through the utilization of digital Internet technologies

Internet promotion the promotion of products to consumers and businesses through electronic media

invention the discovery of new methods and ideas

J

just-in-time (JIT) this concept aims to minimize stocks by organizing a supply system that provides materials and components as they are required

K

key account management an approach to selling that focuses resources on major customers and uses a team selling approach

L

legitimate power power based on legitimate authority, such as line management

licensing a contractual arrangement in which a licensor provides a licensee with certain rights, e.g. to technology access or production rights

life-cycle costs all the components of costs associated with buying, owning and using a physical product or service

lifestyle the pattern of living as expressed in a person's activities, interests and opinions

lifestyle segmentation the grouping of people according to their pattern of living as expressed in their activities, interests and opinions

local consumer culture positioning positioning a brand as associated with a local culture (e.g. local production and consumption of a good)

M

macroenvironment a number of broader forces that affect not only the company but the other actors in the environment, e.g. social, political, technological and economic

macrosegmentation the segmentation of organizational markets by size, industry and location

manufacturer brands brands that are created by producers and bear their chosen brand name

market development to take current products and market them in new markets

market expansion the attempt to increase the size of a market by converting non-users to users of the product and by increasing usage rates

market penetration to continue to grow sales by marketing an existing product in an existing market

market segmentation the process of identifying individuals or organizations with similar characteristics that have significant implications for the determination of marketing strategy

market share analysis a comparison of company sales with total sales of the product, including sales of competitors

market testing the limited launch of a new product to test sales potential

marketing accountability the requirement to justify marketing investment by using marketing metrics

marketing audit a systematic examination of a business's marketing environment, objectives, strategies, and activities with a view to identifying key strategic issues, problem areas and opportunities

marketing concept the achievement of corporate goals through meeting and exceeding customer needs better than the competition

marketing control the stage in the marketing planning process or cycle when performance against plan is monitored so that corrective action, if necessary, can be taken

marketing environment the actors and forces that affect a company's capability to operate effectively in providing products and services to its customers

marketing ethics the moral principles and values that guide behaviour within the field of marketing

marketing information system a system in which marketing information is formally gathered, stored, analysed and distributed to managers in accordance with their informational needs on a regular, planned basis

marketing metrics quantitative measures of the outcomes of marketing activities and expenditures

marketing mix a framework for the tactical management of the customer relationship, including product, place, price, promotion (the 4-Ps); in the case of services three other elements to be taken into account are process, people and physical evidence

marketing objectives there are two types of marketing objective: strategic thrust, which dictates which products should be sold in which markets, and strategic objectives, i.e. product-level objectives, such as build, hold, harvest and divest

marketing orientation companies with a marketing orientation focus on customer needs as the primary drivers of organizational performance

marketing planning the process by which businesses analyse the environment and their capabilities, decide upon courses of marketing action and implement those decisions

marketing research the gathering of data and information on the market

marketing structures the marketing frameworks (organization, training and internal communications) upon which marketing activities are based

marketing systems sets of connected parts (information, planning and control) that support the marketing function

marketing-orientated pricing an approach to pricing that takes a range of marketing factors into account when setting prices

media class decision the choice of prime media, i.e. the press, cinema, television, posters, radio, or some combination of these

media vehicle decision the choice of the particular newspaper, magazine, television spot, poster site, etc.

microenvironment the actors in the firm's immediate environment that affect its capability to operate effectively in its chosen markets—namely, suppliers, distributors, customers and competitors

microsegmentation segmentation according to choice criteria, DMU structure, decision-making process, buy class, purchasing structure and organizational innovativeness

misconception barrier a failure by marketers to understand what customers really value about their service

mobile defence involves diversification or broadening the market by redefining the business

mobile marketing the sending of text messages to mobile phones to promote products and build relationships with consumers

modified rebuy where a regular requirement for the type of product exists and the buying alternatives are known but sufficient change (e.g. a delivery problem) has occurred to require some alteration to the normal supply procedure

money-off promotions sales promotions that discount the normal price

motivation the process involving needs that set drives in motion to accomplish goals

N

new task refers to the first time purchase of a product or input by an organization

niche objective the strategy of targeting a small market segment

O

omnibus survey a regular survey, usually operated by a marketing research specialist company, which asks questions of respondents for several clients on the same questionnaire

operant conditioning the use of rewards to generate reinforcement of response

overt power play the use of visible, open kinds of power tactics

own-label brands brands created and owned by distributors or retailers

P

parallel co-branding the joining of two or more independent brands to produce a combined brand

parallel importing when importers buy products from distributors in one country and sell them in another to distributors who are not part of the manufacturer's normal distribution; caused by big price differences for the same product between different countries

PEEST analysis the analysis of the political/legal, economic, ecological/physical, social/cultural, and technological environments

perception the process by which people select, organize and interpret sensory stimulation into a meaningful picture of the world

perishability a characteristic of services, namely that the capacity of a service business, such as a hotel room, cannot be stored—if it is not occupied, this is lost income that cannot be recovered

personal selling oral communication with prospective purchasers with the intention of making a sale

personality the inner psychological characteristics of individuals that lead to consistent responses to their environment

place the distribution channels to be used, outlet locations, methods of transportation

portal a website that serves as an 'entry point' to the World Wide Web; portals usually offer guidance on using the Internet and search engines that permit keyword searches

portfolio planning managing groups of brands and product lines

position defence building a fortification around existing products, usually through keen pricing and improved promotion

positioning the choice of target market (where the company wishes to compete) and differential advantage (how the company wishes to compete)

positioning strategy the choice of target market (*where* the company wishes to compete) and differential advantage (*how* the company wishes to compete)

pre-emptive defence usually involves continuous innovation and new product development, recognizing that attack is the best form of defence

premiums any merchandise offered free or at low cost as an incentive to purchase

price (1) the amount of money paid for a product; (2) the agreed value placed on the exchange by a buyer and seller

price unbundling pricing each element in the offering so that the price of the total product package is raised

price waterfall the difference between list price and realized or transaction price

product a good or service offered or performed by an organization or individual, which is capable of satisfying customer needs

product-based co-branding the linking of two or more existing brands from different companies or business units to form a product in which the brand names are visible to consumers

product churning a continuous and rapid spiral of new product introductions

product development increasing sales by improving present products or developing new products for current markets

product features the characteristics of a product that may or may not convey a customer benefit

product life cycle a four-stage cycle in the life of a product illustrated as sales and profits curves, the four stages being introduction, growth, maturity and decline

product line a group of brands that are closely related in terms of the functions and benefits they provide

product mix the total set of products marketed by a company

product placement the deliberate placing of products and/or their logos in movies and television, usually in return for money

product portfolio the total range of products offered by the company

production orientation a business approach that is inwardly focused either on costs or on a definition of a company in terms of its production facilities

profile segmentation the grouping of people in terms of profile variables, such as age and socio-economic group, so that marketers can communicate to them

profitability analysis the calculation of sales revenues and costs for the purpose of calculating the profit performance of products, customers and/or distribution channels

project teams the bringing together of staff from such areas as R&D, engineering, manufacturing, finance, and marketing to work on a project such as new product development

promotional mix advertising, personal selling, sales promotions, public relations, direct marketing, and Internet and online promotion

proposal analysis the prediction and evaluation of proposals and demands likely to be made by someone with whom one is negotiating

proprietary-based brand equity is derived from company attributes that deliver value to the brand

prospecting searching for and calling on potential customers

psychographic segmentation the grouping of people according to their lifestyle and personality characteristics

public relations the management of communications and relationships to establish goodwill and mutual understanding between an organization and its public

publicity the communication of a product or business by placing information about it in the media without paying for time or space directly

Q

qualitative research exploratory research that aims to understand consumers' attitudes, values, behaviour and beliefs

R

reasoning a more complex form of cognitive learning where conclusions are reached by connected thought

rebranding the changing of a brand or corporate name

reference group a group of people that influences an individual's attitude or behaviour

referent power power derived by the reference source, e.g. when people identify with and respect the architect of change

relationship marketing the process of creating, maintaining and enhancing strong relationships with customers and other stakeholders

repositioning changing the target market or differential advantage, or both

research brief a written document stating the client's requirements

research proposal a document defining what the marketing research agency promises to do for its client and how much it will cost

retail accordion a theory of retail evolution that focuses on the cycle of retailers widening and then contracting product ranges

retail audit a type of continuous research tracking the sales of products through retail outlets

retail audit data a type of continuous research tracking the sales of products through retail outlets

retail life cycle a theory of retailing evolution that is based on the product life cycle, stating that new types of retailing pass through birth, growth, maturity and decline

retail positioning the choice of target market and differential advantage for a retail outlet

reverse marketing the process whereby the buyer attempts to persuade the supplier to provide exactly what the organization wants

reward power power derived from the ability to provide benefits

rote learning the learning of two or more concepts without conditioning

S

safety (buffer) stocks stocks or inventory held to cover against uncertainty about resupply lead times

sales analysis a comparison of actual with target sales

sales promotion incentives to customers or the trade that are designed to stimulate purchase

salesforce evaluation the measurement of salesperson performance so that strengths and weaknesses can be identified

salesforce motivation the motivation of salespeople by a process that involves needs, which set encouraging drives in motion to accomplish goals

sampling process a term used in research to denote the selection of a sub-set of the total population in order to interview them

secondary research data that has already been collected by another researcher for another purpose

selective attention the process by which people screen out those stimuli that are neither meaningful to them nor consistent with their experiences and beliefs

selective distortion the distortion of information received by people according to their existing beliefs and attitudes

selective distribution the use of a limited number of outlets in a geographical area to sell the products of a supplier

selective retention the process by which people only retain a selection of messages in memory

self-reference criteria the use of one's own perceptions and choice criteria to judge what is important to consumers. In international markets, the perceptions and choice criteria of domestic consumers may be used to judge what is important to foreign consumers

service any deed, performance or effort carried out for the customer

services marketing mix product, place, price, promotion, people, process and physical evidence (the '7-Ps')

simultaneous engineering the involvement of manufacturing and product development engineers in the same development team in an effort to reduce development time

societal marketing focuses on consumers' needs and long-term welfare as keys to satisfying

organizational objectives and responsibilities by taking into account consumers' and societies' wider interests rather than just their short-term consumption

sponsorship a business relationship between a provider of funds, resources or services and an individual, event or organization that offers in return some rights and association that may be used for commercial advantage

stakeholder an individual or group that either (i) is harmed by or benefits from the company, or (ii) whose rights can be violated or have to be respected by the company

stakeholder theory this contends that companies are not managed purely in the interests of their shareholders alone but a broader group including communities associated with the company, employees, customers and suppliers

standardized marketing mix an international marketing strategy for using essentially the same product, promotion, distribution, and pricing in all the company's international markets

straight rebuy refers to a purchase by an organization from a previously approved supplier of a previously purchased item

strategic alliance collaboration between two or more organizations through, for example, joint ventures, licensing agreements, long-term purchasing and supply arrangement, or a joint R&D contract to build a competitive advantage

strategic business unit a business or company division serving a distinct group of customers and with a distinct set of competitors, usually strategically autonomous

strategic focus the strategies that can be employed to achieve an objective

strategic issues analysis an examination of the suitability of marketing objectives and segmentation bases in the light of changes in the marketplace

strategic objectives product-level objectives relating to the decision to build, hold, harvest or divest products

strategic thrust the decision concerning which products to sell in which markets

strategic withdrawal holding on to the company's strengths while getting rid of its weaknesses

strong theory of advertising the notion that advertising can change people's attitudes sufficiently to persuade people who have not previously bought a brand to buy it; desire and conviction precede purchase

supplier analysis an examination of who and where suppliers are located, their competences and shortcomings, the trends affecting them and the future outlook for them

sustainable marketing focuses on reducing environmental damage by creating, producing and delivering sustainable solutions while continuing to satisfy customers and other stakeholders

SWOT analysis a structured approach to evaluating the strategic position of a business by identifying its strengths, weaknesses, opportunities and threats

T

target accounts organizations or individuals whose custom the company wishes to obtain

target audience the group of people at which an advertisement or message is aimed

target market a segment that has been selected as a focus for the company's offering or communications

target marketing the choice of which market segment(s) to serve with a tailored marketing mix

team selling the use of the combined efforts of salespeople, product specialists, engineers, sales managers and even directors to sell products

team sponsorship sponsorship of a team—for example, a football, cricket or motor racing team

telemarketing a marketing communications system whereby trained specialists use telecommunications and information technologies to conduct marketing and sales activities

test marketing the launch of a new product in one or a few geographic areas chosen to be representative of the intended market

total quality management the set of programmes designed to constantly improve the quality of physical products, services and processes

trade marketing marketing to the retail trade

trade-off analysis a measure of the trade-off customers make between price and other product features so that their effects on product preference can be established

transfer pricing the price charged between the profit centres of the same company, sometimes used to take advantage of lower taxes in another country

transition curve the emotional stages that people pass through when confronted with an adverse change

U

undifferentiated marketing a market coverage strategy where a company decides to ignore market segment differences and develops a single marketing mix for the whole market

V

value analysis a method of cost reduction in which components are examined to see if they can be made more cheaply

value chain the set of a firm's activities that are conducted to design, manufacture, market, distribute, and service its products

variability a characteristic of services, namely that, being delivered by people, the standard of their performance is open to variation

vicarious learning learning from others without direct experience or reward

W

weak theory of advertising the notion that advertising can first arouse awareness and interest, nudge some consumers towards a doubting first trial purchase and then provide some reassurance and reinforcement; desire and conviction do not precede purchase

wheel of retailing a theory of retailing development which suggests that new forms of retailing begin as low-cost, cut-price and narrow-margin operations and then trade up until they mature as high-price operators, vulnerable to a new influx of low-cost operators

Companies and Brands Index

Page locators in **bold** refer to main entries and those in *italics* refer to illustrations

Subject and Author Index